American Government and Politics Today

2001–2002 edition

Steffen W. Schmidt
Iowa State University

Mack C. Shelley
Iowa State University

Barbara A. Bardes
University of Cincinnati

WADSWORTH
™
THOMSON LEARNING

Australia • Canada • Mexico • Singapore • Spain
United Kingdom • United States

Publisher: Clark Baxter
Senior Development Editor: Sharon Adams Poore
Assistant Editor: Jennifer Ellis
Senior Marketing Manager: Diane McOscar
Print Buyer: Barbara Britton
Permissions Editor: Joohee Lee
Production: Bill Stryker
Text Designer: Doug Abbott
Art Editor: Bill Stryker
Photo Researcher: Bill Stryker and Megan Ryan

Copy Editor: Pat Lewis
Illustrator: Bill Stryker
Cover Designer: Doug Abbott
Cover Images: Man with flag © Dick Spahr, Liaison Agency; "Vote Aqui" © Bob Daemmrich, Corbis Sygma; "Let your vote be heard" © Bob Daemmrich, Corbis Sygma.
Text and Cover Printer: Von Hoffmann, Inc.
Compositor: Parkwood Composition Service

Library of Congress Cataloging-in-Publication Data
Schmidt, Steffen W.
    American government and politics today / Steffen W. Schmidt,
    Mack C. Shelley II, Barbara A. Bardes. 2001–2002 ed.
    Includes index.
ISBN: 0–534–57152–2
ISSN: 1079–0071
2001–2002 EDITION
    1. United States—Politics and government. I. Shelley, Mack C. 1950–   II. Bardes, Barbara A.   III. Title
JK274.S428   2000
320.973–dc20

Wadsworth/Thomson Learning
10 Davis Drive
Belmont, CA 94002-3098
USA

For more information about our products, contact us:
Thomson Learning Academic Resource Center
1-800-423-0563
http://www.wadsworth.com

International Headquarters
Thomson Learning
International Division
290 Harbor Drive, 2nd Floor
Stamford, CT 06902-7477
USA

UK/Europe/Middle East/South Africa
Thomson Learning
Berkshire House
168-173 High Holborn
London WC1V 7AA
United Kingdom

Asia
Thomson Learning
60 Albert Street, #15-01
Albert Complex
Singapore 189969

Canada
Nelson Thomson Learning
1120 Birchmount Road
Toronto, Ontario M1K 5G4
Canada

Contents in Brief

Part One
The American System 1

CHAPTER 1   Forces of Change in the Twenty-First Century 3

CHAPTER 2   The Constitution 31

CHAPTER 3   Federalism 83

Part Two
Civil Rights and Liberties 113

CHAPTER 4   Civil Liberties 115

CHAPTER 5   Civil Rights: Equal Protection 151

CHAPTER 6   Civil Rights: Beyond Equal Protection 187

Part Three
People and Politics 215

CHAPTER 7   Public Opinion and Political Socialization 217

CHAPTER 8   Interest Groups 247

CHAPTER 9   Political Parties 275

CHAPTER 10   Campaigns, Nominations, and Elections 307

CHAPTER 11   The Media and Cyberpolitics 347

Part Four
Political Institutions 373

CHAPTER 12   The Congress 375

CHAPTER 13   The Presidency 411

CHAPTER 14 The Bureaucracy 447

CHAPTER 15 The Judiciary 477

Part Five
Public Policy 509

CHAPTER 16 Domestic and Economic Policy 511

CHAPTER 17 Foreign and Defense Policy 543

Part Six
State and Local Politics 575

CHAPTER 18 State and Local Government 577

APPENDIX A The Declaration of Independence 607

APPENDIX B How to Read Case Citations and Find Court Decisions 609

APPENDIX C Presidents of the United States 610

APPENDIX D Federalist Papers No. 10, No. 51, and No. 78 613

APPENDIX E Justices of the U.S. Supreme Court since 1900 623

APPENDIX F Party Control of Congress since 1900 627

APPENDIX G Spanish Equivalents for Important Terms in American Government 629

Glossary 635

Index 645

Contents

part 1 The American System 1

CHAPTER 1 Forces of Change in the Twenty-First Century 3

WHAT IF...AMERICANS HAD TO PASS A TEST TO VOTE? 4

Political Change in the United States 5

What Is Politics? 6

The Need for Government and Power 7
Authority and Legitimacy 8
The Question of Power 9

Who Governs? 9
Sources of Political Power 9
Direct Democracy as a Model 10
The Dangers of Direct Democracy 10
Representative Democracy 11

Do We Have a Democracy? 13
Democracy for the Few 13
Democracy for Groups 14

Ideas and Politics: Political Culture 16
The Fundamental Values 17
The Stability of the Culture 18

The Changing Face of America 20
Ethnic Change 20
Other Trends 23

Ideas and Politics: Ideology 24

America's Politics: Issues for the Twenty-First Century 26

MAKING A DIFFERENCE: SEEING DEMOCRACY IN ACTION 27

Key Terms 27
Chapter Summary 28

Selected Print and Electronic Resources 28
LOGGING ON • USING THE INTERNET FOR POLITICAL ANALYSIS

ELECTIONS 2000
More Divided Government 6

E-MOCRACY
Connecting to the
Government 8

POLITICS AND ECONOMICS
The Digital Divide 15

MAKING WAVES
Political Information for Sale 18

CRITICAL PERSPECTIVE
What Do Americans See for the
Twenty-First Century? 19

WHICH SIDE ARE YOU ON?
Should the United States
Encourage the Immigration of
High-Tech Workers? 21

GLOBAL VIEW
Competing Visions of Power 25

CHAPTER **2** The Constitution 31

WHAT IF...CONSTITUTIONAL INTERPRETATION NEVER CHANGED? 32

Initial Colonizing Efforts 33
  Separatists, the *Mayflower,* and the Compact 34
  More Colonies, More Government 35

British Restrictions and Colonial Grievances 35

The Colonial Response: The Continental Congresses 36

Declaring Independence 37
  The Resolution of Independence 37
  July 4, 1776—The Declaration of Independence 37

The Rise of Republicanism 39

The Articles of Confederation:
  Our First Form of Government 39
  Accomplishments under the Articles 40
  Weaknesses of the Articles 40
  Shays's Rebellion and the Need for Revision of the Articles 41

Drafting the Constitution 41
  Who Were the Delegates? 42
  The Working Environment 42
  Factions among the Delegates 42
  Politicking and Compromises 43
  Working toward Final Agreement 46

AN ETHICAL ISSUE
Why Didn't the Founders Ban
Slavery? 46

CRITICAL PERSPECTIVE
Does It Matter What the
Founders Thought? 49

POLITICS AND ECONOMICS
The Motives of the Framers 52

E-MOCRACY
The Internet and Free Speech 53

MAKING WAVES
Shirley Breeze and the Missouri
Women's Network: Resurrecting
the ERA 57

WHICH SIDE ARE YOU ON?
Should the Supreme Court Have
the Final Say on All
Constitutional Questions? 59

The Final Document 48

The Difficult Road to Ratification 50
  The Federalists Push for Ratification 50
  The March to the Finish 51

The Bill of Rights 52

Altering the Constitution: The Formal Amendment Process 54
  Many Amendments Proposed, Few Accepted 55
  Limits on Ratification 55
  The National Convention Provision 56

Informal Methods of Constitutional Change 57
  Congressional Legislation 57
  Presidential Actions 58
  Judicial Review 58
  Interpretation, Custom, and Usage 59

The Constitution: Issues for the Twenty-First Century 60

MAKING A DIFFERENCE:
HOW CAN YOU AFFECT THE U.S. CONSTITUTION? 61

Key Terms 62
Chapter Summary 62

Selected Print and Electronic Resources 62
Logging On • Using the Internet for Political Analysis

APPENDIX TO CHAPTER 2:
THE CONSTITUTION OF THE UNITED STATES 64

CHAPTER 3 Federalism 83

WHAT IF...THE STATES CONTROLLED THE INTERNET? 84

Three Systems of Government 85
A Unitary System 85
A Confederal System 87
A Federal System 87

Why Federalism? 88
A Practical Solution 88
Other Arguments for Federalism 88
Arguments against Federalism 90

The Constitutional Basis for American Federalism 90
Powers of the National Government 90
Powers of the State Governments 92
Concurrent Powers 92
Prohibited Powers 93
The Supremacy Clause 93
Vertical Checks and Balances 93
Horizontal Federalism 95

Defining Constitutional Powers—The Early Years 96
McCulloch v. Maryland (1819) 96
Gibbons v. Ogden (1824) 97

States' Rights and the Resort to Civil War 98
The Shift Back to States' Rights 98
War and the Growth of the National Government 99

The Continuing Dispute over the Division of Power 100
Dual Federalism 100
Cooperative Federalism 100
The New Federalism 104
The Supreme Court and the New Federalism 107

Federalism: Issues for the Twenty-First Century 108

MAKING A DIFFERENCE: WRITING LETTERS TO THE EDITOR 109

Key Terms 110
Chapter Summary 110

Selected Print and Electronic Resources 111
Logging On • Using the Internet for Political Analysis

GLOBAL VIEW
Are Governments Getting
Smaller, Bigger or Both? 86

E-MOCRACY
"Civil Society" in a
Wired World 89

CRITICAL PERSPECTIVE
Should States Make
Foreign Policy? 94

AN ETHICAL ISSUE
Should the Confederate Flag
Be Flown? 99

WHICH SIDE ARE YOU ON?
Should the States Play a Greater
Role in Deciding Who Receives
Donor Organs? 101

ELECTIONS 2000
Trends in Federalism 106

MAKING WAVES
The Shovel Brigade 106

part 2
**Civil Rights
and Liberties 113**

CHAPTER **4** Civil Liberties   115

WHAT IF...YOUR PERSONAL RECORDS WERE PUBLIC? 116

Civil Liberties and the Fear of Government 117

Extending the Bill of Rights to State Governments 117

Freedom of Religion 118
  The Separation of Church and State 119
  The Free Exercise Clause 125

Freedom of Expression 126
  Permitted Restrictions on Expression 126
  The Protection of Symbolic Speech 128
  The Protection of Commercial Speech 128
  Unprotected Speech: Obscenity 128
  Unprotected Speech: Slander 129
  Fighting Words and Hecklers' Veto 130
  Campus Speech Codes 130
  Hate Speech on the Internet 131

Freedom of the Press 132
  Defamation in Writing 132
  A Free Press versus a Fair Trial: Gag Orders 132
  Films, Radio, and TV 133

The Right to Assemble and to
Petition the Government 134

More Liberties under Scrutiny: Matters of Privacy 135
  Privacy Rights in an Information Age 135
  Privacy Rights and Abortion 136
  Privacy Rights and the "Right to Die" 138

The Great Balancing Act:
The Rights of the Accused versus the Rights of Society 140
  Rights of the Accused 140
  Extending the Rights of the Accused 141
  The Exclusionary Rule 143
  The Death Penalty 144

Civil Liberties: Issues for the Twenty-First Century 145

MAKING A DIFFERENCE:
YOUR CIVIL LIBERTIES: SEARCHES AND SEIZURES 146
Key Terms 147
Chapter Summary 147

Selected Print and Electronic Resources 148
  LOGGING ON • USING THE INTERNET FOR POLITICAL ANALYSIS

E-MOCRACY
  Technology in the Schools and
  the Establishment Clause 120

WHICH SIDE ARE YOU ON?
  Should the Ten Commandments
  Be Displayed in Public
  Schools? 123

MAKING WAVES
  Students Lead Football Fans in
  Prayer–Despite Court
  Ruling 124

AN ETHICAL ISSUE
  Should Students Have to
  Subsidize Opposing Views? 131

CRITICAL PERSPECTIVE
  Can Privacy Rights Survive in
  Cyberspace? 138

CHAPTER 5 Civil Rights: Equal Protection 151

WHAT IF...MEDICAL CARE WAS A CIVIL RIGHT? 152

African Americans and the Consequences of Slavery in the United States 153
Ending Constitutional Servitude 154
The Civil Rights Acts of 1865 to 1875 155
The Ineffectiveness of the Civil Rights Laws 157
The End of the Separate-but-Equal Doctrine 158
Reactions to School Integration 160
An Integrationist Attempt at a Cure: Busing 160

The Civil Rights Movement 162
King's Philosophy of Nonviolence 162
Another Approach—Black Power 164

Modern Civil Rights Legislation 164
The Civil Rights Act of 1964 164
The Voting Rights Act of 1965 165
The Civil Rights Act of 1968 and Other Housing-Reform Legislation 166
Increased Political Participation by African Americans 166
Political Participation by Other Minorities 167
Lingering Social and Economic Disparities 167

Immigration and the Civil Rights Agenda 168
The Continued Influx of Immigrants 169
The Problem of Racial Classifications 170

Women's Struggle for Equal Rights 172
Early Women's Political Movements 173
The Modern Women's Movement 174
Women in Politics Today 176

Gender-Based Discrimination in the Workplace 178
Title VII of the Civil Rights Act of 1964 178
Sexual Harassment 179
Wage Discrimination 180

Civil Rights—Equal Protection: Issues for the Twenty-First Century 182

MAKING A DIFFERENCE: CITIZENSHIP AND IMMIGRANT RIGHTS 183

Key Terms 183
Chapter Summary 184

Selected Print and Electronic Resources 185
LOGGING ON • USING THE INTERNET FOR POLITICAL ANALYSIS

CHAPTER 6 Civil Rights: Beyond Equal Protection 187

WHAT IF...ONLY THE TOP 10 PERCENT OF STUDENTS COULD GO TO A PUBLIC COLLEGE? 188

Affirmative Action 189
The *Bakke* Case 190
Further Limitations on Affirmative Action 190

E-MOCRACY
Colorblind on the Web 154

AN ETHICAL ISSUE
Reparations for African Americans? 156

MAKING WAVES
A New Generation of Civil Rights Leaders 168

CRITICAL PERSPECTIVE
Should the Immigration Door Be Shut? 170

WHICH SIDE ARE YOU ON?
Should Racial Categories Be Dropped from the Census? 172

ELECTIONS 2000
Political Leadership by Women 177

GLOBAL VIEW
The Struggle for Women's Rights around the World 178

POLITICS AND ECONOMICS
Debating the Wage Gap 181

State Ballot Initiatives 191
Will Affirmative Action Survive? 191

Bilingual Education 192

Early Language Policies 192
Accommodating Diversity with Bilingual Education 194
The Current Controversy over Bilingual Education 194

Special Protection for Older Americans 194

Age Discrimination in Employment 196
Age, Political Participation, and Public Benefits 197

Securing Rights for Persons with Disabilities 198

The Americans with Disabilities Act of 1990 198
Interpreting and Applying the ADA 200

The Rights and Status of Gay Males and Lesbians 201

State and Local Laws against Gays 201
The Gay Community and Politics 203
Gay Men and Lesbians in the Military 203
Same-Sex Marriages 204
Child Custody and Adoption 206

The Rights and Status of Juveniles 206

Voting Rights and the Young 206
The Rights of Children in Civil and Criminal Proceedings 207

Civil Rights—Beyond Equal Protection: Issues for the Twenty-First Century 210

MAKING A DIFFERENCE: DEALING WITH DISCRIMINATION 211

Key Terms 211
Chapter Summary 211

Selected Print and Electronic Resources 212

Logging On • Using the Internet for Political Analysis

part 3
People and Politics 215

CHAPTER **7** Public Opinion and Political Socialization 217

WHAT IF...COURTS USED PUBLIC OPINION POLLS TO DECIDE CASES? 218

How Powerful Is Public Opinion? 219
Defining Public Opinion 219

Consensus and Division 220
The Qualities of Public Opinion 221

Measuring Public Opinion: Polling Techniques 224

The History of Opinion Polls 224
Sampling Techniques 226

CRITICAL PERSPECTIVE
What Has Affirmative Action Really Accomplished? 192

WHICH SIDE ARE YOU ON?
Should Bilingual Education Be Abandoned? 195

E-MOCRACY
Does the ADA Apply to the Internet? 199

MAKING WAVES
James Dale versus the Boy Scouts 202

AN ETHICAL ISSUE
Should Gay Couples Be Allowed to Marry? 205

GLOBAL VIEW
The Death Penalty for Juveniles 209

E-MOCRACY
What Is a Poll? 225

MAKING WAVES
Going Online to Poll 227

CRITICAL PERSPECTIVE
Is Technology Destroying Opinion Polling? 229

Problems with Polls 227

Political Socialization 232
The Importance of the Family 232
Educational Influence on Political Opinion 233
Peers and Peer Group Influence 233
Religious Influence 234
The Influence of Economic Status and Occupation 234
The Influence of Political Events 234
Opinion Leaders' Influence 235
Media Influence 235
The Influence of Demographic Traits 236
The Gender Gap 237

Political Culture and Public Opinion 237

Public Opinion about Government 238

The Spectrum of Political Beliefs 240

Public Opinion and the Political Process 242

Public Opinion: Issues for the Twenty-First Century 243

**MAKING A DIFFERENCE: BE A
CRITICAL CONSUMER OF OPINION POLLS 244**

Key Terms 245
Chapter Summary 245

Selected Print and Electronic Resources 245
LOGGING ON • USING THE INTERNET FOR POLITICAL ANALYSIS

WHICH SIDE ARE YOU ON?
Should Polling Be
Regulated? 231

ELECTIONS 2000
The Accuracy of the 2000
Polls 231

AN ETHICAL ISSUE
Polls That Mislead 232

POLITICS AND ECONOMICS
The Public and Campaign-
Finance Reform 242

CHAPTER 8 Interest Groups 247

WHAT IF...EVERY LOBBYING CONTACT HAD TO BE REPORTED? 248

The Role of Interest Groups 250
A Nation of Joiners? 250

The Benefits of Interest Groups 251
Solidary Incentives 251
Material Incentives 251
Purposive Incentives 252

Interest Groups and Social Movements 252

Types of Interest Groups 253
Economic Interest Groups 253
Environmental Groups 257
Public-Interest Groups 258
Special Interest Groups 259
Foreign Governments 260

Interest Group Strategies 260
Direct Techniques 261
Indirect Techniques 264

Regulating Lobbyists 268
The Results of the 1946 Act 268
The Reforms of 1995 268

CRITICAL PERSPECTIVE
How Powerful Is Silicon
Valley? 256

WHICH SIDE ARE YOU ON?
Should Foreign Nations Be
Allowed to Lobby the U.S.
Government? 261

MAKING WAVES
A New Kind of Lobbyist 262

ELECTIONS 2000
Interest Groups: The Candidates
of Choice 263

POLITICS AND ECONOMICS
What Does Soft Money
Buy? 266

E-MOCRACY
Interests and the Internet 267

AN ETHICAL ISSUE
Lobbyists as Friends and
Relatives 271

Interest Groups and Representative Democracy 269

Interest Groups: Issues for the Twenty-First Century 270

MAKING A DIFFERENCE: THE GUN CONTROL ISSUE 272

Key Terms 272
Chapter Summary 272

Selected Print and Electronic Resources 273
LOGGING ON • USING THE INTERNET FOR POLITICAL ANALYSIS

CHAPTER 9 Political Parties 275

WHAT IF...EVERYONE HAD TO JOIN A POLITICAL PARTY? 276

What Is a Political Party? 277

Functions of Political Parties in the United States 277

A Short History of Political Parties in the United States 278
The Formative Years: Federalists and Anti-Federalists 278
The Era of Personal Politics 280
National Two-Party Rule: Democrats and Whigs 280
The Post–Civil War Period 280
The Progressive Movement 280
The Modern Era: From the New Deal to the Present 281

E-MOCRACY
Winning Supporters on the
Internet 283

The Three Faces of a Party 282

Party Organization 283
The National Party Organization 284
The State Party Organization 287
Local Party Machinery: The Grassroots 288

POLITICS AND ECONOMICS
Soft Money Floods the Political
Parties 287

The Party and Its Members 289
Differences between the Parties 289

AN ETHICAL ISSUE
Tammany Hall : The
Quintessential Local Political
Machine 288

The Party-in-Government 291

Why Do We Have a Two-Party System? 291
The Historical Foundations of the Two-Party System 292
Self-Perpetuation of the Two-Party System 294
The Political Culture of the United States 294
The Winner-Take-All Electoral System 295
State and Federal Laws Favoring the Two Parties 296

ELECTIONS 2000
Partisan Trends in the 2000
Elections 292

WHICH SIDE ARE YOU ON?
Helping New Parties 297

The Role of Minor Parties in U.S. Political History 296
Historically Important Minor Parties 296
Splinter Minor Parties 298
Other Minor Parties 298
The Impact of Minor Parties 299
The Uncertain Future of Party Identification 300

MAKING WAVES
A New Type of Governor 298

CRITICAL PERSPECTIVE
Is the Time Right for a Third
Party? 302

Political Parties: Issues for the Twenty-First Century 301

MAKING A DIFFERENCE: ELECTING CONVENTION DELEGATES 303

Key Terms 303
Chapter Summary 303

Selected Print and Electronic Resources 304
LOGGING ON • USING THE INTERNET FOR POLITICAL ANALYSIS

CHAPTER 10 Campaigns, Nominations, and Elections 307

WHAT IF...CANDIDATES RECEIVED FREE TELEVISION TIME? 308

The People Who Run for Office 309
Why They Run 310
Who Is Eligible? 311

The Modern Campaign Machine 312
The Changing Campaign 313
The Professional Campaign 314

The Strategy of Winning 315
Candidate Visibility and Appeal 315
The Use of Opinion Polls and Focus Groups 315

Financing the Campaign 316
Regulating Campaign Financing 316
The Federal Election Campaign Act 317
Campaign Financing beyond the Limits 319

Running for President: The Longest Campaign 321
Reforming the Primaries 321
Types of Primaries 322
The Primary as a Springboard to the White House 323
On to the National Convention 324

The Electoral College 325
The Choice of Electors 325
The Electors' Commitment 326
Criticisms of the Electoral College 327
Proposed Reforms 327

How Are Elections Conducted? 328
Office-Block and Party-Column Ballots 328
Voting by Mail 328
Vote Fraud 329

Voting in National, State, and Local Elections 330
The Effect of Low Voter Turnout 331
Factors Influencing Who Votes 332
Why People Do Not Vote 332

Legal Restrictions on Voting 333
Historical Restrictions 333
Current Eligibility and Registration Requirements 335

How Do Voters Decide? 337
Socioeconomic and Demographic Factors 337
Psychological Factors 340

Campaigns, Candidates, and Elections: Issues for the Twenty-First Century 343

MAKING A DIFFERENCE: REGISTERING AND VOTING 344

AN ETHICAL ISSUE
Opposition Research or Dirty Tricks? 314

POLITICS AND ECONOMICS
Raising Money and Making Money on the Internet 317

E-MOCRACY
Voting on the Web is Coming 329

CRITICAL PERSPECTIVE
The Vanishing Voter 334

MAKING WAVES
Getting Out the Vote in California 336

WHICH SIDE ARE YOU ON?
Choosing a Candidate on the Web 342

ELECTIONS 2000
Why Voters Voted as They Did in 2000 343

Key Terms 344
Chapter Summary 345

Selected Print and Electronic Resources 345
Logging On • Using the Internet for Political Analysis

CHAPTER **11** The Media and Cyberpolitics 347

WHAT IF...THE INTERNET REPLACED BROADCAST NEWS? 348

The Media's Functions 349
Entertainment 349
Reporting the News 350
Identifying Public Problems 350
Socializing New Generations 351
Providing a Political Forum 351
Making Profits 352

History of the Media in the United States 352
The Rise of the Political Press 352
The Development of Mass-Readership Newspapers 353
The Popular Press and Yellow Journalism 354
The Age of the Electromagnetic Signal 354
The Revolution in the Electronic Media 356
Talk-Show Politics 356

The Primacy of Television 358

The Media and Political Campaigns 359
Advertising 359
Management of News Coverage 361
Going for the Knockout Punch—Presidential Debates 361
The Media's Impact on the Voters 362

The Media and the Government 363
The Media and the Presidency 363
Setting the Public Agenda 364

Government Regulation of the Media 364
Controlling Ownership of the Media 365
Government Control of Content 366

The Public's Right to Media Access 367

Bias in the Media 367

The Media and Politics: Issues for the Twenty-First Century 369

MAKING A DIFFERENCE: BEING A CRITICAL CONSUMER OF THE NEWS 370

Key Terms 370
Chapter Summary 370

Selected Print and Electronic Resources 371
Logging On • Using the Internet for Political Analysis

GLOBAL VIEW
Media Issues around the World 350

CRITICAL PERSPECTIVE
Is There a Media Monopoly? 353

MAKING WAVES
Pioneering New Internet Media for New Groups 357

E-MOCRACY
The Media and the Internet 358

ELECTIONS 2000
The Role of the Media in the 2000 Elections 362

POLITICS AND ECONOMICS
Should the Government Buy Antidrug Messages? 365

AN ETHICAL ISSUE
Freedom of the Press and the Exit Polls 366

WHICH SIDE ARE YOU ON?
Is the News Biased? 368

part 4
Political Institutions 373

CHAPTER 12   The Congress   375

WHAT IF...MEMBERS OF CONGRESS WERE REQUIRED TO SPEND SIX MONTHS EACH YEAR IN THEIR DISTRICTS? 376

Why Was Congress Created? 377

The Powers of Congress 378
Enumerated Powers 378
The Necessary and Proper Clause 379

The Functions of Congress 379
The Lawmaking Function 379
Service to Constituents 380
The Representation Function 380
The Oversight Function 381
The Public-Education Function 381
The Conflict-Resolution Function 381

House–Senate Differences 382
Size and Rules 382
Debate and Filibustering 383
Prestige 383

Congresspersons and the Citizenry: A Comparison 384

Congressional Elections 384
Candidates for Congressional Elections 384
The Power of Incumbency 386
The Shakeup in the 1994 Elections 387

Congressional Reapportionment 389
Gerrymandering 390
"Minority-Majority" Districts 390

Pay, Perks, and Privileges 391
Special Benefits 392
Permanent Professional Staffs 393
Privileges and Immunities under the Law 394

The Committee Structure 394
The Power of Committees 394
Types of Congressional Committees 395
The Selection of Committee Members 397

The Formal Leadership 397
Leadership in the House 397
Leadership in the Senate 399

E-MOCRACY
Congress Goes Online 382

ELECTIONS 2000
Congressional Characteristics after the 2000 Elections 384

MAKING WAVES
Starting Young 385

WHICH SIDE ARE YOU ON?
Should We Have Congressional Term Limits? 388

ELECTIONS 2000
Party Control of Congress after the 2000 Elections 389

CRITICAL PERSPECTIVE
Gridlock or Constitutional Balance? 392

POLITICS AND ECONOMICS
Bringing Home the Bacon 404

AN ETHICAL ISSUE
Congress Examines Its Own for
Improprieties 406

How Members of Congress Decide 400

How a Bill Becomes Law 401

How Much Will the Government Spend? 401
Preparing the Budget 403
Congress Faces the Budget 405

The Question of Congressional Ethics 406

The Congress: Issues for the Twenty-First Century 406

**MAKING A DIFFERENCE: HOW TO
BE AN INTERN IN WASHINGTON, D.C. 407**

Key Terms 408
Chapter Summary 408

Selected Print and Electronic Resources 409
LOGGING ON • USING THE INTERNET FOR POLITICAL ANALYSIS

CHAPTER 13 The Presidency 411

WHAT IF...WE COULD RECALL THE PRESIDENT? 412

Who Can Become President? 413

The Process of Becoming President 414

The Many Roles of the President 414
Chief of State 415
Chief Executive 415
Commander in Chief 417
Chief Diplomat 419
Chief Legislator 421
Other Presidential Powers 426

E-MOCRACY
The President on the Web 423

POLITICS AND ECONOMICS
The President as Chief
Fund-Raiser 427

CRITICAL PERSPECTIVE
Is the Presidency Becoming Too
Powerful? 428

AN ETHICAL ISSUE
Do We Want Character in Our
President? 431

WHICH SIDE ARE YOU ON?
Should the President Be Sued
While in Office? 436

MAKING WAVES
The White House Fellows 438

The President as Party Chief and Superpolitician 427
The President as Chief of Party 427
Constituencies and Public Approval 428

Special Uses of Presidential Power 432
Emergency Powers 432
Executive Orders 432
Executive Privilege 433
Impoundment of Funds 433

Abuses of Executive Power and Impeachment 434
The Impeachment of Bill Clinton 435

The Executive Organization 436
The Cabinet 437
The Executive Office of the President 437

The Vice Presidency 440
The Vice President's Job 440
Presidential Succession 441
The Twenty-fifth Amendment 442
When the Vice Presidency Becomes Vacant 442

The Presidency: Issues for the Twenty-First Century 443

MAKING A DIFFERENCE: COMMUNICATING WITH THE WHITE HOUSE 444

Key Terms 444
Chapter Summary 445

Selected Print and Electronic Resources 445
LOGGING ON • USING THE INTERNET FOR POLITICAL ANALYSIS

CHAPTER 14   The Bureaucracy 447

WHAT IF...WE HAD A "VIRTUAL" BUREAUCRACY? 448

The Nature of Bureaucracy 449
Public and Private Bureaucracies 449
Bureaucracies Compared 450

Theories of Bureaucracy 451
The Weberian Model 451
The Acquisitive Model 452
The Monopolistic Model 452
The Garbage Can Model 452

The Size of the Bureaucracy 452

The Organization of the Federal Bureaucracy 453
Cabinet Departments 455
Independent Executive Agencies 455
Independent Regulatory Agencies 455
The Purpose and Nature of Regulatory Agencies 455
Government Corporations 458

Staffing the Bureaucracy 459
Political Appointees 459
History of the Federal Civil Service 461

Modern Attempts at Bureaucratic Reform 463
Sunshine Laws 463
Sunset Laws 464
Contracting Out 464
Incentives for Efficiency and Productivity 464
Helping Out the Whistleblowers 465

Bureaucrats as Politicians and Policymakers 466
The Rulemaking Environment 468
Negotiated Rulemaking 469
Bureaucrats Are Policymakers 469

Congressional Control of the Bureaucracy 472
Authorizing Funds 472
Appropriating Funds 472
Congressional Investigations, Hearings, and Reviews 473

The Bureaucracy: Issues for the Twenty-First Century 473

MAKING A DIFFERENCE: WHAT
THE GOVERNMENT KNOWS ABOUT YOU 474

Key Terms 474
Chapter Summary 475

Selected Print and Electronic Resources 475
LOGGING ON • USING THE INTERNET FOR POLITICAL ANALYSIS

GLOBAL VIEW
No More Bribes
to Bureaucrats 450

E-MOCRACY
Government Agencies Tackle
Internet Fraud 458

POLITICS AND ECONOMICS
Rewards for Whistleblowers 466

WHICH SIDE ARE YOU ON?
Do Minorities Really Benefit
from "Environmental
Justice"? 467

MAKING WAVES
Julia "Butterfly" Hill, Tree
Dweller 468

CRITICAL PERSPECTIVE
Has the Bureaucracy Exceeded
Its Lawmaking Mandate? 470

CHAPTER 15 The Judiciary 477

WHAT IF...SUPREME COURT JUSTICES HAD TO CAMPAIGN? 478

The Common Law Tradition 479

Sources of American Law 480
Constitutions 480
Statutes and Administrative Regulations 480
Case Law 480

The Federal Court System 480
Basic Judicial Requirements 481
Types of Federal Courts 481
Parties and Procedures 483

The Supreme Court at Work 485
Which Cases Reach the Supreme Court? 486
Deciding Cases 488
Decisions and Opinions 489

The Selection of Federal Judges 489
Nominating Judicial Candidates 490
Partisanship and Judicial Appointments 492
The Senate's Role 492

The Policymaking Function of the Courts 493
Judicial Review 493
Judicial Activism and Judicial Restraint 495
Ideology and the Rehnquist Court 496
Is the Federal Judiciary Too Powerful? 500

What Checks Our Courts? 500
Executive Checks 500
Legislative Checks 501
Public Opinion 502
Judicial Traditions and Doctrines 503

The Judiciary: Issues for the Twenty-First Century 504

MAKING A DIFFERENCE: CHANGING THE LEGAL SYSTEM 505

Key Terms 505
Chapter Summary 506

Selected Print and Electronic Resources 506
LOGGING ON • USING THE INTERNET FOR POLITICAL ANALYSIS

MAKING WAVES
The Non-English Speaking
Juror 485

E-MOCRACY
Toward a Virtual Classroom 486

AN ETHICAL ISSUE
Should the Supreme Court Hire
More Minority Clerks? 488

ELECTIONS 2000
The Supreme Court and the
2000 Elections 492

CRITICAL PERSPECTIVE
The Politicization of the Judicial
Appointment Process 494

GLOBAL VIEW
Judicial Review 496

WHICH SIDE ARE YOU ON?
Is Judicial Activism Getting Out
of Hand? 497

part 5 Public Policy 509

CHAPTER 16 Domestic and Economic Policy 511

WHAT IF...THERE WERE NO SOCIAL SECURITY? 512

The Policymaking Process 513
Steps in the Policymaking Process 513
Models of the Policymaking Process 515

Poverty and Welfare 516
The Low-Income Population 516
Major Government-Assistance Programs 517
Children Living in Poverty 519
Homelessness—Still A Problem 520

Crime in the Twenty-First Century 521
Crime in American History 521
Crimes Committed by Juveniles 522

Environmental Policy 523
The Government's Response to Air and Water Pollution 523

The Politics of Economic Decision Making 525
The Politics of Taxes and Subsidies 525
Social Security: How Long Will It Last? 528
The Politics of Fiscal and Monetary Policy 530

The Public Debt and the Disappearing Deficit 533
Is the Public Debt a Burden? 534
The Problem of "Crowding Out" 534

Freer World Trade and the World Trade Organization 534
America's Current Competitive Position 535
Opening Up World Trade—The WTO 536

Domestic and Economic Policy: Issues for the Twenty-First Century 537

MAKING A DIFFERENCE: WORKING FOR A CLEANER ENVIRONMENT 539

Key Terms 539
Chapter Summary 540

Selected Print and Electronic Resources 541
LOGGING ON • USING THE INTERNET FOR POLITICAL ANALYSIS

GLOBAL VIEW
Incarceration Worldwide 522

CRITICAL PERSPECTIVE
Does E-Commerce Threaten National Sovereignty? 526

E-MOCRACY
Monetary Policy in the Age of Cybermoney 531

POLITICS AND ECONOMICS
Dealing with the Budget Surplus 535

WHICH SIDE ARE YOU ON?
Granting China Permanent Normal Trade Relations 537

CHAPTER 17 Foreign and Defense Policy 543

WHAT IF...THE UNITED STATES DEFENDED ONLY ITSELF? 544

What Is Foreign Policy? 545
National Security Policy 545
Diplomacy 546

Morality versus Reality in Foreign Policy 546

Who Makes Foreign Policy? 547
Constitutional Powers of the President 547
Informal Techniques of Presidential Leadership 548
Other Sources of Foreign Policymaking 548

Limiting the President's Power 552

Domestic Sources of Foreign Policy 553
Elite and Mass Opinion 553
The Military-Industrial Complex 553

POLITICS AND ECONOMICS
Strange Bedfellows 549

E-MOCRACY
Attacking Government Computer Systems 552

CRITICAL PERSPECTIVE
Is the Nuclear Threat
Increasing? 562

WHICH SIDE ARE YOU ON?
Should the United States Impose
Sanctions? 564

AN ETHICAL ISSUE
The Demands of Ethnic
Nationalism 569

GLOBAL VIEW
Is AIDS a National Security
Threat? 571

The Major Foreign Policy Themes 554
  The Formative Years: Avoiding Entanglements 554
  The Era of Internationalism 555
  Superpower Relations 557

Challenges in World Politics 560
  The Dissolution of the Soviet Union 560
  Nuclear Proliferation 561
  Terrorism 561
  The New Power: China 563
  The Global Economy 565
  Regional Conflicts 566

Foreign and Defense Policy: Issues for the Twenty-First Century 570

MAKING A DIFFERENCE: WORKING FOR HUMAN RIGHTS 572

Key Terms 572
Chapter Summary 572

Selected Print and Electronic Resources 573
  LOGGING ON • USING THE INTERNET FOR POLITICAL ANALYSIS

part 6
State and
Local Politics 575

CHAPTER 18 State and
Local Government 577

WHAT IF...ALL STATES ALLOWED SCHOOL CHOICE? 578

E-MOCRACY
EZ Government on the
Web 579

GLOBAL VIEW
Dealing with Drugs at Home and
Abroad 587

WHICH SIDE ARE YOU ON?
Will of the People or Dollar
Democracy? 588

CRITICAL PERSPECTIVE
Can States Control Betting on
the Internet? 590

The U.S. Constitution and the State Governments 580

State Constitutions 581
  Why Are State Constitutions So Long? 581
  The Constitutional Convention and the Constitutional Initiative 581

The State Executive Branch 582
  A Weak Executive 582
  Reforming the System 582
  The Governor's Veto Power 583

The State Legislature 585
  Legislative Apportionment 585
  Direct Democracy: The Initiative, Referendum, and Recall 586

The State Judiciary 588
  Trial Courts 588
  Appellate Courts 589
  Judicial Elections and Appointments 591

How Local Government Operates 592

The Legal Existence of Local Government 592
Local Governmental Units 593
Consolidation of Governments 595
How Municipalities Are Governed 596
Machine versus Reform in City Politics 598
Governing Metropolitan Areas 599

Paying for State and Local Government 600

State and Local Government Expenditures 600
State and Local Government Revenues 601
Fiscal Policy Lessons 603

State and Local Government: Issues for the Twenty-First Century 603

MAKING A DIFFERENCE: LEARNING ABOUT LOCAL POLITICS AND GOVERNMENT IN YOUR COMMUNITY 604

Key Terms 604
Chapter Summary 605

Selected Print and Electronic Resources 605

LOGGING ON • USING THE INTERNET FOR POLITICAL ANALYSIS

AN ETHICAL ISSUE
The Defiant Ones 596

MAKING WAVES
Taking on Tests 601

APPENDIX A The Declaration of Independence 607

APPENDIX B How to Read Case Citations and Find Court Decisions 609

APPENDIX C Presidents of the United States 610

APPENDIX D Federalist Papers No. 10, No. 51, and No. 78 613

APPENDIX E Justices of the U.S. Supreme Court since 1900 623

APPENDIX F Party Control of Congress since 1900 627

APPENDIX G Spanish Equivalents for Important Terms in American Government 629

Glossary 635

Index 645

Features of Special Interest

- What Do Americans See for the Twenty-First Century? 19
- Does It Matter What the Founders Thought? 49
- Should States Make Foreign Policy? 94
- Can Privacy Rights Survive in Cyberspace? 138
- Should the Immigration Door Be Shut? 170
- What Has Affirmative Action Really Accomplished? 192
- Is Technology Destroying Opinion Polling? 229
- How Powerful Is Silicon Valley? 256
- Is the Time Right for a Third Party? 302
- The Vanishing Voter 334
- Is There a Media Monopoly? 353
- Gridlock or Constitutional Balance? 392
- Is the Presidency Becoming Too Powerful? 428
- Is the Federal Government Becoming Top-Heavy? 460
- Has the Bureaucracy Exceeded Its Lawmaking Mandate? 470
- The Politicization of the Judicial Appointment Process 494
- Does E-Commerce Threaten National Sovereignty? 526
- The Silent Weapons—Chemical and Biological Warfare 596
- Is the Nuclear Threat Increasing? 562
- Can States Control Betting on the Internet? 590

- Connecting to the Government 8
- The Internet and Free Speech 53
- "Civil Society" in a Wired World 89
- Technology in the Schools and the Establishment Clause 120
- Colorblind on the Web 154
- Does the ADA Apply to the Internet? 199
- What Is a Poll? 225
- Interests and the Internet 267
- Winning Supporters on the Internet 283
- Voting on the Web Is Coming 329
- The Media and the Internet 358
- Congress Goes Online 382
- The President on the Web 423
- Government Agencies Tackle Internet Fraud 458
- Toward a Virtual Courtroom 486
- Monetary Policy in the Age of Cybermoney 531
- Attacking Government Computer Systems 552
- EZ Government on the Web 579

- The Digital Divide 15
- The Motives of the Framers 52
- Debating the Wage Gap 181
- The Public and Campaign-Finance Reform 242
- What Does Soft Money Buy? 266
- Soft Money Floods the Political Parties 287
- Raising Money and Making Money on the Internet 317
- Should the Government Buy Antidrug Messages? 365
- Bringing Home the Bacon 404
- The President as Chief Fund-Raiser 427
- Rewards for Whistleblowers 466
- Dealing with the Budget Surplus 535
- Strange Bedfellows 549

- Political Information for Sale 18
- Shirley Breeze and the Missouri Women's Network: Resurrecting the ERA 57
- The Shovel Brigade 106
- Students Lead Football Fans in Prayer—Despite Court Ruling 124
- A New Generation of Civil Rights Leaders 168
- James Dale versus the Boy Scouts 202
- Going Online to Poll 227
- A New Kind of Lobbyist 262
- A New Type of Governor 298
- Getting Out the Vote in California 336
- Pioneering New Internet Media for New Groups 357
- Starting Young 385
- The White House Fellows 438
- Julia "Butterfly" Hill, Tree Dweller 468
- The Non-English-Speaking Juror 485
- Taking on Tests 601

MORE . . .

- Should the United States Encourage the Immigration of High-Tech Workers? 21
- Should the Supreme Court Have the Final Say on All Constitutional Questions? 59
- Should the States Play a Greater Role in Deciding Who Receives Donor Organs? 101
- Should the Ten Commandments Be Displayed in Public Schools? 123
- Should Racial Categories Be Dropped from the Census? 172
- Should Bilingual Education Be Abandoned? 195
- Should Polling Be Regulated? 231
- Should Foreign Nations Be Allowed to Lobby the U.S. Government? 261
- Helping New Parties 297
- Choosing a Candidate on the Web 342
- Is the News Biased? 368
- Should We Have Congressional Term Limits? 388
- Should the President Be Sued While in Office? 436
- Do Minorities Really Benefit from "Environmental Justice"? 467
- Is Judicial Activism Getting Out of Hand? 497
- Granting China Permanent Normal Trade Relations 537
- Should the United States Impose Sanctions? 564
- Will of the People or Dollar Democracy? 588

- Why Didn't the Founders Ban Slavery? 46
- Should the Confederate Flag Be Flown? 99
- Should Students Have to Subsidize Opposing Views? 131
- Reparations for African Americans? 156
- Should Gay Couples Be Allowed to Marry? 205
- Polls That Mislead 232
- Lobbyists as Friends and Relatives 271
- Tammany Hall : The Quintessential Local Political Machine 288
- Opposition Research or Dirty Tricks? 314
- Freedom of the Press and the Exit Polls 366
- Congress Examines Its Own for Improprieties 406
- Do We Want Character in Our President? 431
- Should the Supreme Court Hire More Minority Clerks? 488
- The Demands of Ethnic Nationalism 569
- The Defiant Ones 596

- More Divided Government 6
- Trends in Federalism 106
- Political Leadership by Women 177
- The Accuracy of the 2000 Polls 231
- Interest Groups: The Candidates of Choice 263
- Partisan Trends in the 2000 Elections 292
- Why Voters Voted as They Did in 2000 343
- The Role of the Media in the 2000 Elections 362
- Congressional Characteristics after the 2000 Elections 384
- Party Control of Congress after the 2000 Elections 389
- The Supreme Court and the 2000 Elections 492

- Competing Visions of Power 25
- Are Governments Getting Smaller, Bigger or Both? 86
- The Struggle for Women's Rights around the World 178
- The Death Penalty for Juveniles 209
- Media Issues around the World 350
- No More Bribes to Bureaucrats 450
- Judicial Review 496
- Incarceration Worldwide 522
- Is AIDS a National Security Threat? 571
- Dealing with Drugs at Home and Abroad 587

Preface

On January 20, 2001, when George W. Bush was sworn in as the forty-third president of the United States, he became the second president in this nation's history to ascend to that office without having won the most popular votes. Indeed, for thirty-five days following the elections, it was not clear whether Bush or his opponent, Al Gore, had won the most popular votes in Florida—and thus the election. Ultimately, the United States Supreme Court decided the issue by ruling that votes cast in Florida could not be manually recounted. As a result of the confusing aftermath of the 2000 elections, a major issue facing the nation today is how to bring consistency and credibility to the election process in all of the states.

In addition, many other political issues continue to face this country today. Campaign-financing reform is still pending. New demands are being heard about solving the present and future problems related to Social Security, Medicare, Medicaid, and health care in general. While the 1990s were a period of relative prosperity for Americans, that decade left the nation with a plethora of political issues that must now be faced.

2000 Election Results Included and Analyzed

Our combined teaching experience has been that students respond to up-to-date information about political events. Consequently, we have included all relevant results of the November 2000 presidential elections. In addition, we have analyzed these results in terms of how they will affect our political processes at the national level in the following four years. While we have updated all of the text to be consistent with these election results, in particular we have added the features listed below. Throughout the text, all materials referring to the 2000 elections are accompanied by a special logo.

- *More Divided Government* (Chapter 1).
- *Trends in Federalism* (Chapter 3).
- *Political Leadership by Women* (Chapter 5).
- *The Accuracy of the 2000 Polls* (Chapter 7).
- *Interest Groups: The Candidates of Choice* (Chapter 8).
- *Partisan Trends in the 2000 Elections* (Chapter 9).
- *Why Voters Voted as They Did in 2000* (Chapter 10).
- *The Role of the Media in the 2000 Elections* (Chapter 11).
- *Congressional Characteristics after the 2000 Elections* (Chapter 12).
- *Party Control of Congress after the 2000 Elections* (Chapter 12).
- *The 2000 Elections and the Supreme Court* (Chapter 15).

The Interactive Focus of this Text

Whether it be the problems that face the new president, voter participation, or terrorism, we constantly strive to involve the student reader in the analysis. We make sure that the reader comes to understand that politics is not an abstract process but a very human enterprise, one involving interaction among individuals from all walks of life. We emphasize how different outcomes can affect students' civil rights and liberties, employment opportunities, and economic welfare.

Throughout the text, we encourage the reader to think critically. Virtually all of the features included in this text end with serious questions designed to pique the student's interest. A feature new to this edition—titled *Which Side Are You On?*—directly challenges the reader to find a connection between a controversial issue facing the nation and the reader's personal life. We further encourage interacting with the political system by ending each chapter with a feature titled *Making a Difference* and online exercises (to be discussed shortly) that students can perform to access and analyze political information. In addition, we offer a free, student-oriented supplement called *Thinking Globally, Acting Locally.* This supplement is designed to help students get involved and become active citizens.

VersaBook—An Electronic Version of *American Government and Politics Today*

VersaBook, an electronic version of the 2001–2002 Edition of *American Government and Politics Today* provided by VersaWare, provides students with powerful search functions and multimedia features. VersaBook, which is available at no cost with every copy of the text, allows students to navigate through the text in the standard manner or use the advanced search function to locate topics quickly. Various types of media—including video, animations, and audio—are integrated for a truly unique learning experience. Using the annotation features, students can take notes and highlight material. Links to the Web allow students to access additional material quickly. Web pages and links can be stored in a binder for quick and easy access. Material will be updated by the authors to provide students with the latest information. This e-book version of *American Government and Politics Today* will be available in CD format or online.

The Most Complete Web Connection

Not only has the political world been changing rapidly, but so, too, has the way in which information throughout the world is disseminated. We continue to make sure that our text leads the industry in terms of its integration with the Web. For this edition, you will find the following Web-based resources:

● **The Wadsworth Political Science Resource Center**—at http://politicalscience.wadsworth.com. Here, your students will find information on how to better surf the Web, links to general political Web sites, a career center, news issues, a discussion forum, and more—including the following materials:
- *A Citizen's Survival Guide.*
- *Election Central*, which contains updates and information on elections and links to the hottest election Web sites.
- *Spanish Equivalents for Important Terms in American Government.*
- *A link to the interactive Web site for the America at Odds CD-ROM.*

● **A text-specific site for this book**—accessible through the Wadsworth Political Science Resource Center's site or directly at http://www.wadsworth.com/politics/schmidt01/index.html. The text-specific Web site includes:

- *A link to VersaBook.*
- *Online Instructor's Manual* (password protected).
- *Chapter outlines and objectives* for the student to use.
- *Interactive quizzes* for which the students can submit responses to their professors via e-mail.
- *Links to relevant Web sites.*
- *Internet activities*, which ask students to surf the Web to obtain answers to thought-provoking questions.
- *InfoTrac exercises*, which introduce students to related topics to explore and cite specific articles.

- **InfoTrac College Edition**—an online search engine that will take the student to exactly where he or she needs to go to find relevant information, including full-text articles in important political science journals and other sources. A special icon in the margin indicates that InfoTrac will provide information and links relating to the particular topic being discussed in the text.

- **Logging on**—a section at the end of each chapter that lists and briefly describes important Web sites relating to topics covered in the chapter.

- **Using the Internet for Political Analysis**—a feature concluding each chapter that takes the student through specific exercises on how to use Web resources for a better understanding of American government.

- **American Government Internet Activities**—a free booklet that takes the student on a grand tour of numerous Web sites, each related to a specific major topic in American government studies. The student is asked to perform exercises on the Web for each topic covered.

- **Online testing**—which allows instructors to provide and grade examinations online, using *ExamView*.

- **WebTutor on WebCT**—a content-rich, easy-to-use, Web-based study aid for students that includes presentations of concepts, flashcards with audio clips, Web links, tutorials, discussion questions, and more.

Special Pedagogical Aids and High-Interest Features

The 2001–2002 Edition of *American Government and Politics Today* contains numerous pedagogical aids and high-interest features to assist both students and instructors in the learning/teaching process. The following list summarizes the special elements that can be found in each chapter.

- *Chapter Outline*—a preview of the contents of the chapter.
- *What If . . .* —a discussion of a hypothetical situation that begins with a "Background" section and concludes with a "For Critical Analysis" question.
- *Margin Definitions*—for all important terms.
- *Did You Know . . . ?*—a margin feature presenting various facts and figures that add relevance, humor, and some fun to the learning process.
- *E-mocracy*—a new feature about politics and the Internet.
- *Critical Perspective*—a critical examination of a current issue or theory relating to a topic covered in the chapter.
- *Which Side Are You On?*—a special new feature designed to elicit student responses to controversial issues.

- *Making Waves*—a new feature focusing on individuals or small groups of Americans who are "making waves" in today's political arena.
- *Global View*—a feature that looks at specific developments, events, or government structures in other nations of the world.
- *An Ethical Issue*—a special feature addressing the ethical aspects and implications of selected political events, behavior, and issues.
- *Politics and Economics*—a feature showing the connection between economic interests and political trends or outcomes.
- *Issues for the Twenty-First Century*—a concluding section on issues in American politics that are yet to be resolved.
- *Making a Difference*—a chapter-ending feature showing the student some specific ways in which he or she can become actively involved in American politics.
- *Key Terms*—a chapter-ending list, with page numbers, of all terms in the chapter that were boldfaced and defined in the margins.
- *Chapter Summary*—a point-by-point summary of the chapter text.
- *Selected Print and Electronic Resources*—including suggested readings as well as media resources.
- *Logging on*—a list and brief description of relevant and important Web sites.
- *Using the Internet for Political Analysis*—a specific Internet exercise.

Appendices

Because we know that this book serves as a reference, we have included important documents for the student of American government to have close at hand. A fully annotated copy of the U.S. Constitution appears at the end of Chapter 2, as an appendix to that chapter. In addition, we have included the following appendices:

- The Declaration of Independence.
- How to Read Case Citations and Find Court Decisions.
- The Presidents of the United States.
- Federalist Papers No. 10, No. 51, and No. 78.
- Justices of the U.S. Supreme Court since 1900.
- Party Control of Congress since 1900.
- Spanish Equivalents for Important Terms in American Government.

A Complete Supplements Package

We are proud to be the authors of a text that has the most complete, accessible, and fully integrated supplements package on the market. The text, along with the supplements listed below, constitute a total learning/teaching package for you and your students. For further information on any of these supplements, contact your West/Wadsworth/Thomson Learning sales representative.

Supplements for Instructors

- *Instructor's Manual.*
- *Online Instructors Manual* (password protected).
- *2001 Political Science-Link.*
- *Test Bank.*
- *ExamView.*

- *American Government Transparency Acetates Package*, 2001 Edition.
- *Political Science Video Library.*
- *CNN Today: American Government*, Volumes I and II (VHS videos).

Supplements for Students

- *Study Guide.*
- *WebTutor on WebCT.*
- *American Government: An Introduction Using* MicroCase ExplorIT, *Sixth Edition.*
- *America at Odds* CD-ROM.
- *American Government Internet Activities*, Third Edition.
- *Readings in American Government*, Third Edition.
- *Supplemental government texts for California and Texas.*
- *An Introduction to Critical Thinking and Writing in American Politics.*
- *Handbook of Selected Court Cases.*
- *Thinking Globally, Acting Locally.*
- *Handbook of Selected Legislation and Other Documents.*
- *College Survival Guide: Hints and References to Aid College Students*, Fourth Edition.
- *InfoTrac* College Edition.

For Users of the Previous Edition

As usual, we thank you for your past support of our work. We have made numerous changes to this text for the 2001–2002 Edition, many of which we list below. We have rewritten much of the text, added numerous new features, and updated it to reflect the results of the 2000 elections.

New Special Features

- *E-mocracy.*
- *Which Side Are You On?*
- *Making Waves.*
- *Global View.*
- *An Ethical Issue.*
- *Elections 2000.*
- *Making a Difference.*

New *What If* . . . Features

- "What If . . . Americans Had to Pass a Test to Vote?" (Chapter 1).
- "What If . . . The States Controlled the Internet?" (Chapter 3).
- "What If . . . Your Personal Records Were Public?" (Chapter 4).
- "What If . . . Medical Care Was a Civil Right?" (Chapter 5).
- "What If . . . Only the Top 10 Percent of Students Could Go to a Public College?" (Chapter 6).
- "What If . . . Every Lobbying Contact Had to Be Reported?" (Chapter 8).
- "What If . . . Everyone Had to Join a Political Party?" (Chapter 9).
- "What If . . . Candidates Received Free Television Time?" (Chapter 10).
- "What If . . . The Internet Replaced Broadcast News?" Chapter 11).

- "What If . . . We Could Recall the President?" (Chapter 13).
- "What If . . . We Had a "Virtual" Bureaucracy?" (Chapter 14).
- "What If . . . Supreme Court Justices Had to Campaign?" (Chapter 15).
- "What If . . . There Were No Social Security?" (Chapter 16).
- "What If . . . The United States Defended Only Itself?" (Chapter 17).

New *Critical Perspectives*

Chapter 1: "What Do Americans See for the Twenty-First Century?"

Chapter 3: "Should States Make Foreign Policy?"

Chapter 5: "Should the Immigration Door Be Shut?"

Chapter 6: "What Has Affirmative Action Really Accomplished?"

Chapter 7: "Is Technology Destroying Opinion Polling?"

Chapter 8: "How Powerful Is Silicon Valley?"

Chapter 9: "Is the Time Right for a Third Party?"

Chapter 10: "The Vanishing Voter."

Chapter 11: "Is There a Media Monopoly?"

Chapter 13: "Is the President Becoming Too Powerful?"

Chapter 14: "Has the Bureaucracy Exceeded Its Lawmaking Mandate?"

Chapter 16: "Does E-Commerce Threaten National Sovereignty?"

Chapter 17: "Is the Nuclear Threat Increasing?"

Significant Changes within Chapters

Each chapter contains new features, updated information and tabular data, and, whenever feasible, the most current information available on the problems facing the nation. The effects of emerging technology, including the Internet, are emphasized throughout. Here we list other significant changes made to each chapter.

- Chapter 1—now includes a description of the dominant culture and the pervasive influence of that perspective in data and documents relating to American government and politics.

- Chapter 2—now includes more coverage of John Locke's influence on the founders, as well as greater emphasis on the significance of the federal system established by the Constitution.

- Chapter 3—a subsection on recent Supreme Court rulings on issues relating to state sovereignty and the Eleventh Amendment has been added.

- Chapters 4, 5, and 6—have been extensively revised and rewritten in part to reflect current political, economic, and social trends relating to civil rights issues and the status of minority groups, as well as recent court rulings in significant cases in this area. The discussion of the civil rights movement now discusses the black power movement to show that not all African Americans agreed with Martin Luther King's philosophy of nonviolence. New features in these chapters focus on the most current controversies concerning civil rights and liberties.

● Chapter 7—now includes a discussion of the increasingly significant role of religious groups in the political socialization process and emphasizes the potential impact of changes in the media on political socialization and public opinion.

● Chapter 14—the coverage of whistleblowing has been expanded to discuss the application of the federal False Claims Act of 1986 in detecting and prosecuting fraud against the government.

● Chapter 15—now includes an expanded discussion of basic judicial requirements and emphasizes the significance of the 2000 elections for the future composition of the Supreme Court.

● Chapter 16—combines Chapters 16 and 17 of the previous edition into one chapter on domestic and economic policy. The content has been extensively revised to stress new policy issues raised by technology, the global economy, and other developments.

New Print Supplements

● A new edition of *Readings in American Government.*
● A new edition of transparency acetates.
● A new edition of *American Government Internet Activities.*
● A new edition of *College Survival Guide.*

New Multimedia Supplements

● *VersaBook.*
● *WebTutor* on *WebCT.*
● American Government: An Introduction Using *MicroCase ExplorIT*, Sixth Edition.
● *ExamView.*
● Political Science Video Library.
● New Web resources.
● New CNN videos.

Acknowledgments

Since we started this project a number of years ago, a sizable cadre of individuals has helped us in various phases of the undertaking. The following academic reviewers offered numerous constructive criticisms, comments, and suggestions during the preparation of all previous editions:

Danny M. Adkison
Oklahoma State University

Sharon Z. Alter
William Rainey Harper College, Illinois

William Arp III
Louisiana State University

Kevin Bailey
North Harris Community College, Texas

Evelyn Ballard
Houston Community College

Dr. Charles T. Barber
University of Southern Indiana, Evansville,

Clyde W. Barrow
Texas A&M University

David S. Bell
Eastern Washington University

David C. Benford, Jr.
Tarrant County Junior College

John A. Braithwaite
Coastline College

Lynn R. Brink
North Lake College, Irving, Texas

Barbara L. Brown
Southern Illinois University at Carbondale

Richard G. Buckner
Santa Fe Community College

Kenyon D. Bunch
Fort Lewis College, Durango, Colorado

Ralph Bunch
Portland State University, Oregon

Carol Cassell
University of Alabama

Frank J. Coppa
Union County College, Cranford, New Jersey

Robert E. Craig
University of New Hampshire

Doris Daniels
Nassau Community College, New York

Carolyn Grafton Davis
North Harris County College, Texas

Paul B. Davis
Truckee Meadows Community College,
Nevada

Richard D. Davis
Brigham Young University

Ron Deaton
Prince George's Community College,
Maryland

Marshall L. DeRosa
Louisiana State University, Baton Rouge

Michael Dinneen
Tulsa Junior College, Oklahoma

Gavan Duffy
University of Texas at Austin

George C. Edwards III
Texas A&M University

Mark C. Ellickson
Southwestern Missouri State University,
Springfield

Larry Elowitz
Georgia College

John W. Epperson
Simpson College, Indianola, Indiana

Daniel W. Fleitas
University of North Carolina at Charlotte

Elizabeth N. Flores
Del Mar College, Texas

Joel L. Franke
Blinn College, Brenham, Texas

Barry D. Friedman
North Georgia College

Robert S. Getz
SUNY–Brockport, New York

Kristina Gilbert
Riverside Community College, California

William A. Giles
Mississippi State University

Donald Gregory
Stephen F. Austin State University

Forest Grieves
University of Montana

Dale Grimnitz
Normandale Community College,
Bloomington, Minnesota

Stefan D. Haag
Austin Community College, Texas

Jean Wahl Harris
University of Scranton, Pennsylvania

David N. Hartman
Rancho Santiago College,
Santa Ana, California

Robert M. Herman
Moorpark College, California

Richard J. Herzog
Stephen F. Austin State University,
Nacogdoches, Texas

Paul Holder
McClennan Community College,
Waco, Texas

Michael Hoover
Seminole Community College,
Sanford, Florida

J. C. Horton
San Antonio College, Texas

Robert Jackson
Washington State University

Willoughby Jarrell
Kennesaw College, Georgia

Loch K. Johnson
University of Georgia

Donald L. Jordan
United States Air Force Academy, Colorado

John D. Kay
Santa Barbara City College, California

Charles W. Kegley
University of South Carolina

Bruce L. Kessler
Shippensburg University, Pennsylvania

Jason F. Kirksey
Oklahoma State University

Nancy B. Kral
Tomball College, Texas

Dale Krane
Mississippi State University

Samuel Krislov
University of Minnesota

William W. Lamkin
Glendale Community College

Harry D. Lawrence
Southwest Texas Junior College, Uvaide,
Texas

Ray Leal
Southwest Texas State University, San Marcos

Sue Lee
Center for Telecommunications, Dallas
County Community College District

Carl Lieberman
University of Akron, Ohio

Orma Linford
Kansas State University

James J. Lopach
University of Montana

Eileen Lynch
Brookhaven College, Texas

James D. McElyea
Tulsa Junior College, Oklahoma

William P. McLauchlan
Purdue University, Indiana

William W. Maddox
University of Florida

S. J. Makielski, Jr.
Loyola University, New Orleans

Jarol B. Manheim
George Washington University

J. David Martin
Midwestern State University, Texas

Bruce B. Mason
Arizona State University

Thomas Louis Masterson
Butte College, California

Steve J. Mazurana
University of Northern Colorado

Thomas J. McGaghie
Kellogg Community College, Michigan

Stanley Melnick
Valencia Community College, Florida

Robert Mittrick
Luzurne County Community College,
Pennsylvania

Helen Molanphy
Richland College, Texas

James Morrow
Tulsa Community College

Keith Nicholls
University of Alabama

Stephen Osofsky
Nassau Community College, New York

John P. Pelissero
Loyola University of Chicago

Neil A. Pinney
Western Michigan University

George E. Pippin
Jones County Community College,
Mississippi

Walter V. Powell
Slippery Rock University, Pennsylvania

Michael A. Preda
Midwestern State University, Texas

Mark E. Priewe
University of Texas at San Antonio

Charles Prysby
University of North Carolina

Donald R. Ranish
Antelope Valley College, California

John D. Rausch
Fairmont State University, West Virginia

Curt Reichel
University of Wisconsin

Russell D. Renka
Southeast Missouri State University

Paul Rozycki
Charles Stewart Mott Community College,
Flint, Michigan

Bhim Sandhu
West Chester University, Pennsylvania

Pauline Schloesser
Texas Southern University

Eleanor A. Schwab
South Dakota State University

Len Shipman
Mount San Antonio College, California

Scott Shrewsbury
Mankato State University, Minnesota

Michael W. Sonnlietner
Portland Community College, Oregon

Gilbert K. St. Clair
University of New Mexico

Carol Stix
Pace University, Pleasantville, New York

Gerald S. Strom
University of Illinois at Chicago

John R. Todd
North Texas State University

Ron Velton
Grayson County College, Texas

Benjamin Walter
Vanderbilt University, Tennessee

B. Oliver Walter
University of Wyoming

Mark J. Wattier
Murray State University, Kentucky

Thomas L. Wells
Old Dominion University, Virginia

Jean B. White
Weber State College, Utah

Allan Wiese
Mankato State University, Minnesota

Lance Widman
El Camino College, California

J. David Woodard
Clemson University, South Carolina

Robert D. Wrinkle
Pan American University, Texas

The 2001–2002 Edition of this text is the result of our working closely with reviewers who each offered us penetrating criticisms, comments, and suggestions for how to improve the text. Although we haven't been able to take account of all requests, each of the reviewers listed below will see many of his or her suggestions taken to heart.

Orlando N. Bama, McLennan
Community College, Texas

Frank T. Colon
Lehigh University, Pennsylvania

Frank J. Coppa
Union County College, New Jersey

Gregory Edwards
Amarillo College, Texas

Willie Hamilton
Mount San Jacinto College, California

Paul Holder
McLennan Community College, Texas

Jessie Horton
San Antonio College

George E. Pippin
Jones County Junior College, Mississippi

Renford Reese
California State Polytechnic University–
Pomona

Alton J. Slane
Muhlenberg College, Pennsylvania

Joseph L. Smith
Grand Valley State University, Michigan

Albert C. Waite
Central Texas College

In preparing this edition of *American Politics and Government Today*, we were the beneficiaries of the expert guidance of a skilled and dedicated team of publishers and editors. We would like, first of all, to thank Susan Badger, the president of Wadsworth Publishing Company, for the support she has shown for this project. We have benefited greatly from the supervision and encouragement given by Clark Baxter, editorial director. Sharon Adams Poore, our senior developmental editor, also deserves our thanks for her efforts in coordinating reviews and in many other aspects of project development. We are also indebted to Jennifer Ellis, editorial assistant, for her contribution to this project.

We are grateful to Bill Stryker, our production manager, for a remarkable design and for making it possible to get the text out on time. In addition, our gratitude goes to all of those who worked on the various supplements offered with this text and to Steve Wainwright, who coordinates the Web site and other multimedia offerings. We would also like to thank Diane McOscar, executive marketing manager, for her tremendous efforts in marketing the text.

Many other people helped during the research and editorial stages of this edition as well. Lavina Leed Miller skillfully coordinated the authors' efforts and provided editorial and research assistance from the outset of the project through its final stages. Pat Lewis's copyediting and proofreading abilities contributed greatly to the book. We also thank Sherri Downing-Alfonso and Roxie Lee for their proofreading and other assistance, which helped us to meet our ambitious publishing schedule, and Sue Jasin of K& M Consulting for her contributions to the smooth running of the project.

Any errors, of course, remain our own. We welcome comments from instructors and students alike. Suggestions that we have received on previous editions have helped us to improve this text and to adapt it to the changing needs of instructors and students.

Steffen Schmidt   Mack Shelley   Barbara Bardes

About the Authors

Steffen W. Schmidt

Steffen W. Schmidt is a professor of political science at Iowa State University. He grew up in Colombia, South America, and studied in Colombia, Switzerland, and France. He obtained his Ph.D. from Columbia University, New York, in public law and government.

Schmidt has published six books and over seventy articles in scholarly journals. He is also the recipient of numerous prestigious teaching prizes, including the Amoco Award for Lifetime Career Achievement in Teaching and the Teacher of the Year award. He is a pioneer in the use of Web-based and real-time video courses and is a member of the American Political Science Association's section on Computers and Multimedia. He is on the editorial board of the *Political Science Educator*.

Schmidt has a political talk show on WOI radio, where he is known as Dr. Politics. The show has been broadcast live from various U.S. and international venues.

Schmidt likes to snow ski, ride hunter jumper horses, and race sailboats.

Mack C. Shelley II

Mack C. Shelley II is a professor of political science and statistics at Iowa State University. After receiving his Bachelor's degree from American University in Washington, D.C., he went on to graduate studies at the University of Wisconsin at Madison, where he received a Master's degree and a Ph.D. He taught for two years at Mississippi State University prior to arriving at Iowa State in 1979.

Shelley has published numerous articles, books, and monographs on public policy. In 1993, he was elected co-editor of the *Policy Studies Journal.* His published books include *The Permanent Majority: The Conservative Coalition in the United States Congress; Biotechnology and the Research Enterprise: A Guide to the Literature* (with William F. Woodman and Brian J. Reichel); and *American Public Policy: The Contemporary Agenda* (with Steven G. Koven and Bert E. Swanson).

In his spare time, Shelley has been known to participate in softball, bowling (he was on two championship faculty teams), and horseback riding. When his son was given a pool table for his fourteenth birthday, he took up that game as a pastime.

Barbara A. Bardes

Barbara A. Bardes is a professor of political science and Dean of Raymond Walters College at the University of Cincinnati. She received her Bachelor of Arts degree and Master of Arts degree from Kent State University, and her Ph.D. from the University of Cincinnati. She held a faculty position at Loyola University in Chicago for many years before returning to Cincinnati, her home town, as a college administrator.

Bardes has written articles on public opinion and foreign policy, and on women and politics. She has authored *Thinking about Public Policy, Declarations of Independence: Women and Political Power in Nineteenth Century American Novels,* and (with Robert W. Oldendick) *Public Opinion: Measuring the American Mind.*

Bardes's home is located in a very small hamlet in Kentucky called Rabbit Hash, famous for its 150-year-old General Store. Her hobbies include travel, gardening, needlework, and antique collecting.

part 1

The American System

chapter 1
Forces of Change in the Twenty-First Century

CHAPTER OUTLINE

- Political Change in the United States

- What Is Politics?

- The Need for Government and Power

- Who Governs?

- Do We Have a Democracy?

- Ideas and Politics: Political Culture

- The Changing Face of America

- Ideas and Politics: Ideology

what if...

Americans Had to Pass a Test to Vote?

BACKGROUND

IF AN IMMIGRANT WANTS TO BECOME AN AMERICAN CITIZEN, HE OR SHE MUST MEET A NUMBER OF REQUIREMENTS. THESE REQUIREMENTS INCLUDE UNDERSTANDING THE ENGLISH LANGUAGE AND PASSING A TEST ON THE CONSTITUTION AND U.S. HISTORY.

IN CONTRAST, IF A CITIZEN WANTS TO REGISTER TO VOTE, GENERALLY ALL HE OR SHE MUST DO IS TO FIND THE LOCAL GOVERNMENT REGISTRATION OFFICE, SIGN A CARD OR A SHORT DOCUMENT, AND PRESENT SOME FORM OF IDENTIFICATION TO SHOW THAT THE VOTER LIVES IN THAT STATE. UNDER FEDERAL LAW, THE FORMS FOR VOTER REGISTRATION MUST BE MADE AVAILABLE AT A NUMBER OF LOCATIONS, INCLUDING DRIVER'S LICENSE BUREAUS AND WELFARE OFFICES. REGISTERING TO VOTE IS OBVIOUSLY MUCH SIMPLER THAN BECOMING A CITIZEN.

WHAT IF AMERICANS HAD TO PASS A TEST TO VOTE?

Many studies have shown that Americans actually have very little knowledge about their government or their political representatives. Although voting turnout has declined over the last fifty years, far more people vote than know the name of their congressional representatives or which political party controls Congress.

Furthermore, Americans know very little about what their representatives are empowered to do. When asked about the powers of Congress or the contents of the Constitution, Americans do not have much information. True, Americans do pay attention to political campaigns and make decisions about candidates and issues as elections come closer. Yet requiring Americans to pass a test on their political system before being entitled to vote might produce more informed voters.

WHAT SHOULD A TEST COVER?

If the national government, for example, would require that all voters pass a test before they could vote for a national office such as the presidency or a member of Congress, what should the test cover? It could be argued that the test should stress basic facts, such as the functions of the branches of government or the length of terms of senators and representatives. Perhaps questions on the way that laws are passed or how government regulations are created might be more appropriate. The test that persons who wish to become naturalized citizens must take includes such questions. Some might suggest that it is most important for voters to know something about the office for which they are casting a vote and about the individuals who are seeking their support.

IS A TEST FOR VOTERS LEGAL?

At the present time, it is illegal for a government to require voters to pass literacy tests. Such tests were used as a tool in the southern states to keep African Americans from voting from the period after the Civil War until the civil rights movement of the 1960s. The Voting Rights Act of 1965 outlawed such tests for any voter who had completed the sixth grade in school. A new literacy or history test could be required by an act of Congress, however.

IS A TEST FOR VOTERS DEMOCRATIC?

The question of whether a test for voters is democratic is much more important than whether such a test could be made legal. The theory of democratic government holds that each member of society has an equal vote and an equal voice in making political decisions. In fact, many of the "checks and balances" in the U.S. Constitution were approved by the founders because they knew that many of the voters in their new nation were not well educated. The lack of an education has never been a reason for denying individuals the right to vote, because that right is considered a fundamental tenet of the system rather than a privilege to be earned.

The idea of requiring a test for voters would raise a host of other issues. For example, inevitably questions would arise about who would write the test and who would grade it. Clearly, a required test for voters could be used, again, as a political tool to keep some groups from voting while encouraging others—one of the oldest political maneuvers in the world.

FOR CRITICAL ANALYSIS

1. What kinds of information do you think would be most important for voters to know before voting in a presidential election?
2. If a test for voting were approved, what might be the political impact of such a test on the composition of the electorate?

Politics is about stability and change. Nations, governments, and their people struggle to create policies and laws that will help them address the problems they face. Governments write and rewrite laws and policies to meet the challenges of the worldwide economy or the threat of an energy crisis. People seek change in who represents them in government in order to get the policies they think best. They also try to change the structures and laws of their governments to improve their lives and their communities. They may, in the interests of improving the political process, make a change such as requiring a test for voting (see the *What If . . .* that opens this chapter). They elect new members of Congress and a new president to lead the nation, as they did in the 2000 elections when they kept the Republicans in control of the House of Representatives, split the Senate evenly between the two parties, and divided the popular vote almost equally between Vice President Al Gore and Texas governor George W. Bush in the closest election for many decades.

People and governments also need stability. Agreement on the rules of the road, on the structure of government, and especially on the processes by which change is made gives people the confidence they need to plan for their own futures. If governments change capriciously or suddenly, no family or individual can be sure that their plans are safe. As the results of the 2000 elections showed, the overwhelming majority of members of Congress were returned safely to their seats, and the two major parties attracted millions of voters to their candidates.

As one of the older democratic societies, the United States has a very stable form of government. Many nations in the world, however, are undergoing extreme changes as they try to define their future structures and political systems. Among the nations undergoing the most drastic changes are Russia, Mexico, South Africa, and many of the countries of Southeast Asia and South America.

In this chapter, we will discuss some of the questions and principles that are fundamental to the construction of any political system. Part of the excitement of the American political system is that these issues and principles continue to be debated in the United States as we attempt to balance the forces of stability with the forces of change.

INFOTRAC®
COLLEGE EDITION

Citizenship Test

Political Change in the United States

Due to our electoral system, Americans have the opportunity to change the balance of power in their national government every two years. In 1994, Americans chose to replace a Congress controlled by Democrats with Republican majorities

Two Florida citizens argue outside the Palm Beach County, Florida, elections headquarters in West Palm Beach, Florida. Palm Beach County became the focus of nationwide attention after election day, 2000, when it was learned that thousands of voters had apparently voted unintentionally for Patrick Buchanan rather than Al Gore because of an allegedly confusing ballot layout.

Divided Government
A situation that exists when political party control over the government is divided—for example, when the president is a Democrat and Congress is controlled by Republicans.

INFOTRAC®
COLLEGE EDITION
Washington House tied

Institution
A long-standing, identifiable structure or association that performs certain functions for society.

in both the House of Representatives and the Senate. The result was **divided government,** with a president from one party and a Congress controlled by the other major party. Americans reelected Bill Clinton as president in 1996 and returned a Republican majority to Congress.

More Divided Government

In the 2000 national elections, Americans produced a government that would be as closely divided as any in our history. With a razor-thin edge in the House of Representatives and an evenly divided Senate, Republican members of Congress will be severely constrained in what they can do because of the difficulty in obtaining unity even among their own legislators.

With the popular vote in a virtual tie, the presidential elections came down to which candidate carried the electoral college—Al Gore or George W. Bush. Thus, when Bush was ultimately declared the winner of the electoral college votes, he could not claim a mandate and use that as a tool to persuade the people or the Congress to do his will. Americans, perhaps without intending to do so, created the ultimate in divided government in 2000. The only way any policy change can happen will have to be through collaboration between the branches and between the political parties.

What does this succession of decisions say about Americans and political change? It would appear that as Americans approached the third millennium, they were strongly seeking only moderate change in their governmental system. They were counting on the Republican Congress to limit the actions of a Democratic president, but they still wanted that president to press forward with his agenda.

In terms of government policies, the divided government of the 1990s and early 2000s turned out to be quite effective. In 2000, Americans found themselves living in an incredibly prosperous time, with low inflation and low unemployment rates. During the Clinton years, Americans had supported massive policy changes in the welfare system, in telecommunications laws, and in farm policy. Neither the American public nor the politicians, however, seemed ready to push for serious policy changes in campaign financing, in the Social Security or Medicare system, or in the health-care system. These issues continued to hover on the agenda, waiting for their place in the political debate.

The willingness of Americans to debate new initiatives and to demand changes in the way the government works is at the core of our democratic nation. Change—even revolutionary change—is a tribute to the success of a political system. As Abraham Lincoln put it, "This country with all its institutions, belongs to the people who inhabit it. Whenever they shall grow weary of the existing government, they can exercise their Constitutional right of amending it, or the revolutionary right to dismember or overthrow it."[1]

In the chapters that follow, we will look more closely at the **institutions** of our government and how they have changed over the decades. We will examine how the political processes of the nation work to accomplish those changes. To begin, we will look at why political institutions and processes are necessary in any society and what purposes they serve.

What Is Politics?

Why do nations and people struggle so hard to establish a form of government and continue to expend so much effort in politics to keep that government functioning? Politics and forms of government are probably as old as human soci-

---

[1]First Inaugural Address, March 4, 1861.

ety. There are many definitions of politics, but all try to explain how human beings regulate conflict within their society. As soon as humans began to live in groups, particularly groups that were larger than their immediate families, they found that they needed to establish rules about behavior, property, the privileges of individuals and groups, and how people would survive together. **Politics** can best be understood as the process of, as Harold Lasswell put it, "who gets what, when, and how."[2] To another social scientist, David Easton, politics should be defined as the "authoritative allocation of values."[3] Politics, then, is the struggle or process engaged in by human beings to decide which members of society get benefits or privileges and which are excluded from certain benefits or privileges.

In the early versions of human society, the tribe or village, politics was relatively informal. Tribal elders or hereditary chiefs were probably vested with the power to decide who married whom, who was able to build a hut on the best piece of land, and which young people succeeded them into the positions of leadership. Other societies were "democratic" from the very beginning, giving their members some form of choice of leadership and rules. Early human societies rarely had the concept of property, so few rules were needed to decide who owned which piece of property or who inherited that piece. The concepts of property and inheritance are much more modern. As society became more complex and humans became settled farmers rather than hunters and gatherers, the problems associated with property, inheritance, sales and exchanges, kinship, and rules of behavior became important to resolve. Politics developed into the process by which some of these questions were answered.

Inevitably, conflicts arise in society, because members of a group are distinct individuals with unique needs, values, and perspectives. At least three different kinds of conflicts that may require the need for political processes arise in a society:

1. People may differ over their beliefs, either religious or personal, or over basic issues of right and wrong. The kind of debate that has arisen in recent years on abortion is an example of this kind of conflict.
2. People within a society may differ greatly in their perception of what the society's goals should be. For example, Americans disagree over whether the national government should set national standards for education or whether the direction for schools should come primarily from local school boards and communities.
3. People compete for scarce resources; government benefits and property are examples. The question of who will pay for Medicare benefits, for instance, is really a discussion of whether younger people will pay for the health care of the older persons in the society or whether retirees must pay more for this health insurance.

The Need for Government and Power

If *politics* refers to conflict and conflict resolution, **government** refers to the structures by which the decisions are made that resolve conflicts or allocate values. In early human societies, such as families and small tribes, there was no need for formal structures of government. Decisions were made by acknowledged leaders in those societies. In families, all members may meet together to

DID YOU KNOW...
That the word *politkos* (pertaining to citizen or civic affairs) was used by the Greeks thousands of years ago and that the English word *politics* entered the language around 1529**?**

Politics
According to David Easton, the "authoritative allocation of values" for a society; according to Harold Lasswell, "who gets what, when, and how" in a society.

Government
A permanent structure (institution) composed of decision makers who make society's rules about conflict resolution and the allocation of resources and who possess the power to enforce those rules.

[2]Harold Lasswell, *Politics: Who Gets What, When and How* (New York: McGraw-Hill, 1936).
[3]David Easton, *The Political System* (New York: Knopf, 1953).

decide values and priorities. When a community makes decisions and allocates values through informal rules, politics exists—but not government. In most contemporary societies, these activities continue in many forms. For example, when a church decides to build a new building or hire a new minister, that decision may be made politically, but there is in fact no government. Politics can be found in schools, social groups, and any other organized group. When a society reaches a certain level of complexity, however, it becomes necessary to establish a permanent or semipermanent group of individuals to act for the whole, to become the government.

Governments range in size from the volunteer city council and one or two employees of a small town to the massive and complex structures of the U.S. government or those of any other large, modern nation. Generally, governments not only make the rules but also implement them through the use of police, judges, and other government officials. (See this chapter's *E-mocracy* for a discussion of how government is becoming connected to the citizens in new ways.)

Authority and Legitimacy

In addition to instituting and carrying out laws regulating individual behavior, such as traffic laws and criminal laws, most modern governments also attempt to carry out public policies that are intended to fulfill specific national or state goals. For example, a state may decide that its goal is to reduce teenage consumption

e-mocracy

Connecting to the Government

Will the Internet make Americans feel closer to their government? Or will it make them feel more alienated from government? With more than 50 percent of American households connected to the Internet, more and more citizens are obtaining government services through computers, rather than through personal contact. While this development may result in a more informed citizenry and, in many cases, more efficient services, it is possible that "government by Internet" may make politics even more distant from the ordinary American.

ONLINE GOVERNMENT SERVICES

Virtually all of the American states now have Web pages that offer access to all government departments. Most large cities and all of the departments of the federal government also offer information and assistance via the Internet. Local governments routinely list public meeting schedules and public documents on the Web. The state and national governments also post online all kinds of public reports, statistics, and meeting minutes. You can find information on state parks, the rules for naturalization and immigration, and all of the rulings of the Supreme Court on the Web.

Due to security issues and the high level of technology needed, far fewer interactive applications are available to citizens than can be found in the world of e-commerce. Nevertheless, their number is growing. Increasingly, state and local govern-

ments are allowing citizens use of the Internet for a variety of transactions, such as paying for parking tickets or renewing driver's licenses (see the *E-mocracy* in Chapter 18 for details). In 2000, the federal government launched an interactive Web site (**http://www.firstgov.gov**) that allows Americans to conduct any number of transactions online, including applying for passports, paying off student loans, and filing forms with the Immigration and Naturalization Service.

EFFICIENCY VERSUS THE PERSONAL TOUCH

Although the American public has become used to automated teller machines and phone systems, most people, according to polls, would prefer to speak to a person, whether in the bank or on the telephone. The question about Internet government services, which cannot yet be answered, is the following: Will the efficiency of Internet service increase citizens' satisfaction with their government, or will they be alienated by their inability to have questions answered in person? Additionally, unlike a business, which might decide to do virtually all of its business online, governments must still remain accessible to the large number of citizens who do not have access to computers or the Internet.

FOR CRITICAL ANALYSIS

Which government services—local, state, or national—are most likely to continue to be rendered in person? Which will most likely be rendered online?

of alcohol and the driving accidents caused by such behavior. To do that, the state may institute extremely strong penalties for drinking, along with a statewide education program for teenagers and younger children about the dangers of drinking and driving. The U.S. government has implemented a series of environmental laws meant to improve air and water quality. These laws require citizens to follow certain rules, such as using unleaded gasoline. Federal air-quality regulations have also forced car manufacturers to produce more fuel-efficient vehicles and, in some urban areas, require citizens to take their vehicles through pollution-inspection stations to see if their cars meet government standards.

Why do citizens obey these laws and subject themselves to these regulations? One reason citizens obey government is that it has the **authority** to make such laws. By authority, we mean the ultimate right to enforce compliance with decisions. Americans also believe the laws should be obeyed because they possess **legitimacy**—that is, they are appropriate and rightful. The laws have been made according to the correct and accepted political process by representatives of the people. Therefore, the people accept the laws as legitimate and having political authority.

The Question of Power

Another and perhaps more basic answer as to why we comply with the laws and rules of the government is that we understand that government has the **power** to enforce the law. We obey environmental laws and pay taxes in part because we acknowledge the legitimacy of the law. We also know that the government has the power to coerce our compliance with the law. Governments differ in the degree to which they must rely on coercion to gain **compliance** from their citizens. In authoritarian nations, the use of force is far more common than in democratic nations, where most citizens comply with the law because they accept the authority of the government and its officials. In authoritarian or **totalitarian regimes**, the will of the government is imposed frequently and is upheld by the use of force.

The concept of power also involves the ability of one individual or a group of individuals to influence the actions of another individual or group. We frequently speak of the power of the president to convince Congress to pass laws, or the power of a certain interest group, such as the National Rifle Association, to influence legislation. We also speak frequently of the power of money to influence political decisions. These uses of power are informal and involve using rewards for compliance rather than the threat of coercion. More often than not, political power in the government is a matter of influence and persuasion rather than coercion.

Who Governs?

One of the most fundamental questions of politics has to do with which person or groups of people control society through the government. Who possesses the power to make decisions about who gets what and how the benefits of the society are distributed among the people?

Sources of Political Power

At one extreme is a society governed by a totalitarian regime. In such a political system, a small group of leaders or a single individual—a dictator—makes all political decisions for the society. Every aspect of political, social, and economic

Authority
The features of a leader or an institution that compel obedience, usually because of ascribed legitimacy. For most societies, government is the ultimate authority.

Legitimacy
A status conferred by the people on the government's officials, acts, and institutions through their belief that the government's actions are an appropriate use of power by a legally constituted governmental authority following correct decision-making policies. These actions are regarded as rightful and entitled to compliance and obedience on the part of citizens.

Power
The ability to cause others to modify their behavior and to conform to what the power holder wants.

Compliance
The act of accepting and carrying out authorities' decisions.

Totalitarian Regime
A form of government that controls all aspects of the political and social life of a nation. All power resides with the government. The citizens have no power to choose the leadership or policies of the country.

Oligarchy
Rule by a few members of the elite, who generally make decisions to benefit their own group.

Elite
An upper socioeconomic class that controls political and economic affairs.

Aristocracy
Rule by the best suited, through virtue, talent, or education; in later usage, rule by the upper class.

Anarchy
The condition of having no government and no laws. Each member of the society governs himself or herself.

Democracy
A system of government in which ultimate political authority is vested in the people. Derived from the Greek words *demos* ("the people") and *kratos* ("authority").

Direct Democracy
A system of government in which political decisions are made by the people directly, rather than by their elected representatives; probably possible only in small political communities.

Legislature
A government body primarily responsible for the making of laws.

Initiative
A procedure by which voters can propose a law or a constitutional amendment.

Referendum
An act of referring legislative (statutory) or constitutional measures to the voters for approval or disapproval.

Recall
A procedure allowing the people to vote to dismiss an elected official from state office before his or her term has expired.

Consent of the People
The idea that governments and laws derive their legitimacy from the consent of the governed.

life is controlled by the government. The power of the ruler is total (thus, the term *totalitarianism*).

Many of our terms for describing the distribution of political power are derived from the ancient Greeks, who were the first Western people to study politics systematically. A society in which political decisions were controlled by a small group was called an **oligarchy**, meaning rule by a few members of the **elite**, who generally benefited themselves. Another form of rule by the few was known as **aristocracy**, meaning rule by the most virtuous, most talented, or the best suited to the position. Later in European history, aristocracy meant rule by the titled or the upper classes. In contrast to such a top-down form of control was the form known as **anarchy**, or the condition of no government. Anarchy exists when each individual makes his or her own rules for behavior, and there are no laws and no government.

The Greek term for rule by the people was **democracy.** Although most Greek philosophers were not convinced that democracy was the best form of government, they understood and debated the possibility of such a political system. Within the limits of their culture, some of the Greek city-states operated as democracies.

Direct Democracy as a Model

From the ancient Greek city-states comes a model for governance that has framed the modern debate over whether the people can make decisions about their own government and laws. The Athenian system of government is usually considered the model for **direct democracy** because the citizens of that community debated and voted directly on all laws, even those put forward by the ruling council of the city. The most important feature of Athenian democracy was that the **legislature** was composed of all of the citizens. Women, foreigners, and slaves, however, were excluded because they were not citizens. The outstanding feature of this early form of government was that it required a high level of participation from every citizen; that participation was seen as benefiting the individual and the city-state. The Athenians recognized that although a high level of participation might lead to instability in government, citizens, if informed about the issues, could be trusted to make decisions about the laws governing their community.

Direct democracy also has been practiced in some Swiss cantons and, in the United States, in New England town meetings and in some midwestern township meetings. At New England town meetings, which can include all of the voters who live in the town, important decisions are made for the community—such as levying taxes, hiring city officials, and deciding local ordinances—by majority vote. Some states provide a modern adaptation of direct democracy for their citizens; in most states, representative democracy is supplemented by the **initiative** or the **referendum**—a process by which the people may vote directly on laws or constitutional amendments. The **recall** process, which is available in over one-third of the states, allows the people to vote to remove an official from state office.

The Dangers of Direct Democracy

Although they were aware of the Athenian model, the framers of the U.S. Constitution—for the most part—were opposed to such a system. For many centuries preceding this country's establishment, any form of democracy was considered to be dangerous and to lead to instability. But in the eighteenth and nineteenth centuries, the idea of government based on the **consent of the people** gained increasing popularity. Such a government was the main aspiration of the American Revolution, the French Revolution in 1789, and many subsequent ones. The masses, however, were considered to be too uneducated to govern themselves, too prone to the influence of demagogues (political leaders who manipulate popular prejudices), and too likely to abrogate minority rights.

James Madison defended the new scheme of government set forth in the U.S. Constitution, while warning of the problems inherent in a "pure democracy":

> A common passion or interest will, in almost every case, be felt by a majority of the whole . . . and there is nothing to check the inducements to sacrifice the weaker party or an obnoxious individual. Hence it is that such democracies have ever been spectacles of turbulence and contention, and have ever been found incompatible with personal security or the rights of property; and have in general been as short in their lives as they have been violent in their deaths.[4]

Like many other politicians of his time, Madison feared that pure, or direct, democracy would deteriorate into mob rule. What would keep the majority of the people, if given direct decision-making power, from abusing the rights of minority groups?

Representative Democracy

The framers of the U.S. Constitution chose to craft a **republic,** meaning a government in which the power rests with the people, who elect representatives to govern them and to make the laws and policies. To eighteenth-century Americans, the idea of a republic also meant a government based on common beliefs and virtues that would be fostered within small communities. The rulers were to be amateurs—good citizens—who would take turns representing their fellow citizens, in a way similar to the Greek model.[5]

To allow for change while ensuring a measure of stability, the U.S. Constitution creates a form of republican government known as a **representative democracy.** The people hold the ultimate power over the government through the

Republic
A form of government in which sovereignty rests with the people, who elect agents to represent them in lawmaking and other decisions.

Representative Democracy
A form of government in which representatives elected by the people make and enforce laws and policies.

---

[4]James Madison, in Alexander Hamilton, James Madison, and John Jay, *The Federalist Papers,* No. 10 (New York: Mentor Books, 1964), p. 81. See Appendix D.
[5]See Chapter 2 for a discussion of the founders' ideas.

DID YOU KNOW...
That there are over 500,000 elected officials in the United States, which is more than all the bank tellers in the country**?**

This town meeting in New Hampshire allows every citizen of the town to vote directly and in person for elected officials, for proposed policies, and, in some cases, for the town budget. To be effective, such a form of direct democracy requires that the citizens stay informed about local politics, attend town meetings, and devote time to discussion and decision making.

Universal Suffrage
The right of all adults to vote for their representatives.

Majority
More than 50 percent.

Majority Rule
A basic principle of democracy asserting that the greatest number of citizens in any political unit should select officials and determine policies.

Volunteers register voters in the Spanish Harlem section of New York City. By setting up a table in the neighborhood, the election officials make registration more convenient for voters as well as less threatening. Both political parties often conduct voter registration drives in the months before general elections.

election process, but policy decisions are all made by elected officials. Even this distance between the people and the government was not sufficient. Other provisions in the Constitution made sure that the Senate and the president would be selected by political elites rather than by the people, although later changes to the Constitution allowed the voters to elect members of the Senate directly. This modified form of democratic government came to be widely accepted throughout the Western world as a compromise between the desire for democratic control and the needs of the modern state. The feature at the end of the chapter, *Making a Difference* on page 27, suggests some ways for you to explore how representative democracies work.

Principles of Democratic Government.   All representative democracies rest on the rule of the people as expressed through the election of government officials. In the 1790s, only free white males were able to vote, and in some states they had to be property owners as well. Women did not receive the right to vote in national elections in the United States until 1920, and the right to vote was not really secured by African Americans until the 1960s. Today, **universal suffrage** is the rule.

Granting every person the right to participate in the election of officials recognizes the equal voting power of each citizen. This emphasis on the equality of every individual before the law is central to the American system. Because everyone's vote counts equally, the only way to make fair decisions is by some form of **majority** will. But to ensure that **majority rule** does not become oppressive, modern democracies also provide guarantees of minority rights. If certain democratic principles did not protect minorities, the majority might violate the fundamental rights of members of certain groups, especially groups that are unpopular or dissimilar to the majority population. In the past, the majority has imposed such limitations on African Americans, Native Americans, and Japanese Americans, to name only a few.

One way to guarantee the continued existence of a representative democracy is to hold free, competitive elections. Thus, the minority always has the opportunity to win elective office. For such elections to be totally open, freedom of the press and speech must be preserved so that opposition candidates may present their criticisms of the government.

Elites may have far more power and influence on the political system than do voters from the lower and middle classes. Because they share an educational background from selective schools, a higher income level, and common lifestyles with government policymakers, they are more likely to see government policymakers on a social basis and to form friendships with elected officials.

Constitutional Democracy.   Another key feature of Western representative democracy is that it is based on the principle of **limited government.** Not only is the government dependent on **popular sovereignty,** but the powers of the government are also clearly limited, either through a written document or through widely shared beliefs. The U.S. Constitution sets down the fundamental structure of the government and the limits to its activities. Such limits are intended to prevent political decisions based on the whims or ambitions of individuals in government rather than on constitutional principles.

Limited Government
A form of government based on the principle that the powers of government should be clearly limited either through a written document or through wide public understanding; characterized by institutional checks to ensure that government serves the public rather than private interests.

Popular Sovereignty
The concept that ultimate political authority rests with the people.

Do We Have a Democracy?

The sheer size and complexity of American society seem to make it unsuitable for direct democracy on a national scale. Some scholars suggest that even representative democracy is difficult to achieve in any modern state. They point to the low level of turnout for presidential elections and the even lower turnout for local ones. Polling data have shown that many Americans are neither particularly interested in politics nor well informed. Few are able to name the persons running for Congress in their districts, and even fewer can discuss the candidates' positions. Members of Congress claim to represent their constituents, but few constituents follow the issues, much less communicate their views to their representatives. For the average citizen, the national government is too remote, too powerful, and too bureaucratic to be influenced by one vote.

Democracy for the Few

If ordinary citizens are not really making policy decisions with their votes, who is? One answer suggests that elites really govern the United States. Proponents of **elite theory** see society much as Alexander Hamilton did, who said,

> All communities divide themselves into the few and the many. The first are the rich and the wellborn, the other the mass of the people. . . . The people are turbulent and changing; they seldom judge or determine right. Give therefore to the first class a distinct, permanent share in the government. They will check the unsteadiness of the second, and as they cannot receive any advantage by a change, they therefore will ever maintain good government.

Elite Theory
A perspective holding that society is ruled by a small number of people who exercise power in their self-interest.

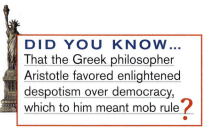

Elite theory describes an American mass population that is uninterested in politics and that is willing to let leaders make the decisions. Some versions of elite theory posit a small, cohesive elite class that makes almost all the important decisions regarding the nation,[6] whereas others suggest that voters choose among competing elites. New members of the elite are recruited through the educational system so that the brightest children of the masses allegedly have the opportunity to join the elite stratum.

In such a political system, the primary goal of the government is stability, because elites do not want any change in their status. Major social and economic change takes place only if elites see their resources threatened. This selfish interest of the elites does not mean, however, that they are necessarily undemocratic or always antiprogressive. Whereas some policies, such as favorable tax-avoidance laws, may be perceived as elitist in nature, other policies benefit many members of the public. Indeed, political scientists Thomas Dye and Harmon Ziegler propose that American elites are more devoted to democratic principles and rights than are most members of the mass public.[7]

Many observers contend that economic and social developments in the last several years have strengthened the perception that America is governed by an elite, privileged group. Wealthier citizens have educational opportunities that poorer individuals believe they cannot afford. Moreover, as you will read in Chapter 10, political campaigns are expensive, and campaign costs have increased steadily each year. Today, candidates for political office, unless they can raise campaign funds from wealthy supporters or interest groups, have to drop out of the race—or not enter it in the first place. Some predict that if present trends continue, we will indeed have a "democracy for the few." (See the feature entitled *Politics and Economics: The Digital Divide* for a discussion of how computers may serve the interests of "the few.")

Democracy for Groups

A different school of thought looks at the characteristics of the American electorate and finds that our form of democracy is based on group interests. Even if the average citizen cannot keep up with political issues or cast a deciding vote in any election, the individual's interests will be protected by groups that represent her or him.

Pluralism
A theory that views politics as a conflict among interest groups. Political decision making is characterized by bargaining and compromise.

Theorists who subscribe to **pluralism** as a way of understanding American politics believe that people are naturally social and inclined to form associations. In the pluralists' view, politics is the struggle among groups to gain benefits for their members. Given the structures of the American political system, group conflicts tend to be settled by compromise and accommodation so that each interest is satisfied to some extent.[8]

Pluralists see public policy as resulting from group interactions carried out within Congress and the executive branch. Because there are a multitude of interests, no one group can dominate the political process. Furthermore, because most individuals have more than one interest, conflict among groups does not divide the nation into hostile camps.

There are a number of flaws in some of the basic assumptions of this theory. Among these are the relatively low number of people who formally join interest groups, the real disadvantages of pluralism for the poorer citizens, and the belief that group decision making always reflects the best interests of the nation.

[6]Michael Parenti, *Democracy for the Few,* 7th ed. (New York: St. Martin's Press, 1995).

[7]Thomas Dye and Harmon Ziegler, *The Irony of Democracy: An Uncommon Introduction to American Politics,* 11th ed. (Orlando, Fla.: Harcourt Brace, 1999).

[8]David Truman, *The Governmental Process: Political Interests and Public Opinion* (New York: Knopf, 1951); and Robert Dahl, *Who Governs?* (New Haven, Conn.: Yale University Press, 1961).

politics and economics

The Digital Divide

By the early 2000s, Internet usage was increasing at a staggering pace. Millions of people around the globe now visit, shop, do business, take care of their personal finances, and find information on the Internet. In the United States, more than 50 percent of all households have access to the Internet from their homes.

AGE AND INCOME DIFFERENCES

One would think that younger Americans who have been exposed to computers and the Internet in school are more likely to use them than are older Americans. In fact, those between thirty-five and fifty-five years of age use computers and the Internet the most; this age group is also very likely to use computers at work and at home. Senior groups in society are much less likely to use computers, however. Only 16 percent of Americans between the ages of seventy and eighty use a computer, and only 4 percent of those eighty years of age and older do so.

The age gap is significant, but the economic gap is much greater. The difference between access to computers and the Internet between poor Americans and those who are better off has been named the "digital divide." Not only is there a divide between rich and poor in the use of computers, but this divide is even greater for families of color. Among families earning $15,000 to $35,000 anually, 32 percent of whites have computers at home while only 19 percent of Hispanic and African American families do. Internet use by families in that income bracket is fairly low, with only 8 percent of African American

families having access to the Internet. In comparison, among households with incomes over $75,000, more than 60 percent of whites and 54 percent of African Americans have Internet access at home.

Computer and Internet use also varies by state and by region. Alaska reports that 62.4 percent of households have computers. Mississippi and West Virginia, in contrast, report that less than 29 percent of all families have computers at home.

IMPLICATIONS OF THE DIGITAL DIVIDE

What difference does it make that some groups are less likely to have computers or use the Internet than others? For one thing, groups without Internet access have far less access to news from varying sources about political and social isues. They cannot connect to their elected representatives via the Internet or take advantage of government services and information that can be found there. Perhaps most importantly, population groups that have less access to computers and the Internet are seriously disadvantaged as potential employees. Without computer skills, members of these families and their children are even less likely to find high-paying jobs or advance in a career.*

FOR CRITICAL ANALYSIS

Should the government make computers available to all American households so that every family can access the Internet?

*For more information on the digital divide, see the Web site of the National Telecommunications and Information Administration at http://www.ntia.doc.gov.

With these flaws in mind, critics see a danger that groups may become so powerful that all policies become compromises crafted to satisfy the interests of the largest groups. The interests of the public as a whole, then, cannot be considered. Critics of pluralism have suggested that a democratic system can be virtually paralyzed by the struggle between interest groups. This struggle results in a condition sometimes called **hyperpluralism,** meaning that groups and their needs control the government and decision making rather than the government's acting for the good of the nation.

Both pluralism and elite theory attempt to explain the real workings of American democracy. Neither approach is complete, nor can either be proved. Viewing the United States as run by elites reminds us that the founders themselves were not great defenders of the mass public. In contrast, the pluralist view underscores both the advantages and the disadvantages of Americans' inclination to join, to organize, and to pursue benefits for themselves. It points out all of the places within the American political system in which interest groups find it comfortable to work. With this knowledge, the system can be adjusted to keep interest groups within the limits of the public good.

Hyperpluralism
A situation that arises when interest groups become so powerful that they dominate the political decision-making structures, rendering any consideration of the greater public interest impossible.

Certain groups within the United States insist on maintaining their own cultural beliefs and practices. The Amish, pictured here, are descended from German religious sects and live in close communities in Pennsylvania, Ohio, Indiana, and Illinois, as well as in other states. The more conservative Amish groups do not use modern conveniences, such as automobiles or electricity, and have resisted immunizations and mandatory schooling for their children.

Political Culture
The collection of beliefs and attitudes toward government and the political process held by a community or nation.

Political Socialization
The process through which individuals learn a set of political attitudes and form opinions about social issues. The family and the educational system are two of the most important forces in the political socialization process.

INFOTRAC®
COLLEGE EDITION

Political Socialization,
Party Identification

Dominant Culture
The values, customs, language, and ideals established by the group or groups in a society that traditionally have controlled politics and government institutions in that society.

Ideas and Politics: Political Culture

The writers of the American constitution believed that the structures they had created would provide for both democracy and a stable political system. They also believed that the nation would be sustained by its **political culture**—a concept defined as a patterned set of ideas, values, and ways of thinking about government and politics. In fact, one of the roles that the founders assigned to women in the early years of the republic was to be the guardians of the political culture and the teachers of our fundamental beliefs to generations of children.

There is considerable consensus among American citizens about certain concepts basic to the U.S. political system. Given that the vast majority of Americans are descendants of immigrants having diverse cultural and political backgrounds, how can we account for this consensus? Primarily, it is the result of **political socialization**—the process by which such beliefs and values are transmitted to new immigrants and to our children. The nation depends on several different agents to transmit to children and newcomers to our nation the precepts of our national culture.

The most obvious source of political socialization is the family. Parents teach their children about the value of participating in the political system through their example and through their approval. One of the primary functions of the public education system in the United States is to teach the values of the political culture to students through history courses, through discussions of political issues, and through the rituals of pledging allegiance to the flag and celebrating national holidays. Traditionally, political parties also have played a role in political socialization as a way to bring new voters to their ranks.

Before we discuss some of the most fundamental concepts of the American political culture, it is important to note that these values can be considered those of the **dominant culture**. The dominant culture in the United States has its roots in Western European civilization. From that civilization, American politics has inherited a bias toward individualism, private property, Judeo-Christian ethics, and, to some extent, the male domination of societal decisions. As the descendants of more recent immigrant groups, especially those from Asian and Islamic nations, become part of the American mainstream, there will be more challenges to the dominant culture. Other cultural heritages honor community or family over individualism and sometimes place far less emphasis on materialism. Additionally, changes in our own society have brought about the breakdown of some values, such as the sanctity of the family structure, and the acceptance of others, such as women pursuing careers in the workplace.

The Fundamental Values

Some nations are very homogeneous, with most of their citizens having the same ethnic and religious background and sharing a common history. Achieving consensus on the basic values of the political culture is fairly easy in these nations. Because the United States is a nation of immigrants, socializing people into the political culture is an important function of the society. Over the two hundred years of its history, however, the people of the United States have formed a deep commitment to certain values and ideas. Among these are liberty, equality, and property.

Liberty. The term **liberty** can be defined as the greatest freedom of individuals that is consistent with the freedom of other individuals in the society. In the United States, our civil liberties include religious freedom—both the right to practice whatever religion one chooses and freedom from any state-imposed religion. Our civil liberties also include freedom of speech—the right to express our opinions freely on matters, including government actions. Freedom of speech is perhaps one of our most prized liberties, because a democracy could not endure without it. These and other basic guarantees of liberty are not found in the body of the U.S. Constitution but in the Bill of Rights, the first ten amendments to the Constitution.

The process of ensuring liberty for all Americans did not end with the adoption of the Bill of Rights but has continued throughout our history. Political issues often turn on how a particular liberty should be interpreted or the extent to which it should be limited in the interests of society as a whole. Some of the most emotionally charged issues today, for example, have to do with whether our civil liberties include the liberty to have an abortion or (for terminally ill persons) to commit assisted suicide.

Equality. The Declaration of Independence states, "All men are created equal." Today, that statement has been amended by the political culture to include groups other than white males—women, African Americans, Native Americans, Asian Americans, and others. The definition of **equality**, however, has been disputed by Americans since the Revolution.[9] Does equality mean simply political equality—the right to register to vote, to cast a ballot, and to run for political office? Does equality mean equal opportunity for individuals to develop their talents and skills? If the latter is the meaning of equality, what should the United States do to ensure equal opportunities for the poor and the disabled? As you will read in later chapters of this book, much of America's politics has concerned just such questions. Although most Americans believe strongly that all persons should have the opportunity to fulfill their potential, many disagree about whether it is the government's responsibility to eliminate economic and social differences. Interestingly, the Internet may provide Americans with a forum in which all are equal—regardless of race, color, ethnic origin, gender, economic status, and the like.

---

[9]Richard J. Ellis, "Rival Visions of Equality in American Political Culture," *Review of Politics,* Vol. 54 (Spring 1992), p. 254.

DID YOU KNOW...
That the Pledge of Allegiance was written by two journalists as a promotional stunt for a children's magazine, *Youth's Companion,* to be recited by children on Columbus Day in 1892?

Liberty
The greatest freedom of individuals that is consistent with the freedom of other individuals in the society.

Equality
A concept that all people are of equal worth.

Property

Anything that is or may be subject to ownership. As conceived by the political philosopher John Locke, the right to property is a natural right superior to human law (laws made by government).

Property. Many Americans probably remember that the "unalienable rights" asserted in the Declaration of Independence are the rights to "life, liberty, and the pursuit of happiness." The inspiration for that phrase, however, came from the writings of an English philosopher, John Locke (1632–1704), who stated that people's rights were to life, liberty, and **property.** In American political culture, the pursuit of happiness and property are considered to be closely related. Our capitalist system is based on private property rights. Indeed, Americans place great value on owning land, acquiring material possessions, and seeking profits through new business ventures. (For a relatively new type of business enterprise, see this chapter's *Making Waves* feature.)

Property can be seen as giving its owner political power and the liberty to do whatever he or she wants. At the same time, the ownership of property immediately creates inequality in society. The desire to own property, however, is so widespread among all classes of Americans that socialist movements, which advocate the redistribution of wealth and property, have had a difficult time securing a wide following here.

Democracy, liberty, equality, and property—these concepts lie at the core of American political culture. Other issues—such as majority rule, popular sovereignty, and **fraternity**—are closely related to them. These fundamental principles are so deeply ingrained in U.S. culture that most Americans rarely question them. (See this chapter's *Critical Perspective* for a discussion of what Americans believe about their nation's future.)

Fraternity

From the Latin *fraternus* (brother), a term that came to mean, in the political philosophy of the eighteenth century, the condition in which each individual considers the needs of all others; a brotherhood. In the French Revolution of 1789, the popular cry was "liberty, equality, and fraternity."

The Stability of the Culture

Political culture plays an important role in holding society together, because the system of ideas at the core of that culture must persuade people to support the existing political process through their attitudes and participation. If people begin to doubt the ideas underlying the culture, they will not transmit those beliefs to their children or support the existing political processes.

Consider that some subgroups, such as Native Americans and the Amish, have made concerted efforts to preserve their language or cultural practices. Many immigrant groups, including Hispanics, Asian Americans, and Caribbean Americans, maintain their language or cultural values within American cities and states. The question is whether these subgroups also subscribe to the values of the American political culture.

making Waves

Political Information for Sale

Traditionally, Internet sites offering information on political candidates, campaign financing, and the like have been dominated by nonprofit and volunteer groups. Given the American penchant for finding opportunities to make profits, however, it should come as no surprise that some people have created for-profit ventures in this area.

Consider the Voter.com Web site (at **http://www.voter.com**), created by twenty-five-year-old Justin Dangel. Dangel's mission is to provide voters with a one-stop Web site at which they can obtain information about all political candidates. A key aspect of this for-profit venture involves collecting voters' political opinions and creating political profiles of the site's users. Then, for a price, candidates and interest groups can use the Web site as a campaign vehicle and direct their political advertising to certain target groups. For example, if one of Voter.com's users indicates that he or she is interested in environmental causes, then an environmental group will be allowed to send e-mail to that user about the group's positions on various issues. Another profit-making possibility is to sell aggregate political information about voter preferences to candidates and other interested parties.

FOR CRITICAL ANALYSIS

Can you see any problems with creating databases of individuals' political beliefs?

critical perspective

What Do Americans See for the Twenty-First Century?

Americans entered the twenty-first century with hopes and fears, and uncertainties and expectations, but not, perhaps, with the opinions expected by the news media and the pundits. Americans, on the whole, did not worry too much about computer problems and did not make a run on the banks on December 31, 1999. They did not travel around the world to celebrate but stayed home with family and friends. They did, however, exhibit a sense of unease about the direction in which America is going, as we will see.

How Strong Is the Economy?

Most Americans are quite aware of the long period of economic prosperity in the 1990s and expect that it will continue. More than 50 percent of American households now hold stocks or bonds, and the average income of all households has shown amazing growth over the last decade. In a *Los Angeles Times* poll taken in November 1999, 83 percent of the respondents said that the economy was doing well. More than seven in ten adults said that their own financial position was secure or fairly secure. Generally, Americans favor using the government surplus for strengthening the Social Security fund. Interestingly enough, Americans have shown only modest interest in any promises to use the surplus for tax reductions.

What Is the Direction of the Nation?

Given the economic prosperity of the United States, it is surprising to learn that many Americans believe that the country is not "going in the right direction." The *Los Angeles Times* poll found that only 42 percent of adults polled said that the country is headed in the right direction, while 47 percent said that it is going in the wrong direction. More liberal Democrats than moderates or Republicans saw the country as going in the right direction. Women and African

WHAT WILL GET BETTER OR WORSE IN THE UNITED STATES BY 2020?

	BETTER	WORSE
Race relations	66%	30%
Medical care	54	43
Quality of life	49	47
Environment	42	55
Moral values	34	62

SOURCES: *Los Angeles Times* Poll, November 22, 1999, http://www.latimes.com/news/timespoll; "Americans Decry Moral Decline," *The Wall Street Journal*, June 24, 1999; *The Polling Report*, http://www.pollingreport.com.

Americans, however, tended to believe that the nation is headed in the wrong direction.

What are the issues that trouble Americans? A *Wall Street Journal* study conducted in mid-1999 found that social issues and family issues cause a great deal of distress and concern to Americans across the board. Among the societal problems that worry Americans are the use of drugs among children (68 percent), violence and sex in the media (51 percent), the declining role of religion (49 percent), and the declining sense of community (47 percent). Americans also believe that significant problems are rooted in the family, including parents' lack of attention to their children (83 percent), high divorce rates (63 percent), and the lack of discipline in schools (56 percent). Americans yearn to have leaders with high moral standards, but they do not trust their political leaders when they talk about social and moral values.

What Do Americans See for the Future?

As the new century began, many different polling groups asked Americans what issues they expected to see in the future and how their world might change. When asked which nation would be the major power of the twenty-first century, 62 percent said the United States and 16 percent said China. Americans believed that war, poverty, environmental degradation, and overpopulation would be problems in the new century. Their greatest hopes for the new century were for world peace (38 percent), for cures for cancer and AIDS (13 percent), and for people to get along better with each other (9 percent).

Perhaps the most interesting data concern the changes Americans anticipated for our nation in the new century. As shown in the table to the left, Americans were quite optimistic about some serious issues. They believed that both "race relations" and the quality of medical care would improve in the next two decades. The majority of those polled, however, believed that the environment and moral values would become worse. Generally, they felt that the quality of life in their own communities would be better.

Americans also think about the technology of the future. When asked about life at the end of the twenty-first century, Americans said that the Internet would still be used, as would printed books and the telephone. They did not think that the post office and cars that run on gasoline would still be around.

FOR CRITICAL ANALYSIS
1. Why do you think that moral and social issues have become so important to Americans?
2. What role will the United States play in bringing greater peace and tolerance to the world?

Studies of immigrant groups and ethnic subgroups generally have shown that they are as supportive of the concepts of American political culture as other Americans are. For example, when asked if they would rather live in the United States than anywhere else, 95 percent of whites said the United States, as did 87 percent of African American respondents and 92 percent of Hispanics. Some surveys have shown that immigrants are even more enthusiastic about American values than are native-born respondents. As shown in Figure 1–1, immigrants are less supportive of holding on to their own culture than are adults in the general population.

The Changing Face of America

The face of America is changing as its citizens age, become more diverse, and generate new needs for laws and policies. Long a nation of growth, the United States has become a middle-aged nation with a low birthrate and an increasing number of older citizens who want services from the government. The 2000 census showed that between 1990 and 2000, the U.S. population grew 13.2 percent, faster than experts expected it to.

Several aspects of this population trend have significant political consequences. As Figure 1–2 shows, the population is aging quickly; the median age (the age at which half the people are older and half are younger) was thirty-five in the year 2000. Even more startling is the fact that almost 13 percent of the population is now sixty-five years old or older. By the year 2050, more than one-fourth of the population will be retired or approaching retirement. If the current retirement and pension systems remain in place, including Social Security, a very large proportion of each worker's wages will have to be deducted to support benefits for the retired (see Chapter 16).

Ethnic Change

The ethnic character of the United States is also changing. Whites have a very low birthrate, whereas African Americans and Hispanics have more children per family. As displayed in Figure 1–3 on page 22, including the effects of immigration, the proportion of whites has decreased, and the proportions of Hispanics, African Americans, and Asian Americans have increased. (For a current issue in immigration policy, see this chapter's *Which Side Are You On?*)

As displayed in Figure 1–3 on page 22

FIGURE 1-1

Immigrants Adopt American Culture

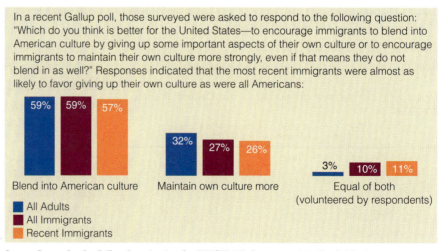

In a recent Gallup poll, those surveyed were asked to respond to the following question: "Which do you think is better for the United States—to encourage immigrants to blend into American culture by giving up some important aspects of their own culture or to encourage immigrants to maintain their own culture more strongly, even if that means they do not blend in as well?" Responses indicated that the most recent immigrants were almost as likely to favor giving up their own culture as were all Americans:

59%   59%   57%
32%   27%   26%
3%   10%   11%

Blend into American culture   Maintain own culture more   Equal of both (volunteered by respondents)

■ All Adults
■ All Immigrants
■ Recent Immigrants

SOURCE: Survey by the Gallup Organization for CNN/*USA Today,* reported in *The Public Perspective,* February/March 1998, p. 52.

which side are you on?

Should the United States Encourage the Immigration of High-Tech Workers?

A bill recently passed by both chambers of Congress raised the visa limit on a temporary basis from about 115,000 to 195,000 annually, but that increase will expire in 2002. Some studies have shown that there are an estimated one million positions that are currently unfilled in the information technology industry.

The computer and software industries would like the visa limit to be raised even higher. They claim that the shortage of American-trained workers is so severe that their research and development efforts will be slowed and their profits affected if they cannot "import" workers. Corporations in other industries that find it difficult to staff their employment needs also support the expansion of visas.

Others say that the estimates of a worker shortage are greatly overblown. The labor unions see an increase in visas as a way to keep American workers from these jobs. Some advocates for the rights of older workers believe that this group will suffer—companies could lay off or fire older, higher-salaried workers and then import foreign workers to perform the same work for lower pay.

Are there other solutions to the shortage of high-tech workers? Could corporations meet industry demands by retraining their own employees or working more closely with colleges and universities to train more workers in information technol-ogy? Or, in a free market economy, should companies be free to hire workers wherever they find them?

DOES IT MATTER?

If you plan to work in the field of information technology, will it matter whether more foreign high-tech workers are allowed to enter the country each year? Why or why not?

GOING ONLINE

To find out more about this debate, try the following Web sites: Communications Workers of America, at **http://www.cwa-legis-pol.org**; *ITAA, at* **http://www.itaa.org**; *and The Public Agenda, at* **http://www. publicagenda.org**.

Although studies show that the various groups in this country share many common values, conflicts between ethnic and racial groups also exist. These conflicts all too often erupt into "hate speech" or "hate crimes," which pose an increasing threat to political stability. There is no reason to assume that these and other divisive forces at work in our society cannot be overcome, but there is also no reason to ignore them. Consider, for example, the results of a recent *Newsweek* poll, in which respondents were asked the following question: "One hundred years from today, will the United States still exist as one nation?" Forty-eight percent of the African American respondents answered "No" to this question, as did 26 percent of white respondents and 38 percent of Hispanic respondents.

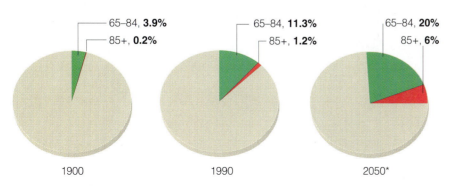

65–84, **3.9%**
85+, **0.2%**

65–84, **11.3%**
85+, **1.2%**

65–84, **20%**
85+, **6%**

1900

1990

2050*

*Data for 2050 are estimates.
SOURCE: U.S. Bureau of the Census.

FIGURE 1-2

The Aging of America

The figures clearly show that the portion of the population over age sixty-five will double by 2050.

FIGURE 1-3

Distribution of the U.S. Population
by Race and Hispanic Origin, 1980
to 2050

By 2050, minorities will constitute about half
of the U.S. population.

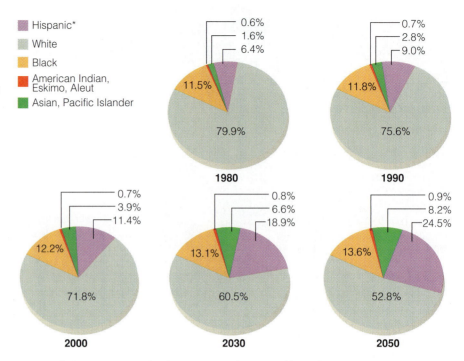

Hispanic*
White
Black
American Indian,
Eskimo, Aleut
Asian, Pacific Islander

1980
0.6%
1.6%
6.4%
11.5%
79.9%

1990
0.7%
2.8%
9.0%
11.8%
75.6%

2000
0.7%
3.9%
11.4%
12.2%
71.8%

2030
0.8%
6.6%
18.9%
13.1%
60.5%

2050
0.9%
8.2%
24.5%
13.6%
52.8%

*Persons of Hispanic origin can be of any race. Data for 2000 and beyond are estimates.
SOURCE: U.S. Bureau of the Census.

Immigrants are also likely to shape American politics in the future. Few
Americans think of the current period in our history as being as volatile as the
early years of the twentieth century, when millions of Europeans immigrated to
the United States. Yet, as Figure 1–4 shows, the percentage of the U.S. population that is foreign-born was about as high by 2000 as it was during the 1930s.

Hispanic Americans join together to support
a political candidate. Like other ethnic
groups, these Hispanic voters seek to have
their concerns heard by the candidates. In
return, political candidates try to show their
appreciation for the culture of the ethnic voters by delivering speeches in their language
or promising more benefits for the group.

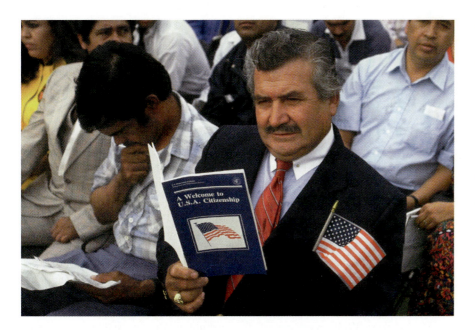

Each year thousands of immigrants are sworn in as new U.S. citizens. The U.S. Constitution in Article I, Section 8, declares that Congress shall have the power to "establish a uniform Rule of Naturalization." Naturalization is the process by which individuals who are not yet citizens become U.S. citizens. Such individuals are called naturalized citizens as opposed to native-born citizens. There are myriad requirements to become a naturalized citizen. Because it is often difficult to do so, many immigrants remain in this country without proper documentation.

In 2000, an estimated 1.7 million persons immigrated to the United States legally, with the greatest number coming from Mexico, but sizable numbers from Asian nations as well. These changes are placing strain on the cohesiveness of U.S. political culture and on the willingness of citizens to support the political structures of the nation.

Other Trends

Other changes in the face of America have more to do with our changing society. More Americans continue to fill the urban places of the nation in comparison with rural areas. By 2000 more than 75 percent of the population lived in an urban environment. Women continued to increase their participation in the educational system. By the beginning of the 1990s, as many women as men had

FIGURE 1-4

Percentage of U.S. Population That Is Foreign-Born 1900–2000

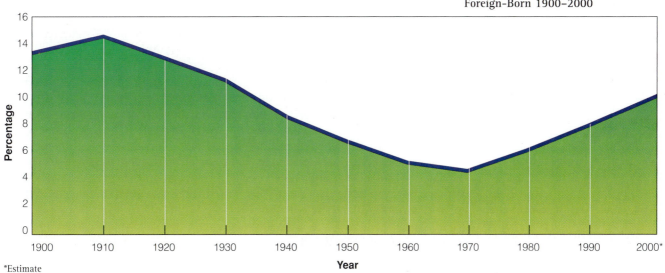

*Estimate

SOURCE: U.S. Bureau of the Census.

For Americans, terrorism always seemed to be a problem for other countries. In the last decade, though, terrorism on American soil has occurred, such as the 1995 bombing of the Alfred P. Murrah Federal Building in Oklahoma City. A crude, but effective, home-made bomb was detonated at the base of this building, killing 168 persons and injuring hundreds of others. It is thought that those convicted of the crime were affiliated with a local militia group.

completed their high school educations, and the percentage of women who had completed college has continued to grow.

Change also continues in the structure of American families, although the traditional two-parent family is still very strong. Just twenty years ago, more than 85 percent of children lived in a two-parent family. Today, 71 percent of children under age eighteen live in two-parent families, and 25 percent live with only one parent. About one-fourth of the children of one-parent families live in poverty.

Other changes also have consequences for social policies. Although the national government has been committed to ending poverty since the mid-1960s, 12.7 percent of all Americans still live in households that have incomes below the official poverty line. Although this number is large, it is below the 22 percent figure recorded in 1960. Far more alarming is the trend in prison populations. Since 1980, the number of persons incarcerated in federal, state, and local prisons and jails has increased from about a half a million to more than 2 million. The number of Americans who lack basic skills is also disturbing; recent national surveys have found that about one-fifth of all Americans are barely literate and have difficulty dealing with simple documents.

Also emerging as a part of the American landscape are citizens' militias or "patriot" groups. While members of these groups might say that they are proud to be Americans, many in these groups view the national government as the enemy—not the protector—of civil rights and liberties. Animosity toward the national government, for whatever reason, is thought to have motivated the 1995 bombing of the Oklahoma City Alfred P. Murrah Federal Building and some other terrorist acts against government bureaucrats, particularly in the West.

Each of these statistics raises political questions for the society as a whole. These facts challenge voters and their representatives to change policies in order to reduce poverty, crime, and illiteracy—if society can agree on how to accomplish these tasks.

Ideas and Politics: Ideology

Ideology
A comprehensive and logically ordered set of beliefs about the nature of people and about the institutions and role of government.

Liberalism
A set of beliefs that includes the advocacy of positive government action to improve the welfare of individuals, support for civil rights, and tolerance for political and social change.

Conservatism
A set of beliefs that includes a limited role for the national government in helping individuals, support for traditional values and lifestyles, and a cautious response to change.

An **ideology** is a closely linked set of beliefs about the goal of politics and the most desirable political order. True ideologies are well-organized theories that can guide virtually every decision that an individual or society can make. As discussed in this chapter's *Global View*, the major ideologies of our time are usually represented as a continuum from the far left to the far right according to their views of the power of government. Few Americans, however, derive their views on politics from the more extreme ideologies. In fact, the U.S. political spectrum has been dominated for decades by two relatively moderate ideological positions: **liberalism** and **conservatism**.

American liberals believe that government should take strong positive action to solve the nation's economic and social problems. They believe that it is the obligation of the government to enhance opportunities for the economic and social equality of all individuals. Liberals tend to support programs to reduce poverty, to endorse progressive taxation to redistribute income from wealthier classes to the poorer, and to rely on government regulation to guide the activities of business and the economy.

Conservatives take a quite different approach to the role of government in the economy, believing that the private sector probably can outperform the government in almost any activity. Believing that the individual is primarily responsible for his or her own well-being, conservatives are less supportive of government initiatives to redistribute income or to craft programs that will change the status of individuals.

In the moral sphere, conservatives tend to support more government regulation of social values and moral decisions than do liberals. Thus, conservatives tend to oppose gay rights legislation and propose stronger curbs on pornography. Liberals usually show greater tolerance for different life choices and oppose government attempts to regulate personal behavior and morals.

Individuals in the society may not accept the full range of either liberal or conservative views. It is not unusual for Americans to be quite liberal on economic issues and supportive of considerable government intervention in the economy while holding conservative views on moral and social issues. Such a mixture of views makes it difficult for American political parties to identify themselves solely with either a conservative or a liberal viewpoint, because such a position may cost them votes on specific issues.

There are also smaller groups of Americans who consider themselves to be communists, socialists, or libertarians, but these groups play a minor role in the national political arena. The limited role played by these and other alternative political perspectives is reinforced by the fact that they receive little positive exposure in classrooms, the media, or public discourse.

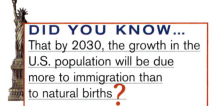

DID YOU KNOW...
That by 2030, the growth in the U.S. population will be due more to immigration than to natural births**?**

global view

Competing Visions of Power

Political ideologies offer their adherents well-organized theories. These theories propose goals for the society and the political means by which those goals can be achieved. At the core of every political ideology is a set of values that guides its theory of governmental power. If we compare political ideologies on the basis of how much power the government should have within a society, we can array them on a continuum from left to right, as shown in the first box below.

For each of these ideological positions, the amount of power granted to the government is intended to achieve a certain set of goals within the society, and the perfect society would completely achieve these values. The values are arrayed in the second box below.

Each of these ideological positions has adherents in the United States. Given widely shared cultural values, however, only two of these belief systems consistently have played a central part in American political debates: liberalism and conservatism.

FOR CRITICAL ANALYSIS

What kinds of activities do you believe the government should control? When is government action most effective? Does answering those questions help you identify with one of the ideological positions described below?

How Much Power Should the Government Have?

MARXISM-LENINISM	SOCIALISM	LIBERALISM	CONSERVATISM	LIBERTARIANISM
Central control of economy and political system.	Active government control of major economic sectors.	Positive government action in economy and to achieve social goals.	Positive government action to support capitalism; action to uphold certain values.	Government action only for defense; almost no regulation of economy or individual behavior.

What Values Should the Government Pursue?

MARXISM-LENINISM	SOCIALISM	LIBERALISM	CONSERVATISM	LIBERTARIANISM
Total equality and security; unity and solidarity.	Economic equality; community.	Political liberty; economic security; equal opportunity.	Political liberty; economic liberty; order.	Total political and economic liberty for individuals.

America's Politics:
Issues for the Twenty-First Century

Although the U.S. government is one of the oldest democratic regimes in the world and its Constitution remains relatively unchanged more than two hundred years after it was written, the U.S. political system has been dynamic since its founding. As you will read in the chapters that follow, Americans have changed their ideas about who votes and who controls the government, expanded their list of rights and liberties, originated and then revised a number of political parties, and significantly altered their view of the role of the national government in their lives and businesses.

As in other parts of the world, in the United States citizens have often pressed to make their government more responsive to the needs of the society and more effective in its functioning. What makes Americans different from the people of those other nations is a long and stable history that encourages them to try to modify the political structures and processes rather than invent totally new ones. Changing the political machinery has brought changes in the past—witness the social legislation of the New Deal in the 1930s and the Great Society in the 1960s—and Americans generally believe that significant change can occur again.

What are some of the American political tasks that remain unfinished as we enter the new century? Clearly, Americans struggle to keep a cohesive society as people become more diverse in terms of ethnic and racial backgrounds, generational expectations, and economic level. How can a wider range of Americans participate in the political process and make the process work for them? What kinds of institutions and policies can meet the demands of world markets, the needs of an aging population, the expectations of a society with instant media access, and the hopes of the youngest generations for jobs and opportunities similar to those given to their parents and grandparents? Many alternatives are up for debate: the decentralization of power to the states, new approaches to retirement security and the protection of privacy rights, universal access to the Internet to connect all Americans, and hundreds more.

The remainder of this book will examine the roots and structures of contemporary American government and politics, with particular attention to the ways in which they have changed over time. At the end of each chapter, we will consider the issues that face the United States at the beginning of the twenty-first century—whether those issues involve the expansion of civil liberties or attempts to curb the power of interest groups. Without a doubt, there is enough unfinished business to last many decades. Also without a doubt, Americans will make political changes as they see fit.

making a difference

Seeing Democracy in Action

One way to begin understanding the American political system is to observe a legislative body in action. There are thousands of elected legislatures in the United States at all levels of government. You might choose to visit the city council, a school board, the township board of trustees, the state legislature, or the U.S. Congress. Before attending a business session of the legislature, try to find out how the members are elected. Look at your state government's Web site. Are they chosen by the "at-large" method of election so that each member represents the whole community, or are they chosen by specific geographic districts or wards? Some other questions you might want to ask are these: Is there a chairperson or official leader who controls the meetings and who may have more power than the other leaders? What are the responsibilities of this legislature? Are the members paid political officials, or do they volunteer their services? Do the officials serve as full-time or part-time employees?

When you visit the legislature, keep in mind the theory of representative democracy. The legislators or council members are elected to represent their constituents (those who voted them into office). Observe how often the members refer to their constituents or to the special needs of their community or electoral district. Listen carefully for the sources of conflict within a community. If there is a

debate, for example, over a zoning proposal that involves the issue of land use, try to figure out why some members oppose the proposal. Perhaps the greatest sources of conflict in local government are questions of taxation and expenditure. It is important to remember that the council or board is also supposed to be working toward the good of the whole; listen for discussions of the community's priorities.

If you want to follow up on your visit and learn more about representative government in action, try to get a brief interview with one of the members of the council or board. In general, legislators are very willing to talk to students, particularly students who also are voters. Ask the member how he or she sees the job of representative. How can the wishes of the constituents be identified? How does the representative balance the needs of the ward or district with the good of the whole community? You also might ask the member how he or she keeps in touch with constituents and informs them of the activities of the council or board. You can write to many legislators via e-mail. You might ask how much e-mail they receive and who actually answers it.

For a different view of democracy in action, watch the activities of the House of Representatives or Senate on one of the C-SPAN channels on cable television. These public television channels show speeches and actions on the floor

of both chambers, broadcast committee hearings when possible, and televise interviews with government officials and the journalists who cover government and politics. If you watch the action on the floor of the House, for example, notice how few members actually are present. Is the member addressing her or his colleagues, or the voters back home? Why do you think members use large charts and graphs? Most observers of Congress believe that members dress differently and use a different speaking style since the proceedings have been televised.

Think about the advantages and disadvantages of representative democracy. Do you think the average citizen would take the time to consider all of the issues that representatives must debate? Do you think that, on the whole, the elected representatives act responsibly for their constituents?

To find out when and where the local legislative bodies meet, look up the number of the city hall or county building in the telephone directory, and call the clerk of council. You might also check cable television listings. In many communities, city council meetings and county board meetings can be seen on public access channels. For information on the structure of your local government, contact the local chapter of the League of Women Voters.

Many cities and almost all state governments have Internet Web sites to investigate. Take a look at some of these, and consider the usefulness of the information provided there to the average citizen.

Key terms

anarchy 10
aristocracy 10
authority 9
compliance 9
consent of the people 10
conservatism 24
democracy 10

direct democracy 10
divided government 6
dominant culture 16
elite 10
elite theory 13
equality 17
fraternity 18

government 7
hyperpluralism 15
ideology 24
initiative 10
institution 6
legislature 10
legitimacy 9

liberalism 24	political culture 16	referendum 10
liberty 17	political socialization 16	representative democracy 11
limited government 13	politics 7	republic 11
majority 12	popular sovereignty 13	totalitarian regime 9
majority rule 12	power 9	universal suffrage 12
oligarchy 10	property 18	
pluralism 14	recall 10	

Chapter summary

1 The willingness of Americans to debate new initiatives and to demand changes in the way the government works is at the core of our democratic nation. Americans worked hard to establish this form of government and continue to expend effort in politics to keep it functioning.

2 *Politics* was defined by Harold Lasswell as the process of "who gets what, when, and how" in a society. David Easton defined it as the "authoritative allocation of values" in a society. The prerogative of government to make allocative decisions is based on authority, legitimacy, and power. Sources of power include direct democracy, a system of government in which political decisions are made by the people directly.

3 Fearing the problems of a direct democracy, the framers of the Constitution set up a representative, or indirect, democracy. The people control the government through the election of representatives. Decisions are made by majority rule, although the rights of minorities are protected.

4 Some scholars believe that most of the power in our society is held by elite leaders who actively influence political decisions, while the masses are apathetic. The pluralist viewpoint, in contrast, suggests that groups representing the different interests of the people struggle for political power. In pluralist theory, the political process is characterized by bargaining and compromise between groups.

5 The American political system is characterized by a set of cultural beliefs that includes liberty, equality, and property. These beliefs are passed on to each generation of Americans through the process of political socialization.

6 The face of America is changing as the population ages and becomes more ethnically diverse. Other changes—including the urbanization of the population, the growing number of women in the work force, and poverty—are also altering the face of the nation.

7 Americans' ideas about how government should act in their lives vary widely. These views may be included in liberal, conservative, or other ideological positions.

Selected print and electronic resources

SUGGESTED READINGS

Beem, Christopher. *The Necessity of Politics: Reclaiming Public Life (Morality and Society)*. Chicago: University of Chicago Press, 1999. This author argues that simply having a healthy civil society is not enough to keep our democracy alive. He believes that society needs politics, political ideas, and a government to exist.

Gamble, Andrew. *Politics and Fate (Themes for the 21st Century)*. Malden, Mass.: Blackwell Publishers, Inc., 2000. The author contends that many people have become disenchanted with the traditional view that politics is a means used by societies to exercise control over their fate. In this book, Gamble comes to the defense of politics, explaining why we cannot do without politics and the political processes.

Haskell, John. *Direct Democracy or Representative Government?: Dispelling the Populist Myth*. Boulder, Colo.: Westview Press, 2000. The author expresses his concern over how the increased use of citizen initiatives, television, and the Internet make direct democracy more possible in this country. He fears that direct democracy will lead to unstable political majorities that are more impulsive and less deliberative than the representative elected bodies envisioned by the founders.

Lasswell, Harold. *Politics: Who Gets What, When and How*. New York: McGraw-Hill, 1936. This classic work defines the nature of politics.

Stanley, Harold W., and Richard G. Niemi. *Vital Statistics on American Politics,* 7th ed. Washington, D.C.: Congressional Quarterly Press, 1999. This valuable reference work contains

over two hundred tables and figures on a wide range of topics covering almost all aspects of American politics.

Tocqueville, Alexis de. *Democracy in America*. Edited by Phillips
Bradley. New York: Vintage Books, 1945. Life in the United
States was described by a French writer who traveled through
the nation in the 1820s.

Wolfe, Alan. *One Nation, After All: How the Middle Class Really
Think about God, Country, and Family*. New York: Viking
Press, 1998. Based on the results of a survey he conducted,
sociologist Alan Wolfe concludes that middle-class Americans
are far less polarized politically, far less judgmental, and much
more tolerant and willing to compromise than is often
thought.

MEDIA RESOURCES

All Things Considered—A daily broadcast of National Public
Radio that provides extensive coverage of political, economic,
and social news stories.

Mr. Smith Goes to Washington—A classic movie, produced in
1939, starring Jimmy Stewart as the honest citizen who goes
to Congress trying to represent his fellow citizens. The movie
dramatizes the clash between representing principles and representing corrupt interests.

Logging on

The World Wide Web is becoming a virtual library, a telephone directory, a contact source, and a vehicle to improve your
learning and understanding of issues. It
therefore is important that you become
familiar with Web resources. To help you
do this, we have included *Logging on* sections at the end of each chapter in this
book. Each of these sections contains a
list of Internet addresses, or uniform
resource locators (URLs), followed by an Internet exercise.
The URLs will help you find information on topics covered
within the chapters, as well as on related topics that you
might find interesting. We hope this feature will lead you to
some of the most interesting and productive Web locations.

The Internet should be approached with care. You
should be very careful in giving out information about
yourself. You also need to use good judgment because the
reliability or intent of any given Web site is often
unknown. Some sites are more concerned with accuracy
than others, and some sites are updated to include current
information, while others are not. Also, realize that sites
come and go continually, so some of the Web sites that we
include in these *Logging on* features may not exist by the
time you read this book.

We also have a powerful and interesting Web site for
the textbook, which you can find at

**http://www.wadsworth.com/politics/
schmidt01/index.html**

This site has many features directly related to the textbook,
including the site's most popular item—the test-review
questions.

You will also want to check out the Wadsworth Political
Science Resource Center for additional information and

learning opportunities. The URL for this site is

http://politicalscience.wadsworth.com

Finally, you may want to visit the home page of Dr.
Politics—offered by Steffen Schmidt, one of the authors of
this book—for some interesting ideas and activities relating to American government and politics. Go to

**http://www.public.iastate.edu/~sws/
homepage.html**

For discussion of current public-policy issues that are
facing the American political system, try the resources at
the Institute for Philosophy and Public Policy at

http://www.puaf.umd.edu/ippp

Information about the rules and requirements for immigration and citizenship can be found at the Web site of the
U.S. Immigration and Naturalization Service:

http://www.ins.usdoj.gov

For a basic "front door" to almost all U.S. government
Web sites, click onto the very useful site maintained by the
University of Michigan:

**http://www.lib.umich.edu/libhome/Documents.
center/govweb.html**

Using the internet for political analysis

Imagine that you are not an American citizen. Try to figure out how you can become an American citizen through the process of naturalization. Log onto the Web site of the Immigration and Naturalization Service using the URL given below and find the topic, Naturalization.

http://www.ins.usdoj.gov

Read the qualifications or eligibility requirements and decide whether you qualify. Then investigate the test materials given on the Web site to see if you would pass the history test to qualify for naturalization. Finally, look through the materials on the Web site and consider whether an immigrant is likely to (1) have a computer, (2) use the Web site, (3) understand the language, and (4) succeed in finding answers to his or her questions.

chapter 2
The Constitution

CHAPTER OUTLINE

- Initial Colonizing Efforts

- British Restrictions and Colonial Grievances

- The Colonial Response: The Continental Congresses

- Declaring Independence

- The Rise of Republicanism

- The Articles of Confederation: Our First Form of Government

- Drafting the Constitution

- The Final Document

- The Difficult Road to Ratification

- The Bill of Rights

- Altering the Constitution: The Formal Amendment Process

- Informal Methods of Constitutional Change

what if...

Constitutional Interpretation Never Changed?

BACKGROUND

OUR CONSTITUTION IS THE OLDEST WRITTEN CONSTITUTION IN THE WORLD TODAY. ONE OF THE REASONS IT HAS ENDURED IS THAT THE FRAMERS USED BROAD ENOUGH LANGUAGE TO ALLOW ROOM FOR INTERPRETATION. THE UNITED STATES SUPREME COURT HAS BECOME THE ULTIMATE DECISION MAKER WHEN IT COMES TO DECIDING WHAT THE SEVEN THOUSAND WORDS IN OUR CONSTITUTION MEAN AND HOW THEY SHOULD BE APPLIED. BUT THE VIEWS OF THE JUSTICES OF THE SUPREME COURT HAVE CHANGED OVER TIME AS SOCIETY HAS CHANGED. AND SOCIETY HAS CHANGED, AT LEAST IN PART, BECAUSE OF CHANGES IN TECHNOLOGY. ISSUES CONCERNING TELEPHONE CONVERSATIONS AND TRANSMISSION OF IDEAS OVER THE INTERNET CERTAINLY WERE NOT EVEN PIPE DREAMS TWO HUNDRED YEARS AGO. BECAUSE THE PRINCIPLES IN OUR CONSTITUTION ARE BROADLY EXPRESSED, THE SUPREME COURT HAS BEEN ABLE TO APPLY THOSE PRINCIPLES TO MEET THE NEEDS OF NEW GENERATIONS. BECAUSE OF ITS FLEXIBILITY AND ADAPTABILITY, OUR CONSTITUTION IS OFTEN REFERRED TO AS A "LIVING CONSTITUTION."

WHAT IF CONSTITUTIONAL INTERPRETATION NEVER CHANGED?

Some students of our Constitution believe that the way the Constitution is interpreted and applied should never change. Assume for a moment that whatever was in the minds of the framers some two hundred years ago remained the backbone of present-day views of the supreme law of the land. What kind of society would we have?

A RESTRICTED VIEW OF THE COMMERCE CLAUSE

Consider first the commerce clause. That clause, which is found in Article I, Section 8, of the Constitution, states that "Congress shall have the power" to "regulate Commerce . . . among the several States." The key to understanding the commerce clause is that it presumably concerns only *interstate* commerce—what goes on between and among the several states. The clause says nothing about Congress regulating activities within states (*intrastate* commerce).

The interpretation of the power of the national government to regulate all commerce has clearly changed since the framers first penned the above words. Over time, the Supreme Court has interpreted the commerce clause to mean that Congress has the power to regulate not only interstate commerce, but also any intrastate commerce that has a "substantial effect" on interstate commerce.

If the Supreme Court had not interpreted the commerce clause so expansively, our nation would be vastly different today. Many of the regulatory activities of the national government would not exist. Indeed, the national government would be a fraction of its size (but perhaps the state and local governments would be larger).

CIVIL RIGHTS AND LIBERTIES

The first ten amendments to the Constitution, the Bill of Rights, lay out the basic rights that all citizens shall enjoy. Many of the crucial issues with respect to our personal rights and liberties were not even conceived of two hundred years ago. Consider the Fourth Amendment right to be free of unreasonable searches and seizures. Originally, searches and seizures had to do with physical elements, items that could be touched or seen. In today's wired world, however, searches and seizures can take the form of police surveillance via electronic means. Over time, the Supreme Court has held that unless certain requirements are met, electronic surveillance constitutes an unreasonable search, in violation of the Fourth Amendment. If the original interpretations of this amendment were still followed, we would probably have much less protection against electronic surveillance.

Consider privacy rights. The framers did not mention a right to privacy in the Bill of Rights. Rather, modern-day interpretations have concluded that a right to privacy is implied by several of the first ten amendments to the Constitution. Further, consider such issues as abortion and assisted suicide. It is almost impossible to imagine how the Constitution as interpreted two hundred years ago could apply to these issues.

Finally, consider that the Declaration of Independence promised equality. Yet the Constitution *implicitly* acknowledged the institution of slavery and gave full political rights only to property-owning white males. The majority of Americans, including women and Native Americans, had no such rights. Had we stayed with the meaning of the Constitution as it was originally understood, certainly most of the political and civil rights enjoyed by the majority of American citizens today would not exist.

FOR CRITICAL ANALYSIS

1. What is the alternative to a "living" Constitution?

2. Why was privacy not as significant an issue two hundred years ago as it is today?

We the People of the United States, in Order to form a more perfect Union, establish Justice, insure domestic Tranquillity, provide for the common defence, promote the general Welfare, and secure the Blessings of Liberty to ourselves and our
Posterity, do ordain and establish this Constitution for the United States of
America.

Every schoolchild in America has at one time or another been exposed to these
famous words from the Preamble to the U.S. Constitution. The document
itself is remarkable. The U.S. Constitution, compared with others in the states
and in the world, is relatively short. Because amending it is difficult (as you will
see later in this chapter), it also has relatively few amendments. Perhaps even
more remarkable is the fact that it has remained largely intact for over two hundred years. In large part, this is because the principles set forth in the
Constitution are sufficiently broad that they can be adapted to meet the needs
of a changing society—as you learned in this chapter's *What If . . . .*

How and why this Constitution was created is a story that has been told and
retold. It is worth repeating, because the historical and political context in which
this country's governmental machinery was formed is essential to understanding American government and politics today. The Constitution was not the result
of completely creative thinking. Many of its provisions were grounded in contemporary political philosophy. The delegates to the Constitutional Convention
in 1787 brought with them two important sets of influences: their political culture and their political experience. In the years between the first settlements in
the New World and the writing of the Constitution, Americans had developed a
political philosophy about how people should be governed and had tried out
numerous forms of government. These experiences gave the founders the tools
with which they constructed the Constitution.

DID YOU KNOW...
That the first English claim to
territory in North America was
made by John Cabot, on behalf
of King Henry VII, on June 24,
1497?

INFOTRAC ®
COLLEGE EDITION

**Supreme Court
Strikes Down Part**

Initial Colonizing Efforts

The first English outpost in North America was set up by Sir Walter Raleigh in
the 1580s for the purpose of harassing the Spanish treasure fleets. The group,
known as the Roanoke Island Colony, stands as one of history's great mysteries:
After a three-year absence to resupply the colony, Raleigh's captain, John White,
returned in 1590 to find signs that the colony's residents apparently had moved

The first British settlers who landed on the
North American continent faced severe tests
of endurance. This woodcut depicts a cold
existence for the settlers in the late 1500s and
early 1600s.

Representative Assembly
A legislature composed of individuals who represent the population.

north to Chesapeake Bay. White was unable to search further, and no evidence of the fate of the "lost colony" has ever been recorded. Local legends in North Carolina maintain that the lost colonists survived and intermarried with the Native Americans, and that their descendants live in the region today. Recent climatological studies may have shed some light on the mystery, however. Scientists at the University of Arkansas, based on the rings of ancient cypress trees still growing in the swamps of that area, concluded that the most extreme drought during the trees' eight-hundred-year history coincided with the attempted settlement on Roanoke Island and lasted for three years.[1]

In 1607, the English government sent over a group of farmers to establish a trading post, Jamestown, in what is now Virginia. The Virginia Company of London was the first to establish successfully a permanent English colony in the Americas. The king of England gave the backers of this colony a charter granting them "full power and authority" to make laws "for the good and welfare" of the settlement. The colonists at Jamestown instituted a **representative assembly,** setting a precedent in government that was to be observed in later colonial adventures.

Jamestown was not a commercial success. Of the 105 men who landed, 67 died within the first year. But 800 new arrivals in 1609 added to their numbers. By the spring of the next year, frontier hazards had cut their numbers to 60. Of the 6,000 people who left England for Virginia between 1607 and 1623, 4,800 perished. The historian Charles Andrews has called this the "starving time for Virginia."[2] The climatological researchers just mentioned suggest that this "starving time" may have been brought about by another severe drought in the Jamestown area, which lasted from 1607 to 1612.

Separatists, the *Mayflower,* and the Compact

The first New England colony was established in 1620. A group of mostly extreme Separatists, who wished to break with the Church of England, came over on the ship *Mayflower* to the New World, landing at Plymouth (Massachusetts). Before going on shore, the adult males—women were not considered to have any

---

[1]D. W. Stahle *et al.,* "The Lost Colony and Jamestown Droughts," *Science,* April 24, 1998.
[2]Charles M. Andrews, *The Colonial Period of American History,* Vol. 1 (New Haven, Conn.: Yale University Press, 1934), p. 110.

The signing of the compact aboard the *Mayflower.* In 1620, the Mayflower Compact was signed by almost all of the men aboard the ship *Mayflower,* just before disembarking at Plymouth, Massachusetts. It stated, "We . . . covenant and combine ourselves togeather into a civil body politick . . . ; and by vertue hearof to enact, constitute, and frame such just and equal laws . . . as shall be thought [necessary] for the generall good of the Colonie."

political status—drew up the Mayflower Compact, which was signed by forty-one of the forty-four men aboard the ship on November 21, 1620. The reason for the compact was obvious. This group was outside the jurisdiction of the Virginia Company of London, which had chartered their settlement in Virginia, not Massachusetts. The Separatist leaders feared that some of the *Mayflower* passengers might conclude that they were no longer under any obligations of civil obedience. Therefore, some form of public authority was imperative. As William Bradford (one of the Separatist leaders) recalled in his accounts, there were "discontented and mutinous speeches that some of the strangers amongst them had let fall from them in the ship; That when they came a shore they would use their owne libertie; for none had power to command them."[3]

The compact was not a constitution. It was a political statement in which the signers agreed to create and submit to the authority of a government, pending the receipt of a royal charter. The Mayflower Compact's historical and political significance is twofold: it depended on the consent of the affected individuals, and it served as a prototype for similar compacts in American history. According to Samuel Eliot Morison, the compact proved the determination of the English immigrants to live under the rule of law, based on the *consent of the people*.[4]

More Colonies, More Government

Another outpost in New England was set up by the Massachusetts Bay Colony in 1630. Then followed Rhode Island, Connecticut, New Hampshire, and others. By 1732, the last of the thirteen colonies, Georgia, was established. During the colonial period, Americans developed a concept of limited government, which followed from the establishment of the first colonies under Crown charters. Theoretically, London governed the colonies. In practice, owing partly to the colonies' distance from London, the colonists exercised a large measure of self-government. The colonists were able to make their own laws, as in the Fundamental Orders of Connecticut in 1639. The Massachusetts Body of Liberties in 1641 supported the protection of individual rights and was made a part of colonial law. In 1682, the Pennsylvania Frame of Government was passed. Along with the Pennsylvania Charter of Privileges of 1701, it established the rationale for our modern Constitution and Bill of Rights. All of this legislation enabled the colonists to acquire crucial political experience. After independence was declared in 1776, the states quickly set up their own constitutions.

British Restrictions and Colonial Grievances

The conflict between Britain and the American colonies, which ultimately led to the Revolutionary War, began in the 1760s when the British government decided to raise revenues by imposing taxes on the American colonies. Policy advisers to Britain's young King George III, who ascended the throne in 1760, decided that it was only logical to require the American colonists to help pay the costs of Britain's defending them during the French and Indian War (1756–1763). The colonists, who had grown accustomed to a large degree of self-government and independence from the British Crown, viewed the matter differently.

---

[3]John Camp, *Out of the Wilderness: The Emergence of an American Identity in Colonial New England* (Middleton, Conn.: Wesleyan University Press, 1990).

[4]See Morison's "The Mayflower Compact" in Daniel J. Boorstin, ed., *An American Primer* (Chicago: University of Chicago Press, 1966), p. 18.

DID YOU KNOW...
That the *Mayflower* was about 90 feet long from stem to stern, had three masts, and weighed about 180 tons?

MILESTONES IN EARLY U.S. POLITICAL HISTORY

1585 English outpost set up on Roanoke Island.
1607 Jamestown established; Virginia Company lands settlers.
1620 Mayflower Compact signed.
1630 Massachusetts Bay Colony set up.
1639 Fundamental Orders of Connecticut adopted.
1641 Massachusetts Body of Liberties adopted.
1682 Pennsylvania Frame of Government passed.
1701 Pennsylvania Charter of Privileges written.
1732 Last of the thirteen colonies established.
1756 French and Indian War declared.
1765 Stamp Act; Stamp Act Congress meets.
1774 First Continental Congress.
1775 Second Continental Congress; Revolutionary War begins.
1776 Declaration of Independence signed.
1777 Articles of Confederation drafted.
1781 Last state signs Articles of Confederation.
1783 "Critical period" in U.S. history begins; weak national government until 1789.
1786 Shays's Rebellion.
1787 Constitutional Convention.
1788 Ratification of Constitution.
1791 Ratification of Bill of Rights.

First Continental Congress
The first gathering of delegates from twelve of the thirteen colonies, held in 1774.

Second Continental Congress
The 1775 congress of the colonies that established an army.

King George III (1738–1820) was king of Great Britain and Ireland from 1760 until his death on January 29, 1820. Under George III, the first attempt to tax the American colonies was made. Ultimately, the American colonies, exasperated at renewed attempts at taxation, proclaimed their independence on July 4, 1776.

In 1764, the Sugar Act was passed. Many colonists were unwilling to pay the required tax. Further regulatory legislation was to come. In 1765, the British Parliament passed the Stamp Act, providing for internal taxation, or, as the colonists' Stamp Act Congress assembled in 1765 called it, "taxation without representation." The colonists boycotted the purchase of English commodities in return. The success of the boycott (the Stamp Act was repealed a year later) generated a feeling of unity within the colonies. The British, however, continued to try to raise revenues in the colonies. When duties on glass, lead, paint, and other items were passed in 1767, the colonists again boycotted English goods. The colonists' fury over taxation climaxed in the Boston Tea Party: colonists dressed as Mohawk Indians dumped almost 350 chests of British tea into the Boston Harbor as a gesture of tax protest. In retaliation, the British Parliament passed the Coercive Acts (the "Intolerable Acts") in 1774, which closed Boston Harbor and placed the government of Boston under direct British control. The colonists were outraged—and they responded.

The Colonial Response: The Continental Congresses

New York, Pennsylvania, and Rhode Island proposed the convening of a colonial congress. The Massachusetts House of Representatives requested that all colonies hold conventions to select delegates to be sent to Philadelphia for such a congress. The **First Continental Congress** was held at Carpenter's Hall on September 5, 1774. It was a gathering of delegates from twelve of the thirteen colonies (Georgia did not attend until 1775). At that meeting, there was little talk of independence. The Congress passed a resolution requesting that the colonies send a petition to King George III expressing their grievances. Resolutions were also passed requiring that the colonies raise their own troops and boycott British trade. The British government condemned the Congress's actions, treating them as open acts of rebellion.

The delegates to the First Continental Congress declared that in every county and city, a committee was to be formed whose mission was to spy on the conduct of friends and neighbors and to report to the press any violators of the trade ban. The formation of these committees was an act of cooperation among the colonies, which represented a step toward the creation of a national government.

By the time the **Second Continental Congress** met in May 1775 (this time all of the colonies were represented), fighting already had broken out between the British and the colonists. One of the main actions of the Second Congress was to establish an army. It did this by declaring the militia that had gathered around Boston an army and naming George Washington as commander in chief. The participants in that Congress still attempted to reach a peaceful settlement with the British Parliament. One declaration of the Congress stated explicitly that "we have not raised armies with ambitious designs of separating from Great Britain, and establishing independent states." But by the beginning of 1776, military encounters had become increasingly frequent.

Public debate was acrimonious. Then Thomas Paine's *Common Sense* appeared in Philadelphia bookstores. The pamphlet was a colonial best seller. (To do relatively as well today, a book would have to sell between eight and ten million copies in its first year of publication.) Many agreed that Paine did make common sense when he argued that

> a government of our own is our natural right: and when a man seriously reflects on the precariousness [instability, unpredictability] of human affairs, he will become convinced, that it is infinitely wiser and safer, to form a constitution of

our own in a cool and deliberate manner, while we have it in our power, than to trust such an interesting event to time and chance.[5]

Students of Paine's pamphlet point out that his arguments were not new—they were common in tavern debates throughout the land. Rather, it was the near poetry of his words—which were at the same time as plain as the alphabet—that struck his readers.

Declaring Independence

The Resolution of Independence

On April 6, 1776, the Second Continental Congress voted for free trade at all American ports for all countries except Great Britain. This act could be interpreted as an implicit declaration of independence. The next month, the Congress suggested that each of the colonies establish state governments unconnected to Britain. Finally, on July 2, the Resolution of Independence was adopted by the Second Continental Congress:

> RESOLVED, That these United Colonies are, and of right ought to be free and independent States, that they are absolved from allegiance to the British Crown, and that all political connection between them and the state of Great Britain is, and ought to be, totally dissolved.

The actual Resolution of Independence was not legally significant. On the one hand, it was not judicially enforceable, for it established no legal rights or duties. On the other hand, the colonies were already, in their own judgment, self-governing and independent of Britain. Rather, the Resolution of Independence and the subsequent Declaration of Independence were necessary to establish the legitimacy of the new nation in the eyes of foreign governments, as well as in the eyes of the colonists themselves. What the new nation needed most were supplies for its armies and a commitment of foreign military aid. Unless it appeared in the eyes of the world as a political entity separate and independent from Britain, no foreign government would enter into a contract with its leaders.

July 4, 1776—The Declaration of Independence

By June 1776, Thomas Jefferson already was writing drafts of the Declaration of Independence in the second-floor parlor of a bricklayer's house in Philadelphia. On adoption of the Resolution of Independence, Jefferson had argued that a declaration putting forth clearly the causes that compelled the colonies to separate from Britain was necessary. The Second Congress assigned the task to him, and he completed his work on the declaration, which enumerated the colonists' major grievances against Britain. Some of his work was amended to gain unanimous acceptance (for example, his condemnation of the slave trade was eliminated to satisfy Georgia and North Carolina), but the bulk of it was passed intact on July 4, 1776. On July 19, the modified draft became "the unanimous declaration of the thirteen United States of America." On August 2, it was signed by the members of the Second Continental Congress.

The Declaration of Independence has become one of the world's most famous and significant documents. The words opening the second paragraph of the Declaration indicate why this is so:

"You know, the idea of taxation with representation doesn't appeal to me very much either."

Drawing by Handelsman; © 1970 The New Yorker Magazine, Inc.

DID YOU KNOW...
That on July 4, 1776, on the day the Declaration of Independence was signed, King George III of Britain wrote in his diary, "Nothing of importance happened today"?

Natural Rights

Rights held to be inherent in natural law, not dependent on governments. John Locke stated that natural law, being superior to human law, specifies certain rights of "life, liberty, and property." These rights, altered to become "life, liberty, and the pursuit of happiness," are asserted in the Declaration of Independence.

Social Contract

A voluntary agreement among individuals to secure their rights and welfare by creating a government and abiding by its rules.

We hold these Truths to be self-evident, that all Men are created equal, that they are endowed by their Creator with certain unalienable Rights, that among these are Life, Liberty, and the Pursuit of Happiness—That to secure these Rights, Governments are instituted among Men, deriving their just Powers from the Consent of the Governed, that whenever any Form of Government becomes destructive of these Ends, it is the Right of the People to alter or abolish it, and to institute new Government.

The assumption that people have **natural rights** ("unalienable Rights"), including the rights to "Life, Liberty, and the Pursuit of Happiness," was a revolutionary concept at that time. Its use by Jefferson reveals the influence of the English philosopher John Locke (1632–1704), whose writings were familiar to educated American colonists, including Jefferson.[6] In his *Two Treatises on Government,* published in 1690, Locke had argued that all people possess certain natural rights, including the rights to life, liberty, and property, and that the primary purpose of government was to protect these rights. Furthermore, government was established by the people through a **social contract**—an agreement among the people to form a government and abide by its rules. As you read earlier, such contracts, or compacts, were not new to Americans. The Mayflower Compact was the first of several documents that established governments or governing rules based on the consent of the governed.

After setting forth these basic principles of government, the Declaration of Independence goes on to justify the colonists' revolt against Britain. Much of the remainder of the document is a list of what "He" (King George III) had done to deprive the colonists of their rights. (See Appendix A at the end of this book for the complete text of the Declaration of Independence.)

Once it had fulfilled its purpose of legitimating the American Revolution, the Declaration of Independence was all but forgotten for many years. According to scholar Pauline Maier, the Declaration did not become enshrined as what she calls "American Scripture" until the nineteenth century.[7]

[6]Not all scholars believe that Jefferson was truly influenced by Locke. For example, Jay Fliegelman states that "Jefferson's fascination with Homer, Ossian, Patrick Henry, and the violin is of greater significance than his indebtedness to Locke." Jay Fliegelman, *Declaring Independence: Jefferson, Natural Language, and the Culture of Performance* (Stanford, Calif.: Stanford University Press, 1993).
[7]See Pauline Maier, *American Scripture: Making the Declaration of Independence* (New York: Knopf, 1997).

Members of the Second Continental Congress adopted the Declaration of Independence on July 4, 1776. Minor changes were made in the document in the following two weeks. On July 19, the modified draft became the "unanimous declaration of the thirteen United States of America." On August 2, the members of the Second Continental Congress signed it. The first official printed version carried only the signatures of the Congress's president, John Hancock, and its secretary, Charles Thompson.

The Rise of Republicanism

Although the colonists had formally declared independence from Britain, the fight to gain actual independence continued for five more years—until the British General Cornwallis surrendered at Yorktown in 1781. In 1783, after Britain formally recognized the independent status of the United States in the Treaty of Paris, Washington disbanded the army. During these years of military struggles, the states faced the additional challenge of creating a system of self-government for an independent United States.

Some colonists in the middle and lower southern colonies had demanded that independence be preceded by the formation of a strong central government. But the anti-Royalists in New England and Virginia, who called themselves Republicans, were against a strong central government. They opposed monarchy, executive authority, and virtually any form of restraint on the power of local groups. These so-called Republicans were a major political force from 1776 to 1780. Indeed, they almost prevented victory over the British by their unwillingness to cooperate with any central authority.

During this time, all of the states adopted written constitutions. Eleven of the constitutions were completely new. Two of them—those of Connecticut and Rhode Island—were old royal charters with minor modifications. Republican sentiment led to increased power for the legislatures. In Pennsylvania and Georgia, **unicameral** (one-body) **legislatures** were unchecked by executive or judicial authority. Basically, the Republicans attempted to maintain the politics of 1776. In almost all states, the legislature was predominant.

The Articles of Confederation: Our First Form of Government

The fear of a powerful central government led to the passage of the Articles of Confederation. The term **confederation** is important; it means a voluntary association of *independent* **states,** in which the member states agree to only limited restraints on their freedom of action. As a result, confederations seldom have an effective executive authority.

In June 1776, the Second Continental Congress began the process of drafting what would become the Articles of Confederation. The final form of the Articles was achieved by November 15, 1777. It was not until March 1, 1781, however, that the last state, Maryland, agreed to ratify what was called the Articles of Confederation and Perpetual Union. Well before the final ratification of the Articles, however, many of them were implemented: the Continental Congress and the thirteen states conducted American military, economic, and political affairs according to the standards and the form specified by the Articles.[8]

Under the Articles, the thirteen original colonies, now states, established on March 1, 1781, a government of the states—the Congress of the Confederation. The Congress was a unicameral assembly of so-called ambassadors from each state, with each state possessing a single vote. Each year, the Congress would choose one of its members as its president, but the Articles did not provide for a president of the United States. The Congress was authorized in Article X to appoint an executive committee of the states "to execute in the recess of Congress, such of the powers of Congress as the United States, in Congress assembled, by the consent of nine [of the thirteen] states, shall from time to time think

DID YOU KNOW...
That the 1776 constitution of New Jersey granted the vote to "all free inhabitants," including women, but the number of women who turned out to vote resulted in male protests and a new law limiting the right to vote to "free white male citizens"**?**

Unicameral Legislature
A legislature with only one legislative body, as compared with a bicameral (two-house) legislature, such as the U.S. Congress. Nebraska is the only state in the union with a unicameral legislature.

Confederation
A political system in which states or regional governments retain ultimate authority except for those powers they expressly delegate to a central government. A voluntary association of independent states, in which the member states agree to limited restraints on their freedom of action.

State
A group of people occupying a specific area and organized under one government; may be either a nation or a subunit of a nation.

---

[8]Robert W. Hoffert, *A Politics of Tensions: The Articles of Confederation and American Political Ideas* (Niwot, Colo.: University Press of Colorado, 1992).

FIGURE 2-1

The Structure of the Confederal Government under the Articles of Confederation

Congress
Congress had one house. Each state had two to seven members, but only one vote. The exercise of most powers required approval of at least nine states. Amendments to the Articles required the consent of all the states.

Committee of the States
A committee of representatives from all the states was empowered to act in the name of Congress between sessions.

Officers
Congress appointed officers to do some of the executive work.

The States

expedient to vest with them." The Congress was also allowed to appoint other committees and civil officers necessary for managing the general affairs of the United States. In addition, the Congress could regulate foreign affairs and establish coinage and weights and measures. But it lacked an independent source of revenue and the necessary executive machinery to enforce its decisions throughout the land. Article II of the Articles of Confederation guaranteed that each state would retain its sovereignty. Figure 2-1 illustrates the structure of the government under the Articles of Confederation; Table 2-1 summarizes the powers—and the lack of powers—of Congress under that system.

Accomplishments under the Articles

Although the Articles of Confederation had many defects, there were also some accomplishments during the eight years of their existence. Certain states' claims to western lands were settled. Maryland had objected to the claims of Massachusetts, New York, Connecticut, Virginia, the Carolinas, and Georgia. It was only after these states consented to give up their land claims to the United States as a whole that Maryland signed the Articles of Confederation. Another accomplishment under the Articles was the passage of the Northwest Ordinance of 1787, which established a basic pattern of government for new territories north of the Ohio River.

Weaknesses of the Articles

Although Congress had the legal right to declare war and to conduct foreign policy, it did not have the right to demand revenues from the states. It could only *ask* for them. Additionally, the actions of Congress required the consent of nine states. Any amendments to the Articles required the unanimous consent of the Congress and confirmation by every state legislature. Furthermore, the Articles did not create a national system of courts.

Basically, the functioning of the government under the Articles depended on the goodwill of the states. Article III of the Articles simply established a "league of friendship" among the states—no national government was intended.

TABLE 2-1

Powers of the Congress of the Confederation

CONGRESS HAD POWER TO	CONGRESS LACKED POWER TO
■ Declare war and make peace. ■ Enter into treaties and alliances. ■ Establish and control armed forces. ■ Requisition men and money from states. ■ Regulate coinage. ■ Borrow money and issue bills of credit. ■ Fix uniform standards of weight and measurement. ■ Create admiralty courts. ■ Create a postal system. ■ Regulate Indian affairs. ■ Guarantee citizens of each state the rights and privileges of citizens in the several states when in another state. ■ Adjudicate disputes between states upon state petition.	■ Provide for effective treaty-making power and control foreign relations; it could not compel states to respect treaties. ■ Compel states to meet military quotas; it could not draft soldiers. ■ Regulate interstate and foreign commerce; it left each state free to set up its own tariff system. ■ Collect taxes directly from the people; it had to rely on states to collect and forward taxes. ■ Compel states to pay their share of government costs. ■ Provide and maintain a sound monetary system or issue paper money; this was left up to the states, and monies in circulation differed tremendously in value.

Probably the most fundamental weakness of the Articles, and the most basic cause of their eventual replacement by the Constitution, concerned the lack of power to raise money for the militia. The Articles lacked any language giving Congress coercive power to raise money (by levying taxes) to provide adequate support for the military forces controlled by Congress. When states refused to send money to support the government (not one state met the financial requests made by Congress under the Articles), Congress resorted to selling off western lands to speculators or issuing bonds that sold for less than their face value. Due to a lack of resources, the Continental Congress was forced to disband the army, even in the face of serious Spanish and British military threats.

Shays's Rebellion and the Need for Revision of the Articles

Because of the weaknesses of the Articles of Confederation, the central government could do little to maintain peace and order in the new nation. The states bickered among themselves and increasingly taxed each other's goods. At times they prevented trade altogether. By 1784, the country faced a serious economic depression. Banks were calling in old loans and refusing to give new ones. People who could not pay their debts were often thrown into prison.

By 1786, in Concord, Massachusetts, the scene of one of the first battles of the Revolution, there were three times as many people in prison for debt as there were for all other crimes combined. In Worcester County, Massachusetts, the ratio was even higher—twenty to one. Most of the prisoners were small farmers who could not pay their debts owing to the disorganized state of the economy.

In August 1786, mobs of musket-bearing farmers led by former revolutionary captain Daniel Shays seized county courthouses and disrupted the trials of the debtors in Springfield, Massachusetts. Shays and his men then launched an attack on the federal arsenal at Springfield, but they were repulsed. Shays's Rebellion demonstrated that the central government could not protect the citizenry from armed rebellion or provide adequately for the public welfare. The rebellion spurred the nation's political leaders to action. As John Jay wrote to Thomas Jefferson,

> Changes are Necessary, but what they ought to be, what they will be, and how and when to be produced, are arduous Questions. I feel for the Cause of Liberty. . . . If it should not take Root in this Soil[,] Little Pains will be taken to cultivate it in any other.[9]

Drafting the Constitution

The Virginia legislature called for a meeting of all the states to be held at Annapolis, Maryland, on September 11, 1786—ostensibly to discuss commercial problems only. It was evident to those in attendance (including Alexander Hamilton and James Madison) that the national government had serious weaknesses that had to be addressed if it were to survive. Among the important problems to be solved were the relationship between the states and the central government, the powers of the national legislature, the need for executive leadership, and the establishment of policies for economic stability.

---

[9]Excerpt from a letter from John Jay to Thomas Jefferson written in October 1786, as reproduced in Winthrop D. Jordan *et al., The United States,* combined ed., 6th ed. (Englewood Cliffs, N.J.: Prentice Hall, 1987), p. 135.

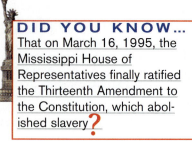

At this Annapolis meeting, a call was issued to all of the states for a general convention to meet in Philadelphia in May 1787 "to consider the exigencies of the union." When the Republicans, who favored a weak central government, realized that the Philadelphia meeting would in fact take place, they approved the convention in February 1787. They made it explicit, however, that the convention was "for the sole and express purpose of revising the Articles of Confederation." Those in favor of a stronger national government—the Federalists, as they were to be called—had different ideas.

The designated date for the opening of the convention at Philadelphia, now known as the Constitutional Convention, was May 14, 1787. Because few of the delegates had actually arrived in Philadelphia by that time, however, it was not formally opened in the East Room of the Pennsylvania State House until May 25.[10] Fifty-five of the seventy-four delegates chosen for the convention actually attended the convention. (Of those fifty-five, only about forty played active roles at the convention.) Rhode Island was the only state that refused to send delegates.

Who Were the Delegates?

Who were the fifty-five delegates to the Constitutional Convention? They certainly did not represent a cross section of eighteenth-century American society. Indeed, most were members of the upper class. Consider the following facts:

1. Thirty-three were members of the legal profession.
2. Three were physicians.
3. Almost 50 percent were college graduates.
4. Seven were former chief executives of their respective states.
5. Six were large plantation owners.
6. Eight were important businesspersons.

They were also relatively young by today's standards: James Madison was thirty-six, Alexander Hamilton was only thirty-two, and Jonathan Dyton of New Jersey was twenty-six. The venerable Benjamin Franklin, however, was eighty-one and had to be carried in on a portable chair borne by four prisoners from a local jail. Not counting Franklin, the average age was just over forty-two.

The Working Environment

The conditions under which the delegates worked for 115 days were far from ideal and were made even worse by the necessity of maintaining total secrecy. The framers of the Constitution felt that if public debate were started on particular positions, delegates would have a more difficult time compromising or backing down to reach agreement. Consequently, the windows were usually shut in the East Room of the State House. Summer quickly arrived, and the air became heavy, humid, and hot by noon of each day. Also, when the windows were open, flies swarmed into the room. The delegates did, however, have a nearby tavern and inn to which they retired each evening. The Indian Queen became the informal headquarters of the delegates.

Factions among the Delegates

We know much about the proceedings at the convention because James Madison kept a daily, detailed personal journal. A majority of the delegates were strong nationalists—they wanted a central government with real power, unlike the cen-

Elbridge Gerry (1744–1814), from Massachusetts, was a patriot during the Revolution. He was a signatory of the Declaration of Independence and later became governor of Massachusetts (1810–1812). He became James Madison's new vice president when Madison was reelected in December 1812.

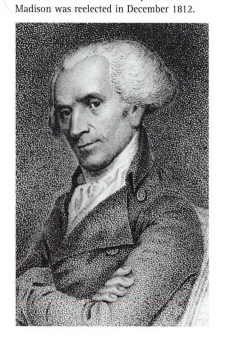

---

[10]The State House was later named Independence Hall. This was the same room in which the Declaration of Independence had been signed eleven years earlier.

George Washington presided over the Constitutional Convention of 1787. Although the convention was supposed to have started on May 14, 1787, few of the delegates had actually arrived in Philadelphia by that date. It formally opened in the East Room of the Pennsylvania State House (later named Independence Hall) on May 25. Only Rhode Island did not send any delegates.

tral government under the Articles of Confederation. George Washington and Benjamin Franklin preferred limited national authority based on a separation of powers. They were apparently willing to accept any type of national government, however, as long as the other delegates approved it. A few advocates of a strong central government, led by Gouverneur Morris of Pennsylvania and John Rutledge of South Carolina, distrusted the ability of the common people to engage in self-government.

Among the nationalists were several monarchists, including Alexander Hamilton, who was chiefly responsible for the Annapolis Convention's call for the Constitutional Convention. In a long speech on June 18, he presented his views: "I have no scruple in declaring . . . that the British government is the best in the world and that I doubt much whether anything short of it will do in America."

Another important group of nationalists were of a more democratic stripe. Led by James Madison of Virginia and James Wilson of Pennsylvania, these democratic nationalists wanted a central government founded on popular support.

Still another faction consisted of nationalists who were less democratic in nature and who would support a central government only if it were founded on very narrowly defined republican principles. This group was made up of a relatively small number of delegates, including Edmund Randolph and George Mason of Virginia, Elbridge Gerry of Massachusetts, and Luther Martin and John Francis Mercer of Maryland.

Most of the other delegates from Maryland, New Hampshire, Connecticut, New Jersey, and Delaware were concerned about only one thing—claims to western lands. As long as those lands became the common property of all of the states, they were willing to support a central government.

Finally, there was a group of delegates who were totally against a national authority. Two of the three delegates from New York quit the convention when they saw the nationalist direction of its proceedings.

Politicking and Compromises

The debates at the convention started on the first day. James Madison had spent months reviewing European political theory. When his Virginia delegation

James Madison (1751–1836) contributed to the colonial cause by bringing to it a deep understanding of government and political philosophy. These resources first proved valuable in 1776, when he helped to draft the constitution for the new state of Virginia. Madison was prominent in disestablishing the Anglican Church when he was a representative of his county in the Virginia legislature from 1784 to 1786. At the Annapolis Convention, he supported New Jersey's motion to hold a federal constitutional convention the following year. Madison earned the title "master builder of the Constitution" because of his persuasive logic during the Constitutional Convention. His contributions to *The Federalist Papers* showed him to be a brilliant political thinker and writer.

Bicameral Legislature
A legislature made up of two chambers, or parts. The U.S. Congress, composed of the House of Representatives and the Senate, is a bicameral legislature.

Supremacy Doctrine
A doctrine that asserts the superiority of national law over state or regional laws. This principle is rooted in Article VI of the Constitution, which provides that the Constitution, the laws passed by the national government under its constitutional powers, and all treaties constitute the supreme law of the land.

Great Compromise
The compromise between the New Jersey and the Virginia plans that created one chamber of the Congress based on population and one chamber that represented each state equally; also called the Connecticut Compromise.

arrived ahead of most of the others, it got to work immediately. By the time George Washington opened the convention, Governor Edmund Randolph of Virginia was immediately able to present fifteen resolutions. In retrospect, this was a masterful stroke on the part of the Virginia delegation. It set the agenda for the remainder of the convention—even though, in principle, the delegates had been sent to Philadelphia for the sole purpose of amending the Articles of Confederation. They had not been sent to write a new constitution.

The Virginia Plan. Randolph's fifteen resolutions proposed an entirely new national government under a constitution. It was, however, a plan that favored the large states, including Virginia. Basically, it called for the following:

1. A **bicameral** (two-house) **legislature,** with the lower chamber chosen by the people and the smaller upper chamber chosen by the lower chamber from nominees selected by state legislatures. The number of representatives would be proportional to a state's population, thus favoring the large states. The legislature could void any state laws.
2. The creation of an unspecified national executive, elected by the legislature.
3. The creation of a national judiciary appointed by the legislature.

It did not take long for the smaller states to realize they would fare poorly under the Virginia plan, according to which Virginia, Massachusetts, and Pennsylvania would form a majority in the national legislature. The debate on the plan dragged on for a number of weeks. It was time for the small states to come up with their own plan.

The New Jersey Plan. On June 15, lawyer William Paterson of New Jersey offered an alternative plan. After all, argued Paterson, under the Articles of Confederation all states had equality; therefore, the convention had no power to change this arrangement. He proposed the following:

1. The fundamental principle of the Articles of Confederation—one state, one vote—would be retained.
2. Congress would be able to regulate trade and impose taxes.
3. All acts of Congress would be the supreme law of the land.
4. Several people would be elected by Congress to form an executive office.
5. The executive office would appoint a Supreme Court.

Basically, the New Jersey plan was simply an amendment of the Articles of Confederation. Its only notable feature was its reference to the **supremacy doctrine,** which was later included in the Constitution.

The "Great Compromise." The delegates were at an impasse. Most wanted a strong national government and were unwilling even to consider the New Jersey plan. But when the Virginia plan was brought up again, the small states threatened to leave. It was not until July 16 that the **Great Compromise** was achieved. Roger Sherman of Connecticut proposed the following:

1. A bicameral legislature in which the House of Representatives would be apportioned according to the number of free inhabitants in each state, plus three-fifths of the slaves.
2. An upper house, the Senate, which would have two members from each state elected by the state legislatures.

This plan, also called the Connecticut Compromise because of the role of the Connecticut delegates in the proposal, broke the deadlock. It did exact a political price, however, because it permitted each state to have equal representation in the Senate. Having two senators represent each state in effect diluted the voting power of citizens living in more heavily populated states and gave the smaller states disproportionate political powers. But the Connecticut Compromise resolved the large-state/small-state controversy. In addition, the Senate acted as part of a checks-and-balances system against the House, which many feared would be dominated by, and responsive to, the masses.

The Three-Fifths Compromise. The Great Compromise also settled another major issue—how to deal with slaves in the representational scheme. Slavery was legal everywhere except in Massachusetts, but it was concentrated in the South. The South wanted slaves to be counted equally in determining representation in Congress. Delegates from the northern states objected. Sherman's three-fifths compromise solved the issue, satisfying those northerners who felt that slaves should not be counted at all and those southerners who wanted them to be counted as free whites. Actually, Sherman's Connecticut plan spoke of three-fifths of "all other persons" (and that is the language in the Constitution itself). It is not hard to figure out, though, who those other persons were.

The slavery issue was not completely eliminated by the three-fifths compromise. Many delegates were opposed to slavery and wanted it banned entirely in the United States. Charles Pinckney of South Carolina led strong southern opposition to the idea of a ban on slavery. Finally, the delegates agreed that Congress could limit the importation of slaves after 1808. The compromise meant that the issue of slavery itself was never addressed. The South won twenty years of unrestricted slave trade and a requirement that escaped slaves in free states be returned to their owners in slave states. (See this chapter's *An Ethical Issue* on page 46 for a further discussion of the founders' views on the slavery question.)

Other Issues. The agrarian South and the mercantile North were in conflict. The South was worried that the northern majority in Congress would pass legislation unfavorable to its economic interests. Because the South depended on exports of its agricultural products, it feared the imposition of export taxes. In return for acceding to the northern demand that Congress be given the power to regulate commerce among the states and with other nations, the South obtained a promise

An American slave market as depicted in a painting from the nineteenth century. The writers of the Constitution did not ban slavery in the United States but did agree to limit the importation of new slaves after 1808. Nowhere are the words *slavery* or *slaves* used in the Constitution. Instead, the Constitution uses such language as "no person held in service" and "all other persons."

that export taxes would not be imposed. Even today, such taxes are prohibited. The United States is among the few countries that do not tax their exports.

There were other disagreements. The delegates could not decide whether to establish only a Supreme Court or to create lower courts as well. They deferred the issue by mandating a Supreme Court and allowing Congress to establish lower courts. They also disagreed over whether the president or the Senate would choose the Supreme Court justices. A compromise was reached with the agreement that the president would nominate the justices and the Senate would confirm the nominations.

These compromises, as well as others, resulted from the recognition that if one group of states refused to ratify the Constitution, it was doomed.

Working toward Final Agreement

The Connecticut Compromise was reached by mid-July. The makeup of the executive branch and the judiciary, however, was left unsettled. The remaining work of the convention was turned over to a five-man Committee of Detail, which presented a rough draft of the Constitution on August 6. It made the executive and judicial branches subordinate to the legislative branch.

The Madisonian Model.   The major issue of **separation of powers** had not yet been resolved. The delegates were concerned with structuring the government to prevent the imposition of tyranny—either by the majority or by a minority. It was Madison who proposed a governmental scheme—sometimes called the **Madisonian model**—to achieve this: the executive, legislative, and judicial powers of gov-

Separation of Powers
The principle of dividing governmental powers among the executive, the legislative, and the judicial branches of government.

Madisonian Model
A structure of government proposed by James Madison in which the powers of the government are separated into three branches: executive, legislative, and judicial.

an ethical issue

Why Didn't the Founders Ban Slavery?

The issue of slavery was debated intensely at the Constitutional Convention. Whether the founders' actions in condoning slavery can be justified ethically remains debatable. Some scholars contend that those delegates who opposed slavery should have made greater efforts to ban the institution outright.* Others claim that the founders ignored the issue because they had no other option. Although several northern states already had taken steps to abolish slavery, it remained entrenched in the southern states, where the 600,000 or more slaves formed an important part of the economy. Delegates from North Carolina, South Carolina, and Georgia argued that their states would never accept the Constitution if slavery was threatened.

ANTISLAVERY SENTIMENTS

Many delegates were against slavery and wanted to ban the institution or at least prohibit slave trading and the further importation of slaves. Indeed, Benjamin Franklin was the president of the Pennsylvania Society for the Abolition of Slavery, the nation's first abolitionist organization. Many other delegates, particularly from the northern states, supported the abolition of slavery. James Madison

and Thomas Jefferson were also opposed to slavery, at least in theory (they both were slave owners).

Given the antislavery sentiment of these delegates, why did they agree to a founding document that implicitly acknowledged the institution of slavery? Why didn't they insist on settling the slavery issue then and there, rather than leaving it for future generations to resolve? Even a number of the delegates' contemporaries considered the compromise on the slavery issue to be a "betrayal" of the Declaration of Independence's promise of equality.

PUTTING THE UNION FIRST

Generally, the antislavery delegates agreed with Madison that "[g]reat as the evil is, a dismemberment of the Union would be worse. . . . If those states should disunite from the other States, . . . they might solicit and obtain aid from foreign powers."[†] Benjamin Franklin also feared that without a compromise on the slavery issue, delegates from some of the southern states would abandon the convention. For this reason, when his Society for the Abolition of Slavery asked him to read at the convention a petition calling for the abolition of slavery, he declined to do so.

FOR CRITICAL ANALYSIS

Do you agree with Madison that "a dismemberment of the Union would be worse" than allowing slavery to continue?

---

*See, for example, Paul Finkelman's criticism of the founders' actions with respect to the slavery issue in *Slavery and the Founders: Race and Liberty in the Age of Jefferson,* 2d ed. (Armonk, N.Y.: M. E. Sharpe, 2000).

[†]Speech before the Virginia ratifying convention on June 17, 1788, as cited in Bruno Leone, ed., *The Creation of the Constitution* (San Diego: Greenhaven Press, 1995), p. 159.

ernment were to be separated so that no one branch had enough power to dominate the others. The separation of powers was by function, as well as by personnel, with Congress passing laws, the president enforcing and administering laws, and the courts interpreting laws in individual circumstances.

Each of the three branches of government would be independent of the others, but they would have to cooperate to govern. According to Madison, in *Federalist Paper* No. 51 (see Appendix D), "the great security against a gradual concentration of the several powers in the same department consists in giving to those who administer each department the necessary constitutional means and personal motives to resist encroachments of the others."

The "constitutional means" Madison referred to is a system of **checks and balances** through which each branch of the government can check the actions of the other branches. For example, Congress can enact laws, but the president has veto power over congressional acts. The Supreme Court has the power to declare acts of Congress and of the executive branch unconstitutional, but the president appoints the justices of the Supreme Court, with the advice and consent of the Senate. (The Supreme Court's power to declare acts unconstitutional was not mentioned in the Constitution, although arguably the framers assumed that the Court would have this power—see the discussion of judicial review later in this chapter.) Figure 2–2 outlines these checks and balances.

Don't Make Harder Govern

Checks and Balances
A major principle of the American government system whereby each branch of the government exercises a check on the actions of the others.

FIGURE 2-2

Checks and Balances
The major checks and balances among the three branches are illustrated here. Some of these checks are not mentioned in the Constitution, such as judicial review—the power of the courts to declare federal or state acts unconstitutional—or the president's ability to refuse to enforce judicial decisions or congressional legislation. Checks and balances can be thought of as a confrontation of powers or responsibilities. Each branch checks the action of another; two branches in conflict have powers that can result in balances or stalemates, requiring one branch to give in or both to reach a compromise.

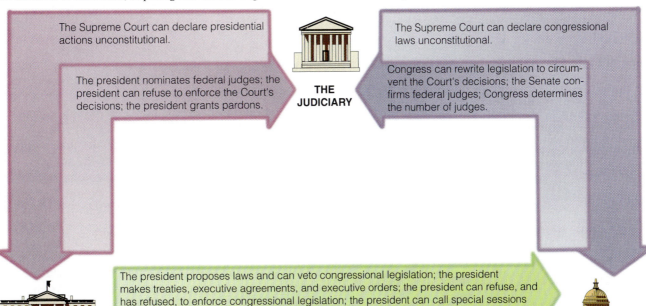

The Executive. Some delegates favored a plural executive made up of representatives from the various regions. This was abandoned in favor of a single chief executive. Some argued that Congress should choose the executive. To make the presidency completely independent of the proposed Congress, however, an **electoral college** was adopted, probably at James Wilson's suggestion. To be sure, the electoral college created a cumbersome presidential election process (see Chapter 10). It could even result in a candidate who came in second in the popular vote becoming president by being the top vote getter in the electoral college. The electoral college insulated the president, however, from direct popular control. The seven-year single term that some of the delegates had proposed was replaced by a four-year term and the possibility of reelection.

The Final Document

On September 17, 1787, the Constitution was approved by thirty-nine delegates. Of the fifty-five who had attended originally, only forty-two remained. Three delegates refused to sign the Constitution. Others disapproved of at least parts of it but signed anyway to begin the ratification debate.

The Constitution that was to be ratified established the following fundamental principles:

1. Popular sovereignty, or control by the people.
2. A republican government in which the people choose representatives to make decisions for them.
3. Limited government with written laws, in contrast to the powerful monarchical British government against which the colonists had rebelled.
4. Separation of powers, with checks and balances among branches to prevent any one branch from gaining too much power.
5. A federal system that allowed for states' rights, because the states feared too much centralized control.

You will read about federalism in detail in Chapter 3. Suffice it to say here that in the **federal system** established by the founders, sovereign powers—ruling powers—are divided between the states and the national government. The Constitution expressly delegated certain powers to the national government. For example, the national government was given the power to regulate commerce among the states. The Constitution also declared that the president is the nation's chief executive and the commander in chief of the armed forces. Additionally, the Constitution made it clear that laws made by the national government take priority over conflicting state laws. At the same time, the Constitution provided for numerous states' rights, including the right to control commerce within state borders and to exercise those governing powers that were not delegated to the national government.

The federal system created by the founders was a novel form of government at that time—no other country in the world had such a system. It was invented by the founders as a compromise solution to the controversy over whether the states or the central government should have ultimate sovereignty. As you will read in Chapter 3, the debate over where the line should be drawn between states' rights and the powers of the national government has characterized American politics ever since. The founders did not go into detail with respect to where this line should be drawn, thus leaving it up to scholars and court judges to divine the founders' intentions. (Some claim that the intentions of the founders should not matter, because today's United States is a far different world, with far different problems, than that in which the framers lived. See this chapter's *Critical Perspective* for a further discussion of this issue.)

Electoral College
A group of persons called electors selected by the voters in each state and Washington, D.C.; this group officially elects the president and vice president of the United States. The number of electors in each state is equal to the number of each state's representatives in both chambers of Congress. The Twenty-third Amendment to the Constitution permits Washington, D.C., to have as many electors as a state of comparable population.

Federal System
A system of government in which power is divided by a written constitution between a central government and regional, or subdivisional governments. Each level must have some domain in which its policies are dominant and some genuine political or constitutional guarantee of its authority.

critical perspective

Does It Matter What the Founders Thought?

Much of the legal debate today over constitutional issues concerns the original meaning of the Constitution. Some argue that the founders' intent is of critical importance in interpreting the Constitution. Others contend that if the Supreme Court always applied constitutional provisions in light of what the founders thought, the Constitution could not be adapted to today's world—which is far different from that of the founders. In any event, the political dimensions of this debate have had grave consequences. For example, how the founders viewed the concept of federalism has had an impact on the issue of states' rights. After all, the Civil War was, in part, fought over this issue. Since the 1990s, the issue of states' rights has become prominent again.

The Founders' Intentions Are Not Really Relevant

Consider the founders' view of democracy. They wanted the general public to be somewhat distant from the government. Hence, they created a representative democracy, not a direct democracy. They also did not override state laws that restricted the vote to property-owning white males. Additionally, they instituted the electoral college so that the public could not elect presidents directly. According to one historian, the founders thought that even the electoral college system gave the public too much power. Yet they were apparently not too worried because they felt that the electors would often be deadlocked, in which case it would be up to the House of Representatives to decide who would be president. James Madison thought the House would have to decide the issue in nine out of every ten elections. George Mason believed a deadlock would occur in forty-nine out of every fifty elections.*

Indeed, even the word *democracy* seemed distasteful to the founders. Historian Charles Beard pointed out that the term was used by conservatives to smear their opponents as late as the mid-1800s. Certainly, the founders rarely—if ever—publicly identified themselves as Democrats. Even Thomas Jefferson, many of whose supporters called themselves Democrats or Democratic Republicans, stated in his 1801 inaugural address, "We are all Republicans—we are all Federalists" (*not* "We are all Democratic Republicans—we are all Federalists"). So, if the founders' views on democracy had prevailed over time, we certainly would not have the democratic form of government we have today.

Consider in addition the founders' view on equality, which are much different than those today. They readily accepted inequality in wealth and property. They were not remotely prepared for the concept of equality as it is understood by most Americans today. Even Jefferson, who advocated freedom for the slaves, did not free his own slaves. Do we really want the views of these individuals to shape our interpretations and applications of the Constitution today?

The Founders' Intentions Should Be Heeded

Three constitutional and political scholars, Alan Brinkley, Kathleen M. Sullivan, and Nelson W. Polsby, argue that the Constitution should be read as it was written, no more no less.† In particular, they argue against the current trend toward *devolution*—the transfer of certain central government powers to the states (see Chapter 3). Many of those who support devolution argue that the framers did not intend the national government to have such extensive powers. Therefore, some powers should be "returned" to state governments. Brinkley, Sullivan, and Polsby, however, argue that such devolution is contrary to the intentions of the founders.

Sullivan, for example, points out that in *Federalist Paper* No. 10 Madison warned against the divisive forces of faction. As a counter to this, Madison argued that we needed to "extend the sphere" of government to national dimensions in order to keep the destructive power of factionalism in check. Madison believed that smaller, homogeneous governmental units were more vulnerable to the tyranny of local majorities. Therefore, according to Sullivan, the attempts to decentralize the national government's powers today are not consistent with the founders' views. Such attempts are also dangerous for the nation. If more and more powers were to be transferred to state and local governments, the result would be an accentuation of "the regional, economic, religious, ethnic, and racial differences that already divide us."

In sum, these scholars argue that enfeebling the federal government is not consistent with what the founders wanted. The result would be a national government with too little power to manage the economy, protect the environment, and address important social issues.

FOR CRITICAL ANALYSIS

1. Is there any way to reconcile the view of those in favor of devolution (transferring more power to the states) with the view held by Brinkley, Sullivan, and Polsby?

2. If a new Constitution were drafted today, would the courts, politicians, and political scientists have more or less difficulty understanding the views of those who wrote it than in understanding the views of the framers of our existing Constitution? Why or why not?

*Richard Shenkman, *Legends, Lives & Cherished Myths of American History* (New York: Harper & Row, 1989), pp. 22–23.

†Alan Brinkley *et al., The New Federalist Papers: Essays in Defense of the Constitution* (New York: W. W. Norton, 1997).

Ratification
Formal approval.

Federalist
The name given to one who was in favor of the adoption of the U.S. Constitution and the creation of a federal union with a strong central government.

Anti-Federalist
An individual who opposed the ratification of the new Constitution in 1787. The Anti-Federalists were opposed to a strong central government.

The Difficult Road to Ratification

The founders knew that **ratification** of the Constitution was far from certain. Indeed, because it was almost guaranteed that many state legislatures would not ratify it, the delegates agreed that each state should hold a special convention. Elected delegates to these conventions would discuss and vote on the Constitution. Further departing from the Articles of Confederation, the delegates agreed that as soon as nine states (rather than all thirteen) approved the Constitution, it would take effect, and Congress could begin to organize the new government.

The Federalists Push for Ratification

The two opposing forces in the battle over ratification were the Federalists and the Anti-Federalists. The **Federalists**—those in favor of a strong central government and the new Constitution—had an advantage over their opponents, called the **Anti-Federalists,** who wanted to prevent the Constitution as drafted from being ratified. In the first place, the Federalists had assumed a positive name, leaving their opposition the negative label of *Anti*-Federalist.[11] More important, the Federalists had attended the Constitutional Convention and knew of all the deliberations that had taken place. Their opponents had no such knowledge, because those deliberations had not been open to the public. Thus, the Anti-Federalists were at a disadvantage in terms of information about the document. The Federalists also had time, power, and money on their side. Communications were slow. Those who had access to the best communications were Federalists—mostly wealthy bankers, lawyers, plantation owners, and merchants living in urban areas, where communication was better. The Federalist campaign was organized relatively quickly and effectively to elect Federalists as delegates to the state ratifying conventions.

The Anti-Federalists, however, had at least one strong point in their favor: they stood for the status quo. In general, the greater burden is placed on those advocating change.

The Federalist Papers. In New York, opponents of the Constitution were quick to attack it. Alexander Hamilton answered their attacks in newspaper columns over the signature "Caesar." When the Caesar letters had little effect, Hamilton switched to the pseudonym Publius and secured two collaborators—John Jay and James Madison. In a very short time, those three political figures wrote a series of eighty-five essays in defense of the Constitution and of a republican form of government. These widely read essays appeared in New York newspapers from October 1787 to August 1788 and were reprinted in the newspapers of other states. Although we do not know for certain who wrote every one, it is apparent that Hamilton was responsible for about two-thirds of the essays. These included the most important ones interpreting the Constitution, explaining the various powers of the three branches, and presenting a theory of judicial review. Madison's *Federalist Paper* No. 10 (see Appendix D), however, is considered a classic in political theory; it deals with the nature of groups—or factions, as he called them. In spite of the rapidity with which *The Federalist Papers* were written, they are considered by many to be perhaps the best example of political theorizing ever produced in the United States.[12]

The Anti-Federalist Response. The Anti-Federalists used such pseudonyms as Montezuma and Philadelphiensis in their replies. Many of their attacks against

---

[11]There is some irony here. At the Constitutional Convention, those opposed to a strong central government pushed for a federal system because such a system would allow states to retain some of their sovereign rights (see Chapter 3). The label *Anti-Federalists* thus contradicted their essential views.

[12]Some scholars believe that *The Federalist Papers* played only a minor role in securing ratification of the Constitution. Even if this is true, they still have lasting value as an authoritative explanation of the Constitution.

the Constitution were also brilliant. They claimed that it was a document written by aristocrats and would lead to aristocratic tyranny. More important, the Anti-Federalists believed that the Constitution would create an overbearing and over-burdening central government hostile to personal liberty. (The Constitution said nothing about freedom of the press, freedom of religion, or any other individual liberty.) They wanted to include a list of guaranteed liberties, or a bill of rights. Finally, the Anti-Federalists decried the weakened power of the states.

The Anti-Federalists cannot be dismissed as a bunch of unpatriotic extremists. They included such patriots as Patrick Henry and Samuel Adams. They were arguing what had been the most prevalent view of the time. This view derived from the French political philosopher Montesquieu (1689–1755), who believed that liberty was only safe in relatively small societies governed by direct democracy or by a large legislature with small districts. The Madisonian view favoring a large republic, particularly expressed in *Federalist Papers* No. 10 and No. 51 (see Appendix D), was actually the more *un*popular view of the time. Madison was probably convincing because citizens were already persuaded that a strong national government was necessary to combat foreign enemies and to prevent domestic insurrections. Still, some researchers believe it was mainly the bitter experiences with the Articles of Confederation, rather than Madison's arguments, that created the setting for the ratification of the Constitution.[13]

The March to the Finish

The struggle for ratification continued. Strong majorities were procured in Delaware, Pennsylvania, New Jersey, Georgia, and Connecticut. After a bitter struggle in Massachusetts, that state ratified the Constitution by a narrow margin on February 6, 1788. By the spring, Maryland and South Carolina had ratified by sizable majorities. Then on June 21 of that year, New Hampshire became the ninth state to ratify the Constitution. Although the Constitution was formally in effect, this meant little without Virginia and New York—the latter did not ratify for yet another month (see Table 2–2). (Was the Constitution actually favored by a majority of citizens at the time? See the feature *Politics and Economics: The Motives of the Framers* on page 52 for a discussion of this issue.)

---

[13]Of particular interest is the view of the Anti-Federalist position contained in Herbert J. Storing, *What the Anti-Federalists Were For* (Chicago: University of Chicago Press, 1981). Storing also edited seven volumes of the Anti-Federalist writings, *The Complete Anti-Federalist* (Chicago: University of Chicago Press, 1981). See also Josephine F. Pacheco, *Antifederalism: The Legacy of George Mason* (Fairfax, Va.: George Mason University Press, 1992).

Frail Precedents
Three-Judge Panels

TABLE 2-2		

Ratification of the Constitution

STATE	DATE	VOTE FOR–AGAINST
Delaware	Dec. 7, 1787	30–0
Pennsylvania	Dec. 12, 1787	43–23
New Jersey	Dec. 18, 1787	38–0
Georgia	Jan. 2, 1788	26–0
Connecticut	Jan. 9, 1788	128–40
Massachusetts	Feb. 6, 1788	187–168
Maryland	Apr. 28, 1788	63–11
South Carolina	May 23, 1788	149–73
New Hampshire	June 21, 1788	57–46
Virginia	June 25, 1788	89–79
New York	July 26, 1788	30–27
North Carolina	Nov. 21, 1789*	194–77
Rhode Island	May 29, 1790	34–32

*Ratification was originally defeated on August 4, 1788, by a vote of 184–84.

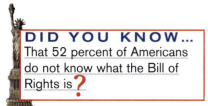

The Bill of Rights

The U.S. Constitution would not have been ratified in several important states if the Federalists had not assured the states that amendments to the Constitution would be passed to protect individual liberties against incursions by the national government. Many of the recommendations of the state ratifying conventions included specific rights that were considered later by James Madison as he labored to draft what became the Bill of Rights. An important right was the right to free speech (see this chapter's *E-mocracy: The Internet and Free Speech*). Although called the Bill of Rights, essentially the first ten amendments to the Constitution were a "bill of limits," because the amendments limited the powers of the national government in regard to the rights and liberties of individuals.

Ironically, a year earlier Madison had told Jefferson, "I have never thought the omission [of the Bill of Rights] a material defect" of the Constitution. But Jefferson's enthusiasm for a bill of rights apparently influenced Madison, as did his desire to gain popular support for his election to Congress. He promised in his campaign letter to voters that, once elected, he would force Congress to "prepare and recommend to the states for ratification, the most satisfactory provisions for all essential rights."

politics and economics

The Motives of the Framers

In 1913, historian Charles Beard published *An Economic Interpretation of the Constitution of the United States,* charging that the Constitution had been produced primarily by wealthy property owners who desired a stronger government able to protect their property rights.* Beard also claimed that the Constitution had been imposed by undemocratic methods to prevent democratic majorities from exercising real power. He pointed out that there was never any popular vote on whether to hold a constitutional convention in the first place. Furthermore, even if such a vote had been taken, state laws generally restricted voting rights to property-owning white males, meaning that most people in the country (white males without property, women, Native Americans, and slaves) were not eligible to vote.

Some political scientists and historians still contend that the Constitution was not favored by a popular majority. The delegates at the various state ratifying conventions had been selected by only 150,000 of the approximately four million citizens of that time. That does not seem very democratic—at least not by today's standards. Some historians have suggested that if a Gallup poll could have been taken at that time, the Anti-Federalists would probably have outnumbered the Federalists.[†]

It is true that some of the delegates to state ratifying conventions from poorer, agrarian areas feared that an elite group of Federalists would run the country just as oppressively as the British had governed the colonies. Amos Singletary, a delegate to the Massachusetts ratifying convention, contended that those

who urged the adoption of the Constitution "expect to get all the power and all the money into their own hands, and then they will swallow up all us little folks . . . just as the whale swallowed Jonah.[‡] Others who were similarly situated, though, felt differently. Jonathan Smith, who was also a delegate to the Massachusetts ratifying convention, regarded a strong national government as a "cure for disorder"—referring to the disorder caused by the rebellion of Daniel Shays and his followers.[§]

Much has been made of the various machinations used by the Federalists to ensure the Constitution's ratification (and they did resort to a variety of devious tactics, including purchasing at least one printing press to prevent the publication of Anti-Federalist sentiments). Yet the perception that a strong central government was necessary to keep order and protect the public welfare appears to have been fairly pervasive among all classes—rich and poor alike.

FOR CRITICAL ANALYSIS

Jonathan Smith posited an example to make his point that the Constitution should be ratified: "Suppose two or three of you had been at the pains to break up a piece of rough land, and sow it with wheat; would you let it lie waste because you could not agree on what sort of a fence to make?" What light, if any, does this sentiment shed on the American political process generally?

[‡]As quoted in Bruno Leone, ed., *The Creation of the Constitution* (San Diego: Greenhaven Press, 1995), p. 215.
[§]*Ibid.,* p. 217.

*Charles A. Beard, *An Economic Interpretation of the Constitution of the United States* (New York: Macmillan, 1913; New York: Free Press, 1986).
[†]Jim Powell, "James Madison—Checks and Balances to Limit Government Power," *The Freeman,* March 1996, p. 178.

Madison had to cull through more than two hundred state recommendations.[14] It was no small task, and in retrospect he chose remarkably well. One of the rights appropriate for constitutional protection that he left out was equal protection under the laws—but that was not commonly regarded as a basic right at that time. It was not until 1868 that an amendment guaranteeing that no state shall deny equal protection to any person was ratified. (The Supreme Court has applied this guarantee to certain actions of the federal government as well.)

The final number of amendments that Madison and a specially appointed committee came up with was seventeen. Congress tightened the language somewhat and eliminated five of the amendments. Of the remaining twelve, two—dealing with the apportionment of representatives and the compensation of the members of Congress—were not ratified immediately by the states. Eventually, Supreme Court decisions led to legislative reforms relating to apportionment. The amendment relating to compensation of members of Congress was ratified 203 years later—in 1992!

On December 15, 1791, the national Bill of Rights was adopted when Virginia agreed to ratify the ten amendments. On ratification, the Bill of Rights became part of the U.S. Constitution. The basic structure of American government had

---

[14]For details on these recommendations, including their sources, see Leonard W. Levy, *Origins of the Bill of Rights* (New Haven, Conn.: Yale University Press, 1999).

e-mocracy

The Internet and Free Speech

One of the most important rights of Americans is freedom of speech. Yet even now, more than two hundred years after the U.S. Bill of Rights was ratified, citizens in some countries do not enjoy this right. Will widespread use of the Internet alter this situation? Some contend that it will.

Consider the People's Republic of China. There, the government prohibits subversive speech against the socialist system or speech that might harm national unity or the "spiritual civilization" that China's political leaders are attempting to build. Enter the Internet. On the one hand, Chinese leaders would like to take advantage of the benefits of the Internet—particularly, the easier exchange of academic, scientific, and business and technical information. On the other hand, they do not want Chinese citizens to be exposed to Western influences that are contrary to the government's political and cultural goals. How do officials promote what they see as good uses of the Internet and at the same time restrict other uses?

To date, the Chinese government has employed various methods to control Internet use. One method is to use filtering software to block electronic pathways to any objectionable sites—including the sites of such Western news organizations as CNN and *Time* magazine. Another method is to ban Internet users from sending or discussing "state secrets"—any information, such as reports of corruption within the Communist Party, that has not been publicly released. A final method is to monitor the online activities of Internet users. None of these methods is foolproof, and the Chinese government may be fighting a losing battle. For example, even today, when only an estimated 8.9 million people in China (less than 1 percent of the country's population) are online, it is difficult to monitor all of these users' activities.[*] As the number of Internet users increases—and it is climbing rapidly—it may become impossible to do so.

Some believe that the Internet, by exposing Chinese citizens to a variety of views on politics and culture, will eventually transform China. According to Steven Calcotte, a technology consultant in Beijing, it already has begun to do so. Calcotte concluded that the first graduates from Beijing University to have had access to e-mail and the Internet have a much different outlook than previous graduates had.[†]

FOR CRITICAL ANALYSIS

Some argue that the Internet is a valuable weapon in the struggle for democracy. Could it also be used to restrict freedoms?

[*]"A Great Wall in Cyberspace," *Los Angeles Times,* February 28, 2000, p. 36.
[†]*The Economist,* February 7, 1998, p. 43.

already been established. Now the fundamental rights and liberties of individuals were protected, at least in theory, at the national level. The proposed amendment that Madison characterized as "the most valuable amendment in the whole lot"—which would have prohibited the states from infringing on the freedoms of conscience, press, and jury trial—had been eliminated by the Senate. Thus, the Bill of Rights as adopted did not limit state power, and individual citizens had to rely on the guarantees contained in the particular state constitution or state bill of rights. The country had to wait until the violence of the Civil War before significant limitations on state power in the form of the Fourteenth Amendment became part of the national Constitution.

Altering the Constitution: The Formal Amendment Process

The U.S. Constitution consists of 7,000 words. It is shorter than every state constitution except that of Vermont, which has 6,880 words. One of the reasons the federal Constitution is short is that the founders intended it to be only a framework for governing, to be interpreted by succeeding generations. One of the reasons it has remained short is because the formal amending procedure does not allow for changes to be made easily. Article V of the Constitution outlines the ways in which amendments may be proposed and ratified (see Figure 2–3).

Two formal methods of proposing an amendment to the Constitution are available: (1) a two-thirds vote in each chamber of Congress or (2) a national convention that is called by Congress at the request of two-thirds of the state legislatures (the second method has never been used).

Ratification can occur by one of two methods: (1) by a positive vote in three-fourths of the legislatures of the various states or (2) by special conventions called in the states for the specific purpose of ratifying the proposed amendment and a positive vote in three-fourths of them. The second method has been used only once, to repeal Prohibition. That situation was exceptional because it involved an amendment (the Twenty-first) to repeal an amendment (the Eighteenth, which had created Prohibition). State conventions were necessary for repeal of the Eighteenth Amendment because the "pro-dry" legislatures in the more conservative states would never have passed the repeal. (Note that Congress determines the method of ratification to be used by all states for each proposed constitutional amendment.)

FIGURE 2-3

The Formal Constitutional Amending Procedure

There are two ways of proposing amendments to the U.S. Constitution and two ways of ratifying proposed amendments. Among the four possibilities, the usual route has been proposal by Congress and ratification by state legislatures.

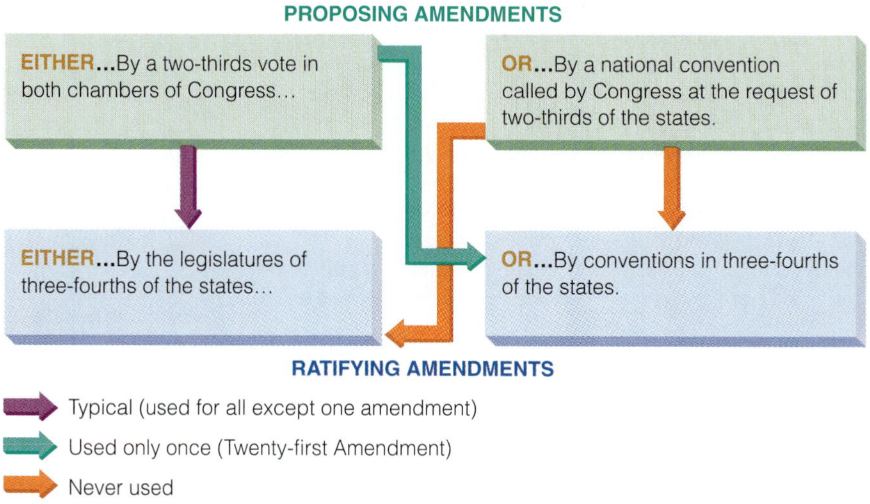

PROPOSING AMENDMENTS

EITHER...By a two-thirds vote in both chambers of Congress...

OR...By a national convention called by Congress at the request of two-thirds of the states.

EITHER...By the legislatures of three-fourths of the states...

OR...By conventions in three-fourths of the states.

RATIFYING AMENDMENTS

➡ Typical (used for all except one amendment)

➡ Used only once (Twenty-first Amendment)

➡ Never used

Many Amendments Proposed, Few Accepted

Congress has considered more than eleven thousand amendments to the Constitution. Only thirty-three have been submitted to the states after having been approved by the required two-thirds vote in each chamber of Congress, and only twenty-seven have been ratified—see Table 2–3. (The full, annotated text of the U.S. Constitution, including its amendments, is presented in a special appendix to this chapter, beginning on page 64.) It should be clear that the amendment process is much more difficult than a graphic depiction such as Figure 2–3 can indicate. Because of competing social and economic interests, the requirement that two-thirds of both the House and Senate approve the amendments is difficult to achieve. Thirty-four senators, representing only seventeen sparsely populated states, could block any amendment. For example, the Republican-controlled House approved the Balanced Budget Amendment within the first one hundred days of the 104th Congress in 1995, but it was defeated in the Senate by one vote.

After approval by Congress, the process becomes even more arduous. Three-fourths of the state legislatures must approve the amendment. Only those amendments that have wide popular support across parties and in all regions of the country are likely to be approved.

Why was the amendment process made so difficult? The framers feared that a simple amendment process could lead to a tyranny of the majority, which could pass amendments to oppress disfavored individuals and groups. The cumbersome amendment process does not seem to stem the number of amendments that are proposed each year in Congress, however, particularly in recent years.

Limits on Ratification

A reading of Article V of the Constitution reveals that the framers of the Constitution specified no time limit on the ratification process. The Supreme Court has held that Congress can specify a time for ratification as long as it is

INFOTRAC®
COLLEGE EDITION

Restraint Key Word in Constitutional Amendments

TABLE   2-3

Amendments to the Constitution

AMENDMENTS	SUBJECT	YEAR ADOPTED	TIME REQUIRED FOR RATIFICATION
1st–10th	The Bill of Rights	1791	2 years, 2 months, 20 days
11th	Immunity of states from certain suits	1795	11 months, 3 days
12th	Changes in electoral college procedure	1804	6 months, 3 days
13th	Prohibition of slavery	1865	10 months, 3 days
14th	Citizenship, due process, and equal protection	1868	2 years, 26 days
15th	No denial of vote because of race, color, or previous condition of servitude	1870	11 months, 8 days
16th	Power of Congress to tax income	1913	3 years, 6 months, 22 days
17th	Direct election of U.S. senators	1913	10 months, 26 days
18th	National (liquor) prohibition	1919	1 year, 29 days
19th	Women's right to vote	1920	1 year, 2 months, 14 days
20th	Change of dates for congressional and presidential terms	1933	10 months, 21 days
21st	Repeal of the Eighteenth Amendment	1933	9 months, 15 days
22d	Limit on presidential tenure	1951	3 years, 11 months, 3 days
23d	District of Columbia electoral vote	1961	9 months, 13 days
24th	Prohibition of tax payment as a qualification to vote in federal elections	1964	1 year, 4 months, 9 days
25th	Procedures for determining presidential disability, presidential succession, and filling a vice presidential vacancy	1967	1 year, 7 months, 4 days
26th	Prohibition of setting minimum voting age above eighteen in any election	1971	3 months, 7 days
27th	Prohibition of Congress's voting itself a raise that takes effect before the next election	1992	203 years

A rally at the U.S. Capitol supporting a constitutional amendment to outlaw the desecration of the American flag.

"reasonable." Since 1919, most proposed amendments have included a requirement that ratification be obtained within seven years. This was the case with the proposed Equal Rights Amendment. When three-fourths of the states had not ratified in that time, however, Congress extended the limit for an additional three years and three months. That extension expired on June 30, 1982, and the amendment still had not been ratified. (See this chapter's *Making Waves* for a further discussion of this proposed amendment.) Another proposed amendment, which would have guaranteed congressional representation to the District of Columbia, fell far short of the thirty-eight state ratifications needed before its August 22, 1985, deadline.

On May 7, 1992, the Michigan state legislature became the thirty-eighth state to ratify the Twenty-seventh Amendment (on congressional compensation)—one of the two "lost" amendments of the twelve that originally were sent to the states in 1789. Because most of the amendments proposed in recent years have been given a time limit of only seven years by Congress, it was questionable for a while whether the amendment would become effective even if the necessary number of states ratified it. Is 203 years too long a lapse of time between the proposal and the final ratification of an amendment? It apparently was not, because the amendment was certified as legitimate by archivist Don Wilson of the National Archives on May 18, 1992.

The National Convention Provision

The Constitution provides that a national convention requested by the legislatures of two-thirds of the states can propose a constitutional amendment. Congress has received approximately 400 convention applications since the Constitution was ratified; every state has applied at least once. Less than 20 applications were submitted during the Constitution's first 100 years, but more than 150 have been filed in the last two decades. No national convention has been held since 1787, and many national political and judicial leaders are uneasy about the prospect of convening a body that conceivably could do as the Constitutional Convention did—create a new form of government. The state legislative bodies that originate national convention applications, however, appear not to be uncomfortable with such a constitutional modification process; more than 230 state constitutional conventions have been held.

Informal Methods of Constitutional Change

Formal amendments are one way of changing our Constitution, and, as is obvious by their small number, they have not been resorted to very frequently. If we discount the first ten amendments (the Bill of Rights), which were adopted soon after the ratification of the Constitution, there have been only seventeen formal alterations of the Constitution in the more than two hundred years of its existence.

But looking at the sparse number of formal constitutional changes gives us an incomplete view. The brevity and ambiguity of the original document have permitted great changes in the Constitution by way of changing interpretations over time. As the United States grew, both in population and territory, new social and political realities emerged. Congress, presidents, and the courts found it necessary to interpret the Constitution's provisions in light of these new realities. The Constitution has proved to be a remarkably flexible document, adapting itself time and again to new events and concerns.

Congressional Legislation

The Constitution gives Congress broad powers to carry out its duties as the nation's legislative body. For example, Article I, Section 8, of the Constitution gives Congress the power to regulate foreign and interstate commerce. Although

making waves

Shirley Breeze and the Missouri Women's Network: Resurrecting the ERA

The Equal Rights Amendment (ERA), which was initially written by suffragist Alice Paul in 1921, reads as follows: "Equality of rights under law shall not be denied or abridged by the United States Constitution or any state on account of sex." The ERA was introduced in Congress time and again, beginning in 1923. By 1972, it finally garnered enough congressional votes in the House and Senate to be submitted to the states for ratification. When the required number of states—thirty-eight (three-fourths of the states)—failed to ratify the amendment within the seven-year limit imposed by Congress, that limit was extended for three more years. In 1982, when the time limit lapsed, the amendment was still three states short of the required number for ratification.

Although many believed that 1982 marked the "death" of the ERA, apparently it is coming back to life. Shirley Breeze, head of the Missouri Women's Network, is spearheading a movement to resurrect the amendment. Breeze and other ERA supporters in

Missouri hope that if three more states ratify the ERA, Congress may make an exception to the ratification time limit. What spurred this strategy was Congress's certification of the Twenty-seventh Amendment, which was ratified 203 years after it had been submitted to the states. Bills to ratify the ERA have been introduced not only in Missouri but also in several other states that did not ratify it earlier, including Illinois, Virginia, and Oklahoma.

Breeze believes that the chances for ratification are good, contending that "if Missouri passes it, two other states will jump on the bandwagon." According to Breeze, "This time it's a different ballgame. A different mood in the country. The ERA is not as threatening as it was, but it's just as important."*

FOR CRITICAL ANALYSIS

Some argue that a constitutional amendment is not necessary to obtain equality of rights under the law for women—because they already have obtained these rights. Do you agree?

*As quoted in Ellen Goodman, "A Glimmer of Hope for the Dormant Equal Rights Amendment," *The Boston Globe,* February 13, 2000, p. E7.

there is no clear definition of foreign commerce or interstate commerce in the Constitution, Congress has cited the *commerce clause* as the basis for passing thousands of laws that have defined the meaning of foreign and interstate commerce. Similarly, Article III, Section 1, states that the national judiciary shall consist of one supreme court and "such inferior courts, as Congress may from time to time ordain and establish." Through a series of acts, Congress has used this broad provision to establish the federal court system of today.

Presidential Actions

Even though the Constitution does not expressly authorize the president to propose bills or even budgets to Congress, presidents since the time of Woodrow Wilson (who served as president from 1913 to 1921) have proposed hundreds of bills to Congress each year. Presidents have also relied on their Article II authority as commander in chief of the nation's armed forces to send American troops abroad into combat, although the Constitution provides that Congress has the power to declare war. Presidents have also conducted foreign affairs by the use of **executive agreements,** which are legally binding documents made between the president and a foreign head of state. The Constitution does not mention such agreements.

Judicial Review

Another way of changing the Constitution—or of making it more flexible—is through the power of judicial review. **Judicial review** refers to the power of U.S. courts to invalidate actions undertaken by the legislative and executive branches of government. A state court, for example, may rule that a statute enacted by the state legislature is unconstitutional. Federal courts (and ultimately, the United States Supreme Court) may rule unconstitutional not only acts of Congress and decisions of the national executive branch but also state statutes, state executive actions, and even provisions of state constitutions.

The Constitution does not specifically mention the power of judicial review. Those in attendance at the Constitutional Convention, however, probably expected that the courts would have some authority to review the legality of acts by the executive and legislative branches. Indeed, Alexander Hamilton, in *Federalist Paper* No. 78 (see Appendix D), explicitly outlined the concept of judicial review. Whether the power of judicial review can be justified constitutionally is a question that has been subject to some debate, particularly in recent years (see this chapter's *Which Side Are You On?* for a further discussion of this issue). For now, suffice it to say that in 1803, the Supreme Court claimed this power for itself in *Marbury v. Madison,*[15] in which the Supreme Court ruled that a particular provision of an act of Congress was unconstitutional.

Through the process of judicial review, the Supreme Court adapts the Constitution to modern situations. Electronic technology, for example, did not exist when the Constitution was ratified. Nonetheless, in the twentieth century the Supreme Court used the Fourth Amendment guarantees against unreasonable searches and seizures to place limits on wiretapping and other electronic eavesdropping methods by government officials. Additionally, the Supreme Court has changed its interpretation of the Constitution in accordance with changing times. It ruled in 1896 that "separate-but-equal" public facilities for African Americans were constitutional; but by 1954 the times had changed, and the Supreme Court

Executive Agreement
A binding international agreement made between chiefs of state that does not require legislative sanction.

Judicial Review
The power of the Supreme Court or any court to declare unconstitutional federal or state laws and other acts of government.

---

[15]1 Cranch 137 (1803). (See Appendix B at the end of this text for information on how court decisions are referenced.) See Chapter 15 for a further discussion of the *Marbury v. Madison* case.

reversed that decision.[16] Woodrow Wilson summarized the Supreme Court's work when he described it as "a constitutional convention in continuous session." Basically, the law is what the Supreme Court says it is at any point in time.

Interpretation, Custom, and Usage

The Constitution has also been changed through its interpretation by both Congress and the president. Originally, the president had a staff consisting of personal secretaries and a few others. Today, because Congress delegates specific tasks to the president and the chief executive assumes political leadership, the executive office staff alone has increased to several thousand persons. The executive branch provides legislative leadership far beyond the intentions of the Constitution.

---

[16]*Brown v. Board of Education of Topeka*, 347 U.S. 483 (1954).

DID YOU KNOW... That some of the framers of the Constitution were influenced by Native American political values, particularly those of the Iroquois Confederacy (the Iroquois concluded a treaty in 1520 that contained wording ["We, the people, to form a union, to establish peace, equity, and order . . . "] very similar to the Preamble to the U.S. Constitution)?

which side are you on?

Should the Supreme Court Have the Final Say on All Constitutional Questions?

Although *judicial review* is an abstract term for an abstract concept, the process has a way of affecting the everyday lives of millions of Americans. As mentioned elsewhere, the power of judicial review allows the judicial branch of government (the courts) to determine whether actions of the other two branches are or are not constitutional. The United States Supreme Court, as the nation's highest court, thus has the final say on what specific provisions of the Constitution mean.

Over the years, the Supreme Court has ruled on the constitutional validity of laws relating to such controversial issues as abortion, physician-assisted suicide, indecent speech on the Internet, term limits for U.S. congresspersons, prayer in public schools, whether votes cast in Florida during the 2000 elections could be manually recounted, and a host of others that you will read about in later chapters of this book. Thus, the unelected judges of the federal courts—and particularly, the nine justices of the Supreme Court—wield extensive influence over national policy.

Some scholars and politicians claim that the founders did not intend the judiciary to exercise such far-reaching powers. After all, Congress was established as the lawmaking branch of government. Although some of the founders had few worries about judicial power (Alexander Hamilton referred to it as the "least dangerous" branch of government because it had no enforcement powers), others had different views. For example, Thomas Jefferson expressed concern over allowing unelected judges to be in charge of interpreting the meaning of the Constitution. In a letter to William Jarvis in 1820, Jefferson wrote, "It is a very dangerous doctrine to consider the judges as the ultimate arbiters of all constitutional questions."

Some people believe that the powers of the judiciary should be curbed—in the interests of maintaining the balance of powers envisioned by the framers. Proposals for doing this include, among other things, removing or limiting the judiciary's power of judicial review and giving Congress the final say on constitutional interpretation. Others argue that the judiciary has proved over time to be an effective guardian of our rights and liberties and that the judicial power should be left alone.

DOES IT MATTER?

Do you believe that Congress would be a better guardian of your constitutional rights and liberties than the Supreme Court has been? Why or why not?

GOING ONLINE

Alexander Hamilton sets forth the doctrine of judicial review, and the reasons why the courts should have this power, in Federalist Paper *No. 78. You can read his essay in Appendix D of this text or find it online at* **http://www.law.emory.edu/FEDERAL**. *Arguments in favor of curbing the courts' use of this power can be found at* **http://www.house.gov/judiciary/22369.htm**.

Citizens protest the availability of pornography on the Internet. How should the First Amendment's guarantee of freedom of speech be applied to materials available on the World Wide Web?

Changes in the ways of doing political business have also altered the Constitution. The Constitution does not mention political parties, yet these informal, "extraconstitutional" organizations make the nominations for offices, run the campaigns, organize the members of Congress, and in fact change the election system from time to time. The emergence and evolution of the party system, for example, have changed the way of electing the president. The Constitution calls for the electoral college to choose the president. Today, the people vote for electors who are pledged to the candidate of their party, effectively choosing the president themselves. Perhaps most strikingly, the Constitution has been adapted from serving the needs of a small, rural republic with no international prestige to providing a framework of government for an industrial giant with vast geographic, natural, and human resources.

The Constitution: Issues for the Twenty-First Century

The U.S. Constitution has been called a "living" constitution because the framers embodied it with sufficient flexibility that its meaning and application could change as the nation and its people changed. As we fully develop the age of technology, information, and communication, this inherent flexibility undoubtedly will be pushed to its limits at times. For example, how can our constitutional right to free speech be applied to electronic communications via the Internet? How can privacy rights be protected in an electronic age? Furthermore, how can any state or national law protect rights in an electronic jurisdiction that is essentially international in scope?

A further issue involves striking a balance between the rights of the fifty sovereign states and the powers of the national government. This has never been easy, and during the 1860s the nation resorted to civil war to resolve the issue. As we enter the twenty-first century, there again seems to be a growing movement toward states' rights and away from national government involvement. We examine the challenges posed by a federal form of government—and how those challenges have been dealt with in the past—in Chapter 3. We return to this theme again in later chapters of this text.

These are just a few of the issues on today's horizon that can only be resolved through constitutional interpretation. Throughout this book, you will read about many more.

making a difference

How Can You Affect the U.S. Constitution?

The Constitution is an enduring document that has survived more than two hundred years of turbulent history. It is also a changing document, however. Twenty-seven amendments have been added to the original Constitution. How can you, as an individual, actively help to rewrite the Constitution?

One of the best ways is to work for (or against) a constitutional amendment. At the time of this writing, national coalitions of interest groups are supporting or opposing proposed amendments concerning prayer in the schools and antiabortion laws. If you want an opportunity to change the Constitution—or to assure that it is not changed—you could work for or with one of the alliances of groups interested in the fate of these amendments.

The following contacts should help you get started on efforts to affect the U.S. Constitution directly.

School Prayer Amendment

The proposed school prayer amendment, or Religious Freedom Amendment, would allow for student-sponsored prayer in public schools.

Supporters of the amendment claim that it is necessary to correct Supreme Court rulings that have strayed from the meaning of the First Amendment's provisions on freedom of religion. To learn more about the arguments in favor of the school prayer amendment, you can contact the Christian Coalition, 1801-L Sara Drive, Chesapeake, VA 23320 (757-424-2630 or 1-800-325-4746). You can access its Web site at

http://www.cc.org

Critics of the amendment claim that the amendment would allow students to impose their religious beliefs on classmates by holding prayers at mandatory school events. For information on this position, contact the American Civil Liberties Union (ACLU), 125 Broad St., New York, NY 10004 (212-549-2500). The ACLU is online at

http://www.aclu.org

Abortion

One of the organizations whose primary goal is to secure the passage of the Human Life Amendment is the American Life League, P.O. Box 1350, Stafford, VA 22555 (540-659-4171). It can be reached online at

http://www.all.org

The Human Life Amendment would recognize in law the "personhood" of the unborn, secure human rights protections for an unborn child from the time of fertilization, and prohibit abortion under any circumstances.

A political action and information organization working on behalf of "pro-choice" issues—that is, the right of women to have control over reproduction—is the National Abortion and Reproductive Rights Action League, 1156 15th St. N.W., Suite 700, Washington, DC 20005 (202-973-3000). Its URL is

http://www.naral.org

Key terms

Anti-Federalist 50	Federalist 50	representative assembly 34
bicameral legislature 44	First Continental Congress 36	Second Continental Congress 36
checks and balances 47	Great Compromise 44	separation of powers 46
confederation 39	judicial review 58	social contract 38
electoral college 48	Madisonian model 46	state 39
executive agreement 58	natural rights 38	supremacy doctrine 44
federal system 48	ratification 50	unicameral legislature 39

Chapter summary

1 An early effort by England to establish North American colonies was unsuccessful. The first permanent English colonies were established at Jamestown in 1607 and Plymouth in 1620. The Mayflower Compact created the first formal government. By the mid-1700s, other British colonies had been established along the Atlantic seaboard from Georgia to Maine.

2 In 1763, the British tried to reassert control over their increasingly independent-minded colonies through a series of taxes and legislative acts. The colonists responded with boycotts of British products and protests. Representatives of the colonies formed the First Continental Congress in 1774. The delegates sent a petition to the British king expressing their grievances. The Second Continental Congress established an army in 1775 to defend colonists against any attacks by British soldiers.

3 On July 4, 1776, the Second Continental Congress approved the Declaration of Independence. Perhaps the most revolutionary aspects of the Declaration were its assumptions that people have natural rights to life, liberty, and the pursuit of happiness; that governments derive their power from the consent of the governed; and that people have a right to overthrow oppressive governments. During the Revolutionary War, all of the colonies adopted written constitutions that severely curtailed the power of executives, thus giving their legislatures predominant powers. By the end of the Revolutionary War, the states had signed the Articles of Confederation, creating a weak central government with few powers. The Articles proved to be unworkable because the national government had no way to assure compliance by the states with such measures as securing tax revenues.

4 General dissatisfaction with the Articles of Confederation prompted delegates to call a convention at Philadelphia in 1787. Although the delegates originally convened with the idea of amending the Articles, the discussions soon focused on creating a constitution for a new form of government. The Virginia plan and the New Jersey plan were offered but did not garner widespread support. A compromise offered by the state of Connecticut helped to break the large-state/small-state disputes dividing the delegates. The final version of the Constitution provided for the separation of powers, checks and balances, and a federal form of government.

5 Fears of a strong central government prompted the addition of the Bill of Rights to the Constitution. The Bill of Rights secured for Americans a wide variety of freedoms, including the freedoms of religion, speech, and assembly. It was initially applied only to the federal government, but amendments to the Constitution following the Civil War made it clear that the Bill of Rights also applied to the states.

6 An amendment to the Constitution may be proposed by either a two-thirds vote in each house of Congress or by a national convention called by Congress at the request of two-thirds of the state legislatures. Ratification can occur by either a positive vote in three-fourths of the legislatures of the various states or by special conventions called in the states for the specific purpose of ratifying the proposed amendment and a positive vote in three-fourths of these state conventions. Informal methods of constitutional change include congressional legislation, presidential actions, judicial review, and changing interpretations of the Constitution.

Selected print and electronic resources

SUGGESTED READINGS

Casper, Gerhard. *Separating Power: Essays on the Founding Period.* Cambridge, Mass.: Harvard University Press, 1997. The author argues that the founders had not fully worked through their principles of constitutional government. Therefore, when scholars and judges try to interpret the Constitution by looking at the intentions of the framers, they run into difficulty.

Finkelman, Paul. *Slavery and the Founders: Race and Liberty in the Age of Jefferson,* 2d ed. Armonk, N.Y.: M. E. Sharpe, 2000. This controversial and provocative book provides a critical account of the founders' attitudes toward slavery and the legal status of slaves in the early years of the nation.

Hamilton, Alexander, James Madison, and John Jay. *The Federalist Papers.* Cambridge, Mass.: Harvard University Press, 1961. The complete set of columns from the *New York Packet* defending the new Constitution is presented.

Levy, Leonard W. *Origins of the Bill of Rights.* New Haven, Conn.: Yale University Press, 1999. The author presents an exciting history of the debates surrounding the origins of the Bill of Rights and the important role played by James Madison in getting Congress to act on the amendments.

MEDIA RESOURCES

In the Beginning–A Bill Moyers program that features discussions with three prominent historians about the roots of the Constitution and its impact on our society.

John Locke–A video exploring the character and principal views of John Locke.

Where America Began–A video tour of American colonial history, including Jamestown, Williamsburg, and Yorktown.

Logging on

For U.S. founding documents, including the Declaration of Independence, the U.S. Constitution, scanned originals of the U.S. Constitution, and *The Federalist Papers,* go to Emory University School of Law's Web site at

http://www.law.emory.edu/FEDERAL

The University of Oklahoma Law Center has a number of U.S. historical documents online, including many of those discussed in this chapter. Go to

http://www.law.ou.edu/hist

The National Constitution Center provides information on the Constitution–including its history, current debates over constitutional provisions, and news articles–at the following site:

http://www.constitutioncenter.org

A study aid for the U.S. Constitution is available at the following Web site, which provides links to many different views for each segment of the Constitution:

http://tcnbp/index.htm

If you want to look at state constitutions, go to

http://www.findlaw.com/casecode/state.html

To find constitutions for other countries, go to

http://www.uni-wuerzburg.de/law/home.html

Using the Internet for political analysis

As noted in this chapter, the U.S. Constitution is one of the most concise in the world. It clearly reflects the basic values of the framers in its emphasis on republican government, liberty, and limited government. Take a look at some modern constitutions by clicking on some of the countries listed at the following site:

http://findlaw.com/12international/ countries/index.html

Choose at least two constitutions from non-Western nations–that is, from Africa, Asia, or the Middle East. Compare these constitutions to that of the United States in terms of guarantees of the people's rights and liberties, the power of the central government, and the relationship between religion and the government.

appendix to chapter 2

The Constitution of the United States of America*

The Preamble

We the People of the United States, in Order to form a more perfect Union, establish Justice, insure domestic Tranquility, provide for the common defence, promote the general Welfare, and secure the Blessings of Liberty to ourselves and our Posterity, do ordain and establish this Constitution for the United States of America.

The Preamble declares that "We the People" are the authority for the Constitution (unlike the Articles of Confederation, which derived their authority from the states). The Preamble also sets out the purposes of the Constitution.

Article I. (Legislative Branch)

The first part of the Constitution is called Article 1; it deals with the organization and powers of the lawmaking branch of the national government, the Congress.

Section 1. Legislative Powers

All legislative Powers herein granted shall be vested in a Congress of the United States, which shall consist of a Senate and House of Representatives.

Section 2. House of Representatives

Clause 1: Composition and Election of Members. The House of Representatives shall be composed of Members chosen every second Year by the People of the several States, and the Electors in each State shall have the Qualifications requisite for Electors of the most numerous Branch of the State Legislature.

Each state has the power to decide who may vote for members of Congress. Within each state, those who may vote for state legislators may also vote for members of the House of Representatives (and, under the Seventeenth Amendment, for U.S. senators). When the Constitution was written, nearly all states limited voting rights to white male property owners or taxpayers at least twenty-one years old. Subsequent amendments granted voting power to African American men, all women, and eighteen-year-olds.

Clause 2: Qualifications. No Person shall be a Representative who shall not have attained to the Age of twenty five Years, and been seven Years a Citizen of the United States, and who shall not, when elected, be an Inhabitant of that State in which he shall be chosen.

Each member of the House must (1) be at least twenty-five years old, (2) have been a U.S. citizen for at least seven years, and (3) be a resident of the state in which she or he is elected.

Clause 3: Apportionment of Representatives and Direct Taxes. Representatives [and direct Taxes][1] shall be apportioned among the several States which may be included within this Union, according to their respective Numbers [which shall be determined by adding to the whole Number of free Persons, including those bound to Service for a Term of Years, and excluding Indians not taxed, three fifths of all other Persons].[2] The actual Enumeration shall be made within three Years after the first Meeting of the Congress of the United States, and within every subsequent Term of ten Years, in such Manner as they shall by Law direct. The Number of Representatives

---

*The spelling, capitalization, and punctuation of the original have been retained here. Brackets indicate passages that have been altered by amendments to the Constitution.

[1]Modified by the Sixteenth Amendment.
[2]Modified by the Fourteenth Amendment.

shall not exceed one for every thirty Thousand, but each State shall have at Least one Representative; and until such enumeration shall be made, the State of New Hampshire shall be entitled to chuse three, Massachusetts eight, Rhode Island and Providence Plantations one, Connecticut five, New York six, New Jersey four, Pennsylvania eight, Delaware one, Maryland six, Virginia ten, North Carolina five, South Carolina five, and Georgia three.

A state's representation in the House is based on the size of its population. Population is counted in each decade's census, after which Congress reapportions House seats. Since early in the twentieth century, the number of seats has been limited to 435.

Clause 4: Vacancies.   When vacancies happen in the Representation from any State, the Executive Authority thereof shall issue Writs of Election to fill such Vacancies.

The "Executive Authority" is the state's governor. When a vacancy occurs in the House, the governor calls a special election to fill it.

Clause 5: Officers and Impeachment.   The House of Representatives shall chuse their Speaker and other Officers; and shall have the sole Power of Impeachment.

The power to impeach is the power to accuse. In this case, it is the power to accuse members of the executive or judicial branch of wrongdoing or abuse of power. Once a bill of impeachment is issued, the Senate holds the trial.

Section 3. The Senate
Clause 1: Term and Number of Members.   The Senate of the United States shall be composed of two Senators from each State [chosen by the Legislature thereof],[3] for six Years; and each Senator shall have one Vote.

Every state has two senators, each of whom serves for six years and has one vote in the upper chamber. Since the Seventeenth Amendment in 1913, all senators are elected directly by voters of the state during the regular election.

Clause 2: Classification of Senators.   Immediately after they shall be assembled in Consequence of the first Election, they shall be divided as equally as may be into three Classes. The Seats of the Senators of the first Class shall be vacated at the Expiration of the second Year, of the second Class at the Expiration of the fourth Year, and of the third Class at the Expiration of the sixth Year, so that one third may be chosen every second Year; [and if Vacancies happen by Resignation, or otherwise, during the

Recess of the Legislature of any State, the Executive thereof may make temporary Appointments until the next Meeting of the Legislature, which shall then fill such Vacancies].[4]

One-third of the Senate's seats are open to election every two years (unlike the House, all of whose members are elected simultaneously).

Clause 3: Qualifications.   No Person shall be a Senator who shall not have attained to the Age of thirty Years, and been nine Years a Citizen of the United States, and who shall not, when elected, be an Inhabitant of that State for which he shall be chosen.

Every senator must be at least thirty years old, a citizen of the United States for a minimum of nine years, and a resident of the state in which he or she is elected.

Clause 4: The Role of the Vice President.   The Vice President of the United States shall be President of the Senate, but shall have no Vote, unless they be equally divided.

The vice president presides over meetings of the Senate but cannot vote unless there is a tie. The Constitution gives no other official duties to the vice president.

Clause 5: Other Officers.   The Senate shall chuse their other Officers, and also a President pro tempore, in the Absence of the Vice President, or when he shall exercise the Office of President of the United States.

The Senate votes for one of its members to preside when the vice president is absent. This person is usually called the president pro tempore because of the temporary situation of the position.

Clause 6: Impeachment Trials.   The Senate shall have the sole Power to try all Impeachments. When sitting for that Purpose, they shall be on Oath or Affirmation. When the President of the United States is tried, the Chief Justice shall preside: And no Person shall be convicted without the Concurrence of two thirds of the Members present.

The Senate conducts trials of officials that the House impeaches. The Senate sits as a jury, with the vice president presiding if the president is not on trial.

Clause 7: Penalties for Conviction.   Judgment in Cases of Impeachment shall not extend further than to removal from Office, and disqualification to hold and enjoy any Office of honor, Trust, or Profit under the United States:

---

[3]Repealed by the Seventeenth Amendment.

[4]Modified by the Seventeenth Amendment.

but the Party convicted shall nevertheless be liable and subject to Indictment, Trial, Judgment, and Punishment, according to Law.

On conviction of impeachment charges, the Senate can only force an official to leave office and prevent him or her from holding another office in the federal government. The individual, however, can still be tried in a regular court.

Section 4. Congressional Elections: Times, Manner, and Places

Clause 1: Elections.   The Times, Places and Manner of holding Elections for Senators and Representatives, shall be prescribed in each State by the Legislature thereof; but the Congress may at any time by Law make or alter such Regulations, except as to the Places of chusing Senators.

Congress set the Tuesday after the first Monday in November in even-numbered years as the date for congressional elections. In states with more than one seat in the House, Congress requires that representatives be elected from districts within each state. Under the Seventeenth Amendment, senators are elected at the same places as other officials.

Clause 2: Sessions of Congress.   [The Congress shall assemble at least once in every Year, and such Meeting shall be on the first Monday in December, unless they shall by Law appoint a different Day.][5]

Congress has to meet every year at least once. The regular session now begins at noon on January 3 of each year, subsequent to the Twentieth Amendment, unless Congress passes a law to fix a different date. Congress stays in session until its members vote to adjourn. Additionally, the president may call a special session.

Section 5. Powers and Duties of the Houses

Clause 1: Admitting Members and Quorum.   Each House shall be the Judge of the Elections, Returns, and Qualifications of its own Members, and a Majority of each shall constitute a Quorum to do Business; but a smaller Number may adjourn from day to day, and may be authorized to compel the Attendance of absent Members, in such Manner, and under such Penalties as each House may provide.

Each chamber may exclude or refuse to seat a member-elect.

*   *The quorum rule requires that 218 members of the House and 51 members of the Senate be present in order to conduct business. This rule is normally not enforced in the handling of routine matters.*

Clause 2: Rules and Discipline of Members.   Each House may determine the Rules of its Proceedings, punish its Members for disorderly Behaviour, and, with the Concurrence of two thirds, expel a Member.

The House and the Senate may adopt their own rules to guide their proceedings. Each may also discipline its members for conduct that is deemed unacceptable. No member may be expelled without a two-thirds majority vote in favor of expulsion.

Clause 3: Keeping a Record.   Each House shall keep a Journal of its Proceedings, and from time to time publish the same, excepting such Parts as may in their Judgment require Secrecy; and the Yeas and Nays of the Members of either House on any question shall, at the Desire of one fifth of those Present, be entered on the Journal.

The journals of the two chambers are published at the end of each session of Congress.

Clause 4: Adjournment.   Neither House, during the Session of Congress, shall, without the Consent of the other, adjourn for more than three days, nor to any other Place than that in which the two Houses shall be sitting.

Congress has the power to determine when and where to meet, provided, however, that both chambers meet in the same city. Neither chamber may recess in excess of three days without the consent of the other.

Section 6. Rights of Members

Clause 1: Compensation and Privileges.   The Senators and Representatives shall receive a Compensation for their services, to be ascertained by Law, and paid out of the Treasury of the United States. They shall in all Cases, except Treason, Felony and Breach of the Peace, be privileged from Arrest during their Attendance at the Session of their respective Houses, and in going to and returning from the same; and for any Speech or Debate in either House, they shall not be questioned in any other Place.

Congressional salaries are to be paid by the U.S. Treasury rather than by the members' respective states. The original salaries were $6 per day; in 1857 they were $3,000 per year. Both representatives and senators currently are paid $141,300 each year.

*   *Treason is defined in Article III, Section 3. A felony is any serious crime. A breach of the peace is any indictable offense less than treason or a felony. Members cannot be arrested for things they say during speeches and debates in Congress. This immunity applies to the Capitol Building itself and not to their private lives.*

Clause 2: Restrictions.   No Senator or Representative shall, during the Time for which he was elected, be

---

[5]Changed by the Twentieth Amendment.

appointed to any civil Office under the Authority of the United States, which shall have been created, or the Emoluments whereof shall have been encreased during such time; and no Person holding any Office under the United States, shall be a Member of either House during his Continuance in Office.

During the term for which a member was elected, he or she cannot concurrently accept another federal government position.

Section 7. Legislative Powers: Bills and Resolutions
Clause 1: Revenue Bills.   All Bills for raising Revenue shall originate in the House of Representatives; but the Senate may propose or concur with Amendments as on other Bills.

All tax and appropriation bills for raising money have to originate in the House of Representatives. The Senate, though, often amends such bills and may even substitute an entirely different bill.

Clause 2: The Presidential Veto.   Every Bill which shall have passed the House of Representatives and the Senate, shall, before it becomes a Law, be presented to the President of the United States; If he approve he shall sign it, but if not he shall return it, with his Objections to the House in which it shall have originated, who shall enter the Objections at large on their Journal, and proceed to reconsider it. If after such Reconsideration two thirds of that House shall agree to pass the Bill, it shall be sent together with the Objections, to the other House, by which it shall likewise be reconsidered, and if approved by two thirds of that House, it shall become a Law. But in all such Cases the Votes of both Houses shall be determined by Yeas and Nays, and the Names of the Persons voting for and against the Bill shall be entered on the Journal of each House respectively. If any Bill shall not be returned by the President within ten Days (Sundays excepted) after it shall have been presented to him, the Same shall be a Law, in like Manner as if he had signed it, unless the Congress by their Adjournment prevent its Return in which Case it shall not be a Law.

When Congress sends the president a bill, he or she can sign it (in which case it becomes law) or send it back to the chamber in which it originated. If it is sent back, a two-thirds majority of each chamber must pass it again for it to become law. If the president neither signs it nor sends it back within ten days, it becomes law anyway, unless Congress adjourns in the meantime.

Clause 3: Actions on Other Matters.   Every Order, Resolution, or Vote to which the Concurrence of the Senate and House of Representatives may be necessary (except on a question of Adjournment) shall be presented to the President of the United States; and before the Same shall take Effect, shall be approved by him, or being disapproved by him, shall be repassed by two thirds of the Senate and House of Representatives, according to the Rules and Limitations prescribed in the Case of a Bill.

The president must either sign or veto everything that Congress passes, except votes to adjourn and resolutions not having the force of law.

Section 8. The Powers of Congress
Clause 1: Taxing.   The Congress shall have Power To lay and collect Taxes, Duties, Imposts and Excises, to pay the Debts and provide for the common Defence and general Welfare of the United States; but all Duties, Imposts and Excises shall be uniform throughout the United States;

Duties are taxes on imports and exports. Impost is a generic term for tax. Excises are taxes on the manufacture, sale, or use of goods.

Clause 2: Borrowing.   To borrow Money on the credit of the United States;

Congress has the power to borrow money, which is normally carried out through the sale of U.S. treasury bonds on which interest is paid. Note that the Constitution places no limit on the amount of government borrowing.

Clause 3: Regulation of Commerce.   To regulate Commerce with foreign Nations, and among the several States, and with the Indian Tribes;

This is the commerce clause, which gives to the Congress the power to regulate interstate and foreign trade. Much of the activity of Congress is based on this clause.

Clause 4: Naturalization and Bankruptcy.   To establish a uniform Rule of Naturalization, and uniform Laws on the subject of Bankruptcies throughout the United States;

Only Congress may determine how aliens can become citizens of the United States. Congress may make laws with respect to bankruptcy.

Clause 5: Money and Standards.   To coin Money, regulate the Value thereof, and of foreign Coin, and fix the Standard of Weights and Measures;

Congress mints coins and prints and circulates paper money. Congress can establish uniform measures of time, distance, weight, and so on. In 1838, Congress adopted the English system of weights and measurements as our national standard.

Clause 6: Punishing Counterfeiters. To provide for the Punishment of counterfeiting the Securities and current Coin of the United States;

Congress has the power to punish those who copy American money and pass it off as real. Currently, the fine is up to $5,000 and/or imprisonment for up to fifteen years.

Clause 7: Roads and Post Offices. To establish Post Offices and post Roads;

Post roads include all routes over which mail is carried—highways, railways, waterways, and airways.

Clause 8: Patents and Copyrights. To promote the Progress of Science and useful Arts, by securing for limited Times to Authors and Inventors the exclusive Right to their respective Writings and Discoveries;

Authors' and composers' works are protected by copyrights established by copyright law, which currently is the 1978 Copyright Act. Copyrights are valid for the life of the author or composer plus fifty years. Inventors' works are protected by patents, which vary in length of protection from three and a half to seventeen years. A patent gives a person the exclusive right to control the manufacture or sale of her or his invention.

Clause 9: Lower Courts. To constitute Tribunals inferior to the supreme Court;

Congress has the authority to set up all federal courts, except the Supreme Court, and to decide what cases those courts will hear.

Clause 10: Punishment for Piracy. To define and punish Piracies and Felonies committed on the high Seas, and Offences against the Law of Nations;

Congress has the authority to prohibit the commission of certain acts outside U.S. territory and to punish certain violations of international law.

Clause 11: Declaration of War. To declare War, grant Letters of Marque and Reprisal, and make Rules concerning Captures on Land and Water;

Only Congress can declare war, although the president, as commander in chief, can make war without Congress's formal declaration. Letters of marque and reprisal authorized private parties to capture and destroy enemy ships in wartime. Since the middle of the nineteenth century, international law has prohibited letters of marque and reprisal, and the United States has honored the ban.

Clause 12: The Army. To raise and support Armies, but no Appropriation of Money to that Use shall be for a longer Term than two Years;

Congress has the power to create an army; the money used to pay for it must be appropriated for no more than two-year intervals. This latter restriction gives ultimate control of the army to civilians.

Clause 13: Creation of a Navy. To provide and maintain a Navy;

This clause allows for the maintenance of a navy. In 1947, Congress created the U.S. Air Force.

Clause 14: Regulation of the Armed Forces. To make Rules for the Government and Regulation of the land and naval Forces;

Congress sets the rules for the military mainly by way of the Uniform Code of Military Justice, which was enacted in 1950 by Congress.

Clause 15: The Militia. To provide for calling forth the Militia to execute the Laws of the Union, suppress Insurrections and repel Invasions;

The militia is known today as the National Guard. Both Congress and the president have the authority to call the National Guard into federal service.

Clause 16: How the Militia Is Organized. To provide for organizing, arming, and disciplining the Militia, and for governing such Part of them as may be employed in the Service of the United States, reserving to the States respectively, the Appointment of the Officers, and the Authority of training the Militia according to the discipline prescribed by Congress;

This clause gives Congress the power to "federalize" state militia (National Guard). When called into such service, the National Guard is subject to the same rules that Congress has set forth for the regular armed services.

Clause 17: Creation of the District of Columbia. To exercise exclusive Legislation in all Cases whatsoever, over such District (not exceeding ten Miles square) as may, by Cession of particular States, and the Acceptance of Congress, become the Seat of the Government of the United States, and to exercise like Authority over all Places purchased by the Consent of the Legislature of the State in which the Same shall be, for the Erection of Forts, Magazines, Arsenals, dock-Yards, and other needful Buildings;–And

Congress established the District of Columbia as the national capital in 1791. Virginia and Maryland had granted land for the District, but Virginia's grant was returned because it was believed it would not be needed. Today, the District covers sixty-nine square miles.

Clause 18: The Elastic Clause.   To make all Laws which shall be necessary and proper for carrying into Execution the foregoing Powers, and all other Powers vested by this Constitution in the Government of the United States, or in any Department or Officer thereof.

This clause—the necessary and proper clause, or the elastic clause—grants no specific powers, and thus it can be stretched to fit different circumstances. It has allowed Congress to adapt the government to changing needs and times.

Section 9. The Powers Denied to Congress

Clause 1: Question of Slavery. The Migration or Importation of such Persons as any of the States now existing shall think proper to admit, shall not be prohibited by the Congress prior to the Year one thousand eight hundred and eight, but a Tax or duty may be imposed on such Importation, not exceeding ten dollars for each Person.

"Persons" referred to slaves. Congress outlawed the slave trade in 1808.

Clause 2: Habeas Corpus.   The privilege of the Writ of Habeas Corpus shall not be suspended, unless when in Cases of Rebellion or Invasion the public Safety may require it.

A writ of habeas corpus is a court order directing a sheriff or other public officer who is detaining another person to "produce the body" of the detainee so the court can assess the legality of the detention.

Clause 3: Special Bills.   No Bill of Attainder or ex post facto Law shall be passed.

A bill of attainder is a law that inflicts punishment without a trial. An ex post facto law is a law that inflicts punishment for an act that was not illegal when it was committed.

Clause 4: Direct Taxes.   [No Capitation, or other direct, Tax shall be laid, unless in Proportion to the Census or Enumeration herein before directed to be taken.][6]

A capitation is a tax on a person. A direct tax is a tax paid directly to the government, such as a property tax. This

clause was intended to prevent Congress from levying a tax on slaves per person and thereby taxing slavery out of existence.

Clause 5: Export Taxes.   No Tax or Duty shall be laid on Articles exported from any State.

Congress may not tax any goods sold from one state to another or from one state to a foreign country. (Congress does have the power to tax goods that are bought from other countries, however.)

Clause 6: Interstate Commerce.   No Preference shall be given by any Regulation of Commerce or Revenue to the Ports of one State over those of another: nor shall Vessels bound to, or from, one State, be obliged to enter, clear, or pay Duties in another.

Congress may not treat different ports within the United States differently in terms of taxing and commerce powers. Congress may not tax goods sent from one state to another. Finally, Congress may not give one state's port a legal advantage over those of another state.

Clause 7: Treasury Withdrawals.   No Money shall be drawn from the Treasury, but in Consequence of Appropriations made by Law; and a regular Statement and Account of the Receipts and Expenditures of all public Money shall be published from time to time.

Federal funds can be spent only as Congress authorizes. This is a significant check on the president's power.

Clause 8: Titles of Nobility.   No Title of Nobility shall be granted by the United States: And no Person holding any Office of Profit or Trust under them, shall, without the Consent of the Congress, accept of any present, Emolument, Office, or Title, of any kind whatever, from any King, Prince, or foreign State.

No person in the United States may hold a title of nobility, such as duke or duchess. This clause also discourages bribery of American officials by foreign governments.

Section 10. Those Powers Denied to the States

Clause 1: Treaties and Coinage.   No State shall enter into any Treaty, Alliance, or Confederation; grant Letters of Marque and Reprisal; coin Money; emit Bills of Credit; make any Thing but gold and silver Coin a Tender in Payment of Debts; pass any Bill of Attainder, ex post facto Law, or Law impairing the Obligation of Contracts, or grant any Title of Nobility.

Prohibiting state laws "impairing the Obligation of Contracts" was intended to protect creditors. (Shays's Rebellion—an attempt to prevent courts from giving effect

---

[6]Modified by the Sixteenth Amendment.

to creditors' legal actions against debtors—occurred only one year before the Constitution was written.)

Clause 2: Duties and Imposts.   No State shall, without the Consent of the Congress, lay any Imports or Duties on Imports or Exports, except what may be absolutely necessary for executing its inspection Laws; and the net Produce of all Duties and Imposts, laid by any State on Imports or Exports, shall be for the Use of the Treasury of the United States; and all such Laws shall be subject to the Revision and Controul of the Congress.

Only Congress can tax imports. Further, the states cannot tax exports.

Clause 3: War.   No State shall, without the Consent of Congress, lay any Duty of Tonnage, keep Troops, or Ships of War in time of Peace, enter into any Agreement or Compact with another State, or with a foreign Power or engage in War, unless actually invaded, or in such imminent Danger as will not admit of delay.

A duty of tonnage is a tax on ships according to their cargo capacity. No states may effectively tax ships according to their cargo unless Congress agrees. Additionally, this clause forbids any state to keep troops or warships during peacetime or to make a compact with another state or foreign nation unless Congress so agrees. States can, in contrast, maintain a militia, but its use has to be limited to internal disorders that occur within a state—unless, of course, the militia is called into federal service.

Article II. (Executive Branch)

Section 1. The Nature and Scope of Presidential Power

Clause 1: Four-Year Term.   The executive Power shall be vested in a President of the United States of America. He shall hold his Office during the Term of four Years, and, together with the Vice President, chosen for the same Term, be elected, as follows.

The president has the power to carry out laws made by Congress, called the executive power. He or she serves in office for a four-year term after election. The Twenty-second Amendment limits the number of times a person may be elected president.

Clause 2: Choosing Electors from Each State.   Each State shall appoint, in such Manner as the Legislature thereof may direct, a Number of Electors, equal to the whole Number of Senators and Representatives to which the State may be entitled in the Congress; but no Senator or Representative, or Person holding an Office of Trust or Profit under the United States, shall be appointed an Elector.

The "Electors" are known more commonly as the "electoral college." The president is elected by electors—that is, representatives chosen by the people—rather than by the people directly.

Clause 3: The Former System of Elections.   [The Electors shall meet in their respective States, and vote by Ballot for two Persons, of whom one at least shall not be an Inhabitant of the same State with themselves. And they shall make a List of all the Persons voted for, and of the Number of Votes for each; which List they shall sign and certify, and transmit sealed to the Seat of the Government of the United States, directed to the President of the Senate. The President of the Senate shall, in the Presence of the Senate and House of Representatives, open all the Certificates, and the Votes shall then be counted. The Person having the greatest Number of Votes shall be the President, if such Number be a Majority of the whole Number of Electors appointed; and if there be more than one who have such Majority, and have an equal Number of Votes, then the House of Representatives shall immediately chuse by Ballot one of them for President; and if no Person have a Majority, then from the five highest on the List the said House shall in like Manner chuse the President. But in chusing the President, the Votes shall be taken by States, the Representation from each State having one Vote; A quorum for this Purpose shall consist of a Member or Members from two thirds of the States, and a Majority of all the States shall be necessary to a Choice. In every Case, after the Choice of the President, the Person having the greater Number of Votes of the Electors shall be the Vice President. But if there should remain two or more who have equal Votes, the Senate shall chuse from them by Ballot the Vice President.][7]

The original method of selecting the president and vice president was replaced by the Twelfth Amendment. Apparently, the framers did not anticipate the rise of political parties and the development of primaries and conventions.

Clause 4: The Time of Elections.   The Congress may determine the Time of chusing the Electors, and the Day on which they shall give their Votes; which Day shall be the same throughout the United States.

Congress set the Tuesday after the first Monday in November every fourth year as the date for choosing electors. The electors cast their votes on the Monday after the second Wednesday in December of that year.

Clause 5: Qualifications for President.   No person except a natural born Citizen, or a Citizen of the United States, at the time of the Adoption of this Constitution,

---

[7]Changed by the Twelfth Amendment.

shall be eligible to the Office of President; neither shall any Person be eligible to that Office who shall not have attained to the Age of thirty five Years, and been fourteen Years a Resident within the United States.

The president must be a natural-born citizen, be at least thirty-five years of age when taking office, and have been a resident within the United States for at least fourteen years.

Clause 6: *Succession of the Vice President.*   [In Case of the Removal of the President from Office, or of his Death, Resignation or Inability to discharge the Powers and Duties of the said Office, the same shall devolve on the Vice President, and the Congress may by Law provide for the Case of Removal, Death, Resignation or Inability, both of the President and Vice President, declaring what Officer shall then act as President, and such Officer shall act accordingly, until the Disability be removed, or a President shall be elected.][8]

This former section provided for the method by which the vice president was to succeed to the presidency, but its wording is ambiguous. It was replaced by the Twenty-fifth Amendment.

Clause 7: *The President's Salary.*   The President shall, at stated Times, receive for his Services, a Compensation, which shall neither be encreased nor diminished during the Period for which he shall have been elected, and he shall not receive within that Period any other Emolument from the United States, or any of them.

The president maintains the same salary during each four-year term. Moreover, she or he may not receive additional cash payments from the government. Originally set at $25,000 per year, it is currently $200,000 a year plus a $50,000 taxable expense account.

Clause 8: *The Oath of Office.*   Before he enter on the Execution of his Office, he shall take the following Oath or Affirmation: "I do solemnly swear (or affirm) that I will faithfully execute the Office of President of the United States, and will to the best of my Ability, preserve, protect and defend the Constitution of the United States."

The president is "sworn in" prior to beginning the duties of the office. Currently, the taking of the oath of office occurs on January 20, following the November election. The ceremony is called the inauguration. The oath of office is administered by the chief justice of the United States Supreme Court.

Section 2. Powers of the President
Clause 1: *Commander in Chief.*   The President shall be Commander in Chief of the Army and Navy of the United States, and of the Militia of the several States, when called into the actual Service of the United States; he may require the Opinion, in writing, of the principal Officer in each of the executive Departments, upon any Subject relating to the Duties of their respective Offices, and he shall have Power to grant Reprieves and Pardons for Offences against the United States, except in Cases of Impeachment.

The armed forces are placed under civilian control because the president is a civilian, but still commander in chief of the military. The president may ask for the help of the heads of each of the executive departments (thereby creating the cabinet). The cabinet members are chosen by the president with the consent of the Senate, but they can be removed without Senate approval.
The president's clemency powers extend only to federal cases. In those cases, he or she may grant a full or conditional pardon, or reduce a prison term or fine.

Clause 2: *Treaties and Appointment.*   He shall have Power, by and with the Advice and Consent of the Senate, to make Treaties, provided two thirds of the Senators present concur; and he shall nominate, and by and with the Advice and Consent of the Senate, shall appoint Ambassadors, other public Ministers and Consuls, Judges of the supreme Court, and all other Officers of the United States, whose Appointments are not herein otherwise provided for, and which shall be established by Law; but the Congress may by Law vest the Appointment of such inferior Officers, as they think proper, in the President alone, in the Courts of Law, or in the Heads of Departments.

Many of the major powers of the president are identified in this clause, including the power to make treaties with foreign governments (with the approval of the Senate by a two-thirds vote) and the power to appoint ambassadors, Supreme Court justices, and other government officials. Most such appointments require Senate approval.

Clause 3: *Vacancies.*   The President shall have Power to fill up all Vacancies that may happen during the Recess of the Senate, by granting Commissions which shall expire at the end of their next Session.

The president has the power to appoint temporary officials to fill vacant federal offices without Senate approval if the Congress is not in session. Such appointments expire automatically at the end of Congress's next term.

Section 3. Duties of the President
He shall from time to time give to the Congress Information of the State of the Union, and recommend to their Consideration such Measures as he shall judge necessary and expedient; he may, on extraordinary Occasions, convene both Houses, or either of them, and in Case of

---

[8]Modified by the Twenty-fifth Amendment.

Disagreement between them, with Respect to the Time of Adjournment, he may adjourn them to such Time as he shall think proper; he shall receive Ambassadors and other public Ministers; he shall take Care that the Laws be faithfully executed, and shall Commission all the Officers of the United States.

Annually, the president reports on the state of the union to Congress, recommends legislative measures, and proposes a federal budget. The State of the Union speech is a statement not only to Congress but also to the American people. After it is given, the president proposes a federal budget and presents an economic report. At any time he or she so chooses, the president may send special messages to Congress while it is in session. The president has the power to call special sessions, to adjourn Congress when its two houses do not agree for that purpose, to receive diplomatic representatives of other governments, and to ensure the proper execution of all federal laws. The president further has the ability to empower federal officers to hold their positions and to perform their duties.

Section 4. Impeachment

The President, Vice President and all civil Officers of the United States, shall be removed from Office on Impeachment for, and Conviction of, Treason, Bribery, or other high Crimes and Misdemeanors.

Treason denotes giving aid to the nation's enemies. The definition of high crimes and misdemeanors is usually given as serious abuses of political power. In either case, the president or vice president may be accused by the House (called an impeachment) and then removed from office if convicted by the Senate. (Note that impeachment does not mean removal, but rather the condition of being accused of treason or high crimes and misdemeanors.)

Article III. (Judicial Branch)

Section 1. Judicial Powers, Courts, and Judges

The judicial Power of the United States, shall be vested in one supreme Court, and in such inferior Courts as the Congress may from time to time ordain and establish. The Judges, both of the supreme and inferior Courts, shall hold their Offices during good Behaviour, and shall, at stated Times, receive for their Services a Compensation, which shall not be diminished during their Continuance in Office.

The Supreme Court is vested with judicial power, as are the lower federal courts that Congress creates. Federal judges serve in their offices for life unless they are impeached and convicted by Congress. The payment of federal judges may not be reduced during their time in office.

Section 2. Jurisdiction

Clause 1: Cases under Federal Jurisdiction.   The judicial Power shall extend to all Cases, in Law and Equity, arising under this Constitution, the Laws of the United States, and Treaties made, or which shall be made, under their Authority;—to all Cases affecting Ambassadors, other public Ministers and Consuls;—to all Cases of admiralty and maritime Jurisdiction;—to Controversies to which the United States shall be a Party;—to Controversies between two or more States; [—between a State and Citizens of another State;—][9] between Citizens of different States;—between Citizens of the same State claiming Lands under Grants of different States, [and between a State, or the Citizens thereof, and foreign States, Citizens or Subjects.][10]

The federal courts take on cases that concern the meaning of the U.S. Constitution, all federal laws, and treaties. They also can take on cases involving citizens of different states and citizens of foreign nations.

Clause 2: Cases for the Supreme Court.   In all Cases affecting Ambassadors, other public Ministers and Consuls, and those in which a State shall be a Party, the supreme Court shall have original Jurisdiction. In all the other Cases before mentioned, the supreme Court shall have appellate Jurisdiction, both as to Law and Fact, with such Exceptions, and under such Regulations as the Congress shall make.

In a limited number of situations, the Supreme Court acts as a trial court and has original jurisdiction. These cases involve a representative from another country or involve a state. In all other situations, the cases must first be tried in the lower courts and then can be appealed to the Supreme Court. Congress may, however, make exceptions. Today the Supreme Court acts as a trial court of first instance on rare occasions.

Clause 3: The Conduct of Trials.   The Trial of all Crimes, except in Cases of Impeachment, shall be by Jury; and such Trial shall be held in the State where the said Crimes shall have been committed; but when not committed within any State, the Trial shall be at such Place or Places as the Congress may by Law have directed.

Any person accused of a federal crime is granted the right to a trial by jury in a federal court in that state in which the crime was committed. Trials of impeachment are an exception.

Section 3. Treason

Clause 1: The Definition of Treason.   Treason against the United States, shall consist only in levying War against

---

[9]Modified by the Eleventh Amendment.
[10]Modified by the Eleventh Amendment.

them, or, in adhering to their Enemies, giving them Aid and Comfort. No Person shall be convicted of Treason unless on the Testimony of two Witnesses to the same overt Act, or on Confession in open Court.

Treason is the making of war against the United States or giving aid to its enemies.

Clause 2: Punishment.   The Congress shall have Power to declare the Punishment of Treason, but no Attainder of Treason shall work Corruption of Blood, or Forfeiture except during the Life of the Person attainted.

Congress has provided that the punishment for treason ranges from a minimum of five years in prison and/or a $10,000 fine to a maximum of death. "No Attainder of Treason shall work Corruption of Blood" prohibits punishment of the traitor's heirs.

Article IV. (Relations among the States)

Section 1. Full Faith and Credit
Full Faith and Credit shall be given in each State to the public Acts, Records, and judicial Proceedings of every other State. And the Congress may by general Laws prescribe the Manner in which such Acts, Records and Proceedings shall be proved, and the Effect thereof.

All states are required to respect one another's laws, records, and lawful decisions. There are exceptions, however. A state does not have to enforce another state's criminal code. Nor does it have to recognize another state's grant of a divorce if the person obtaining the divorce did not establish legal residence in the state in which it was given.

Section 2. Treatment of Citizens
Clause 1: Privileges and Immunities.   The Citizens of each State shall be entitled to all Privileges and Immunities of Citizens in the several States.

A citizen of a state has the same rights and privileges as the citizens of another state in which he or she happens to be.

Clause 2: Extradition.   A Person charged in any State with Treason, Felony, or other Crime, who shall flee from Justice, and be found in another State, shall on Demand of the executive Authority of the State from which he fled, be delivered up, to be removed to the State having Jurisdiction of the Crime.

Any person accused of a crime who flees to another state must be returned to the state in which the crime occurred.

Clause 3: Fugitive Slaves.   [No Person held to Service or Labour in one State, under the Laws thereof, escaping into another, shall, in Consequence of any Law or Regulation therein, be discharged from such Service or Labour, but shall be delivered up on Claim of the Party to whom such Service or Labour may be due.][11]

This clause was struck down by the Thirteenth Amendment, which abolished slavery in 1865.

Section 3. Admission of States
Clause 1: The Process.   New States may be admitted by the Congress into this Union; but no new State shall be formed or erected within the Jurisdiction of any other State; nor any State be formed by the Junction of two or more States, or Parts of States, without the Consent of the Legislatures of the States concerned as well as of the Congress.

Only Congress has the power to admit new states to the union. No state may be created by taking territory from an existing state unless the state's legislature so consents.

Clause 2: Public Land.   The Congress shall have Power to dispose of and make all needful Rules and Regulations respecting the Territory or other Property belonging to the United States; and nothing in this Constitution shall be so construed as to Prejudice any Claims of the United States, or of any particular State.

The federal government has the exclusive right to administer federal government public lands.

Section 4. Republican Form of Government
The United States shall guarantee to every State in this Union a Republican Form of Government, and shall protect each of them against Invasion; and on Application of the Legislature, or of the Executive (when the Legislature cannot be convened) against domestic Violence.

Each state is promised a form of government in which the people elect their representatives. The federal government is bound to protect states against any attack by foreigners or during times of trouble within a state.

Article V. (Methods of Amendment)
The Congress, whenever two thirds of both Houses shall deem it necessary, shall propose Amendments to this Constitution, or on the Application of the Legislatures of two thirds of the several States, shall call a Convention for proposing Amendments, which, in either Case, shall be valid to all Intents and Purposes, as Part of this Constitution, when ratified by the Legislatures of three fourths of the several States, or by Conventions in three

---

[11]Repealed by the Thirteenth Amendment.

fourths thereof, as the one or the other Mode of Ratification may be proposed by the Congress; Provided that no Amendment which may be made prior to the Year One thousand eight hundred and eight shall in any Manner affect the first and fourth Clauses in the Ninth Section of the First Article; and that no State, without its Consent, shall be deprived of its equal Suffrage in the Senate.

Amendments may be proposed in either of two ways: a two-thirds vote of each chamber (Congress) or at the request of two-thirds of the states. Ratification of amendments may be carried out in two ways: by the legislatures of three-fourths of the states or by the voters in three-fourths of the states. No state may be denied equal representation in the Senate.

Article VI. (National Supremacy)

Clause 1: Existing Obligations.   All Debts contracted and Engagements entered into, before the Adoption of this Constitution shall be as valid against the United States under this Constitution, as under the Confederation.

During the Revolutionary War and the years of the Confederation, Congress borrowed large sums. This clause pledged that the new federal government would assume those financial obligations.

Clause 2: Supreme Law of the Land.   This Constitution, and the Laws of the United States which shall be made in Pursuance thereof; and all Treaties made, or which shall be made, under the Authority of the United States, shall be the supreme Law of the Land; and the Judges in every State shall be bound thereby, any Thing in the Constitution or Laws of any State to the Contrary notwithstanding.

This is typically called the supremacy clause; it declares that federal law takes precedence over all forms of state law. No government, at the local or state level, may make or enforce any law that conflicts with any provision of the Constitution, acts of Congress, treaties, or other rules and regulations issued by the president and his or her subordinates in the executive branch of the federal government.

Clause 3: Oath of Office.   The Senators and Representatives before mentioned, and the Members of the several State Legislatures, and all executive and judicial Officers, both of the United States and of the several States, shall be bound by Oath or Affirmation, to support this Constitution; but no religious Test shall ever be required as a Qualification to any Office or public Trust under the United States.

Every federal and state official must take an oath of office promising to support the U.S. Constitution. Religion may not be used as a qualification to serve in any federal office.

Article VII. (Ratification)

The Ratification of the Conventions of nine States shall be sufficient for the Establishment of this Constitution between the States so ratifying the Same.

Nine states were required to ratify the Constitution. Delaware was the first and New Hampshire the ninth.

Done in Convention by the Unanimous Consent of the States present the Seventeenth Day of September in the Year of our Lord one thousand seven hundred and Eighty seven and of the Independence of the United States of America the Twelfth. In witness whereof we have hereunto subscribed our Names,

Go. WASHINGTON
Presid't. and deputy from Virginia

Attest
WILLIAM JACKSON
Secretary

DELAWARE
Geo. Read
Gunning Bedfordjun
John Dickinson
Richard Basset
Jaco. Broom

MASSACHUSETTS
Nathaniel Gorham
Rufus King

CONNECTICUT
Wm. Saml. Johnson
Roger Sherman

NEW YORK
Alexander Hamilton

NEW JERSEY
Wh. Livingston
David Brearley.
Wm. Paterson.
Jona. Dayton

PENNSYLVANIA
B. Franklin
Thomas Mifflin
Robt. Morris
Geo. Clymer
Thos. FitzSimons
Jared Ingersoll
James Wilson.
Gouv. Morris

NEW HAMPSHIRE
John Langdon
Nicholas Gilman

MARYLAND
James McHenry
Dan of St. Thos. Jenifer
Danl. Carroll.

VIRGINIA
John Blair
James Madison Jr.

NORTH CAROLINA
Wm. Blount
Richd. Dobbs Spaight.
Hu. Willaimson

SOUTH CAROLINA
J. Rutledge
Charles Cotesworth Pinckney
Charles Pinckney
Pierce Butler

GEORGIA
William Few
Abr. Baldwin

Articles in addition to, and amendment of the Constitution of the United States of America, proposed by Congress and ratified by the Legislatures of the several states, pursuant to the Fifth Article of the original Constitution.

Amendments to the Constitution of the United States

The Bill of Rights[12]

Amendment I.
Religion, Speech, Assembly, and Petition

Congress shall make no law respecting an establishment of religion, or prohibiting the free exercise thereof; or abridging the freedom of speech, or of the press; or the right of the people peaceably to assemble, and to petition the Government for a redress of grievances.

Congress may not create an official church or enact laws limiting the freedom of religion, speech, the press, assembly, and petition. These guarantees, like the others in the Bill of Rights (the first ten amendments), are not absolute—each may be exercised only with regard to the rights of other persons.

Amendment II.
Militia and the Right to Bear Arms

A well regulated Militia, being necessary to the security of a free State, the right of the people to keep and bear Arms, shall not be infringed.

To protect itself, each state has the right to maintain a volunteer armed force. States and the federal government regulate the possession and use of firearms by individuals.

Amendment III.
The Quartering of Soldiers

No Soldier shall, in time of peace be quartered in any house, without the consent of the Owner, nor in time of war, but in a manner to be prescribed by law.

Before the Revolutionary War, it had been common British practice to quarter soldiers in colonists' homes. Military troops do not have the power to take over private houses during peacetime.

---

[12]On September 25, 1789, Congress transmitted to the state legislatures twelve proposed amendments, two of which, having to do with congressional representation and congressional pay, were not adopted. The remaining ten amendments became the Bill of Rights. In 1992, the amendment concerning congressional pay was adopted as the Twenty-seventh Amendment.

Amendment IV.
Searches and Seizures

The right of the people to be secure in their persons, houses, papers, and effects, against unreasonable searches and seizures, shall not be violated, and no Warrants shall issue, but upon probable cause, supported by Oath or affirmation, and particularly describing the place to be searched, and the persons or things to be seized.

Here the word warrant means "justification" and refers to a document issued by a magistrate or judge indicating the name, address, and possible offense committed. Anyone asking for the warrant, such as a police officer, must be able to convince the magistrate or judge that an offense probably has been committed.

Amendment V.
Grand Juries, Self-incrimination, Double Jeopardy, Due Process, and Eminent Domain

No person shall be held to answer for a capital, or otherwise infamous crime, unless on a presentment or indictment of a Grand Jury, except in cases arising in the land or naval forces, or in the Militia, when in actual service in time of War or public danger; nor shall any person be subject for the same offence to be twice put in jeopardy of life or limb; nor shall be compelled in any criminal case to be a witness against himself, nor be deprived of life, liberty, or property, without due process of law; nor shall private property be taken for public use, without just compensation.

There are two types of juries. A grand jury considers physical evidence and the testimony of witnesses, and decides whether there is sufficient reason to bring a case to trial. A petit jury hears the case at trial and decides it. "For the same offence to be twice put in jeopardy of life or limb" means to be tried twice for the same crime. A person may not be tried for the same crime twice or forced to give evidence against herself or himself. No person's right to life, liberty, or property may be taken away except by lawful means, called the due process of law. Private property taken for use in public purposes must be paid for by the government.

Amendment VI.
Criminal Court Procedures

In all criminal prosecutions, the accused shall enjoy the right to a speedy and public trial, by an impartial jury of the State and district wherein the crime shall have been committed, which district shall have been previously ascertained by law, and to be informed of the nature and cause of the accusation; to be confronted with the witnesses against him; to have compulsory process for obtaining witnesses in his favor, and to have the Assistance of Counsel for his defence.

Any person accused of a crime has the right to a fair and public trial by a jury in the state in which the crime took place. The charges against that person must be so indicated. Any accused person has the right to a lawyer to defend him or her and to question those who testify against him or her, as well as the right to call people to speak in his or her favor at trial.

Amendment VII.
Trial by Jury in Civil Cases

In Suits at common law, where the value in controversy shall exceed twenty dollars, the right of trial by jury shall be preserved, and no fact tried by jury, shall be otherwise re-examined in any Court of the United States, than according to the rules of the common law.

A jury trial may be requested by either party in a dispute in any case involving more than $20. If both parties agree to a trial by a judge without a jury, the right to a jury trial may be put aside.

Amendment VIII.
Bail, Cruel and Unusual Punishment

Excessive bail shall not be required, nor excessive fines imposed, nor cruel and unusual punishments inflicted.

Bail is that amount of money that a person accused of a crime may be required to deposit with the court as a guarantee that she or he will appear in court when requested. The amount of bail required or the fine imposed as punishment for a crime must be reasonable compared with the seriousness of the crime involved. Any punishment judged to be too harsh or too severe for a crime shall be prohibited.

Amendment IX.
The Rights Retained by the People

The enumeration in the Constitution, of certain rights, shall not be construed to deny or disparage others retained by the people.

Many civil rights that are not explicitly enumerated in the Constitution are still held by the people.

Amendment X.
Reserved Powers of the States

The powers not delegated to the United States by the Constitution, nor prohibited by it to the States, are reserved to the States respectively, or to the people.

Those powers not delegated by the Constitution to the federal government or expressly denied to the states belong to the states and to the people. This clause in essence allows the states to pass laws under its "police powers."

Amendment XI
(Ratified on February 7, 1795).
Suits against States

The Judicial power of the United States shall not be construed to extend to any suit in law or equity, commenced or prosecuted against one of the United States by Citizens of another State, or by Citizens or Subjects of any Foreign State.

This amendment has been interpreted to mean that a state cannot be sued in federal court by one of its citizens, by a citizen of another state, or by a foreign country.

Amendment XII
(Ratified on June 15, 1804).
Election of the President

The Electors shall meet in their respective states, and vote by ballot for President and Vice-President, one of whom, at least, shall not be an inhabitant of the same State with themselves; they shall name in their ballots the person voted for as President, and in distinct ballots the person voted for as Vice-President, and they shall make distinct lists of all persons voted for as President, and of all persons voted for as Vice-President, and of the number of votes for each, which lists they shall sign and certify, and transmit sealed to the seat of the government of the United States, directed to the President of the Senate;—The President of the Senate shall, in the presence of the Senate and House of Representatives, open all the certificates and the votes shall then be counted;—The person having the greatest number of votes for President, shall be the President, if such number be a majority of the whole number of Electors appointed; and if no person have such majority, then from the persons having the highest numbers not exceeding three on the list of those voted for as President, the House of Representatives shall choose immediately, by ballot, the President. But in choosing the President, the votes shall be taken by States, the representation from each State having one vote; a quorum for this purpose shall consist of a member or members from two-thirds of the States, and a majority of all States shall be necessary to a choice. [And if the House of Representatives shall not choose a President whenever the right of choice shall devolve upon them, before the fourth day of March next following, then the Vice-President shall act as President, as in the case of the death or other constitutional disability of the President.][13]— The person having the greatest number of votes as Vice-President, shall be the Vice-President, if such number be a

---

[13]Changed by the Twentieth Amendment.

majority of the whole number of Electors appointed, and if no person have a majority, then from the two highest numbers on the list, the Senate shall choose the Vice President; a quorum for the purpose shall consist of two-thirds of the whole number of Senators, and a majority of the whole number shall be necessary to a choice. But no person constitutionally ineligible to the office of President shall be eligible to that of Vice-President of the United States.

The original procedure set out for the election of president and vice president in Article II, Section 1, resulted in a tie in 1800 between Thomas Jefferson and Aaron Burr. It was not until the next year that the House of Representatives chose Jefferson to be president. This amendment changed the procedure by providing for separate ballots for president and vice president.

Amendment XIII
(Ratified on December 6, 1865).
Prohibition of Slavery

Section 1.
Neither slavery nor involuntary servitude, except as a punishment for crime whereof the party shall have been duly convicted, shall exist within the United States, or any place subject to their jurisdiction.

Some slaves had been freed during the Civil War. This amendment freed the others and abolished slavery.

Section 2.
Congress shall have power to enforce this article by appropriate legislation.

Amendment XIV
(Ratified on July 9, 1868).
Citizenship, Due Process, and
Equal Protection of the Laws

Section 1.
All persons born or naturalized in the United States, and subject to the jurisdiction thereof, are citizens of the United States and of the State wherein they reside. No State shall make or enforce any law which shall abridge the privileges or immunities of citizens of the United States; nor shall any State deprive any person of life, liberty, or property, without due process of law; nor deny to any person within its jurisdiction the equal protection of the laws.

Under this provision, states cannot make or enforce laws that take away rights given to all citizens by the federal government. States cannot act unfairly or arbitrarily toward, or discriminate against, any person.

Section 2.
Representatives shall be apportioned among the several States according to their respective numbers, counting the whole number of persons in each State, excluding Indians not taxed. But when the right to vote at any election for the choice of electors for President and Vice President of the United States, Representatives in Congress, the Executive and Judicial officers of a State, or the members of the Legislature thereof, is denied to any of the male inhabitants of such State, being [twenty-one][14] years of age, and citizens of the United States, or in any way abridged, except for participation in rebellion, or other crime, the basis of representation therein shall be reduced in the proportion which the number of such male citizens shall bear to the whole number of male citizens twenty-one years of age in such State.

Section 3.
No person shall be a Senator or Representative in Congress, or elector of President and Vice President, or hold any office, civil or military, under the United States, or under any State, who having previously taken an oath, as a member of Congress, or as an officer of the United States, or as a member of any State legislature, or as an executive or judicial officer of any State, to support the Constitution of the United States, shall have engaged in insurrection or rebellion against the same, or given aid or comfort to the enemies thereof. But Congress may by a vote of two-thirds of each House, remove such disability.

This provision forbade former state or federal government officials who had acted in support of the Confederacy during the Civil War to hold office again. It limited the president's power to pardon those persons. Congress removed this "disability" in 1898.

Section 4.
The validity of the public debt of the United States, authorized by law, including debts incurred for payment of pensions and bounties for services in suppressing insurrection or rebellion, shall not be questioned. But neither the United States nor any State shall assume or pay any debt or obligation incurred in aid of insurrection or rebellion against the United States, or any claim for the loss or emancipation of any slave, but all such debts, obligations and claims shall be held illegal and void.

Section 5.
The Congress shall have power to enforce, by appropriate legislation, the provisions of this article.

---

[14]Changed by the Twenty-sixth Amendment.

Amendment XV
(Ratified on February 3, 1870).
The Right to Vote

Section 1.

The right of citizens of the United States to vote shall not be denied or abridged by the United States or by any State on account of race, color, or previous condition of servitude.

No citizen can be refused the right to vote simply because of race or color or because that person was once a slave.

Section 2.

The Congress shall have power to enforce this article by appropriate legislation.

Amendment XVI
(Ratified on February 3, 1913).
Income Taxes

The Congress shall have power to lay and collect taxes on incomes, from whatever source derived, without apportionment among the several States, and without regard to any census or enumeration.

This amendment allows Congress to tax income without sharing the revenue so obtained with the states according to their population.

Amendment XVII
(Ratified on April 8, 1913).
The Popular Election of Senators

The Senate of the United States shall be composed of two Senators from each State, elected by the people thereof, for six years; and each Senator shall have one vote. The electors in each State shall have the qualifications requisite for electors of the most numerous branch of the State legislatures.

When vacancies happen in the representation of any State in the Senate, the executive authority of such State shall issue writs of election to fill such vacancies: *Provided,* That the legislature of any State may empower the executive thereof to make temporary appointments until the people fill the vacancies by election as the legislature may direct.

This amendment shall not be so construed as to affect the election or term of any Senator chosen before it becomes valid as part of the Constitution.

This amendment modified portions of Article I, Section 3, that related to election of senators. Senators are now elected by the voters in each state directly. When a vacancy

occurs, either the state may fill the vacancy by a special election, or the governor of the state involved may appoint someone to fill the seat until the next election.

Amendment XVIII
(Ratified on January 16, 1919).
Prohibition

Section 1.

After one year from the ratification of this article the manufacture, sale, or transportation of intoxicating liquors within, the importation thereof into, or the exportation thereof from the United States and all territory subject to the jurisdiction thereof for beverage purposes is hereby prohibited.

Section 2.

The Congress and the several States shall have concurrent power to enforce this article by appropriate legislation.

Section 3.

This article shall be inoperative unless it shall have been ratified as an amendment to the Constitution by the legislatures of the several States, as provided in the Constitution, within seven years from the date of the submission hereof to the States by the Congress.[15]

This amendment made it illegal to manufacture, sell, and transport alcoholic beverages in the United States. It was repealed by the Twenty-first Amendment.

Amendment XIX
(Ratified on August 18, 1920).
Women's Right to Vote.

The right of citizens of the United States to vote shall not be denied or abridged by the United States or by any State on account of sex.

Congress shall have power to enforce this article by appropriate legislation.

Women were given the right to vote by this amendment, and Congress was given the power to enforce this right.

Amendment XX
(Ratified on January 23, 1933).
The Lame Duck Amendment

Section 1.

The terms of the President and Vice President shall end at noon on the 20th day of January, and the terms of Senators and Representatives at noon on the 3d day of

---

[15]The Eighteenth Amendment was repealed by the Twenty-first Amendment.

January, of the years in which such terms would have ended if this article had not been ratified; and the terms of their successors shall then begin.

This amendment modified Article I, Section 4, Clause 2, and other provisions relating to the president in the Twelfth Amendment. The taking of the oath of office was moved from March 4 to January 20.

Section 2.

The Congress shall assemble at least once in every year, and such meeting shall begin at noon on the 3d day of January, unless they shall by law appoint a different day.

Congress changed the beginning of its term to January 3. The reason the Twentieth Amendment is called the Lame Duck Amendment is because it shortens the time between when a member of Congress is defeated for reelection and when he or she leaves office.

Section 3.

If, at the time fixed for the beginning of the term of the President, the President elect shall have died, the Vice President elect shall become President. If a President shall not have been chosen before the time fixed for the beginning of his term, or if the President elect shall have failed to qualify, then the Vice President elect shall act as President until a President shall have qualified; and the Congress may by law provide for the case wherein neither a President elect nor a Vice President elect shall have qualified, declaring who shall then act as President, or the manner in which one who is to act shall be selected, and such person shall act accordingly until a President or Vice President shall have qualified.

This part of the amendment deals with problem areas left ambiguous by Article II and the Twelfth Amendment. If the president dies before January 20 or fails to qualify for office, the presidency is to be filled in the order given in this section.

Section 4.

The Congress may by law provide for the case of the death of any of the persons from whom the House of Representatives may choose a President whenever the rights of choice shall have devolved upon them, and for the case of the death of any of the persons from whom the Senate may choose a Vice President whenever the right of choice shall have devolved upon them.

Congress has never created legislation subsequent to this section.

Section 5.

Sections 1 and 2 shall take effect on the 15th day of October following the ratification of this article.

Section 6.

This article shall be inoperative unless it shall have been ratified as an amendment to the Constitution by the legislatures of three-fourths of the several States within seven years from the date of its submission.

Amendment XXI
(Ratified on December 5, 1933).
The Repeal of Prohibition

Section 1.

The eighteenth article of amendment to the Constitution of the United States is hereby repealed.

Section 2.

The transportation or importation into any State, Territory, or possession of the United States for delivery or use therein of intoxicating liquors, in violation of the laws thereof, is hereby prohibited.

Section 3.

This article shall be inoperative unless it shall have been ratified as an amendment to the Constitution by conventions in the several States, as provided in the Constitution, within seven years from the date of the submission hereof to the States by the Congress.

The amendment repealed the Eighteenth Amendment but did not make alcoholic beverages legal everywhere. Rather, they remained illegal in any state that so designated them. Many such "dry" states existed for a number of years after 1933. Today, there are still "dry" counties within the United States, in which alcoholic beverages are illegal.

Amendment XXII
(Ratified on February 27, 1951).
Limitation of Presidential Terms

Section 1.

No person shall be elected to the office of the President more than twice, and no person who has held the office of President, or acted as President, for more than two years of a term to which some other person was elected President shall be elected to the office of President more than once. But this Article shall not apply to any person holding the office of President when this Article was proposed by the Congress, and shall not prevent any person who may be holding the office of President, or acting as President, during the term within which this Article becomes operative from holding the office of President or acting as President during the remainder of such term.

Section 2.

This article shall be inoperative unless it shall have been ratified as an amendment to the Constitution by the legislatures of three-fourths of the several States within seven years from the date of its submission to the States by the Congress.

No president may serve more than two elected terms. If, however, a president has succeeded to the office after the halfway point of a term in which another president was originally elected, then that president may serve for more than eight years, but not to exceed ten years.

Amendment XXIII
(Ratified on March 29, 1961).
Presidential Electors for
the District of Columbia

Section 1.
The District constituting the seat of Government of the United States shall appoint in such manner as the Congress may direct:

A number of electors of President and Vice President equal to the whole number of Senators and Representatives in Congress to which the District would be entitled if it were a State, but in no event more than the least populous State; they shall be in addition to those appointed by the States, but they shall be considered, for the purposes of the election of President and Vice President, to be electors appointed by a State; and they shall meet in the District and perform such duties as provided by the twelfth article of amendment.

Section 2.
The Congress shall have power to enforce this article by appropriate legislation.

Citizens living in the District of Columbia have the right to vote in elections for president and vice president. The District of Columbia has three presidential electors, whereas before this amendment it had none.

Amendment XXIV
(Ratified on January 23, 1964).
The Anti–Poll Tax Amendment

Section 1.
The right of citizens of the United States to vote in any primary or other election for President or Vice President, for electors for President or Vice President, or for Senator or Representative in Congress, shall not be denied or abridged by the United States, or any State by reason of failure to pay any poll tax or other tax.

Section 2.
The Congress shall have power to enforce this article by appropriate legislation.

No government shall require a person to pay a poll tax in order to vote in any federal election.

Amendment XXV
(Ratified on February 10, 1967).
Presidential Disability and
Vice Presidential Vacancies

Section 1.
In case of the removal of the President from office or of his death or resignation, the Vice President shall become President.

Whenever a president dies or resigns from office, the vice president becomes president.

Section 2.
Whenever there is a vacancy in the office of the Vice President, the President shall nominate a Vice President who shall take office upon confirmation by a majority vote of both Houses of Congress.

Whenever the office of the vice presidency becomes vacant, the president may appoint someone to fill this office, provided Congress consents.

Section 3.
Whenever the President transmits to the President pro tempore of the Senate and the Speaker of the House of Representatives his written declaration that he is unable to discharge the powers and duties of his office, and until he transmits to them a written declaration to the contrary, such powers and duties shall be discharged by the Vice President as Acting President.

Whenever the president believes she or he is unable to carry out the duties of the office, she or he shall so indicate to Congress in writing. The vice president then acts as president until the president declares that she or he is again able to properly carry out the duties of the office.

Section 4.
Whenever the Vice President and a majority of either the principal officers of the executive departments or of such other body as Congress may by law provide, transmit to the President pro tempore of the Senate and the Speaker of the House of Representatives their written declaration that the President is unable to discharge the powers and duties of his office, the Vice President shall immediately assume the powers and duties of the office as Acting President.

Thereafter, when the President transmits to the President pro tempore of the Senate and the Speaker of the House of Representatives his written declaration that no inability exists, he shall resume the powers and duties of his office unless the Vice President and a majority of either the principal officers of the executive department or of such other body as Congress may by law provide, transmit within four days to the President pro tempore of the Senate and the Speaker of the House of Representatives their written declaration that the President is unable to discharge the powers and duties of his office. Thereupon Congress shall decide the issue, assembling within forty-eight hours for that purpose if not in session. If the Congress, within twenty-one days after receipt of the latter written declaration, or, if Congress is not in session, within twenty-one days after Congress is required to assemble, determines by two-thirds vote of both Houses that the President is unable to discharge the powers and duties of his office, the Vice President shall continue to discharge the same as Acting President; otherwise, the President shall resume the powers and duties of his office.

Whenever the vice president and a majority of the members of the cabinet believe that the president cannot carry out his or her duties, they shall so indicate in writing to Congress. The vice president shall then act as president. When the president believes that she or he is able to carry out her or his duties again, she or he shall so indicate to the Congress. If, though, the vice president and a majority of the cabinet do not agree, Congress must decide by a two-thirds vote within three weeks who shall act as president.

Amendment XXVI
(Ratified on July 1, 1971).
The Eighteen–Year–Old Vote

Section 1.
The right of citizens of the United States, who are eighteen years of age or older, to vote shall not be denied or abridged by the United States or by any State on account of age.

No one over eighteen years of age can be denied the right to vote in federal or state elections by virtue of age.

Section 2.
The Congress shall have power to enforce this article by appropriate legislation.

Amendment XXVII
(Ratified on May 7, 1992).
Congressional Pay

No law varying the compensation for the services of the Senators and Representatives shall take effect, until an election of representatives shall have intervened.

This amendment allows the voters to have some control over increases in salaries for congressional members. Originally submitted to the states for ratification in 1789, it was not ratified until 203 years later, in 1992.

chapter 3
Federalism

CHAPTER OUTLINE

- Three Systems of Government

- Why Federalism?

- The Constitutional Basis for American Federalism

- Defining Constitutional Powers—The Early Years

- States' Rights and the Resort to Civil War

- The Continuing Dispute over the Division of Power

what if...

The States Controlled the Internet?

BACKGROUND

As you read in Chapter 2, among the powers delegated to the national government by the Constitution was the power to regulate interstate commerce—commerce between and among states and with foreign nations. Known as the *commerce clause,* this constitutional provision has provided the basis for extensive national government regulation of business. State governments, in turn, have the authority to regulate intrastate commerce—commerce taking place within state borders—as well as other rights, including the right to enact laws protecting their citizens' health, safety, and morals.

The Internet, because of its unique nature, understandably has created unique problems for virtually all aspects of American law and government. Clearly, federalism is no exception. One of the questions posed by the advent of the Internet is whether states should be allowed to pass laws regulating the Internet.

WHAT IF STATES REGULATED THE INTERNET?

The diversity of the United States makes it difficult for the national government to pass laws that promote the interests of *all* U.S. citizens. If states regulated the Internet, state legislatures would be able to enact laws consistent with the desires of their constituents—state residents. Those states with more conservative populations might decide to place more stringent restraints on Internet speech. They might make it a crime, for example, for any of their residents to transmit or receive pornographic or indecent materials via the Internet. They might outlaw access to Web sites encouraging violence—such as sites describing how to make homemade bombs. They might ban access to sites maintained by extremist religious cults or groups.

Very likely, the states would also try to find ways to collect sales or use taxes on goods purchased by state residents from Web merchants. As retail business conducted via the Internet displaces traditional in-state sales, states stand to lose significant revenues in sales taxes. Many states have already begun to tax certain components of e-commerce under telecommunications tax laws. For example, some states tax Internet access by adding a fee to the Internet subscription charge. In the wake of resistance to such taxes by business groups, Internet companies, and other groups, the federal government passed legislation in 1998 calling for a three-year moratorium on any new taxes directed specifically to Web-based transactions.

CONSTITUTIONAL ISSUES

Any significant state regulation of the Internet would very likely run into constitutional problems. For one thing, the First Amendment to the Constitution guarantees freedom of speech, and this guarantee is given strong protection by the courts. State constitutions have similar guarantees. The federal government, in the interest of protecting minors, has twice tried to curb indecent and offensive speech on the Internet—through the Communications Decency Act of 1996 and the Child Online Protection Act of 1998. Both acts failed to pass constitutional muster when challenged in court. There is no reason to believe that state laws restraining Internet speech would not be similarly challenged and defeated in court.

If states controlled the Internet, another constitutional issue would be certain to arise: Would state regulation of a network that reaches beyond state borders—and even national borders—violate the commerce clause? For example, suppose that the government of New Jersey, in the interests of protecting its citizens against fraudulent investment schemes, issues a regulation making it illegal for any person to offer securities (corporate stocks) online to people in New Jersey unless that person has registered as a broker in New Jersey and has complied with New Jersey's disclosure requirements and other securities laws. In effect, New Jersey has imposed its regulatory scheme on all other states. Every person in the United States who offers securities online would either have to comply with New Jersey's regulations or risk being required to appear before a court in New Jersey for violating its securities laws.

Under the federal framework established by the founders, states are permitted to regulate activities within their own borders, but not those carried out by citizens in other states.

FOR CRITICAL ANALYSIS

1. Is it possible for any government—national or state—anywhere in the world to regulate the Internet effectively?

2. If the decision were yours to make, would you want the Internet to be regulated? If so, in what way(s)? If not, why not?

There are many separate governments in this country. One national government and fifty state governments, plus local governments, create a grand total of more than 87,500 governments in all! The breakdown can be seen in Table 3–1.

Visitors from France or Spain are often awestruck by the complexity of our system of government. Consider that a criminal action can be defined by state law, by national law, or by both. Thus, a criminal suspect can be prosecuted in the state court system or in the federal court system (or both). Often, economic regulation over exactly the same matter exists at the local level, the state level, and the national level—generating multiple forms to be completed, multiple procedures to be followed, and multiple laws to be obeyed. Numerous programs are funded by the national government but administered by state and local governments.

There are various ways of ordering relations between central governments and local units. *Federalism* is one of these ways. Understanding federalism and how it differs from other forms of government is important in understanding the American political system. Indeed, many political issues today, including the one discussed in this chapter's opening *What If . . .* , would not arise if we did not have a federal form of government in which governmental authority is divided between the central government and various subunits.

Three Systems of Government

There are nearly two hundred independent nations in the world today (see this chapter's *Global View* on the next page for a discussion of how the number of countries has expanded in recent years). Each of these nations has its own system of government. Generally, though, there are three ways of ordering relations between central governments and local units: (1) a unitary system, (2) a confederal system, and (3) a federal system. The most popular, both historically and today, is the unitary system.

A Unitary System

A **unitary system** of government is the easiest to define. Unitary systems allow ultimate governmental authority to rest in the hands of the national, or central, government. Consider a typical unitary system—France. There are departments

Unitary System
A centralized governmental system in which local or subdivisional governments exercise only those powers given to them by the central government.

TABLE 3-1

The Number of Governments in the United States Today

With more than 87,500 separate governmental units in the United States today, it is no wonder that intergovernmental relations in the United States are so complicated. Actually, the number of school districts has decreased over time, but the number of special districts created for single purposes, such as flood control, has increased from only about 8,000 during World War II to nearly 35,000 today.

Federal government		1
State governments		50
Local governments		87,453
Counties	3,043	
Municipalities (mainly cities or towns)	19,372	
Townships (less extensive powers)	16,629	
Special districts (water, sewer, and so on)	34,683	
School districts	13,726	
TOTAL		87,504

Source: U.S. Census Bureau, *Statistical Abstract of the United States, 2001* (Washington, D.C.: U.S. Government Printing Office, 2001).

and municipalities in France. Within the departments and the municipalities are separate government entities with elected and appointed officials. So far, the French system appears to be very similar to the U.S. system, but the similarity is only superficial. Under the unitary French system, the decisions of the governments of the departments and municipalities can be overruled by the national government. The national government also can cut off the funding of many departmental and municipal government activities. Moreover, in a unitary system such as that in France, all questions related to education, police, the use of land, and welfare are handled by the national government.[1] Great Britain, Sweden, Israel, Egypt, Ghana, and the Philippines also have unitary systems of government, as do most countries today.

---

[1]Recent legislation has altered somewhat the unitary character of the French political system.

Are Governments Getting Smaller, Bigger, or Both?

In the last half-century or so, governments around the world have gotten smaller. Consider that the number of nations in the world has more than doubled since the end of World War II (1939–1945). In 1946, there were 74 independent countries in the world; today, there are close to 200. As a result of this explosive growth in the number of independent countries, half of the world's countries now have smaller populations than the state of Massachusetts.*

THE EMERGENCE OF SMALLER NATIONS

One of the reasons for this growth in the number of smaller nations has been the end of colonial rule—particularly in sub-Saharan Africa, which now has forty-eight independent states. Additionally, the dissolution of the Soviet Union in 1991 resulted in the emergence of fifteen smaller, independent nations that formerly were a part of the Soviet Union. Several other nations have also split up. Czechoslovakia became the Czech Republic and Slovakia. Several separate nations split off from Yugoslavia, including Bosnia-Herzegovina, Macedonia, Croatia, and Slovenia.

In a way, the global movement toward democracy may have indirectly encouraged this trend toward smaller countries. In large countries, it is difficult to balance the demands of minorities against the demands of the majority. In a small country with an ethnically homogeneous population, dealing with minority populations is not a problem. The desire to create nations based on cultural, religious, or ethnic identity has propelled many of today's separatist movements. Even in the United States, there are movements toward separatism. Some citizens of Texas would like to see that state become an independent nation. A group called the League of the South is working to promote the eventual secession of the southern states from the Union so that southern traditions can be reflected and protected by government.

A COUNTERMOVEMENT TOWARD BIG GOVERNMENT

Generally, the idea that "smaller is better" seems to be increasingly prevalent. At the same time, the trend toward smaller governments has been paralleled by a movement toward big government. Since the mid-twentieth century, attempts have been under way to create supranational organizations to deal with regional or global problems. The United Nations, for example, was created after World War II to deal with international issues. Today's European Union is the end result of meetings initially undertaken by the European countries in the 1940s. The World Trade Organization, established in 1995, likewise resulted from decades-long meetings over trade relations.

Recently, a regional unit called the Alpine Diamond has been established to deal with issues affecting a small area in Europe where France, Italy, and Switzerland come together. The two million people in that area decided that existing governments could not manage the region's economic development effectively. Larger governmental units are emerging elsewhere as well. In the United States, Georgia created a new "umbrella" government to control transportation and land-use decisions in the Atlanta metropolitan area. The small communities around Pittsburgh are also establishing a larger unit to deal with problems that no longer respect traditional boundaries.

A decade ago, sociologist Daniel Bell predicted that in the twenty-first century, political issues would no longer be national; they would be either global or local. They would have to migrate up or down to a level that could handle them.[†] Perhaps that is what we are seeing today.

FOR CRITICAL ANALYSIS

Can devolution—the transfer of powers from the central government to political subunits within a nation—defuse the urge toward separatism in large nations?

[†]For a further exploration of this issue, see Alan Ehrenhalt, "Look How Government Gets Smaller and Bigger, Too," *International Herald Tribune,* October 5, 1999, p. 8.

*"Little Countries: Small But Perfectly Formed," *The Economist,* January 3, 1998.

A Confederal System

You were introduced to the elements of a **confederal system** of government in Chapter 2, when we examined the Articles of Confederation. A confederation is the opposite of a unitary governing system. It is a league of independent states in which a central government or administration handles only those matters of common concern expressly delegated to it by the member states. The central governmental unit has no ability to make laws directly applicable to individuals unless the member states explicitly support such laws. The United States under the Articles of Confederation and the Confederate States during the American Civil War were confederations.

There are few, if any, confederations in the world today that resemble those that existed in the United States. Switzerland is a confederation of twenty-three sovereign cantons, and several republics of the former Soviet Union formed the Commonwealth of Independent States. Countries also have formed organizations with one another for limited purposes: military/peacekeeping, as in the case of the North Atlantic Treaty Organization or the United Nations; or economic, as in the case of the economic unit created by the North American Free Trade Agreement. These organizations, however, are not true confederations.

A Federal System

The federal system lies between the unitary and confederal forms of government. As mentioned in Chapter 2, in a *federal system,* authority is divided, usually by a written constitution, between a central government and regional, or subdivisional, governments (often called constituent governments). The central government and the constituent governments both act directly on the people through laws and through the actions of elected and appointed governmental officials. Within each government's sphere of authority, each is supreme, in theory. Contrast a federal system with a unitary one in which the central government is supreme and the constituent governments derive their authority from it. Australia, Canada, Mexico, India, Brazil, and Germany are examples of nations with federal systems. See Figure 3–1 for a comparison of the three systems.

Confederal System

A system of government consisting of a league of independent states, each having essentially sovereign powers. The central government created by such a league has only limited powers over the states.

FIGURE 3–1

The Flow of Power in Three Systems of Government

In a unitary system, the flow of power is from the central government to the local and state governments. In a confederal system, the flow of power is in the opposite direction—from the state and local governments to the central government. In a federal system, the flow of power, in principle, goes both ways.

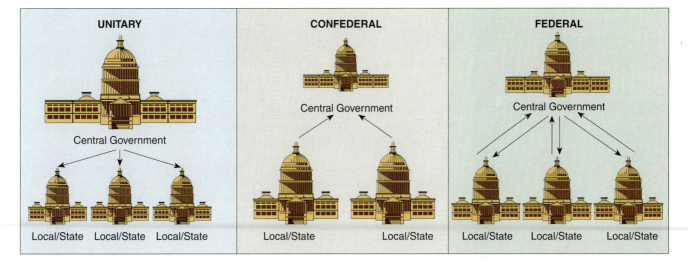

UNITARY	CONFEDERAL	FEDERAL
Central Government	Central Government	Central Government
Local/State Local/State Local/State	Local/State Local/State	Local/State Local/State Local/State

Why Federalism?

Why did the United States develop in a federal direction? We look here at that question as well as at some of the arguments for and against a federal form of government.

A Practical Solution

As you saw in Chapter 2, the historical basis of the federal system was laid down in Philadelphia at the Constitutional Convention, where strong national government advocates opposed equally strong states' rights advocates. This dichotomy continued through to the ratifying conventions in the several states. The resulting federal system was a compromise. The supporters of the new constitution were political pragmatists—they realized that without a federal arrangement, there would be no ratification of the new Constitution. The appeal of federalism was that it retained state traditions and local power while establishing a strong national government capable of handling common problems.

Even if the colonial leaders had agreed on the desirability of a unitary system, the problems of size and regional isolation would have made such a system difficult operationally. At the time of the Constitutional Convention, the thirteen colonies taken together were larger geographically than England or France. Slow travel and communication, combined with geographic spread, contributed to the isolation of many regions within the colonies. For example, it could take up to several weeks for all of the colonies to be informed about one particular political decision.

Other Arguments for Federalism

The arguments for federalism in the United States and elsewhere involve a complex set of factors, some of which we already have noted. First, for big countries, such as the United States, India, and Canada, federalism allows many functions to be "farmed out" by the central government to the states or provinces. The lower levels of government, accepting these responsibilities, thereby can become the focus of political dissatisfaction rather than the national authorities. Second, even with modern transportation and communications systems, the sheer geographic or population size of some nations makes it impractical to locate all political authority in one place. Finally, federalism brings government closer to the people. It allows more direct access to, and influence on, government agencies and policies, rather than leaving the population restive and dissatisfied with a remote, faceless, all-powerful central authority. (As you will read in Chapter 8, one of the benefits of federalism is that citizens have access to government at all levels—local, state, and national. In this chapter's *E-mocracy*, we look at some of the effects of this access to government on "civil society.")

In the United States, federalism historically has yielded many benefits. State governments long have been a training ground for future national leaders. Some presidents made their political mark as state governors. The states themselves have been testing grounds for new government initiatives. As United States Supreme Court justice Louis Brandeis once observed:

> It is one of the happy incidents of the federal system that a single courageous state may, if its citizens choose, serve as a laboratory and try novel social and economic experiments without risk to the rest of the country.[2]

---

[2]*New State Ice Co. v. Liebmann,* 285 U.S. 262 (1932).

INFOTRAC ®
COLLEGE EDITION

Congressional Inconsistencies

Air pollution in Los Angeles, California. In our federal system of government, states have often been the testing grounds for programs later adopted by the federal government for nationwide implementation. Air-pollution control, for example, was initiated in California to cope with the threatening conditions produced by the large population in the area and the famous congestion of automobile traffic.

Examples of programs pioneered at the state level include unemployment compensation, which began in Wisconsin, and air-pollution control, which was initiated in California. Currently, states are experimenting with policies ranging from educational reforms to the medical use of marijuana. Since the passage of the 1996 welfare reform legislation, which gave more control over welfare programs to state governments (see Chapter 16), states have also been experimenting with different methods of delivering welfare assistance.

Additionally, the American way of life always has been characterized by a number of political subcultures, which divide along the lines of race and ethnic origin, wealth, education, and, more recently, age, degree of religious fundamentalism, and sexual preference. The existence of diverse political subcultures would appear to be at odds with a political authority concentrated solely in a central government. Had the United States developed into a unitary system, the various political subcultures certainly would have been less able to influence government behavior (relative to their own regions and interests) than they have been, and continue to be, in our federal system.

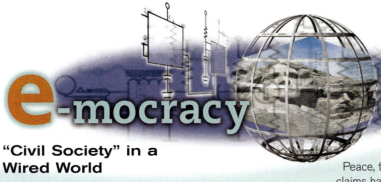

"Civil Society" in a Wired World

It is often said that one of the benefits of federalism is that citizens have access to various levels of government. As you will read in Chapter 8, by forming "interest groups," citizens can wield significant influence at all levels of government. These groups can lobby Congress, state legislatures, or local government bodies to act on their agendas; they can attempt to influence the rules issued by federal, state, or local administrative agencies; and they can submit "friend-of-the-court" briefs before the courts. Interest groups can raise funds to contribute to election campaigns or to advertise their positions on particular campaign issues. In short, the federal form of government established by the founders allows citizens to have extensive access to government.

Interest groups are among the various organizations and associations that are politically influential but independent of the government and outside the control of the state. The term *civil society* is often used to describe the domain of these so-called nongovernmental organizations (NGOs). Although the concept of civil society dates back to the ancient world, its meaning today stems largely from its use by Marxist theorist Antonio Gramsci, who revived the term after World War II (1939–1945) to describe a special nucleus of independent political activists struggling against tyranny. Today, the term is widely used by scholars, writers, politicians, and others who look to civil society to bring pressure on governments to take action on issues ranging from human rights to poverty to the environment to economic development.

In a recent issue of *Foreign Policy*, Thomas Carothers, vice president for global policy at the Carnegie Endowment for International Peace, takes a close look at an aspect of civil society that he claims has received less attention than it deserves: the implications of the Internet for these groups. Carothers observes that this new communication tool has empowered individuals by allowing them to forge connections never before possible. He also emphasizes how these new connections have strengthened the struggle against tyranny on a global level.

Carothers is not totally optimistic, though. He points out that civil society also has a dark side. States may be too compliant in the face of strong pressure groups, and governments may end up taking action or refraining from it on the basis of a small nucleus of advocates. The power of activist groups was clearly evident in the fall of 1999, when a group of demonstrators, organized with the help of the Internet, succeeded in scuttling a new free-trade initiative being considered at a conference of the World Trade Organization in Seattle. In addition, mafias, criminal conspirators, black markets, and other groups engaged in illegal or antisocial conduct can extend their organizations and influence through the Internet.[*]

FOR CRITICAL ANALYSIS

Does a strong civil society necessarily ensure democracy?

[*]"Think Again: Civil Society," *Foreign Policy*, Winter 1999–2000. This article can be accessed online at **http://www.foreignpolicy.com/articles/winter1999–2000**.

Arguments against Federalism

Not everyone thinks federalism is such a good idea. Some see it as a way for powerful state and local interests to block progress and impede national plans. Others see dangers in the expansion of national powers at the expense of the states. President Ronald Reagan said, "The Founding Fathers saw the federalist system as constructed something like a masonry wall. The States are the bricks, the national government is the mortar. . . . Unfortunately, over the years, many people have increasingly come to believe that Washington is the whole wall."[3]

Smaller political units are more likely to be dominated by a single political group, and the dominant groups in some cities and states have resisted implementing equal rights for all minority groups. (This was essentially the argument that James Madison put forth in *Federalist Paper* No. 10, which you can read in Appendix D of this text.) Others point out, however, that the dominant factions in other states have been more progressive than the national government in many areas, such as the environment.

The Constitutional Basis for American Federalism

No mention of the designation "federal system" can be found in the U.S. Constitution. Nor is it possible to find a systematic division of governmental authority between the national and state governments in that document. Rather, the Constitution sets out different types of powers (see Figure 3–2). These powers can be classified as (1) the powers of the national government, (2) the powers of the states, and (3) prohibited powers. The Constitution also makes it clear that if a state or local law conflicts with a national law, the national law will prevail.

Powers of the National Government

The powers delegated to the national government include both expressed and implied powers, as well as the special category of inherent powers. Most of the powers expressly delegated to the national government are found in Article I, Section 8, of the Constitution. These **enumerated powers** include coining money, setting standards for weights and measures, making uniform naturalization laws, admitting new states, establishing post offices, and declaring war. Another important enumerated power is the power to regulate commerce among the states—a topic we deal with later in this chapter.

Enumerated Powers
Powers specifically granted to the national government by the Constitution. The first seventeen clauses of Article I, Section 8, specify most of the enumerated powers of Congress.

The implied powers of the national government are also based on Article I, Section 8, which states that the Congress shall have the power

> [t]o make all Laws which shall be necessary and proper for carrying into Execution the foregoing Powers, and all other Powers vested by this Constitution in the Government of the United States, or in any Department or Officer thereof.

Elastic Clause, or Necessary and Proper Clause
The clause in Article I, Section 8, that grants Congress the power to do whatever is necessary to execute its specifically delegated powers.

This clause is sometimes called the **elastic clause,** or the **necessary and proper clause,** because it provides flexibility to our constitutional system. It gives Congress all of those powers that can be reasonably inferred but that are not expressly stated in the brief wording of the Constitution. The clause was first used in the Supreme Court decision of *McCulloch v. Maryland*[4] (discussed later

---

[3]Text of the address by the president to the National Conference of State Legislatures, Atlanta, Georgia (Washington, D.C.: The White House, Office of the Press Secretary, July 30, 1981), as quoted in Edward Millican, *One United People: The Federalist Papers and the National Idea* (Lexington, Ky.: The University Press of Kentucky, 1990).
[4]4 Wheaton 316 (1819).

in this chapter) to develop the concept of implied powers. Through this concept, the national government has succeeded in strengthening the scope of its authority to meet the numerous problems that the framers of the Constitution did not, and could not, anticipate.

A special category of national powers that is not implied by the necessary and proper clause consists of what have been labeled the inherent powers of the national government. These powers derive from the fact that the United States is a sovereign power among nations, and as such, its national government must be the only government that deals with other nations. Under international law, it is assumed that all nation-states, regardless of their size or power, have an *inherent* right to ensure their own survival. To do this, each nation must have the ability to act in its own interest among and with the community of nations—by, for instance, making treaties, waging war, seeking trade, and acquiring territory. The national government has these powers whether or not they have been enumerated in the Constitution. Some constitutional scholars categorize inherent powers as a third type of power, completely distinct from the delegated powers (both expressed and implied) of the national government.

FIGURE 3-2

The American Federal System—The Division of Powers between the National Government and the State Governments
Here we look at the constitutional powers of both the national government and the state governments together. Then we look at the powers denied by the Constitution to each level of government.

SELECTED CONSTITUTIONAL POWERS

National Government	National and State Governments	State Governments
Expressed • To coin money • To conduct foreign relations • To regulate interstate commerce • To declare war • To raise and support the military • To establish post offices • To establish courts inferior to the Supreme Court • To admit new states	**Concurrent** • To levy and collect taxes • To borrow money • To make and enforce laws • To establish courts • To provide for the general welfare • To charter banks and corporations	**Reserved to the States** • To regulate intrastate commerce • To conduct elections • To provide for public health, safety, and morals • To establish local governments • To ratify amendments to the federal constitution • To establish a state militia
Implied "To make all Laws which shall be necessary and proper for carrying into Execution the foregoing Powers, and all other Powers vested by this Constitution in the Government of the United States, or in any Department or Officer thereof." (Article 1, Section 8, Clause 18)		

SELECTED POWERS DENIED BY THE CONSTITUTION

National Government	National and State Governments	State Governments
• To tax articles exported from any state • To violate the Bill of Rights • To change state boundaries • To suspend the right of *habeas corpus* • To make *ex post facto* laws • To subject officeholders to a religious test	• To grant titles of nobility • To permit slavery • To deny citizens the right to vote because of race, color, or previous servitude • To deny citizens the right to vote because of gender	• To tax imports or exports • To coin money • To enter into treaties • To impair obligations of contracts • To abridge the privileges or immunities of citizens or deny due process and equal protection of the laws

Police Power
The authority to legislate for the protection of the health, morals, safety, and welfare of the people. In the United States, most police power is a reserved power of the states.

Concurrent Powers
Powers held jointly by the national and state governments.

The police power of the states includes the power to create and enforce traffic laws and to regulate commerce within their borders.

Powers of the State Governments

The Tenth Amendment states that the powers not delegated to the United States by the Constitution, nor prohibited by it to the states, are reserved to the states, or to the people. These are the reserved powers that the national government cannot deny to the states. Because these powers are not expressly listed—and because they are not limited to powers that are expressly listed—there is sometimes a question as to whether a certain power is delegated to the national government or reserved to the states. State powers have been held to include each state's right to regulate commerce within its borders and to provide for a state militia. States also have the reserved power to make laws on all matters not prohibited to the states by the national or state constitutions and not expressly, or by implication, delegated to the national government. The states also have **police power**—the authority to legislate for the protection of the health, morals, safety, and welfare of the people. Their police power enables states to pass laws governing such activities as crimes, marriage, contracts, education, traffic laws, and land use.

The ambiguity of the Tenth Amendment has allowed the reserved powers of the states to be defined differently at different times in our history. When there is widespread support for increased regulation by the national government, the Tenth Amendment tends to recede into the background. When the tide turns the other way, as it has in recent years (see the discussion of the new federalism later in this chapter), the Tenth Amendment is resurrected to justify arguments supporting increased states' rights.

Concurrent Powers

In certain areas, the states share **concurrent powers** with the national government. Most concurrent powers are not specifically stated in the Constitution; they are only implied. An example of a concurrent power is the power to tax. The types of taxation are divided between the levels of government. States may not levy a tariff (a set of taxes on imported goods); the federal government may not tax real estate; and neither may tax the facilities of the other. If the state governments did not have the power to tax, they would not be able to function other than on a ceremonial basis. Other concurrent powers include the power to borrow money, to establish courts, and to charter banks and corporations.

Concurrent powers are normally limited to the geographic area of the state and to those functions not delegated by the Constitution exclusively to the national government—such as the coinage of money and the negotiation of treaties.

Prohibited Powers

The Constitution prohibits or denies a number of powers to the national government. For example, the national government has expressly been denied the power to impose taxes on goods sold to other countries (exports). Moreover, any power not delegated expressly or implicitly to the federal government by the Constitution is prohibited to it. For example, the national government cannot create a national public school system. The states are also denied certain powers. For example, no state is allowed to enter into a treaty on its own with another country. (For a discussion of whether states should be making foreign policy via selective purchasing laws, see this chapter's *Critical Perspective* on the next page.)

The Supremacy Clause

The supremacy of the national constitution over subnational laws and actions can be found in the **supremacy clause** of the Constitution. The supremacy clause (Article VI, Clause 2) states the following:

> This Constitution and the Laws of the United States which shall be made in Pursuance thereof; and all Treaties made . . . under the Authority of the United States, shall be the supreme Law of the Land; and the Judges in every State shall be bound thereby, any Thing in the Constitution or Laws of any State to the Contrary notwithstanding.

In other words, states cannot use their reserved or concurrent powers to thwart national policies. All national and state officers, as well as judges, must be bound by oath to support the Constitution. Hence, any legitimate exercise of national governmental power supersedes any conflicting state action.[5] Of course, deciding whether a conflict actually exists is a judicial matter, as you will soon read when we discuss the case of *McCulloch v. Maryland*.

National government legislation in a concurrent area is said to *preempt* (take precedence over) conflicting state or local laws or regulations in that area. One of the ways in which the national government has extended its powers, particularly during the twentieth century, is through the preemption of state and local laws by national legislation. Consider that in the first decade of the twentieth century, fewer than 20 national laws preempted laws and regulations issued by state and local governments. By the beginning of the twenty-first century, this number had risen to nearly 120 (see Figure 3–3 on page 95).

Some political scientists believe that national supremacy is critical for the longevity and smooth functioning of a federal system. Nonetheless, the application of this principle has been a continuous source of conflict. Indeed, as you will see, the most extreme result of this conflict was the Civil War.

Vertical Checks and Balances

Recall from Chapter 2 that one of the concerns of the founders was to prevent the national government from becoming too powerful. For that reason, they

DID YOU KNOW... That, unlike the state and national governments, local governments, which can be created as well as abolished by their state, have no independent existence according to the Constitution?

Supremacy Clause
The constitutional provision that makes the Constitution and federal laws superior to all conflicting state and local laws.

[5]An excellent example of this is President Dwight Eisenhower's disciplining of Arkansas governor Orval Faubus by federalizing the National Guard to enforce the court-ordered desegregation of Little Rock High School.

critical perspective

Should States Make Foreign Policy?

In 1996, the state of Massachusetts passed a law imposing economic sanctions on Burma (Myanmar), a nation ruled by a brutal military regime. The law stated that any company that had business dealings with Burma would not be awarded a state contract unless the company's bid was 10 percent lower than others. The law had the desired effect: several companies–including Apple Computer, Eastman Kodak, and Hewlett-Packard–immediately pulled out of Burma, citing the law as the reason for their withdrawal. Companies that retained their ties with Burma were put on the state's "restricted purchase list," which effectively precluded them from the Massachusetts procurement market. By 1998, this list included nearly 350 U.S. and foreign companies.

Selective Purchasing Laws Are Not New

"Selective purchasing laws"–state and local laws designed to influence foreign events–are largely the product of campaigns led by strongly motivated activist groups. The first such campaign was launched against South Africa in the 1980s to influence that nation's racial policies. In the mid-1990s, activists began to use similar tactics to punish other nations for human rights violations.

Today, in addition to Massachusetts, at least eighteen governments have selective purchasing laws directed at Burma. Massachusetts also has a law targeting companies that do business with the British Army, because of problems in Northern Ireland, and is considering laws imposing sanctions on Indonesia because of human rights violations in East Timor. Oakland, California, has imposed sanctions against Nigeria; and Dade County, Florida, has some against Cuba. U.S. firms that do business in China worry that laws targeting that nation for alleged religious persecution or human rights violations may be next.

Should States Be Making Foreign Policy?

By the late 1990s, the Massachusetts law sanctioning Burma had become the subject of widespread controversy. After the 1996 law was passed, the European Union, Japan, and the Association of Southeast Asian Nations all registered diplomatic protests with the U.S. government, claiming that the law violated World Trade Organization rules that prohibit discrimination in purchases by governments.

Various groups within the United States, including former president Gerald Ford and twenty-seven former cabinet members from both Republican and Democratic administrations, also criticized the Massachusetts law. Foreign policy is the province of the national government, they argued, and state and local trade sanctions are confusing for foreign countries, particularly when they conflict with sanctions imposed by the U.S. government.

The Constitutional Issues

The reason the Massachusetts law has been singled out for publicity is that it is the first such law to be challenged in court. In 1998, the National Foreign Trade Council (NFTC), a nonprofit organization of 580 businesses involved in international trade, sued Massachusetts officials, alleging that the law sanctioning Burma was unconstitutional. The NFTC argued that not only did the law interfere with the federal government's primary authority over foreign affairs, but that it also violated the Constitution's commerce clause, which, as interpreted by the United States Supreme Court, gives Congress the exclusive power "to regulate Commerce with foreign Nations."

The NFTC also claimed that the Massachusetts law violated the supremacy clause of the Constitution, under which federal laws preempt–or take precedence over–conflicting state and local laws. Specifically, the NFTC claimed that the Massachusetts law was preempted by federal sanctions against Burma that were enacted shortly after the law's passage.

Ultimately, the case reached the United States Supreme Court, which ruled in June 2000 that the Massachusetts law was unconstitutional because it conflicted with the earlier, and milder, federal sanctions against Burma.* The Court's decision, of course, will overturn other states' selective-purchasing laws targeted at Burma, but it will not apply to state and local laws that do *not* conflict with federal sanctions. Thus, for cases in which the federal government has not acted, state and local sanctions targeted at foreign countries remain intact–and whether these sanctions are constitutional is a question that remains unanswered.

FOR CRITICAL ANALYSIS

1. Is it appropriate for state and local governments in the United States to issue moral pronouncements, in the form of trade sanctions, on the practices and policies of foreign nations?
2. Suppose that a state establishes a trade policy that rewards nations that have a "good" record with respect to human rights, the environment, labor relations, and so on. Would such a policy also interfere with the federal government's authority over foreign policy?

*Crosby v. National Foreign Trade Council, 120 S.Ct. 2288 (2000).

FIGURE 3-3

Federal Preemption from 1900 to the Present

As this graph shows, the number of federal laws that preempt state authority increased significantly during the twentieth century. The greatest increase has been in the areas of environment, health, and safety.

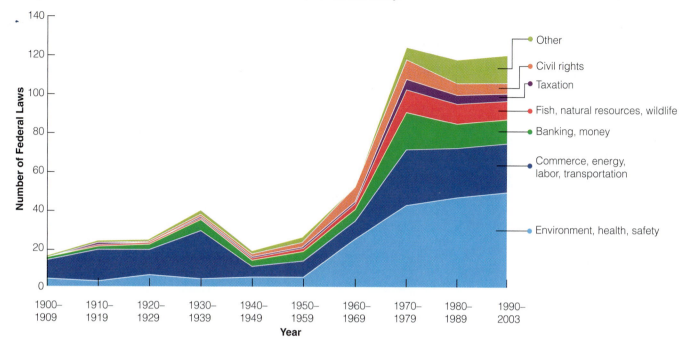

SOURCE: U.S. Advisory Commission on Intergovernmental Relations, plus authors' update.

divided the government into three branches—legislative, executive, judicial. They also created a system of checks and balances that allowed each branch to check the actions of the other branches. The federal form of government created by the founders also involves checks and balances. These are sometimes called "vertical" checks and balances because they involve relationships between the states and the national government.

For example, the reserved powers of the states act as a check on the national government. Additionally, the states' interests are represented in the national legislature (Congress), and the citizens of the various states determine who will head the executive branch (the presidency). The founders also made it impossible for the central government to change the Constitution without the states' consent, as you read in Chapter 2. Finally, national programs and policies are administered by the states, which gives the states considerable control over the ultimate shape of those programs and policies.

The national government, in turn, can check state policies by exercising its constitutional powers under the clauses just discussed, as well as under the commerce clause (to be discussed later). Furthermore, the national government can influence state policies indirectly through federal grants, as you will learn later in this chapter.

INFOTRAC®
COLLEGE EDITION

States' Rights Foreign Policy

Horizontal Federalism

So far we have examined only the relationship between central and state governmental units. The states, however, have numerous commercial, social, and other dealings among themselves. These interstate activities, problems, and policies

Horizontal Federalism
Activities, problems, and policies that require state governments to interact with one another.

make up what can be called **horizontal federalism.** The national Constitution imposes certain "rules of the road" on horizontal federalism, which have had the effect of preventing any one state from setting itself apart from the other states. The three most important clauses relating to horizontal federalism in the Constitution, all taken from the Articles of Confederation, require each state to do the following:

1. Give full faith and credit to every other state's public acts, records, and judicial proceedings (Article IV, Section 1).
2. Extend to every other state's citizens the privileges and immunities of its own citizens (Article IV, Section 2).
3. Agree to return persons who are fleeing from justice in another state back to their home state when requested to do so (Article IV, Section 2).

Interstate Compact
An agreement between two or more states. Agreements on minor matters are made without congressional consent, but any compact that tends to increase the power of the contracting states relative to other states or relative to the national government generally requires the consent of Congress. Such compacts serve as a means by which states can solve regional problems.

Additionally, states may enter into agreements called **interstate compacts**—if consented to by Congress. In reality, congressional consent is necessary only if such a compact increases the power of the contracting states relative to other states (or to the national government). Typical examples of interstate compacts are the establishment of the Port Authority of New York and New Jersey by an interstate compact between New York and New Jersey in 1921 and the regulation of the production of crude oil and natural gas by the Interstate Oil and Gas Compact of 1935.

Defining Constitutional Powers—The Early Years

Recall from Chapter 2 that constitutional language, to be effective and to endure, must have some degree of ambiguity. Certainly, the powers delegated to the national government and the powers reserved to the states contain elements of ambiguity, thus leaving the door open for different interpretations of federalism. Disputes over the boundaries of national versus state powers have characterized this nation from the beginning. In the early 1800s, the most significant disputes arose over differing interpretations of the implied powers of the national government under the necessary and proper clause and the respective powers of the national government and the states in regard to commerce.

Interstate compacts have long been used as a way to address issues that affect more than one state. An interstate compact between New York and New Jersey in 1921 created the Port Authority of New York and New Jersey to develop and maintain harbor facilities in that area, including the Port Authority Bus Terminal shown here. Today, there are over two hundred interstate compacts.

Although political bodies at all levels of government play important roles in the process of settling such disputes, ultimately it is the Supreme Court that casts the final vote. As might be expected, the character of the referee will have an impact on the ultimate outcome of any boundary dispute. From 1801 to 1835, the Supreme Court was headed by Chief Justice John Marshall, a Federalist who advocated a strong central government. We look here at two cases decided by the Marshall Court: *McCulloch v. Maryland*[6] and *Gibbons v. Ogden*.[7] Both cases are considered milestones in the movement toward national government supremacy.

McCulloch v. Maryland (1819)

The U.S. Constitution says nothing about establishing a national bank. Nonetheless, at different times Congress chartered two banks—the First and Second Banks of the United States—and provided part of their initial capital; they were thus national banks. The government of Maryland imposed a tax on the Second Bank's Baltimore branch in an attempt to put that branch out of business. The

---

[6]4 Wheaton 316 (1819).
[7]9 Wheaton 1 (1824).

branch's cashier, James William McCulloch, refused to pay the Maryland tax. When Maryland took McCulloch to its state court, the state of Maryland won. The national government appealed the case to the Supreme Court.

One of the issues before the Court was whether the national government had the implied power, under the necessary and proper clause, to charter a bank and contribute capital to it. The other important question before the Court was the following: If the bank was constitutional, could a state tax it? In other words, was a state action that conflicted with a national government action invalid under the supremacy clause?

Chief Justice John Marshall held that if establishing such a national bank aided the national government in the exercise of its designated powers, then the authority to set up such a bank could be implied. To Marshall, the necessary and proper clause embraced "all means which are appropriate" to carry out "the legitimate ends" of the Constitution. Only when such actions are forbidden by the letter and spirit of the Constitution are they thereby unconstitutional. Having established this doctrine of implied powers, Marshall then answered the other important question before the Court and established the doctrine of national supremacy. Marshall stated that no state could use its taxing power to tax an arm of the national government. If it could, "the declaration that the Constitution . . . shall be the supreme law of the land, is [an] empty and unmeaning [statement]."

Marshall's decision enabled the national government to grow and to meet problems that the Constitution's framers were unable to foresee. Today, practically every expressed power of the national government has been expanded in one way or another by use of the necessary and proper clause.

Gibbons v. Ogden (1824)

One of the more important parts of the Constitution included in Article I, Section 8, is the so-called **commerce clause**, in which Congress is given the power "[t]o regulate Commerce with foreign Nations, and among the several States, and with the Indian Tribes." The meaning of this clause was at issue in *Gibbons v. Ogden*.

The background to the case was as follows. Robert Fulton and Robert Livingston secured a monopoly on steam navigation on the waters in New York State from the New York legislature in 1803. They licensed Aaron Ogden to operate steam-powered ferryboats between New York and New Jersey. Thomas Gibbons, who had obtained a license from the U.S. government to operate boats in interstate waters, decided to compete with Ogden, but he did so without New York's permission. Ogden sued Gibbons. The New York state courts granted Ogden an **injunction**, prohibiting Gibbons from operating in New York waters. Gibbons appealed to the Supreme Court.

There were actually several issues before the Court in this case. The first issue had to do with how the term *commerce* should be defined. New York's highest court had defined the term narrowly to mean only the shipment of goods, or the interchange of commodities, *not* navigation or the transport of people. The second issue was whether the national government's power to regulate interstate commerce extended to commerce within a state (*intra*state commerce) or was limited strictly to commerce among the states (*inter*state commerce). The third issue was whether the power to regulate interstate commerce was a concurrent power (as the New York court had concluded) or an exclusive national power.

Marshall defined *commerce* as *all* commercial intercourse—all business dealings—including navigation and the transport of people. Marshall also held that the commerce power of the national government could be exercised in state jurisdictions, even though it cannot reach *solely* intrastate commerce. Finally, Marshall emphasized that the power to regulate interstate commerce was an

John Marshall (1755–1835) was the fourth chief justice of the Supreme Court. When Marshall took over, the Court had little power and almost no influence over the other two branches of government. Some scholars have declared that Marshall is the true architect of the American constitutional system, because he single-handedly gave new power to the Constitution. Early in his career, he was an attorney and was elected to the first of four terms in the Virginia Assembly. He was instrumental in the fight to ratify the Constitution in Virginia. Prior to being named to the Supreme Court, he won a seat in Congress in 1799 and in 1800 became secretary of state to John Adams.

Commerce Clause
The section of the Constitution in which Congress is given the power to regulate trade among the states and with foreign countries.

Injunction
An order issued by a court to compel or restrain the performance of an act by an individual or entity.

exclusive national power. Marshall held that because Gibbons was duly authorized by the national government to navigate in interstate waters, he could not be prohibited from doing so by a state court.

Marshall's expansive interpretation of the commerce clause in *Gibbons v. Ogden* allowed the national government to exercise increasing authority over all areas of economic affairs throughout the land. Congress did not immediately exploit this broad grant of power. In the 1930s and subsequent decades, however, the commerce clause became the primary constitutional basis for national government regulation—as you will read later in this chapter.

States' Rights and the Resort to Civil War

We usually think of the Civil War simply as the fight to free the slaves, but that issue was closely intertwined with another one. Also at the heart of the controversy that led to the Civil War was the issue of national government supremacy versus the rights of the separate states. Essentially, the Civil War brought to an ultimate and violent climax the ideological debate that had been outlined by the Federalist and Anti-Federalist parties even before the Constitution was ratified.

The Shift Back to States' Rights

As we have seen, while John Marshall was chief justice of the Supreme Court, he did much to increase the power of the national government and to reduce that of the states. During the Jacksonian era (1829–1837), however, a shift back to states' rights began. The question of the regulation of commerce became one of the major issues in federal-state relations. The business community preferred state regulation (or, better yet, no regulation) of commerce.

When Congress passed a tariff in 1828, the state of South Carolina attempted to nullify the tariff (render it void), claiming that in cases of conflict between a state and the national government, the state should have the ultimate authority

The Civil War was not fought over just the question of slavery. Rather, the supremacy of the national government was at issue. Had the South won, presumably any state or states would have the right to secede from the Union.

over its citizens. The concept of **nullification** eventually was used by others to justify the **secession** of the southern states from the Union.

Over the next three decades, the North and South became even more sharply divided—over tariffs that mostly benefited northern industries and over the slavery issue. On December 20, 1860, South Carolina formally repealed its ratification of the Constitution and withdrew from the Union. On February 4, 1861, representatives from six southern states met at Montgomery, Alabama, to form a new government called the Confederate States of America. They wrote a new constitution and adopted a new flag. (See this chapter's feature entitled *An Ethical Issue: Should the Confederate Flag Be Flown?* for a discussion of the stir caused by South Carolina's act of flying the Confederate flag from its statehouse.)

War and the Growth of the National Government

The ultimate defeat of the South in 1865 permanently ended any idea that a state within the Union can successfully claim the right to secede. Ironically, the Civil War—brought about in large part because of the South's desire for increased states' rights—resulted in the opposite: an increase in the political power of the national government.

Thousands of new employees were hired to run the Union war effort and to deal with the social and economic problems that had to be handled in the aftermath of war. A billion-dollar ($1.3 billion, which is over $11 billion in today's dollars) national government budget was passed for the first time in 1865 to cover the increased government expenditures. The first (temporary) income tax was imposed on citizens to help pay for the war. Both the increased national government spending and the nationally imposed income tax were precursors to

DID YOU KNOW...
That Abraham Lincoln, the "Great Emancipator," claimed on taking office that he would not attack slavery as an institution and that he even wanted a constitutional amendment to make the right to own slaves irrevocable**?**

Nullification
The act of nullifying, or rendering void. Prior to the Civil War, southern supporters of states' rights claimed that a state had the right to declare a national law to be null and void and therefore not binding on its citizens, on the assumption that ultimate sovereign authority rested with the several states.

Secession
The act of formally withdrawing from membership in an alliance; the withdrawal of a state from the federal Union.

an ethical issue

Should the Confederate Flag Be Flown?

On Martin Luther King Day in 2000, about 46,000 people joined a protest march to South Carolina's statehouse in Columbia. They were protesting the continued presence of the Confederate battle flag above the statehouse, contending that it was an emblem of slavery and racism. Again in April, a protest march headed toward the capitol, hoping to persuade South Carolina lawmakers to lower the flag.

Defenders of that flag, including a number of South Carolina legislators, contended that the flag is a symbol of the South's distinctive heritage and should be flown. Flag opponents, including the National Association for the Advancement of Colored People (NAACP), responded with banners proclaiming "Your heritage is my slavery!"

In 1962, after the U.S. Congress had called on the states to commemorate the coming centennial of the Civil War, an all-white South Carolina General Assembly voted to raise the Confederate flag over the statehouse. Surviving members of that legislature claimed that the flag was raised as part of the national commemoration activities celebrating the centennial of

the Civil War and that it was to fly only during the centennial celebration. The problem, according to these members, was that the legislation did not contain a date for taking the flag down. Critics claimed that the legislature raised the flag as a form of protest against the national government's civil rights legislation during those years.

In response to the mounting protests, South Carolina legislators finally removed the flag from the capitol building in July 2000. Nonetheless, the flag controversy continues. In part, this is because, as a gesture of compromise with lawmakers who voted against removing the flag, the legislature allowed the flag to be flown elsewhere on statehouse grounds—on a bronze pole in front of a Confederate soldier's monument. Critics, particularly the NAACP, maintain that even in its new location the flag is too visible and should be removed. The debate over the Confederate flag reaches beyond South Carolina. Similar struggles are being waged also in Mississippi and Georgia over the stars and bars in those states' flags.

FOR CRITICAL ANALYSIS

Suppose that the South Carolina legislature had continued to do nothing about the Confederate flag flying over the capitol. Could the citizens of that state do anything to force the issue? Could the U.S. Congress do anything?

the expanded future role of the national government in the American federal system.[8] Civil liberties were curtailed in the Union and in the Confederacy in the name of the wartime emergency. The distribution of pensions and widow's benefits also boosted the national government's social role. The North's victory set the nation on the path to a modern industrial economy and society.

The Continuing Dispute over the Division of Power

Although the outcome of the Civil War firmly established the supremacy of the national government and put to rest the idea that a state could secede from the Union, the war by no means ended the debate over the division of powers between the national government and the states. In fact, many current political issues raise questions relating to states' rights and federalism. (For a discussion of one such issue, see this chapter's feature *Which Side Are You On?*)

The debate over the division of powers in our federal system can be viewed as progressing through at least three stages since the Civil War: dual federalism, cooperative federalism, and the new federalism.

Dual Federalism

Dual Federalism

A system of government in which the states and the national government each remain supreme within their own spheres. The doctrine looks on nation and state as coequal sovereign powers. It holds that acts of states within their reserved powers are legitimate limitations on the powers of the national government.

During the decades following the Civil War, the prevailing doctrine was that of **dual federalism**—a doctrine that emphasizes a distinction between federal and state spheres of government authority. Various images have been used to describe different configurations of federalism over time. Dual federalism is commonly depicted as a layer cake, because the state governments and the national government are viewed as separate entities, like separate layers in a cake.

Generally, in the decades following the Civil War the states exercised their police powers to regulate affairs within their borders, such as intrastate commerce, and the national government stayed out of purely local affairs. The courts tended to support the states' rights to exercise their police powers and concurrent powers in regard to the regulation of intrastate activities. For example, in 1918, the Supreme Court ruled that a 1916 federal law banning child labor was unconstitutional because it attempted to regulate a local problem.[9] In the 1930s, however, the doctrine of dual federalism receded into the background as the nation attempted to deal with the Great Depression.

Cooperative Federalism

Cooperative Federalism

The theory that the states and the national government should cooperate in solving problems.

Franklin D. Roosevelt was inaugurated on March 4, 1933, as the thirty-second president of the United States. In the previous year, nearly 1,500 banks had failed (and 4,000 more would fail in 1933). Thirty-two thousand businesses closed down, and one-fourth of the labor force was unemployed. The national government had been expected to do something about the disastrous state of the economy. But for the first three years of the Great Depression, the national government did very little. That changed with the new Democratic administration's energetic intervention in the economy. FDR's "New Deal" included numerous government spending and welfare programs, in addition to voluminous regulations relating to economic activity.

Some political scientists have described the era since 1937 as characterized by **cooperative federalism,** in which the states and the national government cooper-

---

[8]The future of the national government's powerful role was cemented with the passage of the Sixteenth Amendment (ratified in 1913), which authorized the federal income tax.
[9]*Hammer v. Dagenhart,* 247 U.S. 251 (1918). This decision was overruled in *United States v. Darby,* 312 U.S. 100 (1940).

which side are you on?

Should the States Play a Greater Role in Deciding Who Receives Donor Organs?

As mentioned elsewhere in this chapter, one of the advantages of a federal form of government in a large country such as the United States is that certain functions can be farmed out to state and local governments. Yet deciding which functions are handled better at the state level, rather than the national level, is not always easy. Consider, for example, the distribution of donor organs.

Current Organ-Donation Policy

Currently, an agency of the federal government, the Department of Health and Human Services (HHS) regulates organ-donation policy. The actual management of the distribution of donor organs is contracted out to a privacy agency, the United Network for Organ Sharing (UNOS). From the outset, the UNOS has followed a "local-first" policy—that is, donor organs are distributed to local transplant patients first. This policy was established in the 1980s, at a time when the technology did not exist to preserve a donor organ for transplantation for more

than a few hours. For example, a heart had to be transplanted within three hours; a liver, within eight hours; and a pancreas, within ten hours.

Although advances in preservation techniques have more than doubled those time limits, the policy governing the distribution of donor organs has not changed. Consequently, whether a prospective organ recipient will be allocated an organ that becomes available depends on where the prospective recipient lives. If you live in Pennsylvania, the chances of being allocated an organ are far less than they are in Wisconsin. The waiting time for a liver is 511 days in New York, while it is only 56 days in New Jersey. Furthermore, under the existing policy, patients who are active and not at all in critical condition critical often receive donor organs before those who are in extremely critical health.

Should Donor Organs Go to the Neediest, Not the Nearest?

Should donor organs go to the neediest persons across the nation instead of the geographically nearest? The HHS thinks so, and in early 2000 that agency issued a rule providing for the allocation of donor organs based on this principle.

Others, including some members of Congress, disagree. They argue that a national system will threaten smaller, more rural transplant centers by sending organs to large centers with greater numbers of ill patients. They also worry that giving priority to the neediest (sickest) patients will drive up costs, because these patients need more follow-up care—and may not even recover from the transplantation procedure. For these and other reasons, the House of Representatives recently passed a bill that would allow individual states to play a key role in determining how donor organs are allocated.

DOES IT MATTER?

In your opinion, does it matter whether the national government or state governments control organ-donation policies? Why or why not?

GOING ONLINE

For the chronology of events leading to the HHS's final rule on organ distribution, go to **http://www.hrsa.gov/osp/dot**. *For arguments supporting and opposing the HHS rule, go to* **http://www.house.gov/apps/list/press/pa05_peterson/organ.html** *and* **http://www.house.gov/apps/list/press/mo07_blunt/organdonors.html**, *respectively.*

ate in solving complex common problems. The New Deal programs of Franklin Roosevelt, for example, often involved joint action between the national government and the states. Federal grants (discussed later) were given to the states to help pay for public works projects, housing assistance, welfare programs, unemployment compensation, and other programs. The states, in turn, were required to implement the programs and pay for at least some of the costs involved. The pattern of national-state relationships during these years gave rise to a new metaphor for federalism—that of a marble cake.

Others see the 1930s as the beginning of an era of national supremacy, in which the power of the states has been consistently diminished. Certainly, the 1960s and 1970s saw an even greater expansion of the national government's role in domestic policy. The "Great Society" program of Lyndon Johnson's administration (1963–1969) created the Job Corps, Operation Head Start, Volunteers in Service to America (VISTA), Medicaid, and Medicare. The Civil Rights Act of 1964 prohibited discrimination in public accommodations, employment, and other areas on the basis of race, color, national origin, religion, or gender. The economy was regulated further in the 1970s by national laws protecting consumers, employees, and

In the 1800s, very young children worked in coal mines. Today, child-labor laws prohibit employers from hiring such young workers. Some argue that even in the absence of child-labor laws, few, if any, children would still be working in the mines, because the United States is a much richer country than it was a hundred years ago. Presumably, today's parents, no longer at subsistence income levels, would opt to have their children go to school.

Picket-Fence Federalism
A model of federalism in which specific programs and policies (depicted as vertical pickets in a picket fence) involve all levels of government—national, state, and local (depicted by the horizontal boards in a picket fence).

Categorical Grants-in-Aid
Federal grants-in-aid to states or local governments that are for very specific programs or projects.

Matching Funds
For many categorical grant programs, money that the state must provide to "match" the federal funds. Some programs require the state to raise only 10 percent of the funds, whereas others approach an even share.

Equalization
A method for adjusting the amount of money that a state must provide to receive federal funds. The formula used takes into account the wealth of the state or its ability to tax its citizens.

the environment. Today, few activities are beyond the reach of the regulatory arm of the national government.

The evolving pattern of national-state-local government relationships during the 1960s gave rise to yet another metaphor—**picket-fence federalism,** a concept devised by political scientist Terry Sanford. The horizontal boards in the fence represent the different levels of government (national, state, and local), while the vertical pickets represent the various programs and policies in which each level of government is involved. Officials at each level of government work together to promote and develop the policy represented by each picket.

Federal Grants-in-Aid. As part of the system of cooperative federalism, the national government gives back to the states (and local governments) a significant amount of the tax dollars it collects—an estimated $235 billion a year in fiscal year 2002. Federal grants typically have taken the form of **categorical grants-in-aid,** which are grants to state and local governments designated for very specific programs or projects. For some of the categorical grant programs, the state and local governments must put up a share of the money, usually called **matching funds.** For other types of programs, the funds are awarded according to a formula that takes into account the relative wealth of the state, a process known as **equalization.**

Grants-in-aid in the form of land grants were given to the states even before the ratification of the Constitution. Cash grants-in-aid started in 1808, when Congress gave money to the states to pay for the state militias. It was not until the twentieth century, however, that the federal grants-in-aid program became significant. Grants-in-aid and the restrictions and regulations that accompany them started to mushroom during Roosevelt's administration. The major growth began in the 1960s, however, when the dollar amount of grants-in-aid quadrupled to help pay for the Great Society programs of the Johnson administration. Grants became available in numerous areas, including education, pollution control, conservation, recreation, and highway construction and maintenance.

Nowhere can the shift toward a greater role for the central government in the United States be seen better than in the shift toward increased central government spending as a percentage of total government spending. Figure 3–4 shows

This housing development in Minnesota was one of the many projects sponsored by the New Deal's Works Progress Administration (WPA) in the 1930s. The federal government's efforts to alleviate unemployment (in this case, among construction workers) during the Great Depression signaled a shift from dual federalism to cooperative federalism.

that in 1929, on the eve of the Great Depression, local governments accounted for 60 percent of all government outlays, whereas the federal government accounted for only 17 percent. After Roosevelt's New Deal had been in place for several years during the Great Depression, local governments gave up half their share of the government spending pie, dropping to 30 percent, and the federal government increased its share to 47 percent. Estimates are that in 2001, the federal government accounted for about 60.5 percent of all government spending.

By attaching conditions to federal grants, the national government has been able to exercise substantial control over matters that traditionally have fallen under the purview of state governments. If a state does not comply with a particular requirement, the national government may withhold federal funds for other programs. A classic example of the power of the federal government to sanction the states for lack of compliance occurred during the administration of Ronald Reagan (1981–1989). Reagan threatened to withhold federal highway

FIGURE 3-4

The Shift toward Central Government Spending

Before the Great Depression, local governments accounted for 60 percent of all government spending, with the federal government accounting for only 17 percent. By 2000, federal government spending was up to 60.5 percent, local governments accounted for only 19 percent, and the remainder was spent by state governments.

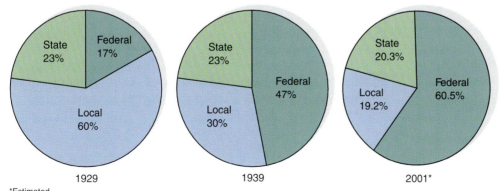

*Estimated.
SOURCE: U.S. Department of Commerce, Bureau of the Census, *Government Finances* (Washington, D.C.: U.S. Government Printing Office, 2001.

President Johnson displays his signature on the War on Poverty bill after he signed it into law in a ceremony in the Rose Garden at the White House on August 20, 1964.

New Federalism
A plan both to limit the national government's power to regulate and to restore power to state governments. Essentially, the new federalism is designed to give the states greater ability to decide for themselves how government revenues should be spent.

Block Grants
Federal programs that provide funds to state and local governments for general functional areas, such as criminal justice or mental-health programs.

funds unless the states raised the minimum drinking age to twenty-one years. The threat of losing federal funds prompted the states to take action, and most of the states soon passed laws establishing twenty-one as the minimum drinking age. Louisiana was the lone holdout. Although it banned minors from purchasing alcohol in order to receive federal funds, it did not prohibit bars and alcohol retailers from *selling* alcohol to minors. Only in 1996, after President Clinton threatened to withhold $1.7 million in federal highway funds from Louisiana, did that state fully comply with the drinking-age mandate.

Cooperative Federalism and the Supreme Court. The full effect of Chief Justice John Marshall's broad interpretation of the commerce clause has only been realized since the 1930s. In the years since then, the commerce clause has been used to justify national regulation of virtually any activity, even what would appear to be a purely local activity. For example, in 1942, the Supreme Court held that wheat production by an individual farmer intended wholly for consumption on his own farm was subject to federal regulation—because the home consumption of wheat reduced the demand for wheat and thus could have a substantial effect on interstate commerce.[10]

The commerce clause has also been used to validate congressional legislation even in what would seem to be social and moral matters—concerns traditionally regulated by the states. For example, in 1964 a small hotel in Georgia challenged the constitutionality of the Civil Rights Act of that year, claiming that Congress had exceeded its authority under the commerce clause by regulating local, intrastate affairs. The Supreme Court held that the 1964 act was constitutional, concluding that "[i]f it is interstate commerce that feels the pinch, it does not matter how local the operation that applies the squeeze."[11] By 1980, the Supreme Court acknowledged that the commerce clause had "long been interpreted to extend beyond activities actually in interstate commerce to reach other activities, while wholly local in nature, which nevertheless substantially affect interstate commerce."[12]

The New Federalism

The third phase of federalism was labeled the **new federalism** by President Richard Nixon (1969–1974). Its goal is to restore to the states some of the powers that have been exercised by the national government since the 1930s. The word *devolution*—which means the transfer of powers to political subunits—is often used in connection with this approach to federalism.

The new federalism has continued, to varying degrees, to the present and is referred to by various names. Some call it "devolutionary federalism." Others have referred to the federalism of the Clinton administration during the 1990s as "new-age federalism." The latter term denotes an approach that continues the devolutionary goals of the new federalism while retaining for the national government the responsibility of overseeing state experiments in finding and implementing solutions to various problems, such as welfare reform.

Tools of the New Federalism—Block Grants.   One of the major tools of the new federalism is the block grant. **Block grants** place fewer restrictions on grants-in-aid given to state and local governments by grouping a number of categorical grants under one broad purpose. Governors and mayors generally prefer block grants because they give the states more flexibility in how the money is spent.

[10]*Wickard v. Filburn,* 317 U.S. 111 (1942).
[11]*Heart of Atlanta Motel v. United States,* 379 U.S. 241 (1964).
[12]*McLain v. Real Estate Board of New Orleans, Inc.,* 444 U.S. 232 (1980).

DID YOU KNOW...
That part of the $4.2 million federal block grants received by four Native American tribes since 1997 goes toward the building of "smoke shops"—stores that sell discounted cigarettes and pipe tobacco**?**

Out of the numerous block grants that were proposed from 1966 until the election of Ronald Reagan in 1980, only five were actually legislated. At the Reagan administration's urging, Congress increased the number to nine. By the beginning of the 1990s, such block grants accounted for slightly over 10 percent of all federal aid programs. With the Republican sweep of Congress in the 1994 elections, block grants again became the focus of attention. Republicans proposed reforming welfare and a number of other federal programs by transforming the categorical grants-in-aid to block grants and transferring more of the policymaking authority to the states. Congress succeeded, in part, in achieving these goals when it passed the welfare reform bill of 1996 (discussed in Chapter 16).

Although state governments desire block grants, Congress generally prefers categorical grants so that the expenditures are targeted according to congressional priorities. These priorities include programs, such as those for disadvantaged groups and individuals, that significantly benefit many voters. As you can see in Figure 3–5, federal grants-in-aid grew rapidly during the Nixon and Ford administrations, as well as during the Carter administration. The rate of growth slowed considerably during the Reagan administration, only to speed up again under Presidents Bush and Clinton.

INFOTRAC® COLLEGE EDITION

HBCU Projects Win Federal Funds

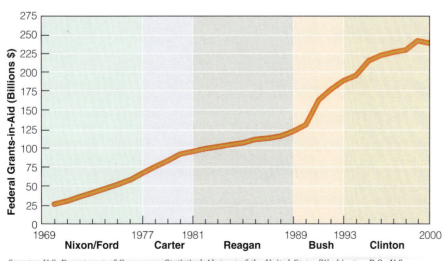

FIGURE 3-5

Federal Grants-in-Aid
Federal grants to state and local governments are an integral part of cooperative federalism. As this figure shows, the amount of funds given to state and local governments in the form of federal grants-in-aid has increased steadily from 1969 to the late 1990s.

SOURCES: U.S. Department of Commerce, *Statistical Abstract of the United States* (Washington D.C.: U.S. Government Printing Office, 2000).

Trends in Federalism

During the 2000 campaigns, the major contenders for the presidential office, Texas governor George W. Bush and Vice President Al Gore, assumed traditional party agendas with respect to federalism. Bush, the Republican candidate, frequently iterated how a vote for Al Gore was essentially a vote for "big government." He emphasized that "the people" should decide for themselves, at the state and local level, what policies and programs should be implemented. Gore, in contrast, emphasized the responsibilities of the federal government with respect to "guaranteeing" certain programs, such as Social Security. As president, Bush is clearly giving state and local governments more responsibilities.

Federal Mandate

A requirement in federal legislation that forces states and municipalities to comply with certain rules.

Federal Mandates.   A major obstacle faced by those who favor returning power to the states concerns **federal mandates**—requirements in federal legislation that force states and municipalities to comply with certain rules. Examples of federal mandates are minimum air and water purity requirements for specific localities and requirements for access by persons with physical disabilities to public buildings, sidewalks, and other areas. (See this chapter's feature *Making Waves* for a discussion of how federal mandates designed to protect endangered species and scarce water resources have affected one locality.) As mentioned earlier, under the supremacy clause of the Constitution, federal laws preempt conflicting state and local laws.

No accurate analysis exists of the overall costs state and local governments have incurred as a result of federal mandates. Certain mandates, however, clearly are very costly. For example, one mandate involves eligibility for Medicaid. Medicaid is the federally subsidized, state-run health-care program for low-income Americans. The estimated cost of the programs for the states was over $70 billion annually by the early 2000s.

One of the major "planks" in the Republican platform of 1994 was a promise to end unfunded mandates to state and local governments. By March 1995, the Republican-controlled 104th Congress had indeed succeeded in passing a bill to regulate the use of such federal mandates. On close analysis,

The Shovel Brigade

Many people are surprised to learn that the U.S. government owns nearly 30 percent of the land in this nation. In the western states, this figure is much higher. In Wyoming, for example, 44 percent of the land is owned by the U.S. government. In Utah, the figure is 57 percent, and in Nevada, it is 87 percent.

Traditionally, the federal government has permitted residents of a state to use federal lands for cattle grazing and other purposes. Over the last decade or so, however, in the interests of preserving endangered species and scarce water resources, the federal government has limited citizens' use of these lands. The result has been a growing hostility in those areas toward the federal government—and particularly toward the federal bureaucrats who enforce federal land-use laws. In the 1990s, rebels in the "Wild West" resorted to violent acts, such as bombing a federal official's vehicle and shooting at a U.S. Forest Service employee.

This ongoing battle was reignited recently when the Forest Service decided not to rebuild a country road on federally owned

land in Elko County, Nevada, after the road had washed away for the umpteenth time. The decision was made after studies showed that rebuilding the road would create pollution runoff harmful to the rare bull trout in the nearby Jarbridge River and thus violate the federal law protecting endangered species. In the fall of 1999, a group of Nevada residents calling themselves the Jarbridge Shovel Brigade decided to rebuild the road themselves. When confronted with a restraining order, the brigade declared war. The brigade grew in size as residents of other states joined the struggle, sending trucks loaded with thousands of shovels to Jarbridge, a nearby town with a population of twenty. So far, there has been no outbreak of violence. In this situation, federal officials have taken steps to avoid confrontations and plan to resolve the issue in court.

FOR CRITICAL ANALYSIS

Some have suggested that federally owned lands should be given to the states so that land-use regulation can be better adapted to state and local needs. Do you agree with this suggestion? Why or why not?

however, the 1995 legislation was mostly symbolic; it accomplished little actual change in the use of unfunded federal mandates. To a great extent, this is because, although the Republicans had sought to repeal previously legislated mandates dealing with such matters as civil rights and discrimination, the compromise bill that President Clinton signed exempts these matters. The act also exempts legislation concerning such issues as constitutional rights, voting rights, and national security. In short, the act exempts the matters that account for many of the most costly unfunded mandates imposed on state and local governments during the last decade.

The Supreme Court and the New Federalism

One of the rallying cries of the new federalism has been that the national government has gone too far in the direction of exercising powers that rightfully belong to the states under the Constitution. To a significant extent, the federal courts have agreed with this contention.

Tenth Amendment Issues.   In 1992, the United States Supreme Court held that requirements imposed on the state of New York under a federal law regulating low-level radioactive waste were inconsistent with the Tenth Amendment and thus unconstitutional. According to the Court, the act's "take title" provision, which required states to accept ownership of waste or regulate waste according to Congress's instructions, exceeded the enumerated powers of Congress. Although Congress can regulate the handling of such waste, "it may not conscript state governments as its agents" in an attempt to enforce a program of federal regulation.[13]

In 1997, the Court revisited this Tenth Amendment issue. In *Printz v. United States*,[14] the Court struck down the provisions of the federal Brady Handgun Violence Prevention Act of 1993 that required state employees to check the backgrounds of prospective handgun purchasers. Said the Court:

> [T]he federal government may neither issue directives requiring the States to address particular problems, nor command the States' officers, or those of their political subdivisions, to administer or enforce a federal regulatory program.

The Court held that the provisions violated "the very principle of separate state sovereignty," which was "one of the Constitution's structural protections of liberty."

Reining in the Commerce Power.   The Supreme Court has also been reining in the powers of the national government under the commerce clause. In a widely publicized 1995 case, *United States v. Lopez*,[15] the Supreme Court held that Congress had exceeded its constitutional authority under the commerce clause when it passed the Gun-Free School Zones Act in 1990. The Court stated that the act, which banned the possession of guns within one thousand feet of any school, was unconstitutional because it attempted to regulate an area that had "nothing to do with commerce, or any sort of economic enterprise." This marked the first time in sixty years that the Supreme Court had placed a limit on the national government's authority under the commerce clause.

In 2000, in *United States v. Morrison*,[16] the Court held that Congress had overreached its authority under the commerce clause when it passed the

INFOTRAC®
COLLEGE EDITION

**States immune suit
Individuals Disabilities
Education Act**

---

[13]New York v. United States, 505 U.S. 144 (1992).
[14]521 U.S. 898 (1997).
[15]514 U.S. 549 (1995).
[16]120 S.Ct. 1740 (2000).

Violence against Women Act in 1994. The Court invalidated a key section of the act that provided a federal remedy for gender-motivated violence, such as rape. The Court noted that in enacting this law Congress had extensively documented that violence against women had an adverse "aggregate" effect on interstate commerce: it deterred potential victims from traveling, from engaging in employment, and from transacting business in interstate commerce. It also diminished national productivity and increased medical and other costs. Nonetheless, the Court held that evidence of an aggregate effect on commerce was not enough to justify national regulation of noneconomic, violent criminal conduct.

State Sovereignty and the Eleventh Amendment.   In its 1999–2000 term, the Supreme Court issued a series of decisions that bolstered the authority of state governments under the Eleventh Amendment to the Constitution. As interpreted by the Court, that amendment precludes lawsuits against state governments for violations of rights established by federal laws unless the states consent to be sued. For example, in a 1999 case, *Alden v. Maine,*[17] the Court held that Maine state employees could not sue the state of Maine for violating the overtime pay requirements of a federal act. According to the Court, state immunity from such lawsuits "is a fundamental aspect of the sovereignty which [the states] enjoyed before the ratification of the Constitution, and which they retain today."

In 2000, in *Kimel v. Florida Board of Regents,*[18] the Court held that the Eleventh Amendment precluded employees of a state university from suing the state to enforce a federal statute prohibiting age-based discrimination. This decision means that although private-sector employees are protected under this federal law, state employees are not.

Federalism: Issues for the Twenty-First Century

The new federalism presumes that state governments should exercise more authority over certain areas that came under national control during the 1930s and subsequent decades. The new federalism, however, has yet to become a reality. Essentially, the issue facing Americans in the twenty-first century is how to deal with the problems that caused the growth of the national government in the first place. Even if the Great Depression had not occurred, we probably still would have witnessed a growth of national-level powers as the country became increasingly populated, industrial, interdependent with other countries, and a world power. With these changes, problems and situations that once were treated locally now have a profound impact on Americans hundreds or even thousands of miles away.

For example, if one state is unable to maintain an adequate highway system, the economy of the entire region may suffer. If another state maintains a substandard educational system, the quality of the work force, the welfare rolls, and the criminal justice agencies in other states may be affected. Environmental pollution does not respect state borders, nor do poverty, crime, and violence. National defense, space exploration, and an increasingly global economy also call for national—not state—action. So the ascendancy of national supremacy had a very logical and very real set of causes. Our more mobile, industrial, and increasingly interdependent nation demanded more uniform and consistent sets

---

[17]527 U.S. 706 (1999).
[18]120 S.Ct. 631 (2000).

of rules, regulations, and governmental programs.

Moreover, cooperative federalism resulted in the growth of a national bureaucracy that became firmly entrenched and that seeks to perpetuate itself (see Chapter 14). The senators and representatives in Congress must heed the wishes of their constituents if they are to retain their positions. They must also heed the wishes of various interest groups (see Chapter 8). Even those groups that vote Republican may pressure Congress to pass national regulatory legislation if such regulation is in the groups' political interest. These political obstacles to the devolutionary goals of the new federalism may be difficult to overcome.

State and local governments also face numerous challenges. State governments have grown in size, as have state populations. As many local governments have realized, state governments find it difficult to create and implement, on a statewide basis, programs that address the diverse needs of different local communities. Indeed, by the late 1990s, many local governments had seized the initiative in dealing with such issues as crime, educational problems, and joblessness. In Chicago, the mayor took over the school system to improve educational performance. The mayor of Milwaukee introduced school vouchers. Mayors in some cities, such as New Orleans, imposed curfews. In the twenty-first century, local governments, along with state governments, may well become significant "laboratories" for experimental new programs and policies.

making a difference

Writing Letters to the Editor

Just about every day an issue concerning federalism is discussed in the media. Advocates of decentralization—a shift of power from federal to state or local governments—argue that we must recognize the rights of states to design their own destinies and master their own fates. Advocates of centralization—more power to the national government—see the shift toward decentralization as undermining the national purpose, common interests, and responsibilities that bind us together in pursuit of national goals.

The big question is how much the national government should do for the people. Is it within the power of the national government to decide what the law should be on abortion? Before 1973, each state set its own laws without interference from the national government. Who should be responsible for the homeless? Should the national government subsidize state and local efforts to help them?

You may have valid, important points to make on these or other issues. One of the best ways to make your point is by writing an effective letter to the editor of your local newspaper (or even to a national newspaper such as the *New York Times*). First, you should familiarize yourself with the kinds of letters that are accepted by the newspapers to which you want to write. Then follow these rules for writing an effective letter:

1. Use a computer, and double-space the lines. If possible, use a spelling checker and grammar checker.

2. Your lead topic sentence should be short, to the point, and powerful.

3. Keep your thoughts on target—choose only one topic to discuss in your letter. Make sure it is newsworthy and timely.

4. Make sure your letter is concise; never let your letter exceed a page and a half in length (double-spaced).

5. If you know that facts were misstated or left out in current news stories about your topic, supply the facts. The public wants to know.

6. Don't be afraid to express moral judgments. You can go a long way by appealing to the readers' sense of justice.

7. Personalize the letter by bringing in your own experiences, if possible.

8. Sign your letter, and give your address (including your e-mail address, if you have one) and your telephone number.

9. Send your letter to the editorial office of the newspaper or magazine of your choice. Virtually all publications now have e-mail addresses and home pages on the Web. The Web sites usually give information on where you can send mail.

10. With appropriate changes, you can send your letter to other newspapers and magazines as well. Make sure, however, that the letters are not exactly the same. If your letter is not published, try again. Eventually, one will be.

Key terms

block grants 104

categorical grants-in-aid 102

commerce clause 97

concurrent powers 92

confederal system 87

cooperative federalism 100

dual federalism 100

elastic clause 90

enumerated powers 90

equalization 102

federal mandate 106

horizontal federalism 96

injunction 97

interstate compact 96

matching funds 102

necessary and proper clause 90

new federalism 104

nullification 99

picket-fence federalism 102

police power 92

secession 99

supremacy clause 93

unitary system 85

Chapter summary

1 There are three basic models for ordering relations between central governments and local units: (a) a unitary system (in which ultimate power is held by the national government), (b) a confederal system (in which ultimate power is retained by the states), and (c) a federal system (in which governmental powers are divided between the national government and the states). A major reason for the creation of a federal system in the United States is that it reflected a compromise between the views of the Federalists (who wanted a strong national government) and those of the Anti-Federalists (who wanted the states to retain their sovereignty), thus making ratification of the Constitution possible.

2 The Constitution expressly delegated certain powers to the national government in Article I, Section 8. In addition to these expressed powers, the national government has implied and inherent powers. Implied powers are those that are reasonably necessary to carry out the powers expressly delegated to the national government. Inherent powers are those held by the national government by virtue of its being a sovereign state with the right to preserve itself.

3 The Tenth Amendment to the Constitution states that powers not delegated to the United States by the Constitution, nor prohibited by it to the states, are reserved to the states, or to the people. In certain areas, the Constitution provides for concurrent powers, such as the power to tax, which are powers that are held jointly by the national and state governments. The Constitution also denies certain powers to both the national government and the states.

4 The supremacy clause of the Constitution states that the Constitution, congressional laws, and national treaties are the supreme law of the land. States cannot use their reserved or concurrent powers to override national policies. Vertical checks and balances allow the states to influence the national government and vice versa.

5 The three most important clauses in the Constitution relating to horizontal federalism require that (a) each state give full faith and credit to every other state's public acts, records, and judicial proceedings; (b) each state extend to every other state's citizens the privileges and immunities of its own citizens; and (c) each state agree to return persons who are fleeing from justice to another state back to their home state when requested to do so.

6 Two landmark Supreme Court cases expanded the constitutional powers of the national government. Chief Justice John Marshall's expansive interpretation of the necessary and proper clause of the Constitution in *McCulloch v. Maryland* (1819) enhanced the implied power of the national government. Marshall's broad interpretation of the commerce clause in *Gibbons v. Ogden* (1824) further extended the constitutional regulatory powers of the national government.

7 At the heart of the controversy that led to the Civil War was the issue of national government supremacy versus the rights of the separate states. The notion of nullification eventually led to the secession of the Confederate states from the Union. But the effect of the South's desire for increased states' rights and the subsequent Civil War was an increase in the political power of the national government.

8 Since the Civil War, federalism has evolved through at least three phases: dual federalism, cooperative federalism, and the new federalism. In dual federalism, each of the states and the federal government remain supreme within their own spheres. The era since the Great Depression has sometimes been labeled one of cooperative federalism, in which states and the national government cooperate in solving complex common problems. Others view it as the beginning of an era of national supremacy, because from the era of Franklin Roosevelt to the present, the national government continually has expanded its regulatory powers and activities.

9 The goal of the *new federalism*, labeled as such by President Nixon, is to decentralize federal programs and return more decision-making authority to the states. A major tool of the new federalism is the block grant, which groups various categorical grants together and gives more authority to the states with respect to the use of federal funds. Curbing unfunded federal mandates is seen as yet another step on the road to a new federalism. The new federalism may take some time to build because of the numerous political obstacles to its implementation.

Selected print and electronic resources

SUGGESTED READINGS

Donahue, John D. *Disunited States*. New York: Basic Books, 1997. The author analyzes current "devolutionary" politics and concludes that devolution may not be in the nation's best interests.

Hamilton, Alexander, James Madison, and John Jay. *The Federalist Papers*. Cambridge, Mass.: Harvard University Press, 1961. These essays remain an authoritative exposition of the founders' views of federalism.

Johnson, Walter. *Soul by Soul: Life inside the Antebellum Slave Market*. Cambridge, Mass.: Harvard University Press, 1999. Slavery, the abolitionist movement, and states' rights principles were intertwined forces leading to the Civil War. In this book, readers are taken inside the New Orleans slave market, the largest in the nation, and shown how 100,000 men, women, and children were packaged, priced, and sold.

Yarbrough, Tinsley E. *The Rehnquist Court and the Constitution*. New York: Oxford University Press, 2000. In this portrait of today's Supreme Court, the author focuses on developing issues, including the Court's use of long-dormant federal principles to curb the national government's authority over the states.

MEDIA RESOURCES

Can the States Do It Better?—A film in which various experts explore the debate over how much power the national government should have and use documentary film footage and other resources to illustrate historical instances of this debate.

Logging on

To learn the founders' views on federalism, you can access *The Federalist Papers* online at

http://www.law.emory.edu/FEDERAL

The following site has links to U.S. state constitutions, *The Federalist Papers,* and international federations, such as the European Union:

http://www.constitution.org/cs_feder.htm

Project Vote Smart's Web site on current issues in American government offers a number of articles on federalism/states' rights. Go to

**http://www.vote-smart.org/issues/
FEDERALISM_STATES_RIGHTS**

The following Web site of the Council of State Governments is a good source for information on state responses to federalism issues:

http://www.statesnews.org

You can find a directory of numerous federalism links at

http://www.gmu.edu

The Brookings Institution's policy analyses and recommendations on a variety of issues, including federalism, can be accessed at

http://www.brook.edu

For a libertarian approach to issues relating to federalism, go to the Cato Institute's Web page at

http://www.cato.org

Using the Internet for political analysis

Almost all state governments have made some part of their organizations and laws available electronically. Use the Internet to compare state issues and policies by pointing your browser to the site maintained by NASIRE, the National Association of State Information Resource Executives:

http://www.nasire.org

Click on StateSearch, and then go to the pages for the Department of Parks or Environmental Resources (the name depends on the state). Compare the hot topics or "What's New" issues of at least two states from different regions of the country. What are the hot issues at the state level? How are those issues unique to that state? Can the state solve the problems alone, or is the issue national in scope? To what extent do you find evidence of national legislation in these state pages?

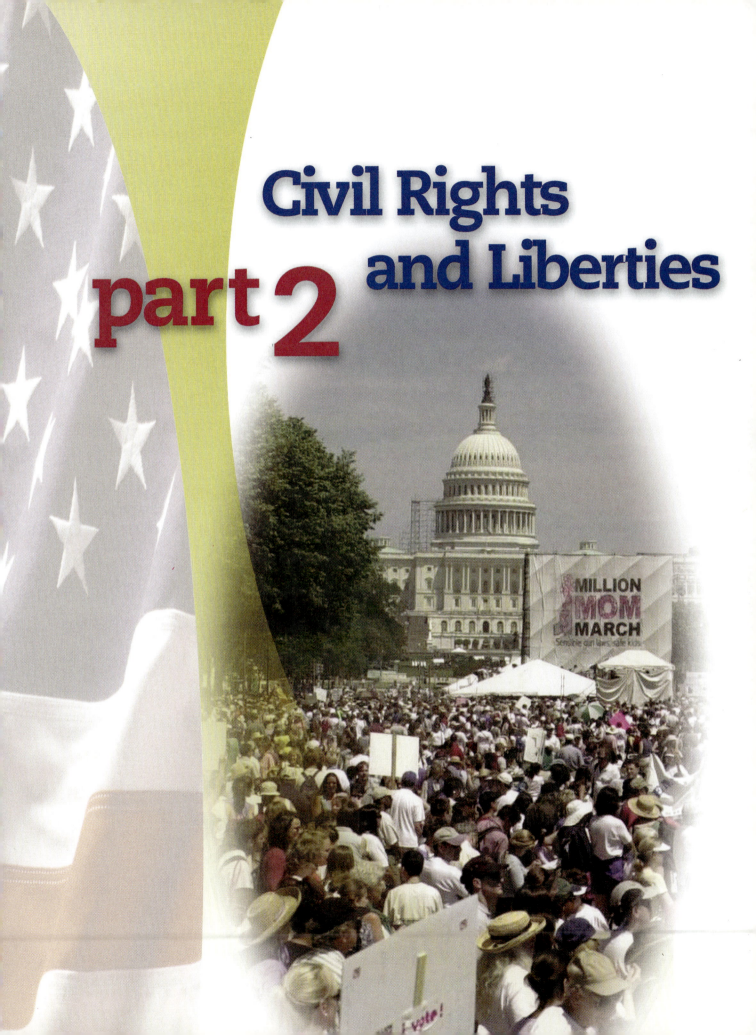

Civil Rights and Liberties

part 2

chapter 4

Civil Liberties

CHAPTER OUTLINE

- Civil Liberties and the Fear of Government

- Extending the Bill of Rights to State Governments

- Freedom of Religion

- Freedom of Expression

- Freedom of the Press

- The Right to Assemble and to Petition the Government

- More Liberties under Scrutiny: Matters of Privacy

- The Great Balancing Act: The Rights of the Accused versus the Rights of Society

what if...

Your Personal Records Were Public?

BACKGROUND

In the past several years, concerns about privacy rights have magnified as more and more personal information about individuals is included in computerized databases, many of which are accessible online. One way to understand the magnitude of the privacy issues raised by computerized databases and the Internet is to imagine what it would be like if there were no privacy. What if anyone, anywhere, at any time could access all of your personal records? How would this affect your life? How would it affect American society generally?

WHAT IF YOUR PERSONAL RECORDS WERE PUBLIC?

Suppose for a moment that all records relating to your personal life—including your bank accounts, tax returns, credit-card bills, medical records, e-mail messages, and investment portfolio—were public. In essence, your life would be an open book. Certainly, crime prevention and detection would be easier. Prosecutors could find out easily if all of your income comes from legitimate sources—such as a salary or dividends on investments. Tax auditors could determine quickly whether you reported all of your income on your tax return. Government investigators could uncover criminal activities and terrorist conspiracies more easily.

At the same time, anyone who wanted to know your income and net worth could find that information in seconds. Direct marketing firms could investigate your spending habits and direct appropriate ads to your mailbox or e-mail address. A prospective employer who is considering you as a candidate for a financial position could easily learn whether you manage your personal finances responsibly. Moreover, someone could easily steal your identity—your Social Security number and credit-card number, for example—and purchase goods under your name, destroy your credit record, and make your life difficult until the matter is straightened out.

A DETERRENT TO PUBLIC SERVICE?

If everyone's personal records were public, the personal lives and activities of government officials could easily be accessed. Citizens and the media could learn about their representative's past history, including the organizations with which they have been affiliated, what they said in e-mail to friends and others, who contributed to their campaigns, and whether they had ever engaged in unethical conduct. This kind of information could help voters decide whether they wanted to support a certain candidate.

At the same time, many good citizens might be deterred from running for public office for fear that some event or activity in their past would be brought to light. For example, a search through a candidate's medical records might reveal past psychiatric consultations or a health condition that the candidate would rather be kept private.

MEDICAL RECORDS

One of the great fears of society today with respect to privacy is that databases containing people's medical records are not sufficiently protected. To understand the reason for this fear, imagine what would happen if medical records were available to the public. Prospective employers could access a job applicant's medical records to learn about the applicant's past and current health status and whether the applicant has a history of alcohol, tobacco, or illegal drug abuse.

Insurance companies could similarly access the health records of insurance applicants to determine their health status and whether they may face significant health risks in the future. For example, suppose that a diagnostic genetic test has shown that the applicant will likely be afflicted with a certain disease in the future. This information could convince the insurance company to tack a significant premium onto the price of the policy for this applicant—or to not insure the applicant at all.

FOR CRITICAL ANALYSIS

1. Suppose that you wanted to run for political office. Would it matter that anyone who wanted to could access your personal records? Would this deter you from running for office?

2. Do you believe, as some people do, that in our wired world privacy is quickly becoming a thing of the past?

Most Americans believe that they have more individual freedom than virtually any other people on earth. For the most part, this opinion is accurate. The freedoms and rights that we take for granted are relatively unknown in some parts of the world. Citizens in many other nations also have few privacy rights—rights that in the United States are among our most prized. Indeed, if the United States suddenly had the same rules, laws, and procedures governing constitutional rights and liberties as some other countries, American jails would be filled overnight with transgressors. Certainly, few people would be discussing privacy rights in hypothetical terms, as we do in the chapter-opening *What If...*, because very likely such rights would not exist.

Civil Liberties and the Fear of Government

Remember from Chapter 2 that to obtain ratification of the Constitution by the necessary nine states, the Federalists had to deal with Americans' fears of a too-powerful national government. The Bill of Rights was the result. These first ten amendments to the U.S. Constitution were passed by Congress on September 25, 1789, and ratified by three-fourths of the states by December 15, 1791. Linked directly to the strong prerevolutionary sentiment for natural rights was the notion that a right was first and foremost a *limitation* on any government's ruling power. Thus, when we speak of **civil liberties** in the United States, we are referring mostly to the specific limitations on government outlined in the Bill of Rights (although there are such limitations in the Constitution's main text itself, including the prohibition against *ex post facto* laws and others found in Section 9 of Article I).

As you read through these chapters, bear in mind that the Bill of Rights, like the rest of the Constitution, is relatively brief. The framers set forth broad guidelines, leaving it up to the courts to interpret these constitutional mandates and apply them to specific situations. Thus, judicial interpretations shape the true nature of the civil liberties and rights that we possess. Because judicial interpretations change over time, so do our liberties and rights. As you will read in the following pages, there have been numerous conflicts over the meaning of such simple phrases as *freedom of religion* and *freedom of the press*. To understand what freedoms we actually have, we need to examine how the courts—and particularly the Supreme Court—have resolved some of those conflicts. One important conflict has to do with whether the national Bill of Rights limited state governments as well as the national government.

Extending the Bill of Rights to State Governments

Most citizens do not realize that, as originally intended, the Bill of Rights limited only the powers of the national government. At the time the Bill of Rights was ratified, there was little concern over the potential of state governments to curb civil liberties. For one thing, state governments were closer to home and easier to control. For another, most state constitutions already had bills of rights. Rather, the fear was of the potential tyranny of the national government. The Bill of Rights begins with the words, "Congress shall make no law . . . ." It says nothing about *states* making laws that might abridge citizens' civil liberties.

State bills of rights were similar to the national one, but there were some differences. Furthermore, each state's judicial system interpreted the rights differently. A citizen in one state, therefore, effectively had a different set of civil

DID YOU KNOW...
That one of the proposed initial constitutional amendments— "No State shall infringe the equal rights of conscience, nor the freedom of speech, nor of the press, nor of the right of trial by jury in criminal cases"— was never sent to the states for approval because the states' rights advocates in the First Congress defeated this proposal?

Civil Liberties
Those personal freedoms that are protected for all individuals and that generally deal with individual freedom. Civil liberties typically involve restraining the government's actions against individuals.

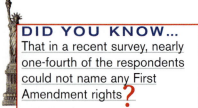

Incorporation Theory
The view that most of the protections of
the Bill of Rights are applied against
state governments through the
Fourteenth Amendment's due process
clause.

rights from a citizen in another state. It was not until after the Fourteenth Amendment was ratified in 1868 that civil liberties guaranteed by the national Constitution began to be applied to the states. Section 1 of that amendment provides, in part, as follows:

No State shall . . . deprive any person of life, liberty, or property, without due process of law.

There was no question that the Fourteenth Amendment applied to state governments. For decades, however, the courts were reluctant to define the liberties spelled out in the national Bill of Rights as constituting "due process of law," which was protected under the Fourteenth Amendment. It was not until 1925, in *Gitlow v. New York*,[1] that the United States Supreme Court held that the Fourteenth Amendment protected the freedom of speech guaranteed by the First Amendment to the Constitution.

Only gradually, and never completely, did the Supreme Court accept the **incorporation theory**—the view that most of the protections of the Bill of Rights are incorporated into the Fourteenth Amendment's protection against state government actions. Table 4–1 shows the rights that the Court has incorporated into the Fourteenth Amendment and the case in which it first applied each protection. As you can see in that table, in the fifteen years following the *Gitlow* decision, the Supreme Court incorporated into the Fourteenth Amendment the other basic freedoms (of the press, assembly, the right to petition, and religion) guaranteed by the First Amendment. These and the later Supreme Court decisions listed in Table 4–1 have bound the fifty states to accept for their respective citizens most of the rights and freedoms that are set forth in the U.S. Bill of Rights. We now look at some of those rights and freedoms, beginning with the freedom of religion.

Freedom of Religion

In the United States, freedom of religion consists of two principal precepts as they are presented in the First Amendment. The first has to do with the separation of church and state, and the second guarantees the free exercise of religion.

---

[1]268 U.S. 652 (1925).

TABLE   4–1

Incorporating the Bill of Rights into the Fourteenth Amendment

Year	Issue	Amendment Involved	Court Case
1925	Freedom of speech	I	*Gitlow v. New York,* 268 U.S. 652.
1931	Freedom of the press	I	*Near v. Minnesota,* 283 U.S. 697.
1932	Right to a lawyer in capital punishment cases	VI	*Powell v. Alabama,* 287 U.S. 45.
1937	Freedom of assembly and right to petition	I	*De Jonge v. Oregon,* 299 U.S. 353.
1940	Freedom of religion	I	*Cantwell v. Connecticut,* 310 U.S. 296.
1947	Separation of state and church	I	*Everson v. Board of Education,* 330 U.S. 1.
1948	Right to a public trial	VI	*In re Oliver,* 333 U.S. 257.
1949	No unreasonable searches and seizures	IV	*Wolf v. Colorado,* 338 U.S. 25.
1961	Exclusionary rule	IV	*Mapp v. Ohio,* 367 U.S. 643.
1962	No cruel and unusual punishment	VIII	*Robinson v. California,* 370 U.S. 660.
1963	Right to a lawyer in all criminal felony cases	VI	*Gideon v. Wainwright,* 372 U.S. 335.
1964	No compulsory self-incrimination	V	*Malloy v. Hogan,* 378 U.S. 1.
1965	Right to privacy	I	*Griswold v. Connecticut,* 381 U.S. 479.
1966	Right to an impartial jury	VI	*Parker v. Gladden,* 385 U.S. 363.
1967	Right to a speedy trial	VI	*Klopfer v. North Carolina,* 386 U.S. 213.
1969	No double jeopardy	V	*Benton v. Maryland,* 395 U.S. 784.

The Separation of Church and State—The Establishment Clause

The First Amendment to the Constitution states, in part, that "Congress shall make no law respecting an establishment of religion." In the words of Thomas Jefferson, the **establishment clause** was designed to create a "wall of separation of Church and State." Perhaps Jefferson was thinking about the religious intolerance that characterized the first colonies. Although many of the American colonies were founded by groups in pursuit of religious freedom, nonetheless they were quite intolerant of religious beliefs that did not conform to those held by the majority of citizens within their own communities. Jefferson undoubtedly was also aware that state religions were the rule; among the original thirteen American colonies, nine of them had official religions.

As interpreted by the Supreme Court, the establishment clause in the First Amendment means at least the following:

> Neither a state nor the federal government can set up a church. Neither can pass laws which aid one religion, aid all religions, or prefer one religion over another. Neither can force nor influence a person to go to or to remain away from church against his will or force him to profess a belief or disbelief in any religion. No person can be punished for entertaining or professing religious beliefs or disbeliefs, for church attendance or nonattendance. No tax in any amount, large or small, can be levied to support any religious activities or institutions, whatever they may be called, or whatever form they may adopt to teach or practice religion. Neither a state nor the federal government can, openly or secretly, participate in the affairs of any religious organizations or groups and vice versa.[2]

The establishment clause covers all conflicts about such matters as the legality of state and local government aid to religious organizations and schools, allowing or requiring school prayers, and the teaching of evolution versus fundamentalist theories of creation.

Aid to Church-Related Schools. Throughout the United States, all property owners except religious, educational, fraternal, literary, scientific, and similar nonprofit institutions must pay property taxes. A large part of the proceeds of such taxes goes to support public schools. But not all school-age children attend public schools. Fully 12 percent attend private schools, of which 85 percent have religious affiliations. Numerous cases have reached the Supreme Court in which the Court has tried to draw a fine line between permissible public aid to students in church-related schools and impermissible public aid to religion.

These issues have arisen most often at the elementary and secondary levels. In a series of cases, the Supreme Court has allowed states to use tax funds for lunches, textbooks, diagnostic services for speech and hearing problems, standardized tests, and transportation for students attending church-operated elementary and secondary schools. In a number of cases, however, the Supreme Court has held state programs helping church-related schools to be unconstitutional. The Court has also denied state reimbursements to religious schools for field trips and for developing achievement tests. (See this chapter's *E-mocracy* on the next page for a discussion of whether public funds can be used to provide all schools, including parochial schools, with computers and Internet links.)

In 1971, in *Lemon v. Kurtzman,*[3] the Court ruled that direct state aid could not be used to subsidize religious instruction. The Court in the *Lemon* case gave

DID YOU KNOW...
That Samuel Argall, governor of Virginia from 1616 to 1618, punished those who failed to attend church with prison terms and forced labor**?**

Establishment Clause
The part of the First Amendment prohibiting the establishment of a church officially supported by the national government. It is applied to questions of state and local government aid to religious organizations and schools, questions of the legality of allowing or requiring school prayers, and questions of the teaching of evolution versus fundamentalist theories of creation.

---

[2]*Everson v. Board of Education,* 330 U.S. 1 (1947).
[3]403 U.S. 602 (1971).

its most general statement on the constitutionality of government aid to religious schools, stating that the aid had to be secular in aim, that it could not have the primary effect of advancing or inhibiting religion, and that the government must avoid "an excessive government entanglement with religion." All laws under the establishment clause are now subject to the three-part *Lemon* test. How the test is applied, however, has varied over the years.

School Vouchers.   Issues concerning the use of public funds for church-related schools are likely to continue as state legislators search for new ways to improve the educational system in this country. An issue that has come to the forefront in recent years has to do with school vouchers. In a voucher system, educational vouchers (state-issued credits) can be used to "purchase" education at any school, public or private.

School districts in several states have been experimenting with voucher systems as a means of improving educational opportunities. The lower courts have reached different conclusions as to the constitutionality of such programs. The Supreme Court, however, has yet to accept for review a case involving a voucher system—or similar programs, such as tax credits, under which public aid is used to defray tuition costs in parochial schools.

The Issue of School Prayer—*Engle v. Vitale.* Do the states have the right to promote religion in general, without making any attempt to establish a particular religion? That is the question in the issue of school prayer and was the precise question presented in 1962 in *Engel v. Vitale,*[4] the so-called Regents' Prayer case in New York. The State Board of Regents of New York had suggested that

----

[4]370 U.S. 421 (1962).

e-mocracy

Technology in the Schools and the Establishment Clause

Federal and state aid to parochial schools has always been controversial. In recent years, it became more so in view of the Clinton administration's plans to link all classrooms, including those in parochial schools, to the Internet. Is it a violation of the establishment clause for the government to provide computers and Internet access to students in parochial schools? This question recently came before the Supreme Court.

At issue in the case was a section of the Educational Consolidation and Improvement Act of 1981. The section allows the federal government to provide special services and instructional equipment to public and private schools, including religious schools. Federal aid to the schools under this act first took the form of textbooks and reference books. Later, the aid was broadened to include computer hardware and software for instructional use, as well as television sets, movie projectors, printers, camcorders, and other types of electronic equipment. Several parents of children attending a public school in Louisiana chal-

lenged the law in court, claiming that it violated the establishment clause. A federal court ruled that the law did not violate the establishment clause. A federal appellate court reversed this decision, and the matter was appealed to the Supreme Court.

Essentially, the question before the Supreme Court turned on whether computers can remain "religiously neutral." During oral argument before the Court in December 1999, the lawyers for the public school parents contended that it would be impossible to tell whether religious schools are using government-provided computers strictly for secular purposes. The lawyer representing the parochial school parents argued that computers can be used for strictly nonreligious purposes. The Supreme Court adopted the latter view and upheld the constitutionality of the act.[*]

FOR CRITICAL ANALYSIS

Would it violate the Constitution if the government discriminated against parochial school students by providing computers and Internet access only to public school students?

[*]*Mitchell v. Helms,* 120 S.Ct. 2530 (2000).

Fundamentalists Vicki Frost and her husband challenged certain textbooks as being too secular and violating their freedom of religion. Other people have argued that public schools cannot teach about religion because that would be a violation of the establishment clause.

a prayer be spoken aloud in the public schools at the beginning of each day. The recommended prayer was as follows:

Almighty God, we acknowledge our dependence upon Thee,
And we beg Thy blessings upon us, our parents, our teachers, and our Country.

Such a prayer was implemented in many New York public schools.

The parents of a number of students challenged the action of the regents, maintaining that it violated the establishment clause of the First Amendment. At trial, the parents lost. The Supreme Court, however, ruled that the regents' action was unconstitutional because "the constitutional prohibition against laws respecting an establishment of a religion must mean at least that in this country it is no part of the business of government to compose official prayers for any group of the American people to recite as part of a religious program carried on by any government." The Court's conclusion was based in part on the "historical fact that governmentally established religions and religious persecutions go hand in hand." In *Abington School District v. Schempp*[5] (1963), the Supreme Court outlawed daily readings of the Bible and recitation of the Lord's Prayer in public schools.

Children pray in school. Such in-school prayer is in violation of Supreme Court rulings based on the First Amendment. A Supreme Court ruling does not necessarily carry with it a mechanism for enforcement everywhere in the United States, however.

The Debate over School Prayer Continues. Although the Supreme Court has ruled repeatedly against officially sponsored prayer and Bible-reading sessions in public schools, other means for bringing some form of religious expression into public education have been attempted. In 1983, the Tennessee legislature passed a bill requiring public school classes to begin each day with a minute of silence. Alabama also had a similar law. In *Wallace v. Jaffree*[6] (1985), the Supreme Court struck down as unconstitutional the Alabama law authorizing one minute of silence in all public schools for prayer or meditation. Applying the three-part *Lemon* test, the Court concluded that the law violated the establishment clause because it was "an endorsement of religion lacking any clearly secular purpose."

Since then, the lower courts have interpreted the Supreme Court's decision to mean that states can require a moment of silence in the schools as long as they make it clear that the purpose of the law is secular, not religious. For example, in 1997, a federal appellate court held that Georgia's "Moment of Quiet Reflection

[5]374 U.S. 203 (1963).
[6]472 U.S. 38 (1985).

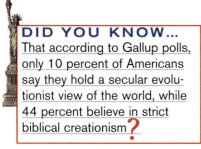

**Teaching Evolution
Kansas High Schools**

in Schools Act" did not violate the establishment clause because the act clearly stated that the moment of silence was "not intended to be and shall not be conducted as a religious service or exercise but shall be considered as an opportunity for a moment of silent reflection on the anticipated activities of the day."[7]

Recently, a number of states have been considering legislation that would allow or require schools to post the Ten Commandments in school buildings. Do such actions violate the establishment clause? Would they do so if the Ten Commandments are part of a display of "historical documents"? For a further discussion of this issue, see this chapter's *Which Side Are You On?*

Prayer outside the Classroom.   The courts have also dealt with cases involving prayer in public schools outside the classroom, particularly prayer during graduation ceremonies. In 1992, in *Lee v. Weisman,*[8] the Supreme Court held that it was unconstitutional for a school to invite a rabbi to deliver a nonsectarian prayer at graduation. The Court said nothing about *students* organizing and leading prayers at graduation ceremonies, however, and since then the lower courts have disagreed on this issue. (See this chapter's *Making Waves* on page 124 for another issue—whether student-led prayers before football games violate the First Amendment.)

Forbidding the Teaching of Evolution.   For many decades, certain religious groups, particularly in the southern states, have opposed the teaching of evolution in the schools. To these groups, evolutionary theory directly counters their religious belief that human beings did not evolve but were created fully formed, as described in the biblical story of the creation. State and local attempts to forbid the teaching of evolution, however, have not passed constitutional muster in the eyes of the United States Supreme Court. For example, in 1968 the Supreme Court held, in *Epperson v. Arkansas,*[9] that an Arkansas law prohibiting the teaching of evolution violated the establishment clause, because it imposed religious beliefs on students. The Louisiana legislature passed a law requiring the teaching of the biblical story of the creation alongside the teaching of evolution. In 1987, in *Edwards v. Aguillard,*[10] the Supreme Court declared that this law was unconstitutional, in part because it had as its primary purpose the promotion of a particular religious belief.

Subsequently, a Louisiana school board required teachers in its district to recite disclaimers that evolution lessons are "not intended to influence or dissuade the Biblical version of Creation or any other concept." In 2000, a federal appellate court held that the disclaimer violated the establishment clause because it was aimed at the "protection and maintenance of a particular religious viewpoint."[11]

Nonetheless, state and local groups around the country, particularly in the so-called Bible Belt, continue their efforts against the teaching of evolution. The Tennessee legislature recently considered a bill that would allow a school to fire any teacher who presents evolution as fact. A proposed amendment to the bill would also protect teachers who want to teach the biblical theories of the creation along with evolution. Alabama has approved a disclaimer to be inserted in biology textbooks, indicating that evolution is "a controversial theory some scientists present as a scientific explanation for the origin of living things." A school district in Georgia adopted a policy that creationism could be taught

[7]*Brown v. Gwinnett County School District,* 112 F.3d 1464 (1997).
[8]505 U.S. 577 (1992).
[9]393 U.S. 97 (1968).
[10]482 U.S. 578 (1987).
[11]*Freiler v. Tangipahoa Parish Board of Education,* 201 F.3d 602 (5th Cir. 2000).

which side are you on?

Should the Ten Commandments Be Displayed in Public Schools?

In February 2000, the Indiana legislature passed a measure that "authorizes the display of the Ten Commandments on real property owned by the state," including public schools. In South Dakota, the state senate passed a bill in March 2000 that permits school districts to allow "any classroom teacher or school administrator" to post "a copy of any religious document or text," including the Ten Commandments. Similar measures are pending in nine other states.

These efforts are, in large part, an outgrowth of the "Hang Ten" project sponsored by the Family Research Council, a conservative religious group. Around the nation, individuals and groups are taking sides in the debate over whether displaying the Ten Commandments in classrooms and other public buildings violates the establishment clause of the First Amendment.

What the Supporters of "Hang Ten" Say

Supporters of the "Hang Ten" project worry that schoolchildren are not being taught the fundamental religious and family values that frame the American way of life. They believe that posting the commandments in classrooms will not harm anyone, and it may help. In the words of South Dakota Democratic senator Jim Lawler, "If kids would just read them from time to time, it couldn't hurt."*

This group also maintains that the Ten Commandments are more than just religious documents. They are also secular in nature because they constitute a part of the official and permanent history of American government. As such, their display does not violate the establishment clause. This was the argument put forth by Kentucky officials when defending displays of the Ten Commandments in several Kentucky county courthouses and school districts. The displays are secular, not religious, in nature, because they also include other historical documents, such as the Mayflower Compact and the Declaration of Independence. In other words, the Ten Commandments are as much a part of American culture as the Declaration of Independence.

What the Opponents Say

Opponents of these laws say that posting the Ten Commandments in public school classrooms is a blatant violation of the First Amendment's establishment clause. Such laws, contend these opponents, mark an unconstitutional government entanglement with the religious life of citizens. The Supreme Court made this clear in its 1980 decision in *Stone v. Graham*.[†] In that case, the Court held

*As quoted in Angie Cannon, "Civics or Religion," *U.S. News & World Report,* February 28, 2000, p. 36.
[†]449 U.S. 39 (1980).

that a Kentucky law requiring that the Ten Commandments be posted in every public school classroom in the state violated the establishment clause.

Interestingly, in *Stone v. Graham,* the Court also addressed the "secular" argument in support of displays including the Ten Commandments. The Court held that even an "avowed" secular purpose is not sufficient to avoid conflict with the First Amendment. The posting of the Ten Commandments, concluded the Court, was "plainly religious in nature."

DOES IT MATTER?

Does it matter whether the Ten Commandments are posted in public schools? Would posting the commandments in public school classrooms have any significant effect on the moral and family values of today's schoolchildren?

GOING ONLINE

For an article discussing Kentucky's defense of that state's current Ten Commandments displays in courthouses and schools, go to the Freedom Forum Online at **http://www.freedom forum.org** *and click on "Religion." For a list of reasons why the Ten Commandments should not be posted in the schools, go to the Web site of Americans United for Separation of Church and State at* **http://www.au.org/pr11499.htm***.*

along with evolution. No doubt, these laws and policies will be challenged on constitutional grounds.

The Supreme Court's "Softened" Approach to Church–State Issues. Some claim that the current Supreme Court is lowering somewhat the barrier between church and state. In 1995, in *Rosenberger v. University of Virginia,*[12] the Court

[12]515 U.S. 819 (1995).

held that the University of Virginia violated the establishment clause when it refused to fund a Christian group's newsletter but granted funds to more than one hundred other student organizations. The Court ruled that the university's policy unconstitutionally discriminated against religious speech. The Court pointed out that the money came from student fees, not general taxes, and was used for the "neutral" payment of bills for student groups. Justice David Souter, who dissented from the majority's conclusion, saw nothing neutral about the Court's decision. He stated, "The Court today, for the first time, approves direct funding of core religious activities by an arm of the state."

The willingness of the Court to accommodate religion was illustrated further in 1997, when the Court decided to review its 1985 decision in *Aguilar v. Felton.*[13] At issue in the *Aguilar* case was the use of federal funds to pay for special educational services for disadvantaged students attending religious schools. The Court held that using federal funds to provide such services on school property violated the establishment clause. When reviewing the *Aguilar* decision in 1997, however, the Court reversed its position. In *Agostini v. Felton,*[14] the Court held that *Aguilar* was "no longer good law." Why? What had happened between 1985 and 1997 to cause the Court to change its mind? Justice Sandra Day O'Connor answered this question in the *Agostini* opinion: What had changed since *Aguilar,* she stated, was "our understanding" of the establishment clause.

These decisions provide striking examples of how constitutional provisions, including the establishment clause, can be interpreted differently by different courts at different times. Note that between 1985 and 1997, the Court's makeup

---

[13]473 U.S. 402 (1985).
[14]521 U.S. 203 (1997).

making waves

Students Lead Football Fans in Prayer—Despite Court Ruling

Prayer and football are both serious business in Texas, and their combination in the fall of 1999, in violation of a federal court ruling, led to equally serious business—before the United States Supreme Court. Joel Allen and Alan Ward, two students at a high school in Stephenville, Texas, knew that the federal appellate court that has jurisdiction over Texas had ruled earlier in the year that students cannot use their school's public address system to lead prayers at sporting events.* The court agreed to allow school prayer at graduation but banned it at football games. In the court's eyes, football games are "hardly the sober type of annual event that can be appropriately solemnized with prayer."

Notwithstanding this ruling, using a public address system, Allen and Ward led the crowd in prayer prior to their school's first football game. "We decided to stand for God and overlook man's laws," said Allen of their decision.[†] They were also following a ninety-year-old tradition in their community of pregame public prayer.

The appellate court's ruling was among a series of conflicting federal court decisions on school prayer. For example, in July 1999, another appellate court ruled that an Alabama school district could not ban student-initiated prayer at school activities, even when attendance is mandatory.[‡] To settle the conflict in the lower courts, the Supreme Court decided to review the Texas case. In July 2000, the Court ruled that public pregame prayers violated the establishment clause of the Constitution. Despite the Court's decision, the controversy over prayer in the schools, including pregame prayers, is unlikely to go away anytime soon.[§]

FOR CRITICAL ANALYSIS

If the government prohibits all forms of religious expression in school, is the government essentially fostering atheism?

[†]As quoted in Robert Bryce, "To Pray—Or Not to Pray," *U.S. News & World Report,* September 13, 1999, p. 26.
[‡]*Chandler v. James,* 180 F.3d 1254 (11th Cir. 1999).
[§]*Santa Fe Independent School District v. Doe,* 120 S.Ct. 2266 (2000).

Doe v. Santa Fe Independent School District, 168 F.3d 806 (5th Cir. 1999).

Here, a group of Hare Krishna adherents are crossing a street singing and playing drums and cymbals. This unfettered expression of their religious belief, and even the proselytization of their faith, is protected by the Constitution. Airport authorities, however, have been allowed to place physical restrictions on Hare Krishna groups to prevent them from approaching travelers. Often, they must stay behind a counter or other structure and not initiate contact with travelers unless invited to do so.

had changed considerably. In fact, six of the nine justices who participated in the 1997 decision were appointed *after* the 1985 decision.

The Free Exercise Clause

The First Amendment constrains Congress from prohibiting the free exercise of religion. Does this **free exercise clause** mean that no type of religious practice can be prohibited or restricted by government? Certainly, a person can hold any religious belief that he or she wants; or a person can have no religious belief. When, however, religious *practices* work against public policy and the public welfare, the government can act. For example, regardless of a child's or parent's religious beliefs, the government can require certain types of vaccinations. Additionally, public school students can be required to study from textbooks chosen by school authorities.

Free Exercise Clause
The provision of the First Amendment guaranteeing the free exercise of religion.

The extent to which government can regulate religious practices always has been subject to controversy. For example, in 1990, in *Oregon v. Smith*,[15] the Supreme Court ruled that the state of Oregon could deny unemployment benefits to two drug counselors who had been fired for using peyote, an illegal drug, in their religious services. The counselors had argued that using peyote was part of the practice of a Native American religion. Many criticized the decision as going too far in the direction of regulating religious practices.

In 1993, Congress responded to the public's criticism by passing the Religious Freedom Restoration Act (RFRA). One of the specific purposes of the act was to overturn the Supreme Court's decision in *Oregon v. Smith*. The act required national, state, and local governments to "accommodate religious conduct" unless the government could show that there was a *compelling* reason not to do so. Moreover, if the government did regulate a religious practice, it had to use the least restrictive means possible.

---

[15]494 U.S. 872 (1990).

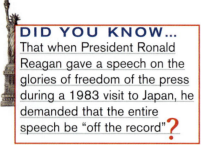

Many people felt that the RFRA went too far in the other direction—it accommodated practices that were contrary to the public policies of state governments. Proponents of states' rights complained that the act intruded into an area traditionally governed by state laws, not the national government. In 1997, in *City of Boerne v. Flores*,[16] the Supreme Court agreed and held that Congress had exceeded its constitutional authority when it passed the RFRA. According to the Court, the act's "sweeping coverage ensures its intrusion at every level of government, displacing laws and prohibiting official actions of almost every description and regardless of subject matter."

Freedom of Expression

Perhaps the most frequently invoked freedom that Americans have is the right to free speech and a free press without government interference. Each of us has the right to have our say, and all of us have the right to hear what others say. For the most part, Americans can criticize public officials and their actions without fear of reprisal or imprisonment by any branch of our government.

Permitted Restrictions on Expression

At various times, restrictions on expression have been permitted. A description of several such restrictions follows.

Clear and Present Danger.   When a person's remarks present a clear and present danger to the peace or public order, they can be curtailed constitutionally. Justice Oliver Wendell Holmes used this reasoning in 1919 when examining the case of a socialist who had been convicted for violating the Espionage Act. Holmes stated:

> The question in every case is whether the words are used in such circumstances and are of such a nature as to create a *clear and present danger* that they will bring about the substantive evils that Congress has a right to prevent. It is a question of proximity and degree. [Emphasis added.][17]

Clear and Present Danger Test
The test proposed by Justice Holmes for determining when government may restrict free speech. Restrictions are permissible, he argued, only when speech presents a "clear and present danger" to the public order.

Thus, according to the **clear and present danger test,** expression may be restricted if evidence exists that such expression would cause a condition, actual or imminent, that Congress has the power to prevent. Commenting on this test, Justice Louis D. Brandeis in 1920 said, "Correctly applied, it will reserve the right of free speech . . . from suppression by tyrannists, well-meaning majorities, and from abuse by irresponsible, fanatical minorities."[18]

The Supreme Court modified the clear and present danger test in a 1951 case, *Dennis v. United States*.[19] At the time, there was considerable tension between the United States and the Soviet Union. The Soviet Union's government was run by the Communist Party. Twelve members of the American Communist Party were convicted of violating a statute that made it a crime to conspire to teach, advocate, or organize the violent overthrow of any government in the United States. The Supreme Court affirmed the convictions, significantly modifying the clear and present danger test in the process. The Court applied a "grave and probable danger rule." Under this rule, "the gravity of the 'evil' discounted by its improbability justifies such invasion of free speech as is necessary to avoid the danger." This rule gave much less protection to free speech than did the clear and present danger test.

INFOTRAC ®
COLLEGE EDITION

Net Endangers Basic American Liberty

---

[16]521 U.S. 507 (1997).
[17]*Schenck v. United States,* 249 U.S. 47 (1919).
[18]*Schaefer v. United States,* 251 U.S. 466 (1920).
[19]341 U.S. 494 (1951).

The Bad-Tendency Rule.   According to the **bad-tendency rule,** speech or other First Amendment freedoms may be curtailed if there is a possibility that such expression might lead to some "evil." In *Gitlow v. New York,*[20] a member of a left-wing group was convicted of violating New York state's criminal anarchy statute when he published and distributed a pamphlet urging the violent over-throw of the U.S. government. In its majority opinion, the Supreme Court held that although the First Amendment afforded protection against state incursions on freedom of expression, Gitlow could be punished legally in this particular instance because his expression would tend to bring about evils that the state had a right to prevent.

No Prior Restraint.   Restraining an activity before that activity has actually occurred is referred to as **prior restraint.** It involves censorship, as opposed to subsequent punishment. Prior restraint of expression would require, for exam-ple, a permit before a speech could be made, a newspaper published, or a movie or TV show exhibited. Most, if not all, Supreme Court justices have been espe-cially critical of any governmental action that imposes prior restraint on expres-sion. The Court clearly expressed this attitude in *Nebraska Press Association v. Stuart,*[21] a case decided in 1976:

> A prior restraint on expression comes to this Court with a "heavy presumption" against its constitutionality. . . . The government thus carries a heavy burden of showing justification for the enforcement of such a restraint.

One of the most famous cases concerning prior restraint was *New York Times v. United States*[22] (1971), the so-called Pentagon Papers case. The *Times* and the *Washington Post* were about to publish the Pentagon Papers, an elaborate secret history of the U.S. government's involvement in the Vietnam War (1964–1975). The secret documents had been obtained illegally by a disillusioned former Pentagon official. The government wanted a court order to bar publication of the documents, arguing that national security was being threatened and that the documents had been stolen. The newspapers argued that the public had a right to know the information contained in the papers and that the press had the right to inform the public. The Supreme Court ruled six to three in favor of the news-papers' right to publish the information. This case affirmed the no prior restraint doctrine.

Typically, prior restraints have been associated with the press. Recently, though, the California Supreme Court issued a ruling that, according to some commentators, amounts to prior restraint in the workplace. The case involved several Hispanic employees who claimed that their supervisor's insults and racist comments had created a hostile work environment. The lower court agreed and awarded damages to the employees. In upholding the ruling, the California Supreme Court took the bold step of issuing a list of offensive words that can no longer be used in any workplace in the state, even among Hispanic Americans themselves. Three justices harshly dissented from the majority opinion, referring to it as "the exception that swallowed the First Amendment."[23] Several media commentators and legal scholars were also astonished at what they referred to as the court's "assault on the First Amendment."[24]

Bad-Tendency Rule
A rule stating that speech or other First Amendment freedoms may be curtailed if there is a possibility that such expres-sion might lead to some "evil."

Prior Restraint
Restraining an action before the activity has actually occurred. It involves cen-sorship, as opposed to subsequent punishment.

---

[20]268 U.S. 652 (1925).
[21]427 U.S. 539 (1976). See also *Near v. Minnesota,* 283 U.S. 697 (1931).
[22]403 U.S. 713 (1971).
[23]*Aguilar v. Avis Rent A Car System,* 21 Cal.4th 121 (1999).
[24]See, for example, Greg Mitchell, "California Court Upholds Hate Speech Gag," *The National Law Journal,* August 16, 1999, p. A6; and John Leo, "Watch What You Say," *U.S. News & World Report,* March 20, 2000, p. 18.

These protesters are burning an American flag as a symbolic expression of their opposition to government policy. Would a constitutional amendment to prohibit such actions place unacceptable limitations on symbolic speech?

Symbolic Speech
Nonverbal expression of beliefs, which is given substantial protection by the courts.

Commercial Speech
Advertising statements, which increasingly have been given First Amendment protection.

The Protection of Symbolic Speech

Not all expression is in words or in writing. Gestures, movements, articles of clothing, and other forms of expressive conduct are considered **symbolic speech.** Such speech is given substantial protection today by our courts. For example, in a landmark decision issued in 1969, *Tinker v. Des Moines School District,*[25] the Supreme Court held that the wearing of black armbands by students in protest against the Vietnam War was a form of speech protected by the First Amendment. The case arose after a school administrator in Des Moines, Iowa, issued a regulation prohibiting students in the Des Moines School District from wearing the armbands. The Supreme Court reasoned that the school district was unable to show that the wearing of the armbands had disrupted normal school activities. Furthermore, the school district's policy was discriminatory, as it banned only certain forms of symbolic speech (the black armbands) and not others (such as lapel crosses and fraternity rings).

In 1989, in *Texas v. Johnson,*[26] the Supreme Court ruled that state laws that prohibited the burning of the American flag as part of a peaceful protest also violated the freedom of expression protected by the First Amendment. Congress responded by passing the Flag Protection Act of 1989, which was ruled unconstitutional by the Supreme Court in June 1990.[27] Congress and President Bush immediately pledged to work for a constitutional amendment to "protect our flag"—an effort that has yet to be successful.

In *R.A.V. v. City of St. Paul, Minnesota*[28] (1992), the Supreme Court ruled that a city statute banning bias-motivated disorderly conduct (in this case, the placing of a burning cross in another's front yard as a gesture of hate) was an unconstitutional restriction of speech. Freedom of speech can also apply to group-sponsored events. In 1995, the Supreme Court held that forcing the organizers of Boston's St. Patrick's Day parade to include gays and lesbians violated the organizers' freedom of speech.[29]

The Protection of Commercial Speech

Commercial speech is usually defined as advertising statements. Can advertisers use their First Amendment rights to prevent restrictions on the content of commercial advertising? Until the 1970s, the Supreme Court held that such speech was not protected at all by the First Amendment. By the mid-1970s, however, more and more commercial speech was brought under First Amendment protection. According to Justice Harry A. Blackmun, "Advertising, however tasteless and excessive it sometimes may seem, is nonetheless dissemination of information as to who is producing and selling what product for what reason and at what price."[30] Generally, the Supreme Court will consider a restriction on commercial speech valid as long as it (1) seeks to implement a substantial government interest, (2) directly advances that interest, and (3) goes no further than necessary to accomplish its objective.

Unprotected Speech: Obscenity

Numerous state and federal statutes make it a crime to disseminate obscene materials. Generally, the courts have not been willing to extend constitutional

---

[25]393 U.S. 503 (1969).
[26]488 U.S. 884 (1989).
[27]*United States v. Eichman,* 496 U.S. 310 (1990).
[28]505 U.S. 377 (1992).
[29]*Hurley v. Irish-American Gay, Lesbian and Bisexual Group of Boston,* 515 U.S. 557 (1995).
[30]*Virginia State Board of Pharmacy v. Virginia Citizens Consumer Council, Inc.,* 425 U.S. 748 (1976).

protections of free speech to what they consider obscene materials. But what is obscenity? Justice Potter Stewart once stated, in *Jacobellis v. Ohio,*[31] a 1964 case, that even though he could not define obscenity, "I know it when I see it." The problem, of course, is that even if it were agreed on, the definition of obscenity changes with the times. Victorians deeply disapproved of the "loose" morals of the Elizabethan Age. The works of Mark Twain and Edgar Rice Burroughs have at times been considered obscene (after all, Tarzan and Jane were not legally wedded).

Definitional Problems. The Supreme Court has grappled from time to time with the problem of specifying an operationally effective definition of obscenity. In 1973, in *Miller v. California,*[32] Chief Justice Warren Burger created a formal list of requirements that currently must be met for material to be legally obscene. Material is obscene if (1) the average person finds that it violates contemporary community standards; (2) the work taken as a whole appeals to a prurient interest in sex; (3) the work shows patently offensive sexual conduct; and (4) the work lacks serious redeeming literary, artistic, political, or scientific merit. The problem, of course, is that one person's prurient interest is another person's medical interest or artistic pleasure. The Court went on to state that the definition of prurient interest would be determined by the community's standards. The Court avoided presenting a definition of obscenity, leaving this determination to local and state authorities. Consequently, the *Miller* case has had widely inconsistent applications.

Protecting Children. In regard to child pornography, the Supreme Court has upheld state laws making it illegal to sell materials showing sexual performances by minors. In 1990, in *Osborne v. Ohio,*[33] the Court ruled that states can outlaw the possession of child pornography in the home. The Court reasoned that the ban on private possession is justified because owning the material perpetuates commercial demand for it and for the exploitation of the children involved.

Pornography on the Internet. Public concern over access to pornographic materials via the Internet led Congress to enact the Communications Decency Act of 1996. The act imposed criminal penalties on those who made "indecent" materials available online to persons under the age of eighteen. In 1997, however, in *Reno v. American Civil Liberties Union,*[34] the Supreme Court held that the act was unconstitutional because it restrained too much protected adult speech. In 1998, Congress made another attempt to regulate the Internet by passing the Child Online Protection Act. This act, which was popularly referred to as "CDA II," made it a crime to make available online any material that is "harmful to minors" unless an age-verification system was used so that minor users could be separated from adult users. Like the 1996 CDA, the 1998 act was immediately blocked in court.[35] A basic problem with any attempt to regulate obscene speech on the Internet is that there are no "community standards" in that medium.

Unprotected Speech: Slander

Can you say anything you want about someone else? Not really. Individuals are protected from **defamation of character**, which is defined as wrongfully hurting a person's good reputation. The law has imposed a general duty on all persons

[31]378 U.S. 184 (1964).
[32]413 U.S. 5 (1973).
[33]495 U.S. 103 (1990).
[34]521 U.S. 844 (1997).
[35]*American Civil Liberties Union v. Reno,* 31 F.Supp.2d 473 (E.D.Pa. 1999).

DID YOU KNOW...
That a local newspaper in Winchester, Indiana, refused to print a proposed antipornography ordinance because the newspaper considered the language of the ordinance too "obscene" to print?

Defamation of Character
Wrongfully hurting a person's good reputation. The law has imposed a general duty on all persons to refrain from making false, defamatory statements about others.

Slander
The public uttering of a false statement that harms the good reputation of another. The statement must be made to, or within the hearing of, persons other than the defamed party.

to refrain from making false, defamatory statements about others. Breaching this duty orally involves the wrongdoing called **slander.** (Breaching it in writing involves the wrongdoing called *libel,* which is discussed later.)

Legally, slander is the public uttering of a false statement that harms the good reputation of another. Slanderous public uttering means that the defamatory statements are made to, or within the hearing of, persons other than the defamed party. If one person calls another dishonest, manipulative, and incompetent when no one else is around, that does not constitute slander. The message is not communicated to a third party. If, however, a third party accidentally overhears defamatory statements, the courts have generally held that this constitutes a public uttering and therefore slander, which is prohibited.

Fighting Words and Hecklers' Veto

Fighting Words
Words that, when uttered by a public speaker, are so inflammatory that they could provoke the average listener to violence; the words are usually of a racial, religious, or ethnic type.

Hecklers' Veto
Boisterous and generally disruptive behavior by listeners to public speakers that, in effect, vetoes the public speakers' right to speak.

The Supreme Court has prohibited types of speech that tend to incite an immediate breach of peace. For example, public speakers may not use **fighting words.** These may include racial, religious, or ethnic slurs that are so inflammatory that they will provoke the "average" listener to fight. Members of a crowd listening to a speech are prohibited from exercising a **hecklers' veto.** The boisterous and disruptive behavior of hecklers poses the threat of disruption or violence, so hecklers are vetoing the essential rights of the speaker.

Campus Speech Codes

In recent years, students have been facing free speech challenges on campuses. One issue has to do with whether a student should have to subsidize, through student activity fees, organizations that promote causes that the student finds objectionable (see this chapter's *An Ethical Issue* for further information on this issue). Another free speech issue relates to campus speech and behavior codes. Some state universities have challenged the boundaries of the protection of free speech provided by the First Amendment with the issuance of such codes. These codes are designed to prohibit so-called hate speech—abusive speech attacking persons on the basis of their ethnicity, race, or other criteria. For example, a University of Michigan code banned "any behavior, verbal or physical, that stigmatizes or victimizes an individual on the basis of race, ethnicity, religion, sex, sexual orientation, creed, national origin, ancestry, age, marital status, handicap" or Vietnam-veteran status. A federal court found that the code violated students' First Amendment rights.[36]

Although the courts generally have held, as in the University of Michigan case, that campus speech codes are unconstitutional restrictions on the right to free speech, such codes continue to exist. For example, the University of North Dakota's code of conduct prohibits speech "intentionally producing psychological discomfort." The University of Minnesota bans speech that shows "insensitivity to the experiences of women." West Virginia University bans speech exhibiting "feelings" about gays that evolve into "attitudes." The University of Connecticut bans "inconsiderate jokes," while Colby College in Waterville, Maine, bans any speech that causes a loss of "self-esteem or a vague sense of danger."[37]

Defenders of such constraints on speech argue that they are necessary not only to prevent violence but also to promote equality among different cultural, ethnic, and racial groups on campus and greater sensitivity to the needs and

[36]*Doe v. University of Michigan,* 721 F.Supp. 852 (1989).
[37]For other examples, see Alan Charles Kors and Harvey Silverglate, *The Shadow University* (New York: HarperCollins, 1999).

feelings of others. Critics worry that campus censorship is fostering the idea that only "good" speech (as defined by the liberal agenda) should be protected by the First Amendment, while "bad" speech (speech opposing that agenda) should be punished.

Hate Speech on the Internet

Campus speech and behavior codes raise a controversial issue: whether rights to free speech can (or should) be traded off to reduce violence in America. This issue extends to hate speech transmitted on the Internet as well, which is a growing concern for many Americans. Those who know how to navigate the online world can find information on virtually any topic, from how to build bombs to how to wage war against the government. Here again, the issue is whether free speech on the Internet should be restrained in the interests of protecting against violence.

Should Students Have to Subsidize Opposing Views?

Should college students have to pay activity fees to support political and social causes with which they do not agree? This question has been raised by students at a number of universities in the last several years. For example, some students at the University of California at Berkeley challenged the use of their student fees to pay for political campaigns to legalize marijuana and to mandate government funding of abortions. Students at the State University of New York claim that they have been forced to pay, through student fees, for lobbying for disarmament and a nuclear arms freeze—which they did not support. At issue in these and similar cases is whether students' free speech rights are being violated.

THE PROS AND CONS OF THE DEBATE

Some claim that using student fees in ways students do not approve violates their free speech rights. Moreover, such uses of student fees force individuals to violate their own consciences with regard to such emotionally charged issues as abortion and homosexuality. They also undermine the educational mission of universities by devaluing the important democratic principles of individualism, dissent, and freedom of speech.

Others, including university administrators and targeted campus groups, argue that a university is a marketplace of ideas. They claim that the use of student fees to fund activities across the political spectrum gives students the opportunity to explore a wide range of ideas and issues. Moreover, if taken to its logical extreme, the idea of permitting students to subsidize only those organizations that meet with their approval ultimately would lead to insufficient funding for many activities and groups on campus—childless students could withhold the portion of their fees that funds child-care activities; Caucasians could withhold fees that support minority groups and vice versa.

THE *SOUTHWORTH* CASE

Because the lower courts arrived at conflicting conclusions on this issue, the Supreme Court addressed the issue in a case brought by Scott Southworth and other students of the University of Wisconsin against the university's board of regents. The students alleged that their mandatory student activity fees—which helped to fund liberal causes with which they disagreed, including gay rights—violated their First Amendment rights of free speech, free association, and free exercise of religion. They argued that they should have the right to choose whether to fund organizations that promoted political and ideological views that were offensive to their personal beliefs.

To the surprise of many, the Supreme Court rejected the students' claim and ruled in favor of the university. The Court stated that "the university may determine that its mission is well served if students have the means to engage in dynamic discussions of philosophical, religious, scientific, social and political subjects in their extracurricular life. If the university reaches this conclusion, it is entitled to impose a mandatory fee to sustain an open dialogue to these ends."*

The Supreme Court's decisions on constitutional issues are final, so the matter is legally resolved—at least for a time. Future Supreme Court justices may view the matter differently. In the meantime, many disagree with the Court's conclusion, so the debate over the proper use of student fees will likely continue for some time to come.

FOR CRITICAL ANALYSIS

"Just as taxpayers should not expect a tax refund when a group with opposing ideas demonstrates in a public square, so students should not expect to be able to opt out of paying for a public forum on campus." Do you agree with this statement? Why or why not?

*Board of Regents of the University of Wisconsin System v. Southworth, 120 S.Ct. 1346 (2000).

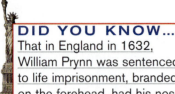

At least one federal court has held that "hate speech" on the Internet is a criminal violation. That case, decided in 1998, involved an engineering student, Richard Machado, who had been attending the University of California's Irvine campus. After being expelled from the university for low grades, Machado sent e-mail messages to some sixty Asian students in which he threatened to "hunt down and kill" them. He was charged under a 1968 act making it a crime to interfere with federally protected activities, such as voting or attending a public school. The jury found that his actions violated that act.

Freedom of the Press

Freedom of the press can be regarded as a special instance of freedom of speech. Of course, at the time of the framing of the Constitution, the press meant only newspapers, magazines, and perhaps pamphlets. As technology has modified the ways in which we disseminate information, the laws touching on freedom of the press been modified. What can and cannot be printed still occupies an important place in constitutional law, however.

Defamation in Writing

Libel

A written defamation of a person's character, reputation, business, or property rights. To a limited degree, the First Amendment protects the press from libel actions.

Libel is defamation in writing (or in pictures, signs, or films, or any other communication that has the potentially harmful qualities of written or printed words). As with slander, libel occurs only if the defamatory statements are observed by a third party. If one person writes another a private letter wrongfully accusing him or her of embezzling funds, that does not constitute libel. It is interesting that the courts have generally held that dictating a letter to a secretary constitutes communication of the letter's contents to a third party, and therefore, if defamation has occurred, the wrongdoer can be sued.

Newspapers are often involved in libel suits. *New York Times Co. v. Sullivan*[38] (1964) explored an important question about libelous statements made about **public figures**—public officials and employees who exercise substantial governmental power, as well as any persons who are generally in the public limelight. The Supreme Court held that only when a statement was made with **actual malice**—that is, with either knowledge of its falsity or a reckless disregard of the truth—against a public official could damages be obtained.

Public Figures

Public officials, movie stars, and generally all persons who become known to the public because of their positions or activities.

Actual Malice

Actual malice in libel cases generally consists of intentionally publishing any written or printed statement that is injurious to the character of another with either knowledge of the statement's falsity or a reckless disregard for the truth.

The standard set by the Court in the *New York Times* case has since been applied to public figures generally. Statements made about public figures, especially when they are made via a public medium, are usually related to matters of general public interest; they are made about people who substantially affect all of us. Furthermore, public figures generally have some access to a public medium for answering disparaging falsehoods about themselves, whereas private individuals do not. For these reasons, public figures have a greater burden of proof (they must prove that the statements were made with actual malice) in defamation cases than do private individuals.

A Free Press versus a Fair Trial: Gag Orders

Another major issue relating to freedom of the press concerns media coverage of criminal trials. The Sixth Amendment to the Constitution guarantees the right of criminal suspects to a fair trial. In other words, the accused have rights. The First Amendment guarantees freedom of the press. What if the two rights appear to be in conflict? Which one prevails?

---

[38]376 U.S. 254 (1964).

Jurors certainly may be influenced by reading news stories about the trial in which they are participating. In the 1970s, judges increasingly issued **gag orders,** which restricted the publication of news about a trial in progress or even a pretrial hearing. In a landmark 1976 case, *Nebraska Press Association v. Stuart,*[39] the Supreme Court unanimously ruled that a Nebraska judge's gag order had violated the First Amendment's guarantee of freedom of the press. Chief Justice Warren Burger indicated that even pervasive adverse pretrial publicity did not necessarily lead to an unfair trial and that prior restraints on publication were not justified. Some justices even went so far as to indicate that gag orders are never justified.

In spite of the *Nebraska Press Association* ruling, the Court has upheld certain types of gag orders. In *Gannett Company v. De Pasquale*[40] (1979), for example, the highest court held that if a judge found a reasonable probability that news publicity would harm a defendant's right to a fair trial, the court could impose a gag rule: "Members of the public have no constitutional right under the Sixth and Fourteenth Amendments to *attend* criminal trials."

The *Nebraska* and *Gannett* cases, however, involved pretrial hearings. Could a judge impose a gag order on an entire trial, including pretrial hearings? In *Richmond Newspapers, Inc. v. Virginia*[41] (1980), the Court ruled that actual trials must be open to the public except under unusual circumstances.

Films, Radio, and TV

As was noted, only in a few cases has the Supreme Court upheld prior restraint of published materials. The Court's reluctance to accept prior restraint is less evident with respect to motion pictures. In the first half of the twentieth century, films were routinely submitted to local censorship boards. In 1968, the Supreme Court ruled that a film can be banned only under a law that provides for a prompt hearing at which the film is shown to be obscene. Today, few local censorship boards exist. Instead, the film industry regulates itself primarily through the industry's rating system.

---

[39]427 U.S. 539 (1976).
[40]443 U.S. 368 (1979).
[41]448 U.S. 555 (1980).

Gag Order
An order issued by a judge restricting the publication of news about a trial in progress or a pretrial hearing in order to protect the accused's right to a fair trial.

Radio "shock jock" Howard Stern apparently offended the sensitivities of the Federal Communications Commission (FCC). That regulatory body fined Stern's radio station owner hundreds of thousands of dollars for Stern's purportedly obscene outbursts on radio. The extent to which the FCC can regulate speech over the air involves the First Amendment. What is considered permissible and acceptable on radio and TV today probably would have been considered "obscene" three decades ago.

Equal Time Rule

A Federal Communications Commission regulation that requires broadcasting stations that give or sell air time to political candidates to make equal amounts of time available to all competing candidates.

Personal Attack Rule

A Federal Communications Commission regulation that requires broadcasting stations, if the stations are used to attack the honesty or integrity of persons, to allow the persons attacked the fullest opportunity to respond.

Radio and television broadcasting has the most limited First Amendment protection. Broadcasting initially received less protection than the printed media because, at that time, the number of airwave frequencies was limited.

In 1934, the national government established the Federal Communications Commission (FCC) to regulate electromagnetic wave frequencies. No one has a right to use the airwaves without a license granted by the FCC. The FCC grants licenses for limited periods and imposes numerous regulations on broadcasting. One of these regulations, called the **equal time rule,** requires any station that gives or sells airtime to a political candidate to make an equal amount of time available for purchase to all competing candidates. Another rule, sometimes referred to as the **personal attack rule,** provides that if a radio or television station is used to attack the honesty or integrity of a person, the station must see to it that the person attacked is afforded the fullest opportunity to respond. The FCC can also impose sanctions on radio or TV stations that broadcast "filthy words," even if the words are not legally obscene.

The Right to Assemble and to Petition the Government

The First Amendment prohibits Congress from making any law that abridges "the right of the people peaceably to assemble and to petition the Government for a redress of grievances." Inherent in such a right is the ability of private citizens to communicate their ideas on public issues to government officials, as well as to other individuals. The Supreme Court has often put this freedom on a par with the freedom of speech and the freedom of the press. Nonetheless, it has allowed municipalities to require permits for parades, sound trucks, and demonstrations, so that public officials may control traffic or prevent demonstrations from turning into riots.

This became a major issue in 1977 when the American Nazi Party wanted to march through the largely Jewish suburb of Skokie, Illinois. The American Civil Liberties Union defended the Nazis' right to march (in spite of its opposition to the Nazi philosophy). The Supreme Court let stand a lower court's ruling that the

With their right to assemble and demonstrate protected by the Constitution, members of the modern Ku Klux Klan march in Wilmington, North Carolina. The police escort is charged with making sure that neither the marchers nor the observers provoke any violence.

city of Skokie had violated the Nazis' First Amendment guarantees by denying them a permit to march.[42]

An issue that has surfaced in recent years is whether communities can prevent gang members from gathering together on the streets without violating their right of assembly or associated rights. Although some actions taken by cities to prevent gang members from gathering together or "loitering" in public places have passed constitutional muster, others have not. For example, in a 1997 case, the California Supreme Court upheld a lower court's order preventing gang members from appearing in public together.[43] In 1999, the United States Supreme Court held that Chicago's "anti-loitering" ordinance violated the constitutional right to due process of law because, among other things, it left too much power to the police to determine what constituted "loitering."[44]

More Liberties under Scrutiny: Matters of Privacy

No explicit reference is made anywhere in the Constitution to a person's right to privacy. The courts did not take a very positive approach toward the right to privacy until relatively recently. For example, during Prohibition, suspected bootleggers' telephones were routinely tapped, and the information obtained was used as a legal basis for prosecution. In *Olmstead v. United States*[45] (1928), the Supreme Court upheld such an invasion of privacy. Justice Louis Brandeis, a champion of personal freedoms, strongly dissented from the majority decision in this case. He argued that the framers of the Constitution gave every citizen the right to be left alone. He called such a right "the most comprehensive of rights and the right most valued by civilized men."

In the 1960s, the highest court began to modify the majority view. In 1965, in *Griswold v. Connecticut*,[46] the Supreme Court overthrew a Connecticut law that effectively prohibited the use of contraceptives, holding that the law violated the right to privacy. Justice William O. Douglas formulated a unique way of reading this right into the Bill of Rights. He claimed that the First, Third, Fourth, Fifth, and Ninth Amendments created "penumbras, formed by emanations from those guarantees that help give them life and substance," and he went on to talk about zones of privacy that are guaranteed by these rights. When we read the Ninth Amendment, we can see the foundation for his reasoning: "The enumeration in the Constitution of certain rights, shall not be construed to deny or disparage others retained by the people." In other words, just because the Constitution, including its amendments, does not specifically talk about the right to privacy does not mean that this right is denied to the people.

Some of today's most controversial issues relate to privacy rights. One of these issues has to do with the protection of privacy rights in today's information age. Other privacy issues concern abortion and the "right to die." (Another important privacy issue has to do with sexual preferences—a topic we examine in Chapter 6 in the context of civil rights.)

Privacy Rights in an Information Age

An important privacy issue, created in part by new technology, is the amassing of information on individuals by government agencies and private businesses,

---

[42]*Smith v. Collin,* 439 U.S. 916 (1978).
[43]*Gallo v. Acuna,* 14 Cal.4th 1090 (1997).
[44]*City of Chicago v. Morales,* 527 U.S. 41 (1999).
[45]277 U.S. 438 (1928). This decision was overruled later in *Katz v. United States,* 389 U.S. 347 (1967).
[46]381 U.S. 479 (1965).

such as marketing firms. The average American citizen has personal information filed away in dozens of agencies—such as the Social Security Administration and the Internal Revenue Service. Because of the threat of indiscriminate use of private information by nonauthorized individuals, Congress passed the Privacy Act in 1974. This was the first law regulating the use of federal government information about private individuals. Under the Privacy Act, every citizen has the right to obtain copies of personal records collected by federal agencies and to correct inaccuracies in such records.

The ease with which personal information can be obtained by using the Internet for marketing and other purposes has led to unique challenges with regard to privacy rights. As discussed in the chapter-opening *What If . . .* feature, some fear that privacy rights with respect to personal information may soon be a thing of the past. In this chapter's *Critical Perspective* on pages 138 and 139, we look further at the issue of privacy rights in cyberspace.

Privacy Rights and Abortion

Historically, abortion was not a criminal offense before the "quickening" of the fetus (the first movement of the fetus in the uterus, usually between the sixteenth and eighteenth weeks of pregnancy). During the last half of the nineteenth century, however, state laws became more severe. By 1973, performance of an abortion was a criminal offense in most states.

Roe v. Wade.   In *Roe v. Wade*[47] (1973), the United States Supreme Court accepted the argument that the laws against abortion violated "Jane Roe's" right to privacy under the Constitution. The Court did not answer the question about when life begins. It simply said that "the right to privacy is broad enough to encompass a woman's decision whether or not to terminate her pregnancy." The

---

[47]410 U.S. 113 (1973). Jane Roe was not the real name of the woman in this case. It is a common legal pseudonym used to protect a person's privacy.

Pro-life groups increased their demonstrations against abortion facilities in the 1990s and early 2000s. The clash between the pro-abortion and the pro-life forces has resulted in several deaths. The Supreme Court has imposed restrictions on what pro-life groups can do in their demonstrations around abortion clinics.

Court held that during the first trimester (three months) of pregnancy, abortion was an issue solely between a woman and her doctor. The state could not limit abortions except to require that they be performed by licensed physicians. During the second trimester, to protect the health of the mother, the state was allowed to specify the conditions under which an abortion could be performed. During the final trimester, the state could regulate or even outlaw abortions except when necessary to preserve the life or health of the mother.

After *Roe,* the Supreme Court issued decisions in a number of cases defining and redefining the boundaries of state regulation of abortion. During the 1980s, the Court twice struck down laws that required a woman who wished to have an abortion to undergo counseling designed to discourage abortions. In the late 1980s and early 1990s, however, the Court took a more conservative approach. Although the Court did not explicitly overturn the *Roe* decision, it upheld state laws that place restrictions on abortion rights. For example, in *Webster v. Reproductive Health Services*[48] (1989), the Court upheld a Missouri statute that, among other things, banned the use of public hospitals or other taxpayer-supported facilities for performing abortions. And, in *Planned Parenthood v. Casey*[49] (1992), the Court upheld a Pennsylvania law that required preabortion counseling, a waiting period of twenty-four hours, and, for girls under the age of eighteen, parental or judicial permission. As a result, abortions are now more difficult to obtain in some states than others.

The Controversy Continues.   Abortion continues to be a divisive issue. Antiabortion forces continue to push for laws banning abortion, to endorse political candidates who support their views, and to organize protests. Because of several episodes of violence attending protests at abortion clinics, in 1994 Congress passed the Freedom of Access to Clinic Entrances Act. The act prohibits protesters from blocking entrances to such clinics. The Supreme Court ruled in 1993 that abortion protesters can be prosecuted under laws governing racketeering,[50] and in 1998 a federal court in Illinois convicted antiabortion protesters under these laws. In 1997, the Supreme Court upheld the constitutionality of prohibiting protesters from entering a fifteen-foot "buffer zone" around abortion clinics and from giving unwanted counseling to those entering the clinics.[51]

In 2000, the Supreme Court again visited the abortion issue when it reviewed a challenge to a Nebraska law banning "partial-birth" abortions. Over thirty other states also ban the controversial procedure. In a partial-birth abortion, which is used during the second trimester of pregnancy, the fetus is brought feet first through the birth canal and aborted by inserting a suction tube into the skull—which remains in the womb—and removing the contents. Abortion rights activists claim that the procedure is among the safest ways to perform an abortion in the second trimester. Opponents argue that it ends the life of a child that might be able to live outside the womb. The Supreme Court invalidated the Nebraska law, thereby upholding the basic premise of *Roe v. Wade*—the right to choose.[52] The Court's ruling will almost certainly affect the validity of similar laws in other states.

In another decision in the same year, the Court upheld a Colorado law requiring demonstrators to stay at least eight feet away from people entering and leaving clinics unless people consented to be approached. The Court concluded

Abortion Trial Again

---

[48] 492 U.S. 490 (1989).
[49] 505 U.S. 833 (1992).
[50] *National Organization of Women v. Joseph Scheidler,* 509 U.S. 951 (1993).
[51] *Schenck v. ProChoice Network,* 519 U.S. 357 (1997).
[52] *Stenberg v. Carhart,* 120 S.Ct. 2597 (2000).

Can Privacy Rights Survive in Cyberspace?

A recent ad in a national publication offered the following service: "Will find anyone you want us to for $69.95." Before the age of the Internet, such an ad would never have appeared. Today, though, there are specialists who can use the Internet to find, well, just about anyone. They also can find information on just about anything and everybody, including individuals' unlisted phone numbers, addresses, driver's license numbers, car registrations, some medical records, military records, criminal records, and the like.

The computer age, coupled with the explosion of information available in cyberspace through the connecting of data banks worldwide, has created a troublesome corollary: an explosion in privacy issues.

We Are All Naked in Cyberspace

In her book *Naked in Cyberspace: How to Find Personal Information Online,** researcher Carole A. Lane made the following claim: "Sitting at my computer, beginning with no more than your name and address, I can find out what you do for a living, the names and ages of your spouse and children, what kind of car you drive, the value of your house and how much taxes you pay on it." Lane is a paid Internet searcher and a member of the Association of Independent Information Professionals. She says that "real privacy as we have known it is fleeting." Others go even further and claim that the Internet has brought about the death of privacy.†

*Wilton, Conn.: Pemberton Press, 1997.

†See, for example, Simson Garfinkel, *Database Nation: The Death of Privacy in the Twenty-First Century* (Cambridge, Mass.: O'Reilly & Associates, 2000).

Consider that if you go into Infospace on the Web, you will find your home address—if you have a listed phone number (as do 112 million Americans). If someone types in your name, that person receives a map of your neighborhood with a little "X" marking your residence. He or she even can get written directions to your house.

Cookies Are Not Just for Eating

You may not know it, but every time you access a Web site, a "tag" may be left in your computer hard drive. Information about you is being stored on your own computer. This procedure is called using a "cookie." Every time you visit a Web site, the server on which it is stored and your computer have to communicate. This communication occurs through a language called http, or hypertext transfer protocol. Many times, the Web sites you access will send out an http command (the cookie) that tells your Internet browser to save part of that communication. So, the next time you visit the same Web site, the saved information is sent back. For the most part, cookies are used simply to tell each Web site how many times you have visited that site before. Cookies can also be used to store a log-in password or a credit-card number if you are buying items, such as CDs. That saves you time in the future because you do not have to key in your password and credit-card number.

Civil libertarians fear that cookies can be used too easily to track your Web-surfing habits. The Web sites that generate such cookies, however, argue that they are harmless and simply enhance your Web surfing. Civil liberties groups are not so sure, and neither is the Federal Trade Commission (FTC). A recent FTC survey of 1,400 Web sites found that although more than 85 percent of the sites collected personal information on visitors, only 14 percent of these sites informed visitors of their information-collecting practices.

that the law's restrictions on speech-related conduct did not violate the free speech rights of abortion protesters.[53]

Privacy Rights and the "Right to Die"

The 1976 case involving Karen Ann Quinlan was one of the first publicized right-to-die cases.[54] The parents of Quinlan, a young woman who had been in a coma for nearly a year and who had been kept alive during that time by a respirator, wanted her respirator removed. In 1976, the New Jersey Supreme Court ruled that

[53]*Hill v. Colorado*, 120 S.Ct. 2480 (2000).
[54]*In re Quinlan*, 70 N.J. 10 (1976).

The Value of Personal Information

In February 1999, Free-PC, a company based in Pasadena, California, announced that it would distribute 10,000 free Compaq computers immediately (and some 90,000 more computers in the future). Within days, the company received more than 1.2 million applications. What did Free-PC expect to get in return? The answer is—information. Those who received the computers had to disclose their ages, incomes, hobbies, and a variety of other details about their lives. They also had to permit their online surfing habits to be tracked.

Online companies realize that profits can be made by gathering and using personal customer information, selling it to third parties, or sharing it with partners. A user's name—and everything connected to it—has become a valuable commodity to be purchased, sold, and otherwise exchanged in today's electronic marketplace for a profit.

Ironically, at a time when the value of personal information is higher than ever, the ability of individuals to control how that information is used is at a low point. A growing concern today is how to protect Internet users' privacy rights. A *Business Week*/Harris poll released on March 20, 2000, shows that 57 percent of U.S. residents favor the passage of some kind of law regulating how personal information is collected and used over the Internet. Analysts of polling data have suggested that unless some legislation is passed, the growth of e-commerce could be slowed because Internet shoppers are wary of giving personal information, including credit-card numbers, to online merchants.

Is Self-Regulation the Solution?

To ward off possible government action, as well as to avoid liability under existing laws for violating Web users' privacy rights, most online businesses are now taking steps to create and implement Web site privacy policies. Such policies include posting notices on their Web sites about the type of information being collected, how it will be used, and the parties to whom it will be disclosed. Some policies allow Web site visitors to access and correct or remove personal information and give visitors an "opt-in" or "opt-out" choice. If a user selects an "opt-out" policy, the personal data collected by the site owner are kept private.

Ultimately, new technology may make privacy a structural component of the Internet. For example, Microsoft and other firms are currently developing software that will enable Web browsers to display a warning if a user visits a Web site that does not have a privacy policy or that collects data the user does not wish to disclose.

Because of these and other efforts, the FTC recently agreed to allow the online industry to regulate itself, with only minimal government oversight. For self-regulation to be effective, however, online companies and privacy organizations will need to agree on uniform privacy policy standards and devise appropriate enforcement mechanisms. These obstacles may be difficult—if not impossible—to overcome.

FOR CRITICAL ANALYSIS

1. Is self-regulation by the online industry a realistic option, or will the government inevitably have to step in to further protect online privacy rights?
2. What benefits do Internet users derive from disclosing personal information to Web merchants?

---

the right to privacy includes the right of a patient to refuse treatment and that patients unable to speak can exercise that right through a family member or guardian. In 1990, the Supreme Court took up the issue. In *Cruzan v. Director, Missouri Department of Health,*[55] the Court stated that a patient's life-sustaining treatment can be withdrawn at the request of a family member only if there is "clear and convincing evidence" that the patient did *not* want such treatment.

Since the 1976 *Quinlan* decision, most states have enacted laws permitting people to designate their wishes concerning life-sustaining procedures in "living wills" or durable health-care powers of attorney. These laws and the Supreme Court's *Cruzan* decision largely have resolved this aspect of the right-to-die controversy.

---

[55]497 U.S. 261 (1990).

In the 1990s, however, another issue surfaced: Do privacy rights include the right of terminally ill people to end their lives through physician-assisted suicide? Until 1996, the courts consistently upheld state laws that prohibited this practice, either through specific statutes or under their general homicide statutes. In 1996, after two federal appellate courts ruled that state laws banning assisted suicide (in Washington and New York) were unconstitutional, the issue reached the Supreme Court. In 1997, in *Washington v. Glucksberg*,[56] the Court stated, clearly and categorically, that the liberty interest protected by the Constitution does not include a right to commit suicide, with or without assistance. To hold otherwise, said the Court, would be "to reverse centuries of legal doctrine and practice, and strike down the considered policy choice of almost every state."

In effect, the Supreme Court left the decision in the hands of the states. Since then, assisted suicide has been allowed in only one state—Oregon.

The Great Balancing Act: The Rights of the Accused versus the Rights of Society

The United States has one of the highest violent crime rates in the world. It is not surprising, therefore, that many citizens have extremely strong opinions about the rights of those accused of criminal offenses. When an accused person, especially one who has confessed to some criminal act, is set free because of an apparent legal "technicality," many people may feel that the rights of the accused are being given more weight than the rights of society and of potential or actual victims. Why, then, give criminal suspects rights? The answer is partly to avoid convicting innocent people, but mostly because all criminal suspects have the right to due process of law and fair treatment.

The courts and the police must constantly engage in a balancing act of competing rights. At the basis of all discussions about the appropriate balance is, of course, the U.S. Bill of Rights. The Fourth, Fifth, Sixth, and Eighth Amendments deal specifically with the rights of criminal defendants. (You will learn about some of your rights under the Fourth Amendment in the *Making a Difference* feature at the end of this chapter.)

Rights of the Accused

The basic rights of criminal defendants are outlined below. When appropriate, the specific constitutional provision or amendment on which a right is based also is given.

Limits on the Conduct of Police Officers and Prosecutors
- No unreasonable or unwarranted searches and seizures (Amend. IV).
- No arrest except on probable cause (Amend. IV).
- No coerced confessions or illegal interrogation (Amend. V).
- No entrapment.
- Upon questioning, a suspect must be informed of her or his rights.

Defendant's Pretrial Rights
- **Writ of *habeas corpus*** (Article I, Section 9).
- Prompt arraignment (Amend. VI).
- Legal counsel (Amend. VI).
- Reasonable bail (Amend. VIII).
- To be informed of charges (Amend. VI).
- To remain silent (Amend. V).

Writ of *Habeas Corpus*

Habeas corpus means, literally, "you have the body." A writ of *habeas corpus* is an order that requires jailers to bring a person before a court or judge and explain why the person is being held in prison.

---

[56]521 U.S. 702 (1997).

Trial Rights

- Speedy and public trial before a jury (Amend. VI).
- Impartial jury selected from a cross section of the community (Amend. VI).
- Trial atmosphere free of prejudice, fear, and outside interference.
- No compulsory self-incrimination (Amend. V).
- Adequate counsel (Amend. VI).
- No cruel and unusual punishment (Amend. VIII).
- Appeal of convictions.
- No double jeopardy (Amend. V).

Extending the Rights of the Accused

During the 1960s, the Supreme Court, under Chief Justice Earl Warren, significantly expanded the rights of accused persons. In a case decided in 1963, *Gideon v. Wainwright*,[57] the Court held that if a person is accused of a felony and cannot afford an attorney, an attorney must be made available to the accused person at the government's expense. Although the Sixth Amendment to the Constitution provides for the right to counsel, the Supreme Court had established a precedent twenty-one years earlier in *Betts v. Brady*,[58] when it held that only criminal defendants in capital cases automatically had a right to legal counsel.

Miranda v. Arizona.   Three years later, the Court issued its decision in *Miranda v. Arizona*.[59] The case involved Ernesto Miranda, who was arrested and charged with the kidnapping and rape of a young woman. After two hours of questioning, Miranda confessed and was later convicted. Miranda's lawyer appealed his conviction, arguing that the police had never informed Miranda that he had a right to remain silent and a right to be represented by counsel. The Court, in ruling in Miranda's favor, enunciated the *Miranda* rights that are now familiar to virtually all Americans:

> Prior to any questioning, the person must be warned that he has a right to remain silent, that any statement he does make may be used against him, and that he has a right to the presence of an attorney, either retained or appointed.

[57]372 U.S. 335 (1963).
[58]316 U.S. 455 (1942).
[59]384 U.S. 436 (1966).

This man is being read his *Miranda* rights by the arresting officer. These rights were established in the 1966 case *Miranda v. Arizona*. The rights concern minimum procedural safeguards. They are also known as the *Miranda* warnings and include informing arrested persons prior to questioning (1) that they have the right to remain silent, (2) that anything they say may be used as evidence against them, and (3) that they have the right to the presence of an attorney.

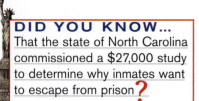

Exceptions to the *Miranda* Rule.   As part of a continuing attempt to balance the rights of accused persons against the rights of society, the Supreme Court has made a number of exceptions to the *Miranda* rule. In 1984, for example, the Court recognized a "public safety" exception to the rule. The need to protect the public warranted the admissibility of statements made by the defendant (in this case, indicating where he placed the gun) as evidence in a trial, even though the defendant had not been informed of his *Miranda* rights.[60]

In 1985, the Court further held that a confession need not be excluded even though the police failed to inform a suspect in custody that his attorney had tried to reach him by telephone.[61] In an important 1991 decision, the Court stated that a suspect's conviction will not be automatically overturned if the suspect was coerced into making a confession. If the other evidence admitted at trial is strong enough to justify the conviction without the confession, then the fact that the confession was obtained illegally can be, in effect, ignored.[62] In yet another case, in 1994, the Supreme Court ruled that a suspect must unequivocally and assertively state his or her right to counsel in order to stop police questioning. Saying, "Maybe I should talk to a lawyer" during an interrogation after being taken into custody is not enough. The Court held that police officers are not required to decipher the suspect's intentions in such situations.[63]

Section 3501 of the Omnibus Crime Control and Safe Streets Act of 1968.
Two years after the Supreme Court's *Miranda* decision, Congress passed the Omnibus Crime Control and Safe Streets Act of 1968. Section 3501 of the act reinstated a rule that had been in effect for 180 years before *Miranda*—namely, that statements by defendants can be used against them as long as the statements were voluntarily made. The Justice Department immediately disavowed Section 3501 as unconstitutional and has continued to hold this position. As a result, Section 3501, although it was never repealed, was not enforced for some thirty-one years.

In 1999, however, a federal appellate court stunned the nation by enforcing the all-but-forgotten provision. According to that court, Congress has the "unquestioned power to establish the rules of procedure and evidence in federal courts," and there is no explicit constitutional requirement that defendants be told of their rights to counsel and to remain silent.[64] The controversial decision was appealed to the Supreme Court, which issued its decision in 2000. The high court held that the *Miranda* warnings were constitutionally based and could not be overruled by a legislative act.[65]

Videotaped Interrogations.   There are no guarantees that *Miranda* will survive indefinitely—particularly in view of the numerous exceptions to the rule and the developments just discussed. Additionally, law enforcement personnel are increasingly using videotapes to record interrogations. According to some scholars, the videotaping of *all* custodial interrogations would satisfy the Fifth Amendment's prohibition against coercion and in the process render the *Miranda* warnings unnecessary.

---

[60]*New York v. Quarles,* 467 U.S. 649 (1984).
[61]*Moran v. Burbine,* 475 U.S. 412 (1985).
[62]*Arizona v. Fulminante,* 499 U.S. 279 (1991).
[63]*Davis v. United States,* 512 U.S. 452 (1994).
[64]*United States v. Dickerson,* 97 F.3d 4750 (4th Cir. 1999).
[65]*Dickerson v. United States,* 120 S.Ct. 2326 (2000).

More and more state and local governments have adopted so-called Megan's laws, laws that inform citizens when criminal sexual offenders move into their neighborhood. Do such laws violate the rights of individuals who have "paid their debt to society," or do they rightfully forewarn a community of potential danger?

The Exclusionary Rule

At least since 1914, judicial policy has prohibited the admission of illegally seized evidence at trials in federal courts. This is the so-called **exclusionary rule.** Improperly obtained evidence, no matter how telling, cannot be used by prosecutors. This includes evidence obtained by police in violation of a suspect's *Miranda* rights or of the Fourth Amendment. The Fourth Amendment protects against unreasonable searches and seizures and provides that a judge may issue a search warrant to a police officer only on probable cause (a demonstration of facts that permit a reasonable belief that a crime has been committed). The question that must be determined by the courts is what constitutes an "unreasonable" search and seizure.

The reasoning behind the exclusionary rule is that it forces police officers to gather evidence properly, in which case their due diligence will be rewarded by a conviction. The exclusionary rule has always had critics who argue that it permits guilty persons to be freed because of innocent errors.

This rule was first extended to state court proceedings in a 1961 Supreme Court decision, *Mapp v. Ohio.*[66] In this case, the Court overturned the conviction of Dollree Mapp for the possession of obscene materials. Police found pornographic books in her apartment after searching it without a search warrant and despite her refusal to let them in.

Over the last several decades, however, the Supreme Court has diminished the scope of the exclusionary rule by creating some exceptions to its applicability. For example, in 1984 the Supreme Court held that illegally obtained evidence could be admitted at trial if law enforcement personnel could prove that they would have obtained the evidence legally anyway.[67] In another case decided in the same year, the Court held that a police officer who used a technically incorrect search warrant form to obtain evidence had acted in good faith and therefore the evidence was admissible at trial. The Court thus created the "good faith" exception to the exclusionary rule.[68]

Exclusionary Rule
A policy forbidding the admission at trial of illegally seized evidence.

INFOTRAC®
COLLEGE EDITION

Exclusionary Rule 20th Century Invention

---

[66]367 U.S. 643 (1961).
[67]*Nix v. Williams,* 467 U.S. 431 (1984).
[68]*Massachusetts v. Sheppard,* 468 U.S. 981 (1984).

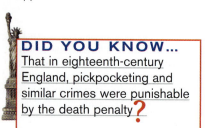

Other exceptions to the rule made by the courts since the 1980s have tended to further weaken criminal defendants' rights and, according to many critics, have allowed law enforcement personnel to exercise power a little too arbitrarily. Who is to say, for example, whether a police officer was acting in "good faith" when obtaining evidence against a criminal suspect? Others argue that these exceptions have not altered the basic fact that the numerous rights of criminal defendants make justice difficult—if not impossible—to obtain.

The Death Penalty

Capital punishment remains one of the most debated aspects of our criminal justice system. Those in favor of the death penalty maintain that it serves as a deterrent to serious crime and satisfies society's need for justice and fair play. Those opposed to the death penalty do not believe it has any deterrent value and hold that it constitutes a barbaric act in an otherwise civilized society. Recent public opinion polls have found that 66 percent of Americans favor the use of the death penalty in murder cases. (Although this is a strong majority, support for the death penalty has declined since 1994, when 80 percent of Americans favored its use.) Thirty-eight states currently provide for the death penalty.

Cruel and Unusual Punishment?   The Eighth Amendment prohibits cruel and unusual punishment. Throughout history, "cruel and unusual" referred to punishments that were more serious than the crimes—the phrase referred to torture and to executions that prolonged the agony of dying. The Supreme Court never interpreted "cruel and unusual" to prohibit all forms of capital punishment in all circumstances. Indeed, a number of states had imposed the death penalty for a variety of crimes and allowed juries to decide when the condemned could be sentenced to death. Many believed, however, and in 1972 the Supreme Court agreed, in *Furman v. Georgia*,[69] that the imposition of the death penalty was random and arbitrary.

The Supreme Court's 1972 decision stated that the death penalty, as then applied, violated the Eighth and Fourteenth Amendments. The Court ruled that capital punishment is not necessarily cruel and unusual if the criminal has killed or attempted to kill someone. In its opinion, the Court invited the states to enact more precise laws so that the death penalty would be applied more consistently. A majority of states have done so. By the 1990s, an increasing number of states were executing death-row inmates. Indeed, by 2000 convicted murderers were being executed at a rate of about one every five days. In the two decades prior to 2001, over 400 convicted murderers were put to death. In 2001, more than 3,600 convicts across the United States were awaiting execution.

Time Limits for Death-Row Appeals.   In 1996, Congress passed the Anti-Terrorism and Effective Death Penalty Act. The law sharply limited federal court access for all defendants convicted in state courts. It also imposed a severe time limit on death-row appeals. The law required federal judges to hear these appeals and issue their opinions within a specified time period. Many are concerned that the shortened appeals process increases the possibility that innocent persons may be put to death. Since 1973, eighty-seven prisoners have been freed from death row after new evidence suggested that they were wrongfully convicted. On average, it takes about seven years to exonerate someone on death row. In recent years, however, the time between conviction and execution has been shortened from an average of ten to twelve years to an average of six to eight years.

---

[69]408 U.S. 238 (1972).

People gather outside a Virginia penitentiary to keep vigil. They are protesting against the execution of a convict.

Civil Liberties:
Issues for the Twenty-First Century

In the twenty-first century, the courts certainly will continue to grapple with several significant issues concerning First Amendment freedoms. One issue concerns the emerging use of the Internet for personal communications and business transactions. Adapting traditional legal concepts and doctrines to the realm of cyberspace—and establishing new laws and guidelines—will take time and will certainly elicit controversy. So will decisions as to whether the Internet should be regulated and who the regulators should be. "Hate speech" and disorderly protests will also force difficult trade-offs to be made between the constitutional guarantee of free speech and society's need to reduce violence.

The desire of many Americans to express their religious beliefs publicly presents an ongoing challenge to courts and legislators, who at some point will need to issue more definitive guidelines on such issues as school prayer, the teaching of evolution, and the use of public funds for education in church-related schools.

How to protect privacy rights in the online environment is an issue that will probably not disappear any time soon. The abortion issue also has yet to be resolved. Although the Supreme Court has upheld state laws banning assisted suicide, state and federal legislators will continue to face controversial demands regarding this practice.

Finally, because crime continues to be a major problem in this country, the rights of accused persons probably will continue to be challenged. As American society looks for new ways to halt crime, it also must attempt to maintain some kind of balance between the rights of accused persons and the rights of those who suffer from criminal wrongdoing. If past experience is any indication, this challenge will continue to exist for generations to come.

making a difference

Your Civil Liberties: Searches and Seizures

What happens if you are stopped by members of the police force? Your civil liberties protect you from having to provide information other than your name and address. Indeed, you are not really required to produce identification, although it is a good idea to show this to the officers. Normally, even if you have not been placed under arrest, the officers have the right to frisk you for weapons, and you must let them proceed. The officers cannot, however, check your person or your clothing further if, in their judgment, no weaponlike object is produced.

The officers may search you only if they have a search warrant or probable cause that they will likely find incriminating evidence if the search is conducted. Normally, it is unwise to resist physically the officers' attempt to search you if they do not have probable cause or a warrant; it is usually best simply to refuse orally to give permission for the search, preferably in the presence of a witness. Also, it is usually advisable to tell the officer as little as possible about yourself and the situation that is under investigation. Being polite and courteous, though firm, is better than acting out of anger or frustration and making the officers irritable. If you

are arrested, it is best to keep quiet until you can speak with a lawyer.

If you are in your car and are stopped by the police, the same fundamental rules apply. Always be ready to show your driver's license and car registration quickly. You may be asked to get out of the car. The officers may use a flashlight to peer inside if it is too dark to see otherwise. None of this constitutes a search. A true search requires either a warrant or probable cause. No officer has the legal right to search your car simply to find out if you may have committed a crime. Police officers can conduct searches that are incident to lawful arrests, however.

If you are in your residence and a police officer with a search warrant appears, you should examine the warrant before granting entry. A warrant that is correctly made out will state the exact place or persons to be searched, a description of the object sought, and the date of the warrant (which should be no more than ten days old), and it will bear the signature of a judge or magistrate. If the search warrant is in order, you should not make any statement. If you believe the warrant to be invalid, you should make it clear orally that you have not con-

sented to the search, preferably in the presence of a witness. If the warrant later is proved to be invalid, normally any evidence obtained will be considered illegal.

Officers who attempt to enter your home without a search warrant can do so only if they are pursuing a suspected felon into the house. Rarely is it advisable to give permission for a warrantless search. You, as the resident, must be the one to give permission if any evidence obtained is to be considered legal. The landlord, manager, or head of a college dormitory cannot give legal permission. A roommate, however, can give permission for a search of his or her room, which may allow the police to search areas where you have personal belongings.

If you find yourself a guest in a location that is being legally searched, you may be legally searched also. But unless you have been placed under arrest, you cannot be compelled to go to the police station or into a squad car.

If you would like to find out more about your rights and obligations under the laws of searches and seizures, you might wish to contact the following organization:

The American Civil Liberties Union
125 Broad St., 18th Floor
New York, NY 10004
1-800-775-ACLU

http://www.aclu.org

Key terms

actual malice 132

bad-tendency rule 127

civil liberties 117

clear and present danger test 126

commercial speech 128

defamation of character 129

equal time rule 134

establishment clause 119

exclusionary rule 143

fighting words 130

free exercise clause 125

gag order 133

hecklers' veto 130

incorporation theory 118

libel 132

personal attack rule 134

prior restraint 127

public figures 132

slander 130

symbolic speech 128

writ of *habeas corpus* 140

Chapter summary

1 To deal with Americans' fears of a too-powerful national government, after the adoption of the U.S. Constitution, Congress proposed a Bill of Rights. These ten amendments to the Constitution were ratified by the states by the end of 1791. The amendments set forth civil liberties—that is, they are limitations on the government.

2 Originally, the Bill of Rights limited only the power of the national government, not that of the states. Gradually, however, the Supreme Court accepted the incorporation theory under which no state can violate the Bill of Rights.

3 The First Amendment protects against government interference with the freedom of religion by requiring a separation of church and state (under the establishment clause) and by guaranteeing the free exercise of religion. Controversial issues relating to the establishment clause include aid to church-related schools, school prayer, the teaching of evolution versus creationism, and school vouchers. The government can interfere with the free exercise of religion only when religious practices work against public policy or the public welfare.

4 The First Amendment protects against government interference with the freedom of speech, which includes symbolic speech (expressive conduct). Restrictions are permitted when expression presents a clear and present danger to the peace or public order, or when expression has a bad tendency (that is, when it might lead to some "evil"). Expression may be restrained before it occurs, but such prior restraint has a "heavy presumption" against its constitutionality. Commercial speech (advertising) by businesses has received limited First Amendment protection. Speech that has not received First Amendment protection includes expression judged to be obscene, utterances considered to be slanderous, and speech constituting fighting words or a hecklers' veto.

5 The First Amendment protects against government interference with the freedom of the press, which can be regarded as a special instance of freedom of speech. Speech by the press that does not receive protection includes libelous statements made with actual malice. Publication of news about a criminal trial may be restricted by a gag order in some circumstances.

6 The First Amendment protects the right to assemble peaceably and to petition the government. Permits may be required for parades, sound trucks, and demonstrations to maintain the public order, and a permit may be denied to protect the public safety.

7 Under the Ninth Amendment, rights not specifically mentioned in the Constitution are not denied to the people. Among these unspecified rights is a right to privacy, which has been implied through the First, Third, Fourth, Fifth, and Ninth Amendments. A major privacy issue today concerns the problem of protecting privacy rights in cyberspace. Questions concerning whether an individual's privacy rights include a right to have an abortion or a "right to die" also continue to elicit controversy.

8 The Constitution includes protections for the rights of persons accused of crimes. Under the Fourth Amendment, no one may be subject to an unreasonable search or seizure or arrested except on probable cause. Under the Fifth Amendment, an accused person has the right to remain silent. Under the Sixth Amendment, an accused person must be informed of the reason for his or her arrest. The accused also has the right to adequate counsel, even if he or she cannot afford an attorney, and the right to a prompt arraignment and a speedy and public trial before an impartial jury selected from a cross section of the community.

9 In *Miranda v. Arizona* (1966), the Supreme Court held that criminal suspects, prior to interrogation by law enforcement personnel, must be informed of certain constitutional rights, including the right to remain silent and the right to counsel.

10 The exclusionary rule forbids the admission in court of illegally seized evidence. There is a "good faith exception" to the exclusionary rule: illegally seized evidence need not be thrown out owing to, for example, a technical defect in a search warrant. Under the Eighth Amendment, cruel and unusual punishment is prohibited. Whether the death penalty is cruel and unusual punishment continues to be debated.

Selected print and electronic resources

SUGGESTED READINGS

Etzioni, Amitai. *The Limits of Privacy.* New York: Basic Books, 1999. The author acknowledges that no society can long remain free without privacy, yet he believes that American communities have other goals that outweigh privacy concerns. His underlying theme is that society must balance individual rights against the common good, and this may require sacrificing some privacy rights.

Foster, James C., and Susan M. Leeson. *Constitutional Law: Cases in Context.* Englewood Cliffs, N.J.: Prentice Hall, 1998. This comprehensive collection of Supreme Court constitutional law cases traces the effects of each case on the American political system.

Heffernan, William C., and John Kleinig, eds. *From Social Justice to Criminal Justice.* New York: Oxford University Press, 2000. In the United States, economically deprived persons come into contact with the criminal justice system in disproportionate numbers. The essays in this collection explore some of the more troubling moral and ethical questions stemming from this situation.

Lewis, Anthony. *Gideon's Trumpet.* New York: Vintage, 1964. This classic work discusses the background and facts of *Gideon v. Wainwright,* the 1963 Supreme Court case in which the Court held that the state must make an attorney available for any person accused of a felony who cannot afford a lawyer.

Shiell, Timothy C. *Campus Hate Speech on Trial.* Lawrence, Kans.: University Press of Kansas, 1998. The author argues that American college campuses, which have traditionally served as forums for the free exchange of ideas, are betraying this tradition by implementing speech codes. Shiell suggests that colleges and universities should put greater emphasis on upholding free speech rights, even if that means tolerating hate speech.

MEDIA RESOURCES

The Chamber—A movie, based on John Grisham's novel by the same name, about a young lawyer who defends a man (his grandfather) who has been sentenced to death and faces imminent execution.

Execution at Midnight—A video presenting the arguments and evidence on both sides of the controversial death-penalty issue.

Gideon's Trumpet—An excellent 1980 film about the *Gideon v. Wainwright* case; Henry Fonda plays the role of the convicted petty thief, Clarence Earl Gideon.

May It Please the Court: The First Amendment—A set of audiocassette recordings and written transcripts of the oral arguments made before the Supreme Court in sixteen key First Amendment cases. Participants in the recording include nationally known attorneys and several Supreme Court justices.

The People versus Larry Flynt—An R-rated 1996 film that clearly articulates the conflict between freedom of the press and how a community defines pornography.

Logging on

At Project Vote Smart's Web site, you can find discussions of major issues, including those involving civil liberties, abortion, and crime. Go to

http://www.vote-smart.org/issues

The American Civil Liberties Union (ACLU), the nation's leading civil liberties organization, provides an extensive array of information and links concerning civil rights issues at

http://www.aclu.org

The Liberty Counsel describes itself as "a nonprofit religious civil liberties education and legal defense organization established to preserve religious freedom." The URL for its Web site is

http://www.lc.org

Summaries and the full text of Supreme Court constitutional law decisions, plus a virtual tour of the Supreme Court, are available at

http://oyez.nwu.edu

If you want to read historic Supreme Court decisions, you can find them, listed by name, at

http://supct.law.cornell.edu:8080/supct

The Center for Democracy and Technology (CDT) focuses on how developments in communications technology are affecting the constitutional liberties of Americans. You can access the CDT's site at

http://www.cdt.org

For a copy of the statement by the American Library Association's Intellectual Freedom Committee concerning the use of filtering software and other issues relating to free speech on the Internet, go to

http://www.ala.org/alaorg/oif/filt_filt_stm.html

You can find current information on privacy issues relating to the Internet at the Electronic Privacy Information Center's Web site. Go to

http://www.epic.org/privacy

For the history of flag protection and the First Amendment, as well as the status of the proposed flag amendment in Congress, go to

http://www.flagamendment.org

Using the Internet for political analysis

Explore the freedom of religious expression that is available to all through the Internet. Use a search engine, such as Yahoo or Alta Vista, to search for Web sites sponsored by "mainline" religious groups and for sites offered by groups that subscribe to less common religious or quasi-religious beliefs or doctrines, such as Scientology, Satanism, atheism, and Zoroastrianism. Examine the home pages of at least three groups. List any of their views or beliefs that may violate current laws, be counter to current political practices, or otherwise have political implications. Do the groups acknowledge their differences with the state or with each other? How can you judge the validity or persuasiveness of this information?

chapter 5

Civil Rights: Equal Protection

CHAPTER OUTLINE

- African Americans and the Consequences of Slavery in the United States

- The Civil Rights Movement

- Modern Civil Rights Legislation

- Immigration and the Civil Rights Agenda

- Women's Struggle for Equal Rights

- Gender-Based Discrimination in the Workplace

what if...

Medical Care Was a Civil Right?

BACKGROUND

IN 1999, THE PRICE OF PRESCRIPTION DRUGS INCREASED FOUR TIMES FASTER THAN THE RATE OF INFLATION. FOR MANY CITIZENS, THE COST OF A VISIT TO A PHYSICIAN'S OFFICE NEARLY DOUBLED. PRIVATE MEDICAL-CARE COSTS ARE PREDICTED TO INCREASE DRAMATICALLY OVER THE NEXT FIVE YEARS, RISING BETWEEN 7 AND 10 PERCENT EACH YEAR. WHILE SUCH FIGURES ARE A CONCERN TO ALL AMERICANS, THEY ARE PARTICULARLY WORRISOME TO THOSE MILLIONS OF AMERICANS WHO DO NOT HAVE HEALTH-CARE INSURANCE.

UNDER THE UNIVERSAL DECLARATION OF HUMAN RIGHTS, THE UNITED NATIONS RECOGNIZES MEDICAL CARE AS A FUNDAMENTAL RIGHT—ONE THAT A GOVERNMENT MUST SECURE FOR ITS CITIZENS. OF COURSE, ALL PERSONS WHO LIVE IN THE UNITED STATES ARE GUARANTEED A CERTAIN MEASURE OF MEDICAL CARE. HOSPITAL EMERGENCY ROOMS, FOR EXAMPLE, NORMALLY ARE REQUIRED TO TREAT ANYONE WHO SHOWS UP AT THEIR DOORS. BUT AMERICANS DO NOT HAVE A RIGHT TO GENERAL MEDICAL CARE.

WHAT IF MEDICAL CARE WAS A CIVIL RIGHT?

The United States is the only industrialized country in the world that relies primarily on the free market for medical care. That is, the quality of the health care an American receives often depends on that person's ability—through personal wealth or an insurance plan—to pay for it. As you will read in this chapter, our civil rights are largely rooted in the Fourteenth Amendment's guarantee of equal treatment under the law for all Americans. If medical care was a civil right, the government would be obligated to make sure that all Americans, rich and poor alike, had equal access to medical care.

If medical care was a civil right, we would probably have a public health system much like our public school system. Anytime we felt we had a medical need, we could see a physician. No money would change hands. This does not mean, however, that medical care would be "free." Taxpayers would share the burden of medical costs, just as taxpayers contribute to the costs of our public school system.

THE SINGLE-PAYER SYSTEM

Most countries that consider medical care a right use the "single-payer" system, in which the single payer is the government. Under this system, after a patient visits a physician or receives treatment, the bill is sent to the government.

If we adopted a single-payer system of national medical insurance, the millions of uninsured Americans mentioned earlier would be covered. Furthermore, private health-insurance companies would go out of business, because they would be unnecessary. Indeed, health-insurance companies and health maintenance organizations (HMOs) that "manage" medical care for their customers are the target of much anger and frustration. Contrary to what one would expect, the recent rise in the ranks of the uninsured has not been among the nation's poor, many of whom are covered by government programs. The fastest-growing group of uninsured persons consists of members of the middle class (those with an annual income ranging from $33,400 to $66,800).

WOULD THE QUALITY OF HEALTH CARE DECLINE?

Given the benefits of a national insurance program, why doesn't the United States adopt one? Part of the answer might be found in Canada's experience with its single-payer system. As you might imagine, when something is considered to be "free," the quantity demanded of that product or service increases. Even with tax rates much higher than those in the United States, the Canadian government finds it impossible to pay for all of the health care its citizens want. In recent years, the Canadian government has had to close hospitals and limit the amount of care that medical professionals can give. As a result hospitals have had to turn away patients or have not given them the quality of care they need.

FOR CRITICAL ANALYSIS

1. Why do you think many physicians' associations are opposed to a single-payer health-care system?

2. Suppose that the United States had a medical system modeled on our public school system. Consumers would be able to choose between receiving public medical care or paying extra for private medical care, just as some families opt to pay more so that their children can attend private schools. Would this type of medical system be fairer than the present system? Why or why not?

The topic of this chapter's opening *What if . . .* feature—the right to receive medical care—certainly was not an issue in the early years of this nation. In spite of the words set forth in the Declaration of Independence that "all Men are created equal," the concept of equal treatment under the law was a distant dream. In fact, the majority of the population in those years had no political rights. As you learned in Chapter 2, the framers of the Constitution permitted slavery to continue. Slaves thus were excluded from the political process. Women also were excluded for the most part, as were Native Americans, African Americans who were not slaves, and even white men who did not own property. Indeed, it has taken this nation more than two hundred years to approach even a semblance of equality among all Americans.

Equality is at the heart of the concept of civil rights. Generally, the term **civil rights** refers to the rights of all Americans to equal treatment under the law, as provided for by the Fourteenth Amendment to the Constitution. Although the terms *civil rights* and *civil liberties* are sometimes used interchangeably, scholars tend to make a distinction between the two. As you learned in Chapter 4, civil liberties are basically *limitations* on government; they specify what the government *cannot* do. Civil rights, in contrast, specify what the government *must* do—to ensure equal protection and freedom from discrimination.

Essentially, the history of civil rights in America is the story of the struggle of various groups to be free from discriminatory treatment. In this chapter, we look at two movements that had significant consequences for the history of civil rights in America: the civil rights movement of the 1950s and 1960s and the women's movement, which began in the mid-1800s and continues today. Each of these movements resulted in legislation that secured important basic rights for all Americans—the right to vote and the right to equal protection under the laws. In the next chapter, we explore a question with serious implications for today's voters and policymakers: What should be the government's responsibility when equal protection under the law is not enough to ensure truly equal opportunities for Americans?

Note that numerous minorities in this nation have suffered—and some continue to suffer—from discrimination. Hispanics, Native Americans, Asian Americans, Arab Americans from Middle Eastern countries, and persons from India have all had to struggle for equal treatment, as have people from various island nations and other countries. The fact that these groups are not singled out for special attention in the following pages should not be construed to mean that their struggle for equality is any less significant than the struggles of those groups that we do discuss. (Some contend that the Internet is helping to create a future "colorblind" society—see the *E-mocracy* on the next page for a discussion of this possibility.)

African Americans and the Consequences of Slavery in the United States

Article I, Section 2, of the U.S. Constitution states that congressional representatives are to be apportioned among the states according to their respective numbers. These numbers were to be obtained by adding to the total number of free persons "three fifths of all other Persons." The "other persons" were, of course, slaves. A slave was thus equal to three-fifths of a white person. As Abraham Lincoln stated sarcastically, "All men are created equal, except Negroes." Before 1863, the Constitution thus protected slavery and made equality impossible in the sense we use the word today. African American leader

DID YOU KNOW...
That by the time of the American Revolution, African Americans made up nearly 25 percent of the American population of about three million?

Civil Rights
Generally, all rights rooted in the Fourteenth Amendment's guarantee of equal protection under the law.

This portrait is of Dred Scott (1795–1858), an American slave who was born in South Hampton County, Virginia, and who later moved with his owner to the state of Illinois, where slavery was illegal. He was the nominal plaintiff in a test case that sought to obtain his freedom on the ground that he lived in the free state of Illinois. Although the Supreme Court ruled against him, he was soon emancipated and became a hotel porter in St. Louis.

Frederick Douglass pointed out that "Liberty and Slavery—opposite as Heaven and Hell—are both in the Constitution."

The constitutionality of slavery was confirmed just a few years before the outbreak of the Civil War in the famous *Dred Scott v. Sanford*[1] case of 1857. The Supreme Court held that slaves were not citizens of the United States, nor were they entitled to the rights and privileges of citizenship. The Court also ruled that the Missouri Compromise, which banned slavery in the territories north of 36° 30' latitude (the southern border of Missouri), was unconstitutional. The *Dred Scott* decision had grave consequences. Most observers contend that the ruling contributed to making the Civil War inevitable.

Ending Constitutional Servitude

With the emancipation of the slaves by President Lincoln's Emancipation Proclamation in 1863 and the passage of the Thirteenth, Fourteenth, and

---

[1] 19 Howard 393 (1857).

e-mocracy

Colorblind on the Web

Almost 10 percent of the U.S. population consists of persons between the ages of sixteen and twenty-two. Half of teenagers and young adults have access to the Internet, and they spend 42 percent more time online than do older adults. Researchers are beginning to look at how "growing up with the Web" will affect future generations, and their findings may have implications for one of the most deep-rooted problems in our society: racism.

THE FIRST "NET-POWERED" GENERATION

In studying the attitudes of what they call the first "Net-powered generation," experts at Forrester Research, Inc.,* found distinct differences between older and younger Americans. Older Americans have "adopted" the Internet, while younger Americans have "internalized" it. That is, while older adults have added the Internet to their preestablished routine, teens and younger adults have integrated the technology into every aspect of their lives.

What does this mean? Specifically, the experts found that the Net-powered generation is much more comfortable communicating online than older generations. On one level, this means that younger Americans are more likely to shop on the Web. On another level, however, it means that they are receptive to forming friendships and personal relations in new ways. The Forrester group found that, for today's youth, building trust does not

require face-to-face interaction. Communications via e-mail or chatrooms, for example, do not seem impersonal to the Net-powered generation, as they often do to older Americans.

COLORBLIND COMMUNICATIONS?

Actually, younger Americans find that corresponding through e-mail is more intimate in many ways than using other forms of communication. A computer screen is colorblind. There is no way to know if the person on the other end of the line is white, African American, or Hispanic. There is no way to tell if she or he speaks with a southern accent or stutters, and online conversations are not hampered by judgments about a person's appearance.

It is too early to proclaim that the Internet will do away with such judgments altogether. Furthermore, because the Internet can be used to hide one's identity, it can also be a safe haven for sending hateful and racist messages. But the Forrester researchers did find that the Net-powered generation has a higher comfort level with diversity than its elders do. Once two people have established an online relationship, the study suggests, the less likely they are to let prejudices concerning race, age, or appearance affect that relationship.

FOR CRITICAL ANALYSIS

What impact do you think the attitudes of the Net-powered generation will have on the way politicians run campaigns and try to attract younger voters?

*You can access the Forrester Research report, as well as other studies on the Internet's impact on American business and society, at **http://www. forrester.com**.

Fifteenth Amendments during the Reconstruction period following the Civil War, constitutional inequality was ended.

The Thirteenth Amendment (1865) states that neither slavery nor involuntary servitude shall exist within the United States. The Fourteenth Amendment (1868) tells us that *all* persons born or naturalized in the United States are citizens of the United States. It states, furthermore, that "[n]o State shall make or enforce any law which shall abridge the privileges or immunities of the citizens of the United States; nor shall any State deprive any person of life, liberty or property, without due process of law; nor deny to any person within its jurisdiction the equal protection of the laws." Note the use of the terms *citizen* and *person* in this amendment. *Citizens* have political rights, such as the right to vote and run for political office. Citizens also have certain privileges or immunities (see Chapter 3). All *persons,* however, including legal *and* illegal immigrants, have a right to due process of law and equal protection under the law.

The Fifteenth Amendment (1870) seems equally impressive: "The right of citizens of the United States to vote shall not be denied or abridged by the United States or by any State on account of race, color, or previous condition of servitude." Pressure was brought to bear on Congress to include in the Fourteenth and Fifteenth Amendments a prohibition against discrimination based on sex, but with no success.

As we shall see, the words of these amendments had little immediate effect. (Nor did a proposal that each emancipated slave should receive "40 acres and a mule"—see the feature *An Ethical Issue: Reparations for African Americans?* on the next page.) Although slavery was legally and constitutionally ended, African American political and social inequality has continued to the present time. In the following sections, we discuss several landmarks in the struggle of African Americans to overcome this inequality.

The Civil Rights Acts of 1865 to 1875

At the end of the Civil War, President Lincoln's Republican Party controlled the national government and most state governments, and the so-called Radical Republicans, with their strong antislavery stance, controlled that party. The Radical Republicans pushed through the Thirteenth, Fourteenth, and Fifteenth Amendments to the Constitution (the "Civil War amendments"). From 1865 to

Abraham Lincoln reads the Emancipation Proclamation on July 22, 1862. The Emancipation Proclamation did not abolish slavery (that was done by the Thirteenth Amendment, in 1865), but it ensured that slavery would be abolished if and when the North won the Civil War. After the Battle of Antietam on September 17, 1862, Lincoln publicly announced the Emancipation Proclamation and declared that all slaves residing in states that were still in rebellion against the United States on January 1, 1863, would be freed once those states came under the military control of the Union Army.

DID YOU KNOW...
That the original Constitution failed to describe the status of a citizen or how this status could be acquired?

1875, they succeeded in getting Congress to pass a series of civil rights acts that were aimed at enforcing these amendments. Even Republicans who were not necessarily sympathetic to a strong antislavery position wanted to undercut Democratic domination of the South. What better way to do so than to guarantee African American suffrage?

The first Civil Rights Act in the Reconstruction period that followed the Civil War was passed in 1866 over the veto of President Andrew Johnson. That act extended citizenship to anyone born in the United States and gave African Americans full equality before the law. The act further authorized the president to enforce the law with national armed forces. Many considered the law to be unconstitutional, but such problems disappeared in 1868 with the adoption of the Fourteenth Amendment.

Among the six other civil rights acts in the nineteenth century, one of the more important was the Enforcement Act of May 31, 1870, which set out specific criminal sanctions for interfering with the right to vote as protected by the Fifteenth Amendment and by the Civil Rights Act of 1866. Equally important was the Civil Rights Act of April 20, 1872, known as the Anti–Ku Klux Klan Act. This act made it a federal crime for anyone to use law or custom to deprive an individual of his or her rights, privi-

an ethical issue

Reparations for African Americans?

During the Civil War (1861–1865), Union general William T. Sherman proposed that each newly liberated slave should receive "40 acres and a mule." That offer was eventually rescinded by President Andrew Johnson, and more than 135 years later the U.S. government has yet to provide any former slaves or their descendants with reparations for the horrors of slavery. After decades in which the issue received little attention, today many prominent politicians, scholars, and journalists are arguing that the federal government has a moral and ethical duty to compensate African Americans for the harms done to them in this nation's past.

THE VALUE OF UNPAID LABOR

"Black people worked long, hard killing days, years, centuries—and they were never *paid*," attorney Randall Robinson writes in *The Debt: What America Owes Blacks*.* "The value of their labor went into others' pockets—plantation owners, Northern entrepreneurs, state treasuries, the United States government . . . . There is a debt here." Just how large that debt is, and to whom it is should be repaid, has yet to be determined. One group of economists has calculated the value of labor supplied by slaves, after adjusting for inflation, at $1.4 trillion. Researchers at Howard University in Washington, D.C., have proposed a plan that would use DNA testing to determine if the ancestors of black Americans came from regions in Africa where traders bought slaves.

COMPENSATION FOR WRONGDOING

In several previous cases, groups of wronged people have been compensated by the government. In 1988, for example, the survivors and descendants of 120,000 Japanese Americans forced into government camps during World War II received $20,000 each, for a total of $1.3 billion in reparations. Six years later the state of Florida paid $2.1 million to the former residents of Rosewood, an African American town that was destroyed by a white lynch mob in 1923. In each of these cases, however, those receiving reparations could point to wrongs done to themselves or to close relatives. Very few African Americans today have a relative as close as a grandparent who was a slave.

AN ALTERNATIVE: PROGRAMS TO HELP BLACKS

For many supporters of reparations for African Americans, the idea of cash payments is beside the point—no amount of money could make up for slavery. They would like to see the U.S. government acknowledge the lasting effects of the legacy of slavery, such as continuing poverty and social decay in African American communities. Instead of doling out the modern equivalent of "40 acres and a mule" to all African Americans, these supporters of reparations for African Americans want the federal government to set up a commission that would come up with broader programs to help blacks. A model is the Indian Claims Commission, created in 1946 to resolve the grievances of Native Americans.

FOR CRITICAL ANALYSIS

"Slavery was a stain on this nation's history, but no living American is responsible for the stain and is therefore not ethically required to pay for it." Analyze this statement.

*New York: Dutton, 2000.

leges, and immunities secured by the Constitution or by any federal law. Section 2 of that act imposed detailed penalties or damages for violation of the act.

The last of these early civil rights acts, known as the Second Civil Rights Act, was passed on March 1, 1875. It declared that everyone is entitled to full and equal enjoyment of public accommodations, theaters, and other places of public amusement, and it imposed penalties for violators. This act, however, was virtually nullified by the *Civil Rights Cases* of 1883 discussed below.

The civil rights acts of the 1870s are of special interest, because they were an indication that congressional power or authority applied both to official, or government, action and to private action. The theory behind the acts was that if a state government failed to act, Congress could act in its absence. Thus, Congress could legislate directly against private individuals who were violating the constitutional rights of other individuals when state officials failed to protect those rights. At the time, this was a novel theory. It was not implemented in practice until the 1960s.

The Ineffectiveness of the Civil Rights Laws

The Reconstruction statutes, or civil rights acts, ultimately did little to secure equality for African Americans in their civil rights. Both the *Civil Rights Cases* and the case of *Plessy v. Ferguson* effectively nullified these acts. Additionally, various voting barriers were erected that prevented African Americans from exercising their right to vote.

The *Civil Rights Cases*.   The Supreme Court invalidated the 1875 Civil Rights Act when it held, in the *Civil Rights Cases*[2] of 1883, that the enforcement clause of the Fourteenth Amendment (which states that "[n]o State shall make or enforce any law which shall abridge the privileges or immunities of citizens") was limited to correcting actions by states in their *official* acts; thus, the discriminatory acts of *private* citizens were not illegal. ("Individual invasion of individual rights is not the subject matter of the Amendment.") The 1883 Supreme Court decision met with widespread approval throughout most of the United States.

In a dissenting opinion, Justice John Marshall Harlan contended that the Thirteenth Amendment gave Congress broad powers to enact laws to ensure the rights of former slaves. According to Justice Harlan, the freedom conferred by that amendment included the freedom from all "badges of slavery."

Twenty years after the Civil War, the nation was all too willing to forget about the Civil War amendments and the civil rights legislation of the 1860s and 1870s. The other civil rights laws that the Court specifically did not invalidate became dead letters in the statute books, although they were never repealed by Congress. At the same time, many former proslavery secessionists had regained political power in the southern states. In the last decades of the nineteenth century, these racists enacted the Jim Crow laws, which will be discussed next in relation to the separate-but-equal doctrine.

***Plessy v. Ferguson*: Separate but Equal.**   A key decision during this period concerned Homer Plessy, a Louisiana resident who was one-eighth African American. In 1892, he boarded a train in New Orleans. The conductor made him leave the car, which was restricted to whites, and directed him to a car for

---

[2] 109 U.S. 3 (1883).

Jim Crow laws required the segregation of the races, particularly in public facilities such as this theater. The name "Jim Crow" came from a nineteenth-century vaudeville character who was called Jim (a common name) Crow (for a black-colored bird). Thus, the name "Jim Crow" was applied to laws and practices affecting African Americans.

Separate-but-Equal Doctrine
The doctrine holding that segregation in schools and public accommodations does not imply that one race is superior to another; and that separate-but-equal facilities do not violate the equal protection clause.

White Primary
A state primary election that restricts voting to whites only; outlawed by the Supreme Court in 1944.

Grandfather Clause
A device used by southern states to exempt whites from state taxes and literacy laws originally intended to disfranchise African American voters. It restricted the voting franchise to those who could prove that their grandfathers had voted before 1867.

Poll Tax
A special tax that must be paid as a qualification for voting. The Twenty-fourth Amendment to the Constitution outlawed the poll tax in national elections, and in 1966 the Supreme Court declared it unconstitutional in all elections.

Literacy Test
A test administered as a precondition for voting, often used to prevent African Americans from exercising their right to vote.

nonwhites. At that time, Louisiana had a statute providing for separate railway cars for whites and African Americans.

Plessy went to court, claiming that such a statute was contrary to the Fourteenth Amendment's equal protection clause. In 1896, the United States Supreme Court rejected Plessy's contention. The Court concluded that the Fourteenth Amendment "could not have been intended to abolish distinctions based upon color, or to enforce social . . . equality." The Court indicated that segregation alone did not violate the Constitution: "Laws permitting, and even requiring their separation in places where they are liable to be brought into contact do not necessarily imply the inferiority of either race to the other."[3] So was born the **separate-but-equal doctrine.**

The only justice to vote against this decision was John Marshall Harlan, a former slaveholder. He stated in his dissent, "Our Constitution is color-blind, and neither knows nor tolerates classes among citizens." Justice Harlan also predicted that the separate-but-equal doctrine would "in time prove to be . . . as pernicious as the decision . . . in the Dred Scott Case."

For more than half a century, the separate-but-equal doctrine was accepted as consistent with the equal protection clause in the Fourteenth Amendment. In practical terms, the separate-but-equal doctrine effectively nullified that clause. *Plessy v. Ferguson* became the judicial cornerstone of racial discrimination throughout the United States. Even though *Plessy* upheld segregated facilities in railway cars only, it was assumed that the Supreme Court was upholding segregation everywhere as long as the separate facilities were equal. The result was a system of racial segregation, particularly in the South, that required separate drinking fountains; separate seats in theaters, restaurants, and hotels; separate public toilets; and separate waiting rooms for the two races—collectively known as Jim Crow laws. "Separate" was indeed the rule, but "equal" was never enforced, nor was it a reality.

Voting Barriers.   The brief enfranchisement of African Americans ended after 1877, when the federal troops that occupied the South during the Reconstruction era were withdrawn. Southern politicians regained control of state governments and, using everything except race as a formal criterion, passed laws that effectively deprived African Americans of the right to vote. By using the ruse that political party primaries were private, southern whites were allowed to exclude African Americans. The **white primary** was upheld by the Supreme Court until 1944 when, in *Smith v. Allwright,*[4] the Court found it to be a violation of the Fifteenth Amendment.

Another barrier to African American voting was the **grandfather clause,** which restricted the voting franchise to those who could prove that their grandfathers had voted before 1867. **Poll taxes** required the payment of a fee to vote; thus, poor African Americans—as well as poor whites—who could not afford to pay the tax were excluded from voting. Not until the Twenty-fourth Amendment to the Constitution was ratified in 1964 was the poll tax eliminated as a precondition to voting. **Literacy tests** also were used to deny the vote to African Americans. Such tests asked potential voters to read, recite, or interpret complicated texts, such as a section of the state constitution, to the satisfaction of local registrars.

The End of the Separate-but-Equal Doctrine

A successful attack on the separate-but-equal doctrine began with a series of lawsuits in the 1930s to admit African Americans to state professional schools.

[3]*Plessy v. Ferguson,* 163 U.S. 537 (1896).
[4]321 U.S. 649 (1944).

By 1950, the Supreme Court had ruled that African Americans who were admitted to a state university could not be assigned to separate sections of classrooms, libraries, and cafeterias. In 1951, Oliver Brown decided that his eight-year-old daughter, Linda Carol Brown, should not have to go to an all-nonwhite elementary school twenty-one blocks from her home, when there was a white school only seven blocks away. The National Association for the Advancement of Colored People (NAACP), formed in 1909, decided to help Oliver Brown. The outcome would have a monumental impact on American society. Actually, Brown's suit was one of a series of cases, first argued in 1952, that contested state laws permitting or requiring the establishment of separate school facilities based on race. Following the death of Chief Justice Frederick M. Vinson and his replacement by Earl Warren, the Supreme Court asked for rearguments.

Brown v. Board of Education of Topeka.   The 1954 unanimous decision in *Brown v. Board of Education of Topeka*[5] established that public school segregation of races violates the equal protection clause of the Fourteenth Amendment. Concluding that separate schools are inherently unequal, Chief Justice Warren stated that "to separate [African Americans] from others of similar age and qualifications solely because of their race generates a feeling of inferiority as to their status in the community that may affect their hearts and minds in a way unlikely ever to be undone." Warren said that separation implied inferiority, whereas the majority opinion in *Plessy v. Ferguson* had said the opposite.

"With All Deliberate Speed."   The following year, in *Brown v. Board of Education*[6] (sometimes called the second *Brown* decision), the Court asked for rearguments concerning the way in which compliance with the 1954 decision should be undertaken. The Supreme Court declared that the lower courts must ensure that African Americans would be admitted to schools on a nondiscriminatory basis "with all deliberate speed." The high court told lower federal courts

INFOTRAC®
COLLEGE EDITION

Jim Crow's Racial Symbolic

---

[5]347 U.S. 483 (1954).
[6]349 U.S. 294 (1955).

that they had to take an activist role in society. The district courts were to consider devices in their desegregation orders that might include "the school transportation system, personnel, [and] revision of school districts and attendance areas into compact units to achieve a system of determining admission to the public schools on a nonracial basis."

Reactions to School Integration

One unlooked-for effect of the "all deliberate speed" decision was that the term *deliberate* was used as a loophole by some officials, who were able to delay desegregation by showing that they were indeed acting with all deliberate speed but still were unable to desegregate. Another reaction to court-ordered desegregation was "white flight." In some school districts, the public school population became 100 percent nonwhite when white parents sent their children to newly established private schools, sometimes known as "segregation academies."

The white South did not let the Supreme Court ruling go unchallenged. Arkansas's Governor Orval Faubus used the state's National Guard to block the integration of Central High School in Little Rock in September 1957. The federal court demanded that the troops be withdrawn. Finally, President Dwight Eisenhower had to federalize the Arkansas National Guard and send it to quell the violence. Central High became integrated.

The universities in the South, however, remained segregated. When James Meredith, an African American student, attempted to enroll at the University of Mississippi in Oxford in 1962, violence flared there, as it had in Little Rock. Two men were killed, and a number of people were injured in campus rioting. President John Kennedy sent federal marshals and ordered federal troops to maintain peace and protect Meredith. One year later, George Wallace, governor of Alabama, promised "to stand in the schoolhouse door" to prevent two African American students from enrolling at the University of Alabama in Tuscaloosa. Wallace was forced to back down when Kennedy federalized the Alabama National Guard.

An Integrationist Attempt at a Cure: Busing

In most parts of the United States, residential concentrations by race have made it difficult to achieve racial balance in schools. Although it is true that a number of school boards in northern districts created segregated schools by drawing school district lines arbitrarily, the residential concentration of African Americans and other minorities in well-defined geographic locations has contributed to the difficulty of achieving racial balance. This concentration results in **de facto** segregation.

Court-Ordered Busing. The obvious solution to both *de facto* and **de jure segregation** seemed to be transporting some African American schoolchildren to white schools and some white schoolchildren to African American schools. Increasingly, the courts ordered school districts to engage in such **busing** across neighborhoods. Busing led to violence in some northern cities, such as in south Boston, where African American students were bused into blue-collar Irish Catholic neighborhoods. Indeed, busing was unpopular with many groups. In the mid-1970s, almost 50 percent of African Americans interviewed were opposed to busing, and approximately three-fourths of the whites interviewed held the same opinion. Nonetheless, through the next decade, the Supreme Court fairly consistently upheld busing plans in the cases it decided.

De Facto Segregation
Racial segregation that occurs because of past social and economic conditions and residential patterns.

De Jure Segregation
Racial segregation that occurs because of laws or administrative decisions by public agencies.

Busing
The transportation of public school students from areas where they live to schools in other areas to eliminate school segregation based on residential patterns.

To remedy *de facto* segregation, the courts often imposed busing requirements on school districts. Busing meant transporting children from white neighborhoods to nonwhite schools, and vice versa. Busing has been one of the most controversial domestic policies in the history of this country. Initially, bused students had to be escorted by police because of potential violence. This scene was photographed in Boston in the 1970s.

Changing Directions.   In an apparent reversal of previous decisions, the Supreme Court in June 1986 let stand (did not accept for review) a lower federal court's decision that allowed the Norfolk, Virginia, public school system to end fifteen years of court-ordered busing of elementary schoolchildren.[7] The Norfolk school board supported the decision because of a drop in enrollment from 32,500 whites attending public schools in 1970, when busing was ordered, to fewer than 14,000 in 1985. In 1991, in *Board of Education v. Dowell,*[8] the Supreme Court instructed a lower court administering a desegregation decree that if school racial concentration was a product of residential segregation that resulted from "private decision making and economics," its effects may be ignored entirely.

In *Freeman v. Pitts,*[9] decided in 1992, the Supreme Court also stressed the importance of "local control over the education of children." In *Freeman,* a Georgia school district, which had once been segregated by law and was operating under a federal court–administered desegregation decree, was allowed to regain partial control over its schools, even though it was judged to have not complied with certain aspects of the decree. In 1995, the Supreme Court ruled in *Missouri v. Jenkins*[10] that the state of Missouri could stop spending money to attract a multiracial student body in urban school districts through major educational improvements. This decision dealt a potentially fatal blow to the use of magnet schools for racial integration.

By the late 1990s, the federal courts had become increasingly unwilling to uphold race-conscious policies designed to further school integration and diversity—outcomes that are not mandated by the Constitution. For example, in one case a school district in Montgomery County, Maryland, had refused to allow a

**Boston Board
Abandons School Busing**

---

[7]*Riddick v. School Board of City of Norfolk,* 627 F.Supp. 814 (E.D.Va. 1984).
[8]498 U.S. 237 (1991).
[9]503 U.S. 467 (1992).
[10]515 U.S. 70 (1995).

white boy to transfer to its magnet program due to the impact his admission would have on the program's "diversity profile." In 1999, a federal appellate court held that the school district's decision not to admit the boy violated the equal protection clause of the Constitution. The Supreme Court declined to review the case, thus letting the decision stand.[11]

The Resurgence of Minority Schools.   Today, schools around the country are again becoming segregated, in large part because of *de facto* segregation. The rapid decline in the relative proportion of whites who live in large cities and high minority birthrates have increased the minority presence in those urban areas. Today, one out of every three African American and Hispanic students goes to a school with more than 90 percent minority enrollment. In the largest U.S. cities, fifteen out of sixteen African American and Hispanic students go to schools with almost no whites.

Generally, Americans are now taking another look at what desegregation means. The attempt to integrate the schools, particularly through busing, has largely failed to improve educational resources and achievement for African American children. In a Gallup poll taken in late 1999, only 26 percent of the respondents thought that minority students would be helped by stepping up integration efforts; 60 percent believed that a better alternative would be to increase funding to minority schools. A full 82 percent of those polled felt that students should be allowed to attend local schools, no matter what their racial composition. Clearly, the goal of racially balanced schools envisioned in the 1954 *Brown v. Board of Education of Topeka* decision is now giving way to the goal of better educated children, even if that means educating them in schools in which the students are of the same race.

The Civil Rights Movement

The *Brown* decision applied only to public schools. Not much else in the structure of existing segregation was affected. In December 1955, a forty-three-year-old African American woman, Rosa Parks, boarded a public bus in Montgomery, Alabama. When the bus became crowded and several white people stepped aboard, Parks was asked to move to the rear of the bus, the "colored" section. She refused, was arrested, and was fined $10; but that was not the end of the matter. For an entire year, African Americans boycotted the Montgomery bus line. The protest was headed by a twenty-seven-year-old Baptist minister, Dr. Martin Luther King, Jr. During the protest period, he went to jail, and his house was bombed. In the face of overwhelming odds, however, King won. In 1956, a federal district court issued an injunction prohibiting the segregation of buses in Montgomery. The era of civil rights protests had begun.

King's Philosophy of Nonviolence

The following year, in 1957, King formed the Southern Christian Leadership Conference (SCLC). King's philosophy of nonviolent civil disobedience was influenced, in part, by the life and teachings of Mahatma Gandhi (1869–1948). Gandhi had led Indian resistance to the British colonial system from 1919 to 1947. He used tactics such as demonstrations and marches, as well as purposeful, public disobedience to unjust laws, while remaining nonviolent. King's followers successfully used these methods to gain wider public acceptance of their cause.

Rosa Parks was born on February 4, 1913, in Tuskegee, Alabama. She was active in the Montgomery Voters' League and the NAACP League Council. After the successful boycott of the Montgomery bus system, which was sparked by her actions, she was fired from her job and moved to Detroit. In 1987, she founded the Rosa Raymond Parks Institute for Self-Development, offering guidance to disadvantaged African Americans.

[11]*Eisenberg v. Montgomery County Public Schools,* 197 F.3d 123 (4th Cir. 1999).

Nonviolent Demonstrations.   For the next decade, African Americans and sympathetic whites engaged in sit-ins, freedom rides, and freedom marches. In the beginning, such demonstrations were often met with violence, but the contrasting image of nonviolent African Americans and violent, hostile whites created strong public support for the civil rights movement. When African Americans in Greensboro, North Carolina, were refused service at a Woolworth's lunch counter, they organized a sit-in that was aided day after day by sympathetic whites and other African Americans. Enraged customers threw ketchup on the protesters. Some spat in their faces. The sit-in movement continued to grow, however. Within six months of the first sit-in the Greensboro Woolworth's, hundreds of lunch counters throughout the South were serving African Americans.

The sit-in technique was also successfully used to integrate interstate buses and their terminals, as well as railroads engaged in interstate transportation. Although buses and railroads that were engaged in interstate transportation were prohibited by law from segregating African Americans from whites, they stopped doing so only after the sit-in protests.

The Birmingham Protest.   The civil rights movement gathered momentum in the 1960s. One of the most famous of the violence-plagued protests occurred in Birmingham, Alabama, in the spring of 1963, when Police Commissioner Eugene "Bull" Connor unleashed police dogs and used electric cattle prods against the protesters. The object of the protest had been to provoke a reaction by local officials so that the federal government would act. People throughout the country viewed the event on national television with indignation and horror. King himself was thrown in jail, and it was during this period that he wrote his famous "Letter from a Birmingham Jail."[12]

The media coverage of the Birmingham protest and the violent response it elicited played a key role in the process of ending Jim Crow conditions in the United States. The ultimate result was the most important civil rights act in the nation's history, the Civil Rights Act of 1964 (to be discussed shortly).

King's March on Washington.   In August 1963, King organized the massive March on Washington for Jobs and Freedom. Before nearly a quarter-million white and African American spectators and millions watching on television, King told the world his dream:

> I have a dream that my four little children will one day live in a nation where they will not be judged by the color of their skin but by the content of their character. . . . When we let freedom ring, when we let it ring from every village and every hamlet, from every state and every city, we will be able to speed up that day when all God's children, black men and white men, Jews and Gentiles, Protestants and Catholics, will be able to join hands and sing in the words of that old Negro Spiritual, "Free at last! Free at last! Thank God almighty, we are free at last!"

[12]A copy of this letter is included in Andrew Carroll, ed., *Letters of a Nation: A Collection of Extraordinary American Letters* (New York: Kodansha America, 1997), pp. 208–226.

Dr. Martin Luther King, Jr., at the August 1963 March on Washington for Jobs and Freedom. Nearly a quarter-million African Americans and sympathetic whites participated in the march. The march is best remembered for King's eloquent "I have a dream" speech and the assembled multitude singing "We Shall Overcome," the anthem of the civil rights movement.

Malcolm X strongly opposed the philosophy of nonviolence espoused by Martin Luther King, Jr., and urged African Americans to "fight back" against white supremacy. Subsequently, several books and a movie by Spike Lee added to the revival of Malcolm X as a symbol of African American identity.

King's dream was not to be realized immediately, however. Eighteen days after his famous speech, four African American girls attending Bible class in the basement room of the Sixteenth Street Baptist Church in Birmingham, Alabama, were killed by a bomb explosion.

Another Approach—Black Power

Not all African Americans agreed with King's philosophy of nonviolence or with the idea that King's strong Christian church background should represent the core spirituality of African Americans. Indeed, Black Muslims and other African American separatists advocated a more militant stance against the politics of cultural assimilation. During the 1950s and 1960s, when King was spearheading nonviolent protests and demonstrations to achieve civil rights for African Americans, black power leaders insisted that African Americans should "fight back" instead of turning the other cheek. Indeed, some would argue that without the fear generated by black militants, a "moderate" like King would not have garnered such widespread support from white America.

Malcolm Little (who became Malcolm X when he joined the Black Muslims in 1952) and other leaders in the black power movement believed that African Americans fell into two groups: the "Uncle Toms," who peaceably accommodated the white establishment, and the "New Negroes," who took pride in their color and culture and who preferred and demanded racial separation as well as power. Malcolm X was assassinated in 1965, but he became an important reference point for a new generation of African Americans and a symbol of African American identity.

Modern Civil Rights Legislation

Police-dog attacks, cattle prods, high-pressure water hoses, beatings, bombings, the March on Washington, and black militance—all of these events and developments led to an environment in which Congress felt compelled to act on behalf of African Americans. The second era of civil rights acts, sometimes referred to as the second Reconstruction period, was under way.

The Civil Rights Act of 1957 established a Civil Rights Commission and a new Civil Rights Division within the Justice Department. The Civil Rights Act of 1960 provided that whenever a pattern or practice of discrimination was documented, the Justice Department could bring suit, even against a state. The act also set penalties for obstructing a federal court order by threat of force and for illegally using and transporting explosives. But the 1960 Civil Rights Act, as well as that of 1957, had little substantive impact.

The same cannot be said about the Civil Rights Acts of 1964 and 1968 or the Voting Rights Act of 1965 (discussed next). With those acts, Congress assumed a leading role in the enforcement of the constitutional notion of equality for *all* Americans, as provided by the Fourteenth and Fifteenth Amendments.

The Civil Rights Act of 1964

As the civil rights movement mounted in intensity, equality before the law came to be "an idea whose time has come," in the words of conservative Senate Minority Leader Everett Dirksen. The Civil Rights Act of 1964, the most far-reaching bill on civil rights in modern times, forbade discrimination on the basis of race, color, religion, gender, and national origin. The major provisions of the act were as follows:

1. It outlawed arbitrary discrimination in voter registration.
2. It barred discrimination in public accommodations, such as hotels and restaurants, whose operations affect interstate commerce.
3. It authorized the federal government to sue to desegregate public schools and facilities.
4. It expanded the power of the Civil Rights Commission and extended its life.
5. It provided for the withholding of federal funds from programs administered in a discriminatory manner.
6. It established the right to equality of opportunity in employment.

Several factors led to the passage of the 1964 act. As noted earlier, there had been a dramatic change in the climate of public opinion owing to violence perpetrated against protesting African Americans and whites in the South. Second, the assassination of President John F. Kennedy in 1963 had, according to some, a significant effect on the national conscience. Many believed the civil rights program to be the legislative tribute that Congress paid to the martyred Kennedy. Congress passed the act only after the longest **filibuster** in the history of the Senate (eighty-three days) and only after **cloture** was imposed for the first time to cut off a civil rights filibuster.

Title VII of the Civil Rights Act of 1964 is the cornerstone of employment-discrimination law. It prohibits discrimination in employment based on race, color, religion, gender, or national origin. Under Title VII, executive orders were issued that banned employment discrimination by firms that received any federal funding. The 1964 Civil Rights Act created a five-member commission, the **Equal Employment Opportunity Commission (EEOC),** to administer Title VII.

The EEOC can issue interpretive guidelines and regulations, but these do not have the force of law. Rather, they give notice of the commission's enforcement policy. The EEOC also has investigatory powers. It has broad authority to require the production of documentary evidence, to hold hearings, and to **subpoena** and examine witnesses under oath.

The Voting Rights Act of 1965

As late as 1960, only 29.1 percent of African Americans of voting age were registered in the southern states, in stark contrast to 61.1 percent of whites. In 1965, Martin Luther King, Jr., took action to change all that. Selma, the seat of Dallas County, Alabama, was chosen as the site to dramatize the voting-rights problem. In Dallas County, only 2 percent of eligible African Americans had registered to vote by the beginning of 1965. King organized a fifty-mile march from Selma to the state capital in Montgomery. He didn't get very far. Acting on orders of Governor George Wallace to disband the marchers, state troopers did so with a vengeance—with tear gas, night sticks, and whips.

Once again the national government was required to intervene to force compliance with the law. President Johnson federalized the National Guard, and the march continued. During the march, the president went on television to address a special joint session of Congress urging passage of new legislation to ensure African Americans the right to vote. The events during the Selma march and Johnson's dramatic speech, in which he invoked the slogan of the civil rights movement ("We shall overcome"), were credited for the swift passage of the Voting Rights Act of 1965.

The Voting Rights Act of 1965 had two major provisions. The first one outlawed discriminatory voter-registration tests. The second major section authorized federal registration of persons and federally administered voting procedures in any political subdivision or state that discriminated electorally

DID YOU KNOW...
That during the Mississippi Summer Project in 1964, organized by students to register African American voters, there were 1,000 arrests, 35 shooting incidents, 30 buildings bombed, 25 churches burned, 80 people beaten, and at least 6 murders **?**

Filibuster
In the Senate, unlimited debate to halt action on a particular bill.

Cloture
A method invoked to close off debate and to bring the matter under consideration to a vote in the Senate.

Equal Employment Opportunity Commission (EEOC)
A commission established by the 1964 Civil Rights Act to (1) end discrimination based on race, color, religion, gender, or national origin in conditions of employment and (2) promote voluntary action programs by employers, unions, and community organizations to foster equal job opportunities.

Subpoena
A legal writ requiring a person's appearance in court to give testimony.

against a particular group. In part, the act provided that certain political subdivisions could not change their voting procedures and election laws without federal approval. The act targeted counties, mostly in the South, in which less than 50 percent of the eligible population was registered to vote. Federal voter registrars were sent to these areas to register African Americans who had been restricted by local registrars. Within one week after the act was passed, forty-five federal examiners were sent to the South. A massive voter-registration drive covered the country.

The Civil Rights Act of 1968 and Other Housing-Reform Legislation

Martin Luther King, Jr., was assassinated on April 4, 1968. Nine days after King's death, President Lyndon Johnson signed the Civil Rights Act of 1968, which forbade discrimination in most housing and provided penalties for those attempting to interfere with individual civil rights (giving protection to civil rights workers, among others). Subsequent legislation added enforcement provisions to the federal government's rules pertaining to discriminatory mortgage-lending practices. Today, all lenders must report to the federal government the race, gender, and income of all mortgage-loan seekers, along with the final decision on their loan applications.

Increased Political Participation by African Americans

As a result of the Voting Rights Act of 1965, its amendments, and the large-scale voter-registration drives in the South, the number of African Americans registered to vote climbed dramatically. By 1980, 55.8 percent of African Americans of voting age in the South were registered. In recent elections, the percentage of voting-age African Americans who have registered to vote is just slightly less than the percentage of voting-age whites who have registered to vote.

Today, there are more than 8,000 African American elected officials in the United States. There are thirty-four African Americans in the 107th Congress.

Reverend Jesse Jackson (shown marching with Patricia Ireland, then president of the National Organization for Women) is one example of the increased political participation of African Americans.

In 1984, the Reverend Jesse Jackson became the first African American candidate to compete seriously for the presidential nomination. In 1989, Virginia became the first state to elect an African American governor. General Colin Powell became the first African American to be appointed chairman of the Joint Chiefs of Staff (in 1989) and, after retiring from the service, secretary of state (in 2001). In 1991, Clarence Thomas became a justice of the Supreme Court, replacing Thurgood Marshall, the first African American justice.

The movement of African American citizens into high elected office has thus been sure, if exceedingly slow. Black Democratic candidates continue to face an uphill fight to gain top political offices, such as governorships and U.S. Senate seats. Yet the same can also be said for white Democratic candidates since the Republican sweep of Congress in 1994. Notably, recent polling data show that most Americans do not consider race a significant factor with regard to presidential candidates. In 1958, when the Gallup poll first asked whether respondents would be willing to vote for an African American as president, only 38 percent of the public said yes. By 2001, this percentage had reached 95 percent.

Political Participation by Other Minorities

As mentioned earlier, the civil rights movement focused primarily on the rights of African Americans. Yet the legislation resulting from the movement ultimately has benefited virtually all minority groups. The Civil Rights Act of 1964, for example, prohibits discrimination against any person because of race, color, or national origin. Subsequent amendments to the Voting Rights Act of 1965 extended its protections to other minorities, including Hispanic Americans, Asian Americans, Native Americans, and Native Alaskans. To further protect the voting rights of minorities, the act now provides that states must make bilingual ballots available in counties where 5 percent or more of the population speaks a language other than English.

The political participation of other minority groups in the United States has also been increasing. Hispanics are gaining political power in several states. Today, over 5 percent of the legislative seats in Arizona, California, Colorado, Florida, New Mexico, and Texas are held by legislators of Hispanic ancestry. At the national level, the percentage of Hispanics in Congress is somewhat lower—they constitute about 3 percent of that institution's members. There is also a Native American in Congress—Senator Ben Nighthorse Campbell (Rep., Colo.), who was elected to the Senate in 1992 after having served in the House from 1987 to 1992.

Even though political participation by minorities has increased dramatically since the 1960s, the number of political offices held by members of minority groups remains disproportionately low compared to their numbers in the overall population. This will likely change in the future due to the continued influx of immigrants, particularly from Mexico. Collectively, Hispanics, African Americans, Native Americans, and Asian Americans are now a majority of the populations in California, Hawaii, and New Mexico. It is estimated that by 2010 minority populations will collectively outnumber whites in Texas and New York as well.

Lingering Social and Economic Disparities

According to Joyce Ladner of the Brookings Institution, one of the problems with the race-based civil rights agenda of the 1950s and 1960s is that it did not envision remedies for cross-racial problems. How, for example, should the nation address problems, such as poverty and urban violence, that affect underclasses in all racial groups? In 1967, when Martin Luther King proposed a Poor

DID YOU KNOW...
That in 1790, according to census data, only two out of every five Americans were of English origin?

People's Campaign, he recognized that a civil rights coalition based entirely on race would not be sufficient to address the problem of poverty among whites as well as blacks. During his 1984 and 1988 presidential campaigns, African American leader Jesse Jackson also acknowledged the inadequacy of a race-based model of civil rights when he attempted to form a "Rainbow Coalition" of minorities, women, and other underrepresented groups, including the poor.[13]

Some contend that government intervention is necessary to eliminate the social and economic disparities that persist within the American population. Others believe that the most effective means of addressing these issues is through coalitions of government groups, private businesses, community-based groups, and individuals. Indeed, a number of civil rights activists today are pursuing the latter strategy (see the feature *Making Waves: A New Generation of Civil Rights Leaders*).

Immigration and the Civil Rights Agenda

Time and again, this nation has been challenged and changed—and culturally enriched—by immigrant groups. All of these immigrants have faced the challenges involved in living in a new and different political and cultural environment. Most

---

[13]Joyce A. Ladner, "A New Civil Rights Agenda," *The Brookings Review,* Vol. 18, No. 2 (Spring 2000), pp. 26–28.

making Waves

A New Generation of Civil Rights Leaders

In the mid-1980s, when Lattie Dorsey returned to her hometown of Atlanta, Georgia, she was shocked to see how much the city had changed during the years that she had been away. The middle-class neighborhoods she had left a decade earlier were now stricken by poverty and violence. Dorsey decided to devote her efforts to turning these neighborhoods around. Eventually, she succeeded in convincing city council members, civic associations, and other groups in the city to help her establish an organization to secure financing for neighborhood redevelopment.

Since 1991, the organization, called the Atlanta Neighborhood Development Partnership, Inc. (ANDP), has raised more than $60 million to help develop and renovate more than six thousand housing units in the inner-city area. ANDP also provides various services to local community-development organizations, including technical assistance and training for residents of neighborhoods where revitalization is taking place. Dorsey, the president and chief executive officer of ANDP, claims that the key to the organization's success is making the business sector understand that what happens in inner-city neighborhoods has

an effect on surrounding areas as well. Businesses that have made major investments in the outlying areas of Atlanta thus have a stake in inner-city redevelopment.

Dorsey is one of a new generation of civil rights activists. Many other individuals, like Dorsey, are moving away from the race paradigm that has long characterized the civil rights movement. Instead, these new leaders are focusing their energies on improving the plight of the poor in America's inner cities. In Boston, Eugene Rivers founded a coalition of government and community groups to disarm gangs and fund rehabilitation services for gang members. Robert Woodson and the organization he heads, the National Neighborhood Enterprise Center, helped the District of Columbia's most violent gangs achieve a truce and placed the members in paying jobs. Bob Moses, a civil rights activist of the 1960s, has refocused his efforts on the needs of the poor: he now teaches math to poor children to help them prepare for a technology-driven society.

FOR CRITICAL ANALYSIS

What, if anything, can the federal government do to reduce poverty, gang violence, and other problems facing inner-city residents?

DID YOU KNOW...
That about two immigrants enter the United States every minute?

of them have had to overcome language barriers, and many have had to deal with discrimination in one form or another because of their color, their inability to speak English fluently, or their customs. The civil rights legislation passed during and since the 1960s has done much to counter the effects of prejudice against immigrant groups by ensuring that they obtain equal rights under the law.

One of the questions facing Americans and their political leaders today concerns the effect of immigration on the economic and social welfare of the United States—see this chapter's *Critical Perspective* on the next two pages for a discussion of this issue. Another issue has to do with the impact of immigration and interracial marriages on the traditional civil rights agenda.

The Continued Influx of Immigrants

Today, immigration rates are the highest they have been since their peak in the early twentieth century. Currently, about one million people a year immigrate to this country, and those who were born on foreign soil now constitute nearly 10 percent of the U.S. population—twice the percentage of thirty years ago.

Clearly, the traditional black-white model of racial and ethnic relations no longer fits the changing ethnic face of America. Consider that since 1977, four out of five immigrants have come from Latin America or Asia. Hispanics are now overtaking African Americans as the nation's largest minority. If current immigration rates continue, by the year 2050 minority groups collectively will constitute the "majority" of Americans. If Hispanics, African Americans, and perhaps Asians were to form coalitions, they could increase their political strength dramatically and would have the numerical strength to make significant changes. According to Ben Wattenberg of the American Enterprise Institute, in the future the "old guard" white majority will no longer dominate American politics.

INFOTRAC®
COLLEGE EDITION

Public Opinion toward Immigrants Immigration Policies

In Los Angeles, Mexican Americans celebrate Cinco de Mayo. Is the United States a nation of many ethnic cultures existing separately, or is it a melting pot of diverse cultures?

critical perspective

Should the Immigration Door Be Shut?

The United States is in the middle of its second "great wave" of immigration. Each year, approximately 700,000 legal immigrants and 275,000 illegal immigrants make their way to American soil. A number of policymakers believe that this number is too high and that the country is paying a steep price for our immigration policies. Many Americans agree: about two-thirds think that too many foreigners are being allowed into the United States. While few think that the immigration door should be completely shut, a large number of Americans would like to see greater restrictions placed on immigration.

This attitude is not necessarily in keeping with America's view of itself as a "nation of immigrants." Indeed, for most of its early history the United States relied heavily on immigrants to populate and cultivate its empty spaces, and the country had an "open-door" policy. That is, anybody who wanted to come to these shores could do so. That policy changed in the 1920s following the first great wave of immigration, when immigration rates were similar to those of today.

Regulating the Flow of Immigrants

To slow the flow of immigrants, in 1921 Congress demanded literacy requirements for immigrants and established quotas based on national origin. This policy, which favored white Europeans, began to change in 1965 as the federal government began to make family unification the centerpiece of its immigration policy. Under today's immigration laws, newcomers are divided into the following categories:

- **Family members.** An American citizen can sponsor a spouse, child, parent, or sibling to receive a U.S. visa. About two-thirds of those who come to this country each year are family members, mostly from South America or Southeast Asia.
- **Workers.** About 140,000 work permits are made available each year. About 80 percent of these permits go to skilled workers, such as technology specialists and scientists.
- **Refugees.** The United States has a long history of allowing those who face oppression in their homelands to seek political asylum in America.
- **Lottery winners.** Each year, about 7 million would-be immigrants participate in a lottery for 50,000 green cards. A certain share of winners is designated for each country.
- **Illegal immigrants.** Currently, about 5 million illegal immigrants–1.9 percent of the U.S. population–are living in the United States. Around 275,000 more arrive annually. The Immigration and Naturalization Service (INS) spends billions of dollars each year to keep immigrants from illegally crossing the borders of Mexico and Canada.

The Case for a Selective Immigration Policy

In his recently published book *Heaven's Door: Immigration Policy and the American Economy,** Harvard economist George J. Borjas claims that the current U.S. immigration policy is harmful to the nation's economic well-being. In contrast to the earlier great wave of immigrants, the new wave includes large numbers of immigrants with few, if any, skills. As a result, these new immigrants have increased inequality in the United States by depressing the economic opportunities of native-born unskilled workers. They also place a fiscal burden on the welfare system, particularly in those states with large immigrant populations, such as California.

According to Borjas, we need to take a hard look at two key questions relating to immigration policy: How many immigrants do

*Ewing, N.J.: Princeton University Press, 1999.

The Problem of Racial Classifications

One of the challenges facing the government today is that the lines separating racial groups are becoming increasingly blurred. About 25 percent of Hispanics marry persons outside their group, as do nearly one-third of the Asians living in America; and many African Americans have both a black and a white heritage. A few years ago, golf professional Tiger Woods emphasized the growing problem of racial identity. When Oprah Winfrey asked Woods about his ethnic status, he said he was not a black but a "Cablinasian"–a combination of Caucasian, black, Indian, and Asian.

we want, and which ones should they be? Borjas goes on to state that the answers to these questions depend on what goal we want to accomplish through immigration. In his opinion, our goal should be to maximize the economic welfare of our native population. To accomplish this goal, he argues, we should shift our immigration policy away from the principle of family reunification toward one that favors skilled workers.

To generate a "more skilled immigrant flow," Borjas suggests that we institute a "point system" similar to that used by Canada. Under Canadian policy, points toward a visa are based on various socioeconomic characteristics, including the applicant's age, education, English-language fluency, relatives already living in the country, and occupation. To enter Canada, a visa applicant must meet a threshold number of points. If the United States used a similar point system, we could easily control the total number of immigrants as well, simply by raising or lowering the threshold number of points. Borjas believes that we should restrict the total number of immigrants to 500,000 a year.

The Case for Open Immigration

Not everybody believes that we should limit immigration. Indeed, some scholars suggest that we should return to the open-door policy of the past. Jacob G. Hornberger and the other editors of *The Case for Free Trade and Open Immigration*[†] argue that immigrants bring a vitality to American society that benefits all citizens, not just culturally and socially but economically as well. Statistics compiled by the U.S. Department of Labor suggest that the economic well-being of

the United States depends to a large extent on immigrant labor. As the native-born population ages over the next decade, American businesses will rely on foreign-born workers to keep the labor pool growing. Without immigrants, the American work force would actually begin to shrink by 2015, with negative results for the economy.

Even though elderly immigrants and refugees rely heavily on government assistance, only 2 percent of working-age, nonrefugee immigrants receive welfare (compared to 3.7 percent of American-born citizens). Using these statistics, Stephen Moore of the Cato Institute concludes that the average immigrant will pay from $20,000 to $80,000 more in taxes than he or she will receive in governmental benefits. Furthermore, immigrants are 50 percent more likely to have a graduate degree than native-born Americans, and nearly one-fourth of all female doctors in the United States are foreign-born. These figures may support Hornberger's contention that immigrants are, for the most part, hard-working, intelligent risk takers who have traded the security of home for the opportunities available in the United States.

FOR CRITICAL ANALYSIS

1. Some observers have suggested that immigrants should be denied social benefits, such as welfare and education, for the first several years they live in the United States. What impact might this policy have on immigration levels?

2. Immigrants are responsible for nearly one-third of our annual population growth. What role should population growth play in the immigration policy debate?

[†]Fairfax, Va.: The Future of Freedom Foundation, 1995.

The blurring of racial distinctions is significant for the civil rights agenda because the U.S. Census Bureau and other federal and state agencies traditionally have used racial classifications to determine who is eligible for certain benefits. Since 1977, for example, the federal government has identified Americans using the following racial categories: black, white, American Indian, Alaskan native, and Asian/Pacific islander. "Hispanic" is a separate category. Yet how can these classifications be applied to the millions of Americans with mixed ethnic and racial backgrounds? In the 2000 census, the government tried to address this problem by allowing respondents to check more than one racial box. Some contend that the government should go even further and drop racial categories from the census entirely (see this chapter's feature *Which Side Are You On?*).

which side are you on?

Should Racial Categories Be Dropped from the Census?

There is no doubt that the United States is becoming a more diverse country. As mentioned elsewhere, each year about one million immigrants arrive from countries all over the world. Additionally, the number of mixed-race marriages that take place each year has risen from 149,000 in 1960 to nearly 1.4 million today. But just how diverse are we? It is the U.S. Census Bureau's job to find out. At the beginning of each decade, the Census Bureau sends out questionnaires to all citizens. The answers to these questions help the government determine the size, shape, and opinions of the American population.

Racial Categories and the 2000 Census

The questionnaires have always included questions about race—in the nation's first census, taken in 1790, the categories included "free white male," "free white female," and "slave." But in 2000, for the first time, respondents were given the choice of checking off multiple boxes from sixty-three different racial combinations and mixtures, instead of being limited to a single box.

By adding the "multibox" option, the Census Bureau acknowledged that tens of millions of Americans do not fit comfortably into one racial "box." In previous decades, a person with a Chinese mother and an African American father, for example, had to choose one or the other if she or he wanted to be counted by the government. In contrast, in the 2000 census a person could check several boxes, such as "white," "Indian," and "African American," to identify his or her "race."

Criticisms of Racial Categories

Some critics believe that attempts to categorize Americans by race are harmful to society as a whole. These critics claim that instead of emphasizing the things that most Americans have in common—such as the desire for good schools, safe streets, and honest politicians—the 2000 census highlights our differences. After all, the argument goes, the ranking of people based on some physical characteristic is the basis of recognized evils such as racism and sexism.

Furthermore, opponents believe it is futile to try to capture the diversity of the population. How much, they ask, does a political refugee from Somalia have in common with an African American whose family has lived in the United States for generations? Finally, scientists point out that from a genetic perspective, all human beings are more than 99.9 percent the same, a fact that is more important than our cultural differences.

How Racial Statistics Are Used

The compilation of racial statistics is not merely an intellectual exercise for the Census Bureau. In order for the federal government to enforce equal protection laws regarding minority groups, it needs to know how many minority group members there are and where they live. Suppose, for example, that a bank was engaged in discriminatory lending practices in a predominantly African American neighborhood. The federal government, in bringing action against that bank, would use census data to back its case.

Census data on the racial composition of the U.S. population are also used to change the boundaries of congressional districts so that minority groups are not severely disadvantaged in congressional elections (see the discussion of redistricting in Chapter 12). Additionally, such information helps the government determine which communities should receive federal funds set aside to improve certain government-provided services, such as education and law enforcement.

DOES IT MATTER?

In your opinion, should the racial identity of an individual or class of individuals be a factor in determining who should receive government assistance?

GOING ONLINE

For further information on the 2000 census, including the uses of population data, go to **http://www.2000.census. gov/iqa/pquse.html**. *Clarence Page, a columnist for the* Chicago Tribune, *believes that the new methods of measuring race are positive for society. To read his views on this issue, go to* **http://www.chicagotribune.com/ news/columnists/page/ 1,1122,SAV-000315008,00.html**. *To learn why some people see the 2000 census as a "multiracial nightmare," go to* **www.sfgate.com/cgi-bin/article. cgi?file=/examiner/archive/1999/ 11/28/NEWS5065.dtl**.

Women's Struggle for Equal Rights

Like African Americans and other minorities, women also have had to struggle for equality. During the first phase of this struggle, the primary goal of women was to obtain the right to vote. Some women had hoped that the founders would provide such a right in the Constitution. In 1776, Abigail Adams wrote to her husband, John Adams, the following words in reference to new laws that would be necessary if a Declaration of Independence was issued:

> I desire you would remember the ladies. . . . If particular care and attention is not paid to the ladies, we are determined to foment a rebellion and will not hold ourselves bound by any laws in which we have no voice or representation.[14]

Despite this request, the founders did not include in the Constitution a provision guaranteeing women the right to vote. Nor did it deny to women—or to any others—this right. Rather, the founders left it up to the states to decide such issues, and, as stated earlier, by and large, the states limited the franchise to adult white males who owned property. That only property owners could vote apparently did not seem unusual to the founders. The prevailing view seems to have been that "the people who own the country ought to govern it," as John Jay phrased it.

Early Women's Political Movements

The first political cause in which women became actively engaged was the slavery abolition movement. Even male abolitionists felt that women should not take an active role on the subject in public, however. When the World Antislavery Convention was held in London in 1840, women delegates were barred from active participation. Responding partly to this rebuff, two American delegates, Lucretia Mott and Elizabeth Cady Stanton, returned from that meeting with plans to work for women's rights in the United States.

In 1848, Mott and Stanton organized the first women's rights convention in Seneca Falls, New York. The three hundred people who attended approved a Declaration of Sentiments: "We hold these truths to be self-evident: that all men *and women* are created equal." In the following twelve years, groups of feminists held seven conventions in different cities in the Midwest and East. With the outbreak of the Civil War, however, advocates of women's rights were urged to put their support behind the war effort, and most agreed.

The Suffrage Issue and the Fifteenth Amendment. "The right of citizens of the United States to vote shall not be denied or abridged by the United States or by any State on account of race, color, or previous condition of servitude." So reads Section 1 of the Fifteenth Amendment to the Constitution, which was ratified in 1870. The campaign for the passage of this amendment split the women's **suffrage** movement. Militant feminists wanted to add "sex" to "race, color, or previous condition of servitude." Other feminists, along with many men, opposed this view; they wanted to separate African American suffrage and women's suffrage to ensure the passage of the amendment. So, although the African American community supported the women's suffrage movement, it became separate from the racial equality movement. Still, some women attempted to vote in the years following the Civil War. One, Virginia Louisa Minor, was arrested and convicted in 1872. She appealed to the Supreme Court, but the Court upheld her conviction.[15]

Women's Suffrage Associations. Susan B. Anthony and Elizabeth Cady Stanton formed the National Woman Suffrage Association in 1869. According

Elizabeth Cady Stanton (1815–1902) was a social reformer and a women's suffrage leader. At her wedding to Henry B. Stanton in 1840, she insisted on dropping the word "obey" from the marriage vows. She wrote *The History of Women's Suffrage,* which was published in 1886.

Suffrage
The right to vote; the franchise.

---

[14]As quoted in Carroll, ed., *Letters of a Nation,* p. 60.
[15]*Minor v. Happersett,* 21 Wall. 162 (1874). The Supreme Court reasoned that the right to vote was a privilege of state, not federal, citizenship. The Court did not consider privileges of state citizenship to be protected by the Fourteenth Amendment.

Susan B. Anthony (1820–1906) was a leader of the women's suffrage movement who was also active in the antialcohol and antislavery movements. In 1869, with Elizabeth Cady Stanton, she founded the National Woman Suffrage Association. In 1888, she organized the International Council of Women and, in 1904, the International Women's Suffrage Alliance, in Berlin.

Feminism
The movement that supports political, economic, and social equality for women.

to their view, women's suffrage was a means to achieve major improvements in the economic and social situation of women in the United States. In other words, the vote was to be used to obtain a larger goal. Lucy Stone, however, felt that the vote was the only major issue. Members of the American Woman Suffrage Association, founded by Stone and others, traveled to each state, addressed state legislatures, wrote, published, and argued their convictions. They achieved only limited success. In 1890, the two organizations quit battling and joined forces. The National American Woman Suffrage Association had only one goal—the enfranchisement of women—but it made little progress.

By the early 1900s, small radical splinter groups were formed, such as the Congressional Union, headed by Alice Paul. This organization worked solely for the passage of an amendment to the U.S. Constitution. Willing to use "unorthodox" means to achieve its goal, this group and others took to the streets; parades, hunger strikes, arrests, and jailings ensued. Finally, in 1920, seventy-two years after the Seneca Falls convention, the Nineteenth Amendment was passed: "The right of citizens of the United States to vote shall not be denied or abridged by the United States or by any State on account of sex." Women were thus enfranchised. Although today it may seem that the United States was slow to give women the vote, it was really not too far behind the rest of the world (see Table 5–1).

The Modern Women's Movement

After gaining the right to vote in 1920, women engaged in little organized political activity until the 1960s. The civil rights movement of that decade resulted in a growing awareness of rights for all groups, including women. Additionally, the publication of Betty Friedan's *The Feminine Mystique* in 1963 focused national attention on the unequal status of women in American life.

In 1966, Friedan and others who were dissatisfied with the lack of aggressive action against gender discrimination by the then-largest women's organizations—the National Federation of Business and Professional Women's Clubs and the League of Women Voters—formed the National Organization for Women (NOW). NOW immediately adopted a blanket resolution designed "to bring women into full participation in the mainstream of American society *now*, exercising all the privileges and responsibilities thereof in truly equal partnership with men."

NOW has been in the forefront of what is often called the *feminist movement*. Historian Nancy Cott contends that the word *feminism* first began to be used around 1910. At that time, **feminism** meant, as it does today, political, social, and economic equality for women—a radical notion that gained little support among members of the suffrage movement. It is difficult to measure the support for feminism today because the term means different things to different people.

TABLE 5–1			
Years, by Country, in Which Women Gained the Right to Vote			
1893: New Zealand	1919: Germany	1945: Italy	1953: Mexico
1902: Australia	1920: United States	1945: Japan	1956: Egypt
1913: Norway	1930: South Africa	1947: Argentina	1963: Kenya
1918: Britain	1932: Brazil	1950: India	1971: Switzerland
1918: Canada	1944: France	1952: Greece	1984: Yemen

SOURCE: Center for the American Woman and Politics.

When the dictionary definition of a feminist—"someone who supports political, economic, and social equality for women"—was read to respondents in a survey, however, 67 percent labeled themselves as feminists.[16]

The initial focus of the modern women's movement was not on expanding the political rights of women. Rather, leaders of NOW and other liberal women's rights advocates sought to eradicate gender inequality through a constitutional amendment.

The Equal Rights Amendment.   The proposed Equal Rights Amendment (ERA), which was first introduced in Congress in 1923 by leaders of the National Women's Party, states as follows: "Equality of rights under the law shall not be denied or abridged by the United States or by any state on account of sex." For years the amendment was not even given a hearing in Congress, but finally it was approved by both chambers and sent to the state legislatures for ratification on March 22, 1972.

As was noted in Chapter 2, any constitutional amendment must be ratified by the legislatures (or conventions) in three-fourths of the states before it can become law. Since the early 1900s, most proposed amendments have required that ratification occur within seven years of Congress's adoption of the amendment. The necessary thirty-eight states failed to ratify the ERA within the seven-year period specified by Congress, even though it was supported by numerous national party platforms, six presidents, and both chambers of Congress. To date, efforts to reintroduce the amendment have not succeeded (see the *Making Waves* feature in Chapter 2 on page 57 for a further discussion of this amendment and its current status).

During the national debate over the ratification of the ERA, a women's countermovement emerged. Many women perceived the goals pursued by NOW and other liberal women's organizations as a threat to their way of life. At the head of the countermovement was Republican Phyllis Schlafly and her conservative organization, Eagle Forum. Eagle Forum's "Stop-ERA" campaign found significant support among fundamentalist religious groups and various other conservative organizations. The campaign was effective in blocking the ratification of the ERA.

Challenging Gender Discrimination in the Courts.   When the ERA failed to be ratified, women's rights organizations began to refocus their efforts. Although NOW continued to press for the ERA, other groups challenged discriminatory statutes and policies in the federal courts, contending that **gender discrimination** violated the Fourteenth Amendment's equal protection clause. Since the 1970s, the Supreme Court has tended to scrutinize gender classifications closely and has invalidated a number of such statutes and policies. For example, in 1977 the Court held that police and firefighting units cannot establish arbitrary rules, such as height and weight requirements, that tend to preclude women from joining those occupations.[17] In 1983, the Court ruled that insurance companies cannot charge different rates for women and men.[18]

A question that the Court has not ruled on is whether women should be allowed to participate in military combat. Generally, the Supreme Court has left this decision up to Congress and the Department of Defense. Although recently

DID YOU KNOW...
That a Gallup poll taken in early 2000 found that 15 percent of the women described themselves as homemakers, but not one man described himself as such**?**

INFOTRAC®
COLLEGE EDITION

Pull together now

Gender Discrimination
Any practice, policy, or procedure that denies equality of treatment to an individual or to a group because of gender.

---

[16]Nancy E. McGlen and Karen O'Connor, *Women, Politics, and American Society,* 2d ed. (Upper Saddle River, N.J.: Prentice Hall, 1998), p. 11.
[17]*Dothard v. Rawlinson,* 433 U.S. 321 (1977).
[18]*Arizona v. Norris,* 463 U.S. 1073 (1983).

A female cadet begins her training at the Virginia Military Institute. In 1996, the Supreme Court ruled that the institute's policy of accepting only males violated the equal protection clause of the Constitution.

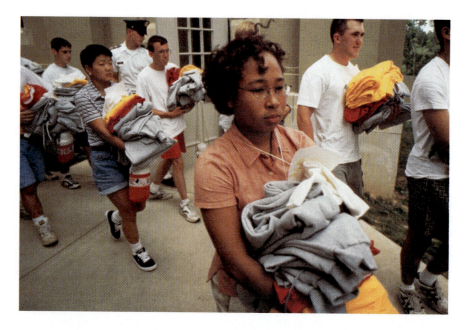

women have been allowed to serve as combat pilots and on naval warships, to date they have not been allowed to join infantry combat units. In regard to military training institutes, however, the Supreme Court held in 1996 that the state-financed Virginia Military Institute's policy of accepting only males violated the equal protection clause.[19]

Expanding Women's Political Opportunities. Following the failure of the ERA, in addition to fighting discrimination in the courts, the women's movement began to work for increased representation in government. Several women's political organizations that are active today concentrate their efforts on getting women elected to political offices. These organizations include the national Women's Political Caucus, the Coalition for Women's Appointments, the Fund for a Feminist Majority, and Black Women Organized for Action.

A variety of women's political action committees, or PACs (see Chapter 10), have also been created and are now important sources of financial support for women candidates. The largest of these PACs is EMILY's List (EMILY stands for "Early Money Is Like Yeast–It Makes the Dough Rise"). This PAC supports Democratic women candidates for congressional offices and governorships. Founded in 1985, EMILY's List now has nearly 50,000 members who contribute funds to be used for political campaigns.

Women in Politics Today

The efforts of women's rights advocates and organizations have helped to increase the number of women holding political offices in all areas of government. The men's club atmosphere still prevails in Congress, however, and no woman has yet held one of the major congressional leadership positions. But the number of women holding congressional seats has increased significantly in recent years. Elections during the 1990s brought more women to Congress than either the Senate or the House had seen before. After the 2000 elections, there were fifty-nine women in the House and thirteen in the Senate. (See the feature *Elections 2000: Political Leadership by Women* for further details on women in today's Congress.)

---

[19]*United States v. Virginia*, 518 U.S. 515 (1996).

Political Leadership by Women

As a result of the 2000 elections, a record number of women—fifty-nine—now hold seats in the U.S. House of Representatives. The fifty-two women incumbents in the House who ran for reelection all retained their seats. Additionally, voters elected seven other women to that chamber. The elections also increased the number of women in the Senate from nine to thirteen. Democratic candidate Hillary Rodham Clinton's victory in New York represented another "first" in women's political history—she became the first former First Lady to ever hold a Senate seat. Jean Carnahan, a Democrat from Missouri who was appointed to the Senate seat won by her late husband, Missouri governor Mel Carnahan (who died in an accident two weeks prior to the election), will face reelection in just two years.

Women also fared well in state races for legislative seats and gubernatorial offices. Today, four governorships are held by women. New Hampshire, Montana, Delaware, and Arizona now all have women governors.

Although no woman has yet been nominated for president by a major political party, in 1984 a woman, Geraldine Ferraro, became the Democratic nominee for vice president. Another woman, Elizabeth Dole, made a serious run at the Republican presidential nomination in the 2000 campaigns. Notably, a recent Gallup poll found that 92 percent of Americans said that they would vote for a qualified woman for president if she was nominated by their party.

An increasing number of women are also being appointed to cabinet posts. Franklin Roosevelt appointed the first woman to a cabinet post—Frances Perkins, who was secretary of labor from 1933 to 1945. His successor, Gerald Ford (1974–1977), appointed a woman as secretary of housing and urban development, and each subsequent president has appointed at least two women to head cabinet departments. President Bill Clinton appointed four women to his cabinet, more than any previous president. One of Clinton's appointees, Secretary of State Madeleine Albright, became the first woman ever to hold an "inner" cabinet post. President George W. Bush appointed three women to cabinet positions and two women to other significant federal offices.

Increasingly, women are sitting on federal judicial benches as well. President Ronald Reagan was credited with a historical first when he appointed Sandra Day O'Connor to the Supreme Court in 1981. President Clinton, during his first term, appointed another woman, Ruth Bader Ginsburg, to the Court.

Women have had more success in gaining political offices in state legislatures and local governments. Several women have been elected to governorships, and about one-fourth of all state legislative seats are now held by women. In some states, including Washington, Colorado, and Nevada, over one-third of these seats are held by women. Additionally, Chicago, Houston, San Francisco, and Minneapolis have had female mayors, as have 17 percent of U.S. cities with populations of more than thirty thousand.

For all their achievements in the political arena, however, the number of women holding political offices remains disproportionately low compared to their participation as voters. In recent elections, the absolute turnout of female voters nationally has been slightly higher than that of male voters. (For a discussion of the political status of women in other countries, see this chapter's *Global View: The Struggle for Women's Rights around the World* on the next page.)

In January 2001, George W. Bush appointee Condoleezza Rice became the first woman to chair the National Security Council and serve as national security adviser to the president. In addition to her substantial academic and political experience in foreign affairs, Rice is an accomplished pianist (her given name comes from the Italian musical term *con dolcezza*, which means "with sweetness").

Gender-Based Discrimination in the Workplace

Traditional cultural beliefs concerning the proper role of women in society continue to be evident not only in the political arena but also in the workplace. Since the 1960s, however, women have gained substantial protection against discrimination by laws mandating equal employment opportunities and equal pay.

Title VII of the Civil Rights Act of 1964

Title VII of the Civil Rights Act of 1964 prohibits gender discrimination in the employment context and has been used to strike down employment policies that discriminate against employees on the basis of gender. Even so-called protective policies have been held to violate Title VII if they have a discriminatory effect. In 1991, for example, the Supreme Court held that a fetal protection policy established by Johnson Controls, Inc., the country's largest producer of automobile batteries, violated Title VII. The policy required all women of childbearing age working in jobs that entailed periodic exposure to lead or other hazardous materials to prove that they were infertile or to transfer to other positions. Women who agreed to transfer often had to accept cuts in pay and reduced job responsibilities. The Court concluded that women who are "as capable of doing their jobs as their male counterparts may not be forced to choose between having a child and having a job."[20]

[20]*United Automobile Workers v. Johnson Controls, Inc.*, 499 U.S. 187 (1991).

global view

The Struggle for Women's Rights around the World

Researcher Camilia Araf-Badr uses an Arabic saying to describe the plight of the Arab women in the part of Israel where she works and lives: "One scoops water from the sea, and another chisels stones." Araf-Badr's comparison of gaining equal rights to carving a path in the stone applies to women in other areas of the world as well. Although the last several decades of the twentieth century saw women's rights emerge as a global issue, progress has been slow.

THE PROBLEM OF VIOLENCE

Most people consider the right to be free from violence as one of the most basic human rights. Women's rights advocates point out that this right is threatened in societies that do not accept the premise that men and women are equal. In some parts of India, for example, a wife is considered the property of her husband, and he can do with her as he pleases. This has led to the practice of dowry killing. (A dowry is a sum of money given to a husband by the bride's family.) In a number of cases, husbands, dissatisfied with the size of dowries, have killed their wives in order to remarry for a "better deal"—a crime that is rarely prosecuted.

In some places, women are also expected to act in certain ways to uphold the "honor" of their family. When they fail to do so, the consequences can be brutal. In 1999, for example, a twenty-seven-year-old Pakistani woman was killed by a "hit man" hired by members of her family, who were upset that she was seeking a divorce. Such "honor killings" are relatively well known not only in Pakistan but also in Iraq, Iran, Palestine, Jordan, and Turkey.

POLITICAL AND ECONOMIC RIGHTS

Violence is by no means the only issue concerning women's rights around the world. In Afghanistan, women have been barred from holding jobs and going to school after the age of eight. In Kuwait, women cannot vote or hold political office. Even in countries that do not legally restrict women's political rights, their political representation may be limited. Only 72 of the 535 members of the U.S. Congress, for example, are women. Low levels of women in the French Parliament have led to calls for legislation that guarantees that equal numbers of men and women will be elected. Furthermore, the low percentage of female professionals in Japan (9.3 percent, compared to 44.3 percent in the United States) led to a series of laws geared toward making the Japanese corporate world a friendlier place for women. The government's commitment to the laws came into question, however, following press reports that the new minister of gender equity had been accused of sexual harassment.

FOR CRITICAL ANALYSIS

The United States has been very critical of such practices as India's dowry killings. Is it fair or appropriate for one country to judge the cultural practices of another? Why or why not?

In 1978, Congress amended Title VII to expand the definition of gender discrimination to include discrimination based on pregnancy. Women affected by pregnancy, childbirth, or related medical conditions must be treated—for all employment-related purposes, including the receipt of benefits under employee-benefit programs—the same as other persons not so affected but similar in ability to work.

Sexual Harassment

The Supreme Court has also held that Title VII's prohibition of gender-based discrimination extends to **sexual harassment** in the workplace. Sexual harassment occurs when job opportunities, promotions, salary increases, and so on are given in return for sexual favors. A special form of sexual harassment, called hostile-environment harassment, occurs when an employee is subjected to sexual conduct or comments that interfere with the employee's job performance or are so pervasive or severe as to create an intimidating, hostile, or offensive environment.

Definitional Problems.   One of the questions faced by employers and employees—as well as the courts—is deciding the point at which offensive conduct in the workplace is so "pervasive or severe" as to create a hostile working environment. In 1993, in *Harris v. Forklift Systems, Inc.,*[21] the Supreme Court attempted to give some guidelines on this issue, as well as on another question: Must a worker claiming to be a victim of hostile-environment harassment establish that the offensive conduct gave rise to serious emotional or psychological effects? Justice O'Connor answered both questions by stating, "So long as the environment would reasonably be perceived, and is perceived, as hostile or abusive, there is no need for it also to be psychologically injurious."

Many have complained that the Court's 1993 decision failed to provide the lower courts with a definitive standard by which to judge hostile-environment claims. Essentially, in some cases, a hostile environment exists whenever an employee claims it exists. According to William Petrocelli, the author of *Sexual Harassment on the Job,*[22] "If you feel you've been sexually harassed, then you have been." Some courts have held that just one incident of sexually offensive conduct—such as a sexist remark by a co-worker or a photo on an employer's desk of his bikini-clad wife—can create a hostile environment.

The Court's Recent Decisions Concerning Harassment.   In 1998, in *Faragher v. City of Boca Raton,*[23] the Court addressed another important question: Should an employer be held liable for its supervisor's sexual harassment of an employee even though the employer was unaware of the harrassment? The Court ruled that the employer in this case was liable but stated that the employer might have avoided such liability if it had taken reasonable care to prevent harassing behavior—which the employer had not done. In another case, *Burlington Industries v. Ellerth,*[24] the Court similarly held that an employer was liable for sexual harassment caused by a supervisor's actions even though the employee had suffered no tangible job consequences as a result of those actions. Again, the Court emphasized that a key factor in holding the employer liable was whether the employer had exercised reasonable care to prevent and promptly correct any sexually harassing behavior.

DID YOU KNOW... That a woman worker at the sewer plant in Palmer, Massachusetts, filed a sexual-harassment complaint against the city after finding a sexually explicit magazine in the plant superintendent's drawer while looking for billing information?

Sexual Harassment
Unwanted physical or verbal conduct or abuse of a sexual nature that interferes with a recipient's job performance, creates a hostile environment, or carries with it an implicit or explicit threat of adverse employment consequences.

---

[21]510 U.S. 17 (1993).
[22]William Petrocelli and Barbara Kate Repa, *Sexual Harassment on the Job: What It Is and How to Stop It,* 3d ed. (Berkeley, Calif.: Nolo Press, 1998).
[23]524 U.S. 725 (1998).
[24]524 U.S. 742 (1998).

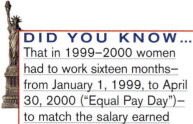

In another 1998 case, *Oncale v. Sundowner Offshore Services, Inc.,*[25] the Supreme Court addressed a further issue: Should Title VII protection be extended to cover situations in which individuals are harassed by members of the same sex? The Court answered this question in the affirmative.

Politics and Sexual Harassment. Twice during the 1990s, claims of sexual harassment had serious political implications. In 1991, law professor Anita Hill charged that Supreme Court nominee Clarence Thomas had sexually harassed her when they both had worked at the Equal Employment Opportunity Commission. Although Thomas was appointed to the Court, Hill's allegations caused a national furor and resulted in a dramatic increase in sexual-harassment claims.

In 1994, Paula Corbin Jones brought a lawsuit against President Clinton, accusing the president of sexually harassing her when she was an employee of the state of Arkansas and he was the governor. She claimed that he made unwanted sexual advances and acted in an obscene manner. A threshold issue in the suit—whether a civil suit could be brought against a sitting president for conduct that occurred before taking office as president—was decided in the affirmative by the Supreme Court in 1997.[26]

The federal court eventually dismissed Jones's lawsuit, concluding that Jones had "failed to demonstrate that she has a case."[27] (Jones appealed this decision, but during the appeal process, she accepted a monetary settlement of $875,000 from the president—thus ending the matter.) Before the suit was dismissed, however, testimony had been gathered that, among other things, pointed to the president's relationship with White House intern Monica Lewinsky. This evidence launched the investigation that ultimately led to President Clinton's impeachment in 1998.

Wage Discrimination

By the year 2010, women will constitute a majority of U.S. workers. Although Title VII and other legislation since the 1960s have mandated equal employment opportunities for men and women, women continue to earn less, on average, than men do. Currently, for every dollar earned by men, women earn about seventy-six cents.

The Equal Pay Act of 1963. The issue of wage discrimination was first addressed during World War II (1939–1945), when the War Labor Board issued an "equal pay for women" policy. In implementing the policy, the board often evaluated jobs for their comparability and required equal pay for comparable jobs. The board's authority ended with the war. Supported by the next three presidential administrations, the Equal Pay Act was finally enacted in 1963 as an amendment to the Fair Labor Standards Act of 1938.

Basically, the Equal Pay Act requires employers to pay equal pay for substantially equal work. In other words, males cannot legally be paid more than females who perform essentially the same job. The Equal Pay Act did not address the fact that certain types of jobs traditionally held by women pay lower wages than the jobs usually held by men. For example, more women than men are sales clerks and nurses, whereas more men than women are construction workers and truck drivers. Even if all clerks performing substantially similar jobs for a com-

In sworn testimony given in relation to Paula Jones's sexual-harassment lawsuit, President Clinton denied having had sexual relations with White House intern Monica Lewinsky, shown here. Clinton also made public denials of any affair with Lewinsky. By the fall of 1998, it became clear that his denials were false, and many people—including several Democrats in Congress—questioned not only his moral integrity but whether he should continue to hold the nation's highest office.

---

[25]523 U.S. 75 (1998).
[26]*Jones v. Clinton,* 520 U.S. 681 (1997).
[27]*Jones v. Clinton,* 990 F.Supp. 657 (E.D.Ark. 1998).

pany earned the same salaries, they would still be earning less than the company's truck drivers.

The Glass Ceiling.   Although increased numbers of women are holding jobs in professions or business enterprises that were once dominated by men, few women hold top positions in their firms. Less than 12 percent of the Fortune 500 companies in America—America's leading corporations—have a woman as one of their five highest-paid executives. In all, according to Census Bureau statistics, men still hold 93 percent of the top corporate management positions in this country. Because the barriers faced by women in the corporate world are subtle and not easily pinpointed, they have been referred to as the "glass ceiling."

In the last decade, however, gender has become less of an issue in the workplace. Women are now breaking through the glass ceiling in far greater numbers than before. In fact, the latest government statistics show that in the last several years more women than men have been promoted to executive positions. (For a further discussion of the "cracks" in the glass ceiling, as well as the gender gap in wages, see this chapter's *Politics and Economics*.)

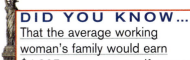

DID YOU KNOW…
That the average working woman's family would earn $4,205 more per year if women were paid as much as men with similar job qualifications?

politics and economics

Debating the Wage Gap

According to government statistics, there is both good news and bad news concerning women in the American workplace. The good news is that the glass ceiling, if not ready to shatter, is showing some cracks. A U.S. Census Bureau study found that 7.1 million women now hold managerial positions in this country—nearly a 30 percent jump from 1993. The bad news is that women still seem far from achieving equal levels of pay.

THE GENDER GAP IN WAGES

When Congress passed the Equal Pay Act in 1963, a woman, on average, made 59 cents for every dollar earned by a man. Figures recently released by the U.S. Department of Labor suggest that women now earn 76 cents for every dollar that men earn. Many are unimpressed by a gain of only 17 cents over more than three decades.

The blame for the disparity in wages has consistently been laid at the feet of a corporate culture that still does not see men and women as deserving of equal pay. Although the salaries of both men and women rose 20 percent between 1993 and 1998, statistics show that men were still paid nearly $18,000 more per year. In response, the federal government has proposed spending $27 million to close the wage gap by making sure that the Equal Pay Act and other relevant laws are more strictly enforced.

A CLOSER LOOK AT THE WAGE GAP

Naomi Lopez, director of the Center for Enterprise and Opportunity at the Pacific Research Institute in San Francisco, believes that the $27 million would be wasted. Lopez and a number of other economists give three reasons why the 76-cents-to-the-dollar figure is misleading.

First, this figure does not account for seniority. Many of today's highest (male) wage earners received their education and training in the 1960s and 1970s, before women were entering the workplace in large numbers. Second, it does not account for job choices. Although women now earn 40 percent of business and law degrees and nearly 50 percent of medical degrees, they are still much more likely than men to enter lower-paying professions, such as public administration. Third, the figure does not account for absenteeism. Because about 80 percent of women will have children at some point in their career, they are more likely to sacrifice higher pay for a profession that will allow them to balance work and family. In fact, one study that compared people between the ages of twenty-seven and thirty-three who have never had children showed that women's earnings were close to 98 percent of men's.[*]

FOR CRITICAL ANALYSIS

Is it inevitable that women should have to choose between a higher-paying job and a family? What steps could companies take to allow women to have both?

[*]Diana Furchgott-Roth, "This Pay Gap Is Phony," *The Washington Post,* January 31, 2000, p. A19.

Civil Rights—Equal Protection: Issues for the Twenty-First Century

To be sure, since the 1950s the gains of African Americans, other minorities, and women have been impressive. The civil rights movement and the legislation it prompted have done much to make equal protection of the laws a reality for minority groups. Nevertheless, these groups remain underrepresented in politics, particularly at the national level. One of the challenges for the new century is how to promote greater political participation among minority groups in American society. Another challenge facing Americans is the need to address the social and economic disparities that persist in this nation, regardless of race.

Certainly, the nation will have to confront the immigration issue at some point in the future. Immigrants who have entered this country since the 1970s—largely from Latin American and Asian nations—have transformed the racial composition of America. This development will likely have a dramatic impact on American politics and government in the years to come. Economist Paul Samuelson says that although immigration policy was a "forgotten issue" during the 2000 presidential campaigns—largely because both major-party candidates were reluctant to take on such a potentially inflammatory issue—immigration, more than any other issue, "will shape America in the twenty-first century.[28]

Finally, although women have much more protection today against gender discrimination in the workplace, the "glass ceiling" will probably remain in place for many years to come. Although this ceiling is showing some cracks, it is far from broken. How to remove this ceiling is a continuing challenge for women's rights groups. Another challenge for women's rights groups and human rights groups generally is how to improve the status of women's rights throughout the world.

---

[28]Paul Samuelson, "Being Choosier about Who We Let In," *Chicago Tribune*, May 5, 2000, p. 25.

making a difference

Citizenship and Immigrant Rights

A great debate has taken place in recent years over the issue of immigrant rights. The questions have included whether illegal immigrants can become citizens, whether employers are liable for hiring illegal immigrants, and whether the economy can absorb so many new workers.

Many organizations are concerned with the way in which illegal immigrants are treated by federal and state police and immigration officials. Such groups want to maintain the nation's commitment to relatively free entry to people of all racial, ethnic, religious, political, and economic backgrounds. Their goals are fair immigration rules, greater protection for resident illegal aliens, and a more pluralistic and tolerant culture.

You can become involved in this national controversy over immigration and citizenship policy in a number of ways. You can pay attention to the often contradictory policies that are proposed in Congress to deal with the problem. If you feel deeply enough about this issue, you might wish to join action organizations that lobby through influencing public opinion or by exerting direct pressure on Congress and the executive branch. You can also lobby your local government to enact laws allowing aliens fleeing persecution to live in your community.

The following groups are generally in favor of the right to immigrate and immigrants' rights:

National Network for Immigrant and Refugee Rights

310 Eighth St., Suite 307
Oakland, CA 94607
510-465-1984

http://www.nnirr.org

National Immigrants' Rights Project
American Civil Liberties Union
125 Broad St.
New York, NY 10004
212-549-2500

http://www.aclu.org/issues/
immigrant/hmir.html

Groups that usually support stricter enforcement of existing immigration laws or a more homogeneous culture include the following:

Federation for American Immigration Reform
1666 Connecticut Ave. N.W.,
Suite 400
Washington, DC 20009
202-328-7004

http://www.fairus.org

U.S. English
1747 Pennsylvania Ave. N.W.,
Suite 1100
Washington, DC 20006
202-833-0100

http://www.us-english.org

Key terms

busing 160

civil rights 153

cloture 165

de facto segregation 160

de jure segregation 160

Equal Employment Opportunity Commission (EEOC) 165

feminism 174

filibuster 165

gender discrimination 175

grandfather clause 158

literacy test 158

poll tax 158

separate-but-equal doctrine 158

sexual harassment 179

subpoena 165

suffrage 173

white primary 158

Chapter summary

1 The civil rights movement started with the struggle by African Americans for equality. Before the Civil War, African Americans were slaves, and slavery was protected by the Constitution and the Supreme Court. African Americans were not considered citizens or entitled to the rights and privileges of citizenship. In 1863 and during the years after the Civil War, the Emancipation Proclamation and the Thirteenth, Fourteenth, and Fifteenth Amendments (the "Civil War amendments") legally and constitutionally ended slavery. From 1865 to 1875, to enforce the Civil War amendments, Congress passed a number of laws (civil rights acts). African Americans gained citizenship, the right to vote, equality before the law, and protection from deprivation of these rights.

2 Politically and socially, African American inequality continued. The *Civil Rights Cases* (1883) and *Plessy v. Ferguson* (1896) effectively nullified the civil rights acts of 1865 to 1875. In the *Civil Rights Cases,* the Supreme Court held that the Fourteenth Amendment did not apply to private invasions of individual rights. In *Plessy,* the Court upheld the separate-but-equal doctrine, declaring that segregation did not violate the Constitution. African Americans were excluded from the voting process through poll taxes, grandfather clauses, white primaries, and literacy tests.

3 Legal segregation was declared unconstitutional by the Supreme Court in *Brown v. Board of Education of Topeka* (1954), in which the Court stated that separation implied inferiority. In *Brown v. Board of Education* (1955), the Supreme Court ordered federal courts to ensure that public schools were desegregated "with all deliberate speed." Segregationists resisted with legal tactics, violence, and "white flight." Integrationists responded with court orders, federal marshals, and busing. Also in 1955, the modern civil rights movement began with a boycott of segregated public transportation in Montgomery, Alabama. Of particular impact was the Civil Rights Act of 1964. The act bans discrimination on the basis of race, color, religion, gender, or national origin in employment and public accommodations. The act created the Equal Employment Opportunity Commission to administer the act.

4 The Voting Rights Act of 1965 outlawed discriminatory voter-registration tests and authorized federal registration of persons and federally administered procedures in any state or political subdivision evidencing electoral discrimination or low registration rates. Subsequent amendments to this act extended its protections to other minorities. As a result of the Voting Rights Act, its amendments, and federal registration drives, African American political participation increased dramatically.

5 The protective legislation passed during and since the 1960s applies not only to African Americans but to other ethnic groups as well. Other minorities have also been increasingly represented in national and state politics, although they have yet to gain representation proportionate to their numbers in the U.S. population.

6 America has always been a land of immigrants and continues to be so. Today, more than one million immigrants from other nations enter the United States each year, and nearly 10 percent of the U.S. population consists of foreign-born persons. The civil rights legislation of the 1960s and later has helped immigrants to overcome some of the effects of prejudice and discrimination against them. One of the pressing issues facing today's political leaders is whether U.S. immigration policy should be changed.

7 In the early history of the United States, women were considered citizens, but by and large they had no political rights. After the first women's rights convention in 1848, the women's movement gained momentum. Women's organizations continued to work toward the goal of the enfranchisement of women. Progress was slow, and it was not until 1920, when the Nineteenth Amendment was ratified, that women finally obtained the right to vote.

8 The modern women's movement began in the 1960s in the wake of the civil rights movement. The National Organization for Women (NOW) was formed in 1966 to bring about complete equality for women in all walks of life. When the efforts to secure the ratification of the Equal Rights Amendment failed, the women's movement began to focus on litigation and increasing the political representation of women to further the goal of gender equality. Although women have found it difficult to gain positions of political leadership, their numbers in Congress and in state and local government bodies increased significantly in the 1990s and early 2000s.

9 Women continue to struggle against gender discrimination in the employment context. Federal government efforts to eliminate gender discrimination in the workplace include Title VII of the Civil Rights Act of 1964, which prohibits, among other things, gender-based discrimination. Title VII has been used to invalidate even "protective" laws or policies, such as fetal protection policies. The Supreme Court has upheld the right of women to be free from sexual harassment on the job, but defining what constitutes sexual harassment, particularly hostile-environment sexual harassment, continues to be a problem. Wage discrimination also continues to be a problem for women, as does the "glass ceiling" that prevents them from rising to the top of their business or professional firms.

Selected print and electronic resources

SUGGESTED READINGS

Delaet, Debra L. *U.S. Immigration Policy in an Age of Rights.* Westport, Conn.: Praeger, 2000. The author explains how civil rights concepts have liberalized U.S. immigration policy over the last several decades, resulting in higher numbers of immigrants.

Jacobson, Matthew Frye. *Whiteness of a Different Color: European Immigrants and the Alchemy of Race.* Cambridge, Mass.: Harvard University Press, 1999. The author takes a close look at the concept of race in American history. He argues that race does not reside in nature but in the contingencies of politics and culture, and that race has been at the core of civic assimilation in this country.

McGlen, Nancy E., and Karen O'Connor. *Women, Politics, and American Society,* 2d ed. Upper Saddle River, N.J.: Prentice Hall, 1998. This is an excellent history of the women's movement in the United States.

Woodward, C. Vann. *The Strange Career of Jim Crow.* New York: Oxford University Press, 1957. This is the classic study of segregation in the southern United States.

MEDIA RESOURCES

Beyond the Glass Ceiling–A CNN-produced program showing the difficulties women face in trying to rise to the top in corporate America.

Dr. Martin Luther King: A Historical Perspective–One of the best documentaries on the civil rights movement, focusing on the life and times of Martin Luther King, Jr.

Frederick Douglass–A documentary about the man who escaped slavery to become a world-famous orator, journalist, diplomat, abolitionist, and civil rights advocate in the mid-1800s.

I Have a Dream–Another film on Martin Luther King, Jr., this one focusing on the 1963 march on Washington and King's "I have a dream" speech, which some consider to be one of the greatest speeches of all time.

Separate but Equal–A video focusing on Thurgood Marshall, the lawyer (and later Supreme Court justice) who took the struggle for equal rights to the Supreme Court, and on the rise and demise of segregation in America.

Logging on

There are an incredible number of resources on the World Wide Web relating to civil rights–and particularly the problem of discrimination. One of the most active and visible civil rights organizations today is the American Civil Liberties Union. You can access its Web site at

http://www.aclu.org

An extensive collection of information on Martin Luther King, Jr., is offered by the Martin Luther King Papers Project at Stanford University. Go to

http://www.stanford.edu/group/King

To learn more about the Equal Employment Opportunity Commission (EEOC) or to find out how to file a complaint with that agency, go to

http://www.eeoc.gov

The National Association for the Advancement of Colored People (NAACP) is online at

http://www.naacp.org

For information on the League of Latin American Citizens (LULAC), go to

http://www.lulac.org

The URL for Women's Web World, which provides information on empowerment and equality for women, is

http://www.feminist.org

To contact the National Organization for Women (NOW) or check out the resources and links it offers, go to

http://www.now.org

You can find an extensive array of political information and news concerning the African American community at

http://www.politicallyblack.com

The National Immigration Forum "embraces and upholds America's tradition as a nation of immigrants." You can access this organization's Web site at

http://www.immigrationforum.org

Using the Internet for political analysis

Sometimes, given all of the laws that have been passed and court cases decided, it may seem that all of the basic issues concerning equality for American citizens have been resolved. To test that assumption, take a look at one of the Web sites listed in the next column and identify at least two or three issues of equal treatment that remain to be resolved.

LatinoLink, at **http://www.latinolink.com**
NAACP Online, at **http://www.naacp.org**
Feminist Majority Online, at **http://www.feminist.org**

chapter 6

Civil Rights: Beyond Equal Protection

CHAPTER OUTLINE

- Affirmative Action

- Bilingual Education

- Special Protection for Older Americans

- Securing Rights for Persons with Disabilities

- The Rights and Status of Gay Males and Lesbians

- The Rights and Status of Juveniles

what if...

Only the Top 10 Percent of Students Could Go to a Public College?

BACKGROUND

AS YOU WILL READ IN THIS CHAPTER, SINCE THE 1960S AFFIRMATIVE ACTION POLICIES HAVE GENERALLY ALLOWED PUBLIC INSTITUTIONS TO CONSIDER RACE AS A FACTOR IN ADMISSIONS DECISIONS. THE GOAL OF AFFIRMATIVE ACTION POLICIES AS IMPLEMENTED ON COLLEGE CAMPUSES IS TWOFOLD: TO MAKE UP FOR THE EFFECTS OF PAST DISCRIMINATION AGAINST MINORITY-GROUPS, WHICH MAKE IT DIFFICULT FOR THESE GROUPS TO COMPETE IN THE EDUCATIONAL MARKETPLACE; AND TO ACHIEVE A CULTURALLY DIVERSE STUDENT BODY SO THAT UNIVERSITY STUDENTS ARE EXPOSED TO A WIDE SPECTRUM OF VIEWS.

OPPONENTS OF AFFIRMATIVE ACTION CONTEND THAT COLLEGE ADMISSIONS POLICIES THAT GIVE PREFERENCE TO SOME GROUPS AND NOT TO OTHERS ARE UNFAIR. INSTEAD, ADMISSIONS POLICIES SHOULD BE BASED ON MERIT.

WHAT IF ONLY THE TOP 10 PERCENT OF STUDENTS COULD GO TO A PUBLIC COLLEGE?

Suppose that only those students who ranked within the top 10 percent of their classes could attend a public college. Who would the "winners" and "losers" be under such a policy? Clearly, students who fell within the top 10 percent of their classes would benefit. But what about the other 90 percent of high school students? What would happen to them?

WHO WOULD BE DISADVANTAGED?

For various reasons, many bright students fail to do well in high school yet earn high grades when they attend college. How could the educational needs of these students be met? Very likely, more private colleges would be established to serve their needs. Yet poorer students might not be willing to pay the tuition rates charged by these institutions. Thus, wealthier students would have an advantage over those who are economically disadvantaged.

High schools in wealthier districts usually have more resources and do a better job of educating their students than do high schools in poorer areas. If the top 10 percent of students from *every* high school were admitted to college, college student bodies would include more students from poorer, rural school districts—where the percentage attending college has always been low. At the same time, students from these areas might find it difficult to overcome their competitive disadvantage in terms of educational preparation. Some argue that universities would have to "dumb down"

their curriculums to accommodate students from these less rigorous high schools.

WHAT ABOUT MINORITY STUDENTS?

How would students from minority groups fare under a "top 10 percent" admissions policy? Clearly, those who fell within the top 10 percent of their high school classes would benefit. After all, it would be clear to everyone that they were admitted to college based on their skills and achievements, not under a "racial preferences" policy.

Moreover, minority students might fare just as well under a 10 percent policy as under affirmative action policies. When a federal appellate court outlawed affirmative action in Texas, that state devised a new policy. It guaranteed that the top 10 percent of high school graduates would be admitted to its leading university, the University of Texas at Austin. So far, the number of African Americans admitted to that university is about the same as under affirmative action admission policies.

Nonetheless, minorities who are *not* in the top 10 percent would have much more limited educational options under a 10 percent policy. They would be less likely to attend top schools and more likely to attend community colleges or less prestigious universities.

FOR CRITICAL ANALYSIS

1. Would a "top 10 percent" policy result in higher performance levels among high school students?

2. If merit were really to be the basis for admission to college, would it be more appropriate to admit students who ranked in the top 10 percent of those taking a statewide achievement test? Why or why not?

This chapter's opening *What If . . .* feature touched on an issue that has long challenged Americans: How can the goal of equality best be achieved? More specifically, does equality mean equality of opportunity or equality of outcome? If social benefits, such as access to higher educational facilities, are based on merit (talent, skills, and achievement), equality of opportunity will exist, because all students have the opportunity to make it to the top of their classes. Yet some degree of inequality will certainly result, because some students have more talents and skills than others.

Remember from the previous chapter that the Civil Rights Act of 1964 prohibited discrimination against any person on the basis of race, color, national origin, religion, or gender. The act also established the right to equal opportunity in employment. A basic problem remained, however: minority groups and women, because of past discrimination, often lacked the education and skills to compete effectively in the marketplace. In 1965, the federal government attempted to remedy this problem by implementing the concept of affirmative action. **Affirmative action** policies attempt to "level the playing field" by giving special preferences in educational admissions and employment decisions to groups that have been discriminated against in the past. These policies go beyond a strict interpretation of the equal protection clause of the Fourteenth Amendment. So do a number of other laws and programs established by the government during and since the 1960s.

In this chapter, we explore the controversy engendered by affirmative action policies and bilingual education programs. We then look at the gains that have been made by older Americans, persons with disabilities, and gay men and lesbians in their struggle for equal treatment. We conclude the chapter with a discussion of the rights and status of children in American society.

Diversity Scam

Affirmative Action
A policy in educational admissions or job hiring that gives special consideration or compensatory treatment to traditionally disadvantaged groups in an effort to overcome present effects of past discrimination.

Affirmative Action

In 1965, President Lyndon Johnson ordered that affirmative action policies be undertaken to remedy the effects of past discrimination. All government agencies, including those of state and local governments, were required to implement such policies. Additionally, affirmative action requirements were imposed on companies that sell goods or services to the federal government and on institutions that receive federal funds. Affirmative action policies were also required whenever

Students at the University of California demonstrate their disagreement with the university's stand on affirmative action. In 1997, the university's board of regents voted to end its affirmative action policy, which had long influenced the university's admissions decisions.

Reverse Discrimination
The charge that affirmative action programs requiring preferential treatment
or quotas discriminate against those
who do not have minority status.

an employer had been ordered to develop such a plan by a court or by the Equal Employment Opportunity Commission because of evidence of past discrimination. Finally, labor unions that had been found to discriminate against women or minorities in the past were required to establish and follow affirmative action plans.

Affirmative action programs have been controversial because they sometimes result in discrimination against majority groups, such as white males (or discrimination against other minority groups that may not be given preferential treatment under a particular affirmative action program). At issue in the current debate over affirmative action programs is whether such programs, because of their inherently discriminatory nature, violate the equal protection clause of the Fourteenth Amendment to the Constitution.

The *Bakke* Case

The first Supreme Court case addressing the constitutionality of affirmative action programs examined a program implemented by the University of California at Davis. Allan Bakke, a Vietnam War veteran and engineer who had been turned down for medical school at the Davis campus of the University of California, discovered that his academic record was better than those of some of the minority applicants who had been admitted to the program. He sued the University of California regents, alleging **reverse discrimination.** The UC–Davis Medical School had held sixteen places out of one hundred for educationally "disadvantaged students" each year, and the administrators at that campus admitted to using race as a criterion for admission for these particular minority slots. At trial in 1974, Bakke said that his exclusion from medical school violated his rights under the Fourteenth Amendment's provision for equal protection of the laws. The trial court agreed. On appeal, the California Supreme Court agreed also. Finally, the regents of the university appealed to the United States Supreme Court.

In 1978, the Supreme Court handed down its decision in *Regents of the University of California v. Bakke.*[1] The Court did not actually rule against affirmative action programs. Rather, it held that Bakke must be admitted to the UC–Davis Medical School because its admissions policy had used race as the sole criterion for the sixteen "minority" positions. Justice Lewis Powell, speaking for the Court, indicated that while race can be considered "as a factor" among others in admissions (and presumably hiring) decisions, race cannot be the sole factor. So affirmative action programs, but not specific quota systems, were upheld as constitutional.

Further Limitations on Affirmative Action

A number of cases decided during the 1980s and 1990s placed further limits on affirmative action programs. In a landmark decision in 1995, *Adarand Constructors, Inc. v. Peña,*[2] the Supreme Court held that any federal, state, or local affirmative action program that uses racial or ethnic classifications as the basis for making decisions is subject to "strict scrutiny" by the courts. Under a strict-scrutiny analysis, to be constitutional, a discriminatory law or action must be narrowly tailored to meet a *compelling* government interest. In effect, the Court's opinion in *Adarand* means that an affirmative action program cannot make use of quotas or preferences for unqualified persons, and once the program has succeeded, it must be changed or dropped.

[1]438 U.S. 265 (1978).
[2]515 U.S. 200 (1995).

In 1996, a federal appellate court went even further. In *Hopwood v. State of Texas*,[3] two white law school applicants sued the University of Texas School of Law in Austin, alleging that they were denied admission because of the school's affirmative action program. The program allowed admissions officials to take race and other factors into consideration when determining which students would be admitted. The federal appellate court held that the program violated the equal protection clause because it discriminated in favor of minority applicants. Significantly, the court directly challenged the *Bakke* decision by stating that the use of race even as a means of achieving diversity on college campuses "undercuts the Fourteenth Amendment." The Supreme Court declined to hear the case, thus letting the lower court's decision stand.

State Ballot Initiatives

In 1996, by a ballot initiative known as Proposition 209, a majority of California voters approved a constitutional amendment that ended all state-sponsored affirmative action programs in that state. The law was immediately challenged in court by civil rights groups and others. These groups claimed that the law violated the Fourteenth Amendment by denying racial minorities and women the equal protection of the law. In 1997, however, a federal appellate court upheld the constitutionality of the amendment. Thus, affirmative action is now illegal in California in all state-sponsored institutions, including state agencies and educational institutions. In 1998, Washington voters also approved a law banning affirmative action in that state.

Will Affirmative Action Survive?

Many groups contend that the time has come for a "colorblind" society in which business firms, government agencies, and educational institutions do not make

---

[3]84 F.3d 720 (5th Cir. 1996).

Citizens in California demonstrate their opposition to Proposition 209, the ballot initiative that ended all state-sponsored affirmative action programs in the state. Why are affirmative action programs more controversial today than they were a decade or so ago?

What Has Affirmative Action Really Accomplished?

Affirmative action programs have now been in effect for several decades. From the outset, these programs have been controversial. Critics claimed that by giving preferences to some groups but not others, affirmative action programs violated the Constitution's mandate of equal protection. Supporters of affirmative action maintained that without such preferential treatment, groups who were disadvantaged by past discrimination would never achieve equality. Largely missing from the debate were factual data supporting either position on the issue.

William G. Bowen and Derek C. Bok helped to fill this "data gap" in the affirmative action debate, at least with respect to race-conscious college admissions, in their recent book, *The Shape of the River: Long-Term Consequences of Considering Race in College and University Admissions.** The core of the Bowen and Bok study is information gleaned from a database assembled by the Andrew W. Mellon Foundation, which is headed by Bowen. The database includes records for over 90,000 students in twenty-eight elite American colleges and universities for the years 1951, 1976, and 1989. The data have been supplemented by follow-up surveys, conducted in 1996

*Ewing, N.J.: Princeton University Press, 1998.

and 1997, of students after they graduated or left college.

Affirmative Action Has Yielded Positive Benefits

Based on their analysis of these data, Bowen and Bok conclude that affirmative action (they prefer the term "racially sensitive") policies at these elite institutions have been beneficial to blacks and not significantly harmful to whites. Eliminating affirmative action would decrease black enrollment at these elite institutions by more than half. As a result, the careers of thousands of blacks would be adversely affected. Although, on average, the black males who entered these schools in 1976 earned $17,000 less than their white counterparts, they earned nearly twice as much ($85,000, on average) as black graduates of less selective institutions and over $20,000 more than white male graduates of less selective schools.

The authors also found that blacks admitted with lower SAT scores than their white classmates would not have been better off at less competitive schools. In fact, the more selective the school, the higher the graduation rate of black students. Furthermore, black graduates from these institutions reported they were happy with their education, were not stigmatized by their classmates for having received racial preferences, and were more likely than their white peers to become actively involved in civic affairs and play key leadership roles within both the black community and the larger society.

Finally, the authors concluded that any reverse discrimination against whites due to these admissions policies was not significant. If

---

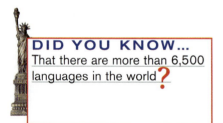

DID YOU KNOW…
That there are more than 6,500 languages in the world?

decisions on the basis of racial and ethnic differences. Nevertheless, affirmative action continues to receive widespread support. Certainly, the Clinton administration was in favor of retaining such policies, perhaps with some modifications, and the Supreme Court, as already indicated, has not yet issued a blanket decision on the matter. (See this chapter's *Critical Perspective* for discussion of recent scholarly examinations of this issue.)

Bilingual Education

The continuous influx of immigrants into this country presents an ongoing challenge—how to overcome language barriers, particularly in the schools. Throughout our history, educators have been faced with the question of how to best educate children who do not speak English or do not speak it very well.

Early Language Policies

In the nineteenth century, the language of instruction was not a significant political issue. Children were taught in a wide variety of languages, depending

critical perspective

preferences were eliminated, the overall admission rate for white students would rise by only 1.5 percentage points.

Critics of Affirmative Action Respond

Perhaps the harshest critics of the Bowen and Bok study are Stephan Thernstrom of Harvard University and Abigail Thernstrom of the Manhattan Institute. In their review of the Bowen and Bok study,[†] the Thernstroms question the study's value because of its extremely narrow focus–the authors looked only at black admissions to elite institutions and made no attempt to place the institutions studied in a national context. The Thernstroms believe that decisions made at the nation's most elite institutions do little to shape the overall structure of opportunity in higher education. They point out that in 1989, the year of the latest sample, only 9 percent of black college students were enrolled in *any* private four-year college or university, and most of these were attending institutions with minimal admissions requirements–and hence no need for preferential policies.

Additionally, the Thernstroms note that Bowen and Bok, former presidents of Princeton and Harvard, respectively, were both key players in launching affirmative action programs at their universities.

In other words, they had an incentive to find that the preferential policies for which they were primarily responsible did, in fact, yield positive benefits.

In their own book, *America in Black and White: One Nation, Indivisible,*[‡] published a year prior to the Bowen and Bok study, the Thernstroms contended that racial preferences threaten progress for blacks. They bolstered their view with a large collection of socioeconomic data. Among other things, these data showed that blacks graduate from high school at about the same rate as whites. Economically, 40 percent of the nation's black citizens considered themselves members of the middle class, and black married couples earned only slightly less, on average, than their white counterparts. With respect to unemployment, about 93 percent of blacks in the labor force had jobs. In addition, residential segregation had dropped dramatically since 1945. These researchers also specifically contended that African Americans had made greater advances in the two decades prior to the civil rights movement than in the years since then.

FOR CRITICAL ANALYSIS

1. Some argue that racial preferences only validate the contention of racists that blacks are inferior. Do you agree with this assertion?
2. In reality, affirmative action programs affect only a very small number of minority members, women, and white males. Why, then, do the programs generate such heated debate?

[†]Stephan Thernstrom and Abigail Thernstrom, "Reflections on the Shape of the River," *UCLA Law Review,* June 1999, pp. 1583–1637.

[‡]New York: Simon & Schuster, 1997.

---

on the wishes of the parents in a particular school district. Some schools provided instruction in German, which was the nation's most common second language at that time. Other schools taught children in Polish, Dutch, or Italian. Some midwestern districts established special "dual-language" schools, where students were taught for half a day in English and half a day in German.

By the beginning of the twentieth century, this open language policy began to change as waves of new immigrants from Europe arrived in the United States. Political leaders in some states began to fear the political effects of what some perceived to be a growing "babel of tongues." By 1915, thirteen states had passed laws requiring basic subjects, such as math, geography, and science, to be taught in English. Anti-German sentiment during World War I (1914–1918) led to further fears of the effects of educating students in a foreign language (particularly German). By the end of the war, thirty-seven states had passed laws restricting foreign-language instruction.

Although most of these restrictive laws were subsequently repealed or struck down by the courts, English-only instruction became the norm throughout the country. Increased immigration from Mexico and Latin American countries during the 1950s, however, caused many educators to be concerned about the language problems facing these immigrants. Spanish had effectively become

DID YOU KNOW...
That proficiency in the English language was not required for naturalization as a U.S. citizen until 1906?

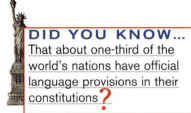

America's second language, yet local school districts in some parts of the Southwest prohibited children from speaking Spanish, even on school playgrounds. In the 1960s, bilingual education programs began to be implemented as a solution to the language problems facing immigrants.

Accommodating Diversity with Bilingual Education

Bilingual education programs teach children in their native language while also teaching them English. To some extent, today's bilingual education programs are the result of the government policies favoring multiculturalism that grew out of the civil rights movement. Multiculturalism involves the belief that the government should accommodate the needs of different cultural groups and should protect and encourage ethnic and cultural differences.

Children attending classes taught in English were frequently encouraged by their teachers as well as their parents to speak English as much as possible, both at school and at home. Children who did so felt distanced from their grandparents and family members who spoke no English and, as a result, felt cut off from their ethnic backgrounds. Bilingual education was premised on the hope that, over time, Hispanic children would become truly bilingual without having to sacrifice their close family relationships and cultural heritage.

Congress authorized bilingual education programs in 1968 when it passed the Bilingual Education Act, which was intended primarily to help Hispanic children learn English. In a 1974 case, *Lau v. Nichols*,[4] the Supreme Court bolstered the claim that children have a right to bilingual education. In that case, the Court ordered a California school district to provide special programs for Chinese students with language difficulties if a substantial number of these children attended school in the district. Today, most bilingual education programs are for Hispanic American children, particularly in areas of the country, such as California and Texas, where there are large numbers of Hispanic residents.

Bilingual education in the fourth grade at Walnut Creek Elementary School in Austin, Texas.

The Current Controversy over Bilingual Education

The bilingual programs established in the 1960s and subsequently have increasingly been coming under attack. Indeed, in 1998 California residents passed a ballot initiative that called for the end of bilingual education programs in that state. The law allowed schools to implement "English-immersion" programs instead. In these programs, students are given intensive instruction in English for a limited period of time and then placed in regular classrooms.

The law was immediately challenged in court on the ground that it unconstitutionally discriminated against non-English-speaking groups. A federal district court, however, concluded that the new law did not violate the equal protection clause and refused to prevent the law's implementation. (For a discussion of the continuing controversy over bilingual education, see this chapter's feature *Which Side Are You On? Should Bilingual Education Be Abandoned?*)

Special Protection for Older Americans

Americans are getting older. In colonial times, about half the population was under the age of sixteen. In 1990, the number of people under the age of sixteen was fewer than one in four, and half the population was thirty-three or older. By the year 2050, at least half could be thirty-nine or older.

---

[4]414 U.S. 563 (1974).

which side are you on?

Should Bilingual Education Be Abandoned?

Today's bilingual education programs have aroused controversy every since their origins in the 1960s. Across the nation, Americans continue to debate how immigrant children can best be educated. Here we look at the views of two opposing groups in this debate.

The English-Only Movement

Among the leading critics of bilingual education are those who push for English-only policies. English-only advocates contend that government policies should emphasize the unity, not the diversity, of American culture. One way to do this is by helping the children of immigrants learn the English language as quickly as possible. In any culture, language is a basic unifying element, and English-only instruction in the schools will help immigrant children be assimilated more rapidly into "American" culture.

The two national groups spearheading the English-only movement—U.S. English and English First—have lobbied government at both the state and federal levels to pass laws making English the official language of government and to reform bilingual education. In response to pressure from these groups, as well as for other reasons, nearly half of the states have passed "English-only" laws that require all official speech, including speech in public schools, to be in English. Congress is also considering a bill that would make English the official language of the U.S. government.

An Alternative Solution: English-Plus

One of the reasons bilingual education has been under attack is that students in some of these programs have lagged in academic achievement. Supporters of bilingual education programs contend that academic underachievement among immigrant children has more to do with issues of status and power than with linguistic factors. In fact, they point to a number of studies that show a positive association between bilingualism and students' linguistic, cognitive, and academic growth.* Rather than abandon bilingual education programs, schools should pursue an "English-plus" approach in teaching immigrant children. An English-plus policy would encourage and help students conserve their native language skills while they learn English.

Supporters of English-plus emphasize the importance of language skills in today's world. Currently, only about 3 percent of American high school graduates and 5 percent of college graduates achieve a meaningful proficiency in a second language. English-plus policies would better prepare students for working and living in a multicultural nation and in an increasingly global environment.[†]

DOES IT MATTER?

Is proficiency in English necessary to be an informed citizen in the United States? Is it necessary to be successful in your community?

GOING ONLINE

To learn more about arguments against bilingual education, visit the Web sites of U.S. English (at **http://www.us-english.org**) *and English First (at* **http://www.englishfirst.org**). *To find articles supporting bilingualism and English-plus policies, go to the Web site of James Crawford, former editor of* Education Week *and a specialist in the politics of language, at* **http://ourworld.compuserve.com/homepages/JWCRAWFORD**.

[†]For a description of the "English-plus" approach, see James Crawford, *Bilingual Education: History, Politics, Theory, and Practice,* 4th ed. (Los Angeles: Bilingual Educational Services, 1999).

*See, for example, the studies discussed in J. Cummins and D. Corson, eds., *Bilingual Education* (Dordrecht, The Netherlands: Kluwer Academic Publishers, 1998).

Today, about 35 million Americans (nearly 13 percent of the population) are aged sixty-five or over. As can be seen in Figure 6–1 on the next page, by the year 2020, this figure is projected to reach about 54 million. By 2040, the portion of the population over age sixty-five will more than double.

Senior citizens face a variety of problems unique to their group. One problem that seems to endure, despite government legislation designed to prevent it, is age discrimination in employment. Others include health care and income security. Since the 1930s, the government has established programs, such as Social Security and Medicare, designed to protect the health and welfare of older Americans. Although we touch on these public benefits in this section, they are explored more fully in Chapter 16.

**Firing Line Reveals Age
Discrimination**

Age Discrimination in Employment

Age discrimination is potentially the most widespread form of discrimination, because anyone—regardless of race, color, national origin, or gender—could be a victim at some point in life. The unstated policies of some companies not to hire or to demote or dismiss people they feel are "too old" have made it difficult for some older workers to succeed in their jobs or continue with their careers. Additionally, older workers have fallen victim at times to cost-cutting efforts by employers. To reduce operational costs, companies may replace older, higher-salaried workers with younger, lower-salaried workers.

The Age Discrimination in Employment Act of 1967. In an attempt to protect older employees from such discriminatory practices, Congress passed the Age Discrimination in Employment Act (ADEA) in 1967. The act, which applies to employers, employment agencies, and labor organizations and covers individuals over the age of forty, prohibits discrimination against individuals on the basis of age unless age is shown to be a bona fide occupational qualification reasonably necessary to the normal operation of the particular business.

Specifically, it is against the law to discriminate by age in wages, benefits, hours worked, or availability of overtime. Employers and unions may not discriminate in providing fringe benefits, such as education or training programs, career development, sick leave, and vacations. It is a violation of the act to publish notices or advertisements indicating an age-preference limitation or discrimination based on age. Even advertisements that imply a preference for youthful workers over older workers are in violation of the law. Requesting age on an application is not illegal but may be closely scrutinized in light of the employer's hiring practices.

To succeed in a suit for age discrimination, an employee must prove that the employer's action, such as a decision to fire the employee, was motivated, at least in part, by age bias. Proof that qualified older employees are generally dis-

FIGURE 6-1

Population Projections: Persons Aged 65 or Older (in Millions)

As shown here, the number of Americans who will be sixty-five years of age or older will grow dramatically during the next decade. The number will more than double between 2005 and 2040. The political power of these older Americans will grow as their numbers increase.

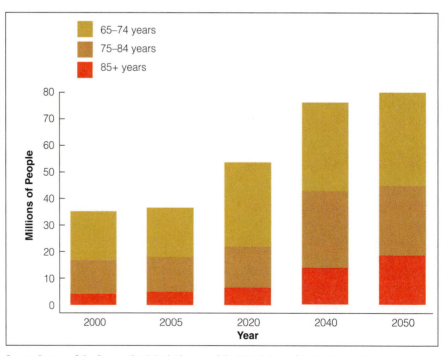

SOURCE: Bureau of the Census, *Statistical Abstract of the United States* (Washington, D.C.: U.S. Government Printing Office, 2000), p. 17.

charged before younger employees or that co-workers continually made unflattering age-related comments about the discharged worker may be enough. In 1996, the Supreme Court held that even if an older worker is replaced by a younger worker falling under the protection of the ADEA—that is, by a younger worker who is also over the age of forty—the older worker is entitled to bring a suit under the ADEA. The Court stated that the issue in all ADEA cases is whether age discrimination has in fact occurred, regardless of the age of the replacement worker.[5]

As discussed in Chapter 3 in the context of federalism, in 2000 the Supreme Court limited the applicability of the ADEA in its decision in *Kimel v. Florida Board of Regents*.[6] The Court held that the sovereign immunity granted the states by the Eleventh Amendment to the Constitution precluded suits against a state by private parties alleging violations of the ADEA. Victims of age discrimination can bring actions under state statutes, however, and most states have laws protecting their citizens from age discrimination.

Mandatory Retirement.   The ADEA, as initially passed, did not address one of the major problems facing older workers—**mandatory retirement** rules, which required employees to retire when they reached a certain age. Mandatory retirement rules often meant that competent, well-trained employees who wanted to continue working were unable to do so. In 1978, in an amendment to the ADEA, Congress prohibited mandatory retirement rules with respect to most employees under the age of seventy. Many states had already passed similar statutes. In 1986, Congress outlawed mandatory retirement rules entirely for all but a few selected occupations, such as firefighting.

Age, Political Participation, and Public Benefits

If we use voter participation as a measure of political involvement, it is clear that political participation increases with age. Generally, the over-sixty-five age group ranks first in voter registration and in actual turnout on election day. Usually, the voting rate in the over-sixty-five category is at least twice that of the youngest voting group (those under twenty-one years of age).

Older Americans work for their interests through a number of large and effective political associations. The largest group is the AARP, formerly known as the American Association of Retired Persons, whose members are limited to those aged fifty and older. Founded in 1958, it has a current membership of more than 33 million. The AARP and the National Retired Teachers' Association have united in a powerful joint effort to ensure beneficial treatment for older Americans by lobbying for legislation at the federal and state levels. They use the same staff in Washington and provide almost the same services to their members, including low-priced group insurance and travel programs.

Because of their voting and lobbying power, Americans over the age of sixty-five receive a disproportionate share of government spending. Almost half of the entire federal budget is spent on Medicare and Social Security. Medicare costs recently have risen at about twice the rate of inflation for the economy as a whole. Many programs, such as Medicare and Social Security, have been tied legislatively to external factors so that spending on them has become, to a large degree, uncontrollable and automatic. Indeed, there is growing concern over whether the government is allocating too many resources to seniors and not enough to the welfare of younger Americans.

DID YOU KNOW...
That in 1922, at age eighty-seven, Rebecca Latimer Felton was the first and oldest woman to serve in the U.S. Senate—although she was appointed as a token gesture and was allowed to serve only one day **?**

Mandatory Retirement
Forced retirement when a person reaches a certain age.

---

[5] *O'Connor v. Consolidated Coil Caterers Corp.*, 517 U.S. 308 (1996).
[6] 120 S.Ct. 145 (2000).

Securing Rights for Persons with Disabilities

Like older Americans, persons with disabilities did not fall under the protective umbrella of the Civil Rights Act of 1964. Remember from Chapter 5 that the 1964 act prohibited discrimination against any person on the basis of race, color, national origin, religion, or gender. As just noted, Congress addressed the problem of age discrimination in 1967. By the 1970s, Congress also began to pass legislation to protect Americans with disabilities. In 1973, Congress passed the Rehabilitation Act, which prohibited discrimination against persons with disabilities in programs receiving federal aid. A 1978 amendment to the act established the Architectural and Transportation Barriers Compliance Board. Regulations for ramps, elevators, and the like in all federal buildings were implemented. Congress passed the Education for All Handicapped Children Act in 1975. It guarantees that all children with disabilities will receive an "appropriate" education. The most significant federal legislation with respect to the rights of persons with disabilities, however, is the Americans with Disabilities Act (ADA), which Congress passed in 1990.

The Americans with Disabilities Act of 1990

The ADA requires that all public buildings and public services be accessible to persons with disabilities. The act also mandates that employers must reasonably accommodate the needs of workers or potential workers with disabilities.

Physical access means ramps; handrails; wheelchair-accessible restrooms, counters, drinking fountains, telephones, and doorways; and more accessible mass transit. In addition, other steps must be taken to comply with the act. Car-rental companies must provide cars with hand controls for disabled drivers. Telephone companies are required to have operators to pass on messages from speech-impaired persons who use telephones with keyboards. A question facing policymakers today is whether the ADA also applies to Internet access—see the feature entitled *E-mocracy: Does the ADA Apply to the Internet?* for a discussion of this issue.

President George Bush signs the 1990 Americans with Disabilities Act. The act requires corporations and public institutions to implement access for disabled Americans and requires employers to accommodate workers with disabilities.

e-mocracy

Does the ADA Apply to the Internet?

The Internet is rapidly taking a central place in American society. But what about sight-impaired persons who are unable to see the words or images on a computer screen or hearing-impaired persons who are unable to hear the audio portion of uncaptioned audio and video clips? What about individuals who are colorblind and thus unable to perceive that certain words on a computer screen are highlighted? How can the needs of persons with disabilities be met in an online environment?

Currently, over 54 million people in the United States suffer from some form of disability. Indeed, most people will experience a period of disability sometime during their lifetime, particularly as they get older. Twenty-five percent of people will experience a period of disability by age fifty-five. What can be done to promote Internet accessibility for Americans with disabilities? According to a U.S. Department of Commerce report, "The transformation of the Internet from a text-based medium to a robust multi-media environment has created a crisis—a growing digital divide in access for people with disabilities."*

TECHNOLOGY IS NOT THE ISSUE

Technology can be—and is already being—developed that will help reduce barriers to Internet participation for persons with disabili-

---

*Cynthia D. Waddell, "The Growing Digital Divide in Access for People with Disabilities: Overcoming Barriers to Participation," report presented at a conference held by the U.S. Department of Commerce in Washington, D.C., on May 25–26, 1999. (This report can be accessed online at **http://www.aasa.dshs.wa.gov/access/waddell.htm**.)

ties. The real issue is not technology but whether the government should require Web site owners, Internet service providers, and others providing various Internet elements, such as browsers, to implement new technology designed to accommodate the needs of persons with disabilities. Central to this debate is whether the Americans with Disabilities Act (ADA) of 1990 can or should be applied to the Internet.

SHOULD THE ADA BE APPLIED TO THE INTERNET?

The question of whether the ADA applies—or should be applied—to the Internet has elicited widespread debate. The U.S. Department of Justice and various advocacy groups claim that the ADA should be applied to require universal access to the Internet by persons with disabilities. Some worry that if the government fails to take action soon—before the Internet develops further—the digital divide may become impossible to bridge.

Others believe that imposing regulations on Internet commerce at this point would be premature and would only slow the growth of Internet development. Still others argue that the ADA cannot be applied to the Internet because the act applies only to "public accommodations." The categories of public accommodations listed in the ADA are all physical places—restaurants, hotels, museums, laundromats, and so on. Clearly, the Internet is not a physical structure.

FOR CRITICAL ANALYSIS

There are few common denominators among Web sites—each site is unique, and different sites have different features, functions, navigation elements, and so on. In view of this diversity, would it even be possible to devise disability-accommodating standards that could be applied across the Web?

The ADA requires employers to "reasonably accommodate" the needs of persons with disabilities unless to do so would cause the employer to suffer an "undue hardship." The ADA defines persons with disabilities as persons who have physical or mental impairments that "substantially limit" their everyday activities. Health conditions that have been considered disabilities under federal law include blindness, alcoholism, heart disease, cancer, muscular dystrophy, cerebral palsy, paraplegia, diabetes, acquired immune deficiency syndrome (AIDS), and the human immunodeficiency virus (HIV) that causes AIDS.

The ADA does not require that *unqualified* applicants with disabilities be hired or retained. If a job applicant or an employee with a disability, with reasonable accommodation, can perform essential job functions, however, then the employer must make the accommodation. Required accommodations may include installing ramps for a wheelchair, establishing more flexible working

The disabled have emerged as a significant political force. Persons with disabilities have held numerous demonstrations, demanding to have their rights upheld in the work force and in society.

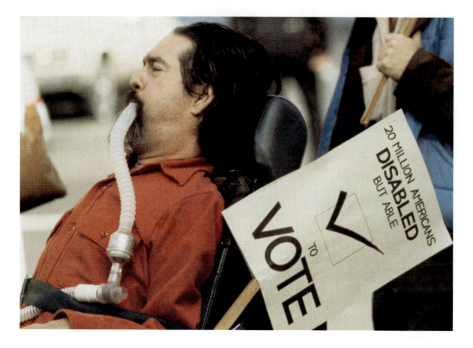

hours, creating or modifying job assignments, and creating or improving training materials and procedures.

Interpreting and Applying the ADA

The ADA has been controversial, not because of its goal—preventing discrimination against persons with disabilities—but because of the difficulties involved in interpreting and applying the act's provisions. For example, what constitutes a physical or mental impairment? At what point does such an impairment "substantially limit" a "major life activity," and what constitutes a major life activity? Finally, what exactly is required to "reasonably accommodate" persons with disabilities, and at what point does accommodation constitute an "undue hardship" for employers?

The courts have had to address these questions, and the outcome of any particular case is not always predictable. For example, in one case an employee came to work toting a loaded gun. The employer, who, like all employers, was required by law to maintain a safe workplace for employees, fired the employee on the spot. The employee took the employer to court, and the jury concluded that the employee's behavior was the result of a mental impairment. Therefore, the employer should not have fired him but accommodated his disability in some way, such as by giving him a leave of absence.

In 1998, the United States Supreme Court for the first time took up a case involving the interpretation of the ADA. The issue was whether HIV, the virus that causes AIDS, could qualify as a disability under the act. The Court held that an HIV infection, even though it has not yet been evidenced by any physical symptoms, is a physical impairment that substantially limits a major life activity. Therefore, persons infected with HIV fall under the protection of the ADA and must be accommodated—unless to do so would constitute a "direct threat" to others.[7]

---

[7]*Bragdon v. Abbott,* 524 U.S. 624 (1998).

Uncertainty about how the act will be applied creates special problems for employers, business owners, and other organizations that must comply with the act's requirements. Despite the ADA's shortcomings, however, many persons suffering from disabilities have benefited from the act, as well as from the changing social attitudes toward them that the act has helped to foster. And a significant number of people with disabilities take advantage of the act's protective provisions. As you can see in Figure 6–2, nearly one-fourth of the complaints filed with the Equal Employment Opportunity Commission in a recent year were for disability-based discrimination.

The Rights and Status of Gay Males and Lesbians

On June 27, 1969, patrons of the Stonewall Inn, a New York City bar popular with gays and lesbians, responded to a police raid by throwing beer cans and bottles because they were angry at what they felt was unrelenting police harassment. In the ensuing riot, which lasted two nights, hundreds of gays and lesbians fought with police. Before Stonewall, the stigma attached to homosexuality and the resulting fear of exposure had tended to keep most gays and lesbians quiescent. In the months immediately after Stonewall, however, "gay power" graffiti began to appear in New York City. The Gay Liberation Front and the Gay Activist Alliance were formed, and similar groups sprang up in other parts of the country. Thus, Stonewall has been called "the shot heard round the homosexual world."

The Stonewall incident marked the beginning of the movement for gay and lesbian rights. Since then, gay men and lesbians have formed thousands of organizations to exert pressure on legislatures, the media, schools, churches, and other organizations to recognize their right to equal treatment. One of the largest gay rights groups today is the Human Rights Campaign Fund, whose goal is to see federal gay rights laws passed. Another major group is the National Gay and Lesbian Task Force, which works toward the repeal of state sodomy laws (laws prohibiting certain forms of sexual activity, including homosexual relationships). The American Civil Liberties Union also actively promotes laws protecting gays and lesbians, as do several other liberal civil rights organizations.

To a great extent, lesbian and gay groups have succeeded in changing public opinion—and state and local laws—relating to their status and rights. Nevertheless, they continue to struggle against age-old biases against homosexuality, often rooted in deeply held religious beliefs, and the rights of gay men and lesbians remain an extremely divisive issue in American society. (See this chapter's *Making Waves: James Dale versus the Boy Scouts* on the next page for a discussion of one controversial issue relating to gay rights.)

State and Local Laws against Gays

Prior to the Stonewall incident in 1969, forty-nine states had sodomy laws (Illinois, which had repealed its sodomy law in 1962, was the only exception). During the 1970s and 1980s, more than half of these laws were either repealed or struck down by the courts.

The trend toward repealing state anti-gay laws ended in 1986 with the Supreme Court's decision in *Bowers v. Hardwick*.[8] In that case, the Court upheld,

[8]478 U.S. 186 (1986).

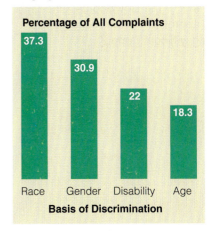

FIGURE 6-2

Charges Filed with the EEOC Alleging Discrimination

Percentage of All Complaints

37.3 Race
30.9 Gender
22   Disability
18.3 Age

Basis of Discrimination

*Percents sum to more than 100 percent because some complaints allege more than one form of discrimination.

SOURCE: Equal Employment Opportunity Commission, 2000.

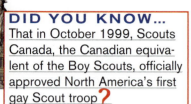

INFOTRAC®
COLLEGE EDITION

Mother Calls More Outreach

by a five-to-four vote, a Georgia law that made homosexual conduct between two adults a crime. Justice Byron White, writing for the majority, stated that "we are quite unwilling" to "announce . . . a fundamental right to engage in homosexual sodomy." Since this decision, however, courts in some states have invalidated state sodomy statutes on the ground that they violate rights guaranteed by state constitutions. For example, in 1998 the Supreme Court of Georgia held that the state's sodomy statute violated the right of privacy as guaranteed by the Georgia constitution's due process clause.[9] Today, sodomy statutes have been repealed or invalidated in all but eighteen states.

In a 1996 case, *Romer v. Evans,*[10] the Supreme Court issued a decision that had a significant impact on the rights of gays and lesbians. The case involved a Colorado state constitutional amendment that invalidated all existing state and local laws protecting homosexuals from discrimination. The Supreme Court held that the amendment violated the equal protection clause of the Constitution because it denied to homosexuals in Colorado—but to no other Colorado residents—"the right to seek specific protection of the law." The Court stated that the equal protection clause simply does not permit Colorado to make homosexuals "unequal to everyone else." Despite the *Romer* decision, in 1998 the Supreme Court declined to review an appellate court decision that left standing an anti-gay amendment to the city charter of Cincinnati.[11]

Today, eleven states[12] and more than 165 cities and counties have special laws protecting lesbians and gay men against discrimination in employment,

---

[9]Powell v. State, 270 Ga. 327 (1998).
[10]517 U.S. 620 (1996).
[11]*Equality Foundation of Greater Cincinnati v. City of Cincinnati* (6th Cir. 1998); unpublished opinion.
[12]California, Connecticut, Hawaii, Massachusetts, Minnesota, Nevada, New Hampshire, New Jersey, Rhode Island, Vermont, and Wisconsin. Maine also had a law protecting gay and lesbian rights until February 1998, when the law was repealed in a referendum.

making waves

James Dale versus the Boy Scouts

When he reached the age of eighteen, Eagle Scout James Dale's membership in the Boy Scouts of America (BSA) automatically expired. He had been an outstanding Scout and registered with the Monmouth (New Jersey) Boy Scout troop to serve as a leader. His registration was approved. Later, while attending Rutgers University, Dale became actively involved in gay rights groups. One of his concerns as a gay activist was the need for gay role models for teenage homosexuals. When the Monmouth Council learned of Dale's activities, it notified Dale that his registration was revoked because the BSA "does not admit avowed homosexuals to membership in the organization."

A year and a half later, after New Jersey had amended its laws to forbid discrimination on the basis of sexual orientation in all places of public accommodation, Dale sued the BSA. He sought damages and his reinstatement as an approved Scout leader. In 1999, the New Jersey Supreme Court ruled that Boy Scout troops serve as places of public accommodation and that

the Monmouth Council had illegally discriminated against Dale. The United States Supreme Court agreed to review the case.

Dale's lawsuit made waves around the country as various organizations—ranging from religious groups and conservative organizations to gay rights alliances and civil rights groups—announced their positions on the issue. Notably, supporters of the Monmouth Council's position included a gay rights group, the Gays and Lesbians for Individual Liberty, which believed that the freedom of all Americans, including gay Americans, would be eroded if the BSA did not have the ability to choose its own leaders and define its own membership criteria. In 2000, the Supreme Court ruled in favor of the BSA. The Court held that as a private organization, the BSA had the right to determine the requirements for becoming a scout leader.[*]

FOR CRITICAL ANALYSIS

If you were a justice on the Supreme Court, how would you have voted on this issue? Why?

[*]*Boy Scouts of America v. Dale,* 120 S.Ct. 2446 (2000).

housing, public accommodations, and credit. Several laws at the national level have also been changed in the past two decades. Among other things, the government has lifted the ban on hiring gays and lesbians and voided a 1952 law prohibiting gays and lesbians from immigrating to the United States. Currently, Congress is considering a bill that would bar workplace discrimination based on sexual orientation.

The Gay Community and Politics

Politicians at the national level have not overlooked the potential significance of homosexual issues in American politics. While conservative politicians generally have been critical of efforts to secure gay and lesbian rights, liberals, by and large, have been speaking out for gay rights in the last two decades. In 1980, the Democratic platform included a gay plank for the first time. Walter Mondale, former vice president of the United States and the Democratic Party nominee for president in 1984, addressed a gay convention and openly bid for the political support of gays and lesbians. The gay community also supported Jesse Jackson's 1988 bid for the presidency and Jackson's Rainbow Coalition.

President Bill Clinton long embraced much of the gay rights agenda and became the first sitting president to address a gay rights organization. In 1997, in a speech intentionally reminiscent of Harry Truman's 1947 speech to an African American civil rights organization, Clinton pledged his support for equal rights for gay and lesbian Americans at a fund-raiser sponsored by the Human Rights Campaign Fund.

In 2000, George W. Bush became the first Republican presidential candidate to meet with a large group of openly gay leaders to discuss their issues. Although Bush asserted that he would continue to oppose gay marriage and adoption, he also said that being openly gay would not disqualify a person from serving in a prominent position in his administration.

Gay Men and Lesbians in the Military

The U.S. Department of Defense traditionally has viewed homosexuality as incompatible with military service. Supporters of gay and lesbian rights have attacked this policy in recent years, and in 1993 the policy was modified. In that year, President Clinton announced that a new policy, generally characterized as "don't ask, don't tell," would be in effect. Enlistees would not be asked about their sexual orientation, and gays and lesbians would be allowed to serve in the military so long as they did not declare that they were gay or lesbian, or commit homosexual acts. Military officials endorsed the new policy, after opposing it initially, but supporters of gay rights were not enthusiastic. Clinton had promised during his presidential campaign to repeal outright the long-standing ban.

Several gays and lesbians who have been discharged from military service have protested their discharges by bringing suit against the Defense Department. In one case, a former Navy lieutenant, Paul Thomasson, was dismissed from the service in 1995 after stating "I am gay" in a letter to his commanding admiral. In 1996, a federal appellate court reviewed the case and concluded that the courts should defer, as they traditionally have, to the other branches of government, especially in military policy. A dissenting judge wrote that Thomasson was being punished for "nothing more than an expression of his state of mind."[13]

DID YOU KNOW...
That Albert Einstein was among six thousand persons in Germany in 1903 who signed a petition to repeal a portion of the German penal code that made homosexuality illegal?

INFOTRAC®
COLLEGE EDITION

Courting Gay Vote

---

[13]*Thomasson v. Perry*, 80 F.3d 915 (4th Cir. 1996).

A widely publicized 1998 case involved the Navy's dismissal of a naval officer, Timothy McVeigh,[14] on the ground that he had entered "gay" on a profile page for his account with America Online (AOL). Naval officers claimed that this amounted to a public declaration of McVeigh's gay status and thus justified his discharge. McVeigh argued that it was not a public declaration. Furthermore, contended McVeigh, the Navy had violated a 1986 federal privacy law governing electronic communications by obtaining information from AOL without a warrant or a court order. In 1998, a federal court judge agreed and ordered the Navy to reinstate McVeigh.[15]

At issue in these cases are the constitutional rights to free speech, privacy, and the equal protection of the laws. Because the lower courts are in disagreement, it is likely that the Supreme Court will rule on the matter in the future.

Same-Sex Marriages

Perhaps one of the most sensitive political issues with respect to the rights of gay and lesbian couples is whether they should be allowed to marry, just as heterosexual couples are. The controversy over this issue was fueled in 1993 when the Hawaii Supreme Court ruled that denying marriage licenses to gay couples might violate the equal protection clause of the Hawaii constitution. The court stated that unless Hawaii could offer a "compelling" reason to maintain this discriminatory practice, it must be abandoned. The Hawaii Supreme Court then sent the case back to the trial court to determine if the state did indeed have such a compelling reason. In 1996, the trial court ruled that the state had failed to meet this burden, and therefore the ban on same-sex marriages violates the state constitution.

In the wake of these events, other states began to worry about whether they would have to treat persons who were legally married in Hawaii as married cou-

---

[14]This is not the Timothy McVeigh who was convicted for the 1995 bombing of the Alfred P. Murrah Federal Building in Oklahoma City.
[15]*McVeigh v. Cohen,* 983 F.Supp. 215 (D.C. 1998).

Gay men and lesbians demonstrate in New York City's Bryant Park in favor of same-sex marriages. They want the state of New York to legalize such marriages.

ples in their states as well. Opponents of gay rights pushed for state laws banning same-sex marriages, and a number of states enacted such laws. At the federal level, Congress passed the Defense of Marriage Act of 1996, which bans federal recognition of lesbian and gay couples and allows state governments to ignore same-sex marriages performed in other states. Ironically, the Hawaii court decisions that gave rise to these concerns have largely come to naught. In 1998, the residents in that state voted for a state constitutional amendment that allows the Hawaii legislature to ban same-sex marriages.

The controversy over gay marriages was recently fueled again by developments in the state of Vermont. See this chapter's feature *An Ethical Issue: Should Gay Couples Be Allowed to Marry?* for a discussion of these developments.

an ethical issue

Should Gay Couples Be Allowed to Marry?

Should gay and lesbian couples have the legal right to marry? Do laws banning such marriages violate the equal protection clause of the U.S. Constitution or state constitutional provisions guaranteeing equal rights? These questions launched a nationwide controversy in the wake of Hawaii court rulings in the 1990s, as discussed elsewhere in this chapter. More recently, developments in the state of Vermont have ignited further controversy.

CIVIL UNIONS FOR GAY COUPLES

In 1999, the Vermont Supreme Court ruled that gay couples are entitled to the same benefits of marriage as opposite-sex couples. The unanimous ruling interpreted the state constitution's "common benefits clause," which is similar to the U.S. Constitution's equal protection clause. The court said that it was up to the legislature to implement the decision. According to the court, the legislature could either allow gay couples to marry or allow them to register as "domestic partners," as long as they would have all the same rights and benefits that married couples have.*

Subsequently, in April 2000, the Vermont legislature passed a law permitting gay and lesbian couples to form "civil unions." Partners forming civil unions will be entitled to receive some three hundred state benefits available to married couples, including the rights to inherit a partner's property, to decide on medical treatment for an incapacitated partner, and to arrange for burial procedures. Vermont civil unions, however, will not be recognized by the federal government and thus will not entitle partners in those unions to any federal benefits, such as spousal Social Security benefits, associated with marriage.

*Baker v. State, 744 A.2d 864 (Vt. 1999).

WHY NOT PERMIT GAY AND LESBIAN COUPLES TO MARRY?

Gay and lesbian groups hailed the Vermont law as a historic step forward on the road to full equality. Yet, according to some, the decision fell short of full equality, which would allow gay couples to become legally "married" just as heterosexual couples can. The Vermont legislature did not take this further step, which the state supreme court had allowed as one of the options.

Polling data show that a strong majority of Americans believe in equal political and economic rights for gays and lesbians. For example, surveys show that about 83 percent of Americans believe that gay and lesbian civil rights should be protected and that the government has not gone far enough to protect these rights. About 58 percent of Americans also state that gay and lesbian spouses should be entitled to certain benefits received by heterosexual spouses—including inheritance rights, Social Security benefits, and job-related benefits, such as health insurance. Notably, however, only about 33 percent of Americans support legally sanctioned marriages for these groups.[†]

Clearly, over the last several decades lesbian and gay groups have succeeded in bringing about significant changes in public opinion—and state and local laws—relating to their status and rights. There now seems to be a broad consensus that gay and lesbian couples should be entitled to equal rights, including many of the tangible benefits of heterosexual spouses. Yet Americans are reluctant to take the further step of extending symbolic equality to gays and lesbians with respect to the institution of marriage and the family.

FOR CRITICAL ANALYSIS

Should the fact that gay marriage is contrary to the majority of Americans' views on what marriage means influence legislators on this issue?

[†]Based on surveys reported in *The Public Perspective*, January/February 2000, pp. 22–31.

Child Custody and Adoption

Gay men and lesbians have also faced difficulties in obtaining child-custody and adoption rights. Courts around the country, when deciding which of two parents should have custody, have wrestled with how much weight, if any, should be given to a parent's sexual orientation. For some time, the courts were split fairly evenly on this issue. In about half the states, courts held that a parent's sexual orientation should not be a significant factor in determining child custody. Courts in other states, however, tended to give more weight to sexual orientation. In one case, a court even went so far as to award custody to a father because the child's mother was a lesbian, even though the father had served eight years in prison for killing his first wife. Today, however, courts in the majority of states no longer deny custody or visitation rights to persons solely on the basis of their sexual orientation.

The last decade has also seen a sharp climb in the number of gay men and lesbians who are adopting children. To date, twenty-two states have allowed lesbians and gay men to adopt children through state-operated or private adoption agencies.

The Rights and Status of Juveniles

Approximately 76 million Americans—almost 30 percent of the total population—are under twenty-one years of age. The definition of children ranges from persons under age sixteen to persons under age twenty-one. However defined, children in the United States have fewer rights and protections than any other major group in society.

The reason for this lack is the common presumption of society and its lawmakers that children are basically protected by their parents. This is not to say that children are the exclusive property of the parents. Rather, an overwhelming case in favor of *not* allowing parents to control the actions of their children must be presented before children can be given authorization to act without parental consent (or before the state can be given authorization to act on children's behalf without regard to their parents' wishes).

Supreme Court decisions affecting children's rights began a process of slow evolution with *Brown v. Board of Education of Topeka,* the landmark civil rights case of 1954 discussed in Chapter 5. In *Brown,* the Court granted children the status of rights-bearing persons. In 1967, in *In re Gault,*[16] the Court expressly held that children have a constitutional right to be represented by counsel at the government's expense in a criminal action. Five years later, the Court acknowledged that "children are 'persons' within the meaning of the Bill of Rights. We have held so over and over again."[17]

Supreme Court decisions affecting the rights of children have also touched on another very controversial issue: abortion. In 1976, the Court recognized a girl's right to have an abortion without consulting her parents.[18] More recently, however, the Court has allowed state laws to dictate whether the child must obtain consent.

Voting Rights and the Young

The Twenty-sixth Amendment to the Constitution, ratified on July 1, 1971, reads as follows:

[16]387 U.S. 1 (1967).
[17]*Wisconsin v. Yoder,* 406 U.S. 205 (1972).
[18]*Planned Parenthood of Central Missouri v. Danforth,* 428 U.S. 52 (1976).

The right of citizens of the United States, who are eighteen years of age or older, to vote shall not be denied or abridged by the United States or by any State on account of age.

Before this amendment was ratified, the age at which citizens could vote was twenty-one. Why did the Twenty-sixth Amendment specify age eighteen? Why not seventeen or sixteen? And why did it take until 1971 to allow those between the ages of eighteen and twenty-one to vote?

There are no easy answers to such questions. One cannot argue simply that those under twenty-one, or those under eighteen for that matter, are "incompetent." Incompetent at what? Certainly, one could find a significant number of seventeen-year-olds who can understand the political issues presented to them as well as can many adults eligible to vote. One of the arguments used for granting suffrage to eighteen-year-olds was that, because they could be drafted to fight in the country's wars, they had a stake in public policy. At the time, the example of the Vietnam War (1964–1975) was paramount.

Have eighteen- to twenty-year-olds used their right to vote? Yes and no. Immediately after the passage of the Twenty-sixth Amendment, the percentage of eighteen- to twenty-year-olds registering to vote was 58 percent (in 1972), and 48.4 percent reported that they had voted. But by the 1996 presidential election, of the 10.7 million Americans in the eighteen-to-twenty voting-age bracket, 45.6 percent were registered, and 31.2 percent reported that they had voted. The 2000 elections showed similar results. In contrast, voter turnout among Americans aged sixty-five or older is very high, usually between 60 and 70 percent.

The Rights of Children in Civil and Criminal Proceedings

Children today have limited rights in civil and criminal proceedings in our judicial system. Different procedural rules and judicial safeguards apply in civil and criminal laws. **Civil law** relates in part to contracts among private individuals or companies. **Criminal law** relates to crimes against society that are defined by society acting through its legislatures.

Civil Rights of Juveniles.   The civil rights of children are defined exclusively by state law with respect to private contract negotiations, rights, and remedies. The legal definition of **majority** varies from eighteen to twenty-one years of age, depending on the state. As a rule, an individual who is legally a minor cannot be held responsible for contracts that he or she forms with others. In most states, only contracts entered into for so-called **necessaries** (things necessary for subsistence, as determined by the courts) can be enforced against minors. Also, when minors engage in negligent behavior, typically their parents are liable. If, for example, a minor destroys a neighbor's fence, the neighbor may bring suit against the child's parent but not against the child.

Civil law also encompasses the area of child custody. Child-custody rulings have traditionally given little weight to the wishes of the child. Courts have maintained the right to act on behalf of the child's "best interests" but have sometimes been constrained from doing so by the "greater" rights possessed by adults. For instance, a widely publicized Michigan Supreme Court ruling awarded legal custody of a two-and-a-half-year-old Michigan resident to an Iowa couple, the child's biological parents. A Michigan couple, who had cared for the child since shortly after its birth and who had petitioned to adopt the child, lost out in the custody battle. The court clearly said that the law had allowed it to consider only the parents' rights and not the child's best interests.

DID YOU KNOW...
That the United Nations Convention on the Rights of the Child calls for the provision of effective legal assistance for children so that their interests can be "heard directly"?

Civil Law
The law regulating conduct between private persons over noncriminal matters. Under civil law, the government provides the forum for the settlement of disputes between private parties in such matters as contracts, domestic relations, and business relations.

Criminal Law
The law that defines crimes and provides punishment for violations. In criminal cases, the government is the prosecutor, because crimes are against the public order.

Majority
Full age; the age at which a person is entitled by law to the right to manage her or his own affairs and to the full enjoyment of civil rights.

Necessaries
In contract law, necessaries include whatever is reasonably necessary for suitable subsistence as measured by age, state, condition in life, and so on.

Common Law
Judge-made law that originated in
England from decisions shaped according to prevailing customs. Decisions
were applied to similar situations and
thus gradually became common to the
nation.

Children's rights and their ability to articulate their rights for themselves in
custody matters were strengthened, however, by several well-publicized rulings
involving older children. In one case, for example, an eleven-year-old Florida
boy filed suit in his own name, assisted by his own privately retained legal
counsel, to terminate his relationship with his biological parents and to have the
court affirm his right to be adopted by foster parents. The court granted his
request, although it did not agree procedurally with the method by which the
boy initiated the suit.[19] The news media characterized the case as the first
instance in which a minor child had "divorced" himself from his parents.

Criminal Rights of Juveniles.   One of the main requirements for an act to be
criminal is intent. The law has given children certain defenses against criminal
prosecution because of their presumed inability to have criminal intent. Under
the **common law,** children up to seven years of age were considered incapable of
committing a crime, because they did not have the moral sense to understand
that they were doing wrong. Children between the ages of seven and fourteen
were also presumed to be incapable of committing a crime, but this presumption
could be challenged by showing that the child understood the wrongful nature
of the act. Today, states vary in their approaches. Most states retain the common
law approach, although age limits vary from state to state. Other states have
simply set a minimum age for criminal responsibility.

All states have juvenile court systems that handle children below the age of
criminal responsibility who commit delinquent acts. The aim of juvenile courts
is allegedly to reform rather than to punish. In states that retain the common
law approach, children who are above the minimum age but are still juveniles
can be turned over to the criminal courts if the juvenile court determines that
they should be treated as adults. Children still do not have the right to trial by
jury or to post bail. Also, in most states parents can still commit their minor
children to state mental institutions without allowing the child a hearing.

---

[19]*Kingsley v. Kingsley,* 623 So.2d 780 (Fla.App. 1993).

This juvenile is being arrested in the same
way that an adult would be, but he does not
have the rights under criminal law of an
adult. Juveniles normally receive less severe
punishment than adults do for similar crimes,
however.

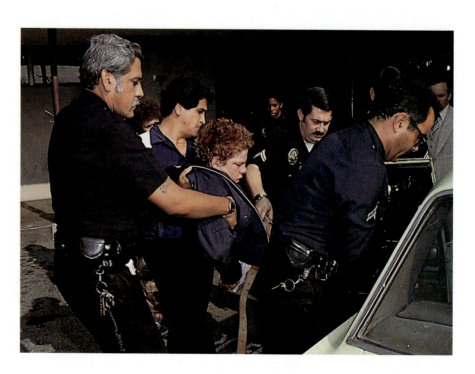

Although minors still do not usually have the full rights of adults in criminal proceedings, they have certain advantages. In felony, manslaughter, murder, armed robbery, and assault cases, juveniles usually are not tried as adults. They may be sentenced to probation or "reform" school for a relatively few years regardless of the seriousness of their crimes. Most states, however, allow juveniles to be tried as adults (often at the discretion of the judge) for certain crimes, such as murder. When they are tried as adults, they are treated to due process of law and tried for the crime, rather than being given the paternalistic treatment reserved for the juvenile delinquent. Juveniles who are tried as adults may also face adult penalties, including the death penalty. Currently, about seventy people are on the nation's death rows for crimes that they committed when they were sixteen or seventeen. (For a cross-national comparison of the use of the death penalty for juvenile offenders, see this chapter's *Global View: The Death Penalty for Juveniles*.)

What to do about crime committed by juveniles is a pressing problem for today's political leaders. One approach to the problem is to treat juveniles as adults, which more and more judges seem to be doing. There appears to be widespread public support for this approach, as well as for lowering the age at which juveniles should receive adult treatment in criminal proceedings. Polling data show that two-thirds of U.S. adults think that juveniles under the age of thirteen who commit murder should be tried as adults. Another approach is to hold parents responsible for the crimes of their minor children (a minority of the states do so under so-called parental-responsibility laws). These are contradictory approaches, to be sure. Yet they perhaps reflect the divided opinion in our society concerning the rights of children versus the rights of parents.

DID YOU KNOW...
That the number of juveniles sent to adult prisons for violent offenses in the United States has tripled since 1985**?**

global View

The Death Penalty for Juveniles

The United States is known throughout the world for the many constitutional protections available to adult criminal suspects. With respect to juvenile offenders, however, the United States does not earn very high scores.

In 1989, the General Assembly of the United Nations adopted the Convention on the Rights of the Child. Article 37 of this convention (agreement) states, "Neither capital punishment nor life imprisonment without possibility of release shall be imposed for offenses committed by a [minor]." Since then, all of the world's nations except the United States and Somalia have signed the convention. In the past several years, China, South Africa, and Russia have all taken steps toward abolishing the death penalty for juveniles. The United States is now one of only a few countries that execute juvenile offenders.*

Various organizations, including Amnesty International, have criticized the United States for its stance on juvenile punishment,

as have various individuals, including the pope of the Roman Catholic Church. Some even contend that prohibition of the juvenile death penalty should be deemed a principle of international law binding on all nations.

Notwithstanding these criticisms, U.S. political leaders and public opinion continue to favor the death penalty for juveniles who commit egregious crimes. Indeed, in the last decade the United States executed six juvenile offenders—more than any other country. Moreover, legislators in some states, including Texas, have been considering legislation that would lower the age at which minors can be sentenced to death—from age fourteen to age eleven, for example. As noted elsewhere, the United States Supreme Court, while aware of the international disapproval of this American practice, has not invalidated laws allowing juveniles to be executed. Rather, it has left this decision to the states.

FOR CRITICAL ANALYSIS

Does the United States have a moral obligation to follow the rest of the world with respect to the use of the death penalty for juvenile offenders?

*Other countries include Iran, Pakistan, Saudi Arabia, and Yemen.

Civil Rights—Beyond Equal Protection: Issues for the Twenty-First Century

As we enter the twenty-first century, the future of civil rights in the United States remains somewhat cloudy. Certainly, the controversy over affirmative action policies has not been resolved one way or the other, and America's political leaders and the courts will continue to address this issue in the coming years. Whether bilingual education programs help or hinder the education of immigrant children is another issue that will extend into the foreseeable future.

The expanding proportion of the American population that is over the age of sixty-five will also lead to political and economic conflicts in the years to come. As senior citizens become a larger percentage of the population, their political power will continue to grow. Undoubtedly, they will clash repeatedly with those who propose cutting or modifying benefits for older Americans or changing the way in which current programs benefiting seniors, such as Social Security and Medicare, are administered. Additionally, persons with disabilities, their employers, and the courts will continue to struggle with what exactly the Americans with Disabilities Act does and does not require.

Although no nation is capable of legislating morality, our government does have a responsibility to create an environment that does not allow state-sanctioned discrimination against any person. Yet gay men and lesbians continue to be subject to anti-gay laws and other discriminatory actions. Clearly, the struggle for equal treatment waged by this group of Americans is far from over.

Finally, the debate over the rights of children has intensified in recent years due to violent crime, including a number of school shootings, committed by teenagers and preteens and the increased awareness of the extent of child abuse in this nation. We can be sure that the controversy over the welfare and rights of children will continue for years to come.

making a difference

Dealing with Discrimination

When you apply for a job, you may be subjected to a variety of possibly discriminatory practices—based on your race, color, gender, religion, age, national origin, sexual preference, or disability. You may also be subjected to a battery of tests, some of which you may feel are discriminatory. At both the state and federal levels, the government continues to examine the fairness and validity of criteria used in job-applicant screening. If you believe that you have been discriminated against by a potential employer, you may wish to consider the following steps:

1. Evaluate your own capabilities, and determine if you are truly qualified for the position.

2. Analyze the reasons that you were turned down. Do you feel that others would agree with you that you have been the object of discrimination, or would they uphold your employer's claim?

3. If you still believe that you have been unfairly treated, you have recourse to several agencies and services.

You should first speak to the personnel director of the company and politely explain that you feel you have not been adequately evaluated. If asked, explain your concerns clearly. If necessary, go into explicit detail, and indicate that you feel that you may have been discriminated against. If a second evaluation is not forthcoming, contact the local branch of your state employment agency. If you still do not obtain adequate help, contact one or more of the following state agencies, usually found by looking in your telephone directory under "State Government" listings.

1. If a government entity is involved, a state ombudsperson or citizen aide who will mediate may be available.

2. You may wish to contact the state civil rights commission, which will at least give you advice even if it does not wish to take up your case.

3. The state attorney general's office will normally have a division dealing with discrimination and civil rights.

4. There may be a special commission or department specifically set up to help you, such as a women's status commission or a commission on Hispanics or Asian Americans. If you are a woman or a member of such a minority group, contact these commissions.

Finally, at the national level, you can contact the American Civil Liberties Union, 125 Broad St., New York, N.Y. 10004-2400, 212-549-2500, or check

http://www.aclu.org

You can also contact the most appropriate federal agency: the Equal Employment Opportunity Commission, 1801 L St. N.W., Washington, DC 20507, 202-663-4900, or go to

http://www.eeoc.gov

Key terms

affirmative action 189

civil law 207

common law 208

criminal law 207

majority 207

mandatory retirement 197

necessaries 207

reverse discrimination 190

Chapter summary

1 Affirmative action programs have been controversial because they can lead to reverse discrimination against majority groups or even other minority groups. In an early case on the issue, *Regents of the University of California v. Bakke* (1978), the Supreme Court held that using race as the sole criterion for admission to a university is improper. Since *Bakke* a number of Supreme Court decisions have further limited affirmative action programs. Recent Supreme Court decisions, particularly *Adarand Constructors, Inc. v. Peña,* and decisions by the lower courts that the Supreme Court has let stand, such as *Hopwood v. State of Texas,* have led some observers to conclude that it will be difficult in the future for any affirmative action program to pass constitutional muster. California voters banned state-sponsored affirmative action in that state in a 1996 ballot initiative known as Proposition 209, which was upheld as constitutional by a federal appellate court. In 1998, voters in the state of Washington ended affirmative action in that state. Whether affirmative action programs will survive the current backlash against them remains to be seen.

2 Bilingual education programs, like affirmative action, have come under attack in recent years. The major criticism against bilingual education programs is that they impede children's ability to learn English quickly and succeed academically.

3 Problems associated with aging and retirement are becoming increasingly important as the number of older persons in the United States increases. The Age Discrimination in Employment Act of 1967 prohibits job-related discrimination against individuals over the age of forty on the basis of age, unless age is shown to be a bona fide occupational qualification reasonably necessary to the normal operation of the business. Amendments to the act prohibit mandatory retirement except in a few selected professions. As a group, older people contribute significantly to American political life, ranking first in voter registration and turnout and being well represented in Congress. Through a variety of organizations, older Americans lobby effectively at both the federal and state levels.

4 In 1973, Congress passed the Rehabilitation Act, which prohibits discrimination against persons with disabilities in programs receiving federal aid. Regulations implementing the act provide for ramps, elevators, and the like in all federal buildings. The Education for All Handicapped Children Act (1975) provides that all children with disabilities should receive an "appropriate" education. The Americans with Disabilities Act of 1990 prohibits job discrimination against persons with physical and mental disabilities, requiring that positive steps be taken to comply with the act's requirements. The act also requires expanded access to public facilities, including transportation, and to services offered by such private concerns as car-rental and telephone companies.

5 Gay and lesbian rights groups, which first began to form in 1969, now number in the thousands. These groups work to promote laws protecting gay men and lesbians from discrimination and to repeal anti-gay laws. Since 1969, sodomy laws have been repealed or struck down by the courts in all but eighteen states. Eleven states and over 165 cities and counties now have laws prohibiting discrimination based on sexual orientation. Gay men and lesbians are no longer barred from federal employment or from immigrating to this country, and Congress is currently considering a bill that would ban employment discrimination against gay men and lesbians. Since 1980, liberal Democrats at the national level have supported gay and lesbian rights and sought electoral support from these groups. The military's "don't ask, don't tell" policy has fueled extensive controversy, as have same-sex marriages and child-custody issues.

6 Although children form a large group of Americans, they have the fewest rights and protections, in part because it is commonly presumed that parents protect their children. The Twenty-sixth Amendment grants the right to vote to those aged eighteen or older. In most states, only contracts entered into for necessaries can be enforced against minors. When minors engage in negligent acts, their parents may be held liable. Minors have some defense against criminal prosecution because of their presumed inability to have criminal intent at certain ages. For those below the age of criminal responsibility, there are state juvenile courts. When minors are tried as adults, they are entitled to the procedural protections afforded to adults and are subject to adult penalties, including the death penalty.

Selected print and electronic resources

SUGGESTED READINGS

Leone, Bruno, *et al.*, eds. *Child Welfare: Opposing Viewpoints.* San Diego, Calif.: Greenhaven Press, 1998. This "issues" book presents opposing viewpoints on various aspects of child welfare.

Roemer, John E. *Equality of Opportunity.* Cambridge, Mass.: Harvard University Press, 1998. Roemer examines the two positions in the affirmative action debate and concludes that both emphasize equal opportunity; they differ over whether equal opportunity should be required before or after the competition (such as for jobs) starts.

Sowell, Thomas. *The Quest for Cosmic Justice.* New York: Free Press, 1999. Sowell takes issue with the idea of social ("cosmic") justice—the liberal notion that people can right all wrongs through such programs as affirmative action and equal pay acts. He claims that such concepts undermine the principles of liberty and justice on which this nation was founded.

Steele, Shelby. *A Dream Deferred: The Second Betrayal of Black Freedom in America.* New York: HarperCollins, 1998. The author, a distinguished black intellectual, contends that affirmative action (a "second betrayal" of black Americans) is less an attempt to create true equality between the races than an attempt by liberals to rid the country of guilt for slavery and segregation (the first betrayal).

MEDIA RESOURCES

Affirmative Action: The History of an Idea—This program explores the historical roots of affirmative action and the current debate over its usefulness.

Shot by a Kid—A film documenting the relationship among children, guns, and violence in four major cities of the United States.

Logging on

For information on, and arguments in support of, affirmative action and the rights of the groups discussed in this chapter, a good source is the American Civil Liberties Union's Web site. Go to:

http://www.aclu.org

The National Organization for Women (NOW) offers online information and updates on the status of women's rights, including affirmative action cases involving women. Go to

http://www.now.org

An excellent source for information on discrimination based on age and disability is the Equal Employment Opportunity Commission's Web site at

http://www.eeoc.gov

You can find information on the Americans with Disabilities Act (ADA) of 1990, including the act's text, at

http://janweb.icdi.wvu.edu/kinder

You can access the Web site of the Human Rights Campaign Fund, the nation's largest gay and lesbian political organization, at

http://www.hrc.org

If you are interested in children's rights and welfare, a good starting place is the Web site of the Child Welfare Institute. Go to

http://www.gocwi.org

Using the Internet for political analysis

Imagine that you are the owner of a new franchise business and are hiring your first employees. Several of the applicants are over the age of sixty-five, and one of them tells you that she has impaired hearing but has a good hearing aid to assist her.

Using one of the Web sites given in the next column, look up Labor and Employment Law and develop some guidelines for your hiring practices that will not violate laws prohibiting discrimination against older Americans and workers with disabilities. Consider the information that you find on the Web. To what extent would you rely on this information when you write an employment manual? What other resources might you also check?

FindLaw, at **http://www.findlaw.com**

Legal Resource Guide, at **http://www.ilrg.com**

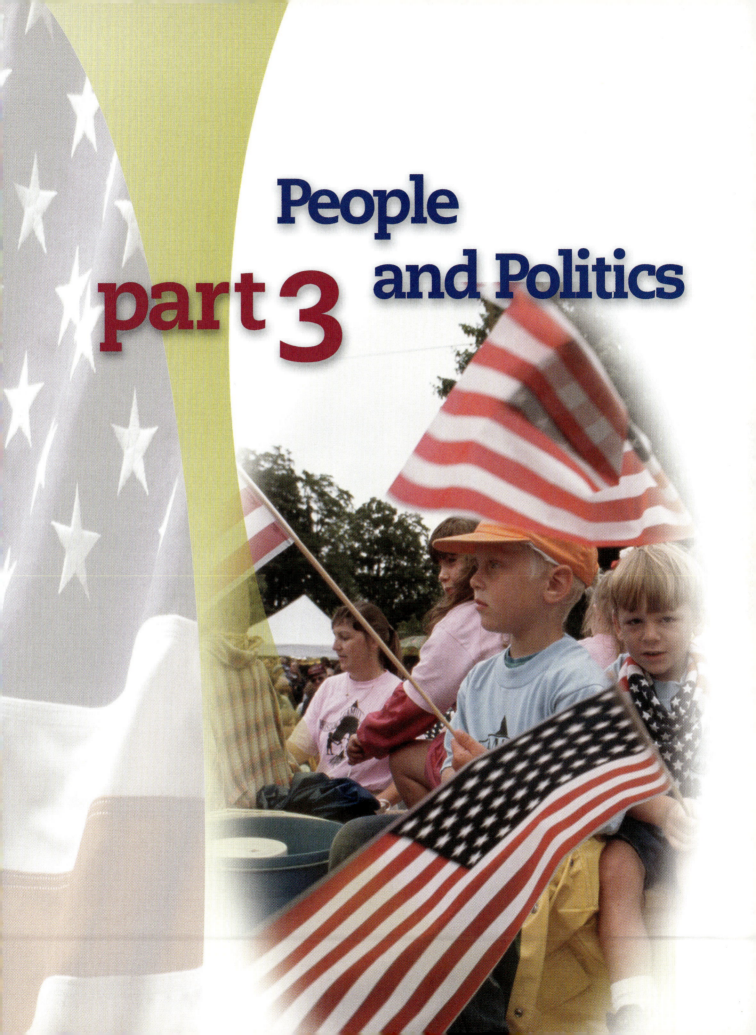

People and Politics

part 3

chapter 7

Public Opinion and Political Socialization

CHAPTER OUTLINE

- How Powerful Is Public Opinion?

- Defining Public Opinion

- Measuring Public Opinion: Polling Techniques

- Political Socialization

- Political Culture and Public Opinion

- Public Opinion about Government

- The Spectrum of Political Beliefs

- Public Opinion and the Political Process

what if...

Courts Used Public Opinion Polls to Decide Cases?

BACKGROUND

IN THE UNITED STATES, THE GUILT OR INNOCENCE OF ANYONE ON TRIAL IS DETERMINED EITHER BY A JUDGE OR A PANEL OF JUDGES OR, ACCORDING TO ANCIENT ENGLISH PRACTICE, A JURY OF THAT PERSON'S PEERS. THE JURY SYSTEM WAS DEVELOPED TO ASSURE ORDINARY PEOPLE THE OPPORTUNITY TO GET A FAIR HEARING FROM OTHER MEMBERS OF SOCIETY. TODAY, THE JURY POOL—A GROUP OF THOSE ELIGIBLE TO BE CHOSEN TO SIT ON A JURY—NORMALLY RESULTS FROM A RANDOM SELECTION OF INDIVIDUALS WHO ARE REGISTERED TO VOTE.

WITH THE ADVENT OF TELEVISED TRIALS AND EXTENSIVE MEDIA COVERAGE OF HIGH-PROFILE CASES, THE POSSIBILITY ARISES THAT THE JURY OR JUDGE MAY BE INFLUENCED BY MEDIA COMMENTARY OR BY REPORTED PUBLIC OPINION ABOUT GUILT OR INNOCENCE. WOULD IT BE FAIRER TO A PERSON ON TRIAL TO HAVE HIS OR HER CASE DECIDED BY A SCIENTIFICALLY CONDUCTED POLL OF PUBLIC OPINION?

WHAT IF COURTS USED PUBLIC OPINION POLLS TO DECIDE CASES?

Given that relatively few individuals ever serve on a jury, scientifically selecting a sample of adult Americans to decide the outcome of a trial might provide a much more representative group to listen to the evidence presented in the court and then make a decision. To give some validity to the opinions, the sample would be much larger than a jury—say, at least 1,200 persons. The opinions expressed by the jury, then, would represent the opinions of all the people living in that jurisdiction and, perhaps more importantly, would include the views of individuals who are excluded from jury duty by employment, infirmity, or their own choice.

How would the public gain enough information to make a decision about a trial? Some trials, of course, are televised. Persons selected to be polled could be asked to watch news summaries of the trial or the trial itself. Or, those charged with devising the poll could give the individuals enough information in the survey to enable them to have an opinion. Today, many prosecutors and defense attorneys use similar kinds of polling to find out what kind of jurors are most likely to be favorable to their clients or how much of an award might be expected if their clients are successful in their suits. Polling "tests" the community's opinion before and during trials. Although today's jurors often are asked *not* to watch news about their trials, inevitably jurors have seen public opinion polls about certain cases, such as that of O. J. Simpson in the mid-1990s, before they begin serving on the jury.

Using a poll of public opinion to try cases would lead to radical changes in the roles of the court, the judge, and the attorneys. The judge might need to coordinate the design of the survey and supervise the provision of information by the attorneys from both sides. There would be little use for charismatic attorneys *in the courtroom.* Instead, attorneys would likely spend even more time on television trying to shape community opinion.

CAN THE PUBLIC JUDGE A TRIAL?

There is a lot of evidence about how the public follows high-profile trials such as that of O. J. Simpson in the mid-1990s or the impeachment trial of President Bill Clinton in 1999. Even though most Americans do not follow the actual transcripts of such trials and may not be knowledgeable about the points of law raised in the courtroom, Americans are quite willing to form opinions about guilt or innocence and to tell them to the pollster. One of the shortcomings of any public opinion poll is the tendency of respondents to answer any question asked whether they have sufficient information to have an opinion or not. Sometimes, respondents just want to end the interview politely, so they answer the questions.

Finally, while the "public jury" might be able to decide guilt or innocence, it might be reluctant to apply the lawful penalty. People may believe the accused is guilty but be very unwilling to approve the death penalty, for example.

FOR CRITICAL ANALYSIS

1. Can you think of some cases, such as those against the tobacco industry that might be suitable to be decided by public opinion?
2. Why might some defendants think that they might have a better chance in the court of public opinion than in a real courtroom? What could they do to sway public opinion to their advantage?

Public opinion polls can give voice to the preferences of the people between elections. These preferences may relate to the distribution of power between the national government and the states, and the future role of the nation in the world. Furthermore, public opinion, whether expressed through scientifically conducted opinion polls or directly over the Internet, can reflect the public's views on specific policy actions in a way that elections cannot. What role, then, does public opinion play in the changing American political system? Is it truly the voice of the people, or is it an instrument to be manipulated by politicians and interest groups? Can political leaders count on public opinion to provide guidance on their actions, or are the results of most opinion polls too ephemeral to be useful?

The very character of public opinion polls may limit their usefulness. After all, the pollster wrote the questions, called the respondents, and perhaps forwarded the results to the politicians. Public opinion, as gathered by polls, is not equivalent to constituents' letters to their representatives or to ballots cast in an election. In fact, polls may be flawed in a number of ways. As the chapter-opening *What If . . .* suggests, however, polls have become a frequent component of the political and judicial process.

Trial Lawyer Can Use Focus Groups

How Powerful Is Public Opinion?

At various times in the recent history of the United States, public opinion has played a powerful role in presidential politics. Beginning in 1965, public opinion became strongly divided over the Vietnam War (1964–1975). Polls and widespread campus demonstrations showed the growing public opposition to the war. Public opinion not only forced President Lyndon Johnson to withdraw from the 1968 presidential race, but it also may have colored the way the public has viewed the use of American troops overseas ever since.

The **Watergate break-in** caused the downfall of President Richard Nixon. As news of the president's role in the cover-up of the crime became known, his popularity, as measured by public opinion polls, fell to 25 percent. Nixon resigned in August 1974.

The influence of public opinion on the fate of President Bill Clinton was quite the opposite. In 1998, throughout the investigation of the scandal concerning his relationship with White House intern Monica Lewinsky, Clinton's approval ratings stayed at incredibly high levels. Even after the House impeached him late in that year, his approval ratings remained high. There can be little doubt that the public's approval of his actions as president and the majority's belief that he should not be removed from office influenced the outcome of the trial in the Senate in early 1999. As you will note from the data in Table 7–1 on the next page, however, public opinion about his personal character and fitness to hold office declined steeply as the investigation progressed.

In most situations, legislators, politicians, and presidents use public opinion to shore up their own arguments. It provides a kind of evidence for their own point of view. If the results of polls do not support their positions, they can either commission their own polls or ignore the polls. Politicians find it more difficult to use public opinion on complex issues, such as changes in Medicare or welfare reform, because such complicated issues cannot be discussed fully in a poll. Thus, public opinion can be useless or useful to political decision makers.

Watergate Break-in
The 1972 illegal entry into the Democratic National Committee offices by participants in Richard Nixon's reelection campaign.

Defining Public Opinion

There is no one public opinion, because there are many different "publics." In a nation of over 275 million people, there may be innumerable gradations of opinion

Those who wish to have legislation passed often muster the forces of public opinion to help convince Congress to pass it. Here you see citizens voicing their opinions on health-care reform.

Public Opinion
The aggregate of individual attitudes or beliefs shared by some portion of the adult population. There is no one public opinion, because there are many different "publics."

Consensus
General agreement among the citizenry on an issue.

TABLE 7–1

Public Opinion and President Clinton: The President versus the Person

DATE	PERCENTAGE APPROVING CLINTON AS PRESIDENT	PERCENTAGE SAYING CLINTON SHARES MORAL VALUES WITH MOST AMERICANS
January 1998	58%	41%
February 1998	72	44
April 1998	67	35
June 1998	60	35
August 1998	67	44
October 1998	65	28
December 1998	65	32
January 1999	69	30

SOURCE: *New York Times*/CBS News Polls, 1998–1999.

on an issue. What we do is describe the distribution of opinions among the public about a particular question. Thus, we define **public opinion** as the aggregate of individual attitudes or beliefs shared by some portion of the adult population.

Often, the public holds quite a range of opinions on a topic, making it difficult to discern what kinds of policies most Americans might support. For example, as Congress debated passing legislation to regulate the tobacco industry, frequent polls asked Americans their views on such policies. Most polls showed that the majority of Americans believed that smoking-related illnesses were the fault of the smokers themselves (67 percent), rather than of the companies (19 percent), yet Americans were divided evenly on whether private suits against the companies by those who had such illnesses should be limited. Americans generally approved of having tobacco companies help pay for health insurance for poor children but were not sure whether those companies should be banned from sponsoring sporting events.

How is public opinion made known in a democracy? In the case of the Vietnam War (1964–1975), it was made known by numerous antiwar protests, countless articles in magazines and newspapers, and continuing electronic media coverage of antiwar demonstrations. Normally, however, public opinion becomes known in a democracy through elections and, in some states, initiatives or referenda (see Chapter 18). Other ways are through lobbying and interest group activities, which are also used to influence public opinion (see Chapter 8). In the age of the Internet, citizens increasingly are able to send their opinions to government officials electronically.

Consensus and Division

There are very few issues on which most Americans agree. The more normal situation is for opinion to be distributed among several different positions. Looking at the distribution of opinion can tell us how divided the public is on a question and give us some indication of whether compromise is possible. The distribution of opinion can also tell us how many individuals have not thought enough about an issue to hold an opinion.

When a large proportion of the American public appears to express the same view on an issue, we say that a **consensus** exists, at least at the moment the poll was taken. Figure 7–1 shows the pattern of opinion that might be called consensual. Issues on which the public holds widely differing attitudes result in **divisive opinion** (see Figure 7–2). If there is no possible middle position on such issues, we expect that the division will continue to generate political conflict.

Figure 7–3 shows a distribution of opinion indicating that most Americans either have no information about the issue or are not interested enough in the issue to formulate a position. Politicians may feel that the lack of knowledge gives them more room to maneuver, or they may be wary of taking any action for fear that opinion will crystallize after a crisis.

Public opinion can be defined most clearly by its effect. As political scientist V. O. Key, Jr., once said, public opinion is what governments "find it prudent to heed."[1] This means that for public opinion to be effective, enough people have to hold a particular view with such strong conviction that a government feels its actions should be influenced by that view.

An interesting question arises as to when *private* opinion becomes *public* opinion. Everyone probably has a private opinion about the competence of the president, as well as private opinions about more personal concerns, such as the state of a neighbor's lawn. We say that private opinion becomes public opinion when the opinion is publicly expressed and if the opinion concerns public issues. When someone's private opinion becomes so strong that the individual is willing to go to the polls to vote for or against a candidate or an issue—or is willing to participate in a demonstration, to discuss the issue at work, to speak out on local television or a radio talk show, or to participate in the political process in any one of a dozen other ways—then that opinion becomes public opinion.

The Qualities of Public Opinion

At the beginning of the Vietnam War in the 1960s, public opinion about its conduct was not very clear, like a camera that is not focused. As the war progressed

---

[1] V. O. Key, Jr., *Public Opinion and American Democracy* (New York: Knopf, 1961), p. 10.

DID YOU KNOW...
That James Madison and others argued in *The Federalist Papers* that because public opinion is potentially dangerous, it should be diffused through a large republic with separation of government powers **?**

Divisive Opinion
Public opinion that is polarized between two quite different positions.

FIGURE 7-1
Consensus Opinion

Question: Do you think it is morally acceptable to clone human beings?

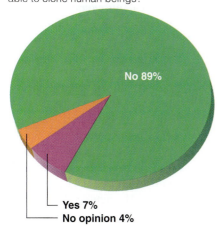

Source: Survey by Yankelovich Partners, Inc., for *Time*/CNN, February 26–27, 1997.

FIGURE 7-2
Divisive Opinion

Question: Do you think it would be a good thing or a bad thing for the tobacco companies in this country to be driven out of business by a lawsuit?

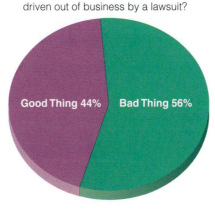

Source: Gallup Organization for CNN/*USA Today,* May 6–7, 1997.

FIGURE 7-3
Nonopinion

Question: Will it be good or bad for the United States if China becomes a member of the World Trade Organization?

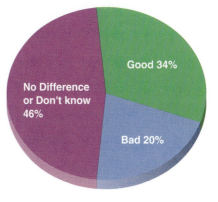

Source: Pew Center for the People and the Press, survey conducted February 9–14, 2000.

Union members protest a cut in benefits. A strike can be seen as an expression of public opinion, but if the union does not get support from others, politicians will feel little effect.

and U.S. involvement deepened, public opinion became increasingly clarified. In that case, as in most cases, public opinion has identifiable qualities that change over time. Political scientists have identified some qualities to describe public opinion: (1) intensity, (2) fluidity, (3) stability, (4) relevance, and (5) political knowledge.

Intensity.   How strongly people are willing to express their private opinions determines the **intensity** of public opinion. Consider, as an example, U.S. relations with Cuba. Normally, most Americans pay little attention to Fidel Castro and Cuba. In 2000, however, Americans and Cubans became consumed with the fate of an orphaned boy rescued from the sea—Elian Gonzalez. Americans held intense opinions about whether he should be sent back to Cuba. Cuban Americans living in Miami, Florida, who usually have very intense opinions about American relations with Cuba, had especially intense opinions about the boy.

Fluidity.   Public opinion can change drastically in a very short period of time. When this occurs, we say that public opinion is fluid. In 1945, at the end of World War II, for example, the American people were about evenly divided in their opinions of the U.S. wartime ally, the Soviet Union. A 1945 Roper poll showed that about 39 percent of Americans saw the Soviets as peace loving, whereas 38 percent felt they were aggressive. During the years of the Cold War (1947 to, roughly, 1985), American opinion about the aims of the Soviet Union was very consistent. Between 13 and 17 percent of the American people believed that the Soviet Union was peace loving, and more than 60 percent saw it as aggressive. As Americans witnessed first the opening of the Soviet Union to Western influences in the late 1980s and then the breakdown of the Soviet Union in 1991, American opinion about the Soviet Union changed quickly. Between 1985 and 1990, the number of Americans who saw the Soviet Union as peace loving increased from 17 to 43 percent.[2] And by 1996, only 12 percent of Americans saw Russia as an enemy of the United States. The **fluidity** of American

Intensity
The strength of a position for or against a public policy or an issue. Intensity is often critical in generating public action; an intense minority can often win on an issue of public policy over a less intense majority.

Fluidity
The extent to which public opinion changes over time.

[2]*The Public Perspective,* August/September, 1997, p. 30.

opinion was a response to the rapidly changing conditions in the Soviet Union and world politics. Such fluidity in public opinion reflects public awareness of government policy and in turn influences government decision making.

Stability.   Many individual opinions remain constant over a lifetime. Taken together, individual opinions that constitute public opinion may also be extremely stable, persisting for many years. Consider the effect of the actions of a series of Democratic administrations on the political attitudes of African Americans. The administration of Franklin Roosevelt (1933–1945) was the first to take a real interest in the situation of African Americans. Harry Truman (1945–1953) desegregated the armed forces. John Kennedy (1961–1963) expressed his support for changes in civil rights laws that were finally passed under President Lyndon Johnson (1963–1969). All of these actions led to the exceptional degree of loyalty that African Americans express for the Democratic Party. Over the last four decades, about 90 percent of African Americans have usually supported the Democratic presidential candidate. Such **stability** in voting trends is remarkable.

Relevance.   Relevant public opinion for most people is simply public opinion that deals with issues concerning them. If a person has a sick parent who is having trouble meeting medical bills, then public opinion that is focused on the issues of Medicare or Medicaid will be relevant for that person. If another person likes to go hunting with his or her children, gun control becomes a relevant political issue. Of course, **relevance** changes according to events. Public concern about inflation, for example, was at an all-time low from the late 1980s to the 1990s and early 2000s. Why? The reason was that the United States had relatively little inflation during that period. Public opinion about the issue of unemployment certainly was relevant during the Great Depression of the 1930s, but not in the 1960s, when the nation experienced 102 months of almost uninterrupted economic growth from 1961 to 1969, or in 2000, when unemployment reached a thirty-year low.

Certain popular books or spectacular events can make a particular issue relevant. A succession of violent acts—including the bombing of the Alfred P. Murrah Federal Building in Oklahoma City in 1995, the bombing of an American

DID YOU KNOW...
That public opinion pollsters typically measure national sentiment among the nearly 200 million adult Americans by interviewing only about 1,500 people?

Stability
The extent to which public opinion remains constant over a period of time.

Relevance
The extent to which an issue is of concern at a particular time. Issues become relevant when the public views them as pressing or of direct concern to daily life.

DID YOU KNOW...
That a radio station in Iowa conducts "The Cess Poll" to assess voters' primary election preferences for president by measuring the drop in water pressure when people express their support for a candidate by flushing their toilets when the candidate's name is read over the air**?**

military compound in Saudi Arabia in 1996, and the bombing of the American embassies in the African countries of Kenya and Tanzania in 1998—made violence and terrorism increasingly relevant for many citizens in the late 1990s.

Political Knowledge.   People are more likely to base their opinions on knowledge about an issue if they have strong feelings about the topic. Just as relevance and intensity are closely related to having an opinion, individuals who are strongly interested in a question will probably take the time to read about it.

Looking at the population as a whole, the level of political information is modest. Survey research tells us that slightly less than 29 percent of adult Americans can give the name of their congresspersons, and just 25 percent can name both U.S. senators from their states. Only 34 percent of adults know that Congress declares war,[3] though almost 70 percent know the majority party in Congress. What these data tell us is that Americans do not expend much effort remembering political facts that may not be important to their daily lives.

Americans are also likely to forget political information quite quickly. Facts that are of vital interest to citizens in a time of crisis lose their significance after the crisis has passed. In the 1985 *New York Times*/CBS News Survey on Vietnam, marking the tenth anniversary of the end of the Vietnam War (1964–1975), 63 percent of those questioned knew that the United States sided with the South Vietnamese in that conflict. Only 27 percent remembered, however, which side in that conflict launched the Tet offensive, which was a major political defeat for American and South Vietnamese forces.

If political information is perceived to be of no use to an individual or is painful to recall, it is not surprising that facts are forgotten. It is disconcerting to learn, however, that Americans have little or no information about policy decisions that have the potential to change our world. In June 1997, for example, 40 percent of Americans had not heard that Hong Kong was reverting to rule by China, and in the same year, as Congress was considering whether to admit new nations to the North Atlantic Treaty Organization (NATO) at a cost of billions of dollars to the United States, 71 percent of those questioned had heard very little or nothing at all about the expansion of NATO.[4] Politicians can use this lack of interest to justify either voting as they see fit or opposing any initiative.

Measuring Public Opinion: Polling Techniques

The History of Opinion Polls

Although some idea of public opinion can be discovered by asking persons we know for their opinions or by reading the "Letters to the Editor" sections in newspapers, most descriptions of the distribution of opinions are based on **opinion polls.** During the 1800s, certain American newspapers and magazines spiced up their political coverage by doing face-to-face straw polls (unofficial polls indicating the trend of political opinion) or mail surveys of their readers' opinions. In the early twentieth century, the magazine *Literary Digest* further developed the technique of opinion polls by mailing large numbers of questionnaires to indi-

Opinion Poll
A method of systematically questioning a small, selected sample of respondents who are deemed representative of the total population. Opinion polls are widely used by government, business, university scholars, political candidates, and voluntary groups to provide reasonably accurate data on public attitudes, beliefs, expectations, and behavior.

[3]Michael X. Delli Carpini and Scott Keeter, "The Public's Knowledge of Politics," in J. David Dennamar, ed., *Public Opinion, the Press, and Public Policy* (Westport, Conn.: Praeger, 1992), p. 29.
[4]*The Public Perspective,* August/September 1997, p. 10.

viduals, many of whom were its own subscribers. From 1916 to 1936, more than 70 percent of the magazine's election predictions were accurate.

Literary Digest's polling activities suffered a major setback in 1936, however, when the magazine predicted, based on more than two million returned questionnaires, that Republican candidate Alfred Landon would win over Democratic candidate Franklin D. Roosevelt. Landon won in only two states. A major problem with the *Digest*'s polling technique was its continuing use of nonrepresentative respondents. In 1936, at the bottom of the Great Depression, the magazine's subscribers were, for one thing, considerably more affluent than the average American. (See this chapter's *E-mocracy: What Is a Poll?* for similar problems with online polling.)

Several newcomers to the public opinion poll industry accurately predicted Roosevelt's landslide victory. The organizations of these newcomers are still active in the poll-taking industry today: the Gallup poll of George Gallup and the Roper poll founded by Elmo Roper. Gallup and Roper, along with Archibald Crossley, developed the modern polling techniques of market research. Using personal interviews with small samples of selected voters (less than a few thousand), they showed that they could predict with accuracy the behavior of the total voting population. We shall see how this is possible.

Government officials during World War II were keenly interested in public opinion about the war effort and about the increasing number of restrictions placed on civilian activities. Improved methods of sampling were used, and by the 1950s, a whole new science of survey research was developed, which soon

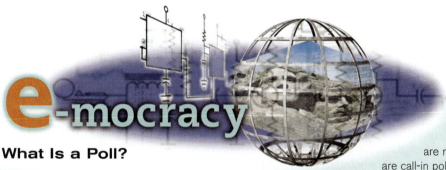

What Is a Poll?

Politicians have long used pseudo-polling techniques to get responses from their constituents. How many times have you received a "poll" by mail from your representative in Congress or your state legislator? Generally, the politician asks for your opinion on current issues. Such polls are not really polls, however, because the responses come only from those who choose to respond. The respondents tend to be either highly loyal supporters of the political decision maker or voters who are quite attentive to the issues and who oppose the legislator's viewpoints across the board.

PSEUDO-POLLS

The Internet has made such pseudo-polling extremely simple and even much more likely to be biased. Now, if you have ever e-mailed your congressional representative or the president, that person can send you a poll via e-mail. The results will, of course, be totally biased because this is a not a random sample. News organizations, interest groups, not-for-profit groups, and online e-zines are now using online polling to gather the opinions of their readers and viewers. All the user has to do is log on to the Web site and click in the box indicating the preferred response. Online polls are much easier for people to respond to than are call-in polls and, in most cases, are free to the user. Yet they are also totally nonscientific because the respondents are all self-selected and, of course, represent only those individuals who have a computer and an online connection.

It is possible, however, for the Internet to provide extremely quick opinion polling for a specified population. Let's say, for example, that you are a member of a national computer users' group or the Association for Public Opinion Research, each of which has the e-mail addresses of most of its members. Online polling of such a population about their presidential preferences or their view of the next convention site can be done by the organization for free and almost overnight. This would certainly increase the democracy within the organization or group. Having such an e-mail list also makes it possible for the group to send thousands of e-mails to an elected official if the group wishes to influence political decisions.

FOR CRITICAL ANALYSIS

Do you think that the public should be informed about whether poll results are scientific or not?

spread to Western Europe, Israel, and other countries. Survey research centers sprang up throughout the United States, particularly at universities. Some of these survey groups are the American Institute of Public Opinion at Princeton, New Jersey; the National Opinion Research Center at the University of Chicago; and the Survey Research Center at the University of Michigan.

Sampling Techniques

How can interviewing fewer than two thousand voters tell us what tens of millions of voters will do? Clearly, it is necessary that the sample of individuals be representative of all voters in the population. Consider an analogy. Let's say we have a large jar containing ten thousand pennies of various dates, and we want to know how many pennies were minted within certain decades (1950–1959, 1960–1969, and so on). One way to estimate the distribution of the dates on the pennies—without examining all ten thousand—is to take a representative sample. This sample would be obtained by mixing the pennies up well and then removing a handful of them—perhaps one hundred pennies. The distribution of dates might be as follows:

- *1950–1959: 5 percent.*
- *1960–1969: 5 percent.*
- *1970–1979: 20 percent.*
- *1980–1989: 30 percent.*
- *1990–present: 40 percent.*

If the pennies are very well mixed within the jar, and if you take a large enough sample, the resulting distribution would probably approach the actual distribution of the dates of all ten thousand coins.

The most important principle in sampling, or poll taking, is randomness. Every penny or every person should have a known chance, and especially an *equal chance,* of being sampled. If this happens, then a small sample should be representative of the whole group, both in demographic characteristics (age, religion, race, living area, and the like) and in opinions. The ideal way to sample the voting population of the United States would be to put all voter names into a jar—or a computer—and randomly sample, say, two thousand of them. Because this is too costly and inefficient, pollsters have developed other ways to obtain good samples. One of the most interesting techniques is simply to choose a random selection of telephone numbers and interview the respective households. This technique produces a relatively accurate sample at a low cost. (One of the problems with online polling is the difficulty of obtaining a random sample—see the feature *Making Waves: Going Online to Poll* for more information on this topic.)

To ensure that the random samples include respondents from relevant segments of the population—rural, urban, Northeast, South, and so on—most survey organizations randomly choose, say, urban areas that they will consider as representative of all urban areas. Then they randomly select their respondents within those areas. A generally less accurate technique is known as *quota sampling.* For this type of poll, survey researchers decide how many persons of certain types they need in the survey—such as minorities, women, or farmers—and then send out interviewers to find the necessary number of these types. This method is often not only less accurate, but it also may be biased if, say, the interviewer refuses to go into certain neighborhoods or will not interview after dark.

Generally, the national survey organizations take great care to select their samples randomly, because their reputations rest on the accuracy of their results.

This woman is participating in a *Los Angeles Times* exit poll after casting her vote in the 2000 elections.

making Waves

Going Online to Poll

Many different polling firms and university survey units have given thought to doing a national poll online. The problems, however, have seemed insurmountable: How can you get a random sample of the entire population when less than 60 percent of American households are connected to the Internet? Wouldn't those who responded to an online survey be so self-selected that they would have opinions quite different from the rest of the public? There is no list of Internet addresses for individuals, so how does one begin to send out messages for a survey?

The Harris Poll, a widely respected national polling organization, conducted online polls during the 1998 elections. While its election predictions were accurate in many states, it made a serious error in one of the southern gubernatorial elections. In January 2000, Harris tested the polling methodology that it had used in 1998. The organization claimed that it had fixed the sampling problem that caused the poor prediction and was going ahead with online polling for 2000.

Many public opinion pollsters criticized the Harris Poll for trying to do public opinion polling online due to the difficulty of getting a random sample. The polling analysts at the Harris organization said that in the year when they conducted parallel online and telephone polling, the results were very similar for the same questions. According to the mathematical assumptions that support random polling, such results should not be the same. So, a scientific argument rages among polling organizations while the Harris Poll and a few others forge ahead into new territory.

FOR CRITICAL ANALYSIS

If polling on the Internet becomes common, how can the ordinary person know which polls are being conducted by legitimate organizations and which are fraudulent polls or scams?

Usually, the Gallup or Roper polls interview about 1,500 individuals, and their results have a very high probability of being correct—within a margin of 3 percentage points. The accuracy with which the Gallup poll has predicted national election results is reflected in Table 7–2 on the next page. (See this chapter's *Critical Perspective* on page 229 for a discussion of how technology and other factors are affecting the accuracy of polling results today.)

Similar sampling techniques are used in many other, nonpolitical situations. For the Nielsen ratings of television programs, for example, representative households are selected by the A. C. Nielsen Company, and a machine is attached to each household's television set. The machine monitors viewing choices twenty-four hours a day and transmits this information to the company's central offices. A one-point drop in a Nielsen rating can mean a loss of revenue of millions of dollars to a television network. A one-point drop indicates that about 800,000 fewer viewers are watching a particular show. As a result, advertisers are unwilling to pay as much for viewing time. Indeed, in many cases advertising rates are based solely on Nielsen ratings. When you consider that only about three thousand families have that little machine attached to their television sets, it is apparent that the science of selecting representative samples has come a long way—at least far enough to convince major advertisers to accept advertising fees based on the results of those samples.

Problems with Polls

Public opinion polls are, as noted above, snapshots of the opinions and preferences of the people at a specific moment in time and as expressed in response to a specific question. Given that definition, it is fairly easy to understand situations in which the polls are wrong. For example, opinion polls leading up to the 1980 presidential election showed President Jimmy Carter defeating challenger Ronald Reagan. Only a few analysts noted the large number of

TABLE 7-2

Gallup Poll Accuracy Record

Year	Gallup Final Survey		Election Results		Deviation
2000	50.0%	Republican	48.0%	Republican	−2.0
1998	49.1	Democratic	53.2	Republican	−4.1
1996	52.0	CLINTON	49.0	CLINTON	−3.0
1994	58.0	Republican	51.0	Republican	+7.0
1992	49.0	CLINTON	43.2	CLINTON	+5.8
1990	54.0	Democratic	54.1	Democratic	−0.1
1988	56.0	BUSH	53.9	BUSH	−2.1
1984	59.0	REAGAN	59.1	REAGAN	−0.1
1982	55.0	Democratic	56.1	Democratic	−1.1
1980	47.0	REAGAN	50.8	REAGAN	−3.8
1978	55.0	Democratic	54.6	Democratic	+0.4
1976	48.0	CARTER	50.0	CARTER	−2.0
1974	60.0	Democratic	58.9	Democratic	+1.1
1972	62.0	NIXON	61.8	NIXON	+0.2
1970	53.0	Democratic	54.3	Democratic	−1.3
1968	43.0	NIXON	43.5	NIXON	−0.5
1966	52.5	Democratic	51.9	Democratic	+0.6
1964	64.0	JOHNSON	61.3	JOHNSON	+2.7
1962	55.5	Democratic	52.7	Democratic	+2.8
1960	51.0	KENNEDY	50.1	KENNEDY	+0.9
1958	57.0	Democratic	56.5	Democratic	+0.5
1956	59.5	EISENHOWER	57.8	EISENHOWER	+1.7
1954	51.5	Democratic	52.7	Democratic	−1.2
1952	51.0	EISENHOWER	55.4	EISENHOWER	−4.4
1950	51.0	Democratic	50.3	Democratic	+0.7
1948	44.5	TRUMAN	49.9	TRUMAN	−5.4
1946	58.0	Republican	54.3	Republican	+3.7
1944	51.5	ROOSEVELT	53.3	ROOSEVELT	−1.8
1942	52.0	Democratic	48.0	Democratic	+4.0
1940	52.0	ROOSEVELT	55.0	ROOSEVELT	−3.0
1938	54.0	Democratic	50.8	Democratic	+3.2
1936	55.7	ROOSEVELT	62.5	ROOSEVELT	−6.8

Note: No congressional poll done in 1986.

SOURCES: *The Gallup Poll Monthly*, November 1992; *Time*, November 21, 1994; *The Wall Street Journal*, November 6, 1996; and authors' update.

critical perspective

Is Technology Destroying Opinion Polling?

Public opinion polling is based on scientific principles that were originally outlined by agricultural statisticians. The accuracy of a poll's predictions depends on polling a truly random sample of the population desired. Technological developments, combined with increasing cynicism among the public, however, may make conducting accurate public opinion polls virtually impossible.

Telephone Polling

In the 1970s, polling moved from in-person, at-your-front-door polling to telephone polling for several reasons. First, telephone polling is much less expensive than sending interviewers out to poll people at their homes. Second, having all interviewers work on the telephone under supervision was a way of overcoming concerns about interviewer safety and reliability. Finally, telephone interviews are extremely quick, allowing the media (and politicians) to poll one night and then report the results within a few hours.

Conducting public opinion polls by telephone is becoming increasingly difficult, however, for several reasons. First, the telemarketing industry has annoyed so many Americans that they either refuse to answer the telephone or use an answering machine or caller-ID system to screen calls. People use these devices because they are tired of marketing calls. As one pollster put it, "Everybody is always trying to sell you something on the phone. Most refusals come within the first thirty seconds when people are not certain it is a legitimate poll."* But when people refuse to answer calls, it becomes impossible for the opinion poll to reach a random sample of telephone subscribers.

Second, Americans' lives are much busier and more chaotic than in the days when telephone polling began. Pollsters have a very difficult time reaching certain households, such as those where all adults work outside the home or those consisting of single individuals with an active social or work life. Reaching individuals who live in retirement homes or other forms of congregate living is also difficult. When pollsters cannot reach these population groups, their telephone polls are not true random samples, and their results may not be accurate.

Perhaps the most important result of these societal and technological changes is a tremendous increase in what pollsters call "nonresponse rates." A nonresponse rate is the proportion of telephone calls

*Don Van Natta, Jr., "Silent Majorities, Polling's 'Dirty Little Secret': No Response," *The New York Times,* November 21, 1999, Section IV, p. 1.

that do not reach a person to respond to the poll.

The rates include unreachable numbers, refusals, answering machines, and call-screening devices. Some industry leaders suggest that the nonresponse rate can be as high as 80 percent; that is, only 20 percent of those who are supposed to be interviewed are actually reached. Such a "nonresponse rate" undercuts confidence in the survey results, because the survey will not meet the criteria for a random sample. Even more important for politics is the fact that polling organizations are not required to report their response rates. Even the *New York Times* does not report its response rates.

Internet Polling

The Internet presents new possibilities and new problems for pollsters. As noted earlier, the Harris Poll has decided to go ahead and do its election polling on the Internet. This organization believes that because so many individuals will respond to its polls, proper weighting of the results will achieve the equivalent of a random sample poll. Many scholars, however, argue that this practice violates the mathematical basis of random samples. An even greater threat to opinion polling, however, is the proliferation of "nonpolls" on the Internet. Almost every television station that maintains a Web site allows anyone to send in his or her opinion. Some companies and organizations send polls to individuals via e-mail. And, of course, there are sites similar to that put up by Mister Poll. This site asks a number of questions on various issues and seeks answers from those who log on. Although the site warns that "none of these polls is scientific," it also has the slogan, "Independent pollsters make all the difference! Make a poll!" Sites such as this one undercut all the efforts of legitimate pollsters to use the Internet scientifically.

Perhaps the greatest threat to the science of polling is that Americans are overwhelmed with polling data. Some results are legitimate and derived from truly scientific work, but many are obtained from cheap, quick, poorly executed polls. How can Americans determine which data are legitimate? If all polls appear equal, will any be believed? If polls and polling come to be regarded as cynical and biased, then the practice of scientific polling is likely to disappear.

FOR CRITICAL ANALYSIS

1. What are the most important benefits of having scientific polling? How would the work of science and government be hurt if polling disappeared?
2. Are accuracy in polling and the perfect random sample truly important?
3. Could legitimate polls on the Internet or by telephone be identified by some "seal of good practice" to help respondents know whether to answer?

President Harry Truman holds up the front page of the *Chicago Daily Tribune* issue that predicted his defeat on the basis of a Gallup poll. The poll had indicated that Truman would lose the 1948 contest for his reelection by a margin of 55.5 to 44.5 percent. Gallup's poll was completed more than two weeks before the election, so it missed the undecided voters. Truman won the election with 49.9 percent of the vote.

What Are Push Polls Anyway

Sampling Error
The difference between a sample's results and the true result if the entire population had been interviewed.

Sampling External Validity

"undecided" respondents to poll questions a week before the election. Those voters shifted massively to Reagan at the last minute, and Reagan won the election.

The famous photo of Harry Truman showing the front page that declared his defeat in the 1948 presidential elections is another tribute to the weakness of polling. Again, the poll that predicted his defeat was taken more than a week before election day.

Sampling Errors. Polls may also report erroneous results because the pool of respondents was not chosen in a scientific manner. That is, the form of sampling and the number of people sampled may be too small to overcome **sampling error,** which is the difference between the sample results and the true result if the entire population had been interviewed. The sample would be biased, for example, if the poll interviewed people by telephone and did not correct for the fact that more women than men answer the telephone and that some populations (college students and very poor individuals, for example) cannot be found so easily by telephone. Unscientific mail-in polls, telephone call-in polls, and polls completed by the workers in a campaign office are usually biased and do not give an accurate picture of the public's views. Because of these and other problems with polls, some have suggested that polling be regulated by the government (see this chapter's *Which Side Are You On? Should Polling Be Regulated?*)

As poll takers get close to election day, they become even more concerned about their sample of respondents. Some pollsters continue to interview eligible voters, meaning those over eighteen and registered to vote. Many others use a series of questions in the poll and other weighting methods to try to identify "likely voters" so that they can be more accurate in their election-eve predictions. When a poll changes its method from reporting the views of eligible voters to reporting those of likely voters, the results are likely to change dramatically.

Poll Questions. Finally, it makes sense to expect that the results of a poll will depend on the questions that are asked. Depending on what question is asked, voters could be said either to support a particular proposal or to oppose it. Furthermore, respondents' answers are also influenced by the order in which questions are asked, the types of answers they are allowed to choose, and, in some cases, by their interaction with the interviewer. To some extent, people try to please the interviewer. They answer questions about which they have no

which side are you on?

Should Polling Be Regulated?

Public opinion polling was once confined to the work of universities and a handful of very large and well-respected polling firms, such as Gallup and Roper. Now, anyone can open a polling shop on the Web or in his or her basement using telephones and a few computers. Currently, polling is, for the most part, completely unregulated. Interviewers are not necessarily trained and certainly not licensed. Polling organizations may be private or public, but they are not regulated in terms of their contracts, operations, or disclosure of results. The media giants that commission polls to obtain results to be reported on the air or in print see polling as part of their news-gathering operation and, therefore, as protected by the First Amendment's guarantee of freedom of the press.

Why Regulate Polls?

What are the concerns that might lead to regulation? The media have agreed among themselves not to release their predictions of election outcomes before the polls close in California, but they do release many other pieces of information from the exit polls during the day. Some of that information may influence voter turnout or votes. Should the media be prohibited from releasing any data until the next day? Polls are often paid for by campaign cash, including the taxpayers' matching funds in the presidential race. Should those polls be public? Additionally, polling can be used to influence voters, particularly through "push polling" (see the feature entitled *An Ethical Issue: Polls That Mislead* on page 232). Should the use of polls to influence voters be prohibited? Should questions used by pollsters be censored or regulated by a government agency?

Are Polls Really All That Powerful?

If you think that polls are or can be too powerful, influencing voters and policy decisions, then more regulations might be appropriate. At the same time, polls have no legal power; they are simply the report of what those who were polled have to say. If polls are seen as having very little power, regulation would seem unwarranted.

DOES IT MATTER?

Would regulating public opinion polls be a true restriction on free speech and deprive the public of the opportunity to debate information that should be freely available?

GOING ONLINE

If you are interested in reading more about the issues that surround polling, especially in an election year, check out USA Today's Web site at **http://www.usatoday.com** *and search "polling." If you would like to read more about the polling industry's view on regulation and see examples of its voluntary standards, go to the Web site for the American Association for Public Opinion Research at* **http://www.aapor.org**.

information and avoid some answers to try to measure up to the interviewer's expectations. Most recently, some campaigns have been using "push polls," in which the respondents are given misleading information in the questions asked to get them to vote against a candidate. Obviously, the answers given are likely to be influenced by such techniques. For a further discussion of push polls, see the feature entitled *An Ethical Issue: Polls That Mislead* on the next page.

Because of these problems, you need to be especially careful when evaluating poll results. For some suggestions on how to be a critical consumer of public opinion polls, see the feature *Making a Difference* at the end of this chapter.

The Accuracy of the 2000 Polls

More polling occurred during the 2000 election campaigns than in any other elections in our history. Each major news outlet polled virtually every week between Labor Day and election day. Although Vice President Gore had a lead in the polls right after the Democratic convention, by mid-October the polls showed, quite correctly, that the race was "too close to call." Because the race was so close, media pundits and news anchors frequently had to report results that fluctuated from week to week. Gore was ahead in one poll, and then the next week, Bush would lead in voter preferences. As noted by some, the polls all had a margin of error between 3 and 4 percent so that, in fact, the final results could go either way. In addition, more careful polling revealed that up to 20 percent of the likely voters were not committed to a candidate until election day. Thus, the pollsters could do little more than "guess" how the undecided voters would divide their ballots in the actual election. They also had to predict whether voter turnout would be greater or less than average and then weigh that factor in their predictions of whether Gore or Bush would win.

Political Socialization

Political Socialization
The process by which people acquire political beliefs and attitudes.

Most Americans are willing to express opinions on political issues when asked. How do individuals acquire these opinions and attitudes? Most views that are expressed as political opinions are acquired through a process known as **political socialization.** By this we mean that people acquire their political attitudes, often including their party identification, through relationships with their families, friends, and co-workers. The most important influences in this process are the following: (1) the family, (2) the educational environment and achievement of the individual, (3) peers, (4) religion, (5) economic status and occupation, (6) political events, (7) opinion leaders, (8) the media, and (9) race and other demographic traits. We discuss each of these influences below, as well as the phenomenon known as the gender gap.

The Importance of the Family

The family is the most important force in political socialization. Not only do our parents' political attitudes and actions affect our adult opinions, but the family also links us to other socialization forces. We acquire our ethnic identity, our notion of social class, our educational opportunities, and our early religious beliefs from our families. Each of these factors can also influence our political attitudes.

Polls That Mislead

Pollsters long have known that the wording of questions can influence the response that a person gives. Different question wordings can provoke extensive political debate about the actual preferences of the public. At one point during the Clinton administration, the president and the congressional Republicans were unable to resolve their differences over the budget for more than six months. Democrats were cheered by poll results that showed that the majority of Americans opposed "cutting funding for Medicare." Republicans countered by showing poll results that indicated that many Americans supported "decreasing the growth in funding for Medicare." Both parties were depending on question wording for building a case for their own positions.

A far more deliberate use of question wording has surfaced recently in election campaigns. In the weeks before a primary or general election, voters are interviewed in what seems to be a legitimate poll. One or more of the questions in the poll, however, give the respondent false or misleading information about the opposing candidate in an effort to influence the respondent's vote. Such surveys have become known as "push polls," because they are intended to push the voter to the candidate whose campaign sponsored the poll. Sometimes the information given in the

question is simply misleading, while on other occasions it has been closer to scandal or gossip. In another variation, push polls can be used to start rumors about a candidate at a time very close to the election when rebuttal of the information is almost impossible.

The prevalence of push polling in early 1996 led to a statement by the American Association for Public Opinion Research condemning such polls and labeling them marketing ploys. Both major parties announced that they would not use such polling techniques.

In the 2000 Republican primary fight in South Carolina, both George W. Bush and John McCain accused the other of unfair tactics. The Bush campaign made more than 200,000 "advocacy" calls asking voters about their likely choice in the election. The calls did use long questions containing information about McCain's record. The Bush camp said the information was accurate, while McCain saw this as "push polling." Push polling, because of its negativity, can be seen as a cause for increased cynicism in politics.

FOR CRITICAL ANALYSIS

How can you tell whether a survey question is worded "neutrally" or whether it might be biased toward a particular response?

How do parents transmit these attachments? Studies suggest that the influence of parents is due to two factors: communication and receptivity. Parents communicate their feelings and preferences to children constantly. Because children have such a strong need for parental approval, they are very receptive to their parents' views.[5]

The clearest legacy of the family is partisan identification. When parents are strong identifiers with a political party, it is likely that their children will identify with the same party. This tendency is strongest if both parents are politically active and share their party identification. Children of independent voters or of families of mixed or weak party attachment are likely to be independent voters when they first vote. When children first cast a ballot, they tend to vote in line with their parents' views. As children get older, however, they are likely to become more and more independent of their parents' political views.

Educational Influence on Political Opinion

From the early days of the republic, schools were perceived to be important transmitters of political information and attitudes. Children in the primary grades learn about their country mostly in patriotic ways. They learn to salute the flag, to say the Pledge of Allegiance, and to celebrate national holidays. Later, in the middle grades, children learn more historical facts and come to understand the structure of government and the functions of the president, judges, and Congress. By high school, students have a more complex understanding of the political system, may identify with a political party, and may take positions on issues.

Generally, education is closely linked to political participation. The more education a person receives, the more likely it is that the person will be interested in politics, be confident in his or her ability to understand political issues, and be an active participant in the political process. Recent polls, however, suggest that younger Americans are not interested in politics. Although up to 49 percent of those between the ages of eighteen and twenty-four may have voted in 1996, as many as one-third of today's college students say that government has no influence on their lives.[6]

Peers and Peer Group Influence

Once a child enters school, the child's friends become an important influence on behavior and attitudes. As young children, and later as adults, friendships and associations in **peer groups** are influential on political attitudes. We must, however, separate the effects of peer group pressure on opinions and attitudes in general from peer group pressure on political opinions. For the most part, associations among peers are nonpolitical. Political attitudes are more likely to be shaped by peer groups when the peer groups are involved directly in political activities.

Individuals who join interest groups based on ethnic identity may find, for example, a common political bond through working for the group's civil liberties and rights. African American activist groups may consist of individuals who join together to support government programs that will aid the African American population. Members of a labor union may feel strong political pressure to support certain pro-labor candidates.

Peer Group
A group consisting of members sharing common relevant social characteristics. These groups play an important part in the socialization process, helping to shape attitudes and beliefs.

---

[5]Barbara A. Bardes and Robert W. Oldendick, *Public Opinion: Measuring the American Mind* (Belmont, Calif.: Wadsworth Publishing Co., 2000), p. 73.
[6]Adam Clymer, "College Students Not Drawn to Voting or Politics," *The New York Times*, January 12, 2000, p. A14.

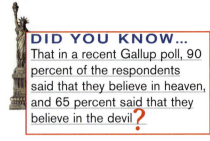

Americans' Belief God

Religious Influence

Religious associations tend to create definite political attitudes, although why this occurs is not clearly understood. Surveys show that Roman Catholic respondents tend to be more liberal on economic issues than are Protestants. Apparently, Jewish respondents are more liberal on all fronts than either Catholics or Protestants. In terms of voting behavior, it has been observed that northern white Protestants are more likely to vote Republican, whereas northern white Roman Catholics more often vote Democratic; everywhere in the United States, Jews mostly vote Democratic.

In the last decade, fundamentalist Christians, sometimes known as evangelical Christians, have played an increasing role in American politics. A recent Pew Center for the People and the Press study found that 42 percent of white evangelical Protestants are Republicans as compared to 35 percent only ten years ago. How do we know that an individual is an evangelical Christian? Public opinion polls use a combination of questions about religious beliefs to identify those with more fundamentalist ideas. These questions include whether the respondent believes in the Bible as the literal truth and sees him- or herself as "born again." These conservative Christians are significant politically because their views are represented by well-organized and well-financed organizations that try to influence elections across the nation.

Sometimes a candidate's religion enters the political picture, as it did in the 1960 presidential election contest between Democrat John Kennedy and Republican Richard Nixon. The fact that Kennedy was a Catholic—the second Catholic to be nominated by a major party—polarized many voters. Among northern whites, Kennedy was supported by 83 percent of voting Catholics and by 93 percent of Jewish voters but by only 28 percent of the Protestants who voted.

The Influence of Economic Status and Occupation

How wealthy you are and the kind of job you hold are also associated with your political views. Social-class differences emerge on a wide range of issues. Poorer people are more inclined to favor government social-welfare programs but are likely to be conservative on social issues such as abortion. The upper middle class is more likely to hold conservative economic views but to be tolerant of social change. People in lower economic strata also tend to be more isolationist on foreign policy issues and are more likely to identify with the Democratic Party and vote for Democratic candidates. Support for civil liberties and tolerance of different points of view tend to be greater among those with higher social status and lower among those with lower social status. Probably, it is educational differences more than the pattern of life at home or work that account for this.

The Influence of Political Events

People's political attitudes may be shaped by political events and the nation's reactions to them. In the 1960s and 1970s, the war in Vietnam—including revelations about the secret bombing in Cambodia—and the Watergate break-in and subsequent cover-up fostered widespread cynicism toward government. In one study of the impact of the Watergate scandal of 1972, Christopher Arterton found that schoolchildren changed their image of President Nixon from a "benevolent" to a "malevolent" leader as the scandal unfolded. Negative views also increased about other aspects of politics and politicians. Members of that age group moderated their views, however, as they matured.[7]

When events produce a long-lasting political impact, **generational effects** result. Voters who grew up in the 1930s during the Great Depression were likely to form lifelong attachments to the Democratic Party, the party of Franklin D. Roosevelt. There was some evidence that the years of economic prosperity under Ronald Reagan during the 1980s may have influenced young adults to identify with the Republican Party. A 1990 poll showed that 52 percent of thirteen- to seventeen-year-olds thought of themselves as Republicans, whereas 32 percent of this age group thought of themselves as Democrats. Although the number of younger voters identifying themselves as Republicans declined in 1992, the group that voted for the first time in 1995 were more likely to be Republican.[8]

Generational effects occur only when the event is a true crisis that changes the life of the nation. The Great Depression of the 1930s was one of those events, as was the Vietnam War. Sustained periods of economic prosperity or decline can influence the youngest generation of voters to feel an attachment to the party in power at the time. Generally, though, events that may seem extremely important in one presidency, such as the impeachment and trial of President Bill Clinton in 1998 and 1999, may have very little if any impact on voters over the long run.

Opinion Leaders' Influence

We are all influenced by those with whom we are closely associated or whom we hold in great respect—friends at school, family members and other relatives, teachers, and so on. In a sense, these people are **opinion leaders,** but on an informal level; that is, their influence over us is not necessarily intentional or deliberate. We are also influenced by formal opinion leaders, such as presidents, lobbyists, congresspersons, news commentators, or religious leaders, who have as part of their jobs the task of swaying people's views. Their interest lies in defining the political agenda in such a way that discussions about policy options will take place on their terms.

Media Influence

Clearly, the **media**—newspapers, television, radio broadcasts, and Internet sources—strongly influence public opinion. This is because the media inform the public about the issues and events of our times and thus have an agenda-setting effect. In other words, to borrow from Bernard Cohen's classic statement on the media and public opinion, the media may not be successful in telling people what to think, but they are "stunningly successful in telling their audience what to think about."[9]

Today, many contend that the media's influence on public opinion is increasing to the point that the media are as influential as the family in regard to public opinion. For example, in her analysis of the role played by the media in American politics,[10] media scholar Doris A. Graber points out that high school students, when asked where they obtain the information on which they base

Generational Effect
A long-lasting effect of events of a particular time period on the political opinions or preferences of those who came of political age at that time.

Opinion Leader
One who is able to influence the opinions of others because of position, expertise, or personality. Such leaders help to shape public opinion.

Media
The technical means of communication with mass audiences.

---

[7]Christopher F. Arterton, "The Impact of Watergate on Children's Attitudes toward Authority," *American Political Science Review,* Vol. 89 (June 1974), pp. 269–288.

[8]*America at the Polls, 1996* (Storrs, Conn.: Roper Center, 1997), pp. 56–57.

[9]*The Press and Foreign Policy* (Princeton, N.J.: Princeton University Press, 1963), p. 81.

[10]See Doris A. Graber, *Mass Media and American Politics,* 5th ed. (Washington, D.C.: Congressional Quarterly Books, 1997).

their attitudes, mention the mass media far more than their families, friends, and teachers. This trend, combined with the increasing popularity of more populist and interactive news sources, such as talk shows and the Internet, may significantly alter the nature of the media's influence on public debate in the future. (See Chapter 11 for a more detailed analysis of the role of the media in American political life.)

The Influence of Demographic Traits

African Americans show a much stronger commitment than do whites to steady or more rapid racial desegregation. African Americans tend to be more liberal than whites on social-welfare issues, civil liberties, and even foreign policy. Party preference and voting among African Americans since the 1930s have supported the Democrats very heavily.

It is somewhat surprising that a person's chronological age has comparatively little impact on political preferences. Still, young adults are somewhat more liberal than older people on most issues, and they are considerably more progressive on such issues as marijuana legalization, pornography, civil disobedience, and racial and gender equality.

Finally, attitudes vary from region to region, although such patterns probably are accounted for mostly by social class and other differences. Regional dif-

In July 2000, nation of Islam leader Louis Farrakhan announced his plans to organize a Million Family March on Washington, scheduled for October 2000, to commemorate the fifth anniversary of the Million Man March on Washington in 1995. In the 1995 march, pictured here, the participants expressed their belief in the importance of individual responsibility, family responsibility, and dedication to the greater community.

ferences are relatively unimportant today. There is still a tendency for the South and the East to be more Democratic than the West and the Midwest. More important than region is a person's residence—urban, suburban, or rural. Big cities tend to be more liberal and Democratic because of their greater concentration of minorities and newer ethnic groups. Smaller communities are more conservative and, in many areas, more Republican.

The Gender Gap

Until the 1980s, there was little evidence that men's and women's political attitudes were very different. The election of Ronald Reagan in 1980, however, soon came to be associated with a **gender gap.** In a May 1983 Gallup poll, 43 percent of the women polled approved of Reagan's performance in office and 44 percent disapproved, versus 49 percent of men who approved and 41 percent who disapproved.

In the 1988 election, the gender gap reappeared, but in a modified form. Although the Democrats hoped that women's votes would add significantly to their totals, a deep split between men and women did not occur. The final polls showed that 54 percent of the men voted for George Bush, as did 50 percent of the women. The 1992 presidential election again found women more likely than men to vote for the Democrats: 46 percent of women voted for Bill Clinton, compared with 41 percent of the men. In 2000, the gender gap persisted. More women (54 percent) than men (42 percent) voted for Al Gore, while more men (53 percent) than women (43 percent) voted for George W. Bush.

Women also appear to hold different attitudes from their male counterparts on a range of issues other than presidential preferences. They are much more likely to oppose capital punishment, as well as the use of force abroad. Studies have also shown that women are more concerned about risks to the environment, more supportive of social welfare, and more supportive of extending civil rights to gay men and lesbians than are men. These differences of opinion appear to be growing and may become an important factor in future elections at national and local levels.[11]

Political Culture and Public Opinion

Americans are divided into a multitude of ethnic, religious, regional, and political subgroups. In many cases, members of these groups hold a particular set of opinions about government policies, about the goals of the society, and about the rights of their group and the rights of others. Given the diversity of American society and the wide range of opinions contained within it, how is it that the political process continues to function without being stalemated by conflict and dissension?

One explanation is rooted in the concept of the American political culture, which can be described as a set of attitudes and ideas about the nation and the government. As discussed in Chapter 1, our political culture is widely shared by Americans of many different backgrounds. To some extent, it consists of symbols, such as the American flag, the Liberty Bell, and the Statue of Liberty. The

Gender Gap
A term most often used to describe the difference between the percentage of votes a candidate receives from women and the percentage of votes the candidate receives from men. The term came into use after the 1980 presidential elections.

Gender Gap Dooms Men

---

[11]Jody Newman, "The Gender Story: Women as Voters and Candidates in the 1996 Elections," in *America at the Polls, 1996* (Storrs, Conn.: Roper Center, 1997), pp. 102–103.

elements of our political culture also include certain shared beliefs about the most important values in the American political system, including (1) liberty, equality, and property; (2) support for religion; and (3) community service and personal achievement. The structure of the government—particularly federalism, the political parties, the powers of Congress, and popular rule—were also found to be important values.[12]

The political culture provides a general environment of support for the political system. If the people share certain beliefs about the system and a reservoir of good feeling exists toward the institutions of government, the nation will be better able to weather periods of crisis, such as Watergate. This foundation of goodwill may combat cynicism and increase the level of participation in elections as well. During the 1960s and 1970s, survey research showed that the overall level of **political trust** declined steeply. A considerable proportion of Americans seemed to feel that they could not trust government officials and that they could not count on officials to care about the ordinary person. This index of political trust reached an all-time low in the early 1990s (see Table 7–3).

Political Trust
The degree to which individuals express trust in the government and political institutions, usually measured through a specific series of survey questions.

Public Opinion about Government

A vital component of public opinion in the United States is the considerable ambivalence with which the public regards many major national institutions. Table 7–4 shows trends from 1975 to 2000 in Gallup public opinion polls asking respondents, at regularly spaced intervals, how much confidence they had in the institutions listed. Over the years, military and religious organizations have ranked highest, but note the decline in confidence in churches following the numerous scandals concerning television evangelists in the late 1980s. Note also the heightened regard for the military after the war in the Persian Gulf in 1991. Not only did the Gulf War give a temporary boost to President Bush's popularity, but it also seemed to inspire patriotism and support for the military throughout the nation. Table 7–4 shows that in 1991, the public had more confidence in the military than it did in the church or organized religion, in newspapers, or in any institution of government. In 1999, confidence in the military increased again, possibly due to the successful military action in Kosovo and the attacks by American aircraft on terrorist camps in Afghanistan.

---

[12]Donald Devine, *Political Culture of the United States* (Boston: Little, Brown, 1972).

TABLE 7-3

Trends in Political Trust

QUESTION: HOW MUCH OF THE TIME DO YOU THINK YOU CAN TRUST THE GOVERNMENT IN WASHINGTON TO DO WHAT IS RIGHT—JUST ABOUT ALWAYS, MOST OF THE TIME, OR ONLY SOME OF THE TIME?

	1964	1968	1972	1974	1976	1978	1980	1982	1984	1986	1988	1990	1992	1994	1996	1998	2000
Percentage saying:																	
Always/Most of the time	76	61	53	36	33	29	25	32	46	42	44	27	23	20	25	34	40
Some of the time	22	36	45	61	63	67	73	64	51	55	54	73	75	79	71	66	59

SOURCES: *New York Times*/CBS News Surveys; the University of Michigan Survey Research Center, National Election Studies; the Pew Research Center for the People and the Press; and the Council for Excellence in Government.

TABLE 7-4

Confidence in Institutions Trend

QUESTION: I AM GOING TO READ A LIST OF INSTITUTIONS IN AMERICAN SOCIETY. WOULD YOU PLEASE TELL ME HOW MUCH CONFIDENCE YOU, YOURSELF, HAVE IN EACH ONE—A GREAT DEAL, QUITE A LOT, SOME, OR VERY LITTLE?

	PERCENTAGE SAYING "GREAT DEAL" OR "QUITE A LOT"														
	1973	1975	1977	1979	1981	1983	1985	1987	1989	1991	1993	1995	1997	1999	2000
Church or organized religion	66%	68%	65%	65%	64%	62%	66%	61%	52%	56%	53%	57%	56%	58%	56%
Military	NA	58	57	54	50	53	61	61	63	69	67	64	60	68	64
U.S. Supreme Court	44	49	46	45	46	42	56	52	46	39	43	44	50	49	47
Banks and banking	NA	NA	NA	60	46	51	51	51	42	30	38	43	41	43	46
Public schools	58	NA	54	53	42	39	48	50	43	35	39	40	40	36	37
Congress	42	40	40	34	29	28	39	NA	32	18	19	21	22	26	24
Newspapers	39	NA	NA	51	35	38	35	31	NA	32	31	30	35	33	37
Big business	26	34	33	32	20	28	31	NA	NA	22	23	21	28	30	29
Television	37	NA	NA	38	25	25	29	28	NA	24	21	33	34	34	36
Organized labor	30	38	39	36	28	26	28	26	NA	22	26	26	23	28	25

NA = Not asked.

SOURCE: Gallup Poll, 2000.

The United States Supreme Court, which many people do not see as a particularly political institution, although it is clearly involved in decisions with vitally important consequences for the nation, has scored well over time, as have banks and banking. Less confidence is expressed in newspapers, big business, television, and organized labor, all of which certainly are involved directly or indirectly in the political process. In 1991, following a scandal involving congressional banking practices and other embarrassments, confidence in Congress fell to a record low of 18 percent. Confidence in Congress has yet to reach the levels reported in the 1970s and 1980s.

Although people may not have much confidence in government institutions, they nonetheless turn to government to solve what they perceive to be the major problems facing the country. Table 7–5, which is based on Gallup polls conducted over the years 1975 to 2000, shows that the leading problems clearly have changed over time. The public tends to emphasize problems that are immediate. It is not at all unusual to see fairly sudden, and even apparently contradictory, shifts

TABLE 7-5

Most Important Problem Trend, 1975 to Present

2000	Morals, family decline	1987	Unemployment, economy
1999	Crime, violence	1986	Unemployment, budget deficit
1998	Crime, violence	1985	Fear of war, unemployment
1997	Crime, violence	1984	Unemployment, fear of war
1996	Budget deficit	1983	Unemployment, high cost of living
1995	Crime, violence	1982	Unemployment, high cost of living
1994	Crime, violence, health care	1981	High cost of living, unemployment
1993	Health care, budget deficit	1980	High cost of living, unemployment
1992	Unemployment, budget deficit	1979	High cost of living, energy problems
1991	Economy	1978	High cost of living, energy problems
1990	War in Middle East	1977	High cost of living, unemployment
1989	War on drugs	1976	High cost of living, unemployment
1988	Economy, budget deficit	1975	High cost of living, unemployment

SOURCES: *New York Times*/CBS News Poll, January 1996; *Gallup Report*, 2000.

in public perceptions of what government should do. In recent years, crime, violence, morals, and the decline of the family reached the top of the problems list.

This gives rise to a critically important question: Is government really responsive to public opinion? A study by political scientists Benjamin I. Page and Robert Y. Shapiro suggests that in fact the national government is very responsive to the public's demands for action.[13] In looking at changes in public opinion poll results over time, Page and Shapiro show that when the public supports a policy change, the following occurs: policy changes in a direction consistent with the change in public opinion 43 percent of the time, policy changes in a direction opposite to the change in opinion 22 percent of the time, and policy does not change at all 33 percent of the time. So, overall, the national government could be said to respond to changes in public opinion about two-thirds of the time. Page and Shapiro also show, as should be no surprise, that when public opinion changes more dramatically—say, by 20 percentage points rather than by just 6 or 7 percentage points—government policy is much more likely to follow changing public attitudes.

The Spectrum of Political Beliefs

Political candidates and officeholders in the United States frequently are identified as liberals or conservatives. These terms refer loosely to a spectrum of political beliefs that commonly are arrayed on a continuum from left to right. Each of the terms has changed its meaning from its origins and continues to change as the issues of political debate change. In the United States, however, the terms most frequently refer to sets of political positions that date from the Great Depression.

Liberals are most commonly understood to embrace national government solutions to public problems, to believe that the national government should intervene in the economy to ensure its health, to support social-welfare programs to assist the disadvantaged, and to be tolerant of social change. Today, liberals are often identified with policies supporting women's rights and civil rights, and opposing increased defense spending.

In contrast, conservatives usually feel that the national government has grown too large, that the private sector needs less interference from the government, that social-welfare programs should be limited, that state and local governments should be able to make their own decisions, and that the nation's defense should be strengthened. Some conservatives express grave concerns about the decline of family life and traditional values in this country; they would not be tolerant of gay rights laws, for example. Senator Paul Wellstone (D., Minn.) is one of the most liberal of the younger Democrats in the Senate, while Senator Orrin Hatch (R., Utah) has stood for conservative values for many years.

When asked, Americans usually are willing to identify themselves on the liberal-conservative spectrum. More individuals are likely to consider themselves moderates than liberals or conservatives. As Table 7–6 shows, there has not been a dramatic change in ideological self-identification since 1976.

Most Americans, however, do not fit into the categories as nicely as do Senator Wellstone and Senator Hatch. Many political leaders, who are quite conscious of their philosophical views and who hold a carefully thought out and a more or less consistent set of political beliefs, can be described as **ideologues**. Partly

Ideologue
An individual whose political opinions are carefully thought out and relatively consistent with one another. Ideologues are often described as having a comprehensive world view.

[13]See the extensive work of Page and Shapiro in Benjamin I. Page and Robert Y. Shapiro, *The Rational Public: Fifty Years of Trends in Americans' Policy Preferences* (Chicago: University of Chicago Press, 1992).

Paul Wellstone (left), a Democratic senator from Minnesota and former political science professor at Carleton College in Northfield, Minnesota, is among the more liberal members of Congress. Orrin Hatch (right), a Republican senator from Utah since 1976, is generally regarded as a leading conservative voice in American politics.

because most citizens are not strongly interested in all political issues and partly because Americans have different stakes in politics, most people have mixed sets of opinions that do not fit into one ideological framework. Election research suggests that only a small percentage of all Americans, perhaps less than 10 percent, could be identified as ideologues. The rest of the public conceives of politics more in terms of the political parties or of economic well-being.

Some critics of the American political system have felt that elections would be more meaningful and that the nation could face important policy problems more

TABLE 7-6

Ideological Self-identification, 1976 to Present

There has been relatively little change in the distribution of liberals and conservatives, even after the elections of self-described liberal or conservative presidents.

YEAR	LIBERAL	MODERATE	CONSERVATIVE	NO OPINION
1976	21%	41%	26%	12%
1977	21	38	29	12
1978	21	35	27	17
1979	21	42	26	12
1980	19	40	31	11
1981	18	43	30	9
1982	17	40	33	11
1984	17	41	31	11
1986	20	45	28	7
1988	18	45	33	4
1990	20	45	28	6
1992	19	41	34	6
1993	18	45	32	5
1994	18	48	34	0
1995	19	39	37	4
1996	17	45	34	4
1997	17	40	39	4
1998	19	40	33	8
1999	20	42	34	4
2000	18	41	41	0

SOURCES: *Gallup Reports;* and *New York Times*/CBS News Surveys.

effectively if Americans were more ideological in their thinking. Public opinion research suggests that for most Americans, political issues are not usually as important as events in their daily lives are. There is no evidence to suggest that forces are in place to turn Americans into highly motivated ideological voters.

Public Opinion and the Political Process

Surveys of public opinion, no matter what fascinating questions they ask or how quickly they get the answers, are not equivalent to elections in the United States. Because not all Americans are equally interested in politics or equally informed, public opinion polls can suggest only the general distribution of opinion on issues. Many times, only a few citizens have formulated preferences, and these preferences will be changed by events.

Politicians, whether in office or in the midst of a campaign, see public opinion as important to their careers. The president, members of Congress, governors, and other elected officials realize that strong support by the public as expressed in opinion polls is a source of power in dealing with other politicians. It is far more difficult for a senator to say no to the president if the president is immensely popular and if polls show approval of the president's policies. Public opinion also helps political candidates identify the most important concerns among the public and may help them shape their campaigns successfully. (For the public's views on the issue of campaign-financing reform, see the feature, *Politics and Economics: The Public and Campaign-Finance Reform*.)

The Public and Campaign-Finance Reform

Despite the campaign-financing scandals of 1996 and the continued efforts to raise as much campaign money as possible in the elections of 2000, there has been no movement in Congress toward reforming the campaign-finance law. John McCain, one of the contenders for the Republican presidential nomination, made campaign-finance reform a major issue during the primary season, but he failed to win the nomination. Both candidates in the general election—Al Gore and George W. Bush—talked about campaign-finance reform, but nothing changed for the 2000 elections.

THE PUBLIC WANTS CAMPAIGN-FINANCE REFORM

Public opinion on the role of money in politics and the need for campaign-finance reform has been fairly consistent. In a 1999 *Newsweek* poll, 59 percent of those polled said that political contributions have too much influence on elections and that this is a major problem for the system. A number of polling firms asked whether government should limit the amount of money that individuals can give to campaigns or whether they should be free to give as much as they want. More than 60 percent of those polled said that there should be limits. When informed that the Supreme Court has said that campaign spending cannot be limited because it is a matter of free speech, 65 percent of the public disagreed with the decision.

WHY CONGRESS DOES NOT ACT

While public opinion data show clearly that most people favor campaign-finance reform and that most are not swayed by the argument that such spending is protected as free speech, other polling data suggest why Congress does not act. When asked whether Congress should make reform a high priority, only 11 percent said it should be a high priority while 41 percent said it should be a low priority. Even more importantly, the public does not support the public financing of campaigns, the remedy most often suggested by reformers. When asked if they favored using tax dollars to pay for campaigns and prohibiting large contributions from individuals and groups, only 37 percent of the public approved of the concept. The public's disapproval of the current state of campaign financing is troubling to policymakers, but, because the public does not really approve of the solution being offered, lawmakers can delay acting on the problem for some time to come.

FOR CRITICAL ANALYSIS

What kind of scandal or misuse of campaign funds might be so serious that the public would accept public financing of campaigns or any other true reform?

Although opinion polls cannot give exact guidance on what the government should do in a specific instance, the opinions measured in polls do set an informal limit on government action. For example, consider the highly controversial issue of abortion. Most Americans are moderates on this issue; they do not approve of abortion as a means of birth control, but they do feel that it should be available under certain circumstances. Yet sizable groups of people express very intense feelings both for and against abortion. Given this distribution of opinion, most elected officials would rather not try to change policy to favor either of the extreme positions. To do so would clearly violate the opinion of the majority of Americans. In this case, as in many others, public opinion does not make public policy; rather, it restrains officials from taking truly unpopular actions. If officials do act in the face of public opposition, the consequences of such actions will be determined at the ballot box.

Public Opinion: Issues for the Twenty-First Century

Public opinion is a vital part of the political process—it identifies issues for resolution, brings public views into political debate, helps choose political candidates, and gives policymakers some idea of what the voters want. Polling, however, the main device for learning public opinion, is facing serious challenges. Instant polls conducted on the Internet undermine the scientific basis of polling, and the reluctance of Americans to answer telephone polls is making polling more difficult than ever before. The public may see polling results as accurately reflecting public views when, in fact, they are not scientific or trustworthy.

The views of the public, whether expressed in poll results or in letters or e-mail, are very important to political leaders. Yet the electronic media, including the Internet, and other instant sources of news may not be providing Americans with enough information to form opinions. In addition, advocacy advertising paid for by interest groups or by political parties makes it even harder for the ordinary citizen to gain enough impartial information to understand political issues. Public opinion in the future, formed by a barrage of news clips, Internet headlines, and politcal advertising, is likely to be even more unstable.

Finally, many Americans worry that the transmission of American political values and culture to the next generation may suffer in the twenty-first century. While the schools continue to teach the basic facts about American history and the Constitution, the real sources of culture for younger people are the electronic media and the entertainment industry. Given the overwhelming influence of popular culture and the growing cynicism and distrust of American voters, it is hard to see how traditional American values can be successfully transmitted to new generations of voters.

making a difference

Be a Critical Consumer of Opinion Polls

Americans are inundated with the results of public opinion polls. The polls, often reported to us through television news, the newspaper, *Time, Newsweek,* or radio, purport to tell us a variety of things: whether the president's popularity is up or down, whether gun control is more popular now than previously, or who is leading the pack for the next presidential nomination.

What must be kept in mind with this blizzard of information is that not all poll results are equally good or equally believable. As a critical consumer, you need to be aware of what makes one set of public opinion poll results valid and other results useless or even dangerously misleading.

Selection of the Sample

How were the people who were interviewed selected? Pay attention only to opinion polls that are based on scientific, or random, samples, in which a known probability was used to select every person who was interviewed. These *probability samples,* as they are also called, can take a number of different forms. The simplest to understand is known as a *random sample,* in which everybody had a known, and possibly an equal, chance of being chosen to be interviewed. As a rule, do not give credence to the results of opinion polls that consist of shopping-mall interviews. The main problem with this kind of opinion taking, which is a special version of a so-called *accidental sample,* is that not everyone had an equal chance of being in the mall when the interview took place. Also, it is almost certain that the people in the mall are not a reasonable cross section of a community's entire population (shopping malls

would tend to attract people who are disproportionately younger, female, mobile, and middle class).

Probability samples are useful (and nonprobability samples are not) for the following reason: when you know the odds that the particular sample would have been chosen randomly from a larger population, you can calculate the range within which the real results for the whole population would fall if everybody had been interviewed. Well-designed probability samples will allow the pollster to say, for example, that he or she is 95 percent sure that 61 percent of the public, plus or minus 4 percentage points, supports national health insurance. It turns out that if you want to become twice as precise about a poll result, you would need to collect a sample four times as large. This tends to make accurate polls quite expensive and difficult to collect. Typically, the Gallup organization seldom interviews more than about 1,500 respondents.

Interview Method

There are other important points to keep in mind when you see opinion poll results. How were people contacted for the poll—by mail, by telephone, in person in their homes, or in some other way (such as via the Internet)? By and large, because of its lower cost, polling firms have turned more and more to telephone interviewing. This method usually can produce highly accurate results. Its disadvantage is that telephone interviews typically need to be short and to deal with questions that are fairly easy to answer. Interviews in person are better for getting useful information about why a

particular response was given to a question. They take much longer to complete, however, and are not as useful if results must be generated quickly. Results from mailed questionnaires should be taken with a grain of salt. Usually, only a small percentage of people complete them and send them back.

Nonpolls

Be particularly critical of telephone "call-in" polls or "Internet polls." When viewers or listeners of television or radio shows are encouraged to call in their opinions to an 800 telephone number, the call is free, but the polling results are useless. Users of the Internet also have an easy way to make their views known. Only people who are interested in the topic will take the trouble to respond, however, and that group, of course, is not representative of the general public. Polls that use 900 numbers are perhaps even more misleading. The only respondents to those polls are those who care enough about the topic to pay for a call. Both types of polls are likely to be manipulated by interest groups or supporters of a political candidate, who will organize their supporters to make calls and reinforce their own point of view. Remember, when seeing the results of any poll, to take a moment and try to find out how the poll was conducted.

Key terms

consensus 220

divisive opinion 221

fluidity 222

gender gap 237

generational effect 235

ideologue 240

intensity 222

media 235

opinion leader 235

opinion poll 224

peer group 233

political socialization 232

political trust 238

public opinion 220

relevance 223

sampling error 230

stability 223

Watergate break-in 219

Chapter summary

1 Public opinion is the aggregate of individual attitudes or beliefs shared by some portion of the adult population. It has at least five special qualities: (a) intensity—the strength of an opinion; (b) fluidity—the extent to which opinion changes; (c) stability—the extent to which opinion remains constant; (d) relevance—the extent to which an issue is of concern at a particular time; and (e) political knowledge. Consensus issues are those on which most people agree, whereas divisive issues are those about which people strongly disagree.

2 Most descriptions of public opinion are based on the results of opinion polls. The accuracy of polls is based on sampling techniques that ensure randomness in the selection of respondents. Polls only measure opinions held on the day they are taken and will not reflect rapidly changing opinions. Certain methodological problems may reduce the accuracy of polls.

3 Opinions and attitudes are produced by a combination of socialization, information, and experience. Young peo-ple, for example, are likely to be influenced by their parents' political party identification. Education has an effect on opinions and attitudes, as do peer groups, religious affiliation, and economic status. Political events may have generational effects, shaping the opinions of a particular age group. Opinion leaders, the media, ethnicity, and gender also affect political views.

4 A political culture exists in the United States because so many Americans hold similar attitudes and beliefs about how the government and the political system should work. In addition, most Americans are able to identify themselves as liberals, moderates, or conservatives, even though they may not articulate a consistent philosophy of politics, or ideology.

5 Public opinion can play an important part in the political system by providing information to candidates, by indicating support or opposition to the president and Congress, and by setting limits on government action through public pressure.

Selected print and electronic resources

SUGGESTED READINGS

Asher, Herbert. *Polling and the Public: What Every Citizen Should Know*, 3d ed. Washington, D.C.: Congressional Quarterly Press, 1995. This brief introduction to the science of polling for the citizen as consumer pays special attention to the use of polls by the media and by political candidates.

Bardes, Barbara A., and Robert W. Oldendick. *Public Opinion: Measuring the American Mind*. Belmont, Calif.: Wadsworth Publishing Co., 2000. This examination of public opinion polling looks at the uses of public opinion data and recent technological issues in polling in addition to providing excellent coverage of public opinion on important issues over a period of decades.

Delli Carpini, Michael X., and Scott Keeter. *What Americans Know about Politics and Why It Matters*. New Haven, Conn.: Yale University Press, 1996. The authors provide an extensive discussion of all the known data about the amount of political knowledge possessed by Americans and how they come to possess it.

Fishkin, James S. *The Voice of the People: Public Opinion and Democracy*. New Haven, Conn.: Yale University Press, 1995. In this provocative work, Fishkin lays out his proposal for a deliberative poll and discusses the theoretical framework for using such a gathering for understanding public opinion on major issues.

Gaubatz, Kathlyn Taylor. *Crime in the Public Mind*. Ann Arbor, Mich.: University of Michigan Press, 1995. This volume explores in depth American attitudes toward criminals and the criminal justice system. The author compares the views of those who support "tougher" policies toward crime with those who oppose such policies.

Langston, Thomas S. *With Reverence and Contempt: How Americans Think about Their President*. Baltimore, Md.: Johns Hopkins University Press, 1995. This is a qualitative study of how Americans regard the president and the presidency. The author looks at the topic both historically and in terms of reforms that might improve the relationship between the people and the president.

MEDIA RESOURCES

Wag the Dog–A 1997 film that provodes a very cynical look at the importance of public opinion. The film, which features Dustin Hoffman and Robert DeNiro, follows the efforts of a presidential political consultant who stages a foreign policy crisis to divert public opinion from a sex scandal in the White House.

Vox Populi: Democracy in Crisis–A PBS special focusing on why public confidence in government, which has plummeted during recent decades, still has not recovered despite the current economic boom.

Logging on

If you do a search on Yahoo using "Public AND Opinion," you'll get, among other things, some lists under "Government: Politics: Political Opinion: . . ." After the colon, they list different options: Conservative, Liberal/Progressive, or Libertarian. These contain numerous links to other sources.

Yale University Library, one of the great research institutions, has a Social Science Library and Information Services. If you want to roam around some library sources of public opinion data, this is an interesting site to visit. Go to

http://www.library.yale.edu/socsci/opinion

According to its home page, the mission of National Election Studies (NES) "is to produce high quality data on voting, public opinion, and political participation that serves the research needs of social scientists, teachers, students, and policymakers concerned with understanding the theoretical and empirical foundations of mass politics in a democratic society." This is a good place to obtain information related to public opinion. Find it at

http://www.umich.edu/~nes

The Polling Report Web site offers polls and their results organized by topic. It is up to date and easy to use. Go to

http://www.pollingreport.com

Using the Internet for political analysis

To sharpen your skills in using public opinion data, point your browser to one of the sites noted in the *Logging on* or to one maintained by one of the national newspapers. Pick a subject or topic on which the site maintains public opinion polling results (often you must use the Contents button for this). Then try to identify and consider the following types of information: First, how large was the sample, and how big is the "confidence" interval cited in the study? Do you know who commissioned the poll and to whom the results were given? Second, examine at least three questions and responses, and answer the following questions: How might the wording of the question have influenced the responses? How can you tell if the survey respondents had any information about the question asked? Was the number of respondents who couldn't answer the question significant? Can you tell if respondents could answer the question without much information? Finally, consider how much a political leader might learn from this poll.

chapter 8

Interest Groups

CHAPTER OUTLINE

- The Role of Interest Groups
- The Benefits of Interest Groups
- Interest Groups and Social Movements
- Types of Interest Groups
- Interest Group Strategies
- Regulating Lobbyists
- Interest Groups and Representative Democracy

what if...

Every Lobbying Contact Had to Be Reported?

BACKGROUND

Regulating those who try to influence congresspersons or state legislators has always been difficult. The right to lobby or to try to influence any governmental official is protected by the First Amendment to the Constitution, which gives every citizen the right to "assemble and petition the government" for the resolution of his or her grievances. This right pertains to individuals, to groups, and to organizations, such as large corporations and labor unions.

The problem is, how can we make sure that those who lobby or influence political officials are not using any sort of corrupt means to do so or corrupting the government in any way? Congress has imposed registration requirements on lobbyists, and lobbyists or organizations must file a report about the issues that they are trying to influence and their general activities. They need not precisely identify the officials they tried to influence, however.

WHAT IF EVERY LOBBYING CONTACT HAD TO BE REPORTED?

One possible way to manage the increasing efforts of groups, corporations, and foreign nations to influence legislation in Washington would be to require that members of Congress and the administration record or register every contact they have with a lobbyist. Alternatively, every lobbyist who is registered with Congress would be required to list daily every contact that she or he has with a public official. Congress could establish an Internet site that lists, by member of Congress and by member of the administration, all of the contacts made by lobbyists, no matter what the occasion.

The definition of lobbying contacts covered by the legislation should be very broad. Cocktail parties after work, telephone calls, scheduled appointments and meetings, golf matches, weddings, and funerals would be included as long as the registered lobbyist met with any political official. The legislation could require a brief mention of the topic discussed at any meeting or, more simply, list the organizations that the lobbyist represents.

INCREASING PUBLIC INFORMATION

The advantage of such a regulation would be that all of the contacts between lobbyists and members of Congress or the administration would be publicly disclosed. The public, the media, and all of the members of the government would have equal access to this information. Most importantly, the voters and constituents of a political official would have a public record of that official's activities and contacts.

Reporting such contacts might, in fact, slow down the process of raising money through afternoon cocktail parties held for the benefit of legislators. Lobbyists are invited to these benefits and pay for their tickets, and there is no doubt that attempts to influence legislation take place at these events. If all such events were publicized quickly on the Internet, members of Congress might be less apt to give or to attend these parties.

THE LOSS OF PRIVACY

Requiring that all contacts between lobbyists and public officials be reported would reduce the privacy and freedom of movement of those involved. Nevertheless, so long as there is no attempt to limit the number of contacts or the kinds of conversations that are held, such legislation would not violate the Constitution. In many cases, though, it is truly very difficult to separate lobbying activities from personal social relationships. If a senator invites an old friend, perhaps a former senator, to his son's wedding, is that really a lobbying contact?

Additionally, gathering this information could be a logistical nightmare. It would require the recording of millions of contacts weekly and the building of a database that would allow individuals to understand what took place.

Finally, how many individuals would actually access these data and find out for themselves what their political representatives are doing? Would the media scan the reports and present the information to the public in a helpful format? If no one uses the data except political opponents during a campaign, then lobbyists or political officials would be no more accountable than they are now.

FOR CRITICAL ANALYSIS

1. What could you learn from a complete listing of all lobbyists' contacts with a particular official? Would you know whether the lobbyist actually influenced any votes or other actions of the official?
2. Is it fair for political officials to lose their personal privacy and their social contacts to provide such information to the voters?
3. To what extent do you think such information would become part of public debates or political campaigns?

The debate over the regulation of tobacco began more than thirty years ago, when it was first proposed that the health risks of smoking be identified. The range of **interest groups** participating in the debate has expanded greatly since those early days when the major groups were the tobacco companies and the federal government. Among the crowd at or near the table during the recent negotiations were representatives from the tobacco companies; the attorneys general of more than twenty states; members of the Food and Drug Administration; hundreds of lawyers representing clients; and legislators. Also present were **lobbyists** representing health groups, including the American Medical Association; children's groups; farmers; asbestos companies; and drug companies. Many of these groups also claimed to represent large segments of the American public—smokers, nonsmokers, and the taxpayers.

The tobacco negotiations presented complicated issues for the political system: If the price of tobacco were raised, would smoking among teens be reduced? Could regulating the advertising and availability of tobacco products reduce teen smoking? What would happen to the farmers who depended on the tobacco crop? Who should pay for the health costs of cigarette smoking? How would the settlement affect the industry and employees, the tax revenues of the government, health costs, and the general health of society? All of these issues would eventually be resolved either in state legislatures or in Congress.

The final tobacco settlement was negotiated between the tobacco companies and the state governments: the tobacco companies agreed to send billions of dollars to the states in reparation for the money spent by the states in treating the tobacco-related illnesses of their citizens. Because the settlement did not specify how the money would be spent, lobbying about where the dollars would flow began in all fifty state houses. Cities, school districts, hospitals, highway construction firms, and many more groups lined up for funds.

The final decisions about how the tobacco industry will be regulated, however, still rest with Congress and the president. Consequently, the tobacco companies continue to spend money in hopes of influencing the outcome. In the 1998 election cycle, the tobacco industry gave more than $6 million to congressional campaigns. In addition, the tobacco companies continue to lobby for their interests, including conducting a public relations campaign that emphasizes their contributions to charitable causes. As long as the tobacco industry exists, lobbying by that industry will continue.

Interest Group

An organized group of individuals sharing common objectives who actively attempt to influence policymakers in all three branches of the government and at all levels.

Lobbyist

An organization or individual who attempts to influence the passage, defeat, or contents of legislation and the administrative decisions of government.

Lobbying activity becomes most intense the day a vote is being taken on an important issue. Not surprisingly, lobbyists are often found in the lobbies of Congress.

The Role of Interest Groups

As the negotiations for a tobacco settlement and for the future regulation of the industry demonstrate, the American system of government and politics provides a wealth of opportunities for those affected by government action to voice their views and to try to influence policymakers.

Interest groups take many forms. They include ordinary people who make their points in Congress and the statehouses of America. When a businessperson contacts her state representative about a proposed change in the law, she is lob-bying the government. When farmers descend on Washington, D.C., on tractors or Americans with disabilities gather in the corridors of city hall, they are also interest groups lobbying their representatives. Protected by the First Amendment's guarantee of the right to assemble and petition the government for the redress of grievances, individuals have joined together in voluntary associations to try to influence the government ever since the Boston Tea Party (see Chapter 2), which involved, after all, an eighteenth-century trade issue.

As pluralist theories suggest, the structure of American government invites the participation of interest groups. The governmental system has many points of access or places in the decision-making process at which interest groups may focus an attack. If a bill opposed by a group passes the Senate, the lobbying efforts shift to the House of Representatives or to the president to seek a veto. If, in spite of all efforts, the legislation passes, the group may even lobby the executive agency or bureau that is supposed to implement the law and hope to influence the way in which the legislation is applied. In some cases, interest groups carry their efforts into the court system, either by filing lawsuits or by filing briefs as "friends of the court." The constitutional features of separation of powers and checks and balances encourage interest groups in their efforts.

A Nation of Joiners?

Alexis de Tocqueville observed in 1834 that "in no country of the world has the principle of association been more successfully used or applied to a greater mul-titude of objectives than in America."[1] The French traveler was amazed at the degree to which Americans formed groups to solve civic problems, establish social relationships, and speak for their economic or political interests. Perhaps James Madison, when he wrote *Federalist Paper* No. 10 (see Appendix D), had already judged the character of his country's citizens similarly. He supported the creation of a large republic with several states to encourage the formation of many interests. The multitude of interests, in Madison's view, would work to dis-courage the formation of an oppressive larger minority or majority interest.

Surely, neither Madison nor de Tocqueville foresaw the formation of more than a hundred thousand associations in the United States. Poll data show that more than two-thirds of all Americans belong to at least one group or associa-tion. While the majority of these affiliations could not be classified as "interest groups" in the political sense, Americans do understand the principles of work-ing in groups. As noted in Chapter 1, some scholars maintain that this penchant for group action supports a pluralist interpretation of American politics, in which most government policies become the work of group conflict and com-promise. (The tobacco settlement, discussed earlier, illustrates this principle.) Some critics might say that the drive to organize interests can go too far, result-ing in "hyperpluralism," meaning that so many powerful interests are compet-ing that no real policy change can take place. Furthermore, it is possible that

Alexis de Tocqueville (1805–1859), a French social historian and traveler, commented on Americans' predilection for joining groups.

---

[1]Alexis de Tocqueville, *Democracy in America,* Vol. 1, edited by Phillips Bradley (New York: Knopf, 1980), p. 191.

interest groups can become so powerful that the needs and demands of ordinary citizens can be ignored (see the discussion of interest groups and representative democracy later in this chapter).

The Benefits of Interest Groups

One puzzle that has fascinated political scientists is why some people join interest groups, whereas many others do not. Everyone has some interest that could benefit from government action. For many groups, however, those remain unorganized interests, or latent interests.

According to the theory of Mancur Olson, it may be that it simply is not rational for individuals to join most groups. He introduces the idea of the "collective good." This concept refers to any public benefit that, if available to any member of the community, cannot be denied to any other member, whether or not he or she participated in the effort to gain the good.

Although collective benefits are usually thought of as coming from such public goods as clean air or national defense, benefits are also bestowed by the government on subsets of the public. Price subsidies to dairy farmers and loans to college students are examples. Olson uses economic theory to propose that it is not rational for interested individuals to join groups that work for group benefits. In fact, it is often more rational for the individual to wait for others to procure the benefits and then share them.

If so little incentive exists for individuals to join together, why are there thousands of interest groups lobbying in Washington? According to the logic of collective action, if the contribution of an individual *will* make a difference to the effort, then it is worth it to the individual to join. Thus, smaller groups, which seek benefits for only a small proportion of the population, are more likely to enroll members who will give time and money to the cause. Larger groups, which represent general public interests (the women's movement or the American Civil Liberties Union, for example), will find it relatively more difficult to get individuals to join. People need an incentive—material or otherwise—to join.[2]

Solidary Incentives

Interest groups offer **solidary incentives** for their members. Solidary incentives include companionship, a sense of belonging, and the pleasure of associating with others. Although originally the National Audubon Society was founded to save the snowy egret from extinction, most members join today to learn more about birds and to meet and share their pleasure with other individuals who enjoy bird watching as a hobby. Even though the incentive might be solidary for many members, this organization nonetheless also pursues an active political agenda, working to preserve the environment and to protect endangered species. Most members may not play any part in working toward larger, more national goals unless the organization can convince them to take political action or unless some local environmental issue arises.

Solidary Incentive
A reason or motive having to do with the desire to associate with others and to share with others a particular interest or hobby.

Material Incentives

For other individuals, interest groups offer direct **material incentives.** A case in point is the AARP (formerly the American Association of Retired Persons), which

Material Incentive
A reason or motive having to do with economic benefits or opportunities.

---

[2]For further reading on this complex and interesting theory, see Mancur Olson, *The Logic of Collective Action* (Cambridge, Mass.: Harvard University Press, 1965).

provides discounts, insurance plans, and organized travel opportunities for its members. Because of its exceptionally low dues ($10 annually) and the benefits gained through membership in the AARP, it has become the largest—and a very powerful—interest group in the United States. The AARP can claim to represent the interests of millions of senior citizens and can show that they actually have joined the group. For most seniors, the material incentives outweigh the membership costs.

Many other interest groups offer indirect material incentives for their members. Such groups as the American Dairy Association or the National Association of Automobile Dealers do not give discounts or freebies to their members, but they do offer indirect benefits and rewards by, for example, protecting the material interests of their members from government policymaking that is injurious to their industry or business.

Purposive Incentives

Purposive Incentive
A reason or motive having to do with ethical beliefs or ideological principles.

Interest groups also offer the opportunity for individuals to pursue political, economic, or social goals through joint action. Such **purposive incentives** offer individuals the satisfaction of taking action for the sake of their beliefs or principles. The individuals who belong to groups focusing on the abortion issue have joined those groups because they are concerned about the question of whether abortions should be made available to the public. People join such groups because they feel strongly enough about the issues to support the groups' work with money and time.

Interest Groups and Social Movements

Social Movement
A movement that represents the demands of a large segment of the public for political, economic, or social change.

Interest groups are often spawned by mass **social movements.** Such movements represent demands by a large segment of the population for change in the political, economic, or social system. Social movements are often the first expression of latent discontent with the contemporary system. They may be the authentic voice of weaker or oppressed groups in society that do not have the means or

Former President Bill Clinton is shown here addressing the American Association of Retired Persons (AARP), which has become one of the most powerful lobbying groups in America. As the population grows older, a larger percentage of Americans are over the age of fifty. Any president knows the importance of keeping such an important interest group happy. Through its lobbying efforts, the AARP has been effective in preventing any significant reductions in Social Security benefits.

standing to organize as interest groups. For example, the women's movement of the nineteenth century suffered social disapproval from most mainstream political and social leaders. Because women were unable to vote or take an active part in the political system, it was difficult for women who desired greater freedoms to organize formal groups. After the Civil War, when more women became active in professional life, the first real women's rights group, the National Woman Suffrage Association, came into being.

African Americans found themselves in an even more disadvantaged situation after the end of the Reconstruction period. Not only were they unable to exercise political rights in many southern and border states, but also participation in any form of organization could lead to economic ruin, physical harassment, or even death. The civil rights movement of the 1950s and 1960s was clearly a social movement. Although several formal organizations worked to support the movement—including the Southern Christian Leadership Conference, the National Association for the Advancement of Colored People, and the Urban League—only a social movement could generate the kinds of civil disobedience that took place in hundreds of towns and cities across the country.

Social movements are often precursors of interest groups. They may generate interest groups with specific goals that successfully recruit members through the incentives the group offers. In the case of the women's movement of the 1960s, the National Organization for Women was formed out of a demand to end gender-segregated job advertising in newspapers.

Types of Interest Groups

Thousands of groups exist to influence government. Among the major types of interest groups are those that represent the main sectors of the economy—business, agricultural, government, and labor groups. In more recent years, a number of "public-interest" organizations have been formed to represent the needs of the general citizenry, including some "single-issue" groups. The interests of foreign governments and foreign businesses are also represented in the American political arena. The memberships of some major interest groups are shown in Table 8–1 on the next page.

Economic Interest Groups

Numerous interest groups have been formed to promote economic interests. These groups include business, agricultural, labor, public employee, and professional organizations.

Business Interest Groups. Thousands of trade and business organizations attempt to influence government policies. Some groups target a single regulatory unit, whereas others try to effect major policy changes. Three large business groups are consistently effective: (1) the National Association of Manufacturers (NAM), (2) the U.S. Chamber of Commerce, and (3) the Business Roundtable. The annual budget of the NAM is more than $22 million, which it collects in dues from about 14,000 relatively large corporations. Sometimes called the National Chamber, the U.S. Chamber of Commerce represents nearly 200,000 companies. Dues from its members, which include about 3,000 state and local chambers of commerce, exceed $30 million a year. Separately, two hundred of the largest corporations in the United States send their chief executive officers to the Business Roundtable. This organization is based in New York, but it does its lobbying in Washington, D.C. Established in 1972, the Roundtable was designed to promote

TABLE 8-1

Characteristics of Selected Interest Groups

NAME (FOUNDED)	MEMBERS (INDIVIDUALS OR AS NOTED)
Business/Economic	
Business Roundtable (1972)	200 corporations (10 million employees)
The Conference Board, Inc. (1916)	3,000 labor unions, colleges & universities, etc.
National Association of Manufacturers (1895)	14,000 companies
U.S. Chamber of Commerce (1912)	200,000 companies, state & local chambers of commerce, etc.
Civil/Constitutional Rights	
AARP (1958)	33,000,000
American Civil Liberties Union (1920)	275,000
Amnesty International USA (1961)	over 1 million
Handgun Control, Inc. (1974)	500,000
Leadership Conference on Civil Rights, Inc. (1950)	180 national organizations
League of United Latin American Citizens (LULAC) (1929)	115,000
Mexican-American Legal Defense and Educational Fund (1968)	—
NAACP Legal Defense and Educational Fund, Inc. (1940)	—
National Abortion Rights Action League (1969)	500,000
National Association for the Advancement of Colored People (1909)	over 500,000
National Gay and Lesbian Task Force (1973)	35,000
National Organization for Women, Inc. (1966)	300,000
National Rifle Association of America (1871)	3,400,000
National Right to Life Committee, Inc. (1973)	—
National Urban League (1910)	1,600,000
Planned Parenthood Federation of America, Inc. (1916)	—
Women's Legal Defense Fund (1971)	1,500
Community/Grassroots	
The American Society for the Prevention of Cruelty to Animals (1866)	475,000
Association of Community Organizations for Reform Now (ACORN) (1970)	over 125,000
Mothers Against Drunk Driving (1980)	3 million
National Anti-Vivisection Society (1929)	—
Environmental	
Environmental Defense Fund (1967)	300,000
Greenpeace USA (1971)	244,000
Izaak Walton League of America (1922)	50,000
League of Conservation Voters (1970)	over 1 million
National Audubon Society (1905)	550,000
National Wildlife Federation (1936)	4,500,000
The Nature Conservancy (1951)	over 1 million
Sierra Club (1892)	550,000
The Wilderness Society (1935)	200,000
World Wildlife Fund (1948)	over 1 million
International Affairs	
Accuracy in Media (1969)	25,000
American Israel Public Affairs Committee (1954)	55,000
Human Rights Watch (1978)	—

SOURCE: Foundation for Public Affairs, *Public Interest Profiles 1995–1996* (Washington, D.C.: Congressional Quarterly Press, 1995), and authors' update.

a more aggressive view of business interests in general, cutting across specific industries. Dues paid by the member corporations are determined by the companies' wealth. One of the newer interest groups is discussed in this chapter's *Critical Perspective* on the next page.

Agricultural Interest Groups.   American farmers and their workers represent about 2 percent of the U.S. population. In spite of this, farmers' influence on legislation beneficial to their interests has been enormous. Farmers have succeeded in their aims because they have very strong interest groups. They are geographically dispersed and therefore have many representatives and senators to speak for them. The American Farm Bureau Federation, established in 1919, has over 4.9 million members. It was instrumental in getting government guarantees of "fair" prices during the Great Depression in the 1930s.[3] Another important agricultural special interest organization is the National Farmers' Union (NFU).

Labor Interest Groups.   Interest groups representing the **labor movement** date back to at least 1886 when the American Federation of Labor (AFL) was formed. In 1955, the AFL joined forces with the Congress of Industrial Organizations (CIO). Today, the combined AFL-CIO is an enormous union with a membership exceeding 13 million workers. In a sense, the AFL-CIO is a union of unions.

The political arm of the AFL-CIO is the Committee on Political Education (COPE). COPE's activities are funded by voluntary contributions from union members. COPE has been active in state and national campaigns since 1956.

Other unions are also active politically. One of the most widely known is the International Brotherhood of Teamsters, which was led by Jimmy Hoffa until his expulsion in 1967 because of alleged ties with organized crime. The Teamsters Union was established initially in 1903 and today has a membership of 1.5 million.

Another independent union is the Automobile, Aerospace, and Agricultural Implement Workers of America (formerly United Automobile Workers), founded in 1935. It now has a membership of 760,000. Also very active in labor lobbying is the United Mine Workers union, representing about 130,000 members.

The role of unions in American society has weakened in recent years, as witnessed by a decline in union membership (see Figure 8–1). In the age of

Northwest Airlines pilots picket at the Minneapolis airport during their 1998 strike.

Labor Movement
Generally, the full range of economic and political expression of working-class interests; politically, the organization of working-class interests.

---

[3]The Agricultural Adjustment Act of 1933 (declared unconstitutional) was replaced by the 1937 Agricultural Adjustment Act and later changed and amended several times.

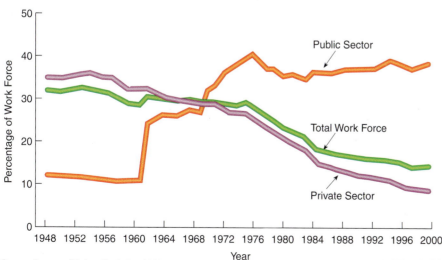

SOURCE: Bureau of Labor Statistics, 2000.

FIGURE **8–1**

Decline in Union Membership, 1948 to Present

As shown in this figure, the percentage of the total work force that is represented by labor unions has declined precipitously over the last two decades. Note, however, that in contrast to the decline in union membership in the private sector, the percentage of government workers who are unionized has increased significantly.

critical perspective

How Powerful Is Silicon Valley?

The youngest major industry in the world is information technology. The industry is centered in Silicon Valley, California, with outposts in northern Virginia, Massachusetts, and a few other states. Although primitive computers have existed since the 1930s, only when computing and the Internet became part of the mainstream of American life did the growth and influence of the information technology industry begin to explode. Since 1993, for example, the industry has created more than one million new jobs.

Silicon Valley Enters Politics

For most of its young life, Silicon Valley avoided politics. Its leaders were very young, uninterested in politics, and devoted to innovation in their enterprises. In 1992, the leadership generally supported the candidacies of Bill Clinton and Al Gore because they advocated freedom for the industry to grow. Since that time, the information technology industry has become far more sophisticated in its view of Washington, D.C. The Republicans, who took control of Congress in 1994, are more supportive than Democrats of freedom from government restraints on the Internet—except in matters of pornography and the protection of children on the Internet. The Democrats, who tend to be more supportive than Republicans of freedom of speech in general, have been more willing to regulate the industry, including preventing the export of certain encryption software overseas. Additionally, the Clinton administration pursued Microsoft in federal court as a monopoly. For these and other reasons, the information technology industry rapidly recruited lobbyists and established a presence in Washington. It created several lobbying alliances and now issues a high-tech scorecard on members of Congress.

Will Silicon Valley Become Too Powerful?

Why should the entry of Silicon Valley into national politics arouse concern? First, the industry generally views growth as its paramount concern; any attempt to regulate, slow, or put any conditions on its development is seen as negative. While the industry has provided tremendous job growth and improved productivity in American business, the nation faces a number of issues in regard to information technology. Why, for example, is it necessary for the industry to import employees from overseas instead of hiring Americans? Is it possible that these companies' substantial profits come from monopolistic practices?

The power of the information technology industry is multifaceted. First, it has generated billions of dollars in profit and created thousands of millionaires within its companies. These individuals have the financial power to be major campaign contributors, although they have not done so yet. Many of the leaders of the industry are on the list of America's billionaires. The industry, recognizing the power of such achievements, has decided to use its leaders as personal lobbyists on Capitol Hill.

Second, the industry now employs millions of people across the nation. In California alone, it employs more than 750,000 individuals. Close behind are the employment figures in Texas, New York, and Illinois. These workers are also voters and will have influence on their respective members of Congress.

Perhaps the greatest concern with Silicon Valley is its potential for power in the future. The telecommunications industry is in the process of deregulation. Seeing the potential for control over virtually all forms of media, companies have been striving to form alliances and buy out other companies so that they can supply Internet services and content (news, entertainment, shopping, sports) directly to consumers. The market and advertising potential of these combined companies is beyond imagination. The merger of America Online (AOL) and Time Warner is only the first of these mega-mergers between an Internet company and those who entertain us and provide the news. The question yet to be answered is whether such mega-mergers can be trusted to include alternative views in the news and to maintain any competition in the marketplace of ideas.

For members of Congress or the president, the political ramifications of opposing the desires of these information technology and media giants could be astonishing. What power will they wield as they continue to buy television networks and newspapers and provide the content to their own e-news? Will they have the power to influence elections and government decision making, or will they voluntarily keep competition alive?

FOR CRITICAL ANALYSIS

1. What are the most important goals of the companies in Silicon Valley?
2. What aspects of the information technology industry do you think will need some form of government regulation?
3. Should mega-mergers of Internet companies and entertainment and news companies be permitted?

automation and with the rise of the **service sector,** blue-collar workers in basic industries (autos, steel, and the like) represent a smaller and smaller percentage of the total working population. Because of this decline in the industrial sector of the economy, national unions are looking to nontraditional areas for their membership, including migrant farm workers, service workers, and, most recently, public employees—such as police officers; firefighting personnel; and teachers, including college professors. Indeed, public-sector unions are the fastest growing labor organizations.

Public Employee Interest Groups.   The degree of unionization in the private sector has declined since 1965, but this has been offset partially by growth in the unionization of public employees. Figure 8–1 on page 255 shows the growth in the public-sector work force. With a total work force of more than 7.1 million, these unions are likely to continue expanding.

Both the American Federation of State, County, and Municipal Employees and the American Federation of Teachers are members of the AFL-CIO's Public Employee Department. Originally, the public employee unions started out as social and professional organizations. Over the years, they have become quite militant and are often involved in strikes. Many of these strikes are illegal, because certain public employees do not have the right to strike and essentially sign a contract so stating. In August 1981, the Professional Air Traffic Controllers Organization (PATCO) went on strike in defiance of a court order. President Ronald Reagan, convinced that public opinion was on his side, fired the strikers. Supervisors, nonstrikers, military personnel, and new trainees were rounded up to handle the jobs vacated by the 16,000 terminated air traffic controllers.

A powerful interest group lobbying on behalf of public employees is the National Education Association (NEA), a nationwide organization of about 2.5 million administrators, teachers, and others connected with education. The NEA lobbies intensively for increased public funding of education. The NEA sponsors regional and national conventions each year and has an extensive program of electronic media broadcasts, surveys, and the like.

Interest Groups of Professionals.   Numerous professional organizations exist, including the American Bar Association, the Association of General Contractors of America, the Institute of Electrical and Electronic Engineers, the Screen Actors Guild, and others. Some professional groups, such as lawyers and doctors, are more influential than others due to their social status. Lawyers have a unique advantage—a large number of members of Congress share their profession. In terms of money spent on lobbying, however, one professional organization stands head and shoulders above the rest—the American Medical Association (AMA). Founded in 1847, it is now affiliated with more than 2,000 local and state medical societies and has a total membership of 300,000. The AMA spent an estimated $3 million in 2000 presidential campaign contributions in its efforts to influence legislation.

Environmental Groups

Environmental interest groups are not new. We have already mentioned the National Audubon Society, which was founded in 1905 to protect the snowy egret from the commercial demand for hat decorations. The patron of the Sierra Club, John Muir, worked for the creation of national parks more than ninety years ago. But the blossoming of national environmental groups with mass memberships did not occur until the 1970s. Since the first Earth Day, organized

DID YOU KNOW...
That the National Audubon Society, one of the leading environmental lobbying organizations, currently has about 550,000 members?

Service Sector
The sector of the economy that provides services—such as food services, insurance, and education—in contrast to the sector of the economy that produces goods.

INFOTRAC®
COLLEGE EDITION

Think Locally, Act Globally

The *Rainbow Warrior,* the flagship of Greenpeace, is both a symbol for the environmental interest group and a resource that can be used for actions at sea to protect the environment. The *Rainbow Warrior* has acted to save dolphins, to protest oil spills, and to stop Japanese and Russian whaling.

Public Interest

The best interests of the collective, overall community; the national good, rather than the narrow interests of a self-serving group.

Ralph Nader began the movement to create public-interest groups through the publication, in 1965, of his book *Unsafe at Any Speed,* which criticized General Motors for underplaying the dangers of its Corvair automobile. Since that time, he has founded a number of not-for-profit public-interest groups that track business and governmental actions in specific policy arenas. In 2000, he was the presidential candidate for the Green Party.

in 1972, many interest groups have sprung up to protect the environment in general or unique ecological niches. The groups range from the National Wildlife Federation, with a membership of more than 4.5 million and an emphasis on education, to the fairly elite Environmental Defense Fund, with a membership of 300,000 and a focus on influencing federal policy. Other groups include the Nature Conservancy, which seeks members' contributions so the organization can buy up threatened natural areas and either give them to state or local governments or manage them itself, and the more radical Greenpeace Society and Earth First.

Public-Interest Groups

Public interest is a difficult term to define because, as we noted earlier, there are many publics in our nation of over 275 million. It is almost impossible for one particular public policy to benefit everybody, which makes it practically impossible to define the public interest. Nonetheless, over the past few decades, a variety of law and lobbying organizations have been formed "in the public interest."

Nader Organizations. The best-known and perhaps the most effective public-interest groups are those organized under the leadership of consumer activist Ralph Nader. Nader's rise to the top began after the publication, in 1965, of his book *Unsafe at Any Speed,* a lambasting critique of the purported attempt by General Motors (GM) to keep from the public detrimental information about its rear-engine Corvair. Partly as a result of Nader's book, Congress began to consider testimony in favor of an automobile safety bill. GM made a clumsy attempt to discredit Nader's background. Nader sued, the media exploited the story, and when GM settled out of court for $425,000, Nader became the recognized champion of consumer interests. Since then, Nader has turned over much of his income to the more than sixty public-interest groups that he has formed or sponsored. In 2000, Nader ran for president on the ticket of the Green Party.

Other Public-Interest Groups. Partly in response to the Nader organizations, numerous conservative public-interest law firms have sprung up that are often pitted against the consumer groups in court. Some of these are the Mountain

States Legal Defense Foundation, the Pacific Legal Foundation, the National Right-to-Work Legal Defense Foundation, the Washington Legal Foundation, and the Mid-Atlantic Legal Foundation.

One of the largest public-interest groups is Common Cause, founded in 1968, whose goal is to reorder national priorities toward "the public" and to make governmental institutions more responsive to the needs of the public. Anyone willing to pay dues of $20 a year can become a member. Members are polled regularly to obtain information about local and national issues requiring reassessment. Some of the activities of Common Cause have been (1) helping to ensure the passage of the Twenty-sixth Amendment (giving eighteen-year-olds the right to vote), (2) achieving greater voter registration in all states, (3) supporting the complete withdrawal of all U.S. forces from South Vietnam in the 1970s, and (4) promoting legislation that would limit campaign spending.

Other public-interest groups are active on a wide range of issues. The goal of the League of Women Voters, founded in 1920, is to educate the public on political matters. Although generally nonpartisan, it has lobbied for the Equal Rights Amendment and for government reform. The Consumer Federation of America is an alliance of about two hundred local and national organizations interested in consumer protection. The American Civil Liberties Union dates back to World War I (1914–1918), when, under a different name, it defended draft resisters. It generally enters into legal disputes related to Bill of Rights issues.

Special Interest Groups

Special interest groups, being narrowly focused, may be able to call more attention to their respective causes because they have simple and straightforward goals and because their members tend to care intensely about the issues. Thus, such groups can easily motivate their members to contact legislators or to organize demonstrations in support of their policy goals.

A number of interest groups focus on just one issue. The abortion debate has created various groups opposed to abortion (such as Right to Life) and groups in favor of abortion (such as the National Abortion Rights Action League). Other

Reprinted courtesy of Larry Wright and the *Detroit News.*

The job of lobbyists never stops. These Washington lobbyists are scrutinizing news reports to ascertain the positions of members of Congress on policy issues that will have an impact on the interests that the lobbyists represent. While many critics of lobbyists and interest groups argue that they distort the actions of government, the First Amendment prohibits the government from regulating their speech.

Direct Technique
An interest group activity that involves interaction with government officials to further the group's goals.

Indirect Technique
A strategy employed by interest groups that uses third parties to influence government officials.

single-issue groups are the National Rifle Association, the Right to Work Committee (an anti-union group), and the Hudson Valley PAC (a pro-Israel group).

Other groups represent particular groups of Americans who share a common characteristic, such as age or ethnicity. Such interest groups lobby for legislation that may benefit their members in terms of rights or just represent a viewpoint.

The AARP, as mentioned earlier, is one of the most powerful interest groups in Washington, D.C., and, according to some, the strongest lobbying group in the United States. It is certainly the nation's largest interest group, with a membership of over thirty-three million. The AARP has accomplished much for its members over the years. It played a significant role in the creation of Medicare and Medicaid, as well as in obtaining cost-of-living increases in Social Security payments. Today, though, the AARP is under attack. In part, this is because of the changed circumstances of today's older Americans. Whereas they were once among the poorer groups of our society, today they are, on average, among the country's wealthiest citizens. In other words, they no longer need special legislation to protect their welfare to the extent that they once did. Nonetheless, the AARP continues to pressure Congress for legislation that benefits this group of Americans.

Foreign Governments

Home-grown interests are not the only players in the game. Washington, D.C., is also the center for lobbying by foreign governments as well as private foreign interests. Large research and lobbying staffs are maintained by governments of the largest U.S. trading partners, such as Japan, South Korea, Canada, and the European Union (EU) countries. Even smaller nations, such as those in the Caribbean, engage lobbyists when vital legislation affecting their trade interests is considered. Frequently, these foreign interests hire former representatives or former senators to promote their positions on Capitol Hill. As discussed in the feature *Which Side Are You On?* lobbying by foreign nations is intense and rarely visible to the general public.

Interest Group Strategies

Interest groups employ a wide range of techniques and strategies to promote their policy goals. Although few groups are successful at persuading Congress and the president to endorse their programs completely, many are able to prevent—or at least weaken—legislation injurious to their members from being considered. The key to success for interest groups is the ability to have access to government officials. To achieve this, interest groups and their representatives try to cultivate long-term relationships with legislators and government officials. The best of such relationships are based on mutual respect and cooperation. The interest group provides the official with excellent sources of information and assistance, and the official in turn gives the group opportunities to express its views.

The techniques used by interest groups may be divided into direct and indirect techniques. With **direct techniques,** the interest group and its lobbyists approach the officials personally to press their case. With **indirect techniques,** in contrast, the interest group uses the general public or individuals to influence the government on behalf of the interest group.

which side are you on?

Should Foreign Nations Be Allowed to Lobby the U.S. Government?

Foreign nations and foreign-owned corporations and unions are permitted to lobby the U.S. government and are subject to the same registration requirements as domestic interests. Foreign corporations and noncitizens generally are not allowed to donate to political campaigns, however—although the 1996 election brought to light numerous ways that this restriction can be circumvented. Many foreign nations and corporations employ former senators and representatives to represent their interests in Congress and in agencies of the executive branch.

Is it fair to the American people for foreign companies and nations to be lobbying for trade agreements or other provisions that will increase their imports to this country? Labor unions long opposed the North American Free Trade Agreement (NAFTA) on the ground that it would allow American companies to shift manufacturing to Mexico and cost Americans their jobs. The same logic applies to trade. Because China has been granted trade concessions, will cheaper Chinese clothing adversely affect the American garment industry? Trade protectionists say that Congress should first represent American interests. Free trade advocates claim that opening trade to all nations expands the market for American goods and should increase jobs.

Foreign nations also lobby the U.S. Congress and executive branch on national security issues. Although most Americans pay very little attention to conflicts between other nations, those nations vie for support, foreign aid, military assistance, and favor from the U.S. government. Both India and Pakistan have now developed and tested nuclear weapons and the missile technology to deliver the weapons. Both nations have launched serious lobbying efforts in Washington, D.C., to obtain attention and support from the United States. Should such nations, which are virtually at war, be allowed to lobby members of Congress to get the United States involved in their disputes? Israel, Greece, and Taiwan have long maintained similar efforts to advance their interests.

DOES IT MATTER?

Does it matter to you personally whether foreign nations are allowed to lobby for economic and security interests, or should their lobbying be restricted or prohibited? What about foreign corporations, including foreign corporations that own American companies, such as DaimlerChrysler?

GOING ONLINE

For some background on these issues, check the following Web sites: **http://www.policy.com** *and* **http://www.foreignpolicy.com.**

Direct Techniques

Lobbying, publicizing ratings of legislative behavior, and providing campaign assistance are the three main direct techniques used by interest groups.

Lobbying Techniques.   As might be guessed, the term *lobbying* comes from the activities of private citizens regularly congregating in the lobbies of legislative chambers before a session to petition legislators. In the latter part of the nineteenth century, railroad and industrial groups openly bribed state legislators to pass legislation beneficial to their interests, giving lobbying a well-deserved bad name. Today, standard lobbying techniques still include buttonholing (detaining and engaging in conversation) senators and representatives in state capitols and in Washington, D.C., while they are moving from their offices to the voting chambers. (For an example of a new type of lobbyist, see this chapter's *Making Waves* on the next page.) Lobbyists, however, do much more than that.

Lobbyists engage in an array of activities to influence legislation and government policy. These include, at a minimum, the following:

1. Engaging in private meetings with public officials, including the president's advisers, to make known the interests of the lobbyist's clients. Although acting on behalf of their clients, often lobbyists furnish needed information to senators and representatives (and government agency appointees) that they could not

hope to obtain on their own. It is to the lobbyist's advantage to provide accurate information so that the policymaker will rely on this source in the future.

2. Testifying before congressional committees for or against proposed legislation being considered by Congress.

3. Testifying before executive rulemaking agencies—such as the Federal Trade Commission or the Consumer Product Safety Commission—for or against proposed rules.

4. Assisting legislators or bureaucrats in drafting legislation or prospective regulations. Often, lobbyists furnish legal advice on the specific details of legislation.

5. Inviting legislators to social occasions, such as cocktail parties, boating expeditions, and other events, including conferences at exotic locations. Most lobbyists feel that contacting legislators in a more relaxed social setting is effective.

6. Providing political information to legislators and other government officials. Often, the lobbyists will have better information than the party leadership about how other legislators are going to vote. In this case, the political information they furnish may be a key to legislative success.

7. Supplying nominations for federal appointments to the executive branch.

The Ratings Game.   Many interest groups attempt to influence the overall behavior of legislators through their rating systems. Each year, the interest group selects those votes on legislation that it feels are most important to the organization's goals. Each legislator is given a score based on the percentage of times that he or she voted in favor of the group's position. The usual scheme ranges from 0 to 100 percent. If a legislator has a score of, for example, 90 percent on the Americans for Democratic Action (ADA) rating, it means that he or she supported that group's position to a high degree. A legislator with such a high ADA score is usually considered to be very liberal. In 1999, the ADA classified twenty-one of the forty-five Democratic senators as "Heroes" because they earned perfect scores of 100. Twenty-eight of the fifty-five Republicans fell into the ADA's "Zeros" category because of their "zero" scores. Such large numbers of "Heroes" and "Zeros" reflected the extreme partisanship and ideological division that characterized the Senate that year.

making waves

A New Kind of Lobbyist

As the information technology industry exploded during the 1990s, most of the leaders of the new businesses in Silicon Valley avoided contact with Washington, D.C., and the politics of influence. Generally, they were very young, and because their industry had little contact with government regulation, they saw no reason to get involved in lobbying. One of the industry leaders, Stephen Case, chief executive officer (CEO) of America Online (which is now known as AOL/Time Warner), took a different path.

Case joined AOL, a struggling Internet access company, in 1983. Although the company nearly failed several times in the intervening years, Case has been a pioneer both in building relationships with powerful political leaders and in building his company's business. When members of Congress first began to write legislation to control pornography on the Internet, Case hired lobbyists to work against such legislation. At the same time, AOL began developing software to allow parents to control their children's access to the Internet. Case was among the first software leaders to cooperate with the government in tracking down sexual predators who used the Internet.

From his headquarters in northern Virginia—not Silicon Valley—Case was the first to see the need for intensive lobbying of Congress and the executive branch to protect his company's interests. He established personal relationships with important members of Congress and with political officials, including President Bill Clinton. At the same time, he supported charity work and built a positive image for his firm by such measures as appointing former general Colin Powell to his board. Clearly, Stephen Case is providing new directions for his rapidly growing industry.

FOR CRITICAL ANALYSIS

What are some of the issues involving Internet companies that are likely to come before Congress and the executive branch?

Other groups that use rating systems range from the American Conservative Union to the League of Conservation Voters (an environmental group). Each year, the latter group identifies the twelve legislators having what it sees as the worst records on environmental issues and advertises them as the "Dirty Dozen."

Campaign Assistance.   Interest groups have additional strategies to use in their attempts to influence government policies. Groups recognize that the greatest concern of legislators is to be reelected, so they focus on the legislators' campaign needs. Associations with large memberships, such as labor unions or the National Education Association, are able to provide workers for political campaigns, including precinct workers to get out the vote, volunteers to put up posters and pass out literature, and people to staff telephone banks for campaign headquarters.

In many states where certain interest groups have large memberships, candidates vie for the groups' endorsements in the campaign. Gaining those endorsements may be automatic, or it may require that the candidates participate in debates or interviews with the interest groups. Endorsements are important because an interest group usually publicizes its choices in its membership publication and because the candidate can use the endorsement in her or his campaign literature. Traditionally, labor unions such as the AFL-CIO and the Teamsters have endorsed Democratic Party candidates. Republican candidates, however, often try to persuade union locals at least to refrain from any endorsement. Making no endorsement can then be perceived as disapproval of the Democratic Party candidate.

Interest Groups: The Candidates of Choice

As expected, interest groups played a significant role in the 2000 elections, in both the presidential and congressional campaigns. Big business and especially the tobacco, oil, and health-care industries were eager to help Republicans get elected and thus reduce the threat of more regulation for their business ventures. Although both Bush and Gore downplayed their views on abortion, the abortion rights forces argued that a Gore presidency would ensure a friendly Supreme Court with respect to protecting a woman's right to choose. The National Rifle Association weighed in heavily in states where hunting is a popular sport, sponsoring ads opposing Gore and Democrats who would support stricter gun laws. On election day, the rank and file of organized labor put forward an effective "get out the vote" campaign, probably winning Pennsylvania, Michigan, and Wisconsin for Vice President Gore.

PACs and Political Campaigns.   In the last two decades, the most important form of campaign help from interest groups has become the political contribution from a group's **political action committee (PAC).** The 1974 Federal Election Campaign Act and its 1976 amendments allow corporations, labor unions, and other interest groups to set up PACs to raise money for candidates. For a PAC to be legitimate, the money must be raised from at least fifty volunteer donors and must be given to at least five candidates in the federal election. PACs can contribute up to $5,000 to each candidate in each election. Each corporation or each union is limited to one PAC. As you might imagine, corporate PACs obtain funds from executives in their firms, and unions obtain PAC funds from their members.

The number of PACs has grown significantly since 1977, as has the amount they spend on elections. There were about 1,000 PACs in 1976; by 1998, there were more than 4,500 (see Figure 8–2 on the next page). Total spending by PACs

Political Action Committee (PAC)
A committee set up by and representing a corporation, labor union, or special interest group. PACs raise and give campaign donations on behalf of the organizations or groups they represent.

grew from $19 million in 1973 to an estimated $470 million in 1997–1998. Of all of the campaign money spent by House candidates in 1998, about 32 percent came from PACs.[4]

Interest groups funnel PAC money to the candidates they think can do the most good for them. Frequently, they make the maximum contribution of $5,000 per election to candidates who face little or no opposition. The summary of PAC contributions given in Figure 8–3 shows that the great bulk of campaign contributions goes to incumbent candidates rather than to challengers. Table 8–2 shows the amounts contributed by the top twenty PACs.

Some PACs give most of their contributions to candidates of one party. Other PACs, particularly corporate PACs, tend to give money to Democrats in Congress as well as to Republicans, because Democratic incumbents may again chair important committees or subcommittees. Why, might you ask, would business leaders give to Democrats who may be more liberal than themselves? Interest groups see PAC contributions as a way to ensure access to powerful legislators, even though the groups may disagree with the legislators some of the time. PAC contributions are, in a way, an investment in a relationship. (For a further discussion of this issue, see the feature *Politics and Economics: What Does Soft Money Buy?* on page 266.)

The campaign-finance regulations clearly limit the amount that a PAC can give to any one candidate, but there is no limit on the amount that a PAC can spend on issue advocacy, either on behalf of a candidate or party or in opposition to one (see Chapter 10).

Indirect Techniques

Interest groups can try to influence government policy by working through third parties—who may be constituents, the general public, or other groups. Indirect techniques mask the interest group's own activities and make the effort

FIGURE 8-2

PAC Growth, 1977 to 2001

This figure shows the significant increase in PACs since 1977 as well as the large number of corporate PACs relative to PACs that are sponsored by other types of organizations.

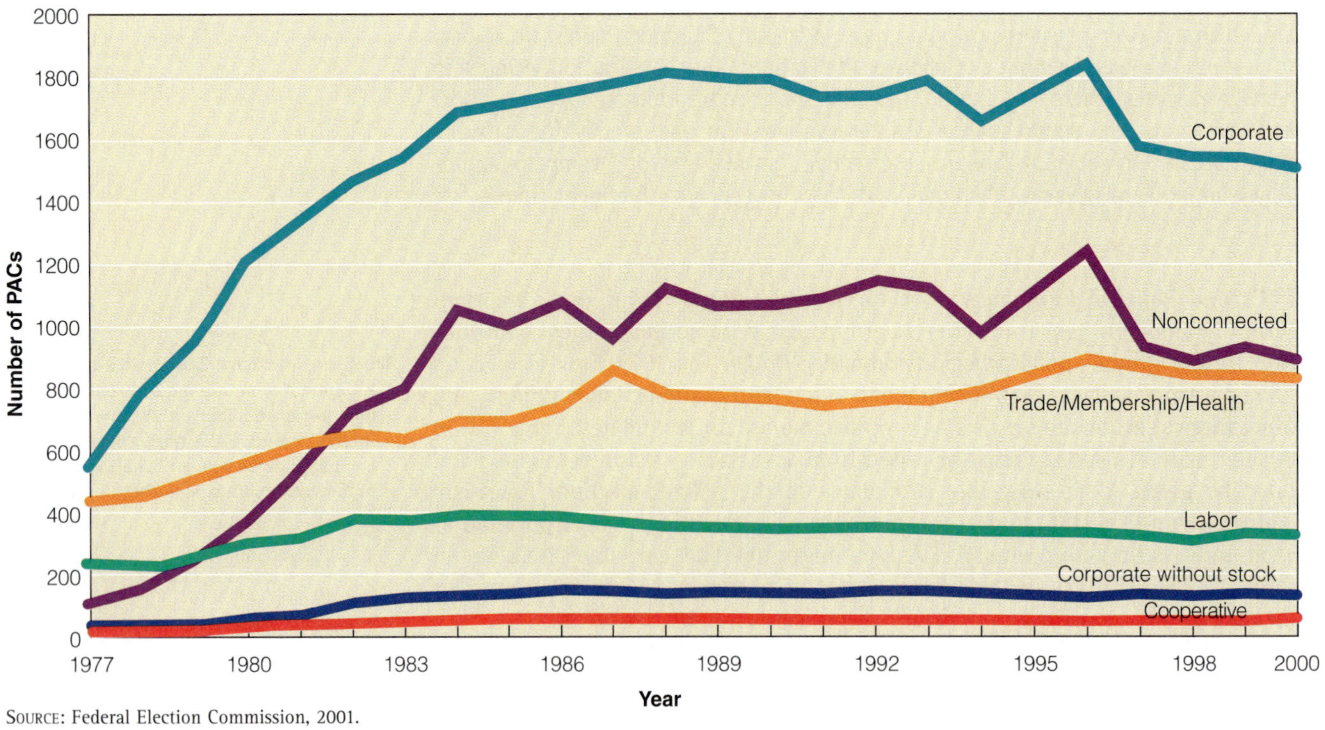

SOURCE: Federal Election Commission, 2001.

FIGURE 8-3

**PAC Contributions to Congressional
Candidates, 1988 to 2000**

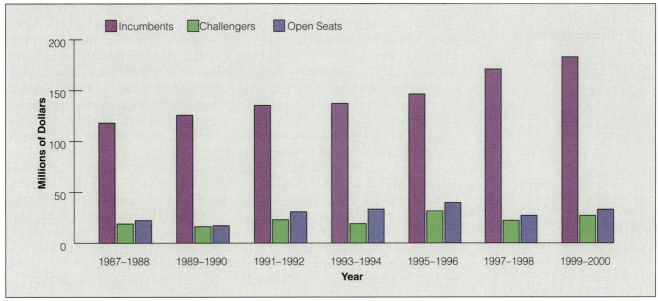

SOURCE: *Federal Election Commission Report,* 2001.

TABLE 8-2

The Top Twenty PAC Contributors, 1999–2000 Election Cycle

RANK	CONTRIBUTOR	TOTAL CONTRIBUTIONS	TO DEMOCRATS	TO REPUBLICANS
1	American Federation of State, County, and Municipal Employees	$8,521,119	98%	1%
2	Service Employees International Union	$6,163,010	96%	4%
3	AT&T	$5,044,318	42%	58%
4	Carpenters & Joiners Union	$4,754,083	94%	6%
5	Microsoft Corp.	$4,611,476	47%	52%
6	Bank of America	$4,428,333	82%	18%
7	International Brotherhood of Electrical Workers	$4,285,034	98%	2%
8	Goldman Sachs Group	$4,073,857	69%	31%
9	United Food & Commercial Workers Union	$3,909,161	99%	1%
10	Communications Workers of America	$3,871,385	99%	0%
11	National Association of Realtors	$3,842,950	41%	59%
12	Citigroup, Inc.	$3,775,316	54%	46%
13	SBC Communications	$3,717,716	45%	55%
14	Association of Trial Lawyers of America	$3,618,750	90%	10%
15	MBNA America Bank	$3,545,555	14%	86%
16	Philip Morris	$3,508,950	19%	81%
17	Verizon Communications	$3,478,220	36%	63%
18	American Federation of Teachers	$3,271,555	99%	1%
19	United Parcel Service	$3,136,569	26%	73%
20	Laborers Union	$3,125,565	93%	7%

SOURCE: Federal Election Commission, 2001.

Letters, We Get Letters
Grassroot Lobbying

Climate Control
The use of public relations techniques to create favorable public opinion toward an interest group, industry, or corporation.

appear to be spontaneous. Furthermore, legislators and government officials are often more impressed by contacts from constituents than from an interest group's lobbyist.

Generating Public Pressure.   In some instances, interest groups try to produce a "ground swell" of public pressure to influence the government. Such efforts may include advertisements in national magazines and newspapers, mass mailings, television publicity, and demonstrations. The Internet and satellite links make communication efforts even more effective (see this chapter's feature *E-mocracy: Interests and the Internet* for a discussion of this topic). Interest groups may commission polls to find out what the public's sentiments are and then publicize the results. The intent of this activity is to convince policymakers that public opinion overwhelmingly supports the group's position.

Some corporations and interest groups also engage in a practice that might be called **climate control**. With this strategy, public relations efforts are aimed at improving the public image of the industry or group and are not necessarily related to any specific political issue. Contributions by corporations and groups in support of public television programs, sponsorship of special events, and commercials extolling the virtues of corporate research are examples of climate control. By building a reservoir of favorable public opinion, groups believe it less likely that their legislative goals will be met with opposition by the public.

Using Constituents as Lobbyists.   One of the most effective interest group activities is the use of constituents to lobby for the group's goals. In the "shotgun" approach, the interest group tries to mobilize large numbers of constituents to write, phone, or send e-mail to their legislators or the president. Often, the group provides postcards or form letters for constituents to fill out and mail. These efforts are only effective on Capitol Hill when there is an extraordinary number of responses, because legislators know that the voters did not initiate the communications on their own.

politics and economics

What Does Soft Money Buy?

American organizations spent more than $480 million in soft money contributions to political campaigns in the 2000 election cycle. (As you will learn in Chapter 10, the term *soft money* refers to contributions to political parties and other political committees that are not regulated by the campaign-finance laws.) The goal of these contributions was to elect members of Congress and other officials who would be friendly to business. A recent study by the Business-Industry Political Action Committee (BIPAC) found that soft money did not have much impact on who was elected. Of course, in 2000 Democrats actually gained seats in the House of Representatives, often defeating candidates who were more business-friendly.

ACCESS TO LEGISLATORS

Soft money contributions are successful in one very important way, however: winning candidates are more likely to grant access to companies that have been strong supporters. Legislators are likely to hear from and listen to companies that are soft money contributors. Because of the importance of such access, many industries—including telecommunications, agriculture, banking, insurance, and real estate—give almost equally to Republicans and Democrats so that access is assured no matter which party is in control of Congress.

OTHER SPENDING OPTIONS

The BIPAC study suggested, however, that companies should rethink their funding strategy to follow the model of labor unions. Companies should target more of their spending on political activities to registering voters, especially their own employees and their families; educating those voters on the issues that affect business; and then getting out the vote. Winning more votes for business-friendly candidates is the most effective way for companies to influence the makeup of Congress. Such activities cost money, of course, but they cost only a fraction of what is given away in soft money contributions.

FOR CRITICAL ANALYSIS

Do you think employees would welcome pressure from their employer to register and vote?

A more influential variation of this technique uses only important constituents. Known as the "rifle" technique, or the "Utah plant manager's theory," the interest group contacts an influential constituent, such as the manager of a local plant in Utah, to contact the senator from Utah.[5] Because the constituent is seen as being responsible for many jobs or other resources, the legislator is more likely to listen carefully to the constituent's concerns about legislation than to a paid lobbyist.

Building Alliances.   Another indirect technique used by interest groups is to form an alliance with other groups concerned about the same legislation. Often, these groups will set up a paper organization with an innocuous name to represent their joint concerns. In one case, for example, environmental, labor, and consumer groups, formed an alliance called the Citizens Trade Campaign to oppose the passage of the North American Free Trade Agreement in 1993. Members of such an alliance share expenses and multiply the influence of their individual groups by combining their efforts. Other advantages of such an alliance are that it looks as if larger public interests are at stake, and it blurs the

---

[5]Kay Lehman Schlozman and John T. Tierney, *Organized Interests and American Democracy* (New York: Harper & Row, 1986), p. 293.

Interests and the Internet

The Internet may have a strong equalizing effect in the world of lobbying and government influence. The first organizations to use electronic means to reach their constituents and drum up support for action were the large economic coalitions, including the Chamber of Commerce and the National Association of Manufacturers. Groups such as these, as well as those representing a single product such as tobacco, quickly realized that they could set up Web sites and mailing lists to provide information more rapidly to their members. Members could check the Web every day to see how legislation was developing in Congress or anywhere in the world. National associations could send e-mail to all of their members with one keystroke, mobilizing them to contact their representatives in Congress.

SPECIAL INTEREST GROUPS GO ONLINE

The next interest groups to become "wired" were the large "special interests," such as the National Rifle Association, the religious right, and other groups with strongly committed members. Like the business interests, they use the Web to provide information to their members and to spur members to take action. For example, the Christian Coalition maintains a Web site that allows members to customize letters to their legislators online and send them electronically. These and other groups believe that swamping a member's office with e-mail is less burdensome to congressional staff than "snail mail" or telephone calls and just as effective in voicing their concerns.

A BOON FOR SMALL GROUPS

Recently, it has become obvious that the Internet can level the playing field for small organizations. In the weeks before President Clinton designated millions of acres of Utah as the Grand Staircase–Escalante National Monument, a very small group called the Southern Utah Wilderness Alliance used its Web site to trigger thousands of letters to the White House supporting the action. Low-budget organizations that rely on volunteer time and energy can build Web sites and mailing lists that are as effective as those of large lobbying groups. E-mail is virtually free compared to standard mailing costs, and the communication link is instantaneous. As Rob Portman, a Republican member of Congress from Ohio, noted, "It's real-time. You get the message more quickly."*

Interest groups have different views on the efficacy of Internet communications. Most believe that to be effective, groups and constituents still need to make direct contact with legislators. Small groups that cannot travel to Washington view the matter differently: they now have a way to make their voices heard.

FOR CRITICAL ANALYSIS

Think about the reaction of a legislator who is trying to decide how to vote on an issue. Which form of communication— e-mail, telephone calls, mail, or personal visits—would likely be most effective in swaying the legislator's vote?

*As quoted in David Hosansky, "Phone Banks to E-Mail," *Congressional Quarterly Weekly Report,* November 29, 1997, p. 2942.

specific interests of the individual groups involved. These alliances also are efficient devices for keeping like-minded groups from duplicating one another's lobbying efforts.

Regulating Lobbyists

Congress made its first attempt to control lobbyists and lobbying activities through Title III of the Legislative Reorganization Act of 1946, otherwise known as the Federal Regulation of Lobbying Act. The act actually provided for public disclosure more than for regulation, and it neglected to specify which agency would enforce its provisions. The 1946 legislation defined a lobbyist as any person or organization that received money to be used principally to influence legislation before Congress. Such persons and individuals were supposed to "register" their clients and the purposes of their efforts, and report quarterly on their activities.

The legislation was tested in a 1954 Supreme Court case, *United States v. Harriss*,[6] and was found to be constitutional. The Court agreed that the lobbying law did not violate due process, freedom of speech or of the press, or the freedom to petition. The Court narrowly construed the act, however, holding that it applied only to lobbyists who were influencing federal legislation *directly*.

The Results of the 1946 Act

The result of the act was that a minimal number of individuals registered as lobbyists. National interest groups, such as the National Rifle Association and the American Petroleum Institute, could employ hundreds of staff members who were, of course, working on legislation but only register one or two lobbyists who were engaged *principally* in influencing Congress. There were no reporting requirements for lobbying the executive branch, federal agencies, the courts, or congressional staff. Approximately seven thousand individuals and organizations registered annually as lobbyists, although most experts estimated that ten times that number were actually employed in Washington to exert influence on the government.

The Reforms of 1995

The reform-minded Congress of 1995–1996 overhauled the lobbying legislation, fundamentally changing the ground rules for those who seek to influence the federal government. Lobbying legislation, passed in 1995, included the following provisions:

1. A lobbyist is defined as anyone who spends at least 20 percent of his or her time lobbying members of Congress, their staffs, or executive-branch officials.
2. Lobbyists must register with the clerk of the House and the secretary of the Senate within forty-five days of being hired or of making their first contact. The registration requirement applies to organizations that spend more than $20,000 in one year or to individuals who are paid more than $5,000 annually for their work.
3. Semiannual reports must disclose the general nature of the lobbying effort, specific issues and bill numbers, the estimated cost of the campaign, and a list of the branches of government contacted. The names of the individuals contacted need not be reported.
4. Representatives of U.S.–owned subsidiaries of foreign-owned firms and lawyers who represent foreign entities also are required to register for the first time.
5. The requirements exempt "grassroots" lobbying efforts and those of tax-exempt organizations, such as religious groups.

---

[6]347 U.S. 612 (1954).

The 1995 law was expected to increase the number of registered lobbyists by three to ten times what it was then. It made the connections between organizations and specific issues much clearer in the reporting process. The major exemption for grassroots campaigns, however, was expected to cause interest groups to divert major resources to organizing the folks back home so that they can exert pressure on Congress.

Concurrently with the debate on the 1995 law, both the House and the Senate adopted new rules on gifts and travel expenses: the House adopted a flat ban on gifts, and the Senate limited gifts to $50 in value and to no more than $100 in gifts from a single source in a year. There are exceptions for gifts from family members and for home-state products and souvenirs, such as T-shirts and coffee mugs. Both chambers ban all-expenses-paid trips, golf outings, and other such junkets. An exception applies for "widely attended" events, however, or if the member is a primary speaker at an event. These gift rules stopped the broad practice of taking members of Congress to lunch or dinner, but the various exemptions and exceptions undoubtedly will cause much controversy as individual cases are decided by the Senate and House Ethics Committees in future years.

INFOTRAC®
COLLEGE EDITION

How Become Top Banana

Interest Groups and Representative Democracy

The significant role played by interest groups in shaping national policy has caused many to question whether we really have a democracy at all. To be sure, most interest groups have a middle-class or upper-class bias. Members of interest groups can afford to pay the membership fees, are generally fairly well educated, and normally participate in the political process to a greater extent than the "average" American. Furthermore, leaders of interest groups tend to constitute an "elite within an elite" in the sense that they usually are from a higher social class than their members. The most powerful interest groups—those with the most resources and political influence—are primarily business, trade, or professional groups. In contrast, public interest groups or civil rights groups make up only a small percentage of the interest groups lobbying Congress.

Remember from Chapter 1 that the elite theory of politics presumes that most Americans are uninterested in politics and are willing to let a small, elite group of citizens make decisions for them. Pluralist theory, in contrast, views politics as a struggle among various interest groups to gain benefits for their members. The pluralist approach views compromise among various competing interests as the essence of political decision making. In reality, neither theory describes American politics very accurately. If interest groups led by elite, upper-class individuals are the dominant voices in Congress, then what we see is a conflict among elite groups—which would support the elitist theory, not a pluralist approach.

The results of lobbying efforts—congressional legislation—do not always favor the interests of the most powerful groups, however. In part, this is because not all interest groups have an equal influence on government. Each group has a different combination of resources to use in the policymaking process. While some groups are composed of members who have high social status and enormous economic resources, such as the National Association of Manufacturers, other groups derive influence from their large memberships. The AARP, for example, has more members than any other interest group. Its large membership allows it to wield significant power over legislators. Still other groups, such as environmentalists, have causes that can claim strong public support even from people who have no direct stake in the issue. Groups such as the National Rifle Association are well organized and have highly motivated members. This enables them to channel a stream of mail or electronic messages toward Congress with a few days' effort.

"A very special interest to see you, Senator."

Even the most powerful interest groups do not always succeed in their demands. Whereas the National Chamber of Commerce may be accepted as having a justified interest in the question of business taxes, many legislators might feel that the group should not engage in the debate over the future of Social Security. In other words, groups are seen as having a legitimate concern in the issues closest to their interests but not necessarily in broader issues. This may explain why some of the most successful groups are those that focus on very specific issues—such as tobacco farming, funding of abortions, or handgun control—and do not get involved in larger conflicts.

Complicating the question of interest group influence is the fact that many groups' lobbyists are former colleagues, friends, or family members of current members of Congress. Do these lobbyists wield more influence over congressional policymaking than the wishes of constituents? For a discussion of this question and similar issues, see the feature *An Ethical Issue: Lobbyists as Friends and Relatives.*

Interest Groups: Issues for the Twenty-First Century

The role of interest groups in American politics has been in question since the writing of the Constitution. James Madison, among many others, worried about how to control the "mischiefs of faction" while recognizing that the very business of a democracy is to resolve the conflicts between interests. Today, the power of interest groups is probably greater than ever before. PACs sponsored by interest groups are able to raise and spend huge amounts of money to support candidates and parties. Politicians admit that such support buys access, if not influence. Groups use modern technology, and increasingly the Internet, to rally their members. And Congress seems unable to get beyond the adjudication of interests to write policy for the good of all.

In the future, Americans will consider whether to limit the role that interest groups can play in campaigns and elections either by reducing the financial support these groups can give or by eliminating that influence altogether through some public financing scheme. Then, all taxpayers would support campaigns rather than special groups. It is unlikely that there will be any attempt to limit severely the contact that groups have with political decision makers, because their right to access is protected by the First Amendment to the Constitution. Lobbyists could, however, be required to report every contact publicly; interest groups could be required to make public the amount that they spend on attempts to influence government; or the use of the media by specialized groups for their own interest could be regulated.

The existence of interest groups, nonetheless, has great advantages for a democracy. By participating in such groups, individual citizens are empowered to influence government in ways far beyond the ballot. Groups do increase the interest and participation of voters in the system. And, without a doubt, these groups can protect the rights of minorities through their access to all branches of the government. Thus, the future could see a continued expansion of interest groups. No doubt, numerous groups, particularly among segments of society that have been left out of the debate, will take advantage of the Internet to promote their interests at lower cost. In any event, given the structure of the government with its pluralist enticements for group struggle, it is unlikely that these political associations will disappear soon.

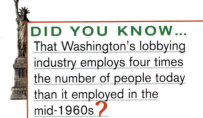

INFOTRAC®
COLLEGE EDITION

Mother's Milk, Elections

an ethical issue

Lobbyists as Friends and Relatives

Anyone can be hired to represent the interests of a group or company to members of Congress or the executive branch. In fact, though, many of the individuals who are most sought after as lobbyists are former members of the House, former senators, former employees of Congress or the White House, or relatives of sitting members of Congress.

Why are these individuals so valuable as lobbyists? Former members of Congress have certain privileges on Capitol Hill, including the right to meet in rooms restricted to members of Congress. More important, former members of Congress and their aides are thought to have a wide network of friends and colleagues on Capitol Hill with whom they can meet and socialize. One of the most powerful lobbying groups in Washington, D.C., is the law firm of Verner, Liipfert, Bernhard, McPherson & Hand, which employs former senators Bob Dole (Republican) and George Mitchell (Democrat), and former Texas governor Ann Richards (Democrat). Among the relatives of members of Congress or other officials in the lobbying business in 2000 were Anthony Podesta, brother of an adviser to President Clinton; Linda Hall Daschle, wife of Senate minority leader Tom Daschle; and Randy DeLay, brother of House whip Tom DeLay.

The activities of these prominent Washingtonians raise some ethical issues. One issue concerns whether members of Congress are using their time in public service to build up their credentials for higher paying jobs as lobbyists later on. Another issue has to do with public trust: How should the Kansas constituents of former senator Bob Dole see his activities as a lobbyist for causes that he might have opposed when he was their senator? And, most important, do former members of Congress and current family members have special access to their colleagues based on social ties that makes their lobbying efforts more effective than the efforts of voters or constituents back home? Is it ethical for a member of Congress to be swayed by her or his friendship with a former colleague instead of making a personal decision based on facts or on constituent preferences? One of the chief assets that lobbyists have is the trust of their colleagues, trust that earns them a very good living.

FOR CRITICAL ANALYSIS

Do you think that it is possible for members of Congress to listen to the arguments of old friends and colleagues impartially? Do you think that prior commitments and friendships might have an impact on political decisions?

making a difference

The Gun Control Issue

Is the easy availability of handguns a major cause of crime? Do people have a right to possess firearms to defend home and hearth? These questions are part of a long-term and heated battle between organized pro-firearm and anti-firearm camps. The disagreements run deeply and reflect strong sentiments on both sides. The fight is fueled by the one million gun incidents occurring in the United States each year—the murders, suicides, assaults, accidents, robberies, and injuries in which guns are involved. In 1999, the Columbine High School shootings in Colorado brought the debate to a fever pitch.

New issues in the debate concern child safety features on guns and the regulation of gun dealers who sell firearms at gun shows. Proponents of gun control seek safety locks and more restrictions on gun purchases—if not a ban on them entirely—while decreasing existing arsenals of privately owned weapons. Proponents of firearms claim that firearms are a cherished tradition, a constitutional right, and a vital defense need for individuals. They contend that the problem lies not in the sale and ownership of the weapons themselves but in the criminal use of firearms.

The National Coalition to Ban Handguns favors a total ban, taking the position that handguns "serve no valid purpose, except to kill people." Such a ban is opposed by the National Rifle Association of America (NRA). The NRA, founded in 1871, is currently one of the most powerful single-issue groups on the American political scene, representing the seventy million gun owners in the United States. The NRA claims, among other things, that a gun law won't reduce the number of crimes. It is illogical to assume, according to the NRA, that persons who refuse to obey laws prohibiting rape, murder, and other crimes will obey a gun law.

A matter of particular concern to many Americans is the increase in crimes involving guns among younger Americans. Many proponents of gun control insist that controlling the purchase of weapons would reduce the availability of guns to children. In response to these efforts, some states have passed laws that hold adults liable for not locking away their firearms. In addition, a number of cities have sued gun manufacturers for not controlling the flow of their products to unscrupulous dealers who sell guns to criminals and gang members in inner-city areas.

Tougher gun control laws are on the legislative agenda in Congress and in most states. To find out more about the NRA's position, contact that organization at the following address:

The National Rifle Association
11250 Waples Mill Rd.
Fairfax, VA 22030
703-267-1000

http://www.nra.org

If, however, you are concerned with the increase in gun-related crimes and feel that stricter gun laws are necessary, you can get involved through the following organizations:

The Coalition to Stop Gun Violence
1000 16th St. N.W., Suite 603
Washington, DC 20036
202-530-0340

http://www.gunfree.org

Handgun Control, Inc.
1225 I St. N.W.
Suite 1100
Washington, DC 20006
202-898-0792

http://www.handguncontrol.org

Key terms

climate control 266

direct technique 260

indirect technique 260

interest group 249

labor movement 255

lobbyist 249

material incentive 251

political action committee
  (PAC) 263

public interest 258

purposive incentive 252

service sector 257

social movement 252

solidary incentive 251

Chapter summary

1 An interest group is an organization whose members share common objectives and who actively attempt to influence government policy. Interest groups proliferate in the United States because they can influence government at many points in the political structure and because they offer solidary, material, and purposive incentives to their members. Interest groups are often created out of social movements.

2 Major types of interest groups include business, agricultural, labor, public employee, professional, and environmental groups. Other important groups may be considered public-interest groups. In addition, special interest groups and foreign governments lobby the government.

3 Interest groups use direct and indirect techniques to influence government. Direct techniques include testifying before committees and rulemaking agencies, providing information to legislators, rating legislators' voting records, and making campaign contributions. Contributions are often made through political action committees, or PACs. Most PAC money is given to incumbents to ensure access for the group. Indirect techniques to influence government include campaigns to rally public sentiment, letter-writing campaigns, efforts to influence the climate of opinion, and the use of constituents to lobby for the group's interest.

4 The 1946 Legislative Reorganization Act was the first attempt to control lobbyists and their activities through registration requirements. The Supreme Court narrowly construed the act as applying only to lobbyists who directly seek to influence federal legislation.

5 In 1995, Congress approved new legislation requiring anyone who spends 20 percent of his or her time influencing legislation to register. Also, any organization spending $20,000 or more and any individual who is paid more than $5,000 annually for his or her work must register. Semiannual reports must include the name of clients, the bills in which they are interested, and the branches of government contacted. Grassroots lobbying and the lobbying efforts of tax-exempt organizations are exempt from the rules.

Selected print and electronic resources

SUGGESTED READINGS

Berry, Jeffrey M. *The Interest Group Society,* 3d ed. New York: Longman, 1997. This is an excellent overview and discussion of the ways in which interest groups and lobbies participate in the political system.

Biersack, Robert, Clyde Wilcox, and Paul Herrnson, eds. *After the Revolution: PACs, Lobbies, and the Republican Congress.* Reading, Mass.: Addison-Wesley, 1999. This collection of essays examines the lobbying tactics of a number of quite different interest groups.

Cammisa, Anne Marie. *Governments as Interest Groups: Intergovernmental Lobbying and the Federal System.* Westport, Conn.: Praeger Publishers, 1995. This book looks closely at the way state and local governments lobby Congress and the executive branch in regard to the writing of national policy that affects local governments. Housing policy, welfare policy, and child-care policy are examined with respect to the impact of state and local lobbying.

Goldstein, Kenneth M. *Interest Groups, Lobbying, and Participation in America.* Port Chester, N.Y.: Cambridge University Press, 1999. What motivates individuals to participate in interest groups? This volume looks at how leaders of interest groups recruit new members.

Kollman, Ken. *Outside Lobbying: Public Opinion and Interest Group Strategies.* Ewing, N.J.: Princeton University Press, 1998. This volume focuses on how groups rally public support for their positions.

Mollenkamp, Carrick, Adam Levy, Joseph Menn, and Jeffrey Rothfeder. *The People vs. Big Tobacco: How the States Took on the Cigarette Giants.* New York: Bloomberg Press, 1998. This book is a careful account of the conflicts and legal battles that led to the tobacco settlement.

Wilson, James Q. *Political Organizations* (with a new introduction to the 1974 edition). Princeton, N.J.: Princeton University Press, 1995. This is one of the classic works on the formation and membership of interest groups in American society. Wilson looks closely at the motivations of a group's members and the relationship of the members to the leaders of a group.

MEDIA RESOURCES

Norma Rae–A 1979 film about an attempt by a northern union organizer to unionize workers in the southern textile industry; stars Sally Field.

Silkwood–A 1979 film focusing on the story of a nuclear plant worker who attempted to investigate safety issues at the plant and ended up losing her job; stars Meryl Streep and Cher.

Washington under the Influence–A segment of the PBS series *On the Issues,* produced in 1993, in which ABC news correspondent Jeff Greenfield follows the trail of lobbyists, press leaks, and PAC money as a corporation faces Senate hearings following allegations that the company's popular product causes injury.

Logging on

Interest groups have established literally hundreds of sites that you can investigate. A good starting point is the Web site of Internet Public Library (IPL) Associations on the Net, which provides efficient access to more than six hundred professional and trade associations. Go to

http://www.ipl.org/ref/AON

There are numerous Web sites on the tobacco controversy. The following site offers links to many of them:

http://www.tobaccoresolution.com

Gun control opponents may want to visit the National Rifle Association's site at

http://www.nra.org

If you are interested in human rights worldwide, you can go to the site of Human Rights Watch at

http://www.hrw.org

There are a number of sites to visit to find information concerning environmental issues. The Environmental Defense Fund's site is

http://www.edf.org

You can also go to the National Resource Defense Council's site for information on environmental issues. Its URL is

http://www.nrdc.org

Using the Internet for political analysis

"Today in Perspective" is a site that allows you to look at both sides of an issue. Access this site at

http://www.iquest.net/~gtemp

Choose an issue, and compare the information resources given for both sides of that issue. Then critique the site for the breadth and depth of coverage on the issue. What other information might you need to form an opinion?

chapter 9
Political Parties

CHAPTER OUTLINE

- What Is a Political Party?

- Functions of Political Parties in the United States

- A Short History of Political Parties in the United States

- The Three Faces of a Party

- Party Organization

- The Party and Its Members

- The Party-in-Government

- Why Do We Have a Two-Party System?

- The Role of Minor Parties in U.S. Political History

what if...

Everyone Had to Join a Political Party?

BACKGROUND

AMERICAN POLITICAL PARTIES ARE VOLUNTARY ORGANIZATIONS. IN FACT, POLITICAL PARTIES IN THIS COUNTRY DO NOT CHARGE DUES OR SEND OUT MEMBERSHIP CARDS. IN SOME STATES, THEY DO TRY TO LIMIT PARTICIPATION IN POLITICAL PARTY CAUCUSES AND IN PRIMARY ELECTIONS TO PARTY MEMBERS IN ORDER TO BETTER CONTROL THE NOMINATING PROCESS. OTHER STATES, HOWEVER, ALLOW ANYONE—REPUBLICAN, DEMOCRAT, OR INDEPENDENT—TO VOTE IN THEIR PRIMARY ELECTIONS. POLITICAL PARTIES DO PLAY A VERY IMPORTANT ROLE IN THE SYSTEM BY FINDING AND NOMINATING CANDIDATES FOR OFFICE. THEY ALSO ORGANIZE POLITICAL CAMPAIGNS AND GET OUT THE VOTE AT EVERY LEVEL OF GOVERNMENT. IS IT FAIR AND IS IT HEALTHY FOR THE COUNTRY TO HAVE ONLY SOME OF THE PEOPLE INVOLVED IN THESE IMPORTANT PROCESSES? SHOULD ALL AMERICANS BE REQUIRED TO JOIN A POLITICAL PARTY?

WHAT IF JOINING A POLITICAL PARTY WAS REQUIRED?

The federal government could possibly require that all American citizens aged eighteen and older register a political party preference in order to vote. The government does, after all, require all males to register with the Selective Service, all parents of newborns to get Social Security numbers, and all individuals to pay taxes and to respond to the census. In the same way, the government could require all Americans, on reaching the age of eighteen, to choose a political party identity and register it at the local courthouse or other office.

To gain adherents, the political party organizations would have to be "recognized" officially by the federal government. They would probably have to file papers about their forms of organization and finances. Any organization that enlisted a specified number of registered voters would then be recognized as a party. The government might then support the parties with a tax check-off, similar to the one for presidential campaigns, based on the number of registered voters.

STRONGER PARTIES, STRONGER PLATFORMS

American political parties are usually viewed as weaker than their European counterparts because they lack a dues structure and have a rather weak relationship with their party members. If party membership were required, it is likely that members would play a greater role in selecting the leadership of the party and, perhaps, in writing the party platform, or statement of principles.

To encourage individuals to sign up, the parties would probably try to be more distinctive and truly offer prospective members a choice. Parties would seek support from eighteen-year-olds and newly nationalized citizens who agreed with their platforms. Each party would also be more likely to choose candidates who would follow its platform because the members would more closely identify with the party's principles. Those holding political offices would also be more likely to follow the party platform in order to win renomination.

Having more coherent, more disciplined parties would likely spur the formation of several new parties, because moderates and independents might not want to join the more coherent Democratic and Republican Parties. Special interests, such as farmers or environmentalists, might decide to form new parties to represent their concerns.

THE FREEDOM TO CHOOSE

Forcing everyone to join a political party, while increasing participation in the system, would also limit a basic American freedom—the freedom *not* to vote or support a party. One way that American voters demonstrate their unhappiness with the choices offered by the political parties is by not voting and not participating in the political process. Another way that Americans actually control the direction of political parties in the society is by voting against candidates and parties that are "off the track." In fact, the large independent, or swing, vote forces the parties to pay attention to those voters. Political parties constantly attempt to find candidates and structure campaign messages that will not only keep the votes of their own members but also attract independent voters. This forces the parties to moderate their more extreme positions and be attentive to the needs of a majority of voters, not just their members. If every American were forced to be a member of a political party, the parties would need to be more extreme, rather than more moderate, to attract members.

FOR CRITICAL ANALYSIS

1. Would requiring membership in a political party violate an individual's rights to privacy and freedom of expression?

2. Would required membership in political parties give the parties too much power over their candidates and officeholders?

What Is a Political Party?

Around election time, the polls and the media concentrate on the state of the political parties. Every poll asks the question, "Do you consider yourself to be a Republican, a Democrat, or an independent?" Most Americans are able to answer that question, and the number of persons who identify themselves as **independents** now exceeds 30 percent. If, as was suggested in the *What If . . .* that opens this chapter, all Americans were required to join a political party, there would likely be several middle-of-the-road parties that would woo independents.

Independent
A voter or candidate who does not identify with a political party.

In the United States, being a member of a political party does not require paying dues, passing an examination, or swearing an oath of allegiance. If nothing is really required to be a member of a political party, what, then, is a political party?

A **political party** might be formally defined as a group of political activists who organize to win elections, to operate the government, and to determine public policy. This definition explains the difference between an interest group and a political party. Interest groups do not want to operate government, and they do not put forth political candidates—even though they support candidates who will promote their interests if elected or reelected. Another important distinction is that interest groups tend to sharpen issues, whereas American political parties tend to blur their issue positions to attract voters.

Political Party
A group of political activists who organize to win elections, to operate the government, and to determine public policy.

Political parties differ from **factions,** which are smaller groups that are trying to obtain certain benefits for themselves.[1] Factions generally preceded the formation of political parties in American history, and the term is still used to refer to groups within parties that follow a particular leader or share a regional identification or an ideological viewpoint. The Republican Party sometimes is seen as having a northeastern "moderate" faction that holds more moderate positions than the dominant conservative majority of the party. Factions are subgroups within parties that may try to capture a nomination or get a position adopted by the party. The key difference between factions and parties is that factions do not have a permanent organization, whereas political parties do.

Faction
A group or bloc in a legislature or political party acting together in pursuit of some special interest or position.

Supporters of Al Gore and Joseph Lieberman lead the cheers for their presidential and vice presidential candidates during the 2000 Democratic National Convention.

Functions of Political Parties in the United States

Political parties in the United States engage in a wide variety of activities, many of which are discussed in this chapter. Through these activities, parties perform a number of functions for the political system. These functions include the following:

1. *Recruiting candidates for public office.* Because it is the goal of parties to gain control of government, they must work to recruit candidates for all elective offices. Often this means recruiting candidates to run against powerful incumbents or for unpopular jobs. Yet if parties did not search out and encourage political hopefuls, far more offices would be uncontested, and voters would have limited choices.

2. *Organizing and running elections.* Although elections are a government activity, political parties actually organize the voter-registration drives, recruit the volunteers to work at the polls, provide most of the campaign activity to stimulate interest in the election, and work to increase participation.

---

[1]See the comments on factions by James Madison in Chapter 2.

3. *Presenting alternative policies to the electorate.* In contrast to factions, which are often centered on individual politicians, parties are focused on a set of political positions. The Democrats or Republicans in Congress who vote together do so because they represent constituencies that have similar expectations and demands.

4. *Accepting responsibility for operating the government.* When a party elects the president or governor and members of the legislature, it accepts the responsibility for running the government. This includes staffing the executive branch with loyal party supporters and developing linkages among the elected officials to gain support for policies and their implementation.

5. *Acting as the organized opposition to the party in power.* The "out" party, or the one that does not control the government, is expected to articulate its own policies and oppose the winning party when appropriate. By organizing the opposition to the "in" party, the opposition party forces debate on the policy alternatives.

Students of political parties, such as Leon D. Epstein, point out that the major functions of American political parties are carried out by a small, relatively loose-knit **cadre,** or nucleus, of party activists.[2] This is quite a different arrangement from the more highly structured, mass-membership party organization typical of certain European working-class parties. American parties concentrate on winning elections rather than on signing up large numbers of deeply committed, dues-paying members who believe passionately in the party's program.

Cadre
The nucleus of political party activists carrying out the major functions of American political parties.

A Short History of Political Parties in the United States

Political parties in the United States have a long tradition dating back to the 1790s (see Figure 9–1). The function and character of these political parties, as well as the emergence of the two-party system itself, have much to do with the unique historical forces operating from this country's beginning as an independent nation. Indeed, James Madison linked the emergence of political parties to the form of government created by our Constitution.

Generally, we can divide the evolution of our nation's political parties into six periods:

1. The creation of parties, from 1789 to 1812.
2. The era of one-party rule, or personal politics, from 1816 to 1824.
3. The period from Andrew Jackson's presidency to just prior to the Civil War, from 1828 to 1860.
4. The post–Civil War period, from 1864 to 1892.
5. The progressive period, from 1896 to 1928.
6. The modern period, from 1932 to the present.

The Formative Years: Federalists and Anti-Federalists

The first partisan political division in the United States occurred prior to the adoption of the Constitution. The **Federalists** pushed for the adoption of the Constitution, whereas the **Anti-Federalists** were against ratification.

In September 1796, George Washington, who had served as president for almost two full terms, decided not to run again. In his farewell address, he made a somber assessment of the nation's future. Washington felt that the country

Federalists
The first American political party, led by Alexander Hamilton and John Adams. Many of its members had strongly supported the adoption of the new Constitution and the creation of the federal union.

Anti-Federalists
Those who opposed the adoption of the Constitution because of its centralist tendencies and attacked the failure of the Constitution's framers to include a bill of rights.

---

[2]*Political Parties in Western Democracies* (New Brunswick, N.J.: Transaction, 1980).

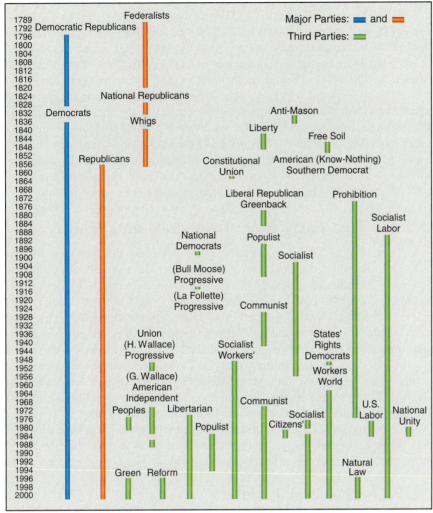

SOURCES: Congressional Quarterly, *Congressional Quarterly's Guide to U.S. Elections,* 2d ed. (Washington, D.C.: Congressional Quarterly Press, 1985), p. 224; *Congressional Quarterly Weekly Report* (1988), p. 3184; and J. David Gillespie, *Politics at the Periphery* (Columbia, S.C.: University of South Carolina Press, 1993); updated by authors.

FIGURE **9-1**

American Political Parties since 1789

The chart indicates the years that parties either ran presidential candidates or held national conventions. The life span for many political parties can only be approximated, because parties existed at the state or local level before they ran candidates in presidential elections, and parties continued to exist at local levels long after they ceased running presidential candidates. Not every party fielding a presidential candidate is represented in the chart.

might be destroyed by the "baneful effects of the spirit of party." He viewed parties as a threat to both national unity and the concept of popular government. Early in his career, Thomas Jefferson did not like political parties either. In 1789, he stated, "If I could not go to heaven but with a party, I would not go there at all."[3]

What Americans found out during the first decade or so after the ratification of the Constitution was that not even a patriot-king such as George Washington could govern by consensus. During this period, it became obvious to many that something more permanent than a faction would be necessary to identify candidates for the growing number of citizens who would be participating in elections. Thus, according to many historians, the world's first democratic political parties were established in this country. In 1800, when the Federalists lost the presidential election to the Democratic Republicans (also known as the Jeffersonian Republicans), one of the first peaceful transfers of power from one party to another was achieved.

Thomas Jefferson, founder of the Democratic Republicans. His election to the presidency in 1800 was decided in the House of Representatives, because no candidate won a majority of the electoral votes.

---

[3]Letter to Francis Hopkinson written from Paris while Jefferson was minister to France. In John P. Foley, ed., *The Jeffersonian Cyclopedia* (New York: Russell & Russell, 1967), p. 677.

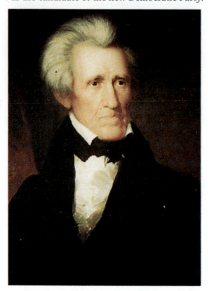

Andrew Jackson earned the name "Old Hickory" for his exploits during the War of 1812. In 1828, Jackson was elected president as the candidate of the new Democratic Party.

Era of Personal Politics
The years from 1816 to 1828, when attention centered on the character of individual candidates rather than on party identification.

Era of Good Feeling
The years from 1817 to 1825, when James Monroe was president and there was, in effect, no political opposition.

Democratic Party
One of the two major American political parties evolving out of the Democratic (Jeffersonian) Republican group supporting Thomas Jefferson.

Whig Party
One of the foremost political organizations in the United States during the first half of the nineteenth century, formally established in 1836. The Whig Party was dominated by the same anti-Jackson elements that organized the National Republican faction within the Democratic (Jeffersonian) Republicans and represented a variety of regional interests. It fell apart as a national party in the early 1850s.

Republican Party
One of the two major American political parties, which emerged in the 1850s as an antislavery party. It was created to fill the vacuum caused by the disintegration of the Whig Party.

The Era of Personal Politics

From 1816 to 1828, a majority of U.S. voters regularly elected Democratic Republicans to the presidency and to Congress. Two-party competition did not really exist. This was the so-called **era of personal politics,** when attention centered on the character of individual candidates rather than on party identification. Although during elections the Democratic Republicans opposed the Federalists' call for a stronger, more active central government, they acquired the Louisiana Territory and Florida, established a national bank, enforced a higher tariff (tax on imports), and resisted European intrusion into the Western Hemisphere. Because there was no real political opposition to the dominant Democratic Republicans and thus little political debate, the administration of James Monroe (1817–1825) came to be known as the **era of good feeling.**

National Two-Party Rule: Democrats and Whigs

During the era of personal politics, one-party rule did not prevent the Democratic Republican factions from competing against each other. Indeed, there was quite a bit of intraparty rivalry. Finally, in 1824 and 1828, Democratic Republicans who belonged to the factions of Henry Clay and John Quincy Adams split with the rest of the party to oppose Andrew Jackson in those elections. Jackson's supporters and the Clay-Adams bloc formed separate parties, the **Democratic Party** and the **Whig Party,** respectively. That same Democratic Party is now the oldest continuing political party in the Western world.

The Whigs were those Democratic Republicans who were often called the "National Republicans." At the national level, the Whigs were able to elect two presidents—William Henry Harrison in 1840 and Zachary Taylor in 1848. The Whigs, however, were unable to maintain a common ideological base when the party became increasingly divided over the issue of slavery in the late 1840s. During the 1850s, the Whigs fell apart as a national party.

The Post–Civil War Period

The existing two-party system was disrupted by the election of 1860, in which there were four major candidates. Abraham Lincoln, the candidate of the newly formed **Republican Party,** was the victor with a majority of the electoral vote, although with only 39.9 percent of the popular vote. This newly formed Republican Party—not to be confused with the Democratic Republicans—was created in the mid-1850s from the various groups that sought to fill the vacuum left by the disintegration of the Whigs. It took the label of Grand Old Party, or GOP. Its first national convention was held in 1856, but its presidential candidate, John C. Frémont, lost.

After the end of the Civil War, the South became heavily Democratic (the Solid South), and the North became heavily Republican. This era of Republican dominance was highlighted by the election of 1896, when the Republicans, emphasizing economic development and modernization under William McKinley, resoundingly defeated the Democratic and Populist candidate, William Jennings Bryan. The Republicans' control was solidified by winning over the urban working-class vote in northern cities. From the election of Abraham Lincoln until the election of Franklin D. Roosevelt in 1932, the Republicans won all but four presidential elections.

The Progressive Movement

In 1912, a major schism occurred in the Republican Party when former Republican president Theodore Roosevelt campaigned for the presidency as a Progressive.

Consequently, there were three significant contenders in that presidential contest. Woodrow Wilson was the Democratic candidate, William Howard Taft was the regular Republican candidate, and Roosevelt was the Progressive candidate. The Republican split allowed Wilson to be elected. The Wilson administration, although Democratic, ended up enacting much of the Progressive Party's platform. Left without any reason for opposition, the Progressive Party collapsed in 1921.

Republican Warren Harding's victory in 1920 reasserted Republican domination of national politics until the Republicans' defeat by Franklin D. Roosevelt in 1932, in the depths of the Great Depression.

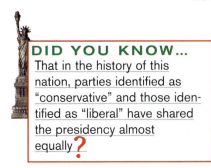

The Modern Era: From the New Deal to the Present

Franklin D. Roosevelt was elected in 1932 and reelected in 1936, 1940, and 1944. The impact of his successive Democratic administrations and the New Deal that he crafted is still with us today. Roosevelt used his enormous personal appeal to unify Democrats under his leadership, and he established direct communication between the president and the public through his radio fireside chats.[4] It wasn't until 1940 that the Republicans made even a small dent in the Democratic strength, when Wendell Willkie reduced Roosevelt's popular vote to 54.8 percent from the 60.5 percent and the 57.4 percent of the two previous elections.

In April 1945, Roosevelt died; Vice President Harry Truman became president through succession and, in 1948, through election. The New Deal coalition, under Truman's revised theme of the Fair Deal, continued. Not until Republican Dwight Eisenhower won the 1952 election did the Democrats lose their control of the presidency. Eisenhower was reelected in 1956.

From 1960 through 1968, the Democrats, led first by John F. Kennedy and then by Lyndon B. Johnson, held national power. Republicans again gained control of the presidency with Richard Nixon's victory in 1968 and retained it in 1972, but they lost prestige and public support after the Watergate scandal forced Nixon's resignation on August 8, 1974. For this and other reasons, the Democrats were back in power after the presidential elections in 1976. But Democratic president Jimmy Carter was unable to win reelection against Ronald Reagan in 1980. The Republicans also gained control of the Senate in 1980 and retained it in the elections of 1982 and 1984. The 1984 reelection of Ronald Reagan appeared to some pollsters to signal the resurgence of the Republican Party as a competitive force in American politics as more people declared themselves to be Republicans than had done so in the previous several decades.

The election of George Bush in 1988 may have signaled the beginning of a true era of **divided government.** Republican Bush won the presidency, but his Republican Party lost seats in the House and Senate to Democrats. In 1992, Democrat Bill Clinton won the presidency, with Democratic control of the House and Senate, but his party actually lost congressional seats, presaging the Democrats' debacle in 1994 when the Republicans took control of both the House and the Senate. In 1996, Bill Clinton was reelected, but the voters returned Republicans to control in Congress. Republicans also controlled most of the governorships in the states. After the 2000 elections, divided government took on a new meaning. Although Republican George W. Bush won the presidency, Congress became almost evenly divided, with the Republicans holding a slim majority only in the House. Indeed, some observers speculated that such a strongly divided Congress could make it difficult to avoid endless stalemates.

Divided Government
A situation in which one major political party controls the presidency and the other controls the chambers of Congress, or in which one party controls a state governorship and the other controls the state legislature.

---

[4]One of the warm, informal talks by Franklin D. Roosevelt to a few million of his intimate friends—via the radio (see Chapter 11). Roosevelt's fireside chats were so effective that succeeding presidents have been urged by their advisers to emulate him by giving more radio and television reports to the nation.

William McKinley campaigns in 1896 on a platform draped with the flag. A century later candidates were still using the same type of decorations.

The Three Faces of a Party

Although American parties are known by a single name and, in the public mind, have a common historical identity, each party really has three major components. The first component is the **party-in-the-electorate.** This phrase refers to all those individuals who claim an attachment to the political party. They need not be members in the sense that they pay dues or even participate in election campaigns. Rather, the party-in-the-electorate is the large number of Americans who feel some loyalty to the party or who use partisanship as a cue to decide who will earn their vote. (See this chapter's *E-mocracy* for a discussion of how parties use the Internet to attract members.) As discussed in Chapter 7, most Americans who actually identify with one of the parties acquired that affiliation either as a result of their family upbringing or by coming of age during the era of their party's dominance. Party membership is not really a rational choice; rather, it is an emotional tie somewhat analogous to identifying with a region or a baseball team. Although individuals may hold a deep loyalty to or identification with a political party, there is no need for members of the party-in-the-electorate to speak out publicly, to contribute to campaigns, or to vote a straight party ticket. Needless to say, the party leaders pay close attention to the affiliation of their members in the electorate.

The second component, the **party organization,** provides the structural framework for the political party by recruiting volunteers to become party leaders; identifying potential candidates; and organizing caucuses, conventions, and election campaigns for its candidates. It is the party organization and its active workers that keep the party functioning between elections, as well as make sure that the party puts forth electable candidates and clear positions in the elections. When individuals accept paid employment for a political party, they are considered party professionals. Among that group are campaign consultants; fund-

Party-in-the-Electorate
Those members of the general public who identify with a political party or who express a preference for one party over the other.

Party Organization
The formal structure and leadership of a political party, including election committees; local, state, and national executives; and paid professional staff.

raisers; local, state, and national executives; and national staff members. If the party-in-the-electorate declines in numbers and loyalty, the party organization must try to find a strategy to rebuild the grassroots following.

The **party-in-government** is the third component of American political parties. The party-in-government consists of those elected and appointed officials who identify with a political party. Generally, elected officials cannot also hold official party positions within the formal organization. Executives such as the president, governors, and mayors often have the informal power to appoint party executives, but their duties in office preclude them from active involvement in the party organization most of the time.

Ties to a political party are essential to the functioning of government and the operation of the political process in the United States. Republican representatives, senators, and governors expect to receive a hearing at a Republican-controlled White House if they request it. In return, Republican presidents call on party loyalty when they ask the legislators to support their programs. Finally, the electorate at the polls is asked to judge the party-in-government by its policies and candidates. American political parties, although not nearly as ideological as many European parties, do claim to present alternative positions to the voters. If the party organization and the party-in-government are in conflict, the party-in-the-electorate is likely to look for other party leadership to articulate its preferences.

DID YOU KNOW...
That the political party with the most seats in the House of Representatives chooses the speaker of the House, makes any new rules it wants, gets a majority of the seats on each important committee and chooses their chairs, and hires most of the congressional staff**?**

Party-in-Government
All of the elected and appointed officials who identify with a political party.

Party Organization

In theory, each of the American political parties has a standard, pyramid-shaped organization (see Figure 9–2 on page 284). The pyramid, however, does not

Winning Supporters on the Internet

Both the Republican Party and the Democratic Party recognized the potential of the Internet in the late 1990s. Each party put up Web pages and tried to attract voters through the Internet. Their early efforts were fairly primitive, with Web pages devoted to the national party organization and national contests. Candidates for office and their opponents, however, were much more inventive. In 1996 and 1998, some congressional candidates began to answer e-mail and raise funds via their Internet sites. Candidates in statewide races quickly realized that they could communicate more efficiently with their poll workers, fund-raisers, and local party organizers via the Internet than by telephone or snail mail.

Jesse Ventura's Reform Party campaign in 1998 (discussed on page 298) showed the other political parties how powerful this new medium can be. The Internet is tailor-made for minor parties, which can have as big a presence as the major parties through innovative and interactive Web sites. The major parties now have organizations and home pages that are targeted at specific groups, such as younger voters, seniors, union members, and independents.

Those who use the Internet for political information need to do so with some caution, however. There is no "secure site" for political party Web sites. Besides the parties' official sites, there are also satirical sites mimicking the parties, sites distributing misleading information, and sites that are raising money for their own causes rather than the political parties. Because it is so easy to design a home page and post it, the number of party and campaign sites in an election year will number in the thousands.

FOR CRITICAL ANALYSIS

How could an ordinary voter determine whether a political party's Web site is authentic? What information would you look for to verify a political party's site?

A Theoretical Structure of the American Political Party

Each "layer" of an American political party is representative of a level of government, from local to national. Although there are linkages between the layers, each is fairly independent of the others in terms of financing, supporters, nominations, and platform. No one level of the party has real control over any other level.

National Chairperson and National Committee

National Convention and Delegates

State Chairperson/Committee

County Chairperson/Committee

Ward or Township Chairperson/Committee

Precinct Chairperson/Committee

INFOTRAC® COLLEGE EDITION

Can Bush Get Serious

accurately reflect the relative power and strengths of the individual parts of the party organization. If it did, the national chairperson of the Democratic Party or the Republican Party, along with the national committee, could simply dictate how the organization was to be run, just as if it were ExxonMobil Corporation or Ford Motor Company.

In reality, the formal structure of political parties resembles a layer cake with autonomous strata more than it does a pyramid. Malcolm E. Jewell and David M. Olson point out that "there is no command structure within political parties. Rather, each geographic unit of the party tends to be autonomous from the other units at its same geographic level."[5]

The National Party Organization

Each party has a national organization, the most clearly institutional part of which is the **national convention,** held every four years. The convention is used to nominate the presidential and vice presidential candidates. In addition, the **party platform** is written, ratified, and revised at the national convention. The platform sets forth the party's position on the issues and makes promises to initiate certain policies if the party wins the presidency.

After the convention, the platform frequently is neglected or ignored by party candidates who disagree with it. Because candidates are trying to win votes from a wide spectrum of voters, it is counterproductive to emphasize the fairly narrow and sometimes controversial goals set forth in the platform. The work of Gerald M. Pomper has shown, however, that once elected, the parties do try to carry out platform promises and that roughly three-fourths of the promises eventually become law.[6] Of course, some general goals, such as economic prosperity, are included in the platforms of both parties.

The party convention provides the most striking illustration of the difference between the ordinary members of a party, or party identifiers, and those individuals who are party activists. As a series of studies by the *New York Times* shows, delegates to the national party conventions are quite dissimilar from ordinary

National Convention
The meeting held every four years by each major party to select presidential and vice presidential candidates, to write a platform, to choose a national committee, and to conduct party business. In theory, the national convention is at the top of a hierarchy of party conventions (the local and state conventions are below it) that consider candidates and issues.

Party Platform
A document drawn up by the platform committee at each national convention, outlining the policies, positions, and principles of the party; it is then submitted to the entire convention for approval.

[5]Malcolm E. Jewell and David M. Olson, *American State Political Parties and Elections*, rev. ed. (Homewood, Ill.: Dorsey Press, 1982), p. 73.
[6]Gerald M. Pomper and Susan S. Lederman, *Elections in America: Control and Influence in Democratic Politics*, 2d ed. (New York: Longman, 1980).

party identifiers. Delegates to the Democratic National Convention, as shown in Table 9–1, are far more liberal than are ordinary Democratic voters. In the same fashion, Republican voters are not nearly as conservative as are delegates to the Republican National Convention. Why does this happen? In part, it is because a person, to become a delegate, must gather votes in a primary election from party members who care enough to vote in a primary or be appointed by party leaders. Furthermore, the primaries generally pit candidates against each other on intraparty issues. Delegates who are pledged to those candidates are also likely to hold positions on the issues that are far different from those of the other major party. Often, the most important activity for the convention is making peace between the delegates who support different candidates and helping them accept a party platform that will appeal to the general electorate.

DID YOU KNOW...
That the Democrats and Republicans each had exactly one woman delegate at their conventions in 1900?

TABLE 9–1

Convention Delegates and Voters: How Did They Compare on the Issues in 2000?

PERCENTAGE OF . . .	DEMOCRATIC DELEGATES	DEMOCRATIC VOTERS	ALL VOTERS	REPUBLICAN VOTERS	REPUBLICAN DELEGATES
SCOPE OF GOVERNMENT					
Government should do more to . . .					
. . . solve the nation's problems	73	44	33	21	4
. . . regulate the environmental and safety practices of businesses	60	61	50	37	8
SOCIAL ISSUES					
Abortion should be generally available	71	48	36	25	14
The penalty for murder should be death rather than life term	20	46	51	55	60
Favor programs to help minorities get ahead due to past discrimination	83	59	51	44	29
Favor child safety locks on guns	94	81	84	76	48
CAMPAIGN FINANCE					
Favor limit to individual contributions to campaigns	58	39	37	36	34
Favor banning soft money for political parties	47	68	64	60	24
GOVERNMENT SPENDING					
Favor Medicare prescription benefit	58	39	37	36	34
Allow people to invest part of Social Security on own	23	44	53	61	89
IDEOLOGY					
Political ideology is . . .					
. . . very liberal	14	6	4	1	<1
. . . somewhat liberal	20	28	19	10	1
. . . moderate	56	46	43	38	34
. . . somewhat conservative	2	12	19	28	27
. . . very conservative	2	4	12	21	30

SOURCE: *The New York Times*, August 14, 2000, p. A17.

National Committee
A standing committee of a national political party established to direct and coordinate party activities during the four-year period between national party conventions.

**Both Parties
Rake Record Cash**

Terry McAuliffe (left), the national chairman of the Democratic National Committee, and Jim Gilmore (right), the national chairman of the Republican National Committee. Is the function of a national party chairperson similar to the function of a chairperson of a corporate board of directors?

Choosing the National Committee. At the national convention, each of the parties formally chooses a national standing committee, elected by the individual state parties. This **national committee** is established to direct and coordinate party activities during the following four years. The Democrats include at least two members, a man and a woman, from each state, from the District of Columbia, and from the several territories. Governors, members of Congress, mayors, and other officials may be included as at-large members of the national committee. The Republicans, in addition, add state chairpersons from every state carried by the Republican Party in the preceding presidential, gubernatorial, or congressional elections. The selections of national committee members are ratified by the delegations to the national convention.

One of the jobs of the national committee is to ratify the presidential nominee's choice of a national chairperson, who in principle acts as the spokesperson for the party. Even though we have placed the national committee at the top of the hierarchy of party organization (refer back to Figure 9–2 on page 284), it has very little direct influence. Basically, the national chairperson and the national committee simply plan the next campaign and the next convention, obtain financial contributions, and publicize the national party.

Picking a National Chairperson. In general, the party's presidential candidate chooses the national chairperson. (If that candidate loses, however, the chairperson is often changed.) The major responsibility of the chairperson is the management of the national election campaign. In some cases, a strong national chairperson has considerable power over state and local party organizations. There is no formal mechanism with which to exercise direct control over subnational party structures, however. The national chairperson does such jobs as establish a national party headquarters, raise campaign funds and distribute them to state parties and to candidates, and appear in the media as a party spokesperson.

The national chairperson, along with the national committee, attempts basically to maintain some sort of liaison among the different levels of the party organization. The fact is that the real strength and power of a national party are at the state level. The national party, however, is now able to raise significant amounts of "soft money" contributions and funnel these funds to state parties. This chapter's feature *Politics and Economics* describes how these funds are used.

The State Party Organization

There are fifty states in the Union, plus the territories and the District of Columbia, and an equal number of party organizations for each major party. Therefore, there are more than a hundred state parties (and even more, if we include local parties and minor parties). Because every state party is unique, it is impossible to describe what an "average" state political party is like. Nonetheless, state parties have several organizational features in common.

This commonality can be described in one sentence: each state party has a chairperson, a committee, and a number of local organizations. In principle, each **state central committee**—the principal organized structure of each political party within each state—has a similar role in the various states. The committee, usually composed of those members who represent congressional districts, state legislative districts, or counties, has responsibility for carrying out the policy decisions of the party's state convention, and in some states the state committee will direct the state chairperson with respect to policymaking.

Also, like the national committee, the state central committee has control over the use of party campaign funds during political campaigns. Usually, the state central committee has little, if any, influence on party candidates once they are elected. In fact, state parties are fundamentally loose alliances of local interests and coalitions of often bitterly opposed factions.

State parties are also important in national politics because of the **unit rule,** which awards electoral votes in presidential elections as an indivisible bloc (except in Maine and Nebraska). Presidential candidates concentrate their efforts in states in which voter preferences seem to be evenly divided or in which large numbers of electoral votes are at stake.

State Central Committee
The principal organized structure of each political party within each state. This committee is responsible for carrying out policy decisions of the party's state convention.

Unit Rule
All of a state's electoral votes are cast for the presidential candidate receiving a plurality of the popular vote in that state.

politics and economics

Soft Money Floods the Political Parties

As you will read in Chapter 10, the laws regulating campaign financing limit the amounts of money that individuals can give directly to candidates. There are no limits, however, on the amounts that individuals and companies can give to party committees and other "uncoordinated" activities. Both the Democrats and the Republicans have become extremely skillful in raising these "soft money" dollars; in 2000, the Democrats raised almost $243 million, while the Republicans raised more than $244 million.

What do the parties do with all this soft money? They transfer it to committees in congressional districts or in states that engage in issue advocacy. Because these are supposedly "uncoordinated" activities and are not controlled by a candidate or her or his campaign, the soft money can be used for massive television campaigns. So long as the advertising does not explicitly ask voters to vote for a specific candidate, soft money can be spent to create the ad, pay for running it, and cover any other

expenses. Usually, this type of advertising provides negative information about the opponent or spreads fear about an issue, such as Medicare or Social Security. A political party's efforts to defeat its opposition may also be buttressed by the issue advocacy ads of interest groups that share the party's views. For example, when a Republican House member refused to sign a term limits pledge, the interest group Americans for Term Limits spent almost $400,000 to try to defeat him. Although ads include the name of such a campaign's sponsor, voters have no idea that the money raised for these campaigns is unregulated and could be contributed by a few very wealthy individuals or companies.*

FOR CRITICAL ANALYSIS

How could a voter know whether an ad is part of a candidate's campaign or is sponsored by an interest group or the opposition party?

*For a more detailed look at this type of advertising and the role of the political parties, see "The Long Shadow of Soft Money and Issue Advocacy Ads," *Campaigns and Elections,* May 1999, p. 22.

Local Party Machinery: The Grassroots

The lowest layer of party machinery is the local organization, supported by district leaders, precinct or ward captains, and party workers. Much of the work is coordinated by county committees and their chairpersons. At the end of the nineteenth century, the institution of **patronage**—rewarding the party faithful with government jobs or contracts—held the local organization together. For immigrants and the poor, the political machine often furnished important services and protections. The big-city machine was the archetypal example, and Tammany Hall, or the Tammany Society, which dominated New York City government for nearly two centuries, was perhaps the highest refinement of this political form. (See this chapter's *An Ethical Issue*.)

Patronage
Rewarding faithful party workers and followers with government employment and contracts.

Tammany Hall: The Quintessential Local Political Machine

The Tammany Society dominated New York City politics for nearly two centuries. Founded in 1786 with the express purpose of engaging in cultural, social, and patriotic activities, the society evolved into a major political force and became known as Tammany Hall. In the beginning, it organized and provided social services for the foreign born, who made up the bulk of the Democratic Party in New York City.

One of its more notorious leaders was William Tweed, head of the so-called Tweed ring, whose scandals were unearthed by the *New York Times* in 1871. Readers were entertained and horrified by stories of millions of dollars in kickbacks received from giving out government contracts, of how civil and criminal violations were being overlooked, and of phony leases and padded bills that were paid to members of the Tweed ring. As a result of the exposé, Tweed was imprisoned; but the other members of the ring managed to flee the country (as very wealthy men and women). Richard Crocker took over the leadership of Tammany Hall in 1886 and kept it until 1901.

Tammany Hall's influence declined when its slate of candidates was defeated in a reform movement in 1901. It was not until Franklin D. Roosevelt's victory in 1932, however, that Tammany lost its political clout almost completely—but only for a couple of decades. In the 1950s, there was a short-lived resurgence in the influence of the Tammany Society. It has enjoyed no political influence in New York City politics since then.

TWEEDLEDEE AND SWEEDLEDUM.
(A New Christmas Pantomime at the Tammany Hall.)
Clown (to Pantaloon). " Let's Blind them with *this*, and then take *some more*."

FOR CRITICAL ANALYSIS

What kinds of organizations today provide the services that political machines did in the past?

The last big-city local political machine to exercise a great deal of power was run by Chicago's Mayor Richard J. Daley, who was also an important figure in national Democratic politics. Daley, as mayor, ran the Chicago Democratic machine from 1955 until his death in 1976. The Daley organization, largely Irish in candidate origin and voter support, was split by the successful candidacy of African American Democrat Harold Washington in the racially divisive 1983 mayoral election. The current mayor of Chicago, Richard M. Daley, son of the former mayor, today heads a party organization that includes many different groups in the electorate.

City machines are now dead, mostly because their function of providing social services (and reaping the reward of votes) has been taken over by state and national agencies. This trend began in the 1930s, when the social legislation of the New Deal established Social Security and unemployment insurance. The local party machine has little, if anything, to do with deciding who is eligible to receive these benefits.

Local political organizations, whether located in cities, in townships, or at the county level, still can contribute a great deal to local election campaigns. These organizations are able to provide the foot soldiers of politics—individuals who pass out literature and get out the vote on election day, which can be crucial in local elections. In many regions, local Democratic and Republican organizations still exercise some patronage, such as awarding courthouse jobs, contracts for street repair, and other lucrative construction contracts. The constitutionality of awarding—or not awarding—contracts on the basis of political affiliation increasingly is subject to challenge, however. The Supreme Court has ruled that hiring and firing individuals because of their political affiliation is an infringement of the employees' First Amendment rights to free expression.[7] Local party organizations are also the most important vehicles for recruiting young adults into political work, because political involvement at the local level offers activists many opportunities to gain experience.

INFOTRAC®
COLLEGE EDITION

Continuing Judicial Assault Patronage

The Party and Its Members

The two major American political parties are often characterized as being too much like Tweedledee and Tweedledum, the twins in Lewis Carroll's *Through the Looking Glass*. When both parties nominate moderates for the presidency, the similarities between the parties seem to outweigh their differences. Yet the political parties do generate strong conflict for political offices throughout the United States, and there are significant differences between the parties, both in the characteristics of their members and in their platforms. (See the *Critical Perspective* presented later in this chapter on page 302 for a different view on the current state of the political parties.)

Differences between the Parties

Although Democrats and Republicans are not divided along religious or class lines to the extent that some European parties are, certain social groups are more likely to identify with each party. Since the New Deal of Franklin D. Roosevelt, the Democratic Party has appealed to the more disadvantaged groups in society. African American voters are far more likely to identify with the Democrats, as are members of union households, Jewish voters, and individuals who have less

---

[7]*Rutan v. Republican Party of Illinois*, 497 U.S. 62 (1990).

than a high school education. Republicans draw more of their support from college graduates, upper-income families, and professionals or businesspersons. In recent years, more women than men have tended to identify themselves as Democrats rather than as Republicans.

The coalition of minorities, the working class, and various ethnic groups has been the core of Democratic Party support since the presidency of Franklin D. Roosevelt. The social programs and increased government intervention in the economy that were the heart of Roosevelt's New Deal were intended to ease the strain of economic hard times on these groups. This goal remains important for many Democrats today. In general, Democratic identifiers are more likely to approve of social-welfare spending, to support government regulation of business, to approve of measures to improve the situation of minorities, and to support assistance to the elderly with their medical expenses. Republicans are more supportive of the private marketplace, and many Republicans feel that the federal government should be involved in fewer social programs.

Public opinion polls that ask the public which party they trust to handle certain issues reaffirm the loyalties of various groups. As shown in Figure 9–3, a majority of those polled think that Republicans are more likely to keep military defenses strong, have high ethical standards, reduce crime, and reduce taxes. Democrats are seen as having quite an advantage with respect to protecting Social Security and Medicare, protecting the environment, and improving the health-care system. These are the issues that are most attractive to Democratic voters.

FIGURE 9–3

Which Party Is Better?

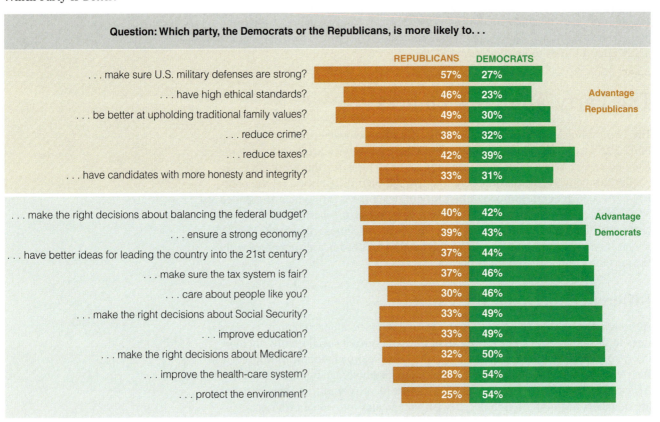

SOURCE: *New York Times*/CBS News survey, November 4–7, 1999, as reported in *The New York Times*, November 10, 1999, p. A19.

Note that in 1999, Democrats were seen as slightly more likely than Republicans to "ensure a strong economy." This is a bit of a reversal from the years of Ronald Reagan and George Bush, when Republicans were perceived to have an advantage on economic issues. The strong performance of the nation's economy during the Clinton presidency apparently increased voters' confidence in the ability of the Democratic Party to address economic issues effectively.

The Party-in-Government

After the election is over and the winners are announced, the focus of party activity shifts from getting out the vote to organizing and controlling the government. As you will see in Chapter 12, party membership plays an important role in the day-to-day operations of Congress, with partisanship determining everything from office space to committee assignments and power on Capitol Hill. For the president, the political party furnishes the pool of qualified applicants for political appointments to run the government. Although it is uncommon to do so, presidents can and occasionally do appoint executive personnel, such as cabinet secretaries, from the opposition party. As we note in Chapter 13, there are not as many of these appointed positions as presidents might like, and presidential power is limited by the permanent bureaucracy. Judicial appointments, however, offer a great opportunity to the winning party. For the most part, presidents are likely to appoint federal judges from their own party.

All of these party appointments suggest that the winning political party, whether at the national, state, or local level, has a great deal of control in the American system. Because of the checks and balances and the relative lack of cohesion in American parties, however, such control is an illusion. In fact, many Americans, at least implicitly, prefer a "divided government," with the executive and legislative branches controlled by different parties. The trend toward **ticket splitting**—splitting votes between the president and members of Congress—has increased sharply since 1952. This practice may indicate a lack of trust in government or the relative weakness of party identification among many voters. Voters seem comfortable with having a president affiliated with one party and a Congress controlled by the other.

When it comes to how many Americans think that divided government is the best way to govern, the answer varies somewhat depending on what the pollsters ask. When asked if it is a good idea for Congress and the White House to be in different hands to provide a check on one another, 52 percent of Americans agree, according to a *Los Angeles Times* poll.[8] When asked if it is better to have different parties in control to prevent either one from going too far, about 60 percent said it is better to have different parties. Only 28 percent of those polled by the *Wall Street Journal* felt that divided government harmed the country.[9]

Ticket Splitting
Voting for candidates of two or more parties for different offices. For example, a voter splits her ticket if she votes for a Republican presidential candidate and for a Democratic congressional candidate.

Why Do We Have a Two-Party System?

Although it is difficult to imagine a political system in the United States with four, five, six, or seven major political parties, other democratic systems have three-party, four-party, or even ten-party systems. In some European nations, parties are

[8]*The Los Angeles Times,* November 22, 1999.
[9]*The Wall Street Journal,* December 16, 1999, p. A12.

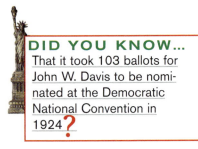

Two-Party System
A political system in which only two parties have a reasonable chance of winning.

clearly tied to ideological positions; parties that represent Marxist, socialist, liberal, conservative, and ultraconservative positions appear on the political continuum. Some nations have political parties that represent regions of the nation that have separate cultural identities, such as the French-speaking and German-speaking regions of Switzerland. Some parties are rooted in religious differences. In some Muslim nations, political parties are based on differences between factions of Islam. Parties also exist that represent specific economic interests—agricultural, maritime, or industrial—and some, such as monarchist parties, speak for alternative political systems.

The United States has a **two-party system,** and that system has been around from about 1800 to the present. Considering the range of political ideology among voters and the variety of local and state party machines, the fact that we still have just two major political parties is somewhat unusual.

There are several reasons why two major parties have dominated the political landscape in the United States for almost two centuries. These reasons have to do with (1) the historical foundations of the system, (2) the self-perpetuation of the parties, (3) the commonality of views among Americans, (4) the winner-take-all electoral system, and (5) state and federal laws favoring the two-party system.

Partisan Trends in the 2000 Elections

Although the 2000 presidential elections were perhaps the most closely contested in American history, neither party made any inroads into the other's base of core voters. Voters who identify with the Republican Party voted for Governor Bush, and Democratic Party identifiers supported Vice President Gore. The independents who voted for one of the two major party candidates split very evenly. The more interesting stories of 2000 were the impact of the Green Party and the failure of the Reform Party. Ralph Nader's run for the presidency on the Green Party ticket attracted considerable attention. Although the party did not secure the necessary 5 percent of the national vote to receive federal funding in the next election, Nader was successful in getting many voters to think seriously about how to build a third party. Pat Buchanan, formerly among the most conservative of Republicans, failed to get voters to choose the Reform Party in order to support his ideas.

The Historical Foundations of the Two-Party System

As we have seen, the first two opposing groups in U.S. politics were the Federalists and the Anti-Federalists. The Federalists, who remained in power and solidified their identity as a political party, represented those with commercial interests, including merchants, shipowners, and manufacturers. The Federalists supported the principle of a strong national government. The Anti-Federalists, who gradually became known as the Democratic Republicans, represented artisans and farmers. They strongly supported states' rights. These interests were also fairly well split along geographic lines, with the Federalists dominant in the North and the Democratic Republicans dominant in the South.

Two relatively distinct sets of interests continued to characterize the two different parties. During Andrew Jackson's time in power, eastern commercial interests were pitted against western and southern agricultural and frontier interests. Before the Civil War, the major split again became North versus South. The split was ideological (over the issue of slavery), as well as economic (the

Northeast's industrial interests versus the agricultural interests of the South). After the Civil War, the Republicans found most of their strength in the Northeast, and the Democrats, among white voters in the Solid South. The period from the Civil War to the 1920s has been called one of **sectional politics**.

In the early 1970s, Kevin Phillips, a well-known commentator, predicted that migration from the North and the general conservative attitudes of southern white voters would lead to Republican control in the once solidly Democratic South. As the maps in Figure 9–4 on the next page show, the Republican Party now has control of the majority of southern governorships, Senate seats, and House seats. Only in the state legislatures are Democrats still in control. Republicans were able to capture the national offices first because the campaigns for these offices were often statewide (for the Senate) or covered larger areas (House seats). This meant that more of the newcomers to the region were included, and political conflicts were more national in nature. State legislatures often reflect very local interests as well as the power of local party organizations—which remain, to a great extent, Democratic in the southern states.

Today, sectional politics has largely given way to **national politics**, which focuses on the concerns of the nation as a whole. The contemporary period can also be described as one of **class politics**, with the Republicans generally finding support among groups of higher economic status and the Democrats appealing more to working-class constituencies and the poor.

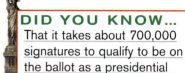

Sectional Politics
The pursuit of interests that are of special concern to a region or section of the country.

National Politics
The pursuit of interests that are of concern to the nation as a whole.

Class Politics
Political preferences based on income level, social status, or both.

Drawing by Steiner © 1994 The New Yorker Magazine, Inc.

"The euonymus likes partial shade and does equally well under Republican and Democratic Administrations."

FIGURE 9-4

The Rise of the Republican South

In the years following the Civil War, the South, resentful of defeat by the Union, became solidly Democratic. As the figure shows, however, in recent years the "Solid South" has been giving way to a Republican South, except in state legislatures.

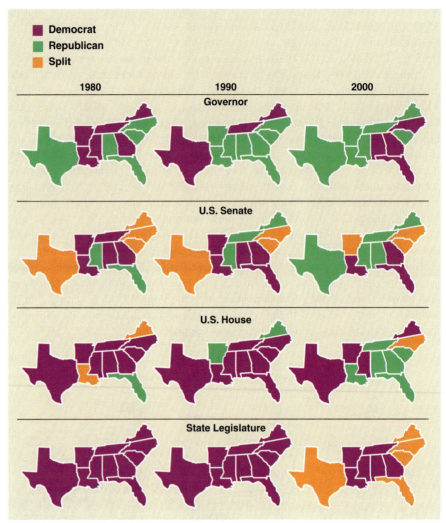

SOURCE: *The New York Times,* March 16, 1998; *The New York Times,* November 9, 2000.

Self-Perpetuation of the Two-Party System

As we saw in Chapter 7, most children identify with the political party of their parents. Children learn at a fairly young age to think of themselves as either Democrats or Republicans. Relatively few are taught to think of themselves as Libertarians or Socialists or even independents. This generates a built-in mechanism to perpetuate a two-party system. Also, many politically oriented people who aspire to work for social change consider that the only realistic way to capture political power in this country is to be either a Republican or a Democrat.

The Political Culture of the United States

Another determining factor in the perpetuation of our two-party system is the commonality of goals among Americans. Most Americans want continuing material prosperity. They also believe that this goal should be achieved through individual, rather than collective, initiative. There has never been much support for the idea of limiting the ownership of private property or equalizing everyone's income. Most Americans take a dim view of such proposals. Private property is considered a basic American value, and the ability to acquire and use it the way one wishes commonly is regarded as a basic American right. Thus, socialist parties have found limited support.

Another reason we have had a basic consensus about our political system and the two major parties is that we have managed largely to separate religion from politics. Religion was an issue in 1928, when Governor Alfred Smith of New York became the first Roman Catholic to be nominated for the presidency (he was defeated by Republican Herbert Hoover), and again in 1960, when John F. Kennedy was running for president. But religion has never been a dividing force triggering splinter parties. There has never been a major Catholic party or a Protestant party or a Jewish party or a Muslim party.

The major division in American politics has been economic. As we mentioned earlier, the Democrats have been known—at least since the 1920s—as the party of the working class. They have been in favor of government intervention in the economy and more government redistribution of income from the wealthy to those with lower incomes. The Republican Party has been known in modern times as the party of the middle and upper classes and commercial interests, in favor of fewer constraints on the market system and less redistribution of income.

Not only does the political culture support the two-party system, but also the parties themselves are adept at making the necessary shifts in their platforms or electoral appeal to gain new members. Because the general ideological structure of the parties is so broad, it has been relatively easy for them to change their respective platforms or to borrow popular policies from the opposing party or from minor parties to attract voter support. Both parties perceive themselves as being broad enough to accommodate every group in society. The Republicans try to gain support from the African American community, and the Democrats strive to make inroads among professional and business groups.

This handbill was used in the election campaign of 1860. Handbills served the same purpose as today's direct-mail advertisements, appealing directly to the voters with the candidate's message.

The Winner-Take-All Electoral System

At virtually every level of government in the United States, the outcome of elections is based on the **plurality**, winner-take-all principle. A plurality system is one in which the winner is the person who obtains the most votes, even if a majority (over 50 percent of the votes) is not obtained. Whoever gets the most votes gets everything. Because most legislators in the United States are elected from single-member districts in which only one person represents the constituency, the candidate who finishes second in such an election receives nothing for the effort.

The winner-take-all system also operates in the **electoral college** (see Chapter 10). In virtually all of the states, the electors are pledged to presidential candidates chosen by their respective national party conventions. During the popular vote in November, in each of the fifty states and in the District of Columbia, the voters choose one slate of electors from those on the state ballot. If the slate of electors wins a plurality in a state, then usually *all* the electors so chosen cast their ballots for the presidential and vice presidential candidates of the winning party. This means that if a particular candidate's slate of electors receives a plurality of, say, 40 percent of the votes in a state, that candidate will receive all the state's electoral votes. Minor parties have a difficult time competing under such a system, even though they may influence the final outcome of the election. Because voters know that minor parties cannot succeed, they often will not vote for minor-party candidates, even if the voters are ideologically in tune with them.

Not all countries, or even all states in the United States, use the plurality, winner-take-all electoral system. Some hold run-off elections until a candidate obtains at least one vote over 50 percent of the votes. Such a system also may be used in countries with multiple parties. Small parties hope to be able to obtain a sufficient number of votes at least to get into a run-off election.

Plurality
The total votes cast for a candidate who receives more votes than any other candidate but not necessarily a majority. Most national, state, and local electoral laws provide for winning elections by a plurality vote.

Electoral College
A group of persons called electors who are selected by the voters in each state. This group officially elects the president and the vice president of the United States. The number of electors in each state is equal to the number of each state's representatives in both chambers of Congress.

Many other nations use a system of proportional representation with multi-member districts. If, during the national election, party X obtains 12 percent of the vote, party Y gets 43 percent of the vote, and party Z gets the remaining 45 percent of the vote, then party X gets 12 percent of the seats in the legislature, party Y gets 43 percent of the seats, and party Z gets 45 percent of the seats. Because even a minor party may still obtain at least a few seats in the legislature, the smaller parties have a greater incentive to organize under such electoral systems than they do in the United States.

State and Federal Laws Favoring the Two Parties

Many state and federal election laws offer a clear advantage to the two major parties. In some states, the established major parties need to gather fewer signatures to place their candidates on the ballot than minor parties or independent candidates do. The criterion for determining how many signatures will be required is often based on the total party vote in the last general election, thus penalizing a new political party that did not compete in that election.

At the national level, minor parties face different obstacles. All of the rules and procedures of both houses of Congress divide committee seats, staff members, and other privileges on the basis of party membership. A legislator who is elected on a minor-party ticket, such as the Liberal Party of New York, must choose to be counted with one of the major parties to get a committee assignment. The Federal Election Commission (FEC) rules for campaign financing also place restrictions on minor-party candidates. Such candidates are not eligible for federal matching funds in either the primary or the general election. (See this chapter's *Which Side Are You On?* for a discussion of campaign financing for minor parties.) In the 1980 election, John Anderson, running for president as an independent, sued the FEC for campaign funds. The commission finally agreed to repay part of his campaign costs after the election in proportion to the votes he received.

The Role of Minor Parties in U.S. Political History

Minor parties have a difficult, if not impossible, time competing within the American two-party political system. Nonetheless, minor parties have played an important role in our political life. Frequently, dissatisfied groups have split from major parties and formed so-called **third parties,**[10] which have acted as barometers of changes in the political mood. Such barometric indicators have forced the major parties to recognize new issues or trends in the thinking of Americans. Political scientists also believe that third parties have acted as a safety valve for dissident political groups, perhaps preventing major confrontations and political unrest. Additionally, parties may be formed to represent a particular ethnic group, such as Hispanics, or groups such as gays and lesbians.

Historically Important Minor Parties

Most minor parties that have endured have had a strong ideological foundation that is typically at odds with the majority mindset. Ideology has at least two

Third Party
A political party other than the two major political parties (Republican and Democratic). Usually, third parties are composed of dissatisfied groups that have split from the major parties. They act as indicators of political trends and as safety valves for dissident groups.

**Easy Being
Green Party Convention**

---

[10]The term *third party* is erroneous, because sometimes there have been third, fourth, fifth, and even sixth parties, and so on. Because it has endured, however, we will use the term here.

which side are you on?

Helping New Parties

Under current federal law, the Federal Election Commission (FEC) provides matching funds to the major-party candidates, if they meet certain conditions, and equal sums of money (more than $30 million) to each major party for its fall campaign. The Republicans and the Democrats also get public dollars to help fund their national nominating conventions. Third (minor) parties or new parties do not receive any of these up-front funds from the FEC. Third-party candidates may also be excluded from any national presidential debates.

Since the independent candidacy of John Anderson in 1980, the FEC has given funding, after the election, to third-party candidates who gained a specified proportion of the vote. Of course, such funding after the fact is of no help to a party trying to mount a national campaign. Should the FEC award funds for conventions and for the national campaign to minor-party candidates? Providing such funding would certainly give minor parties a much better chance of competing in the race. It would recognize their voters and members as legitimate. Of course, such financing could spawn even more minor parties and encourage them to organize to gain the funding, something the Democrats and Republicans do not want.

DOES IT MATTER?

Think about your own political views. If a third party, such as the Reform Party, could run a national campaign, would you be likely to vote for its candidate rather than for the Democratic or Republican candidate?

GOING ONLINE

If you are interested in third parties and want to see how they solicit support, try the Web pages of the Reform Party (at **http://www.reformparty.org***); the Libertarian Party (at* **http://www.lp.org***); and the Green Party (two factions at* **http://www.greenparties.org** *and* **http://www.greens.org***, respectively).*

---

functions. First, the members of the minor party regard themselves as outsiders and look to one another for support; ideology provides tremendous psychological cohesiveness. Second, because the rewards of ideological commitment are partly psychological, these minor parties do not think in terms of immediate electoral success. A poor showing at the polls therefore does not dissuade either the leadership or the grassroots participants from continuing their quest for change in American society. Some of the notable third parties include the following:

1. The Socialist Labor Party, started in 1877.
2. The Socialist Party, founded in 1901.
3. The Communist Party, started in 1919 as the radical left wing that split from the Socialist Party.
4. The Socialist Workers' Party, formerly a Trotskyite group, started in 1938.
5. The Libertarian Party, formed in 1972 and still an important minor party.
6. The Reform Party, founded in 1996.

As we can see from their labels, several of these minor parties have been Marxist oriented. The most successful was Eugene Debs's Socialist Party, which captured 6 percent of the popular vote for president in 1912 and elected more than a thousand candidates at the local level. About eighty mayors were affiliated with the Socialist Party at one time or another. It owed much of its success to the corruption of big-city machines and to antiwar sentiment. The other, more militant parties of the left (the Socialist Labor, Socialist Workers', and Communist Parties) have never enjoyed wide electoral success. At the other end

Eugene V. Debs was the founder of the Socialist Party and a candidate for president on that ticket five times. Despite its longevity, the party has had little impact on the American political system.

of the ideological spectrum, the Libertarian Party supports a *laissez-faire* capitalist economic program, combined with a hands-off policy on regulating matters of moral conduct. The Reform Party, founded by H. Ross Perot in 1996, seeks to reform the political process and reduce the size of government. See the *Making Waves* feature for a discussion of the most prominent Reform Party officeholder, Governor Jesse Ventura of Minnesota.

Splinter Minor Parties

Splinter Party
A new party formed by a dissident faction within a major political party. Usually, splinter parties have emerged when a particular personality was at odds with the major party.

The most successful minor parties have been those that split from major parties. The impetus for these **splinter parties,** or factions, has usually been a situation in which a particular personality was at odds with the major party. The most famous spin-off was the Bull Moose Progressive Party, which split from the Republican Party in 1912 over the candidate chosen to run for president. Theodore Roosevelt rallied his forces and announced the formation of the Bull Moose Progressive Party, leaving the regular Republicans to support William Howard Taft. Although the party was not successful in winning the election for Roosevelt, it did succeed in splitting the Republican vote so that Democrat Woodrow Wilson won.

Among the Democrats, there have been three splinter third parties since the late 1940s: (1) the Dixiecrat (States' Rights) Party of 1948, (2) Henry Wallace's Progressive Party of 1948, and (3) the American Independent Party supporting George Wallace in 1968. The strategy employed by Wallace in the 1968 election was to attempt to deny Richard Nixon or Hubert Humphrey the necessary majority in the electoral college. Many political scientists believe that Humphrey still would have lost to Nixon in 1968 even if Wallace had not run, because most Wallace voters would probably have given their votes to Nixon. The American Independent Party emphasized mostly racial issues and, to a lesser extent, foreign policy. Wallace received 9.9 million popular votes and forty-six electoral votes.

Other Minor Parties

Numerous minor parties have coalesced around specific issues or aims. The Free Soil Party, active from 1848 to 1852, was dedicated to preventing the spread of slavery. The goal of the Prohibition Party, started in 1869, was to ban the sale of liquor.

making Waves

A New Type of Governor

In 1998, three candidates ran for the governorship of Minnesota: Hubert ("Skip") Humphrey III, the son of the late vice president; Norm Coleman, the mayor of St. Paul, Minnesota; and Jesse Ventura, a talk show host and former wrestler. Most of the media discounted Ventura's candidacy and, according to the polls before the election, he was unlikely to win. Ventura used the radio and the Internet, as well as some clever television ads, to publicize his campaign and his political views. He won the three-way race quite handily, shocking political commentators and the leaders of both parties in Minnesota.

Pundits predicted that Minnesotans would soon tire of the flamboyant and outspoken Ventura. Yet the first polls after the election showed that 72 percent of the voters approved of his performance; six months later, his approval rating reached 73

percent. Ventura got some of his initiatives through the legislature and lost others, but his support, especially among younger voters, less educated voters, and moderates, continues to be extremely strong.

The question remains: Is Governor Ventura so well liked because of his personality and commonsense approach to politics, or is his popularity a sign that the Reform Party was gaining strength at the time of his election? Most observers would say that Ventura's popularity is rooted in his personality and his style of governing. Ventura would no doubt agree. On February 11, 2000, he announced his resignation from the Reform Party, which he said had become "hopelessly dysfunctional" as a result of squabbling among the party's leaders.

FOR CRITICAL ANALYSIS

Can Republican or Democratic candidates adopt Ventura's political style and political views successfully?

Theodore Roosevelt, president of the United States from 1901 to 1909, became president after William McKinley was assassinated. Roosevelt was reelected in 1904. In 1912, unable to gain the nomination of the Republican Party, Roosevelt formed a splinter group named the Bull Moose Progressive Party but was unsuccessful in his efforts to win the presidency.

Some minor parties have had specific economic interests as their reason for being. When those interests are either met or made irrelevant by changing economic conditions, these minor parties disappear. Such was the case with the Greenback Party, which lasted from 1876 to 1884. It was one of the most prominent farmer-labor parties that favored government intervention in the economy. Similar to the Greenbacks, but with broader support, was the Populist Party, which lasted from about 1892 to 1908. Farmers were the backbone of this party, and agrarian reform was its goal. In 1892, it ran a presidential candidate, James Weaver, who received one million popular votes and twenty-two electoral votes. The Populists, for the most part, joined with the Democrats in 1896, when both parties endorsed the Democratic presidential candidate, William Jennings Bryan.

The Impact of Minor Parties

Minor parties clearly have had an impact on American politics. What is more difficult to ascertain is how great that impact has been. Simply by showing that third-party issues were taken over some years later by a major party really does not prove that the third party instigated the major party's change. The case for the importance of minor parties may be strongest for the splinter parties. These parties do indeed force a major party to reassess its ideology and organization. There is general agreement that Teddy Roosevelt's Progressive Party in 1912 and

DID YOU KNOW...
That 72 percent of Americans between the ages of eighteen and twenty-nine favor the formation of a third political party**?**

Robert La Follette's Progressive Party in 1924 caused the major parties to take up business regulation as one of their major issues.

Minor parties also can have a serious impact on the outcomes of an election. Although Bill Clinton might well have won the 1992 election in any case, the campaign of H. Ross Perot left its imprint on American politics. Perot was not the candidate of a third party; rather, he was antiparty, attacking both major political parties for being ineffective and beholden to special interests. Perot had a very strong appeal to young voters, independent voters, and disaffected party identifiers. His share of the total vote, 14 percent, could have changed the outcome of the election. In 1996, Perot started the Reform Party, but he received only 8 percent of the vote, not enough to affect the election.

Although the Reform Party had elected one governor, Jesse Ventura of Minnesota, it had little impact in the 2000 presidential elections because its nominee, Pat Buchanan, was too conservative for most of the party's members. Instead, the Green Party gathered 3 percent of the vote for its nominee, Ralph Nader, taking some votes away from Democrat Al Gore. The Green Party was successful, however, in raising awareness of the role a third party might have in addressing issues and policies.

Calling the U.S. system a two-party system is an oversimplification. The nature and names of the major parties have changed over time, and smaller parties almost always have enjoyed a moderate degree of success. Whether they are splinters from the major parties or expressions of social and economic issues not addressed adequately by factions within the major parties, the minor parties attest to the vitality and fluid nature of American politics.

The Uncertain Future of Party Identification

Party Identification
Linking oneself to a particular political party.

Figure 9–5 shows trends in **party identification,** as measured by standard polling techniques from 1937 to the present. What is evident is the rise of the independent voter combined with a relative strengthening of support for the Republican Party, so that the traditional Democratic advantage in party identification is relatively small today.

Carol Miller, a member of the Green Party, recently won 17 percent of the vote in a special election for New Mexico's Third District congressional seat. Using a populist and environmentalist platform, the Green Party has garnered enough votes in New Mexico elections since 1994 to allow the Republicans to win three major races in a state having a Democratic majority.

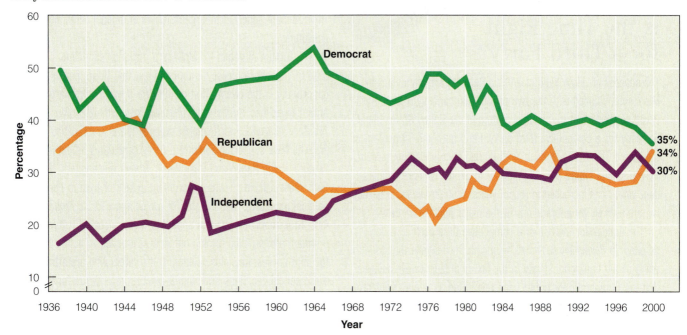

FIGURE 9-5

Party Identification from 1937 to the Present

SOURCES: *Gallup Report*, August 1995; *New York Times*/CBS poll, June 1996; *Gallup Report*, February 1998; and authors' update.

In the 1940s, only about 20 percent of voters classified themselves as independents. By 1975, this percentage had increased to about 33 percent, and more recent polls show it holding steady at about that level. At times, the Democrats have captured the loyalty of about half the electorate, and the Republicans, until 1960, had more than 30 percent support. By the 1990s, the Democrats could count on less than 40 percent of the electorate and the Republicans, on about 30 percent.

Not only have ties to the two major parties weakened in the last three decades, but also voters are less willing to vote a straight ticket—that is, to vote for all the candidates of one party. The percentage of voters who engage in ticket splitting increased from 12 percent in 1952 to more than 38 percent in the presidential election of 1996. This trend, along with the increase in the number of voters who call themselves independents, suggests that parties have lost much of their hold on the loyalty of the voters. (See this chapter's *Critical Perspective* on the next page for a discussion of whether voters are ready for a third party.)

Political Parties: Issues for the Twenty-First Century

American political parties face a number of issues as they look to the next decade and beyond. First and foremost is their relationship to the voters: What can the parties offer to individuals to induce them to become loyal party members? Political parties are rarely able to offer individuals the social relationship or ability to achieve political goals that they could at various times in the past.

Political parties have been weakened by the growing independence of political candidates and the ability of those candidates to raise their own funds and to run their own campaigns. If parties do not become essential to the process of recruiting candidates to run for office and supporting them while holding office,

critical perspective

Is the Time Right for a Third Party?

The success of Jesse Ventura and his Reform Party candidacy in Minnesota, coupled with the two presidential campaigns of H. Ross Perot, suggests that the political system in the United States might be ready for a competitive third party. Perot garnered 14 percent of the vote in the 1992 elections, with no real gain in election turnout. As you saw in Figure 9–5, the number of people who are independent voters has increased in recent years. Younger voters, in particular, are unlikely to embrace one of the major political parties.

The outlook for the rise of a competitive third party is widely debated. In *Reinventing Democrats,** Kenneth Baer details the strengthening of the Democratic Party in the last two decades. He believes that the Democratic Party has been reinvented as a more moderate, more successful party following the efforts of the Democratic Leadership Council, a group of southern moderate Democrats. The Democratic Party has reformulated its agenda to include more moderate proposals while at the same time holding on to union members and to minority voters, especially African Americans. In Baer's view, the Democratic Party is strong and now has the capacity to be a majority party in the United States.

Many commentators believe that the Republican Party may have been weakened, in part due to the unsuccessful leadership of the House by former House speaker Newt Gingrich and the House Republicans' impeachment of President Clinton in 1998. At the time of the impeachment, the approval rating of the Republicans was quite low, and, as shown earlier in this chapter in Figure 9–3 on page 290, the Republican Party is seen as less likely than the Democratic Party to be able to solve major domestic problems. The

*Kenneth S. Baer, *Reinventing Democrats* (Lawrence, Kans.: University Press of Kansas, 2000).

Republican primary elections of 2000 attracted huge turnouts, however, and the candidacy of Senator John McCain appealed to large numbers of independents and former nonvoters.

The turnout of voters for McCain, a maverick candidate, and the base of support for Jesse Ventura suggest that there may well be an opportunity in the twenty-first century for a major third party in American politics. In *Democracy Unbound: Progressive Challenges to the Two Party System,*† David Reynolds explores the characteristics of voters who have supported such third-party candidates as Jesse Ventura, Ralph Nader, and Ross Perot. Among these voters, Reynolds finds mass discontent with government, a lack of trust in current political processes, and a desire for a new approach to American politics. Grassroots activists can appeal to these alienated voters, many of whom are not even turning out to cast a ballot, to build support for third parties. Reynolds, looking at the voters who are attracted to these candidates, finds evidence of a widespread desire for fundamental change.

For millions of Americans, a third party might be the stimulus for them to return to the political system. To be successful, however, a party must not only field a candidate for president who can truly challenge the current major parties but also win seats in the House of Representatives and at the state level. In addition, it must create an organization to carry on its business and create loyalty and support among its voters. To date, very few third parties have made such an impact on American politics, but the time may be right for one to do so.

FOR CRITICAL ANALYSIS

1. Why is it necessary for a political party to win seats in the House or the Senate to become a major force in American politics?
2. What kinds of issues are likely to mobilize the millions of nonvoters and independents to support a third party?

†David Reynolds, *Democracy Unbound: Progressive Challenges to the Two Party System* (Boston: South End Press, 1997).

then the parties' future is quite limited. Not only will they be unable to gain the loyalty of their officeholders, but also they will be unable to promise the voters that candidates elected on either the Republican or the Democratic ticket will behave in predictable ways on the issues.

Finally, do the political parties actually stand for different positions on the issues? The popularity of Ross Perot in 1992 and 1996 demonstrated the readiness of Americans to support a candidate on the basis of his stand against the established parties and candidates. A majority of Americans believe that a third party would be a healthful development for the nation and would give them more choices when they vote. If the political parties are not able to recruit new voters and hold their loyalty, they may be greatly weakened by the rise of new parties and the fluidity of independent voters.

making a difference

Electing Convention Delegates

The most exciting political party event, staged every four years, is the national convention. Surprising as it might seem, there are opportunities for the individual voter to become involved in nominating delegates to the national convention or to become such a delegate. For both the Republican and Democratic Parties, most delegates must be elected at the local level—either the congressional district or the state legislative district. These elections take place at the party primary election or at a neighborhood or precinct caucus level. If the delegates are elected in a primary, persons who want to run for these positions must file petitions with the board of elections in advance of the election. If you are interested in committing yourself to a particular presidential candidate and running for the delegate position, check with the local county committee or with the party's national committee about the rules you must follow.

It is even easier to get involved in the grassroots politics of presidential caucuses. In some states—Iowa being the earliest and most famous one—delegates are first nominated at the local precinct caucus. According to the rules of the Iowa caucuses, anyone can participate in a caucus if he or she is eighteen years old, a resident of the precinct, and registered as a party member. These caucuses, in addition to being the focus of national media attention in January or February, select delegates to the county conventions who are pledged to specific presidential candidates. This is the first step toward the national convention.

At both the county caucus and the convention levels, both parties try to find younger members to fill some of the seats. Contact the state or county political party to find out when the caucuses or primaries will be held. Then gather local supporters and friends, and prepare to join in an occasion during which political persuasion and debate are practiced at their best.

For further information about these opportunities (some states hold caucuses and state conventions in every election year), contact the state party office or your local state legislator for specific dates and regulations. Or write to the national committee for its informational brochures on how to become a delegate.

Republican National Committee
Republican National Headquarters
310 First St. S.E.
Washington, DC 20003
202-863-8500

http://www.rnc.org

Democratic National Committee
Democratic National Headquarters
430 Capital St. S.E.
Washington, DC 20003
202-863-8000

**http://www.democrats.org
/index.html**

Key terms

Anti-Federalists 279

cadre 278

class politics 293

Democratic Party 280

divided government 281

electoral college 295

era of good feeling 280

era of personal politics 280

faction 277

Federalists 279

independent 277

national committee 286

national convention 284

national politics 293

party identification 300

party-in-government 283

party-in-the-electorate 282

party organization 282

party platform 284

patronage 288

political party 277

plurality 295

Republican Party 280

sectional politics 293

splinter party 298

state central committee 287

third party 296

ticket splitting 291

two-party system 292

unit rule 287

Whig Party 280

Chapter summary

1 A political party is a group of political activists who organize to win elections, operate the government, and determine public policy. Political parties perform a number of functions for the political system. These functions include recruiting candidates for public office, organizing and running elections, presenting alternative policies to the voters, assuming responsibility for operating the government, and acting as the opposition to the party in power.

2 The evolution of our nation's political parties can be divided into six periods: (a) the creation and formation of political parties from 1789 to 1812; (b) the era of one-party rule, or personal politics, from 1816 to 1824; (c) the period from Andrew Jackson's presidency to the Civil War, from 1828 to 1860; (d) the post–Civil War period, from 1864 to 1892, ending with solid control by the modern Republican Party; (e) the progressive period, from 1896 to 1928; and (f) the modern period, from 1932 to the present.

3 A political party is composed of three components: the party-in-the-electorate, the party organization, and the party-in-government. Each party component maintains linkages to the others to keep the party strong. In theory, each of the political parties has a pyramid-shaped organization with a hierarchical command structure. In reality, each level of the party—local, state, and national—has considerable autonomy. The national party organization is responsible for holding the national convention in presidential election years, writing the party platform, choosing the national committee, and conducting party business.

4 The party-in-government comprises all of the elected and appointed officeholders of a party. The linkage of party members is crucial to building support for programs among the branches and levels of government.

5 Although it may seem that the two major American political parties do not differ substantially on the issues, each has a different core group of supporters. The general shape of the parties' coalitions reflects the party divisions of Franklin Roosevelt's New Deal. It is clear, however, that party leaders are much further apart in their views than are the party followers.

6 Two major parties have dominated the political landscape in the United States for almost two centuries. The reasons for this include (a) the historical foundations of the system, (b) the self-perpetuation of the parties, (c) the commonality of views among Americans, (d) the winner-take-all electoral system, and (e) state and federal laws favoring the two-party system. Minor parties have emerged from time to time, often as dissatisfied splinter groups from within major parties, and have acted as barometers of changes in political moods. Splinter parties, or factions, usually have emerged when a particular personality was at odds with the major party, as when Teddy Roosevelt's differences with the Republican Party resulted in the formation of the Bull Moose Progressive Party. Numerous other minor parties, such as the Prohibition Party, have formed around single issues.

7 From 1937 to the present, independent voters have formed an increasing proportion of the electorate, with a consequent decline of strongly Democratic or strongly Republican voters. Minor parties have also had a serious impact on the outcome of elections. In 1992, for example, the candidacy of H. Ross Perot drew enough support to change the outcome of the presidential elections. In 1998, a Reform Party candidate won the governorship in Minnesota.

Selected print and electronic resources

SUGGESTED READINGS

Baer, Kenneth S. *Reinventing Democrats*. Lawrence, Kans.: University Press of Kansas, 2000. This book traces the movement of the Democratic Party to a more moderate, centrist position under the leadership of southern moderates such as Bill Clinton.

Beck, Paul Allen. *Party Politics in America*, 8th ed. New York: Longman, 1998. This excellent text covers the role of parties in the late twentieth century, the changes in campaign financing, and the role of parties in the life of the voter.

Bibby, John, and L. Sandy Maisel. *Two Parties—or More? The American Party System*. Boulder, Colo.: Westview Press, 1998. Two well-known scholars of American politics discuss the factors that define the party system and look at the historical record of third-party efforts. They use the Perot candidacies to discuss whether a third party might be successful today.

Feulner, Edwin J., Jr., ed. *Leadership for America: The Principles of Conservatism*. Dallas, Tex.: Spence Publishing Co., 2000. This collection of essays explores the major principles of conservatism and their importance for American political leadership and democratic government.

Horowitz, David. *The Art of Political War and Other Radical Pursuits*. Dallas, Tex.: Spence Publishing Co., 2000. The author, a former left-wing radical, contends that the Democratic Party's electoral dominance in recent years is due not to the issues that it supports or to its "theft" of Republican issues but to its greater mastery of "the art of political war."

Reynolds, David. *Democracy Unbound: Progressive Challenges to the Two Party System*. Boston: South End Press, 1997. The author explores the roots of discontent within the electorate that support the formation of political parties.

MEDIA RESOURCES

A Third Choice—A film that examines America's experience with third parties and independent candidates throughout American political history.

Logging on

The Democratic Party is online at

http://www.democrats.org/index.html

The Republican National Committee is at

http://www.rnc.org

The Libertarian Party has a Web site at

http://www.lp.org/lp.html

The Socialist Party in the United States can be found at

http://sp-usa.org

The Pew Research Center for the American People and the Press offers survey data online on how the parties fared during the most recent elections, voter typology, and numerous other issues. To access this site, go to

http://www.people-press.org

Using the Internet for political analysis

Access the home pages of both the Democratic and Republican Parties using the URLs given in the *Logging on.* List at least three major differences in the policies and approaches to government of the two parties. Then look at the home page for one of the other parties—such as the Libertarian, Socialist Workers', Green, or Populist Party— and compare the policy positions you find there with those of the major parties. What other kinds of information truly differentiate the major parties from the minor ones? To what extent do the two major parties manage to ignore or minimize the importance of any other parties? How do the goals of the major parties differ from those of the minor parties?

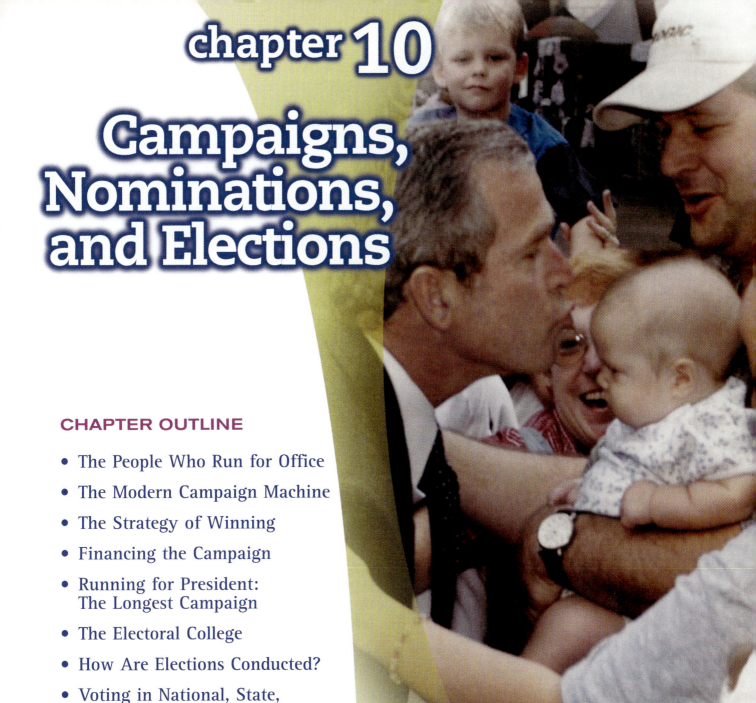

chapter 10

Campaigns, Nominations, and Elections

CHAPTER OUTLINE

- The People Who Run for Office
- The Modern Campaign Machine
- The Strategy of Winning
- Financing the Campaign
- Running for President: The Longest Campaign
- The Electoral College
- How Are Elections Conducted?
- Voting in National, State, and Local Elections
- Legal Restrictions on Voting
- How Do Voters Decide?

what if...

Candidates Received Free Television Time?

BACKGROUND

MORE THAN $3 BILLION WAS SPENT ON THE 2000 PRESIDENTIAL AND CONGRESSIONAL CAMPAIGNS. A LARGE PROPORTION OF THAT AMOUNT WAS SPENT ON TELEVISION ADVERTISING—ON DESIGNING AND PRODUCING ADVERTISING AND PAYING FOR THE AIRTIME. BY THE TIME ELECTION DAY ARRIVED, MOST AMERICANS WERE SURE THAT THE CANDIDATES HAD FOCUSED TOO MUCH ON POLITICAL ADVERTISING AND NOT ENOUGH ON THEIR POLICY POSITIONS.

AT ONE TIME, TELEVISION STATIONS WERE REQUIRED TO GIVE EQUAL TIME TO CANDIDATES, BUT THAT FEDERAL COMMUNICATIONS COMMISSION RULE HAS BEEN DROPPED. TODAY, CANDIDATES OBTAIN TELEVISION TIME THROUGH PAID ADVERTISING AND MAKING NEWS.

WHAT IF CANDIDATES RECEIVED FREE TELEVISION TIME?

A number of nations provide free television time for political candidates of all major parties. Some countries also allow a limited amount of paid advertising, while others permit no paid advertising. The free time is made available in short thirty-second spots or in longer periods that allow candidates to answer questions or speak on more specific issues.

Because all airwaves are essentially controlled by the national government on behalf of the people and are leased or sold to private companies subject to regulation, Congress could mandate that television stations and cable companies give a specified amount of free time to all candidates for the presidency and for the House and the Senate. Candidates could then decide whether they wanted to use the time for live appearances or for campaign advertisements or videos. Congress could also sharply limit paid advertising in campaigns.

CHANGING AMERICAN CAMPAIGNS

Based on the examples of other countries, free television time would certainly offer benefits to both incumbent candidates and challengers. On the one hand, free airtime would benefit incumbents because voters are already familiar with their names and their views. On the other hand, although challengers would have a harder time getting name recognition, they would no longer be disadvantaged when it comes to raising money to pay for advertising.

Campaigns would need fewer contributions, and the need for unregulated or soft money contributions would decrease. Senators and members of the House might spend less time raising funds. Funds would still be needed to run the campaign and to design and film advertising but not to pay for airtime.

Without unregulated issue ads, there would be less negative campaigning. Because interest groups and party committees could not run issue ads "against opponents," candidates would put more emphasis on persuading voters of the correctness of their own positions and less emphasis on pointing out the failings of their opponents.

NOTHING IS COMPLETELY FREE

Giving free television time to all federal candidates would raise a host of issues, however. The television networks, news networks, online news services, and cable companies oppose such legislation because they make significant profits on political advertising. Local affiliates of the networks make a profit on such advertising as well. To compensate these media companies for the loss of paid advertising, the federal government would likely pay some minimum airtime rate.

Taking away the right of candidates or issue advocacy groups to advertise freely on television would face a strong constitutional challenge. Does every candidate have the right to spend unlimited amounts of his or her own money to get elected? The Supreme Court has said yes to that in general. Can spending on television time be limited? That question involving freedom of speech has not yet been answered. How could private individuals or groups be prohibited from buying time to advertise their political views?

FOR CRITICAL ANALYSIS

1. Do you think that limiting television advertising by candidates and parties would violate freedom of speech?

2. What are the most important types of information that voters need to make good decisions? Would they be more likely to get such information if candidates were given free television time?

3. Are candidates likely to use free advertising time for positive or negative messages?

Political campaigns are at the heart of a democratic political system. When voters go to the polls and choose between candidates who have presented their views on leadership and policy, the citizens are exercising the fundamental right to choose the leadership of the nation and, thus, to direct national policy. The same process is repeated at every level of government in the United States: on election day, voters choose members of the town council, the county prosecuting attorney, state legislators, governors, and members of Congress, depending on the year in the political cycle. In each of these venues, candidates depend on their campaigns to sway the voters and win the election.

It is because of the importance of campaigns in our democratic system that Americans are becoming increasingly concerned about campaign costs and convinced of the need for campaign-finance reform. As discussed in the chapter-opening *What If . . .* feature, a large portion of campaign war chests goes toward political advertising on television. Free airtime for candidates has been proposed as one way to reduce the costs of campaigning. You will read about other proposed reforms later in this chapter.

The People Who Run for Office

For democracy to work, there must be candidates for office, and for voters to have a choice, there must be competing candidates for most offices. The presidential campaign provides the most colorful and exciting look at these candidates and how they prepare to compete for the highest office in the land. The men and women who wanted to be candidates in the 2000 presidential campaign faced a long and obstacle-filled path. First, they needed to raise enough money to tour the nation, particularly the states with early **presidential primaries**, to see if they had enough local supporters. Then, they needed funds to start up an organization, devise a plan to win primary votes, and win the party's nomination at the national convention. Finally, they needed funds to finance a successful campaign for president. Always, at every turn, was the question of whether they would have enough funds to wage a campaign.

Presidential Primary
A statewide primary election of delegates to a political party's national convention to help a party determine its presidential nominee. Such delegates are either pledged to a particular candidate or unpledged.

Al Gore rallies voters during his 2000 presidential campaign. Such large public events are carefully staged to gain maximum television exposure for a candidate while at the same time encouraging those in the audience to vote for the candidate.

Why They Run

People who choose to run for office can be divided into two groups—those who are "self-starters" and those who are recruited. The volunteers, or self-starters, get involved in political activities to further their careers, to carry out specific political programs, or in response to certain issues or events. The campaign of Senator Eugene McCarthy in 1968 to deny Lyndon Johnson's renomination was rooted in McCarthy's opposition to the Vietnam War. H. Ross Perot's runs for the presidency in 1992 and in 1996 were a response to public alienation and discontent with the major parties' candidates.

Issues are important, but self-interest and personal goals—status, career objectives, prestige, and income—are central in motivating some candidates to enter political life. Political office is often seen as the steppingstone to achieving certain career goals. A lawyer or an insurance agent may run for office only once or twice and then return to private life with enhanced status. Other politicians may aspire to long-term political office—for example, county offices such as commissioner or sheriff sometimes offer attractive opportunities for power, status, and income and are in themselves career goals. Finally, we think of ambition as the desire for ever more important offices and higher status. Politicians who run for lower offices and then set their sights on Congress or a governorship may be said to have "progressive" ambitions.[1]

We tend to pay far more attention to the flamboyant politician or to the personal characteristics of those with presidential ambitions than to their colleagues who compete for lower offices. But it is important to note that there are far more opportunities to run for office than there are citizens eager to take advantage of them. To fill the slate of candidates for election to such jobs as mosquito-abatement district commissioner, the political party must recruit individuals to run. The problem of finding candidates is compounded in states or cities where the majority party is so dominant that the minority-party candidates have virtually no chance of winning. In these situations, candidates are recruited by party leaders on the basis of loyalty to the organization and civic duty.

---

[1]See the discussion of this topic in Linda Fowler, *Candidates, Congress, and the American Democracy* (Ann Arbor, Mich.: University of Michigan Press, 1993), pp. 56–59.

Dwight D. Eisenhower campaigns for president in 1952. Why do few presidential candidates take the time to ride in parades today?

Who Is Eligible?

There are few constitutional restrictions on who can become a candidate in the United States. As detailed in the Constitution, the formal requirements for a national office are as follows:

1. *President.* Must be a natural-born citizen, have attained the age of thirty-five years, and be a resident of the country for fourteen years by the time of inauguration.
2. *Vice president.* Must be a natural-born citizen, have attained the age of thirty-five years, and not be a resident of the same state as the candidate for president.
3. *Senator.* Must be a citizen for at least nine years, have attained the age of thirty by the time of taking office, and be a resident of the state from which elected.
4. *Representative.* Must be a citizen for at least seven years, have attained the age of twenty-five by the time of taking office, and be a resident of the state from which elected.

The qualifications for state legislators are set by the state constitutions and likewise relate to age, place of residence, and citizenship. (Usually, the requirements for the upper chamber of a legislature are somewhat higher than those for the lower chamber.) The legal qualifications for running for governor or other state office are similar.

Who Runs?   In spite of these minimal legal qualifications for office at both the national and state levels, a quick look at the slate of candidates in any election—or at the current members of the U.S. House of Representatives—will reveal that not all segments of the population take advantage of these opportunities. Holders of political office in the United States are overwhelmingly white and male. Until this century, politicians were also predominantly of northern European origin and predominantly Protestant. Laws enforcing segregation in the South and many border states, as well as laws that effectively denied voting rights, made it impossible to elect African American public officials in many areas in which African Americans constituted a significant portion of the population. As a result of the passage of major civil rights legislation in the last several decades, the number of African American public officials has increased throughout the United States.

Until recently, women generally were considered to be appropriate candidates only for lower-level offices, such as state legislator or school board member. The last ten years have seen a tremendous increase in the number of women who run for office, not only at the state level but for the U.S. Congress as well. Figure 10–1 on the next page shows the increase in female candidates. (In 2000, 128 women ran for Congress, and 64 were elected.) Whereas African Americans were restricted from running for office by both law and custom, women generally were excluded by the agencies of recruitment—parties and interest groups—because they were thought to have no chance of winning or because they had not worked their way up through the party organization. Women also had a more difficult time raising campaign funds. Today, it is clear that women are just as likely as men to participate in many political activities, and a majority of Americans say they would vote for a qualified woman or for an African American for president of the United States.

Professional Status.   Not only are candidates for office more likely to be male and white than female or African American, but they are also likely to be professionals, particularly lawyers. Political campaigning and officeholding are simply easier for some occupational and economic groups than for others,

One of the many "firsts" of the 2000 elections was the campaign of a former First Lady for a seat in Congress. Hillary Clinton succeeded in garnering enough votes to win a contest in New York for one of that state's seats in the U.S. Senate.

FIGURE 10-1

Women Running for Congress

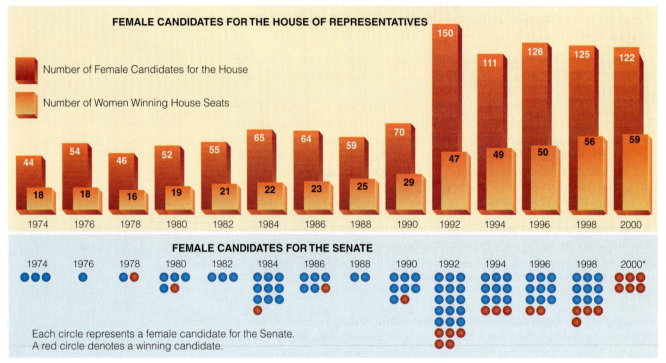

*A seventh woman, Jean Carnahan, was appointed to the Senate seat won by her late husband, Missouri governor Mel Carnahan, who died in a car accident two weeks before the election.

and political involvement can make a valuable contribution to certain careers. Lawyers, for example, have more flexible schedules than do other professionals, can take time off for campaigning, and can leave their jobs to hold public office full-time. Furthermore, holding political office is good publicity for their professional practice, and they usually have partners or associates to keep the firm going while they are in office. Perhaps most important, many jobs that lawyers aspire to—federal or state judgeships, state attorney offices, or work in a federal agency—can be attained by political appointment. Such appointments most likely go to loyal partisans who have served their party by running for and holding office. Personal ambitions, then, are well served for certain groups by entering the political arena, whereas it could be a sacrifice for others whose careers demand full-time attention for many years.

The Modern Campaign Machine

American political campaigns are extravagant, year-long events that produce campaign buttons and posters for collectors, hours of film and sound to be relayed by the media, and, eventually, winning candidates who become the public officials of the nation. Campaigns are also enormously expensive; the total expenditures for 2000 were estimated to be several billion dollars for all congressional and local races in that year. Political campaigns exhaust candidates, their staff members, and the journalists covering the campaign—to say nothing of the public's patience.

These campaign workers have volunteered their time to support the candidacy of Congresswoman Loretta Sanchez, a Democrat from California who was reelected to her third term in 2000. Political parties and candidates at all levels would have a difficult time conducting their campaigns without such volunteers. Volunteering for a campaign is one way to participate actively in the political process, to learn more about it, and to take advantage of one's rights as a citizen.

The Changing Campaign

Campaigns seem to be getting longer and more excessive each year. The goal of all the frantic activity is the same for all campaigns—to convince voters to choose a candidate or a slate of candidates for office. Part of the reason for the increased intensity of campaigns in the last decade is that they have changed from being centered on the party to being centered on the candidate. The candidate-centered campaign emerged in response to several developments: changes in the electoral system, the increased importance of television in campaigns, technological innovations such as computers, and the increased cost of campaigning.

To run a successful and persuasive campaign, the candidate's organization must be able to raise funds for the effort, get coverage from the media, produce and pay for political commercials and advertising, schedule the candidate's time effectively with constituent groups and prospective supporters, convey the candidate's position on the issues, conduct research on the opposing candidate, and get the voters to go to the polls. (See this chapter's *An Ethical Issue* on the next page for a discussion of how political research has changed.) When party identification was stronger among voters and before the advent of television campaigning, a strong party organization on the local, state, or national level could furnish most of the services and expertise that the candidate needed. Political parties provided the funds for campaigning until the 1970s. Parties used their precinct organizations to distribute literature, register voters, and get out the vote on election day. Less effort was spent on advertising for a single candidate's positions and character, because the party label communicated that information to many of the voters.

One of the reasons that campaigns no longer depend on parties is that fewer people identify with them (see Chapter 9), as is evident from the increased number of independent voters. In 1952, about 22 percent of the voters were independent voters, whereas in 2000, between 27 and 31 percent classified themselves as independents, depending on the survey. Independent voters include not only voters who are well educated and issue oriented but also many voters who are not very interested in politics or well informed about candidates or issues.

A volunteer campaign worker uses the telephone to collect polling information from potential voters.

The Professional Campaign

Whether the candidate is running for the state legislature, for the governor's office, for the U.S. Congress, or for the presidency, every campaign has some fundamental tasks to accomplish. What is most striking about today's campaigns is that most of these tasks are now put into the hands of paid professionals rather than volunteers or amateur politicians.

Political Consultant
A paid professional hired to devise a campaign strategy and manage a campaign. Image building is the crucial task of the political consultant.

The most sought-after and possibly the most criticized campaign expert is the **political consultant,** who, for a large fee, devises a campaign strategy, thinks up a campaign theme, and possibly chooses the campaign colors and candidate's portrait for all literature to be distributed. The paid consultant monitors the campaign's progress, plans all media appearances, and coaches the candidate for debates. The consultants and the firms they represent are not politically neutral; most will work only for candidates from one party or only for candidates of a particular ideological persuasion.

Political consultants began to displace volunteer campaign managers in the 1960s, about the same time that television became a force in campaigns. Some of the first "superfirms" of consultants operated in California; Ronald Reagan engaged one of these pioneer firms, Spencer-Roberts, to organize his first campaign for governor of California. Several new generations of political consultants have succeeded these early firms. In the 1990s, the most sought-after firms included those of Roger Ailes (worked for Republicans), James Carville and Paul Begala (Democrats), and Bob Teeter (Republicans). Following the 1992 campaign, a documentary film about the Clinton campaign, featuring the president's consultants (Carville and Begala) and campaign staff, was released under the title *The War*

Opposition Research or Dirty Tricks?

Political campaigns have long engaged in "opposition research," meaning research on the opposing candidate. Traditionally, a campaign staffer would be assigned to find answers to several straightforward research questions: Was the candidate's biography truthful, especially in terms of educational degrees, military service, and professional credentials? Did the candidate raise money from "interesting" sources? Had the candidate formerly taken any political positions that would now be embarrassing? All research depended on public records. Any discovery about the opponent might be disclosed to the press or used in a debate.

It appears that the goals and methods of opposition research have recently taken a turn for the worse. Although most campaigns still do the traditional research, many candidates and party committees now hire private investigators to research an opposing candidate's past, as well as spy on the person daily. Private investigators use cameras to spy on candidates, sift through their trash, pose as journalists asking questions, or take volunteer positions in a campaign to gain information.

The Internet and access to public records through computers have made investigative work even easier. Private investigators can request and often receive telephone records, bank records

(through credit checks), driving records, and, of course, court records. Take the case of a Maine Republican, W. John Hathaway, who was running in the primary for the senatorial nomination. Another candidate, fearing a loss in the primary, engaged a private detective firm to look for records of charges of sexual misconduct against a minor involving Hathaway. After detectives found the public court records, the news was leaked, and two major newspapers ran headlines about the charges of Hathaway's sexual misconduct with a babysitter. What the papers did *not* print was that two attorneys general had investigated the claims and dismissed them with no prejudice against Hathaway, who was never officially charged. The question is not whether the information was public but how it was handled and given to the press. As information sources become even more available, state and national governments will be considering what use should be made of public records and where the line separating ethical from unethical conduct should be drawn.

FOR CRITICAL ANALYSIS

Should certain records, such as divorce proceedings or court charges that were dismissed, be private, or are candidates for office to be stripped of all privacy?

Room, a reference to the center of campaign planning. The Clinton campaign perfected a "rapid response" strategy that countered every charge by the opposition candidate with another more negative attack.

As more and more political campaigns are run exclusively by professional campaign managers, critics of the campaign system are becoming increasingly vociferous. Their worry is that political consultants are more concerned with plotting campaign strategy and developing the candidate's image than with developing positions on issues. Thomas Edmonds, a conservative consultant, believes that candidates are changing, too. He notes that "most modern candidates are more interested in sound bites [very brief, memorable comments] than they are in position papers. They are more interested in how to manipulate the message than what the message really is."[2]

> **DID YOU KNOW...**
> That during Boris Yeltsin's 1996 campaign for the presidency of Russia, his campaign managers hired a team of six American political consultants?

The Strategy of Winning

The goal of every political campaign is the same: to win the election. In the United States, unlike some European countries, there are no rewards for a candidate who comes in second; the winner takes all. The campaign organization must plan a strategy that maximizes the candidate's chances of winning. In American politics, candidates are guided by this basic wisdom: they seek to capture all the votes of their party members, to convince a majority of the independent voters to vote for them, and to gain a few votes from members of the other party. To accomplish these goals, candidates must consider their visibility, their message, and their campaign strategy.

Candidate Visibility and Appeal

One of the most important concerns is how well known the candidate is. If she or he is a highly visible incumbent, there may be little need for campaigning except to remind the voters of the officeholder's good deeds. If, however, the candidate is an unknown challenger or a largely unfamiliar character attacking a well-known public figure, the campaign must devise a strategy to get the candidate before the public.

In the case of the independent candidate or the candidate representing a minor party, the problem of name recognition is serious. There are usually a number of third-party candidates in each presidential election. Such candidates must present an overwhelming case for the voter to reject the major-party candidate. Both the Democratic and the Republican candidates use the strategic ploy of labeling third-party candidates as "not serious" and therefore not worth the voter's time.

The Use of Opinion Polls and Focus Groups

One of the major sources of information for both the media and the candidates is opinion polls. Poll taking is widespread during the primaries. Presidential hopefuls have private polls taken to make sure that there is at least some chance they could be nominated and, if nominated, elected. Also, because the party nominees depend on polls to fine-tune their campaigns, during the presidential campaign itself continual polls are taken. Polls are taken not only by the regular pollsters—Roper, Harris, Gallup, and others—but also privately by each candidate's campaign organization. These private polls, as opposed to the independent public

---

[2]"The Political Campaign Industry," *Campaigns and Elections*, December/January 1994, p. 46.

Tracking Poll
A poll taken for the candidate on a nearly daily basis as election day approaches.

Focus Group
A small group of individuals who are led in discussion by a professional consultant to gather opinions and responses to candidates and issues.

Corrupt Practices Acts
A series of acts passed by Congress in an attempt to limit and regulate the size and sources of contributions and expenditures in political campaigns.

George W. Bush attends a fund-raising event during the 2000 election campaign.

polls conducted by Gallup and others, are for the exclusive and secret use of the candidate and his or her campaign organization.

As the election approaches, many candidates use **tracking polls**, which are polls taken almost every day, to find out how well they are competing for votes. Tracking polls, by indicating how well the campaign is going, enable consultants to fine-tune the advertising and the candidate's speeches in the last days of the campaign.

Another tactic is to use a **focus group** to gain insights into public perceptions of the candidate. Professional consultants organize a discussion of the candidate or of certain political issues among ten to fifteen ordinary citizens. The citizens are selected from certain target groups in the population—for example, working men, blue-collar men, senior citizens, or young voters. The group discusses personality traits of the candidate, political advertising, and other candidate-related issues. The conversation is videotaped (and often observed from behind a mirrored wall). Focus groups are expected to reveal more emotional responses to candidates or the deeper anxieties of voters—feelings that consultants believe often are not tapped by more impersonal telephone surveys. The campaign then can shape its messages to respond to these feelings and perceptions.

Financing the Campaign

In a book published in 1932 entitled *Money in Elections,* Louise Overacker had the following to say about campaign financing:

> The financing of elections in a democracy is a problem which is arousing increasing concern. Many are beginning to wonder if present-day methods of raising and spending campaign funds do not clog the wheels of our elaborately constructed mechanism of popular control, and if democracies do not inevitably become [governments ruled by small groups].[3]

Although writing more than sixty years ago, Overacker touched on a sensitive issue in American political campaigns—the connection between money and elections. It is estimated that over $3 billion was spent at all levels of campaigning in the 1999–2000 election cycle. At the federal level alone, a total of more than $500 million is estimated to have been spent in races for the House of Representatives, $300 million in senatorial races, and $800 million in the presidential campaign. Except for the presidential campaign in the general election, all of the other money had to be provided by the candidates and their families, borrowed, or raised by contributions from individuals or PACs (as discussed in Chapter 8). For the general presidential campaign, some of the money comes from the federal government. (See this chapter's *Politics and Economics* for the impact of the Internet on campaign finance.)

Regulating Campaign Financing

The way in which campaigns are financed has changed dramatically in the last two and a half decades, and today candidates and political parties, when trying to increase their funding sources, must operate within the constraints imposed by complicated laws regulating campaign financing.

There have been a variety of federal **corrupt practices acts** designed to regulate campaign financing. The first, passed in 1925, limited primary and general

---

[3]Louise Overacker, *Money in Elections* (New York: Macmillan, 1932), p. vii.

election expenses for congressional candidates. In addition, it required disclosure of election expenses and, in principle, put controls on contributions by corporations. Numerous loopholes were found in the restrictions on contributions, and the acts proved to be ineffective.

The **Hatch Act** (Political Activities Act) of 1939 was passed in another attempt to control political influence buying. That act forbade a political group to spend more than $3 million in any campaign and limited individual contributions to a political group to $5,000. Of course, such restrictions were easily circumvented by creating additional political groups.

In the 1970s, Congress passed legislation that reshaped the nature of campaign financing. In 1971, it passed a law reforming the process. Then in 1974, in the wake of the Watergate scandal (see Chapter 7), Congress enacted further reforms.

The Federal Election Campaign Act

The Federal Election Campaign Act (FECA) of 1971, which became effective in 1972 essentially replaced all past laws and instituted a major reform. The act

DID YOU KNOW...
That a candidate can buy lists of all the voters in a precinct, county, or state for only about 2 cents per name from a commercial firm?

Hatch Act
An act passed in 1939 that prohibited a political group from spending more than $3 million in any campaign and limited individual contributions to a committee to $5,000. The act was designed to control political influence buying.

politics and economics

Raising Money and Making Money on the Internet

While the vast information resources on the Internet are virtually free to most users once they have access to the Web, the Internet and its dot.com businesses have become a source of enormous wealth to entrepreneurs. In the realm of politics, the Internet is becoming a way for businesses to make profits and for candidates to raise funds.

Political campaigns attempt to convince voters to pick one candidate over another, but these persuasive efforts are not cheap. Political campaigns raise money to pay for advertising, creative design work, mailing lists, Web sites, direct-mail and telephone campaigns, and much more. Internet entrepreneurs quickly saw that potential voters and potential donors could be reached more efficiently and effectively using the Internet than by using "snail mail." Campaign consultants estimate the target audience for direct-mail donations at about 12 million adults, most of whom are aged sixty or over. The potential donor base on the Internet may be millions more and tends to consist of persons who are younger, more affluent, and more interested in politics. Experts also suggest that the cost of using the Internet is lower and the rate of positive responses is much higher than for direct mail. Consequently, candidates are spending more money to hire firms to do Internet solicitations for political contributions.

Internet firms not only conduct e-mail fund-raising and voting campaigns but also operate sites providing political information

for voters. They then solicit banner ads and "hot links" from candidates, charging them for advertising on the information sites. At least one of these political Internet firms has sold stock to become a public company, although investors are concerned that the political season is limited.

Do individuals give money via the Internet? By the middle of October in the pre-primary months of 1999, the leading candidates had raised only 1.1 percent of their contributions online. John McCain's victory in the New Hampshire primary, however, showed how powerful the Internet can be. As the television cameras recorded his victory statement, all of the placards in the crowd advertised his Web site. Within twenty-four hours, McCain's campaign raised more than $1.5 million through donations via that site. Political consultants and other candidates were stunned. Moreover, Internet contributions that are made via credit card mean cash in the campaign's coffers within twenty-four to thirty-six hours. In contrast, checks that come via mail take a week or more to become spendable funds. Clearly, the use of the Internet in political campaigns both to make money and to raise money is still in its infancy, with many new uses yet to be discovered.

FOR CRITICAL ANALYSIS

Does the campaign business—direct mail, Internet sites, advertising, and so on—encourage the raising of more soft money and more campaign-finance abuse?

placed no limit on overall spending but restricted the amount that could be spent on mass-media advertising, including television. It limited the amount that candidates and their families could contribute to their own campaigns and required disclosure of all contributions and expenditures in excess of $100. In principle, the FECA limited the role of labor unions and corporations in political campaigns. It also provided for a voluntary $1 check-off on federal income tax returns for general campaign funds to be used by major-party presidential candidates (first applied in the 1976 campaign).

For many, however, the act did not go far enough. Amendments to the FECA passed in 1974, did the following:

1. *Created the Federal Election Commission.* This commission consists of six nonpartisan administrators whose duties are to enforce compliance with the requirements of the act.

2. *Provided public financing for presidential primaries and general elections.* Any candidate running for president who is able to obtain sufficient contributions in at least twenty states can obtain a subsidy from the U.S. Treasury to help pay for primary campaigns. Each major party was given $15 million for its national convention in 2000. The major-party candidates have federal support for almost all of their expenses, provided they are willing to accept campaign-spending limits.

3. *Limited presidential campaign spending.* Any candidate accepting federal support has to agree to limit campaign expenditures to the amount prescribed by federal law.

4. *Limited contributions.* Citizens can contribute up to $1,000 to each candidate in each federal election or primary; the total limit of all contributions from an individual to all candidates is $25,000 per year. Groups can contribute up to a maximum of $5,000 to a candidate in any election.

5. *Required disclosure.* Each candidate must file periodic reports with the Federal Election Commission, listing who contributed, how much was spent, and for what the money was spent.

The 1971 act had also limited the amount that each individual could spend on his or her own behalf. The Supreme Court declared the provision unconstitutional in 1976, in *Buckley v. Valeo*,[4] stating that it was unconstitutional to restrict in any way the amount congressional candidates or their immediate families could spend on their own behalf: "The candidate, no less than any other person, has a First Amendment right to engage in the discussion of public issues and vigorously and tirelessly to advocate his own election."

Further amendments to the FECA in 1976 allowed corporations, labor unions, and special interest groups to set up PACs to raise money for candidates. For a PAC to be legitimate, the money must be raised from at least fifty volunteer donors and must be given to at least five candidates in the federal election. Each corporation or each union is limited to one PAC. As you might imagine, corporate PACs obtain funds from executives, employees, and stockholders in their firms, and unions obtain PAC funds from their members.[5]

Campaign Financing beyond the Limits

Within a few years after the establishment of the tight limits on contributions, new ways to finance campaigns were developed that skirt the reforms and make it possible for huge sums of money to be raised, especially by the major political parties.

Contributions to Political Parties.   Candidates, PACs, and political parties have found ways to generate **soft money**—that is, campaign contributions to political parties that escape the rigid limits of federal election law. Although federal law limits contributions that are spent on elections, there are no limits on contributions to political parties for party activities such as voter education or voter-registration drives. This loophole has enabled the parties to raise millions of dollars from corporations and individuals. It has not been unusual for such corporations as Time Warner to give more than half a million dollars to the Democratic National Committee and for the tobacco companies to send more than a million dollars to the Republican Party.[6] As shown in Table 10–1, nearly five times as much soft money was raised in the 1999–2000 election cycle as in the 1993–1994 election cycle. The parties then spend this money for the convention, for registering voters, and for advertising to promote the general party position. The parties also send a great deal of the money to state and local party organizations, which use it to support their own tickets.

Independent Expenditures.   Business corporations, labor unions, and other interest groups discovered that it was legal to make **independent expenditures** in

Follow Money
Hard Money Soft Money

Soft Money
Campaign contributions that evade contribution limits by being given to parties and party committees to help fund general party activities.

Independent Expenditures
Nonregulated contributions from PACs, ideological organizations, and individuals. The groups may spend funds on advertising or other campaign activities so long as those expenditures are not coordinated with those of a candidate.

---

[4]424 U.S. 1 (1976).
[5]See Paul Allen Beck, *Party Politics in America*, 8th ed. (New York: Longman Publishers, 1997), p. 285.
[6]Beck, *Party Politics in America*, pp. 293–294.

TABLE 10-1				
Soft Money Raised by Political Parties, 1994 to 2000				
	1993–1994	**1995–1996**	**1997–1998**	**1999–2000**
Democratic Party	$ 45.6 million	$122.3 million	$ 92.8 million	$243.0 million
Republican Party	59.5 million	141.2 million	131.6 million	244.4 million
Total	105.1 million	263.5 million	224.4 million	487.4 million

SOURCE: *Congressional Quarterly Weekly Report*, September 6, 1997, p. 2065, and authors' update.

Taiwanese Buddhist leader Hsing Yun greets then Vice President Al Gore at the Hsi Lai Temple, which is the largest Buddhist monastery in the Western Hemisphere. Gore's appearance at the temple, initially characterized by him as a "community event," became a source of controversy once it was discovered that $140,000 in campaign money was raised at the event. The appearance was also sensitive because of its potentially negative impact on U.S. relations with China.

Long Shadow
Soft Money Issue Advocacy

an election campaign so long as the expenditures were not coordinated with those of the candidate or political party. Hundreds of unique committees and organizations blossomed to take advantage of this campaign tactic. Although a 1990 United States Supreme Court decision, *Austin v. Michigan State Chamber of Commerce,*[7] upheld the right of the states and the federal government to limit independent, direct corporate expenditures (such as for advertisements) on behalf of *candidates,* the decision did not stop business and other types of groups from making independent expenditures on *issues.*

Indeed, issue advocacy–spending unregulated money on advertising that promotes positions on issues rather than candidates–has become a prevalent tactic in recent years. Consider some examples. Prior to the 1996 campaign, Clinton's candidacy was greatly enhanced by a series of issue ads that accused the Republicans of wanting to damage Medicare if they were elected. These ads were developed and paid for by unregulated funds and were sponsored by organizations that were not directly connected with the president's own campaign. The Christian Coalition, which is incorporated, annually raises millions of dollars to produce and distribute voter guidelines and other direct-mail literature to describe candidates' positions on various issues and to promote its agenda. Although promoting issue positions is very close to promoting candidates who support those positions, the courts repeatedly have held, in accordance with the *Buckley v. Valeo* decision mentioned earlier, that interest groups have a First Amendment right to advocate their positions.

The Supreme Court clarified, in a 1996 decision,[8] that political parties may also make independent expenditures on behalf of candidates–as long as the par-

---

[7]494 U.S. 652 (1990).
[8]*Colorado Republican Federal Campaign Committee v. Federal Election Commission,* 518 U.S. 604 (1996).

ties do so *independently* of the candidates. In other words, the parties must not coordinate such expenditures with the candidates' campaigns or let the candidates know the specifics of how party funds are being spent.

Bundling.   Yet another way to maximize contributions to a candidate or a party is through the practice of **bundling**—collecting $1,000 contributions from a number of individuals in the same firm or family and then sending the quite large check to the candidate of choice. While this practice is in complete compliance with the law, it makes the candidate or party more aware of the source of the funding.

The effect of all of these strategies is to increase greatly the amount of money spent for campaigns and party activities. Critics of the system continue to wonder whether the voice of the individual voter or the small contributor is drowned in the flood of big contributions. Although Congress has considered reform measures every year, none has been approved.

Bundling
The practice of adding together maximum individual campaign contributions to increase their impact on the candidate.

Running for President: The Longest Campaign

The American presidential election is the culmination of two different campaigns linked by the parties' national conventions. The presidential primary campaign lasts officially from January until June of the election year, and the final presidential campaign heats up around Labor Day.

Primary elections were first mandated in 1903 in Wisconsin. The purpose of the primary was to open the nomination process to ordinary party members and to weaken the influence of party bosses in the nomination process. Until 1968, however, there were fewer than twenty primary elections for the presidency. They were generally **"beauty contests"** in which the contending candidates for the nomination competed for popular votes, but the results had little or no impact on the selection of delegates to the national convention. National conventions were meetings of the party elite—legislators, mayors, county chairpersons, and loyal party workers—who were mostly appointed to their delegations. National conventions saw numerous trades and bargains among competing candidates, and the leaders of large blocs of delegate votes could direct their delegates to support a favorite candidate.

"Beauty Contest"
A presidential primary in which contending candidates compete for popular votes but the results have little or no impact on the selection of delegates to the national convention, which is made by the party elite.

Reforming the Primaries

In recent decades, the character of the primary process and the make-up of the national convention have changed dramatically. The mass public, rather than party elites, now generally controls the nomination process, owing to extraordinary changes in the party rules. After the disruptive riots outside the doors of the 1968 Democratic convention in Chicago, many party leaders pushed for serious reforms of the convention process. They saw the general dissatisfaction with the convention, and the riots in particular, as stemming from the inability of the average party member to influence the nomination system.

The Democratic National Committee appointed a special commission to study the problems of the primary system. Referred to as the McGovern-Fraser Commission, the group over the next several years formulated new rules for delegate selection that had to be followed by state Democratic Parties.

Demonstrations outside the 1968 Democratic convention in Chicago. The demonstrations influenced the party to reform its delegate selection rules.

The reforms instituted by the Democratic Party, which were imitated in most states by the Republicans, revolutionized the nomination process for the presidency. The most important changes require that most convention delegates not be nominated by the elites in either party; they must be elected by the voters in primary elections, in caucuses held by local parties, or at state conventions. Delegates are mostly pledged to a particular candidate, although the pledge is not always formally binding at the convention. The delegation from each state must also include a proportion of women, younger party members, and representatives of the minority groups within the party. At first, virtually no special privileges were given to elected party officials, such as senators or governors. In 1984, however, many of these officials returned to the Democratic convention as **superdelegates.**

Superdelegate
A party leader or elected official who is given the right to vote at the party's national convention. Superdelegates are not elected at the state level.

Types of Primaries

Not only do the states and state parties use different devices for nominations, but they also may hold different types of primary elections. Among the most likely to be seen are those discussed here.

Closed Primary.   In a *closed primary,* the selection of a party's candidates in an election is limited to avowed or declared party members. In other words, voters must declare their party affiliation, either when they register to vote or at the primary election. A closed-primary system tries to make sure that registered voters cannot cross over into the other party's primary in order to nominate the weakest candidate of the opposing party or to affect the ideological direction of that party.

Open Primary.   An *open primary* is a primary in which voters can vote in either party primary without disclosing their party affiliation. Basically, the voter makes the choice in the privacy of the voting booth. The voter must, however, choose one party's list from which to select candidates. Open primaries place no restrictions on independent voters.

Blanket Primary.   A *blanket primary* is one in which the voter may vote for candidates of more than one party. Alaska, Louisiana, and Washington all have blanket primaries. Blanket-primary campaigns may be much more costly because each candidate for every office is trying to influence all the voters, not just those in his or her party.

In 2000, the United States Supreme Court issued a decision that will alter significantly the use of the blanket primary. The case arose when political parties in California challenged the constitutionality of a 1996 ballot initiative authorizing the use of the blanket primary in that state. The parties contended that the blanket primary violated their First Amendment right of association. Because the nominees represent the party, they argued, party members—not the general electorate—should have the right to choose the party's nominee. The Supreme Court ruled in favor of the parties, holding that the blanket primary violated parties' First Amendment associational rights.[9]

The Court's ruling called into question the constitutional validity of blanket primaries in other states as well. The question before these states now is how to devise a primary election system that will both comply with the Supreme Court's ruling yet offer independent voters a chance to participate in the primary elections.

Run-off Primary.   Some states have a two-primary system. If no candidate receives a majority of the votes in the first primary, the top two candidates must compete in another primary, called a *run-off primary*.

The Primary as a Springboard to the White House

As soon as politicians and potential presidential candidates realized that winning as many primary elections as possible guaranteed the party's nomination for president, their tactics changed dramatically. Candidates running in the 2000 primaries, such as John McCain, concentrated on building organizations in states that held early, important primary elections. Candidates realized that winning early primaries, such as the New Hampshire election in February, or finishing first in the Iowa **caucus** meant that the media instantly would label the winner as the **front-runner**, thus increasing the candidate's media exposure and increasing the pace of contributions to his or her campaign fund.

The states and state political parties began to see that early primaries had a much greater effect on the outcome of the presidential election and, accordingly, began to hold their primaries earlier in the season to secure that advantage. While New Hampshire held on to its claim as the "first" primary, other states moved to the next week. The southern states decided to hold their primaries on the same date, known as **Super Tuesday,** in the hopes of nominating a moderate southerner at the Democratic convention. When California, which had held the last primary (in June), moved its primary to March, the primary season was curtailed drastically. Due to this process of **front-loading** the primaries, in 2000 the presidential nominating process was over in March, with both George W. Bush and Al Gore having enough convention delegate votes to win their respective nominations. This meant that the campaign was essentially without news until the conventions in August, a gap that did not appeal to the politicians or the media. Both parties discussed whether more changes in the primary process were necessary.

---

[9]*California Democratic Party v. Jones*, 120 S.Ct. 2402 (2000).

DID YOU KNOW...
That you can be listed on the New Hampshire primary ballot merely by paying a $1,000 filing fee?

Caucus
A closed meeting of party leaders to select party candidates or to decide on policy; also, a meeting of party members designed to select candidates and propose policies.

Front-Runner
The presidential candidate who appears to have the most momentum at a given time in the primary season.

Super Tuesday
The date on which a number of presidential primaries are held, including those of most of the southern states.

Front-Loading
The practice of moving presidential primary elections to the early part of the campaign, to maximize the impact of certain states or regions on the nomination.

On to the National Convention

Presidential candidates have been nominated by the convention method in every election since 1832. The delegates are sent from each state and are apportioned on the basis of state representation. Extra delegates are allowed to attend from states that had voting majorities for the party in the preceding elections. Parties also accept delegates from the District of Columbia, the territories, and certain overseas groups.

At the convention, each political party uses a **credentials committee** to determine which delegates may participate. The credentials committee usually prepares a roll of all delegates entitled to be seated. Controversy may arise when rival groups claim to be the official party organization for a county, district, or state. The Mississippi Democratic Party split along racial lines in 1964 at the height of the civil rights movement in the Deep South. Separate all-white and mixed white and African American sets of delegates were selected, and both factions showed up at the national convention. After much debate on party rules, the committee decided to seat the pro–civil rights delegates and exclude those who represented the traditional "white" party.

Because delegates generally arrive at the convention committed to presidential candidates, no convention since 1952 has required more than one ballot to choose a nominee. Since 1972, candidates have usually come into the convention with enough committed delegates to win.

The typical convention lasts only a few days. The first day consists of speech making, usually against the opposing party. During the second day, there are committee reports, and during the third day, there is presidential balloting. On

Credentials Committee
A committee used by political parties at their national conventions to determine which delegates may participate. The committee inspects the claim of each prospective delegate to be seated as a legitimate representative of his or her state.

Delegates to the 2000 Democratic National Convention in Los Angeles, California, nominated Al Gore for president and Joseph Lieberman for vice president. Because the television networks have cut their coverage of the conventions, both parties planned their major speeches much more carefully in 2000 to maximize viewer interest.

the fourth day, a vice presidential candidate is usually nominated, and the presidential nominee gives the acceptance speech.

In 2000, the outcome of the two conventions was so predictable that the national networks televised the convention proceedings for no more than two hours each evening. The convention planners concentrated on showing off the most important speeches during that prime-time period. Gavel-to-gavel coverage was available at several Internet sites.

DID YOU KNOW...
That forty-two states do not indicate on the ballot that the voter is casting a ballot for the electors rather than for the president and vice president directly?

The Electoral College

Most voters who vote for the president and vice president think that they are voting directly for a candidate. In actuality, they are voting for **electors** who will cast their ballots in the electoral college. Article II, Section 1, of the Constitution outlines in detail the number and choice of electors for president and vice president. The framers of the Constitution wanted to avoid the selection of president and vice president by the excitable masses. Rather, they wished the choice to be made by a few supposedly dispassionate, reasonable men (but not women).

Elector
A person on the partisan slate that is selected early in the presidential election year according to state laws and the applicable political party apparatus. Electors cast ballots for president and vice president. The number of electors in each state is equal to that state's number of representatives in both chambers of Congress.

The Choice of Electors

Each state's electors are selected during each presidential election year. The selection is governed by state laws and by the applicable party apparatus. After the national party convention, the electors are pledged to the candidates chosen. The total number of electors today is 538, equal to 100 senators, 435 members of the House, plus 3 electors for the District of Columbia (subsequent to the Twenty-third Amendment, ratified in 1961). Each state's number of electors equals that state's number of senators (two) plus its number of representatives. The graphic in Figure 10–2 shows how the electoral votes are apportioned by state.

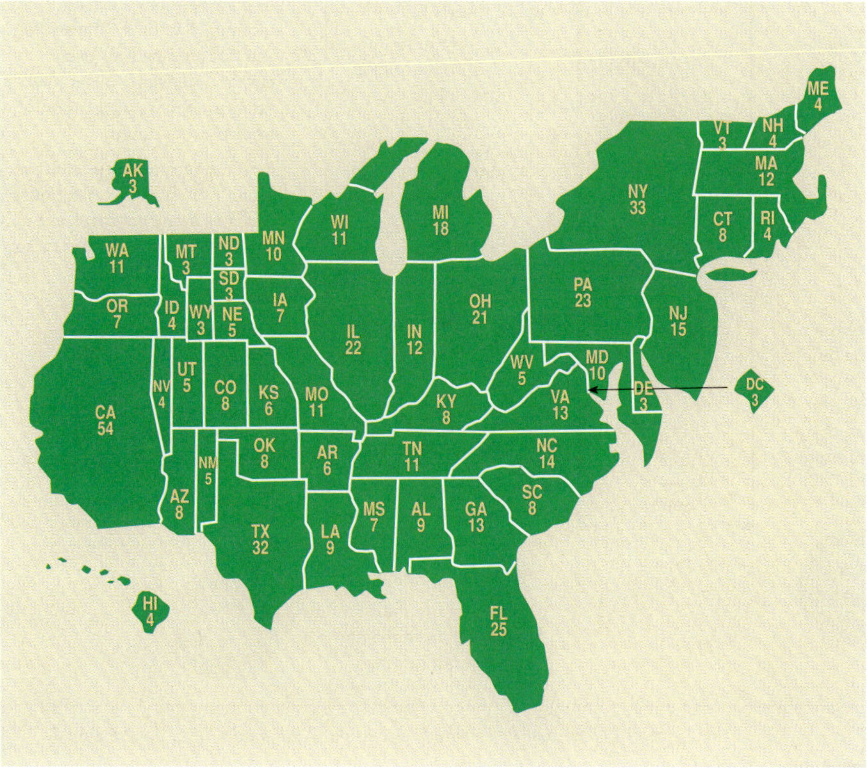

FIGURE 10–2
State Electoral Votes in 2000
The map of the United States shown here is distorted to show the relative weight of the states in terms of electoral votes in 2000. Considering that a candidate must win 270 electoral votes to be elected, presidential candidates plan their visits around the nation to maximize their exposure in the most important states. As vice president, Al Gore visited California numerous times in anticipation of the 2000 elections.

The Electors' Commitment

If a plurality of voters in a state chooses one slate of electors, then those electors are pledged to cast their ballots on the first Monday after the second Wednesday in December in the state capital for the presidential and vice presidential candidates for the winning party.[10] The Constitution does not, however, require the electors to cast their ballots for the candidate of their party.

The ballots are counted and certified before a joint session of Congress early in January. The candidates who receive a majority of the electoral votes (270) are certified as president-elect and vice president–elect. According to the Constitution, in cases in which no candidate receives a majority of the electoral votes, the election of the president is decided in the House from among the candidates with the three highest number of votes (decided by a plurality of each state delegation), each state having one vote. The selection of the vice president is determined by the Senate in a choice between the two highest candidates, each senator having one vote. Congress was required to choose the president and vice president in 1801 (Thomas Jefferson and Aaron Burr), and the House chose the president in 1825 (John Quincy Adams). The entire process is outlined in Figure 10–3.

[10]In Maine and Nebraska, electoral votes are based on congressional districts. Each district chooses one elector. The remaining two electors are chosen statewide.

FIGURE 10-3

How Presidents and
Vice Presidents Are Chosen

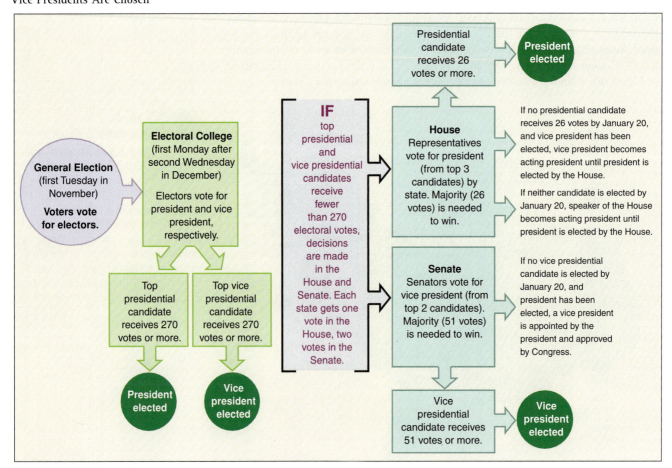

SOURCE: Adapted from Michael J. Glennon, *When No Majority Rules: The Electoral College and Presidential Succession* (Washington, D.C.: Congressional Quarterly Press, 1993), p. 20.

It is possible for a candidate to become president without obtaining a major-ity of the popular vote. There have been numerous minority presidents in our history, including Abraham Lincoln, Woodrow Wilson, Harry Truman, John F. Kennedy, Richard Nixon (in 1968), and Bill Clinton. Such an event can always occur when there are third-party candidates.

Perhaps more distressing is the possibility of a candidate's being elected when the opposing candidate receives a larger share of the popular vote. This occurred on four occasions—in the elections of John Quincy Adams in 1824, Rutherford B. Hayes in 1876, Benjamin Harrison in 1888, and George W. Bush in 2000, all of whom won elections without obtaining a plurality of the popular vote.

Criticisms of the Electoral College

Besides the possibility of a candidate's becoming president even though his or her major opponent obtains more popular votes, there are other complaints about the electoral college. The idea of the Constitution's framers was to have electors use their own discretion to decide who would make the best president. But electors no longer perform the selecting function envisioned by the founders, because they are committed to the candidate who has a plurality of popular votes in their state in the general election.[11]

One can also argue that the current system, which gives all of the electoral votes to the candidate who has a statewide plurality, is unfair to other candi-dates and their supporters. The current system of voting also means that presi-dential campaigning will be concentrated in those states that have the largest number of electoral votes and in those states in which the outcome is likely to be close. All of the other states generally get second-class treatment during the presidential campaign.

It can also be argued that there is something of a less-populous-state bias in the electoral college, because including Senate seats in the electoral vote total partly offsets the edge of the more populous states in the House. A state such as Alaska (with two senators and one representative) gets an electoral vote for roughly each 183,000 people (based on the 1990 census), whereas Iowa gets one vote for each 397,000 people, and New York has a vote for every 545,000 inhabitants.

Proposed Reforms

Many proposals for reform of the electoral college system have been advanced. The most obvious is to get rid of it completely and simply allow candidates to be elected on a popular-vote basis; in other words, have a direct election, by the people, for president and vice president. This was proposed as a constitutional amendment by President Jimmy Carter in 1977, but it failed to achieve the required two-thirds majority in the Senate in a 1979 vote. An earlier effort in 1969 passed the House but was defeated in the Senate due to the efforts of sen-ators from less populous states and the South. In early 2001, such an amend-ment was again introduced in Congress.

Another proposed reform would eliminate the electors but retain the elec-toral vote, which would be given on a proportional basis rather than on a unit (winner-take-all) basis. This method was endorsed by President Richard Nixon in 1969.

---

[11]Note, however, that there have been revolts by so-called *faithless electors*—in 1796, 1820, 1948, 1956, 1960, 1968, 1972, 1976, and 1988.

DID YOU KNOW...
That Texas's "LBJ Law" permits a U.S. senator to run for reelec-tion to the Senate and run for president or vice president in the same election?

Australian Ballot
A secret ballot prepared, distributed, and tabulated by government officials at public expense. Since 1888, all states have used the Australian ballot rather than an open, public ballot.

Office-Block, or Massachusetts, Ballot
A form of general election ballot in which candidates for elective office are grouped together under the title of each office. It emphasizes voting for the office and the individual, rather than for the party.

Party-Column, or Indiana, Ballot
A form of general election ballot in which candidates for elective office are arranged in one column under their respective party labels and symbols. It emphasizes voting for the party, rather than for the office or individual.

Coattail Effect
The influence of a popular candidate on the electoral success of other candidates on the same party ticket. The effect is increased by the party-column ballot, which encourages straight-ticket voting.

The major parties are not in favor of eliminating the electoral college, fearing that it would give minor parties a more influential role. Also, less populous states are not in favor of direct election of the president, because they feel they would be overwhelmed by the large urban vote.

How Are Elections Conducted?

The United States uses the **Australian ballot**—a secret ballot that is prepared, distributed, and counted by government officials at public expense. Since 1888, all states have used the Australian ballot. Before that, many states used the alternatives of oral voting and differently colored ballots prepared by the parties. Obviously, knowing which way a person was voting made it easy to apply pressure to change his or her vote, and vote buying was common.

Office-Block and Party-Column Ballots

There are two types of ballots in use in the United States in general elections. The first, called an **office-block ballot,** or sometimes a **Massachusetts ballot,** groups all the candidates for each elective office under the title of each office. Politicians dislike the office-block ballot, because it places more emphasis on the office than on the party; it discourages straight-ticket voting and encourages split-ticket voting.

A **party-column ballot** is a form of general election ballot in which the candidates are arranged in one column under their respective party labels and symbols. It is also called the **Indiana ballot.** In some states, it allows voters to vote for all of a party's candidates for local, state, and national offices by simply marking a single "X" or by pulling a single lever. Most states use this type of ballot. As it encourages straight-ticket voting, majority parties favor this form. When a party has an exceptionally strong presidential or gubernatorial candidate to head the ticket, the use of the party-column ballot increases the **coattail effect.**

Voting by Mail

Although voting by mail has been accepted for absentee ballots for many decades, particularly for those who are doing business away from home or for members of the armed forces, only recently have several states offered mail ballots to all of their voters. The rationale for going to the mail ballot is to make voting easier and more accessible to the voters, particularly in an era when voters are likely to hold jobs and commute some distance from home to work. A startling result came in the spring 1996 special election in Oregon to replace Senator Bob Packwood: turnout in the election was 66 percent, and the mail ballot saved the state more than $1 million. In the 2000 presidential elections, in which Oregon voters were allowed to mail in their ballots, voter participation was over 80 percent.

There are arguments both for and against mail balloting across the nation. Some commentators, including Norman Ornstein,[12] suggest that mail balloting subverts the whole process. In part, this is because the voter casts her or his ballot at any time, perhaps before any debates or other dialogues are held between candidates. Thus, the voter may be casting an uninformed ballot. Furthermore, Ornstein believes that although the Oregon elections so far have shown no evidence of corruption, balloting by mail presents an exceptional opportunity for vote fraud. Others, however, see the mail ballot as the best way to increase voter

A student casts his vote.

---

[12]Norman Ornstein, "Vote-by-Mail: Is It Good for Democracy?" *Campaigns and Elections,* May 1996, p. 47.

Election judges check the registration of each voter before giving out the ballot. Most local election boards require judges from both political parties at each precinct.

participation at a time when many are too busy to vote or have little interest in the process. The next step in making voting easier will be Internet voting (see the *E-mocracy* feature for a further discussion of this possibility).

Vote Fraud

Vote fraud is something regularly suspected but seldom proved. Voting in the nineteenth century, when secret ballots were rare and people had a cavalier attitude toward the open buying of votes, was probably much more conducive to fraud than

e-mocracy

Voting on the Web Is Coming

What seems more logical and effective as a way to increase voter information and turnout than voting on the Internet? Students who are away at universities could easily become more involved in local and state politics by voting on the Internet. Businesspersons and military personnel who are posted in foreign countries could easily cast their votes. The fastest-growing community of Internet users, senior citizens, could overcome the barriers of illness and accessibility by voting online.

Voting via the Internet is coming soon. The Democratic Party of Arizona contracted with private firms to conduct its 2000 primary voting on the Internet. One firm organized the election on the Web, while the other devised security measures to ensure each voter's identity. The Pentagon conducted a pilot test of Internet voting for members of the armed forces in the 2000 general elections. Military personnel who were voters in Florida, Missouri, South Carolina, or Utah could take part in this pilot project.

Although Internet voting seems like a great idea, it also raises many concerns. After almost a year of study, the state of California said that caution is important because of the security issues involved. The first issue is to prevent vote fraud by making sure that each voter casts only one electronic ballot. Just as important is the need to protect the secrecy of the ballot after the vote is cast. Although most people agree that making the ballot available on the Internet would increase turnout and appeal to many nonvoters, Democrats are not as excited about Internet voting as Republicans are because computers and the Internet are more accessible to wealthier voters. Finally, there are the security concerns raised by hackers: If computer hackers can gain entry to the Internet sites of major newspapers and major online providers, what will prevent them from altering votes and election outcomes?

FOR CRITICAL ANALYSIS

How might electronic voting via the Internet affect election outcomes?

Delirium Democracy

modern elections are. An investigation by Larry J. Sabato and Glenn R. Simpson, however, revealed that the potential for vote fraud is high in many states, particularly through the use of phony voter registrations and absentee ballots.[13]

Recent changes in the election laws of California, for example, make it very difficult to remove a name from the polling list even if the person has not cast a ballot for the prior two years. Thus, many persons are still on the rolls even though they no longer reside in California. Enterprising political activists can use these names for absentee ballots. Other states have registration laws that are meant to encourage easy registration and voting. Such laws can be taken advantage of by those who seek to vote more than once. Since the passage of the "motor voter" law in 1993, all states have been required to allow voters to register by mail. It may be necessary to develop new processes to verify that registrations or ballots sent by mail come from legitimate voters.

Voting in National, State, and Local Elections

In 2000, there were 200 million eligible voters. Of that number, 101 million actually went to the polls. The participation rate during the 2000 presidential elections was only 50.7 percent of eligible voters, up slightly from the 49.2 percent of the eligible voters who cast ballots in 1996 (see Table 10–2).

---

[13]Larry J. Sabato and Glenn R. Simpson, *Dirty Little Secrets: The Persistence of Corruption in American Politics* (New York: Random House, 1996).

TABLE 10-2

Elected by a Majority?

Most presidents have won a majority of the votes cast in the election. We generally judge the extent of their victory by whether they have won more than 51 percent of the votes. Some presidential elections have been proclaimed *landslides,* meaning that the candidates won by an extraordinary majority of votes cast. As indicated below, however, no modern president has been elected by more than 38 percent of the total voting-age electorate.

YEAR–WINNER (PARTY)	PERCENTAGE OF TOTAL POPULAR VOTE	PERCENTAGE OF VOTING-AGE POPULATION
1932–Roosevelt (D)	57.4	30.1
1936–Roosevelt (D)	60.8	34.6
1940–Roosevelt (D)	54.7	32.2
1944–Roosevelt (D)	53.4	29.9
1948–Truman (D)	49.6	25.3
1952–Eisenhower (R)	55.1	34.0
1956–Eisenhower (R)	57.4	34.1
1960–Kennedy (D)	49.7	31.2
1964–Johnson (D)	61.1	37.8
1968–Nixon (R)	43.4	26.4
1972–Nixon (R)	60.7	33.5
1976–Carter (D)	50.1	26.8
1980–Reagan (R)	50.7	26.7
1984–Reagan (R)	58.8	31.2
1988–Bush (R)	53.4	26.8
1992–Clinton (D)	43.3	23.1
1996–Clinton (D)	49.2	23.2
2000–Bush (R)	47.8	24.9

SOURCES: *Congressional Quarterly Weekly Report,* January 31, 1989, p. 137; *New York Times,* November 5, 1992; *New York Times,* November 7, 1996; and *New York Times,* November 12, 2000.

Figure 10–4 shows **voter turnout** for presidential and congressional elections from 1900 to 2000. The last "good" year of turnout for the presidential elections was 1960, when almost 65 percent of the eligible voters actually voted. Each of the peaks in the figure represents voter turnout in a presidential election. Thus, we can also see that voting for U.S. representatives is greatly influenced by whether there is a presidential election in the same year.

The same is true at the state level. When there is a race for governor, more voters participate both in the general election for governor and in the election for state representatives. Voter participation rates in gubernatorial elections are also greater in presidential election years. The average turnout in state elections is about 14 percentage points higher when a presidential election is held.

Now consider local elections. In races for mayor, city council, county auditor, and the like, it is fairly common for only 25 percent or less of the electorate to vote. Is something amiss here? It would seem obvious that people would be more likely to vote in elections that directly affect them. At the local level, each person's vote counts more (because there are fewer voters). Furthermore, the issues—crime control, school bonds, sewer bonds, and so on—touch the immediate interests of the voters. The facts, however, do not fit the theory. Potential voters are most interested in national elections, when a presidential choice is involved. Otherwise, voter participation in our representative government is very low (and, as we have seen, it is not overwhelmingly great even at the presidential level).

The Effect of Low Voter Turnout

There are two schools of thought concerning low voter turnout. Some view the decline in voter participation as a clear threat to our representative democratic government. Fewer and fewer individuals are deciding who wields political power in our society. Also, low voter participation presumably signals apathy about our political system in general. It also may signal that potential voters simply do not want to take the time to learn about the issues. When only a handful of people

DID YOU KNOW...
That in Agust 2000, six people offered to sell their votes for president on eBay, the online auction site (eBay quickly canceled the bidding)**?**

Voter Turnout
The percentage of citizens taking part in the election process; the number of eligible voters that actually "turn out" on election day to cast their ballots.

FIGURE 10–4

Voter Turnout for Presidential and Congressional Elections, 1900 to 2000
The peaks represent turnout in presidential election years; the troughs represent turnout in off-presidential-election years.

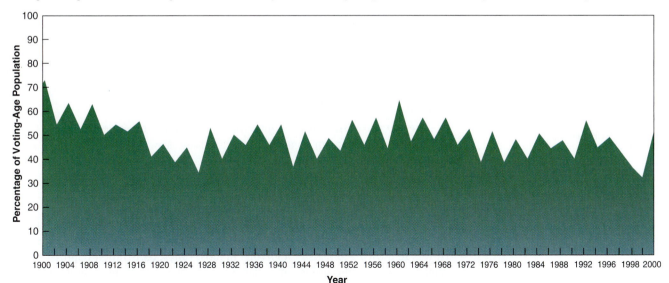

SOURCES: Historical Data Archive, Inter-university Consortium for Political and Social Research: U.S. Department of Commerce, *Statistical Abstract of the United States: 1980,* 101st ed. (Washington, D.C.: U.S. Government Printing Office, 1980), p. 515; William H. Flanigan and Nancy H. Zingale, *Political Behavior of the American Electorate,* 5th ed. (Boston: Allyn and Bacon, 1983), p. 20; *Congressional Quarterly,* various issues; and authors' update.

do take the time, it will be easier, say the alarmists, for an authoritarian figure to take over our government.

Others are less concerned about low voter participation. They believe that a decline in voter participation simply indicates more satisfaction with the status quo. Also, they believe that representative democracy is a reality even if a very small percentage of eligible voters vote. If everyone who does not vote believes that the outcome of the election will accord with his or her own desires, then representative democracy is working. The nonvoters are obtaining the type of government—with the type of people running it—that they want to have anyway.

Factors Influencing Who Votes

A clear association exists between voter participation and the following characteristics: age, educational attainment, minority status, income level, and the existence of two-party competition.

1. *Age.* Look at Table 10-3, which shows the breakdown of voter participation by age group for the 1996 presidential election. It would appear from these figures that age is a strong factor in determining voter turnout on election day. The reported turnout increases with older age groups. Greater participation with age is very likely due to the fact that older voters are more settled in their lives, are already registered, and have had more time to experience voting as an expected activity.

2. *Educational attainment.* Education also influences voter turnout. In general, the more education you have, the more likely you are to vote. This pattern is clearly evident in the 1996 election results, as we can see in Table 10-4. Reported turnout was over 30 percentage points higher for those who had some college education than it was for people who had never been to high school.

3. *Minority status.* Race is important, too, in determining the level of voter turnout. Whites in 1996 voted at a 56.0 percent rate, whereas the African American turnout rate was 50.6 percent.

4. *Income levels.* Differences in income can also lead to differences in voter turnout. Wealthier people tend to be overrepresented in the electorate. In 1996, turnout among whites varied from less than 40 percent of those with annual family incomes under $15,000 to about 70 percent for people with annual family incomes of $50,000 or more.

5. *Two-party competition.* Another factor in voter turnout is the extent to which elections are competitive within a state. More competitive states generally have higher turnout rates, and turnout increases considerably in states where there is a highly competitive race in a particular year. As the 1998 congressional elections showed, turnout can be increased through targeted get-out-the-vote drives among minority voters.

The foregoing statistics reinforce one another. White voters are likely to be wealthier than African American voters, who are also less likely to have obtained a college education.

Why People Do Not Vote

For many years, political scientists believed that one reason why voter turnout in the United States was so much lower than in other Western nations was that it was so difficult to register and vote. In most states, registration required a special trip to a public office far in advance of elections. Many experts are now advancing other explanations for low U.S. voter turnout, however.

TABLE 10-3

Voting in the 1996 Presidential Elections by Age Group (in Percentages)

AGE	REPORTED TURNOUT
18–24	32.4
25–44	49.2
45–64	64.4
65 and over	67.0

SOURCE: U.S. Bureau of the Census, October 17, 1997, www.census.gov.

TABLE 10-4

Voting in the 1996 Presidential Elections by Education Level (in Percentages)

YEARS OF SCHOOL COMPLETED	REPORTED TURNOUT
8 years or less	29.9
9–11 years	33.8
12 years	49.1
1–3 years of college	60.5
4+ years of college	72.6

SOURCE: U.S. Bureau of the Census, October 17, 1997; www.census.gov/.

Political Withdrawal.   Ruy A. Teixeira believes that the factor that has contributed most significantly to the decline in voting turnout since 1960 is not the "cost" of voting but the increasing social and political disconnectedness of American society. Teixeira's study shows that the barriers to voting have been reduced considerably since 1960, yet turnout continues to decrease. It is true that as the population has become more educated and wealthier, turnout has increased among some groups. But with the decline of church membership, social memberships, and community identity, along with the extraordinary increase in political cynicism and distrust, fewer and fewer citizens feel involved enough in their community to be interested in voting.[14]

The Rational Ignorance Effect.   Another explanation of low voter turnout suggests that citizens are making a logical choice in not voting. If citizens believe that their votes will not affect the outcome of an election, then they have little incentive to seek the information they need to cast intelligent votes. The lack of incentive to obtain costly (in terms of time, attention, and so on) information about politicians and political issues has been called the **rational ignorance effect.** That term may seem contradictory, but it is not. Rational ignorance is a condition in which people purposely and rationally decide not to obtain information—to remain ignorant.

Why, then, do even one-third to one-half of U.S. citizens bother to show up at the polls? One explanation is that most citizens receive personal satisfaction from the act of voting. It makes them feel that they are good citizens and that they are doing something patriotic. Even among voters who are registered and who plan to vote, if the cost of voting goes up (in terms of time and inconvenience), the number of eligible voters who actually vote will fall. In particular, bad weather on election day means that, on average, a smaller percentage of eligible voters will go to the polls.

Campaign Effects.   Some analysts suggest that the length of the campaigns and the amount of negative advertising actually drive voters away from the polls. As discussed in this chapter's *Critical Perspective* on the next page, a major study is under way to look at the impact of campaigns and media coverage on voter interest and turnout.

Legal Restrictions on Voting

Legal restrictions on voter registration have existed since the founding of the nation. Most groups in the United States have been concerned with the suffrage issue at one time or another.

Historical Restrictions

In colonial times, only white males who owned property with a certain minimum value were eligible to vote, leaving a far greater number of Americans ineligible than eligible to take part in the democratic process. Because many government functions are in the economic sphere and concern property rights and the distribution of income and wealth, some of the founders of our nation felt it was appropriate that only people who had an interest in property should vote on these issues. The idea of extending the vote to all citizens was, according to South Carolina delegate Charles Pinckney, merely "theoretical nonsense."

DID YOU KNOW... That computer software now exists that can identify likely voters and likely campaign donors by town, neighborhood, and street?

Rational Ignorance Effect
When people purposely and rationally decide not to become informed on an issue because they believe that their vote on the issue is not likely to be a deciding one; a lack of incentive to seek the necessary information to cast an intelligent vote.

[14]Ruy A. Teixeira, *The Disappearing American Voter* (Washington, D.C.: Brookings Institution, 1992), p. 57.

critical perspective

The Vanishing Voter

Turnout for American elections has been quite low since the early 1960s and shows no sign of increasing. Young people, in particular, show little attachment to the political system, and voter turnout is quite low for this group. Senior citizens and those between the ages of forty-five and sixty are the most likely to vote. Scholars and observers of the political scene have begun to ask whether the length and structure of political campaigns actually discourage Americans from being interested in politics.

Many researchers have documented that the news media tend to provide much more news about "the horse race," or which candidates are ahead in the polls, than about the actual policy positions of the candidates. The emphasis on the race and the lack of information about why a citizen should care enough to vote for one of the candidates may also depress turnout. Still other campaign watchers suggest that negative campaigning depresses voter turnout. By the time a citizen has to cast a ballot, most of the information about all of the candidates is so negative that no candidate is appealing. While some research supports the view that negative campaigning decreases turnout, other research suggests that negative campaigning may actually increase interest in the campaign.

The 2000 elections provided an opportunity for a year-long study of the voting public and its reaction to the presidential campaigns. Directed by Thomas Patterson of the Joan Shorenstein Center on the Press, Politics, and Public Policy at Harvard University, the study surveyed Americans every week for one year before the 2000 presidential elections. The Vanishing Voter study asked the respondents which candidates, if any, they had chosen as their preference, whether they were paying attention to the campaigns, and whether they were talking about the campaigns with others.

The most important early findings of the study are that most Americans think that the campaigns are too long and that they do not make up their minds about candidates very early. Americans generally pay little attention to the campaigns in the early days, and despite the news coverage of the Iowa caucuses and the New Hampshire primary in 2000, only about a third of those polled were "involved" in discussions of the campaigns.

The Vanishing Voter project also found that vast amounts of news coverage did not increase interest in the campaigns. This suggests that the media are, indeed, making news out of the campaigns to fill their pages and newscasts, even when the public is not interested. Polls following the New Hampshire primary, which receives the most intense coverage of all the early events, did result in an increase in interest. Less than half of the respondents, however, could correctly identify the Republican winner, John McCain. Interest in the New Hampshire primary was lowest among the youngest group of respondents.

The principal assumption underlying the Vanishing Voter study, as stated by Marvin Kalb, former newsman and director of the Center's Washington office, is that "elections are punctuated by moments when citizens sit up, take notice, and actively listen, learn and decide." What the project found during the primary phase of the presidential campaigns is that most Americans paid attention only sporadically to the campaign news coverage and that the majority did not choose a candidate during this time period.*

After weekly polling of the American electorate, the Vanishing Voter project created quite a portrait of the voters and how their views on politics are shaped. As the 2000 elections drew near, the surveys found that nonvoters and voters share the same criticisms of the way the media cover campaigns: it seems like theater or entertainment to most. They differ, however, in that nonvoters are much more cynical about government and politicians than are voters. As Mr. Patterson puts it, "All the polls, the spin, the attack ads, the money and the negative news have soured Americans on the way we choose our president."

FOR CRITICAL ANALYSIS

1. What are the consequences for democracy if citizens are uninterested in the presidential campaigns?
2. If the primary season is too long and does not actually interest educated Americans, should the system be changed?

*The Vanishing Voter study is online at http://www.vanishingvoter.org.

The logic behind this restriction of voting rights to property owners was questioned seriously by Thomas Paine in his pamphlet *Common Sense*:

> Here is a man who today owns a jackass, and the jackass is worth $60. Today the man is a voter and goes to the polls and deposits his vote. Tomorrow the jackass dies. The next day the man comes to vote without his jackass and cannot vote at all. Now tell me, which was the voter, the man or the jackass?[15]

[15]Thomas Paine, *Common Sense* (London: H. D. Symonds, 1792), p. 28.

The writers of the Constitution allowed the states to decide who should vote. Thus, women were allowed to vote in Wyoming in 1870 but not in the entire nation until the Nineteenth Amendment was ratified in 1920.

By about 1850, most white adult males in virtually all the states could vote without any property qualification. North Carolina was the last state to eliminate its property test for voting—in 1856.

Extension of the franchise to black males occurred with the passage of the Fifteenth Amendment in 1870. This enfranchisement was short-lived, however, as the "redemption" of the South by white racists rolled back these gains by the end of the century. As discussed in Chapter 5, it was not until the 1960s that African Americans, both male and female, were able to participate in large numbers in the electoral process. Women received full national voting rights with the Nineteenth Amendment in 1920. The most recent extension of the franchise occurred when the voting age was reduced to eighteen by the Twenty-sixth Amendment in 1971. Young people, however, have a low turnout, leading to efforts such as those described in the *Making Waves* feature on page 336.

INFOTRAC ®
COLLEGE EDITION

Drivers wanted motor voter

Current Eligibility and Registration Requirements

Voting requires **registration,** and to register, a person must satisfy the following voter qualifications, or legal requirements: (1) citizenship, (2) age (eighteen or older), and (3) residency—the duration varies widely from state to state and with types of elections. Since 1972, states cannot impose residency requirements of more than thirty days. In addition, most states disqualify people who are mentally incompetent, prison inmates, convicted felons, and election-law violators.

Each state has different qualifications for voting and registration. In 1993, Congress passed the "motor voter" bill, which requires that states provide voter-registration materials when people receive or renew driver's licenses, that all states allow voters to register by mail, and that voter-registration forms be made available at a wider variety of public places and agencies. In general, a person must register well in advance of an election, although voters in Maine, Minnesota, Oregon, and Wisconsin are allowed to register up to, and on, election day.

Registration
The entry of a person's name onto the list of eligible voters for elections. Registration requires meeting certain legal requirements relating to age, citizenship, and residency.

Voter registration is an important part of our political process. These workers are helping a citizen register to vote in the next election. The requirements for voter registration vary across states.

Signs in English and Spanish encourage voters to register for the next election. The Supreme Court has ruled that registration materials and ballots must be available in other languages if a specified proportion of the citizens speak a language other than English.

making waves

Getting Out the Vote in California

Turnout is lower in poorer neighborhoods throughout the United States and especially among young minority group members. Some have dropped out of school and have had little education about politics. Most have little opportunity to gain information about candidates, and almost all see very little relevance in the claims and counterclaims of candidates running for office at the state or national level.

During the 2000 campaigns, one effort to increase voter registration and turnout in south Los Angeles and other poor neighborhoods was led by a group that calls itself The Third Eye. This group, which was headed by young African Americans, used concerts and hip-hop music to appeal to younger Californians and give them the message that politics is important and that they can make a difference through voting. By using music and entertainers that attract young people, The Third Eye was able to get a political message into the community. This tactic was pioneered by MTV in the 1992 presidential election with its Rock the Vote campaign, which targeted voters eighteen to twenty-five years old. For more information about the movement to involve young people, see the home page of Rock the Vote at http://www.rockthevote.org.

FOR CRITICAL ANALYSIS

If younger Americans are stimulated to register and vote by MTV or their favorite musicians, is their involvement in politics likely to be temporary or long-standing? What might influence younger voters to stay involved?

Some argue that registration requirements are responsible for much of the nonparticipation in our political process. Certainly, since their introduction in the late nineteenth century, registration laws have had the effect of reducing the voting participation of African Americans and immigrants. There also is a partisan dimension to the debate over registration and nonvoting. Republicans generally fear that an expanded electorate would help to elect more Democrats.

The question arises as to whether registration is really necessary. If it decreases participation in the political process, perhaps it should be dropped altogether. Still, as those in favor of registration requirements argue, such requirements may prevent fraudulent voting practices, such as multiple voting or voting by noncitizens.

DID YOU KNOW...
That noncitizens were allowed to vote in some states until the early 1920s?

How Do Voters Decide?

Political scientists and survey researchers have collected much information about voting behavior. This information sheds some light on which people vote and why people decide to vote for particular candidates. We have already discussed factors influencing voter turnout. Generally, the factors that influence voting decisions can be divided into two groups: (1) socioeconomic and demographic factors and (2) psychological factors.

Socioeconomic and Demographic Factors

As Table 10–5 on the next two pages indicates, a number of socioeconomic and demographic factors appear to influence voting behavior, including (1) education, (2) income and **socioeconomic status,** (3) religion, (4) ethnic background, (5) gender, (6) age, and (7) geographic region. These influences all reflect the voter's personal background and place in society. Some factors have to do with the family into which a person is born: race, religion (for most people), and ethnic background. Others may be the result of choices made throughout an individual's life: place of residence, educational achievement, or profession. It is also clear that many of these factors are related. People who have more education are likely to have higher incomes and to hold professional jobs. Similarly, children born into wealthier families are far more likely to complete college than children from poorer families. Furthermore, some of these demographic factors relate to psychological factors—as we shall see.

Socioeconomic Status
A category of people within a society who have similar levels of income and similar types of occupations.

Education.   Having a college education tends to be associated with voting for Republicans, but this is not always the case. For example, college graduates voted 44 percent for Democrat Bill Clinton and 39 percent for Republican George Bush. Typically, those with less education are more inclined to vote for the Democratic nominee. In 1984, Democrat Walter Mondale received 43 percent and Republican Ronald Reagan, 57 percent of the vote from high school graduates, whereas those with only a grade school education voted 51 percent for Mondale and 49 percent for Reagan.

Income and Socioeconomic Status.   If we measure socioeconomic status by profession, then those of higher socioeconomic status—professionals and businesspersons, as well as white-collar workers—tend to vote Republican more than Democratic. Manual laborers, factory workers, and especially union members are more likely to vote Democratic (but see Table 10–6 on page 340). The effects of income are much the same. The higher the income, the more likely it is that a person will vote Republican. But there are no hard and fast rules. Some very poor individuals are devoted Republicans, just as some extremely wealthy people support the Democratic Party.

TABLE　10-5

Vote by Groups in Presidential Elections since 1968 (in Percentages)

| | 1968 | | | 1972 | | 1976 | | | 1980 | | | 1984 | |
	HUMPHREY (DEM.)	NIXON (REP.)	WALLACE (IND.)	MCGOVERN (DEM.)	NIXON (REP.)	CARTER (DEM.)	FORD (REP.)	MCCARTHY (IND.)	CARTER (DEM.)	REAGAN (REP.)	ANDERSON (IND.)	MONDALE (DEM.)	REAGAN (REP.)
NATIONAL	43.0	43.4	13.6	38	62	50	48	1	41	51	7	41	59
SEX													
Male	41	43	16	37	63	53	45	1	38	53	7	36	64
Female	45	43	12	38	62	48	51	*	44	49	6	45	55
RACE													
White	38	47	15	32	68	46	52	1	36	56	7	34	66
Nonwhite	85	12	3	87	13	85	15	*	86	10	2	87	13
EDUCATION													
College	37	54	9	37	63	42	55	2	35	53	10	39	61
High school	42	43	15	34	66	54	46	*	43	51	5	43	57
Grade school	52	33	15	49	51	58	41	1	54	42	3	51	49
OCCUPATION													
Professional	34	56	10	31	69	42	56	1	33	55	10	34	66
White collar	41	47	12	36	64	50	48	2	40	51	9	47	53
Manual	50	35	15	43	57	58	41	1	48	46	5	46	54
AGE (Years)													
Under 30	47	38	15	48	52	53	45	1	47	41	11	40	60
30–49	44	41	15	33	67	48	49	2	38	52	8	40	60
50 and older	41	47	12	36	64	52	48	*	41	54	4	41	59
RELIGION													
Protestants	35	49	16	30	70	46	53	*	39	54	6	39	61
Catholics	59	33	8	48	52	57	42	1	46	47	6	39	61
POLITICS													
Republicans	9	86	5	5	95	9	91	*	8	86	5	4	96
Democrats	74	12	14	67	33	82	18	*	69	26	4	79	21
Independents	31	44	25	31	69	38	57	4	29	55	14	33	67
REGION													
East	50	43	7	42	58	51	47	1	43	47	9	46	54
Midwest	44	47	9	40	60	48	50	1	41	51	7	42	58
South	31	36	33	29	71	54	45	*	44	52	3	37	63
West	44	49	7	41	59	46	51	1	35	54	9	40	60
MEMBERS OF LABOR UNION FAMILIES	56	29	15	46	54	63	36	1	50	43	5	52	48

*Less than 1 percent.

NOTE: Results do not include votes for all minor-party candidates.

Religion. In the United States, Protestants have traditionally voted Republican, and Catholics and Jews have voted Democratic. As with the other patterns discussed, however, this one is somewhat fluid. Republican Richard Nixon obtained 52 percent of the Catholic vote in 1972, and Democrat Lyndon Johnson won 55 percent of the Protestant vote in 1964. The Catholic vote was evenly split between Democrat Jimmy Carter and Republican Ronald Reagan in 1980 but went heavily for Reagan in 1984. In 1996, Republican candidate Bob Dole obtained fewer votes from Catholics than did Democratic candidate Bill Clinton.

Ethnic Background. Traditionally, the Irish have voted for Democrats. So, too, have voters of Slavic, Polish, and Italian heritages. But Anglo-Saxon and northern European ethnic groups have voted for Republican presidential candidates. These patterns were disrupted in 1980, when Ronald Reagan obtained much of his support from several of the traditionally Democratic ethnic groups, with the help of fundamentalist religious groups.

TABLE   10-5

Vote by Groups in Presidential Elections since 1968 (in Percentages)—continued

	1988		1992			1996			2000	
	DUKAKIS (DEM.)	BUSH (REP.)	CLINTON (DEM.)	BUSH (REP.)	PEROT (IND.)	CLINTON (DEM.)	DOLE (REP.)	PEROT (REF.)	GORE (DEM.)	BUSH (REP.)
NATIONAL	45	53	43	38	19	49	41	8	48	48
SEX										
Male	41	57	41	38	21	43	44	10	42	53
Female	49	50	46	37	17	54	38	7	54	43
RACE										
White	40	59	39	41	20	43	46	9	42	54
Nonwhite	86	12	NA	NA	NA	NA	NA	NA	NA	NA
EDUCATION										
College	43	56	44	39	18	44	46	8	48	48
High school	49	50	43	36	20	51	35	13	48	49
Grade school	56	43	56	28	NA	59	28	11	59	39
OCCUPATION										
Professional	40	59	NA	NA	NA	NA	NA	NA	NA	NA
White collar	42	57	NA	NA	NA	NA	NA	NA	NA	NA
Manual	50	49	NA	NA	NA	NA	NA	NA	NA	NA
AGE (Years)										
Under 30	47	52	44	34	22	54	34	10	48	46
30–49	45	54	42	38	20	48	41	9	NA	NA
50 and older	49	50	50	38	12	48	44	7	NA	NA
RELIGION										
Protestants	33	66	33	46	21	36	53	10	42	56
Catholics	47	52	44	36	20	53	37	9	50	47
POLITICS										
Republicans	8	91	10	73	17	13	80	6	8	91
Democrats	82	17	77	10	13	84	10	5	86	11
Independents	43	55	38	32	30	43	35	17	45	47
REGION										
East	49	50	47	35	NA	55	34	9	56	39
Midwest	47	52	42	37	NA	48	41	10	48	49
South	41	58	42	43	NA	46	46	7	43	55
West	46	52	44	34	NA	48	40	8	48	46
MEMBERS OF LABOR UNION FAMILIES	57	42	55	24	NA	59	30	9	59	37

*Less than 1 percent.

NOTE: Results do not include votes for all minor-party candidates.

SOURCES: *Gallup Report,* November 1984, p. 32; *New York Times,* November 10, 1988, p. 18; *New York Times,* November 15, 1992, p. B9; *New York Times,* November 10, 1996, p. 16; *New York Times,* November 12, 2000, Section 4, p. 4.

African Americans voted principally for Republicans until Democrat Franklin Roosevelt's New Deal in the 1930s. Since then, they have largely identified with the Democratic Party. Indeed, Democratic presidential candidates have received, on average, more than 80 percent of the African American vote since 1956.

Gender.   As discussed in Chapter 7, until relatively recently there seemed to be no fixed pattern of voter preference by gender in presidential elections. One year, more women than men would vote for the Democratic candidate; another year, more men than women would do so. Some political analysts believe that a "gender gap" became a major determinant of voter decision making in the 1980 presidential election. Ronald Reagan obtained 15 percentage points more than Jimmy Carter among male voters, whereas women gave about an equal number of votes to each candidate. In 1984, the gender gap amounted to 9 percentage points nationally, with 64 percent of male voters casting their ballots for Ronald

Reagan and 55 percent of female voters doing the same. In 2000, 54 percent of women and 42 percent of men voted for Al Gore, the Democrat, constituting a gender gap of 12 percentage points. Similarly, 53 percent of men and 43 percent of women voted for the Republican candidate, George W. Bush, showing a gender gap of 10 percentage points.

Age.   Age clearly seems to relate to an individual's voting behavior. Younger voters have tended to vote Democratic, whereas older voters have tended to vote Republican. Only the voters under age thirty clearly favored Jimmy Carter during the Carter-Reagan election in 1980. This trend was reversed in 1984 and 1988, when voters under thirty voted heavily for Ronald Reagan and then for George Bush. In 1992, Bill Clinton won back the young voters by 10 percentage points, a margin that expanded to nearly 20 percentage points in 1996. In 2000, this margin decreased to only 2 percentage points. Voters under the age of thirty split their votes almost evenly between Al Gore (48 percent) and George Bush (46 percent).

Geographic Region.   As we noted in Chapter 9, the former Solid (Democratic) South has crumbled in national elections. In 1972, Republican Richard Nixon obtained 71 percent of the southern vote, whereas Democrat George McGovern obtained only 29 percent. Ronald Reagan drew 52 percent of the southern vote in 1980, however, and 63 percent in 1984.

Democrats still draw much of their strength from large northern and eastern cities. Rural areas tend to be Republican (and conservative) throughout the country except in the South, where the rural vote still tends to be heavily Democratic. On average, the West has voted Republican in presidential elections. Except for the 1964 election between Barry Goldwater and Lyndon Johnson, and again in the 1992 and 1996 elections, the Republicans have held the edge in western states in every presidential election since 1956.

Psychological Factors

In addition to socioeconomic and demographic explanations for the way people vote, at least three important psychological factors play a role in voter decision

---

TABLE **10-6**

How Democratic Are Labor Voters?

Although union members are more likely to identify themselves as Democrats than Republicans and labor organizations are far more likely to support Democratic candidates, the data below show that in seven of thirteen presidential elections, Republicans have captured at least 40 percent of the votes from union households.

UNION HOUSEHOLDS VOTING REPUBLICAN FOR PRESIDENT

YEAR	CANDIDATES	PERCENTAGE
1952	Eisenhower vs. Stevenson	44%
1956	Eisenhower vs. Stevenson	57
1960	Kennedy vs. Nixon	36
1964	Johnson vs. Goldwater	17
1968	Nixon vs. Humphrey	44
1972	Nixon vs. McGovern	57
1976	Carter vs. Ford	36
1980	Reagan vs. Carter	45
1984	Reagan vs. Mondale	43
1988	Bush vs. Dukakis	41
1992	Clinton vs. Bush	32
1996	Clinton vs. Dole	30
2000	Gore vs. Bush	37

SOURCES: *CQ Researcher,* June 28, 1996, p. 560; *New York Times,* November 10, 1996, p. 16; and authors' update.

A number of factors determine how voters make decisions at the polling place. Aside from the many demographic influences that come into play, there are also psychological factors that help shape the way voters make decisions when they enter the voting booth.

making. These factors, which are rooted in attitudes and beliefs held by voters, are (1) party identification, (2) perception of the candidates, and (3) issue preferences.

Party Identification.   With the possible exception of race, party identification has been the most important determinant of voting behavior in national elections. As we pointed out in Chapter 7, party affiliation is influenced by family and peer groups, by age, by the media, and by psychological attachment. During the 1950s, independent voters were a little more than 20 percent of the eligible electorate. In the middle to late 1960s, however, party identification began to weaken, and by the mid-1990s, independent voters constituted over 30 percent of all voters. In 2000, the estimated proportion of independent voters was between 26 and 33 percent. Independent voting seems to be concentrated among new voters, particularly among new young voters. Thus, we can still say that party identification for established voters is an important determinant in voter choice.

Perception of the Candidates.   The image of the candidate also seems to be important in a voter's choice for president. To some extent, voter attitudes toward candidates are based on emotions (such as trust) rather than on any judgment about experience or policy. In 2000, voters seemed to be attracted to candidates of high integrity and honesty.

Issue Preferences.   Issues make a difference in presidential and congressional elections. Although personality or image factors may be very persuasive, most voters have some notion of how the candidates differ on basic issues or at least know that the candidates want a change in the direction of government policy. As discussed in this chapter's *Which Side Are You On?* feature on the following page, the Internet provides new information resources to help voters determine candidates' views on various issues.

Historically, economic issues have the strongest influence on voters' choices. When the economy is doing well, it is very difficult for a challenger, particularly at the presidential level, to defeat the incumbent. In contrast, increasing infla-

which side are you on?

Choosing a Candidate on the Web

The World Wide Web is surely the richest possible source for finding information on political candidates. Individual candidates now have their own home pages on which they include everything from their views on issues to recipes for apple pie and pictures of the family pet. Other sites provide critical analyses of a candidate's positions or humorous interpretations of the candidate's views. Some sites, such as Project Vote Smart, attempt to gather information on all of the candidates, congressional and presidential, to allow the voter to do research starting from one site. In addition, Internet users can do their own research by accessing news and library resources from around the world.

A new generation of Web sites attempts to match users with particular candidates. These sites ask users to record their views on a variety of issues and then match each individual's views to those of the candidate who is closest in philosophy. This sounds like an easy way to narrow the search for the right candidate. Choosing a candidate, however, is not like choosing a vacation or a digital camera. Should you select a president, for example, by picking the one person who matches your individual requirements? How should you figure in the needs of the country at this time? Should you consider the needs of other voters or other people in the population that you think deserve attention, such as children or the elderly? Is it a good idea to think about whether the individual has a record of getting legislation passed or administering a large organization? Can the sum of important factors in voting be found in an Internet match?

DOES IT MATTER?

What would the voting outcome be if all voters picked the candidate who matched all of their views most closely? Would there be more votes for third-party candidates? Would more people not vote because they were unable to find a match?

GOING ONLINE

Try the match at **http://www.selectsmart.com** *or* **http://www.GoVote.com**. *For a more traditional site, go to* **http://www.vote-smart.org**.

Issue Voting
Voting for a candidate based on how he or she stands on a particular issue.

tion, rising unemployment, or high interest rates are likely to work to the disadvantage of the incumbent. Studies of how economic conditions affect the vote differ in their conclusions. Some indicate that people vote on the basis of their personal economic well-being, whereas other studies seem to show that people vote on the basis of the nation's overall economic health.

Foreign policy issues become more prominent in a time of crisis. Although the parties and candidates have differed greatly over policy toward trade with China, for example, foreign policy issues are truly influential only when armed conflict is a possibility. Clearly, public dissension over the war in Vietnam had an effect on elections in 1968 and 1972.

Some of the most heated debates in American political campaigns take place over the social issues of abortion, the role of women, the rights of lesbians and gay males, and prayer in the public schools. In general, presidential candidates would prefer to avoid such issues, because voters who care about these questions are likely to be offended if a candidate does not share their views.

From time to time, drugs, crime, and corruption become important campaign issues. The Watergate affair cost the Republicans a number of congressional seats in 1974, and its aftereffects probably defeated Gerald Ford in 1976. If the president or high officials are involved in truly criminal or outrageous conduct, the issue will undoubtedly influence voters.

All candidates try to set themselves apart from their opposition on crucial issues in order to attract voters. What is difficult to ascertain is the extent to which issues overshadow partisan loyalty or personality factors in the voters' minds. It appears that some campaigns are much more issue oriented than others. Some research has shown that **issue voting** was most important in the presidential elections of 1964, 1968, and 1972, was moderately important in 1980, and was less important in the 1990s and early 2000s.

Why Voters Voted as They Did in 2000

The incredibly close presidential elections in 2000 reflected some real divisions within the American electorate. Some of the divisions were related to the characteristics of the voters: African Americans were highly likely to vote for Al Gore, while wealthier voters chose George W. Bush. Jewish voters were much more likely to vote for the Gore-Lieberman ticket, and better educated Americans were more likely to vote for the Bush-Cheney combination. The election outcomes, however, were decided by voters' views on the issues and on national priorities. Those voters who felt that tax cuts should be a priority voted for Bush, while those who felt that prescription drug coverage and fixing Social Security were top priorities voted for Gore. Exit polls showed that the voters pretty clearly understood how the candidates differed and voted accordingly. The messages put forward by the candidates about their views on the role of government versus the role of the individual helped voters to make up their mind. While President Clinton was not an issue for most voters, those who had an unfavorable view of him were very likely to vote for George W. Bush.

Campaigns, Candidates, and Elections: Issues for the Twenty-First Century

Few areas in American politics seem to be in such need of change and reform as campaigns, voting, and elections. Every four years, polls show that the majority of Americans are dissatisfied with the length of campaigns, with vicious campaign strategies, with the caliber of candidates, and with the influence of campaign contributions on the system. Yet very few serious reforms result, in part, because reforms might affect the people in office, and after the campaign fury subsides, most citizens are willing to get on with their personal business and allow the officials elected in that campaign to take office and hold political authority.

The cost of waging a national or statewide campaign continues to rise due to the need to obtain media coverage, to use new technologies, and to hire many campaign professionals. The issue of how campaigns are to be financed in the future while still preserving freedom of speech and press for all, including candidates, will continue to demand the attention of American voters and politicians.

The Internet will play an even greater role in campaigns of the future, forcing society to deal with such issues as the truthfulness of the content of Web publications and the security of one's interactions with the Internet. In addition, the success of mail balloting in Oregon suggests that in the future, the American political system may embrace new forms of voting, such as mail voting, telephone balloting, or Internet voting, that are more in keeping with society today.

Perhaps the most important issue for the future is the increasing cynicism of the American electorate with regard to government and politics. As voter participation falls and cynicism rises, the nation will need to address the issues that have sapped the public's confidence not only in the government but also in the democratic electoral system that we use to choose our government.

making a difference

Registering and Voting

In nearly every state, before you are allowed to cast a vote in an election, you must first register. Registration laws vary considerably from state to state, and, depending on how difficult a state's laws make it to register, some states have much higher rates of registration and voting participation than do others.

What do you have to do to register and cast a vote? Most states require that you meet minimum residence requirements. In other words, you must have lived in the state in which you plan to be registered for a specified period of time. You may retain your previous registration, if any, in another state, and you can cast an absentee vote if your previous state permits that. The minimum-residency requirement is very short in some states, such as one day in Alabama or ten days in New Hampshire and Wisconsin. No state requires more than thirty days. Other states with voter residency requirements have minimum-day requirements between these extremes. Twenty states do not have any minimum-residency requirement at all.

Nearly every state also specifies a closing date by which you must be registered before an election. In other words, even if you have met a residency require-ment, you still may not be able to vote if you register too close to the day of the election. The closing date is different in certain states (Connecticut, Delaware, and Louisiana) for primary elections than for other elections. The closing date for registration varies from election day itself (Maine, Minnesota, Oregon, and Wisconsin) to thirty days before the election (Arizona). Delaware specifies the third Saturday in October as the closing date. In North Dakota, no registration is necessary.

In most states, your registration can be revoked if you do not vote within a certain number of years. This process of automatically "purging" the voter-registration lists of nonactive voters happens every two years in about a dozen states, every three years in Georgia, every four years in more than twenty other states, every five years in Maryland and Rhode Island, every eight years in North Carolina, and every ten years in Michigan. Ten states do not require this purging at all.

What you must do to register and remain registered to vote varies from state to state and even from county to county within a state. In general, you must be a citizen of the United States, at least eighteen years old on or before election day, and a resident of the state in which you intend to register.

Using Iowa as an example, you normally would register through the local county auditor or when you obtain your driver's license (under the "motor voter" law of 1993). If you moved to a new address within the state, you would also have to change your registration to vote by contacting the auditor. Postcard regis-trations must be postmarked or delivered to the county auditor no later than the twenty-fifth day before an election. Party affiliation may be changed or declared when you register or reregister, or you may change or declare a party at the polls on election day. Postcard registra-tion forms in Iowa are available at many public buildings, from labor unions, at political party headquarters, at the county auditors' offices, or from campus groups. Registrars who will accept registrations at other locations may be located by call-ing your party headquarters or your county auditor.

For more information on voting regis-tration, contact your county or state offi-cials, party headquarters, labor union, or local chapter of the League of Women Voters. The Web site for the League of Women Voters is

http://www.lwv.org

Key terms

Australian ballot 328

"beauty contest" 321

bundling 321

caucus 323

coattail effect 328

corrupt practices acts 316

credentials committee 324

elector 325

focus group 316

front-loading 323

front-runner 323

Hatch Act 317

independent expenditures 319

issue voting 343

office-block, or Massachusetts, ballot 328

party-column, or Indiana, ballot 328

political consultant 314

presidential primary 321

rational ignorance effect 333

registration 335

socioeconomic status 337

soft money 319

superdelegate 322

Super Tuesday 323

tracking poll 316

voter turnout 331

Chapter summary

1   People may choose to run for political office to further their careers, to carry out specific political programs, or in response to certain issues or events. The legal qualifications for holding political office are minimal at both the state and local levels, but holders of political office still are predominantly white and male and are likely to be from the professional class.

2   American political campaigns are lengthy and extremely expensive. In the last decade, they have become more candidate centered rather than party centered in response to technological innovations and decreasing party identification. Candidates have begun to rely less on the party and more on paid professional consultants to perform the various tasks necessary to wage a political campaign. The crucial task of professional political consultants is image building. The campaign organization devises a campaign strategy to maximize the candidate's chances of winning. Candidates use public opinion polls to gauge their popularity and to test the mood of the country.

3   The amount of money spent in financing campaigns is steadily increasing. A variety of corrupt practices acts have been passed to regulate campaign finance. The Federal Election Campaign Acts of 1972 and 1974 instituted major reforms by limiting spending and contributions; the acts allowed corporations, labor unions, and interest groups to set up political action committees (PACs) to raise money for candidates. New techniques, including contributions to the parties, independent expenditures, and bundling, have been created to raise money.

4   Following the Democratic convention of 1968, the McGovern-Fraser Commission was appointed to study the problems of the primary system. It formulated new rules, which were adopted by all Democrats and by Republicans in many states. These reforms opened up the nomination process for the presidency to all voters.

5   A presidential primary is a statewide election to help a political party determine its presidential nominee at the national convention. Some states use the caucus method of choosing convention delegates. The primary campaign recently has been shortened to the first few months of the election year.

6   In making a presidential choice on election day, the voter technically does not vote directly for a candidate but chooses between slates of presidential electors. The slate that wins the most popular votes throughout the state gets to cast all the electoral votes for the state. The candidate receiving a majority (270) of the electoral votes wins. Both the mechanics and the politics of the electoral college have been sharply criticized. There have been many proposed reforms, including a proposal that direct elections be held in which candidates would be elected on a popular-vote basis.

7   The United States uses the Australian ballot, a secret ballot that is prepared, distributed, and counted by government officials. The office-block ballot groups candidates according to office. The party-column ballot groups candidates according to their party labels and symbols.

8   Voter participation in the United States is low (and generally declining) compared with that of other countries. Some view the decline in voter turnout as a threat to representative democracy, whereas others believe it simply indicates greater satisfaction with the status quo. There is an association between voting and a person's age, education, minority status, and income level. Another factor affecting voter turnout is the extent to which elections are competitive within a state.

9   In colonial times, only white males with a certain minimum amount of property were eligible to vote. The suffrage issue has concerned, at one time or another, most groups in the United States. Currently, to be eligible to vote, a person must satisfy registration, citizenship, and specified age and residency requirements. Each state has different qualifications. It is argued that these requirements are responsible for much of the nonparticipation in the political process in the United States.

10   Socioeconomic or demographic factors that influence voting decisions include (a) education, (b) income and socioeconomic status, (c) religion, (d) ethnic background, (e) gender, (f) age, and (g) geographic region. Psychological factors that influence voting decisions include (a) party identification, (b) perception of candidates, and (c) issue preferences.

Selected print and electronic resources

SUGGESTED READINGS

Bike, William S. *Winning Political Campaigns: A Comprehensive Guide to Electoral Success.* New York: Denali Press, 1998. This is a guide to politics for any aspiring officeholder or candidate.

Conway, M. Margaret, Gertrude A. Steuernagel, and David W. Ahern. *Women and Political Participation.* Washington, D.C.: CQ Press, 1997. This volume examines the changing role of women in the political system, including the increase in participation and officeholding by women.

Davis, James W. *U.S. Presidential Primaries and the Caucus-Convention System: A Sourcebook.* New York: Greenwood Press, 1997. A comprehensive source book on the history of the American electoral system, this work provides analyses of primaries, polls, and campaign-finance regulations.

Hill, Kevin A., and John E. Hughes. *Cyberpolitics: Citizen Activism in the Age of the Internet: People, Passions and Power.* Lanham, Md.: Rowman & Littlefield Publishing Group, 1998. The authors look at who uses the Internet, what kinds of information they look for, and how people "talk" on the Internet about politics.

Lupia, Arthur, and Mathew D. McCubbins. *The Democratic Dilemma.* New York: Cambridge University Press, 1998. Using advances in psychology and economics to inform their work, the authors investigate the question of how citizens with little information make reasonable choices in a democratic system.

Witcover, Jules. *No Way to Pick a President.* New York: Farrar, Straus & Giroux, 2000. Witcover, a veteran Washington newspaper reporter, outlines the troubles that plague presidential elections—campaign finance, the electoral college, and voter alienation—and then proposes some changes.

MEDIA RESOURCES

The Candidate—Starring the young Robert Redford, this 1972 film produced by Warner Brothers effectively investigates and satirizes the decisions that a candidate for the U.S. Senate must make. It's a political classic.

The War Room—Using video coverage taped throughout Bill Clinton's 1992 campaign for the presidency, this 1993 documentary shows the strategic decisions behind the scenes in the campaign. Footage shows Clinton's strategists, including James Carville and George Stephanopoulos, pulling out all the stops for their candidate.

All the King's Men—A classic film, produced in 1949 and based on a best-selling novel by Robert Penn Warren, that traces the rise to power of a southern politician (played by Broderick Crawford) and parallels the life of Huey Long, the governor of Louisiana during the Great Depression of the 1930s.

Campaigns and Elections Video Library—A series of videos, made available in 1998 by the periodical *Campaigns and Elections*, that include the best campaign ads of specific election cycles, the best overall ads, and the classic ads of all time.

Bulworth—A satirical look at a Senate candidate who tells the truth. The film, starring Warren Beatty, was released in 1999.

Logging on

For detailed information about current campaign election laws and for the latest filings of finance reports, see the site maintained by the Federal Election Commission at

http://www.fec.gov

To find excellent reports on where the money comes from and how it is spent in campaigns, be sure to view the site maintained by the Center for Responsive Politics at

http://www.opensecrets.org

You can learn about the impact of different voting systems on election strategies and outcomes at the following Web site:

http://www.igc.org/cvd

Another excellent site for investigating voting records and campaign-finance information is that of Project Vote Smart. Go to

http://www.vote-smart.org

For a site that gives you information about political races around the nation and about controversial issues, go to ElectNet at

http://www.EL.com

Using the Internet for political analysis

Point your browser at either the Federal Election Commission site (**http://www.fec.org**) or the Center for Responsive Politics site (**http://www.opensecrets.org**). Choose the campaign-finance records of at least three individual candidates or members of Congress. Print out those records, and then compare the types of donors that are listed. Can you find enough information about campaign donations to have some idea of what policy positions are held by the candidates? What does the donor list tell you about each person's role and importance in Congress?

chapter 11

The Media and Cyberpolitics

CHAPTER OUTLINE

- The Media's Functions

- History of the Media in the United States

- The Primacy of Television

- The Media and Political Campaigns

- The Media and the Government

- Government Regulation of the Media

- The Public's Right to Media Access

- Bias in the Media

what if...

The Internet Replaced Broadcast News?

BACKGROUND

FROM THE BEGINNING OF RADIO BROADCASTING UNTIL THE DEVELOPMENT OF CABLE TELEVISION IN THE 1980S, THE ELECTRONIC MEDIA HAVE BEEN DOMINATED BY LARGE NATIONAL NETWORKS. AS TELEVISION CAME TO DOMINATE THE NEWS INDUSTRY, NEWSPAPERS STRUGGLED TO KEEP THEIR READERS. MOST CITIES AND TOWNS NO LONGER HAVE COMPETING NEWSPAPERS. WITH THE RISE OF CABLE TELEVISION AND THE ARRIVAL OF THE INTERNET, MANY PEOPLE, IN THE UNITED STATES AND AROUND THE WORLD, HAVE MULTIPLE NEWS OUTLETS FROM WHICH TO CHOOSE.

TELEVISION NETWORKS AND MOST NEWSPAPERS ARE TRYING TO WIN BACK THEIR FORMER VIEWERS AND READERS BY ESTABLISHING THEIR OWN WEB SITES ON THE INTERNET. UNLIKE THE EVENING NETWORK NEWS, HOWEVER, THE INTERNET IS ACCESSIBLE TO USERS AT ANY TIME DAY OR NIGHT. IN ADDITION, VIRTUALLY ANYONE WITH A COMPUTER AND TELEPHONE LINE CAN BECOME A BROADCASTER AND HAVE HIS OR HER OWN NEWSCAST.

WHAT IF THE INTERNET REPLACED BROADCAST NEWS?

It took radio thirty-eight years to reach 50 million listeners. The Internet had more than that number of users in just four years. Clearly, the Internet is on the way to becoming the most popular way for people to communicate, do business, and seek information, including the news that they may have received previously via television. At the same time that the Internet is growing, audience shares for network television are dropping. Cable television continues to increase its share and, in some markets, also offers high-speed Internet connections.

Given the rapid spread of Internet use among the public and the growth of high-speed connections for businesses and households, the Internet could easily replace broadcast news in the United States. Imagine everyone getting the headlines on her or his personal, handheld device. Families would get the news via a permanently connected computer that could instantly retrieve the home page for a news source.

What would the news industry be like if the Internet supplanted television networks? The networks and cable companies would, of course, have their own Web sites. They might, in fact, have multiple Web sites so that users could log on to news about sports, politics, business, or style separately. Users could also choose hundreds of alternative news sites, however: the cost of setting up an Internet site is so low that most towns and cities would offer many local sites, and thousands of newscasts would be available from third-party political groups or special interests, such as environmentalists.

What would happen to the news anchors and news-gathering organizations maintained by the networks? Although it would be possible to receive "video" of the news anchors over the Internet, "live broadcasts" would become obsolete. Why should users watch an old newscast on video when they can get breaking news from the Internet? News-gathering, however, would become much more important because users want instant access to breaking stories.

WOULD THE INTERNET BE BIASED?

The Internet has the potential to open the news to hundreds of different viewpoints. No longer could the public charge the media with bias toward either political party. Users could find virtually any political position or viewpoint on Internet broadcasts of news.

In addition, news broadcasts via the Internet could do a much better job of representing minority populations or other groups in the United States that have less access to the broadcast business. One would find Web sites hosted by African Americans, women, people with disabilities, Greek Americans, Turkish Americans, and so on. Internet journalists would cover events around the world with digital cameras and post pictures on the Web instantly. Americans could see firsthand the oppression of people in some countries and learn about different cultures and political policies around the world.

Nonetheless, the Internet, by its nature, would be biased as a news source. Although Web sites provided by major news organizations would be edited for content and their news sources checked for accuracy, hundreds of Web sites would have no editing or checking of facts. Many individuals and groups would maintain Web sites to put forward their own views of the news and of public issues. Individual users would have to be much more critical of news sources to be sure of their accuracy. The Internet would provide many opportunities for hateful speech and the spreading of lies about individuals or specific groups.

FOR CRITICAL ANALYSIS

1. If all Americans had access to the Internet, would anyone want to watch network news? What would they want to see covered in such broadcasts?

2. How could people be assured that Internet news was factual and accurate?

The study of people and politics—of how people gain the information that they need to be able to choose between political candidates, to organize for their own interests, and to formulate opinions on the policies and decisions of the government—needs to take into account the role played by the media in the United States. Historically, the printed media played the most important role in informing public debate. The printed media developed, for the most part, our understanding of how news is to be reported. Today, however, more than 90 percent of all Americans use television news as their primary source of information. In addition, the Internet has become a source for political communication and fund-raising. About 50 percent of American households now have computers, and 40 percent use the Internet for communications and information. As Internet use grows, the system of gathering and sharing news and information is changing from one in which the media have a primary role to one in which the individual citizen may play a greater role. The chapter-opening *What If . . .* explores some of the possible consequences of such a change for the future. With that future in mind, it is important to analyze the current relationship between the media and politics.

The Media's Functions

The mass media perform a number of different functions in any country. In the United States, we can list at least six. Almost all of them can have political implications, and some are essential to the democratic process. These functions are as follows: (1) entertainment, (2) reporting the news, (3) identifying public problems, (4) socializing new generations, (5) providing a political forum, and (6) making profits. It is important to keep in mind that almost all newspapers and radio and television outlets are owned by private corporations. We will examine the growing influence of corporate giants on the media in the *Critical Perspective* presented later in this chapter on page 353.

Entertainment

By far the greatest number of radio and television hours are dedicated to entertaining the public. The battle for prime-time ratings indicates how important successful entertainment is to the survival of networks and individual stations.

President Clinton arrives at the International Press Center, in Thurmont, Maryland, during the Middle East summit talks at Camp David in July 2000. Clinton's role in hosting the negotiations at Camp David gained him worldwide media attention, as did his trip to Japan, in the middle of the negotiations, to participate in a G–8 conference—a meeting attended by the representatives of the world's leading industrialized nations.

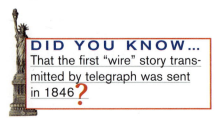

Although there is no direct linkage between entertainment and politics, network dramas often introduce material that may be politically controversial and that may stimulate public discussion. Made-for-TV movies have focused on many controversial topics, including AIDS, incest, and wife battering.

Reporting the News

A primary function of the mass media in all their forms—newspapers and magazines, radio, television, cable, and online news services—is the reporting of news. The media convey words and pictures about events, facts, personalities, and ideas. The protections of the First Amendment are intended to keep the flow of news as free as possible, because it is an essential part of the democratic process. If citizens cannot get unbiased information about the state of their communities and their leaders' actions, how can they make voting decisions? Perhaps the most incisive comment about the importance of the media was made by James Madison, who said, "A people who mean to be their own governors must arm themselves with the power knowledge gives. A popular government without popular information or the means of acquiring it, is but a prologue to a farce or a tragedy or perhaps both."[1] Not all nations accept this premise of democratic thought, however, as explained in this chapter's *Global View*.

Identifying Public Problems

Public Agenda

Issues that commonly are perceived by members of the political community as meriting public attention and governmental action. The media play an important role in setting the public agenda by focusing attention on certain topics.

The power of information is important not only in revealing what the government is doing but also in determining what the government ought to do—in other words, in setting the **public agenda**. The mass media identify public issues, such as the placement of convicted sex offenders in new homes and neighborhoods. The media then influence the passage of legislation, such as "Megan's Law," which requires police to notify neighbors about the release and/or resettlement of certain offenders. American journalists also work in a long tradition of uncovering public wrongdoing, corruption, and bribery and of bringing such wrongdoing to the public's attention. Closely related to this investigative function is that of presenting policy alternatives. Public policy is often complex and

[1]As quoted in "Castro vs. (Some) Censorship," *The New York Times*, November 22, 1983, p. 24.

global **View**

Media Issues around the World

For all of our complaining about bias in the media and the superficiality of American news, the United States has more freedom of expression than many other nations. Although the national networks might be criticized for their staunch support of corporate America, the Internet, low-frequency radio, and many other outlets permit the free expression of radical and sometimes distasteful views.

Censorship of newspapers is still quite common around the world. The governments of Iraq and Iran routinely censors and shut down newspapers for political content, as does the government of China. Many nations censor television and movies for sexual content on the ground that it violates the mores of their societies. In virtually any nation that has an authoritarian govern-

ment, newspapers are carefully watched and censorship measures imposed if they express too much opposition to the government.

The Internet has provided a new and extremely useful tool for opposition groups throughout the world. Using just text or text and pictures, opposition media can transmit information about their political situation throughout the world. The Chinese government, for just that reason, has tightly controlled the Internet. No unfavorable news is to be sent out to China by dissidents. Western citizens can follow the degree of censorship and control of the media by government through a number of Web sites, including the one maintained by Mediachannel.

FOR CRITICAL ANALYSIS

Why does the Internet pose such a threat to authoritarian governments? Why do most governments need Internet access to improve their economies?

The town meeting of yesterday has given way to the electronic town meeting of today. Here, then Vice President Al Gore answers a question asked by a citizen in another location but whose image and voice were transmitted through videoconferencing telecommunications equipment. As telecommunications that include video and voice become better and cheaper, politicians will be able to use the electronic town-meeting concept more and more.

difficult to make entertaining, but programs devoted to public policy increasingly are being scheduled for prime-time television. Most networks produce shows with a "news magazine" format that sometimes include segments on foreign policy and other issues.

Socializing New Generations

As mentioned in Chapter 7, the media, and particularly television, strongly influence the beliefs and opinions of all Americans. Because of this influence, the media play a significant role in the political socialization of the younger generation, as well as immigrants to this country. Through the transmission of historical information (sometimes fictionalized), the presentation of American culture, and the portrayal of the diverse regions and groups in the United States, the media teach young people and immigrants about what it means to be an American. TV talk shows, such as *Oprah,* sometimes focus on controversial issues (such as abortion or assisted suicide) that relate to basic American values (such as liberty). Many children's shows are designed not only to entertain young viewers but also to instruct them in the traditional moral values of American society. In recent years, the public has become increasingly concerned about the level of violence depicted on children's programs and on other shows during prime time.

Providing a Political Forum

As part of their news function, the media also provide a political forum for leaders and the public. Candidates for office use news reporting to sustain interest in their campaigns, whereas officeholders use the media to gain support for their policies or to present an image of leadership. Presidential trips abroad are an outstanding way for the chief executive to get colorful, positive, and exciting news coverage that makes the president look "presidential." The media also offer a way for citizens to participate in public debate, through letters to the editor,

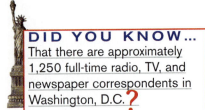

televised editorials, or electronic mail. The question of whether more public access should be provided will be discussed later in this chapter.

Making Profits

Most of the news media in the United States are private, for-profit corporate enterprises. One of their goals is to make profits—for employee salaries, for expansion, and for dividends to the stockholders who own the companies. Profits are made, in general, by charging for advertising. Advertising revenues usually are related directly to circulation or to listener/viewer ratings. (Recent developments in the area of media ownership, particularly with respect to corporate mergers and the potential for monopoly control of the news, are discussed in this chapter's *Critical Perspective*.)

Several well-known outlets are publicly owned—public television stations in many communities and National Public Radio. These operate without extensive commercials, are locally supported, and are often subsidized by the government and corporations.

Added up, these factors form the basis for a complex relationship among the media, the government, and the public. Throughout the rest of this chapter, we examine some of the many facets of this relationship. Our purpose is to set a foundation for understanding how the media influence the political process.

History of the Media in the United States

Many years ago Thomas Jefferson wrote, "Were it left to me to decide whether we should have a government without newspapers, or newspapers without a government, I should not hesitate a moment to prefer the latter."[2] Although the media have played a significant role in politics since the founding of this nation, they were not as overwhelmingly important in the past as they are today. For one thing, politics was controlled by a small elite who communicated personally. For another, during the early 1800s and before, news traveled slowly. If an important political event occurred in New York, it was not known until five days later in Philadelphia; ten days later in the capital cities of Connecticut, Maryland, and Virginia; and fifteen days later in Boston.

Roughly three thousand newspapers were being published by 1860. Some of these, such as the *New York Tribune,* were mainly sensation mongers that concentrated on crimes, scandals, and the like. The *New York Herald* specialized in self-improvement and what today would be called practical news. Although sensational and biased reporting often created political divisiveness (this was true particularly during the Civil War), many historians believe that the growth of the printed media played an important role in unifying the country.

The Rise of the Political Press

Americans may cherish the idea of a nonpartisan press, but in the early years of the nation's history, the number of politically sponsored newspapers was significant. The sole reason for the existence of such periodicals was to further the interests of the politicians who paid for their publication. As chief executive of our government during this period, George Washington has been called a "firm

INFOTRAC®
COLLEGE EDITION

FCC eyes AOL-TW

---

[2]As quoted in Richard M. Clurman, "The Media Learn a Lesson," *The New York Times,* December 2, 1983, p. A2.

Is There a Media Monopoly?

For decades, Republican politicians have complained about a liberal bias in the media, while Democratic candidates have suggested that the corporate character of newspapers makes them biased in favor of Republicans–at least in terms of endorsements on the editorial page. The recent explosion of mergers and acquisitions in the media business suggests, however, that the real source of bias in the media in the future will be corporate and that the real danger is media monopoly.

Merger Mania

Within the past decade, all of the prime-time television networks have been purchased by major American corporations and have become part of corporate conglomerates. The Turner Broadcasting/CNN network was also purchased by a major corporation, Time Warner; and Fox Television is already part of Rupert Murdoch's publishing and media empire. In addition to these mergers and acquisitions, many of these corporations have formed partnerships with computer software makers, such as Microsoft, for joint electronic publishing ventures. In January 2000, America Online (AOL) announced its acquisition of Time Warner. This merger combined the world's largest media company with the world's largest online company.

Corporate Control

Critics are very concerned that these corporations may exercise censorship over materials that might be damaging to their corporate profits and that news and information might have a bias toward their corporate business interests. One such critic, Dan Kennedy, gives evidence of corporate control in two instances: the *Jim Hightower Show,* a Texas populist talk show, was canceled soon after Disney acquired Capital Cities, presumably because Hightower had been critical of the corporate takeover on the air; and CBS's lawyers, in an attempt to avoid public and expensive lawsuits, forced *60 Minutes* to cancel an interview with a tobacco researcher who was going to talk about his research.*

Critics suggest that the corporate perspective involves very subtle forms of bias, including the suppression of news that could hurt the parent corporation, the refusal to deal with certain issues because they might potentially provoke unpopular lawsuits, and a movement toward less controversial, pure entertainment "news"–because it will offend fewer viewers.

Corporate Monopoly

The new company formed by the AOL–Time Warner merger, for example, is able to control content on networks, on the Internet, and in popular magazines. Each form of media can advertise the others and control the content to benefit its own interest. Because these major corporations control a very large percentage of local television stations, as well as other media producers (books, cable, music, movie studios), their viewpoints could become pervasive, truly limiting freedom of the press and depriving citizens of full debate on public issues.

FOR CRITICAL ANALYSIS

1. What kinds of viewpoints might be suppressed by these corporate conglomerates?
2. How can a reader or viewer determine whether a story might be biased toward the corporation's profits?

*Dan Kennedy, "Merger Mania," *The Boston Phoenix,* December 5, 1995, http://www.bostonphoenix.com.

---

believer" in **managed news.** Although acknowledging that the public had a right to be informed, he felt that some matters should be kept secret and that news that might damage the image of the United States should not be published. Washington, however, made no attempt to control the press.

Managed News
Information generated and distributed by the government in such a way as to give government interests priority over candor.

The Development of Mass-Readership Newspapers

Two inventions in the nineteenth century led to the development of mass-readership newspapers. The first was the high-speed rotary press; the second was the telegraph. Faster presses meant lower per-unit costs and lower subscription prices. By 1848, the Associated Press had developed the telegraph into a nationwide apparatus for the dissemination of all types of information on a systematic basis.

" INTERESTING.....IT'S LIKE A PORTABLE 500K FILE and YOU DON'T HAVE TO WAIT FOR IT TO DOWNLOAD.... AND YOU SAY IT'S CALLED A NEWSPAPER ?"

Reprinted with special permission of King Features Syndicate.

Along with these technological changes came a growing population and increasing urbanization. Daily newspapers could be supported by a larger, more urban population, even if the price per paper was only a penny. Finally, the burgeoning, diversified economy encouraged the growth of advertising, which meant that newspapers could obtain additional revenues from merchants who seized the opportunity to promote their wares to a larger public.

The Popular Press and Yellow Journalism

Yellow Journalism
A term for sensationalistic, irresponsible journalism. Reputedly, the term is short for "Yellow Kid Journalism," an allusion to the cartoon "The Yellow Kid" in the old *New York World,* a newspaper especially noted for its sensationalism.

Students of the history of journalism have ascertained a change, in the last half of the 1800s, not in the level of biased news reporting but in its origin. Whereas politically sponsored newspapers had expounded a particular political party's point of view, the post–Civil War mass-based newspapers expounded whatever political philosophy the owner of the newspaper happened to have.

Even if newspaper owners did not have a particular political axe to grind, they often allowed their editors to engage in sensationalism and what is known as **yellow journalism.** The questionable or simply personal activities of a prominent businessperson, politician, or socialite were front-page material. Newspapers, then as now, made their economic way by maximizing readership. As the *National Enquirer* demonstrates with its current circulation of more than five million, sensationalism is still rewarded by high levels of readership.

The Age of the Electromagnetic Signal

KDKA-Pittsburgh broadcasts the presidential-election returns in 1920.

The first scheduled radio program in the United States featured politicians. On the night of November 2, 1920, KDKA-Pittsburgh transmitted the returns of the presidential-election race between Warren G. Harding and James M. Cox. The listeners were a few thousand people tuning in on very primitive, homemade sets.

By 1924, there were nearly 1,400 radio stations. But it wasn't until 8 P.M. on November 15, 1926, that the electronic media came into their own in the United States. On that night, the National Broadcasting Company (NBC) made its debut with a four-hour program broadcast by twenty-five stations in twenty-one cities. Network broadcasting had become a reality.

In a cartoon attacking yellow journalism, William Randolph Hearst (left) and Joseph Pulitzer (right) are lampooned for emphasizing scandal and gossip in news coverage.

Even with the advent of national radio in the 1920s and television in the late 1940s, many politicians were slow to understand the significance of the **electronic media.** The 1952 presidential campaign was the first to involve a real role for television. Television coverage of the Republican convention helped Dwight Eisenhower win over delegates and secure the nomination. His vice presidential running mate, Richard Nixon, put the TV time to good use. Accused of hiding a secret slush fund, Nixon replied to his critics with his famous "Checkers" speech. He denied the attacks, cried real tears, and said that the only thing he ever received from a contributor for his personal use was his dog, Checkers. It was a highly effective performance.

Today, television dominates the campaign strategy of every would-be national politician, as well as that of every elected official. Politicians think of ways to continue to be newsworthy, thereby gaining access to the electronic media. Attacking the president's programs is one way of becoming newsworthy; other ways include holding highly visible hearings on controversial subjects, going on "fact-finding" trips, and gimmicks (such as a walking tour of a state). President Clinton's 1992 presidential campaign perfected the technique of "instant response," meaning that every attack was answered immediately, usually with a counterattack on the opponent.

Electronic Media
Communication channels that involve electronic transmissions, such as radio, television, and, to an increasing extent, the Internet.

How Monica Story Played

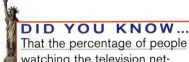

Narrowcasting
Broadcasting that is targeted to one small sector of the population.

The Revolution in the Electronic Media

Just as technological change was responsible for the end of politically sponsored periodicals, technology is increasing the number of alternative news sources today. The advent of pay TV, cable TV, subscription TV, satellite TV, and the Internet has completely changed the electronic media landscape. When there were basically only three TV networks, it was indeed a "wasteland," as former Federal Communications Commission chairman Newton Minnow once claimed. But now, with hundreds, if not thousands, of potential outlets for specialized programs, the electronic media are becoming more and more like the printed media in catering to specialized tastes. This is sometimes referred to as **narrowcasting.** Both cable television and the Internet offer the public unparalleled access to specialized information on everything from gardening and home repair to sports and religion. Most viewers are able to choose among several sources for their favorite type of programming. As detailed in the *Making Waves* feature, new groups can have control as well.

In recent years, narrowcasting has become increasingly prevalent. Consumers watch only those shows and channels that they like, and the networks' audiences are declining. Between 1982 and 2001 network television's share of the audience fell from 72 percent to 55 percent. At the same time, the percentage of households having access to the Internet grew from zero to more than 50 percent, with 20 percent of all households belonging to an online service. (For some implications of news publication on the Internet, see the feature *E-mocracy: The Media and the Internet* on page 358.)

Talk-Show Politics

In the realm of politics, the multiple news outlets have given rise to literally thousands of talk shows, whether on television, radio, or the Internet. By 2000, there were more than two dozen national television talk shows; their hosts ranged from Jerry Springer, who is regarded as a sensationalist, to Larry King, whose show has become a political necessity for candidates. Ross Perot actually announced his candidacy for the presidency in the 1992 election on *Larry King Live*.

CNN's Larry King, left, interviews Republican presidential candidate and Texas governor George W. Bush and his wife, Laura, for his show, *Larry King Live,* on July 20, 2000, in Austin, Texas.

The real blossoming of "talk" has occurred on the radio. The number of radio stations that program only talk shows has increased from about 300 in 1989 to more than 1,200 today. The topics of talk shows range from business and investment to psychology to politics. There has been considerable criticism of the political talk shows, especially those hosted by Rush Limbaugh, G. Gordon Liddy, and other conservatives. Critics contend that such shows increase the level of intolerance and irrationality in American politics. The listeners to those shows are self-selected and tend to share the viewpoint of the host. Similarly,

making waves

Pioneering New Internet Media for New Groups

The Internet clearly offers opportunities for communication and business to groups within American society that have not had access to ownership or control of the media. Young entrepreneurs are leading the way in opening Internet sites to women and minority groups. Candice Carpenter, whose experiences include working at Time Life Video and serving as former president of QVC, a cable shopping network, started iVillage as an Internet site for women in 1995. The site, which offers information about child care, health, and working moms' issues and provides chat groups for women, is immensely popular. As a corporate leader, Carpenter, now forty-seven years old, allows employees to take a month's leave to rest after they have been with the company for only three years.

Fernando J. Espuelas, age thirty-three, started Media Network in 1996 to provide a media company for Spanish- and Portuguese-speaking Americans. These groups, which have no national network devoted to their views, can get news, Internet service, and e-commerce services from Espuelas's company. This upstart company is also providing services throughout North and South America. Espuelas, reflecting on the success of his company, says, "Well, what happens in ten years and what happens in twenty years? Which is kind of a ridiculous thing to think about on the Internet."*

These young Internet entrepreneurs and others are providing access to news and services to groups that have not been targeted by major media companies. Their success will attract others who will market to groups within American society that may have previously been left out of the news business. One of the consequences of such specialized news media is that their clients will see politics in terms of their own issues and not think about the impact on society as a whole. Of course, that is what the national media have been doing for many decades.

FOR CRITICAL ANALYSIS

Do media companies that target one or two specialized demographic or ethnic groups work to reduce the sense of a national culture and a national political system?

*"Online Pioneers: The Buzz Never Stops," *The New York Times,* November 21, 1999, Section 3, p. 14.

the Internet makes it possible for a Web site to be highly ideological or partisan and to encourage chat with others of the same persuasion. One of the potential hazards of narrowcasting of this kind is that people will be less open to dialogue with those whose opinions differ from their own and that more extremism in politics may result.

The Primacy of Television

Television is the most influential medium. It also is big business. National news TV personalities such as Peter Jennings may earn in excess of several million dollars per year from their TV news–reporting contracts alone. They are paid so much because they command large audiences, and large audiences command high prices for advertising on national news shows. Indeed, news *per se* has become a major factor in the profitability of TV stations. In 1963, the major networks—ABC, CBS, and NBC—devoted only eleven minutes daily to national news. By 2000, the amount of time on the networks devoted to news-type programming had increased to about three hours. In addition, a

e-mocracy

The Media and the Internet

When the Internet became accessible to millions of Americans through their personal computers and the introduction of browsers that enable people to search the Web quickly, the established news media, such as the *New York Times* and *Washington Post,* were less than eager to embrace this technology. They worried that if people could read the paper free on the Internet or get online updates on sports events, they would stop buying newspapers. The three major broadcasting networks were also leery of this technology and feared that it would lure people away from television. The quick adaptation to the Web by some news outlets such as CNN and the rapid development of electronic news resources, however, forced the major players to develop their own Web sites. In addition, the popularity of the Web became clear when, for example, millions of people around the world watched a robot vehicle scan the surface of Mars via pictures that NASA broadcast on the Internet.

Today, the media are well represented online in at least three major ways. First, the major news organizations, including the big networks—national and local radio and television stations, and national and local newspapers—have all developed Web sites. In some cases, most of a daily newspaper is available via the Internet. The major media are still struggling to figure out how to make a profit through advertising or the sale of their information on the Web.

Far more exciting is the second type of media on the Web—the purely Web-based publications. Like a crowd of rowdy children in the play yard, e-zines (magazines on the Web) are more likely to be outspoken, to have advanced graphics and interactive features, and, in some cases, to be overtly political than their print cousins are. Among the most popular are *Slate* (**http://Slate.msn.com**), *Daily Muse* (**http://www.cais.com/aschnedr/muse.htm**), *Hotwired* (**http://www.hotwired.com**),

Salon (**http://www.salonmagazine.com**), *news.com* (**http://www.news.com**) and, of course, *MSNBC* (**www.msnbc.com**), and *CNN.com* (**http://www.cnn.com**).

Of course, as soon as Congress released Independent Counsel Kenneth Starr's report on the Clinton-Lewinsky investigation in 1998 (see Chapter 5), both the standard newspapers and the electronic publications provided instant access to the report on the Web. The release of the report by the *New York Times* was interrupted by hackers who replaced the front page of the Web version of the newspaper with nude photos of women. All e-zines fear such hacker invasions of their sites.

Because it is relatively simple for anyone or any organization to put up a home page or Web site, a wide variety of sites have appeared that critique the news media or give alternative interpretations of the news and the way it is presented. These sites are essential for the future usefulness of the Web for a number of reasons. For one thing, news on the Web is only made valid by its provider, and the nation's major news organizations have a history of editing and publishing news that has been verified (Webmasters may have no such standards). Of even more importance to the phenomenon of online media is the sponsorship of Web sites by corporations. *Slate,* for example, is the creation of Microsoft Corporation. Other sites are also sponsored by corporations. How does the ordinary user know when the news provided by these online e-zines is biased toward corporate interests? How does one get access to another view of the political interests involved? In fact, the unregulated nature of the Internet has given rise to many Web sites that make it difficult to distinguish reality from fantasy in their telling of history or the news of the day.

FOR CRITICAL ANALYSIS

How can online news sites develop standards that assure the user of the authenticity of the information they provide?

twenty-four-hour-a-day news cable channel—CNN—started operating in 1980. With the addition of CNN-Headline News, CNBC, and other news-format cable channels and shows since the 1980s, the amount of news-type programming continues to increase. In recent years, all of the major networks have also added Internet sites to try to capture that market, but they face hundreds of competitors on the Internet.

Television's influence on the political process today is recognized by all who engage in it. Its special characteristics are worthy of attention. Television news is often criticized for being superficial, particularly compared with the detailed coverage available in the *New York Times*, for example. In fact, television news is constrained by its peculiar technical characteristics, the most important being the limitations of time; stories must be reported in only a few minutes.

The most interesting aspect of television is, of course, the fact that it relies on pictures rather than words to attract the viewer's attention. Therefore, the videotapes or slides that are chosen for a particular political story have exaggerated importance. Viewers do not know what other photos may have been taken or events recorded—they note only those appearing on their screens. Television news can also be exploited for its drama by well-constructed stories. Some critics suggest that there is pressure to produce television news that has a "story line," like a novel or movie. The story should be short, with exciting pictures and a clear plot. In the extreme case, the news media are satisfied with a **sound bite,** a several-second comment selected or crafted for its immediate impact on the viewer.

It has been suggested that these formatting characteristics—or necessities—of television increase its influence on political events. (Newspapers and news magazines are also limited by their formats, but to a lesser extent.) As you are aware, real life is usually not dramatic, nor do all events have a neat or an easily understood plot. Political campaigns are continuing events, lasting perhaps as long as two years. The significance of their daily turns and twists is only apparent later. The "drama" of Congress, with its 535 players and dozens of important committees and meetings, is also difficult for the media to present. What television needs is dozens of daily three-minute stories.

Sound Bite
A brief, memorable comment that easily can be fit into news broadcasts.

The Media and Political Campaigns

All forms of the media—television, newspapers, radio, magazines, and online services—have an enormous political impact on American society. Media influence is most obvious during political campaigns. News coverage of a single event, such as the results of the Iowa caucuses or the New Hampshire primary, may be the most important factor in having a candidate be referred to in the media as the "front-runner" in presidential campaigns. It is not too much of an exaggeration to say that almost all national political figures, starting with the president, plan all public appearances and statements to snag media coverage.

Because television is the primary news source for the majority of Americans, candidates and their consultants spend much of their time devising strategies to use television to their benefit. Three types of TV coverage are generally used in campaigns for the presidency and other offices: advertising, management of news coverage, and campaign debates.

INFOTRAC®
COLLEGE EDITION

Six Surefire Ways
Make Campaign Coverage

Advertising

Perhaps one of the most effective political ads of all time was a short, thirty-second spot created by President Lyndon Johnson's media adviser. In this ad, a little girl stood in a field of daisies. As she held a daisy, she pulled the petals off

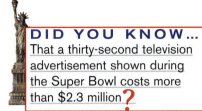

and quietly counted to herself. Suddenly, when she reached number ten, a deep bass voice cut in and began a countdown: "10, 9, 8, 7, 6 . . . ." When the voice intoned "zero," the unmistakable mushroom cloud of an atomic bomb began to fill the screen. Then President Johnson's voice was heard: "These are the stakes. To make a world in which all of God's children can live, or to go into the dark. We must either love each other or we must die." At the end of the commercial, the message read, "Vote for President Johnson on November 3."

To understand how effective this daisy girl commercial was, you must know that Johnson's opponent was Barry Goldwater, a Republican conservative candidate known for his expansive views on the role of the U.S. military. The ad's implication was that Goldwater would lead the United States into nuclear war. Although the ad was withdrawn within a few days, it has a place in political campaign history as the classic negative campaign announcement. The ad's producer, Tony Schwartz, describes the effect in this way: "It was comparable to a person going to a psychiatrist and seeing dirty pictures in a Rorschach pattern. The daisy commercial evoked Goldwater's pro-bomb statements. They were like dirty pictures in the audience's mind."[3]

Since the daisy girl advertisement, negative advertising has come into its own. Candidates vie with one another to produce "attack" ads and then to counterattack when the opponent responds. The public claims not to like negative advertising, but as one consultant put it, "Negative advertising works." Any advertising "works" when viewers or listeners remember an ad. It is clear that negative ads are more memorable than ones that praise the candidate's virtues. Negative advertising, which supporters and independents remember longer than positive advertising, works well. No vote gain is expected anyway from members of the other party or supporters of the candidate under attack.

President Lyndon Johnson's "Daisy Girl" ad contrasted the innocence of childhood with the horror of an atomic attack.

[3]As quoted in Kathleen Hall Jamieson, *Packaging the Presidency: A History and Criticism of Presidential Campaign Advertising,* 3d ed. (New York: Oxford University Press, 1996), p. 200.

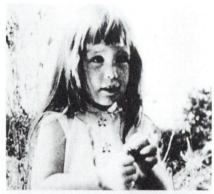

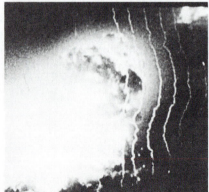

As noted in Chapter 10, "advocacy ads," which argue for or against a policy or an issue (and, indirectly, for or against candidates who support that policy or issue), are another form of political advertising. These ads are paid for by soft money and are very effective at conveying political messages to voters.

Management of News Coverage

Using political advertising to get a message across to the public is a very expensive tactic. Coverage by the news media, however, is free; it simply demands that the campaign ensure that coverage takes place. In recent years, campaign managers have shown increasing sophistication in creating newsworthy events for journalists to cover. As Doris Graber points out, "To keep a favorable image of their candidates in front of the public, campaign managers arrange newsworthy events to familiarize potential voters with their candidates' best aspects."[4]

To take advantage of the media's interest in campaign politics, whether at the presidential level or perhaps in a Senate race, the campaign staff tries to influence the quantity and type of coverage the campaign receives. First, it is important for the campaign staff to understand the technical aspects of media coverage—camera angles, necessary equipment, timing, and deadlines—and to plan their political events to accommodate the press. Second, the campaign organization learns that political reporters and their sponsors—networks or newspapers—are in competition for the best stories and can be manipulated through the granting of favors, such as a personal interview with the candidate. Third, an important task for the scheduler in the campaign is the planning of events that will be photogenic and interesting enough for the evening news. A related goal, although one that is more difficult to attain, is to convince reporters that a particular interpretation of an event is correct.

Today, the art of putting the appropriate **spin** on a story or event is highly developed. Each presidential candidate's press advisers, often referred to as **spin doctors,** try to convince the journalists that their interpretations of the political events are correct. For example, in the 2000 primaries George W. Bush's camp played down his loss to John McCain in the Michigan primary by using the spin that Michigan independents who normally vote Democratic voted in the Republican primary to defeat Bush. Journalists began to report on the different spins and on how the candidates tried to manipulate campaign news coverage.

Spin
An interpretation of campaign events or election results that is most favorable to the candidate's campaign strategy.

Spin Doctor
A political campaign adviser who tries to convince journalists of the truth of a particular interpretation of events.

Going for the Knockout Punch—Presidential Debates

Perhaps of equal importance to political advertisements is the performance of the candidate in a televised presidential debate. After the first such debate in 1960, in which John Kennedy, the young senator from Massachusetts, took on the vice president of the United States, Richard Nixon, candidates became aware of the great potential of television for changing the momentum of a campaign. In general, challengers have much more to gain from debating than do incumbents. Challengers hope that the incumbent may make a mistake in the debate and undermine the "presidential" image. Incumbent presidents are loath to debate their challengers, because it puts their opponents on an equal footing with them.

A family watches the 1960 Kennedy-Nixon debates on television. After the debate, TV viewers thought Kennedy had won, whereas radio listeners thought Nixon had won.

[4]Doris Graber, *Mass Media and American Politics,* 5th ed. (Washington, D.C.: Congressional Quarterly Press, 1997), p. 59.

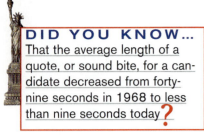

Betting Substance Sells

After some negotiating about the structure and timing of debates, Vice President Al Gore and Governor George W. Bush met for three public debates, and their respective vice presidential candidates met for one. The three presidential debates each featured a different format: one formal debate, one moderated discussion between them, and one "town meeting" style debate. Vice President Gore was criticized for being too aggressive in one debate, and Governor Bush was criticized for either being too passive or being uninformative. The real issue was style—that is, whether a candidate could be calm under pressure, likeable, and not make any big mistakes. The debates were, in terms of voter influence, a draw.

The crucial fact about the practice of televising debates is that, although debates are justified publicly as an opportunity for the voters to find out how candidates differ on the issues, what the candidates want is to capitalize on the power of television to project an image. They view the debate as a strategic opportunity to improve their own images or to point out the failures of their opponents. Candidates are very aware not only that the actual performance is important but also that the morning-after interpretation of the debate by the news media may play a crucial role in what the public thinks. Regardless of the risks of debating, the potential for gaining votes is so great that candidates undoubtedly will continue to seek televised debates.

The Media's Impact on the Voters

The question of how much influence the media have on voting behavior is difficult to answer. Generally, individuals watch television, read newspapers, or log on to a Web site with certain preconceived ideas about political issues and candidates. These attitudes and opinions act as a kind of perceptual screen that filters out information that makes people feel uncomfortable or that does not fit with their own ideas.

Voters watch campaign commercials and news about political campaigns with "selective attentiveness." That is, they tend to watch those commercials that support the candidates they favor and tend to pay attention to news stories about their own candidates. This selectivity also affects their perceptions of the content of the news story or commercial and whether it is remembered. Apparently, the media are most influential with those persons who have not formed an opinion about political candidates or issues. Studies have shown that the flurry of television commercials and debates immediately before election day has the most impact on those voters who are truly undecided. Few voters who have already formed their opinions change their minds under the influence of the media.

The Role of the Media in the 2000 Elections

As in prior years, the media continued to focus on the "horse race" aspects of the 2000 elections. While some media outlets did present careful analyses of the issues and critiques of the candidates' advertising spots, most of the television coverage focused on the ever-present polls. Both presidential candidates took advantage of every opportunity to be on prime time television: they visited with Oprah, David Letterman, and Larry King, among others. In fact, the news programs were shocked when a national poll indicated that some 20 percent of the voters said that they learned about politics from the late night talk shows. The media's worst hour came on election night. All of the networks and cable news operations vied with each other to "call" the states for one or the other of the presidential candidates. Because they were using data from exit polls rather than actual vote counts, a number of states were "too close to call," and several were called mistakenly and later changed. Whether the rush to declare the election over had any impact on the outcome is uncertain.

The Media and the Government

The mass media not only wield considerable power when it comes to political campaigns, but they also, in one way or another, can wield power over the affairs of government and over government officials. Perhaps the most notable example in modern times concerns the activities of *Washington Post* reporters Bob Woodward and Carl Bernstein. These two reporters were assigned to cover the Watergate break-in, and they undertook an investigation that eventually led to the resignation of President Richard Nixon.

The Media and the Presidency

A love-hate relationship clearly exists between the president and the media. During the administration of John F. Kennedy, the president was seen in numerous photos scanning the *New York Times*, the *Washington Post*, and other newspapers each morning to see how the press tallied his successes and failures. This led to frequent jocular comments about his speed-reading ability.

In the United States, the prominence of the president is accentuated by a **White House press corps** that is assigned full-time to cover the presidency. These reporters even have a lounge in the White House where they spend their days, waiting for a story to break. Most of the time, they simply wait for the daily or twice-daily briefing by the president's **press secretary.** Because of the press corps's physical proximity to the president, the chief executive cannot even take a brief stroll around the presidential swimming pool without its becoming news. Perhaps no other nation allows the press such access to its highest government official. Consequently, no other nation has its airwaves and print media so filled with absolute trivia regarding the personal lives of the chief executive and his family.

President Franklin D. Roosevelt brought new spirit to a demoralized country and led it through the Great Depression through his effective use of the media, particularly through his radio broadcasts. His radio "fireside chats" brought hope to millions. Roosevelt's speeches were masterful in their ability to forge a common

White House Press Corps
A group of reporters assigned full-time to cover the presidency.

Press Secretary
The individual responsible for representing the White House before the media. The press secretary writes news releases, provides background information, sets up press conferences, and so on.

President Franklin D. Roosevelt, the first president to fully exploit the airwaves for his benefit, reported to the nation through radio "fireside chats."

A family friend holds six-year-old Cuban citizen Elian Gonzalez in a closet as an immigration agent armed with an MP-5 submachine gun attempts to grab him. In the early morning of April 22, 2000, the federal government raided the Miami, Florida, home of the boy's relatives in order to resolve a custody dispute. This photo ran in hundreds of newspapers across the country, causing many citizens to question the use of force in this situation. Elian subsequently returned to Cuba with his father.

emotional bond among his listeners. His decisive announcement in 1933 on the reorganization of the banks, for example, calmed a jittery nation and prevented the collapse of the banking industry, which was threatened by a run on banks, from which nervous depositors were withdrawing their assets. His famous Pearl Harbor speech, following the Japanese attack on the U.S. Pacific fleet on December 7, 1941 ("a day that will live in infamy"), mobilized the nation for the sacrifices and effort necessary to win World War II.

Perhaps no president exploited the electronic media more effectively than did Ronald Reagan. The "great communicator," as he was called, was never more dramatic than in his speech to the nation following the October 1983 U.S. invasion of the Caribbean island of Grenada. In this address, the president, in an almost flawless performance, appeared to many to have decisively laid to rest the uncertainty and confusion surrounding the event.

The relationship between the media and the president is most often reciprocal: each needs the other to thrive. Because of this co-dependency, both the media and the president work hard to exploit the other. The media need news to report, and the president "may" need coverage. For example, although the struggle over the custody of the young Cuban boy, Elian Gonzalez, received extraordinary media coverage, President Clinton stayed out of the news, leaving Attorney General Janet Reno to provide "news" to the media. With no good political solution to the case, most other politicians also avoided being on the news.

Setting the Public Agenda

Given that government officials have in front of them an array of problems with which they must deal, the process of setting the public agenda is constant. To be sure, what goes on the public agenda for discussion, debate, and, ultimately, policy action depends on many factors—not the least being each official's personal philosophy.

According to a number of studies, the media play an important part in setting the public agenda. Evidence is strong that whatever public problems receive the most media treatment will be cited by the public in contemporary surveys as the most important problems. Although the media do not make policy decisions, they do determine to a significant extent the policy issues that need to be decided—and this is an important part of the political process. Because those who control the media are not elected representatives of the people, the agenda-setting role of the media necessarily is a controversial one. The relationship of the media to agenda setting remains complex, though, because politicians are able to manipulate media coverage to control some of its effects, as well as to exploit the media to further their agendas with the public. For an example of one way the government might control the news, see this chapter's *Politics and Economics* feature.

Government Regulation of the Media

The United States has perhaps the freest press in the world. Nonetheless, regulation of the media does exist, particularly of the electronic media. Many aspects of this regulation were discussed in Chapter 4, when we examined First Amendment rights and the press.

Controlling Ownership of the Media

The First Amendment does not mention electronic media, which did not exist when the Bill of Rights was written. For many reasons, the government has much greater control over the electronic media than it does over printed media. Through the Federal Communications Commission (FCC), which regulates communications by radio, television, wire, and cable, the number of radio stations has been controlled for many years, in spite of the fact that technologically we could have many more radio stations than now exist. Also, the FCC created a situation in which the three major TV networks have dominated the airwaves.

Most FCC rules have dealt with ownership of news media, such as how many stations a network can own. Recently, the FCC has decided to auction off hundreds of radio frequencies, allowing the expansion of cellular telephone applications.

In 1996, Congress passed, and the president signed, an act that has far-reaching implications for the communications industry—the Telecommunications Act of 1996. The act ended the rule that kept telephone companies from entering the cable business and other communications markets. What this means is that a single corporation—whether AT&T or Disney—can offer long-distance and local telephone services, cable television, satellite television, Internet services, and, of course, libraries of films and entertainment. The race is on for companies to control media ownership and to develop all the needed technology. As discussed in this chapter's *Critical Perspective* on page 353, already the Disney Company has purchased ABC/Capital Cities Company, and AOL has merged with Time Warner. Consumers can now choose among multiple competitors for all these services delivered to the home. A single entity may own a television network; the studios that produce shows, news, and movies; and the means to deliver that content to the home via

politics and economics

Should the Government Buy Antidrug Messages?

As part of the campaign to stop illegal drug use and the drug business in the United States, Congress has approved millions of dollars for media campaigns against drugs at the local and national level. In 1997, the nation's drug czar, General Barry R. McCaffrey, was authorized by Congress to spend $1 billion for a campaign against drugs. Congress further required that any advertising time be purchased at half the regular price.

At the time this policy began, the national media—the networks and cable television—were charging top prices for advertising on their prime-time shows and did not want to give General McCaffrey a discount for antidrug advertising. The government offered the networks another option: they could embed antidrug messages in their programs instead of giving discounts on advertising time. Newspapers could write and distribute antidrug messages in their school editions.

The question then became, How much antidrug publicity was equal to a certain amount of advertising time or space? General McCaffrey's office became a kind of government editorial board. It reviewed scripts for television shows and decided which news stories were "on strategy" and thus qualified as financial discounts for advertising. The government office also provided guid-

ance and instruction about antidrug messages to network writers and newspaper editors.

Max Frankel, former publisher of the *New York Times,* criticizes this financial arrangement on a number of grounds.* First, the practice was kept secret by all involved. Americans who watched network shows or browsed newspaper Web sites had no way of knowing that the antidrug messages found in those places were, in fact, advertising for the government and had been edited by the government. In addition, the media, eager to gain the advertising dollars, went along with this practice, including hiding their relationship with the government. The arrangement goes against the policies of earlier times, when Congress expressly forbade some government agencies, such as the Voice of America and the Central Intelligence Agency, from sending any anti-Communist messages within the United States on the ground that such messages were government propaganda.

FOR CRITICAL ANALYSIS

If the government and the media keep their relationship secret, how can a citizen find out if the government is sponsoring certain kinds of messages through the newspapers and television?

*Max Frankel, "Plots for Hire: Media Mercenaries Join the War on Drugs," *The New York Times Magazine,* February 2, 2000, p. 32.

cable, satellite, or the Internet. The question to be faced in the future is how to assure competition in the delivery of the news so that citizens have access to multiple points of view from the media.

Government Control of Content

In general, the broadcasting industry has avoided government regulation of content by establishing its own code. This code consists of a set of rules developed by the National Association of Broadcasters (the lobby for the TV and radio industry) that regulate the amount of sex, violence, nudity, profanity, and so forth that is allowed on the air. (High rates of violent crime among teens have again brought the attention of Congress to media programming.) It should be noted that abiding by the code is voluntary on the part of networks and stations.

Since 1980, there has been continued public debate over whether the government should attempt to control polling and the "early calling" of presidential elections by the television networks. On election night in 1980, before numerous states had closed their polls, the networks predicted, based on exit polls, that Ronald Reagan had been elected. The concern expressed by many was that voters on their way to vote might not bother because the victor had already been declared. It was feared that the resulting drop in turnout would particularly affect state and local races. Because some types of voters, such as factory workers, are more likely to vote late in the day, the outcomes of elections and referenda might be seriously affected.

In 1984, the networks were careful to say that they would not project winners in any state until the polling places *in that state* were closed. With the different time zones and with a concentration of population in the Northeast and Midwest, however, the networks were able to project a winner by 8:00 P.M. eastern time, which was 5:00 P.M. on the West Coast. As discussed in the feature *An Ethical Issue: Freedom of the Press and the Exit Polls,* the Internet allows for even earlier release of polling data to the public.

Some legislators and citizens have called for a ban on exit polls or on releasing them before *all* polling

Freedom of the Press and the Exit Polls

The major networks and newspapers have been conducting exit polls during election days for more than twenty years. Ever since the 1980 election, when they "called the winner" before the voting ended in California, the networks have promised to withhold their election predictions in a state until voting ends there. Today, the major networks and newspapers all get their exit polling data from a cooperative polling service called Voters News Service (VNS). Although all of the partners in this service agree not to call the winners until after voting polls are closed, they do give extensive hints of how the election is going throughout the afternoon. These hints are based on the VNS data that are fed to the partners as the information is gathered and analyzed.

During the 2000 presidential primary season, the major networks got quite a shock when the online magazine *Slate* obtained exit polling data through leaks from a major media source and other news-gathering organizations and published the results on its Web site during the New Hampshire primary. It also published early results during the voting day in the South Carolina and Michigan presidential primaries. The networks,

through VNS, then went to court to stop the online magazine from publishing exit poll results in future primaries. VNS claimed that one company's "hot news" can be protected from another. Additionally, VNS imposed new rules on its customers, sending out numbers in the next set of primaries at 4:00 P.M. instead of at 2:00 P.M., to stop the leaks.

Other online magazines were undaunted by the VNS legal threat. The *National Review* and the *Drudge Report* continued to post leaked data during the Virginia primary. Their theory was that information obtained by legitimate news-gathering techniques, including leaks from other organizations, was protected by the Constitution as freedom of the press. They denied that the data gathered by VNS were actually "owned" by its media partners and therefore protected as a form of property. Which side will win out in the long run remains to be seen. Congress may settle the issue by simply outlawing exit polling on election day, as it has threatened to do in the past.

FOR CRITICAL ANALYSIS

Should polling data gathered by the news media be considered private property or news that the public can access? How do polling data differ from other news gathered by a newspaper or network?

places in the continental United States are closed. Others have called for a federal law establishing a uniform closing time for voting so that voting would end at the same time all over the country, and thus exit polls could not be a factor. In any event, although turnout has been lower than expected in many western states, studies suggest that the early announcement of election results based on exit polls has little effect on election outcomes.

The Telecommunications Act of 1996 included two provisions that allow for some government control of the content of the media. One provision required that television manufacturers include a "V-chip" in each set. The V-chip allows parents to block programs that include violence or sexual conduct from being viewed on their televisions. The other provision prohibited the transmission of indecent or patently offensive materials on the Internet in such a way that minors could access those materials. Responding to immediate legal challenges to this portion of the new law, two federal district courts held in 1996 that the provision blocking certain content from the Internet was unconstitutional. One court stated that this section was "profoundly repugnant" to the First Amendment's guarantee of free speech. In 1997, the Supreme Court agreed that the provision restrained too much protected adult speech and was therefore unconstitutional. Further regulation of the Internet is obviously a matter of constitutional debate (see Chapter 4).

The Public's Right to Media Access

Does the public have a right to **media access?** Both the FCC and the courts gradually have taken the stance that citizens do have a right of access to the media, particularly the electronic media. The argument is that the airwaves are public, but because they are used for private profit, the government has the right to dictate how they are used. It does so in many ways. Recall from Chapter 4 that in addition to the equal-time rule for candidates—under which broadcasters who sell airtime to political candidates must make equal time available to opposing candidates on equal terms—the FCC has also promulgated the personal attack rule. This rule allows individuals (or groups) airtime to reply to attacks that have previously been aired.

Technology is giving more citizens access to the electronic media and, in particular, to television. As more cable operators have more airtime to sell, some of that time will remain unused and will be available for public access. At the same time, the Internet makes media access by the public very easy, although not everyone has the resources to take advantage of it.

Media Access
The public's right of access to the media. The Federal Communications Commission and the courts gradually have taken the stance that citizens do have a right to media access.

Bias in the Media

Many studies have been undertaken to try to identify the sources and direction of **bias** in the media, and these studies have reached different conclusions. For example, in a classic study conducted in the 1980s, the researchers found that media producers, editors, and reporters (the "media elite") had a notably liberal and "left-leaning" bias in their news coverage.[5] Other studies, however, have concluded that there is a pro-Republican and pro-conservative bias in the overall stance of newspapers and major networks. Still other studies assert that the

Bias
An inclination or a preference that interferes with impartial judgment.

[5]S. Robert Lichter, Stanley Rothman, and Linda S. Lichter, *The Media Elite* (New York: Adler and Adler, 1986).

press is "apolitical." For example, Calvin F. Exoo, in his study of politics in the media, suggests that journalists are neither liberal nor conservative. Rather, they are constrained by both the pro-America bias of the media ownership and the journalists' own code of objectivity. Most are more interested in improving their career prospects by covering the winning candidate and pleasing their editors to get better assignments than they are in discussing public policies.[6] Thus, the bias in the media is toward not criticizing the American system and on producing "news" that will attract viewers and readers without threatening the American way of life. This analysis would support Thomas E. Patterson's view that the real bias of the news media is to emphasize bad news and cynicism rather than any partisan position.[7] (See the public's views on media bias in this chapter's *Which Side Are You On?*)

Increasingly, the media are being criticized for their failure to provide any context—biased or not—for news events. According to one critic, the focus on the "brief now" of events tends to magnify the trivial and trivialize the important. The media convey the sense that

---

[6]Calvin F. Exoo, *The Politics of the Mass Media* (St. Paul: West, 1994), pp. 49–50.
[7]Thomas E. Patterson, *Out of Order* (New York: Knopf, 1993).

which side are you on?

Is the News Biased?

Losing candidates and many voters often claim that the news media are biased toward the other side. Researchers have looked for this "bias" in the news for decades. Although the vast majority of news journalists identify themselves as Democrats, corporations that are likely to be pro-Republican own most news organizations.

Do People Perceive a Partisan Bias?

According to a recent study by the Pew Center for the People and the Press, about 69 percent of Americans see news coverage as having a "fair amount" of political bias. That is a decrease of 7 percentage points from ten years ago, however, and those respondents did not seem to think that the bias favors either party. Forty-eight percent of those polled said that there is no partisan bias. Among those who found a great deal of bias in the media more thought that it favors Democrats over Republicans. More than 40 percent of Americans polled thought that the media are too hard on female candidates and on those

who are behind in the race. When people were asked which of various news sources they considered unbiased, the largest percentage (31 percent) named C-SPAN. The respondents viewed their daily newspaper as the source most likely to be biased, with only 18 percent regarding it as unbiased.

Is There a Bias toward the System?

All of this research is based on the most widely used sources of news. Others in society, however, say that the whole news-gathering system is biased toward maintaining the status quo, meaning that it is biased toward supporting corporate America and its aims. Although some newspapers criticize the capitalist system or present other points of view, "alternative" news sources are hard to find and expensive for the publishers to maintain. The Internet is a much easier place for alternative news organizations to provide their points of view. For example, the demonstrations in Seattle against the World Trade Organization in 1999 seemed to surprise the news media, but

they were expected by the alternative news Web sites. Similarly, although some major news outlets covered the demonstrations against the World Bank in Washington, D.C., in May 2000, the amount of coverage was minimal. On the alternative news Web sites, these demonstrations were well covered and, in fact, were coordinated with May Day celebrations around the world.

DOES IT MATTER?

Does it matter whether the news media are somewhat biased toward one political party or another or toward leading candidates rather than the dark horses in the race? Or is it more important that the media are biased toward the system as we know it and ignore news about events and organizations that are attacking the system?

GOING ONLINE

You can read more about the study by the Pew Center by going to its Web site at __http://www.people-press.org__. *An alternative way of presenting the news can be found at the Web site of the Independent Media Center at* __http://www.indymedia.org__.

life is just a sequence of random events in a world that "cannot be understood, shaped or controlled."[8]

The Media and Politics: Issues for the Twenty-First Century

The power of the media and their impact on American society clearly are a controversial and important subject. To what extent the mass media help to clarify issues and to contribute to a more enlightened public, as opposed to distorting and oversimplifying reality, is a topic hotly debated in the United States. The increasing dependence of campaigns and candidates on the media makes this an era of symbolic politics and weakened political attachments. At the same time, the greatly expanded number of media outlets, including cable television and online services, has offered Americans more freedom to choose what they watch and read.

By 2001, the Internet had made available literally hundreds of sites allowing voters to read about candidates and "chat" with politicians, journalists, and other voters. Voters could view home pages that were advertisements for candidates and seek information about almost any topic from the great libraries of the nation. Although this interactive political forum was beyond the reach of those Americans who are not connected to the Internet, the vigor and intensity of these Internet exchanges suggest that Americans are willing and eager to express themselves in the arena of national politics. The same lesson was demonstrated in debates in which ordinary citizens, rather than journalists, were allowed to ask the questions. At the same time, the number of partisan talk shows and cable TV channels is increasing, so Americans can choose to listen only to media outlets that support their own positions. Obviously, how to harness the potential of the mass media to allow for national debate about the good of the nation is an issue yet to be resolved.

---

[8]James Fallows, *Breaking the News: How the Media Undermine American Democracy* (New York: Pantheon Books, 1996).

making a difference

Being a Critical Consumer of the News

Television and newspapers provide an enormous range of choice for Americans who want to stay informed. Still, critics of the media argue that a substantial amount of programming and print is colored either by the subjectivity of editors and producers or by the demands of profit making. Few Americans take the time to become critical consumers of the news, either in print or on the TV screen.

To become a critical news consumer, you must practice reading a newspaper with a critical eye toward editorial decisions. For example, ask yourself what stories are given prominence on the front page of the paper, and which ones merit a photograph. What is the editorial stance of the newspaper? Most American papers tend to have moderate to conservative editorial pages. Who are the columnists given space on the "op-ed" page, the page opposite the paper's own editorial page? For a contrast to most daily papers, occasionally pick up an outright political publication such as the *National Review* or the *New Republic* and take note of the editorial positions.

Watching the evening news can be far more rewarding if you look at how much the news depends on video effects. You will note that stories on the evening news tend to be no more than three minutes long, that stories with excellent videotape get more attention, and that considerable time is taken up with "happy talk" or human interest stories that tap the emotions of the audience.

Another interesting study you might make is to compare the evening news with the daily paper on a given date. You will see that the paper is perhaps half a day behind the news but that the print story contains far more information. Headlines must take the place of videotape in grabbing your attention.

You can also be a more active consumer by voicing your views and suggestions to the producers of television news or to the editors of newspapers and magazines through letters, by telephone, and by electronic mail. These persons are often responsive to criticism and open to constructive suggestions; you might be surprised to find them so accessible.

If you wish to obtain more information on the media and take an active role as a consumer of the news, you can contact one of the following organizations:

National Association of Broadcasters
1771 N St. N.W.
Washington, DC 20036
202-429-5300

http://www.nab.org

National Newspaper Association
1010 N. Glebe Rd., Suite 450
Arlington, VA 22209
1-800-829-4NNA
info@nna.org

http://www.nna.org

Accuracy in Media
(a conservative group)
4455 Connecticut Ave. N.W.,
Suite 330
Washington, DC 20008
202-364-4401

http://www.aim.org

People for the American Way
(a liberal group)
2000 M St. N.W., Suite 400
Washington, DC 20036
202-467-4999

http://www.pfaw.org

Key terms

bias 367
electronic media 355
managed news 353
media access 367
narrowcasting 356
press secretary 363
public agenda 350
sound bite 359
spin 361
spin doctor 361
White House press corps 363
yellow journalism 354

Chapter summary

1 The media are enormously important in American politics today. They perform a number of functions, including (a) entertainment, (b) news reporting, (c) identifying public problems, (d) socializing new generations, (e) providing a political forum, and (f) making profits.

2 The media have always played a significant role in American politics. In the 1800s and earlier, however, news traveled slowly, and politics was controlled by a small group whose members communicated personally. The high-speed rotary press and the telegraph led to self-supported newspapers and mass readership.

3 The electronic media (television, radio, and the Internet) are growing in significance in the area of communications. New technologies, such as cable television and the Internet, are giving broadcasters the opportunity to air a greater number of specialized programs.

4 The media wield enormous political power during political campaigns and over the affairs of government and government officials by focusing attention on their actions. Today's political campaigns use political advertising and expert management of news coverage. Of equal importance for presidential candidates is how they appear in presidential debates.

5 The relationship between the media and the president is close; each has used the other—sometimes positively, sometimes negatively. The media play an important role in investigating the government, in getting government officials to understand better the needs and desires of American society, and in setting the public agenda.

6 The media in the United States, particularly the electronic media, are subject to government regulation, although the United States has possibly the freest press in the world. Most Federal Communications Commission rules have dealt with ownership of TV and radio stations. Recent legislation has removed many rules about co-ownership of several forms of media.

7 Studies of bias in the media have reached different conclusions. Some detect a conservative bias, while others find a more liberal stance. Still other studies conclude that the media are apolitical. Recently, the media have been criticized for being biased in favor of cynicism and "bad news," as well as for not providing any context—biased or unbiased—for the events they report.

Selected print and electronic resources

SUGGESTED READINGS

Cook, Timothy E. *Governing with the News: The News Media as Political Institution*. Chicago: University of Chicago Press, 1998. Cook reviews the history of the media and examines their position today as a powerful part of government. He looks at the interactions of the various offices and branches of government with the news media and suggests reforms to make the media more accountable in their role as a political partner in government.

Dautrich, Kenneth, and Thomas H. Hartley. *How the News Media Fail American Voters: Causes, Consequences, and Remedies*. New York: Columbia University Press, 1999. How American voters actually use the media and the causes of voters' frustration with the media are the topics of this book. The authors analyze the impact of the media on the voters and vice versa.

Davis, Richard, and Diana Marie Owen. *New Media and American Politics*. New York: Oxford University Press, 1998. The authors critique many of the new media outlets, including e-zines, cable outlets, talk radio, and the Internet. They ask whether these new media actually do reflect the needs and desires of American voters.

Ferguson, Charles H. *High Stakes, No Prisoners: A Winner's Tale of Greed and Glory in the Internet Wars*. New York: Random House, 1998. This is an insider's description of the fast-paced, entrepreneurial world of Silicon Valley, which also looks at how the Internet and its businesses are challenging society.

Graber, Doris A. *Media Power in Politics*. Washington, D.C.: Congressional Quarterly Books, 2000. In this collection of essays, many of which are newly written, the author explores the mass media's ability to shape political agendas and the ways in which the mass media have profoundly changed American politics.

Kurtz, Howard. *Spin Cycle: Inside the Clinton Propaganda Machine*. New York: Free Press, 1998. Kurtz, a member of the Washington press corps, writes about the ways that the Clinton administration tried to manipulate press coverage of its activities. Kurtz portrays the press corps as fundamentally distrustful of the president.

MEDIA RESOURCES

Broadcast News—A 1987 film starring Holly Hunter, Albert Brooks, and William Hurt as the members of a television news team. The film examines the ways that news broadcasts are created and satirizes the role of the handsome news anchor.

Citizen Kane—A film, based on the life of William Randolph Hearst and directed by Orson Welles, that has been acclaimed as one of the best movies ever made. Welles himself stars as the newspaper tycoon. The film also stars Joseph Cotten and Alan Ladd. Oscar-winning best film in 1941.

All the President's Men—A film, produced by Warner Brothers in 1976, starring Dustin Hoffman and Robert Redford as the two *Washington Post* reporters, Bob Woodward and Carl Bernstein, who broke the story on the Watergate scandal. The film is an excellent portrayal of the *Washington Post* newsroom and the decisions that editors make in such situations.

Logging on

The Web site of the *American Journalism Review* is a joint venture between that magazine and News Link Associates, an online research and consulting firm. This site includes features from the magazine and original content created specifically for online reading. Additionally, it provides numerous links to various publications. Go to

http://ajr.newslink.org

The *Drudge Report* home page, posted by Matt Drudge, provides a handy guide to the Web's best spots for news and opinions. Its mission is one-click access to breaking news and recent columns. It provides links to specific columnists and opinion pages for magazines and major daily newspapers. Go to

http://www.drudgereport.com

The American Review Web page critiques the media, promotes media activism, and calls for media reform. Its URL is

http://www.AmericanReview.net

To view *Slate,* the e-zine of politics and culture published by Microsoft, go to

http://Slate.msn.com

An AP-like system for college newspapers is Uwire, offered by Northwestern University and intended to provide college papers with a reliable source of information that directly affects their readers. You can access Uwire at

http://www.uwire.com

For an Internet site that provides links to news media around the world, including alternative media, go to

http://www.mediachannel.org

Using the Internet for political analysis

Compare the print version of a major national newspaper—such as the *New York Times, Los Angeles Times, Wall Street Journal, Washington Post,* or *USA Today*—with its online edition from the same day. How do the two versions differ? What decisions did the editors make in regard to picture choice, headlines, placement, and length of the stories that suggest a different audience for the online edition? How does the newspaper raise revenue from each of these editions? How does the way you read the paper vary between the two editions? Which format do you think is better for generating political dialogue, and why? If you could design your own online newspaper, what features would it include?

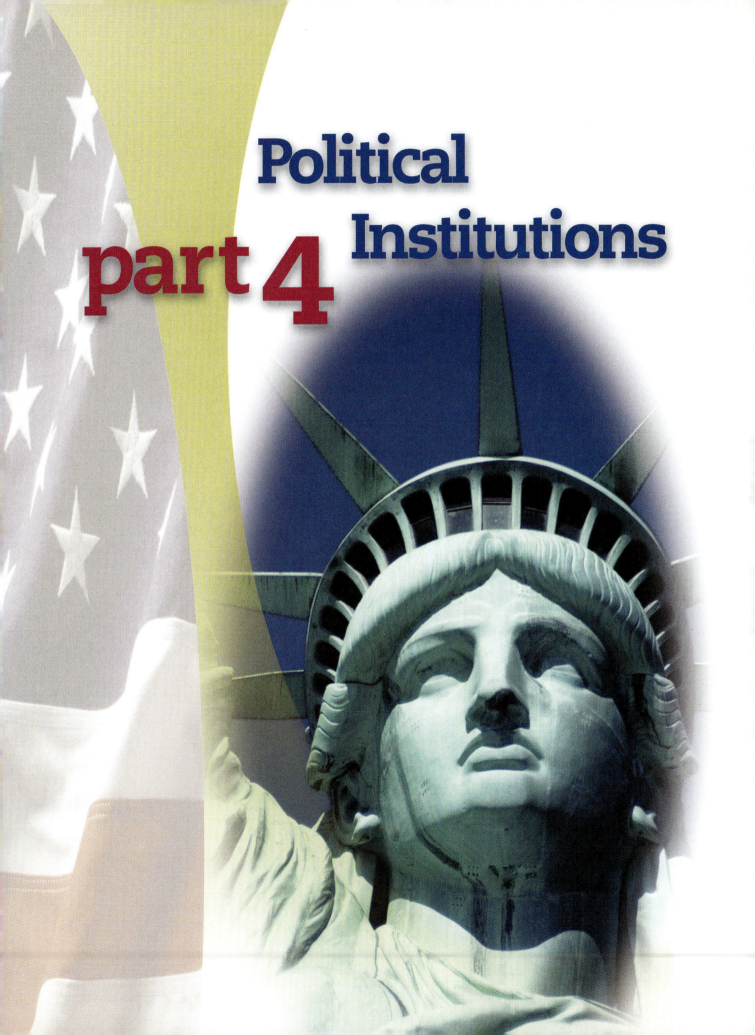

part **4**

Political Institutions

chapter 12
The Congress

CHAPTER OUTLINE

- Why Was Congress Created?

- The Powers of Congress

- The Functions of Congress

- House-Senate Differences

- Congresspersons and the Citizenry: A Comparison

- Congressional Elections

- Congressional Reapportionment

- Pay, Perks, and Privileges

- The Committee Structure

- The Formal Leadership

- How Members of Congress Decide

- How a Bill Becomes Law

- How Much Will the Government Spend?

- The Question of Congressional Ethics

what if...

Members of Congress Were Required to Spend Six Months Each Year in Their Districts?

BACKGROUND

MEMBERS OF CONGRESS SPEND FAR MORE TIME IN WASHINGTON TALKING TO LOBBYISTS AND OTHER MEMBERS THAN THEY DO AT HOME. IN FACT, ALTHOUGH INCUMBENT MEMBERS OF CONGRESS ARE VERY DIFFICULT TO DEFEAT, A FEW OF THEM ARE CHALLENGED SUCCESSFULLY EACH ELECTION BY NEWCOMERS WHO POINT TO THE MEMBERS' WASHINGTON TOWN HOUSES AND HEAVY INVOLVEMENT WITH POLITICS "INSIDE THE BELTWAY."

SOME CONTEND THAT CONGRESS-PERSONS SHOULD SPEND MORE TIME IN THEIR HOME DISTRICTS. AFTER ALL, MEMBERS OF CONGRESS ARE ELECTED TO REPRESENT THE VIEWS OF THOSE WHO ELECTED THEM—THEIR CONSTITUENTS. HOW CAN MEMBERS OF CONGRESS LEARN THEIR CONSTITUENTS' VIEWS IF THOSE MEMBERS ARE INVOLVED IN WASHINGTON POLITICS FOR MOST OF THE YEAR?

WHAT IF MEMBERS OF CONGRESS WERE REQUIRED TO SPEND SIX MONTHS EACH YEAR IN THEIR DISTRICTS?

Requiring members of Congress to be in their districts for six months each year certainly would strengthen their relationship with the voters. The voters would have far more opportunities to meet with the members and express their views. It is likely that members would be even more immersed in problem solving for ordinary citizens than they are now. It is also very likely that local interests might be perceived as more powerful than they are now, and national lobbyists would have to compete with local demands. Having spent so much time listening to the concerns of local workers, for example, a member of Congress might be more aware of the impact of international trade on his or her constituents.

Spending more time in the district could have the effect of reducing the legislator's tie to his or her political party. Strong state and regional interests would be likely to force the legislator to vote against the party's position if that position was contrary to constituent interests. If the legislator cultivated good constituency relations, the time spent at home probably would strengthen the power of incumbency. After all, it is much harder for voters to reject someone who has met with them and who may have helped their families or towns on an issue than it is to reject someone who is always in Washington, D.C. A new person often can get to Congress only by running for an open seat.

GETTING THE LEGISLATIVE WORK DONE

Could members of Congress complete the budget and all legislation in six months so they could go home? To be sure, most legislation could move faster than it does, particularly if members would be willing to delegate more power to committees or to the leadership. One of the problems of a speedier legislative process in Washington, D.C., however, is that not all issues might be raised or all interests considered in the process of writing legislation. Part of a representative democracy involves allowing all who have opinions to contribute to the legislative process. Shortening the time spent in Washington might reduce the amount of influence that the public has on the process. Furthermore, speeding up legislation could, in the long run, produce laws that soon would need to be reconsidered or amended. Time does allow difficult issues to be worked out.

Finally, sending members of Congress home for six months each year would transfer a great deal of power to the president and to the members of the executive branch to act without a counterbalance. While Americans might like their representatives to spend more time at home, they also are unlikely to place their trust in the executive branch for six months each year.

FOR CRITICAL ANALYSIS

1. Which local interests might receive stronger representation if members spent more time at home? Which interests would be unaffected?

2. Do you think that members of Congress could transact some of their business via electronic communications systems? Is face-to-face deliberation really necessary?

Most Americans spend little time thinking about the Congress of the United States, and when they do, their opinions are frequently unflattering. For many years, the public's approval rating of Congress as a whole was about 30 percent. With the strong economy of the late 1990s and early 2000s, Congress's approval ratings climbed to between 40 percent and 50 percent in most polls. The majority of voters, however, expressed even higher approval ratings (in the range of 60 percent to 70 percent) for the members of Congress from their districts. This is one of the paradoxes of the relationship between the people and Congress. Members of the public hold the institution in relatively low regard while expressing satisfaction with their individual representatives.

Part of the explanation for these seemingly contradictory appraisals is that members of Congress spend considerable time and effort serving their **constituents.** If the federal bureaucracy makes a mistake, the senator's or representative's office tries to resolve the issue. What most Americans see of Congress, therefore, is the work of their own representatives in their home states. As suggested in this chapter's opening *What If . . .*, the tie between members of Congress and the voters might be even further strengthened if the members were at home more of the time.

Congress, however, was created to work not just for local constituents but also for the nation as a whole. Understanding the nature of the institution and the process of lawmaking is an important part of understanding how the policies that shape our lives are made.

Why Was Congress Created?

The founders of the American republic believed that the bulk of the power that would be exercised by a national government should be in the hands of the legislature. As you will recall from Chapter 2, the authors of the Constitution were strongly influenced by their fear of tyrannical kings and powerful, unchecked rulers. They were also aware of how ineffective the confederal Congress had been during its brief existence under the Articles of Confederation.

The leading role envisioned for Congress in the new government is apparent from its primacy in the Constitution. Article I deals with the structure, the powers, and the operation of Congress, beginning in Section 1 with an application of the basic principle of separation of powers: "All legislative Powers herein granted shall be vested in a Congress of the United States, which shall consist of a Senate and House of Representatives." These legislative powers are spelled out in detail in Article I and elsewhere.

The **bicameralism** of Congress—its division into two legislative houses—was in part an outgrowth of the Connecticut Compromise, which tried to balance the large-state population advantage, reflected in the House, and the small-state demand for equality in policymaking, which was satisfied in the Senate. Beyond that, the two chambers of Congress also reflected the social class biases of the founders. They wished to balance the interests and the numerical superiority of the common citizens with the property interests of the less numerous landowners, bankers, and merchants. This goal was achieved by providing in Sections 2 and 3 of Article I that members of the House of Representatives should be elected directly by "the People," whereas members of the Senate were to be chosen by the elected representatives sitting in state legislatures, who were more likely to be members of the elite. (The latter provision was changed in 1913 by the passage of the Seventeenth Amendment, which provides that senators also are to be elected directly by the people.)

The logic of separate constituencies and separate interests underlying the bicameral Congress was reinforced by differences in length of tenure. Members of the House were required to face the electorate every two years, whereas

DID YOU KNOW... That a miniature Capitol Hill exists beneath a wing of the Greenbrier Hotel in West Virginia, complete with dormitories and legislative chambers for members to use in case of nuclear war?

Constituent
One of the people represented by a legislator or other elected or appointed official.

Bicameralism
The division of a legislature into two separate assemblies.

senators could serve for a much more secure term of six years—even longer than the four-year term provided for the president. Furthermore, the senators' terms were staggered so that only one-third of the senators would face the electorate every two years, along with all of the House members.

The Powers of Congress

The Constitution is both highly specific and extremely vague about the powers that Congress may exercise. The first seventeen clauses of Article I, Section 8, specify most of the **enumerated powers** of Congress—that is, powers expressly given to that body.

Enumerated Powers

Enumerated Power
A power specifically granted to the national government by the Constitution. The first seventeen clauses of Article I, Section 8, specify most of the enumerated powers of Congress.

The enumerated, or expressed, powers of Congress include the right to impose taxes and import tariffs; borrow money; regulate interstate commerce and international trade; establish procedures for naturalizing citizens; make laws regulating bankruptcies; coin (and print) money and regulate its value; establish standards of weights and measures; punish counterfeiters; establish post offices and postal routes; regulate copyrights and patents; establish the federal court system; punish pirates and others committing illegal acts on the high seas; declare war; raise and regulate an army and a navy; call up and regulate the state militias to enforce laws, to suppress insurrections, and to repel invasions; and govern the District of Columbia.

The most important of the domestic powers of Congress, listed in Article I, Section 8, are the rights to collect taxes, to spend, and to regulate commerce, whereas the most important foreign policy power is the power to declare war. Other sections of the Constitution give Congress a wide range of further powers. Generally, Congress is also able to establish rules for its own members, to regulate the electoral college, and to override a presidential veto.

Some functions are restricted to only one chamber. Under Article II, Section 2, the Senate must advise on, and consent to, the ratification of treaties and must accept or reject presidential nominations of ambassadors, Supreme Court

Representative William Jefferson, a Democrat from Louisiana, shakes hands with a constituent during a visit to his home district. Jefferson represents the Second District in Louisiana, which includes most of the city of New Orleans. After a tough fight to win his seat in 1990, Jefferson has been reelected with ease.

justices, and "all other Officers of the United States." But the Senate may delegate to the president, the courts, or department heads the power to make lesser appointments. Congress may regulate the extent of the Supreme Court's authority to review cases decided by the lower courts, regulate relations between states, and propose amendments to the Constitution.

The amendments to the Constitution provide for other congressional powers. Congress must certify the election of a president and a vice president or itself choose these officers if no candidate has a majority of the electoral vote (Twelfth Amendment). It may levy an income tax (Sixteenth Amendment) and determine who will be acting president in case of the death or incapacity of the president or vice president (Twentieth Amendment, Sections 3 and 4, and Twenty-fifth Amendment, Sections 2, 3, and 4). In addition, Congress explicitly is given the power to enforce, by appropriate legislation, the provisions of several other amendments.

The Necessary and Proper Clause

Beyond these numerous specific powers, Congress enjoys the right under Article I, Section 8 (the "elastic," or "necessary and proper," clause), "[t]o make all Laws which shall be necessary and proper for carrying into Execution the foregoing Powers [of Article I], and all other Powers vested by this Constitution in the Government of the United States, or in any Department or Officer thereof." As discussed in Chapter 3, this vague statement of congressional responsibilities set the stage for a greatly expanded role for the national government relative to the states. It also constitutes, at least in theory, a check on the expansion of presidential powers.

The Functions of Congress

The Constitution provides the foundation for congressional powers. Yet a complete understanding of the role that Congress plays requires a broader study of the functions that the national legislature performs for the American political system.

Congress, as an institution of government, is expected by its members, by the public, and by other centers of political power to perform a number of functions. Our perceptions of how good a job Congress is doing overall are tied closely to evaluations of whether and how it fulfills certain specific tasks. These tasks include lawmaking, service to constituents, representation, oversight, public education, and conflict resolution.

The Lawmaking Function

The principal and most obvious function of any legislature is **lawmaking.** Congress is the highest elected body in the country charged with making binding rules for all Americans. Lawmaking requires decisions about the size of the federal budget, about health-care reform and gun control, and about the long-term prospects for war or peace. This does not mean, however, that Congress initiates most of the ideas for legislation that it eventually considers. Most of the bills that Congress acts on originate in the executive branch, and many other bills are traceable to interest groups and political party organizations. Through the processes of compromise and **logrolling** (offering to support a fellow member's bill in exchange for that member's promise to support your bill in the future), as well as debate and discussion, backers of legislation attempt to fashion a winning majority coalition.

DID YOU KNOW...
That fewer than three in ten people can name the House member from their district, and fewer than half can name even one of the two senators from their state?

Lawmaking
The process of deciding the legal rules that govern society. Such laws may regulate minor affairs or establish broad national policies.

Logrolling
An arrangement in which two or more members of Congress agree in advance to support each other's bills.

Service to Constituents

Individual members of Congress are expected by their constituents to act as brokers between private citizens and the imposing, often faceless federal government. **Casework** is the usual form taken by this function of providing service to constituents. The legislator and her or his staff spend a considerable portion of their time in casework activity, such as tracking down a missing Social Security check, explaining the meaning of particular bills to people who may be affected by them, promoting a local business interest, or interceding with a regulatory agency on behalf of constituents who disagree with proposed agency regulations.

Legislators and many analysts of congressional behavior regard this **ombudsperson** role as an activity that strongly benefits the members of Congress. A government characterized by a large, confusing bureaucracy and complex public programs offers innumerable opportunities for legislators to come to the assistance of (usually) grateful constituents. Morris P. Fiorina suggests somewhat mischievously that senators and representatives prefer to maintain bureaucratic confusion in order to maximize their opportunities for performing good deeds on behalf of their constituents:

> Some poor, aggrieved constituent becomes enmeshed in the tentacles of an evil bureaucracy and calls upon Congressman St. George to do battle with the dragon. . . . In dealing with the bureaucracy, the congressman is not merely one vote of 435. Rather, he is a nonpartisan power, someone whose phone call snaps an office to attention. He is not kept on hold. The constituent who receives aid believes that his congressman and his congressman alone got results.[1]

The Representation Function

If constituency service carries with it nothing but benefits for most members of Congress, the function of **representation** is less certain and even carries with it some danger that the legislator will lose his or her bid for reelection. Generally, representation means that the many competing interests in society should be represented in Congress. It follows that Congress should be a body acting slowly and deliberately and that its foremost concern should be to maintain a carefully crafted balance of power among competing interests.

How is representation to be achieved? There are basically two points of view on this issue.

The Trustee View of Representation.   The first approach to the question of how representation should be achieved is that legislators should act as **trustees** of the broad interests of the entire society and that they should vote against the narrow interests of their constituents as their conscience and their perception of national needs dictate. For example, a number of Republican legislators supported strong laws regulating the tobacco industry in spite of the views of some of their constituents.

The Instructed-Delegate View of Representation.   Directly opposed to the trustee view of representation is the notion that the members of Congress should behave as **instructed delegates.** That is, they should mirror the views of the majority of the constituents who elected them to power in the first place. On the surface, this approach is plausible and rewarding. For it to work, however, we must assume that constituents actually have well-formed views on the issues that are decided in Congress and, further, that they have clear-cut preferences

---

Casework
Personal work for constituents by members of Congress.

Ombudsperson
A person who hears and investigates complaints by private individuals against public officials or agencies.

Representation
The function of members of Congress as elected officials in representing the views of their constituents.

Trustee
In regard to a legislator, one who acts according to her or his conscience and the broad interests of the entire society.

Instructed Delegate
A legislator who is an agent of the voters who elected him or her and who votes according to the views of constituents regardless of personal assessments.

---

[1]Morris P. Fiorina, *Congress: Keystone of the Washington Establishment,* 2d ed. (New Haven, Conn.: Yale University Press, 1989), pp. 44, 47.

about these issues. Neither condition is likely to be satisfied very often. Most people generally do not have well-articulated views on major issues.

Generally, most legislators hold neither a pure trustee view nor a pure instructed-delegate view. Typically, they combine both perspectives in a pragmatic mix.

The Oversight Function

Oversight of the bureaucracy is essential if the decisions made by Congress are to have any force. **Oversight** is the process by which Congress follows up on the laws it has enacted to ensure that they are being enforced and administered in the way Congress intended. This is done by holding committee hearings and investigations, changing the size of an agency's budget, and cross-examining high-level presidential nominees to head major agencies. Also, until 1983, Congress could refuse to accede to proposed rules and regulations by resorting to the **legislative veto.** This allowed one, or sometimes both, chambers of Congress to disapprove of an executive rule within a specified period of time by a simple majority vote and thereby prevent its enforcement. The legislative veto was created by 1932 legislation that directed the president to restructure the executive branch. In 1983, however, the Supreme Court ruled that such a veto violated the separation of powers mandated by the Constitution, because the president had no power to veto the legislative action. Thus, the legislative veto was declared unconstitutional.[2]

Senators and representatives increasingly see their oversight function as a critically important part of their legislative activities. In part, oversight is related to the concept of constituency service, particularly when Congress investigates alleged arbitrariness or wrongdoing by bureaucratic agencies.

Oversight
The responsibility Congress has for following up on laws it has enacted to ensure that they are being enforced and administered in the way Congress intended.

Legislative Veto
A provision in a bill reserving to Congress or to a congressional committee the power to reject an action or regulation of a national agency by majority vote; declared unconstitutional by the Supreme Court in 1983.

The Public-Education Function

Educating the public is a function that is exercised whenever Congress holds public hearings, exercises oversight over the bureaucracy, or engages in committee and floor debate on such major issues and topics as political assassinations, aging, illegal drugs, or the concerns of small businesses. In so doing, Congress presents a range of viewpoints on pressing national questions. Congress also decides what issues will come up for discussion and decision; **agenda setting** is a major facet of its public-education function. Congressional documents are now available online at the following Web site: http://thomas.loc.gov. Most members of Congress now have Web pages as well—see the feature *E-mocracy: Congress Goes Online* on the next page.

Agenda Setting
Determining which public-policy questions will be debated or considered by Congress.

The Conflict-Resolution Function

Congress is commonly seen as an institution for resolving conflicts within American society. Organized interest groups and representatives of different racial, religious, economic, and ideological interests look on Congress as an access point for airing their grievances and seeking help. This puts Congress in the role of trying to resolve the differences among competing points of view by passing laws to accommodate as many interested parties as possible. To the extent that Congress meets pluralist expectations in accommodating competing interests, it tends to build support for the entire political process by all branches of government.

INFOTRAC®
COLLEGE EDITION

Report Criticizes Federal Oversight

---

[2]*Immigration and Naturalization Service v. Chadha,* 454 U.S. 812 (1983).

House-Senate Differences

Congress is composed of two markedly different—but coequal—chambers. Although the Senate and the House of Representatives exist within the same legislative institution, each has developed certain distinctive features that clearly distinguish life on one end of Capitol Hill from conditions on the other (the Senate wing is on the north side of the Capitol building, and the House wing is on the south side). A summary of these differences is given in Table 12–1.

Size and Rules

The central difference between the House and the Senate is simply that the House is much larger than the Senate. The House has 435 representatives, plus delegates from the District of Columbia, Puerto Rico, Guam, American Samoa, and the Virgin Islands, compared with just 100 senators. This size difference means that a greater number of formal rules are needed to govern activity in the House, whereas correspondingly looser procedures can be followed in the less crowded Senate. This difference is most obvious in the rules governing debate on the floors of the two chambers.

Rules Committee
A standing committee of the House of Representatives that provides special rules under which specific bills can be debated, amended, and considered by the House.

The Senate normally permits extended debate on all issues that arise before it. In contrast, the House operates with an elaborate system in which its **Rules Committee** normally proposes time limitations on debate for any bill, and a majority of the entire body accepts or modifies those suggested time limits. As a consequence of its stricter time limits on debate, the House, despite its greater size, often is able to act on legislation more quickly than the Senate.

e-mocracy

Congress Goes Online

After the Republican victory in 1994, Speaker Newt Gingrich declared, "Information . . . [will be] available to every citizen in the country at the same moment that it is available to the highest-paid Washington lobbyist." Congress, like most institutions, did not move that quickly, but by 2000, almost all congressional committees had Web sites. Many committees, in addition to posting basic schedules and agendas, posted documents and reports as soon as they were issued.

Virtually all senators and almost all representatives also now have their own Web sites. These sites, which are supported by public funds, do have some restrictions. According to the rules of both chambers, the Web sites may not contain material that is "personal and unrelated to . . . official business." This rule, however, is difficult to interpret for many members. If a constituent seeks a senator's favorite recipe, for example, is posting that recipe personal? Representative Peter DeFazio (D., Ore.) says that his constituents love the photos of his dog, his 1963 Dodge Dart, and his recipe for home-brewed beer.

Having a Web site and an e-mail address has advantages and disadvantages. Representative Anna G. Eshoo (D., Cal.) notes, "Everyone in the legislative office has total access to you 24 hours a day."* But a member's Web site can provide important services to constituents. Some congressional members' sites, for example, allow constituents to apply for internships in Washington, D.C., apply for appointments to military academies, order flags, order tours of the Capitol, and register complaints electronically. Congresswoman Eshoo's "virtual office" also allows voters to send e-mail and offers forms from the Veterans Affairs Department and the Social Security Administration for constituent problem solving.

Congressional use of the Web came of age in 1998 when the House Judiciary Committee placed the entire text of Kenneth Starr's report online (see Chapter 11). A few days later, President Clinton's videotaped testimony was also on the Web. Millions of people around the world accessed the Web to view this information.

By 2001, more than one hundred members of Congress had joined the Congressional Internet Caucus. This bipartisan group was formed to support the growth of the Internet and to educate their colleagues about issues related to the information age.

FOR CRITICAL ANALYSIS

How can a voter distinguish between straightforward information on a congressional Web site and political and partisan persuasion?

*Jonathan Weisman, "Lawmakers Gingerly Step into the Information Age," *Congressional Quarterly Weekly Report,* November 29, 1997, p. 2935.

TABLE 12-1

Differences between the House and the Senate

House*	Senate*
Members chosen from local districts	Members chosen from an entire state
Two-year term	Six-year term
Originally elected by voters	Originally (until 1913) elected by state legislatures
May impeach (indict) federal officials	May convict federal officials of impeachable offenses
Larger (435 voting members)	Smaller (100 members)
More formal rules	Fewer rules and restrictions
Debate limited	Debate extended
Less prestige and less individual notice	More prestige and more media attention
Originates bills for raising revenues	Has power to advise the president on, and to consent to, presidential appointments and treaties
Local or narrow leadership	National leadership
More partisan	Less party loyalty

*Some of these differences, such as the term of office, are provided for in the Constitution. Others, such as debate rules, are not.

Debate and Filibustering

According to historians, the Senate tradition of unlimited debate, which is known as **filibustering,** dates back to 1790, when a proposal to move the U.S. capital from New York to Philadelphia was stalled by such time-wasting tactics. This unlimited-debate tradition—which also existed in the House until 1811—is not absolute, however.

Under Senate Rule 22, debate may be ended by invoking **cloture,** or shutting off discussion on a bill. Amended in 1975 and 1979, Rule 22 states that debate may be closed off on a bill if sixteen senators sign a petition requesting it and if, after two days have elapsed, three-fifths of the entire membership (sixty votes, assuming no vacancies) vote for cloture. After cloture is invoked, each senator may speak on a bill for a maximum of one hour before a vote is taken.

In 1979, the Senate extended Rule 22 to provide that a final vote must take place within one hundred hours of debate after cloture has been imposed. It further limited the use of multiple amendments to stall postcloture final action on a bill.

Filibustering
In the Senate, unlimited debate to halt action on a particular bill.

Cloture
A method to close off debate and to bring the matter under consideration to a vote in the Senate.

Prestige

As a consequence of the greater size of the House, representatives generally cannot achieve as much individual recognition and public prestige as can members of the Senate. Senators, especially those who openly express presidential ambitions, are better able to gain media exposure and to establish careers as spokespersons for large national constituencies. To obtain recognition for his or her activities, a member of the House generally must do one of two things. He or she might survive in office long enough to join the ranks of the leadership on committees or within the party. Alternatively, the representative could become an expert on some specialized aspect of legislative policy—such as tax laws, the environment, or education.

INFOTRAC®
COLLEGE EDITION

While Congress Plays Games, Americans Suffer Vote Fraud

Congresspersons and the Citizenry: A Comparison

Government institutions are given life by the people who work in them and shape them as political structures. Who, then, are the members of Congress, and how are they elected?

Members of the U.S. Senate and the U.S. House of Representatives are not typical American citizens. As can be seen in Table 12–2, members of Congress are older than most Americans, partly because of constitutional age requirements and partly because a good deal of political experience normally is an advantage in running for national office. Members of Congress are also disproportionately white, male, Protestant, and trained in higher-status occupations. Lawyers are by far the largest occupational group among congresspersons, although the proportion of lawyers in the House is lower now than it was in the past.

Congressional Characteristics after the 2000 Elections

The 2000 congressional elections brought some changes to the characteristics of Congress, mostly by the addition of more women to the Senate. Of the total body of one hundred senators, thirteen are now female. Perhaps the most attention will be focused on the new senator from New York, Hillary Rodham Clinton, the first First Lady to be elected in her own right. In comparison to the gains for women, the number of minority legislators remains about the same as in the 106th Congress. The legislators continue to get somewhat younger and to have a wider range of occupations.

Congressional Elections

The process of electing members of Congress is decentralized. Congressional elections are operated by the individual state governments, which must conform to the rules established by the U.S. Constitution and by national statutes. The Constitution states that representatives are to be elected every second year by popular ballot, and the number of seats awarded to each state is to be determined by the results of the decennial census. Each state has at least one representative, with most congressional districts having about half a million residents. Senators are elected by popular vote (since the passage of the Seventeenth Amendment) every six years; approximately one-third of the seats are chosen every two years. Each state has two senators. Under Article I, Section 4, of the Constitution, state legislatures are given control over "[T]he Times, Places and Manner of holding Elections for Senators and Representatives"; however, "the Congress may at any time by Law make or alter such Regulations."

Candidates for Congressional Elections

Candidates for congressional seats may be self-selected, or, in districts where one party is very strong, they may be recruited by the local minority-party leadership.[3] Candidates may resemble the voters of the district in terms of ethnicity or religion, but they are also likely to be very successful individuals who have been active in politics before. Additionally, with respect to House seats, they are likely

---

[3]See the work of Gary Jacobson, *The Politics of Congressional Elections*, 4th ed. (New York: Longman Publishers, 1997).

TABLE 12-2

Characteristics of the 107th Congress, 2001–2003

CHARACTERISTIC	U.S. POPULATION (2000)*	HOUSE	SENATE
Age (median)	35.8	54.4	59.8
Percentage minority	28.6	13.7	3
Religion			
Percentage church members	61.0	98	99
Percentage Roman Catholic	39.0	28.7	24
Percentage Protestant	56.0	60	58
Percentage Jewish	4.0	6.4	10
Percentage female	51.1	13.6	13
Percentage with college degrees	21.4	93	94
Occupation			
Percentage lawyers	2.8	36	53
Percentage blue-collar workers	20.1	0	0
Family income			
Percentage of families earning over $50,000 annually	22.0	100	100
Personal wealth			
Percentage of population with assets over $1 million	0.7	16	33

*Estimates based on 1990 census; they do not reflect Census 2000 counts.

to have local ties to their districts. Candidates most likely choose to run because they believe they would enjoy the job and its accompanying status. They also may be thinking about a House seat as a steppingstone to future political office as a senator, governor, or presidential candidate. (See this chapter's *Making Waves* for the story of two very young members of the House.)

making Waves

Starting Young

How do you get elected to Congress before you turn thirty? There are many paths to the House of Representatives: the two youngest members of Congress have taken different routes to the House, but both seem likely to have long political careers.

In 1996, at the age of twenty-six, Congressman Harold E. Ford was elected to the House by a margin of 61 percent to 27 percent. He represents the Ninth District in Tennessee, which includes the city of Memphis. Ford, who is African American, succeeded his father in office. Harold Ford, Sr., first won a seat in the state legislature at the age of twenty-five and won his House seat in 1974. He held the seat for twenty-two years. The younger Ford attended the elite St. Albans School in Washington, D.C., and graduated from the University of Pennsylvania. He worked on his father's campaigns, on the Clinton transition team in 1992, and for Secretary of Commerce Ron Brown. When his father announced retirement plans, the younger Ford was a natural choice for the seat. He had to defeat a rival in the primary but has won both of his general elections handily. Congressman Ford has established a reputation as a moderate southern Democrat.

Congressman Paul Ryan was the second youngest member of the House of Representatives in the 106th Congress (1999–2001). This Republican won election to Congress from the

First District of Wisconsin in 1998, at the age of twenty-eight. (He is five months older than Congressman Ford.) Although it was his first election in a district that can be closely contested, Ryan won in 1998 by a margin of 57 percent to 43 percent. In 2000, he was reelected with 66 percent of the vote. The Ryan family has long been prominent in Janesville, Wisconsin, where they have been in the construction business for five generations. Ryan evidently acquired his interest in politics in school, graduating from Miami University, Ohio, as a political science major. While in college, he worked for Senator Robert Kasten of Wisconsin. After graduation, he went to Washington to work for Senator Sam Brownback of Kansas and as a speechwriter for prominent Republicans. When it seemed that the incumbent congressperson would run for a Senate seat, Ryan returned home to work for his family's business and get involved in local politics. He won his first election as a conservative Republican running against a single mom who suggested that he was too young to serve in Congress.*

FOR CRITICAL ANALYSIS

Is it possible for someone young to get elected to Congress without family political ties or family wealth?

*Michael Barone and Grant Ujifusa, *The Almanac of American Politics 2000* (Washington, D.C.: National Journal, 1999), p. 1739.

TABLE 12-3

Midterm Gains and Losses by the
Party of the President, 1942 to 1998

SEATS GAINED OR LOST BY THE PARTY OF THE PRESIDENT IN THE HOUSE OF REPRESENTATIVES	
1942	−45 (D.)
1946	−55 (D.)
1950	−29 (D.)
1954	−18 (R.)
1958	−47 (R.)
1962	−4 (D.)
1966	−47 (D.)
1970	−12 (R.)
1974	−48 (R.)
1978	−15 (D.)
1982	−26 (R.)
1986	−5 (R.)
1990	−8 (R.)
1994	−52 (D.)
1998	+5 (D.)

Direct Primary
An intraparty election in which the voters select the candidates who will run on a party's ticket in the subsequent general election.

Party Identifier
A person who identifies with a political party.

Congressional campaigns have changed considerably in the past two decades. Like all other campaigns, they are much more expensive, with the average cost of a winning Senate campaign now being $5 million and a winning House campaign averaging more than $770,000. Campaign funds include direct contributions regulated by law (as discussed in Chapter 10), political action committee (PAC) contributions, and "soft money" funneled through the national and state party committees. Once in office, legislators spend some time almost every day raising funds for their next campaign.

Most candidates for Congress must win the nomination through a **direct primary,** in which **party identifiers** vote for the candidate who will be on the party ticket in the general election. To win the primary, candidates may take more liberal or more conservative positions to get the votes of party identifiers. In the general election, they may moderate their views to attract the votes of independents and voters from the other party.

Presidential Effects.   Congressional candidates are always hopeful that a strong presidential candidate on the ticket will have "coattails" that will sweep in senators and representatives of the same party. In fact, coattail effects have been quite limited, appearing only in landslide elections such as Lyndon Johnson's victory over Barry Goldwater in 1964. Members of Congress who are from contested districts or who are in their first term are more likely to experience the effect of midterm elections, which are held in the even-numbered years in between presidential contests. In these years, voter turnout falls sharply, and the party controlling the White House normally loses seats in Congress. Additionally, voters in midterm elections often are responding to incumbency issues, because there is no presidential campaign. The result is a fragmentation of party authority and a loosening of ties between Congress and the president. Table 12–3 shows the pattern for midterm elections since 1942.

The Power of Incumbency

The power of incumbency in the outcome of congressional elections cannot be overemphasized. Table 12–4 shows that the overwhelming majority of representatives and a smaller proportion of senators who decide to run for reelection

TABLE 12-4

The Power of Incumbency

	PRESIDENTIAL-YEAR ELECTIONS						MIDTERM ELECTIONS						
	1980	1984	1988	1992	1996	2000	1974	1978	1982	1986	1990	1994	1998
House													
Number of incumbent candidates	398	409	409	368	382	400	391	382	393	393	407	382	401
Reelected	361	390	402	325	359	394	343	358	352	385	391	347	394
Percentage of total	90.7	95.4	98.3	88.9	93.4	98.5	87.7	93.7	90.1	98.0	96.1	90.8	98.2
Defeated	37	19	7	43	23	6	48	24	39	8	16	35	8
In primary	6	3	1	19	2	0	8	5	10	2	1	1	1
In general election	31	16	6	24	21	6	40	19	29	6	15	34	7
Senate													
Number of incumbent candidates	29	29	27	28	21	29	27	25	30	28	32	26	29
Reelected	16	26	23	23	19	24	23	15	28	21	31	24	26
Percentage of total	55.2	89.6	85	82.1	90	82.7	85.2	60.0	93.3	75.0	96.9	92.3	89.6
Defeated	13	3	4	5	2	5	4	10	2	7	1	2	3
In primary	4	0	0	1	1	0	2	3	0	0	0	0	0
In general election	9	3	4	4	1	5	2	7	2	7	1	2	3

SOURCES: Norman Ornstein, Thomas E. Mann, and Michael J. Malbin, *Vital Statistics on Congress, 1993–1994* (Washington, D.C.: Congressional Quarterly Press, 1994), pp. 56–57; *Congressional Quarterly Weekly Report,* November 7, 1992, pp. 3551, 3576; and authors' update.

are successful. This conclusion holds for both presidential-year and midterm elections. David R. Mayhew argues that the pursuit of reelection is the strongest motivation behind the activities of members of Congress. The reelection goal is pursued in three major ways: by *advertising,* by *credit claiming,* and by *position taking.*[4] Advertising includes using the mass media, making personal appearances with constituents, and sending newsletters—all to produce a favorable image and to make the incumbent's name a household word. Members of Congress try to present themselves as informed, experienced, and responsive to people's needs. Credit claiming focuses on the things a legislator claims to have done to benefit his or her constituents—by fulfilling the congressional casework function or bringing money for mass transit to the district, for example. Position taking occurs when an incumbent explains her or his voting record on key issues; makes public statements of general support for presidential decisions; or indicates that she or he specifically supports positions on key issues, such as gun control or anti-inflation policies. Position taking carries with it certain risks, as the incumbent may lose support by disagreeing with the attitudes of a large number of constituents. (One way to limit the power of incumbency is by limiting the terms of members of Congress—see the feature *Which Side Are You On?* on the next page.)

The Shakeup in the 1994 Elections

The 1994 midterm elections swept the Democratic majority in both chambers of Congress out of power and brought in a Republican majority in a nationwide change of government that surprised and shocked the members of Congress and

Citizens display signs that show their support for term limits for members of Congress. The movement toward establishing term limits gathered steam in the early 1990s, and by 1994 more than twenty states had passed laws imposing such limits on members of Congress elected in those states. In 1995, however, the Supreme Court held that these laws were unconstitutional. Because the Constitution did not provide for limiting the number of terms a congressperson could serve, term limits could be established only by a constitutional amendment. The Court's decision did not end the controversy over this issue, however, as this photo indicates.

---

[4]David R. Mayhew, *Congress: The Electoral Connection* (New Haven, Conn.: Yale University Press, 1974).

which side are you on?

Should We Have Congressional Term Limits?

The heated debate over term limits has continued for more than a decade. The idea that legislators should serve a limited number of terms in office started as a grass-roots campaign on the West Coast. With its own organization, U.S. Term Limits, the movement spread across the country, often winning statewide referenda. Currently, eighteen states limit the terms of their state lawmakers. Three other states passed similar laws that have been found unconstitutional by their respective state supreme courts. By 1994, more than twenty states had passed laws limiting the terms of their congressional representatives as well. In 1995, however, the United States Supreme Court held that those laws were unconstitutional because the U.S. Constitution does not mention term limits. Only a constitutional amendment could impose such limits.

Why Term Limits?

Advocates of term limits say that the original idea of the founders was to have amateur legislators who were representative of the common people and who were not career politicians. Such amateur lawmakers are more likely to be in touch with the needs and issues of the mass of voters. In addition, lawmakers who know that they cannot make a career in office are not as likely to become the pawns of special interests, because they will not have a long-lasting relationship with such interests or lobbying groups.

All of the advantages of term limits would be enhanced if limits were applied to members of Congress. Clearly, relationships with special interests would be greatly weakened.

Arguments against Term Limits

Opponents of term limits look to the future with trepidation: they have found that in states that impose term limits on state lawmakers the result is "amateur" lawmakers who have almost no knowledge of the issues that face the state or of prior policy decisions. Each new crop of legislators must be educated about state issues. Imagine having a Congress in which virtually no member understood the budget or defense policy.

Another side effect of term limits in the states that have adopted them is the weakening of leadership or party control. Since the legislators are arriving with a known end to their legislative career, they are very unlikely to accept guidance from either the political party or the elected leadership of the state assembly. Votes on state policies become very unpredictable and, in some cases, capricious. Needless to say, most career politicians find this a difficult situation.

DOES IT MATTER?

Do you think that members of Congress would be more in touch with the needs of the citizenry if they were subject to term limits? Could such members gain enough expertise in policy to serve their constituents well?

GOING ONLINE

A number of Web sites offer information about the term limits question. U.S. Term Limits, the organization that backs this movement, has a Web site at **http://www.termlimits.org**. *Americans Back in Charge, at* **http://www.townhall.com**, *also supports term limits. The CATO Institute offers policy papers on this issue at* **http://www.cato.org**. *Common Cause, the citizen's lobbying group, argues against term limits at its site, at* **http://www.commoncause.org**. *If you would like to read the text of the Supreme Court decision about congressional term limits, U.S. Term Limits v. Thornton, go to FindLaw, at* **http://www.findlaw.com**, *and select "Supreme Court Decisions."*

the parties themselves. According to exit polls taken on election day, Republican candidates for Congress won the votes of their own party identifiers, of the majority of independents, and of those who had voted for independent candidate H. Ross Perot in 1992, but of very few Democratic voters. Republicans captured the votes of white males, with a gender gap of about 8 percent. Republicans won 19 more seats in the South, giving them a 73–64 seat majority in that region. In Washington, the speaker of the House, Tom Foley, was defeated, the first speaker to be denied reelection since 1862. In total, the Democrats lost 52 seats, with 190 incumbents reelected and 35 defeated. All Republican incumbents in the House were reelected.

The 1994 elections resulted in a "divided" government, which was reaffirmed by the voters in subsequent elections. The *Critical Perspective* beginning on page 392 presents some of the issues raised by a government with no majority.

Party Control of Congress after the 2000 Elections

The 107th Congress may face tremendous obstacles to its work due to the extremely narrow majorities held by the Republicans in both chambers. The Senate is evenly divided, with fifty Democrats and fifty Republicans. The Republicans have nominal control over the Senate, however, because Vice President Dick Cheney can cast a vote to break a tied vote in the Senate. In the House, less than a dozen seats divide the parties, with the Republicans holding the majority. The close margins mean that the defection of only one or two members from the party's position will defeat legislation. And, of course, it will be impossible to build a two-thirds majority to override a presidential veto.

Because new elections are only two years away, there is even less incentive to work together in the 107th Congress. Each party will be looking ahead to the 2002 elections and planning ways to capture more seats. Democrats are so close to control that they will be highly motivated to raise campaign funds for the next election, and Republicans will be seeking any possible way to increase their margin of control. For some members, it will be easier to wait until the 108th Congress rather than fight for issues in this one.

Congressional Reapportionment

By far the most complicated aspects of the mechanics of congressional elections are the issues of **reapportionment** (the allocation of seats in the House to each state after each census) and **redistricting** (the redrawing of the boundaries of the districts within each state).[5] In a landmark six-to-two vote in 1962, the Supreme Court made reapportionment a **justiciable** (that is, a reviewable) **question** in the Tennessee case of *Baker v. Carr*[6] by invoking the Fourteenth Amendment principle that no state can deny to any person "the equal protection of the laws." This principle was applied directly in the 1964 ruling, *Reynolds v. Sims*,[7] when the Court held that *both* chambers of a state legislature must be apportioned with equal populations in each district. This "one person, one vote" principle was applied to congressional districts in the 1964 case of *Wesberry v. Sanders*,[8] based on Article I, Section 2, of the Constitution, which requires that congresspersons be chosen "by the People of the several States."

Severe malapportionment of congressional districts prior to *Wesberry* had resulted in some districts containing two or three times the populations of other districts in the same state, thereby diluting the effect of a vote cast in the more populous districts. This system generally had benefited the conservative populations of rural areas and small towns and harmed the interests of the more heavily populated and liberal urban areas. In fact, suburban areas have benefited the most from the *Wesberry* ruling, as suburbs account for an increasingly larger proportion of the nation's population, and cities include a correspondingly smaller segment of the population.

Reapportionment
The allocation of seats in the House of Representatives to each state after each census.

Redistricting
The redrawing of the boundaries of the congressional districts within each state.

Justiciable Question
A question that may be raised and reviewed in court.

---

[5]For an excellent discussion of these issues, see *Congressional Districts in the 1990s* (Washington, D.C.: Congressional Quarterly Press, 1993).
[6]369 U.S. 186 (1962). The term *justiciable* is pronounced juhs-*tish*-a-buhl.
[7]377 U.S. 533 (1964).
[8]376 U.S. 1 (1964).

Gerrymandering
The drawing of legislative district boundary lines for the purpose of obtaining partisan or factional advantage. A district is said to be gerrymandered when its shape is manipulated by the dominant party in the state legislature to maximize electoral strength at the expense of the minority party.

Congressional Reapportionment

Gerrymandering

Although the general issue of reapportionment has been dealt with fairly successfully by the one person, one vote principle, the **gerrymandering** issue has not yet been resolved. This term refers to the legislative boundary-drawing tactics that were used by Elbridge Gerry, the governor of Massachusetts, in the 1812 elections (see Figure 12–1). A district is said to have been gerrymandered when its shape is altered substantially by the dominant party in a state legislature to maximize its electoral strength at the expense of the minority party. This can be achieved either by concentrating the opposition's voter support in as few districts as possible or by diffusing the minority party's strength by spreading it thinly across many districts.

In 1986, the Supreme Court heard a case that challenged gerrymandered congressional districts in Indiana. The Court ruled for the first time that redistricting for the political benefit of one group could be challenged on constitutional grounds. In this specific case, *Davis v. Bandemer,*[9] the Court, however, did not agree that the districts were drawn unfairly, because it could not be proved that a group of voters would consistently be deprived of its influence at the polls as a result of the new districts.

"Minority-Majority" Districts

The Supreme Court had declared as unconstitutional districts that are uneven in population or that violate norms of size and shape to maximize the advantage of one party. In the early 1990s, however, the federal government encouraged another type of gerrymandering that made possible the election of a minority representative from a "minority-majority" area. Under the mandate of the Voting Rights Act of 1965, the Justice Department issued directives to states after the 1990 census instructing them to create congressional districts that would max-

---

[9]478 U.S. 109 (1986).

FIGURE 12–1

The Original Gerrymander
The practice of "gerrymandering"—the excessive manipulation of the shape of a legislative district to benefit a certain incumbent or party—is probably as old as the republic, but the name originated in 1812. In that year, the Massachusetts legislature carved out of Essex County a district that historian John Fiske said had a "dragonlike contour." When the painter Gilbert Stuart saw the misshapen district, he penciled in a head, wings, and claws and exclaimed, "That will do for a salamander!" Editor Benjamin Russell replied, "Better say a Gerrymander" (after Elbridge Gerry, then governor of Massachusetts).

SOURCE: *Congressional Quarterly's Guide to Congress,* 3d ed. (Washington, D.C.: Congressional Quarterly Press, 1982), p. 695.

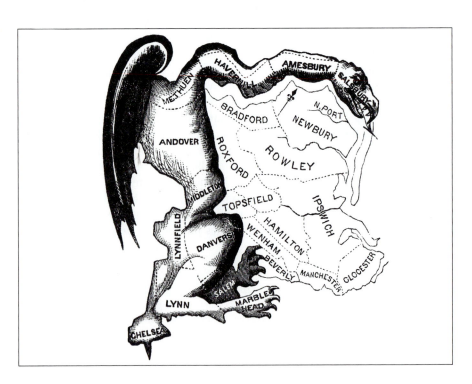

imize the voting power of minority groups—that is, create districts in which
minority voters were the majority. One such district—the Twelfth District of
North Carolina—was 165 miles long, following Interstate 85 for the most part
(see Figure 12–2). According to a local joke, the district was so narrow that a car
traveling down the interstate highway with both doors open would kill most of
the voters in the district.

Many of these "minority-majority" districts were challenged in court by citizens who claimed that to create districts based on race or ethnicity alone violates the equal protection clause of the Constitution. In 1995, the Supreme Court
agreed with this argument when it declared that Georgia's new Eleventh District
was unconstitutional. The district stretched from Atlanta to the Atlantic, splitting eight counties and five municipalities along the way. The Court referred to
the district as a "monstrosity" linking "widely spaced urban centers that have
absolutely nothing to do with each other." The Court went on to say that when
a state assigns voters on the basis of race, "it engages in the offensive and
demeaning assumption that voters of a particular race, because of their race,
think alike, share the same political interests, and will prefer the same candidates
at the polls." The Court also chastised the Justice Department for concluding that
race-based districting was mandated under the Voting Rights Act of 1965:
"When the Justice Department's interpretation of the Act compels race-based
districting, it by definition raises a serious constitutional question."[10] In subsequent rulings, the Court affirmed its position that when race is the dominant factor in the drawing of congressional district lines, the districts are
unconstitutional.

In 2000, the Supreme Court also limited the federal government's authority
to invalidate changes in state and local elections on the basis that the changes
were discriminatory. The case involved a proposed school redistricting plan in
Louisiana. The Court held that the federal approval for the plan could not be
withheld simply because the plan was discriminatory. Rather, the test was
whether the plan left racial and ethnic minorities worse off than they were
before.[11]

Pay, Perks, and Privileges

Compared with the average American citizen, members of Congress are well
paid. In 2001, annual congressional salaries were $145,100. Legislators also have
many benefits that are not available to most workers.

---

[10]*Miller v. Johnson,* 515 U.S. 900 (1995).
[11]*Reno v. Bossier Parish School Board,* 120 S.Ct. 886 (2000).

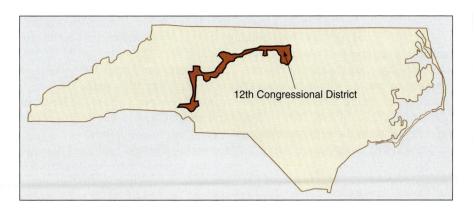

FIGURE 12–2
The Twelfth District of North Carolina
The Twelfth District, which was
declared unconstitutional by the
United States Supreme Court in 1996,
was created to facilitate the election of
a minority representative. It snaked
through North Carolina along
Interstate 85.

critical perspective

Gridlock or Constitutional Balance?

By the end of George Bush's presidency in 1993, the relationship between Congress and the president was frequently described as one of gridlock. The term described the political standoff between Bush and the Democratic majority in Congress. Few of the bills that the president introduced could be passed, and he successfully vetoed a number of bills that the Democrats in Congress passed. In fact, the Democratic Party used Bush's presidential term to try to convince the electorate that it was time, after twelve years, to put a Democrat in the White House, because the Democratic-controlled Congress would work more effectively with a Democratic administration.

Constitutional Checks and Balances

The relationship between the president and Congress is structured constitutionally to prevent either branch from being totally dominant. Because of checks and balances, including the veto, the veto override, the nomination and treaty processes, and the different constituencies and terms in office of members of the House and the Senate, presidential success with Congress is difficult to achieve. Some presidents of the same party as the majority in Congress have had great success after landslide elections, such as Franklin Roosevelt in 1933 and Lyndon Johnson in 1965. This happened, in part, because many new Democrats were elected with the president. Sometimes, as in Ronald Reagan's case, a president who does not control the chambers of Congress still can have great legislative suc-

cess. Reagan's personal electoral victory and great popularity with the public seemed to generate congressional cooperation.

Remember that checks and balances were put into the Constitution to assure exactly what has happened—to make sure that it would not be too easy for an electoral majority, either for the president or in Congress, to make changes too quickly. In fact, opinion polls in 1997 found that 67 percent of the public approved of a divided government, believing that it kept the political parties and the government from gaining too much power.*

*Hart and Teeter poll for NBC News/*Wall Street Journal,* reported in *The Public Perspective,* February/March 1998, p. 48.

The Occurrence of Divided Government Following Presidential and Midterm Elections, 1864–2000

	ELECTIONS RESULTING IN DIVIDED GOVERNMENT		
ELECTION YEARS	% PRESIDENTIAL ELECTIONS	% MIDTERM ELECTIONS	% ALL ELECTIONS
1864–1894	25 (2/8)	75 (6/8)	50 (8/16)
1896–1966	6 (1/18)	28 (5/18)	17 (6/36)
1968–2000	66 (6/9)	88 (7/8)	77 (13/17)

Note: The numbers in parentheses are the actual number of elections in the category that resulted in divided government and the total number of presidential or midterm elections held in that period.

SOURCES: James E. Campbell, *The Presidential Pulse of Congressional Elections* (Lexington, Ky.: University Press of Kentucky, 1993), p. 212; and authors' update.

Special Benefits

Members of Congress benefit in many ways from belonging to a select group. They have access to private Capitol Hill gymnasium facilities; get low-cost haircuts; receive free, close-in parking at the National and Dulles Airports near Washington; and get six free parking spaces per member in Capitol Hill garages—plus one free outdoor Capitol parking slot. They also avoid parking tickets because of their congressional license plates and, until 1994, were not required to comply with most labor laws in dealing with their staffs. They eat in a subsidized dining room and take advantage of free plants from the Botanical Gardens for their offices, free medical care, an inexpensive but generous pension plan, liberal travel allowances, and special tax considerations.

Members of Congress are also granted generous **franking** privileges that permit them to mail newsletters, surveys, and other letters to their constituents. The annual cost of congressional mail has risen from $11 million in 1971 to almost

Franking
A policy that enables members of Congress to send material through the mail by substituting their facsimile signature (frank) for postage.

critical perspective

Divided Government and Legislative Deadlock

Historically, there have been cycles of divided government, as shown in the accompanying table, with higher proportions before 1894 and since 1968. The question for consideration is whether a "unified" government is more likely than a "divided government" to pass legislation.

In 1992, the voters were presented with a choice between a continuation of divided government, a Democratic-controlled government, or (in the case of H. Ross Perot) a nonpartisan presidency. The voters opted for a Democratic-controlled government, with Bill Clinton at its helm. At the end of his first year in office, President Bill Clinton declared that "gridlock was over." He saluted the effectiveness of the Democratic leadership in Congress in passing his tax increase/deficit reduction plan; the family leave plan; the national service plan; and the North American Free Trade Agreement (NAFTA). The president vetoed no bills in 1993.

Scholars, however, suggest that the election of a president who is of the same party as the majority in Congress does not guarantee smooth sailing. Both David Mayhew and Roger Davidson argue that historically divided government is not related to deadlock in legislation.[†] Republicans Dwight Eisenhower, Richard Nixon, Ronald Reagan, and George Bush all were able to pass important legislation with Democratic control of one or both chambers of Congress. Democratic

[†]David Mayhew, *Divided We Govern* (New Haven: Yale University Press, 1991); and Roger Davidson, "The Presidency and Three Eras of the Modern Congress," in *Divided Democracy*, ed. by James A. Thurber (Washington, D.C.: Congressional Quarterly Press, 1991).

President Jimmy Carter, with a Democratic majority, had as much difficulty as any other president.

President Bill Clinton's chance to work with a Democratic Congress ended abruptly with the 1994 election. For the first year after the election of the Republican-controlled House and Senate, the president and Congress seemed to be truly ineffective. The fight over the passage of the federal budget brought some areas of the government to a halt before the president and the congressional leadership were able to forge a deal. Actually, Clinton gained in popularity when he vetoed Republican bills that he felt he could not approve, and the Republicans in Congress gained in respect when they were able to pass major bills after compromising with their Democratic colleagues.

The second Clinton term saw the continuation of divided government, although the Republican majority in the House was cut to a very narrow margin by the 1998 elections. Notably, although the relationship between the Republicans in Congress and the president was extremely bitter, especially during the impeachment process, the two branches were able to pass a number of important laws. These accomplishments included a reform of banking laws, a new telecommunications law, new farming legislation, and the balanced budget. Some issues, such as Social Security and health insurance, remained too contentious for either party or branch of government to tackle during the second Clinton term. The general public, according to the polls, just wanted the president and Congress to solve the nation's problems and spend less time on political name calling.

FOR CRITICAL ANALYSIS

1. Does divided government make it impossible for Congress and the president to deal with major national problems?
2. How do the personality and style of the president and congressional leaders influence the degree of gridlock between the two branches?

$60 million today. Typically, the costs for these mailings rise enormously during election years.

Permanent Professional Staffs

More than 35,000 people are employed in the Capitol Hill bureaucracy. About half of them are personal and committee staff members. The personal staff includes office clerks and secretaries; professionals who deal with media relations, draft legislation, and satisfy constituency requests for service; and staffers who maintain local offices in the member's home district or state.

The average Senate office on Capitol Hill employs about thirty staff members, and twice that number work on the personal staffs of senators from the most populous states. House office staffs typically are about half as large as those of the Senate. The number of staff members has increased dramatically since 1960. With the bulk of those increases coming in assistance to individual members,

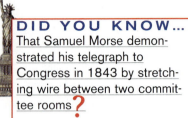

some scholars question whether staff members are really advising on legislation or are primarily aiding constituents and gaining votes in the next election. Electronic communications, however, have greatly increased constituents' contacts with the legislators; staff members respond to these contacts.

Congress also benefits from the expertise of the professional staffs of agencies that were created to produce information for members of the House and Senate. The Congressional Research Service (CRS), a section of the Library of Congress, furnishes a computer-based record of the contents and current legislative status of major bills that are under consideration. This record can be reviewed by staff members using computer terminals available in most offices. The General Accounting Office (GAO) audits spending by federal agencies, investigates agency practices, and makes policy recommendations to Congress, especially concerning the financial activities of the government. The Congressional Budget Office (CBO) advises Congress on the anticipated effect on the economy of government expenditures and estimates the cost of proposed policies.

Privileges and Immunities under the Law

Members of Congress also benefit from a number of special constitutional protections. Under Article I, Section 6, of the Constitution, they "shall in all Cases, except Treason, Felony and Breach of the Peace, be privileged from Arrest during their Attendance at the Session of their respective Houses, and in going to and returning from the same; and for any Speech or Debate in either House, they shall not be questioned in any other Place." The arrest immunity clause is not really an important provision today. The "speech or debate" clause, however, means that a member may make any allegations or other statements he or she wishes in connection with official duties and normally not be sued for libel or slander or otherwise be subject to legal action.

Congresswoman Connie Morella of Maryland sits at her desk while speaking with her staff in her Washington, D.C., office. Congressional staff members serve as researchers, help write speeches for their legislators, answer the mail, and assist constituents in getting their problems solved. Today, staff members spend more and more of their time answering e-mail and working on their legislators' Web sites.

The Committee Structure

Most of the actual work of legislating is performed by the committees and subcommittees within Congress. Thousands of bills are introduced in every session of Congress, and no single member can possibly be adequately informed on all the issues that arise. The committee system is a way to provide for specialization, or a division of the legislative labor. Members of a committee can concentrate on just one area or topic—such as taxation or energy—and develop sufficient expertise to draft appropriate legislation when needed. The flow of legislation through both the House and the Senate is determined largely by the speed with which the members of these committees act on bills and resolutions.

The Power of Committees

Commonly known as "little legislatures," committees usually have the final say on pieces of legislation.[12] Committee actions may be overturned on the floor by the House or Senate, but this rarely happens. Legislators normally defer to the expertise of the chairperson and other members of the committee who speak on the floor in defense of a committee decision. Chairpersons of committees exercise control over the scheduling of hearings and formal action on a bill. They also decide which subcommittee will act on legislation falling within their com-

---

[12]The term *little legislatures* is from Woodrow Wilson, *Congressional Government* (New York: Meridian Books, 1956 [first published in 1885]).

mittee's jurisdiction.

Committees only very rarely are deprived of control over a bill—although this kind of action is provided for in the rules of each chamber. In the House, if a bill has been considered by a standing committee for thirty days, the signatures of a majority (218) of the House membership on a **discharge petition** can pry a bill out of an uncooperative committee's hands. From 1909 to 2000, however, although over nine hundred such petitions were made, only slightly more than two dozen resulted in successful discharge efforts. Of those, twenty passed the House.[13]

Types of Congressional Committees

Over the past two centuries, Congress has created several different types of committees, each of which serves particular needs of the institution.

Standing Committees.   By far the most important committees in Congress are the **standing committees**—permanent bodies that are established by the rules of each chamber of Congress and that continue from session to session. A list of the standing committees of the 107th Congress is presented in Table 12-5. In addition, most of the standing committees have created several subcommittees to carry out their work. In the 106th Congress, there were 68 subcommittees in the Senate and 85 in the House.[14]

Each standing committee is given a specific area of legislative policy jurisdiction, and almost all legislative measures are considered by the appropriate standing committees. Because of the importance of their work and the traditional

---

[13]*Congressional Quarterly's Guide to Congress,* 3d ed. (Washington, D.C.: Congressional Quarterly Press, 1982), p. 426; and authors' update.

[14]*Congressional Directory* (Washington, D.C.: U.S. Government Printing Office, various editions).

DID YOU KNOW...
That the House members' gym has no locker room for female members, and women must call ahead to warn the men that they are coming to use the gym?

Discharge Petition
A procedure by which a bill in the House of Representatives may be forced out of a committee (discharged) that has refused to report it for consideration by the House. The discharge petition must be signed by an absolute majority (218) of representatives and is used only on rare occasions.

Standing Committee
A permanent committee within the House or Senate that considers bills within a certain subject area.

TABLE 12-5

Standing Committees of the 107th Congress, 2001–2003

HOUSE COMMITTEES	SENATE COMMITTEES
Agriculture	Agriculture, Nutrition, and Forestry
Appropriations	Appropriations
Armed Services	Armed Services
Banking and Financial Services	Banking, Housing, and Urban Affairs
Budget	Budget
Commerce	Commerce, Science, and Transportation
Education and the Workforce	Energy and Natural Resources
Government Reform	Environment and Public Works
House Administration	Finance
International Relations	Foreign Relations
Judiciary	Governmental Affairs
Resources	Health, Education, Labor, and Pensions
Rules	Indian Affairs
Science and Technology	Judiciary
Small Business	Rules and Administration
Standards of Official Conduct	Small Business
Transportation and Infrastructure	Veterans' Affairs
Veterans' Affairs	
Ways and Means	

A committee hearing in Congress. Starting from the chair of the committee in the center, Democratic senators sit on the left in order of seniority, while Republicans take the seats on the right in order of seniority.

influence of their members in Congress, certain committees are considered to be more prestigious than others. If a congressperson seeks to be influential, she or he will usually aspire to a seat on the Appropriations Committee in either chamber, the Ways and Means Committee in the House, the House Education and the Workforce Committee, or the Senate Foreign Relations Committee.

Each member of the House generally serves on two standing committees, except when the member sits on the Appropriations, Rules, or Ways and Means Committee—in which case he or she serves on only that one standing committee. Each senator may serve on two major committees and one minor committee (only the Rules and Administration Committee and the Veterans' Affairs Committee are considered minor).

Select Committee
A temporary legislative committee established for a limited time period and for a special purpose.

Select Committees.   A **select committee** normally is created for a limited period of time and for a specific legislative purpose. For example, a select committee may be formed to investigate a public problem, such as child nutrition or aging. Select committees are disbanded when they have reported to the chamber that created them. They rarely create original legislation.

Joint Committee
A legislative committee composed of members from both chambers of Congress.

Joint Committees.   A **joint committee** is formed by the concurrent action of both chambers of Congress and consists of members from each chamber. Joint committees, which may be permanent or temporary, have dealt with the economy, taxation, and the Library of Congress.

Conference Committee
A special joint committee appointed to reconcile differences when bills pass the two chambers of Congress in different forms.

Conference Committees.   Special types of joint committees—**conference committees**—are formed for the purpose of achieving agreement between the House and the Senate on the exact wording of legislative acts when the two chambers pass legislative proposals in different forms. No bill can be sent to the White House to be signed into law unless it first passes both chambers in identical form. Sometimes called the "third house" of Congress, conference committees are in a position to make significant alterations in legislation and frequently become the focal point of policy debates.

The House Rules Committee.   Because of its special "gatekeeping" power over the terms on which legislation will reach the floor of the House of

Representatives, the House Rules Committee holds a uniquely powerful position. A special committee rule sets the time limit on debate and determines whether and how a bill may be amended. This practice dates back to 1883. The Rules Committee has the unusual power to meet while the House is in session, to have its resolutions considered immediately on the floor, and to initiate legislation on its own.

The Selection of Committee Members

In the House, representatives are appointed to standing committees by the Steering Committee of their party. Majority-party members with longer terms of continuous service on a standing committee are given preference when the committee chairperson—as well as holders of other significant posts in Congress—is selected. This is not a law but an informal, traditional process. The **seniority system,** although deliberately unequal, provides a predictable means of assigning positions of power within Congress.

The general pattern until the 1970s was that members of the House or Senate who represented **safe seats** would be reelected continually and eventually would accumulate enough years of continuous committee service to enable them to become the chairpersons of their committees.

In the 1970s, a number of reforms in the chairperson selection process somewhat modified the seniority system. The reforms introduced the use of a secret ballot in electing House committee chairpersons and established rules for the selection of subcommittee chairpersons that resulted in a greater dispersal of authority within the committees themselves. In 1995, Speaker Newt Gingrich introduced a set of reforms that restored power to committee chairpersons. In addition, the Republicans passed a rule limiting the term of a committee chairperson to six years.

The Formal Leadership

The limited amount of centralized power that exists in Congress is exercised through party-based mechanisms. Congress is organized by party. When the Democratic Party, for example, wins a majority of seats in either the House or the Senate, Democrats control the official positions of power in that chamber, and every important committee has a Democratic chairperson and a majority of Democratic members. The same process holds when Republicans are in the majority.

We consider the formal leadership positions in the House and Senate separately, but you will note some broad similarities in the way leaders are selected and in the ways they exercise power in the two chambers.

Leadership in the House

The House leadership is made up of the speaker, the majority and minority leaders, and the party whips.

The Speaker.   The foremost power holder in the House of Representatives is the **speaker of the House.** The speaker's position is technically a nonpartisan one, but in fact, for the better part of two centuries, the speaker has been the official leader of the majority party in the House. When a new Congress convenes in January of odd-numbered years, each party nominates a candidate for speaker. In one of the very rare instances of perfect party cohesion, all Democratic members of the

Seniority System
A custom followed in both chambers of Congress specifying that members with longer terms of continuous service will be given preference when committee chairpersons and holders of other significant posts are selected.

Safe Seat
A district that returns the legislator with 55 percent of the vote or more.

Speaker of the House
The presiding officer in the House of Representatives. The speaker is always a member of the majority party and is the most powerful and influential member of the House.

DID YOU KNOW...
That the Constitution does not require that the speaker of the House of Representatives be an elected member of the House**?**

House ordinarily vote for their party's nominee, and all Republicans support their alternative candidate.

The influence of modern-day speakers is based primarily on their personal prestige, persuasive ability, and knowledge of the legislative process–plus the acquiescence or active support of other representatives. The major formal powers of the speaker include the following:

1. Presiding over meetings of the House.
2. Appointing members of joint committees and conference committees.
3. Scheduling legislation for floor action.
4. Deciding points of order and interpreting the rules with the advice of the House parliamentarian.
5. Referring bills and resolutions to the appropriate standing committees of the House.

A speaker may take part in floor debate and vote, as can any other member of Congress, but recent speakers usually have voted only to break a tie.

In general, the powers of the speaker are related to his or her control over information and communications channels in the House. This is a significant power in a large, decentralized institution in which information is a very important resource. With this control, the speaker attempts to ensure the smooth operation of the chamber and to integrate presidential and congressional policies.

In 1975, the powers of the speaker were expanded when the House Democratic Caucus gave its party's speaker the power to appoint the Democratic Steering Committee, which determines new committee assignments for House party members.

The election of Newt Gingrich, Republican of Georgia, as speaker in 1994 put a forceful man into an office that had not exercised much direct power, especially for Republicans. Gingrich began his term by hand-picking some of the committee chairpersons so they would work with him, overriding the seniority rule. On occasion, he overruled committee chairpersons, appointed task forces to take issues away from certain members, forced members to debate issues in the Republican Conference, and, by exercising his formal powers, kept extremely tight control of the agenda. Gingrich's strong personality, however, was unpopular with voters, and his tactics lost support among some Republican legislators. After the loss of Republican House seats in the 1998 elections, Gingrich announced that he would resign from the speaker's position rather than provoke a divisive fight within the party. Dennis Hastert of Illinois became speaker of the House in 1999.

Majority Leader of the House
A legislative position held by an important party member in the House of Representatives. The majority leader is selected by the majority party in caucus or conference to foster cohesion among party members and to act as spokesperson for the majority party in the House.

The Majority Leader. The **majority leader of the House** is elected by a caucus of party members to foster cohesion among party members and to act as a spokesperson for the party. The majority leader influences the scheduling of debate and generally acts as the chief supporter of the speaker. The majority leader cooperates with the speaker and other party leaders, both inside and outside Congress, to formulate the party's legislative program and to guide that program through the legislative process in the House. The Democrats recruit future speakers from that position.

Minority Leader of the House
The party leader elected by the minority party in the House.

The Minority Leader. The **minority leader of the House** is the candidate nominated for speaker by a caucus of the minority party. Like the majority leader, the leader of the minority party has as her or his primary responsibility the maintaining of cohesion within the party's ranks. The minority leader works for cohesion among the party's members and speaks on behalf of the president if the minority party controls the White House. In relations with the majority party, the minority leader consults with both the speaker and the majority leader on recognizing members who wish to speak on the floor, on House rules and procedures, and on the scheduling of legislation. Minority leaders have no actual power in these areas, however.

Whips.   The formal leadership of each party includes assistants to the majority and minority leaders, who are known as **whips.** The whips assist the party leaders by passing information down from the leadership to party members and by ensuring that members show up for floor debate and cast their votes on important issues. Whips conduct polls among party members about the members' views on major pieces of legislation, inform the leaders about whose vote is doubtful and whose is certain, and may exert pressure on members to support the leaders' positions.

Whip
An assistant who aids the majority or minority leader of the House or the Senate majority or minority floor leader.

Leadership in the Senate

The Senate is less than one-fourth the size of the House. This fact alone probably explains why a formal, complex, and centralized leadership structure is less necessary in the Senate than it is in the House.

The two highest-ranking formal leadership positions in the Senate are essentially ceremonial in nature. Under the Constitution, the vice president of the United States is the president (that is, the presiding officer) of the Senate and may vote to break a tie. The vice president, however, only rarely is present for a meeting of the Senate. The Senate elects instead a **president *pro tempore*** ("pro tem") to preside over the Senate in the vice president's absence. Ordinarily, the president pro tem is the member of the majority party with the longest continuous term of service in the Senate. The president pro tem is mostly a ceremonial position. Junior senators take turns actually presiding over the sessions of the Senate.

The real leadership power in the Senate rests in the hands of the **majority floor leader,** the **minority floor leader,** and their respective whips. The Senate majority and minority leaders have the right to be recognized first in debate on the floor and generally exercise the same powers available to the House majority and minority leaders. They control the scheduling of debate on the floor in conjunction with the majority party's Policy Committee, influence the allocation of committee assignments for new members or for senators attempting to transfer to a new committee, influence the selection of other party officials, and participate in selecting members of conference committees. The leaders are expected to mobilize support for partisan legislative initiatives or for the proposals of a president who belongs to the same party. The leaders act as liaisons with the White House when the president is of their party, try to get the cooperation of committee chairpersons, and seek to facilitate the smooth functioning of the Senate through the senators' unanimous consent. Floor leaders are elected by their respective party caucuses.

Senate party whips, like their House counterparts, maintain communication within the party on platform positions and try to ensure that party colleagues are present for floor debate and important votes. The Senate whip system is far less elaborate than its counterpart in the House, simply because there are fewer members to track.

A list of the formal party leaders of the 107th Congress is presented in Table 12–6 on the following page. Party leaders are a major source of influence over the decisions about public issues that senators and representatives must make every day.

Just Man GOP Needed

President *Pro Tempore*
The temporary presiding officer of the Senate in the absence of the vice president.

Majority Floor Leader
The chief spokesperson of the majority party in the Senate, who directs the legislative program and party strategy.

Minority Floor Leader
The party officer in the Senate who commands the minority party's opposition to the policies of the majority party and directs the legislative program and strategy of his or her party.

TABLE 12-6
Party Leaders in the 107th Congress, 2001–2003

POSITION	INCUMBENT	PARTY/ STATE	LEADER SINCE
House			
Speaker	J. Dennis Hastert	R., Ill.	Jan. 1999
Majority leader	Dick Armey	R., Tex.	Jan. 1995
Majority whip	Tom DeLay	R., Tex.	Jan. 1995
Chairperson of the Republican Conference	J. C. Watts	R., Okla.	Jan. 1999
Minority leader	Richard Gephardt	D., Mo.	Jan. 1995
Minority whip	David Bonior	D., Mich.	Jan. 1995
Chairperson of the Democratic Caucus	Martin Frost	D., Tex.	Jan. 2001
Senate			
President *pro tempore*	Strom Thurmond	R., S.C.	Jan. 1995
Majority floor leader	Trent Lott	R., Miss.	June 1996
Assistant majority leader	Don Nickles	R., Okla.	June 1996
Secretary of the Republican Conference	Rick Santorum	R., Pa.	Jan. 2001
Minority floor leader	Tom Daschle	D., S.Dak.	Jan. 1995
Assistant floor leader	Harry Reid	D., Nev.	Jan. 1999
Secretary of the Democratic Conference	Barbara Mikulski	D., Md.	Jan. 1995

How Members of Congress Decide

Why congresspersons vote as they do is difficult to know with any certainty. One popular perception of the legislative decision-making process is that legislators take cues from other trusted or more senior colleagues. This model holds that because most members of Congress have neither the time nor the incentive to study the details of most pieces of legislation, they frequently arrive on the floor with no clear idea about what they are voting on or how they should vote. Their decision is simplified, according to the cue-taking model, by quickly checking how key colleagues have voted or intend to vote. More broadly, verbal and non-verbal cues can be taken from fellow committee members and chairpersons, party leaders, state delegation members, or the president.

Most people who study the decision-making process in Congress agree that the single best predictor for how a member will vote is the member's party affiliation. Republicans tend to vote similarly on issues, as do Democrats. Of course, even though liberals predominate among the Democrats in Congress and conservatives predominate among the Republicans, the parties still may have internal disagreements about the proper direction that national policy should take. This was generally true for the civil rights legislation of the 1950s and 1960s, for example, when the greatest disagreement was between the conservative southern wing and the liberal northern wing of the Democratic Party.

One way to measure the degree of party unity in Congress is to look at how often a majority of one party votes against the majority of members from the other party. Table 12–7 displays the percentage of all votes in the House and the Senate when this type of party voting has occurred.

Regional differences, especially between northern and southern Democrats, may overlap and reinforce basic ideological differences among members of the same party. One consequence of the North-South split among Democrats has been the **conservative coalition** policy alliance between southern Democrats and Republicans. This conservative, cross-party grouping formed regularly on votes during the Reagan years but has virtually disappeared since then, because many southern states and districts are now represented by conservative Republicans.

How a Bill Becomes Law

Each year, Congress and the president propose and approve many laws. Some are budget and appropriation laws that require extensive bargaining but must be passed for the government to continue to function. Other laws are relatively free of controversy and are passed with little dissension between the branches of government. Still other proposed legislation is extremely controversial and reaches to the roots of differences between Democrats and Republicans and between the executive and legislative branches.

As detailed in Figure 12–3 on the next page, each law begins as a bill, which must be introduced in either the House or the Senate. Often, similar bills are introduced in both chambers. If it is a "money bill," however, it must start in the House. In each chamber, the bill follows similar steps. It is referred to a committee and its subcommittees for study, discussion, hearings, and rewriting. When the bill is reported out to the full chamber, it must be scheduled for debate (by the Rules Committee in the House and by the leadership in the Senate). After the bill has been passed in each chamber, if it contains different provisions, a conference committee is formed to write a compromise bill, which must be approved by both chambers before it is sent to the president to sign or veto.

How Much Will the Government Spend?

The Constitution is extremely clear about where the power of the purse lies in the national government: all money bills, whether for taxing or spending, must originate in the House of Representatives. Today, much of the business of Congress is concerned with approving government expenditures through the budget process and with raising the revenues to pay for government programs. As you will see in the feature *Politics and Economics: Bringing Home the Bacon,* on page 404 some budget bills directly benefit constituents.

From 1922, when Congress required the president to prepare and present to the legislature an **executive budget,** until 1974, the congressional budget process was so disjointed that it was difficult to visualize the total picture of government finances. The president presented the executive budget to Congress in January. It was broken down into thirteen or more appropriations bills. Some time later, after all of the bills were debated, amended, and passed, it was more or less possible to estimate total government spending for the next year.

Frustrated by the president's ability to impound funds and dissatisfied with the entire budget process, Congress passed the Budget and Impoundment Control Act of 1974 to regain some control over the nation's spending. The act required the president to spend the funds that Congress had appropriated, frustrating the president's

TABLE 12-7

Party Voting in Congress

This table lists the percentage of all roll calls in which a majority of Democratic legislators voted against a majority of Republican legislators.

YEAR	HOUSE	SENATE
2000	43.1	48.7
1999	47.1	62.8
1998	55.5	55.7
1997	50.4	50.3
1996	56.4	62.4
1995	73.0	69.0
1994	61.8	51.7
1993	65.0	67.0
1992	64.0	53.0
1991	55.0	49.0
1990	49.0	54.0
1989	55.0	35.0
1988	47.0	42.0
1987	64.0	41.0
1986	57.0	52.0
1985	61.0	50.0
1984	47.1	40.0
1983	55.6	43.6
1982	36.4	43.4
1981	37.4	47.8
1980	37.6	45.8
1979	47.3	46.7
1978	33.2	45.2
1977	42.2	42.4
1976	35.9	37.2
1975	48.4	47.8
1974	29.4	44.3
1973	41.8	39.9

SOURCE: *CQ Weekly Report.*

Conservative Coalition
An alliance of Republicans and southern Democrats that can form in the House or the Senate to oppose liberal legislation and support conservative legislation.

Executive Budget
The budget prepared and submitted by the president to Congress.

FIGURE 12-3

How a Bill Becomes Law

This illustration shows the most typical way in which proposed legislation is enacted into law. Most legislation begins as similar bills introduced into each chamber of Congress. The process is illustrated here with two hypothetical bills. House bill No. 100 (HR 100) and Senate bill No. 200 (S 200). The path of HR 100 is shown on the left, and that of S 200, on the right.

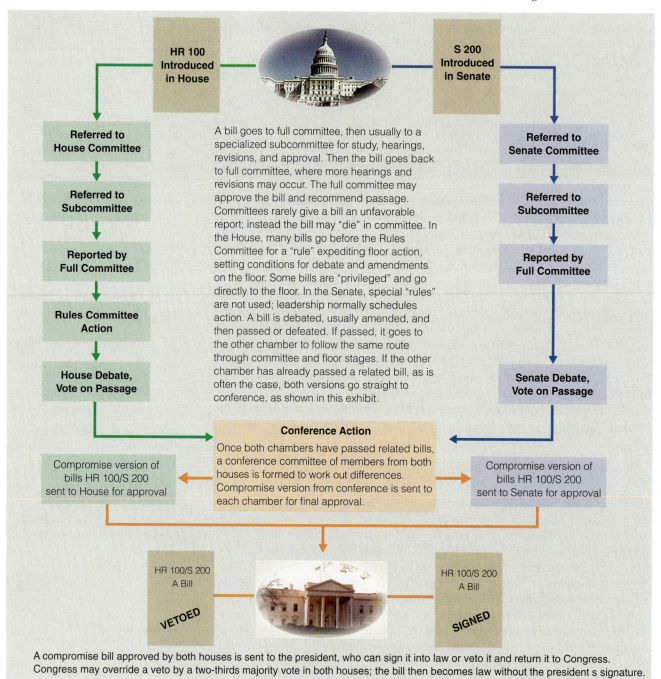

A bill goes to full committee, then usually to a specialized subcommittee for study, hearings, revisions, and approval. Then the bill goes back to full committee, where more hearings and revisions may occur. The full committee may approve the bill and recommend passage. Committees rarely give a bill an unfavorable report; instead the bill may "die" in committee. In the House, many bills go before the Rules Committee for a "rule" expediting floor action, setting conditions for debate and amendments on the floor. Some bills are "privileged" and go directly to the floor. In the Senate, special "rules" are not used; leadership normally schedules action. A bill is debated, usually amended, and then passed or defeated. If passed, it goes to the other chamber to follow the same route through committee and floor stages. If the other chamber has already passed a related bill, as is often the case, both versions go straight to conference, as shown in this exhibit.

Conference Action
Once both chambers have passed related bills, a conference committee of members from both houses is formed to work out differences. Compromise version from conference is sent to each chamber for final approval.

A compromise bill approved by both houses is sent to the president, who can sign it into law or veto it and return it to Congress. Congress may override a veto by a two-thirds majority vote in both houses; the bill then becomes law without the president s signature.

ability to kill programs of which the president disapproved by withholding funds. The other major accomplishment of the act was to force Congress to examine total national taxing and spending at least twice in each budget cycle.

The budget cycle of the federal government is described in the following subsections. (See Figure 12–4 for a graphic illustration of the budget cycle.)

FIGURE 12–4
The Budget Cycle

FIGURE 12–4
The Budget Cycle

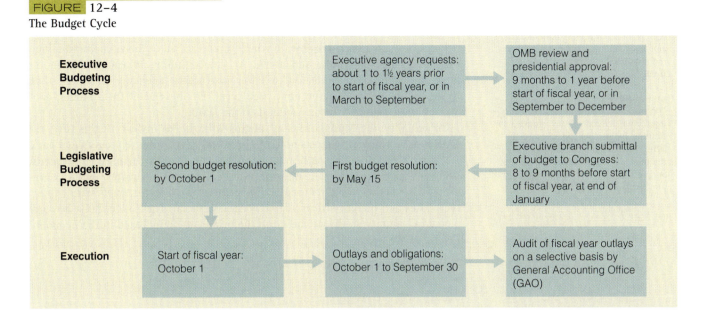

Executive Budgeting Process		Executive agency requests: about 1 to 1½ years prior to start of fiscal year, or in March to September → OMB review and presidential approval: 9 months to 1 year before start of fiscal year, or in September to December
Legislative Budgeting Process	Second budget resolution: by October 1 ← First budget resolution: by May 15 ←	Executive branch submittal of budget to Congress: 8 to 9 months before start of fiscal year, at end of January
Execution	Start of fiscal year: October 1 →	Outlays and obligations: October 1 to September 30 → Audit of fiscal year outlays on a selective basis by General Accounting Office (GAO)

Preparing the Budget

The federal government operates on a **fiscal year (FY)** cycle. The fiscal year runs from October through September, so that fiscal 2002, or FY02, runs from October 1, 2001, through September 30, 2002. Eighteen months before a fiscal year starts, the executive branch begins preparing the budget. The Office of Management and Budget (OMB) receives advice from the Council of Economic Advisers (CEA) and the Treasury Department. The OMB outlines the budget and then sends it to the various departments and agencies. Bargaining follows, in which—to use only two of many examples—the Department of Health and Human Services argues for more welfare spending, and the armed forces argue for fewer defense spending cuts.

Fiscal Year (FY)

The twelve-month period that is used for bookkeeping, or accounting, purposes. Usually, the fiscal year does not coincide with the calendar year. For example, the federal government's fiscal year runs from October 1 through September 30.

President Bill Clinton signs the Highway Transportation Act on June 8, 1998. Surrounding him at the signing are Democratic and Republican leaders of the House and the Senate who worked on getting the legislation passed. Even though the president had criticized the bill for some of its "pork barrel" projects, he eventually joined the bipartisan coalition that supported the legislation.

Spring Review

The time every year when the Office of Management and Budget requires federal agencies to review their programs, activities, and goals and submit their requests for funding for the next fiscal year.

Fall Review

The time every year when, after receiving formal federal agency requests for funding for the next fiscal year, the Office of Management and Budget reviews the requests, makes changes, and submits its recommendations to the president.

Even though the OMB has only six hundred employees, it is known as one of the most powerful agencies in Washington. It assembles the budget documents and monitors the agencies throughout each year. Every year, it begins the budget process with a **spring review,** in which it requires all of the agencies to review their programs, activities, and goals. At the beginning of each summer, the director of the OMB sends out a letter instructing agencies to submit their requests for funding for the next fiscal year. By the end of the summer, each agency must submit a formal request to the OMB.

In actuality, the "budget season" begins with the **fall review.** At this time, the OMB looks at budget requests and, in almost all cases, routinely cuts them back. Although the OMB works within guidelines established by the president, specific decisions often are left to the director and the director's associates. By the beginning of November, the director's review begins. The director meets with cabinet secretaries and budget officers. Time becomes crucial. The budget must be completed by January so that it can go to the printer to be included in the *Economic Report of the President.*

Bringing Home the Bacon

Although no member of Congress actually endorses wasteful government spending, almost all members of the House and Senate know the value of expanding government spending in their own district or state. Much federal government spending on programs is mandated by law: spending on highways is based on a formula, as is federal spending on job training and many other programs. Some government spending, though, is specifically designated for the city, institution, or organization that will receive the federal largess. This kind of spending has been known for generations as "pork."

BRINGING HOME THE BACON

Members of Congress regularly brag to their constituents on their success in "bringing home the bacon," or getting their share of the "pork barrel." Some kinds of legislation are more likely than others to contain pork barrel projects. Military spending bills, transportation appropriations, and agricultural appropriation bills are all likely to include funds for projects that are earmarked for a particular supplier. One public-interest group, the Citizens against Government Waste (CAGW), tries to monitor pork barrel projects and releases its findings via the Internet and other publications. In the view of CAGW, fiscal year 2000 appropriations were the most pork-laden in the nation's history. Its research found more than $14.6 billion in earmarked projects across eight appropriations bills.

What kinds of projects might be considered "pork" for the district? In the 2000 legislation, the state of Georgia received $100,000 to develop a test for the pungency, or smell, of Vidalia onions. New York and California teamed up to get $1.1 million for a Viticulture Consortium to assist their wine industries. The Pentagon received more than $1.6 billion to build a helicopter

carrier, although the military had not requested one. The ship construction will take place in Senator Trent Lott's home state of Mississippi.

While granting subsidies and federal dollars that will enhance economic development in a state seems defensible, this legislation also earmarked funds for a number of very local projects. Included in the 2000 appropriations, for example, were $500,000 for a water taxi for Savannah, Georgia; $250,000 for trolley cars for New Haven, Connecticut; $400,000 for the bus barn for Kalispell, Montana; and $1 million for a transportation center for White Plains, New York. Individual members of Congress will, of course, claim credit for these federal disbursements.

PORK FOR UNIVERSITIES

You may be surprised to learn that many of these pork projects are earmarked directly for colleges and universities. The FY2000 bills included $1 million for a National Welfare to Work Center at the University of Illinois, $1 million for a study on growing vegetables in a vacuum to Texas Tech University, $2.5 million for Florida International University to simulate windstorms, and $400,000 to study tributyltin-based ship-bottom paints for Old Dominion University in Virginia. All of these studies are likely to produce interesting and useful results, but the practice of earmarking money for a specific university undercuts the usually rigorous competition for federal research monies. The earmarked funds do, however, provide excellent results for the members of Congress who have managed to get the project into the budget. What will be attacked as pork in another person's district is always a vital initiative at home.

FOR CRITICAL ANALYSIS

Do you think there is any harm in earmarking relatively small amounts of federal dollars for universities, cities, and states through these pork barrel projects? Are taxpayers and voters well served by this practice?

Congress Faces the Budget

In January, nine months before the fiscal year starts, the president takes the OMB's proposed budget, approves it, and submits it to Congress. Then the congressional budgeting process takes over. Congressional committees and subcommittees look at the proposals from the executive branch. The Congressional Budget Office (CBO) advises the different committees on economic matters, just as the OMB and the CEA advise the president.

Budget Resolutions.   The **first budget resolution** by Congress is supposed to be passed in May. It sets overall revenue goals and spending targets. During the summer, bargaining among all the concerned parties takes place. Spending and tax laws that are drawn up during this period are supposed to be guided by the May congressional budget resolution.

By September, Congress is supposed to pass its **second budget resolution,** one that will set "binding" limits on taxes and spending for the fiscal year beginning October 1. Bills passed before that date that do not fit within the limits of the budget resolution are supposed to be changed.

In actuality, between 1978 and 1996, Congress did not pass a complete budget by October 1. In other words, generally, Congress does not follow its own rules. Budget resolutions are passed late, and when they are passed, they are not treated as binding. In each fiscal year that starts without a budget, every agency operates on the basis of **continuing resolutions,** which enable the agencies to keep on doing whatever they were doing the previous year with the same amount of funding. Even continuing resolutions have not always been passed on time.

Budget Battles.   Dealing with the budget is a recurring nightmare for Congress and the president. George Bush's 1990 budget battle, which forced him to raise taxes, may have cost him the presidency in 1992. President Bill Clinton won his first big budget fight in 1993 by a margin of one vote in the Senate, cast by Vice President Al Gore to break the tie, and by a single vote in the House. Clinton's deficit reduction package included large new taxes on the rich, on gasoline, and on tobacco.

The Republican sweep of 1994 changed the budget dynamics completely in the 104th Congress. The Republicans in the House, who had pledged to balance the budget as part of the Contract with America, tried to force the president to accept a budget with cuts in domestic spending. President Clinton resisted the pressure. By October 1, 1995, only two of the thirteen bills needed to finance government for fiscal year 1996 had been passed. When the president and Congress could not agree on the spending bills, the government partially "shut down" twice over the next three months. Finally, after painstakingly working out the budget for each of the remaining bills, the FY96 budget was completed in April 1996, seven months after it was due.

The 1996 elections made the lessons of the budget stalemate perfectly clear: the president was reelected easily, and the Republican majority lost some of its margin in Congress. The public, according to polls, believed that Congress was more responsible for the partial government shutdowns than was the president, and the public did not approve of such tactics.

With these lessons in mind, the 105th Congress set to work on a proposal to balance the budget. After months of negotiations, the president and Congress agreed on a five-year plan to balance the budget, which included $95 billion in budget cuts and trimmed spending by more than $250 billion over five years. The Republicans were even more willing to compromise on the budget during the 106th Congress because they had only a five-vote majority.

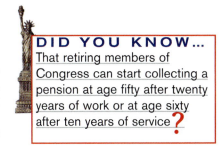

DID YOU KNOW...
That retiring members of Congress can start collecting a pension at age fifty after twenty years of work or at age sixty after ten years of service**?**

First Budget Resolution
A resolution passed by Congress in May that sets overall revenue and spending goals for the following fiscal year.

Second Budget Resolution
A resolution passed by Congress in September that sets "binding" limits on taxes and spending for the next fiscal year beginning October 1.

Continuing Resolution
A temporary law that Congress passes when an appropriations bill has not been decided by the beginning of the new fiscal year on October 1.

The Question of Congressional Ethics

Ethics is the most serious public relations problem confronting Congress today. Perhaps nothing has so tarnished the public's perception of Congress as the revelations concerning the abuse of staff members, the misuse of public funds, and the personal indiscretions and corruption of members of that institution. (For more details, see this chapter's *An Ethical Issue.*) The effects can be seen in Congress's approval rating, which, by 2000, was about 40 percent, compared with the president's rating of nearly 60 percent.

Congress's response to revelations of member misconduct has been mixed. The House Democratic Caucus in June 1980 voted 160 to 0 to require that chairpersons of committees or subcommittees be stripped of their posts automatically if they have been censured or indicted on a felony charge carrying a prison sentence of at least two years. This rule can be waived, however, by the same caucus.

Public financing of congressional campaigns may offer a partial solution to recurring problems of financial misconduct. Nonetheless, Congress has refused to impose spending limits on its members' campaigns.

The Congress: Issues for the Twenty-First Century

To many voters, the House and the Senate seem like arcane institutions that spend too much time in political battles with each other and with the president. Too little legislation that matters to the people seems to be produced by Congress, and too many members of Congress seem to hold office just to satisfy their own ambitions. In addition, too much money seems to be spent in congressional campaigns. One of the results of the public's cynical attitude toward Congress is the popularity of term limits for elected officials. Depending on how term limits are perceived to be working in the

Congress Examines Its Own for Improprieties

Public approval of Congress as a body continues to be relatively low, in part because of the succession of ethical problems and improprieties that have become public. Both the House and the Senate have attempted to deal with the ethical lapses of their respective members through internal processes, but the public perception continues to be that many members are involved in shady dealings that the ordinary citizen finds hard to justify.

The most flamboyant ethical problems for elected representatives concern sexual misconduct involving staff members or constituents. A widely publicized Senate case involved Senator Robert Packwood of Oregon, who was accused of sexually harassing a number of women. Packwood admitted some of his guilt, citing abuse of alcohol as the reason for his misbehavior. Packwood resigned in September 1995, after the Senate Ethics Committee voted to expel him from the Senate.

Both the House and the Senate have also dealt with the ethical problems that arise when a member takes advantage of his

or her office for personal benefit. Several House members—including Jim Wright, a former speaker, and Tony Coelho, a former Democratic whip—resigned from Congress after investigations of their personal finances. Even the former speaker of the House, Newt Gingrich, got into trouble in 1997. Gingrich was reprimanded by the House Ethics Committee and fined $300,000 for using money from a tax-exempt foundation to underwrite a televised college course that he taught and a televised "town hall" on politics that he led.

Ethical conduct seemed to reach a new low during the investigation of the Clinton-Lewinsky affair in 1998 when various members of Congress, including Henry Hyde (R., Ill.), were accused of having had extramarital affairs. Shortly after being named speaker, Robert Livingston (R., La.) acknowledged having had an affair and then resigned from the House. While these disclosures did not violate the House ethics code, there were political consequences for some of these members.

FOR CRITICAL ANALYSIS

Do you think that the public's perception of congressional behavior is influenced by media coverage?

states, there could be a renewed push for a constitutional amendment to establish term limits for members of Congress.

Another problem facing Congress relates to the underrepresentation of minority groups in that institution. The Supreme Court has made it clear that racial gerrymandering to increase minority representation in Congress is not an acceptable solution to this problem. Finding alternative solutions may be one of the most difficult challenges facing Congress—and American society—today.

Given the complexity of national problems and the attempts by hundreds of interest groups to influence congressional action, both the House and the Senate continue to try to meet the expectations of the people in the media age. The president continues to garner far more credit for whatever legislation is enacted, while Congress tries to find a way to balance interests and produce policies that meet modern needs. The members of Congress, however, continue to go home to their districts and, in most cases, build trusting relationships with their constituents—which helps build support for the institution as a whole.

INFOTRAC®
COLLEGE EDITION

Monica Lewinsky Affair Could Open Members

making a difference

How to Be an Intern in Washington, D.C.

In the nineteenth century, John Stuart Mill, a British political philosopher and economist, wrote, "There are many truths of which the full meaning cannot be realized until personal experience has brought it home." Hundreds of students each year flock to Washington, D.C., for a summer, a semester, or a full year to gain personal experience in one of the myriad institutions of the nation's capital. For those with "Potomac fever," an internship in Washington earning college credit while working is an extraordinary opportunity. If you are interested in a Washington experience, here are some things to keep in mind.

First, make sure that you discuss your internship plan with your faculty adviser. He or she will have useful tips. Some colleges have strict rules on who may obtain credit for internships, what preparation is necessary, in what year students are allowed to participate in internships, and other such matters. Internships are most useful if you are in your junior or senior year.

There are several ways to plan an internship. First, contact an existing program, such as the following:

The Washington Center
2000 M St. N.W., Suite 750
Washington, D.C. 20036
1-800-486-8921

http://www.twc.edu

Such an organization will assist you in finding a suitable internship in government, the private sector, foundations, and nonprofit or volunteer organizations, as well as in considering other opportunities. "Organized" internship programs will also find you housing and usually provide field trips, special seminars, internship advisers, and other support. Ask if your college or university is affiliated with a Washington program or has an internship program of its own.

Second, find your own internship. There are several avenues for identifying and pursuing opportunities. Contact the local office of your representative or senator, which is usually listed in the telephone directory under "United States Government." Many members of Congress have internship coordinators and large, well-supervised programs. Some even may be able to pay part of your expenses.

Always make sure that you explore in detail what a specific job offers. Think carefully about internships that are glorified secretarial jobs in which all you do is typing and filing. A good internship should give you an insider's view of how a profession works. It should furnish some real "hands-on" opportunities to do research, deal with the public, learn about legislation, and watch government officials in action.

Remember that most internships are nonpaying. Make sure that you understand all the costs involved. Arrange for financing through your college, a guaranteed student loan, personal savings, or family support.

Finally, keep in mind that there are also internships in most members' district offices close to home. Such jobs may not have the glamour of Washington, but they may offer excellent opportunities for political experience.

A very useful booklet with which you should start is *Storming Washington: An Intern's Guide to National Government,* by Stephen E. Frantzich. It is available from the following source:

American Political Science Association
1527 New Hampshire Ave. N.W.
Washington, DC 20036
202-483-2512

http://www.apsanet.org

Key terms

agenda setting 381	fiscal year (FY) 403	party identifier 386
bicameralism 377	franking 392	president *pro tempore* 399
casework 380	gerrymandering 390	reapportionment 389
cloture 383	instructed delegate 380	redistricting 389
conference committee 396	joint committee 396	representation 380
conservative coalition 401	justiciable question 389	Rules Committee 382
constituent 377	lawmaking 379	safe seat 397
continuing resolution 405	legislative veto 381	second budget resolution 405
direct primary 386	logrolling 379	select committee 396
discharge petition 395	majority floor leader 399	seniority system 397
enumerated power 378	majority leader of the House 398	speaker of the House 397
executive budget 401	minority floor leader 399	spring review 404
fall review 404	minority leader of the House 398	standing committee 395
filibustering 383	ombudsperson 380	trustee 380
first budget resolution 405	oversight 381	whip 399

Chapter summary

1 The authors of the Constitution, believing that the bulk of national power should be in the legislature, set forth the structure, power, and operation of Congress. The Constitution states that Congress will consist of two chambers. Partly an outgrowth of the Connecticut Compromise, this bicameral structure established a balanced legislature, with the membership in the House of Representatives based on population and the membership in the Senate based on the equality of states.

2 The first seventeen clauses of Article I, Section 8, of the Constitution specify most of the enumerated, or expressed, powers of Congress, including the right to impose taxes, to borrow money, to regulate commerce, and to declare war. Besides its enumerated powers, Congress enjoys the right to "make all Laws which shall be necessary and proper for carrying into Execution the foregoing Powers, and all other Powers vested by this Constitution in the Government of the United States, or in any Department or Officer thereof." This is called the elastic, or necessary and proper, clause.

3 The functions of Congress include (a) lawmaking, (b) service to constituents, (c) representation, (d) oversight, (e) public education, and (f) conflict resolution.

4 There are 435 members in the House of Representatives and 100 members in the Senate. Owing to its larger size, the House has a greater number of formal rules. The Senate tradition of unlimited debate, or filibustering, dates back to 1790 and has been used over the years to frustrate the passage of bills. Under Senate Rule 22, cloture can be used to shut off debate on a bill.

5 Members of Congress are not typical American citizens. They are older than most Americans; disproportionately white, male, and Protestant; and more likely to be trained in professional occupations.

6 Congressional elections are operated by the individual state governments, which must abide by rules established by the Constitution and national statutes. The process of nominating congressional candidates has shifted from party conventions to the direct primaries currently used in all states. The overwhelming majority of incumbent representatives and a smaller proportion of senators who run for reelection are successful. The most complicated aspect of the mechanics of congressional elections is reapportionment—the allocation of legislative seats to constituencies. The Supreme Court's "one person, one vote" rule has been applied to equalize the populations of state legislative and congressional districts.

7 Members of Congress are well paid and enjoy other benefits, including franking privileges. Members of Congress have personal and committee staff members available to them and also benefit from a number of legal privileges and immunities.

8 Most of the actual work of legislating is performed by committees and subcommittees within Congress. Legislation introduced into the House or Senate is assigned to the appropriate standing committees for review. Select committees are created for a limited period of time for a specific legislative purpose. Joint committees are formed by the concurrent action of both chambers and consist of members from each chamber. Conference committees are special joint committees set up to achieve agreement between the House and the Senate on the exact wording of legislative acts passed by both chambers in different forms. The seniority rule specifies that longer-serving members will be given preference when committee chairpersons and holders of other important posts are selected.

9 The foremost power holder in the House of Representatives is the speaker of the House. Other leaders are the House majority leader, the House minority leader, and the majority and minority whips. Formally, the vice president is the presiding officer of the Senate, with the majority party choosing a senior member as the president *pro tempore* to preside when the vice president is absent. Actual leadership in the Senate rests with the majority floor leader, the minority floor leader, and their respective whips.

10 A bill becomes law by progressing through both chambers of Congress and their appropriate standing and joint committees to the president.

11 The budget process for a fiscal year begins with the preparation of an executive budget by the president. This is reviewed by the Office of Management and Budget and then sent to Congress, which is supposed to pass a final budget by the end of September. Since 1978, Congress has not followed its own time rules.

12 Ethics is the most serious public relations problem facing Congress. Financial misconduct, sexual improprieties, and other unethical behavior on the part of several House and Senate members have resulted in a significant lowering of the public's regard for the institution of Congress. Despite congressional investigations of ethical misconduct and, in some cases, reprimands of members of Congress, the overall view of the public is that Congress has little control over the actions of its members with respect to ethics.

Selected print and electronic resources

SUGGESTED READINGS

Barone, Michael, and Grant Ujifusa. *The Almanac of American Politics, 2000.* Washington, D.C.: National Journal, 1999. This book, which is published biannually, is a comprehensive summary of current political information on each member of Congress, his or her state or congressional district, recent congressional election results, key votes, ratings by various organizations, sources of campaign contributions, and records of campaign expenditures.

Brown, Sherrod. *Congress from the Inside: Observations from the Majority and the Minority.* Kent, Ohio: Kent State University Press, 1999. Brown, an incumbent congressperson from Ohio, provides an insider's view of the struggles that take place within the House. When elected, Brown was a member of the majority. After 1994, he became a member of the minority, thus giving him a new viewpoint on life in Congress.

Clayton, Dewey M. *African Americans and the Politics of Congressional Redistricting (Race and Politics).* Hamden, Conn.: Garland Publishing, 2000. This book gives a detailed look at the role of race in the drawing of congressional districts from the Civil War to the present.

Cook, Rhodes. *How Congress Gets Elected.* Washington, D.C.: Congressional Quarterly Press, 1999. This is an authoritative source on the legal and political issues that affect the way congressional elections are conducted and the results of those elections. Topics include reapportionment, redistricting, and campaign financing, among others.

Davidson, Roger H., and Walter J. Oleszek. *Congress and Its Members,* 7th ed. Washington, D.C.: Congressional Quarterly Press, 2000. This updated classic looks carefully at the "two Congresses," the one in Washington and the role played by congresspersons at home.

MEDIA SOURCES

Mr. Smith Goes to Washington—A 1939 film in which Jimmy Stewart plays the naïve congressman who is quickly educated in Washington. A true American political classic.

The Seduction of Joe Tynan—A 1979 film in which Alan Alda plays a young senator who must face serious decisions about his political role and his private life.

Logging on

To find out about the schedule of activities taking place in Congress, use the following Web sites:

http://www.senate.gov

http://www.house.gov

The Congressional Budget Office is online at

http://www.cbo.gov

The URL for the Government Printing Office is

http://www.access.gpo.gov

For the real inside facts on what's going on in Washington, D.C., you can look at the following resources:

RollCall, the newspaper of the Capitol:

http://www.rollcall.com

Congressional Quarterly, a publication that reports on Congress:

http://www.cq.com

The Hill, which investigates various activities of Congress:

http://www.hillnews.com

Using the Internet for political analysis

Point your browser to one of the general guides to Congress given at the following Web sites:

http://www.house.gov

http://www.senate.gov

Look up the Web pages of at least three different members of the House or the Senate. Try to pick members from each of the major parties. Compare the Web pages on the following issues:

1. Which page appears to provide the most assistance to constituents?

2. How much partisan information is included on the Web page?

3. To what extent is the member of Congress giving information about her or his policy stands?

4. To what extent is the member trying to build trust and loyalty through providing personal information and services?

chapter 13
The Presidency

CHAPTER OUTLINE

- Who Can Become President?

- The Process of Becoming President

- The Many Roles of the President

- The President as Party Chief and Superpolitician

- Special Uses of Presidential Power

- Abuses of Executive Power and Impeachment

- The Executive Organization

- The Vice Presidency

what if...

We Could Recall the President?

BACKGROUND

THE IMPEACHMENT AND TRIAL OF PRESIDENT BILL CLINTON IN 1998–1999 STIMULATED A NATIONAL DIALOGUE ON WHETHER IT WAS APPROPRIATE TO REMOVE A SITTING PRESIDENT WHO HAD BEEN DULY ELECTED BY THE AMERICAN PEOPLE. OF COURSE, THE U.S. CONSTITUTION PROVIDES FOR IMPEACHMENT TO DO JUST THAT. THE STANDARD FOR IMPEACHMENT, CONVICTION, AND REMOVAL FROM OFFICE IS VERY HIGH: THE HOUSE OF REPRESENTATIVES MUST VOTE TO IMPEACH, AND TWO-THIRDS OF THE SENATORS MUST VOTE TO CONVICT. NEVER HAS THIS HAPPENED. THE FOUNDERS INTENTIONALLY MADE IMPEACHMENT AND CONVICTION DIFFICULT BECAUSE IT WOULD BE SUCH A GRAVE STEP.

MANY STATES, HOWEVER, PROVIDE FOR THE RECALL OF ELECTED OFFICIALS IN THEIR CONSTITUTIONS. UNDER THIS PROCESS, IF THE VOTERS OF A STATE OR LOCAL COMMUNITY GATHER A SUFFICIENT NUMBER OF LEGITIMATE SIGNATURES ON A PETITION TO REMOVE A SPECIFIC ELECTED OFFICIAL, A SPECIAL ELECTION MUST BE HELD IN WHICH CITIZENS VOTE ON WHETHER TO REMOVE THAT OFFICIAL FROM OFFICE. NO FINDING OF BLAME OR GUILT FOR A CRIME IS NECESSARY FOR REMOVAL.

WHAT IF WE COULD RECALL THE PRESIDENT?

The U.S. Constitution allows for only the impeachment, not the recall, of the chief executive, the vice president, and federal judges. Impeachment allows members of Congress to decide whether a president should be removed from office. If recall were added to the Constitution through an amendment, the whole nation would be involved in the decision.

If the process were similar to that used by the states, voters could sign petitions seeking a special national election to vote on the recall of the president. Then, a special national election would be held to decide the issue. This would be a much clearer test of how people feel about an official than the various public opinion polls that made news during the Clinton impeachment process.

A RECALL COULD BE USEFUL

The recall process could be a useful tool to keep government officials accountable. If they knew that they could be removed from office when enough citizens were really dissatisfied with their conduct, they might pay closer attention to public needs. The recall process would involve a large number of citizens gathering signatures, discussing the conduct of government officials, and turning out to vote. An extensive campaign would be held before the election to educate the voters. Information technology might play an important role in the process, from the recording of signatures to the vote itself.

Furthermore, the recall would be based on the public's view that the president was failing to perform the duties of the office or to fulfill campaign promises. Thus, the recall process would indicate that the public disapproved of the presi-

A RECALL COULD BE VERY HARMFUL

A national recall process also could involve significant disadvantages. Imagine the kind of campaigning that would take place prior to a recall election. Those who initiated the recall would use the media to bring out every unpleasant fact about the president, while the president and his or her consultants would use every aspect of the executive office to fight the recall. Smears, lies, and character assassination would be likely.

In addition, having a recall process in place would be very destabilizing to the political system. The president and the administration might follow public opinion polls even more slavishly if their fates rested on recall petitions. The governments of other nations would be wary of dealing with the American president if they perceived that an unpopular chief executive was about to be removed from office. If the American political system is seen as partisan now, it would only be more so with a recall process in place.

IS RECALL LIKELY?

Given that recall could be implemented only through a constitutional amendment, a recall process is highly unlikely to be in place anytime soon. Such an amendment would have to be approved by two-thirds of the members of the House and the Senate and signed by the president before being sent to state legislatures. If there is one certainty in politics, it is that elected officials are very unlikely to create a mechanism that makes their own removal any easier.

FOR CRITICAL ANALYSIS

1. Can you think of a president or vice president who, due to his unpopularity, would have been a candidate for removal through recall? Do you think that the voters felt strongly enough to carry out the process?

2. Given the responsibilities of the president, do you think it would be good for the country to be able to recall the chief executive for unpopularity or partisan reasons?

The writers of the Constitution created the presidency of the United States without any models on which to draw. Nowhere else in the world was there a democratically selected chief executive. What the founders did not want was a king. In fact, given their previous experience with royal governors in the colonies, many of the delegates to the Constitutional Convention wanted to create a very weak executive who could not veto legislation. Other delegates, especially those who had witnessed the need for a strong leader in the Revolutionary army, believed a strong executive to be necessary for the republic. The delegates, after much debate, created a chief executive who had enough powers granted in the Constitution to balance those of the Congress.[1]

The power exercised by each president who has held the office has been scrutinized and judged by historians, political scientists, the media, and the public. Indeed, it would seem that Americans are fascinated by presidential power and by the persons who hold the office. Recent experience with impeachment have also led Americans to consider why a president should be removed. (See the *What If . . .* that opens this chapter for some ideas about removal.) In this chapter, after looking at who can become president and at the process involved, we examine closely the nature and extent of the constitutional powers held by the president.

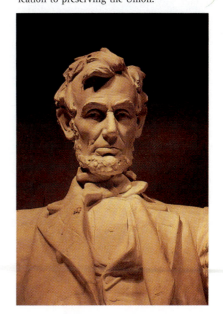

DID YOU KNOW...
That George Washington's salary of $25,000 in 1789 was the equivalent of about $600,000 in today's dollars?

Who Can Become President?

The requirements for becoming president, as outlined in Article II, Section 1, of the Constitution, are not overwhelmingly stringent:

> No person except a natural born Citizen, or a Citizen of the United States, at the time of the Adoption of this Constitution, shall be eligible to the Office of President; neither shall any Person be eligible to that Office who shall not have attained to the Age of thirty-five Years, and been fourteen Years a Resident within the United States.

The only question that arises about these qualifications relates to the term "natural born Citizen." Does that mean only citizens born in the United States and its territories? What about a child born to a U.S. citizen (or to a couple who are U.S. citizens) while visiting or living in another country? Although the question has not been dealt with directly by the Supreme Court, it is reasonable to expect that someone would be eligible if her or his parents were Americans. The first presidents, after all, were not even American citizens at birth, and others were born in areas that did not become part of the United States until later. These questions were debated when George Romney, who was born in Chihuahua, Mexico, made a serious bid for the Republican presidential nomination in the 1960s.[2]

The great American dream is symbolized by the statement that "anybody can become president of this country." It is true that in modern times, presidents have included a haberdasher (Harry Truman—for a short period of time), a peanut farmer (Jimmy Carter), and an actor (Ronald Reagan). But if you examine Appendix C, you will see that the most common previous occupation of presidents in this country has been the legal profession. Out of forty-three presidents, twenty-six have been lawyers, and many have been wealthy.

Although the Constitution states that the minimum-age requirement for the presidency is thirty-five years, most presidents have been much older than that

Abraham Lincoln is usually classified as one of the greatest presidents because of his dedication to preserving the Union.

---

[1]Forrest McDonald, *The American Presidency: An Intellectual History* (Lawrence, Kans.: University Press of Kansas, 1994), p. 179.

[2]George Romney was governor of Michigan from 1963 to 1969. Romney was not nominated, and the issue remains unresolved.

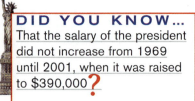
when they assumed office. John F. Kennedy, at the age of forty-three, was the youngest elected president, and the oldest was Ronald Reagan, at age sixty-nine. The average age at inauguration has been fifty-four. There has clearly been a demographic bias in the selection of presidents. All have been male, white, and Protestant, except for John F. Kennedy, a Roman Catholic. Presidents have been men of great stature—such as George Washington—and men in whom leadership qualities were not so pronounced—such as Warren Harding.

The Process of Becoming President

Major and minor political parties nominate candidates for president and vice president at national conventions every four years. As discussed in Chapter 10, the nation's voters do not elect a president and vice president directly but rather cast ballots for presidential electors, who then vote for president and vice president in the electoral college.

Because the election is governed by a majority in the electoral college, it is conceivable that someone could be elected to the office of the presidency without having a plurality of the popular vote cast. Indeed, in three cases, candidates won elections even though their major opponents received more popular votes. In elections when more than two candidates were running for office, many presidential candidates have won with less than 50 percent of the total popular votes cast for all candidates—including Abraham Lincoln, Woodrow Wilson, Harry S. Truman, John F. Kennedy, and Richard Nixon. In the 1992 election, Bill Clinton, with only 43 percent of the vote, defeated incumbent George Bush. Independent candidate H. Ross Perot garnered a surprising 19 percent of the vote. Remember from Chapter 10 that no president has won a majority of votes from the entire voting-age population.

Twelfth Amendment
An amendment to the Constitution, adopted in 1804, that specifies the separate election of the president and vice president by the electoral college.

On occasion, the electoral college has failed to give any candidate a majority. At this point, the election is thrown into the House of Representatives. The president is then chosen from among the three candidates having the most electoral college votes. Only two times in our past has the House had to decide on a president. Thomas Jefferson and Aaron Burr tied in the electoral college in 1800. This happened because the Constitution had not been explicit in indicating which of the two electoral votes was for president and which was for vice president. In 1804, the **Twelfth Amendment** clarified the matter by requiring that the president and vice president be chosen separately. In 1824, the House again had to make a choice, this time among William H. Crawford, Andrew Jackson, and John Quincy Adams. It chose Adams, even though Jackson had more electoral and popular votes.

From left to right, the first cabinet—Henry Knox, Thomas Jefferson, Edmund Randolph, Alexander Hamilton—and the first president, George Washington.

The Many Roles of the President

The Constitution speaks briefly about the duties and obligations of the president. Based on a brief list of powers and the precedents of history, the presidency has grown into a very complicated job that requires balancing at least five constitutional roles. These are (1) chief of state, (2) chief executive, (3) commander in chief of the armed forces, (4) chief diplomat, and (5) chief legislator of the United States. Here we examine each of these significant presidential functions, or roles. It is worth noting that one person plays all these roles simultaneously and that the needs of these roles may at times come into conflict.

Chief of State

Every nation has at least one person who is the ceremonial head of state. In most democratic governments, the role of **chief of state** is given to someone other than the chief executive, who is the head of the executive branch of government. In Britain, for example, the chief of state is the queen. In France, the prime minister is the chief executive, and the chief of state is the president. But in the United States, the president is both chief executive and chief of state. According to William Howard Taft, as chief of state the president symbolizes the "dignity and majesty" of the American people.

As chief of state, the president engages in a number of activities that are largely symbolic or ceremonial, such as the following:

- Decorating war heroes.
- Throwing out the first ball to open the baseball season.
- Dedicating parks and post offices.
- Receiving visiting chiefs of state at the White House.
- Going on official state visits to other countries.
- Making personal telephone calls to astronauts.
- Representing the nation at times of national mourning, such as after the 1998 bombing of two American embassies in Africa.

Many students of the American political system believe that having the president serve as both the chief executive and the chief of state drastically limits the time available to do "real" work. Not all presidents have agreed with this conclusion, however—particularly those presidents who have been able to blend skillfully these two roles with their role as politician. Being chief of state gives the president tremendous public exposure, which can be an important asset in a campaign for reelection. When that exposure is positive, it helps the president deal with Congress over proposed legislation and increases the chances of being reelected—or getting the candidates of the president's party elected.

Chief Executive

According to the Constitution, "The executive Power shall be vested in a President of the United States of America. . . . [H]e may require the Opinion, in writing, of the principal Officer in each of the executive Departments, upon any Subject relating to the Duties of their respective Offices . . . and he shall nominate, and by and with the Advice and Consent of the Senate, shall appoint . . . Officers of the United States. . . . [H]e shall take Care that the Laws be faithfully executed."

As **chief executive,** the president is constitutionally bound to enforce the acts of Congress, the judgments of federal courts, and treaties signed by the United States. The duty to "faithfully execute" the laws has been a source of constitutional power for presidents. To assist in the various tasks of the chief executive, the president has a federal bureaucracy (see Chapter 14), which currently consists of about 2.8 million federal civilian employees.

The Powers of Appointment and Removal. You might think that the president, as head of the largest bureaucracy in the United States, wields enormous power. The president, however, only nominally runs the executive bureaucracy, for most government positions are filled by **civil service** employees.[3] Therefore, even though the president has **appointment power,** it is not very extensive, being

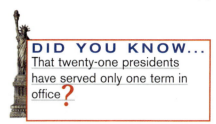

Chief of State
The role of the president as ceremonial head of the government.

Chief Executive
The role of the president as head of the executive branch of the government.

Civil Service
A collective term for the body of employees working for the government. Generally, civil service is understood to apply to all those who gain government employment through a merit system.

Appointment Power
The authority vested in the president to fill a government office or position. Positions filled by presidential appointment include those in the executive branch and the federal judiciary, commissioned officers in the armed forces, and members of the independent regulatory commissions.

---

[3]See Chapter 14 for a discussion of the Civil Service Reform Act.

DID YOU KNOW...
That Thomas Jefferson was the first president to be inaugurated in Washington, D.C., where he walked to the Capitol from a boarding house, took the oath, made a brief speech in the Senate chamber, and then walked back home?

limited to cabinet and subcabinet jobs, federal judgeships, agency heads, and about two thousand lesser jobs. This means that most of the 2.8 million federal employees owe no political allegiance to the president. They are more likely to owe loyalty to congressional committees or to interest groups representing the sector of the society that they serve. Table 13–1 shows what percentage of the total employment in each executive department is available for political appointment by the president.

The president's power to remove from office officials who are not doing a good job or who do not agree with the president is not explicitly granted by the Constitution and has been limited. In 1926, however, a Supreme Court decision prevented Congress from interfering with the president's ability to fire those executive-branch officials whom the president had appointed with Senate approval.[4] There are ten agencies whose directors the president can remove at any time. These agencies include the Arms Control and Disarmament Agency, the Commission on Civil Rights, the Environmental Protection Agency, the General Services Administration, the Postal Service, and the Small Business Administration. In addition, the president can remove all heads of cabinet departments, all individuals in the Executive Office of the President, and all political appointees listed in Table 13–1.

Harry Truman spoke candidly of the difficulties a president faces in trying to control the executive bureaucracy. On leaving office, he referred to the problems that Dwight Eisenhower, as a former general of the army, was going to have: "He'll sit here and he'll say do this! do that! and nothing will happen. Poor Ike—it won't be a bit like the Army. He'll find it very frustrating."[5]

---

[4]*Meyers v. United States,* 272 U.S. 52 (1926).

[5]Quoted in Richard E. Neustadt, *Presidential Power: The Politics of Leadership* (New York: Wiley, 1960), p. 9.

TABLE 13–1

Total Civilian Employment in Cabinet Departments Available for Political Appointment by the President

Executive Department	Total Number of Employees	Political Appointments Available	Percentage
Agriculture	93,201	439	0.47
Commerce	75,433	446	0.59
Defense	679,762	466	0.07
Education	4,743	186	3.92
Energy	15,583	433	2.78
Health and Human Services	61,508	391	0.64
Housing and Urban Development	10,218	156	1.53
Interior	66,042	240	0.36
Justice	124,846	501	0.40
Labor	15,903	188	1.18
State	31,085	1,066	3.43
Transportation	63,540	274	0.43
Treasury	153,675	231	0.15
Veterans Affairs	217,311	315	0.14
TOTAL	1,612,850	5,332	0.33

Sources: *Policy and Supporting Positions* (Washington, D.C.: Government Printing Office, 1996); U.S. Office of Personnel Management, 2000.

The Power to Grant Reprieves and Pardons.   Section 2 of Article II of the Constitution gives the president the power to grant **reprieves** and **pardons** for offenses against the United States except in cases of impeachment. All pardons are administered by the Office of the Pardon Attorney in the Department of Justice. In principle, pardons are granted to remedy a mistake made in a conviction.

The Supreme Court upheld the president's power to grant reprieves and pardons in a 1925 case concerning the pardon granted by the president to an individual convicted of contempt of court. The judiciary had contended that only judges had the authority to convict individuals for contempt of court when court orders were violated and that the courts should be free from interference by the executive branch. The Supreme Court simply stated that the president could grant reprieves or pardons for all offenses "either before trial, during trial, or after trial, by individuals, or by classes, conditionally or absolutely, and this without modification or regulation by Congress."[6] In a controversial decision, President Gerald Ford pardoned former president Richard Nixon for his role in the Watergate affair before any charges were brought in court. After his defeat in the 1992 presidential election, George Bush also exercised the right of executive pardon for six former members of the Reagan administration who had been charged with various offenses relating to the Iran-*contra* affair. The affair concerned the secret sale of arms to Iran and the use of proceeds to aid insurgents (the *contras*) in Nicaragua in their struggle against that country's Communist government. In 1999, President Clinton granted executive clemency to sixteen Puerto Rican nationalists who had been convicted of plotting terrorism. Just before George W. Bush's inauguration in 2001, Clinton announced pardons for more than one hundred persons.

Commander in Chief

The president, according to the Constitution, "shall be Commander in Chief of the Army and Navy of the United States, and of the Militia of the several States, when called into the actual Service of the United States." In other words, the

---

[6]*Ex parte Grossman*, 267 U.S. 87 (1925).

Reprieve
The presidential power to postpone the execution of a sentence imposed by a court of law; usually done for humanitarian reasons or to await new evidence.

Pardon
The granting of a release from the punishment or legal consequences of a crime; a pardon can be granted by the president before or after a conviction.

INFOTRAC®
COLLEGE EDITION

Together We Must Stop Terrorism

The two presidential contenders in the 2000 race for the presidency, George W. Bush (left) and Al Gore (right), don military caps during their campaigns. Presidential candidates generally try to identify with the military and show their pride in having served in uniform.

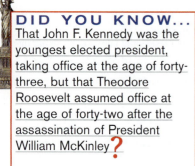

Commander in Chief
The role of the president as supreme commander of the military forces of the United States and of the state National Guard units when they are called into federal service.

armed forces are under civilian, rather than military, control.

Certainly, those who wrote the Constitution had George Washington in mind when they made the president the **commander in chief**. Although we no longer expect our president to lead the troops into battle, presidents as commanders in chief have wielded dramatic power. Harry Truman made the awesome decision to drop atomic bombs on Hiroshima and Nagasaki in 1945 to force Japan to surrender and thus bring to an end World War II. Lyndon Johnson ordered bombing missions against North Vietnam in the 1960s, and he personally selected some of the targets. Richard Nixon decided to invade Cambodia in 1970. Ronald Reagan sent troops to Lebanon and Grenada in 1983 and ordered U.S. fighter planes to attack Libya in 1986. George Bush sent troops to Panama in 1989 and to the Middle East in 1990. Bill Clinton sent troops to Haiti in 1994 and to Bosnia in 1995, ordered missile attacks on alleged terrorist bases in 1998, and sent American planes to bomb Serbia in 1999.

The president is the ultimate decision maker in military matters. Everywhere he goes, so too goes the "football"—a briefcase filled with all the codes necessary to order a nuclear attack. Only the president has the power to order the use of nuclear force.

As commander in chief, the president has probably exercised more authority than in any other role. Constitutionally, Congress has the sole power to declare war, but the president can send the armed forces into a country in situations that are certainly the equivalent of war. When William McKinley ordered troops into Peking to help suppress the Boxer Rebellion in 1900, he was sending them into a combat situation. Harry Truman dispatched troops to Korea as part of a "police action" in 1950. Kennedy, Johnson, and Nixon waged an undeclared war in Southeast Asia, where more than 58,000 Americans were killed and 300,000 were wounded. In none of these situations did Congress declare war.

In an attempt to gain more control over such military activities, in 1973

President George W. Bush is shown here working in the Oval Office. This oval-shaped office in the White House, with its immense seal of the United States in the carpet, is often used to represent the power of the presidency and of the United States. Indeed, common references to "the Oval Office" mean specifically the president who is in power at that time.

Congress passed the **War Powers Resolution**—over President Nixon's veto—requiring that the president consult with Congress when sending American forces into action. Once they are sent, the president must report to Congress within forty-eight hours. Unless Congress approves the use of troops within sixty days or extends the sixty-day time limit, the forces must be withdrawn. The War Powers Resolution was tested in the fall of 1983, when Reagan requested that troops be left in Lebanon. The resulting compromise was a congressional resolution allowing troops to remain there for eighteen months. Shortly after the resolution was passed, however, more than 240 sailors and Marines were killed in the suicide bombing of a U.S. military housing compound in Beirut. That event provoked a furious congressional debate over the role American troops were playing in the Middle East, and all troops were withdrawn shortly thereafter.

In spite of the War Powers Resolution, the powers of the president as commander in chief are more extensive today than they were in the past. These powers are linked closely to the president's powers as chief diplomat, or chief crafter of foreign policy.

Chief Diplomat

The Constitution gives the president the power to recognize foreign governments; to make treaties, with the **advice and consent** of the Senate; and to make special agreements with other heads of state that do not require congressional approval. In addition, the president nominates ambassadors. As **chief diplomat,** the president dominates American foreign policy, a role that has been supported numerous times by the Supreme Court.

Diplomatic Recognition.   An important power of the president as chief diplomat is that of **diplomatic recognition,** or the power to recognize—or refuse to recognize—foreign governments. In the role of ceremonial head of state, the president has always received foreign diplomats. In modern times, the simple act of receiving a foreign diplomat has been equivalent to accrediting the diplomat and officially recognizing his or her government. Such recognition of the legitimacy of another

War Powers Resolution
A law passed in 1973 spelling out the conditions under which the president can commit troops without congressional approval.

Advice and Consent
The power vested in the U.S. Senate by the Constitution (Article II, Section 2) to give its advice and consent to the president on treaties and presidential appointments.

Chief Diplomat
The role of the president in recognizing foreign governments, making treaties, and making executive agreements.

Diplomatic Recognition
The president's power, as chief diplomat, to acknowledge a foreign government as legitimate.

In his roles of chief of state and chief diplomat, the U.S. president frequently visits or receives foreign diplomats and heads of state. During their 2000 presidential campaigns, each major party candidate offered a preview of his presidential role by being photographed while greeting the newly elected president of Mexico, Vicente Fox.

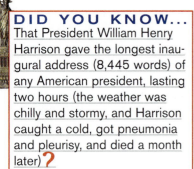

DID YOU KNOW...
That President William Henry Harrison gave the longest inaugural address (8,445 words) of any American president, lasting two hours (the weather was chilly and stormy, and Harrison caught a cold, got pneumonia and pleurisy, and died a month later)❓

I N F O T R A C ®
COLLEGE EDITION

National Security Rejects Test Ban

country's government is a prerequisite to diplomatic relations or negotiations between that country and the United States.

Deciding when to recognize a foreign power is not always simple. The United States, for example, did not recognize the Soviet Union until 1933—sixteen years after the Russian Revolution of 1917. It was only after all attempts to reverse the effects of that revolution—including military invasion of Russia and diplomatic isolation—had proved futile that Franklin Roosevelt extended recognition to the Soviet government. U.S. presidents faced a similar problem with the Chinese Communist revolution. In December 1978, long after the Communist victory in China, Jimmy Carter granted official recognition to the People's Republic of China.[7]

A diplomatic recognition issue that faced the Clinton administration involved recognizing a former enemy—the Republic of Vietnam. Many Americans, particularly those who believed that Vietnam had not been forthcoming in the efforts to find the remains of missing American soldiers or to find out about former prisoners of war, opposed any formal relationship with that nation. After the U.S. government had negotiated with the Vietnamese government for many years over the missing-in-action issue and engaged in limited diplomatic contacts for several years, President Clinton announced on July 11, 1995, that the United States would recognize the government of Vietnam and move to establish normal diplomatic relations.

Proposal and Ratification of Treaties.   The president has the sole power to negotiate treaties with other nations. These treaties must be presented to the Senate, where they may be modified and must be approved by a two-thirds vote. After ratification, the president can approve the senatorial version of the treaty. Approval poses a problem when the Senate has tacked on substantive amendments or reservations to a treaty, particularly when such changes may require reopening negotiations with the other signatory governments. Sometimes a president may decide to withdraw a treaty if the senatorial changes are too extensive—as Woodrow Wilson did with the Versailles Treaty in 1919. Wilson felt that the senatorial reservations would weaken the treaty so much that it would be ineffective. His refusal to accept the senatorial version of the treaty led to the eventual refusal of the United States to join the League of Nations.

President Jimmy Carter was successful in lobbying for the treaties that provided for the return of the Panama Canal to Panama by the year 2000 and neutralizing the canal. He was unsuccessful, however, in his attempts to gain ratification of the Strategic Arms Limitation Treaty, known as SALT II. That treaty, which provided for limits on nuclear-armed long-range bombers and intercontinental ballistic missiles, encountered fierce opposition from Senate conservatives and from the subsequent Reagan administration.

President Bill Clinton won a major political and legislative victory in 1993 by persuading Congress to ratify the North American Free Trade Agreement (NAFTA). In so doing, he had to overcome opposition from Democrats and most of organized labor. In 1998, he worked closely with Senate Republicans to ensure Senate approval of the Chemical Weapons Convention (see Chapter 17). In 2000, the president won a major legislative victory when Congress voted to establish permanent trade relations with China.

---

[7]The Nixon administration first encouraged new relations with the People's Republic of China by allowing a cultural exchange of ping-pong teams.

Executive Agreements.   Presidential power in foreign affairs is enhanced greatly by the use of **executive agreements** made between the president and other heads of state. Such agreements do not require Senate approval, although the House and Senate may refuse to appropriate the funds necessary to implement them. Whereas treaties are binding on all succeeding administrations, executive agreements are not binding without each new president's consent.

Among the advantages of executive agreements are speed and secrecy. The former is essential during a crisis; the latter is important when the administration fears that open senatorial debate may be detrimental to the best interests of the United States or to the interests of the president.[8] There have been far more executive agreements (about 9,000) than treaties (about 1,300). Many executive agreements contain secret provisions calling for American military assistance or other support. For example, Franklin Roosevelt (1933–1945) used executive agreements to bypass congressional isolationists in trading American destroyers for British Caribbean naval bases and in arranging diplomatic and military affairs with Canada and Latin American nations.

Chief Legislator

Constitutionally, presidents must recommend to Congress legislation that they judge necessary and expedient. Not all presidents have wielded their powers as **chief legislator** in the same manner. President John Tyler was almost completely unsuccessful in getting his legislative programs implemented by Congress. Presidents Theodore Roosevelt, Franklin Roosevelt, and Lyndon Johnson, however, saw much of their proposed legislation put into effect.

In modern times, the president has played a dominant role in creating the congressional agenda. In the president's annual **State of the Union message,** which is required by the Constitution (Article II, Section 3) and is usually given

---

[8]The Case Act of 1972 requires that all executive agreements be transmitted to Congress within sixty days after the agreement takes effect. Secret agreements are transmitted to the foreign relations committees as classified information.

Executive Agreement
An international agreement made by the president, without senatorial ratification, with the head of a foreign state.

Chief Legislator
The role of the president in influencing the making of laws.

State of the Union Message
An annual message to Congress in which the president proposes a legislative program. The message is addressed not only to Congress but also to the American people and to the world. It offers the opportunity to dramatize policies and objectives and to gain public support.

U.S. President Jimmy Carter, Egyptian President Anwar el-Sadat, and Israeli Prime Minister Menachem Begin sign the Camp David accords, bringing peace between Egypt and Israel.

Each year the president presents the State of the Union message, which is required by Article II, Section 3, of the Constitution and is usually given in late January, shortly after Congress reconvenes. Because the floor of the House of Representatives is so much larger than that of the Senate, the State of the Union speech is given there. Attendees include all members of Congress, plus usually the justices of the U.S. Supreme Court, the heads of most of the executive departments, and certain others, such as the chairman of the Federal Reserve Board of Governors. The press, of course, is in attendance, too.

in late January shortly after Congress reconvenes, the president as chief legislator presents his program. The message gives a broad, comprehensive view of what the president wishes the legislature to accomplish during its session. It is as much a message to the American people and to the world as it is to Congress. Its impact on public opinion can determine the way in which Congress responds to the president's agenda.

Getting Legislation Passed.   The president can propose legislation. Congress, however, is not required to pass any of the administration's bills. How, then, does the president get those proposals made into law? One way is by exercising the power of persuasion. The president writes to, telephones, and meets with various congressional leaders; makes public announcements to force the weight of public opinion onto Congress in favor of a legislative program; and, as head of the party, exercises legislative leadership through the congresspersons of the president's party. (See this chapter's *E-mocracy* for a discussion of the president's leadership in expanding access to the Internet.)

To be sure, a president whose party represents a majority in both chambers of Congress may have an easier time getting legislation passed than does a president who faces a hostile Congress. But one of the ways in which a president who faces a hostile Congress still can wield power is through the ability to veto legislation.

Saying No to Legislation.   The president has the power to say no to legislation through use of the veto, by which the White House returns a bill unsigned to Congress with a **veto message** attached.[9] Because the Constitution requires that every bill passed by the House and the Senate be sent to the president before it becomes law, the president must act on each bill:

1. If the bill is signed, it becomes law.
2. If the bill is not sent back to Congress after ten congressional working days, it becomes law without the president's signature.

Veto Message
The president's formal explanation of a veto when legislation is returned to Congress.

_____
[9]*Veto* in Latin means "I forbid."

3. The president can reject the bill and send it back to Congress with a veto message setting forth objections. Congress then can change the bill, hoping to secure presidential approval and repass it. Or it can simply reject the president's objections by overriding the veto with a two-thirds roll-call vote of the members present in each house.

4. If the president refuses to sign the bill and Congress adjourns within ten working days after the bill has been submitted to the president, the bill is killed for that session of Congress. If Congress wishes the bill to be reconsidered, the bill must be reintroduced during the following session. This is called a **pocket veto.**

Presidents employed the veto power infrequently until the administration of Andrew Johnson, but it has been used with increasing vigor since then (see Table 13–2 on page 424). The total number of vetoes from George Washington through Bill Clinton's eighth year in office was 2,532, with about two-thirds of those vetoes being exercised by Grover Cleveland, Franklin Roosevelt, Harry Truman, and Dwight Eisenhower.

After the 1994 congressional elections, Bill Clinton faced a Republican-controlled Congress. He used the veto very effectively to force the Republicans to rewrite their legislative proposals to gain his approval. The Republicans, not having enough votes to overturn Clinton's veto, modified some proposals during subsequent years in order to enact them into law.

The Line-Item Veto.   Ronald Reagan lobbied strenuously for Congress to give another tool to the president—the **line-item veto.** Reagan saw the ability to veto

DID YOU KNOW...
That the expression "O.K.," which is used worldwide, was coined in the presidential campaign of 1840 in reference to Martin Van Buren, who was called "Old Kinderhook" after his birthplace (his New York supporters formed the "O.K." club and shouted the expression at political rallies and parades)**?**

Pocket Veto
A special veto power exercised by the chief executive after a legislative body has adjourned. Bills not signed by the chief executive die after a specified period of time. If Congress wishes to reconsider such a bill, it must be reintroduced in the following session of Congress.

Line-Item Veto
The power of an executive to veto individual lines or items within a piece of legislation without vetoing the entire bill.

The President on the Web

The Clinton administration was the first to provide access to the White House via the Internet. Early in his first term, President Bill Clinton supported making many White House documents available on the Web site for the White House. Additionally, correspondence with the president and the First Lady quickly moved from ordinary handwritten letters to e-mail. During the Clinton presidency, most agencies of the government as well as congressional offices also began to provide access and information on the Internet.

In 1999, Clinton became the first U.S. president to "chat" live online with Americans. Sitting in front of a laptop computer at George Washington University, the president (whose video image was in a program window) answered questions from those in the chat room. The chat room was limited to fifty thousand participants by its sponsor, Excite.com, but the president's numbers were equal to those drawn by such individuals and groups as Shania Twain and The Cure. The event went flawlessly, in contrast to Al Gore's first online chat in 1994, when the transmission broke up in midsession.

The chat included other political leaders from across the country, including the mayor of Bethlehem, Pennsylvania, the mayor of San Jose, California, and the governor of New Hampshire, who

also answered queries online. Unlike Clinton, who according to his aides surfed the Net occasionally but was not very computer literate, the mayor of Bethlehem, who is only thirty-four years old, uses e-mail daily to communicate with city officials and the public.

In the last two years of his term, President Clinton also addressed the problem of the so-called digital divide, which has arisen because urban, well-to-do Americans are more likely to have access to the Internet and all forms of information technology than are poor families and those living in rural areas. In his view, the president should take a leadership role in making the Internet accessible to all Americans and in convincing dot.com corporations to work toward this goal. Although many corporate leaders welcome presidential support for the Internet, they would prefer that access to it be driven by the market and that the government neither regulate nor interfere with the growth of their industry.

FOR CRITICAL ANALYSIS

Is it the role of the U.S. president to promote the use of the Internet and to make sure that all Americans have access to this technology?

specific spending provisions of legislation that he was sent by Congress as the only way that the president could control overall congressional spending. In 1996, Congress passed a law providing for the line-item veto. Signed by President Clinton, the law granted the president the power to rescind any item in an appropriations bill unless Congress passed a "disapproval" bill, which could be vetoed. The law did not take effect until after the 1996 election.

TABLE 13-2
Presidential Vetoes, 1789 to Present

YEARS	PRESIDENT	REGULAR VETOES	VETOES OVERRIDDEN	POCKET VETOES	TOTAL VETOES
1789–1797	Washington	2	0	0	2
1797–1801	J. Adams	0	0	0	0
1801–1809	Jefferson	0	0	0	0
1809–1817	Madison	5	0	2	7
1817–1825	Monroe	1	0	0	1
1825–1829	J. Q. Adams	0	0	0	0
1829–1837	Jackson	5	0	7	12
1837–1841	Van Buren	0	0	1	1
1841–1841	Harrison	0	0	0	0
1841–1845	Tyler	6	1	4	10
1845–1849	Polk	2	0	1	3
1849–1850	Taylor	0	0	0	0
1850–1853	Fillmore	0	0	0	0
1853–1857	Pierce	9	5	0	9
1857–1861	Buchanan	4	0	3	7
1861–1865	Lincoln	2	0	5	7
1865–1869	A. Johnson	21	15	8	29
1869–1877	Grant	45	4	48	93
1877–1881	Hayes	12	1	1	13
1881–1881	Garfield	0	0	0	0
1881–1885	Arthur	4	1	8	12
1885–1889	Cleveland	304	2	110	414
1889–1893	Harrison	19	1	25	44
1893–1897	Cleveland	42	5	128	170
1897–1901	McKinley	6	0	36	42
1901–1909	T. Roosevelt	42	1	40	82
1909–1913	Taft	30	1	9	39
1913–1921	Wilson	33	6	11	44
1921–1923	Harding	5	0	1	6
1923–1929	Coolidge	20	4	30	50
1929–1933	Hoover	21	3	16	37
1933–1945	F. Roosevelt	372	9	263	635
1945–1953	Truman	180	12	70	250
1953–1961	Eisenhower	73	2	108	181
1961–1963	Kennedy	12	0	9	21
1963–1969	L. Johnson	16	0	14	30
1969–1974	Nixon	26*	7	17	43
1974–1977	Ford	48	12	18	66
1977–1981	Carter	13	2	18	31
1981–1989	Reagan	39	9	28	67
1989–1993	Bush	37	1	0	37
1993–2001	Clinton	37†	2	0	37
TOTAL		1,493	106	1039	2,532

*Two pocket vetoes by President Nixon, overruled in the courts, are counted here as regular vetoes.
†President Clinton's line-item vetoes are not included.

SOURCES: Louis Fisher, *The Politics of Shared Power: Congress and the Executive,* 2d ed. (Washington, D.C.: Congressional Quarterly Press, 1987), p. 30; *Congressional Quarterly Weekly Report,* October 17, 1992, p. 3249; and authors' update.

President Clinton used the line-item veto on several occasions, beginning on August 11, 1997. While his early vetoes were of little consequence to the members of Congress, the next set of vetoes—of thirty-eight military construction projects—caused an uproar in Congress and the passage of a disapproval bill to rescind the vetoes. The act also was challenged in court as an unconstitutional delegation of legislative powers to the executive branch. In 1998, by a six-to-three vote, the United States Supreme Court agreed and overturned the act. The Court stated that "there is no provision in the Constitution that authorizes the president to enact, to amend or to repeal statutes."[10]

Congress's Power to Override Presidential Vetoes.   A veto is a clear-cut indication of the president's dissatisfaction with congressional legislation. Congress, however, can override a presidential veto, although it rarely exercises this power. Consider that two-thirds of the members of each chamber who are present must vote to override the president's veto in a roll-call vote. This means that if only one-third plus one of the members voting in one of the chambers of Congress do not agree to override the veto, the veto holds. It was not until the administration of John Tyler that Congress overrode a presidential veto. In the first sixty-five years of American federal government history, out of thirty-three regular vetoes, Congress overrode only one, or about 3 percent. Overall, only about 7 percent of all vetoes have been overridden.

Measuring the Success or Failure of a President's Legislative Program.   One way of determining a president's strength is to evaluate that president's success as chief legislator. A strong president may be one who has achieved much of the administration's legislative program; a weak president has achieved little. Using these definitions of strong and weak, it is possible to rank presidents according to their legislative success.

---

[10]*Clinton v. City of New York*, 524 U.S. 417 (1998).

Figure 13–1 shows the percentages of presidential victories measured by congressional votes in situations in which the president took a clear-cut position. Based on this information, John Kennedy appears to have been the most successful president in recent years until President Clinton, whose high success rate (86.4 percent) in the first two years of his presidency tumbled to 36 percent after the Republican victory in the 1994 elections. During his second term, Clinton's "success rate" hovered between 50 and 55 percent. Such data provide a statistical measure but do not indicate the importance of the legislation, the bills not introduced, or whether the president was perceived as a successful national leader regardless of this measure.

Other Presidential Powers

The powers of the president just discussed are called **constitutional powers,** because their basis lies in the Constitution. In addition, Congress has established by law, or statute, numerous other presidential powers—such as the ability to declare national emergencies. These are called **statutory powers.** Both constitutional and statutory powers have been labeled the **expressed powers** of the president, because they are expressly written into the Constitution or into law.

Presidents also have what have come to be known as **inherent powers.** These depend on the loosely worded statement in the Constitution that "the executive Power shall be vested in a President" and that the president should "take Care that the Laws be faithfully executed." The most common example of inherent powers are those emergency powers invoked by the president during wartime. Franklin Roosevelt used his inherent powers to move the Japanese living in the United States into internment camps for the duration of World War II.

Clearly, modern U.S. presidents have numerous powers at their disposal. According to some critics, among the powers exercised by modern presidents are certain powers that rightfully belong to Congress but that Congress has yielded to the executive branch—see the *Critical Perspective* on pages 428–429 for a discussion of this issue.

Constitutional Power
A power vested in the president by Article II of the Constitution.

Statutory Power
A power created for the president through laws enacted by Congress.

Expressed Power
A constitutional or statutory power of the president, which is expressly written into the Constitution or into statutory law.

Inherent Power
A power of the president derived from the loosely worded statement in the Constitution that "the executive Power shall be vested in a President" and that the president should "take Care that the Laws be faithfully executed"; defined through practice rather than through constitutional or statutory law.

FIGURE 13-1

Presidential Support on Congressional Votes, 1953 to Present

Most presidents have their greatest successes in the first years of their terms in office.

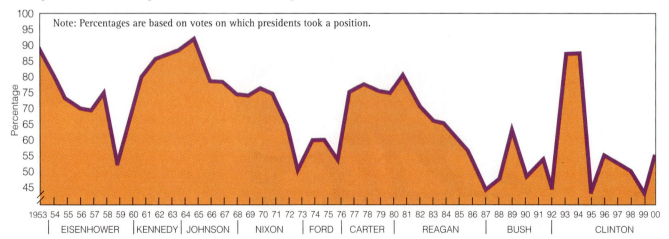

SOURCE: *CQ Weekly Report,* various issues.

The President as Party Chief and Superpolitician

Presidents are by no means above political partisanship, and one of their many roles is that of chief of party. Although the Constitution says nothing about the function of the president within a political party (the mere concept of political parties was abhorrent to most of the authors of the Constitution), today presidents are the actual leaders of their parties.

The President as Chief of Party

As party leader, the president chooses the national committee chairperson and can try to discipline party members who fail to support presidential policies. One way of exerting political power within the party is by **patronage**—appointing individuals to government or public jobs. This power was more extensive in the past, before the establishment of the civil service in 1883 (see Chapter 14), but the president still retains impressive patronage power. As we noted earlier, the president can appoint several thousand individuals to jobs in the cabinet, the White House, and the federal regulatory agencies.

Patronage
Rewarding faithful party workers and followers with government employment and contracts.

Perhaps the most important role that the president played for his party in the late 1990s and early 2000s was that of fund-raiser. Because of the ability of political parties to accept unregulated contributions in the form of "soft money" (see Chapter 10 for details on these contributions), the president is able to raise large amounts of money for the political party through appearances at dinners, speaking engagements, and other social occasions. In addition, the Clinton White House (expanding prior practice) sponsored social events in the executive mansion for prospective donors, although contributions were not directly solicited there. (See this chapter's *Politics and Economics* for a discussion of fund-raising activity.)

Presidents have a number of other ways of exerting influence as party chief. The president may make it known that a particular congressperson's choice for

politics and economics

The President as Chief Fund-Raiser

Throughout his presidency, Bill Clinton played an extremely important role for the Democratic Party as the fund-raiser in chief. Over the eight years of his term, he and his vice president, Al Gore, raised as much as $500 million in campaign contributions. Although a portion of the funds raised for the 1996 campaign was spent to reelect Clinton and Gore, a great deal of the money was spent to support Democratic candidates for the House of Representatives and the Senate.

In 2000, when Vice President Gore faced his own presidential campaign, the fund-raising kicked into high gear for both parties. After raising unprecedented amounts of money for his primary campaign, in April 2000 George W. Bush, the Republican nominee, hosted a dinner in Washington, D.C., that raised $21.3 million. With 1,500 guests at the dinner, the average dinner ticket was about $15,000. Only two weeks later, the Democrats hosted a much more "democratic" fund-raiser in a basketball arena in Washington, D.C. The 12,000 guests were treated to superstar

entertainment and speeches by the president and vice president. Democrats extolled the diversity of the crowd: tickets ranged from a few hundred dollars to $250,000. Those who paid $250,000 had dined with the president at the White House on the previous night.

Some of the fund-raising that preceded the 1996 election later came under scrutiny for its legality. Investigations looked into illegal contributions from China and the practice of allowing high-level contributors to spend a "night in the Lincoln bedroom." Both parties pledged to work for campaign-financing reform. Ironically, Al Gore, while speaking at an event where more than $25 million in soft money was raised, promised that a campaign-financing bill would be "the first bill I will send to the U.S. Congress" if elected president.

FOR CRITICAL ANALYSIS

What kinds of changes would have to be made in the American election system for both parties to agree to limits on campaign fund-raising?

critical perspective

Is the President Becoming Too Powerful?

When the framers crafted the U.S. Constitution more than 210 years ago, they created a balance of powers among the three branches of the national government. Today, some people claim that Congress has upset this balance of powers by yielding too many powers to the presidency that rightfully should be exercised by the legislative branch. For example, as discussed elsewhere in the chapter, critics of the Line Item Veto Act of 1996 contended that giving line-item veto power to the president essentially transferred legislative power to the executive branch. Some argue that Congress has also yielded its powers to the presidency through (1) the passage of the War Powers Resolution of 1973, (2) the acceptance of "near treaties" without Senate approval, (3) the delegation of increasingly broad regulatory powers to the administrative branch of government, and (4) the acceptance of the president's wide use of executive orders.

The War Powers Resolution

Only Congress has the ability to declare war. Nevertheless, numerous presidents have sent American troops into action without a congressional declaration of war. Truman sent troops to Korea in 1950. Presidents Kennedy, Johnson, and Nixon sent hundreds of thousands of troops to Vietnam in the 1960s and 1970s. In 1973, Congress attempted to gain control over military activities by passing the War Powers Resolution. That resolution requires the president to consult with Congress when sending American troops into action. After they are sent, the president has to report to Congress within two days. Congress then has to approve the use of troops within sixty days or

extend the sixty-day limit. Otherwise, the U.S. forces must be withdrawn.

Critics of the War Powers Resolution argue that it has had little effect on presidential use of the military throughout the world. According to some, the president today seems to take for granted the unlimited use of the military for humanitarian purposes, as when troops were sent to Somalia, Haiti, and Bosnia, for example. Political scientists Louis Fisher and David Gray Adler suggest that although the idea behind the resolution was to curb presidential powers, in effect, it allows the president to engage in war for up to ninety days without congressional approval. According to these authors, "Seldom has a statute misfired to such an extent on a basic purpose. The resolution does violence to the intent of the Framers and has not in any sense insured the collective judgment of Congress and the president in the use of military force."*

Near Treaties

Article II, Section 2, Clause 2, of the Constitution requires that any treaty signed by the president be ratified by a two-thirds favorable vote in the Senate to become effective. President Clinton found a way around this constitutional requirement, according to his critics, by calling what are essentially treaties by some other name. For example, an agreement signed by the president that gives Russia a voice in North Atlantic Treaty Organization (NATO) decisions whenever such decisions bear on the national security of Russia was called a "founding act" instead of a treaty. Other agreements were titled "political agreements" or "memorandums of understanding." By not calling these agreements treaties, the president was able to avoid the necessity of asking the Senate for its advice and consent. At least one member of Congress, Senator Jesse Helms (R., N.C.), has

*Louis Fisher and David Gray Adler, "The War Powers Resolution: Time to Say Goodbye," *Political Science Quarterly,* No. 113 (Spring 1998).

---

federal judge will not be appointed unless that member of Congress is more supportive of the president's legislative program.[11] The president may agree to campaign for a particular program or for a particular candidate. Presidents also reward loyal supporters in Congress with funding for local projects, tax breaks for regional industries, and other forms of "pork." (See the *Politics and Economics* feature in Chapter 12 for a discussion of these appropriations.)

Constituencies and Public Approval

All politicians worry about their constituencies, and presidents are no exception. Presidents, however, have numerous constituencies. In principle, they are beholden to the entire electorate—the public of the United States—even to those

[11]"Senatorial courtesy" (see Chapter 15) often puts the judicial appointment in the hands of the Senate, however.

critical perspective

argued against the legality of such "near" treaties without congressional approval.

Broad Regulatory Powers

One of the duties of the president, as set forth in Article II, Section 3, of the Constitution, is to "take Care that the Laws be faithfully executed." When Congress passes laws to regulate certain practices, such as occupational safety, it falls to the administrative branch to enforce the laws.

Typically, a law passed by Congress authorizes an agency in the executive branch to "fill in the gaps" in the law by making and implementing specific rules and regulations (see Chapter 14). The Occupational Safety and Health Administration, for example, has the authority to make and implement rules to increase safety in the workplace. These rules have the force of law. Generally, the broader the language of an act, the more gaps there are to fill by agency rulemaking. Each year, administrative agency rules fill between fifty thousand and one hundred thousand pages of the *Federal Register,* the government publication in which agency rules are initially published.

Some contend that Congress, by enacting broad legislation to regulate the economy, delegates too much lawmaking authority to the executive branch. After all, the Constitution authorizes only the legislative branch to create laws. Yet administrative agencies, to which the Constitution does not specifically refer, make rules that are as legally binding as the laws passed by Congress.

Executive Orders

The Clinton administration made broad use of the president's power to make policy decisions without the approval of Congress by issuing executive orders and proclamations. For example, using power granted to the chief executive under past legislation, President Clinton proclaimed that millions of acres in Utah (the Escalante wilderness) that had been under federal management would be a national monument. Although many environmentalists were pleased, many local residents and conservatives were angered. In 1999, the president directed the U.S. Forest Service to make up to 50 million acres of national forest off-limits to any development. National monuments were also declared in Nevada, California, and Arizona.

Why are these presidential declarations significant? In the case of the national monuments and the Forest Service lands, the president decided, as a matter of his administration's policy, to remove these lands from potential use by mining, ranching, or other economic interests and place them under strict protection. By doing so, he changed the economic situation in those states and, in the eyes of some members of Congress, circumvented the intent of Congress when it originally enacted legislation concerning those lands. Some members of Congress have proposed legislation that would restrict executive orders to those provided for by Congress. Inasmuch as the Supreme Court struck down the legislative veto (see Chapter 12), it is uncertain whether restrictions on executive orders pursuant to legislation would be constitutional either.

FOR CRITICAL ANALYSIS

1. Senate approval is required for any treaty negotiated by the president. Should executive agreements negotiated by the president with other heads of state be subject to the same requirement? Why or why not?
2. Has Congress, by authorizing executive agencies to make legally binding rules, delegated too much of its lawmaking powers to those agencies? Do you see any reasonable alternative to delegating such authority to agencies?

---

who did not vote. They are certainly beholden to their party constituency, because its members put them in office. The president's constituencies also include members of the opposing party whose cooperation the president needs. Finally, the president has to take into consideration a constituency that has come to be called the **Washington community.** This community consists of individuals who—whether in or out of political office—are intimately familiar with the workings of government, thrive on gossip, and measure on a daily basis the political power of the president.

All of these constituencies are impressed by presidents who maintain a high level of public approval, partly because this is very difficult to accomplish. Presidential popularity, as measured by national polls, gives the president an extra political resource to use in persuading legislators or bureaucrats to pass legislation. After all, refusing to do so might be going against public sentiment. President Clinton showed significant strength in the public opinion polls for a

Washington Community
Individuals regularly involved with politics in Washington, D.C.

second-term chief executive, as Figure 13–2 indicates. To the surprise of his critics, after news of a potential scandal involving a White House intern (Monica Lewinsky) broke, President Clinton's job approval ratings improved. His ratings remained high even after he admitted publicly, in August 1998, that he had engaged in inappropriate sexual conduct with Lewinsky. (See the feature *An Ethical Issue* for a discussion of ethics and the presidency.)

The presidential preoccupation with public opinion has been criticized by at least one scholar as changing the balance of national politics. Since the early twentieth century, presidents have spoken more to the public and less to Congress. In the nineteenth century, only 7 percent of presidential speeches were addressed to the public; since 1900, 50 percent have been addressed to the pub-

FIGURE 13-2

Public Popularity of Modern Presidents

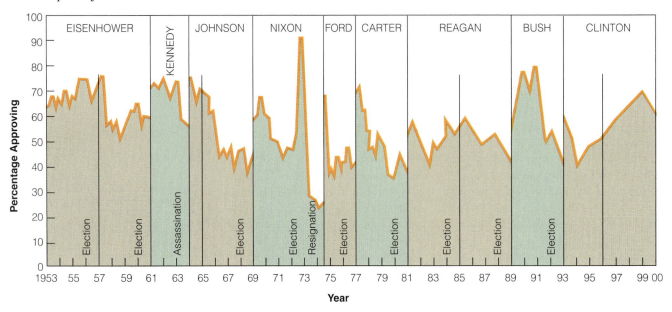

SOURCES: *Public Opinion,* February/March 1988, pp. 36–39; and Gallup Polls, 1992 through 2000.

lic. Samuel Kernell has proposed that the style of presidential leadership has changed since World War II, owing partly to the influence of television.[12] Presidents frequently go over the heads of Congress and the political elites, taking their cases directly to the people. This strategy, which Kernell dubbed "going public," gives the president additional power through the ability to persuade and manipulate public opinion. By identifying their own positions so clearly, presidents make compromises with Congress much more difficult and weaken the legislators' positions. Given the increasing importance of the media as the major source of political information for citizens and elites, presidents will continue to use public opinion as part of their arsenal of weapons to gain support from Congress and to achieve their policy goals.

---

[12]Samuel Kernell, *Going Public: New Strategies of Presidential Leadership,* 3d ed. (Washington, D.C.: Congressional Quarterly Press, 1997).

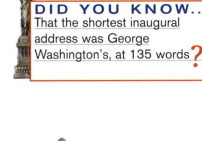

INFOTRAC®
COLLEGE EDITION

Does Macroeconomics Matter

Do We Want Character in Our President?

One of the strangest phenomena of the Clinton impeachment proceedings during 1998 and 1999 was the disjuncture between the president's job approval ratings and the public's assessment of his character. For many decades, analysts of the presidency have emphasized the importance of character in the chief executive. According to past theories, presidents should be trusted by the people and by other leaders to tell the truth, to be reliable, and to keep their word. Presidents should be models of behavior for young people. Presidents should act consistently and make decisions for the good of the nation, not for their own political gains.

THE CLINTON PARADOX

Public opinion analysts were stunned by the results of their polls as the accusations against the president in the Lewinsky scandal mounted. As it became clear through the testimony of both parties that the president and the intern had had an inappropriate relationship, the popularity of the president soared. Although the polls showed that most Americans believed that Clinton had engaged in the affair, the polls also showed that Americans were happy with the job he was doing as president. His job approval rating was about 58 percent in 1997; as the allegations mounted, his rating climbed, reaching 69 percent at the time of the impeachment vote in the House. At the same time, his rating for handling the economy reached 81 percent approval.

While the television anchors and newspaper columnists struggled to explain Clinton's popularity, the members of Congress and other politicians realized that it meant that the American people did not want the president removed from office through impeachment.

Although Americans supported the president's job performance, they had reservations about his character and trustworthiness. The percentage of people who thought that President Clinton was honest and trustworthy fell from 40 percent in 1996 to 24 percent in January 1999. When asked, in January 1999, whether the president shared the respondents' personal values, 62 percent said no. Sixty-four percent of those polled did not feel that the president showed good judgment, and 68 percent believed that the president provided weak or very weak moral leadership for the country.*

ETHICS AND FUTURE PRESIDENTS

Does the Clinton experience show that Americans no longer seek character in their presidents? It is very difficult to answer this question. Americans still seem quite willing to make judgments about the character and ethics of their presidents and of those who seek the office. They also seem to want to distinguish between presidents in office during a time of prosperity and candidates for the presidency. Finally, the fact that Clinton's moral failing was sexual and fairly common in American society seemed to make it less serious for many Americans. If he had clearly broken the law, his approval ratings might have reflected a different judgment. Some president watchers think that the public will never hold the chief executive accountable again for moral behavior, but others believe that public expectations may get higher, at least in the short term.

FOR CRITICAL ANALYSIS

What moral and ethical values should be most important in the president of the United States?

*Frank Newport, "The Best of Times, the Worst of Times: A Sanguine Public Assessment of Bill Clinton in Crisis," *The Public Perspective,* August/September 1999, pp. 22–23.

Special Uses of Presidential Power

Presidents have at their disposal a variety of special powers and privileges not available in other branches of the U.S. government. These include (1) emergency powers, (2) executive orders, (3) executive privilege, and, until relatively recently, (4) impoundment of funds.

Emergency Powers

Emergency Power
An inherent power exercised by the president during a period of national crisis, particularly in foreign affairs.

If you were to read the Constitution, you would find no mention of the additional powers that the executive office may exercise during national emergencies. Indeed, the Supreme Court has indicated that an "emergency does not create power."[13] But it is clear that presidents have used their inherent powers during times of emergency, particularly in the realm of foreign affairs. The **emergency powers** of the president were first enunciated in the Supreme Court's decision in *United States v. Curtiss-Wright Export Corp.*[14] In that case, President Franklin Roosevelt, without authorization by Congress, ordered an embargo on the shipment of weapons to two warring South American countries. The Court recognized that the president may exercise inherent powers in foreign affairs and that the national government has primacy in foreign affairs.

Examples of emergency powers are abundant, coinciding with real or contrived crises in domestic and foreign affairs. Abraham Lincoln's suspension of civil liberties at the beginning of the Civil War (1861–1865), his calling of the state militias into national service, and his subsequent governance of conquered areas and even of areas of northern states were justified by claims that such actions were essential to preserve the Union. Franklin Roosevelt declared an "unlimited national emergency" following the fall of France in World War II (1939–1945) and mobilized the federal budget and the economy for war.

President Harry Truman authorized the federal seizure of steel plants and their operation by the national government in 1952 during the Korean War. Truman claimed that he was using his inherent emergency power as chief executive and commander in chief to safeguard the nation's security, as the ongoing steel mill strike threatened the supply of weapons to the armed forces. The Supreme Court did not agree, holding that the president had no authority under the Constitution to seize private property or to legislate such action.[15] According to legal scholars, this was the first time a limit was placed on the exercise of the president's emergency powers.

Executive Orders

Executive Order
A rule or regulation issued by the president that has the effect of law. Executive orders can implement and give administrative effect to provisions in the Constitution, to treaties, and to statutes.

Federal Register
A publication of the executive branch of the U.S. government that prints executive orders, rules, and regulations.

Congress allows the president (as well as administrative agencies) to issue **executive orders** that have the force of law. These executive orders can do the following: (1) enforce legislative statutes, (2) enforce the Constitution or treaties with foreign nations, and (3) establish or modify rules and practices of executive administrative agencies.

An executive order, then, represents the president's legislative power. The only apparent requirement is that under the Administrative Procedure Act of 1946, all executive orders must be published in the *Federal Register,* a daily publication of the U.S. government. Executive orders have been used to establish some procedures for appointing noncareer administrators, to implement national affirmative action regulations, to restructure the White House bureaucracy, to

---

[13]*Home Building and Loan Association v. Blaisdell,* 290 U.S. 398 (1934).
[14]299 U.S. 304 (1936).
[15]*Youngstown Sheet and Tube Co. v. Sawyer,* 343 U.S. 579 (1952).

ration consumer goods and to administer wage and price controls under emergency conditions, to classify government information as secret, and to regulate the export of restricted items.

Executive Privilege

Another inherent executive power that has been claimed by presidents concerns the ability of the president and the president's executive officials to refuse to appear before, or to withhold information from, Congress or the courts. This is called **executive privilege,** and it relies on the constitutional separation of powers for its basis. Critics of executive privilege believe that it can be used to shield from public scrutiny actions of the executive branch that should be open to Congress and to the American public.

Limits to executive privilege went untested until the Watergate affair in the early 1970s. Five men had broken into the headquarters of the Democratic National Committee and were caught searching for documents that would damage the candidacy of the Democratic nominee, George McGovern. Later investigation showed that the break-in was planned by members of Richard Nixon's campaign committee and that Nixon and his closest advisers had devised a strategy for impeding the investigation of the crime, using the Central Intelligence Agency for illegal activities. After it became known that all of the conversations held in the Oval Office had been tape-recorded on a secret system, Nixon was ordered to turn over the tapes to the special prosecutor. Nixon refused to do so, claiming executive privilege. He argued that "no president could function if the private papers of his office, prepared by his personal staff, were open to public scrutiny." In 1974, in one of the Supreme Court's most famous cases, *United States v. Nixon,*[16] the justices unanimously ruled that Nixon had to hand over the tapes to the Court. The Court held that executive privilege could not be used to prevent evidence from being heard in criminal proceedings.

The claim of executive privilege was also raised by the Clinton administration as a defense against the aggressive investigation of Clinton's relationship with Monica Lewinsky by Independent Counsel Kenneth Starr. The Clinton administration claimed executive privilege for several presidential aides who might have discussed the situation with the president. In addition, President Clinton asserted that his White House counsel did not have to testify before the Starr grand jury due to attorney-client privilege. Finally, the Department of Justice claimed that members of the Secret Service who guard the president could not testify about his activities due to a "protective function privilege" inherent in their duties.

The federal judge overseeing the case denied the claims of privilege, so both sides appealed to the Supreme Court for an expedited hearing. The Court refused to accept the case and sent it to a federal appeals court for a hearing. The appellate court upheld the lower court's decision.

Impoundment of Funds

By law, the president proposes a budget, and Congress approves it. But there is no provision in the Constitution that requires the president, as chief executive, to *spend* all of the funds appropriated by Congress, and many presidents prior to the 1970s did not do so. The question of whether the president is required to spend all appropriated funds came to a head during the Nixon administration after a number of confrontations over this issue between the Republican president and an antagonistic, Democratic-controlled Congress. When Nixon vetoed appropriation

DID YOU KNOW... That President Jimmy Carter was the first president to hold a phone-in television broadcast, with Walter Cronkite as the moderator?

Executive Privilege
The right of executive officials to refuse to appear before, or to withhold information from, a legislative committee. Executive privilege is enjoyed by the president and by those executive officials accorded that right by the president.

[16]318 U.S. 683 (1974).

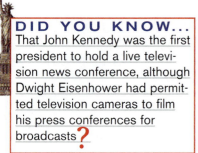

bills, Congress often overrode his veto. In retaliation, Nixon refused to spend the appropriated funds, claiming that he wanted to reduce overall federal spending.

As part of its Budget and Impoundment Control Act of 1974, Congress required that the president spend all appropriated funds, although Congress gave the president some leeway. A president who is not going to spend all appropriated funds must tell Congress, and only if Congress agrees within forty-five days can the president withhold spending. If the president simply wishes to delay spending, this must be indicated to Congress. If Congress does not agree, it can pass a resolution requiring the immediate spending of the appropriated funds. The Supreme Court in 1975 unanimously ruled that the president had to spend money appropriated by Congress because of his constitutional obligation to "take care that the laws be faithfully executed."[17]

Abuses of Executive Power and Impeachment

Presidents normally leave office either because their first term has expired and they do not seek (or win) reelection or because, having served two full terms, they are not allowed to be elected for a third term (owing to the Twenty-second Amendment, passed in 1951). Eight presidents have died in office. But there is still another way for a president to leave office—by **impeachment.** Articles I and II of the Constitution authorize the House and Senate to remove the president, the vice president, or other civil officers of the United States for crimes of "Treason, Bribery, or other high Crimes and Misdemeanors." Remember from Chapter 12 that according to the Constitution, the impeachment process begins in the House, which impeaches (accuses) the federal officer involved. If the House votes to impeach the officer, it draws up articles of impeachment and submits them to the Senate, which conducts the actual trial.

Impeachment
As authorized by Articles I and II of the Constitution, an action by the House of Representatives and the Senate to remove the president, vice president, or civil officers of the United States from office for crimes of "Treason, Bribery, or other high Crimes and Misdemeanors."

In the history of the United States, no president has ever been impeached and also convicted—and thus removed from office—by means of this process. President Andrew Johnson, who succeeded to the office after the assassination of Abraham Lincoln, was seen by the Radical Republicans as too lenient toward the southern states. When Congress passed a law denying the president the right to remove cabinet officers, Johnson defied the law by firing his secretary of war. The House voted to impeach him and submitted eleven articles of impeachment to the Senate. After a three-month trial in the Senate, Johnson was acquitted by one vote. Seven Republicans, convinced that the impeachment articles were politically motivated, crossed party lines to vote for acquittal.

More than a century later, the House Judiciary Committee investigated President Richard Nixon for his involvement in the cover-up of the Watergate break-in of 1972. After months of testimony, including the discovery of tapes made of presidential conversations in the Oval Office, the House committee approved three articles of impeachment against President Nixon. The charges were obstruction of justice, the abuse of power, and the failure to respond to the committee's subpoenas. Six Republicans voted with the committee's Democrats to approve the articles. Convinced that he had little hope of surviving the trial in the Senate, Nixon resigned on August 9, 1974, before the full House voted on the articles.

In both of these cases, charges that the impeachment process was totally political were common. The Nixon case, because of the taped evidence, became more clearly one of provable offense.

Richard Nixon (right) leaves the White House after his resignation on August 9, 1974. Next to him are his wife, Pat, Betty Ford, and Gerald Ford, the new president.

---
[17]*Train v. City of New York,* 420 U.S. 35 (1975).

The Impeachment of Bill Clinton

The second president to be impeached but not convicted by the Senate was President Bill Clinton. In September 1998, Independent Counsel Kenneth Starr sent the findings of his investigation of the president on the charges of perjury and obstruction of justice to Congress. The Republican majority in the House of Representatives then began to organize itself for the possible impeachment of the president, releasing some of the documents to the public. After the 1998 elections, in which the Republicans lost five House seats, the House Judiciary Committee presented four charges to the House for consideration. The House approved two of the charges against Clinton: lying to the grand jury about his affair with Monica Lewinsky (by a vote of 228 to 206); and obstruction of justice (by a vote of 221 to 212). The other two charges were rejected by the House.

Soon after the new Congress convened in 1999, the Senate received the articles of impeachment from the House of Representatives. Chief Justice William Rehnquist presided over the trial, although he had virtually no power to make any procedural or substantive decisions. Soon after the House team of prosecutors and the president's defense team made their opening presentations, a motion was made to dismiss the charges for lack of evidence. When forty-one senators, all Democrats, voted to dismiss, it was clear to all that it would be impossible to obtain the two-thirds vote of the Senate required for conviction. The House team requested the right to call witnesses, and the Senate, unwilling to completely constrain their colleagues, allowed them to interview several witnesses on videotape, tapes that were shown on the Senate floor.

On several occasions during the trial and for three days before the final vote, the Senate debated behind closed doors. Although many liberals and members of the media decried this secrecy, no public outcry against it arose. Finally, on February 12, 1999, the Senate voted on the articles of impeachment: Article I, which charged perjury, was defeated by a vote of forty-five to fifty-five, and Article II, which charged obstruction of justice, was defeated by a fifty-fifty vote (thus falling far short of the two-thirds vote needed for conviction). On both votes, Republican senators joined Democrats to defeat the charges. The president was acquitted. How history will treat the impeachment of President Clinton in relationship to his accomplishments in office will be answered in the years after he leaves office. (Consider the strain that involvement in legal issues places on the president in the feature *Which Side Are You On?* on the next page.)

DID YOU KNOW...
That only two U.S. presidents and their wives are buried together at Arlington National Cemetery—John Kennedy and his wife, Jacqueline Kennedy Onassis; and William Taft and his wife, Helen Herron Taft?

INFOTRAC®
COLLEGE EDITION

Clinton Misuse
Executive Privilege

On the day after Labor Day in 1998, Independent Counsel Kenneth Starr sent his report to Congress indicating that the president might have committed impeachable offenses. Accompanying the report were thirty-six boxes of supporting material. Much more material became available in subsequent weeks.

which side are you on?

Should the President Be Sued While in Office?

In 1994, Paula Jones, a former employee of the state of Arkansas, filed a sexual-harassment suit against President Bill Clinton, who had been governor of Arkansas at the time of the alleged incident. The president's attorneys claimed that the president could not be sued in a civil matter, even though the incident had happened before he became president, because the president should be immune from such suits. The Clinton team argued that forcing a sitting president to become a litigant in such a civil suit would put the nation at risk: the president's performance of his duties as chief executive would necessarily be interrupted as he prepared for and engaged in a trial. The attorneys representing Jones argued that protecting a president from legal responsibility in such suits would set a precedent that would extend presidential privilege too far.

The appeals court agreed with the Jones team, and the Clinton attorneys appealed the decision to the United States Supreme Court. In the case of *Jones v. Clinton,** the high court agreed with Jones. The Supreme Court disagreed with Clinton's claim that the suit would take up too much of the president's time and that allowing this suit would encourage many more. As a direct result of this opinion, the president gave a deposition in the case, which was later shown to be false by his own testimony before the grand jury in the Monica Lewinsky affair. As more than one commentator suggested, if Clinton had settled out of court with Jones, the Supreme Court decision would never have been made.

The question remains: Is the well-being of the United States threatened when the president acts as a litigant in a civil suit? In the Clinton case, there is no hard evidence to suggest that the time he spent with his attorneys preparing for his testimony substantially damaged the nation. In fact, the president's approval ratings were at their highest when these issues were in court. Some newspaper accounts, however, suggest that the president did have to make some very serious decisions about U.S. intervention in Kosovo during the impeachment crisis—decisions that may have been made without his full concentration. In a more serious crisis, could the president's involvement in a court case lead him to the wrong decision?

DOES IT MATTER?

Do Americans have a right to the full attention of their chief executive? Should presidents be protected from such distractions as minor court cases and similar issues?

GOING ONLINE

If you would like to read the text of the Supreme Court decision in Jones v. Clinton, *you can locate it at* **http://www.findlaw.com**. *Interesting discussions of how this case weakened the presidency can be found at the site of the Brookings Institution,* **http://www.brook.edu**.

*520 U.S. 681 (1997).

INFOTRAC ®
COLLEGE EDITION

Do We Need a Twenty-Eighth Amendment?

The Executive Organization

Gone are the days when presidents answered their own mail, as George Washington did. It was not until 1857 that Congress authorized a private secretary for the president, to be paid by the federal government. Woodrow Wilson typed most of his correspondence, even though he did have several secretaries. At the beginning of Franklin Roosevelt's long tenure in the White House, the entire staff consisted of thirty-seven employees. It was not until the New Deal and World War II that the presidential staff became a sizable organization.

Today, the executive organization includes a White House Office staff of about 600, including some workers who are part-time employees and others who are detailed from their departments to the White House. Not all of these employees have equal access to the president, nor are all of them likely to be equally concerned about the administration's political success. The more than 350 employees who work in the White House Office itself are closest to the president. They often include many individuals who worked in the president's campaign. These assistants are most concerned with preserving the president's reputation. Also included in the president's staff are a number of councils and advisory organizations, such as the National Security Council. Although the individuals who hold staff positions in these offices are appointed by the president, they are really more concerned with their own area than with the president's overall success. The group of appointees who perhaps are least helpful to the president is the cabinet, each member of which is the principal officer of a government department.

The Cabinet

Although the Constitution does not include the word *cabinet,* it does state that the president "may require the Opinion, in writing, of the principal Officer in each of the executive Departments." Since the time of George Washington, there has been an advisory group, or **cabinet,** to which the president turns for counsel. Originally, the cabinet consisted of only four officials—the secretaries of state, treasury, and war, and the attorney general. Today, the cabinet numbers thirteen secretaries and the attorney general. (See Table 13–1 on page 416 for the names of the cabinet departments and Chapter 14 for a detailed discussion of these units.)

The cabinet may consist of more than the secretaries of the various departments. The president at his or her discretion can, for example, ascribe cabinet rank to the National Security adviser, to the ambassador to the United Nations, or to others. Because neither the Constitution nor statutory law requires the president to consult with the cabinet, its use is purely discretionary. Some presidents have relied on the counsel of their cabinets more than others. Dwight Eisenhower frequently turned to his cabinet for advice on a wide range of governmental policies—perhaps because he was used to the team approach to solving problems from his experience in the U.S. Army. Other presidents solicited the opinions of their cabinets and then did what they wanted to do anyway. Lincoln supposedly said—after a cabinet meeting in which a vote was seven nays against his one aye—"Seven nays and one aye, the ayes have it."

In general, few presidents have relied heavily on the advice of their cabinet members. Jimmy Carter thought he could put his cabinet to good use and held regular cabinet meetings for the first two years of his tenure. Then he fired three cabinet members and forced two others to resign, while reorganizing his "inner government." He rarely met with the members of his cabinet thereafter. In recent years, the growth of other parts of the executive branch has rendered the cabinet less significant as an advisory board to the president.

Often, a president will use a **kitchen cabinet** to replace the formal cabinet as a major source of advice. The term *kitchen cabinet* originated during the presidency of Andrew Jackson, who relied on the counsel of close friends who often met with him in the kitchen of the White House. A kitchen cabinet is a very informal group of advisers, who usually are friends of the president with whom the president worked before being elected.

It is not surprising that presidents meet with their cabinet heads only reluctantly. Often, the departmental heads are more responsive to the wishes of their own staffs or to their own political ambitions than they are to the president. They may be more concerned with obtaining resources for their departments than with helping presidents achieve their goals. So there is often a strong conflict of interest between presidents and their cabinet members. It is likely that formal cabinet meetings are held more out of respect for the cabinet tradition than for their problem-solving value.

The Executive Office of the President

When President Franklin Roosevelt appointed a special committee on administrative management, he knew that the committee would conclude that the president needed help. Indeed, the committee proposed a major reorganization of the executive branch. Congress did not approve the entire reorganization, but it did

Cabinet
An advisory group selected by the president to aid in making decisions. The cabinet currently numbers thirteen department secretaries and the attorney general. Depending on the president, the cabinet may be highly influential or relatively insignificant in its advisory role.

Kitchen Cabinet
The informal advisers to the president.

**Executive Office of
the President (EOP)**
Established by President Franklin D.
Roosevelt by executive order under the
Reorganization Act of 1939, the EOP
currently consists of ten staff agencies
that assist the president in carrying out
major duties.

create the **Executive Office of the President (EOP)** to provide staff assistance for
the chief executive and to help coordinate the executive bureaucracy. Since that
time, a number of agencies have been created within the EOP to supply the president with advice and staff help. These agencies are as follows:

- White House Office (1939).
- Council of Economic Advisers (1946).
- National Security Council (1947).
- Office of the United States Trade Representative (1963).
- Council on Environmental Quality (1969).
- Office of Management and Budget (1970).
- Office of Science and Technology Policy (1976).
- Office of Administration (1977).
- Office of National Drug Control Policy (1988).
- Office of Policy Development (1993).

Several of the offices within the EOP are especially important, including the
White House Office, the Council of Economic Advisers, the Office of Management
and Budget, and the National Security Council. (As described in this chapter's
Making Waves, there are opportunities for young Americans to serve in EOP
positions.)

White House Office
The personal office of the president,
which tends to presidential political
needs and manages the media.

The White House Office.   One of the most important of the agencies within the
EOP is the **White House Office**, which includes most of the key personal and political advisers to the president. Among the jobs held by these aides are those of
legal counsel to the president, secretary, press secretary, and
appointments secretary. Often, the individuals who hold
these positions are recruited from the president's

making Waves

The White House Fellows

If you are interested in getting close to the center of power in
Washington, D.C., you should consider applying for the White
House Fellows program. For more than twenty years, a national,
nonpartisan competition has been held annually to nominate
White House Fellows. The selection criteria specify that the
applicants be U.S. citizens, be out of school and working in their
chosen profession, and have shown early achievement in their
careers. After a screening process, the final group of applicants
is interviewed, and eleven are chosen each year. They are then
assigned as assistants to high-level government officials and
paid at the rate of top-level civil servants.

SOME RECENT FELLOWS

Recent White House Fellows included Esther Benjamin, age
thirty, who has master's degrees in economics and international
affairs. Born in Sri Lanka, she moved to the United States at the
age of thirteen. She founded the Good Samaritan Fund to
finance education for victims of the civil war in her home country.
Her White House assignment was in the Department of Labor.

Melissa Goldstein, age twenty-nine, of Florence, Alabama,
interned in the Office of the Vice President during 1999–2000.
She has used her professional training as an attorney to work in

the field of medical ethics and consult with the National
Bioethics Advisory Commission. She also volunteers legal
services for clinics and hospitals.

Lance Wyatt of Los Angeles, a doctor, was assigned to the
Department of Veterans Affairs during his White House Fellows
year. At the age of thirty-two, Wyatt was a senior resident in general surgery. He is a co-founder of a worldwide organization
committed to providing health care to indigent adults and
children.

OUTSTANDING ALUMNI

The White House Fellows program targets outstanding young
adults and gives them an extraordinary experience in the offices
of top government officials. It includes individuals from all walks
of life. The alumni of the program include military leaders such as
General Colin Powell and General Wesley Clarke, the chief executive officers of Levi Strauss and Company and R. H. Macy and
Company, and the head of the Girl Scouts of America. Some, of
course, have political ambitions; Congressmen Joe Barton (R.,
Tex.) and Thomas Campbell (R., Calif.) and Senator Sam
Brownback (R., Kan.) are also graduates of the program.

CRITICAL ANALYSIS

*Do you think that it is worthwhile for some young Americans to
have this opportunity? Does it pay off in service to the country?*

campaign staff. Their duties—mainly protecting the president's political interests—are similar to campaign functions. In all recent administrations, one member of the White House Office has been named **chief of staff**. This person, who is responsible for coordinating the office, is one of the president's chief advisers.

Employees of the White House Office have been both envied and criticized. The White House Office, according to most former staffers, grants its employees access and power. They are able to use the resources of the White House to contact virtually anyone in the world by telephone, cable, fax, or electronic mail as well as to use the influence of the White House to persuade legislators and citizens. Because of this influence, staffers are often criticized for overstepping the bounds of the office. It is the appointments secretary who is able to grant or deny senators, representatives, and cabinet secretaries access to the president. It is the press secretary who grants to the press and television journalists access to any information about the president. White House staff members are closest to the president and may have considerable influence over the administration's decisions. Often, when presidents are under fire for their decisions, the staff is accused of keeping the chief executive too isolated from criticism or help. Presidents insist that they will not allow the staff to become too powerful, but given the difficulty of the office, each president eventually turns to staff members for loyal assistance and protection.

The Council of Economic Advisers.   The Employment Act of 1946 created a three-member **Council of Economic Advisers (CEA)** to advise the president on economic matters. The council's advice serves as the basis for the president's annual economic report to Congress. Each of the three members is appointed by the president and can be removed at will. In principle, the CEA was also created to advise the president on economic policy, but for the most part the function of the CEA has been to prepare the annual report.

The Office of Management and Budget.   The **Office of Management and Budget (OMB)** was originally the Bureau of the Budget, which was created in 1921 within the Department of the Treasury. Recognizing the importance of this agency, Franklin Roosevelt moved it into the White House Office in 1939. Richard Nixon reorganized the Bureau of the Budget in 1970 and changed its name to reflect its new managerial function. It is headed by a director, who must make up the annual federal budget that the president presents to Congress each January for approval. In principle, the director of the OMB has broad fiscal powers in planning and estimating various parts of the federal budget, because all agencies must submit their proposed budget to the OMB for approval. In reality, it is not so clear that the OMB truly can affect the greater scope of the federal budget. The OMB may be more important as a clearinghouse for legislative proposals initiated in the executive agencies.

The National Security Council.   The **National Security Council (NSC)** is a link between the president's key foreign and military advisers and the president. Its members consist of the president, the vice president, and the secretaries of state and defense, plus other informal members. The NSC has the resources of the National Security Agency (NSA) at its disposal in giving counsel to the president. (The NSA protects U.S. government communications and produces foreign intelligence information.) Included in the NSC is the president's special assistant for national security affairs. Richard Nixon had Henry Kissinger in this post; Jimmy Carter had the equally visible Zbigniew Brzezinksi. In the Reagan years, staff members of the NSC, including Lieutenant Colonel Oliver North and Admiral John Poindexter, were the focus of national media attention because of their involvement in the Iran-*contra* affair (discussed earlier in this chapter).

Chief of Staff
The person who is named to direct the White House Office and advise the president.

Council of Economic Advisers (CEA)
A staff agency in the Executive Office of the President that advises the president on measures to maintain stability in the nation's economy; established in 1946.

Office of Management and Budget (OMB)
A division of the Executive Office of the President created by executive order in 1970 to replace the Bureau of the Budget. The OMB's main functions are to assist the president in preparing the annual budget, to clear and coordinate all departmental agency budgets, to help set fiscal policy, and to supervise the administration of the federal budget.

National Security Council (NSC)
A staff agency in the Executive Office of the President established by the National Security Act of 1947. The NSC advises the president on domestic and foreign matters involving national security.

The Vice Presidency

The Constitution does not give much power to the vice president. The only formal duty is to preside over the Senate—which is rarely necessary. This obligation is fulfilled when the Senate organizes and adopts its rules and when the vice president is needed to decide a tie vote. In all other cases, the president pro tem manages parliamentary procedures in the Senate. The vice president is expected to participate only informally in senatorial deliberations, if at all.

The Vice President's Job

Vice presidents have traditionally been chosen by presidential nominees to balance the ticket to attract groups of voters or appease party factions. If a presidential nominee is from the North, it is not a bad idea to have a vice presidential nominee who is from the South or the West. If the presidential nominee is from a rural state, perhaps someone with an urban background would be most suitable as a running mate. Presidential nominees who are strongly conservative or strongly liberal would do well to have vice presidential nominees who are more in the middle of the political road.

In recent presidential elections, vice presidents have been selected for other reasons. Bill Clinton picked Al Gore to be his running mate in 1992 even though both were southern and moderates. The ticket appealed to younger voters and moderates, both of which were crucial to the election. In 2000, both vice presidential selections were intended to shore up the respective presidential candidates' "perceived weaknesses." Republican George W. Bush, who was subject to criticism for his lack of government experience and his "lightweight" personality, chose Dick Cheney, a former member of Congress who had also served as secretary of defense. Democrat Al Gore chose Senator Joe Lieberman of Connecticut, demonstrating his willingness to "take a chance" on a Jewish running mate. Significantly, Lieberman had been the first Democratic senator to criticize Bill Clinton's behavior in the Lewinsky case (see Chapter 5), thus bringing some moral authority to the Gore candidacy.[18]

---

[18]Note, though, that Lieberman did not vote against Clinton during the impeachment proceedings that followed an investigation of the Lewinsky scandal.

After taking office in 1993, Vice President Gore became known for his aggressive efforts to strengthen environmental-protection policies on a global basis. He also took a special interest in areas of emerging technology and was instrumental in providing subsidies to public schools for Internet use.

Vice presidents infrequently have become elected presidents in their own right. John Adams and Thomas Jefferson were the first to do so. Then Martin Van Buren was elected president in 1836 after he had served as Andrew Jackson's vice president for the previous eight years. In 1988, George Bush was elected to the presidency after eight years as Ronald Reagan's vice president.

The job of vice president is not extremely demanding, even when the president gives some specific task to the vice president. Typically, vice presidents spend their time supporting the president's activities. All of this changes, of course, if the president becomes disabled or dies in office.

Presidential Succession

Eight vice presidents have become president because of the death of the president. John Tyler, the first to do so, took over William Henry Harrison's position after only one month. No one knew whether Tyler should simply be a caretaker until a new president could be elected three and a half years later or whether he actually should be president. Tyler assumed that he was supposed to be the chief executive and he acted as such—although he was commonly referred to as "His Accidency." On all occasions since then, vice presidents taking over the position of the presidency because of the incumbent's death have assumed all of the presidential powers.

But what should a vice president do if a president becomes incapable of carrying out necessary duties while in office? When James Garfield was shot in 1881, he stayed alive for two and a half months. What was Vice President Chester Arthur's role?

This question was not addressed in the original Constitution. Article II, Section 1, says only that "in Case of the Removal of the President from Office,

DID YOU KNOW...
That President Richard Nixon served 56 days without a vice president, and that President Gerald Ford served 132 days without a vice president?

INFOTRAC ®
COLLEGE EDITION

2000 Democratic Nomination

An attempted assassination of Ronald Reagan occurred on March 31, 1981. In the foreground, press secretary James Brady lies seriously wounded. In the background, two men bend over President Reagan.

or of his Death, Resignation, or Inability to discharge the Powers and Duties of the said Office, the same shall devolve on the Vice President." There have been many instances of presidential disability. When Dwight Eisenhower became ill a second time in 1958, he entered into a pact with Richard Nixon that provided that the vice president could determine whether the president was incapable of carrying out his duties if the president could not communicate. John Kennedy and Lyndon Johnson entered into similar agreements with their vice presidents. Finally, in 1967, the **Twenty-fifth Amendment** was passed, establishing procedures in case of presidential incapacity.

The Twenty-Fifth Amendment

According to the Twenty-fifth Amendment, when the president believes that he is incapable of performing the duties of office, he must inform Congress in writing. Then the vice president serves as acting president until the president can resume his normal duties. When the president is unable to communicate, a majority of the cabinet, including the vice president, can declare that fact to Congress. Then the vice president serves as acting president until the president resumes his normal duties. If a dispute arises over the return of the president's ability to discharge his normal functions, a two-thirds vote of Congress is required to decide whether the vice president shall remain acting president or whether the president shall resume his duties.

Although President Reagan did not formally invoke the Twenty-fifth Amendment during his surgery for the removal of a cancerous growth in his colon on July 13, 1985, he followed its provisions in temporarily transferring power to the vice president, George Bush. At 10:32 A.M., before the operation began, Reagan signed letters to the speaker of the House and the president pro tem of the Senate directing that the vice president "shall discharge those powers and duties in my stead commencing with the administration of anesthesia to me." In the early evening of that same day, Reagan transmitted another letter to both officials announcing that he was again in charge. During this period, Vice President Bush signed no bills and took no actions as acting president. Although the Reagan administration claimed that the president's action set no precedents, most legal experts saw Reagan's acts as the first official use of the Twenty-fifth Amendment.

When the Vice Presidency Becomes Vacant

The Twenty-fifth Amendment also addresses the issue of how the president should fill a vacant vice presidency. Section 2 of the amendment simply states, "Whenever there is a vacancy in the office of the Vice President, the President shall nominate a Vice President who shall take office upon confirmation by a majority vote of both Houses of Congress." This is exactly what occurred when Richard Nixon's vice president, Spiro Agnew, resigned in 1973 because of his alleged receipt of construction contract kickbacks during his tenure as governor of Maryland. Nixon turned to Gerald Ford as his choice for vice president. After extensive hearings, both chambers of Congress confirmed the appointment. Then, when Nixon resigned on August 9, 1974, Ford automatically became president and nominated as his vice president Nelson Rockefeller. Congress confirmed Ford's choice. For the first time in the history of the country, both the president and the vice president were individuals who were not elected to their positions.

The question of who shall be president if both the president and vice president die is answered by the Succession Act of 1947. If the president and vice

Twenty-fifth Amendment
An amendment to the Constitution adopted in 1967 that establishes procedures for filling vacancies in the two top executive offices and that makes provisions for situations involving presidential disability.

Spiro Agnew was Richard Nixon's vice president from 1969 to 1973. Agnew resigned amid allegations of income tax evasion in connection with money he received when he was governor of Maryland.

president die, resign, or are disabled, the speaker of the House will act as president, after resigning from Congress. Next in line is the president pro tem of the Senate, followed by the cabinet officers in the order of the creation of their departments (see Table 13–3).

The Presidency: Issues for the Twenty-First Century

During the twentieth century, the responsibilities of world leadership and the growth of government led to enormous changes in the American presidency. The office changed from being that of "chief clerk" to being leader of the most powerful military force in the Western world and the chief operating officer of a huge organization that affects the lives of everyone in the nation. The relationship between the president and the electorate also changed, most notably through the growth of television as the major news source for most Americans. Presidential staffs work continuously to gain favorable images and reports on television and in the other media. It may be that our nation's fixation on image and popularity keeps us from considering the substance of public policy and tackling the work of making real policy choices.

Additionally, Congress, faced with impossible tasks in regulating the huge economy and overseeing the government, has delegated much of its lawmaking power to the president. After President Clinton and the Republican Congress had tested "gridlock" through the partial shutdowns of government in 1995, both the president and the majority Republicans found that their respective standing with the public was improved by cooperation in the legislative process. Because it appears that the public approves such "divided government," presidents in the future will need to work out their relationship with the opposition in Congress to be able to pursue their policy goals.

Finally, the impact of the Clinton presidency on future presidents will only be known in the coming years. In the lawsuit brought against him by Paula Jones for sexual harassment, Clinton claimed that a sitting president could not be sued for past conduct. The Supreme Court held otherwise, thus setting a precedent that previously did not exist. Additionally, during Kenneth Starr's investigation of the Lewinsky affair, the president claimed various privileges in an attempt to prevent his White House counsel and members of the Secret Service from giving testimony about Clinton and his activities. It may be that President Clinton, by claiming these privileges and having them denied by the courts, has, in the long run, weakened the presidency. Future presidents may be reluctant to rely for advice on White House counsel, knowing that such communication may not be privileged. Future presidents will also face the possibility that they may be called to testify before a grand jury.

TABLE 13-3

Line of Succession to the Presidency of the United States

1. Vice president
2. Speaker of the House of Representatives
3. Senate president *pro tempore*
4. Secretary of state
5. Secretary of the treasury
6. Secretary of defense
7. Attorney general
8. Secretary of the interior
9. Secretary of agriculture
10. Secretary of commerce
11. Secretary of labor
12. Secretary of health and human services
13. Secretary of housing and urban development
14. Secretary of transportation
15. Secretary of energy
16. Secretary of education
17. Secretary of veterans affairs

making a difference

Communicating with the White House

Writing to the president of the United States has long been a way for citizens to express their political opinions. The most traditional form of communication is, of course, by letter. Letters to the president should be addressed to:

The President of the United States
The White House
1600 Pennsylvania Avenue N.W.
Washington, D.C. 20500

If you wish to write to the First Lady, letters may be sent to her at the same address. Will you get an answer? Almost certainly. The White House mail room is staffed by volunteers and paid employees who sort the mail for the president and tally the public's concerns. You may receive a standard response to your com-

ments or a more personal, detailed response.

You can also call the White House on the telephone and leave a message for the president or First Lady. To call the switchboard, call 202-456-1414, a number publicized by former Secretary of State James Baker when he told the Israelis publicly, "When you're serious about peace, call us at . . . ." The switchboard received more than eight thousand calls in the next twenty-four hours.

The White House also has a round-the-clock comment line, which you can reach at 202-456-1111. When you call that number, an operator will take down your comments and forward them to the president's office. Again, the operators tally the calls to give the president a measurement of opinion on specific topics.

In this electronic age, the White House has been aggressive in its use of the Internet and the World Wide Web. The home page for the White House is listed in the *Logging on* feature at the end of this chapter. It is always designed to be entertaining and to convey information about the president. You can, however, easily send your comments and ideas to the White House via e-mail. Send comments to the president to

President@whitehouse.gov

Address e-mail to the First Lady at

First.Lady@whitehouse.gov

You will receive an electronic response to your mail from the White House staff. Due to the extremely heavy e-mail load, you will only receive one response per day regardless of how many messages you send.

Key terms

advice and consent 419

appointment power 415

cabinet 437

chief diplomat 419

chief executive 415

chief legislator 421

chief of staff 439

chief of state 415

civil service 415

commander in chief 418

constitutional power 426

Council of Economic Advisers (CEA) 439

diplomatic recognition 419

emergency power 432

executive agreement 421

Executive Office of the President (EOP) 438

executive order 432

executive privilege 433

expressed power 426

Federal Register 432

impeachment 434

inherent power 426

kitchen cabinet 437

line-item veto 423

National Security Council (NSC) 439

Office of Management and Budget (OMB) 439

pardon 417

patronage 427

pocket veto 423

reprieve 417

State of the Union message 421

statutory power 426

Twelfth Amendment 414

Twenty-fifth Amendment 442

veto message 422

War Powers Resolution 419

Washington community 429

White House Office 438

Chapter summary

1 The office of the presidency in the United States, combining as it does the functions of chief of state and chief executive, is unique. The framers of the Constitution were divided over whether the president should be a weak executive controlled by the legislature or a strong executive.

2 The requirements for the office of the presidency are outlined in Article II, Section 1, of the Constitution. The president's roles include both formal and informal duties. The president is chief of state, chief executive, commander in chief, chief diplomat, chief legislator, and party chief.

3 As chief of state, the president is ceremonial head of the government. As chief executive, the president is bound to enforce the acts of Congress, the judgments of the federal courts, and treaties. The chief executive has the power of appointment and the power to grant reprieves and pardons.

4 As commander in chief, the president is the ultimate decision maker in military matters. As chief diplomat, the president recognizes foreign governments, negotiates treaties, signs agreements, and nominates and receives ambassadors.

5 The role of chief legislator includes recommending legislation to Congress, lobbying for the legislation, approving laws, and exercising the veto power. The president also has statutory powers written into law by Congress. The president is also leader of his or her political party. Presidents use their power to persuade and their access to the media to fulfill this function.

6 Presidents have a variety of special powers not available to other branches of the government. These include emergency power, executive power, executive privilege, and impoundment of funds.

7 Abuses of executive power are dealt with by Articles I and II of the Constitution, which authorize the House and Senate to impeach and remove the president, vice president, or other officers of the federal government for crimes of "Treason, Bribery or other high Crimes and Misdemeanors."

8 The president gets assistance from the cabinet and from the Executive Office of the President (including the White House Office).

9 The vice president is the constitutional officer assigned to preside over the Senate and to assume the presidency in case of the death, resignation, removal, or disability of the president. The Twenty-fifth Amendment, passed in 1967, established procedures to be followed in case of presidential incapacity and when filling a vacant vice presidency.

Selected print and electronic resources

SUGGESTED READINGS

Gelderman, Carol. *All the Presidents' Words: The Bully Pulpit and the Creation of the Virtual Presidency.* New York: Walker & Company, 1997. Gelderman examines the speeches of the presidents, demonstrating how the goals of presidential speeches have shifted from true speech making and powerful rhetoric to "spin" and "staying on message."

Greenstein, Fred I. *The Presidential Difference: Leadership Style from Roosevelt to Clinton.* Old Tappan, N.J.: Free Press, 2000. In this book, an eminent presidential scholar examines and discusses the leadership styles of eleven chief executives. Greenstein assesses each president in several categories including organization, skill, vision, and emotional intelligence.

Kernell, Samuel. *Going Public: New Strategies of Presidential Leadership,* 3d ed. Washington, D.C.: Congressional Quarterly Press, 1997. Kernell updates his classic work on how presidents go "over the head of Congress" to the people and includes examples from the Clinton presidency.

Kunhardt, Peter W., and Philip B. Kunhardt, III. *The American President.* New York: Riverhead Books, 1999. Although this book is aimed at general readership, it contains hundreds of facts and interesting anecdotes about the presidents from Washington to Clinton.

McDonald, Forrest. *The American Presidency: An Intellectual History.* Lawrence, Kans.: University Press of Kansas, 1994. This intellectual history traces the development of the presidency and its powers from the early colonial governors through the American Revolution, the Constitutional Convention, and the early presidents.

Pious, Richard M. *The Presidency.* Boston: Allyn and Bacon, 1996. In this comprehensive look at the presidency, the author uses examples from many presidencies, including the Clinton administration, to illustrate his discussions of presidential influence.

Posner, Richard A. *An Affair of State: The Investigation, Impeachment, and Trial of President Clinton.* Cambridge, MA: Harvard University Press, 1999. The author, a federal judge, examines the investigation, impeachment, and trial of President Clinton from a careful legal point of view. He discusses a number of topics including whether a president can pardon himself and other fascinating nuances of the Clinton impeachment trial.

Reich, Robert B. *Locked in the Cabinet.* New York: Random House, 1998. This memoir is a lively, anecdote-filled account of life in Washington, D.C., during Reich's four years as secretary of labor

MEDIA RESOURCES

Sunrise at Campobello—An excellent portrait of one of the greatest presidents, Franklin Delano Roosevelt, produced in 1960 and starring Ralph Bellamy.

LBJ: A Biography—An acclaimed biography of Lyndon Johnson that covers his rise to power, his presidency, and the events of the Vietnam War, which ended his presidency; produced in 1991 as part of PBS's *The American Experience* series.

Nixon—An excellent 1995 film exposing the events of Richard Nixon's troubled presidency; Anthony Hopkins plays the embattled but brilliant chief executive.

Logging on

This is a site from which you can obtain extensive information on the White House and the presidency:

http://www.whitehouse.gov

The Library of Congress White House page is a great source of information and has numerous presidency-related links. The URL is

http://lcweb.loc.gov/global

The White House archives at Texas A&M are helpful for researching documents and other academic resources. You can reach these archives at

http://www.tamu.edu/whitehouse

Inaugural addresses of American presidents from Washington to Clinton can be found at

www.bartleby.com/index.html

Using the Internet for political analysis

Take a look at the activities of the president of the United States by clicking on the White House at

http://www.whitehouse.gov

and the Government Documents site, SunSITE, at

http://metalab.unc.edu/govdocs.html

Try to find the president's schedule for a day or a week, or read at least two speeches he has given within the last few months. After you have read these documents, decide which role the president was playing when he engaged in certain activities or made certain statements: commander in chief, chief legislator, and so on.

You then might want to search a site such as that of the *Congressional Quarterly* at

http://www.cq.com

or AllPolitics at

http://www.cnn.com/ALLPOLITICS

and look at articles from the same date as the president's speech for an alternative view of what he was proposing.

chapter 14
The Bureaucracy

CHAPTER OUTLINE

- The Nature of Bureaucracy
- Theories of Bureaucracy
- The Size of the Bureaucracy
- The Organization of the Federal Bureaucracy
- Staffing the Bureaucracy
- Modern Attempts at Bureaucratic Reform
- Bureaucrats as Politicians and Policymakers
- Congressional Control of the Bureaucracy

what if...

We Had a "Virtual" Bureaucracy?

BACKGROUND

THE INTERNET HAS BECOME AN INTE-GRAL PART OF OUR SOCIETY, INCLUDING THE GOVERNMENT. ADMINISTRATIVE AGENCIES AT ALL LEVELS OF GOVERN-MENT NOW HAVE WEB SITES ON WHICH THEY PROVIDE A HOST OF INFORMA-TION, RANGING FROM THE LAWS THEY ADMINISTER AND THE DATA THEY COL-LECT TO VARIOUS FORMS USED BY CITIZENS DEALING WITH THE AGENCIES. THE INTERNAL REVENUE SERVICE NOW ALLOWS CITIZENS TO FILE THEIR TAX RETURNS ELECTRONICALLY. A NUMBER OF COURTS AROUND THE NATION PER-MIT LAWSUITS TO BE FILED VIA THE INTERNET. STATE AND LOCAL GOVERN-MENTS ARE EXPERIMENTING WITH THE DELIVERY OF A NUMBER OF DIFFERENT TYPES OF GOVERNMENT SERVICES VIA THE WEB (SEE, FOR EXAMPLE, THE *E-MOCRACY* FEATURES IN CHAPTER 1 AND CHAPTER 18).

THERE IS LITTLE DOUBT THAT THE GOVERNMENT'S USE OF THE WEB WILL CONTINUE TO EXPAND. BUT WHAT IF WE HAD A VIRTUAL BUREAU-CRACY IN WHICH GOVERNMENT AGEN-CIES WERE REQUIRED TO CONDUCT *ALL* OF THEIR ACTIVITIES AND FUNC-TIONS ONLINE? HOW WOULD THIS ALTER THE OPERATIONS OF THE SO-CALLED FOURTH BRANCH OF GOVERNMENT—THE BUREAUCRACY?

WHAT IF WE HAD A "VIRTUAL" BUREAUCRACY

If all government agency functions had to be conducted online, we would have a truly "faceless" bureaucracy. A person who wanted to apply for Medicare, for example, would not go to the nearest Social Security office for assistance. Rather, he or she would go to the Social Security Administration's Web site, fill out the relevant forms, and submit them to the agency online. If the person needed assistance, he or she might be asked to e-mail an agency representative, who would then send a return message with the appropriate response. Alternatively, the agency might make a "chat room" available so that online "conversations" between agency representatives and clients could take place.

Clearly, doing business with the government solely via the Internet would mean that there would no longer be any personal, face-to-face interaction. Yet "wired" government would offer an obvious advantage: citizens would not have to spend time driving to government offices, waiting in lines for assistance, and so on.

VIRTUAL GOVERNMENT WOULD BE COST-EFFECTIVE

If all government services were delivered online, the cost of government would certainly be reduced. Consider the federal bureaucracy. Many agencies in the federal government have regional and local offices around the country, in addition to their offices in Washington, D.C. By performing all of its functions online, the federal bureaucracy could save the costs of obtaining and maintaining these regional and local offices.

If the bureaucracy were totally online, the government might also be able to cut its work force significantly. Currently, many government employees spend a good deal of their time help-ing citizens in face-to-face transactions. In an online bureaucracy, citizens would access agency forms and information online, and they would need less assistance. Also, employees would need to spend little, if any, time filling out paperwork, sending snail-mail, and so on.

EFFECTS ON POLICYMAKING

We can speculate that a virtual bureaucracy could have significant consequences for policy-making. Bureaucrats are pressured by lobbyists representing special interests, just as members of Congress are. Additionally, as you will read later in this chapter, agency representatives are often participants in "iron triangles"—three-way networks among legislators, bureaucrats, and interest groups—that play a key role in govern-ment policymaking.

If bureaucrats were restricted to online com-munications with these groups, there might be more "openness" in government. A private con-versation between a lobbyist and a bureaucrat over lunch is one thing; an online conversation via e-mail or in an agency "chat room" is quite another—because the agency's backup storage devices would have a more or less permanent record of all that was said. Similarly, there would be digital records of any official communications between members of Congress and bureau-crats. Certainly, the way deals are made among these groups would change.

FOR CRITICAL ANALYSIS

1. Do you think that a virtual bureaucracy will ever become a reality in this country? Why or why not?
2. Can you think of any significant drawbacks to having a virtual bureaucracy?

Virtually every modern president, at one time or another, has proclaimed that his administration was going to "fix government." As you can see in Table 14–1, all modern presidents also have put forth plans to end government waste and inefficiency. While none has come out in favor of a virtual bureaucracy, a possibility discussed in this chapter's opening *What If . . .* , they all have declared their intention to reform the bureaucracy. Their success has been, in a word, underwhelming. Presidents have been generally powerless to affect the structure and operation of the federal bureaucracy significantly.

The bureaucracy has been called the "fourth branch of government," even though you will find no reference to the bureaucracy in the original Constitution or in the twenty-seven amendments that have been passed since 1787. But Article II, Section 2, of the Constitution gives the president the power to appoint "all other Officers of the United States, whose Appointments are not herein otherwise provided for." Article II, Section 3, states that the president "shall take Care that the Laws be faithfully executed, and shall Commission all the Officers of the United States." Constitutional scholars believe that the legal basis for the bureaucracy rests on these two sections in Article II.

The Nature of Bureaucracy

A **bureaucracy** is the name given to a large organization that is structured hierarchically to carry out specific functions. Generally, most bureaucracies are characterized by an organization chart. The units of the organization are divided according to the specialization and expertise of the employees.

Bureaucracy
A large organization that is structured hierarchically to carry out specific functions.

Public and Private Bureaucracies

We should not think of bureaucracy as unique to government. Any large corporation or university can be considered a bureaucratic organization. The fact is that the handling of complex problems requires a division of labor. Individuals must concentrate their skills on specific, well-defined aspects of a problem and depend on others to solve the rest of it.

Public or government bureaucracies differ from private organizations in some important ways, however. A private corporation, such as Microsoft, has a single set of leaders, its board of directors. Public bureaucracies, in contrast, do not have a single set of leaders. Although the president is the chief administrator of the federal system, all bureaucratic agencies are subject to the desires of Congress for their funding, staffing, and, indeed, their continued existence. Furthermore, public bureaucracies supposedly serve the citizen rather than the stockholder.

TABLE 14–1

Selected Presidential Plans to End Government Inefficiency

PRESIDENT	NAME OF PLAN
Lyndon Johnson (1963–1969)	Programming, Planning, and Budgeting Systems
Richard Nixon (1969–1974)	Management by Objectives
Jimmy Carter (1977–1981)	Zero-Based Budgeting
Ronald Reagan (1981–1989)	President's Private Sector Survey on Cost Control (the Grace Commission)
George Bush (1989–1993)	Right-Sizing Government
Bill Clinton (1993–2001)	"From Red Tape to Results: Creating a Government That Works Better and Costs Less"

One other important difference between private corporations and government bureaucracies is that government bureaucracies are not organized to make a profit. Rather, they are supposed to perform their functions as efficiently as possible to conserve the taxpayers' dollars. Perhaps it is this aspect of government organization that makes citizens hostile toward government bureaucracy when they experience inefficiency and red tape.

These characteristics, together with the prevalence and size of the government bureaucracies, make them an important factor in American life.

Bureaucracies Compared

The federal bureaucracy in the United States enjoys a greater degree of autonomy than do federal or national bureaucracies in most other countries. Much of the insularity that is commonly supposed to characterize the bureaucracy in this country may stem from the sheer size of the government organizations needed to implement a budget that exceeds $1.8 trillion. Because the lines of authority often are not well defined, some bureaucracies may be able to operate with a significant degree of autonomy.

The federal nature of the American government also means that national bureaucracies regularly provide financial assistance to their state counterparts. Both the Department of Education and the Department of Housing and Urban Development, for example, distribute funds to their counterparts at the state level. In contrast, most bureaucracies in European countries have a top-down command structure so that national programs may be implemented directly at the lower level. This is due not only to the small size of most European countries but also to the fact that public ownership of such things as telephone companies, airlines, railroads, and utilities is far more common in Europe than in the United States. (For a discussion of another way in which the U.S. bureaucracy differs from bureaucracies in other countries, see the feature *Global View: No More Bribes to Bureaucrats.*)

The fact that the U.S. government owns relatively few enterprises does not mean, however, that its bureaucracies are comparatively powerless. Indeed,

global view

No More Bribes to Bureaucrats

In many foreign countries, the government exercises extensive control over trade and industry, and thus decisions on most major construction and manufacturing contracts are made by government bureaucrats. In these nations, making side payments ("gifts") to government officials in exchange for favorable business contracts is an age-old custom and, until recently, typically was not considered unethical. Indeed, languages around the world have a word designating such payments—including "ghagshish" in the Middle East, "suborno" in South America, "dash" in West Africa, "podkup" in Russia, and "kickbacks" in the United States.

In 1977, the U.S. Congress passed the Foreign Corrupt Practices Act (FCPA), which prohibits Americans doing business abroad from bribing foreign officials to secure advantageous contracts. In effect, the law put U.S. businesspersons at a relative disadvantage in the international marketplace. Consider that in a recent two-year period, according to the U.S.

Department of Commerce, American companies lost more than one hundred international contracts, valued at $45 billion, because they (but not their competitors) were prohibited from bribing foreign officials.

For twenty years, the FCPA was the only law of its kind in the world, despite attempts by U.S. political leaders to convince other nations to pass similar legislation. That situation started to change in the late 1990s, however, when the members of the Organization for Economic Cooperation and Development (OECD) signed a convention (treaty) that made the bribery of foreign public officials a serious crime. Each of the twenty-six industrialized nations that belong to the OECD is obligated to enact legislation in accordance with the treaty. The agreement will not only improve the ethical climate in international trade but also level the playing field for U.S. businesspersons.

FOR CRITICAL ANALYSIS

What is the difference between bribing a public official and contributing to a politician's campaign in the hope of gaining favorable treatment?

there are numerous **administrative agencies** in the federal bureaucracy—such as the Environmental Protection Agency, the Nuclear Regulatory Commission, and the Securities and Exchange Commission—that extensively regulate private companies even though they virtually never have an ownership interest in those companies.

Theories of Bureaucracy

Several theories have been offered to help us understand better the ways in which bureaucracies function. Each of these theories focuses on specific features of bureaucracies.

The Weberian Model

The classic model, or **Weberian model,** of the modern bureaucracy was proposed by the German sociologist Max Weber.[1] He argued that the increasingly complex nature of modern life, coupled with the steadily growing demands placed on governments by their citizens, made the formation of bureaucracies inevitable. According to Weber, most bureaucracies—whether in the public or private sector—are hierarchically organized and governed by formal procedures. The power in a bureaucracy flows from the top downward. Decision-making processes in bureaucracies are shaped by detailed technical rules that promote similar decisions in similar situations. Bureaucrats are specialists who attempt to resolve problems through logical reasoning and data analysis instead of "gut feelings" and guesswork. Individual advancement in bureaucracies is supposed to be based on merit rather than political connections. Indeed, the modern bureaucracy, according to Weber, should be an apolitical organization.

---

[1]Max Weber, *Theory of Social and Economic Organization,* ed. Talcott Parsons (New York: Oxford University Press, 1974).

Administrative Agency
A federal, state, or local government unit established to perform a specific function. Administrative agencies are created and authorized by legislative bodies to administer and enforce specific laws.

Weberian Model
A model of bureaucracy developed by the German sociologist Max Weber, who viewed bureaucracies as rational, hierarchical organizations in which power flows from the top downward and decisions are based on logical reasoning and data analysis.

The Department of Agriculture inspects meat-packing facilities throughout the United States, certifying the quality and condition of the meat to be sold. Why is it necessary for the U.S. government to have administrative agencies such as the Department of Agriculture?

Acquisitive Model
A model of bureaucracy that views top-level bureaucrats as seeking constantly to expand the size of their budgets and the staffs of their departments or agencies so as to gain greater power and influence in the public sector.

Monopolistic Model
A model of bureaucracy that compares bureaucracies to monopolistic business firms. Lack of competition within a bureaucracy leads to inefficient and costly operations. Because bureaucracies are not penalized for inefficiency, there is no incentive to reduce costs or use resources more productively.

Garbage Can Model
A model of bureaucracy that characterizes bureaucracies as rudderless entities with little formal organization in which solutions to problems are based on trial and error rather than rational policy planning.

The Acquisitive Model

Other theorists do not view bureaucracies in terms as benign as Weber's. Some believe that bureaucracies are acquisitive in nature. Proponents of the **acquisitive model** argue that top-level bureaucrats will always try to expand, or at least to avoid any reductions in, the size of their budgets. Although government bureaucracies are not-for-profit enterprises, bureaucrats want to maximize the size of their budgets and staffs, because these things are the most visible trappings of power in the public sector. These efforts are also prompted by the desire of bureaucrats to "sell" their products—national defense, public housing, agricultural subsidies, and so on—to both Congress and the public.

The Monopolistic Model

Because government bureaucracies seldom have competitors, some theorists have suggested that bureaucratic organizations may be explained best by using a **monopolistic model**. The analysis is similar to that used by economists to examine the behavior of monopolistic firms. Monopolistic bureaucracies—like monopolistic firms—essentially have no competitors and act accordingly. Because monopolistic bureaucracies usually are not penalized for chronic inefficiency, they have little reason to adopt cost-saving measures or to make more productive uses of their resources. Some economists have argued that such problems can be cured only by privatizing certain bureaucratic functions.

The Garbage Can Model

The image of a bumbling, rudderless organization is offered by proponents of the **garbage can model** of bureaucracy. This theory presupposes that bureaucracies rarely act in any purposeful or coherent manner but instead bumble along aimlessly in search of solutions to particular problems. This model views bureaucracies as having relatively little formal organization. The solutions to problems are obtained not by the smooth implementation of well-planned policies but instead by trial and error. Choosing the right policy is tricky, because usually it is not possible to determine in advance which solution is best. Thus, bureaucrats may have to try one, two, three, or even more policies before they obtain a satisfactory result.

The Size of the Bureaucracy

In 1789, the new government's bureaucracy was minuscule. There were three departments—State (with nine employees), War (with two employees), and Treasury (with thirty-nine employees)—and the Office of the Attorney General (which later became the Department of Justice). The bureaucracy was still small in 1798. At that time, the secretary of state had seven clerks and spent a total of $500 (about $5,900 in 2001 dollars) on stationery and printing. In that same year, the Appropriations Act allocated $1.4 million to the War Department (or $16.4 million in 2001 dollars).[2]

Times have changed, as we can see in Figure 14–1, which lists the various federal agencies and the number of civilian employees in each. Excluding the military, approximately 2.8 million government employees constitute the federal bureaucracy. That number has remained relatively stable for the last several decades. It is somewhat deceiving, however, because there are many

---

[2]Leonard D. White, *The Federalists: A Study in Administrative History, 1789–1801* (New York: Free Press, 1948).

FIGURE 14-1
Federal Agencies and Their Respective Numbers of Civilian Employees

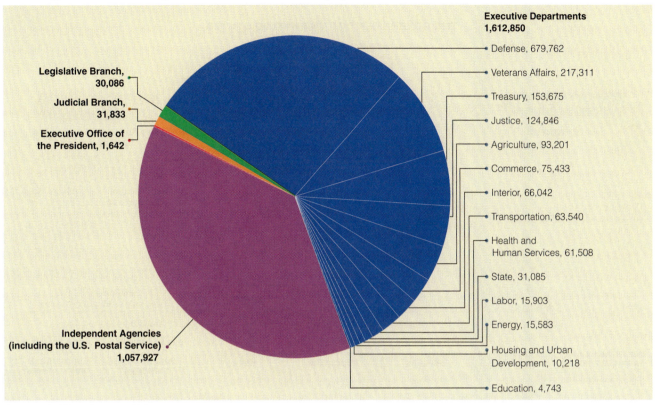

SOURCE: U.S. Office of Personnel Management, 2000.

others working directly or indirectly for the federal government as subcontractors or consultants and in other capacities. In fact, according to some studies, the federal work force vastly exceeds the number of official federal workers.[3]

The figures for federal government employment are only part of the story. Figure 14-2 shows the growth in government employment at the federal, state, and local levels. Since 1970, this growth has been mainly at the state and local levels. If all government employees are counted, then, more than 15 percent of all civilian employment is accounted for by government.

The costs of the bureaucracy are commensurately high and growing. The share of the gross national product taken up by all government spending was only 8.5 percent in 1929. Today, it exceeds 40 percent.

The Organization of the Federal Bureaucracy

Within the federal bureaucracy are a number of different types of government agencies and organizations. Figure 14-3 on the next page outlines the several bureaucracies within the executive branch, as well as the separate organizations that provide services to Congress, to the courts, and directly to the president. In

[3]See, for example, Paul C. Light, *The True Size of Government* (Washington, D.C.: Brookings Institution Press, 1999).

FIGURE 14-2
Government Employment at the Federal, State, and Local Levels

There are more local government employees than federal and state employees combined.

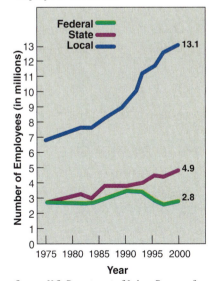

SOURCE: U.S. Department of Labor, Bureau of Labor Statistics, *Monthly Labor Review,* various issues. Data for state and local government employment in 2000 are estimates.

FIGURE 14-3

Organization Chart of the Federal Government

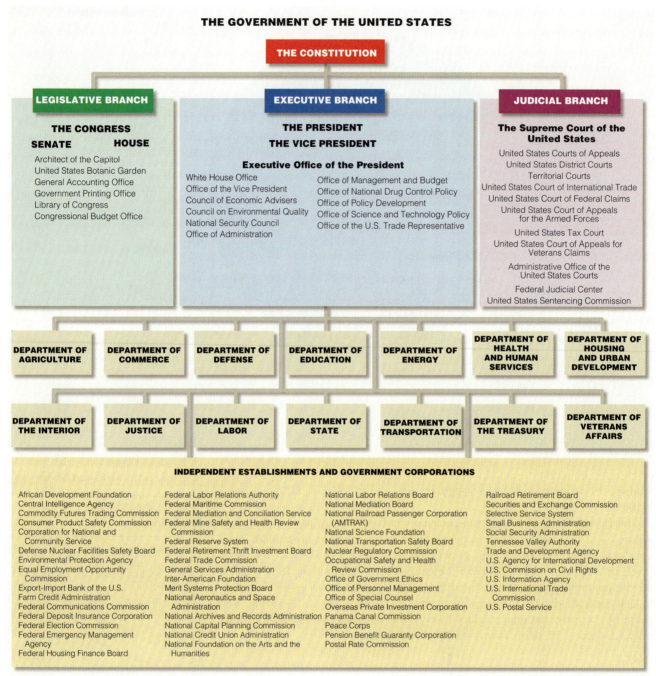

THE GOVERNMENT OF THE UNITED STATES

THE CONSTITUTION

LEGISLATIVE BRANCH

THE CONGRESS
SENATE   HOUSE

Architect of the Capitol
United States Botanic Garden
General Accounting Office
Government Printing Office
Library of Congress
Congressional Budget Office

EXECUTIVE BRANCH

THE PRESIDENT
THE VICE PRESIDENT

Executive Office of the President

White House Office   Office of Management and Budget
Office of the Vice President   Office of National Drug Control Policy
Council of Economic Advisers   Office of Policy Development
Council on Environmental Quality   Office of Science and Technology Policy
National Security Council   Office of the U.S. Trade Representative
Office of Administration

JUDICIAL BRANCH

**The Supreme Court of the
United States**

United States Courts of Appeals
United States District Courts
Territorial Courts
United States Court of International Trade
United States Court of Federal Claims
United States Court of Appeals
for the Armed Forces
United States Tax Court
United States Court of Appeals for
Veterans Claims
Administrative Office of the
United States Courts
Federal Judicial Center
United States Sentencing Commission

DEPARTMENT OF AGRICULTURE | **DEPARTMENT OF COMMERCE** | **DEPARTMENT OF DEFENSE** | **DEPARTMENT OF EDUCATION** | **DEPARTMENT OF ENERGY** | **DEPARTMENT OF HEALTH AND HUMAN SERVICES** | **DEPARTMENT OF HOUSING AND URBAN DEVELOPMENT**

DEPARTMENT OF THE INTERIOR | **DEPARTMENT OF JUSTICE** | **DEPARTMENT OF LABOR** | **DEPARTMENT OF STATE** | **DEPARTMENT OF TRANSPORTATION** | **DEPARTMENT OF THE TREASURY** | **DEPARTMENT OF VETERANS AFFAIRS**

INDEPENDENT ESTABLISHMENTS AND GOVERNMENT CORPORATIONS

African Development Foundation
Central Intelligence Agency
Commodity Futures Trading Commission
Consumer Product Safety Commission
Corporation for National and
  Community Service
Defense Nuclear Facilities Safety Board
Environmental Protection Agency
Equal Employment Opportunity
  Commission
Export-Import Bank of the U.S.
Farm Credit Administration
Federal Communications Commission
Federal Deposit Insurance Corporation
Federal Election Commission
Federal Emergency Management
  Agency
Federal Housing Finance Board

Federal Labor Relations Authority
Federal Maritime Commission
Federal Mediation and Conciliation Service
Federal Mine Safety and Health Review
  Commission
Federal Reserve System
Federal Retirement Thrift Investment Board
Federal Trade Commission
General Services Administration
Inter-American Foundation
Merit Systems Protection Board
National Aeronautics and Space
  Administration
National Archives and Records Administration
National Capital Planning Commission
National Credit Union Administration
National Foundation on the Arts and the
  Humanities

National Labor Relations Board
National Mediation Board
National Railroad Passenger Corporation
  (AMTRAK)
National Science Foundation
National Transportation Safety Board
Nuclear Regulatory Commission
Occupational Safety and Health
  Review Commission
Office of Government Ethics
Office of Personnel Management
Office of Special Counsel
Overseas Private Investment Corporation
Panama Canal Commission
Peace Corps
Pension Benefit Guaranty Corporation
Postal Rate Commission

Railroad Retirement Board
Securities and Exchange Commission
Selective Service System
Small Business Administration
Social Security Administration
Tennessee Valley Authority
Trade and Development Agency
U.S. Agency for International Development
U.S. Commission on Civil Rights
U.S. Information Agency
U.S. International Trade
  Commission
U.S. Postal Service

SOURCE: *United States Government Manual, 2000/01* (Washington, D.C.: U.S. Government Printing Office, 2000), p. 22.

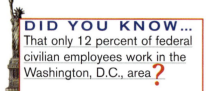

DID YOU KNOW...
That only 12 percent of federal
civilian employees work in the
Washington, D.C., area **?**

Chapter 13, we discussed those agencies that are considered to be part of the Executive Office of the President.

The executive branch, which employs most of the bureaucrats, has four major types of bureaucratic structures. They are (1) cabinet departments, (2) independent executive agencies, (3) independent regulatory agencies, and (4) government corporations. Each has a distinctive relationship to the president, and some have unusual internal structures, overall goals, and grants of power.

Cabinet Departments

The fourteen **cabinet departments** are the major service organizations of the federal government. They can also be described in management terms as **line organizations.** This means that they are directly accountable to the president and are responsible for performing government functions, such as printing money or training troops. These departments were created by Congress when the need for each department arose. The first department to be created was State, and the most recent one was Veterans Affairs, established in 1988. A president might ask that a new department be created or an old one abolished, but the president has no power to do so without legislative approval from Congress.

Each department is headed by a secretary (except for the Justice Department, which is headed by the attorney general) and has several levels of undersecretaries, assistant secretaries, and so on.

Presidents theoretically have considerable control over the cabinet departments, because presidents are able to appoint or fire all of the top officials. Even cabinet departments do not always respond to the president's wishes, though. One reason that presidents are frequently unhappy with their departments is that the entire bureaucratic structure below the top political levels is staffed by permanent employees, many of whom are committed to established programs or procedures and who resist change. As we can see from Table 14-2 on the next page, each cabinet department employs thousands of individuals, only a handful of whom are under the control of the president. The table also describes the functions of each of the cabinet departments.

Independent Executive Agencies

Independent executive agencies are bureaucratic organizations that are not located within a department but report directly to the president, who appoints their chief officials. When a new federal agency is created—the Environmental Protection Agency, for example—Congress decides where it will be located in the bureaucracy. In this century, presidents often have asked that a new organization be kept separate or independent rather than added to an existing department, particularly if a department may in fact be hostile to the agency's creation. Table 14-3 on page 457 describes the functions of several selected independent executive agencies.

Independent Regulatory Agencies

The **independent regulatory agencies** are typically responsible for a specific type of public policy. Their function is to make and implement rules and regulations in a particular sector of the economy to protect the public interest. The earliest such agency was the Interstate Commerce Commission (ICC), which was established in 1887 when Americans began to seek some form of government control over the rapidly growing business and industrial sector. This new form of organization, the independent regulatory agency, was supposed to make technical, nonpolitical decisions about rates, profits, and rules that would be for the benefit of all and that did not require congressional legislation. In the years that followed the creation of the ICC, other agencies were formed to regulate communication (the Federal Communications Commission), nuclear power (the Nuclear Regulatory Commission), and so on. (The ICC was abolished on December 30, 1995.)

The Purpose and Nature of Regulatory Agencies

The regulatory agencies are administered independently of all three branches of government. They were set up because Congress felt it was unable to handle the

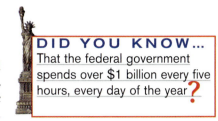

DID YOU KNOW...
That the federal government spends over $1 billion every five hours, every day of the year?

Cabinet Department
One of the fourteen departments of the executive branch (State, Treasury, Defense, Justice, Interior, Agriculture, Commerce, Labor, Health and Human Services, Housing and Urban Development, Education, Energy, Transportation, and Veterans Affairs).

Line Organization
With respect to the federal government, an administrative unit that is directly accountable to the president.

Independent Executive Agency
A federal agency that is not part of a cabinet department but reports directly to the president.

Independent Regulatory Agency
An agency outside the major executive departments charged with making and implementing rules and regulations to protect the public interest.

TABLE 14-2

Executive Departments

Department and Year Established	Principal Functions	Most Important Subagencies
State (1789) (31,085 employees)	Negotiates treaties; develops foreign policy; protects citizens abroad.	Passport Agency; Bureau of Diplomatic Security; Foreign Service; Bureau of Human Rights and Humanitarian Affairs; Bureau of Consular Affairs.
Treasury (1789) (153,675 employees)	Pays all federal bills; borrows money; collects federal taxes, mints coins and prints paper currency; operates the Secret Service; supervises national banks.	Internal Revenue Service; Bureau of Alcohol, Tobacco, and Firearms; U.S. Secret Service; U.S. Mint; Customs Service.
Interior (1849) (66,042 employees)	Supervises federally owned lands and parks; operates federal hydroelectric power facilities; supervises Native American affairs.	U.S. Fish and Wildlife Service; National Park Service; Bureau of Indian Affairs; Bureau of Land Management.
Justice (1870)* (124,846 employees)	Furnishes legal advice to the president; enforces federal criminal laws; supervises the federal corrections systems (prisons).	Federal Bureau of Investigation; Drug Enforcement Administration; Bureau of Prisons; Immigration and Naturalization Service.
Agriculture (1889) (93,201 employees)	Provides assistance to farmers and ranchers; conducts research to improve agricultural activity and to prevent plant disease; works to protect forests from fires and disease.	Soil Conservation Service; Agricultural Research Service; Food and Safety Inspection Service; Federal Crop Insurance Corporation; Farmers Home Administration.
Commerce (1913)† (75,433 employees)	Grants patents and trademarks; conducts a national census; monitors the weather; protects the interests of businesses.	Bureau of the Census; Bureau of Economic Analysis; Minority Business Development Agency; Patent and Trademark Office; National Oceanic and Atmospheric Administration; U.S. Travel and Tourism Administration.
Labor (1913) (15,903 employees)	Administers federal labor laws; promotes the interests of workers.	Occupational Safety and Health Administration (OSHA); Bureau of Labor Statistics; Employment Standards Administration; Office of Labor-Management Standards.
Defense (1947)‡ (679,762 employees)	Manages the armed forces (army, navy, air force, and marines); operates military bases; is responsible for civil defense.	National Guard; National Security Agency; Joint Chiefs of Staff; Departments of the Air Force, Navy, Army.
Housing and Urban Development (1965) (10,218 employees)	Deals with the nation's housing needs; develops and rehabilitates urban communities; promotes improvement in city streets and parks.	Office of Block Grant Assistance; Emergency Shelter Grants Program; Office of Urban Development Action Grants; Office of Fair Housing and Equal Opportunity.
Transportation (1967) (63,540 employees)	Finances improvements in mass transit; develops and administers programs for highways, railroads, and aviation; is involved with offshore maritime safety.	Federal Aviation Administration; Federal Highway Administration; National Highway Traffic Safety Administration; U.S. Coast Guard; Federal Transit Administration.
Energy (1977) (15,583 employees)	Is involved in the conservation of energy and resources; analyzes energy data; conducts research and development.	Office of Civilian Radioactive Waste Management; Bonneville Power Administration; Office of Nuclear Energy; Energy Information Administration; Office of Conservation and Renewable Energy.
Health and Human Services (1979)§ (61,508 employees)	Promotes public health; enforces pure food and drug laws; is involved in health-related research.	Food and Drug Administration; Administration for Children and Families; Health Care Financing Administration; Public Health Service.
Education (1979)§ (4,743 employees)	Coordinates federal programs and policies for education; administers aid to education; promotes educational research.	Office of Special Education and Rehabilitation Service; Office of Elementary and Secondary Education; Office of Postsecondary Education; Office of Vocational and Adult Education.
Veterans Affairs (1988) (217,311 employees)	Promotes the welfare of veterans of the U.S. armed forces.	Veterans Health Administration; Veterans Benefits Administration; National Cemetery Systems.

*Formed from the Office of the Attorney General (created in 1789).
†Formed from the Department of Commerce and Labor (created in 1903).
‡Formed from the Department of War (created in 1789) and the Department of Navy (created in 1798).
§Formed from the Department of Health, Education, and Welfare (created in 1953).

TABLE 14-3

Selected Independent Executive Agencies

NAME	DATE FORMED	PRINCIPAL FUNCTIONS
Central Intelligence Agency (CIA)*	1947	Gathers and analyzes political and military information about foreign countries so that the United States can improve its own political and military status; conducts activities outside the United States, with the goal of countering the work of intelligence services operated by other nations whose political philosophies are inconsistent with our own.
General Services Administration (GSA) (14,116 employees)	1949	Purchases and manages all property of the federal government; acts as the business arm of the federal government in overseeing federal government spending projects; discovers overcharges in government programs.
National Science Foundation (NSF) (1,254 employees)	1950	Promotes scientific research; provides grants to all levels of schools for instructional programs in the sciences.
Small Business Administration (SBA) (4,423 employees)	1953	Protects the interests of small businesses; provides low-cost loans and management information to small businesses.
National Aeronautics and Space Administration (NASA) (18,460 employees)	1958	Is responsible for the U.S. space program, including the building, testing, and operating of space vehicles.
Environmental Protection Agency (EPA) (18,240 employees)	1970	Undertakes programs aimed at reducing air and water pollution; works with state and local agencies to help fight environmental hazards.

*The CIA will not release information on the number of employees who work for this agency (because it is "classified information").

complexities and technicalities required to carry out specific laws in the public interest. The regulatory commissions in fact combine some functions of all three branches of government—executive, legislative, and judicial. They are legislative in that they make rules that have the force of law. They are executive in that they provide for the enforcement of those rules. They are judicial in that they decide disputes involving the rules they have made. (For some recent actions of independent agencies with respect to the enforcement of agency rules against Internet fraud, see this chapter's *E-mocracy* on the next page.)

Regulatory agency members are appointed by the president with the consent of the Senate, although they do not report to the president. By law, the members of regulatory agencies cannot all be from the same political party. Presidents can influence regulatory agency behavior by appointing people of their own parties or people who share their political views when vacancies occur, in particular when the chair is vacant. Members may be removed by the president only for causes specified in the law creating the agency. Table 14–4 on page 459 describes the functions of selected independent regulatory agencies.

Agency Capture.   Over the last several decades, some observers have concluded that these agencies, although nominally independent, may in fact not always be so. They also contend that many independent regulatory agencies have been **captured** by the very industries and firms that they were supposed to regulate. The results have been less competition rather than more competition, higher prices rather than lower prices, and less choice rather than more choice for consumers.

Deregulation and Reregulation.   During the presidency of Ronald Reagan in the 1980s, some significant deregulation (the removal of regulatory restraints— the opposite of regulation) occurred, much of which had started under President

DID YOU KNOW...
That the Commerce Department's U.S. Travel and Tourism Administration recently gave away $440,000 in so-called disaster relief to western ski resort operators because there hadn't been enough snow?

INFOTRAC®
COLLEGE EDITION

CIA Breach Confidence

Capture
The act of gaining direct or indirect control over agency personnel and decision makers by the industry that is being regulated.

Jimmy Carter. For example, President Carter appointed a chairperson of the Civil Aeronautics Board (CAB) who gradually eliminated regulation of airline fares and routes. Then, under Reagan, the CAB was eliminated on January 1, 1985. During the Bush administration, calls for *re*regulation of many businesses increased. Indeed, under President Bush, the Americans with Disabilities Act of 1990, the Civil Rights Act of 1991, and the Clean Air Act Amendments of 1991, all of which increased or changed the regulation of many businesses, were passed. Additionally, the Cable Reregulation Act of 1992 was passed. Under President Clinton, the Interstate Commerce Commission was eliminated, and there was deregulation of the banking and telecommunications industries, and many other sectors of the economy. At the same time, there was extensive regulation to protect the environment. Additionally, in the late 1990s and the early 2000s, major attempts to institute general regulatory reform were made in Congress. So far, no significant legislation of that nature has been passed.

Government Corporations

Government Corporation

An agency of government that administers a quasi-business enterprise. These corporations are used when activities are primarily commercial. They produce revenue for their continued existence, and they require greater flexibility than is permitted for departments and agencies.

Another form of bureaucratic organization in the United States is the **government corporation.** Although the concept is borrowed from the world of business, distinct differences exist between public and private corporations.

A private corporation has shareholders (stockholders) who elect a board of directors, who in turn choose the corporate officers, such as president and vice president. When a private corporation makes a profit, it must pay taxes (unless it avoids them through various legal loopholes). It either distributes part or all of the after-tax profits to shareholders as dividends or plows the profits back into the corporation to make new investments.

e-mocracy

Government Agencies Tackle Internet Fraud

The expanding world of e-commerce has created many benefits for American consumers. It has also led to some challenging problems, including fraud conducted via the Internet. In the past few years, a number of federal agencies have been tackling this problem.

One of these agencies is the Federal Trade Commission (FTC). The FTC is an administrative agency established by Congress in 1914 to enforce laws prohibiting unfair and deceptive trade practices, including deceptive advertising. For years, the FTC has fought deceptive advertising in printed materials and in radio and television broadcasts. Since the late 1990s, it has spent a considerable portion of its resources on fighting deceptive advertising on the Internet. The FTC has moved particularly quickly on commercial Internet fraud schemes. It has even provided "hot links" on Web sites that it has targeted. A hot link takes the user to the FTC's own Web site, where the complaint, restraining order, and other documents in the case can be read and downloaded.

Another agency fighting online fraud and false advertising is the Securities and Exchange Commission (SEC). The SEC has initiated actions against dozens of entities that have perpetrated

online investment scams. One fraudulent scheme involved twenty thousand investors, who together lost more than $3 million. Some cases have involved false claims about the earnings potential of home business programs, such as the claim that one could "earn $4,000 or more each month." Others have concerned promises of "guaranteed credit repair."

The Department of Transportation (DOT) and the Food and Drug Administration (FDA) have also investigated purported online violators of advertising and disclosure laws. The DOT fined Virgin Airlines for failing to disclose the true price of a flight that it advertised on the Web. The FDA has not yet brought any actions against apparent online violators of regulations governing drug advertising, however. One issue that the FDA has yet to resolve is the distinction between advertising and labeling. Also, the Consumer Product Safety Commission has created what it calls a one-stop Web site that provides information to help consumers avoid the most obvious fraud problems on the Web and elsewhere.

FOR CRITICAL ANALYSIS

Given the seemingly infinite number of Web sites, are government agency "watchdogs" fighting a losing battle in trying to control fraud and deceptive advertising on the Internet?

TABLE 14-4
Selected Independent Regulatory Agencies

NAME	DATE FORMED	PRINCIPAL FUNCTIONS
Federal Reserve System Board of Governors (Fed) (1,641 employees)	1913	Determines policy with respect to interest rates, credit availability, and the money supply.
Federal Trade Commission (FTC) (994 employees)	1914	Prevents businesses from engaging in unfair trade practices; stops the formation of monopolies in the business sector; protects consumer rights.
Securities and Exchange Commission (SEC) (2,855 employees)	1934	Regulates the nation's stock exchanges, in which shares of stocks are bought and sold; requires full disclosure of the financial profiles of companies that wish to sell stocks and bonds to the public.
Federal Communications Commission (FCC) (1,974 employees)	1934	Regulates all communications by telegraph, cable, telephone, radio, and television.
National Labor Relations Board (NLRB) (1,873 employees)	1935	Protects employees' rights to join unions and bargain collectively with employers; attempts to prevent unfair labor practices by both employers and unions.
Equal Employment Opportunity Commission (EEOC) (2,642 employees)	1964	Works to eliminate discrimination based on religion, gender, race, color, national origin, age, or disability; examines claims of discrimination.
Federal Election Commission (FEC) (347 employees)	1974	Ensures that candidates and states follow the rules established by the Federal Election Campaign Act.
Nuclear Regulatory Commission (NRC) (2,833 employees)	1974	Ensures that electricity-generating nuclear reactors in the United States are built and operated safely; regularly inspects the operations of such reactors.

A government corporation has a board of directors and managers, but it does not have any stockholders. We cannot buy shares of stock in a government corporation. If the government corporation makes a profit, it does not distribute the profit as dividends. Also, if it makes a profit, it does not have to pay taxes; the profits remain in the corporation. Table 14–5 on the next page describes the functions of selected government corporations.

Staffing the Bureaucracy

There are two categories of bureaucrats: political appointees and civil servants. As noted earlier, the president is able to make political appointments to most of the top jobs in the federal bureaucracy. The president also can appoint ambassadors to the most important foreign posts. All of the jobs that are considered "political plums" and that usually go to the politically well connected are listed in *Policy and Supporting Positions,* a book published by the Government Printing Office after each presidential election. This has been informally (and appropriately) called "The Plum Book." The rest of the individuals who work for the national government belong to the civil service and obtain their jobs through a much more formal process.

Political Appointees

To fill the positions listed in "The Plum Book," the president and the president's advisers solicit suggestions from politicians, businesspersons, and other prominent individuals. Appointments to these positions offer the president a way to pay off

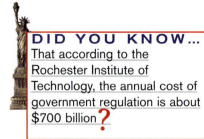

outstanding political debts. But the president must also take into consideration such things as the candidate's work experience, intelligence, political affiliations, and personal characteristics. Presidents have differed over the importance they attach to appointing women and minorities to plum positions. Presidents often use ambassadorships, however, to reward selected individuals for their campaign contributions.

Political appointees are in some sense the aristocracy of the federal government. But their powers, although appearing formidable on paper, are often exaggerated. Like the president, a political appointee will occupy her or his position for a comparatively brief time. Political appointees often leave office before the president's term actually ends. The average term of service for political appointees is less than two years. As a result, most appointees have little background for their positions and may be mere figureheads. Often, they only respond to the paperwork that flows up from below. Additionally, the professional civil servants who make up the permanent civil service but serve under a normally temporary political appointee may not feel compelled to carry out their current boss's directives quickly, because they know that he or she will not be around for very long.

This inertia is compounded by the fact that it is extremely difficult to discharge civil servants. In recent years, less than one-tenth of 1 percent of federal employees have been fired for incompetence. Because discharged employees may appeal their dismissals, many months or even years may pass before the issue is resolved conclusively. This occupational rigidity helps to ensure that most political appointees, no matter how competent or driven, will not be able to exert much meaningful influence over their subordinates, let alone implement dramatic changes in the bureaucracy itself. Of course, there are exceptions. Under the Civil Service Reform Act of 1978, for example, senior employees can be transferred within their departments and receive salary bonuses and other benefits as incentives for being productive and responsive to the goals and policy preferences of their politically appointed superiors.

I N F O T R A C ®
COLLEGE EDITION

Civil Service Commission

Selected Government Corporations

NAME	DATE FORMED	PRINCIPAL FUNCTIONS
Tennessee Valley Authority (TVA) (13,287 employees)	1933	Operates a Tennessee River control system and generates power for a seven-state region and for the U.S. aeronautics and space programs; promotes the economic development of the Tennessee Valley region; controls floods and promotes the navigability of the Tennessee River.
Federal Deposit Insurance Corporation (FDIC) (7,347 employees)	1933	Insures individuals' bank deposits up to $100,000; oversees the business activities of banks.
Export-Import Bank of the United States (Ex-Im Bank) (416 employees)	1933	Promotes the sale of American-made goods abroad; grants loans to foreign purchasers of American products.
National Railroad Passenger Corporation (AMTRAK) (23,000 employees)	1970	Provides a balanced national and intercity rail passenger service network; controls 23,000 miles of track with 505 stations.
U.S. Postal Service* (867,863 employees)	1970	Delivers mail throughout the United States and its territories; is the largest government corporation.

*Formed from the Office of the Postmaster General in the Department of the Treasury (created in 1789).

History of the Federal Civil Service

When the federal government was formed in 1789, it had no career public servants but rather consisted of amateurs who were almost all Federalists. When Thomas Jefferson took over as president, he found that few in his party were holding federal administrative jobs, so he fired more than one hundred officials and replaced them with members of the so-called **natural aristocracy**—that is, with his own Jeffersonian (Democratic) Republicans. For the next twenty-five years, a growing body of federal administrators gained experience and expertise, becoming in the process professional public servants. These administrators stayed in office regardless of who was elected president. The bureaucracy had become a self-maintaining, long-term element within government.

To the Victor Belong the Spoils.   When Andrew Jackson took over the White House in 1828, he could not believe how many appointed officials (appointed before he became president, that is) were overtly hostile toward him and his Democratic Party. The bureaucracy—indeed an aristocracy—considered itself the only group fit to rule. But Jackson was a man of the people, and his policies were populist in nature. As the bureaucracy was reluctant to carry out his programs, Jackson did the obvious: he fired federal officials—more than had all his

Natural Aristocracy
A small ruling clique of a society's "best" citizens, whose membership is based on birth, wealth, and ability. The Jeffersonian era emphasized government rule by such a group.

U.S. Postal Service employees sort the mail during the night shift at an Austin, Texas, post office. The postal service is the largest single employer in the United States.

Spoils System
The awarding of government jobs to political supporters and friends; generally associated with President Andrew Jackson.

Merit System
The selection, retention, and promotion of government employees on the basis of competitive examinations.

Pendleton Act
(Civil Service Reform Act)
The law, as amended over the years, that remains the basic statute regulating federal employment personnel policies. It established the principle of employment on the basis of merit and created the Civil Service Commission to administer the personnel service.

Civil Service Commission
The initial central personnel agency of the national government; created in 1883.

predecessors combined. The **spoils system**—an application of the principle that to the victor belong the spoils—reigned. The aristocrats were out, and the common folk were in. The spoils system was not, of course, a Jacksonian invention. Thomas Jefferson, too, had used this system of patronage in which the boss, or patron, rewards those who worked to get him or her elected.

The Civil Service Reform Act of 1883. Jackson's spoils system survived for a number of years, but it became increasingly corrupt. Also, the size of the bureaucracy increased by 300 percent between 1851 and 1881. Reformers began to look to the example of several European countries, which had established a professional civil service that operated under a **merit system** in which job appointments were based on competitive examinations. The cry for civil service reform became louder.

In 1883, the **Pendleton Act**—or **Civil Service Reform Act**—was passed, bringing to a close the period of Jacksonian spoils. The act established the principle of employment on the basis of open, competitive examinations and created the **Civil Service Commission** to administer the personnel service. Only 10 percent of federal employees were initially covered by the merit system. Later laws, amendments, and executive orders, however, increased the coverage to more than 90 percent of the federal civil service. The effects of these reforms were felt at all levels of government, including city governments run by political machines—for example, New York's Tammany Hall.

The Supreme Court put an even heavier lid on the spoils system in *Elrod v. Burns*[4] in 1976 and *Branti v. Finkel*[5] in 1980. In those two cases, the Court used the First Amendment to forbid government officials from discharging or threatening to discharge public employees solely for not being supporters of the political party in power unless party affiliation is an appropriate requirement for the position. Additional curbs on political patronage were added in *Rutan v. Republican Party of Illinois*[6] in 1990. The Court's ruling effectively prevented the use of partisan political considerations as the basis for hiring, promoting, or transferring most public employees. An exception was permitted, however, for senior policymaking positions, which usually go to officials who will support the programs of the elected leaders.

---

[4]427 U.S. 347 (1976).
[5]445 U.S. 507 (1980).
[6]497 U.S. 62 (1990).

On September 19, 1881, President James A. Garfield was assassinated by a disappointed office seeker, Charles J. Guiteau. The long-term effect of this event was to replace the spoils system with a permanent career civil service, with the passage of the Pendleton Act in 1883, which established the Civil Service Commission.

The Hatch Act of 1939.   The growing size of the federal bureaucracy created the potential for political manipulation. In principle, a civil servant is politically neutral. But civil servants certainly know that it is politicians who pay the bills through their appropriations and that it is politicians who decide about the growth of agencies. In 1933, when President Franklin D. Roosevelt set up his New Deal, a virtual army of civil servants was hired to staff the numerous new agencies that were created. Because the individuals who worked in these agencies owed their jobs to the Democratic Party, it seemed natural for them to campaign for Democratic candidates. The Democrats controlling Congress in the mid-1930s did not object. But in 1938, a coalition of conservative Democrats and Republicans took control of Congress and forced through the **Hatch Act**—or the **Political Activities Act**—of 1939.

The main provision of this act is that civil service employees cannot take an active part in the political management of campaigns. It also prohibits the use of federal authority to influence nominations and elections and outlaws the use of bureaucratic rank to pressure federal employees to make political contributions.

In 1972, a federal district court declared the Hatch Act prohibition against political activity to be unconstitutional. The United States Supreme Court, however, reaffirmed the challenged portion of the act in 1973, stating that the government's interest in preserving a nonpartisan civil service was so great that the prohibitions should remain.[7]

The Civil Service Reform Act of 1978.   In 1978, the Civil Service Reform Act abolished the Civil Service Commission and created two new federal agencies to perform its duties. To administer the civil service laws, rules, and regulations, the act created the Office of Personnel Management (OPM). The OPM is empowered to recruit, interview, and test potential government workers and determine who should be hired. The OPM makes recommendations to the individual agencies as to which persons meet the standards (typically, the top three applicants for a position), and the agencies generally decide whom to hire. To oversee promotions, employees' rights, and other employment matters, the act created the Merit Systems Protection Board (MSPB). The MSPB evaluates charges of wrongdoing, hears employee appeals from agency decisions, and can order corrective action against agencies and employees.

Modern Attempts at Bureaucratic Reform

As long as the federal bureaucracy exists, there will continue to be attempts to make it more open, efficient, and responsive to the needs of U.S. citizens. The most important actual and proposed reforms in the last several decades include sunshine and sunset laws, contracting out, and more protection for so-called whistleblowers.

Sunshine Laws

In 1976, Congress enacted the **Government in the Sunshine Act.** It required for the first time that all multiheaded federal agencies—about fifty of them—hold their meetings regularly in public session. The bill defined *meetings* as almost any gathering, formal or informal, of agency members, including conference telephone calls. The only exceptions to this rule of openness are discussions of matters such as court proceedings or personnel problems, and these exceptions are specifically listed in the bill. Sunshine laws now exist at all levels of government.

---

[7]*United States Civil Service Commission v. National Association of Letter Carriers,* 413 U.S. 548 (1973).

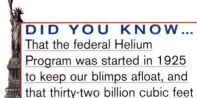

Hatch Act
(Political Activities Act)
The act that prohibits the use of federal authority to influence nominations and elections or the use of rank to pressure federal employees to make political contributions. It also prohibits civil service employees from active involvement in political campaigns.

INFOTRAC®
COLLEGE EDITION

Government Civil Service Reform

Government in the Sunshine Act
A law that requires all multiheaded federal agencies to conduct their business regularly in public session.

Sunset Legislation
A law requiring that an existing program be reviewed regularly for its effectiveness and be terminated unless specifically extended as a result of this review.

Contracting Out
The replacement of government services with services provided by private firms.

Sunset Laws

A potential type of control on the size and scope of the federal bureaucracy consists of **sunset legislation,** which would place government programs on a definite schedule for congressional consideration. Unless Congress specifically reauthorized a particular federally operated program at the end of a designated period, it would be terminated automatically; that is, its sun would set.

The idea of sunset legislation—the first hint at the role of the bureaucracy in the legislative process—was initially suggested by Franklin D. Roosevelt when he created the plethora of New Deal agencies. His assistant, William O. Douglas, recommended that each agency's charter should include a provision allowing for its termination in ten years. Only an act of Congress could revitalize it. Obviously, the proposal was never adopted. It was not until 1976 that a state legislature—Colorado's—adopted sunset legislation for state regulatory commissions, giving them a life of six years before their suns set. Today, most states have some type of sunset law.

Contracting Out

One approach to bureaucratic reform is **contracting out,** which occurs when government services are replaced by services from the private sector. For example, the government might contract with private firms to operate prisons. Supporters of contracting out argue that some services could be provided more efficiently by the private sector. Another scheme is to furnish vouchers to "clients" in lieu of services. For example, it has been proposed that instead of federally supported housing assistance, the government should offer vouchers that recipients could use to "pay" for housing in privately owned buildings.

The contracting-out strategy has been most successful on the local level. Municipalities, for example, can form contracts with private companies for such things as trash collection. Such an approach is not a cure-all, however, as there are many functions, particularly on the national level, that cannot be contracted out in any meaningful way. For example, the federal government could not contract out all of the Defense Department's functions to private firms.

Incentives for Efficiency and Productivity

An increasing number of state governments are beginning to experiment with a variety of schemes to run their operations more efficiently and capably. They focus on maximizing the efficiency and productivity of government workers by providing incentives for improved performance.[8] For example, many governors, mayors, and city administrators are considering ways in which government can be made more entrepreneurial. Some of the more promising measures have included such tactics as permitting agencies that do not spend their entire budgets to keep some of the difference and rewarding employees with performance-based bonuses.

At the federal level, the Government Performance and Results Act of 1997 was designed to improve efficiency in the federal work force. The act required that all government agencies (except the Central Intelligence Agency) describe their new goals and establish methods for determining whether those goals are met. Goals may be broadly crafted (for example, reducing the time it takes to

---

[8] See, for example, David Osborne and Ted Gaebler, *Reinventing Government: How the Entrepreneurial Spirit Is Transforming the Public Sector* (Reading, Mass.: Addison-Wesley, 1992); and David Osborne and Peter Plastrik, *Banishing Bureaucracy: The Five Strategies for Reinventing Government* (Reading, Mass.: Addison-Wesley, 1997).

test a new drug before allowing it to be marketed) or narrowly crafted (for example, reducing the number of times a telephone rings before it is answered).

Efforts to improve bureaucratic efficiency are supported by the assertion that although society and industry have changed enormously in the past century, the form of government used in Washington, D.C., and in most states has remained the same. Some observers believe that the nation's diverse economic base cannot be administered competently by traditional bureaucratic organizations. Consequently, government must become more responsive to cope with the increasing number of demands placed on it. Political scientists Joel Aberbach and Bert Rockman take issue with this contention. They argue that the bureaucracy has changed significantly over time in response to changes desired by various presidential administrations. In their opinion, many of the problems attributed to the bureaucracy are, in fact, a result of the political decision-making process. Therefore, attempts to "reinvent" government by reforming the bureaucracy are misguided.[9]

Other analysts have suggested that the problem lies not so much with traditional bureaucratic organizations as with the people who run them. According to policy specialist Taegan Goddard and journalist Christopher Riback, what needs to be "reinvented" is not the machinery of government but public officials. After each election, new appointees to bureaucratic positions may find themselves managing complex, multimillion-dollar enterprises, yet they often are untrained for their jobs. According to these authors, if we want to reform the bureaucracy, we should focus on preparing newcomers for the task of "doing" government.[10]

Helping Out the Whistleblowers

The term **whistleblower** as applied to the federal bureaucracy has a special meaning: it is someone who blows the whistle on a gross governmental inefficiency or illegal action. Whistleblowers may be clerical workers, managers, or even specialists, such as scientists. The 1978 Civil Service Reform Act prohibits reprisals against whistleblowers by their superiors, and it set up the Merit Systems Protection Board as part of this protection. Many federal agencies also have toll-free hotlines that employees can use anonymously to report bureaucratic waste and inappropriate behavior. About 35 percent of all calls result in agency action or follow-up.

Further protection against whistleblowing was provided in 1989, when Congress passed the Whistle-Blower Protection Act. That act established an independent agency, the Office of Special Counsel (OSC), to investigate complaints brought by government employees who have been demoted, fired, or otherwise sanctioned for reporting government fraud or waste. There is little evidence, though, that potential whistleblowers truly have received more protection as a result of these endeavors. More than 40 percent of the employees who turned to the OSC for assistance in a recent three-year period stated that they were no longer employees of the government agencies on which they blew the whistle.

Some state and federal laws encourage employees to blow the whistle on their employers' wrongful actions by providing monetary incentives to the whistleblowers. At the federal level, for example, the False Claims Act of 1986 allows a whistleblower who has disclosed information relating to a fraud perpetrated against the U.S. government to receive a monetary award. If the government chooses to prosecute the case, the whistleblower receives between 15 and 25 percent of the proceeds. If the government declines to intervene, the whistleblower can bring suit

DID YOU KNOW...
That federal officials spent $333,000 building a deluxe, earthquake-proof outhouse for hikers in Pennsylvania's remote Delaware Water Gap recreation area**?**

Whistleblower
Someone who brings to public attention gross governmental inefficiency or an illegal action.

---

[9] Joel D. Aberbach and Bert A. Rockman, *In the Web of Politics: Three Decades of the U.S. Federal Executive* (Washington, D.C.: Brookings Institution Press, 2000).

[10] Taegan D. Goddard and Christopher Riback, *You Won—Now What? How Americans Can Make Democracy Work from City Hall to the White House* (New York: Scribner, 1998).

on behalf of the government and will receive between 25 and 30 percent of the proceeds. (For a further discussion of this act and the controversy it has generated, see this chapter's *Politics and Economics: Rewards for Whistleblowers*.)

Bureaucrats as Politicians and Policymakers

Enabling Legislation
A statute enacted by Congress that authorizes the creation of an administrative agency and specifies the name, purpose, composition, functions, and powers of the agency being created.

Because Congress is unable to oversee the day-to-day administration of its programs, it must delegate certain powers to administrative agencies. Congress delegates the power to implement legislation to agencies through what is called **enabling legislation.** For example, the Federal Trade Commission was created by the Federal Trade Commission Act of 1914, the Equal Employment Opportunity Commission was created by the Civil Rights Act of 1964, and the Occupational Safety and Health Administration was created by the Occupational Safety and Health Act of 1970. The enabling legislation generally specifies the name, purpose, composition, functions, and powers of the agency.

In theory, the agencies should put into effect laws passed by Congress. Laws are often drafted in such vague and general terms, however, that they provide little guidance to agency administrators as to how the laws

politics and economics

Rewards for Whistleblowers

Fraud against the federal government is nothing new, nor are attempts to curb the problem—as noted elsewhere in this chapter. Indeed, an early attempt by the government to deal with the problem dates back to the Civil War years. In 1863, as a result of investigations of the fraudulent use of federal funds, Congress passed the False Claims Act (FCA). As amended in 1986, the act provides that any person can sue an individual or a company for defrauding the government through false claims.

INCENTIVES FOR WHISTLEBLOWERS

A whistleblower who brings such a suit technically is acting on behalf of the U.S. government, which sometimes intervenes in the suit and always gets at least 70 percent of the proceeds of any settlement or verdict. The whistleblower gets the rest, which usually amounts to between 15 and 25 percent of the recovered amount.

For example, in one case an employee of General Electric Corporation (GE) who blew the whistle on his employer's fraudulent use and embezzlement of government funds was awarded over $13 million—about 23 percent of the $59 million recovered in the suit against GE. Recently, an engineer who worked for FMC Corporation contended that FMC had defrauded the government of billions of dollars by producing a military machine (a vehicle that is part tank, part armored troop carrier) that was likely to fail in combat. The engineer's main accusation was that the machine, which was supposed to float, would sink. A jury believed him and levied a $310 million judgment against FMC, up to 30 percent ($93 million) of which will go to the engineer—and his lawyers—if the amount of damages is not reduced on appeal.

THE CONTROVERSY OVER THE FCA

Some consider the FCA to be a powerful weapon against fraud on the government. Others argue that the whistleblowers are merely bounty hunters and that a higher percentage of the amounts recovered should go to the government. Still others criticize the FCA's provisions on legal grounds. They contend that whistleblowers should not be able to bring such lawsuits because they do not have "standing to sue." As you will read in Chapter 15, standing to sue is a basic judicial requirement. To have standing, a person must have suffered a harm, or have been threatened by a harm, from the action about which he or she is complaining. Whistleblowers in cases brought under the FCA do not have standing if they have suffered no harm, or threatened harm, from their employers' fraud against the government.

The controversy over the standing issue, which goes to the core of the FCA, was recently resolved by the United States Supreme Court. The case was brought by Jonathan Stevens, a former state attorney who accused a Vermont agency of fraudulently filling out time cards for work done under a federal grant. A key issue before the Supreme Court was whether Stevens had standing to sue, given that he did not claim that he suffered any injury as a result of the fraud. The Supreme Court held that Stevens acquired standing because, technically, the government had "assigned" (transferred) to Stevens its right to sue Vermont for the fraud.[*]

FOR CRITICAL ANALYSIS

In all, since 1986 whistleblowers have received nearly $442 million in lawsuits brought under the FCA. Do you agree with some of the act's critics that more of these dollars should go into the federal treasury? Why or why not?

[*]*Vermont Agency of Natural Resources v. United States ex rel. Stevens,* 120 S.Ct.1858 (2000).

which side are you on?

Do Minorities Really Benefit from "Environmental Justice"?

About 60 percent of the people who live in Romeville, Louisiana, are unemployed and have low incomes. Not surprisingly, when the community learned that Shintech Corporation planned to establish a $700 million polyvinyl chloride plant in their area, many residents welcomed the prospect of the new job opportunities that would be created.

The project was approved by Louisiana's Department of Environmental Quality, and it looked as though construction would soon be under way. The Environmental Protection Agency (EPA), however, had other ideas. Concluding that blacks would suffer disproportionately from allegedly cancer-causing emissions from the plant, in 1997 the EPA ordered that construction be delayed. To avoid further hassles with the EPA, the company decided to locate its plant in a nearby community that was largely white.

The EPA's concern with "environmental justice" began in 1993, when the agency's director, Carol Browner, created the Office of Environmental Justice within the EPA. One of the purposes of the new office was to oversee studies on the effects of industrial pollutants on poorer, mostly black communities. In the following year, the White House supported Browner's initiative by requiring all federal administrative agencies to consider the health and environmental effects of their decisions on minority and low-income communities.

Environmental activists and civil rights groups applauded the EPA's decision with respect to the Shintech facility. But Louisiana officials, as well as many residents of Romeville, were enraged at the EPA's action. According to Louisiana's director of economic development, Kevin Reilly, it was "demeaning and despicable for these people to play the race card," especially when the plant would have provided economic benefits for poor people and blacks. Additionally, a study reported in the *Journal of the Louisiana Medical Society* found that the project would not have created the significant health risk that the EPA claimed it would.*

Others criticized the EPA for intruding too extensively into state and local affairs. For example, a number of state and local groups, including the U.S. Conference of Mayors, the National Association of Counties, and the Environmental Council of the States, have demanded that the EPA withdraw its policy, which has disrupted several job-creating projects.

*Pranay Gupte and Bonner R. Cohen, "Carol Browner, Master of Mission Creep," *Forbes*, October 20, 1997, p. 175.

Carol Browner, head of the EPA.

DOES IT MATTER?

Should it matter whether those whose health may be jeopardized by an industrial plant's purported cancer-causing emissions are black or white?

GOING ONLINE

For arguments in support of environmental justice, go to the the following Web sites: **http://www-personal.umich.edu/ ~jrajzer/nre/index.html** *and* **http://www.tsulaw.edu/environ/ enviropg.htm.** *For arguments against environmental justice, go to these Web sites:* **http://www.junkscience. com/news/payne.html** *and* **http:// www. ncpa.org/pl/enviro/oct98g. html**.

should be put into effect. This means that the agencies themselves must decide how best to carry out the wishes of Congress.

The discretion given to administrative agencies is not accidental. Congress has long realized that it lacks the technical expertise and the resources to monitor the implementation of its laws. Hence, the administrative agency is created to fill the gaps. This gap-filling role requires the agency to formulate administrative rules (regulations) to put flesh on the bones of the law. But it also forces the agency itself to assume the role of an unelected policymaker. (For an example of an Environmental Protection Agency policy decision, see the feature *Which Side Are You On? Do Minorities Really Benefit from "Environmental Justice"?*)

Green Redlining

The Rulemaking Environment

Rulemaking does not occur in a vacuum. Suppose that Congress passes a new air-pollution law. The Environmental Protection Agency (EPA) might decide to implement the new law by a technical regulation relating to factory emissions. This proposed regulation would be published in the *Federal Register,* a daily government publication, so that interested parties would have an opportunity to comment on it. Individuals and companies that opposed parts or all of the rule might then try to convince the EPA to revise or redraft the regulation. Some parties might try to persuade the agency to withdraw the proposed regulation altogether. In any event, the EPA would consider these comments in drafting the final version of the regulation following the expiration of the comment period.

Once the final regulation has been published in the *Federal Register,* the regulation might be challenged in court by a party having a direct interest in the rule, such as a company that could expect to incur significant costs in complying with it. The company could argue that the rule misinterprets the applicable law or goes beyond the agency's statutory purview. An allegation by the company that the EPA made a mistake in judgment probably would not be enough to convince the court to throw out the rule. The company instead would have to demonstrate that the rule itself was "arbitrary and capricious." To meet this standard, the company would have to show that the rule reflected a serious flaw in the EPA's judgment—such as a steadfast refusal by the agency to consider reasonable alternatives to its rule. (In addition to complying with EPA rules, businesses are often pressured to engage in environmentally friendly actions by publicity generated by individuals or interest groups—see, for example, this chapter's *Making Waves: Julia "Butterfly" Hill, Tree Dweller.*)

A budget package signed by the president in 1996 provided some regulatory relief. When an agency now issues a new rule, it has to wait sixty days (instead of only thirty days, as was previously required) before enforcing the rule. During that waiting period, businesses, individuals, and state and local governments can ask Congress to overturn the regulation rather than having to sue the agency after the rule takes effect.

making Waves

Julia "Butterfly" Hill, Tree Dweller

A number of federal agencies have authority to regulate specific environmental matters. The most well known of these agencies is, of course, the Environmental Protection Agency, which is charged with coordinating federal environmental policy. These agencies have issued a host of regulations to protect the environment, and businesses must comply with these rules or face penalties. But what if a company that allegedly is destroying an environmental resource is acting within legal limits?

In this situation, powerful environmental interest groups may bring pressure to bear on the company—through adverse publicity, for example—in an effort to change its behavior. Rarely does a single individual have the power and resources to alter a company's business practices. Julia "Butterfly" Hill is an exception to this rule.

From December 10, 1997, to December 18, 1999, Hill lived in a 180-foot-tall ancient redwood tree named "Luna" to make a point. She and several earlier tree sitters occupied the tree to keep it and other nearby trees from being cut down by the Pacific Lumber Company, which owns the land. The national media attention she gathered brought results: Pacific Lumber agreed to save the area in exchange for her exit from the tree. In Hill's view, individuals can and do make a difference.

FOR CRITICAL ANALYSIS

One could speculate that Hill's efforts would have been in vain had she not gained national media attention. Generally, do you think that the media play too great a role in the policymaking process? Why or why not?

Negotiated Rulemaking

Since the end of World War II (1939–1945), companies, environmentalists, and other special interest groups have challenged government regulations in court. In the 1980s, however, the sheer wastefulness of attempting to regulate through litigation became more and more apparent. Today, a growing number of federal agencies encourage businesses and public-interest groups to become directly involved in the drafting of regulations. Agencies hope that such participation may help to prevent later courtroom battles over the meaning, applicability, and legal effect of the regulations.

Congress formally approved such a process, which is called *negotiated rulemaking,* in the Negotiated Rulemaking Act of 1990. The act authorizes agencies to allow those who will be affected by a new rule to participate in the rule-drafting process. If an agency chooses to engage in negotiated rulemaking, it must publish in the *Federal Register* the subject and scope of the rule to be developed, the parties that will be affected significantly by the rule, and other information. Representatives of the affected groups and other interested parties then may apply to be members of the negotiating committee. The agency is represented on the committee, but a neutral third party (not the agency) presides over the proceedings. Once the committee members have reached agreement on the terms of the proposed rule, notice of the proposed rule is published in the *Federal Register,* followed by a period for comments by any person or organization interested in the proposed rule. Negotiated rulemaking often is conducted under the condition that the participants promise not to challenge in court the outcome of any agreement to which they were a party.

Bureaucrats Are Policymakers

Theories of public administration once assumed that bureaucrats do not make policy decisions but only implement the laws and policies promulgated by the president and legislative bodies. Many people continue to make this assumption. A more realistic view, which is now held by most bureaucrats and elected officials, is that the agencies and departments of government play important roles in policymaking. As we have seen, many government rules, regulations, and programs are in fact initiated by the bureaucracy, based on its expertise and scientific studies. How a law passed by Congress eventually is translated into concrete action—from the forms to be filled out to decisions about who gets the benefits—usually is determined within each agency or department. Even the evaluation of whether a policy has achieved its purpose usually is based on studies that are commissioned and interpreted by the agency administering the program. Indeed, some contend that the bureaucracy has exceeded its regulatory authority—see this chapter's *Critical Perspective* beginning on the next page for a discussion of this issue.

The bureaucracy's policymaking role often has been depicted by what has been called the "iron triangle." Recently, the concept of an "issue network" has been viewed as a more accurate description of the policymaking process.

Iron Triangles.   In the past, scholars often described the bureaucracy's role in the policymaking process by using the concept of an **iron triangle**—a three-way alliance among legislators in Congress, bureaucrats, and interest groups in a given policy area. The presumption was that policy development depended on how a policy affected each component of the iron triangle.

Consider as an example the development of agricultural policy. The Department of Agriculture has over 93,200 employees working directly for the federal government and thousands of others who, directly or indirectly, work as contractors, subcontractors, or consultants to the department. Now consider that various interest, or client, groups are concerned with what the federal government does for

Iron Triangle
The three-way alliance among legislators, bureaucrats, and interest groups to make or preserve policies that benefit their respective interests.

critical perspective

Has the Bureaucracy Exceeded Its Lawmaking Mandate?

During the course of the twentieth century, the national government's regulatory arm reached into virtually every sector of American business activity. Despite the devolutionary trend in recent years (see Chapter 3) and various attempts at deregulation, the federal bureaucracy remains a vast edifice. Of increasing concern today is the extent to which this so-called fourth branch of government makes national policy. After all, the founders' intention was that Congress would be the lawmaking branch of government. The job of the executive branch was to enforce laws, not make them. Yet through their rulemaking function, administrative agencies issue rules that are as binding as any laws passed by Congress.

A New Executive State?

Christopher DeMuth, head of the American Enterprise Institute, contends that Congress has been far too lax in overseeing the work of the agencies to which it delegates lawmaking powers. He cites several examples of how the legislative branch of government, through administrative agency rulemaking, has created what he calls a "new executive state." He claims, for instance, that the Clean Air Act of 1970, which was at first just a "thin skeleton of congressional senti-ments," has been largely written by the Environmental Protection Agency (EPA) through the issuance of various rules. He also asserts that the executive branch has used Title IX of the Civil Rights Act of 1964 (relating to discrimination in educational institutions) as an "excuse" for writing rules that compel many colleges to abolish some men's sports to achieve equal expenditures and participation in men's and women's sports. Yet Congress mentioned no such requirement in Title IX.

Additionally, federal agencies have been levying taxes—a power that, under the Constitution, only Congress can exercise. As an example, DeMuth points to a rule issued by the Federal Communications Commission (FCC), which requires a tax on long-distance services—now producing more than $5 billion annually—to help fund the provision of computers in schools and other projects.

The latest innovation in "executive taxation," according to DeMuth, is "recoupment" litigation—lawsuits brought by federal and/or state agencies against certain industries, such as the tobacco industry, to recoup (recover) expenses paid for by government in treating, for example, tobacco-related health problems. According to DeMuth, "As a legal matter the cases are travesties. The government already collects more in tobacco taxes than it pays in smoking-related medical expenses." Yet Congress and state legislatures have clearly stepped aside and allowed state and federal administrative agencies to take actions on these issues.[*]

[*]Christopher C. DeMuth, "After the Ascent: Politics and Government in the Super-Affluent Society," Francis Boyer Lecture, American Enterprise Institute, Washington, D.C., February 15, 2000.

farmers. These include the American Farm Bureau Federation, the National Cattleman's Association, the National Milk Producers Association, the Corn Growers Association, and the Citrus Growers Association. Finally, go directly to Congress, and you will see that there are two major congressional committees concerned with agriculture—the House Committee on Agriculture and the Senate Committee on Agriculture, Nutrition, and Forestry—each of which has several subcommittees.

Clearly, it is in the Department of Agriculture's interest to support policies that enhance the department's budget and powers. Consider that the secretary of agriculture cannot even buy a desk lamp if Congress does not approve the appropriations for the department's budget. Therefore, the department will lend whatever support it can to those members of Congress who are in charge of deciding which agricultural programs should be cut, maintained, or created and what amount of funds should be allocated to the department.

Various agricultural interest groups will lobby Congress to develop policies that benefit their groups' interests. Members of Congress cannot afford to ignore the wishes of interest groups, because those groups are potential sources of voter support and campaign contributions. Therefore, the legislators involved in the

critical perspective

Agency Powers and the Courts

Traditionally, the courts have given fairly wide latitude to agencies in their rulemaking activities. Generally, the courts have held that the exercise of lawmaking powers by administrative agencies is justified under several constitutional provisions. For example, Article I, Section 1, which grants all legislative powers to Congress, also requires Congress to oversee the implementation of all laws. Article I, Section 8, gives Congress the power to make all laws necessary for executing its specified powers. The courts interpret these passages, under what is known as the *delegation doctrine,* as granting Congress the power to establish administrative agencies that can create rules for implementing those laws. Additionally, as mentioned elsewhere, Article II, Section 3, requires the president to "take Care that the Laws be faithfully executed."

According to some observers, a recent Supreme Court decision may indicate a greater willingness on the part of the Court to rein in the bureaucrats' policymaking powers. The case involved rules issued by the Food and Drug Administration (FDA) pursuant to a policy adopted by the agency in 1996. Under that policy, nicotine would be regulated as a drug, and the new rules called for restrictions on the marketing and sale of tobacco products to youth. A number of tobacco companies sued the agency, contending that the FDA lacked the authority to regulate tobacco. The Supreme Court looked closely at the wording of the statutory authority for the rules–the Federal Food, Drug, and Cosmetic Act–and concluded that Congress had not explicitly authorized the FDA to regulate tobacco products. Therefore, the FDA had exceeded its regulatory authority.[†]

According to James O'Reilly of the University of Cincinnati College of Law, the decision represents "a very significant threat to the ability of regulatory bodies . . . to fill the interstices, the gaps, in what Congress has not addressed" when enacting laws.[‡] Others, however, feel that the Court's ruling was narrow in scope and will not be extended beyond the specific question at issue in the case–the FDA's ability to regulate tobacco.

FOR CRITICAL ANALYSIS

1. Traditionally, the courts have generally deferred to decisions made by government agencies. Why is this?

2. Should Congress exercise more oversight over the rulemaking activities of agencies? If not, is there any way to narrow the scope of agencies' rulemaking powers, other than through judicial review?

[†]*Food and Drug Administration v. Brown & Williamson Tobacco Corp.,* 120 S.Ct. 1291 (2000).
[‡]As quoted in Marcia Coyle, "More to FDA Ruling Than Tobacco," *The National Law Journal,* April 3, 2000, p. A4.

---

iron triangle will work closely with interest group lobbyists when developing new policy. The legislators also will work closely with the Department of Agriculture, which, in implementing a policy, can develop rules that benefit—or are not adverse to—certain industries or groups.

To be sure, this is a much simplified picture of how the iron triangle works. But you can see how the interests of government agencies, legislators, and interest groups are all involved in the policymaking process. At times, iron triangles have completely thwarted efforts by the president to get the administration's programs enacted.

Issue Networks. With the growth in the complexity of the government, including expansion in the size of the bureaucracy, the increased number of subcommittees in Congress, and the proliferation of interest groups, policymaking also has become more complex. Often, different interest groups concerned about a certain area, such as agriculture, will have conflicting demands, which makes agency decision making difficult. Additionally, government agencies often are controlled by more than one legislative group. Finally, divided government in recent years has meant that departments may be pressured by the president to

Issue Network

A group of individuals or organizations—which may consist of legislators or legislative staff members, interest group leaders, bureaucrats, the media, scholars, and other experts—that supports a particular policy position on a given issue, such as one relating to the environment, taxation, or consumer safety.

Authorization

A formal declaration by a legislative committee that a certain amount of funding may be available to an agency. Some authorizations terminate in a year; others are renewable automatically without further congressional action.

Appropriation

The passage, by Congress, of a spending bill, specifying the amount of authorized funds that actually will be allocated for an agency's use.

While the National Aeronautics and Space Administration works to build support for its programs in the future, many question the need for such an expensive public program as the space shuttle.

take one approach and by legislators to take another. Today, policymaking typically involves a complex attempt to balance many conflicting demands.

Although iron triangles still exist, often they are inadequate as descriptions of how policy is actually made. Many scholars now use the term "issue network" to describe the policymaking process. An **issue network** consists of a group of individuals or organizations that support a particular policy position on the environment, taxation, consumer safety, or some other issue. Typically, an issue network includes legislators and/or their staff members, interest groups, bureaucrats, scholars and other experts, and representatives from the media. Members of a particular issue network work together to influence the president, members of Congress, administrative agencies, and the courts to change public policy on a specific issue. Each policy issue may involve conflicting positions taken by two or more issue networks.

Congressional Control of the Bureaucracy

Although Congress is the ultimate repository of political power under the Constitution, many political pundits doubt whether Congress can meaningfully control the federal bureaucracy. These commentators forget that Congress, as already mentioned, specifies in an agency's "enabling legislation" the powers of the agency and the parameters within which it can operate. Additionally, Congress has the power of the purse and could, theoretically, refuse to authorize or appropriate funds for a particular agency. Whether Congress would actually take such a drastic measure would depend on the circumstances. It is clear, however, that Congress does have the legal authority to decide whether to fund or not to fund administrative agencies. Congress also can exercise oversight over agencies through investigations and hearings.

Authorizing Funds

Once an agency is created by enabling legislation, Congress must authorize funds for it. The **authorization** is a formal declaration by the appropriate legislative committee that a certain amount of funding may be available to the agency. The authorization itself may terminate in a year, or it may be renewed automatically without further action by Congress. Authorizations for the National Aeronautics and Space Administration (NASA) must be periodically renewed; Social Security, in contrast, is funded through a permanent authorization. Periodic authorizations enable Congress to exercise greater control over the spending programs of an agency, whereas permanent authorizations free Congress from the task of having to review the authorization each year. The drawback of permanent authorizations is that they can become almost impossible to control politically.

Appropriating Funds

After the funds are authorized, they must be appropriated by Congress. The appropriations committees of both the House and the Senate forward spending bills to their respective bodies. The **appropriation** of funds occurs when the final bill is passed. Congress is not required to appropriate the entire authorized amount. It may appropriate less if it so chooses. If the appropriated funds are substantially less than the authorized amount, however, it may signal that the agency's agenda soon may be revamped by Congress.

Congressional Investigations, Hearings, and Review

Congressional committees conduct investigations and hold hearings to oversee an agency's actions, reviewing them to ensure compliance with congressional intentions. The agency's officers and employees can be ordered to testify before a committee about the details of an action. Through these oversight activities, especially in the questioning and commenting by members of the House or Senate during the hearings, Congress indicates its positions on specific programs and issues. Congress can also ask the General Accounting Office (GAO) to investigate particular agency actions. The Congressional Budget Office (CBO) also conducts oversight studies. The results of a GAO or CBO study may encourage Congress to hold further hearings or make changes in the law. Even if a law is not changed explicitly by Congress, however, the views expressed in any investigations and hearings are taken seriously by agency officials, who often act on those views.

In 1996, Congress passed the Congressional Review Act. The act created special procedures that could be used to express congressional disapproval of particular agency actions. These procedures have been rarely used, however. Since the act's passage, the executive branch has issued over 15,000 regulations. Yet only eight resolutions of disapproval have been introduced, and none of these was passed by either chamber.

The Bureaucracy:
Issues for the Twenty-First Century

There probably will be continued attempts to reform the bureaucracy as long as we have a representative democratic form of government. The way members of the House and Senate get reelected and the role lobbyists play in that process, however, practically guarantee that the bureaucracy will never be reformed completely.

This does not mean that we will not see some improvements. Indeed, competition in the private marketplace is forcing changes on some federal government institutions. For example, the efficiency of private overnight delivery services, such as FedEx, Airborne, and United Parcel Service (UPS), has forced many changes on the U.S. Postal Service. Increasingly, the use of electronic communications, such as e-mail, also has put added pressure on the U.S. Postal Service to become more efficient. Such changes are bound to continue as communications technology improves.

The actual job of the federal bureaucracy, of course, will never disappear. Federal agencies are the primary means by which the laws of Congress are put into practice. The "gap-filling" power of federal agencies gives them significant discretion to make policy. Such policymaking has certain advantages: bureaucrats are often specialists in their fields and are more knowledgeable than members of Congress about specific issues relating to the legislation passed by Congress. At the same time, if bureaucratic policymaking becomes too extensive, the result is rule by nonelected agency personnel, rather than rule by the governed, through congressional representatives. Whether agency lawmaking powers should be curbed—and, if so, how this is to be done—is an issue that will likely continue to challenge Americans and their political leaders for years to come.

DID YOU KNOW...
That each year, federal administrative agencies produce rules that fill 7,500 pages in the *Code of Federal Regulations*?

making a difference

What the Government Knows about You

The federal government collects billions of pieces of information on tens of millions of Americans each year. These data are stored in files and gigantic computers and often are exchanged among agencies. You probably have at least several federal records (for example, those in the Social Security Administration; the Internal Revenue Service; and, if you are a male, the Selective Service).

The 1966 Freedom of Information Act (FOIA) requires that the federal government release, at your request, any identifiable information it has in the administrative agencies of the executive branch. This information can be about you or about any other subject. Ten categories of material are exempted, however (classified material, confidential material dealing with trade secrets, internal personnel rules, personal medical files, and

the like). To request material, you must write directly to the Freedom of Information Act officer at the agency in question (say, the Department of Education). You must also have a relatively specific idea about the document or information you wish to obtain.

A second law, the Privacy Act of 1974, gives you access specifically to information the government may have collected about you. This is a very important law, because it allows you to review your records on file with federal agencies (for example, with the Federal Bureau of Investigation) and to check those records for possible inaccuracies. Cases do exist in which the records of two people with similar or the same names have become confused. In some cases, innocent persons have had the criminal records of another person erroneously inserted into their files.

If you wish to look at any records or find out if an agency has a record on you, write to the agency head or Privacy Act officer, and address your letter to the specific agency. State that "under the provisions of the Privacy Act of 1974, 5 U.S.C. 522a, I hereby request a copy of (or access to) _____." Then describe the record that you wish to investigate.

The American Civil Liberties Union (ACLU) has published a booklet, called *A Step-by-Step Guide to Using the Freedom of Information Act,* that offers basic information about the FOIA, sample letters, and federal government agency addresses. You can access this booklet online at

http://www.aclu.org/ library/foia.html

or you can order it from the ACLU at the following address:

ACLU Publications
P.O. Box 186
Wye Mills, MD 21679
1-800-775-ACLU

Key terms

acquisitive model 452

administrative agency 451

appropriation 472

authorization 472

bureaucracy 449

cabinet department 455

capture 457

Civil Service Commission 462

contracting out 464

enabling legislation 466

garbage can model 452

government corporation 458

Government in the Sunshine Act 463

Hatch Act (Political Activities Act) 463

independent executive agency 455

independent regulatory agency 455

iron triangle 469

issue network 472

line organization 455

merit system 462

monopolistic model 452

natural aristocracy 461

Pendleton Act (Civil Service Reform Act) 462

spoils system 462

sunset legislation 464

Weberian model 451

whistleblower 465

Chapter summary

1 Presidents have long complained about their inability to control the federal bureaucracy. There is no reference to the bureaucracy itself in the Constitution, but Article II gives the president the power to appoint officials to execute the laws of the United States. Most scholars cite Article II as the constitutional basis for the federal bureaucracy.

2 Bureaucracies are rigid hierarchical organizations in which the tasks and powers of lower-level employees are defined clearly. Job specialties and extensive procedural rules set the standards for behavior. Bureaucracies are the primary form of organization of most major corporations and universities.

3 Several theories have been offered to explain bureaucracies. The Weberian model posits that bureaucracies have developed into centralized hierarchical structures in response to the increasing demands placed on governments by their citizens. The acquisitive model views top-level bureaucrats as pressing for ever greater funding, staffs, and privileges to augment their own sense of power and security. The monopolistic model focuses on the environment in which most government bureaucracies operate, stating that bureaucracies are inefficient and excessively costly to operate because they often have no competitors. Finally, the garbage can model posits that bureaucracies are rudderless organizations that flounder about in search of solutions to problems.

4 Since the founding of the United States, the federal bureaucracy has grown from 50 to about 2.8 million employees (excluding the military). Federal, state, and local employees together make up over 15 percent of the nation's civilian labor force. The federal bureaucracy consists of fourteen cabinet departments, as well as numerous independent executive agencies, independent regulatory agencies, and government corporations. These entities enjoy varying degrees of autonomy, visibility, and political support.

5 A self-sustaining federal bureaucracy of career civil servants was formed during Thomas Jefferson's presidency. Andrew Jackson implemented a spoils system through which he appointed his own political supporters. A civil service based on professionalism and merit was the goal of the Civil Service Reform Act of 1883. Concerns that the civil service be freed from the pressures of politics prompted the passage of the Hatch Act in 1939. Significant changes in the administration of the civil service were made by the Civil Service Reform Act of 1978.

6 There have been many attempts to make the federal bureaucracy more open, efficient, and responsive to the needs of U.S. citizens. The most important reforms have included sunshine and sunset laws, contracting out, strategies to provide incentives for increased productivity and efficiency, and protection for whistleblowers.

7 Congress delegates much of its authority to federal agencies when it creates new laws. The bureaucrats who run these agencies may become important policymakers, because Congress has neither the time nor the technical expertise to oversee the administration of its laws. In the agency rulemaking process, a proposed regulation is published. A comment period follows, during which interested parties may offer suggestions for changes. Because companies and other organizations have challenged many regulations in court, federal agencies now are allowed to involve parties that will be affected by new regulations in the rule-drafting process.

8 Congress exerts ultimate control over all federal agencies, because it controls the federal government's purse strings. It also establishes the general guidelines by which regulatory agencies must abide. The appropriations process may also provide a way to send messages of approval or disapproval to particular agencies, as do congressional hearings and investigations relating to agency actions.

Selected print and electronic resources

SUGGESTED READINGS

Downs, Anthony. *Inside Bureaucracy.* Boston: Little, Brown, 1967. In this classic work on the bureaucracy, Downs provides an economist's explanation of why the bureaucracy is what it is and why bureaucrats and their agencies conduct themselves as they do.

Foerstel, Herbert N. *Freedom of Information and the Right to Know: The Origins and Applications of the Freedom of Information Act.* Westport, Conn.: Greenwood Publishing Group, 1999. The author, a strong advocate for freer access to

information in the hands of the government, explores the origins of the American belief that citizens in a democracy have a right to know what their government is doing. He looks closely at the Freedom of Information Act, its use, and the continuing impediments to the "right to know."

Hill, Michael. *The Policy Process in the Modern State.* Englewood Cliffs, N.J.: Prentice Hall, 1998. This overall view of the policymaking process includes a discussion of the role played by bureaucrats in policymaking.

Osborne, David, and Peter Plastrik. *Banishing Bureaucracy: The Five Strategies for Reinventing Government.* Reading, Mass.: Addison-Wesley, 1997. The author of *Reinventing Government* (1992), David Osborne, joined by Peter Plastrik, goes a step further in promoting an entrepreneurial model of government in which market principles are applied to government administration.

Reinhart, Bruce A. *In the Middle of a Muddle: How Not to Reinvent Government.* Washington, D.C.: Brookings Institution Press, 1999. The author offers an insider's perspective into the workings of the Department of Education. He also illustrates what can go wrong when political appointees try to restructure organizations that they do not understand.

MEDIA RESOURCES

Men in Black—A 1997 science-fiction comedy about an unofficial government agency that regulates the immigration of aliens from outer space who are living on earth.

Missiles of October—A movie retelling the events of October 1962, when the Kennedy administration decided to blockade Cuba to force the Soviet Union to remove its missiles from Cuba. The 1974 film, starring William Devane and Ralph Bellamy, gives an excellent inside view of policymaking involving the State Department, the Defense Department, and the president.

1984—A 1984 adaptation of George Orwell's well-known novel about the bureaucratic world of the future, starring John Hurt and Richard Burton; a superb fable of government versus individual values.

Logging on

Numerous links to many federal agencies and information on the federal government can be found at the Web site of Federal World. Go to

http://www.fedworld.gov

The Federal Web Locator is an excellent site to access if you want to find information on the bureaucracy. Its URL is

http://www.infoctr.edu/fwl

The *Federal Register,* which is the official publication for executive-branch documents, is online at

http://www.gpo.ucop.edu/search

Another government publication that you might want to examine is the *United States Government Manual,* which describes the origins, purposes, and administrators of every federal department and agency. To access this publication online, go to

http://www.gpo.ucop.edu/catalog/govman.html

If you want to find telephone numbers for government agencies and personnel, you can go to

http://www.info.gov/fed_directory/ phone.shtml

"The Plum Book," which lists the bureaucratic positions that can be filled by presidential appointment, is online at

http://www.louisville.edu/library/ekstrom/ govpubs/federal/plum.html

Using the Internet for political analysis

Be a critical consumer of government information on the World Wide Web. Go to a government locator page, such as FedWorld (cited above), or to the Center for Information Law and Policy at

http://www.law.vill.edu

and compare the Web pages of at least three federal departments or agencies. Answer the following questions for each Web page:

1. Do you get the basic information about the department or agency, including its goals, locations, size, budget, and how citizens can gain access to the agency?

2. Can you tell from the page who the primary clients of the agency are? For example, are the agency's primary clients governments, ordinary citizens, businesses, or labor unions?

3. Is the page well designed, up to date, and easy for the average citizen to use?

4. What is the most valuable information on the page for you?

chapter 15
The Judiciary

CHAPTER OUTLINE

- The Common Law Tradition
- Sources of American Law
- The Federal Court System
- The Supreme Court at Work
- The Selection of Federal Judges
- The Policymaking Function of the Courts
- What Checks Our Courts?

what if...

Supreme Court Justices Had to Campaign?

BACKGROUND

THE NINE JUSTICES WHO SIT ON THE BENCH OF THE SUPREME COURT ARE NOT ELECTED TO THEIR POSTS. RATHER, THEY ARE APPOINTED BY THE PRESIDENT (AND CONFIRMED BY THE SENATE). THEY ALSO HOLD THEIR OFFICES FOR LIFE, BARRING GROSS MISCONDUCT. NEVERTHELESS, THESE JUSTICES ARE AMONG THE MOST IMPORTANT "POLICYMAKERS" OF THIS NATION BECAUSE THEY HAVE THE FINAL SAY ON HOW THE U.S. CONSTITUTION—THE "SUPREME LAW OF THE LAND"—SHOULD BE INTERPRETED.

IN RECENT YEARS, THE SUPREME COURT HAS BEEN STRONGLY CRITICIZED BY SOME FOR BEING TOO REMOTE FROM THE REAL WORLD OF POLITICS AND FOR MAKING POLICY DECISIONS ON ISSUES WITHOUT REGARD FOR THE PRACTICAL CONSEQUENCES OF THOSE DECISIONS. WOULD THE JUSTICES ACT DIFFERENTLY IF THEY WERE ELECTED AND THEREFORE HAD TO CAMPAIGN FOR THEIR POSITIONS ON THE COURT?

WHAT IF SUPREME COURT JUSTICES HAD TO CAMPAIGN?

Under the existing system, once approved by the Senate and seated on the high court's bench, a justice is free to decide cases as he or she wishes. Because they hold their offices for life, Supreme Court justices do not need to worry about job security. If, however, the justices were elected and had to campaign for election and reelection, the situation could change dramatically.

For one thing, very likely the justices would have to devote a substantial amount of their time to their campaigns, just as members of Congress do. This would take time away from their judicial work, and decisions might receive significantly less deliberation than under the current system. Additionally, if the justices had to run for reelection in order to maintain their seats on the high court, it is only natural that public opinion and particularly the wishes of major campaign contributors would come into play.

INTEREST GROUPS AND CAMPAIGN COSTS

If state judicial campaigns and elections can serve as a guide, it is likely that interest groups that made sizable contributions to the justices' campaigns would wield at least some influence over the justices' decisions. In the thirty-nine states where members of the judiciary are elected, judges increasingly are using their discretion in deciding cases to satisfy public opinion and campaign contributors. Typically, the largest donors to state judicial campaigns are attorneys, parties, or interest groups involved in civil litigation before the judges they are helping to elect.

In a survey of Texas judges sponsored by that state's supreme court, 48 percent of the judges responded that campaign contributions were "fairly influential" or "very influential" in guiding their decisions. In fact, the degree to which elected state judges are influenced by their political and financial supporters has caused some to claim that justice is increasingly "for sale."

POLITICAL IDEOLOGY

Humorist Finley Peter Dunne once said that "th' Supreme Court follows th' iliction returns." In other words, Democratic presidents tend to appoint liberal judges and justices to federal benches, and Republican presidents tend to appoint conservative judges and justices. Ultimately, then, the federal judiciary, including the Supreme Court, does change in response to election returns, but this process takes time.

Justices on the nation's highest court, because they are at the top of the judicial career ladder, sometimes end up sitting on the Supreme Court for decades. If these justices were elected, the ideological complexion of the Court probably would change much more quickly. A voting bloc of liberal or conservative justices might be short-lived, with new alliances being formed after the next election. As a result, the decisions made by the Court, as the final interpreter of the Constitution, might not be very "final." If the next election brought in justices with different ideological views, the Court could overturn the precedents set by the Court during the previous term. Of course, staggered terms could be used, as in the Senate, to ensure more continuity in judicial decision making.

FOR CRITICAL ANALYSIS

1. Should Supreme Court justices be influenced by public opinion when making their decisions? Why or why not?
2. If Supreme Court justices were elected, would their decisions be less authoritative? Explain.

As indicated in this chapter's opening *What If . . . ,* the justices of the Supreme Court are not elected but rather are appointed by the president and confirmed by the Senate. The same is true for all other federal court judges. This fact does not mean that the federal judiciary is apolitical, however. Indeed, our courts play a larger role in making public policy than courts in any other country in the world today.

As Alexis de Tocqueville, a nineteenth-century French commentator on American society, noted, "scarcely any political question arises in the United States that is not resolved, sooner or later, into a judicial question."[1] Our judiciary forms part of our political process. The instant that judges interpret the law, they become actors in the political arena—policymakers working within a political institution. As such, the most important political force within our judiciary is the United States Supreme Court.

How do courts make policy? Why do the federal courts play such an important role in American government? The answers to these questions lie, in part, in our colonial heritage. Most of American law is based on the English system, particularly the English common law tradition. In that tradition, the decisions made by judges constitute an important source of law.

The Common Law Tradition

In 1066, the Normans conquered England, and William the Conqueror and his successors began the process of unifying the country under their rule. One of the ways they did this was to establish the king's courts, or *curiae regis.* Before the conquest, disputes had been settled according to local custom. The king's courts sought to establish a common or uniform set of rules for the whole country. As the number of courts and cases increased, portions of the more important decisions of each year were gathered together and recorded in *Year Books.* Judges settling disputes similar to ones that had been decided before used the *Year Books* as the basis for their decisions. If a case was unique, judges had to create new laws, but they based their decisions on the general principles suggested by earlier cases. The body of judge-made law that developed under this system is still used today and is known as the **common law.**

The practice of deciding new cases with reference to former decisions—that is, according to **precedent**—became a cornerstone of the English and American judicial systems and is embodied in the doctrine of ***stare decisis*** (pronounced *ster*-ay dih-*si*-ses), a Latin phrase that means "to stand on decided cases." The doctrine of *stare decisis* obligates judges to follow the precedents set previously by their own courts or by higher courts that have authority over them.

For example, a lower state court in California would be obligated to follow a precedent set by the California Supreme Court. That lower court, however, would not be obligated to follow a precedent set by the supreme court of another state, because each state court system is independent. Of course, when the United States Supreme Court decides an issue, all of the nation's other courts are obligated to abide by the Court's decision—because the Supreme Court is the highest court in the land.

The doctrine of *stare decisis* provides a basis for judicial decision making in all countries that have common law systems. Today, the United States, Britain, and thirteen other countries have common law systems. Generally, those countries that were once colonies of Great Britain, including Australia, Canada, India, and New Zealand, have retained their English common law heritage since they achieved independence.

INFOTRAC®
COLLEGE EDITION

**Scalia Contra
Common Law Adjudication**

Common Law
Judge-made law that originated in England from decisions shaped according to prevailing custom. Decisions were applied to similar situations and gradually became common to the nation.

Precedent
A court rule bearing on subsequent legal decisions in similar cases. Judges rely on precedents in deciding cases.

Stare Decisis
To stand on decided cases; the judicial policy of following precedents established by past decisions.

---

[1]Alexis de Tocqueville, *Democracy in America* (New York: Harper & Row, 1966), p. 248.

Sources of American Law

The body of American law includes the federal and state constitutions, statutes passed by legislative bodies, administrative law, and case law—the legal principles expressed in court decisions.

Constitutions

The constitutions of the federal government and the states set forth the general organization, powers, and limits of government. The U.S. Constitution is the supreme law of the land. A law in violation of the Constitution, no matter what its source, may be declared unconstitutional and thereafter cannot be enforced. Similarly, the state constitutions are supreme within their respective borders (unless they conflict with the U.S. Constitution or federal laws and treaties made in accordance with it). The Constitution thus defines the political playing field on which state and federal powers are reconciled. The idea that the Constitution should be supreme in certain matters stemmed from widespread dissatisfaction with the weak federal government that had existed previously under the Articles of Confederation adopted in 1781.

Statutes and Administrative Regulations

Although the English common law provides the basis for both our civil and criminal legal systems, statutes (laws enacted by legislatures) increasingly have become important in defining the rights and obligations of individuals. Federal statutes may relate to any subject that is a concern of the federal government and may cover areas ranging from hazardous waste to federal taxation. State statutes include criminal codes, commercial laws, and laws relating to a variety of other matters. Cities, counties, and other local political bodies also pass statutes, which are called ordinances. These ordinances may deal with such issues as zoning proposals and public safety. Rules and regulations issued by administrative agencies are another source of law. Today, much of the work of the courts consists of interpreting these laws and regulations and applying them to circumstances in cases before the courts.

Case Law

Case Law
The rules and principles announced in court decisions. Case law includes judicial interpretations of common law principles and doctrines as well as interpretations of constitutional law, statutory law, and administrative law.

Because we have a common law tradition, in which the doctrine of *stare decisis* plays an important role, the decisions rendered by the courts also form an important body of law, collectively referred to as **case law**. Case law includes judicial interpretations of common law principles and doctrines as well as interpretations of the types of law just mentioned—constitutional provisions, statutes, and administrative agency regulations. As you learned in previous chapters, it is up to the courts, and particularly the Supreme Court, to decide what a constitutional provision or a statutory phrase means. In doing so, the courts, in effect, establish law. (We will discuss this policymaking function of the courts in more detail later in the chapter.)

The Federal Court System

The United States has a dual court system. There are state courts and federal courts. Each of the fifty states, as well as the District of Columbia, has its own fully developed, independent system of courts, which we will examine in Chapter 18. Here we focus on the federal courts.

Basic Judicial Requirements

In either court system, state or federal, before a case can be brought before a court, certain requirements must be met. Two important requirements relate to jurisdiction and standing to sue.

Jurisdiction.   A state court can exercise **jurisdiction** (the authority of the court to hear and decide a case) over the residents of a particular geographic area, such as a county or district. A state's highest court, or supreme court, has jurisdictional authority over all residents within the state. Because the Constitution established a federal government with limited powers, federal jurisdiction is also limited.

Article III, Section 1, of the U.S. Constitution limits the jurisdiction of the federal courts to cases that involve either a federal question or diversity of citizenship. A **federal question** arises when a case is based, at least in part, on the U.S. Constitution, a treaty, or a federal law. A person who claims that her or his rights under the Constitution, such as the right to free speech, have been violated could bring a case in a federal court. **Diversity of citizenship** exists when the parties to a lawsuit are from different states or (more rarely) when the suit involves a U.S. citizen and a government or citizen of a foreign country. The amount in controversy must be at least $75,000 before a federal court can take jurisdiction in a diversity case, however.

Standing to Sue.   Another basic judicial requirement is standing to sue, or a sufficient "stake" in a matter to justify bringing suit. The party bringing a lawsuit must have suffered a harm, or have been threatened by a harm, as a result of the action that led to the dispute in question. Standing to sue also requires that the controversy at issue be a **justiciable** (pronounced just-*tish*-a-buhl) **controversy**—a controversy that is real and substantial, as opposed to hypothetical or academic. In other worlds, a court will not give advisory opinions on hypothetical questions.

Jurisdiction
The authority of a court to decide certain cases. Not all courts have the authority to decide all cases. Where a case arises and what its subject matter is are two jurisdictional factors.

Federal Question
A question that pertains to the U.S. Constitution, acts of Congress, or treaties. A federal question provides a basis for federal jurisdiction.

Diversity of Citizenship
A basis for federal court jurisdiction over a lawsuit that involves citizens of different states or (more rarely) citizens of a U.S. state and citizens or subjects of a foreign country. The amount in controversy must be at least $75,000 before a federal court can take jurisdiction in such cases.

Justiciable Controversy
An actual dispute that raises questions about the law and that is appropriate for resolution before a court.

Types of Federal Courts

As you can see in Figure 15–1, the federal court system is basically a three-tiered model consisting of (1) U.S. district courts and various specialized courts of limited

FIGURE 15–1

The Federal Court System

Trial Court
The court in which most cases usually begin and in which questions of fact are examined.

General Jurisdiction
Exists when a court's authority to hear cases is not significantly restricted. A court of general jurisdiction normally can hear a broad range of cases.

Limited Jurisdiction
Exists when a court's authority to hear cases is restricted to certain types of claims, such as tax claims or bankruptcy petitions.

Appellate Court
A court having jurisdiction to review cases and issues that were originally tried in lower courts.

jurisdiction (not all of the latter are shown in the figure), (2) intermediate U.S. courts of appeals, and (3) the United States Supreme Court.

U.S. District Courts.   The U.S. district courts are trial courts. **Trial courts** are what their name implies—courts in which trials are held and testimony is taken. The U.S. district courts are courts of **general jurisdiction,** meaning that they can hear cases involving a broad array of issues. Federal cases involving most matters typically are heard in district courts. (The other courts on the lower tier of the model shown in Figure 15–1 are courts of **limited jurisdiction,** meaning that they can try cases involving only certain types of claims, such as tax claims or bankruptcy petitions.)

There is at least one federal district court in every state. The number of judicial districts can vary over time, primarily owing to population changes and corresponding case loads. Currently, there are ninety-four federal judicial districts. A party who is dissatisfied with the decision of a district court judge can appeal the case to the appropriate U.S. court of appeals, or federal **appellate court.** Figure 15–2 shows the jurisdictional boundaries of the district courts (which are state boundaries, unless otherwise indicated by dotted lines within a state), as well as of the U.S. courts of appeals.

U.S. Courts of Appeals.   There are thirteen U.S. courts of appeals—also referred to as U.S. circuit courts of appeals. Twelve of these courts, including the U.S. Court of Appeals for the District of Columbia, hear appeals from the federal district courts located within their respective judicial circuits (geographic areas over which they exercise jurisdiction). The Court of Appeals for the Thirteenth Circuit, called the Federal Circuit, has national appellate jurisdiction over certain types of cases, such as cases involving patent law and those in which the U.S. government is a defendant.

Note that when an appellate court reviews a case decided in a district court, the appellate court does not conduct another trial. Rather, a panel of three or more judges reviews the record of the case on appeal, which includes a transcript of the trial proceedings, and determines whether the trial court committed an error. Usually, appellate courts do not look at questions of *fact* (such as whether a party did, in fact, commit a certain action, such as burning a flag) but at questions of *law* (such as whether the act of flag burning is a form of speech protected by the First Amendment to the Constitution). An appellate court will challenge a trial court's finding of fact only when the finding is clearly contrary to the evidence presented at trial or when there is no evidence to support the finding.

A party can petition the United States Supreme Court to review an appellate court's decision. The likelihood that the Supreme Court will grant the petition is slim, however, because the Court reviews only a very few of the cases decided by the appellate courts. This means that decisions made by appellate judges usually are final.

The United States Supreme Court.   The highest level of the three-tiered model of the federal court system is the United States Supreme Court. When the Supreme Court came into existence in 1789, it had five justices. In the following years, more justices were added, and since 1837 there have been nine justices on the Court.

According to the language of Article III of the U.S. Constitution, there is only one national Supreme Court. All other courts in the federal system are considered "inferior." Congress is empowered to create other inferior courts as it deems necessary. The inferior courts that Congress has created include the federal courts of appeals and the district courts, as well as the federal courts of limited jurisdiction.

Although the Supreme Court can exercise original jurisdiction (that is, act as a trial court) in certain cases, such as those affecting foreign diplomats and those in which a state is a party, most of its work is as an appellate court. The Court hears appeals not only from the federal appellate courts but also from the highest state courts. Note, though, that the United States Supreme Court can review a state supreme court decision only if a federal question is involved. Because of its importance in the federal court system, we will look more closely at the Supreme Court in the next section.

Parties and Procedures

In most lawsuits, the parties are the plaintiff (the person or organization that initiates the lawsuit) and the defendant (the person or organization against whom the lawsuit is brought). There may be numerous plaintiffs and defendants in a single lawsuit. In the last several decades, many lawsuits have been brought by interest groups (see Chapter 8). Interest groups play an important role in our judicial system, because they **litigate**—bring to trial—or assist in litigating most cases of racial or gender-based discrimination, virtually all civil liberties cases, and more than one-third of the cases involving business matters. Interest groups also file **amicus curiae** (pronounced ah-*mee*-kous *kur*-ee-eye) **briefs,** or "friend of the court" briefs, in more than 50 percent of these kinds of cases.

Sometimes, interest groups or other plaintiffs will bring a **class-action suit,** in which whatever the court decides will affect all members of a class similarly

Litigate
To engage in a legal proceeding or seek relief in a court of law; to carry on a lawsuit.

Amicus Curiae Brief
A brief (a document containing a legal argument supporting a desired outcome in a particular case) filed by a third party, or *amicus curiae* (Latin for "friend of the court"), who is not directly involved in the litigation but who has an interest in the outcome of the case.

Class-Action Suit
A lawsuit filed by an individual seeking damages for "all persons similarly situated."

FIGURE 15–2

Geographic Boundaries of Federal District Courts and Circuit Courts of Appeals

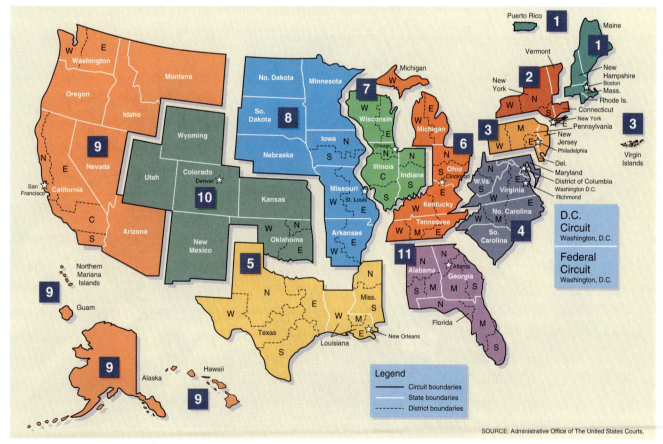

SOURCE: Administrative Office of The United States Courts.

situated (such as users of a particular product manufactured by the defendant in the lawsuit). The strategy of class-action lawsuits was pioneered by such groups as the National Association for the Advancement of Colored People (NAACP), the Legal Defense Fund, and the Sierra Club, whose members believed that the courts—rather than Congress—would offer the most sympathetic forum for their views.

Both the federal and the state courts have established procedural rules that shape the litigation process. These rules are designed to protect the rights and interests of the parties, to ensure that the litigation proceeds in a fair and orderly manner, and to identify the issues that must be decided by the court—thus saving court time and costs. Court decisions may also apply to trial procedures. For example, the Supreme Court has held that the parties' attorneys cannot discriminate against prospective jurors on the basis of race or gender. Some lower courts have also held that people cannot be excluded from juries because of their sexual orientation or religion. (For another issue relating to jury selection, see this chapter's *Making Waves: The Non-English-Speaking Juror.*)

The parties must comply with procedural rules and with any orders given by the judge during the course of the litigation. When a party does not follow a court's order, the court can cite him or her for contempt. A party who commits *civil* contempt (failing to comply with a court's order for the benefit of another party to the proceeding) can be taken into custody, fined, or both, until the party complies with the court's order. A party who commits *criminal* contempt (obstructing the administration of justice or bringing the court into disrespect) also can be taken into custody and fined but cannot avoid punishment by complying with a previous order.

A jury is being sworn in. Most jury trials have between six and twelve jurors. Some trials are held without juries.

Throughout this text, you have read about how technology is affecting all areas of government. The judiciary is no exception. Today's courts are becoming increasingly "wired," and there is little doubt that in the future we will see more court proceedings being conducted via the Internet—as discussed in this chapter's feature *E-mocracy: Toward a Virtual Courtroom* on the next page.

The Supreme Court at Work

The Supreme Court, by law, begins its regular annual term on the first Monday in October and usually adjourns in late June or early July of the next year. Special sessions may be held after the regular term is over, but only a few cases are decided in this way. More commonly, cases are carried over until the next regular session.

Of the total number of cases that are decided each year, those reviewed by the Supreme Court represent less than one-half of 1 percent. Included in these, however, are decisions that profoundly affect our lives. In recent years, the United States Supreme Court has decided issues involving capital punishment, affirmative action programs, religious freedom, assisted suicide, abortion, busing, term limits for congresspersons, sexual harassment, pornography, states' rights, limits on federal jurisdiction, and numerous other matters with significant consequences for the nation. Because the Supreme Court exercises a great deal of discretion over the types of cases it hears, it can influence the nation's policies by issuing decisions in some types of cases and refusing to hear appeals in others, thereby allowing lower court decisions to stand.

making Waves

The Non-English-Speaking Juror

In January 2000, forty-three-year-old carpenter Benito Casillas made waves when he turned up in court, as ordered, to serve on a jury in the Doña Ana County Courthouse in New Mexico. The problem was, the trial would be conducted in English, a language that Casillas did not understand. No matter, said the court, an interpreter would be provided.

Courts in all states commonly provide interpreters for non-English-speaking witnesses or defendants. But only in New Mexico does the state constitution, in a provision that has been on the books since 1912, state that people cannot be excluded from jury duty simply because they do not speak or read English. Despite this provision, people who could not speak English were routinely excluded from jury duty in New Mexico—until 1998, when the New Mexico Supreme Court upheld the provision. As a result of the court's decision, courts in New Mexico now must provide interpreters for non-English-speaking jurors, such as Casillas.

Providing interpreters for non-English-speaking jurors certainly enlarges the number of prospective jurors in New Mexico. Hispanics account for nearly half of New Mexico's population. In Doña Ana County, approximately 100,000 of the county's 169,000 residents are Hispanic. According to John Greacen, director of the administrative office of the New Mexico court system, the state supreme court's 1998 ruling was "not a bad thing" but "a recognition that we are living in a truly multicultural society, and the courts simply have to adjust to that fact."*

FOR CRITICAL ANALYSIS

"Non-English-speaking jurors should not be allowed to sit on juries because there is no way of guaranteeing that the interpreter's translation of trial proceedings is accurate." Analyze this statement.

*As quoted in Guillermo X. Garcia, "N.M. Carpenter Becomes First Non-English-Speaking Juror," *USA Today,* February 4, 2000, p. 4A.

Which Cases Reach the Supreme Court?

Many people are surprised to learn that in a typical case, there is no absolute right of appeal to the United States Supreme Court. The Court's appellate jurisdiction is almost entirely discretionary—the Court can choose which cases it will decide. The justices never explain their reasons for hearing certain cases and not others, so it is difficult to predict which case or type of case the Court might select. Chief Justice William Rehnquist, in his description of the selection process in *The Supreme Court: How It Was, How It Is,*[2] said that the decision of whether or not to accept a case "strikes me as a rather subjective decision, made up in part of intuition and in part of legal judgment."

Factors That Bear on the Decision.   Factors that bear on the decision include whether a legal question has been decided differently by various lower courts and needs resolution by the highest court, whether a lower court's decision conflicts with an existing Supreme Court ruling, and whether the issue could have significance beyond the parties to the dispute. For example, the justices probably decided to review the sexual-harassment case brought by Paula Jones against President Clinton (see Chapter 5) because it also involved an important question—whether a president should have to defend himself against a lawsuit while in office.

---

[2]William H. Rehnquist, *The Supreme Court: How It Was, How It Is* (New York: Morrow, 1987).

e-mocracy

Toward a Virtual Courtroom

Most courts in the United States now have sites on the Web. Of course, it is up to each court to decide what to make available at its site. Some courts display only the names of court personnel and office phone numbers. Others add court rules and forms. Some include judicial decisions, although generally the sites do not include archives of old decisions. Instead, decisions are available online for only a limited time. For example, California keeps opinions online for sixty days. Generally, except for the decisions of the United States Supreme Court and some opinions in classic cases, few court decisions that predate the 1990s are available online free of charge.

At some point in the future, we may see the use of *virtual courtrooms,* in which judicial proceedings take place totally via the Internet. Already, a number of courts allow court documents, such as those initiating a lawsuit, to be filed electronically.

ELECTRONIC FILING

The federal court system first experimented with an electronic filing system in January 1996, in an asbestos case heard by a federal court in Ohio. Currently, more than a dozen federal courts permit attorneys to file documents electronically in certain types of cases. At last count, more than 130,000 documents in approximately 10,000 cases had been filed electronically in federal courts.

State and local courts also are setting up electronic court filing systems. Since late 1997, the Pima County, Arizona, court system has been accepting filings of litigation documents via e-mail. In 1998, the supreme court of the state of Washington also began to accept online filing of litigation documents. Electronic filing projects are also being developed in other states, including Kansas, Virginia, Utah, and Michigan. Notably, the judicial branch of the state of Colorado recently decided to implement the first statewide court e-filing system in the United States. When implementation is complete, an Internet-based service will allow all Colorado civil courts to accept legal filings electronically. In California, Florida, and a few other states, some court clerks offer docket information and other searchable databases online.

VIRTUAL COURTROOMS

In the future, it is possible that litigation will also be conducted entirely via the Internet. The parties to a case could meet online to make their arguments and present their evidence. This might be done with e-mail submissions, through video cameras, in designated "chat" rooms, at closed sites, or through the use of any other Internet facility. These courtrooms could be efficient and economical. It is possible that we will also see the use of virtual lawyers, judges, and juries.

FOR CRITICAL ANALYSIS

Some are concerned that people will have less respect for the law if litigation is conducted via the Internet instead of in traditional courtrooms. Do you agree? Why or why not?

In the 1999–2000 term, the justices decided to review a number of cases relating to states' rights and the scope of the national government's regulatory powers. Very likely, the Court accepted these cases for review because of the growing sentiment, shared by several Supreme Court justices, that the national government has overreached its regulatory authority at the expense of states' rights and because of the significance of these issues for American government.

Another factor is whether the solicitor general is pressuring the Court to take a case. The solicitor general, a high-ranking presidential appointee within the Justice Department, represents the national government in the Supreme Court and promotes presidential policies in the federal courts. He or she decides what cases the government should ask the Supreme Court to review and what position the government should take in cases before the Court. The influence wielded by solicitors general over the Court's decision making has led some to refer to the solicitor general as the "Tenth Justice."

Granting Petitions for Review. If the Court decides to grant a petition for review, it will issue a **writ of *certiorari*** (pronounced sur-shee-uh-*rah*-ree). The writ orders a lower court to send the Supreme Court a record of the case for review. More than 90 percent of the petitions for writs of *certiorari* are denied. A denial is not a decision on the merits of a case, nor does it indicate agreement with the lower court's opinion. (The judgment of the lower court remains in force, however.) Therefore, denial of the writ has no value as a precedent. The

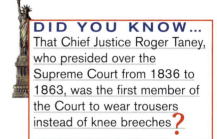

Writ of *Certiorari*
An order issued by a higher court to a lower court to send up the record of a case for review. It is the principal vehicle for United States Supreme Court review.

In her chambers, Justice Ruth Bader Ginsburg works on her case load with one of her law clerks. Each justice has four law clerks, who typically are culled from the "best and the brightest" graduates from U.S. law schools. Some critics of the Supreme Court's practices argue that the clerks have too much power and influence over the Court's decision making.

Rule of Four
A United States Supreme Court procedure requiring four affirmative votes to hear the case before the full Court.

Oral Arguments
The verbal arguments presented in person by attorneys to an appellate court. Each attorney presents reasons to the court why the court should rule in her or his client's favor.

Court will not issue a writ unless at least four justices approve of it. This is called the **rule of four**.[3]

Deciding Cases

Once the Supreme Court grants *certiorari* in a particular case, the justices do extensive research on the legal issues and facts involved in the case. (Of course, some preliminary research was necessary before deciding to grant the petition for review.) Each justice is entitled to four law clerks, who undertake much of the research and preliminary drafting necessary for the justice to form an opinion.[4] (A question debated in recent years has to do with whether the Supreme Court should hire more minority law clerks—see this chapter's feature *An Ethical Issue* for a discussion of this topic.)

The Court normally does not hear any evidence, as is true with all appeals courts. The Court's consideration of a case is based on the abstracts, the record, and the briefs. The attorneys are permitted to present **oral arguments**. The Court hears oral arguments on Monday, Tuesday, Wednesday, and sometimes Thursday, usually for seven two-week sessions scattered from the first week in October to the end of April or the first week in May. All statements and the justices' questions are tape-recorded during these sessions. Unlike the practice in most courts, lawyers addressing the Supreme Court can be (and often are) questioned by the justices at any time during oral argument.

The justices meet to discuss and vote on cases in conferences held each Wednesday and Friday throughout the term. In these conferences, in addition to deciding cases currently before the Court, the justices decide which new petitions for *certiorari* to grant. These conferences take place in the oak-paneled chamber and are strictly private—no stenographers, tape recorders, or video cameras are allowed. Two pages used to be in attendance to wait on the justices

---

[3]The "rule of four" is modified when seven or fewer justices participate, which occurs from time to time. When that happens, as few as three justices can grant *certiorari*.

[4]For a former Supreme Court law clerk's account of the role these clerks play in the high court's decision-making process, see Edward Lazarus, *Closed Chambers: The First Eyewitness Account of the Epic Struggles inside the Supreme Court* (New York: Times Books, 1998).

an ethical issue

Should the Supreme Court Hire More Minority Clerks?

Although minority representation on the lower federal courts increased during the last decade, the same cannot be said about the Supreme Court. John Paul Stevens, the most liberal voice on the Court, is the only justice who has hired more than one African American law clerk during his tenure. Clarence Thomas, the Court's only black justice, has had only one black clerk during his tenure on the Court. In all, less than 2 percent of the 428 clerks hired by current justices during their respective tenures have been African American. Since 1998, when the media first reported these numbers, the Court has faced strong criticism from civil rights groups for failing to hire more minority clerks.

Chief Justice William Rehnquist defends the Court's clerk-hiring practices by stating that the low number of minorities hired is due to their low representation in the "talent pool"—which, for the most part, consists of graduates from eight elite law schools. As the demographic makeup of the pool changes, the underrepresentation of minorities will also change, claims Rehnquist. That day may one day come, say those who criticize the Court's hiring practices, but in the meantime isn't there something that the Court can do to rectify this demographic imbalance?

Thomas Brennan, president of the Thomas Cooley Law School in Lansing, Michigan, recently proposed a solution. He suggests that the Court should enlarge the pool to include students from each of the nation's 175 accredited law schools. Each school could nominate a top student to be included in a national "dean's list." The justices could then at least consider applicants from this list and see if they are qualified. To date, the Supreme Court has preferred to continue with its current system.

FOR CRITICAL ANALYSIS

Should Supreme Court justices give more priority to minority representation when hiring law clerks? Why or why not?

while they were in conference, but fear of information leaks caused the Court to stop this practice.[5]

Decisions and Opinions

When the Court has reached a decision, its opinion is written. The **opinion** contains the Court's ruling on the issue or issues presented, the reasons for its decision, the rules of law that apply, and other information. In many cases, the decision of the lower court is **affirmed,** resulting in the enforcement of that court's judgment or decree. If the Supreme Court feels that a reversible error was committed during the trial or that the jury was instructed improperly, however, the decision will be **reversed.** Sometimes the case will be **remanded** (sent back to the court that originally heard the case) for a new trial or other proceeding. For example, a lower court might have held that a party was not entitled to bring a lawsuit under a particular law. If the Supreme Court holds to the contrary, it will remand (send back) the case to the trial court with instructions that the trial go forward.

The Court's written opinion sometimes is unsigned; this is called an opinion *per curiam* ("by the court"). Typically, the Court's opinion will be signed by all the justices who agree with it. Usually, when in the majority, the chief justice will write the opinion. Whenever the chief justice is in the minority, the senior justice on the majority side decides who writes the opinion.

When all justices unanimously agree on an opinion, the opinion is written for the entire Court (all the justices) and can be deemed a **unanimous opinion.** When there is not a unanimous opinion, a **majority opinion** is written, outlining the views of the majority of the justices involved in the particular case. Often, one or more justices who feel strongly about making or emphasizing a particular point that is not made or emphasized in the unanimous or majority written opinion will write a **concurring opinion.** That means the justice writing the concurring opinion agrees (concurs) with the conclusion given in the majority written opinion, but for different reasons. Finally, in other than unanimous opinions, one or more dissenting opinions are usually written by those justices who do not agree with the majority. The **dissenting opinion** is important because it often forms the basis of the arguments used years later that cause the Court to reverse the previous decision and establish a new precedent.

Shortly after the opinion is written, the Supreme Court announces its decision from the bench. At that time, the opinion is made available to the public at the office of the clerk of the Court. The clerk also releases the opinion for online publication (see the *Logging on* section at the end of this chapter for the Supreme Court's official Web site, as well as other Web sites that publish Supreme Court opinions). Ultimately, the opinion is published in the *United States Reports,* which is the official printed record of the Court's decisions.

The Selection of Federal Judges

All federal judges are appointed. The Constitution, in Article II, Section 2, states that the president appoints the justices of the Supreme Court with the advice and consent of the Senate. Congress has provided the same procedure for staffing other federal courts. This means that the Senate and the president jointly decide who shall be a federal judge, no matter what the level.

---

[5]It turned out that one supposed information leak came from lawyers making educated guesses.

DID YOU KNOW...
That today, a federal appellate judge will typically turn out fifty signed opinions each year, while the nine Supreme Court justices combined issue about seventy-five signed opinions per year?

Opinion
The statement by a judge or a court of the decision reached in a case tried or argued before it. The opinion sets forth the law that applies to the case and details the legal reasoning on which the ruling was based.

Affirm
To declare that a court ruling is valid and must stand.

Reverse
To annul or make void a court ruling on account of some error or irregularity.

Remand
To send a case back to the court that originally heard it.

Unanimous Opinion
A court opinion or determination on which all judges agree.

Majority Opinion
A court opinion reflecting the views of the majority of the judges.

Concurring Opinion
A separate opinion, prepared by a judge who supports the decision of the majority of the court but who wants to make or clarify a particular point or to voice disapproval of the grounds on which the decision was made.

Dissenting Opinion
A separate opinion in which a judge dissents from (disagrees with) the conclusion reached by the majority on the court and expounds his or her own views about the case.

Senatorial Courtesy
In regard to federal district court judgeship nominations, a Senate tradition allowing a senator of the president's political party to veto a judicial appointment in his or her state simply by indicating that the appointment is personally not acceptable. At that point, the Senate may reject the nomination, or the president may withdraw consideration of the nominee.

There are over 850 federal judgeships in the United States. Once appointed to such a judgeship, a person holds that job for life. Judges serve until they resign, retire voluntarily, or die. Federal judges who engage in blatantly illegal conduct may be removed through impeachment, although such action is extremely rare.

Nominating Judicial Candidates

Judicial candidates for federal judgeships are suggested to the president by the Department of Justice, senators, other judges, the candidates themselves, and lawyers' associations and other interest groups. In selecting a candidate to nominate for a judgeship, the president considers not only the person's competence but also other factors, including the person's political philosophy (as will be discussed shortly), ethnicity, and gender.

The nomination process—no matter how the nominees are obtained—always works the same way. The president makes the actual nomination, transmitting the name to the Senate. The Senate then either confirms or rejects the nomination. To reach a conclusion, the Senate Judiciary Committee (operating through subcommittees) invites testimony, both written and oral, at its various hearings. In the case of federal district court judgeships, a practice used in the Senate, called **senatorial courtesy**, is a constraint on the president's freedom to appoint whomever the administration chooses. Senatorial courtesy allows a senator of the president's political party to veto a judicial appointment in her or his state.

Federal District Court Judgeship Nominations.   Although the president nominates federal judges, the nomination of federal district court judges typically originates with a senator or senators of the president's party from the state in which there is a vacancy. If the nominee is deemed unqualified, as a matter of political courtesy the president will discuss with the senator or senators who originated the nomination whether the nomination should be withdrawn. Also, when a nomination is unacceptable politically to the president, the president will consult with the appropriate senator or senators, indicate that the nomination is unacceptable, and work with the senator or senators to seek an alternative candidate.

Federal Courts of Appeals Appointments.   There are many fewer federal courts of appeals appointments than federal district court appointments, but they are more important. This is because federal appellate judges handle more important matters, at least from the point of view of the president, and therefore presidents take a keener interest in the nomination process for such judgeships. Also, appointments to the U.S. courts of appeals have become "steppingstones" to the Supreme Court. Typically, the president culls the Circuit Judge Nominating Commission's list of nominees for potential candidates. The president may also use this list to oppose senators' recommendations that may be unacceptable politically to the president.

Supreme Court Appointments.   As we have described, the president nominates Supreme Court justices.[6] As you can see in Table 15–1, which summarizes the background of all Supreme Court justices to 2000, the most common occupational background of the justices at the time of their appointments has been private legal practice or state or federal judgeships. Those nine justices who were

[6]For a discussion of the factors that may come into play during the process of nominating Supreme Court justices, see David A. Yalof, *Pursuit of Justices: Presidential Politics and the Selection of Supreme Court Nominees* (Chicago: University of Chicago Press, 1999).

TABLE 15-1

Background of Supreme Court Justices to 2001

	NUMBER OF JUSTICES (108 = TOTAL)
Occupational Position before Appointment	
Private legal practice	25
State judgeship	21
Federal judgeship	28
U.S. attorney general	7
Deputy or assistant U.S. attorney general	2
U.S. solicitor general	2
U.S. senator	6
U.S. representative	2
State governor	3
Federal executive post	9
Other	3
Religious Background	
Protestant	83
Roman Catholic	11
Jewish	6
Unitarian	7
No religious affiliation	1
Age on Appointment	
Under 40	5
41–50	31
51–60	58
61–70	14
Political Party Affiliation	
Federalist (to 1835)	13
Democratic Republican (to 1828)	7
Whig (to 1861)	1
Democrat	44
Republican	42
Independent	1
Educational Background	
College graduate	92
Not a college graduate	16
Gender	
Male	106
Female	2
Race	
Caucasian	106
Other	2

SOURCE: Congressional Quarterly, *Congressional Quarterly's Guide to the U.S. Supreme Court* (Washington, D.C.: Congressional Quarterly Press, 1996); and authors' update.

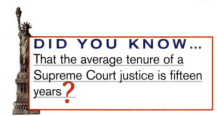

DID YOU KNOW...
That the average tenure of a Supreme Court justice is fifteen years?

in federal executive posts at the time of their appointments held the high offices of secretary of state, comptroller of the treasury, secretary of the navy, post-master general, secretary of the interior, chairman of the Securities and Exchange Commission, and secretary of labor. In the "Other" category under "Occupational Position before Appointment" in Table 15–1 are two justices who were professors of law (including William H. Taft, a former president) and one justice who was a North Carolina state employee with responsibility for organizing and revising the state's statutes.

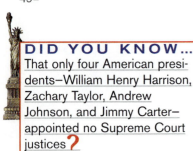

Partisanship and Judicial Appointments

Ideology plays an important role in the president's choices for judicial appointments. As a result, presidential appointments to the federal judiciary have had an extremely partisan distribution. The justices' partisan attachments have been mostly the same as those of the president who appointed them. There have been some exceptions, however. Nine nominal Democrats have been appointed by Republican presidents, three Republicans by Democratic presidents, and one Democrat by Whig president John Tyler.[7]

Presidents see their federal judiciary appointments as the one sure way to institutionalize their political views long after they have left office. By 1993, for example, Presidents Reagan and Bush together had appointed nearly three-quarters of all federal court judges. This preponderance of Republican-appointed federal judges strengthened the legal moorings of the conservative social agenda on a variety of issues, ranging from abortion to civil rights. Nevertheless, President Bill Clinton had the opportunity to appoint about two hundred federal judges, thereby shifting the ideological makeup of the federal judiciary. Also, Clinton's appointees matched more closely the actual U.S. demographics than did the appointees of his predecessors. By the end of his presidency, Clinton had appointed more women and members of minority groups to federal judgeships than any other president.

The 2000 Elections and the Supreme Court

While never a major campaign issue, the future of the Supreme Court certainly played a role in the 2000 elections. Some observers predicted that at least three and perhaps even four justices would be retiring within the newly elected president's first term. Thus, the new president, through judicial appointments to the high court, would be able to exercise considerable influence over the future ideological makeup and decisions of the Court. Several Democratic candidates, including Al Gore, emphasized that pro-choice groups should vote Democratic, because "a woman's right to choose" hung in the balance. Others, however, including several Supreme Court scholars, thought that talk of judicial appointments was premature—after all, none of the justices had even mentioned retirement. Furthermore, as many presidents have learned, there is no guarantee that once appointed to the bench, a justice's decisions will please the president.

The Senate's Role

Ideology also plays a large role in the Senate's confirmation hearings, and presidential nominees to the Supreme Court have not always been confirmed. In fact, almost 20 percent of presidential nominations to the Supreme Court have been either rejected or not acted on by the Senate. Numerous acrimonious battles over Supreme Court appointments have ensued when the Senate and the president have not seen eye to eye about political matters.

The U.S. Senate had a long record of refusing to confirm the president's judicial nominations from the beginning of Andrew Jackson's presidency in 1829 to the end of Ulysses Grant's presidency in 1877. During a fairly long period of relative acquiescence to presidential nominations on the part of the Senate, from 1894 until 1968, only three nominees were not confirmed. From 1968 through 1986, however, two presidential nominees to the highest court were rejected.

---

[7]Actually, Tyler was a member of the Democratic Party who ran with William H. Harrison on the Whig ticket. When Harrison died, much to the surprise of the Whigs, Tyler—a Democrat—became president, although they tried to call him "acting president." Thus, some historians would quibble over the statement that Tyler was a Whig.

Both were Nixon appointees, rejected because of questions about their racial attitudes. In 1987, two of President Ronald Reagan's nominees failed to be confirmed—Robert Bork was rejected for his views on the Constitution, and Douglas Ginsburg withdrew his nomination when it was reported that he had used marijuana in the 1970s.

President George Bush had little difficulty securing the Senate's confirmation of his nomination of David Souter to fill the void on the Court left when Justice William Brennan retired in 1989. Bush's second nominee, Clarence Thomas, underwent an extremely volatile confirmation hearing in 1991, replete with charges of sexual harassment leveled at him by his former aide, Anita Hill. Despite Hill's dramatic and televised allegations, however, Thomas's nomination was confirmed.

In 1993, President Clinton had little trouble gaining approval for his nominee to take the seat left vacant by Justice Byron White. Ruth Bader Ginsburg became the second female Supreme Court justice. In 1994, Clinton nominated Stephen Breyer, a federal court of appeals judge, to fill the seat of retiring Supreme Court Justice Harry Blackmun. Breyer, who was seen by many as a consensus builder who might effectively pull together justices with divergent views, was confirmed without significant opposition.

President Clinton found it more difficult to secure Senate approval for his judicial nominations to the lower courts, however, just as he had difficulty with nominations to executive-branch posts. In fact, during the late 1990s the duel between the Senate and the president aroused considerable concern about the consequences of the increasingly partisan and ideological tension over federal judicial appointments. As a result of Senate delays in confirming nominations, the number of judicial vacancies mounted, as did the backlog of cases pending in the federal courts. (See this chapter's *Critical Perspective* on pages 494 and 495 for a further discussion of this issue.)

The Policymaking Function of the Courts

The partisan battles over judicial appointments reflect an important reality in today's American government: the importance of the judiciary in national politics. Because appointments to the federal benches are for life, the ideology of judicial appointees can affect national policy for years to come. Although the primary function of judges in our system of government is to interpret and apply the laws, inevitably judges make policy when carrying out this task. One of the major policymaking tools of the federal courts is their power of judicial review.

Judicial Review

Remember from Chapter 2 that the power of the courts to determine whether a law or action by the other branches of government is constitutional is known as the power of *judicial review*. This power of the judiciary enables the judicial branch to act as a check on the other two branches of government, in line with the checks and balances system established by the U.S. Constitution.

The power of judicial review is not mentioned in the Constitution, however. Rather, it was established by the United States Supreme Court's decision in *Marbury v. Madison*.[8] In that case, in which the Court declared that a law passed by Congress violated the Constitution, the Court claimed such a power for the courts:

---

[8]5 U.S. 137 (1803).

INFOTRAC®
COLLEGE EDITION

Must Joe Robinson Die

Demonstrators protest the possible confirmation of Judge Clarence Thomas in 1991, after Professor Anita Hill charged him with sexually harassing her while she was his employee. After long and difficult hearings on the subject, the Senate voted to confirm Thomas's nomination.

critical perspective

The Politicization of the Judicial Appointment Process

There used to be an implicit understanding that the president had a popular mandate to appoint as federal judges men and women whose views were compatible with those of the president. In effect, judicial appointments were part of an electoral spoils system. Although the U.S. Senate has the power of advice and consent in all federal judicial appointments, for most of this country's history the Senate did not interfere with the president's choices unless a nominee was clearly unfit to carry out the job. The Senate was also fairly prompt in confirming judicial appointments.

Times have changed. Today, the Senate needs approximately seven months to confirm a judicial nomination, compared to about one month in the early 1980s. These delays resulted in part from divided government. But they also have been ascribed to the bitter partisan battles between President Clinton and the Republican-led Senate. By 1997, President Clinton was accusing the Republican majority in Congress of politicizing the judicial appointment process. His proof: the unfilled vacancies on the federal bench. During 1997, for example, more than one hundred federal judgeships were vacant. Thirty of those were ranked as "judicial emergencies" because they had remained empty for more than eighteen months. Nine months into that year, only nine federal judges had been approved by the Senate. Also during that year, a record wait of 183 days from nomination to confirmation occurred.

The results of these delays include significantly increased case loads for the federal bench as well as increased delays in settling cases. In some areas, the period between filing the last brief and a court hearing is two hundred days—60 percent longer than average. Additionally, there is a growing backlog of federal cases. The number of suits waiting three years or more to be heard has increased to over sixteen thousand. The federal judiciary has asked Congress for legislation to add fifty-five judgeships to the federal court system, even though Congress increased the size of the federal judiciary as recently as 1990.

Rehnquist's Report on the Federal Judiciary

By late 1997, the vacancy situation had become so bad that Chief Justice Rehnquist, in his year-end *Report on the Federal Judiciary*, stated that judicial vacancies were aggravating the problem of "too few judges and too much work." He argued that "vacancies cannot remain at such high levels indefinitely without eroding the quality of justice that has been traditionally associated with the Federal judiciary." His plea was simple: the president should nominate candidates with reasonable promptness, and the Senate should act within a reasonable time to confirm or reject them.*

Have Partisan Republicans Been to Blame?

During Clinton's tenure as president, the view seemed to be that Republicans were trying to prevent Clinton from appointing liberal activist jurists. Some Republicans did, in fact, implicitly "declare war" on Clinton's judicial choices. They delved into everything written by Clinton judicial nominees in an effort to dig up evidence of liberal judicial activism. At least one researcher, Professor Emeritus Gideon Kanner of Loyola Law School (Los Angeles), however, does not believe that the current politicization of Supreme Court nominees is a recent phenomenon. He goes back to the 1930s to find its roots.

*The New York Times, National Edition, January 1, 1998, p. A15.

It is emphatically the province and duty of the Judicial Department to say what the law is. Those who apply the rule to a particular case, must of necessity expound and interpret that rule. If two laws conflict with each other, the courts must decide on the operation of each.

If a federal court declares that a federal or state law or policy is unconstitutional, the court's decision affects the application of the law or policy only within that court's jurisdiction. For this reason, the higher the level of the court, the greater the impact of the decision on society. Because of the Supreme Court's national jurisdiction, its decisions can have a significant impact. For example, when the Supreme Court held that an Arkansas state constitutional amendment limiting the terms of congresspersons was unconstitutional, laws establishing term limits in twenty-three other states also were invalidated.[9]

[9]*U.S. Term Limits v. Thornton,* 514 U.S. 779 (1995).

critical perspective

When President Franklin Roosevelt proposed numerous New Deal laws during his first few months in office, he found a hostile Supreme Court, one that struck down many of the new laws as unconstitutional. He came up with a solution. He threatened to "pack the court" with additional judges selected on the basis of their support for his New Deal philosophy. The nine justices of the Supreme Court at that time got the message. They no longer ruled against New Deal legislation. According to Professor Gideon Kanner, from that day on, "an ideologically compliant judiciary was thus legitimized with a bang."†

Professor Kanner then points out that the Warren Court—the Court presided over by Chief Justice Earl Warren from 1953 to 1969—contributed greatly to the politicization of the federal judicial process in general, and therefore to the nomination process. Warren frequently would interrupt carefully legally reasoned arguments to ask, "Yes, but is it fair?" By stressing what is fair as opposed to what is law, according to Kanner, the Warren Court created among politicians and the public a dichotomous view of judges. Those who were liberal were considered to be "fair"; those who were conservative were considered to be "mean spirited." The end result is an intense scrutiny of federal judicial nominees by whichever party is in power in Congress.

Reagan, Bork, Bush, Thomas, and Senate Democrats

The most blatantly political battle over a Supreme Court justice nominee since the mid-1980s occurred in 1987, when President Ronald

Reagan nominated Robert Bork to be on the Supreme Court. A respected legal scholar and federal circuit judge, Bork fell prey to hostile Democrats during the Senate hearings to evaluate his nomination. The proceedings were bitter, and the criticisms of Bork were often petty. Even the videos he and his wife checked out from the local rental store were mentioned. In the end, the Senate rejected his nomination.

The nationally televised spectacle of the grilling of Clarence Thomas in 1991 further cemented the notion of the legitimacy of the politicization of the federal judicial nominating process. Later, at the end of the Bush administration, 102 vacant federal judgeships were blocked by Senate Democrats. Thus, Kanner concludes, it should come as no surprise that during Clinton's tenure as president, the Republican majority in the Senate delayed scheduling of floor debates and votes on judicial nominations.

Whether political battles over judicial appointments will occur in the coming years is uncertain. Given the strongly divided Congress resulting from the 2000 elections, it is likely that any judicial appointee with a liberal or a conservative bent will face prolonged proceedings in, and possible rejection by, the Senate. Probably the only candidates to pass Senate muster will have to be in the center of the ideological spectrum.

FOR CRITICAL ANALYSIS
1. Why are federal judicial appointments seemingly so important to both the president and the party in power in Congress?
2. What might result if Senate confirmation were not required for presidential appointments of federal judges?

†Gideon Kanner, "Don't Forget Who Brought Politics to the Bench," *The National Law Journal*, February 2, 1998, p. A20.

Some claim that the power of judicial review gives unelected judges and justices on federal court benches too much influence over national policy. Despite continued attacks on the legitimacy of judicial review, courts continue to exercise the power. (Judicial review is also practiced by courts in other countries around the world—see this chapter's *Global View* on page 496 for details.)

Judicial Activism and Judicial Restraint

Judicial scholars like to characterize different judges and justices as being either activist or restraintist. The doctrine of **judicial activism** rests on the conviction that the federal judiciary should take an active role in using its powers to check the activities of Congress, state legislatures, and administrative agencies when those government bodies exceed their authority. One of the Supreme Court's most activist eras was the period from 1953 to 1969 when the Court was headed

Judicial Activism
A doctrine holding that the Supreme Court should take an active role in using its powers to check the activities of Congress, state legislatures, and administrative agencies when those government bodies exceed their authority.

Judicial Restraint
A doctrine holding that the Supreme Court should defer to the decisions made by the elected representatives of the people in the legislative and executive branches.

by Chief Justice Earl Warren. The Warren Court propelled the civil rights movement forward by holding, among other things, that laws permitting racial segregation violated the equal protection clause.

In contrast, the doctrine of **judicial restraint** rests on the assumption that the courts should defer to the decisions made by the legislative and executive branches, because members of Congress and the president are elected by the people whereas members of the federal judiciary are not. Because administrative agency personnel normally have more expertise than the courts do in the areas regulated by the agencies, the courts likewise should defer to agency rules and decisions. In other words, under the doctrine of judicial restraint, the courts should not thwart the implementation of legislative acts and agency rules unless they are clearly unconstitutional.

Judicial activism sometimes is linked with liberalism, and judicial restraint with conservatism. In fact, a conservative judge can be activist, just as a liberal judge can be restraintist—and vice versa. In the 1950s and 1960s, the Supreme Court was activist and liberal. Some observers believe that the Rehnquist Court, with its conservative majority, has become increasingly activist since the 1990s. Some go even further and claim that judicial activism on the federal courts, including the Supreme Court, is getting out of hand—see this chapter's *Which Side Are You On?* for an exploration of this issue.

Ideology and the Rehnquist Court

William H. Rehnquist became the sixteenth chief justice of the Supreme Court in 1986, after fifteen years as an associate justice. He was known as a strong anchor of the Court's conservative

global View

Judicial Review

The concept of judicial review was pioneered by the United States. As noted elsewhere, the U.S. Constitution does not explicitly mention that the Supreme Court may rule actions of the other branches of government invalid on the grounds that they violate the Constitution. Yet the Court's 1803 assertion in *Marbury v. Madison* that it had this power became widely accepted in this country. Some maintain that one of the reasons the doctrine was readily accepted was that it fit in well with the checks and balances designed by the founders, who were as concerned about the tyranny of popular majorities as they were with giving the people a voice in government.

JUDICIAL REVIEW VERSUS POPULAR SOVEREIGNTY

Ironically, these same concerns prompted European countries to go in the opposite direction, at least initially. Judicial review was perceived as a force contrary to popular sovereignty. As representatives of the people, parliaments should not have their actions invalidated by unelected court judges. These attitudes later changed, however, with the rise of fascist and totalitarian governments in the 1920s and 1930s. It became clear that "popular" leaders, such as Adolf Hitler in Germany and Benito Mussolini in Italy, could be far more dangerous to individual lib-

erty than any court. As a result, the courts came to be viewed, as in the United States, as protectors of civil rights and liberties.

JUDICIAL REVIEW ACROSS NATIONS

Today, all established constitutional democracies have some type of judicial review—the power to rule on the constitutionality of laws—but its form varies from country to country. For example, Canada's Supreme Court can exercise judicial review only if a law does not include a provision explicitly prohibiting such review. France has a Constitutional Council that rules on the constitutionality of laws before the laws take effect. The president, prime minister, and the heads of the two chambers of parliament can refer laws to the council for prior review. Prior review is also an option in Germany and Italy, if requested by the national or a regional government. In contrast, the United States Supreme Court does not give advisory opinions; rather, there must be an actual dispute concerning an issue before the Supreme Court can render a decision on the matter.

FOR CRITICAL ANALYSIS

In any country in which a constitution sets forth the basic powers and structure of government, some government branch or unit has to decide whether laws enacted by government are consistent with that constitution. Is this task best handled by the courts? Can you think of a better alternative?

which side are you on?

Is Judicial Activism Getting Out of Hand?

In recent years, federal judges, including Supreme Court justices, have come under attack for being too activist and "legislating from the bench" on policy issues. Steve Forbes, a conservative candidate running for the presidency during the early stages of the 2000 campaigns, stated that judicial activism was "out of control and must be stopped." Orrin Hatch, the chair of the Senate Judiciary Committee, has repeatedly warned against "activist judges." One bill introduced in Congress, but never passed, would have permitted activist judges to be impeached. Other proposals would, among other things, limit the federal courts' power of judicial review, a power that allows the federal courts to invalidate actions taken by the other two branches of government.

Activism on the High Court?

Critics of the extensive powers of the federal judiciary are particularly concerned with what they perceive as an activist majority on today's Supreme Court. In a number of five-to-four decisions, the conservative majority on the Court has invalidated provisions of laws passed by Congress. Some of these decisions, claim these critics, rest on shaky grounds.

As an example, they point to the Court's decisions on state sovereign immunity (see Chapter 3), a concept not included in the Constitution but inferred by the Court. Even one of the Court's own members—liberal justice John Paul Stevens—has charged the majority with judicial activism. In his dissent from the majority's opinion in one of these sovereign immunity cases, he stated, "The kind of judicial activism manifested in [recent cases on state sovereignty issues] represents such a radical departure from the proper role of this court that it should be opposed whenever possible."*

The Case for Judicial Independence

Others are less worried about the federal courts' decisions on policy matters. They argue that the courts, particularly the Supreme Court, have long been the protectors of liberty. The nation's founders intended the judicial branch to act as a check on the other branches of government to prevent a possible "tyranny of the majority" in Congress. The courts' power of judicial review is thus an essential judicial power and is a mainstay of our liberty.

Moreover, if the federal courts are making policy, it is because Congress drafts ambiguous laws that leave too much room for judicial interpretation. For example, it has been left to the Supreme Court to decide whether employers are liable for sexual harassment in the workplace of which the employers are unaware. Had Congress been more specific on this issue in the Civil Rights Act

*Kimel v. Florida Board of Regents, 120 S.Ct. 631 (2000).

of 1964, the Court would not have had to decide this issue. Similarly, it has been left to the Court to decide what exactly qualifies as a "disability" under the Americans with Disabilities Act of 1990. There are literally hundreds of other examples of the specifics of regulatory policy being left for the courts to determine. According to Robert A. Katzman, a scholar of judicial and legislative process at Georgetown Law Center and the Brookings Institution, "the pattern is that Congress doesn't want to face up to its responsibilities and then blames the court afterward for its decisions."†

DOES IT MATTER?

What might result if the courts' power of judicial review were limited or abolished?

GOING ONLINE

To access Justice Stevens's critical comments on the Supreme Court's decisions relating to state sovereignty, go to **http://www.usscplus.com/ current**, *click to view the cases in alphabetical order, and scroll down the list to Kimel v. Florida Board of Regents. For arguments for and against curbing the federal courts' powers, go to* **http:// www.senate.gov/cgi-bin/ ashcroft.cgi** *and* **http://www. nispac.org/~nis/activism/judac2. html**, *respectively. For a summary of bills introduced in Congress that could affect judicial independence, go to* **http://www.constitutionproject. org/cic_facts_federal.html**.

†As quoted in Fred Barbash, "Congress Didn't, So the Court Did," *The Washington Post*, July 5, 1998, p. C1.

wing. With Rehnquist's appointment as chief justice, it seemed to observers that the Court necessarily would become more conservative.

This, in fact, has happened. The Court began to take a rightward shift shortly after Rehnquist became chief justice, and the Court's rightward movement continued as other conservative appointments to the bench were made during the Reagan and Bush administrations. Today, three of the justices (William Rehnquist, Antonin Scalia, and Clarence Thomas) are notably conservative in their views. Four of the justices (John Paul Stevens, David Souter, Ruth Bader Ginsburg, and Stephen Breyer) hold liberal-to-moderate views. The middle of the Court is now occupied by two moderate-to-conservative justices, Sandra Day

INFOTRAC® COLLEGE EDITION

Rehnquist's Call

Critics Taking Aim
Judicial Activism

O'Connor and Anthony Kennedy. O'Connor and Kennedy usually provide the "swing votes" on the Court in controversial cases. The ideological alignments on the Court vary, however, depending on the issues involved in particular cases.

Certainly, today's Supreme Court has moved far from the liberal positions taken by the Court under Earl Warren (1953–1969) and under Warren Burger (1969–1986). Since the mid-1990s, the Court has issued numerous conservative rulings, many of which you have already read about in this text.

Federalist Issues. Several of these rulings reflect a conservative approach to constitutional law with respect to states' rights and other federalist issues. For example, in 1995 the Court curbed—for the first time in sixty years—the national government's constitutional power under the commerce clause to regulate intrastate activities. The Court held that a federal law regulating the possession of guns in school zones had nothing to do with interstate commerce, and therefore Congress had overreached its powers by attempting to regulate this activity.[10] In 1997, the Court again upheld states' rights when it invalidated portions of the federal gun control law. The Court stated that the federal government lacked constitutional authority to require state officials to perform background checks on prospective gun purchasers.[11]

In 2000, the Court held that Congress had overreached its authority under the commerce clause when it included a federal remedy for gender-motivated violence, such as rape or stalking, in the Federal Violence against Women Act of 1994. The Court concluded that the effect of such violence on interstate commerce was not sufficient to justify national regulation of noneconomic, violent criminal conduct.[12]

In view of the Court's support for states' rights, many scholars were surprised when the Court involved itself in the dispute over the manual recounting of the Florida votes after the 2000 elections. Nonetheless, in an historic decision, the Court reversed the Florida supreme court's order to manually recount the votes in selected Florida counties—a decision that effectively handed the presidency to George W. Bush.[13]

Civil Rights Issues. In regard to civil rights issues, the Rehnquist Court's generally conservative ("strict") interpretation of the Constitution has had mixed results. In one decision, the Court refused to extend the constitutional right to privacy to include the right of terminally ill persons to end their lives through physician-assisted suicide. Therefore, a state law banning this practice did not violate the Constitution.[14] (Essentially, the Court left it up to the states to decide whether to ban—or to permit—assisted suicide; to date, only one state, Oregon, has passed a law permitting the practice.) In another decision, the Court held that a federal statute expanding religious liberties was an unconstitutional attempt by Congress to rewrite the Constitution.[15]

In regard to sexual harassment, the Court issued a series of decisions in 1998 that gave added protection to employees and employers alike. On the one hand, the Court made it easier for harassment victims (including victims of same-gender harassment) to bring claims against their employers. On the other hand, the Court made it clear that employers who were unaware of incidents of harass-

---

[10]*United States v. Lopez,* 514 U.S. 549 (1995).
[11]*Printz v. United States,* 521 U.S. 898 (1997).
[12]*United States v. Morrison,* 120 S.Ct. 2706 (2000).
[13]*Bush v. Gore,* 121 S.Ct. 525 (2000).
[14]*Washington v. Glucksberg,* 521 U.S. 702 (1997).
[15]*City of Boerne v. Flores,* 521 U.S. 507 (1997).

The Rehnquist Court
LIBERAL/MODERATE

John Paul Stevens

David Souter

Ruth Bader Ginsburg

Stephen Breyer

SWING VOTES

Sandra Day O'Connor

Anthony Kennedy

CONSERVATIVE

William Rehnquist

Antonin Scalia

Clarence Thomas

ment in their workplaces could escape liability for those actions if they could demonstrate that they had effective antiharassment policies and procedures in place.[16]

In early 2000, the Court rendered a decision in a case challenging the constitutionality of the federal Driver's Privacy Protection Act of 1994. The act restricted the sale of personal information gathered by states when they issue driver's licenses. Many thought that the key issue in the case was drivers' privacy and hoped that the decision might open the door to tighter federal laws protecting privacy rights. The Court, however, barely mentioned the privacy

[16]*Faragher v. City of Boca Raton,* 524 U.S. 725 (1998); *Burlington Industries v. Ellerth,* 524 U.S. 742 (1998); *Oncale v. Sundowner Offshore Services,* 523 U.S. 75 (1998). These decisions are discussed more fully in Chapter 5.

issue. Rather, it ruled that the act was constitutional because (1) drivers' personal data had become articles of interstate commerce and (2) the act did not "commandeer" states into enforcing federal law.[17]

Is the Federal Judiciary Too Powerful?

The extensive influence over national policy wielded by today's federal courts, particularly the Supreme Court, could not possibly have been foreseen by the founders. Indeed, many of the founders had few worries about judicial power. In *Federalist Paper* No. 78, Alexander Hamilton expressed the opinion that the judiciary (meaning the Supreme Court, which was the only court designated in the Constitution) was the "least dangerous branch" of government because it had no enforcement powers. If the Court rendered a decision that was unacceptable to the other branches of government or to the public, there was no way the Court itself could enforce that decision.

In its earliest years, the Court did indeed lack stature and influence. The first Supreme Court chief justice, John Jay, refused to serve a second term because he thought the Court would never play an important role in American society. Jay became governor of New York instead. The next chief justice, Oliver Ellsworth, resigned his position to become an envoy to France. In 1801, when the federal capital was moved to Washington, no one remembered to include the Supreme Court in the plans. As a result, the Court met in the office of the clerk of the Senate until 1935.

Today, in contrast, the federal court system is an extensive network of courts located around the nation. More than 850 judges preside over these courts, including the nine justices of the United States Supreme Court. The policymaking role of the Supreme Court has been mentioned elsewhere in this chapter. But bear in mind that, because the highest court accepts relatively few cases for review, the decisions of the federal appellate courts are also usually final. In other words, decisions made by these courts concerning particular issues, unless reversed by the Supreme Court, apply in the states that fall within their jurisdictions.

As you read earlier in this chapter's *Which Side Are You On?* feature on page 497, a question being debated today is whether the powers of the federal courts should be curbed. Often overlooked in the debate is the fact that a number of checks on the courts already exist.

What Checks Our Courts?

Our judicial system is probably the most independent in the world. But the courts do not have absolute independence, for they are part of the political process. Political checks limit the extent to which courts can exercise judicial review and engage in an activist policy. These checks are exercised by the executive branch, the legislature, the public, and, finally, the judiciary itself.

Executive Checks

President Andrew Jackson was once supposed to have said, after Chief Justice John Marshall made an unpopular decision, that "John Marshall has made his decision; now let him enforce it."[18] This purported remark goes to the heart of **judicial implementation**—the enforcement of judicial decisions in such a way that

Judicial Implementation
The way in which court decisions are translated into action.

[17]*Reno v. Condon,* 120 S.Ct. 666 (2000).
[18]The decision referred to was *Cherokee Nation v. Georgia,* 30 U.S. 1 (1831).

those decisions are translated into policy. The Supreme Court simply does not have any enforcement powers, and whether a decision will be implemented depends on the cooperation of the other two branches of government. Rarely, though, will a president refuse to enforce a Supreme Court decision, as President Jackson did. To take such an action could mean a significant loss of public support, because of the Supreme Court's stature in the eyes of the nation.

More commonly, presidents exercise influence over the judiciary by appointing new judges and justices as federal judicial seats become vacant. Additionally, as mentioned earlier, the U.S. solicitor general plays a significant role in the federal court system, and the person holding this office is a presidential appointee.

Executives at the state level also may refuse to implement court decisions with which they disagree. A notable example of such a refusal occurred in Arkansas after the Supreme Court ordered schools to desegregate "with all deliberate speed" in 1955.[19] Arkansas governor Orval Faubus refused to cooperate with the decision and used the state's National Guard to block the integration of Central High School in Little Rock. Ultimately, President Dwight Eisenhower had to federalize the Arkansas National Guard and send federal troops to Little Rock to quell the violence that had erupted.

Legislative Checks

Courts may make rulings, but often the legislatures at local, state, and federal levels are required to appropriate funds to carry out the courts' rulings. A court, for example, may decide that prison conditions must be improved, but it is up to the legislature to authorize the funds necessary to carry out such a ruling. When such funds are not appropriated, the court that made the ruling, in effect, has been checked.

Courts' rulings can be overturned by constitutional amendments at both the federal and state levels. Many of the amendments to the U.S. Constitution (such as the Fourteenth, Fifteenth, and Twenty-sixth Amendments) check the state courts' ability to allow discrimination, for example. Proposed constitutional amendments that were created by a desire to reverse courts' decisions on school prayer and abortion have failed.

---

[19]*Brown v. Board of Education*, 349 U.S. 294 (1955)—the second *Brown* decision.

A handful of pro-prayer advocates show their support for student-led prayer before football games outside the football stadium before Santa Fe High School's first football game on Friday, September 1, 2000, in Santa Fe, Texas. It was the first home football game for Santa Fe since the Supreme Court ruled that student-led prayer over a public address system is not allowed at football games.

Finally, Congress or a state legislature can rewrite (amend) old laws or enact new ones to overturn a court's rulings if the legislature concludes that the court is interpreting laws or legislative intentions erroneously. For example, Congress passed the Civil Rights Act of 1991 in part to overturn a series of conservative rulings in employment-discrimination cases. In 1993, Congress enacted the Religious Freedom Restoration Act (RFRA), which broadened religious liberties, after Congress concluded that a 1990 Supreme Court ruling restricted religious freedom to an unacceptable extent.[20]

According to political scientist Walter Murphy, "A permanent feature of our constitutional landscape is the ongoing tug and pull between elected government and the courts."[21] Certainly, today's Supreme Court and the other two branches of government have been at odds on several occasions in the last decade. Consider the battle over religious rights and the RFRA. On signing the RFRA, President Clinton stated that the act was necessary to reverse the Court's erroneous interpretation of the Constitution in its 1990 decision. According to the president, the elected government's view of religious liberty was "far more consistent with the intent of the founders than [was] the Supreme Court."[22] The Supreme Court responded in kind. In 1997, it invalidated the RFRA, declaring that the act represented an unconstitutional attempt by Congress to add new rights to the Constitution.[23] The Court proclaimed horror at the prospect that "[s]hifting legislative majorities could change the Constitution."

Public Opinion

Public opinion plays a significant role in shaping government policy, and certainly the judiciary is not excepted from this rule. For one thing, persons affected by a Supreme Court decision that is noticeably at odds with their views may simply ignore it. Prayers were banned in public schools in 1962, yet it was widely known that the ban was (and still is) ignored in many southern districts. What can the courts do in this situation? Unless someone complains about the prayers and initiates a lawsuit, the courts can do nothing.

The public also can pressure state and local government officials to refuse to enforce a certain decision. As already mentioned, judicial implementation requires the cooperation of government officials at all levels, and public opinion in various regions of the country will influence whether or not such cooperation is forthcoming.

Additionally, the courts themselves necessarily are influenced by public opinion to some extent. After all, judges are not "islands" in our society; their attitudes are influenced by social trends, just as the attitudes and beliefs of all persons are. Courts generally tend to avoid issuing decisions that they know will be noticeably at odds with public opinion. In part, this is because the judiciary, as a branch of the government, prefers to avoid creating divisiveness among the public. Also, a court—particularly the Supreme Court—may lose stature if it decides a case in a way that markedly diverges from public opinion. Given that it has no enforcement powers, the Court's authority is linked to its stature in the eyes of the public.

---

[20]*Employment Division, Department of Human Resources of Oregon v. Smith,* 494 U.S. 872 (1990).
[21]As quoted in Neal Devins, "The Last Word Debate: How Social and Political Forces Shape Constitutional Values," *American Bar Association Journal,* October 1997, p. 48.
[22]*Ibid.*
[23]*City of Boerne v. Flores,* 521 U.S. 507 (1997).

Judicial Traditions and Doctrines

Supreme Court justices (and other federal judges) typically exercise self-restraint in fashioning their decisions. In part, this restraint stems from their knowledge that the other two branches of government and the public can exercise checks on the judiciary, as previously discussed. To a large extent, however, this restraint is mandated by various judicially established traditions and doctrines. For example, in exercising its discretion to hear appeals, the Supreme Court will not hear a meritless appeal just so it can rule on the issue. Also, when reviewing a case, the Supreme Court typically narrows its focus to just one issue or one aspect of an issue involved in the case. The Court rarely makes broad, sweeping decisions on issues. Furthermore, the doctrine of *stare decisis* acts as a restraint because it obligates the courts, including the Supreme Court, to follow established precedents when deciding cases. Only rarely will courts overrule a precedent.

Other judicial doctrines and practices also act as restraints. As already mentioned, the courts will hear only what are called justiciable disputes—disputes that arise out of actual cases. In other words, a court will not hear a case that involves a merely hypothetical issue. Additionally, if a political question is involved, the Supreme Court often will exercise judicial restraint and refuse to rule on the matter. A **political question** is one that the Supreme Court declares should be decided by the elected branches of government—the executive branch, the legislative branch, or those two branches acting together. For example, the Supreme Court has refused to rule on the controversy regarding the rights of gays and lesbians in the military, preferring instead to defer to the executive branch's decisions on the matter. Generally, fewer questions are deemed political questions by the Supreme Court today than in the past.

Higher courts can reverse the decisions of lower courts. Lower courts can act as a check on higher courts, too. Lower courts can ignore—and have ignored—Supreme Court decisions. Usually, this is done indirectly. A lower court might

Political Question
An issue that a court believes should be decided by the executive or legislative branch.

conclude, for example, that the precedent set by the Supreme Court does not apply to the exact circumstances in the case before the court; or the lower court may decide that the Supreme Court's decision was ambiguous with respect to the issue before the lower court. The fact that the Supreme Court rarely makes broad and clear-cut statements on any issue facilitates different interpretations of the Court's decisions by the lower courts.

The Judiciary: Issues for the Twenty-First Century

The judiciary remains one of the most active and important institutions in American political life. Particularly at the federal level, judicial decision making through the years has affected the way all of us live and work. As the ultimate decision maker on constitutional issues, the Supreme Court will continue to play a significant policymaking role in American government. Whether the policy-making powers of the Supreme Court and other courts in the federal judiciary are too extensive and should be curbed, as some scholars and politicians suggest, remains a controversial issue.

Since the 1980s, there has been a trend toward a noticeably more conservative federal judiciary. Some have argued that this "conservative" legacy of the Reagan-Bush years will remain effective for years to come. The judicial appointments of Bill Clinton, however, will have a significant effect on the ideological leanings of the federal judiciary for years to come. When he took office, over one hundred judicial openings in the lower federal courts existed. By the time he left office, he had appointed more than two hundred federal court judges, including two Supreme Court justices. George W. Bush, however, will appoint federal judges who are more likely to agree with his views.

Given the possible retirement of some of the Supreme Court justices in the next few years (three of them are over seventy years old), the composition of the Court may change. Few believe, however, that the change will be radical. As mentioned in the *Critical Perspective* earlier in this chapter, a Senate so strongly divided in terms of partisanship will not likely confirm the appointment of any judicial appointee with strong ideological leanings.

A number of key constitutional issues will continue to be brought before the federal judiciary. These issues include affirmative action programs, congressional redistricting to maximize minority representation, indecent speech on the Internet, privacy rights, and a variety of other civil rights issues, as well as questions involving states' rights. The work of the judiciary in this sense will always remain unfinished. Even when an issue seems to be "resolved," it may come up again many years later. After all, the Supreme Court decision in *Roe v. Wade* appeared to have put an end to discussion about restrictions on abortion. Yet the issue continues to come before the courts and is currently being settled there, as well as through decisions and movements in public opinion. In a dynamic nation with a changing population, we can never expect issues to be resolved once and for all.

making a difference

Changing the Legal System

The U.S. legal system may seem all powerful and too complex to be influenced by one individual, but its power nonetheless depends on our support. A hostile public has many ways of resisting, modifying, or overturning statutes and rulings of the courts. Sooner or later a determined majority will prevail. Even a determined minority can make a difference. As Alexander Hamilton suggested in *The Federalist Papers,* the people will always hold the scales of justice in their hands, and ultimately all constitutional government depends on their firmness and wisdom.

One example of the kind of pressure that can be exerted on the legal system began with a tragedy. On a spring afternoon in 1980, thirteen-year-old Cari Lightner was hit from behind and killed by a drunk driver while walking in a bicycle lane. The driver turned out to be a forty-seven-year-old man with two prior drunk-driving convictions. He was at that time out on bail for a third arrest. Cari's mother, Candy, quit her job as a real estate agent to form Mothers Against Drunk Driving (MADD) and launched a personal campaign to stiffen penalties for drunk-driving convictions.

The organization now has three million members and supporters. Outraged by the thousands of lives lost every year because of drunk driving, the group not only seeks stiff penalties against drunk drivers but also urges police, prosecutors, and judges to crack down on such violators. MADD, by becoming involved, has gotten results. Owing to its efforts and the efforts of other citizen-activist groups, many states have responded with stiffer penalties and deterrents. If you feel strongly about this issue and want to get involved, contact the following organization:

MADD
511 E. John Carpenter Freeway
Suite 700
Irving, TX 75062
214-744-6233

http://www.madd.org

Several other organizations have been formed by people who want to change or influence the judicial system. A few of them follow:

HALT—An Organization of
Americans for Legal Reform
1612 K St. N.W., Suite 510
Washington, DC 20006
1-800-FOR-HALT

http://www.halt.org

National Legal Center for
the Public Interest
1000 Sixteenth St. N.W.
Washington, DC 20036
202-296-1683

http://www.nlcpi.org/

If you want information about the Supreme Court, contact the following by telephone or letter:

Clerk of the Court
The Supreme Court
of the United States
1 First St. N.E.
Washington, DC 20543
202-479-3000

You can access online information about the Supreme Court at the following site:

http://oyez.nwu.edu

Key terms

affirm 489

amicus curiae brief 483

appellate court 482

case law 480

class–action suit 483

common law 479

concurring opinion 489

dissenting opinion 489

diversity of citizenship 481

federal question 481

general jurisdiction 482

judicial activism 495

judicial implementation 500

judicial restraint 496

jurisdiction 481

justiciable controversy 481

limited jurisdiction 482

litigate 483

majority opinion 489

opinion 489

oral arguments 488

political question 503

precedent 479

remand 489

reverse 489

rule of four 488

senatorial courtesy 490

stare decisis 479

trial court 482

unanimous opinion 489

writ of *certiorari* 487

Chapter summary

1 American law is rooted in the common law tradition, which was part of our legal heritage from England. The common law doctrine of *stare decisis* (which means "to stand on decided cases") obligates judges to follow precedents established previously by their own courts or by higher courts in their jurisdiction. Precedents established by the United States Supreme Court, the highest court in the land, are binding on all lower courts. Fundamental sources of American law include the U.S. Constitution and state constitutions, statutes enacted by legislative bodies, regulations issued by administrative agencies, and case law.

2 Article III, Section 1, of the U.S. Constitution limits the jurisdiction of the federal courts to cases involving (a) a federal question—which is a question based, at least in part, on the U.S. Constitution, a treaty, or a federal law; and (b) diversity of citizenship—which arises when a lawsuit is between parties of different states or involves a foreign citizen or government. The federal court system is basically a three-tiered model consisting of (a) U.S. district (trial) courts and various lower courts of limited jurisdiction; (b) U.S. courts of appeals; and (c) the United States Supreme Court. Cases may be appealed from the district courts to the appellate courts. In most cases, the decisions of the federal appellate courts are final because the Supreme Court hears relatively few cases.

3 The Supreme Court begins its annual term on the first Monday in October and usually adjourns in late June or early July of the next year. A special session may be held, but this rarely occurs. The Court's decision to review a case is influenced by many factors, including the significance of the parties and issues involved and whether the solicitor general is pressing the Court to take the case. After a case is accepted, the justices (a) undertake research (with the help of their law clerks) on the issues involved in the case, (b) hear oral arguments from the parties, (c) meet in conference to discuss and vote on the issue, and (d) announce the opinion, which is then released for publication.

4 Federal judges are nominated by the president and confirmed by the Senate. Once appointed, they hold office for life, barring gross misconduct. The nomination and confirmation process, particularly for Supreme Court justices, is often extremely politicized. Democrats and Republicans alike realize that justices may occupy seats on the Court for decades and naturally want to have persons appointed who share their basic views. Nearly 20 percent of all Supreme Court appointments have been either rejected or not acted on by the Senate.

5 In interpreting and applying the law, judges inevitably become policymakers. The most important policymaking tool of the federal courts is the power of judicial review. This power was not mentioned specifically in the Constitution, but John Marshall claimed the power for the Court in his 1803 decision in *Marbury v. Madison*. Judges who take an active role in checking the activities of the other branches of government sometimes are characterized as "activist" judges, and judges who defer to such activities sometimes are regarded as "restraintist" judges. The Warren Court of the 1950s and 1960s was activist in a liberal direction, whereas today's Rehnquist Court seems to be increasingly activist in a conservative direction. Several politicians and scholars argue that judicial activism has gotten out of hand. A question being debated today is whether the policymaking powers of the federal courts should be curbed.

6 Checks on the powers of the federal courts include executive checks, legislative checks, public opinion, and judicial traditions and doctrines.

Selected print and electronic resources

SUGGESTED READINGS

Lazarus, Edward. *Closed Chambers: The First Eyewitness Account of the Epic Struggles inside the Supreme Court.* New York: Times Books, 1998. Lazarus, who served as a clerk to former Supreme Court Justice Harry Blackmun during the Court's 1988–1989 term, gives an eyewitness account of some of the significant ideological struggles waged within the Court, among both law clerks and the justices.

Scalia, Antonin. *A Matter of Interpretation: Federal Courts and the Law.* Ewing, N.J.: Princeton University Press, 1997. Supreme Court Justice Antonin Scalia presents his views on a number of topics, including the distinction between adjudicating and legislating. He contends that the Supreme Court too often engages in making new law rather than interpreting the Constitution.

Segal, Jeffrey, and Harold J. Spaeth. *Majority Rule or Minority Will: Adherence to Precedent on the U.S. Supreme Court.* Cambridge, Mass.: Harvard University Press, 1999. These two constitutional scholars examine the influence of precedents (prior decisions on issues being considered by the Court) in Supreme Court decision making. They conclude that although the justices cite precedents to support their legal reasoning, in fact, because there are always precedents to support either side of an issue, following precedent does not mean that the justices are influenced by precedent.

Tushnet, Mark. *Taking the Constitution Away from the Courts.* Ewing, N.J.: Princeton University Press, 1999. In this book, a serious constitutional scholar proposes that a constitutional amendment be adopted to overrule *Marbury v. Madison* (1803), in which the Supreme Court assumed the power of judicial review. The author believes that constitutional interpretation should be decided by the voters and their elected representatives rather than by judges.

MEDIA RESOURCES

Court TV—This TV channel covers high-profile trials, including those of O. J. Simpson, the Unabomber, British nanny Louise Woodward, and Timothy McVeigh. (You can learn how to access Court TV from your area at its Web site—see the *Logging on* section below for its URL.)

First Monday in October—A 1981 movie with a light touch that centers on the appointment of the first woman to the United States Supreme Court.

Gideon's Trumpet—A 1980 film starring Henry Fonda as the small-time criminal, James Earl Gideon, which makes clear the path that a case takes to the Supreme Court and the importance of cases decided there.

The Magnificent Yankee—A 1950 movie, starring Louis Calhern and Ann Harding, that traces the life and philosophy of Oliver Wendell Holmes, Jr., one of the Supreme Court's most brilliant justices.

Marbury v. Madison—A thirty-minute video on this famous 1803 case that established the principle of judicial review.

Logging on

The home page of the federal courts is a good starting point if you are learning about the federal court system in general. At this site, you can even follow the "path" of a case as it moves through the federal court system. Go to

http://www.uscourts.gov

To access the Supreme Court's official Web site, on which Supreme Court decisions are made available within hours of their release, go to

http://supremecourtus.gov

Several Web sites offer searchable databases of Supreme Court decisions. You can access Supreme Court cases since 1970 at FindLaw's site:

http://www.findlaw.com

The following Web site also offers an easily searchable index to Supreme Court opinions, including some important historic decisions:

http://supct.law.cornell.edu/supct/index.html

You can find information on the justices of the Supreme Court, as well as their decisions, at

http://oyez.nwu.edu

Court TV's Web site offers information ranging from its program schedule and how you can find Court TV in your area to famous cases and the wills of famous people. For each case it includes on the site, it gives a complete history as well as selected documents filed with the court and court transcripts. You can access this site at

http://www.courttv.com

Using the Internet for political analysis

Go to one of the sites on the Web that organizes the Supreme Court's cases, such as the federal courts site or the Cornell site given above. Then look up the list of Supreme Court decisions for a recent time period—say, three months. Select three cases, and read the summary of each case. Try to categorize the federal or constitutional issue that was decided in each case. To whom is the decision important? Does the decision change the relationship between the ordinary citizen and the government? What other kinds of information would make this site more useful to you?

part 5

Public Policy

chapter 16
Domestic and Economic Policy

CHAPTER OUTLINE

- The Policymaking Process

- Poverty and Welfare

- Crime in the Twenty-First Century

- Environmental Policy

- The Politics of Economic Decision Making

- The Public Debt and the Disappearing Deficit

- Freer World Trade and the World Trade Organization

what if...

There Were No Social Security?

BACKGROUND

OUR SOCIAL SECURITY SYSTEM WAS CREATED MORE THAN SIX DECADES AGO. IN 1935, DURING THE DEPTHS OF THE GREAT DEPRESSION, BANK FAILURES AND A STOCK MARKET CRASH HAD WIPED OUT THE SAVINGS OF MILLIONS OF AMERICANS. THE COUNTRY TURNED TO THE FEDERAL GOVERNMENT TO CREATE A SAFETY NET FOR THE NATION'S ELDERLY. PAYROLL TAXES TO FUND SOCIAL SECURITY PAYMENTS WERE STARTED THEN.

RIGHT AFTER WORLD WAR II, WHICH ENDED IN 1945, PAYROLL TAXES FROM FORTY-TWO WORKERS SUPPORTED ONE SOCIAL SECURITY RECIPIENT. BY 1960, ONLY NINE WORKERS FUNDED EACH RETIREE'S SOCIAL SECURITY BENEFITS. TODAY, ABOUT THREE WORKERS PROVIDE FOR EACH RETIREE'S SOCIAL SECURITY AND MEDICARE BENEFITS. IF CURRENT TRENDS CONTINUE, BY 2030 ONLY TWO WORKERS WILL BE AVAILABLE TO PAY THE SOCIAL SECURITY AND MEDICARE BENEFITS DUE EACH RECIPIENT. BY THE MIDDLE OF THE TWENTY-FIRST CENTURY, THE PAYROLL TAX RATE WILL RISE TO 40 PERCENT FROM TODAY'S APPROXIMATELY 16 PERCENT—IF NOTHING IS CHANGED.

WHAT IF THERE WERE NO SOCIAL SECURITY?

Suppose that Congress abolished Social Security for all those, say, below the age of eighteen and those who will be born in years to come. Current beneficiaries of Social Security would not be affected, at least for a while. In time, though, Congress might be tempted to reduce Social Security benefits, or at least not increase them.

HOW WOULD PEOPLE PAY FOR RETIREMENT?

If there were no Social Security benefits, the way people would create their own retirement funds would depend largely on whether Congress also eliminated the payroll tax currently assessed. If Congress eliminated the tax, working Americans would have almost 16 percent more income. Presumably, Congress would also increase or add to current tax-free retirement savings programs that allow retirement funds to grow over time without the earnings being taxed.

The combination of tax-free private pension accounts and reduced (or eliminated) payroll taxes would certainly encourage many, if not most, working Americans to save more. That is to say, those workers entering the labor force after the change in law would have a double incentive to create their own private pension plans. Some political scientists and economists argue that this increased saving would provide more funds for increased investment, thereby leading to more economic growth.

WHEN PROBLEMS MIGHT ARISE

The first hint of problems with such a system (or the lack of Social Security completely, as it were) would occur when today's teenagers would be retiring. So, in about forty-five years the nation might discover that an alarmingly large percentage of those who had been working had not provided adequately for their own retirements. Although a callous observer might contend that people's failure to save should be no one's problem but their own, compassionate Americans and their political representatives might think otherwise. Thus, elimination of Social Security for today's young people and for generations that follow might result in increased welfare payments.

As an alternative, the government might require that all workers put a certain percentage of their salaries into their own private pension plans. In essence, then, the government would be replacing Social Security with a forced-saving plan based wholly in the private sector.

DON'T FORGET MEDICARE

Tightly linked to Social Security is our Medicare system. In fact, Medicare taxes are paid with Social Security taxes. If Medicare were also eliminated for young people today and for generations that follow, then all Americans aged eighteen and younger, as well as future generations, would have to plan to pay for private health insurance to cover medical expenses during their retirement years. Starting forty-five years from now, those Americans who choose not to spend money on health insurance during their retirement might become burdens on the state if they became ill. Again, it is possible that the federal and state governments might have to provide more welfare payments for these people.

As with the alternative of forced saving above, the government could eliminate Medicare but at the same time require that everyone purchase a medical insurance policy just as most states require all drivers to carry automobile insurance.

FOR CRITICAL ANALYSIS

1. What groups in American society might be in favor of eliminating Social Security?
2. What political forces might prevent Social Security from ever being eliminated?

This chapter's opening *What If . . .* touched on an important federal government policy dilemma—how to handle the increasing demands placed on the Social Security system as our population ages. Whatever policy decision is made with respect to Social Security, some groups will be better off and some groups will be hurt. All economic policymaking generally involves such a dilemma.

Part of the public-policy debate in our nation involves domestic problems. **Domestic policy** can be defined as all of the laws, government planning, and government actions that affect each individual's daily life in the United States. Consequently, the span of such policies is enormous. Domestic policies range from relatively simple issues, such as what the speed limit should be on interstate highways, to more complex issues, such as how best to protect our environment. Many of our domestic policies are formulated and implemented by the federal government, but many others are the result of the combined efforts of federal, state, and local governments.

In this chapter we look at domestic policy issues concerned with e-commerce, poverty and welfare, and the environment. We also examine national economic policies undertaken solely by the federal government. Before we start our analysis, we must look at how public policies are made.

Domestic Policy
Public plans or courses of action that concern issues of national importance, such as poverty, crime, and the environment.

The Policymaking Process

How does any issue get resolved? First, of course, the issue has to be identified as a problem. Often, policymakers simply have to open their local newspapers—or letters from their constituents—to discover that a problem is brewing. Like most Americans, however, policymakers receive much of their information from the national media. Finally, different lobbying groups provide information to members of Congress.

One challenging policy issue today is whether Internet transactions should be taxed. During the 1990s, the potential tax revenues from burgeoning e-commerce did not escape the attention of state governments. In fact, by 1997 most states had extended their telecommunications tax laws to cover at least some of the components of e-commerce. For example, about a dozen states had imposed some form of access tax on Internet services, such as a fee added to the Internet subscription charge. Some jurisdictions attempted to tax the transfer of data downloaded by users. Other states, including Texas and New York, imposed sales taxes on a broad array of e-commerce components, including software that is downloaded electronically and Internet access.

In response to concerns over Internet taxation, Congress passed the Internet Tax Freedom Act of 1998. This act provides a good example of the steps involved in the policymaking process.

Steps in the Policymaking Process

No matter how simple or how complex the problem, those who make policy follow a number of steps. Based on observation, we can divide the process of policymaking into at least five steps: agenda building, agenda formulation, agenda adoption, agenda implementation, and agenda evaluation.

Agenda Building.   First of all, the issue must get on the agenda. In other words, Congress must become aware that an issue requires congressional action. Agenda building may occur through a crisis, technological change, or mass media campaigns, as well as through the efforts of strong political personalities and effective lobbying groups.

With respect to the Internet Tax Freedom Act of 1998, a number of groups were pressuring Congress to take action. Not surprisingly, Internet companies,

A packer for Kozmo.com prepares an order for delivery in New York. Kozmo.com, an e-commerce firm, is trying to rebound from multimillion-dollar losses with a streamlined delivery operation that employs a former Marine logistics officer, a revamped warehouse, and more nimble software.

various business coalitions, and other groups resisted such taxation and lobbied Congress to prohibit the states from imposing further fees and taxes on Internet access and transactions. They claimed that the taxes so far imposed were unfair and discriminatory. They also argued that attempts to tax Internet transactions would constrain the growth of e-commerce—a position taken by the Clinton administration as well. Still others believed that if cyberspace was to be subject to taxation, the states had at least to develop a more uniform taxation scheme.

State lobbying groups, such as the National Governors Association (NGA), wanted Congress to allow the states to tax certain Internet components and transactions. Of particular concern to the states were the sales tax revenues they were losing due to sales conducted via the Internet. In-state sales could be taxed, because states have the authority to tax intrastate commerce (see Chapter 3). But what if a merchant located in another state sold goods to in-state residents via the Web? Under traditional law, the state could not require out-of-state sellers to collect sales taxes on transactions with in-state buyers unless a seller had a sufficient "nexus" (connection) with the state. Such a nexus could be established by having physical sales outlets in the state.

Agenda Formulation.   Next, various policy proposals are discussed among government officials and the public. Such discussions may take place in the printed media, on television, and in the halls of Congress. Congress holds hearings, the president voices the administration's views, and the topic may even become a campaign issue. With respect to the Internet Tax Freedom Act, members of Congress worked closely with representatives of state governments, the Clinton administration, and interest groups voicing the concerns of businesses providing Internet access and involved in Web transactions.

One of the major challenges facing all of these participants was that in view of the rapidly changing technological environment, any position taken by Congress on the issue might be premature. A decision to tax—or not to tax—Internet components and transactions could have consequences that were hard to foresee. As a result, most of the policy proposals called for legislation that would give Congress time to consider the issue.

Agenda Adoption.   The third step in the policymaking process involves choosing a specific strategy from among the proposals that have been discussed. In 1997, Representative Christopher Cox (R., Calif.) introduced a bill designed to establish a moratorium on Internet taxes to give Congress and the states time to study the issue. Months of intense negotiations with state and local government leaders followed. State and local governments wanted a time limit on the moratorium. They also wanted to be able to continue to collect the taxes already in effect and to guard against the erosion of their revenues in the future.

The Internet Tax Freedom Act, which was signed into law by President Bill Clinton on October 1, 1998, reflected a compromise between state and local concerns and the national interest in not stifling the growth of the Internet. The act called for a three-year moratorium on Internet taxation. During that time, the states that had already levied Internet-related taxes could continue to collect them. The act also established a commission to study e-commerce taxation issues. The commission was to report its findings to Congress within eighteen months.

Agenda Implementation.   The fourth step in the policy process involves the implementation of the policy alternative chosen by Congress. Government action must be implemented by bureaucrats, the courts, police, and individual citizens. With respect to the Internet Tax Freedom Act, however, the only policy to be implemented was the decision to establish a commission to study the issue of Internet taxes. An Advisory Commission on Electronic Commerce (ACEC)—consisting of representatives from the federal government, state and local governments, businesses in the e-commerce industry, and consumer groups—was formed immediately after the act's passage. The commission was ordered to report its findings to Congress within eighteen months—by April 2000.

Agenda Evaluation.   After a policy has been implemented, increasingly groups are undertaking policy evaluation. Groups inside and outside government conduct studies to determine what actually happens after a policy has been implemented for a given period of time. Based on this "feedback" and the perceived success or failure of the policy, a new round of policymaking initiatives will be undertaken to correct and hopefully improve on the effort. The evaluation of the Internet Tax Freedom Act necessarily followed a different course. In this case, the feedback was solely from the ACEC, which submitted its report to Congress in April 2000.

In its report, the commission made a number of recommendations to Congress. Based on these recommendations, Congress quickly introduced legislation that would extend the moratorium on Internet-related taxes for another five years, beginning in 2001. Congress also introduced a bill to implement another recommendation of the commission: the repeal of the "luxury tax" on telephones, which was imposed in 1898 to fund the Spanish-American War. Other recommendations made by the commission will be considered by Congress in the future.

Generally, the commission shared Congress's general concern that designing a tax policy for the twenty-first century was arguably one of the most important challenges facing the nation. Therefore, any regulation of the Internet through taxation will require careful deliberation by Congress, and extending the moratorium would give Congress the necessary time to do this.

Models of the Policymaking Process

It is worth noting that although the flow of the policy process is well understood, there are competing models of how and for whose benefit that process works. Two of these models—the power elite model and the bureaucratic politics model—are rooted in the elitist and pluralist theories that you read about in Chapter 1. Table 16–1 provides a brief summary of these and of a number of other competing models of the policymaking process.

TABLE 16–1

Selected Models of the Policymaking Process

1. The Bureaucratic Politics Model. In the bureaucratic politics model, the relative power of the large bureaucracies in Washington determines which policy becomes part of the national agenda and which is implemented. This theory of American politics is based on the struggle among competing interest groups.

2. The Power Elite, or Elitism, Model. Powerful economic interests determine the outcome of policy struggles, according to the power elite, or elitism, model. The rich and those who know the rich determine what gets done. More important, the power elite decides what items do *not* get on the public agenda and which items get removed if they are already on it.

3. The Marxist Model. Closely aligned with the power elite model is the Marxist model of public policymaking, in which the ruling class institutes public policy, often at the expense of the working class. The Marxist solution is revolution and the seizure of government by the working class.

4. The Incrementalist Model. Public policy evolves through small changes or adjustments, according to the incrementalist model. Consequently, policymakers examine only a few alternatives in trying to solve national problems. A good public-policy decision is made when there is agreement among contesting interests, and agreement is obtained most easily when changes are minimal.

5. The Rationalist Model. The rationalist model, sometimes thought of as a pure textbook abstraction, hypothesizes a rational policymaker who sets out to maximize his or her own self-interest, rather than determining what the public, or collective, interest might be. Rational policymakers will rank goals and objectives according to their benefit to the policymakers. Such a model is often viewed as an alternative to the incrementalist model. This model is sometimes known as the theory of public choice.

6. The Systems Model. The most general, and perhaps the most ambitious, approach to modeling public policymaking is a systems approach, in which policy is a product of the relationships between the institutions of government and the socioeconomic-political environment. Such a model has (a) inputs from public opinion and crises; (b) a political process including legislative hearings, debates, court deliberations, party conventions, and so on; (c) a set of policy outputs consisting of legislation, appropriations, and regulations; and (d) policy outcomes, which may provide, for example, more job security, less unemployment, more research on AIDS, and so on.

Income Transfer
A transfer of income from some individuals in the economy to other individuals. This is generally done by way of the government. It is a transfer in the sense that no current services are rendered by the recipients.

Poverty and Welfare

Throughout the world, historically poverty has been accepted as inevitable. Even today, little has been done on an international level to eliminate worldwide poverty. The United States and other industrialized nations, however, have sustained enough economic growth in the past several hundred years to eliminate *mass* poverty. In fact, considering the wealth and high standard of living in the United States, the persistence of poverty here appears bizarre and anomalous. How can there still be so much poverty in a nation of so much abundance? And what can be done about it?

A traditional solution has been **income transfers**. These are methods of transferring income from relatively well-to-do to relatively poor groups in society, and as a nation, we have been using such methods for a long time. Today, a vast array of welfare programs exists for the sole purpose of redistributing income. We know, however, that these programs have not been entirely successful. Before we examine the problems posed by the welfare system, let's look at the concept of poverty in more detail and at the characteristics of the poor.

The Low-Income Population

We can see in Figure 16–1 that the number of individuals classified as poor fell rather steadily from 1959 through 1969. Then, for about a decade, the number of poor leveled off, until the recession of 1981 to 1982. The number then fell somewhat until the early 1990s, when it began to increase—until 1994. Since then, it has fallen steadily.

Defining Poverty.   The threshold income level, which is used to determine who falls into the poverty category, was originally based on the cost of a nutritionally adequate food plan designed by the U.S. Department of Agriculture for emergency or temporary use. The threshold was determined by multiplying the food-plan cost times three, on the assumption that food expenses constitute approximately one-third of a poor family's expenditures. In 1969, a federal interagency committee examined the calculations of the threshold and decided to set new standards. Until then, annual revisions of the threshold level had been based only on price changes in the food budget. After 1969, the adjustments were made on the basis of changes in the consumer price index (CPI). The CPI is based on the average prices of a specified set of goods and services bought by wage earners in urban areas.

FIGURE 16–1

The Official Number of Poor in the United States
The number of individuals classified as poor fell steadily from 1959 through 1969. From 1970 to 1981, the number stayed about the same. It then increased during the 1981–1982 recession. The number of poor then fell somewhat, until the early 1990s, when it began to increase. Since 1994, the number has fallen steadily.

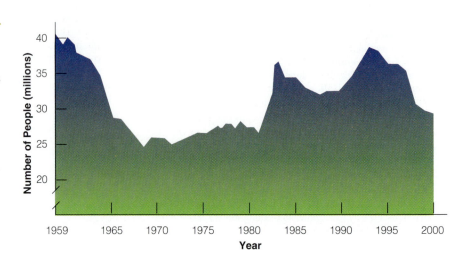

The low-income poverty threshold thus represents an absolute measure of income needed to maintain a specified standard of living as of 1963, with the constant-dollar value, or purchasing-power value, increased year by year in relation to the general increase in prices. For 2000, for example, the official poverty level for a family of four was about $17,500. It has gone up since then by the amount of the change in the CPI during the intervening period. (The poverty level varies with family size and location.)

Transfer Payments as Income.   The official poverty level is based on pretax income, including cash but not **in-kind subsidies**—food stamps, housing vouchers, and the like. If we correct poverty levels for such benefits, the percentage of the population that is below the poverty line drops dramatically. Some economists argue that the way in which the official poverty level is calculated makes no sense in a nation that redistributed annually over $900 billion in cash and noncash transfers in the past few years.

Major Government–Assistance Programs

Welfare assistance to the poor traditionally has taken a variety of forms. Through a number of welfare programs, hundreds of billions of dollars have been transferred to the poor over the last several decades. With the passage in 1996 of the Personal Responsibility and Work Reconciliation Act, popularly known as the Welfare Reform Act, Congress made significant changes in the nation's welfare system. Notably, the states gained more responsibility for establishing welfare rules and managing the welfare program.

Temporary Assistance to Needy Families.   Prior to the Welfare Reform Act of 1996, the basic welfare program in the United States was known as Aid to Families with Dependent Children (AFDC). This program provided aid for children who did not receive financial support from the father. The 1996 welfare reform legislation abolished the AFDC program and replaced it with a program called **Temporary Assistance to Needy Families (TANF)**. Under the TANF program, the U.S. government turns over to the states, in the form of block grants (see

DID YOU KNOW...
That the Greenville County Department of Social Services in South Carolina wrote to a food-stamp recipient, "Your food stamps will be stopped . . . because we received notice that you passed away. May God bless you. You may reapply if there is a change in your circumstances."**?**

In-Kind Subsidy
A good or service—such as food stamps, housing, or medical care—provided by the government to lower-income groups.

Temporary Assistance to Needy Families (TANF)
A state-administered program in which grants from the national government are given to the states, which use the funds to provide assistance to those eligible to receive welfare benefits. The TANF program was created by the Welfare Reform Act of 1996 and replaced the former AFDC program.

These two teenage mothers could be subject to the provisions of the 1996 welfare reform law, which limits their eligibility for federal assistance to two years. States may choose to extend assistance for a longer period of time, however. Although the goal of the law was to get people into employment, it did not provide the child-care benefits usually needed by mothers to allow them to accept jobs.

Chapter 3), funds targeted for welfare assistance. The states, not the national government, now have to meet the costs of any increased welfare spending. For example, if a state wishes to increase the amount of TANF payments to individuals over what the national government gives it, the state has to pay for the additional costs.

One of the basic aims of the Welfare Reform Act was to reduce welfare spending by all governments in the long run. To do this, the act made two significant changes in the basic welfare program. One change involved limiting most welfare recipients to only two years of welfare assistance. After two years, welfare payments must be discontinued unless the recipient is working, either at a public service job or in the private sector. The bill also limited lifetime welfare assistance to five years. (The federally established five-year limit can be avoided by the states, however, if they use their own funds to pay for continued welfare benefits.)

With respect to reducing the welfare rolls, the 1996 act has been stunningly successful. Nationwide, the number of people receiving welfare assistance through the TANF program has declined by at least 50 percent since the act's passage. In some states, the percentage of decline has been significantly higher. In Idaho, for example, the number of people on welfare dropped by 85 percent. At the same time, some people give the Welfare Reform Act low marks because it has forced many former welfare recipients to take jobs at low wage rates. In other words, these critics contend that the welfare changes have not much improved the plight of poor people. Rather, they have provided business with a pool of cheap labor. Certainly, the poverty rate has remained fairly stable in the last several years, as you can see in Figure 16–2.

Supplemental Security Income (SSI)

A federal program established to provide assistance to elderly persons and disabled persons.

Other Forms of Government Assistance.   The **Supplemental Security Income (SSI)** program was established in 1974 to provide a nationwide minimum income for elderly persons and persons with disabilities who do not qualify for Social Security benefits. The SSI program is one of the fastest-growing programs in the United States. When it started, it cost less than $8 billion annually. Today, that figure is about $35 billion.

FIGURE 16–2

Welfare Spending and the Poverty Rate

Welfare spending increased dramatically from the late 1960s to the late 1990s, when it began to decline. Nevertheless, the measured poverty rate has remained relatively stable.

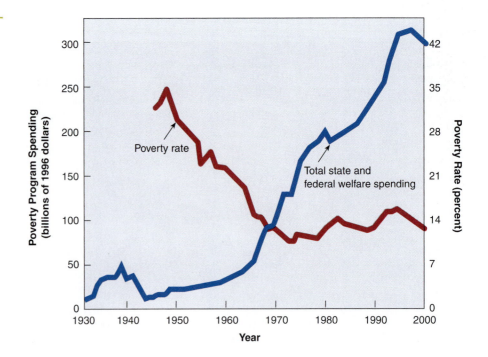

The government also issues **food stamps,** coupons that can be used to purchase food. Food stamps are available for low-income individuals and families. Recipients must prove that they qualify by showing that they do not have very much income (or no income at all). In 1964, about 367,000 Americans were receiving food stamps. In 2001, the number of those receiving food stamps was estimated at more than 28 million. The annual cost of funding food stamps jumped from $860,000 in 1964 to an estimated $30 billion in 2001. Workers on strike, and even some college students, are eligible to receive food stamps. The food-stamp program has become a major part of the welfare system in the United States, although it was started in 1964 mainly to shore up the nation's agricultural sector by distributing surplus food through retail channels.

The **earned-income tax credit (EITC) program** was created in 1975 to help low-income workers by giving back part or all of their Social Security taxes. Since its creation, the EITC program has grown remarkably. Currently, more than 20 percent of all taxpayers claim an EITC, and an estimated $23 billion a year is rebated to taxpayers through the program. The EITC has generated controversy in recent years, however, for two reasons. First, although it was designed to reward hard-working Americans who work full-time, in fact many part-time workers benefit from the program. According to the General Accounting Office (GAO), the average recipient of EITC rebates works only 1,300 hours per year, whereas the normal working year exceeds 2,000 hours. Second, the program has not had a significant effect on poverty. The GAO claims that the EITC program has decreased the poverty rate by less than one percentage point.

Children Living in Poverty

Today, nearly 19 percent of American children live in poverty. While the poverty rate for this group has declined in the past several years (it was 22.7 percent in 1993), it has done so at a slower rate than might be expected, given the health of the economy and the reduction in the unemployment rate during this same period of time.

Young Children in Poverty.   For young children—those under the age of six—the poverty rate is about 22 percent. About 10 percent of young children live in extreme poverty, in families with seriously inadequate incomes. Indeed, America's youngest children are more likely to live in poverty than Americans in any other age group. Moreover, the poverty rate for young children is often two to three times higher than that of other major Western industrialized nations.

According to researchers at Columbia University's National Center for Children in Poverty, extreme poverty during the first five years of life has a much more negative effect on a child's future life chances than extreme poverty experienced later in childhood. An important question for policymakers, though, is whether poverty alone is the cause of this negative effect.

Poverty's Effect on Children.   F. Scott Fitzgerald once wrote that the rich "are different from you and me"; Ernest Hemingway replied, "Yes, they have more money." Are the children of low-income families the same as everyone else, except that they have less money? This has been a major policy question for years. Some have argued that children of very poor families fail in society because their parents are unlike other parents. The policy implications of this debate are crucial, for if children from poor families are just like everyone else, then reducing poverty rates will lead to higher success rates in the economic and social world for such children.

Food Stamps
Coupons issued by the federal government to low-income individuals to be used for the purchase of food.

Earned-Income Tax Credit (EITC) Program
A government program that helps low-income workers by giving back part or all of their Social Security taxes.

Two studies cast doubts on such a possibility.[1] According to researcher Susan Mayer, even if our poverty policies doubled the income of the poorest 20 percent of families, childbearing by teenagers would drop only 2 percent. The high school dropout rate would only decrease from 17.3 percent to about 16 percent. Mayer argues that the parents' skills, honesty, diligence, and health may matter more to children's prospects than whether the family is in poverty. She says that "although children's opportunities are unequal, income inequality is not the primary reason."

This research has implications with respect to the long-run effects of the Welfare Reform Act of 1996. On the one hand, income losses to families previously receiving welfare payments may not damage children that much if unequal incomes are not at the heart of the problem. On the other hand, large income losses could be a problem because, according to other research, the children of poor parents who obtain larger income transfers show increased aptitudes in educational achievements up to about age five. Thus, if the Welfare Reform Act ultimately results in dramatic losses in income to poor families, early child development may suffer.

Homelessness—Still a Problem

The plight of the homeless remains a problem. Indeed, some observers argue that the Welfare Reform Act of 1996 has increased the numbers of homeless persons. There are no hard statistics on the homeless, but estimates of the number of people without a home on any given night in the United States range from a low of 230,000 to as many as 750,000 people.

It is difficult to estimate how many people are homeless because the number depends on how the homeless are defined. There are *street people*—those who sleep in bus stations, parks, and other areas. Many of these people are youthful runaways. There are the so-called *sheltered homeless*—those who sleep in government-supported or privately funded shelters. Many of these individu-

Liz's Story

---

[1]Susan Mayer, *What Money Can't Buy: Family Income and Children's Life Chances* (Cambridge, Mass.: Harvard University Press, 1997); and Greg J. Duncan and Jeanne Brooks-Gunn, eds., *Consequences of Growing up Poor* (New York: Russell Sage Foundation, 1997).

Less than one hundred yards from the White House, a homeless man sleeps, with his head on a cart containing all of his possessions. What should (or can) the government do to help the homeless?

als used to live with their families or friends. While street people are almost always single, the sheltered homeless include numerous families with children. Homeless families are the fastest-growing subgroup of the homeless population.

As a policy issue, how to handle the homeless problem pits liberals against conservatives. Conservatives argue that there are not really that many homeless and that most of them are alcoholics, drug users, or mentally ill. Conservatives argue that these individuals should be dealt with either by the mental-health system or the criminal justice system. In contrast, many liberals argue that homelessness is caused by a reduction in welfare benefits and by excessively priced housing. They want more shelters to be built for the homeless.

Recently, cities have been attempting to "criminalize" homelessness. Many municipalities have outlawed sleeping on park benches and sidewalks, as well as panhandling and leaving personal property on public property. In some cities, police sweeps remove the homeless, who then become part of the criminal justice system.

Since 1993, the U.S. Department of Housing and Urban Development has spent nearly $5 billion on programs designed to combat homelessness. Yet because there is so much disagreement about the number of homeless persons, the reasons for homelessness, and the possible cures for the problem, there has been no consistent government policy. Whatever policies have been adopted usually have been attacked by one group or another.

DID YOU KNOW...
That a University of Southern California evaluation of a gang prevention program discovered that when the program lost funding, the gang broke up and its crime rate declined?

Crime in the Twenty-First Century

The issue of crime has been on the national agenda for years now. Virtually all polls taken in the United States in the last few years show that crime is one of the major concerns of the public. Although crime rates have fallen, on average, in the last several years, the public's concern has not been misplaced.

Crime in American History

In every period in the history of this nation, people have voiced their apprehension about crime. Some criminologists argue that crime was probably as frequent around the time of the American Revolution as it is currently. During the Civil War, mob violence and riots erupted in numerous cities. After the Civil War, people in San Francisco were told that "no decent man is in safety to walk the streets after dark; while at all hours, both night and day, his property is jeopardized by incendiarism and burglary."[2] In 1886, *Leslie's Weekly* reported that "Each day we see ghastly records of crime . . . murder seems to have run riot and each citizen asks . . . 'who is safe?'" From 1860 to 1890, the crime rate rose twice as fast as the population.[3] In 1910, one author stated that "crime, especially in its more violent forms and among the young, is increasing steadily and is threatening to bankrupt the Nation."[4]

From 1900 to the 1930s, social violence and crime increased dramatically. Labor union battles and racial violence were common. Only during the three-decade period from the mid-1930s to the early 1960s did the United States experience, for the first time in its history, stable or slightly declining overall crime rates.

What most Americans are worried about is violent crime. From the mid-1980s to 1994, its rate rose relentlessly. The murder rate per 100,000 people in 1964

---

[2]President's Commission on Law Enforcement and Administration of Justice, *Challenge of Crime in a Free Society* (Washington, D.C.: Government Printing Office, 1967), p. 19.
[3]Richard Shenkman, *Legends, Lies & Cherished Myths of American History* (New York: HarperCollins, 1988), p. 158.
[4]President's Commission, *Challenge of Crime*, p. 19.

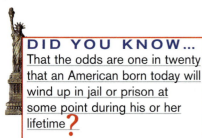

DID YOU KNOW...
That the odds are one in twenty that an American born today will wind up in jail or prison at some point during his or her lifetime**?**

was 4.9, whereas in 1994 it was estimated at 9.3, an almost 100 percent increase. Since 1995, however, violent crime rates have declined each year. Some argue that the cause of this decline in crime rates is the booming economy the United States has enjoyed since about 1993. Others claim that the $3 billion of additional funds the federal government has spent to curb crime in the last few years has led to less crime. Still others argue that an increase in the number of persons who are jailed or imprisoned is responsible for the reduction in crime. (For a comparison of U.S. incarceration rates compared with those of other nations, see this chapter's *Global View*.)

Crimes Committed by Juveniles

A disturbing aspect of crime is the number of serious crimes committed by juveniles, although the number of such crimes is also dropping. The political response to this rise in serious juvenile crimes has been varied. Some cities have established juvenile curfews. Several states have begun to try more juveniles as adults, particularly juveniles who have been charged with homicides. Still other states are operating "boot camps" to try to "shape up" the less violent juvenile criminals. Additionally, victims of juvenile crime and victims' relatives are attempting to pry open the traditionally secret juvenile court system.[5]

Some worry that the decline in serious juvenile crimes is only temporary. The number of youths between the ages of fifteen and seventeen will rise from about nine million today to almost thirteen million in the year 2010. It is thus understandable that there is grave concern about preventing an even worse juvenile crime problem in the years to come.

I N F O T R A C ®
COLLEGE EDITION

**Prisons New
Growth Industry**

---

[5]See Chapter 6 for details on the rights of juveniles in our legal system.

global **view**

Incarceration Worldwide

The United States is known as "the home of the free and the land of the brave." It therefore may surprise many Americans to discover that the United States has the highest incarceration rate of any country in the world today except for Russia. In the United States, nearly 1.4 million convicts are locked up in 1,500 state and federal prisons. An additional 626,000 are housed in the nation's 3,300 jails. Just look at the figure in this feature. Despite comparable crime rates, the United States incarcerates five times as many of its citizens as Canada does, and seven times as many as most European democracies.

FOR CRITICAL ANALYSIS

Why does the U.S. prison population continue to rise even though the number of violent crimes committed each year has fallen?

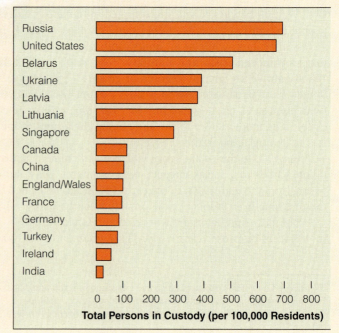

SOURCE: FBI, Bureau of Justice Statistics, The Sentencing Project.

Environmental Policy

Human actions may create unwanted side effects—including the destruction of the environment and the ecology (the total pattern of environmental relationships). Every day, humans, through their actions, emit pollutants into the air and the water. Each year, the world atmosphere receives twenty million metric tons of sulfur dioxide, eighteen million metric tons of ozone pollutants, and sixty million metric tons of carbon monoxide.

The Government's Response to Air and Water Pollution

The government has been responding to pollution problems since before the American Revolution, when the Massachusetts Bay Colony issued regulations to try to stop the pollution of Boston Harbor. In the nineteenth century, states passed laws controlling water pollution after scientists and medical researchers convinced most policymakers that dumping sewage into drinking and bathing water caused disease. At the national level, the Federal Water Pollution Control Act of 1948 provided research and assistance to the states for pollution-control efforts, but little was done. In 1952, the first state air-pollution law was passed in Oregon. The federal Air Pollution Control Act of 1955 gave some assistance to states and cities. Table 16–2 describes the major environmental legislation in the United States.

TABLE   16-2

Major Federal Environmental Legislation

1899 Refuse Act. Made it unlawful to dump refuse into navigable waters without a permit. A 1966 court decision made all industrial wastes subject to this act.

1948 Federal Water Pollution Control Act. Set standards for the treatment of municipal water waste before discharge. Revisions to this act were passed in 1965 and 1967.

1955 Air Pollution Control Act. Authorized federal research programs for air-pollution control.

1963 Clean Air Act. Assisted local and state governments in establishing control programs and coordinated research.

1965 Clean Air Act Amendments. Authorized the establishment of federal standards for automobile exhaust emissions, beginning with 1968 models.

1965 Solid Waste Disposal Act. Provided assistance to local and state governments for control programs and authorized research in this area.

1965 Water Quality Act. Authorized the setting of standards for discharges into waters.

1967 Air Quality Act. Established air-quality regions, with acceptable regional pollution levels. Required local and state governments to implement approved control programs or be subject to federal controls.

1969 National Environmental Policy Act. Established the Council for Environmental Quality (CEQ) for the purpose of coordinating all federal pollution-control programs. Authorized the establishment of the Environmental Protection Agency (EPA) to implement CEQ policies on a case-by-case basis.

1970 Clean Air Act Amendments. Authorized the Environmental Protection Agency to set national air-pollution standards and restricted the discharge of six major pollutants into the lower atmosphere. Automobile manufacturers were required to reduce nitrogen oxide, hydrocarbon, and carbon monoxide emissions by 90 percent (in addition to the 1965 requirements) during the 1970s.

1972 Federal Water Pollution Control Act Amendments. Set national water-quality goal of restoring polluted waters to swimmable, fishable waters by 1983.

1972 Federal Environmental Pesticide Control Act. Required that all pesticides used in interstate commerce be approved and certified as effective for their stated purpose. Required certification that they were harmless to humans, animal life, animal feed, and crops.

1974 Clean Water Act. Originally called the Safe Drinking Water Act, this law set (for the first time) federal standards for water suppliers serving more than twenty-five people, having more than fifteen service connections, or operating more than sixty days a year.

1976 Resource Conservation and Recovery Act. Encouraged the conservation and recovery of resources. Put hazardous waste under government control. Prohibited the opening of new dumping sites. Required that all existing open dumps be closed or upgraded to sanitary landfills by 1983. Set standards for providing technical, financial, and marketing assistance to encourage solid waste management.

1977 Clean Air Act Amendments. Postponed the deadline for automobile emission requirements.

1980 Comprehensive Environmental Response, Compensation, and Liability Act. Established a "Superfund" to clean up toxic waste dumps.

1990 Clean Air Act Amendments. Provided for precise formulas for new gasoline to be burned in the smoggiest cities, further reduction in carbon monoxide and other exhaust emissions in certain areas that still have dangerous ozone levels in the year 2003, and a cap on total emissions of sulfur dioxide from electricity plants. Placed new restrictions on toxic pollutants.

1990 Oil Pollution Act. Established liability for the clean-up of navigable waters after oil-spill disasters.

1996 Food Quality and Protection Act. Amended the Federal Food, Drug, and Cosmetic Act of 1938 to regulate the use of pesticides in the cultivation and marketing of food products.

1999 Chemical Safety Information, Site Security, and Fuels Regulatory Relief Act. Established new provisions to regulate risk management plans at certain chemical and fuel facilities to reduce the risk of chemical explosions and to lessen the vulnerability of these facilities to criminal and terrorist activities.

Environmental Impact Statement (EIS)

As a requirement mandated by the National Environmental Policy Act, a report that must show the costs and benefits of major federal actions that could significantly affect the quality of the environment.

The National Environmental Policy Act.   The year 1969 marked the start of the most concerted national government involvement in solving pollution problems. In that year, the conflict between oil exploration interests and environmental interests literally erupted when a Union Oil Company's oil well six miles off the coast of Santa Barbara, California, exploded, releasing 235,000 gallons of crude oil. The result was an oil slick, covering an area of eight hundred square miles, that washed up on the city's beaches and killed plant life, birds, and fish. Hearings in Congress revealed that the Interior Department did not know which way to go in the energy-environment trade-off. Congress did know, however, and passed the National Environmental Policy Act in 1969. This landmark legislation established, among other things, the Council for Environmental Quality. Also, it mandated that an **environmental impact statement (EIS)** be prepared for all major federal actions that significantly affected the quality of the environment. The act gave citizens and public-interest groups concerned with the environment a weapon against the unnecessary and inappropriate use of natural resources by the government.

The Clean Air Act of 1990.   The most comprehensive government attempt at cleaning up our environment occurred in 1990. After years of lobbying by environmentalists and counterlobbying by industry, the Clean Air Act of 1990 was passed. This act amended the 1963 Clean Air Act, which had also been amended in 1970 and 1977. The 1990 amendments required automobile manufacturers to cut new automobiles' exhaust emissions of nitrogen oxide by 60 percent and emissions of other pollutants by 35 percent. By 1998, all new automobiles had to meet this standard. Regulations that will go into effect beginning with 2004 model cars call for cutting nitrogen oxide tailpipe emissions by nearly 10 percent by 2007. For the first time, sport utility vehicles and light trucks were required to meet the same emission standards as automobiles.

Stationary sources of air pollution were also made subject to more regulation under the 1990 act. The act required 110 of the oldest coal-burning power plants in the United States to cut their emissions by 40 percent by the year 2001. Controls were placed on other factories and businesses in an attempt to reduce ground-level ozone pollution in ninety-six cities to healthful levels by 2005 (except in Los Angeles, which has until 2010 to meet the standards). The act also required that the production of chlorofluorocarbons (CFCs) be stopped completely by the year 2002. CFCs are thought to deplete the ozone layer and increase global warming. CFCs are used in air-conditioning and other refrigeration units.

A number of urban areas have a landfill problem. The price of landfill has been going up in many of the major cities for many years. Nationwide, in contrast, the average per-ton price of landfill has gone down. In other words, people in many regions of the United States pay less today to dump their garbage into landfills than they did ten years ago.

In 1997, in light of evidence that very small particles (2.5 microns, or millionths of a meter) of soot might affect our health as significantly as larger particles, the Environmental Protection Agency (EPA) issued new particulate standards for motor vehicle exhaust systems and other sources of pollution. The EPA also established a more rigorous standard for ozone, which is formed when sunlight combines with pollutants from cars and other sources. Ozone is the basic ingredient of smog. The EPA's new standards, however, have been challenged in the courts.

The Politics of Economic Decision Making

Nowhere are the principles of public policymaking more obvious than in the area of economic decisions undertaken by the federal government. The president and Congress (and to a growing extent, the judiciary) are faced constantly with questions concerning economic policy. Consider some of them:

1. Should federal income taxes be lowered, given that the federal government no longer has a budget deficit?
2. Should Social Security and Medicare taxes be raised to cover the inevitable growth in the number of recipients for those two programs?
3. Should the Federal Reserve change interest rates to counteract a possible slowing or overheating of the economy?
4. Should Congress restrict imports to improve our balance of trade?

There are no clear-cut answers to such questions. Each policy action carries with it costs and benefits, known as **policy trade-offs.** The costs are typically borne by one group and the benefits enjoyed by another group. (Economic policymakers have faced even more challenges as a result of the rapid growth in e-commerce—See this chapter's *Critical Perspective* on the following pages for a discussion of this topic.)

Policy Trade-Offs
The cost to the nation of undertaking any one policy in terms of all of the other policies that could have been undertaken. For example, an increase in the expenditures on one federal program means either a reduction in expenditures on another program or an increase in federal taxes (or the deficit).

The Politics of Taxes and Subsidies

Taxes are not just given to us from above. Rather, they are voted on by members of Congress. Members of Congress also vote on *subsidies,* which are a type of negative taxes that benefit certain businesses and individuals. An examination of the Internal Revenue Code, encompassing thousands of pages, thousands of sections, and thousands of subsections, gives some indication that our tax system is not very simple.

We begin our analysis with the premise that in the world of taxes and subsidies, the following is always true: *For every action on the part of the government, there will be a reaction on the part of the public.* Eventually, the government will react with another action, followed by the public's further reaction. The **action-reaction syndrome** is a reality that has plagued government policymakers since the beginning of this nation.

Action-Reaction Syndrome
For every action on the part of government, there is a reaction on the part of the affected public. Then the government attempts to counter the reaction with another action, which starts the cycle all over again.

TABLE 16-3

2000 Tax Rates for Single Persons and Married Couples

SINGLE PERSONS		MARRIED COUPLES	
MARGINAL TAX BRACKET	MARGINAL TAX RATE	MARGINAL TAX BRACKET	MARGINAL TAX RATE
$ 0-$ 26,250	15 %	$ 0-$ 43,850	15 %
$ 26,250-$ 63,550	28	$ 43,850-$105,950	28
$ 63,550-$132,600	31	$105,950-$161,450	31
$132,600-$288,350	36	$161,450-$288,350	36
$288,350 and above	39.6	$288,350 and above	39.6

critical perspective

Does E-Commerce Threaten National Sovereignty?

In any nation, the concept of sovereignty is quite well defined. Part of that concept has to do with the police power of government. In the United States, the police power enjoyed by federal, state, and local governments may be in conflict, but no one doubts that at some level, a governmental agency or other institution has this power. A key element of national sovereignty is the police power to regulate commerce. This involves, among other things, the regulation of pharmaceuticals, safety, and the like. Often closely intertwined with police power is the sovereign power to tax. Each state and municipality has specific powers to tax the sale of goods and sometimes services. Many governments also tax personal and corporate income.

Sovereignty at Bay

Over three decades ago, Raymond Vernon wrote *Sovereignty at Bay.*[*] The author concluded that "[c]oncepts such as national sovereignty and national economic strength appear curiously devoid of meaning." At that time, Vernon and a slew of other authors believed that large, multinational enterprises and the globalization of production would reduce the strength of sovereign states as well as national markets. In subsequent years, these predictions failed to prove accurate. Nonetheless, today some people believe that the predictions have taken on a new vitality because of the rapid expansion—or rather, explosion—of commerce via the Internet.

Taxes at the Forefront

One of the reasons given for the dramatic increase in e-commerce in the United States is the federal government's legislation that imposed

[*]Raymond Vernon, *Sovereignty at Bay* (New York: Basic Books, 1971).

a moratorium on the taxation of Internet sales and services. This moratorium will last until 2001; and it will likely be extended by Congress until 2006.

But consider an even larger source of revenues for governments, particularly national governments—income taxes on both individuals and corporations. The government that is deprived of its ability to tax income is a government that loses its power. Governments must know where income is earned, however, before they can tax it. In addition, governments must have authority over activities in the locations where income is earned.

Even simple sales transactions are often hard to trace in the expanding world of e-commerce. If a U.S. customer orders a product from a Peruvian company with a Guatemalan factory and uses funds in an offshore bank to pay for the purchase, the transaction becomes difficult, if not impossible, to tax. Where did the transaction actually take place? Where was the product ordered? As more corporations become spread out throughout the world and as communications and encryption become more sophisticated, multinational e-commerce transactions will become commonplace and even more complicated. Thus, governments will lose, little by little, their ability to tax such transactions.

Trying to Control the Uncontrollable

Among the major police power activities of sovereign governments is the regulation of pharmaceuticals. Most countries place restrictions on who can sell pharmaceuticals and how they may be purchased. The United States has relatively strict laws on the subject. Prescriptions are required for most significant drugs.

Enter the Internet age. Would you like to buy some antibiotics without going to your physician? Web-based offshore pharmacies will be glad to oblige you. Indeed, you can purchase just about any pharmaceutical without a prescription on the Internet. U.S. regulators have attempted to crack down on offshore pharmacies but can do so only when the foreign government agrees to work with the U.S.

Tax Rates and Tax Loopholes. People are not assessed a lump-sum tax each year; each family does not just pay $1,000 or $10,000 or $20,000. Rather, individuals and businesses pay taxes based on tax rates. (Table 16–3 shows the 2000 tax rates for individuals and married couples.) The higher the tax rate—the action on the part of the government—the greater the public's reaction to that tax rate. Again, it is all a matter of costs and benefits. If the tax rate on all the income you make is 15 percent, that means that any method you can use to reduce your taxable income by one dollar saves you fifteen cents in tax liabilities that you owe the federal government. Therefore, those individuals paying a 15 percent rate have a relatively small incentive to avoid paying taxes. But consider individuals who were faced with a tax rate of 94 percent in the 1940s. They had a tremendous incentive to find legal ways to reduce their taxable incomes. For every dolfor sums less than a few dollars are not worthwhile for a company to undertake. But many small transactions might take place on the Internet if people could use a common currency. That is why beenz were created.

authorities. For example, the U.S. government convinced the Thai government to close down a couple of Web-based pharmacies in that country. Given that the Web knows no national boundaries, however, other Web-based pharmacies in other countries will step in to fill the void. In most places in the world, the United States has no jurisdictional authority and will obtain no cooperation from foreign governments on such matters.

A Potential Decline in the Authority over Monetary Matters

Today, virtually all countries in the world have their own central banks and their own currencies. One exception is the European Union (EU), some members of which have agreed to adopt a uniform currency called the euro. In any case, the Web-based economy may still use national currencies for bookkeeping purposes. But, and this is important, it is now possible to create money without being part of a nation's banking system. Specifically, as encryption systems and secure methods for delivery and use of Web-created money improve, the ability of nontraditional banking entities to affect the supply of money and credit in the economy increases. Perhaps not tomorrow, but within the next decade, national monetary authorities, such as the U.S. Federal Reserve System, may have less and less control over money and credit.

It is even possible for specially created Internet "money" to replace national currencies. Twenty-five to thirty million transactions (small, of course) have occurred using an Internet-created money called beenz (go to http://www.beenz.com for information on this development). Beenz were created out of thin air to facilitate the purchase of small-value items over the Internet. Credit-card transactions

Does National Sovereignty Remain King?

According to writer William Pfaff of the Los Angeles Times Syndicate, despite all the global changes and the Internet, national sovereignty remains king.[†] He argues that the globalization of business and markets may seem uncontrollable simply because that is the prevailing political-economic ideology. During the Clinton administration, there was a strong push for global market deregulation. But, Pfaff notes, whenever deregulation has threatened national interests or state power, reregulation has been imposed. Nations still possess the power to regulate or to override global forces that might weaken their sovereignty. He points out that we have created new international institutions—thus lessening national sovereignty—*only* when we find them convenient. Until the United States was willing to support a permanent war crimes tribunal, for example, it did not get off the ground.

FOR CRITICAL ANALYSIS

1. When we refer to losing sovereignty, what do we really mean? Specifically, who is actually affected by a loss in national sovereignty?
2. Why should the average citizen be worried about whether her or his national government is losing some of its sovereign power?

[†]"Despite Global Changes, National Sovereignty Remains King," *International Herald Tribune,* March 30, 2000, p. 6.

---

lar of income that was somehow deemed nontaxable, these taxpayers would reduce tax liabilities by ninety-four cents.

So, individuals and corporations facing high tax rates will always react by making concerted attempts to get Congress to add **loopholes** to the tax law that allow them to reduce their taxable incomes. When the Internal Revenue Code imposed very high tax rates on high incomes, it also provided for more loopholes. Special provisions enabled investors in oil and gas wells to reduce their taxable incomes. Loopholes allowed people to shift income from one year to the next. Other loopholes allowed individuals to avoid some taxes completely by forming corporations outside the United States.

These same principles apply to other interest groups. As long as one group of taxpayers sees a specific benefit from getting the law changed and that benefit

Loophole
A legal method by which individuals and businesses are allowed to reduce the tax liabilities owed to the government.

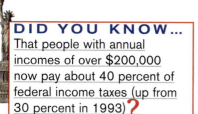

INFOTRAC ®
COLLEGE EDITION

**Shop Till You
Drop Tax Moratoria**

Regressive Tax
A tax system in which tax rates go down as income goes up.

Medicare Expenditures as a Percentage of Total National Income

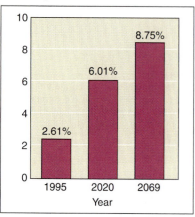

means a lot of money per individual, the interest group will aggressively support lobbying activities and the election and reelection of members of Congress who will push for special tax loopholes. In other words, if enough benefits are to be derived from influencing tax legislation, such influence will be exerted by the affected parties.

Why We Probably Will Never Have a Truly Simple Tax System. The federal government was running large deficits in the late 1980s, and these continued until the late 1990s. When faced with the prospect of having to cut the growth of federal government spending, Congress balked. Instead, it raised tax rates. This occurred under the Bush administration in 1990 and under the Clinton administration in 1993. Indeed, at the upper end of income earners, the tax rate paid on each extra dollar earned went up from 28 percent in 1986 to 39.6 percent in 1993. That was an increase in the effective tax rate of 41.4 percent.

In response, the action-reaction syndrome certainly went into effect. As tax rates went up, those who were affected spent more time and effort to get Congress to legislate special exceptions, exemptions, loopholes, and the like, so that the *full* impact of such tax-rate increases would not be felt by richer Americans. As a result, the U.S. tax code became more complicated than it was before.

Social Security: How Long Will It Last?

Closely related to the question of taxes in the United States is the viability of the Social Security system. Social Security taxes came into existence when the Federal Insurance Contribution Act (FICA) was passed in 1935. When the FICA tax was first levied, it was 1 percent of earnings up to $3,000. By 1963, the percentage rate had increased to 3.625 percent. As of 2000, a 6.2 percent rate was imposed on each employee's wages up to a maximum of $76,200 to pay for Social Security. In addition, employers must pay in ("contribute") an equal percentage. Also, there is a combined employer/employee 2.9 percent tax rate assessed for Medicare on all wage income, with no upper limit.

Social Security Is a Regressive Tax. When people with higher incomes pay lower tax rates than people with lower incomes, we call it a **regressive tax.** Social Security taxes are regressive, because once individuals' incomes exceed the maximum taxable amount, they pay no more Social Security taxes. The Medicare portion of the FICA tax is no longer regressive, because it applies to all wage income, but the Social Security portion remains regressive. A person earning a million dollars in a year pays the same total Social Security taxes as a person earning $76,200.

The Grim Future of the Social Security System. Several years ago, Senator Bob Kerrey (D., Neb.) stated that "we are damning our children to a very grim future if we continue to hide our heads in the sand." He was referring to the projected "bankruptcy" of the Social Security system sometime around the year 2010. After that date, Social Security taxes will have to be raised, Social Security benefits will have to be dramatically curtailed, or spending on other federal programs will have to be reduced. Medicare appears to be in even worse shape. As the number of Americans aged sixty-five and older increases from about thirty-five million today to forty-five million in the year 2010, and to seventy-five million in the year 2040, Medicare expenditures as a percentage of total national income are expected to grow dramatically, as can be seen in Figure 16-3.

The Real Problem. The real problem with the Social Security system is that people who pay into Social Security think that they are actually paying into a fund,

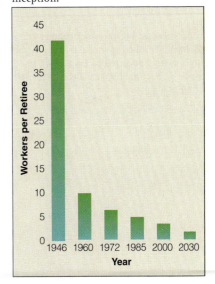
perhaps with their name on it. This is what you do when you pay into a private pension plan. It is not the case, however, with the federal Social Security system. That system is basically a pay-as-you-go transfer system in which those who are working are paying benefits to those who are retired.

Currently, the number of people who are working relative to the number of people who are retiring is declining, as you can see in Figure 16–4. Therefore, those who work will continue to have to pay more of their incomes in Social Security taxes in order to pay for the benefits of those who retire. In the year 2025, when the retirement of the baby boomer generation is complete, benefits are projected to cost almost 25 percent of taxable payroll income in the economy. Today this figure is only 16 percent. In today's dollars, that amounts to more than a trillion dollars of additional taxes annually.

As long as Congress continues to increase Social Security benefits while at the same time the labor force grows less rapidly than the number of retirees, financial strain will plague the Social Security system. Social Security also will continue to be a political issue, as well as a focal point of lobbying efforts, particularly by groups that represent older Americans.

The Debate over Privatization.   Clearly, what to do about the Social Security dilemma is a major issue facing today's policymakers. One possible solution would be to partially privatize the Social Security system by allowing workers to invest a specified portion of their Social Security payroll taxes in the stock market. Although such a solution would have been unthinkable in past decades, today there is growing support for the idea of reaping greater returns on Social security contributions through private investments. Indeed, in the 2000 presidential campaigns, Republican contender George W. Bush's proposal that Social Security be partially privatized in this way drew significant support.

A number of groups oppose the concept of partial privatization, however, fearing that many Americans would mismanage their investments or not invest wisely. During the 2000 campaigns, Democratic candidate Al Gore attacked

FIGURE 16–4

Workers per Retiree

The average number of workers per Social Security retiree has declined dramatically since the program's inception.

SOURCES: Social Security Administration and authors' estimates.

Fiscal Policy
The use of changes in government spending or taxation to alter national economic variables, such as the rate of unemployment.

Monetary Policy
The use of changes in the amount of money in circulation to alter credit markets, employment, and the rate of inflation.

Bush's proposal by claiming that the diversion of Social Security funds into individual stock portfolios could jeopardize the welfare of future retirees, who would be at the mercy of the volatile stock market. Opponents of partial privatization also worry that such a step could be a first step down the slippery slope toward full privatization—and no government guarantees with respect to Social Security.

Certainly, changing from a public system to a private system faces enormous political roadblocks in the United States. Yet regardless of how the Social Security problem is solved, it must be solved—because there is no way to stop the aging of the population.

The Politics of Fiscal and Monetary Policy

Changes in the tax code sometimes form part of an overall fiscal policy change. **Fiscal policy** is defined as the use of changes in government expenditures and taxes to alter national economic variables, such as the rate of inflation, the rate of unemployment, the level of interest rates, and the rate of economic growth. The federal government also controls **monetary policy,** defined as the use of changes in the amount of money in circulation so as to affect interest rates, credit markets, the rate of inflation, and employment. Fiscal policy is the domain of Congress and the president. Monetary policy, as we shall see, is much less under the control of Congress and the president, because the monetary authority in the United States, the Federal Reserve System, or the Fed, is an independent agency not directly controlled by either Congress or the president.

Fiscal Policy: Theory and Reality. The theory behind fiscal policy changes is relatively straightforward: When the economy is going into a recession (a period of rising unemployment), the federal government should stimulate economic activity by increasing government expenditures, by decreasing taxes, or both. When the economy is becoming overheated with rapid increases in employment and rising prices (a condition of inflation), fiscal policy should become contractionary, reducing government expenditures and increasing taxes. That particular view of fiscal policy was first implemented in the 1930s and became popular again during the 1960s. It was an outgrowth of the economic theories of the English economist John Maynard Keynes. Keynes's ideas, published during the Great Depression of the 1930s, influenced the economic policymakers guiding President Franklin D. Roosevelt's New Deal.

Wall Street during the stock market crash of 1929. Another spectacular drop in the stock market occurred in October of 1987. Stock prices tumbled yet again in the fall of 1998.

Keynes believed that the forces of supply and demand operated too slowly in a serious recession and that government should step in to stimulate the economy. Such actions thus are guided by **Keynesian economics.** Keynesian (pronounced *kayn*-zeean) economists believe, for example, that the Great Depression resulted from a serious imbalance in the economy. The public was saving more than usual, and businesses were investing less than usual. According to Keynesian theory, at the beginning of the depression, the government should have filled the gap that was created when businesses began limiting their investments. The government could have done so by increasing government spending or cutting taxes.

Monetary Policy: Politics and Reality. The theory behind monetary policy, like that behind fiscal policy, is relatively straightforward. In periods of recession and high unemployment, we should stimulate the economy by expanding the rate of growth of the money supply. (The money supply is defined loosely as checking account balances and currency—see the feature *E-mocracy: Monetary Policy in the Age of Cybermoney* for a discussion of how "e-money" presents a challenge to monetary policymakers.) An easy-money policy is supposed to lower interest rates and induce consumers to spend more and producers to invest more. With

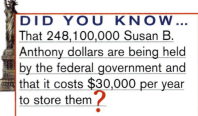

Keynesian Economics
An economic theory, named after English economist John Maynard Keynes, that gained prominence during the Great Depression of the 1930s. It is typically associated with the use of fiscal policy to alter national economic variables—for example, increased government spending during times of economic downturns.

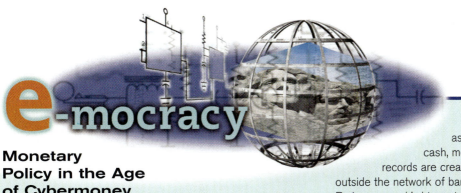

Monetary Policy in the Age of Cybermoney

The technological revolution is changing the nature of financial services, including banking and investing, in fundamental ways. Traditional concepts of branches, networks, and payment systems do not apply in cyberspace. A bank or an investment broker with a home office in Kansas, for example, can do business with a customer anywhere in the world. In fact, an online financial institution does not even need a physical office—a Web page is enough.

E-MONEY

One of the most important ways that the new technology is changing the nature of financial services is the method by which payments are made. Electronic money, or *e-money,* includes a number of alternatives to traditional means of payment. In one type of e-money, a balance of funds is recorded on a magnetic stripe on a card; each time the card is used, a computer terminal debits funds from the balance. Another type uses a microprocessor chip embedded in a so-called *smart card.* A smart card is safer than a magnetic-stripe card because it can be encrypted to protect the value on the card from theft. A smart card is also more versatile because it can function simultaneously as a credit card, a debit card, a stored value card, and a personal information card, such as a driver's license.

E-money is sometimes referred to as *e-cash* because it can be used like cash, meaning that no personally identifiable records are created. E-cash moves about completely outside the network of banks, checks, and paper currency. Perhaps e-cash's biggest play will be on the Internet, where electronic commerce is growing daily. People will be able to download money to their PCs or to palm-sized electronic wallets. People will be able to zap money to Internet merchants.

E-MONEY AND MONETARY POLICY

With the growth of e-cash, the traditional definition of money will certainly no longer hold. The Federal Reserve will have even less ability to control the money supply. Furthermore, e-cash may create problems if it is stored in computer systems. What if the systems crash? Additionally, electronic counterfeiting may be a serious problem. Computer hackers who break into e-cash systems might be able to steal money from thousands or even hundreds of thousands of people all at once. Finally, e-cash may allow for an increased amount of tax evasion and money laundering.

Clearly, the concept of digital money roaming the globe at the speed of light does not bode well for the future of effective monetary policy in the United States or elsewhere. It will be difficult for our Federal Reserve System to have any control over the flows of digitally created cybermoney.

FOR CRITICAL ANALYSIS

Why should it matter whether the Federal Reserve System can or cannot regulate e-cash?

rising inflation, we should do the reverse: reduce the rate of growth of the amount of money in circulation. Interest rates should rise, choking off some consumer spending and some business investment. But the world is never so simple as the theory we use to explain it. If the nation experiences stagflation–rising inflation *and* rising unemployment–expansionary monetary policy (expanding the rate of growth of the money supply) will lead to even more inflation. Ultimately, the more money there is in circulation, the higher prices will be–there will be inflation.

The Monetary Authority–The Federal Reserve System.   Congress established our modern central bank, the Federal Reserve System, in 1913. It is governed by a board of governors consisting of seven members, including the very powerful chairperson. All of the governors, including the chairperson, are nominated by the president and approved by the Senate. Their appointments are for fourteen years.

Through the Federal Reserve System, called the Fed, and its **Federal Open Market Committee (FOMC),** decisions about monetary policy are made eight times a year. The Board of Governors of the Federal Reserve System is independent. The president can attempt to convince the board, and Congress can threaten to merge the Fed with the Treasury, but as long as the Fed retains its independence, its chairperson and governors can do what they please. Hence, talking about "the president's monetary policy" or "Congress's monetary policy" is inaccurate. To be sure, the Fed has, on occasion, yielded to presidential pressure, and for a while the Fed's chairperson felt constrained to follow a congressional resolution requiring him to report monetary targets over each six-month period. But now, more than ever before, the Fed remains one of the truly independent sources of economic power in the government.

Monetary Policy and Lags.   Monetary policy does not suffer from the lengthy time lags that affect fiscal policy, because the Fed can, within a very short period, put its policy into effect. Nonetheless, researchers have estimated that it takes almost fourteen months for a change in monetary policy to become effec-

Federal Open Market Committee (FOMC)
The most important body within the Federal Reserve System. The FOMC decides how monetary policy should be carried out by the Federal Reserve System.

Alan Greenspan, the chairman of the Federal Reserve. The Federal Reserve is responsible for our nation's monetary policy. Greenspan is often called to testify before various congressional committees. He frequently finds himself in the "hot seat" when interest rates are rising.

tive, measured from the time the economy either slows down or speeds up too much to the time the economy feels the policy change. This means that by the time monetary policy goes into effect, a different policy might be appropriate.

In the 1990s, few commentators were able to complain about monetary policy. Inflation had almost disappeared by the end of the decade, which also saw the unemployment rate drop to its lowest level in thirty-five years. There used to be criticism of the Fed's actions in the financial press and even from politicians. This is not so today. There used to be discussions of eliminating the independence of the Fed and merging it with the Treasury. This is not so today. There used to be a fear that inflation was always "waiting in the wings." This is also not so today. The only real question is the following: How much longer will low unemployment and low inflation coexist?

The Public Debt and the Disappearing Deficit

Until the late 1990s, the federal government had run a deficit—spent more than it received—in every year except two since 1960. Every time a budget deficit occurred, the federal government issued debt instruments in the form of **U.S. Treasury bonds.** The sale of these bonds to corporations, private individuals, pension plans, foreign governments, foreign businesses, and foreign individuals added to the **public debt,** or **national debt,** defined as the total amount owed by the federal government. Thus, the relationship between the annual federal government budget deficit and the public debt is clear: if the public debt is, say, $4 trillion this year and the federal budget deficit is $150 billion during the year, then at the end of the year the public debt will be $4.15 trillion. Table 16–4 shows what has happened to the net public debt over time.

It would seem that until recently the nation increasingly was mortgaging its future. But this table does not take into account two important variables: inflation and increases in population. A better way to examine the relative importance of the public debt is to compare it to total national output. We do this in Figure 16–5. There you see that, as a percentage of total national output, the public debt reached its peak during World War II and fell steadily thereafter until the mid-1970s. Since then, except for a slight reduction in 1990, it continued to rise until 1995, when it again started to fall.

TABLE 16–4

Net Public Debt of the Federal Government

YEAR	TOTAL (BILLIONS OF CURRENT DOLLARS)
1940	$ 42.7
1945	235.2
1950	219.0
1960	237.2
1970	284.9
1980	709.3
1990	2,410.1
1992	2,998.6
1993	3,247.5
1994	3,432.1
1995	3,603.4
1996	3,747.1
1997	3,900.0
1998	3,870.0
1999	3,632.9
2000	3,448.6
2001	3,200.3*

*Estimate.

SOURCE: U.S. Office of Management and Budget.

U.S. Treasury Bond
Evidence of debt issued by the federal government; similar to corporate bonds but issued by the U.S. Treasury.

Public Debt, or National Debt
The total amount of debt carried by the federal government.

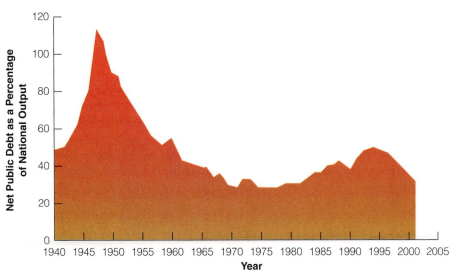

FIGURE 16–5

Net Public Debt as a Percentage of National Output
The public debt as a percentage of national output reached its peak during World War II and then dropped consistently until about 1975. It then grew steadily—until the mid-1990s, when it again started to fall.

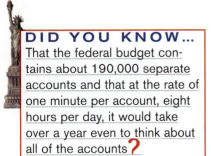

**Federal Reserve
Holds Theory**

Public Debt Financing
The government's spending more than it receives in taxes and paying for the difference by issuing U.S. Treasury bonds, thereby adding to the public debt.

Is the Public Debt a Burden?

We often hear about the burden of the public debt. Some argue that the government eventually is going to go bankrupt, but that, of course, cannot happen. As long as the government has the ability to pay the interest on the public debt through taxation, it will never go bankrupt. What happens is that when Treasury bonds come due, they are simply "rolled over." That is, if a $1 million Treasury bond comes due today, the U.S. Treasury pays it off and sells another $1 million bond.

What about the interest payments? Interest payments are paid by taxes, so what we are really talking about is taxing some people to pay interest to others who loaned money to the government. This cannot really be called a burden to all of society. There is one hitch, however. Not all of the interest payments are paid to Americans. A significant amount is paid to foreigners, because foreigners own nearly 37 percent of the public debt. This raises the fear of too much foreign control of U.S. assets. So it is no longer the case that we "owe it all to ourselves."

The Problem of "Crowding Out"

Although it may be true that we owe the public debt to ourselves (except for what is owed to foreigners), another issue is involved. A large public debt is made up of a series of annual federal government budget deficits. Each time the federal government runs a deficit, we know that it must go into the financial marketplace to borrow the money. This process, in which the U.S. Treasury sells U.S. Treasury bonds, is called **public debt financing.** Public debt financing, in effect, "crowds out" private borrowing. Consider that to borrow, say, $100 billion, the federal government must bid for loanable funds in the marketplace, just as any business does. It bids for those loanable funds by offering to pay higher interest rates. Consequently, interest rates are increased when the federal government runs large deficits and borrows money to cover them. Higher interest rates can stifle or slow business investment, which reduces the rate of economic growth.

Of course, the problem of crowding out is now a moot issue because the federal budget deficit virtually disappeared by the end of 1998. Some forecasts indicate that in the absence of big tax cuts or increases in the rate of government expenditures, there may be federal budget surpluses for years into the future. (See this chapter's *Politics and Economics* for a discussion of the challenge posed by budget surpluses.)

Freer World Trade and the World Trade Organization

At the close of World War II in 1945, the United States was clearly the most powerful and influential nation on earth. Japan, Europe, and the Soviet Union were all in shambles. From the end of the war through most of the 1960s, America retained its economic hegemony. Over the next twenty-five years, however, U.S. dominance in the global marketplace was challenged. Japan rose from its wartime defeat to become one of the top world economic powers. Some of its Pacific Rim neighbors—Taiwan, Hong Kong, Singapore, Malaysia, and Thailand—also started to catch up.

On the other side of the world, the fifteen countries of the former European Community (EC) became one consumer market—the European Union, or EU—on December 31, 1992. For the first time in more than a hundred years, the U.S.

economy slipped to second place, behind the 360-million-consumer economy of the EU. Adding to the EU's formidable economic power is the untapped low-cost labor that is available from the former republics of the Soviet Union and from Eastern Europe.

America's Current Competitive Position

It was very fashionable in the 1980s and even for much of the 1990s to argue that America had lost its competitive edge in the world economy. Numerous reports showed that we were lagging behind European countries and particularly Asian countries—such as Japan, Indonesia, Malaysia, Thailand, Hong Kong, South Korea, and Taiwan. Today, one rarely reads anything about problems with America's global competitiveness. Why? The reason is that the Asian economies went into near collapse in the late 1990s, and Europe has been stagnating. At the same time, the U.S. economy has been booming—millions of jobs have been added every year, the unemployment rate has dropped to low levels, and we are living in an era without much inflation. The economy is so strong that the United States has to import skilled laborers from other countries, particularly for the information-technology sector.

It is true that the United States still faces a deficit in its balance of trade. But that does not mean that America has lost its global competitiveness—far from it. It simply means that the rest of the world wants to invest here. A few short years ago, only 15 percent of the net U.S. public debt was owned by foreigners, while

politics and economics

Dealing with the Budget Surplus

As late as 1997, commentators frequently remarked that the federal budget deficit was a "permanent" part of our economic landscape. They argued that Congress and the president were never able to "spend within their means." Just about every year since the mid-1980s, somebody in Congress introduced a constitutional amendment to balance the federal budget. A funny thing happened on the way to the forum, however—the federal budget deficit virtually disappeared by the end of 1998, and since then the government has experienced budget surpluses.

A NEW CHALLENGE

As a result of budget surpluses, today's lawmakers face a different challenge: How should surplus revenues be used? Answers to this question have ranged from tax cuts to shoring up Social Security to paying off some of the government's accumulated debt from years past. Generally, Republicans place greater emphasis on reducing taxes, while Democrats are concerned with setting more funds aside for domestic spending and debt reduction. Indeed, during the latter years of the Clinton presidency, the U.S. Treasury used annual budget surpluses to pay off part of the national debt, and some forecasts indicated the possibility of completely paying off the debt by 2013.

IS RUNNING BUDGET SURPLUSES GOOD FOR THE ECONOMY?

A number of economists—many of whom had argued previously against large government deficits—now argue against running big federal surpluses. Their concern is the possibility of ill effects on economic growth. When the government runs a surplus, the government saves *on behalf* of private individuals and adds to the total flow of saving in the economy. It channels unspent tax revenues to financial markets. So far, the government has saved by repurchasing some of its debt. In principle, it could save by buying privately placed debt, such as corporate bonds or stocks.

What critics of government surpluses question is the government's ability to channel surplus funds to the most productive uses. They worry that government saving may not be allocated as efficiently as private saving. In other words, too much government saving may be directed to activities with low rates of return. If this happens, they argue, persistent government surpluses will lead to lower rates of economic growth than the nation could otherwise achieve.

FOR CRITICAL ANALYSIS

Some critics contend that attaining high rates of return on saving entails taking risks that are inappropriate for government institutions to take. Do you agree? Why or why not?

A scene from Jakarta, Indonesia, during riots precipitated by the disastrous economic situation in 1998. Many Asian countries suffered a dramatic decline in their well-being during this period.

today it is nearly 37 percent. Asians, particularly in Japan, find U.S. interest rates attractive and want to invest in our government and corporate bonds. They also want to buy real estate in the United States and stocks in U.S. companies. For every dollar of capital that foreigners invest in the United States, there has to be a dollar of trade deficit, for that is an accounting-identity requirement.

In any event, the United States remains the premier world economic power, although this position should not be taken for granted. Many countries have been economic powerhouses, only to find themselves years later way down on the ladder of developed countries.

Opening Up World Trade—The WTO

In general, over the last decade the United States has been in the forefront of those trying to ease restrictions on international trade. In particular, the United States had been an active participant in the negotiations for reducing **tariffs** (taxes on imports) as part of the World Trade Organization (WTO).

The origins of a worldwide trade liberalization policy date to 1947, when the General Agreement on Tariffs and Trade, or GATT, was signed. Under GATT, countries met periodically to negotiate tariff reductions that would be mutually advantageous to all members. The 117 member nations of GATT accounted for between 85 and 90 percent of all world trade. The final round of GATT meetings in 1994 created the World Trade Organization (WTO). The WTO replaced GATT.

The establishment of the WTO will result in a roughly 40 percent cut in tariffs worldwide. Agricultural subsidies will eventually be reduced and eventually eliminated. Protection of patents will be extended worldwide.

The WTO raises serious political issues, however (see this chapter's *Which Side Are You On?* for one issue). Although the WTO has arbitration boards to settle international disputes over trade issues, no country has a veto. Opponents argue that a "vetoless" America will repeatedly be outvoted by the mercantile countries of Western Europe and East Asia. Some activist groups maintain that the unelected WTO international trade bureaucrats based in Geneva, Switzerland, are weakening environmental health and consumer safety laws when such laws affect international trade flows. Another criticism is that member nations of the WTO are obligated to pursue favorable trade relations with other member nations regardless of a nation's record with respect to human rights.

Tariff
A tax on imported goods.

which side are you on?

Granting China Permanent Normal Trade Relations

Until 2000, every year Congress had to debate whether to renew its relatively open trade policy with China. Finally, in 2000, both the House and the Senate voted to grant permanent normal trade relations (PNTR) with China. Particularly in the House, the debate and lobbying were often intense and acrimonious.

It Was about Human Rights, at Least for Some

The objections most often raised against establishing PNTR with China involved China's human rights record. The Clinton administration stated in its annual review of human rights that China had a "poor human rights record [that] deteriorated markedly throughout [1999] as the government intensified efforts to suppress dissent." Opponents to the bill argued that establishing normal trade relations would essentially put America's stamp of approval on a nation that violates human rights every day of the year. They compared China's human rights record to that of Nazi Germany and argued that we would never have established such trade relationships with the Nazis.

Some opponents also argued that national security might be threatened. After all, they pointed out, China had used its export earnings to upgrade its weapons systems. Reducing trade barriers will have the effect of increasing both exports and imports in China.

Finally, labor unions strongly opposed granting China any permanent trade benefits. Unions see relatively less expensive Chinese labor as a threat to their members.

Economics and Government

Supporters of permanently normalizing trade with China argued that the gains from trade are mutual—it's the first thing one learns in a beginning economics course. Evidence of benefits from increased international trade have been quite obvious since the passsage of the North American Free Trade Agreement among the United States, Mexico, and Canada. As trade barriers have been lowered throughout the world, world trade has increased dramatically, as have living standards in many countries.

Because trade normalization will force China to reduce its taxes on imports (tariffs) through 2005, American exporters expect to see gains. In particular, farm exports, especially of beef and pork, should expand by over $2 billion per year.

Political and social change in China may also be a long-run result of normalized trade. As President Clinton put it, "We will be exporting more than our products. By this agreement we will also export one of our most cherished values—economic freedom." The reasoning is that as trade increases between the two countries, China's leaders will be forced to loosen controls over the Chinese population. There is certainly evidence that Soviet society became more open when trade increased between the former Soviet Union and the West. Whether the West can anticipate the fall of communism in China as a result of the trade agreement remains to be seen.

DOES IT MATTER?

Are you at all concerned about the government's willingness to pursue trade relationships with China despite the country's record on human rights issues? Explain.

GOING ONLINE

To find arguments favoring PNTR with China, go to the Web site of the U.S. Chamber of Commerce at **http://www.uschamber.org/traderoots/china/pntrvote.html**. *For arguments against PNTR with China, access a speech on this issue by House minority leader Dick Gephardt (D., Mo.) at* **http://democraticleader.house.gov/media/speeches/readSpeech.asp?ID=19**.

Domestic and Economic Policy: Issues for the Twenty-First Century

It seems strange that programs to reduce poverty are still on the domestic policy agenda. After all, the federal government started its "war on poverty" back in the early 1960s. By some estimates, we have transferred well over a trillion dollars to eliminate poverty since then. Yet poverty remains a blight on the record of one of the world's richest countries—the United States.

Another domestic policy issue that certainly will continue to challenge policymakers is the level of crime and violence in the United States. There is little indication that this problem will be solved in the foreseeable future. Although crime rates have declined significantly since the mid-1990s, they are still much higher than they were two decades ago. We probably will see continuing attempts to control crime. No doubt, we also will hear political candidates stress that our high crime rates are a reflection of the breakdown of American values and family structure.

Political issues will continue to swirl around Social Security. Older Americans will continue to make Social Security a focal point of their lobbying efforts, as they have in the past, and policymakers will continue to consider alternatives to the current system.

The independence of the Federal Reserve System probably will be an issue, also. Many in Congress resent the Fed's ability to alter economic policy without consulting legislators. Debates over the effectiveness of the Fed's policies will never end, because even economists disagree.

The United States has enjoyed a relatively long period of economic growth. If for any reason a recession were to occur and jobs were to become scarce, the current debates over domestic and economic policy would become much sharper and the issues far more contentious than they currently are.

making a difference

Working for a Cleaner Environment

Energy undoubtedly will be among the more important domestic issues in the coming decades. Ultimately, every energy policy involves environmental questions. Not only is this issue central to our every-day lives, but also, it is argued, the fate of the planet may hang in the balance as today's policymakers make decisions about energy production and environmental protection. To make things more complicated, these parallel struggles of coping with energy problems and preserving our environment tend to work at cross-purposes. In the pursuit of secure and abundant energy, the interests of clean air, water, and land—as well as people—sometimes are sacrificed.

When objectives clash, difficult political trade-offs must be made. To a large group of environmentalists in this country, the choice is clear: if we want to improve or even preserve our quality of life, we must stop environmental degradation.

Environmental groups work on a host of issues, ranging from solar power to mass transit and from wildlife preservation to population control. If you feel strongly about these or other environmental issues and want to get involved, contact the following groups:

Environmental Defense Fund
257 Park Ave. South
New York, NY 10010
800-684-3322

http://www.edf.org

National Environmental Policy Institute
1401 K St. N.W., Suite M–103
Washington, DC 20005
202-833-5977

http://www.nepi.org

Friends of the Earth
1025 Vermont Ave. N.W., Suite 300
Washington, DC 20005
202-783-7400

http://www.foe.org

Greenpeace USA
702 H St. N.W.
Washington, DC 20001
800-326-0959

http://www.greenpeaceusa.org

League of Conservation Voters
1920 L St. N.W., Suite 800
Washington, DC 20036
202-785-8683

http://www.lcv.org

National Audubon Society
700 Broadway
New York, NY 10003
212-979-3000

http://www.audubon.org/nas

National Parks Conservation Association
1300 Nineteenth St. N.W., Suite 300
Washington, DC 20036
800-628-7275

http://www.npca.org

National Wildlife Federation
8925 Leesburg Pike
Vienna, VA 22184
703-790-7000

http://www.nwf.org

Natural Resources Defense Council
40 West 20th St.
New York, NY 10011
212-727-2700

http://www.nrdc.org

Sierra Club
85 Second St.
San Francisco, CA 94105
415-977-5500

http://www.sierraclub.org

Wilderness Society
900 Seventh St. N.W.
Washington, DC 20006
202-833-2300

http://www.wilderness.org

Key terms

action-reaction syndrome 525

domestic policy 513

earned-income tax credit (EITC) program 519

environmental impact statement (EIS) 524

Federal Open Market Committee (FOMC) 532

fiscal policy 530

food stamps 519

income transfer 516

in-kind subsidy 517

Keynesian economics 531

loophole 527

monetary policy 530

policy trade-offs 524

public debt, or national debt 533

public debt financing 534

regressive tax 528

Supplemental Security Income (SSI) 518

tariff 536

Temporary Assistance to Needy Families (TANF) 517

U.S. Treasury bond 533

Chapter summary

1 Domestic policy consists of all of the laws, government planning, and government actions that affect the lives of American citizens. Policies are created in response to public problems or public demand for government action. Major policy problems now facing this nation include the taxation of e-commerce, poverty and welfare, crime, the environment, and Social Security.

2 The policymaking process is initiated when policymakers become aware—through the media or from their constituents—of a problem that needs to be addressed by the legislature and the president. The process of policymaking includes five steps: agenda building, agenda formulation, agenda adoption, agenda implementation, and agenda evaluation. All policy actions necessarily result in both costs and benefits for society.

3 In spite of the wealth of the United States, a significant number of Americans live in poverty or are homeless. The low-income poverty threshold represents an absolute measure of income needed to maintain a specified standard of living as of 1963, with the constant-dollar, or purchasing-power, value increased year by year in relation to the general increase in prices. The official poverty level is based on pretax income, including cash, and does not take into consideration in-kind subsidies (food stamps, housing vouchers, and so on).

4 The 1996 Welfare Reform Act transferred more control over welfare programs to the states, limited the number of years people can receive welfare assistance, and imposed work requirements on welfare recipients. The reform act succeeded in reducing the number of welfare recipients in the United States by at least 50 percent. Despite the reform, poverty rates have not significantly changed.

5 There is widespread concern in this country about violent crime, and particularly, the large number of crimes that are committed by juveniles. The overall rate of violent crime, including crimes commited by juveniles, has been declining since 1995, however.

6 Pollution problems continue to plague the United States and the world. Since the nineteenth century, a number of significant federal acts have been passed in an attempt to curb the pollution of our environment. The National Environmental Policy Act of 1969 established the Council for Environmental Quality. That act also mandated that environmental impact statements be prepared for all legislation or major federal actions that might significantly affect the quality of the environment. The Clean Air Act amendments of 1990 constituted the most significant government attempt at cleaning up our environment.

7 In the area of taxes and subsidies (negative taxes), policymakers have long had to contend with what is known as the action-reaction syndrome. For every action on the part of the government, there will be a reaction on the part of the public, to which the government will react with another action, to which the public will again react, and so on. In regard to taxes, as a general rule, individuals and corporations that pay the highest tax rates will react to those rates by pressuring Congress into creating exceptions and tax loopholes (loopholes allow high-income earners to reduce their taxable incomes). This action on the part of Congress results in a reaction from another interest group—consisting of those who want the rich to pay more taxes. In response, higher tax rates are imposed on the rich, and so the cycle continues.

8 Closely related to the question of taxes is the viability of the Social Security system. As the number of people who are working relative to the number of people who are retiring declines, those who work will have to pay more Social Security taxes to pay for the benefits of those who retire.

9 Fiscal policy is the use of changes in government expenditures and taxes to alter national economic variables, such as the rate of inflation or unemployment. Monetary policy is defined as the use of changes in the amount of money in circulation so as to affect interest rates, credit markets, the rate of inflation, and employment. Fiscal policy economics usually means increasing government spending during recessionary periods and increasing taxes during inflationary boom periods. The problem with fiscal policy and monetary policy is the lag between the time a problem occurs in the economy and the time when policy changes are actually felt in the economy.

10 Whenever the federal government spends more than it receives, it runs a deficit. The deficit is met by U.S. Treasury borrowing. This adds to the public debt of the federal government. Those who oppose large increases in government spending argue that one effect of the federal deficit is the crowding out of private investment. The federal budget deficit virtually disappeared by 1998, however, and since then the budget has showed a surplus.

11 The United States remains the foremost world economic power. It has also been an active participant in the World Trade Organization (WTO), whose aim is to increase trade among nations by reducing tariffs worldwide. The WTO has been criticized in recent years by activist groups concerned with the organization's impact on worldwide concerns, such as environmental health, human rights, and consumer safety.

Selected print and electronic resources

SUGGESTED READINGS

Benedick, Richard Elliot. *Ozone Diplomacy: New Directions in Safeguarding the Planet.* Enlarged edition. Cambridge, Mass.: Harvard University Press, 1998. The author, an experienced diplomat, gives an insider's view of some of the international efforts that have been made to address environmental issues.

Friedman, Milton, and Walter Heller. *Monetary versus Fiscal Policy.* New York: Norton, 1969. This is a classic presentation of the pros and cons of monetary and fiscal policy given by a noninterventionist (Friedman) and an advocate of federal government intervention in the economy (Heller).

Miller, Roger LeRoy, *et al. The Economics of Public Issues,* 12th ed. Reading, Mass.: Addison-Wesley, 2001. Chapters 4, 12, 15–17, 22, 26, 28, and 29–31 are especially useful. The authors use short essays of three to seven pages to explain the purely economic aspects of numerous social problems, including health care, the environment, and poverty.

Peterson, Peter G. *Gray Dawn: How the Coming Age Wave Will Transform America–And the World.* New York: Times Books, 1999. As populations age and decline, will economies decline as well? The author explores this question and its ramifications for policymakers and suggests possible solutions to the "gray dawn" of the twenty-first century.

The President's Council of Economic Advisers. *Economic Report of the President.* Washington, D.C.: U.S. Government Printing Office, published annually. This volume contains a wealth of details concerning current monetary and fiscal policy and what is happening to the economy.

Wallach, Lori, Michelle Sforza, and Ralph Nader. *Whose Trade Organization? Corporate Globalization and the Erosion of Democracy.* Washington, D.C.: Public Citizen, 1999. This book explores the effects of the rules and actions of the World Trade Organization (WTO) on the global environment, public health and safety, labor, and human rights.

MEDIA RESOURCES

America's Promise: Who's Entitled to What?–A four-part series that examines the current state of welfare reform and its impact on immigrant and other populations.

Crimes and Punishments: A History–A controversial documentary that traces the often brutal history of criminal punishment from the medieval era through today.

Rollover–A 1981 film starring Jane Fonda as a former film star who inherits a multimillion-dollar empire when her husband is mysteriously murdered and Kris Kristofferson as a financial troubleshooter who helps her try to save the company. The film offers an insider's view of the politics of currency crises.

Young Criminals, Adult Punishment–An ABC program that examines the issue of whether the harsh sentences given out to adult criminals, including capital punishment, should also be applied to young violent offenders.

Logging on

You can find further information on most of the issues discussed in this chapter at Project Vote Smart's Web site. Go to

http://www.vote-smart.org/issues

For current statistics on poverty in the United States, go to

http://www.census.gov

The National Governors Association offers information on the current status of welfare reform among the various states at

http://www.nga.org

The Federal Bureau of Investigation offers information about crime rates at its Web site:

http://www.fbi.gov

You can also find statistics and other information on crime in the United States at the Web site of the Bureau of Justice Statistics. Go to

http://www.ojp.usdoj.gov/bjs

To find more information on poverty in the United States and the latest research on this topic, go to the site of the Institute for Research on Poverty at

http://www.ssc.wisc.edu/irp

You can keep up with actions taken by the Federal Reserve by checking the home page of the Federal Reserve Bank of San Francisco at

http://www.frbsf.org

For further information on Social Security, access the Social Security Administration's home page at

http://www.ssa.gov

For information on the 2001 budgets of the U.S. government, go to

http://www.cnie.org/nle/info-14.html

Using the Internet for political analysis

Take your turn at proposing a federal budget, balanced or not. Check out the Web site for the National Budget Simulation at

http://garnet.berkeley.edu:3333/budget/budget.html

Play the game at this Web site, which allows you to simulate budget cuts by categories of spending. You will decide what should be cut and see what difference it makes in the overall budget. This site provides other budget information through the Economic Democracy Information Network.

If you would like more input into the budget, you might access the Web site for the Concord Coalition at

http://www.concordcoalition.org

There, you can take part in a poll on what to do with any budget surplus in the coming years.

chapter 17
Foreign and Defense Policy

CHAPTER OUTLINE

- What Is Foreign Policy?

- Morality versus Reality in Foreign Policy

- Who Makes Foreign Policy?

- Limiting the President's Power

- Domestic Sources of Foreign Policy

- The Major Foreign Policy Themes

- Challenges in World Politics

what if...

The United States Defended Only Itself?

BACKGROUND

Since World War II (1939–1945), the United States has frequently sent military forces to defend other nations from attack. The Korean War (1950–1953), the Vietnam War (1964–1975), and the Persian Gulf War (1991) are examples of such actions. Officially, in the Korean and Gulf Wars, the United States sent troops to carry out the resolutions of the Security Council of the United Nations, to which this nation belongs.

Although the United States may not often be called on to uphold its obligations to the North Atlantic Treaty Organization (NATO) or under various other duly approved treaties, the nation is obligated under a number of different treaties to provide troops to defend another nation if that nation is attacked. Because of these treaty obligations, the United States has kept military bases active around the globe and expended huge sums of money for military preparedness.

WHAT IF THE UNITED STATES DEFENDED ONLY ITSELF?

For more than 150 years, the United States approached global affairs from an isolationist perspective, avoiding any mutual defense alliances. What if the United States returned to that sort of posture, maintaining military forces only to defend U.S. soil and U.S. citizens?

With an isolationist policy, organizing the U.S. military effort would be much simpler and cheaper. American airbases and naval bases around the world would be closed, and the hundreds of thousands of Americans stationed overseas would be brought home. Expenditures for military weapons would probably concentrate on missile defenses and coastal defenses, utilizing high technology instead of massive numbers of military personnel. Much of the U.S. defense effort would probably be carried out by the National Guard and reserve contingents, because a large standing army would not be necessary.

The domestic political discussion about the use of troops and the president's role as commander in chief would also change, because the conditions for using troops would be extremely clear: only when the United States or its citizens are under attack.

WOULD WARS BREAK OUT AROUND THE GLOBE?

If the United States returned to a "fortress America" posture, it is possible that a number of wars might break out around the globe. One of the reasons for NATO and other mutual defense pacts, as well as for the United Nations, is that they raise the stakes for an aggressor nation. Any nation that starts a war must plan for massive retaliation by a group of nations bound in a defensive alliance. If the United States were to

pull out of its alliances, many of them might fall apart.

Another real possibility would be an increase in terrorist attacks, threats by rogue nations, and civil wars. Although the United States has not adopted the role of global police officer, it has been able to persuade its allies to join together to intimidate nations such as Libya and Iraq through threats and joint military attacks. If NATO ceased to exist, it is not clear that any European nation acting alone would assume leadership in stopping civil wars and other types of conflicts.

Other nations, however, might become the world's leaders in the pursuit of peace. Or, possibly, the United Nations could become a truly powerful force for peace, uniting its many members to enforce the peace as it was founded to do.

HOW COULD THE UNITED STATES PULL OUT OF ITS COMMITMENTS?

If the United States decided to follow an isolationist policy, it would have to renounce its commitments to treaties, such as the NATO alliance, probably by vote of Congress. The United States could be pressured to relinquish its seat on the United Nations Security Council and might, to be safe, give up membership in the United Nations altogether. If the United States did not withdraw, it might be subject to sanctions or other actions for failing to follow through on commitments made by the United Nations. For all of this to happen, the president and Congress would have to be very sure that the American public supported a return to isolationism even as more and more Americans and their companies are going global.

FOR CRITICAL ANALYSIS

1. Do you think that U.S. interests could be sufficiently protected if the United States decided to defend only U.S. soil and U.S. citizens against aggression?

2. Is there any other way for the United States to reduce its obligations and troop commitments abroad and encourage other nations to take leadership roles?

mericans view a world that is changing so rapidly that their first response can be to turn inward and focus on domestic problems. Presidents and members of Congress also are tempted to pay less attention to foreign affairs in the post-**Cold War** world. The instability of world politics, however, which has been fueled by the disintegration of the Soviet Union in 1991, the rise of ethnic nationalism, the continuing threat of terrorism, and the existence of multiple regional "hot spots," presents serious threats to American security.

Without a guiding theme to foreign policy—the containment of communism—the creation and implementation of foreign policy and a national security strategy have become much more complex. The United States has lowered defense spending and concentrated on the domestic economy. Without the need to compete with the Soviet Union in different regions of the world, the United States could decide not to become engaged in regional conflicts. It could end foreign aid as a further signal that the United States is looking inward. The chapter-opening *What If . . .* suggests the consequences of such an isolationist position.

The Clinton administration, which focused on domestic policies, including welfare reform, was criticized for not developing an equally clearly focused foreign policy. Yet it is certainly not clear what the right policy should be toward Bosnia, Rwanda, Haiti, Pakistan, or North Korea, to name just a few trouble spots. It is clear, however, that in times of crisis the nation still needs guiding principles for action.

Cold War
The ideological, political, and economic impasse that existed between the United States and the Soviet Union following World War II.

What Is Foreign Policy?

As the cultural, military, and economic interdependence of the nations of the world has increased, it has become even more important for the United States to establish and carry out foreign policies to deal with external situations and to carry out its own national goals. By **foreign policy,** we mean both the goals the government wants to achieve in the world and the techniques and strategies to achieve them. For example, if one national goal is to achieve stability in Eastern Europe and to encourage the formation of pro-American governments there, U.S. foreign policy in that area may be carried out using various techniques, including **diplomacy, economic aid, technical assistance,** or military intervention. Sometimes foreign policies are restricted to statements of goals or ideas, such as helping to end world poverty, whereas at other times foreign policies are comprehensive efforts to achieve particular objectives.

In the United States, the **foreign policy process** usually originates with the president and those agencies that provide advice on foreign policy matters. Foreign policy formulation often is affected by congressional action and national public debate.

Foreign Policy
A nation's external goals and the techniques and strategies used to achieve them.

Diplomacy
The total process by which states carry on political relations with each other; settling conflicts among nations by peaceful means.

Economic Aid
Assistance to other nations in the form of grants, loans, or credits to buy the assisting nation's products.

Technical Assistance
The sending of experts with technical skills in such areas as agriculture, engineering, or business to aid other nations.

Foreign Policy Process
The steps by which external goals are decided and acted on.

National Security Policy

As one aspect of overall foreign policy, **national security policy** is designed primarily to protect the independence and the political integrity of the United States. It concerns itself with the defense of the United States against actual or potential (real or imagined) enemies, domestic or foreign.

U.S. national security policy is based on determinations made by the Department of Defense, the Department of State, and a number of other federal agencies, including the **National Security Council (NSC).** The NSC acts as an advisory body to the president, but it has increasingly become a rival to the State Department in influencing the foreign policy process.

National Security Policy
Foreign and domestic policy designed to protect the independence and political and economic integrity of the United States; policy that is concerned with the safety and defense of the nation.

National Security Council (NSC)
A board created by the 1947 National Security Act to advise the president on matters of national security.

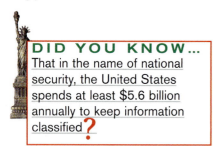

Isolateralism or Unilationism?

Moral Idealism
A philosophy that sees all nations as willing to cooperate and agree on moral standards for conduct.

Political Realism
A philosophy that sees each nation acting principally in its own interest.

Diplomacy

Diplomacy is another aspect of foreign policy. Diplomacy includes all of a nation's external relationships, from routine diplomatic communications to summit meetings among heads of state. More specifically, diplomacy refers to the settling of disputes and conflicts among nations by peaceful methods. Diplomacy is the set of negotiating techniques by which a nation attempts to carry out its foreign policy.

Diplomacy may or may not be successful, depending on the willingness of the parties to negotiate. For example, in 1993, after years of refusing to negotiate or even recognize each other's existence, Israel and representatives of the Palestine Liberation Organization (the PLO) reached an agreement under which Israel returned control of Jericho and part of the West Bank to the Palestinians. The 1993 agreement left open the possibility of a Palestinian state.

Morality versus Reality in Foreign Policy

From the earliest years of the republic, Americans have felt that their nation had a special destiny. The American experiment in democratic government and capitalism, it was thought, would provide the best possible life for men and women and be a model for other nations. As the United States assumed greater status as a power in world politics, Americans came to believe that the nation's actions on the world stage should be guided by American political and moral principles. As Harry Truman stated, "The United States should take the lead in running the world in the way that it ought to be run."

This view of America's mission has led to the adoption of many foreign policy initiatives that are rooted in **moral idealism**, a philosophy that sees the world as fundamentally benign and other nations as willing to cooperate for the good of all.[1] In this perspective, nations should come together and agree to keep the peace, as President Woodrow Wilson (1913–1921) proposed for the League of Nations. Nations should see the wrong in violating the human rights of ethnic or religious minorities and should work to end such injustice. Many of the foreign policy initiatives taken by the United States have been based on this idealistic view of the world, but few of these actions have been very successful.

The Peace Corps, however, which was created by President John Kennedy in 1961, is one example of an effort to spread American goodwill and technology that has achieved some of its goals. The Clinton administration's actions in 1994 to return the democratically elected president of Haiti to power were rooted partly in moral conviction, although elements within the U.S. government regarded President Jean-Bertrand Aristide as unstable or left-leaning. Foreign policy based on moral imperatives often is unsuccessful because it assumes that other nations agree with American views of morality and politics.

In opposition to the moral perspective is **political realism.** Realists see the world as a dangerous place in which each nation strives for its own survival and interests. Foreign policy decisions must be based on a cold calculation of what is best for the United States without regard for morality. Realists believe that the United States must be prepared militarily to defend itself, because all other nations are, by definition, out to improve their own situations. A strong defense will show the world that the United States is willing to protect its interests. The practice of political realism in foreign policy allows the United States to sell weapons to military dictators who will support its policies, to support American

---

[1]Charles W. Kegley, Jr., and Eugene Wittkopf, *American Foreign Policy, Pattern and Process,* 3d ed. (New York: St. Martin's Press, 1987), p. 73.

business around the globe, and to repel terrorism through the use of force. Political realism leads, for example, to a policy of not negotiating with terrorists who take hostages, because such negotiations simply will lead to the taking of more hostages.

It is important to note that the United States never has been guided by only one of these principles. Instead, both moral idealism and political realism affect foreign policymaking. Sometimes, U.S. policy blends the two, granting aid to a nation that is a major trading partner and then attaching conditions that are rooted in morality to that aid. President Clinton wrestled with the situation in Bosnia to try to find a way for the United States to practice a pragmatic policy based on moral principles. Strongly opposed to using U.S. troops to establish peace in Bosnia, the president tried to convince the warring parties—the Bosnian Serbs and the Bosnian Muslims—to negotiate and accept a cease-fire. Finally, under pressure from the United States, the warring parties hammered out an agreement to divide the territory into ethnic nations. The United States and other nations in the North Atlantic Treaty Organization (NATO) guaranteed military forces to patrol the new boundaries for a period of time.

Who Makes Foreign Policy?

Is foreign policy made by the president, by Congress, or by joint executive and congressional action? There is no easy answer to this question, because, as constitutional authority Edwin S. Corwin once observed, the U.S. Constitution created an "invitation to struggle" between the president and Congress for control over the foreign policy process. Let us look first at powers given to the president by the Constitution.

President Franklin D. Roosevelt signs the declaration of war against Japan on December 8, 1941.

Constitutional Powers of the President

The Constitution confers on the president broad powers that are either explicit or implied in key constitutional provisions. Article II vests the executive power of the government in the president. The presidential oath of office given in Article II, Section 1, requires that the president "solemnly swear" to "preserve, protect and defend the Constitution of the United States."

In addition, and perhaps more important, Article II, Section 2, designates the president as "Commander in Chief of the Army and Navy of the United States." Starting with Abraham Lincoln, all presidents have interpreted this authority dynamically and broadly. Indeed, since George Washington's administration, the United States has been involved in at least 125 undeclared wars that were conducted under presidential authority. For example, Harry Truman ordered U.S. armed forces in the Pacific to enter into North Korea's conflict with South Korea. Dwight Eisenhower threatened China and North Korea with nuclear weapons if the Korean peace talks were not successfully concluded. Bill Clinton sent troops to Haiti and Bosnia.

Article II, Section 2, of the Constitution also gives the president the power to make treaties, provided that two-thirds of the senators present concur. Presidents usually have been successful in getting treaties through the Senate. In addition to this formal treaty-making power, the president makes use of executive agreements (discussed in Chapter 13). Since World War II (1939–1945), executive agreements have accounted for almost 95 percent of the understandings reached between the United States and other nations.

Executive agreements have a long and important history. Significant in their long-term effects were the several agreements Franklin Roosevelt reached with the Soviet Union and other countries, especially at Yalta, during World War II.

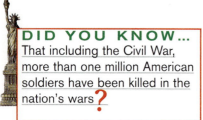

The government of South Vietnam and the government of the United States, particularly under Dwight Eisenhower, John Kennedy, and Lyndon Johnson, made a series of executive agreements in which the United States promised support. All in all, since 1946 over eight thousand executive agreements with foreign countries were made. There is no way to get an accurate count, because perhaps as many as several hundred of these agreements have been secret.

An additional power conferred on the president in Article II, Section 2, is the right to appoint ambassadors, other public ministers, and consuls. In Section 3 of that article, the president is given the power to recognize foreign governments through receiving their ambassadors.

Informal Techniques of Presidential Leadership

Other broad sources of presidential power in the U.S. foreign policy process are tradition, precedent, and the president's personality. The president can employ a host of informal techniques that give the White House overwhelming superiority within the government in foreign policy leadership.

First, the president has access to information. More information is available to the president from the Central Intelligence Agency (CIA), the State Department, and the Defense Department than to any other governmental official. This information carries with it the ability to make quick decisions—and that ability is used often. Second, the president is a legislative leader who can influence the amount of funds that are allocated for different programs. Third, the president can influence public opinion. President Theodore Roosevelt once made the following statement:

> People used to say to me that I was an astonishingly good politician and divined what the people are going to think. . . . I did not "divine" how the people were going to think; I simply made up my mind what they ought to think and then did my best to get them to think it.[2]

Presidents are without equal with respect to influencing public opinion, partly because of their ability to command the media. Depending on their skill in appealing to patriotic sentiment (and sometimes fear), they can make people think that their course in foreign affairs is right and necessary. President Clinton, for example, worked intensely to secure the passage of the China Trade Bill in 2000 (see this chapter's *Politics and Economics* for a discussion of how he achieved this legislative victory). Public opinion often seems to be impressed by the president's decision to make a national commitment abroad. Presidents normally, although certainly not always, receive the immediate support of the American people when reacting to (or creating) a foreign policy crisis.

Finally, the president can commit the nation morally to a course of action in foreign affairs. Because the president is the head of state and the leader of one of the most powerful nations on earth, once the president has made a commitment for the United States, it is difficult for Congress or anyone else to back down on that commitment.

Other Sources of Foreign Policymaking

There are at least four foreign policymaking sources within the executive branch, in addition to the president. These are (1) the Department of State, (2) the National Security Council, (3) the intelligence community and informational programs, and (4) the Department of Defense.

---

[2]Sidney Warren, *The President as World Leader* (New York: McGraw-Hill, 1964), p. 23.

The Department of State.   In principle, the State Department is the executive agency that is most directly concerned with foreign affairs. It supervises U.S. relations with the nearly two hundred independent nations around the world and with the United Nations and other multinational groups, such as the Organization of American States. It staffs embassies and consulates throughout the world. It has more than 31,000 employees. This number may sound impressive, but it is small compared with, say, the Department of Health and Human Services with its more than 61,000 employees. Also, the State Department had an annual operating budget of only $5.7 billion in fiscal year 2001—one of the smallest budgets of the cabinet departments.

Newly elected presidents usually tell the American public that the new secretary of state is the nation's chief foreign policy adviser. Nonetheless, the State Department's preeminence in foreign policy has declined dramatically since World War II. The State Department's image within the White House Executive Office and Congress (and even foreign governments) is quite poor—a slow, plodding, bureaucratic maze of inefficient, indecisive individuals. There is even a story about how Premier Nikita Khrushchev of the Soviet Union urged President

politics and economics

Strange Bedfellows

One of the hallmarks of the Clinton administration's foreign policy was its commitment to free trade and expanded markets for American business and products. Early in President Clinton's first term, Congress approved the North American Free Trade Agreement (NAFTA), opening a free trade zone from Mexico to Canada. Although some American companies took advantage of NAFTA to move their factories south of the border where labor costs were lower, the increase in American exports to Mexico and Canada seemed to outweigh any job losses.

At the end of his second term, Clinton engaged in a concerted effort to change U.S. trade relations with the People's Republic of China. American relations with China had turned rocky after the Chinese government harshly suppressed the political reform movement at Tiananmen Square in 1989. The United States withdrew normal trade privileges from China at that time and, for the next ten years, required that Congress reapprove the granting of "most-favored-nation" status (essentially, normal trade relations) to China each year. Every year that approval process reopened a debate in Congress over the Chinese government's repression of religious freedom and political reform, its use of slave labor, and its threat against Taiwan.

THE CHINA TRADE BILL

In 1999, the Clinton administration reached agreement with China on a set of trade accords that could allow China to join the World Trade Organization. For China, to do that, the United States would have to grant permanent most-favored-nation status to China. The administration anticipated that the Senate would pass the China Trade Bill but expected that the vote in the House of

Representatives would be very close. The debate raged for weeks in the spring of 2000. Amnesty International and other groups supporting human rights, religious groups, and American labor lined up against the bill. Most businesses, most state governors, and most farm organizations favored the bill. The administration staked its legacy on it.

UNLIKELY ALLIANCES

The lobbying effort was intense and, in the language of politics, created strange bedfellows. Here was the Democratic president of the United States working closely in alliance with the Republican House members who had impeached him. Businesses that normally supported only Republicans worked with the president to lobby for the bill's passage. Human rights groups that normally supported Clinton worked against him. Labor unions tried to pressure their representatives to vote against the bill, claiming that it would allow China to use slave labor and would cost American jobs. One of the weaknesses in organized labor's strategy, however, was the defection of some unions. Workers in the telecommunications, satellite, and telephone industries and aircraft workers at Boeing Corporation and the makers of aircraft engines supported the bill because their products were sought by China.

At the end of the debate, the China Trade Bill passed the House by a margin of forty votes, with a majority of Republicans and a minority of Democrats joining forces to pass the bill. The Senate subsequently passed the bill, which was signed into law by the president in October 2000.

FOR CRITICAL ANALYSIS

If a Democratic member of Congress voted for the China Trade Bill, would labor unions really withhold their support from that member and support the Republican challenger in the upcoming election?

Negative Constituents
Citizens who openly oppose government foreign policies.

In January 2001, Colin Powell, a former U.S. Army general and chairman of the Joint Chiefs of Staff, assumed his responsibilities as secretary of state in the George W. Bush administration. Powell is the first African American to hold that position.

Intelligence Community
The government agencies that are involved in gathering information about the capabilities and intentions of foreign governments and that engage in activities to further U.S. foreign policy aims.

John Kennedy to formulate his own views rather than to rely on State Department officials who, according to Khrushchev, "specialized in why something had not worked forty years ago."[3] In any event, since the days of Franklin Roosevelt, the State Department sometimes has been bypassed and often has been ignored when crucial decisions are made.

It is not surprising that the State Department has been overshadowed in foreign policy. It has no natural domestic constituency as does, for example, the Department of Defense, which can call on defense contractors for support. Instead, the State Department has what might be called **negative constituents**—U.S. citizens who openly oppose American foreign policy. One of the State Department's major functions, administering foreign aid, often elicits criticisms. Also, within Congress, the State Department is often looked on as an advocate of unpopular and costly foreign involvement. It is often called "the Department of Bad News."

The National Security Council.   The job of the National Security Council (NSC), created by the National Security Act of 1947, is to advise the president on the integration of "domestic, foreign, and military policies relating to the national security." Its larger purpose is to provide policy continuity from one administration to the next. As it has turned out, the NSC—consisting of the president, the vice president, the secretaries of state and defense, the director of emergency planning, and often the chairperson of the joint chiefs of staff and the director of the CIA—is used in just about any way the president wants to use it.

The role of national security adviser to the president seems to adjust to fit the player. Some advisers have come into conflict with heads of the State Department. Henry A. Kissinger, Nixon's flamboyant and aggressive national security adviser, rapidly gained ascendancy over William Rogers, the secretary of state, in foreign policy. When Jimmy Carter became president, he appointed Zbigniew Brzezinski as national security adviser. Brzezinski competed openly with Secretary of State Cyrus Vance (who apparently had little power). In the Clinton administration, Madeleine Albright played a global role as secretary of state, while Sandy Berger, the national security adviser, became a close counselor of the president during his second term.

The Intelligence Community.   No discussion of foreign policy would be complete without some mention of the **intelligence community**. This consists of the forty or more government agencies or bureaus that are involved in intelligence activities, informational and otherwise. On January 24, 1978, President Carter issued Executive Order 12036, in which he formally defined the official major members of the intelligence community. They are as follows:

1. Central Intelligence Agency (CIA).
2. National Security Agency (NSA).
3. Defense Intelligence Agency (DIA).
4. Offices within the Department of Defense.
5. Bureau of Intelligence and Research in the Department of State.
6. Federal Bureau of Investigation (FBI).
7. Army intelligence.
8. Air Force intelligence.
9. Department of the Treasury.
10. Drug Enforcement Administration (DEA).
11. Department of Energy.

---

[3]Theodore C. Sorensen, *Kennedy* (New York: Harper & Row, 1965), pp. 554–555.

The CIA was created as part of the National Security Act of 1947. The National Security Agency and the Defense Intelligence Agency were created by executive order. Until recently, Congress voted billions of dollars for intelligence activities with little knowledge of how the funds were being used. Intelligence activities consist mostly of overt information gathering, but covert actions also are undertaken. Covert actions, as the name implies, are done secretly, and rarely does the American public find out about them. In the late 1940s and early 1950s, the CIA covertly subsidized anti-Communist labor unions in Western Europe. The CIA covertly aided in the overthrow of the Mossadegh regime in Iran, which allowed the restoration of the shah in 1953. The CIA also helped to overthrow the Arbenz government of Guatemala in 1954 and apparently was instrumental in destabilizing the Allende government in Chile from 1970 to 1973.

During the mid-1970s, the "dark side" of the CIA was at least partly uncovered when the Senate undertook an investigation of its activities. One of the major findings of the Senate Select Committee on Intelligence was that the CIA had routinely spied on American citizens domestically—supposedly, a strictly prohibited activity. Consequently, the CIA came under the scrutiny of six, and later eight, oversight committees within Congress, which restricted the scope of its activity. By 1980, however, the CIA had regained much of its lost power to engage in covert activities. In the early 1990s, as relationships with the states of the former Soviet Union eased, the attention of the CIA and other agencies began to turn from military to economic intelligence. During the first Clinton administration, the CIA's reputation was damaged when a high-ranking agent, Aldrich Ames, was convicted of spying against the United States. The agency was further embarrassed in 1998 when it failed to detect India's preparations to detonate several nuclear devices. On the heels of that development and Pakistan's subsequent entry into the ranks of nuclear powers, a highly critical report highlighted the CIA's failure to gather intelligence.

The Department of Defense.   The Department of Defense (DOD) was created in 1947 to bring all of the various activities of the American military establishment under the jurisdiction of a single department headed by a civilian secretary of

INFOTRAC®
COLLEGE EDITION

Code Red: Internet Security

The Pentagon—a five-sided building—has become the symbol of the Department of Defense. It has six million square feet of floor space and over seventeen miles of corridors.

defense. At the same time, the joint chiefs of staff, consisting of the commanders of each of the military branches and a chairperson, was created to formulate a unified military strategy.

Although the Department of Defense is larger than any other federal department, it has declined in size since the fall of the Soviet Union in 1991. In the last ten years, the total number of civilian employees has been reduced by about 400,000, to the current number of about 679,700. Military personnel have also been reduced from 2.1 million in 1985 to about 1.4 million today. The defense budget has remained relatively flat in recent years, although those in active military service have received some increases in pay. Given the reduced budget and the cut in uniformed personnel, it is more difficult than ever for the Defense Department to maintain a high level of readiness. (For another challenge facing the Defense Department, see this chapter's *E-mocracy* below.)

Limiting the President's Power

A new interest in the balance of power between Congress and the president on foreign policy questions developed during the Vietnam War (1964–1975). Sensitive to public frustration over the long and costly war and angry at Richard Nixon for some of his other actions as president, Congress attempted to establish some limits on the power of the president in setting foreign and defense policy. In 1973, Congress passed the War Powers Resolution over President Nixon's veto. The act limited the president's use of troops in military action without congressional approval (see Chapter 12). Most presidents, however, have not interpreted the "consultation" provisions of the act as meaning that Congress should be consulted before military action is taken. Instead, Presidents Ford, Carter, Reagan, Bush, and Clinton ordered troop movements and then informed congressional leaders. Critics note that it is

e-mocracy

Attacking Government Computer Systems

Although the incidents frequently are not reported in the media, attacks on the government's computer systems occur often and are sometimes extremely successful. During the Persian Gulf War (1991), European computer hackers were able to access U.S. military computers at several dozen sites and gain information. In 1996, hackers caused mischief at the computers of the Central Intelligence Agency and the Justice Department and destroyed the Air Force's home page. In early 1998, computer hackers accessed a whole series of nonclassified sites, caused major university and National Aeronautics and Space Administration computers to crash, and defaced military base home pages. It is clear from these episodes that the electronic network used by the U.S. military and intelligence organizations is quite susceptible to access by amateurs, criminals, and spies.

Military and defense sites are not the only ones targeted by hackers: perhaps even more damage could be caused by interruptions to the global economic and banking system. During

1997, a survey of banks, universities, and companies showed that more than 60 percent had been accessed "illegitimately" during that year alone. In 2000, a series of computer viruses crippled businesses around the world. One of the most destructive, the "I Love You" virus, was eventually traced to a graduate student in the Philippines whose thesis had been rejected.

The potential consequences of successful attacks on government or business computer systems are almost too great to contemplate. Among the networks that, if impaired or destroyed, could bring down the nation's activities are those that connect the military services; guide satellites for communications and defense; launch missiles; guide submarines; and control all air traffic, credit-card transactions, interbank transactions, utility grids throughout the nation, and generally all telecommunications. The U.S. military establishment, acutely aware of this possibility, has initiated planning for "information warfare."

FOR CRITICAL ANALYSIS

How can the government build up a defense system to protect against hackers without violating the privacy and rights of legitimate users of the Internet?

quite possible for a president to commit troops to a situation from which the nation could not withdraw without incurring heavy losses, whether or not Congress is consulted.

Congress also has exerted its authority to limit or deny the president's requests for military assistance to Angolan rebels and to the government of El Salvador, and requests for new weapons, such as the B-1 bomber. In general, Congress has been far more cautious in supporting the president in situations where military involvement of American troops is possible.

At times, Congress can take the initiative in foreign policy. In 1986, Congress initiated and passed a bill instituting economic sanctions against South Africa to pressure that nation into ending its policy of racial segregation (apartheid). President Reagan vetoed the bill, but the veto was overridden by large majorities in both the House and the Senate.

Domestic Sources of Foreign Policy

The making of foreign policy is often viewed as a presidential prerogative because of the president's constitutional power in that area and the resources of the executive branch that the president controls. Foreign policymaking is also influenced by a number of other sources, however, including elite and mass opinion and the military-industrial complex.

Elite and Mass Opinion

Public opinion influences the making of U.S. foreign policy through a number of channels. Elites in American business, education, communications, labor, and religion try to influence presidential decision making through several strategies. Some individuals, such as former secretary of state Henry Kissinger, had a long-standing interest in foreign policy and were asked to advise the president privately. Several elite organizations, such as the Council on Foreign Relations and the Trilateral Commission, work to increase international cooperation and to influence foreign policy through conferences, publications, and research.

The members of the American elite establishment also exert influence on foreign policy through the general public by encouraging debate over foreign policy positions, publicizing the issues, and using the media. Generally, the efforts of the president and the elites are most successful with the segment of the population called the **attentive public.** This sector of the mass public, which probably constitutes 10 to 20 percent of all citizens, is more interested in foreign affairs than most Americans. These Americans are also likely to transmit their opinions to the less interested members of the public through conversation and local leadership.

Attentive Public
That portion of the general public that pays attention to policy issues.

The Military-Industrial Complex

Civilian fear of the relationship between the defense establishment and arms manufacturers (the **military-industrial complex**) dates back many years. During President Eisenhower's eight years in office, the former five-star general of the army experienced firsthand the kind of pressure that could be brought against him and other policymakers by arms manufacturers. Eisenhower decided to give the country a solemn and, as he saw it, necessary warning of the consequences of this influence. On January 17, 1961, in his last official speech, he said,

> In the councils of government, we must guard against the acquisition of unwarranted influence, whether sought or unsought, by the military-industrial complex.

Military-Industrial Complex
The mutually beneficial relationship between the armed forces and defense contractors.

The potential for the disastrous rise of misplaced power exists and will persist. . . . Only an alert and knowledgeable citizenry can compel the proper meshing of the huge industrial and military machinery of defense with our peaceful methods and goals, so that security and liberty may prosper together.[4]

The Pentagon has supported a large sector of our economy through defense contracts. It also has supplied retired army officers as key executives to large defense-contracting firms. Perhaps the Pentagon's strongest allies have been members of Congress whose districts or states benefited from the economic power of military bases or contracts. After the Cold War ended in the late 1980s, the defense industry looked abroad for new customers. Sales of some military equipment to China raised serious issues for the Clinton administration.

The Major Foreign Policy Themes

Although some observers might suggest that U.S. foreign policy is inconsistent and changes with the current occupant of the White House, the long view of American diplomatic ventures reveals some major themes underlying foreign policy. In the early years of the nation, presidents and the people generally agreed that the United States should avoid foreign entanglements and concentrate instead on its own development. From the beginning of the twentieth century until today, one major theme has been increasing global involvement, with the United States taking an active role in assisting the development of other nations, dominating the world economy, and, in some cases, acting as a peacemaker. The major theme of the post–World War II years was the containment of communism. In the following brief review of American diplomatic history, these three themes predominate. The theme for the twenty-first century, now that there are multiple strong nations and only one superpower, has not yet emerged.

The Formative Years: Avoiding Entanglements

Foreign policy was largely negative during the formative years of the United States. Remember that the new nation was operating under the Articles of Confederation. The national government had no right to levy and collect taxes, no control over commerce, no right to make commercial treaties, and no power to raise an army (the Revolutionary army was disbanded in 1783). The government's lack of international power was made clear when the United States was unable to recover American hostages who had been seized in the Mediterranean by Barbary pirates but ignominiously had to purchase the hostages in a treaty with Morocco.

The founders of this nation had a basic mistrust of corrupt European governments. George Washington said it was the U.S. policy "to steer clear of permanent alliances," and Thomas Jefferson echoed this sentiment when he said America wanted peace with all nations but "entangling alliances with none." This was also a logical position at a time when the United States was so weak militarily that it could not influence European development directly. Moreover, being protected by oceans that took weeks to traverse certainly allowed the nation to avoid entangling alliances. During the 1700s and 1800s, the United States generally stayed out of European conflicts and politics.

---

[4]*Congressional Almanac* (Washington, D.C.: Congressional Quarterly Press, 1961), pp. 938–939.

The Monroe Doctrine.   President James Monroe, in his message to Congress on December 2, 1823, stated that this country would not accept foreign intervention in the Western Hemisphere. In return, the United States would not meddle in European affairs. The **Monroe Doctrine** was the underpinning of the U.S. **isolationist foreign policy** toward Europe, which continued throughout the nineteenth century.

In this hemisphere, however, the United States pursued an actively expansionist policy. The nation purchased Louisiana in 1803, annexed Texas in 1845, gained half of Mexico's territory in the 1840s, purchased Alaska in 1867, and annexed Hawaii in 1898.

The Spanish-American War and World War I.   The end of the isolationist policy started with the Spanish-American War in 1898. Winning that war gave the United States possession of Guam, Puerto Rico, and the Philippines (which gained independence in 1946). On the heels of that war came World War I (1914–1918). In his reelection campaign of 1916, President Woodrow Wilson ran on the slogan "He kept us out of war." Nonetheless, on April 6, 1917, the United States declared war on Germany. It was evident to Wilson that without help, the Allies would be defeated, and American property and lives, already under attack, increasingly would be endangered. In the 1920s, the United States did indeed go "back to normalcy," as President Warren G. Harding urged it to do. U.S. military forces were largely disbanded, defense spending dropped to about 1 percent of total national income, and the nation entered a period of isolationism.

The Era of Internationalism

Isolationism was permanently shattered and relegated to its place in history by the bombing of the U.S. naval base at Pearl Harbor, Hawaii, on December 7, 1941. The surprise attack by the Japanese resulted in the deaths of 2,403 American servicemen and the wounding of 1,143 others. Eighteen warships were sunk or seriously damaged, and 188 planes were destroyed at the airfields. The

Monroe Doctrine
The policy statement included in President James Monroe's 1823 annual message to Congress, which set out three principles: (1) European nations should not establish new colonies in the Western Hemisphere, (2) European nations should not intervene in the affairs of independent nations of the Western Hemisphere, and (3) the United States would not interfere in the affairs of European nations.

Isolationist Foreign Policy
Abstaining from an active role in international affairs or alliances, which characterized U.S. foreign policy toward Europe during most of the nineteenth century.

Managing Domestic and Foreign Policies

This painting shows President James Monroe explaining the Monroe Doctrine to a group of government officials. Essentially, the Monroe Doctrine made the Western Hemisphere the concern of the United States.

Soviet leader Joseph Stalin, U.S. President Franklin Roosevelt, and British Prime Minister Winston Churchill met at Yalta from February 4 to 11, 1945, to resolve their differences over the shape that the international community would take after World War II.

The atomic bomb explodes over Nagasaki, Japan, on August 9, 1945.

American public was outraged. President Franklin Roosevelt asked Congress to declare war on Japan immediately, and the United States entered World War II. This unequivocal response was certainly due to the nature of the provocation. American soil had not been attacked by a foreign power since the burning of Washington, D.C., by the British in 1814.

The United States was the only major participating country to emerge from World War II with its economy intact, and even strengthened. The Soviet Union, Japan, Italy, France, Germany, Britain, and a number of minor participants in the war were all economically devastated. The United States was also the only country to have control over operational nuclear weapons. President Harry Truman had personally made the decision to use two atomic bombs, on August 6 and August 9, 1945, to end the war with Japan. (Historians still dispute the necessity of this action, which ultimately killed more than 100,000 Japanese civilians and left an equal number permanently injured.) The United States truly had become the world's superpower.

The Cold War. The United States had become an uncomfortable ally of the Soviet Union after Adolf Hitler's invasion of Soviet territory. Soon after the war ended, relations between the Soviet Union and the West deteriorated. The Soviet Union wanted a weakened Germany, and to achieve this, it insisted that the country be divided in two, with East Germany becoming a buffer against the West. Little by little, the Soviet Union helped to install Communist governments in Eastern European countries, which began to be referred to collectively as the

Soviet bloc. In response, the United States encouraged the rearming of Western Europe. The Cold War had begun.[5]

In Fulton, Missouri, on March 5, 1946, Winston Churchill, in a striking metaphor, declared that from the Baltic to the Adriatic Sea "an iron curtain has descended across the [European] continent." The term **iron curtain** became even more appropriate when the Soviet Union built a wall separating East Berlin from West Berlin on August 17 and 18, 1961.

Containment Policy. In 1947, a remarkable article was published in *Foreign Affairs*. The article was signed by "X." The actual author was George F. Kennan, chief of the policy-planning staff for the State Department. The doctrine of **containment** set forth in the article became—according to many—the Bible of Western foreign policy. "X" argued that whenever and wherever the Soviet Union could successfully challenge Western institutions, it would do so. He recommended that our policy toward the Soviet Union be "firm and vigilant containment of Russian expansive tendencies."[6]

The containment theory was expressed clearly in the **Truman Doctrine**, which was enunciated by President Harry Truman in his historic address to Congress on March 12, 1947. In that address, he announced that the United States must help countries in which a Communist takeover seemed likely, and he proposed a Greek-Turkish aid program specifically to counter Soviet influence in the eastern Mediterranean area. Truman proposed $400 million in aid to those two countries. He put the choice squarely before Congress—it either must support those measures required to preserve peace and security abroad or risk widespread global instability and perhaps World War III.[7]

Superpower Relations

During the Cold War, there was never any direct military confrontation between the United States and the Soviet Union. Rather, confrontations among "client" nations were used to carry out the policies of the superpowers. Only on occasion did the United States directly enter into a conflict in a significant way. Two such occasions were in Korea and Vietnam.

In 1950, North Korean troops were embroiled in a war with South Korea. President Truman asked for and received a Security Council order from the United Nations (UN) for the North Koreans to withdraw their troops. The Soviet Union was absent from the council on that day, protesting the exclusion of the People's Republic of China from the UN, and did not participate in the discussion. Truman then authorized the use of American forces in support of the South Koreans. For the next three years, American troops were engaged in a land war in Asia, a war that became a stalemate and a political liability to President Truman. One of Dwight Eisenhower's major 1952 campaign promises was to end the Korean War—which he did. An armistice was signed on July 27, 1953. (American troops have been stationed in South Korea ever since, however.)

U.S. involvement in Vietnam began shortly after the end of the Korean conflict. When the French army in Indochina was defeated by the Communist forces of Ho Chi Minh and the two Vietnams were created in 1954, the United States

Soviet Bloc
The Eastern European countries that installed Communist regimes after World War II.

Iron Curtain
The term used to describe the division of Europe between the Soviet Union and the West; popularized by Winston Churchill in a speech portraying Europe as being divided by an iron curtain, with the nations of Eastern Europe behind the curtain and increasingly under Soviet control.

Containment
A U.S. diplomatic policy adopted by the Truman administration to "build situations of strength" around the globe to contain Communist power within its existing boundaries.

Truman Doctrine
The policy adopted by President Harry Truman in 1947 to halt Communist expansion in southeastern Europe.

---

[5]See John Lewis Gaddis, *The United Nations and the Origins of the Cold War* (New York: Columbia University Press, 1972).

[6]X, "The Sources of Soviet Conduct," *Foreign Affairs*, July 1947, p. 575.

[7]*Public Papers of the Presidents of the United States: Harry S. Truman, 1947* (Washington, D.C.: U.S. Government Printing Office, 1963), pp. 176–180.

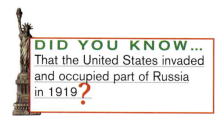

assumed the role of supporting the South Vietnamese government against North Vietnam. President John Kennedy sent 16,000 "advisers" to help South Vietnam, and after Kennedy's death, President Lyndon Johnson greatly increased the scope of that support. American forces in Vietnam at the height of the U.S. involvement totaled more than 500,000 troops. More than 58,000 Americans were killed, and 300,000 were wounded, in the conflict. The debate over U.S. involvement in Vietnam divided the American electorate and, as mentioned previously, spurred congressional efforts to limit the ability of the president to commit forces to armed combat.

The Cuban Missile Crisis.   With the two superpowers having enough nuclear bombs to destroy the world, a confrontation between the United States and the Soviet Union was unthinkable. Perhaps the closest the two nations came to such a confrontation was the Cuban missile crisis in 1962. The Soviets placed missiles ninety miles off the U.S. coast in response to Cuban fears of an American invasion and to try to balance the American nuclear advantage. President Kennedy and his advisers rejected the possibility of armed intervention, setting up a naval blockade around the island instead. When Soviet vessels, apparently carrying nuclear warheads, appeared near Cuban waters, the tension reached its height. After intense negotiations between Washington and Moscow, the Soviet ships turned around on October 25, and on October 28 the Soviet Union announced the withdrawal of its missile operations from Cuba. In exchange, the United States agreed not to invade Cuba and to remove some of its own missiles that were located near the Soviet border in Turkey.

Détente

A French word meaning the relaxation of tensions. The term characterizes U.S.–Soviet policy as it developed under President Richard Nixon and Secretary of State Henry Kissinger. Détente stressed direct cooperative dealings with Cold War rivals but avoided ideological accommodation.

Strategic Arms Limitation Treaty (SALT I)

A treaty between the United States and the Soviet Union to stabilize the nuclear arms competition between the two countries. SALT I talks began in 1969, and agreements were signed on May 26, 1972.

A Period of Détente.   The French word **détente** means a relaxation of tensions. By the end of the 1960s, it was clear that some efforts had to be made to reduce the threat of nuclear war between the United States and the Soviet Union. The Soviet Union gradually had begun to catch up in the building of strategic nuclear delivery vehicles in the form of bombers and missiles, thus balancing the nuclear scales. Each nation acquired the military capacity to destroy the other with nuclear weapons.

As the result of protracted negotiations, in May 1972, the United States and the Soviet Union signed the **Strategic Arms Limitation Treaty (SALT I)**. That treaty "permanently" limited the development and deployment of antiballistic missiles (ABMs), and it limited for five years the number of offensive missiles each country could deploy. To further reduce tensions, under the policy of Secretary of State Henry Kissinger and President Nixon, new scientific and cultural exchanges were arranged with the Soviets, as well as new opportunities for Jewish emigration out of the Soviet Union.

The policy of détente was not limited to U.S. relationships with the Soviet Union. Seeing an opportunity to capitalize on increasing friction between the Soviet Union and the People's Republic of China, Kissinger secretly began negotiations to establish a new relationship with that nation. President Nixon eventually visited the People's Republic of China and set the stage for the formal diplomatic recognition of that country, which occurred during the Carter administration (1977–1981).

The Reagan-Bush Years.   President Ronald Reagan took a hard line against the Soviet Union during his first term, proposing the strategic defense initiative (SDI), or "Star Wars," in 1983. SDI was designed to serve as a space-stationed defense against enemy missiles. Reagan and others in his administration argued that the program would deter nuclear war by shifting the emphasis of defense strategy from offensive to defensive weapons systems.

President Richard Nixon signs SALT I, a Cold War agreement with the Soviet Union, in 1972. The Soviet Union dissolved in late December 1991. Consequently, do you think that the member republics of the former Soviet Union should have to abide by the SALT I agreement?

In November 1985, President Reagan and Mikhail Gorbachev, the Soviet leader, held summit talks in Geneva. The two men agreed to reestablish cultural and scientific exchanges and to continue the arms control negotiations. Progress toward an agreement was slow, however.

In 1987, representatives of the United States and the Soviet Union continued work on an arms reduction agreement. Although there were setbacks throughout the year, the negotiations resulted in a historic agreement signed by Reagan and Gorbachev in Washington, D.C., on December 8, 1987. The terms of the Intermediate-Range Nuclear Force (INF) Treaty, which was ratified by the Senate, required the superpowers to dismantle a total of four thousand intermediate-range missiles within the first three years of the agreement.

George Bush continued the negotiations with the Soviet Union after he became president. The goal of both nations was to reduce the number of nuclear weapons and the number of armed troops in Europe. The developments in Eastern Europe, the drive by the Baltic republics for independence, the unification of Germany, and the dissolution of the Soviet Union (in December 1991) made the process much more complex, however. American strategists worried as much about who now controlled the Soviet nuclear arsenal as about completing the treaty process. In 1992, the United States signed the Strategic Arms Reduction Treaty (START) with four former Soviet republics—Russia, Ukraine, Belarus, and Kazakhstan—to reduce the number of long-range nuclear weapons.

Challenges in World Politics

The end of the Cold War, the dissolution of the Soviet Union, the economic unification of Europe, and the political changes in Eastern Europe have challenged U.S. foreign policy in ways that were unimaginable a few years ago. The United States had no contingency plans for these events. Also, predicting the consequences of any of these changes for world politics is all but impossible. Furthermore, such sweeping changes mean not only that the United States must adjust its foreign policy to deal with new realities but also that it must consider adjustments in the American military and intelligence establishments.

The Dissolution of the Soviet Union

After the fall of the Berlin Wall in 1989, it was clear that the Soviet Union had relinquished much of its political and military control over the states of Eastern Europe that formerly had been part of the Soviet bloc. Sweeping changes within the Soviet Union had been proposed by Gorbachev, and talks to reduce nuclear armaments were proceeding. No one expected the Soviet Union to dissolve into separate states as quickly as it did, however. While Gorbachev tried to adjust the Soviet constitution and political system to allow greater autonomy for the republics within the union, demands for political, ethnic, and religious autonomy grew. In August 1991, the Soviet military tried to slow the process by arresting Gorbachev. Led by Boris Yeltsin, then president of Russia, efforts to preserve the Soviet state were thwarted.

The result of the failed attempt to gain control by military leaders was to hasten the process of creating an independent Russian state led by Yeltsin. On the day after Christmas in 1991, the Soviet Union was officially dissolved. A few months later, a majority of the former republics had joined a loose federation called the Commonwealth of Independent States, although a few of the larger republics, including Georgia and Ukraine, refused to join. Another uprising in Russia, this time led by anti-Yeltsin members of the new parliament who wanted to restore the Soviet Union immediately, failed in 1993.

In 2000, Yeltsin resigned due to poor health. He named Vladimir Putin, architect of the Russian military effort against the breakaway ethnic movement in the province of Chechnya, as acting president. A few months later, Putin won the presidency in a national election.

President Clinton (right) reaches out to shake hands with Russian president Vladimir Putin (left) during a meeting on September 6, 2000, at the Waldorf Astoria Hotel. The presidents were in New York for the United Nations Millennium Summit.

Nuclear Proliferation

The dissolution of the Soviet Union brought a true lowering of tensions between the major powers in the world. The United States and Russia agreed to continue negotiating the dismantling of nuclear warheads and delivery systems. The problems of nuclear proliferation were far from solved, however. As shown in Table 17–1, more than thirty-two thousand warheads are known to be in stock worldwide; other nations do not report the extent of their nuclear stockpiles. In 1999, the Senate rejected the Comprehensive Nuclear Test Ban Treaty, which had been presented to it for ratification by the Clinton administration. For a discussion of how this action affected the nuclear threat, see this chapter's *Critical Perspective* on the next page.

Terrorism

Dissident groups, rebels, and other revolutionaries always have engaged in some sort of terrorism to gain attention and to force their enemies to the bargaining table. Over the last two decades, terrorism has continued to threaten world peace and the lives of ordinary citizens.

Terrorism can be a weapon of choice in domestic or civil strife. The conflict in the Middle East between Israel and the Arab states has been lessened by a series of painfully negotiated agreements between Israel and some of the other states. In recent years, Israel and the Palestinians have tried to reach agreement on some of their differences. Those opposed to the peace process, however, have continued to disrupt the negotiations through assassinations, mass murders, and bomb blasts in the streets of major cities within Israel. At this point, most of the terrorist attacks are carried out by groups (either Israeli or Arab) that reject the peace process. Similar "domestic" terrorist acts were used to disrupt talks between Britain and Ireland over the fate of Northern Ireland. The terrorist acts did not stop the peace process in Ireland, however, which culminated in a vote supporting the agreement in 1998. Terrorist acts by rebels or separatist groups have also occurred in Sri Lanka (the Tamils), Paris (Algerian extremists), Russia (Chechen rebels), and Japan (secret cults).

In other cases, terrorist acts are planned against the civilians of foreign nations to make an international statement and to frighten the citizens of a faraway land. Perhaps one of the most striking of these attacks was that launched against Israeli

---

TABLE 17–1

The Nuclear Club

LOCATION	KNOWN AND SUSPECTED NUMBER OF WARHEADS
Official estimates:	
United States	10,920*
Former Soviet Union	20,000*
France	450
China	400
Britain	185
Unofficial estimates:	
Israel	100
India	40–50
Pakistan	10–20
Nations that are capable of building weapons and/or suspected of having a nuclear program:	
Algeria, Argentina, Brazil, Iran, Iraq, Libya, North Korea, South Africa, and Syria.	

*Up to half are retired and will be dismantled.

SOURCE: *The Wall Street Journal*, October 15, 1999, p. A8.

Is the Nuclear Threat Increasing?

Since the 1980s, the United States and Russia have negotiated a series of agreements and treaties aimed at reducing the threat that their nuclear arsenals pose to the world. The superpowers agreed to begin retiring and dismantling their nuclear warheads and to permit the other nation to conduct inspections. This progress toward decreasing nuclear arsenals has not, however, been extended to some of the other critical regions of the globe.

Nuclear Proliferation Threats

The efforts of North Korea, India, and Pakistan to develop nuclear weapons have been a particular cause of concern. In 1994, North Korea opposed the efforts of the International Atomic Energy Commission to inspect parts of its nuclear power plant, particularly at a time when fuel rods were to be changed. The international inspectors suspected that spent fuel would be reprocessed to make a nuclear bomb or warhead. When North Korea continued to resist international pressure to comply with inspection, the United States sought approval for sanctions on the nation from the United Nations. Former U.S. president Jimmy Carter went to North Korea in mid-1994 and negotiated a deal by which the North Koreans would give up their nuclear power plant in exchange for a new one. In the summer of 1998, however, the United States obtained information that North Korea was developing an underground nuclear arms site.

Concerns over nuclear proliferation intensified in 1998 when both India and Pakistan detonated nuclear devices within a few weeks of each other. Even though the newly elected government of India had declared its intent to pursue nuclear weapons, the American intelligence establishment did not take this declaration seriously. The Indian government proceeded to conduct two sets of tests, exploding a total of five devices. India claimed that the development of the weapons was necessary due to its long history of war with Pakistan.

After the tests, President Clinton imposed sanctions on India and then urged Pakistan not to follow suit. Two weeks later, the Pakistani government also conducted successful nuclear tests, claiming that they were necessary for its national security. Given that China has already joined the "nuclear club," the possibility of one of these three powers using a nuclear device in war seemed to the rest of the world to be a real threat.

The Nuclear Test Ban Treaty

The United States continues to try to influence late arrivals to the "nuclear club" through a combination of rewards and punishments. In some cases, the United States has promised aid to a nation to gain cooperation, but in the case of Iraq, the United States encouraged Israel to destroy an Iraqi power plant that produced nuclear fuel. In late 1999, however, one of the weapons of moral suasion used by the United States disappeared.

President Clinton presented the Comprehensive Nuclear Test Ban Treaty to the Senate for ratification in 1999. The treaty, formed in 1996, prohibits all nuclear test explosions worldwide and established a global network of monitoring stations. Twenty-six nations have ratified the treaty. Among those that had not ratified it by late 1999 were China, Israel, Russia, India, and Pakistan.

In a defeat for the Clinton administration, the U.S. Senate rejected the treaty on October 14, 1999. The vote was according to party lines, with most Republicans rejecting the treaty. The Republicans asserted that the treaty's monitoring mechanisms were flawed and that some nations with nuclear capability might sign the treaty but continue to test undetected. The Democrats claimed that the defeat of the treaty would lead to further development of nuclear capability by nations that had not ratified the agreement and thus would increase the nuclear threat. Perhaps the most obvious effect of the defeat was that the United States could not use its ratification to persuade India and Pakistan to sign and ratify the treaty as well.

Will the defeat of the treaty increase the nuclear threat? It is possible that ratifying the treaty might bring a false sense of security to the United States and other signatories. If they relied on the treaty to halt nuclear proliferation and the monitoring system failed, a nation that violated the treaty by testing might gain an advantage. At the same time, however, perhaps pressure from nations that had ratified the treaty would be instrumental in influencing some nations to stop testing. In that case, the United States, clearly the strongest "influencer," lost all of its moral authority to lobby nations to join the treaty.

FOR CRITICAL ANALYSIS

1. Is there any real assurance that a nation that wishes to develop a nuclear capability will not do so or test its weapons?
2. Why doesn't the United States pressure nations such as China and Israel to reveal the real extent of their nuclear capabilities?

Although India has historically taken a neutral position in world affairs, it has engaged in military conflicts with Pakistan and China on its borders. When the Indian government followed through on its promise to develop and test nuclear weapons, there was widespread support for that action among Indian citizens, as shown here. Nuclear testing in both India and Pakistan in 1998 caught the U.S. intelligence community off guard—it had no knowledge that the tests would be conducted.

athletes at the Munich Olympics in 1972. Others have included ship hijackings, airplane hijackings, and the bombing of the World Trade Center in New York. In the 1990s, two other incidents brought the fear of terrorism home to Americans. In 1996, radical elements in Saudi Arabia bombed an American military compound there, killing a number of American military personnel. In 1998, terrorist bombings of two American embassies in Africa killed 257 people, including 12 Americans, and injured over 5,500 others. In 2000, a terrorist bombing of the *USS Cole,* while it was refueling in a port in Yemen, killed seventeen sailors and injured many others.

What can nations do to prevent terrorism? The best defense of nations is to be vigilant. This includes stronger security measures and a commitment to intelligence gathering. The Clinton administration requested a strengthening of U.S. intelligence capabilities in 1996, but that proposal met with opposition from civil liberties groups as well as conservative Republicans. The Clinton administration also used sanctions, as discussed in this chapter's *Which Side Are You On?* on the next page. The problem that faces a democracy that upholds liberty for its citizens is how to balance the needs of increased surveillance for criminals against the rights of citizens to be free of police spying and record keeping.

The New Power: China

Since Nixon's visit to China, American policy has been to gradually engage the Chinese in diplomatic and economic relationships in the hope of turning the nation toward a more pro-Western and capitalistic system. In 1989, however, when Chinese students engaged in extraordinary demonstrations against the government, the Chinese government crushed the demonstrations, killing a number of students and protesters and imprisoning others for political crimes.

Nevertheless, the Clinton administration continued the policy of diplomatic outreach to the Chinese, in part because China had allowed free enterprise in many regions of the country and had the potential to be a major trading partner of the United States. China was granted **most-favored-nation status** for tariffs and

Most-Favored-Nation Status
A status granted by an international treaty by which each member nation must treat other members at least as well as it treats the country that receives its most favorable treatment.

which side are you on?

Should the United States Impose Sanctions?

The United States has faced a very different world since the end of the Cold War which lasted from 1947 to, roughly, 1985. No longer are most disputes framed by the threat of the Soviet Union. Instead, the security of the United States and of other nations is often threatened by the terrorist activities of rogue nations or by nations that attack their neighbors, destabilizing a region of the world. In addition, some nations continue to defy world opinion, keeping brutal dictators in power or engaging in genocide against part of their own citizenry.

The Use of Sanctions

The use of sanctions as a tool of foreign policy became popular after multilateral sanctions applied against South Africa helped to force the nation's white-controlled government to negotiate with the opposition African National Congress and end officially sanctioned racial segregation (apartheid) in 1992. Sanctions came to be seen as a way for the United States, alone or in coalition with other nations, to try to force a nation to change its ways without resorting to the use of force. In some cases, sanctions are imposed to encourage people of a nation to demand political change from their government. In other cases, the sanctions are intended to force a government to comply with some aspect of international law; for example, sanctions have

been imposed on Iraq to force it to comply with the agreements it made after the 1991 Persian Gulf War. In addition to South Africa and Iraq, sanctions have been imposed against Myanmar, formerly Burma, for its political repression and against Libya for engaging in terrorism. Because sanctions are a nonmilitary tool, they remain popular.

The Cost of Sanctions

Economic sanctions are intended to put political pressure on a regime by denying a nation critical materials and access to very important trading partners. Sanctions that restrict trade with a nation can be extremely costly in terms of trade opportunities lost, however. A study by the Institute for International Economics found that sanctions cost U.S. businesses between $15 billion and $20 billion in a recent year and affected more than 200,000 American workers.

Are Sanctions Effective?

Because of the incredible changes that have taken place in South Africa—a peaceful end to civil strife, the end of apartheid, and the installation of a new, multiethnic regime—there is a tendency to see sanctions as being extremely effective. In other cases, it is less clear that sanctions have had the intended results, however. In the case of Libya, the United States recently lifted sanctions imposed because of that nation's terrorist activity. The leader of Libya, Muammar Qaddafi, is

still in control of the country.

The Iraqi situation has proved even more troublesome. Human rights observers report that thousands of Iraqi children have died from malnutrition and from diseases for which the nation lacks medicine. Not only has the ruler, Saddam Hussein, stayed in office, but he and his family have grown even more wealthy. They control much of the black market in goods smuggled into Iraq in defiance of the embargo. They sell the goods at inflated prices to those who have money while other sectors of Iraqi society suffer from the impact of the sanctions. Furthermore, several of the allies of the United States in the Persian Gulf War believe that sanctions have done as much as they can to influence Hussein and should be lifted. These nations are suffering economic losses from the sanctions as well.

DOES IT MATTER?

Should the United States continue to use sanctions as a foreign policy tool even though they cost Americans jobs and trade opportunities, or is the importance of sanctions as a nonmilitary tool worth the cost?

GOING ONLINE

To find out more about the debate over sanctions, try the Web site, **http://www.policy.com**. *For the U.S. government's position on sanctions, go to the site of the State Department,* **http://www.state.gov**. *Position papers on sanctions are also available at the Brookings Institution's site,* **http://www.brookings.edu**.

trade policy on a year-to-year basis. In 2000, over objections from organized labor and human rights groups, Congress approved a permanent grant of most-favored-nation status to China (see the *Politics and Economics* feature presented earlier in this chapter on page 549).

In 1997, China seemed to be conscious of Western concerns when it took over the government of Hong Kong in ceremonies that promised a continuation of the previous government and economic system in the former British colony. Although the new government did impose an appointed assembly, it was careful to preserve the free enterprise system of Hong Kong.

The Chinese-American connection eventually reached domestic politics in the United States when campaign-finance investigations showed that a number of

In August 1998, bombs exploded virtually simultaneously in the U.S. embassies in Kenya and Tanzania. Pictured here is the embassy in Nairobi, Kenya, moments after the bombing. The administration believed that the bombs were planted by Muslim terrorists, perhaps under the direction of a Saudi millionaire who has verbally declared war on Americans. These two attacks on relatively low-security installations killed far more citizens of the two African nations than they did Americans.

Chinese Americans had made large contributions to the 1996 Clinton reelection campaign. Some of the contributions were illegal and were returned by the Democratic Party. There were also accusations that a presidential waiver given to Loral Corporation to sell technology to China was granted soon after Loral's chief executive made a major contribution to the campaign. Congressional investigations into the transfer of technology to China came at about the time that intelligence revealed China's missile technology to the world. In 1998, President Clinton traveled to China for a state visit amid protests about U.S.–China policy.

The Global Economy

Although the United States derives only about 10 percent of its total national income from world trade, it is deeply dependent on the world economy. A serious stock market crash in 1987 showed how closely other markets watch the economic situation of the United States and, conversely, how U.S. markets follow those of London and Japan. In 1997 and 1998, when several Asian economies experienced serious problems, the American business community, now dependent on Asian concerns for materials, products, and customers, showed some signs of weakness, at least for a short period of time. The Asian economies—among them South Korea and Thailand—received aid from the

International Monetary Fund on the condition that they impose severe restrictions on their economies and people. In Indonesia, the failing economy brought down President Suharto, who had held that office for thirty years, and led to increased cries for reform among that nation's people.

Furthermore, since the 1980s, the United States has become a debtor nation, meaning that we owe more to foreigners than foreigners owe to us. The reason for this is a large trade deficit and the willingness of foreign individuals and nations to finance part of the U.S. national debt by purchasing U.S. government securities. Because the United States imports more goods and services than it exports, it has a net trade deficit. These imports include BMWs, Sonys, Toshibas, and Guccis, as well as cheaper products such as shoes manufactured in Brazil and clothes from Taiwan.

No one can predict how a unified Europe will affect world trade. With the European Union having become one economic "nation" on December 31, 1992, some expect Europe will gradually close some markets to outside economic powers. By 2000, the European Union had become a major trading partner of the United States, however.

Regional Conflicts

The United States has played a role—sometimes alone, sometimes in conjunction with other powers—in many regional conflicts. During the 1990s, the United States became involved in conflicts in countries and regions around the globe.

Haiti and Cuba.   The Caribbean nation of Haiti became a focal point of U.S. policy in the 1990s. The repressive military regime there ousted the democratically elected president Jean-Bertrand Aristide in 1992. The Clinton administration announced that it would support sanctions and other measures to reinstate Aristide in office. At the same time, the administration tried to stem the tide of refugees who tried to reach Florida by sea from the island nation. Although Clinton had promised in his campaign to admit the Haitian "boat people," he maintained the Bush policy of returning them to their native land. By 1994, he announced that the United States would at least listen to pleas for political asylum if refugees could reach Jamaica or other Caribbean islands. The Clinton administration also increased the sanctions on Haiti in 1994 and then sent

INFOTRAC®
COLLEGE EDITION

Haiti Puts Hex

troops to Haiti to assist in the reinstatement of President Aristide. The troops were withdrawn in 1999, leaving Haiti as poor and politically corrupt as before.

The United States continued to face problems with Cuba. In the last days of the summer of 1994, Fidel Castro threatened to "swamp" the United States with Cuban refugees. True to his word, he allowed thousands to leave the island on anything that would float. President Clinton was forced to rescind the U.S. open-door policy for Cuban refugees. He ordered the Coast Guard to return all refugees picked up at sea to the U.S. naval base at Guantánamo in Cuba. Then U.S. and Cuban authorities reached an agreement under which the United States would accept 20,000 legal Cuban immigrants a year. In exchange, Castro agreed to police Cuba's shores to prevent an exodus of Cuban refugees.

In 1996, another incident occurred. Cuban military aircraft shot down two planes flown by anti-Castro American residents who were searching for Cubans escaping by sea. The United States, refusing to accept Cuba's explanation that the two planes were in Cuban territorial waters, retaliated by passing the Helms-Burton Act. The act, which punished owners of foreign firms (and their family members) for investing in formerly American-owned business firms that had been nationalized by Cuba, sparked international opposition.

Tensions between the United States and Cuba increased tremendously in late 1999 and 2000 after a little boy, Elian Gonzalez, survived a boat wreck in which his mother died. They had been crossing from Cuba to join Miami relatives. With his mother dead, Elian became the prize in a political tug of war between Castro and the Cuban American population in Miami.

The Middle East.   The United States has also played a role in the Middle East. As a long-time supporter of Israel, the United States has undertaken to persuade the Israelis to agree to negotiations with the Palestinians who live in the territories occupied by the state of Israel. The conflict, which began in 1948, has been extremely hard to resolve. One reason is that it requires all the Arab states in the region to recognize Israel's right to exist. Another reason is that resolution of the conflict would require Israel to make some settlement with the Palestine Liberation Organization (PLO), which has launched attacks on Israel from within and outside its borders and which Israel has regarded as a terrorist organization. In December 1988, the United States began talking directly to the

Cuban President Fidel Castro waves his hat to the congregation as he arrives at the Riverside Church in New York on September 8, 2000. Castro made this appearance while he was in the United States to attend the United Nations Millennium Summit.

The Israeli-Palestinian agreements of 1993 have been only partially implemented due to continued Israeli settlements in the West Bank and continued Palestinian attacks against Israelis. In May 1998, U.S. Secretary of State Madeleine Albright met with Yasser Arafat, leader of the Palestinian Authority, in London to try to restart the negotiations between the two sides.

PLO, and in 1991, under great pressure from the United States, the Israelis opened talks with representatives of the Palestinians and other Arab states.

In 1993, the Israeli-Palestinian peace talks reached a breakthrough, with both parties agreeing to set up Palestinian territories in the West Bank and Gaza. The historic agreement, signed in Cairo on May 4, 1994, put in place a process by which the Palestinians would assume self-rule in the Gaza Strip and in the town of Jericho. In the months that followed, Israeli troops withdrew from much of the occupied territory, Palestinians assumed police duties, and many Palestinian prisoners were freed by the Israelis. During an election campaign speech in 1995, however, Israeli prime minister Yitzhak Rabin, a key figure in the negotiations for peace, was assassinated by a right-wing Israeli student who opposed the peace process. Although peace negotiations continued, they have recently been jeopardized by Palestinian uprisings and counterattacks by the Israelis.

U.S. Response to Iraq's Invasion of Kuwait.   On August 2, 1990, the Middle East became the setting for a major challenge to the authority of the United States and its ability to buy oil from its allies there. President Saddam Hussein of Iraq initially sent more than 100,000 troops into the neighboring oil sheikdom of Kuwait, occupying the entire nation. Within less than two days, President George Bush took the position that the annexation of Kuwait must not be tolerated by the Western world and that the oil fields of Saudi Arabia must be protected. At the formal request of the king of Saudi Arabia, American troops were dispatched to set up a defensive line at the Kuwaiti border. In addition, the president announced an economic boycott of Iraq (supported by the United Nations) and sent American carrier groups to seal off the Iraqi ports, cutting off shipments of oil.

Bush continued to send troops—including reserve units called up from the United States—to Saudi Arabia. By the end of 1990, more than half a million troops were in place. After the United Nations approved a resolution authorizing the use of force if Saddam Hussein did not respond to sanctions, the U.S. Congress reluctantly also approved such an authorization. On January 17, 1991, two days after the deadline for President Hussein to withdraw, the coalition forces launched a massive air attack on Iraq. After several weeks of almost unopposed aerial bombardment, the ground offensive began. Iraqi troops retreated from Kuwait a few days later, and the Persian Gulf War ended within another week.

American tanks carry out maneuvers in Saudi Arabia during Operation Desert Shield. Subsequently, in early 1991, the United States, together with a coalition of other nations, instituted Operation Desert Storm—the Persian Gulf "hot war" that lasted for only one hundred hours on the ground, following prolonged air attacks. Such maneuvers were undertaken again in Kuwait in the fall of 1994, when Saddam Hussein moved troops close to the Kuwaiti border.

After the end of the armed conflict, many Americans criticized the Bush administration for not sending troops to Baghdad, where they might have deposed Saddam Hussein. Others faulted the effort for raising the expectations of the Kurdish people that the United States would eliminate President Hussein if they revolted. The war also created an environmental disaster owing to the destruction of the oil fields by the Iraqis when they retreated from Kuwait.

Eastern Europe.   Eastern Europe, a region that had been extremely stable while under Soviet domination, suddenly became an unknown quantity in U.S. policy. With the decision of the Soviet Union to allow free elections and non-Marxist governments in Eastern Europe, these nations took separate paths to becoming self-governing states with mixed or market-oriented economies. Some nations immediately held elections; some struggled first to repair damaged economies; and still others attempted to deal with ethnic tensions within their populations.

It is difficult to overestimate the potential for civil disorder in these nations, particularly with regard to ethnic differences. (See this chapter's feature *An Ethical Issue.*) The world watched in 1991 as Yugoslavia split into a number of independent states. As former provinces of Yugoslavia—Slovenia, Croatia, and Bosnia and Herzegovina—tried to declare independence, Serbian military and government leaders launched attacks on their neighbors. The fighting was caused by historic conflicts and by strong ethnic and religious differences.

The fighting was fiercest in the former province of Bosnia, where Serbs and Muslims launched attacks on each other's villages and cities. News reports suggested that many women were raped and that the men were sent to camps to

The Demands of Ethnic Nationalism

The slaughter of civilians in Rwanda in 1994 and the fighting between Serbian and Muslim Bosnians are but a prelude of things to come. As new states are created from the wreckage of the Soviet Union and as postcolonial states mature, more and more people identifying with ethnic subnationalities will be claiming the right to sovereignty as new states or, at a minimum, the right to international protection for their culture and identity.

According to one commentator, the first wave of twentieth-century nationalism followed World War II, when colonial powers such as Great Britain and France allowed their former colonies to become independent states. At that time, the new states, including India, Pakistan, and Vietnam, fought to establish national unity against the colonial powers.*

Since that time, several more waves of ethnic nationalism have followed, as people of ethnic nationalities within these new nations (and within old nations) have claimed independence or the need for greater rights within the nation. The response of the world's international organizations has also changed; they now support human rights in every case.

The result has been an explosion of ethnic conflicts in developing nations, in the states of the former Soviet Union, and even in

*Joane Nagel, "Ethnic Nationalism: Politics, Ideology, and the World Order," *International Journal of Comparative Sociology*, Vol. 34 (1993), p. 107.

the industrialized nations. A few years ago, the *Los Angeles Times* listed fifty-three separate ethnic conflicts in the world. Although Rwanda was mentioned, at that time, the mass killings of more than half a million people had not yet occurred. In India, at least twenty thousand people have been killed in violence between the Sikhs and the Hindu government. In Azerbaijan, three thousand deaths have occurred since 1988. In Sri Lanka, twenty thousand Tamils have died in their revolt against the Buddhist Sinhalese. In Iraq, persecution of the Kurds and the "marsh Arabs" continues. Within Russia, Chechen rebels successfully fended off Russian troops sent to subdue their uprising. In late 1996, ethnic strife in Rwanda again erupted into violence.

The international community faces an ethical dilemma in these situations. Should all peoples who claim an ethnic identity be protected, either by outside forces or through the creation of a separate political entity? If that is the case, what is the right of a nation as a whole to protect its sovereignty and its borders for the good of all the citizens? It cannot be correct morally to allow the oppression of one group by another, but can outsiders intervene in the domestic affairs of a nation? Finally, the solution cannot be separate states for each people. Such a solution would produce a world of nations too small to survive and would require large-scale migrations of peoples back to their homelands.

FOR CRITICAL ANALYSIS

What can the United States and other members of the world community do to curb increasing ethnic violence?

force their families to leave their homes. The United States and European nations forced the Serbs to withdraw their weapons from the province and to begin a process for permanent disengagement. With guarantees from the United States and other NATO allies, the warring parties began the process of establishing separate ethnic provinces and returning to their home villages. Troops from the United States and other European nations patrolled the new borders and assisted in the process. Prospects for a lasting peace after the troops leave are not great due to the degree of ethnic hatred in this region.

By 1998 the situation in the Balkans had again become violent as ethnic Albanians sought independence for the Kosovo region of Serbia. The United States and several European powers launched a bombing campaign against Serbia to force an end to the Serbs' war against the ethnic Albanians in Kosovo. Although Serbia capitulated, the bombing left the Serbian leadership in power and forced thousands of Kosovars to resettle.

Africa.   The continent of Africa witnessed both great strides for freedom and savage civil strife during the mid-1990s. In South Africa, the first all-race elections were held—mostly in an orderly and peaceful manner—and Nelson Mandela was elected as the first president under a new constitution. Most South African constituencies took part in the election and seemed ready to support the new black-majority regime. The economic sanctions applied by the United States had helped bring the white South African government to a position of economic hardship and led, in part, to its negotiations with Mandela and his African National Congress Party.

In central Africa, another situation arose that seemed to be totally beyond the influence of the United States, France, or the United Nations. After a plane crash that killed the presidents of Rwanda and of neighboring Burundi, civil war erupted in Rwanda. The political war between the government and the rebel forces was complicated by a terrible ethnic struggle between the Hutu and Tutsi tribes. Observers estimated that more than half a million people were killed within a few weeks, with many bodies dumped in the rivers. About 250,000 refugees arrived in Uganda, setting up a small city in less than a week. Over a million others fled into neighboring Zaire. The United Nations called for troops to assist in relief efforts, but only France responded (and pulled out shortly thereafter). The United States played virtually no part in this situation until small military and civilian contingents were sent to assist with the refugee crisis. Unrest continued in Africa in 2000, especially in Congo and Sierra Leone. Perhaps an even greater threat to world stability, however, comes from disease. See this chapter's *Global View* for a discussion of the impact of HIV/AIDS on national security.

Foreign and Defense Policy: Issues for the Twenty-First Century

No president or secretary of state can predict the future of world politics. There is simply no way of knowing whether the states of the former Soviet Union will be a source of future conflicts, whether ethnic tensions will erupt in more nations, or whether the United Nations will be able to assemble an effective peacekeeping force. Nonetheless, it is necessary for U.S. leaders to try to plan for the future. The United States needs to plan a strategy for self-defense rather than a strategy for confronting Russia. Among the foreign policy issues to be considered, it is vitally important for the United States to plan an economic strategy that will increase U.S. exports and hold imports steady—in order to reduce the trade deficit. The severe downturns in several Asian economies in the late 1990s, showed that modern capitalist systems can experience problems.

Other issues that need to be resolved include the role that the United States sees for the United Nations, the degree to which the United States must keep a vital intelligence service, the strategies for supporting American interests in the Western Hemisphere and throughout the world, and the degree to which the United States will play an active role in the world. Without the structure of the Cold War, it is likely that foreign policy for the United States, as well as for other leading nations, will need to be much more flexible than it has been in the past to deal with changing conditions and complex situations.

From the perspective of the twenty-first century, the international experiences of the 1990s—and of the whole twentieth century—may be seen as a time of transition. The events of the last century created the economic and social basis for the United States to change from a nation focused primarily on domestic policy to a major player on the world stage. During the next decades, that role is likely to grow, perhaps making possible a new variety of world politics.

global view

Is AIDS a National Security Threat?

The spread of AIDS (acquired immune deficiency syndrome) and the human immunodeficiency virus (HIV), the virus that causes AIDS, has been a topic of world concern for almost two decades. At first AIDS was seen as a grave threat to the health of all Americans and the populations of other Western societies where it seemed to be spreading like wildfire. Later, scientists realized that HIV came from Africa and began to investigate the extent of the infection on that continent. The disease was found across sub-Saharan Africa and in Asia as well.

President Clinton hugs youth peer educator Tayo Akinmuwagun before speaking to health-care providers at the Nigerian National Center for Women Development in Abuja on August 27, 2000. Akinmuwagun made an impassioned plea to the president to help the children of Africa with AIDS.

PROGRESS ONLY IN THE WEST

In the United States and Europe, medical advances have led to a drastic reduction in the number of deaths from HIV/AIDS. In the United States, deaths from HIV infections fell by 47 percent between 1996 and 1997. The disease fell from eighth to fourteenth on the list of leading causes of death. Similar progress against the disease has been reported for most of the nations of Western Europe. In addition, massive educational campaigns targeted at those population groups most likely to contract the disease have greatly improved efforts to prevent the disease.

In the rest of the world, the story is quite different.

HIV infections have spread to millions of people in Africa and Asia. The disease infects one-fourth of the populations in Botswana and Zimbabwe in sub-Saharan Africa. Millions of adults die from the disease, leaving orphaned children. Millions of children are also infected by the disease and will die at an early age. Developing nations have neither the resources to mount the vast educational campaigns needed to slow the spread of the disease nor enough funds to provide the new medications to those who are already sick. In some nations, pregnant women cannot get the drug AZT, which prevents the spread of the disease to their unborn children. The extent of the disease is so great that the United Nations has lowered its estimates of the world population in 2050 by almost half a billion due to anticipated deaths from HIV/AIDS.

AIDS AS A MAJOR THREAT

Some argue that the spread of HIV/AIDS and the millions of deaths that it will cause pose a security risk to the United States and to other Western nations. The Security Council of the United Nations devoted a session to this issue in the spring of 2000. The epidemic in Africa is taking a huge economic toll on these nations, both because of the cost of caring for patients and because the work force is shrinking. Poor nations may soon find themselves embroiled in civil war or at the mercy of aggressive neighbors. A report released by the U.S. Central Intelligence Agency suggests that the deaths of the educated elites in many of these nations will lead to a vacuum in leadership, one that could be filled by military coups and other nondemocratic forms of leadership. Although the Clinton administration put forth this view, some members of the Senate argued that HIV/AIDS is still much more of a health threat than a national security threat. Whether the industrialized nations should give more aid and assistance to the nations that have large numbers of victims of the disease continues to be a matter for debate in the United States and abroad.

FOR CRITICAL ANALYSIS

Should the United States take a much more active role in helping developing nations deal with their HIV/AIDS epidemic, or would such aid be better spent elsewhere in the world or at home?

making a difference

Working for Human Rights

In many countries throughout the world, human rights are not protected to the extent that they are in the United States. In some nations, people are imprisoned, tortured, or killed because they oppose the current regime. In other nations, certain ethnic or racial groups are oppressed by the majority population. In nations such as Somalia, where civil war has caused starvation among millions of people, international efforts to send food relief to the refugee camps were hampered by the fighting among rival factions that raged within that country.

What can you do to work for the improvement of human rights in other nations? One way is to join one of the national and international organizations listed to the right that attempt to keep watch over human rights violations. By publicizing human rights violations, these organizations try to pressure nations into changing their tactics. Sometimes, such organizations are able to apply enough pressure and cause enough embarrassment that some victims may be freed from prison or allowed to emigrate.

Another way to work for human rights is to keep informed about the state of affairs in other nations and to write personally to those governments or to their embassies, asking them to cease these violations. Again, the organizations listed in the next column have newsletters or other publications to keep you aware of developments in other nations.

If you want to receive general information about the position of the United States on human rights violations, you could begin by contacting the State Department:

U.S. Department of State
Bureau of Democracy,
Human Rights, and Labor
2201 C St. N.W.
Washington, DC 20520
202-647-4000

http://www.state.gov/www/ global/human_rights/index.html

You can also contact the United Nations:

United Nations
777 United Nations Plaza
New York, NY 10017
212-963-1234

http://www.un.org

The following organizations are well known for their watchdog efforts in countries that violate human rights for political reasons:

Amnesty International U.S.A.
322 Eighth Ave., Fl. 10
New York, NY 10001
212-807-8400

http://www.amnesty-usa.org

American Friends Service Committee
1501 Cherry St.
Philadelphia, PA 19102
215-241-7000

http://www.afsc.org

Key terms

attentive public 553

Cold War 557

containment 557

détente 558

diplomacy 545

economic aid 545

foreign policy 545

foreign policy process 545

intelligence community 550

iron curtain 557

isolationist foreign policy 555

military-industrial complex 553

Monroe Doctrine 555

moral idealism 546

most-favored-nation status 563

National Security Council (NSC) 545

national security policy 545

negative constituents 550

political realism 546

Soviet bloc 557

Strategic Arms Limitation Treaty (SALT I) 558

technical assistance 545

Truman Doctrine 557

Chapter summary

1 Foreign policy includes national goals and the techniques used to achieve them. National security policy, which is one aspect of foreign policy, is designed to protect the independence and the political and economic integrity of the United States. Diplomacy involves the nation's external relationships and is an attempt to resolve conflict without resort to arms. Sometimes U.S. foreign policy is based on moral idealism. At other times, U.S. policies stem from political realism.

2 The formal power of the president to make foreign policy derives from the U.S. Constitution, which makes the president responsible for the preservation of national security and designates the president as commander in chief of the army and navy. Presidents have interpreted this authority broadly. They also have the power to make treaties and executive agreements. In principle, the State Department is the executive agency most directly involved with foreign affairs. The National Security Council (NSC) advises the president on the integration of "domestic, foreign, and military policies relating to the national security." The intelligence community consists of forty or more government agencies engaged in intelligence activities varying from information gathering to covert actions. In response to presidential actions in the Vietnam War, Congress attempted to establish some limits on the power of the president in foreign policy by passing the War Powers Resolution in 1973.

3 Three major themes have guided U.S. foreign policy. In the early years of the nation, isolationism was the primary focus. With the start of the twentieth century, this view gave way to global involvement. From the end of World War II through the 1980s, the major goal was to contain communism and the influence of the Soviet Union.

4 During the 1700s and 1800s, the United States had little international power and generally stayed out of European conflicts and politics. The nineteenth century has been called the period of isolationism. The Monroe Doctrine of 1823 stated that the United States would not accept foreign intervention in the Western Hemisphere and would not meddle in European affairs. The United States pursued an actively expansionist policy in the Americas and the Pacific area during the nineteenth century, however.

5 The end of the policy of isolationism toward Europe started with the Spanish-American War of 1898. U.S. entanglement in European politics became more extensive when the United States entered World War I on April 6, 1917. World War II marked a lasting change in American foreign policy. The United States was the only major country to emerge from the war with its economy intact and the only country with operating nuclear weapons.

6 Soon after the close of World War II, the uncomfortable alliance between the United States and the Soviet Union ended, and the Cold War began. A policy of containment, which assumed an expansionist Soviet Union, was enunciated in the Truman Doctrine. Following the frustrations of the Vietnam War and the apparent arms equality of the United States and the Soviet Union, the United States was ready for détente. As the arms race escalated, arms control became a major foreign policy issue. Although President Ronald Reagan established a tough stance toward the Soviet Union in the first term of his administration, the second term saw serious negotiations toward arms reduction, culminating with the signing of the Intermediate-Range Nuclear Force Treaty in 1987. Negotiations toward further arms reduction continued in the Bush administration. The Strategic Arms Reduction Treaty, which limited long-range nuclear missiles, was signed in 1992 with Russia and several other states of the former Soviet Union.

7 Nuclear proliferation continues to be an issue due to the breakup of the Soviet Union and the loss of control over its nuclear arsenal, along with the continued efforts of other nations to gain nuclear warheads. The number of warheads is known to be more than thirty-two thousand.

8 The United States is dependent on the world economy, as shown by the vulnerability of its stock market to world forces, its status as a debtor nation, and its significant trade deficit. The effects of a united Europe on world trade are yet to be fully realized.

9 Ethnic tensions and political instability in many regions of the world provide challenges to the United States. The nations of Central America and the Caribbean, including Haiti, require American attention because of their proximity. Negotiations have brought agreement in the Middle East and South Africa, whereas civil wars have torn apart Rwanda and Yugoslavia.

Selected print and electronic resources

SUGGESTED READINGS

Adams, James. *The Next World War: Computers Are the Weapons and the Front Line Is Everywhere.* New York: Simon & Schuster, 2000. The author gives a clear history of the evolution of "information warfare," in which hackers or others break into a nation's computer system to disrupt and cripple its military defenses.

Bernstein, Richard, and Ross H. Munro. *The Coming Conflict with China.* New York: Knopf, 1997. These authors take the position that it is important for the United States to be aware of the magnitude of Chinese power and to deal with China as a great nation. In their view, the rivalry between the United States and China is very natural and will require the United States to take a "containment" stance toward Chinese national goals.

Friedman, Thomas L. *The Lexus and the Olive Tree: Understanding Globalization.* Des Plaines, Ill.: Bantam Doubleday, 2000. Written by a *New York Times* reporter, this book examines the trend toward globalization. The author focuses on the difference in goals between nations that seek material wealth and those that seek less tangible assets.

Fromkin, David. *Kosovo Crossing: American Ideals Meet Reality on the Balkan Battlefields.* New York: The Free Press, 2000. In this discussion of the U.S. intervention in Kosovo, the author argues that sometimes vital national interests may suggest that intervention is a mistake. He looks at the military and humanitarian options in these situations.

Kull, Steven, and I. M. Destler. *Misreading the Public: The Myth of a New Isolationism.* Washington, D.C.: Brookings Institution Press, 1999. The authors discuss whether the American public is really seeking isolationism and why the public is reluctant to have Americans involved in military situations overseas. They rely on several sources of poll data to support their analysis.

Martin, Hans-Peter, and Harald Schumann. *The Global Trap: Globalization and the Assault on Prosperity and Democracy.* New York: Oxford University Press, 1997. This analysis of globalization, written by Europeans, shows how the global companies exploit their workers and avoid the regulations of their own nations.

Tanter, Raymond. *Rogue Regimes: Terrorism and Proliferation.* New York: Oxford University Press, 1997. A noted scholar of international relations examines the threats posed to peace and security by the so-called rogue states.

MEDIA RESOURCES

On the Beach—A film starring Gregory Peck, Ava Gardner, and Anthony Perkins that examines the lives of survivors of a nuclear holocaust living in Australia, the only nation to escape the blast.

Dr. Strangelove or How I Learned to Stop Worrying and Love the Bomb—A classic portrayal of a crazed general who is trying to start a nuclear war, produced in 1964 and starring Peter Sellers, who plays three roles; the film also stars George C. Scott and James Earl Jones.

The Mouse That Roared—An outrageous 1959 comedy that satirizes how Americans treat nations that they defeat. Peter Sellers leads the army of a very tiny nation that invades the United States in order to be defeated but ends up winning the war.

Logging on

For an overall look at the theory and practice of international relations, look at the Web site maintained by the Institute of World Politics at

http://www.iwp.edu

The University of Michigan also maintains a Web site with information about regions throughout the world. Go to

http://henry.ugl.lib.umich.edu/libhome/ Documents.center/foreign.html

The International Relations and Security Network, which is maintained by the Swiss government, contains

information about human rights, national security, and other issues at

http://www.fsk.ethz.ch

If you are interested in the intelligence community, you might want to look at the Web site maintained by Loyola University at

http://www.loyola.edu/dept/politics/home.html

For information about visas, politics, business opportunities, and travel warnings, access the Web site maintained by the Department of State at

http://www.state.gov/index.html

Using the Internet for political analysis

Go to the home page maintained by the United Nations at

http://www.un.org

and look over at least three of its divisions. Find out what kind of work those divisions do, and then identify the issues that might be controversial in the United States. Try

to find the budget of the United Nations, and consider whether the United States should pay the back dues that it owes to this organization. Should the United States support all of the activities that you find on this Web site, or should the United States choose to support only those that are compatible with American ideals and goals?

part 6

State and Local Politics

chapter 18
State and Local Government

CHAPTER OUTLINE

- The U.S. Constitution and the State Governments

- State Constitutions

- The State Executive Branch

- The State Legislature

- The State Judiciary

- How Local Government Operates

- Paying for State and Local Government

what if...

All States Allowed School Choice?

BACKGROUND

THERE IS A GROWING SENSE IN THIS COUNTRY THAT OUR EDUCATIONAL SYSTEM IS DECLINING. ROUTINELY, U.S. STUDENTS TEST POORLY IN ACHIEVEMENT, PARTICULARLY IN MATH AND SCIENCE, COMPARED TO STUDENTS IN SUCH COUNTRIES AS JAPAN, RUSSIA, AND GERMANY.

NOT SURPRISINGLY, MANY OBSERVERS OF THE EDUCATIONAL SCENE BELIEVE THAT THE FAULT LIES IN OUR PUBLIC SCHOOL SYSTEM. THEY ARGUE THAT A CHANGE MUST BE MADE AND THAT THE EASIEST WAY TO MAKE SUCH A CHANGE INVOLVES SCHOOL CHOICE. CURRENTLY, PARENTS NORMALLY ARE REQUIRED TO SEND THEIR CHILDREN TO A PUBLIC SCHOOL IN THE PARTICULAR DISTRICT WHERE THE FAMILY'S PHYSICAL RESIDENCE IS LOCATED. GENERALLY, ONLY FAMILIES THAT WISH TO SPEND FROM $3,000 TO $10,000 A YEAR FOR TUITION AT PRIVATE SCHOOLS (IN ADDITION TO THE PROPERTY TAXES THEY PAY TO SUPPORT THEIR LOCAL PUBLIC SCHOOL DISTRICT) HAVE A CHOICE.

WHAT IF ALL STATES ALLOWED SCHOOL CHOICE?

The concept of school choice sometimes involves open districts, meaning that parents can choose to send their children to public schools outside their districts. The aspect of school choice that generates substantial controversy, however, usually involves giving families vouchers, representing state funds, that can be used at any school, public or private. In other words, a voucher would be worth some specified amount of money, such as $5,000, but only if it were redeemed by a bona fide public or private school.

Under such a system, parents would determine where their children went to school. The children could attend the same local public school, a public school in another district, or a private school anywhere. Private schools might accept the vouchers as full payment for tuition fees or request that additional fees be paid.

COMPETITION WOULD BECOME EVIDENT

Certainly, competition for students would develop. Public schools would have to compete not only among themselves (which they currently do in areas that have open districts) but also with private schools. Private schools would have to compete with all schools, including new competitors in the educational marketplace.

Some critics of school choice, particularly public school teachers and administrators, are uncomfortable with treating public education like a business. Because of the competitive environment that would be created by school choice, some public schools might not be able to keep and attract enough students to survive. These schools, unless further subsidized by state and local governments, would "go bankrupt" and disappear.

THE CONSTITUTIONAL ISSUE

Other critics of school vouchers claim that such programs are unconstitutional because they allow state funds to be used to pay for education at religious schools. For example, in a voucher program set up in Cleveland, Ohio, children from low-income families received state funds, in the form of vouchers, to attend the school of their choice. Most of the four thousand children in the program left public schools to attend Catholic educational institutions.

According to those who challenged the program, the use of tax dollars to support religious education violated the establishment clause of the First Amendment to the Constitution, which requires the separation of church and state (see Chapter 4). An Ohio court agreed and invalidated the program. Florida's plan to introduce statewide school choice met with a similar fate.

FOR CRITICAL ANALYSIS

1. Why are teachers' unions, such as the National Education Association, so adamantly against school choice?

2. Given that the goal of our public school system is universal education, do you see school choice as hurting or helping students from low-income families? Explain.

As you read in this chapter's *What If . . .* , it is up to the individual states to determine whether to allow school choice. There is no federal law that determines the issue, at least not yet. Within each state, even if a law allowing school choice were passed, local governments, particularly school boards, no doubt would have a large say in determining exactly how school choice would be made available in their particular areas.

This is true with respect to many state—and federal—policies. Typically, it is the local governing units in this country that give a human face to particular policies, such as welfare reform, and that deal directly with the people affected by those policies. Indeed, many people, when they think of government, think of local agencies or sets of individuals—such as city councils, city or county commissioners, school boards, libraries, zoning boards, fire and police departments, and so on—and not their state government or the federal government. (Whether this will change as more and more government services are delivered via the Web—see, for example, this chapter's *E-mocracy: EZ Government on the Web*—remains to be seen.) Because they shape the environments in which all Americans live, the more than eighty-seven thousand local governmental units in the United States play a vital role in our federal system.

From a practical point of view, it is impossible to understand American politics and government today without a knowledge of how state and local governments operate—the topic of this chapter. We begin by examining the constitutional powers of the states as set forth by the founders in the U.S.

> **DID YOU KNOW...**
> That the Louisiana legislature passed a law requiring students from kindergarten through fifth grade to address teachers as "sir" and "ma'am"?

e-mocracy

EZ Government on the Web

Politicians have been trying for years to make government more efficient. Perhaps the answer is just a click away. Instead of waiting in long lines or negotiating through frustrating telephone services, many Americans now have the option of dealing with their local and state governments in cyberspace. In Riverside, California, tax bills are payable through the Internet. In Atlanta, citizens can pay parking tickets, renew their driver's licenses, and obtain building permits by going online. Also, a physician in Maryland can renew his or her license by visiting a state government site.

Today, businesses and individuals do about $600 billion in transactions with federal, state, and local governments each year. A tiny fraction—less than 1 percent—of these funds changes hands over the Internet. But that amount will increase sharply over the next decade, providing a number of benefits to taxpayers. Besides being more convenient, a "virtual government" would be less costly. The state of Maryland, for example, saved $1.6 million when 40 percent of its 250,000 professionals renewed their licenses online. Arizona saves $5 every time a citizen renews her or his vehicle registration via the Internet. Eventually, those savings are passed on to the taxpayer.

For the most part, private companies handle online government services. A number of firms have sprung up over the past several years in anticipation of tapping this large market. The largest, Atlanta-based ezgov.com, charges customers $3 to $5 each time they access the company's technology to pay a government bill. Furthermore, ezgov.com offers Web surfers a significant amount of government-related information. At the firm's home page (http://www.ezgov.com), users can enter their home zip code and receive data about their federal, state, and local legislators. They can also find tips on how to write letters to politicians and start grassroots campaigns. One of ezgov.com's founders says that the company wants to "put government at the fingertips of every United States citizen."

The day when such a statement is more than sales talk may come sooner than expected: in 2000, Arizona Democrats were able to cast their votes in the state's Democratic presidential primary over the Internet.

FOR CRITICAL ANALYSIS

Experts speak of the "technology gap" that is growing in this country between those who have Internet access and those, mostly in low-income communities, who do not. If such a technology gap exists, how might the online government services discussed in this feature widen it?

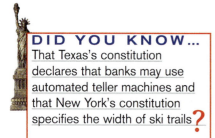

Police Power
  Authority to promote and safeguard the health, morals, safety, and welfare of the people.

Constitution. As you will see, local governments were not mentioned in the Constitution. The founders left their existence in the hands of state government.

The U.S. Constitution and the State Governments

We live in a federal system in which there are fifty separate state governments and one national government. The U.S. Constitution reserves a broad range of powers for state governments. It also prohibits state governments from engaging in certain activities. The U.S. Constitution does not say explicitly what the states actually may do. Rather, state powers are simply reserved, or residual: states may do anything that is not prohibited by the Constitution or anything that is not expressly within the realm of the national government.

The major reserved powers of the states are the powers to tax, spend, and regulate intrastate commerce, or commerce within a given state. The states also have general **police power,** meaning they can impose their will on their citizens in the areas of safety (through, say, traffic laws), health (immunizations), welfare (child-abuse laws), and morals (regulation of pornographic materials).

Restrictions on state and local governmental activity are implied by the Constitution in Article VI, Clause 2:

> This Constitution, and the Laws of the United States which shall be made in Pursuance thereof; and all Treaties made, or which shall be made, under the Authority of the United States, shall be the supreme Law of the Land; and the Judges in every State shall be bound thereby, any Thing in the Constitution or Laws of any State to the Contrary notwithstanding.

In other words, it is the U.S. Constitution that is the supreme law of the land. No state or local law can be in conflict with the Constitution, with laws made by the national Congress, or with treaties entered into by the national government. Judicially, the United States Supreme Court has been the final arbiter of conflicts arising between the national government and state governments.

Public education is one of the primary functions of state and local government. In recent years, a number of states have begun school-reform efforts, often delegating more control over local schools to parents and to the community.

State Constitutions

The U.S. Constitution is a model of brevity, although at the cost of specificity. State constitutions, however, typically are excessively long and detailed. The U.S. Constitution has endured for two hundred years and has been amended only twenty-seven times. State constitutions are another matter. Louisiana has had eleven constitutions; Georgia, ten; South Carolina, seven; and Alabama, Florida, and Virginia, six. The number of amendments that have been submitted to voters borders on the absurd. For example, by 2001, the citizens of Alabama had adopted nearly 600 amendments to their state constitution.

Why Are State Constitutions So Long?

According to historians, the length and mass of detail of many state constitutions reflect the loss of popular confidence in state legislatures between the end of the Civil War and the early 1900s. During that period, forty-two states adopted or revised their constitutions. Those constitutions adopted before or after that period are shorter and contain fewer restrictions on the powers of state legislatures. Another equally important reason for the length and detail of state constitutions is that state constitution makers apparently have had a difficult time distinguishing between constitutional and statutory law. Does the Louisiana constitution need an amendment to declare Huey Long's birthday a legal holiday? Is it necessary for the constitution of South Dakota to authorize a cordage and twine plant at the state penitentiary? Does the California constitution need to discuss the tax-exempt status of the Huntington Library and Art Gallery? The U.S. Constitution contains no such details. It leaves to the legislature the nuts-and-bolts activity of making specific statutory laws.

In all fairness to the states, their courts do not interpret their constitutions as freely as the United States Supreme Court interprets the U.S. Constitution. Therefore, the states feel compelled to be more specific in their own constitutions. Additionally, the framers of state constitutions may feel compelled to fill in the gaps left by the very brief federal constitution.

The Constitutional Convention and the Constitutional Initiative

Two of the several ways to effect constitutional changes are the state constitutional convention and the constitutional initiative. As of 2001, over 230 state constitutional conventions had been used to write an entirely new constitution or to attempt to amend an existing one. A major feature of the constitutions of eighteen states permits those constitutions to be amended by **constitutional initiatives**.[1] An initiative allows citizens to place a proposed amendment on the ballot without calling a constitutional convention. The number of signatures required to get a constitutional initiative on the ballot varies from state to state; it is usually between 5 and 10 percent of the total number of votes cast for governor in the last election. The initiative process has been used most frequently in California and Oregon. Relatively few initiative amendments are approved by the electorate.

Constitutional Initiative
An electoral device whereby citizens can propose a constitutional amendment through petitions signed by the required number of registered voters.

---

[1]These states are Arizona, Arkansas, California, Colorado, Florida, Illinois, Massachusetts, Michigan, Mississippi, Missouri, Montana, Nebraska, Nevada, North Dakota, Ohio, Oklahoma, Oregon, and South Dakota.

The State Executive Branch

All state governments in the United States have executive, legislative, and judicial branches. Here the similarity with the federal government ends. State governments do not always have strong executive branches.

A Weak Executive

During the colonial period, governors were appointed by the Crown and had the power to call the colonial assembly (the colonial legislative body) into session, recommend legislation, exercise veto power, and dissolve the assembly. The colonial governor acted as commander in chief of the colony's military forces and was also the head of the judiciary.

Not surprisingly, the colonies' revolt against British rule centered on the all-powerful colonial governors. When the first states were formed after the Declaration of Independence, hostility toward the governor's office ensured a weak executive branch and an extremely strong legislative branch. By the 1830s, however, the state executive office had become more important. Since Andrew Jackson's presidency, all governors (except in South Carolina) have been elected directly by the people. Simultaneously, there was an effort to democratize state government by popularly electing other state government officials as well.

Under the tenets of Jacksonian democracy, the more public officials who are elected (and not appointed), the more democratic (and better) the system will be. Even today, some states have numerous state offices with independently elected officials. The direct election of so many executive officials makes it likely that no one will have much power, because each official is working to secure his or her own political support. Only if the elected officials happen to be able to work together cohesively can they get much done.

A slight majority of the states require that the candidates for governor and lieutenant governor run for election as a team. In some states where this is not required, however, the voters have at times chosen a governor from one political party and a lieutenant governor from another. As a result, the governor may be unwilling to leave the state in order to prevent the lieutenant governor from exerting power during the governor's travels.

Reforming the System

Most states follow the practice of electing numerous executive officials. Nonetheless, governors have exercised the authority of their office with increasing frequency in recent years. Governors have become a significant force in legislative policymaking. The governor, in theory, enjoys the same advantage that the president has over Congress in his or her ability to make policy decisions and to embody these in a program on which the state legislative body can act. How the governor exercises this ability often depends on her or his powers of persuasion. A strong personality can make for a strong executive office. Personal skill, the strength of political parties and special interest groups, and the governor's use of the media can affect how much actual power she or he has.

Reorganization of the state executive branch to achieve greater efficiency has been attempted numerous times and in many states. There are some obstacles to reorganizing state executive branches. Voters do not want to lose their ability to influence politics directly. Both the voters and the legislators fear that reorganization will concentrate too much authority in the hands of the governor. Finally, many believe that numerous governmental functions, such as control of the highway program, should remain administrative rather than political.

Despite the fragmentation of executive power and doubts about the concentration of power in an executive's hands, the trend toward modernization has increased the powers of many of the states' highest executives. Based on a governor's ability to make major appointments, formulate a state budget, veto legislation, and exercise other powers, the National Governors Association ranks the governors of at least twenty-five states as powerful or very powerful executives. Only eleven states are assessed as giving their executives little or very little power.

Moreover, state governors—as well as legislators—are playing increasingly important roles as the states assume more authority over programs, such as welfare, that for decades have been controlled by the national government. The devolutionary trend of the 1990s and early 2000s has allowed governors to become models of leadership on a number of issues affecting national politics, including crime, welfare, and education. A state governorship also may be a steppingstone to the U.S. presidency. Sixteen of the nation's first forty-two presidents (38 percent), including several recent presidents (Jimmy Carter, Ronald Reagan, and Bill Clinton), served as state governors before assuming the presidential office. For these reasons, elections to state governorships tend to receive more national attention than in the past.

The Governor's Veto Power

The veto power gives the president of the United States immense leverage. Simply the threat of a presidential veto often means that legislation will not be passed by Congress. In some states, governors have strong veto power, but in other states, governors have no veto power at all. Some states give the governor veto power but allow only five days in which to exercise it. Thirteen states give the governor pocket veto power (see Chapter 13).

In forty-three states, the governor has some form of **item veto** power on appropriations. If the governor in such a state does not particularly like one item, or line, in an appropriations bill, he or she can veto that item. In twelve states, the governor can reduce the amount of the appropriation but cannot reduce it to zero. Nineteen states give governors the ability to use the item veto on more than just appropriations.

Item Veto
The power exercised by the governors of most states to veto particular sections or items of an appropriations bill, while signing the remainder of the bill into law.

TABLE 18-1

Characteristics of State Legislatures

	SEATS IN SENATE	LENGTH OF TERM	SEATS IN HOUSE	LENGTH OF TERM	YEARS SESSIONS ARE HELD	SALARY*
Alabama	35	4	105	4	Annual	$10(d)†
Alaska	20	4	40	2	Annual	24,012†
Arizona	30	2	60	2	Annual	24,000
Arkansas	35	4	100	2	Odd	12,500†
California	40	4	80	2	Even	99,000†
Colorado	35	4	65	2	Annual	30,000†
Connecticut	36	2	151	2	Annual	21,788
Delaware	21	4	41	2	Annual	29,574†
Florida	40	4	120	2	Annual	26,388†
Georgia	56	2	180	2	Annual	11,348†
Hawaii	25	4	51	2	Annual	32,000†
Idaho	35	2	70	2	Annual	14,760†
Illinois	59	‡	118	2	Annual	50,803†
Indiana	50	4	100	2	Annual	11,600†
Iowa	50	4	100	2	Annual	20,758
Kansas	40	4	125	2	Annual	72(d)†
Kentucky	38	4	100	2	Even	107(d)†
Louisiana	39	4	105	4	Annual	16,800†
Maine	35	2	151	2	Even	10,500§
Maryland	47	4	141	4	Annual	30,591†
Massachusetts	40	2	160	2	Annual	46,410†
Michigan	38	4	110	2	Annual	55,054†
Minnesota	67	4	134	2	Odd	31,140†
Mississippi	52	4	122	4	Annual	10,000†
Missouri	34	4	163	2	Annual	26,803
Montana	50	4	100	2	Odd	60(d)†
Nebraska"	49	4	—	—	Annual	12,000†
Nevada	21	4	42	2	Odd	130(d)†
New Hampshire	24	2	400	2	Annual	200(b)
New Jersey	40	4	80	2	Annual	35,000
New Mexico	42	4	70	2	Annual	—†
New York	61	2	150	2	Annual	79,500†
North Carolina	50	2	120	2	Odd	13,951†
North Dakota	49	4	98	4	Odd	111(d)†
Ohio	33	4	99	2	Annual	42,427
Oklahoma	48	4	101	2	Annual	38,400†
Oregon	30	4	60	2	Odd	14,496
Pennsylvania	50	4	203	2	Annual	59,245†
Rhode Island	50	2	100	2	Annual	10,768
South Carolina	46	4	124	2	Annual	10,400†
South Dakota	35	2	70	2	Annual	12,000#
Tennessee	33	4	99	2	Odd	16,500†
Texas	31	4	150	2	Odd	7,200†
Utah	29	4	75	2	Annual	100(d)†
Vermont	30	2	150	2	Odd	536(w)
Virginia	40	4	100	2	Annual	18,000†
Washington	49	4	98	2	Annual	28,300†
West Virginia	34	4	100	2	Annual	15,000
Wisconsin	33	4	99	2	Annual	41,809†
Wyoming	30	4	60	2	Annual	125(d)†

*Salaries annual unless otherwise noted as (d)—per day, (b)—biennium, or (w)—per week.
†Plus *per diem* living expenses.
‡Terms vary from two to four years.
§For odd year; $7,500 for even year.
"Unicameral legislature.
#For 2 years

SOURCE: Adapted from Council of State Governments, *Book of the States, 2000–2001.*

The State Legislature

Although there has been a move in recent years to increase the power of governors, state legislatures are still an important force in state politics and state governmental decision making. The task of these assemblies is to legislate on such matters as taxes and the regulation of business and commerce, highways, school systems and the funding of education, and welfare payments. Allocation of funds and program priorities are vital issues to local residents and communities, and conflicts between regions within the state or between the cities and the rural areas are common.

State legislatures have been criticized for being unprofessional and less than effective. It is true that state legislatures sometimes spend their time considering trivial legislation (such as the official state pie in Florida), and lobbyists often have too much influence in state capitals. At the same time, state legislators are often given few resources with which to work. In many states, legislatures are limited to meeting only part of the year, and in some the pay is a disincentive to real service. In a number of states, state legislators are paid less than $10,000 per year. A complete list of state legislators' salaries, as well as other characteristics of state legislatures, is given in Table 18–1 on the previous page.

We have seen earlier how a bill becomes a law in the U.S. Congress. A similar process occurs at the state level. Figure 18–1 traces how an idea becomes a law in the Florida legislature. Similar steps are followed in other states (note that Nebraska has a unicameral legislature, however, so there is no second chamber process).

Legislative Apportionment

Drawing up legislative districts—state as well as federal—has long been subject to gerrymandering—creative cartography designed to guarantee that one political party maintains control of a particular voting district. Malapportionment is

> **DID YOU KNOW...**
> That the most expensive ballot initiative in history was California's Proposition 5 (the opposing sides of the 1998 proposition, which permitted video slot machines and card games on Indian reservations, spent a total of approximately $100 million)?

FIGURE 18–1

How an Idea Becomes a Law

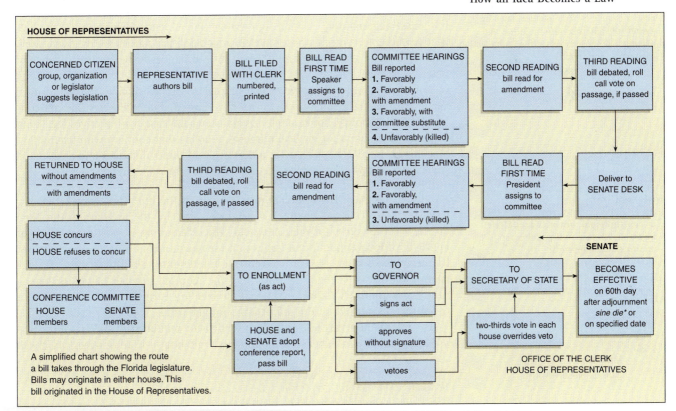

A simplified chart showing the route a bill takes through the Florida legislature. Bills may originate in either house. This bill originated in the House of Representatives.

Sine die means "without assigning a day for a further meeting."

SOURCE: Allen Morris and Joan Perry Morris, compilers, *The Florida Handbook, 1999–2000*, 27th ed. (Tallahassee, Fla.: Peninsular Publishing Co., 2000).

the skewed distribution of voters in a state's legislative districts. The United States Supreme Court ruled in 1962 that malapportioned state legislatures violate the equal protection clause of the Fourteenth Amendment.[2] In a series of cases that followed, the Court held that legislative districts must be as nearly equal as possible in terms of population, and the grossest examples of state legislative malapportionment were eliminated.[3] The Supreme Court, however, allowed "benevolent, bipartisan gerrymandering" in certain states. Indeed, in 1977, the Supreme Court held that a state had an obligation imposed under the 1965 Voting Rights Act to draw district boundaries to maximize minority legislative representation.[4] Thus, each decade, state and federal legislative districts must be redrawn to ensure that every person's vote is roughly equal and that minorities are represented adequately.

By the mid-1990s, however, the Supreme Court had reversed its position on what has been called "racial gerrymandering." In a series of cases, the Court held that voting districts that are redrawn with the goal of maximizing the electoral strength and representation of minority groups violate the equal protection clause.[5] (See Chapter 12 for a more detailed discussion of this issue.)

Direct Democracy: The Initiative, Referendum, and Recall

There is a major difference between the legislative process as outlined in the U.S. Constitution and the legislative process as outlined in the various state constitutions. Many states exercise a type of direct democracy through the initiative, the referendum, and the recall—procedures that allow voters to control the government directly.

The Initiative.   One technique lets citizens bypass legislatures by proposing new statutes or changes in government for citizen approval. Most states that permit the citizen **legislative initiative** require that the initiative's backers circulate a petition to place the issue on the ballot and that a certain percentage of the registered voters in the last gubernatorial election sign the petition. Twenty-four states use the legislative initiative, typically those states in which political parties are relatively weak and nonpartisan groups are strong. Legislative initiatives have involved a range of issues, including crime victims' rights, campaign contributions, corporate spending on ballot questions, affirmative action, physician-assisted suicide, and the medical use of marijuana. In some cases, voters have passed state initiatives that are contrary to federal policy. For example, several states have passed initiatives legalizing the use of marijuana for medical purposes, a policy that conflicts with federal law. (See this chapter's *Global View* for a discussion of these initiatives and attempts in some other countries to legalize the use of drugs in certain circumstances.)

The Referendum.   The **referendum** is similar to the initiative, except that the issue (or constitutional change) is proposed first by the legislature and then directed to the voters for their approval. The referendum is most often used for approval of local school bond issues and for amendments to state constitutions. In a number of states that provide for the referendum, a bill passed by the legislature may be suspended by obtaining the required number of voters' signatures on petitions. A statewide referendum election is then held. If a majority of the voters disapprove of the bill, it is no longer valid.

The referendum was not initially intended for regular use, and indeed it was used infrequently in the past. Its opponents argue that it is an unnecessary check

Legislative Initiative
A procedure by which voters can propose a change in state or local laws by gathering signatures on a petition and placing a proposed law on the ballot for the voters' approval.

Referendum
An electoral device whereby legislative or constitutional measures are referred by the legislature to the voters for approval or disapproval.

Minneapolis Seeks Referendum

---

[2] *Baker v. Carr,* 369 U.S. 186 (1962).
[3] *Reynolds v. Sims,* 377 U.S. 533 (1964); and other cases.
[4] *United Jewish Organizations of Williamsburg v. Cary,* 430 U.S. 144 (1977).
[5] *Miller v. Johnson,* 515 U.S. 900 (1995); *Shaw v. Hunt,* 517 U.S. 899 (1996); and *Bush v. Vera,* 517 U.S. 952 (1996).

on representative government and that it weakens legislative responsibility. In recent years, the referendum has become increasingly popular as citizens have attempted to control their state and local governments. Interest groups have been active in sponsoring the petition drives necessary to force a referendum. Over two-thirds of the states provide for the referendum.

The Recall.   The right of citizens to recall, or remove, elected officials is not exercised frequently. **Recall** is a provision written into the constitutions of fifteen states. It allows voters to remove elected state officials, including the governor, before the expiration of their terms of office. In the case of judges, the recall can terminate a lifetime appointment.

Citizens begin the recall process by circulating petitions demanding a statewide vote to remove the offending officeholder. The number of signatures required to bring about the election ranges from 10 to 40 percent of the last vote for the office in question. If the required number of signatures is obtained, the question of whether to remove the incumbent is decided in a general election.

The recall and the initiative are examples of "pure democracy," in which the people as a whole vote directly on important issues. Such measures are distinct in theory and in practice from the norms of "representative democracy," in which the people govern only indirectly, through their elected representatives. (For a discussion of the initiative process and the controversy it has engendered, see this chapter's feature *Which Side Are You On?* on the next page.)

DID YOU KNOW...
That by 2001, at least twenty-three state legislatures had enacted some form of law making English the official language of those states?

Recall
A procedure enabling voters to remove an elected official from office before his or her term has expired.

global View

Dealing with Drugs at Home and Abroad

Seven states—Alaska, Arizona, California, Maine, Nevada, Oregon, and Washington—and Washington, D.C., have passed ballot initiatives legalizing marijuana, or cannabis, for medical use. Proponents of "medical pot" claim that tetrahydrocannabol (THC), the primary active ingredient in marijuana, can alleviate the pain and suffering associated with conditions such as cancer, insomnia, arthritis, migraine headaches, and acquired immune deficiency syndrome (AIDS).

Opponents of medical marijuana point to the large number of health risks associated with the drug, including bronchitis, emphysema, and lung cancer. The federal government, for its part, has threatened to arrest and revoke the prescription license of any doctor that tells her or his patient to use cannabis. On at least one occasion, this threat has been carried out.

DRUG PROGRAMS IN SWITZERLAND AND THE NETHERLANDS

The United States is not the only country struggling with the issue of illegal drugs and their possible health benefits. For several years, health officials in Switzerland have overseen an experimental program that provides heroin addicts with heroin, the use of which is otherwise illegal in the country. The goals of the program are to slow the spread of the AIDS virus via dirty needles and reduce crime associated with heroin use. Swiss experts reasoned that it was better for addicts to pick up the drug at government-run clinics, where they could get clean needles and counseling, than for them to buy it on the street.

Similar attitudes in the Netherlands have led to that country's marijuana policy. Though the drug is illegal, Dutch police are not allowed to arrest someone for the sale or possession of fewer than five grams of cannabis. In addition, approximately 1,200 "coffee shops" are allowed to sell marijuana. The Dutch authorities believe these coffee shops keep users off the streets and reduce the risk that they will move on to "harder" drugs, such as cocaine and heroin.

IN ENGLAND, JURIES DECIDE THE ISSUE

In England, jurors have taken the issue into their own hands. Taxi driver Alan Blythe was acquitted of a criminal charge for growing marijuana in his home after he was able to prove that smoking the drug eased the pain his wife suffered as a result of multiple sclerosis. Several other English juries have followed suit, causing some British legal experts to predict that such rulings will become a trend.

It is highly unlikely that these European examples will influence American drug policy. Despite the ballot initiatives mentioned earlier, public opinion in the United States is strongly against more lenient drug laws. With regard to marijuana, federal law will no doubt continue to hold that *any* use of the drug is a criminal activity.

FOR CRITICAL ANALYSIS

What role does the supremacy clause of the Constitution (see Chapter 3) play in attempts by states to permit the use of medical marijuana and the federal government's refusal to allow them to do so?

which side are you on?

Will of the People or Dollar Democracy?

The voter initiative has been around since the nineteenth century—it is a product of the grassroots politicking that was characteristic of an earlier era in American politics. According to some, such initiatives represent politics at its best—citizens proposing and voting on laws tailored to the needs of their state or local region. Twenty-four states permit voter initiatives, and they are particularly popular in the western states, such as Arizona, California, Oregon, and Washington.

The Use of Initiatives

California first used the voter initiative in 1911, but it became widely popular in the state only after 1978, when Californians voted in favor of a controversial initiative referred to as Proposition 13. This proposition capped local property tax rates and cut $5 billion in taxes statewide—something that California politicians said could not be done. Since Proposition 13, some of the state's most significant legislation has come about through the initiative process. In 1994, Californians voted to deny social benefits, such as education, to illegal immigrants. (This law was eventually invalidated by the courts.) Two years later, they passed an initiative outlawing affir-mative action. In 1998, a ballot initiative was used to repeal bilingual education, and in 2000 voters approved Proposition 22, which denies equal marital rights to same-sex couples.

Similarly, other states (and cities) are using voter initatives to settle controversial issues. For example, Oregon citizens passed an initiative legalizing physician-assisted suicide, and Arizona citizens supported a measure to make English the official language of the state.

The Controversy over the Initiative Process

Those who favor ballot initiatives see them as backlash against a political system that does not represent the will of the people. It is no coincidence, say supporters, that the popularity of initiatives has risen as the percentage of Americans who vote in local and national elections has dropped. Many citizens, the argument goes, mistrust what they see as an impossibly complex lawmaking system that favors wealthy special interests and denies them a voice.

Critics of ballot initiatives claim that it is naïve to think that the initiative process represents the triumph of grassroots politicking. On the contrary, the process has come to be dominated by large, often national interest groups that funnel millions of dollars into advertising the merits (or faults) of particular initiatives. In California, it costs approximately $1 million just to gather the signatures necessary to get an initiative on the ballot. Furthermore, note the critics, the process bypasses the traditional research and deliberation that legislators undertake before enacting new laws. Instead, initiatives often call for radical departures from existing law without exploring the consequences. Some commentators, for example, contend that Proposition 13 shifted the property tax burden from corporations to individual homeowners, hardly the intent of its supporters.

DOES IT MATTER?

Should it matter whether state initiatives are financed by national interest groups? Why or why not?

GOING ONLINE

To access opposing viewpoints on the initiative process in the context of California's Proposition 209 concerning affirmative action, go to **http://www.thirteen.org/federalist/opinion-prop.html**. *For a collection of articles exploring the financing of ballot initiatives, see* **http://www.policy.com/issuewk/1998/1030_41/detail99.html**. *To visit the home page of the Ballot Initiative Strategy Center, go to* **http://www.ballot.org**.

**Drug Crime
Impact State Courts**

The State Judiciary

Each of the fifty states, as well as the District of Columbia, has its own separate court system (which is in addition to the federal courts—see Chapter 15). Figure 18-2 shows a sample state court system. Like the federal court system, it has several tiers, including trial courts, intermediate courts of appeal, and a supreme court.

Trial Courts

All states have major trial courts, commonly called circuit courts, district courts, or superior courts. The number of judges and their terms in office vary widely. As in the federal court system, the trial courts are of two types: those having limited jurisdiction and those having general jurisdiction.[6] (For some jurisdictional challenges faced by state courts today, see this chapter's *Critical Perspective* on pages 590 and 591.) Cases heard before these courts can be appealed to the state appellate court and ultimately to the state supreme court.

Appellate Courts

About three-fourths of the states have intermediate appellate courts between the trial courts of original jurisdiction and the highest state appellate court, or the supreme court. These are usually called courts of appeal. Salaries of state judges vary widely, but higher pay is given to appellate and supreme court members.

[6]See Chapter 15 for a definition of these terms.

FIGURE 18-2

A Sample State Court System

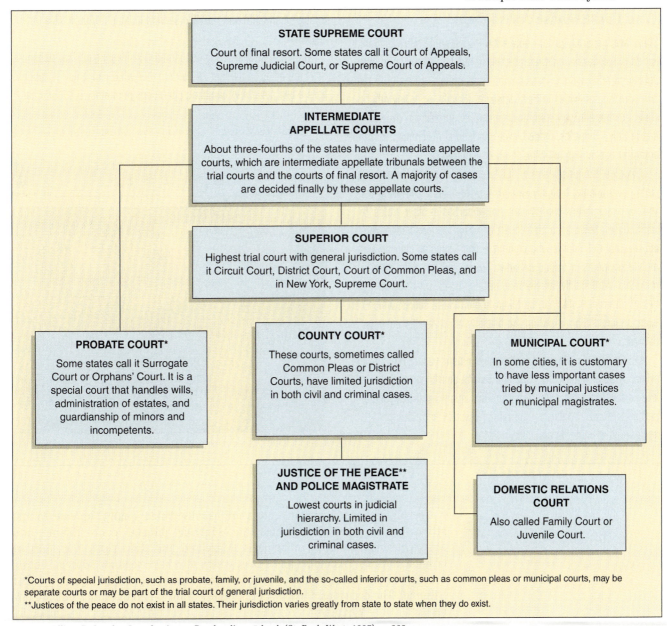

STATE SUPREME COURT
Court of final resort. Some states call it Court of Appeals, Supreme Judicial Court, or Supreme Court of Appeals.

INTERMEDIATE APPELLATE COURTS
About three-fourths of the states have intermediate appellate courts, which are intermediate appellate tribunals between the trial courts and the courts of final resort. A majority of cases are decided finally by these appellate courts.

SUPERIOR COURT
Highest trial court with general jurisdiction. Some states call it Circuit Court, District Court, Court of Common Pleas, and in New York, Supreme Court.

PROBATE COURT*
Some states call it Surrogate Court or Orphans' Court. It is a special court that handles wills, administration of estates, and guardianship of minors and incompetents.

COUNTY COURT*
These courts, sometimes called Common Pleas or District Courts, have limited jurisdiction in both civil and criminal cases.

MUNICIPAL COURT*
In some cities, it is customary to have less important cases tried by municipal justices or municipal magistrates.

JUSTICE OF THE PEACE AND POLICE MAGISTRATE**
Lowest courts in judicial hierarchy. Limited in jurisdiction in both civil and criminal cases.

DOMESTIC RELATIONS COURT
Also called Family Court or Juvenile Court.

*Courts of special jurisdiction, such as probate, family, or juvenile, and the so-called inferior courts, such as common pleas or municipal courts, may be separate courts or may be part of the trial court of general jurisdiction.
**Justices of the peace do not exist in all states. Their jurisdiction varies greatly from state to state when they do exist.

SOURCE: William P. Statsky, *Introduction to Paralegalism*, 5th ed. (St. Paul: West, 1997), p. 329.

critical perspective

Can States Control Betting on the Internet?

At one time, few states permitted gambling in any form. Even by 1976, only thirteen states had lotteries, two states had approved off-track wagering, and there were no casinos outside Nevada. Today, in contrast, thirty-seven states have lotteries, twenty-eight states have casinos, and twenty-two states allow off-track betting. Moreover, the advent of the Internet has given Americans unprecedented access to gambling facilities.

Who Can Exercise Jurisdiction?

State laws generally govern only activities within a state's borders. For example, Texas could not attempt to regulate gambling in New Jersey. In other words, Texas has no constitutional authority to regulate gambling activities in New Jersey or Nevada, or in any other state. Furthermore, no state government has jurisdiction over activities in other countries. Indeed, even the federal government has little authority concerning activities in other countries.

Likewise, the jurisdiction of state courts, the judicial branches of state governments, typically extends only to disputes involving persons within a state's borders, and not to parties in other states. In some states, however, a state court can exercise jurisdiction over out-of-state defendants who commit wrongs—such as causing automobile accidents or selling defective goods—that harm the state's residents. Additionally, as you read in Chapter 15, suits between parties of different states can be taken to the federal courts, which can exercise jurisdiction based on the diversity of citizenship between the parties.

In other words, although a state government cannot regulate the affairs of other states, the state and federal courts can and do regulate—at least to some extent—matters that might extend beyond a particular state's borders by permitting lawsuits to be brought against out-of-state defendants.

Online Gambling

Today, virtually any person, even a twelve-year-old with a credit card, can play blackjack on the Internet. Often, the gambling entity resides in some offshore location, such as the Cayman Islands or even Finland or Iceland.

Online gambling has created thorny jurisdictional issues for both state governments and the federal government. To understand why, consider an example. Assume that a resident of Missouri logs on the Internet and pulls up a gambling site. He or she then places a bet via a credit card. The home Web site server of the gambling company is on the Caribbean island of Grenada. The gambling company has a bona fide license in Grenada to operate the Web site. The interacting electronic links between the home server and the gambler would go through many different possible servers located in Africa, Asia, or anywhere.

The state of Missouri is concerned that illegal gambling transactions are occurring within its borders, but what can it do? It cannot pass a law governing gambling operations in another U.S. state, let

One of the many Internet sites that allow individuals to engage in online gambling.

The highest state appellate courts are usually called simply supreme courts, although they are also labeled the supreme judicial court (Maine and Massachusetts), the court of appeals (Maryland and New York), the court of criminal appeals (Oklahoma and Texas, which also have separate supreme courts for appeals in noncriminal cases), or the supreme court of appeals (West Virginia). The decisions of each state's highest court on all questions of state law are final. Only when issues of federal law are involved can a decision made by a state's highest court be overruled by the United States Supreme Court.

The Problem of Enforcement

Assume for a moment that this law is passed. How can it be enforced? It is impossible to keep track of thousands of Internet gambling sites and the estimated one million people who use them. The same issue has already arisen with respect to online pornography sites, which draw significantly more hits than gambling sites. No government, including the federal government, can monitor every action by every user of the Internet. Furthermore, one industry group believes that the amount wagered online will reach $3 billion by 2002. Given the potential profits, at least some operators will probably find creative ways to circumvent any restrictions.

Surprisingly, the single most devastating blow against Internet gambling was struck not by the government, but by Cynthia Haines of northern California. After piling up $115,000 in charges using credit cards to gamble at online casinos, Haines sued the credit-card companies, claiming that she did not have to pay because in California, as in many other states, gambling debts are void—that is, they cannot be legally collected. Therefore, it would be illegal for credit-card companies to try to get their money back from her. In the end, Haines did not have to honor a penny of her debt. If more consumers follow her lead, credit-card companies will likely refuse to process gambling transactions. Given that credit cards are used in about 90 percent of online gambling transactions, this would deal a serious blow to Internet gambling.

FOR CRITICAL ANALYSIS
1. Which business groups in America would be in favor of making online betting illegal, and why?
2. Does the fact that the American Psychiatric Association considers obsessive gambling to be a mental illness justify state and federal efforts to prohibit Internet gambling? Why or why not?

alone Grenada. It could try to bring a criminal action in court against the gambling company for conducting illegal gambling operations "within" its state, but then a jurisdictional problem arises. How can a Missouri court or even a federal court exercise jurisdiction over a foreign entity? Complicating the issue is the fact that the online transactions could have involved servers in twenty different jurisdictions. Clearly, jurisdictional concepts that have traditionally been linked to geographic borders are difficult to apply to the non-physical landscape of the Internet.

Can the Government Regulate Online Gambling?

Because gambling in any form is widely considered a social ill, jurisdictional problems have not discouraged government entities from trying to regulate betting on the Internet. The Illinois legislature amended its criminal code to prohibit a person from operating or maintaining an Internet gambling site within state lines. A trial court in New York ruled that citizens who engage in gambling on an Antigua-based Internet site are violating state law. The court held that it had jurisdiction over a business located on the Caribbean island because that business was providing an obvious service to New York citizens.

The federal government is also trying its hand at controlling Internet betting. The Department of Justice has charged twenty-two offshore Internet gaming operators with violating the same laws that make it illegal to bet over the telephone in the United States. The U.S. Congress, for its part, is moving slowly but surely toward passing the Internet Gambling Prohibition Act. Although the House and Senate must resolve differences in their respective versions of the act, the final product will probably, among other conditions, impose a fine (ranging from $10,000 to $20,000) or a prison term (for up to two years) on operators of Internet gambling facilities.

Judicial Elections and Appointments

State court judges are either elected or appointed, depending on the state and (often) on the level of court involved—the procedures vary widely from state to state. In some states, including Delaware, the procedure is similar to the way federal judges are appointed—the judges are appointed by the governor and confirmed by the upper chamber of the legislature. In other states, all state court judges are elected, either on a partisan ballot (as in Arkansas) or on a nonpartisan

This volunteer is working to make sure that a local referendum is passed in California. A referendum is an issue or constitutional change that is proposed first by the legislature and then directed to the voters for their approval. An initiative, in contrast, lets citizens bypass legislatures completely by proposing new statutes or changes in government for citizen approval.

ballot (as in Kentucky). In several states, judges in some of the lower courts are elected, while those in the appellate courts are appointed. Additionally, depending on the state, judges who are appointed may have to run for reelection if they wish to serve a second term.

How Local Government Operates

Local governments are difficult to describe because of their great dissimilarities and because, if we include municipalities, counties, towns, townships, and special districts, there are so many of them. We limit the discussion here to the most important types and features of local governments.

The Legal Existence of Local Government

As mentioned earlier, the U.S. Constitution makes no mention of local governments. Article IV, Section 4, states that "[t]he United States shall guarantee to every State in this Union a Republican Form of Government." Actually, then, the states do not even have to have local governments. Consequently, every local government is a creature of the state. The state can create a local government, and the state can terminate the right of a local government to exist. Indeed, states often have abolished entire counties, school districts, cities, and special districts. Since World War II (1939–1945), almost twenty thousand school districts have gone out of existence as they were consolidated with other school districts.

Because the local government is the legal creation of the state, does that mean the state can dictate everything the local government does? For many years that seemed to be the case. The narrowest possible view of the legal status of local governments follows **Dillon's rule**, outlined by Judge John F. Dillon in his *Commentaries on the Law of Municipal Corporations* in 1872. He stated that municipal corporations may possess only powers "granted in express words . . . [that are] necessarily or fairly implied in or incident to the powers expressly

Dillon's Rule
The narrowest possible interpretation of the legal status of local governments, outlined by Judge John F. Dillon, who in 1872 stated that a municipal corporation can exercise only those powers expressly granted by state law.

granted."[7] Cities governed under Dillon's rule have sometimes been dominated by the state legislatures, depending on the extent of authority granted to the cities by the legislatures. Those communities wishing to obtain the status of a municipal corporation have simply petitioned the state legislature for a **charter.**

In a revolt against state legislative power over municipalities, the home rule movement began. It was based on **Cooley's rule,** derived from an 1871 decision by Michigan judge Thomas Cooley stating that cities should be able to govern themselves.[8] Since 1900, about four-fifths of the states have allowed **municipal home rule,** but only with respect to local concerns for which no statewide interests are involved. A municipality must choose to become a **home rule city;** otherwise, it operates as a **general law city.** In the latter case, the state makes certain general laws relating to cities of different sizes, which are designated as first-class cities, second-class cities, or towns. Once a city, by virtue of its population, receives such a ranking, it follows the general law put down by the state. Only if it chooses to be a home rule city can it avoid such state government restrictions. In most states, only cities with populations of 2,500 or more can choose home rule.

Local Governmental Units

There are four major types of local governmental units: municipalities, counties, towns and townships, and special districts.

Municipalities.   A municipality is a political entity created by the people of a city or town to govern themselves locally. Currently, there are over nineteen thousand municipalities within the fifty states. Almost all municipalities are fairly small cities. Only about two hundred cities have populations over one hundred thousand, and only ten cities (New York, Los Angeles, Chicago, Houston, Philadelphia, San Diego, Phoenix, San Antonio, Dallas, and Detroit) have populations over a million. City expenditures are primarily for water supply and other utilities, police and fire protection, and education. About three-fourths of municipal tax revenues come from property taxes. Municipalities rely very heavily on financial assistance from both the federal and state governments.

Counties.   The difference between a **county** and a municipality is that a county may not be created at the behest of its inhabitants. The state sets up counties on its own initiative to serve as political extensions of the state government. Counties apply state law and administer state business at the local level.

Counties, of which there are over three thousand within the United States, vary greatly in both size and population. San Bernardino County in California is the largest geographically, with 20,102 square miles. New York County in New York is the smallest, with less than 22 square miles. County populations range from millions of residents, as in Los Angeles County, to fewer than a hundred residents, as in Kalawao County, Hawaii.

County governments' responsibilities include zoning, building regulations, health, hospitals, parks, recreation, highways, public safety, justice, and record keeping. Typically, when a municipality is established within a county, the county withdraws most of its services from the municipality; for example, the municipal police force takes over from the county police force. County governments are extremely complex entities, a product of the era of Jacksonian democracy and its effort to bring government closer to the people. There is no easy

Charter
A document issued by a government that grants to a person, a group of persons, or a corporation the right to carry on one or more specific activities. A state government can grant a charter to a municipality allowing that group of persons to carry on specific activities.

Cooley's Rule
The view that cities should be able to govern themselves, presented in an 1871 Michigan decision by Judge Thomas Cooley.

Municipal Home Rule
The power vested in a local unit of government to draft or change its own charter and to manage its own affairs.

Home Rule City
A city with a charter allowing local voters to frame, adopt, and amend their own charter.

General Law City
A city operating under general state laws that apply to all local governmental units of a similar type.

County
The chief governmental unit set up by the state to administer state law and business at the local level. Counties are drawn up by area, rather than by rural or urban criteria.

---

[7]John F. Dillon, *Commentaries on the Law of Municipal Corporations,* 5th ed. (Boston: Little, Brown, 1911), Vol. 1, Sec. 237.
[8]*People v. Hurlbut,* 24 Mich. 44 (1871).

New England Town
A governmental unit in the New England states that combines the roles of city and county in one unit.

Town Meeting
The governing authority of a New England town. Qualified voters may participate in the election of officers and in the passage of legislation.

Town Manager System
A form of city government in which voters elect three selectpersons, who then appoint a professional town manager, who in turn appoints other officials.

Selectperson
A member of the governing group of a town.

Township
A rural unit of government based on federal land surveys of the American frontier in the 1780s. Townships have declined significantly in importance.

Unincorporated Area
An area not located within the boundary of a municipality.

TABLE 18-2

Local Governments
in the United States

Counties	3,043
Municipalities (mainly cities and towns)	19,372
Townships (less extensive powers)	16,629
Special districts (water supply, fire protection, hospitals, libraries, parks and recreation, highways, sewers, and so on)	34,683
School districts	13,726
Total	87,453

SOURCE: U.S. Bureau of the Census, *Statistical Abstract of the United States, 2000* (Washington, D.C.: U.S. Government Printing Office, 2000).

way to describe their operation in summary form. Indeed, the county has been called by one scholar "the dark continent of American politics."[9]

Towns and Townships.   A unique governmental creation in the New England states is the **New England town**—not to be confused with the word *town* when used as just another name for a city. In Maine, Massachusetts, New Hampshire, Vermont, and Connecticut, the unit called the town combines the roles of city and county in one governing unit. A New England town typically consists of one or more urban settlements and the surrounding rural areas. Consequently, counties have little importance in New England. In Connecticut, for example, they are simply geographic units.

From the New England town is derived the tradition of the **town meeting**, an annual meeting at which direct democracy was—and continues to be—practiced. Each resident of a town is summoned to the annual meeting at the town hall. Those who attend levy taxes, pass laws, elect town officers, and appropriate money for different activities.

Normally, few residents show up for town meetings today unless an item of high interest is on the agenda or unless family members want to be elected to office. The town meeting takes a day or more, and few citizens are able to set aside such a large amount of time. Because of the declining interest in town meetings, many New England towns have adopted a **town manager system:** the voters simply elect three **selectpersons,** who then appoint a professional town manager. The town manager in turn appoints other officials.

Townships operate somewhat like counties. Where they exist, there may be several dozen within a county. They perform the same functions that the county would otherwise perform. Indiana, Iowa, Kansas, Michigan, Minnesota, New Jersey, New York, Ohio, Pennsylvania, and Wisconsin all have numerous townships. A township is not the same thing as a New England town, because it is meant to be a rural government rather than a city government. Moreover, it is never the principal unit of local government, as are New England towns. The boundaries of most townships are based on federal land surveys that began in the 1780s, mapping the land into six-mile squares called townships. They were then subdivided into thirty-six blocks of one square mile each, called sections. Along the boundaries of each section, a road was built.

Although townships have few functions left to perform in many parts of the nation, they are still politically important in others. In some metropolitan areas, townships are the political unit that provides most public services to residents who live in suburban **unincorporated areas.**

Special Districts and School Districts.   The most numerous local government units are special districts. Currently, there are nearly thirty-five thousand special districts (see Table 18–2). Special districts are one-function governments that usually are created by the state legislature and governed by a board of directors. Special districts may be called authorities, boards, corporations—or simply districts.

One important feature of special districts is that they cut across geographic and governmental boundaries. Sometimes special districts even cut across state lines. For example, the Port of New York Authority was established by an interstate compact between New Jersey and New York in 1921 to develop and operate the harbor facilities in the area. A mosquito control district may cut across both municipal and county lines. A metropolitan transit district may provide bus service to dozens of municipalities and to several counties.

---

[9]Henry S. Gilbertson, *The County, the "Dark Continent of American Politics"* (New York: National Short Ballot Association, 1917).

A billboard in Blue Earth, Minnesota, supports a referendum to increase taxes to pay for a new school. There are over 13,000 school districts in the United States today.

School districts, although listed separately in Table 18–2, are essentially a type of special district. Except for school districts, the typical citizen is not very aware of most special districts. Indeed, most citizens do not know who furnishes their weed control, mosquito control, water, or sewage control. Part of the reason for the low profile of special districts is that most special district administrators are appointed, not elected, and therefore receive little public attention.

Consolidation of Governments

With over eighty thousand separate and often overlapping governmental units within the United States, the trend toward consolidation in recent years is understandable. **Consolidation** is the union of two or more governmental units to form a single unit. Typically, a state constitution or a state statute will designate consolidation procedures.

Consolidation is often recommended for metropolitan-area problems, but to date there have been few consolidations within metropolitan areas. The most successful consolidations have been **functional consolidations**—particularly of city and county police, health, and welfare departments. In some cases, functional consolidation is a satisfactory alternative to the complete consolidation of governmental units. The most successful form of functional consolidation was started in 1957 in Dade County, Florida. The county government, now called Miami-Dade, is a union of twenty-six municipalities. Each municipality has its own governmental entity, but the county government has the authority to furnish water, planning, mass transit, and police services and to set minimum standards of performance. The governing body of Miami-Dade is an elected board of county commissioners, which appoints an executive mayor. (Miami-Dade mayor Alex Penelas recently made national headlines because of his actions in the Elian Gonzalez case—see this chapter's *An Ethical Issue: The Defiant Ones* on the next page for details.)

A special type of consolidation is the **council of government (COG),** a voluntary organization of counties and municipalities that attempts to tackle areawide problems. More than two hundred COGs have been established, mainly since 1966. The impetus for their establishment was, and continues to be, federal government

Consolidation
The union of two or more governmental units to form a single unit.

Functional Consolidation
The cooperation of two or more units of local government in providing services to their inhabitants.

Council of Government (COG)
A voluntary organization of counties and municipalities concerned with areawide problems.

grants. COGs are an alternative means of treating major regional problems that various communities are unwilling to tackle on a consolidated basis either by true consolidation of governmental units or by functional consolidation.

The power of COGs is advisory only. Each member unit simply selects its council representatives, who report back to the unit after COG meetings. Nonetheless, today several COGs have begun to have considerable influence on regional policy. These include the Metropolitan Washington Council of Governments, the Supervisors' Inter-County Commission in Detroit, and the Association of Bay Area Governments in San Francisco.

How Municipalities Are Governed

We can divide municipal representative governments into four general types of plans: (1) the commission plan, (2) the council-manager plan, (3) the mayor-administrator plan, and (4) the mayor-council plan.

The Commission Plan.   The commission form of municipal government consists of a commission of three to nine members who have both legislative and executive powers. The salient aspects of the commission plan are as follows:

1. Executive and legislative powers are concentrated in a small group of individuals, who are elected at large on a (normally) nonpartisan ballot.

2. Each commissioner is individually responsible for heading a particular municipal department, such as the department of public safety.

an ethical issue

The Defiant Ones

Miami–Dade County (Florida) mayor Alex Penelas, surrounded by more than twenty other local politicians, spoke with conviction. "It is very clear," he said, "that we will not lend our respective resources—police or otherwise—to assist the federal government in any way, shape, or form to repatriate Elian Gonzalez to Cuba." If any violence were to break out in the community over the next few days, the mayor added, "we are holding the federal government responsible."

Six-year-old Elian Gonzalez was found floating in an inner tube off the coast of South Florida on Thanksgiving Day, 1999. His mother and stepfather had died in an attempt to reach Miami from Cuba. Elian was allowed to stay with relatives in Miami on a temporary basis. Eventually, however, the Immigration and Naturalization Service (INS) and the U.S. Department of Justice decided that U.S. law required Elian to be returned to the care of his father, who still lived in Cuba. In response, members of Miami's Cuban exile community formed a "human chain" around the home where Elian was staying.

THE ETHICAL DEBATE

Penelas and other community members felt that they were ethically justified in their stance against the federal government. To send the boy back to live under the Communist regime of Fidel Castro—known in Cuban sections of Miami as "Castro's hell"— would be unconscionable, regardless of federal law. They saw

themselves walking in the footsteps of Martin Luther King, Jr., and others in the civil rights movement who used civil disobedience to bring national attention to unjust laws.

The majority of Miami's non-Cuban population disagreed. They did not see the INS's efforts to return a boy to his father as unjust. Penelas was heavily criticized for his statements, which seemed to hint that Miami police would stand idle in the face of civil unrest. To give the incident historical perspective, commentators raised the image of Orval Faubus, the Arkansas governor who ignored federal law by failing to provide police protection for the first African American student to enter Little Rock's Central High School in 1957.

WAS IT JUST POLITICS?

Some observers believe that Penelas and his peers were acting with an eye toward politics rather than ethics. Among Miami's politically active Cuban American community, more than 90 percent of those polled did not want to see Elian go back to Cuba. If the mayor had cooperated with the federal government, his political future in Miami might well have been in jeopardy. Penelas, for his part, insisted that he was not supporting violence. He also stressed that he was acting out of concern for Elian's well-being. "It's not about politics," Penelas said. "It's about how you feel."

FOR CRITICAL ANALYSIS

Under what circumstances, if any, do you believe local politicians are justified in resisting or ignoring the laws of the United States?

3. The commission is collectively responsible for passing ordinances and controlling spending.
4. The mayor (an office that is only ceremonial) is selected from the members of the commission.

The commission plan, originating in Galveston, Texas, in 1901, had its greatest popularity during the first twenty years of the twentieth century. It appealed to municipal government reformers. They looked on it as a type of business organization that would eliminate the problems they believed to be inherent in the long ballot and in partisan municipal politics. Unfortunately, vesting both legislative and executive power in the hands of a small group of individuals means that there are no checks and balances on administration and spending. Also, because the mayoral office is ceremonial, there is no provision for strong leadership. Not surprisingly, only about one hundred cities today use the commission plan—Tulsa, Salt Lake City, Mobile, Topeka, and Atlantic City are a few of them.

The Council-Manager Plan.   In the council-manager form of municipal government, a city council appoints a professional manager, who acts as the chief executive. He or she typically is called the city manager. In principle, the manager is there simply to see that the general directions of the city council are carried out. The important features of the council-manager plan are as follows:

1. A professional, trained manager can hire and fire subordinates and is responsible to the council.
2. The council or commission consists of five to seven members, elected at large on a nonpartisan ballot.
3. The mayor may be chosen from within the council or from outside, but he or she has no executive function. As with the commission plan, the mayor's job is largely ceremonial. The city manager works for the council, not the mayor (unless, of course, the mayor is part of the council).

Today, about two thousand cities use the council-manager plan. About one-third of the cities with populations of more than 5,000 and about one-half of the cities with populations of more than 25,000 operate with this type of plan. Only four large cities with populations of more than 500,000—Cincinnati, Dallas, San Antonio, and San Diego—have adopted this plan.

The major defect of the council-manager scheme, as with the commission plan, is that there is no single, strong political executive leader. It is therefore not surprising that large cities rarely use such a plan.

The Mayor-Administrator Plan.   The mayor-administrator plan is often used in large cities where there is a strong mayor. It is similar to the council-manager plan except that the political leadership is vested in the mayor. The mayor is an elected chief executive. She or he appoints an administrative officer, whose function is to free the mayor from routine administrative tasks, such as personnel direction and budget supervision.

The Mayor-Council Plan.   The mayor-council form of municipal government is the oldest and most widely used. The mayor is an elected chief executive, and the council is the legislative body. Virtually all councils are unicameral except in Everett, Massachusetts. There are typically five to nine members of the council except in very large cities, such as Chicago, which has fifty members. Council members are popularly elected for terms as long as six, but normally four, years.

The mayor-council plan can either be a strong-mayor type or a weak-mayor type. In the *strong mayor–council plan,* the mayor is the chief executive and has virtually complete control over hiring and firing employees, as well as preparing the budget. The mayor exercises strong and positive leadership in the

DID YOU KNOW... That because Texas was the only state to enter the Union after having sovereign status, it is the only state that can fly its state flag at the same height as the U.S. flag**?**

Patronage
Rewarding faithful party workers and followers with government employment and contracts.

formation of city policies. The *weak mayor–council plan* separates executive and legislative functions completely. The mayor is elected as chief executive officer; the council is elected as the legislative body. This traditional division of powers allows for checks and balances on spending and administration.

About 50 percent of American cities use some form of the mayor-council plan. Most recently, the mayor-council plan has lost ground to the council-manager plan in small and middle-sized cities.

Machine versus Reform in City Politics

For much of the late nineteenth and early twentieth centuries, many major cities were run by "the machine." The machine was an integrated political organization. Each city block within the municipality had an organizer, each neighborhood had a political club, each district had a leader, and all of these parts of the machine had a boss—such as William Tweed in New York (see the feature on Tammany Hall in Chapter 9), Richard Daley in Chicago, Edward Crump in Memphis, or Tom Pendergast in Kansas City. The machine became a popular form of city political organization in the 1840s, when the first waves of European immigrants came to the United States to work in urban factories. Those individuals, often lacking the ability to communicate in English, needed help; and the machine was created to help them.[10] The urban machine drew on the support of the dominant ethnic groups to forge a strong political institution that was able to keep the boss (usually the mayor) in office year after year. The machine was oiled by **patronage**—rewarding faithful party workers and followers with government employment and contracts. The party in power was often referred to as the patronage party.[11]

According to sociologist Robert Merton, the machine offered personalized assistance to the needy, helped to establish local businesses, opened avenues of

---

[10]See Harvey W. Zorbaugh, *The Gold Coast and the Slum: A Sociological Study of Chicago's Near North Side* (Chicago: University of Chicago Press, 1929).
[11]See, for example, Harold F. Gosnell, *Machine Politics: Chicago Model* (Chicago: University of Chicago Press, 1937).

A citizen addresses the city council of the city of Gloucester, Massachusetts. What are some of the problems facing city governments today?

upward social mobility for the underprivileged, and afforded a locus of strong political authority and responsibility.[12] Others, however, viewed party machines and the behind-the-scenes government that they often involved as contrary to our principles of government. In their classic work on city politics, Edward Banfield and James Q. Wilson also gave a critical appraisal of machine politics:

> [M]achine government is, essentially, a system of organized bribery. The destruction of machines . . . permit[s] government on the basis of appropriate motives, that is, public-regarding ones. In fact it has other highly desirable consequences—especially greater honesty, impartiality, and (in routine matters) efficiency.[13]

When the last of the big-city bosses, Mayor Richard Daley of Chicago, died in December 1976, with him died an era. The big-city machine began to be in serious trouble in the 1960s, when community activists organized to work for a more professional and efficient municipal government. Soon, a government of administrators rather than politicians began to appear. Fewer offices were elective; more were appointive.

Switching from a political to an administrative form of urban government was a way to break up the centralized urban political machine. In some cities, the results have been beneficial to most citizens. In others, decentralization has gone so far that there is no strong leader who can pull together discordant factions to create and follow a coherent policy. Consequently, in cities with a greatly decentralized government typified by numerous independent commissions and boards, a lot that should be done does not get done, particularly when an areawide problem is involved. This is an especially severe problem for less economically privileged people, who used to be able to rely on machine-sponsored activities and on the machine's political clout to help them compete against wealthier citizens for a share of the city's services. Reform is in some ways a middle-class preoccupation, whereas the less advantaged may find themselves better served by machine politics.

Governing Metropolitan Areas

Large cities are often faced with problems that develop in part from a shrinking employment base. When employers move out of a city, there is a smaller tax base, and more people are out of work. Less tax revenue means less money to pay for schools and to meet other municipal obligations, including fighting crime and assisting those who are out of work. These developments feed on themselves, leading to more crime, more poverty, an even smaller job base, and other problems.

But crime, as well as such problems as traffic congestion and pollution, is not contained within municipal political boundaries. For this reason, solutions are sometimes sought by governing a metropolitan area as a whole. Annexation by a city of the surrounding suburbs is one solution; consolidation of city and county governments into one government is another. People who live in the suburbs often oppose such measures, however, particularly when they and the residents of a city are of different races or social classes, or have different political agendas.

A third attempt to deal with problems that spread beyond limited political boundaries is represented by a system of metropolitan government. With this method, a single entity, such as a county, concerns itself with the problems of an entire metropolitan area, and smaller entities, such as individual city governments, concern themselves with local matters. People who live in the suburbs

---

[12]Robert Merton, *Social Theory and Social Structure* (Glencoe, Ill.: Free Press, 1957), pp. 71–81.
[13]Edward C. Banfield and James Q. Wilson, *City Politics* (New York: Vintage Books, 1963), p. 12.

often oppose this solution, however, for the same reasons that they oppose other measures: they want to preserve their communities and lifestyles as they are.

A fourth solution is the creation of special districts, each of which is concerned with a specific service—an area's water supply or public transportation system, for example. Special districts are more popular than the other solutions, in part because they can deal with a single matter relatively more efficiently without concern for social issues or class conflict.

Paying for State and Local Government

Examining the spending habits of a household often gives relevant information about the personalities and priorities of the household members. Examination of the expenditure patterns of state and local governments likewise can be illuminating.

State and Local Government Expenditures

Table 18–3 shows state expenditures, expressed in percentages, for the latest fiscal year for which data are available. Table 18–4 shows the same data for local governments. There is a clear-cut pattern. State and city expenditures are concentrated in the areas of education, public welfare, highways, health, and police protection.

Education is the biggest category of expenditure, particularly at the local level. Contrast this expenditure pattern with that of the federal government, which allocates only about 4 percent of its budget to education. In 2000, state and local expenditures exceeded $1 trillion. Despite these expenditures, state and local governments are finding that their educational programs are not always producing the desired outcome—well-educated students. As mentioned in the chapter-opening *What If . . .* feature, several states have been implementing various types of educational reforms, such as school choice. For another example of how states are trying to improve educational achievement, see this chapter's feature *Making Waves: Taking on Tests*.

Concerned citizens meet with police and city council members regarding crime, drugs, and gang violence in Austin, Texas.

TABLE 18-3	
State Expenditures (in percentages)	
EXPENDITURE	**PERCENTAGE**
Education	31.7
Public welfare	22.4
Insurance trust	9.8
Health and hospitals	6.9
Highways	6.8
Corrections	3.3
Governmental administration	3.3
Interest on general debt	2.9
Natural resources	1.5
Utilities	.9
Police	.9
Parks and recreation	.5
Liquor stores	.3
Other	8.8

SOURCE: U.S. Bureau of the Census, 2000.

TABLE 18-4	
Local Expenditures (in percentages)	
EXPENDITURE	**PERCENTAGE**
Education	41.9
Health and hospitals	8.6
Governmental administration	5.4
Police	5.4
Public welfare	5.1
Interest on general debt	5.0
Highways	4.5
Sewerage	3.2
Housing and community development	2.8
Fire protection	2.6
Parks and recreation	2.2
Solid waste management	2.0
Corrections	1.7
Natural resources	0.4
Other	9.2

SOURCE: U.S. Bureau of the Census, 2000.

State and Local Government Revenues

State and local expenditures have to be paid for somehow. Until the twentieth century, almost all state and local expenditures were paid for by state and local revenues raised within state borders. Starting in the twentieth century, however, federal grants to state and local governmental units began to pay some of these costs.

making waves

Taking on Tests

The high school sophomore stood outside city hall in Cambridge, Massachusetts, waving a sign that read, "Be a Hero Take a Zero." Nearly three hundred "heroes" followed her advice on that spring day by refusing to take the Massachusetts Comprehensive Assessment System (MCAS). The MCAS is a standardized test that was created to evaluate students and schools. The main problem with the MCAS, wrote protester Daniel Elitzer, is that "Different people learn in different ways. Why should all students be assessed the same way?"

Standardized tests have long been used to measure student achievement. Increasingly, though, schools are requiring their students to pass such tests before they can be promoted to a higher grade or graduate from high school. Nearly twenty states now use standardized test scores to determine whether students move from one grade to the next. By 2003, students in twenty-six states, including Massachusetts, will not receive their high school diploma unless they pass a standardized exam. State education officials created the tests in response to complaints—particularly from businesses and universities—that American high school graduates do not have the basic skills needed to compete in today's economy.

The Massachusetts protesters insist that the MCAS and other, similar tests are not the answer to this problem. These protesters and other critics of such exams complain that the exams place too much emphasis on memorization at the expense of critical thinking. Such tests also discriminate against students in less rigorous school systems. Critics further worry that as a result of these testing requirements, schools will abandon subjects that are not tested, such as art and music. At least one lawmaker was listening to the Massachusetts protesters. Senator Paul Wellstone (D., Minn.) called the boycotters "very courageous" and introduced legislation in Congress to punish states that rely too heavily on standardized tests to measure student achievement.

FOR CRITICAL ANALYSIS

If you could design a plan for school improvement, how would you measure student achievement—by standardized tests or by some other means?

General Sales Tax

A tax levied as a proportion of the retail price of a commodity at the point of sale.

Property Tax

A tax on the value of real estate. This tax is limited to state and local governments and is a particularly important source of revenue for local governments.

INFOTRAC®
COLLEGE EDITION

Sales Tax No Longer Makes Sense

Figure 18–3 shows the percentages of revenues in various categories received by state and local governments. By far the most important tax at the state level is the **general sales tax.** Whereas the federal government obtains about 45 percent of its total revenues from the personal income tax, states obtain only about 16 percent in this way. By 2001, there were still seven states that did not have a personal income tax. Other taxes assessed by states include corporate income taxes and fees, permits, and licenses at both the state and local governmental level, as well as inheritance and gift taxes at the state level. At the local level, the most important tax is the **property tax.** About 90 percent of property tax revenues are raised by local governments. Generally, the types of taxes that states levy vary widely from state to state.

A tremendous amount of variation also exists in the total amounts of state and local taxes collected. Among the states receiving the highest amounts in tax revenues are California and New York. Those levying the lowest taxes are North Dakota, South Dakota, and Wyoming.

Nontax revenue includes federal grants to state and local governments. Today, federal grants to state and local governments total about $235 billion annually and provide about 20 percent of state government income. The grants are not always without "strings," however. Federal programs in such areas as education, highway construction, health care, and law enforcement may dispense cash subject to certain conditions. For example, the funds may be used only for a specific purpose or only if matching funds are contributed (see Chapter 3).

Profits generated by publicly operated businesses are another source of revenue for state and local governments. Publicly operated businesses include toll roads and bridges, as well as water, electric power, and mass transportation systems. More than a third of the states sell liquor through state-operated stores that earn profits. Other state-operated businesses include Washington's ferries and North Dakota's commercial banks. Some states receive lease payments for public lands, and some cities rent space in publicly owned buildings.

Other nontax revenue sources include court fines and interest on loans and investments. In the 1980s, state-run lotteries became an increasingly popular way to raise money. By 2001, nearly three-fourths of the states and the District of Columbia sponsored lotteries. It is expected that the rest of the states will soon follow.

FIGURE 18–3
State and Local Government Revenues

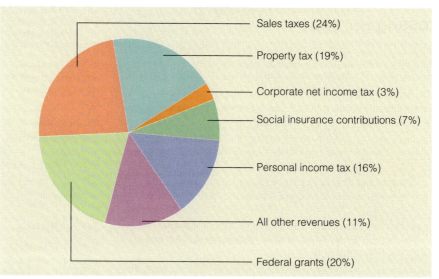

Sales taxes (24%)

Property tax (19%)

Corporate net income tax (3%)

Social insurance contributions (7%)

Personal income tax (16%)

All other revenues (11%)

Federal grants (20%)

SOURCE: U.S. Bureau of the Census, 2000.

Fiscal Policy Lessons

In the 1980s, when state budgets more than doubled, most states tried to close the gap between state income and spending by raising taxes. Many of these states continued this policy into the early 1990s. The states that approved the largest tax increases in the early 1990s, however, also approved the greatest increases in spending.

By 1999, it became clear that states' attempts to reduce their budget deficits by increasing taxes were not especially successful at lowering those deficits. In fact, many states actually harmed, rather than helped, their economies. This was the lesson learned by such states as California, Connecticut, New Jersey, Pennsylvania, and Rhode Island.

At the same time, states such as Massachusetts, Michigan, Mississippi, and Virginia attempted to balance their budgets by cutting spending instead of raising taxes. This policy proved more successful, resulting in balanced budgets and improved state economies. By the mid-1990s, many of these states were proposing state tax cuts to encourage the development of business and further improve their local economies.

By 2000, a number of states—including Arizona, California, Indiana, Minnesota, North Carolina, South Carolina, Texas, and Washington—experienced budget surpluses of half a billion dollars or more. Not surprisingly, cries for state tax cuts were heard throughout the nation. Significant state tax cuts were enacted in over one-third of the states. While the tax cuts generally did not represent major reductions in general state revenues, they did indicate a change in the trend toward ever-increasing taxes.

State and Local Government: Issues for the Twenty-First Century

The states face a broad array of problems, the solutions to which no longer can be found in Washington, D.C. Specifically, as the federal government continues to give the states more responsibilities, the states are expected to solve more problems—such as crime, education, and welfare—than they had in previous years. At the same time, some states are attempting to lure population and businesses by reducing taxes. The friction between the need to solve problems and the need to expand the business base will continue to challenge state governments for years to come. As e-commerce expands, the states and the national government will have to decide how sales of goods over the Internet will be taxed. As discussed in Chapter 16, the outcome of this debate will have a significant impact on state revenues.

Local governments will continue to be expected to solve the local problems of crime, pollution, congestion, and the like. Many municipalities have seen their tax bases decline as residents move to the suburbs. Nonetheless, fiscal help from the state and federal governments is less available today than ever before. Consequently, local governments must continue to seek ways to streamline the provision of public services, perhaps by more contracting out or by better management.

State and local governments also will continue to search for new ways to meet the pressing challenge of how to improve the quality of education and at the same time keep educational expenditures in check. States across the nation are experimenting with various systems, including school vouchers (discussed in this chapter's *What If . . .*), in their attempt to meet this challenge. How the states resolve the educational issues confronting them certainly will have a significant effect on America's future electorate.

making a difference

Learning about Local Politics and Government in Your Community

What government does or fails to do in the areas of education, health, employment, and crime affects you, your family, and your friends. Your sense of adventure, concern, curiosity, or injustice may urge you to take an active part in the government of a society with which you might not be particularly content. Yet getting involved on the national level may seem complicated, and national issues may not be of immediate concern. You may not even know exactly where you stand on many of those issues.

Every week, however, decisions are being made in your community that directly affect your local environment, transportation, education, health, employment, rents, schools, utility rates, freedom from crime, and overall quality of life. The local level is a good place to begin discovering who you are politically.

Many neighborhoods have formed neighborhood associations for the purposes of protecting their interests. One way to learn about issues that directly affect you (such as whether a street in your neighborhood should be widened or a park created) is to attend a local neighborhood association meeting. Another way to familiarize yourself with local political issues is to attend a city council meeting. Think about the issues being discussed. How do these issues and their outcomes concern you as an individual? What is your position on each issue?

If you are interested in education and educational reform, you can attend a school board meeting. Typically, the board will devote a substantial amount of time to budgetary decisions. Pay close attention to how the board feels school funds should be allocated. What are the board's primary concerns and priorities? Do you agree with the board's views? Find out if the school district is considering proposals to implement innovative educational programs.

Virtually all communities have groups that are working to improve the environment at the state or local level. At the local level, environmental issues may concern efforts to beautify the city (by restricting billboards or yard signs, for example) or to implement recycling programs to control waste. State environmental organizations may need volunteers to go door-to-door in your community to distribute information on their lobbying efforts before the state legislature, to gather signatures for petitions, and the like. If you look in the Yellow Pages under "Environment" or "Environmental," you probably will find a listing of several local and state organizations to contact.

Getting involved in a campaign for a local or state office is another way to learn about political issues that affect your community or your state. You also can participate at the local level in campaigns by candidates seeking national office, such as candidates running for Congress. Working at the "grassroots" level for a political candidate gives you firsthand knowledge of how the politics of democracy actually work.

Finally, to observe the judicial branch of government at work, you can observe proceedings in your local courts. An important court at the local level is the small claims court. Small claims courts hear disputes involving claims under a certain amount, such as $1,000 or $2,500 (the amount varies from state to state). Lawyers are not required, and many small claims courts do not permit lawyers. Other local courts are described in Figure 18–2 on page 589. For information on your local courts and on when you can attend court proceedings, call the courthouse clerk.

A recycling program in Portland, Oregon, is an example of a local government's successful effort in tackling of a policy problem.

Key terms

charter 593

consolidation 595

constitutional initiative 581

Cooley's rule 593

council of government (COG) 595

county 593

Dillon's rule 592

functional consolidation 595

general law city 593

general sales tax 602

home rule city 593

item veto 583

legislative initiative 586

municipal home rule 593

New England town 594

patronage 598

police power 580

property tax 602

recall 587

referendum 586

selectperson 594

town manager system 594

town meeting 594

township 594

unincorporated area 594

Chapter summary

1 The United States has more than eighty-seven thousand separate governmental units. State and local governments perform a wide variety of highly visible functions, such as education, police and fire protection, and so on.

2 Under the U.S. Constitution, powers not delegated expressly to the federal government are reserved to the states. The states may exercise taxing, spending, and general police powers. State constitutions are often very long, owing to the desire of their framers to include much of what we would consider statutory law because of a loss of popular confidence in state legislatures at the end of the nineteenth century. Other reasons include state courts' reluctance to interpret state constitutions as freely as the United States Supreme Court interprets the U.S. Constitution.

3 In colonial America, the governors of the colonies were vested with extensive powers. Following the Revolutionary War, most states established forms of government in which the governor was given extremely limited powers. After Andrew Jackson's presidency, however, all governors (except in South Carolina) were elected directly by the people. Most governors have the right to exercise some sort of veto power; some enjoy item veto power.

4 State legislatures deal with matters such as taxes, schools, highways, and welfare. They also must redraw state and federal legislative districts each decade to ensure that every person's vote is roughly equal to that of others

and that minorities are adequately represented in both the state legislature and Congress. Voters may exercise some direct control over state government through the use of the initiative, referendum, and recall. Every state has its own court system. Most such systems have several levels of courts—including trial courts, intermediate courts of appeal, and a supreme court.

5 There are over nineteen thousand municipalities in the United States, most of which are small cities. The more than three thousand counties in this country are merely extensions of state authority and apply state laws at the local level. Many of the functions of municipalities and counties are combined in towns or townships, particularly in the New England area. Municipalities may be governed by a commission consisting of members with executive and legislative powers, or they may be administered according to a council-manager, mayor-administrator, or mayor-council plan. Most major cities used to be run by political machines, which freely dispensed favors to supporters. In recent decades, however, machine politics has fallen into disfavor, particularly among the middle class.

6 State and local government spending is concentrated in the areas of education, public welfare, highways, health, and police protection. State services are funded primarily by sales taxes, whereas local services are financed by property taxes.

Selected print and electronic resources

SUGGESTED READINGS

Banfield, Edward C., and James Q. Wilson. *City Politics.* New York: Vintage Books, 1963. A classic work describing competing interests and ideas in city life.

Bartlett, Randall. *The Crisis of America's Cities.* New York: M. E. Sharpe, 1999. This book offers a colorful overview of America's urban history and the crises facing metropolitan areas today. The author predicts that cities will continue to lose jobs, population, and economic activity to suburbs and "edge cities" on their peripheries.

Coppa, Frank J. *County Government: A Guide to Efficient and Accountable Government.* Westport, Conn.: Praeger, 2000. The author gives an excellent review of the historical foundations of county government in the United States. In addition, he shows how charter reform can address the issues that face local governments.

Solamine, Michael E., and James L. Walker. *Respecting State Courts: The Inevitability of Judicial Federalism.* Westport, Conn.: Greenwood Press, 1999. The authors make a case for

the value of judicial federalism—the division of judicial power between the federal and state court systems. They emphasize the important role played by state courts in implementing federal civil rights, interpreting their own state constitutions, and dealing with special problems, such as the death penalty.

Waste, Robert J. *Independent Cities: Rethinking U.S. Urban Policy.* Cambridge, Mass.: Harvard University Press, 1998. Public-policy specialist Robert Waste examines the problems confronting American cities and appraises solutions ranging from revamping current policies to implementing radical new approaches.

MEDIA RESOURCES

Can the States Do It Better?—A program examining devolution—shifting federal powers back to the states—and what this means for the states with respect to, among other things, school reform.

The Last Hurrah—A film based, in part, on the career of James Curley (1874–1958) of Massachusetts, who played a leading role in creating and running Boston's political machine in the first half of the twentieth century. When Curley was convicted of mail fraud and sent to prison in 1947, he refused to resign as mayor and maintained his office while in jail.

Our Town—A 1980 film based on Thornton Wilder's play about day-to-day life and politics in a small, picturesque community—Peterborough ("Grover's Corners" in the play) in New Hampshire.

Logging on

If you are interested in state law codes (statutes) and state court cases, go to

http://www.findlaw.com/ casecode/state.html

Information on state governments, including their constitutional powers, education, and finances, can be accessed online at

http://www.vote-smart.org/reference/primer

Another excellent source for information on state governments is the following Web site:

http://www.statesnews.org

You can access the *Book of the States,* a biennial publication of the Council of State Governments from this site, or access it directly at

http://www.statesnews.org/publications/bos.html

The National Governors Association offers a wide variety of information on issues and data relating to state governments at

http://www.nga.org

The National Conference of State Legislators is a good source for state information as well. Its URL is

http://www.ncsl.org

You can find a wealth of data on state and local governments at the "Map Stats" site of the U.S. Census Bureau by simply clicking on states and counties on the maps. Go to

http://www.census.gov/datamap/www/index.html

Piper Resources offers a Web site with numerous links to state and local government resources. You can access this site at

http://www.piperinfo.com/index.cfm

Using the Internet for political analysis

As you are aware, each state has its own approach to taxation, government, and the work force. Go to the home pages of several different states, and then try to find their departments of economic development. Compare how states describe their tax advantages and other virtues to try to "sell" themselves to businesses that are relocating. Seek out the sales pitches that the states make for new businesses and then compare these marketing efforts across states. Which state do you think would be most favorable to business? Which states are able to offer the best business climate? Which states have few advantages for business? How does the political climate in a state influence its business climate? Do the states make a serious effort to attract workers or those with other, nonbusiness interests?

appendix A

The Declaration of Independence

In Congress, July 4, 1776

A Declaration by the Representatives of the United States of America, in General Congress assembled. When in the Course of human Events, it becomes necessary for one People to dissolve the Political Bands which have connected them with another, and to assume among the Powers of the Earth, the separate and equal Station to which the Laws of Nature and of Nature's God entitle them, a decent Respect to the Opinions of Mankind requires that they should declare the causes which impel them to the Separation.

We hold these Truths to be self-evident, that all Men are created equal, that they are endowed by their Creator with certain unalienable Rights, that among these are Life, Liberty, and the Pursuit of Happiness—That to secure these Rights, Governments are instituted among Men, deriving their just Powers from the Consent of the Governed, that whenever any Form of Government becomes destructive of these Ends, it is the Right of the People to alter or to abolish it, and to institute new Government, laying its Foundation on such Principles, and organizing its Powers in such Forms, as to them shall seem most likely to effect their Safety and Happiness. Prudence, indeed, will dictate that Governments long established should not be changed for light and transient Causes; and accordingly all Experience hath shewn, that Mankind are more disposed to suffer, while Evils are sufferable, than to right themselves by abolishing the Forms to which they are accustomed. But when a long Train of Abuses and Usurpations, pursuing invariably the same Object, evinces a Design to reduce them under absolute Despotism, it is their Right, it is their Duty, to throw off such Government, and to provide new Guards for their future Security. Such has been the patient Sufferance of these Colonies; and such is now the Necessity which constrains them to alter their former Systems of Government. The History of the present King of Great-Britain is a History of repeated Injuries and Usurpations, all having in direct Object the Establishment of an absolute Tyranny over these States. To prove this, let Facts be submitted to a candid World.

He has refused his Assent to Laws, the most wholesome and necessary for the public Good.

He has forbidden his Governors to pass Laws of immediate and pressing Importance, unless suspended in their Operation till his Assent should be obtained; and when so suspended, he has utterly neglected to attend to them.

He has refused to pass other Laws for the Accommodation of large Districts of People, unless those People would relinquish the Right of Representation in the Legislature, a Right inestimable to them, and formidable to Tyrants only.

He has called together Legislative Bodies at Places unusual, uncomfortable, and distant from the Depository of their Public Records, for the sole Purpose of fatiguing them into Compliance with his Measures.

He has dissolved Representative Houses repeatedly, for opposing with manly Firmness his Invasions on the Rights of the People.

He has refused for a long Time, after such Dissolutions, to cause others to be elected; whereby the Legislative Powers, incapable of Annihilation, have returned to the People at large for their exercise; the State remaining in the mean time exposed to all the Dangers of Invasion from without, and Convulsions within.

He has endeavoured to prevent the Population of these States; for that Purpose obstructing the Laws for Naturalization of Foreigners; refusing to pass others to encourage their Migrations hither, and raising the Conditions of new Appropriations of Lands.

He has obstructed the Administration of Justice, by refusing his Assent to Laws for establishing Judiciary Powers.

He has made Judges dependent on his Will alone, for the Tenure of their offices, and the Amount and payment of their Salaries.

He has erected a Multitude of new Offices, and sent hither Swarms of Officers to harrass our People, and eat out their Substance.

He has kept among us, in Times of Peace, Standing Armies, without the consent of our Legislatures.

He has affected to render the Military independent of, and superior to the Civil Power.

He has combined with others to subject us to a Jurisdiction foreign to our Constitution, and unacknowledged by our Laws; giving his Assent to their Acts of pretended Legislation:

For quartering large Bodies of Armed Troops among us:

For protecting them, by a mock Trial, from Punishment for any Murders which they should commit on the Inhabitants of these States:

For cutting off our Trade with all Parts of the World:

For imposing Taxes on us without our Consent:

For depriving us, in many cases, of the Benefits of Trial by Jury:

For transporting us beyond Seas to be tried for pretended Offences:

For abolishing the free System of English Laws in a neighbouring Province, establishing therein an arbitrary Government, and enlarging its Boundaries, so as to render it at once an Example and fit Instrument for introducing the same absolute Rule into these Colonies:

For taking away our Charters, abolishing our most valuable Laws, and altering fundamentally the Forms of our Governments:

For suspending our own Legislatures, and declaring themselves invested with Power to legislate for us in all Cases whatsoever.

He has abdicated Government here, by declaring us out of his Protection and waging War against us.

He has plundered our Seas, ravaged our Coasts, burnt our towns, and destroyed the Lives of our People.

He is, at this Time, transporting large Armies of foreign Mercenaries to compleat the works of Death, Desolation, and Tyranny, already begun with circumstances of Cruelty and Perfidy, scarcely paralleled in the most barbarous Ages, and totally unworthy the Head of a civilized Nation.

He has constrained our fellow Citizens taken Captive on the high Seas to bear Arms against their Country, to become the Executioners of their Friends and Brethren, or to fall themselves by their Hands.

He has excited domestic Insurrections amongst us, and has endeavoured to bring on the Inhabitants of our Frontiers, the merciless Indian Savages, whose known Rule of Warfare, is an undistinguished Destruction, of all Ages, Sexes and Conditions.

In every state of these Oppressions we have Petitioned for Redress in the most humble Terms: Our repeated Petitions have been answered only by repeated Injury. A Prince, whose Character is thus marked by every act which may define a Tyrant, is unfit to be the Ruler of a free People.

Nor have we been wanting in Attentions to our British Brethren. We have warned them from Time to Time of Attempts by their Legislature to extend an unwarrantable Jurisdiction over us. We have reminded them of the Circumstances of our Emigration and Settlement here. We have appealed to their native Justice and Magnanimity, and we have conjured them by the Ties of our common Kindred to disavow these Usurpations, which, would inevitably interrupt our Connections and Correspondence. They too have been deaf to the Voice of Justice and of Consanguinity. We must, therefore, acquiesce in the Necessity, which denounces our Separation, and hold them, as we hold the rest of Mankind, Enemies in War, in Peace, Friends.

We, therefore, the Representatives of the UNITED STATES OF AMERICA, in General Congress Assembled, appealing to the Supreme Judge of the World for the Rectitude of our Intentions, do, in the Name, and by the Authority of the good People of these Colonies, solemnly Publish and Declare, That these United Colonies are, and of Right ought to be, Free and Independent States; that they are absolved from all Allegiance to the British Crown, and that all political Connection between them and the State of Great-Britain, is and ought to be totally dissolved; and that as Free and Independent States, they have full Power to levy War, conclude Peace, contract Alliances, establish Commerce, and to do all other Acts and Things which Independent States may of right do. And for the support of this declaration, with a firm Reliance on the Protection of divine Providence, we mutually pledge to each other our lives, our Fortunes, and our sacred Honor.

appendix B

How to Read Case Citations and Find Court Decisions

Many important court cases are discussed in references in footnotes throughout this book. Court decisions are recorded and published. When a court case is mentioned, the notation that is used to refer to, or to cite, the case denotes where the published decision can be found.

State courts of appeals decisions are usually published in two places, the state reports of that particular state and the more widely used *National Reporter System* published by West Publishing Company. Some states no longer publish their own reports. The *National Reporter System* divides the states into the following geographic areas: Atlantic (A. or A.2d, where *2d* refers to *Second Series*), South Eastern (S.E. or S.E.2d), South Western (S.W. or S.W.2d), North Western (N.W. or N.W.2d), North Eastern (N.E. or N.E.2d), Southern (So. or So.2d), and Pacific (P. or P.2d).

Federal trial court decisions are published unofficially in *West's Federal Supplement* (F.Supp.), and opinions from the circuit courts of appeals are reported unofficially in West's *Federal Reporter* (F., F.2d, or F.3d). Opinions from the United States Supreme Court are reported in the *United States Reports* (U.S.), the *Lawyers' Edition of the Supreme Court Reports* (L.Ed.), West's *Supreme Court Reporter* (S.Ct.), and other publications. The *United States Reports* is the official publication of United States Supreme Court decisions. It is published by the federal government. Many early decisions are missing from these volumes. The citations of the early volumes of the *U.S. Reports* include the names of the actual reporters, such as Dallas, Cranch, or Wheaton. *McCulloch v. Maryland,* for example, is cited as 17 U.S. (4 Wheat.) 316. Only after 1874 did the present

citation system, in which cases are cited based solely on their volume and page numbers in the *United States Reports,* come into being. The *Lawyers' Edition of the Supreme Court Reports* is an unofficial and more complete edition of Supreme Court decisions. West's *Supreme Court Reporter* is an unofficial edition of decisions dating from October 1882. These volumes contain headnotes and numerous brief editorial statements of the law involved in the case.

State courts of appeals decisions are cited by giving the name of the case; the volume, name, and page number of the state's official report (if the state publishes its own reports); the volume, unit, and page number of the *National Reporter;* and the volume, name, and page number of any other selected reporter. Federal court citations are also listed by giving the name of the case and the volume, name and page number of the reports. In addition to the citation, this textbook lists the year of the decision in parentheses. Consider, for example, the case *United States v. Curtiss-Wright Export Co.,* 299 U.S. 304 (1936). The Supreme Court's decision of this case may be found in volume 299 of the *United States Reports* on page 304. The case was decided in 1936.

Today, many courts, including the United States Supreme Court, publish their opinions online. This makes it much easier for students to find and read cases, or summaries of cases, that have significant consequences for American government and politics. To access cases via the Internet, use the URLs given in the *Logging on* at the end of Chapter 15.

appendix C

Presidents of the United States

	Term of Service	Age at Inauguration	Political Party	College or University	Occupation or Profession
1. George Washington	1789–1797	57	None		Planter
2. John Adams	1797–1801	61	Federalist	Harvard	Lawyer
3. Thomas Jefferson	1801–1809	57	Democratic-Republican	William and Mary	Planter, Lawyer
4. James Madison	1809–1817	57	Democratic-Republican	Princeton	Lawyer
5. James Monroe	1817–1825	58	Democratic-Republican	William and Mary	Lawyer
6. John Quincy Adams	1825–1829	57	Democratic-Republican	Harvard	Lawyer
7. Andrew Jackson	1829–1837	61	Democrat		Lawyer
8. Martin Van Buren	1837–1841	54	Democrat		Lawyer
9. William H. Harrison	1841	68	Whig	Hampden-Sydney	Soldier
10. John Tyler	1841–1845	51	Whig	William and Mary	Lawyer
11. James K. Polk	1845–1849	49	Democrat	U. of N. Carolina	Lawyer
12. Zachary Taylor	1849–1850	64	Whig		Soldier
13. Millard Fillmore	1850–1853	50	Whig		Lawyer
14. Franklin Pierce	1853–1857	48	Democrat	Bowdoin	Lawyer
15. James Buchanan	1857–1861	65	Democrat	Dickinson	Lawyer
16. Abraham Lincoln	1861–1865	52	Republican		Lawyer
17. Andrew Johnson	1865–1869	56	Nat/I. Union†		Tailor
18. Ulysses S. Grant	1869–1877	46	Republican	U.S. Mil. Academy	Soldier
19. Rutherford B. Hayes	1877–1881	54	Republican	Kenyon	Lawyer
20. James A. Garfield	1881	49	Republican	Williams	Lawyer
21. Chester A. Arthur	1881–1885	51	Republican	Union	Lawyer
22. Grover Cleveland	1885–1889	47	Democrat		Lawyer
23. Benjamin Harrison	1889–1893	55	Republican	Miami	Lawyer
24. Grover Cleveland	1893–1897	55	Democrat		Lawyer
25. William McKinley	1897–1901	54	Republican	Allegheny College	Lawyer
26. Theodore Roosevelt	1901–1909	42	Republican	Harvard	Author
27. William H. Taft	1909–1913	51	Republican	Yale	Lawyer
28. Woodrow Wilson	1913–1921	56	Democrat	Princeton	Educator
29. Warren G. Harding	1921–1923	55	Republican		Editor
30. Calvin Coolidge	1923–1929	51	Republican	Amherst	Lawyer
31. Herbert C. Hoover	1929–1933	54	Republican	Stanford	Engineer
32. Franklin D. Roosevelt	1933–1945	51	Democrat	Harvard	Lawyer
33. Harry S. Truman	1945–1953	60	Democrat		Businessman
34. Dwight D. Eisenhower	1953–1961	62	Republican	U.S. Mil. Academy	Soldier
35. John F. Kennedy	1961–1963	43	Democrat	Harvard	Author
36. Lyndon B. Johnson	1963–1969	55	Democrat	Southwest Texas State	Teacher
37. Richard M. Nixon	1969–1974	56	Republican	Whittier	Lawyer
38. Gerald R. Ford‡	1974–1977	61	Republican	Michigan	Lawyer
39. James E. Carter, Jr.	1977–1981	52	Democrat	U.S. Naval Academy	Businessman
40. Ronald W. Reagan	1981–1989	69	Republican	Eureka College	Actor
41. George H. W. Bush	1989–1993	64	Republican	Yale	Businessman
42. Bill Clinton	1993–2001	46	Democrat	Georgetown	Lawyer
43. George W. Bush	2001–	54	Republican	Harvard	Businessman

*Church preference; never joined any church.
†The National Union Party consisted of Republicans and War Democrats. Johnson was a Democrat.
**Inaugurated Dec. 6, 1973, to replace Agnew, who resigned Oct. 10, 1973.
‡Inaugurated Aug. 9, 1974, to replace Nixon, who resigned that same day.
§Inaugurated Dec. 19, 1974, to replace Ford, who became president Aug. 9, 1974.

appendix C

Presidents of the United States

Religion	Born	Died	Age at Death	Vice President	
1. Episcopalian	Feb. 22, 1732	Dec. 14, 1799	67	John Adams	(1789–1797)
2. Unitarian	Oct. 30, 1735	July 4, 1826	90	Thomas Jefferson	(1797–1801)
3. Unitarian*	Apr. 13, 1743	July 4, 1826	83	Aaron Burr	(1801–1805)
				George Clinton	(1805–1809)
4. Episcopalian	Mar. 16, 1751	June 28, 1836	85	George Clinton	(1809–1812)
				Elbridge Gerry	(1813–1814)
5. Episcopalian	Apr. 28, 1758	July 4, 1831	73	Daniel D. Tompkins	(1817–1825)
6. Unitarian	July 11, 1767	Feb. 23, 1848	80	John C. Calhoun	(1825–1829)
7. Presbyterian	Mar. 15, 1767	June 8, 1845	78	John C. Calhoun	(1829–1832)
				Martin Van Buren	(1833–1837)
8. Dutch Reformed	Dec. 5, 1782	July 24, 1862	79	Richard M. Johnson	(1837–1841)
9. Episcopalian	Feb. 9, 1773	Apr. 4, 1841	68	John Tyler	(1841)
10. Episcopalian	Mar. 29, 1790	Jan. 18, 1862	71		
11. Methodist	Nov. 2, 1795	June 15, 1849	53	George M. Dallas	(1845–1849)
12. Episcopalian	Nov. 24, 1784	July 9, 1850	65	Millard Fillmore	(1849–1850)
13. Unitarian	Jan. 7, 1800	Mar. 8, 1874	74		
14. Episcopalian	Nov. 23, 1804	Oct. 8, 1869	64	William R. King	(1853)
15. Presbyterian	Apr. 23, 1791	June 1, 1868	77	John C. Breckinridge	(1857–1861)
16. Presbyterian*	Feb. 12, 1809	Apr. 15, 1865	56	Hannibal Hamlin	(1861–1865)
				Andrew Johnson	(1865)
17. Methodist*	Dec. 29, 1808	July 31, 1875	66		
18. Methodist	Apr. 27, 1822	July 23, 1885	63	Schuyler Colfax	(1869–1873)
				Henry Wilson	(1873–1875)
19. Methodist*	Oct. 4, 1822	Jan. 17, 1893	70	William A. Wheeler	(1877–1881)
20. Disciples of Christ	Nov. 19, 1831	Sept. 19, 1881	49	Chester A. Arthur	(1881)
21. Episcopalian	Oct. 5, 1829	Nov. 18, 1886	57		
22. Presbyterian	Mar. 18, 1837	June 24, 1908	71	Thomas A. Hendricks	(1885)
23. Presbyterian	Aug. 20, 1833	Mar. 13, 1901	67	Levi P. Morton	(1889–1893)
24. Presbyterian	Mar. 18, 1837	June 24, 1908	71	Adlai E. Stevenson	(1893–1897)
25. Methodist	Jan. 29, 1843	Sept. 14, 1901	58	Garret A. Hobart	(1897–1899)
				Theodore Roosevelt	(1901)
26. Dutch Reformed	Oct. 27, 1858	Jan. 6, 1919	60	Charles W. Fairbanks	(1905–1909)
27. Unitarian	Sept. 15, 1857	Mar. 8, 1930	72	James S. Sherman	(1909–1912)
28. Presbyterian	Dec. 29, 1856	Feb. 3, 1924	67	Thomas R. Marshall	(1913–1921)
29. Baptist	Nov. 2, 1865	Aug. 2, 1923	57	Calvin Coolidge	(1921–1923)
30. Congregationalist	July 4, 1872	Jan. 5, 1933	60	Charles G. Dawes	(1925–1929)
31. Friend (Quaker)	Aug. 10, 1874	Oct. 20, 1964	90	Charles Curtis	(1929–1933)
32. Episcopalian	Jan. 30, 1882	Apr. 12, 1945	63	John N. Garner	(1933–1941)
				Henry A. Wallace	(1941–1945)
				Harry S. Truman	(1945)
33. Baptist	May 8, 1884	Dec. 26, 1972	88	Alben W. Barkley	(1949–1953)
34. Presbyterian	Oct. 14, 1890	Mar. 28, 1969	78	Richard M. Nixon	(1953–1961)
35. Roman Catholic	May 29, 1917	Nov. 22, 1963	46	Lyndon B. Johnson	(1961–1963)
36. Disciples of Christ	Aug. 27, 1908	Jan. 22, 1973	64	Hubert H. Humphrey	(1965–1969)
37. Friend (Quaker)	Jan. 9, 1913	Apr. 22, 1994	81	Spiro T. Agnew	(1969–1973)
				Gerald R. Ford**	(1973–1974)
38. Episcopalian	July 14, 1913			Nelson A. Rockefeller§	(1974–1977)
39. Baptist	Oct. 1, 1924			Walter F. Mondale	(1977–1981)
40. Disciples of Christ	Feb. 6, 1911			George H. W. Bush	(1981–1989)
41. Episcopalian	June 12, 1924			J. Danforth Quayle	(1989–1993)
42. Baptist	Aug. 19, 1946			Albert A. Gore	(1993–2001)
43. Methodist	July 6, 1946			Dick Cheney	(2001–)

611

appendix D

Federalist Papers No. 10, No. 51, and No. 78

In 1787, after the newly drafted U.S. Constitution was submitted to the thirteen states for ratification, a major political debate ensued between the Federalists (who favored ratification) and the Anti-Federalists (who opposed ratification). Anti Federalists in New York were particularly critical of the Constitution, and in response to their objections, Federalists Alexander Hamilton, James Madison, and John Jay wrote a series of eighty-five essays in defense of the Constitution. The essays were published in New York newspapers and reprinted in other newspapers throughout the country.

For students of American government, the essays, collectively known as The Federalist Papers, *are particularly important because they provide a glimpse of the founders' political philosophy and intentions in designing the Constitution—and, consequently, in shaping the American philosophy of government.*

We have included in this appendix three of these essays: Federalist Papers No. 10, No. 51, and No. 78. Each essay has been annotated by the authors to indicate its importance in American political thought and to clarify the meaning of particular passages.

Federalist Paper No. 10

Federalist Paper No. 10, penned by James Madison, has often been singled out as a key document in American political thought. In this essay, Madison attacks the Anti-Federalists' fear that a republican form of government will inevitably give rise to "factions"—small political parties or groups united by a common interest—that will control the government. Factions will be harmful to the country because they will implement policies beneficial to their own interests but adverse to other people's rights and to the public good.

In this essay, Madison attempts to lay to rest this fear by explaining how, in a large republic such as the United States, there will be so many different factions, held together by regional or local interests, that no single one of them will be dominate national politics.

Madison opens his essay with a paragraph discussing how important it is to devise a plan of government that can control the "instability, injustice, and confusion" brought about by factions.

Among the numerous advantages promised by a well-constructed Union, none deserves to be more accurately developed than its tendency to break and control the violence of faction. The friend of popular governments never finds himself so much alarmed for their character and fate as when he contemplates their propensity to this dangerous vice. He will not fail, therefore, to set a due value on any plan which, without violating the principles to which he is attached, provides a proper cure for it. The instability, injustice, and confusion introduced into the public councils have, in truth, been the mortal diseases under which popular governments have everywhere perished, as they continue to be the favorite and fruitful topics from which the adversaries to liberty derive their most specious declamations. The valuable improvements made by the American constitutions on the popular models, both ancient and modern, cannot certainly be too much admired; but it would be an unwarrantable partiality to contend that they have as effectually obviated the danger on this side, as was wished and expected. Complaints are everywhere heard from our most considerate and virtuous citizens, equally the friends of public and private faith and of public and personal liberty, that our governments are too unstable, that the public good is disregarded in the conflicts of rival parties, and that measures are too often decided, not according to the rules of justice and the rights of the minor party, but by the superior force of an interested and overbearing majority. However anxiously we may wish that these complaints had no foundation, the evidence of known facts will not permit us to deny that they are in some degree true. It will be found, indeed, on a candid review of our situation, that some of the distresses under which we labor have been erroneously charged on the operation of our governments; but it will be found, at the same time, that other causes will not alone account for many of our heaviest misfortunes; and, particularly, for that prevailing and increasing distrust of public engagements and alarm for private rights which are echoed from one end of the continent to the other. These must be chiefly, if not wholly, effects of the unsteadiness and injustice with which a factious spirit has tainted our public administration.

Madison now defines what he means by the term faction.

By a faction I understand a number of citizens, whether amounting to a majority or minority of the whole, who are united and actuated by some common impulse of passion, or of interest, adverse to the rights of other citizens, or the permanent and aggregate interests of the community.

Madison next contends that there are two methods by which the "mischiefs of factions" can be cured: by removing the causes of faction or by controlling their effects. In the following paragraphs, Madison explains how liberty itself nourishes factions. Therefore, to abolish factions would involve abolishing liberty—a cure "worse than the disease."

There are two methods of curing the mischiefs of faction: the one, by removing its causes; the other, by controlling its effects.

There are again two methods of removing the causes of faction: the one, by destroying the liberty which is essential to its existence; the other, by giving to every citizen the same opinions, the same passions, and the same interests.

It could never be more truly said than of the first remedy that it was worse than the disease. Liberty is to faction what air is to fire, an aliment without which it instantly expires. But it could not be a less folly to abolish liberty, which is essential to political life, because it nourishes faction than it would be to wish the annihilation of air, which is essential to animal life, because it imparts to fire its destructive agency.

The second expedient is as impracticable as the first would be unwise. As long as the reason of man continues fallible, and his is at liberty to exercise it, different opinions will be formed. As long as the connection subsists between his reason and his self-love, his opinions and his passions will have a reciprocal influence on each other; and the former will be objects to which the latter will attach themselves. The diversity in the faculties of men, from which the

rights of property originate, is not less an insuperable obstacle to a uniformity of interests. The protection of these faculties is the first object of government. From the protection of different and unequal faculties of acquiring property, the possession of different degrees and kinds of property immediately results; and from the influence of these on the sentiments and views of the respective proprietors ensues a division of the society into different interests and parties.

The latent causes of faction are thus sown in the nature of man; and we see them everywhere brought into different degrees of activity, according to the different circumstances of civil society. A zeal for different opinions concerning religion, concerning government, and many other points, as well of speculation as of practice; an attachment to different leaders ambitiously contending for pre-eminence and power; or to persons of other descriptions whose fortunes have been interesting to the human passions, have, in turn, divided mankind into parties, inflamed them with mutual animosity, and rendered them much more disposed to vex and oppress each other than to co-operate for their common good. So strong is this propensity of mankind to fall into mutual animosities that where no substantial occasion presents itself the most frivolous and fanciful distinctions have been sufficient to kindle their unfriendly passions and excite their most violent conflicts. But the most common and durable source of factions has been the various and unequal distribution of property. Those who hold and those who are without property have ever formed distinct interests in society. Those who are creditors, and those who are debtors, fall under a like discrimination. A landed interest, a manufacturing interest, a mercantile interest, a moneyed interest, with many lesser interests, grow up of necessity in civilized nations, and divide them into different classes, actuated by different sentiments and views. The regulation of these various and interfering interests forms the principal task of modern legislation and involves the spirit of party and faction in the necessary and ordinary operations of government.

No man is allowed to be a judge in his own cause, because his interest would certainly bias his judgment, and, not improbably, corrupt his integrity. With equal, nay with greater reason, a body of men are unfit to be both judges and parties at the same time; yet what are many of the most important acts of legislation but so many judicial determinations, not indeed concerning the rights of single persons, but concerning the rights of large bodies of citizens? And what are the different classes of legislators but advocates and parties to the causes which they determine? Is a law proposed concerning private debts? It is a question to which the creditors are parties on one side and the debtors on the other. Justice ought to hold the balance between them. Yet the parties are, and must be, themselves the judges; and the most numerous party, or in other words, the most powerful faction must be expected to prevail. Shall domestic manufacturers be encouraged, and in what degree, by restrictions on foreign manufacturers? Are questions which would be differently decided by the landed and the manufacturing classes, and probably by neither with a sole regard to justice and the public good. The apportionment of taxes on the various descriptions of property is an act which seems to require the most exact impartiality; yet there is, perhaps, no legislative act in which greater opportunity and temptation are given to a predominant party to trample on the rules of justice. Every shilling with which they overburden the inferior number is a shilling saved to their own pockets.

It is in vain to say that enlightened statesmen will be able to adjust these clashing interests and render them all subservient to the public good. Enlightened statesmen will not always be at the helm. Nor, in many cases, can such an adjustment be made at all without taking into view indirect and remote considerations, which will rarely prevail over the immediate interest which one party may find in disregarding the rights of another or the good of the whole.

The inference to which we are brought is that the *causes* of faction cannot be removed and that relief is only to be sought in the means of controlling its *effects*.

Having concluded that "the causes of factions cannot be removed," Madison now looks in some detail at the other method by which factions can be cured—by controlling their effects. This is the heart of his essay. He begins by positing a significant question: How can you have self-government without risking the possibility that a ruling faction, particularly a majority faction, might tyrannize over the rights of others?

If a faction consists of less than a majority, relief is supplied by the republican principle, which enables the majority to defeat its sinister views by regular vote. It may clog the administration, it may convulse the society; but it will be unable to execute and mask its violence under the forms of the Constitution. When a majority is included in a faction, the form of popular government, on the other hand, enables it to sacrifice to its ruling passion or interest both the public good and the rights of other citizens. To secure the public good and private rights against the danger of such a faction, and at the same time to preserve the spirit and the form of popular government, is then the great object to which our inquiries are directed. Let me add that it is the great desideratum by which alone this form of government can be rescued from the opprobrium under which it has so long labored and be recommended to the esteem and adoption of mankind.

Madison now sets forth the idea that one way to control the effects of factions is to ensure that the majority is rendered incapable of acting in concert in order to "carry into effect schemes of oppression." He goes on to state that in a democracy, in which all citizens participate personally in government decision making, there is no way to prevent the majority from communicating with each other and, as a result, acting in concert.

By what means is this object attainable? Evidently by one of two only. Either the existence of the same passion or interest in a majority at the same time must be prevented, or the majority, having such coexistent passion or interest, must be rendered, by their number and local situation, unable to concert and carry into effect schemes of oppression. If the impulse and the opportunity be suffered to coincide, we well know that neither moral nor religious motives can be relied on as an adequate control. They are not found to be such on the injustice and violence of individuals, and lose their efficacy in proportion to the number combined together, that is, in proportion as their efficacy becomes needful.

From this view of the subject it may be concluded that a pure democracy, by which I mean a society consisting of a small number of citizens, who assemble and administer the government in person, can admit of no cure for the mischiefs of faction. A common passion or interest will, in almost every case, be felt by a majority of the whole; a communication and concert results from the form of government itself; and there is nothing to check the inducements to sacrifice the weaker party or an obnoxious individual. Hence it is that such democracies have ever been spectacles of turbulence and contention; have ever been found incompatible with personal security or the rights of property; and have in general been as short in their lives as they have been violent in their deaths. Theoretic politicians, who have patronized this species of government, have erroneously supposed that by reducing mankind to a perfect equality in their political rights, they would at the same time be perfectly equalized and assimilated in their possessions, their opinions, and their passions.

Madison now moves on to discuss the benefits of a republic with respect to controlling the effects of factions. He begins by defining a republic and then pointing out the "two great points of difference" between a republic and a democracy: a republic is governed by a small body of elected representatives, not by the people directly; and a republic can extend over a much larger territory and embrace more citizens than a democracy can.

A republic, by which I mean a government in which the scheme of representation takes place, opens a different prospect and promises the cure for which we are seeking. Let us examine the points in which it varies from pure democracy, and we shall comprehend both the nature of the cure and the efficacy which it must derive from the Union.

The two great points of difference between a democracy and a republic are: first, the delegation of the government, in the latter, to a small number of citizens elected by the rest; secondly, the greater number of citizens and greater sphere of country over which the latter may be extended.

In the following four paragraphs, Madison explains how in a republic, particularly a large republic, the delegation of authority to elected representatives will increase the likelihood that those who govern will be "fit" for their positions and that a proper balance will be achieved between local (factional) interests and national interests. Note how he stresses that the new federal Constitution, by dividing powers between state governments and the national government, provides a "happy combination in this respect."

The effect of the first difference is, on the one hand, to refine and enlarge the public views by passing them through the medium of a chosen body of citizens, whose wisdom may best discern the true interest of their country and whose patriotism and love of justice will be least likely to sacrifice it to temporary or partial considerations. Under such a regulation it may well happen that the public voice, pronounced by the representatives of the people, will be more consonant to the public good than if pronounced by the people themselves, convened for the purpose. On the other hand, the effect may be inverted. Men of factious tempers, of local prejudices, or of sinister designs, may, by intrigue, by corruption, or by other means, first obtain the suffrages, and then betray the interests of the people. The question resulting is, whether small or extensive republics are most favorable to the election of proper guardians of the public weal; and it is clearly decided in favor of the latter by two obvious considerations.

In the first place it is to be remarked that however small the republic may be the representatives must be raised to a certain number in order to guard against the cabals of a few; and that however large it may be they must be limited to a certain number in order to guard against the confusion of a multitude. Hence, the number of representatives in the two cases not being in proportion to that of the constituents, and being proportionally greatest in the small republic, it follows that if the proportion of fit characters be not less in the large than in the small republic, the former will present a greater option, and consequently a greater probability of a fit choice.

In the next place, as each representative will be chosen by a greater number of citizens in the large than in the small republic, it will be more difficult for unworthy candidates to practice with success the vicious arts by which elections are too often carried; and the suffrages of the people being more free, will be more likely to center on men who possess the most attractive merit and the most diffusive and established characters.

It must be confessed that in this, as in most other cases, there is a mean, on both sides of which inconveniencies will be found to lie. By enlarging too much the number of electors, you render the representative too little acquainted with all their local circumstances and lesser interests; as by reducing it too much, you render him unduly attached to these, and too little fit to comprehend and pursue great and national objects. The federal Constitution forms a happy combination in this respect; the great and aggregate interests being referred to the national, the local and particular to the State legislatures.

Madison now looks more closely at the other difference between a republic and a democracy—namely, that a republic can encompass a larger territory and more citizens than a democracy can. In the remaining paragraphs of his essay, Madison concludes that in a large republic, it will be difficult for factions to act in concert. Although a factious group—religious, political, economic, or otherwise—may control a local or regional government, it will have little chance of gathering a national following. This is because in a large republic, there will be numerous other factions whose work will offset the work of any one particular faction ("sect"). As Madison phrases it, these numerous factions will "secure the national councils against any danger from that source."

The other point of difference is the greater number of citizens and extent of territory which may be brought within the compass of republican than of democratic government; and it is this circumstance principally which renders factious combinations less to be dreaded in the former than in the latter. The smaller the society, the fewer probably will be the distinct parties and interests composing it; the fewer the distinct parties and interests, the more frequently will a majority be found of the same party; and the smaller the number of individuals composing a majority, and the smaller the compass within which they are placed, the more easily will they concert and execute their plans of oppression. Extend the sphere and you take in a greater variety of parties and interests; you make it less probable that a majority of the whole will have a common motive to invade the rights of other citizens; or if such a common motive exists, it will be more difficult for all who feel it to discover their own strength and to act in unison with each other. Besides other impediments, it may be remarked that, where there is a consciousness of unjust or dishonorable purposes, communication is always checked by distrust in proportion to the number whose concurrence is necessary.

Hence, it clearly appears that the same advantage which a republic has over a democracy in controlling the effects of faction is enjoyed by a large over a small republic—is enjoyed by the Union over the States composing it. Does this advantage consist in the substitution of representatives whose enlightened views and virtuous sentiments render them superior to local prejudices and to schemes of injustice? It will not be denied that the representation of the Union will be most likely to possess these requisite endowments. Does it consist in the greater security afforded by a greater variety of parties, against the event of any one party being able to outnumber and oppress the rest? In an equal degree does the increased variety of parties comprised within the Union increase this security. Does it, in fine, consist in the greater obstacles opposed to the concert and accomplishment of the secret wishes of an unjust and interested majority? Here again the extent of the Union gives it the most palpable advantage.

The influence of factious leaders may kindle a flame within their particular States but will be unable to spread a general conflagration through the other States. A religious sect may degenerate into a political faction in a part of the Confederacy; but the variety of sects dispersed over the entire face of it must secure the national councils against any danger from that source. A rage for paper money, for an abolition of debts, for an equal division of property, or for any other improper or wicked project, will be less apt to pervade the whole body of the Union than a particular member of it, in the same proportion as such a malady is more likely to taint a particular county or district than an entire State.

In the extent and proper structure of the Union, therefore, we behold a republican remedy for the diseases most incident to republican government. And according to the degree of pleasure and pride we feel in being republicans ought to be our zeal in cherishing the spirit and supporting the character of federalists.

Publius
(James Madison)

Federalist Paper No. 51

Federalist Paper No. 51, also authored by James Madison, is another classic in American political theory. Although the Federalists wanted a strong national government, they had not abandoned the traditional American view, particularly notable during the revolutionary era, that those holding powerful government positions could not be trusted to put national interests and the common good above their own personal interests. In this essay, Madison explains why the separation of the national government's powers into three branches—executive, legislative, and judicial—and a federal structure of government offer the best protection against tyranny.

To what expedient, then, shall we finally resort, for maintaining in practice the necessary partition of power among the several departments as laid down in the Constitution? The only answer that can be given is that as all these exterior provisions are found to be inadequate the defect must be supplied, by so contriving the interior structure of the government as that its several constituent parts may, by their mutual relations, be the means of keeping each other in their proper places. Without presuming to undertake a full development of this important idea I will hazard a few general observations which may perhaps place it in a clearer light, and enable us to form a more correct judgment of the principles and structure of the government planned by the convention.

In the next two paragraphs, Madison stresses that for the powers of the different branches (departments) of government to be truly separated, the personnel in one branch should not be dependent on another branch for their appointment or for the "emoluments" (compensation) attached to their offices.

In order to lay a due foundation for that separate and distinct exercise of the different powers of government, which to a certain extent is admitted on all hands to be essential to the preservation of liberty, it is evident that each department should have a will of its own; and consequently should be so constituted that the members of each should have as little agency as possible in the appointment of the members of the others. Were this principle rigorously adhered to, it would require that all the appointments for the supreme executive, legislative, and judiciary magistracies should be drawn from the same fountain of authority, the people, through channels having no communication whatever with one another. Perhaps such a plan of constructing the several departments would be less difficult in practice than it may in contemplation appear. Some difficulties, however, and some additional expense would attend the execution of it. Some deviations, therefore, from the principle must be admitted. In the constitution of the judiciary department in particular, it might be inexpedient to insist rigorously on the principle: first, because peculiar qualifications being essential in the members, the primary consideration ought to be to select that mode of choice which best secures these qualifications; second, because the permanent tenure by which the appointments are held in that department must soon destroy all sense of dependence on the authority conferring them.

It is equally evident that the members of each department should be as little dependent as possible on those of the others for the emoluments annexed to their offices. Were the executive magistrate, or the judges, not independent of the legislature in this particular, their independence in every other would be merely nominal.

In the following passages, which are among the most widely quoted of Madison's writings, he explains how the separation of the powers of government into three branches helps to counter the effects of personal ambition on government. The separation of powers allows personal motives to be linked to the constitutional rights of a branch of government. In effect, rivaling personal interests in each branch will help to keep the powers of the three government branches separate and, in so doing, will help to guard the public interest.

But the great security against a gradual concentration of the several powers in the same department consists in giving to those who administer each department the necessary constitutional means and personal motives to resist encroachments of the others. The provision for defense must in this, as in all other cases, be made commensurate to the danger of attack. Ambition must be made to counteract ambition. The interest of the man must be connected with the constitutional rights of the place. It may be a reflection on human nature that such devices should be necessary to control the abuses of government. But what is government itself but the greatest of all reflections on human nature? If men were angels, no government would be necessary. If angels were to govern men, neither external nor internal controls on government would be necessary. In framing a government which is to be administered by men over men, the great difficulty lies in this: you must first enable the government to control the governed; and in the next place oblige it to control itself. A dependence on the people is, no doubt, the primary control on the government; but experience has taught mankind the necessity of auxiliary precautions.

This policy of supplying, by opposite and rival interests, the defect of better motives, might be traced through the whole system of human affairs, private as well as public. We see it particularly displayed in all the subordinate distributions of power, where the constant aim is to divide and arrange the several offices in such a manner as that each may be a check on the other—that the private interest of every individual may be a sentinel over the public rights. These inventions of prudence cannot be less requisite in the distribution of the supreme powers of the State.

Madison now addresses the issue of equality between the branches of government. The legislature will necessarily predominate, but if the executive is given an "absolute negative" (absolute veto power) over legislative actions, this also could lead to an abuse of power. Madison concludes that the division of the legislature into two "branches" (parts, or chambers) will act as a check on the legislature's powers.

But it is not possible to give to each department an equal power of self-defense. In republican government, the legislative authority necessarily predominates. The remedy for this inconveniency is to divide the legislature into different branches; and to render them, by different modes of election and different principles of action, as little connected with each other as the nature of their common functions and their common dependence on the society will admit. It may even be necessary to guard against dangerous encroachments by still further precautions. As the weight of the legislative authority requires that it should be thus divided, the weakness of the executive may require, on the other hand, that it should be fortified. An absolute negative on the legislature appears, at first view, to be the natural defense with which the executive magistrate should be armed. But perhaps it would be neither altogether safe nor alone sufficient. On ordinary occasions it might not be exerted with the requisite firmness, and on extraordinary

occasions it might be perfidiously abused. May not this defect of an absolute negative be supplied by some qualified connection between this weaker department and the weaker branch of the stronger department, by which the latter may be led to support the constitutional rights of the former, without being too much detached from the rights of its own department?

If the principles on which these observations are founded be just, as I persuade myself they are, and they be applied as a criterion to the several State constitutions, and to the federal Constitution, it will be found that if the latter does not perfectly correspond with them, the former are infinitely less able to bear such a test.

In the remainder of the essay, Madison discusses how a federal system of government, in which powers are divided between the states and the national government, offers "double security against tyranny.

There are, moreover, two considerations particularly applicable to the federal system of America, which place that system in a very interesting point of view.

First. In a single republic, all the power surrendered by the people is submitted to the administration of a single government; and the usurpations are guarded against by a division of the government into distinct and separate departments. In the compound republic of America, the power surrendered by the people is first divided between two distinct governments, and then the portion allotted to each subdivided among distinct and separate departments. Hence a double security arises to the rights of the people. The different governments will control each other, at the same time that each will be controlled by itself.

Second. It is of great importance in a republic not only to guard the society against the oppression of its rulers, but to guard one part of the society against the injustice of the other part. Different interests necessarily exist in different classes of citizens. If a majority be united by a common interest, the rights of the minority will be insecure. There are but two methods of providing against this evil: the one by creating a will in the community independent of the majority—that is, of the society itself; the other, by comprehending in the society so many separate descriptions of citizens as will render an unjust combination of a majority of the whole very improbable, if not impracticable. The first method prevails in all governments possessing an hereditary or self-appointed authority. This, at best, is but a precarious security; because a power independent of the society may as well espouse the unjust views of the major as the rightful interests of the minor party, and may possibly be turned against both parties. The second method will be exemplified in the federal republic of the United States. Whilst all authority in it will be derived from and dependent on the society, the society itself will be broken into so many parts, interests and classes of citizens, that the rights of individuals, or of the minority, will be in little danger from interested combinations of the majority. In a free government the security for civil rights must be the same as that for religious rights. It consists in the one case in the multiplicity of interests, and in the other in the multiplicity of sects. The degree of security in both cases will depend on the number of interests and sects; and this may be presumed to depend on the extent of country and number of people comprehended under the same government. This view of the subject must particularly recommend a proper federal system to all the sincere and considerate friends of republican government, since it shows that in exact proportion as the territory of the Union may be formed into more circumscribed Confederacies, or States, oppressive combinations of a majority will be facilitated; the best security, under the republican forms, for the rights of every class of citizen, will be diminished; and consequently the stability and independence of some member of the government, the only other security, must be proportionally increased. Justice is the end of government. It is the end of civil society. It ever has been and ever will be pursued until it be obtained, or until liberty be lost in the pursuit. In a society under the forms of which the stronger faction can readily unite and oppress the weaker, anarchy may as truly be said to reign as in a state of nature, where the weaker individual is not secured against the violence of the stronger; and as, in the latter state, even the stronger individuals are prompted, by the uncertainty of their condition, to submit to a government which may protect the weak as well as themselves; so, in the former state, will the more powerful factions or parties be gradually induced, by a like motive, to wish for a government which will protect all parties, the weaker as well as the more powerful. It can be little doubted that if the State of Rhode Island was separated from the Confederacy and left to itself, the insecurity of rights under the popular form of government within such narrow limits would be displayed by such reiterated oppressions of factious majorities that some power altogether independent of the people would soon be called for by the voice of the very factions whose misrule had proved the necessity of it. In the extended republic of the United States, and among the great variety of interests, parties, and sects which it embraces, a coalition of a majority of the whole society could seldom take place on any other principles than those of justice and the general good; whilst there being thus less danger to a minor from the will of a major party, there must be less pretext, also, to provide for the security of the former, by introducing into the government a will not dependent on the latter, or, in other words, a will independent of the society itself. It is no less certain than it is important, notwithstanding the contrary opinions which have been entertained, that the larger the society, provided it lie within a practicable sphere, the more duly capable it will be of self-government. And happily for the republican cause, the practicable sphere may be carried to a very great extent by a judicious modification and mixture of the *federal principle.*

Publius
(James Madison)

Federalist Paper No. 78

In this essay, Alexander Hamilton looks at the role of the judicial branch (the courts) in the new government fashioned by the Constitution's framers. The essay is historically significant because, among other things, it provides a basis for the courts' power of judicial review, which was not explicitly set forth in the Constitution (see Chapters 3 and 15).

After some brief introductory remarks, Hamilton explains why the founders decided that federal judges should be appointed and given lifetime tenure. Note how he describes the judiciary as the "weakest" and "least dangerous" branch of government. Because of this, claims Hamilton, "all possible care" is required to enable the judiciary to defend itself against attacks by the other two branches of government. Above all, the independence of the judicial branch should be secured, because if judicial powers were combined with legislative or executive powers, there would be no liberty.

WE PROCEED now to an examination of the judiciary department of the proposed government.

In unfolding the defects of the existing Confederation, the utility and necessity of a federal judicature have been clearly pointed out. It is the less necessary to recapitulate the considerations there urged, as the propriety of the institution in the abstract is not disputed; the only questions which have been raised being relative to the manner of constituting it, and to its extent. To these points, therefore, our observations shall be confined.

The manner of constituting it seems to embrace these several objects: 1st. The mode of appointing the judges. 2d. The tenure by which they are to hold their places. 3d. The partition of the judiciary authority between different courts, and their relations to each other.

First. As to the mode of appointing the judges; this is the same with that of appointing the officers of the Union in general, and has been so fully discussed in the last two numbers, that nothing can be said here which would not be useless repetition.

Second. As to the tenure by which the judges are to hold their places; this chiefly concerns their duration in office; the provisions for their support; the precautions for their responsibility.

According to the plan of the convention, all judges who may be appointed by the United States are to hold their offices during good behavior; which is conformable to the most approved of the State constitutions and among the rest, to that of this State. Its propriety having been drawn into question by the adversaries of that plan, is no light symptom of the rage for objection, which disorders their imaginations and judgments. The standard of good behavior for the continuance in office of the judicial magistracy, is certainly one of the most valuable of the modern improvements in the practice of government. In a monarchy it is an excellent barrier to the despotism of the prince; in a republic it is a no less excellent barrier to the encroachments and oppressions of the representative body. And it is the best expedient which can be devised in any government, to secure a steady, upright, and impartial administration of the laws.

Whoever attentively considers the different departments of power must perceive, that, in a government in which they are separated from each other, the judiciary, from the nature of its functions, will always be the least dangerous to the political rights of the Constitution; because it will be least in a capacity to annoy or injure them. The Executive not only dispenses the honors, but holds the sword of the community. The legislature not only commands the purse, but prescribes the rules by which the duties and rights of every citizen are to be regulated. The judiciary, on the contrary, has no influence over either the sword or the purse; no direction either of the strength or of the wealth of the society; and can take no active resolution whatever. It may truly be said to have neither force nor will, but merely judgment; and must ultimately depend upon the aid of the executive arm even for the efficacy of its judgments.

This simple view of the matter suggests several important consequences. It proves incontestably, that the judiciary is beyond comparison the weakest of the three departments of power; that it can never attack with success either of the other two; and that all possible care is requisite to enable it to defend itself against their attacks. It equally proves, that though individual oppression may now and then proceed from the courts of justice, the general liberty of the people can never be endangered from that quarter; I mean so long as the judiciary remains truly distinct from both the legislature and the Executive. For I agree, that "there is no liberty, if the power of judging is not separated from the legislative and executive powers." And it proves, in the last place, that as liberty can have nothing to fear from the judiciary alone, but would have everything to fear from its union with either of the other departments; that as all the effects of such a union must ensue from a dependence of the former on the latter, notwithstanding a nominal and apparent separation; that as, from the natural feebleness of the judiciary, it is in continual jeopardy of being overpowered, awed, or influenced by its co-ordinate branches; and that as nothing can contribute so much to its firmness and independence as permanency in office, this quality may therefore be justly regarded as an indispens-

able ingredient in its constitution, and, in a great measure, as the citadel of the public justice and the public security.

Hamilton now stresses that the "complete independence of the courts" is essential in a limited government, because it is up to the courts to interpret the laws. Just as a federal court can decide which of two conflicting statutes should take priority, so can that court decide whether a statute conflicts with the Constitution. Essentially, Hamilton sets forth here the theory of judicial review—the power of the courts to decide whether actions of the other branches of government are (or are not) consistent with the Constitution. Hamilton points out that this "exercise of judicial discretion, in determining between two contradictory laws," does not mean that the judicial branch is superior to the legislative branch. Rather, it "supposes" that the power of the people (as declared in the Constitution) is superior to both the judiciary and the legislature.

The complete independence of the courts of justice is peculiarly essential in a limited Constitution. By a limited Constitution, I understand one which contains certain specified exceptions to the legislative authority; such, for instance, as that it shall pass no bills of attainder, no ex-post-facto laws, and the like. Limitations of this kind can be preserved in practice no other way than through the medium of courts of justice, whose duty it must be to declare all acts contrary to the manifest tenor of the Constitution void. Without this, all the reservations of particular rights or privileges would amount to nothing. Some perplexity respecting the rights of the courts to pronounce legislative acts void, because contrary to the Constitution, has arisen from an imagination that the doctrine would imply a superiority of the judiciary to the legislative power. It is urged that the authority which can declare the acts of another void, must necessarily be superior to the one whose acts may be declared void. As this doctrine is of great importance in all the American constitutions, a brief discussion of the ground on which it rests cannot be unacceptable.

There is no position which depends on clearer principles, than that every act of a delegated authority, contrary to the tenor of the commission under which it is exercised, is void. No legislative act, therefore, contrary to the Constitution, can be valid. To deny this, would be to affirm, that the deputy is greater than his principal; that the servant is above his master; that the representatives of the people are superior to the people themselves; that men acting by virtue of powers, may do not only what their powers do not authorize, but what they forbid.

If it be said that the legislative body are themselves the constitutional judges of their own powers, and that the construction they put upon them is conclusive upon the other departments, it may be answered, that this cannot be the natural presumption, where it is not to be collected from any particular provisions in the Constitution. It is not otherwise to be supposed, that the Constitution could intend to enable the representatives of the people to substitute their will to that of their constituents. It is far more rational to suppose, that the courts were designed to be an intermediate body between the people and the legislature, in order, among other things, to keep the latter within the limits assigned to their authority. The interpretation of the laws is the proper and peculiar province of the courts. A constitution is, in fact, and must be regarded by the judges, as a fundamental law. It therefore belongs to them to ascertain its meaning, as well as the meaning of any particular act proceeding from the legislative body. If there should happen to be an irreconcilable variance between the two, that which has the superior obligation and validity ought, of course, to be preferred; or, in other words, the Constitution ought to be preferred to the statute, the intention of the people to the intention of their agents.

Nor does this conclusion by any means suppose a superiority of the judicial to the legislative power. It only supposes that the power of the people is superior to both; and that where the will of the legislature, declared in its statutes, stands in opposition to that of the people, declared in the Constitution, the judges ought to be governed by the latter rather than the former. They ought to regulate their decisions by the fundamental laws, rather than by those which are not fundamental.

This exercise of judicial discretion, in determining between two contradictory laws, is exemplified in a familiar instance. It not uncommonly happens, that there are two statutes existing at one time, clashing in whole or in part with each other, and neither of them containing any repealing clause or expression. In such a case, it is the province of the courts to liquidate and fix their meaning and operation. So far as they can, by any fair construction, be reconciled to each other, reason and law conspire to dictate that this should be done; where this is impractable, it becomes a matter of necessity to give effect to one, in exclusion of the other. The rule which has obtained in the courts for determining their relative validity is, that the last in order of time shall be preferred to the first. But this is a mere rule of construction, not derived from any positive law, but from the nature and reason of the thing. It is a rule not enjoined upon the courts by legislative provision, but adopted by themselves, as consonant to truth the propriety, for the direction of their conduct as interpreters of the law. They thought it reasonable, that between the interfering acts of an equal authority, that which was the last indication of its will should have the preference.

But in regard to the interfering acts of a superior and subordinate authority, of an original and derivative power, the nature and reason of the thing indicate the converse of that rule as proper to be followed. They teach us that the prior act of a superior ought to be preferred to the subsequent act of an inferior and subordinate authority; and that

accordingly, whenever a particular statute contravenes the Constitution, it will be the duty of the judicial tribunals to adhere to the latter and disregard the former.

It can be of no weight to say that the courts, on the pretense of a repugnancy, may substitute their own pleasure to the constitutional intentions of the legislature. This might as well happen in the case of two contradictory statutes; or it might as well happen in every adjudication upon any single statute. The courts must declare the sense of the law; and if they should be disposed to exercise will instead of judgment, the consequence would equally be the substitution of their pleasure to that of the legislative body. The observation, if it prove anything, would prove that there ought to be no judges distinct from that body.

If, then, the courts of justice are to be considered as the bulwarks of a limited Constitution against legislative encroachments, this consideration will afford a strong argument for the permanent tenure of judicial offices, since nothing will contribute so much as this to that independent spirit in the judges which must be essential to the faithful performance of so arduous a duty.

The independence of the judges is equally requisite to guard the Constitution and the rights of individuals from the effects of those ill humors, which the arts of designing men, or the influence of particular conjunctures, sometimes disseminate among the people themselves, and which, though they speedily give place to better information, and more deliberate reflection, have a tendency, in the meantime, to occasion dangerous innovations in the government, and serious oppressions of the minor party in the community. Though I trust the friends of the proposed Constitution will never concur with its enemies, in questioning that fundamental principle of republican government, which admits the right of the people to alter or abolish the established Constitution, whenever they find it inconsistent with their happiness, yet it is not to be inferred from this principle, that the representatives of the people, whenever a momentary inclination happens to lay hold of a majority of their constituents, incompatible with the provisions of the existing Constitution, would, on that account, be justifiable in a violation of those provisions; or that the courts would be under a greater obligation to connive at infractions in this shape, than when they had proceeded wholly from the cabals of the representative body. Until the people have, by some solemn and authoritative act, annulled or changed the established form, it is binding upon themselves collectively, as well as individually; and no presumption, or even knowledge, of their sentiments, can warrant their representatives in a departure from it, prior to such an act. But it is easy to see, that it would require an uncommon portion of fortitude in the judges to do their duty as faithful guardians of the Constitution, where legislative invasions of it had been instigated by the major voice of the community.

But it is not with a view to infractions of the Constitution only, that the independence of the judges may be an essential safeguard against the effects of occasional ill humors in the society. These sometimes extend no farther than to the injury of the private rights of particular classes of citizens, by unjust and partial laws. Here also the firmness of the judicial magistracy is of vast importance in mitigating the severity and confining the operation of such laws. It not only serves to moderate the immediate mischiefs of those which may have been passed, but it operates as a check upon the legislative body in passing them; who, perceiving that obstacles to the success of iniquitous intention are to be expected from the scruples of the courts, are in a manner compelled, by the very motives of the injustice they meditate, to qualify their attempts. This is a circumstance calculated to have more influence upon the character of our governments, than but few may be aware of. The benefits of the integrity and moderation of the judiciary have already been felt in more States than one; and though they may have displeased those whose sinister expectations they may have disappointed, they must have commanded the esteem and applause of all the virtuous and disinterested. Considerate men, of every description, ought to prize whatever will tend to beget or fortify that temper in the courts; as no man can be sure that he may not be to-morrow the victim of a spirit of injustice, by which he may be a gainer to-day. Any every man must now feel, that the inevitable tendency of such a spirit is to sap the foundations of public and private confidence, and to introduce in its stead universal distrust and distress.

That inflexible and uniform adherence to the rights of the Constitution, and of individuals, which we perceive to be indispensable in the courts of justice, can certainly not be expected from judges who hold their offices by a temporary commission. Periodical appointments, however regulated, or by whomsoever made, would, in some way or other, be fatal to their necessary independence. If the power of making them was committed either to the Executive or legislature, there would be danger of an improper complaisance to the branch which possessed it; if to both, there would be an unwillingness to hazard the displeasure of either; if to the people, or to persons chosen by them for the special purpose, there would be too great a disposition to consult popularity, to justify a reliance that nothing would be consulted but the Constitution and the laws.

Hamilton points to yet another reason why lifetime tenure for federal judges will benefit the public: effective judgments rest on a knowledge of judicial precedents and the law, and such knowledge can only be obtained through experience on the bench. A "temporary duration of office," according to Hamilton, would "discourage individuals [of 'fit character'] from quitting a lucrative practice to serve on the bench" and ultimately would "throw the administration of justice into the hands of the less able, and less well qualified."

There is yet a further and a weightier reason for the permanency of the judicial offices, which is deducible from the nature of the qualifications they require. It has been frequently remarked, with great propriety, that a voluminous code of laws is one of the inconveniences necessarily connected with the advantages of a free government. To avoid an arbitrary discretion in the courts, it is indispensable that they should be bound down by strict rules and precedents, which serve to define and point out their duty in every particular case that comes before them; and it will readily be conceived from the variety of controversies which grow out of the folly and wickedness of mankind, that the records of those precedents must unavoidably swell to a very considerable bulk, and must demand long and laborious study to acquire a competent knowledge of them. Hence it is, that there can be but few men in the society who will have sufficient skill in the laws to qualify them for the stations of judges. And making the proper deductions for the ordinary depravity of human nature, the number must be still smaller of those who unite the requisite integrity with the requisite knowledge. These considerations apprise us, that the government can have no great option between fit character; and that a temporary duration in office, which would naturally discourage such characters from quitting a lucrative line of practice to accept a seat on the bench, would have a tendency to throw the administration of justice into hands less able, and less well qualified, to conduct it with utility and dignity. In the present circumstances of this country, and in those in which it is likely to be for a long time to come, the disadvantages on this score would be greater than they may at first sight appear; but it must be confessed, that they are far inferior to those which present themselves under other aspects of the subject.

Upon the whole, there can be no room to doubt that the convention acted wisely in copying from the models of those constitutions which have established good behavior as the tenure of their judicial offices, in point of duration; and that so far from being blamable on this account, their plan would have been inexcusably defective, if it had wanted this important feature of good government. The experience of Great Britain affords an illustrious comment on the excellence of the institution.

Publius
(Alexander Hamilton)

appendix E

Justices of the U.S. Supreme Court since 1900

Chief Justices

Name	Years of Service	State App't From	Appointing President	Age App't	Political Affiliation	Educational* Background
Fuller, Melville Weston	1888–1910	Illinois	Cleveland	55	Democrat	Bowdoin College; studied at Harvard Law School
White, Edward Douglass	1910–1921	Louisiana	Taft	65	Democrat	Mount St. Mary's College; Georgetown College (now University)
Taft, William Howard	1921–1930	Connecticut	Harding	64	Republican	Yale; Cincinnati Law School
Hughes, Charles Evans	1930–1941	New York	Hoover	68	Republican	Colgate University; Brown; Columbia Law School
Stone, Harlan Fiske	1941–1946	New York	Roosevelt, F.	69	Republican	Amherst College; Columbia
Vinson, Frederick Moore	1946–1953	Kentucky	Truman	56	Democrat	Centre College
Warren, Earl	1953–1969	California	Eisenhower	62	Republican	University of California, Berkeley
Burger, Warren Earl	1969–1986	Virginia	Nixon	62	Republican	University of Minnesota; St. Paul College of Law (Mitchell College)
Rehnquist, William Hubbs	1986–	Virginia	Reagan	62	Republican	Stanford; Harvard; Stanford University Law School

*Source: Educational background information derived from Elder Witt, Guide to the *U.S. Supreme Court,* 2d ed. (Washington, D.C.: Congressional Quarterly Press, Inc., 1990) Reprinted with the permission of the publisher.

Associate Justices

Name	Years of Service	State App't From	Appointing President	Age App't	Political Affiliation	Educational* Background
Harlan, John Marshall	1877–1911	Kentucky	Hayes	61	Republican	Centre College; studied law at Transylvania University
Gray, Horace	1882–1902	Massachusetts	Arthur	54	Republican	Harvard College; Harvard Law School
Brewer, David Josiah	1890–1910	Kansas	Harrison	53	Republican	Wesleyan University; Yale; Albany Law School
Brown, Henry Billings	1891–1906	Michigan	Harrison	55	Republican	Yale; studied at Yale Law School and Harvard Law School
Shiras, George, Jr.	1892–1903	Pennsylvania	Harrison	61	Republican	Ohio University; Yale; studied law at Yale and privately
White, Edward Douglass	1894–1910	Louisiana	Cleveland	49	Democrat	Mount St. Mary's College; Georgetown College (now University)

Associate Justices (continued)

Name	Years of Service	State App't From	Appointing President	Age App't	Political Affiliation	Educational* Background
Peckham, Rufus Wheeler	1896–1909	New York	Cleveland	58	Democrat	Read law in father's firm
McKenna, Joseph	1898–1925	California	McKinley	55	Republican	Benicia Collegiate Institute, Law Dept.
Holmes, Oliver Wendell, Jr.	1902–1932	Massachusetts	Roosevelt, T.	61	Republican	Harvard College; studied law at Harvard Law School
Day, William Rufus	1903–1922	Ohio	Roosevelt, T.	54	Republican	University of Michigan; University of Michigan Law School
Moody, William Henry	1906–1910	Massachusetts	Roosevelt, T.	53	Republican	Harvard; Harvard Law School
Lurton, Horace Harmon	1910–1914	Tennessee	Taft	66	Democrat	University of Chicago; Cumberland Law School
Hughes, Charles Evans	1910–1916	New York	Taft	48	Republican	Colgate University; Brown University; Columbia Law School
Van Devanter, Willis	1911–1937	Wyoming	Taft	52	Republican	Indiana Asbury University; University of Cincinnati Law School
Lamar, Joseph Rucker	1911–1916	Georgia	Taft	54	Democrat	University of Georgia; Bethany College; Washington and Lee University
Pitney, Mahlon	1912–1922	New Jersey	Taft	54	Republican	College of New Jersey (Princeton); read law under father
McReynolds, James Clark	1914–1941	Tennessee	Wilson	52	Democrat	Vanderbilt University; University of Virginia
Brandeis, Louis Dembitz	1916–1939	Massachusetts	Wilson	60	Democrat	Harvard Law School
Clarke, John Hessin	1916–1922	Ohio	Wilson	59	Democrat	Western Reserve University; read law under father
Sutherland, George	1922–1938	Utah	Harding	60	Republican	Brigham Young Academy; one year at University of Michigan Law School
Butler, Pierce	1923–1939	Minnesota	Harding	57	Democrat	Carleton College
Sanford, Edward Terry	1923–1930	Tennessee	Harding	58	Republican	University of Tennessee; Harvard; Harvard Law School
Stone, Harlan Fiske	1925–1941	New York	Coolidge	53	Republican	Amherst College; Columbia University Law School
Roberts, Owen Josephus	1930–1945	Pennsylvania	Hoover	55	Republican	University of Pennsylvania; University of Pennsylvania Law School
Cardozo, Benjamin Nathan	1932–1938	New York	Hoover	62	Democrat	Columbia University; two years at Columbia Law School
Black, Hugo Lafayette	1937–1971	Alabama	Roosevelt, F.	51	Democrat	Birmingham Medical College; University of Alabama Law School
Reed, Stanley Forman	1938–1957	Kentucky	Roosevelt, F.	54	Democrat	Kentucky Wesleyan University; Foreman Yale; studied law at University of Virginia and Columbia University; University of Paris
Frankfurter, Felix	1939–1962	Massachusetts	Roosevelt, F.	57	Independent	College of the City of New York; Harvard Law School
Douglas, William Orville	1939–1975	Connecticut	Roosevelt, F.	41	Democrat	Whitman College; Columbia University Law School

Associate Justices (continued)

NAME	YEARS OF SERVICE	STATE APP'T FROM	APPOINTING PRESIDENT	AGE APP'T	POLITICAL AFFILIATION	EDUCATIONAL* BACKGROUND
Murphy, Frank	1940–1949	Michigan	Roosevelt, F.	50	Democrat	University of Michigan; Lincoln's Inn, London; Trinity College
Byrnes, James Francis	1941–1942	South Carolina	Roosevelt, F.	62	Democrat	Read law privately
Jackson, Robert Houghwout	1941–1954	New York	Roosevelt, F.	49	Democrat	Albany Law School
Rutledge, Wiley Blount	1943–1949	Iowa	Roosevelt, F.	49	Democrat	University of Wisconsin; University of Colorado
Burton, Harold Hitz	1945–1958	Ohio	Truman	57	Republican	Bowdoin College; Harvard University Law School
Clark, Thomas Campbell	1949–1967	Texas	Truman	50	Democrat	University of Texas
Minton, Sherman	1949–1956	Indiana	Truman	59	Democrat	Indiana University College of Law; Yale Law School
Harlan, John Marshall	1955–1971	New York	Eisenhower	56	Republican	Princeton; Oxford University; New York Law School
Brennan, William J., Jr.	1956–1990	New Jersey	Eisenhower	50	Democrat	University of Pennsylvania; Harvard Law School
Whittaker, Charles Evans	1957–1962	Missouri	Eisenhower	56	Republican	University of Kansas City Law School
Stewart, Potter	1958–1981	Ohio	Eisenhower	43	Republican	Yale; Yale Law School
White, Byron Raymond	1962–1993	Colorado	Kennedy	45	Democrat	University of Colorado; Oxford University; Yale Law School
Goldberg, Arthur Joseph	1962–1965	Illinois	Kennedy	54	Democrat	Northwestern University
Fortas, Abe	1965–1969	Tennessee	Johnson, L.	55	Democrat	Southwestern College; Yale Law School
Marshall, Thurgood	1967–1991	New York	Johnson, L.	59	Democrat	Lincoln University; Howard University Law School
Blackmun, Harry A.	1970–1994	Minnesota	Nixon	62	Republican	Harvard; Harvard Law School
Powell, Lewis F., Jr.	1972–1987	Virginia	Nixon	65	Democrat	Washington and Lee University; Washington and Lee University Law School; Harvard Law School
Rehnquist, William H.	1972–1986	Arizona	Nixon	48	Republican	Stanford; Harvard; Stanford University Law School
Stevens, John Paul	1975–	Illinois	Ford	55	Republican	University of Colorado; Northwestern University Law School
O'Connor, Sandra Day	1981–	Arizona	Reagan	51	Republican	Stanford; Stanford University Law School
Scalia, Antonin	1986–	Virginia	Reagan	50	Republican	Georgetown University; Harvard Law School
Kennedy, Anthony M.	1988–	California	Reagan	52	Republican	Stanford; London School of Economics; Harvard Law School
Souter, David Hackett	1990–	New Hampshire	Bush	51	Republican	Harvard; Oxford University
Thomas, Clarence	1991–	District of Columbia	Bush	43	Republican	Holy Cross College; Yale Law School
Ginsburg, Ruth Bader	1993–	District of Columbia	Clinton	60	Democrat	Cornell University; Columbia Law School
Breyer, Stephen, G.	1994–	Massachusetts	Clinton	55	Democrat	Stanford University; Oxford University; Harvard Law School

appendix F
Party Control of Congress since 1900

CONGRESS	YEARS	PRESIDENT	MAJORITY PARTY IN HOUSE	MAJORITY PARTY IN SENATE
57th	1901–1903	T. Roosevelt	Republican	Republican
58th	1903–1905	T. Roosevelt	Republican	Republican
59th	1905–1907	T. Roosevelt	Republican	Republican
60th	1907–1909	T. Roosevelt	Republican	Republican
61st	1909–1911	Taft	Republican	Republican
62d	1911–1913	Taft	Democratic	Republican
63d	1913–1915	Wilson	Democratic	Democratic
64th	1915–1917	Wilson	Democratic	Democratic
65th	1917–1919	Wilson	Democratic	Democratic
66th	1919–1921	Wilson	Republican	Republican
67th	1921–1923	Harding	Republican	Republican
68th	1923–1925	Coolidge	Republican	Republican
69th	1925–1927	Coolidge	Republican	Republican
70th	1927–1929	Coolidge	Republican	Republican
71st	1929–1931	Hoover	Republican	Republican
72d	1931–1933	Hoover	Democratic	Republican
73d	1933–1935	F. Roosevelt	Democratic	Democratic
74th	1935–1937	F. Roosevelt	Democratic	Democratic
75th	1937–1939	F. Roosevelt	Democratic	Democratic
76th	1939–1941	F. Roosevelt	Democratic	Democratic
77th	1941–1943	F. Roosevelt	Democratic	Democratic
78th	1943–1945	F. Roosevelt	Democratic	Democratic
79th	1945–1947	Truman	Democratic	Democratic
80th	1947–1949	Truman	Republican	Democratic
81st	1949–1951	Truman	Democratic	Democratic
82d	1951–1953	Truman	Democratic	Democratic
83d	1953–1955	Eisenhower	Republican	Republican
84th	1955–1957	Eisenhower	Democratic	Democratic
85th	1957–1959	Eisenhower	Democratic	Democratic
86th	1959–1961	Eisenhower	Democratic	Democratic
87th	1961–1963	Kennedy	Democratic	Democratic
88th	1963–1965	Kennedy/Johnson	Democratic	Democratic
89th	1965–1967	Johnson	Democratic	Democratic
90th	1967–1969	Johnson	Democratic	Democratic
91st	1969–1971	Nixon	Democratic	Democratic
92d	1971–1973	Nixon	Democratic	Democratic
93d	1973–1975	Nixon/Ford	Democratic	Democratic
94th	1975–1977	Ford	Democratic	Democratic
95th	1977–1979	Carter	Democratic	Democratic
96th	1979–1981	Carter	Democratic	Democratic
97th	1981–1983	Reagan	Democratic	Republican
98th	1983–1985	Reagan	Democratic	Republican
99th	1985–1987	Reagan	Democratic	Republican
100th	1987–1989	Reagan	Democratic	Democratic
101st	1989–1991	Bush	Democratic	Democratic
102d	1991–1993	Bush	Democratic	Democratic
103d	1993–1995	Clinton	Democratic	Democratic
104th	1995–1997	Clinton	Republican	Republican
105th	1997–1999	Clinton	Republican	Republican
106th	1999–2001	Clinton	Republican	Republican
107th	2001–2003	Bush	Republican	Republican

appendix G

Spanish Equivalents for Important Terms in American Government

Acid Rain: Lluvia Acida
Acquisitive Model: Modelo Adquisitivo
Actionable: Procesable, Enjuiciable
Action-reaction Syndrome: Sídrome de Acción y Reacción
Actual Malice: Malicia Expresa
Administrative Agency: Agencia Administrativa
Advice and Consent: Consejo y Consentimiento
Affirmative Action: Acción Afirmativa
Affirm: Afirmar
Agenda Setting: Agenda Establecida
Aid to Families with Dependent Children (AFDC): Ayuda para Familias con Niños Dependientes
Amicus Curiae **Brief:** Tercer persona o grupo no involucrado en el caso, admitido en un juicio para hacer valer el intéres público o el de un grupo social importante.
Anarchy: Anarquía
Anti-Federalists: Anti-Federalistas
Appellate Court: Corte de Apelación
Appointment Power: Poder de Apuntamiento
Appropriation: Apropiación
Aristocracy: Aristocracia
Attentive Public: Público Atento
Australian Ballot: Voto Australiano

Authority: Autoridad
Authorization: Autorización

Bad-Tendency Rule: Regla de Tendencia-mala
"Beauty Contest": Concurso de Belleza
Bicameralism: Bicameralismo
Bicameral Legislature: Legislatura Bicameral
Bill of Rights: Declaración de Derechos
Blanket Primary: Primaria Comprensiva
Block Grants: Concesiones de Bloque
Bureaucracy: Burocracia
Busing: Transporte público

Cabinet: Gabinete, Consejo de Ministros
Cabinet Department: Departamento del Gabinete
Cadre: El núcleo de activistas de partidos políticos encargados de cumplir las funciones importantes de los partidos políticos americanos.
Canvassing Board: Consejo encargado con la encuesta de una violación.
Capture: Captura, toma
Casework: Trabajo de Caso
Categorical Grants-in-Aid: Concesiones Categóricas de Ayuda
Caucus: Reunión de Dirigentes

Challenge: Reto
Checks and Balances: Chequeos y Equilibrio
Chief Diplomat: Jefe Diplomático
Chief Executive: Jefe Ejecutivo
Chief Legislator: Jefe Legislador
Chief of Staff: Jefe de Personal
Chief of State: Jefe de Estado
Civil Law: Derecho Civil
Civil Liberties: Libertades Civiles
Civil Rights: Derechos Civiles
Civil Service: Servicio Civil
Civil Service Commission: Comisión de Servicio Civil
Class-action Suit: Demanda en representación de un grupo o clase.
Class Politics: Política de Clase
Clear and Present Danger Test: Prueba de Peligro Claro y Presente
Climate Control: Control de Clima
Closed Primary: Primaria Cerrada
Cloture: Cierre al voto
Coattail Effect: Effecto de Cola de Chaqueta
Cold War: Guerra Fría
Commander in Chief: Comandante en Jefe
Commerce Clause: Clausula de Comercio
Commercial Speech: Discurso Comercial
Common Law: Ley Común, Derecho Consuetudinario
Comparable Worth: Valor Comparable
Compliance: De acuerdo

Concurrent Majority: Mayoría Concurrente

Concurring Opinion: Opinión Concurrente

Confederal System: Sistema Confederal

Confederation: Confederación

Conference Committee: Comité de Conferencia

Consensus: Concenso

Consent of the People: Consentimiento de la Gente

Conservatism: Calidad de Conservador

Conservative Coalition: Coalición Conservadora

Consolidation: Consolidación

Constant Dollars: Dólares Constantes

Constitutional Initiative: Iniciativa Constitucional

Constitutional Power: Poder Constitucional

Containment: Contenimiento

Continuing Resolution: Resolució Contínua

Cooley's Rule: Régla de Cooley

Cooperative Federalism: Federalismo Cooperativo

Corrupt Practices Acts: Leyes Contra Acciones Corruptas

Council of Economic Advisers (CEA): Consejo de Asesores Económicos

Council of Government (COG): Consejo de Gobierno

County: Condado

Credentials Committee: Comité de Credenciales

Criminal Law: Ley Criminal

De Facto **Segregation:** Segregación de Hecho

De Jure **Segregation:** Segregación Cotidiana

Defamation of Character: Defamación de Carácter

Democracy: Democracia

Democratic Party: Partido Democratico

Dillon's Rule: Régla de Dillon

Diplomacy: Diplomácia

Direct Democracy: Democracia Directa

Direct Primary: Primaria Directa

Direct Technique: Técnica Directa

Discharge Petition: Petición de Descargo

Dissenting Opinion: Opinión Disidente

Divisive Opinion: Opinión Divisiva

Domestic Policy: Principio Político Doméstico

Dual Citizenship: Ciudadanía Dual

Dual Federalism: Federalismo Dual

Détente: No Spanish equivalent.

Economic Aid: Ayuda Económica

Economic Regulation: Regulación Económica

Elastic Clause, or Necessary and Proper Clause: Cláusula Flexible o Cláusula Propia Necesaria

Elector: Elector

Electoral College: Colegio Electoral

Electronic Media: Media Electronica

Elite: Elite (el selecto)

Elite Theory: Teoría Elitista (de lo selecto)

Emergency Power: Poder de Emergencia

Enumerated Power: Poder Enumerado

Environmental Impact Statement (EIS): Afirmación de Impacto Ambiental

Equality: Igualdad

Equalization: Igualación

Equal Employment Opportunity Commission (EEOC): Comisión de Igualdad de Oportunidad en el Empleo

Era of Good Feeling: Era de Buen Sentimiento

Era of Personal Politics: Era de Política Personal

Establishment Clause: Cláusula de Establecimiento

Euthanasia: Eutanasia

Exclusionary Rule: Regla de Exclusión

Executive Agreement: Acuerdo Ejecutivo

Executive Budget: Presupuesto Ejecutivo

Executive Office of the President (EOP): Oficina Ejecutiva del Presidente

Executive Order: Orden Ejecutivo

Executive Privilege: Privilegio Ejecutivo

Expressed Power: Poder Expresado

Extradite: Entregar por Extradición

Faction: Facción

Fairness Doctrine: Doctrina de Justicia

Fall Review: Revision de Otoño

Federalist: Federalista

Federal Mandate: Mandato Federal

Federal Open Market Committee (FOMC): Comité Federal de Libre Mercado

Federal Register: Registro Federal

Federal System: Sistema Federal

Federalists: Federalistas

Fighting Words: Palabras de Provocación

Filibuster: Obstrucción de iniciativas de ley

Fireside Chat: Charla de Hogar

First Budget Resolution: Resolució Primera Presupuesta

First Continental Congress: Primér Congreso Continental

Fiscal Policy: Politico Fiscal

Fiscal Year (FY): Año Fiscal

Fluidity: Fluidez

Food Stamps: Estampillas para Comida

Foreign Policy: Politica Extranjera

Foreign Policy Process: Proceso de Politica Extranjera

Franking: Franqueando

Fraternity: Fraternidad

Free Exercise Clause: Cláusula de Ejercicio Libre

Full Faith and Credit Clause: Cláusula de Completa Fé y Crédito

Functional Consolidation: Consolidación Funcional

Gag Order: Orden de Silencio

Garbage Can Model: Modelo Bote de Basura

Gender Gap: Brecha de Género

General Law City: Regla General Urbana

General Sales Tax: Impuesto General de Ventas

Generational Effect: Efecto Generacional

Gerrymandering: División arbitraria de los distritos electorales con fines políticos.
Government: Gobierno
Government Corporation: Corporación Gubernamental
Government in the Sunshine Act: Gobierno en la acta: Luz del Sol
Grandfather Clause: Clausula del Abuelo
Grand Jury: Gran Jurado
Great Compromise: Grán Acuerdo de Negociación

Hatch Act (Political Activities Act): Acta Hatch (acta de actividades politicas)
Hecklers' Veto: Veto de Abuchamiento
Home Rule City: Regla Urbana
Horizontal Federalism: Federalismo Horizontal
Hyperpluralism: Hiperpluralismo

Ideologue: Ideólogo
Ideology: Ideología
Image Building: Construcción de Imágen
Impeachment: Acción Penal Contra un Funcionario Público
Inalienable Rights: Derechos Inalienables
Income Transfer: Transferencia de Ingresos
Incorporation Theory: Teoría de Incorporación
Independent: Independiente
Independent Candidate: Candidato Independiente
Independent Executive Agency: Agencia Ejecutiva Independiente
Independent Regulatory Agency: Agencia Regulatoria Independiente
Indirect Technique: Técnica Indirecta
Inherent Power: Poder Inherente
Initiative: Iniciativa
Injunction: Injunción, Prohibición Judicial
Institution: Institución
Instructed Delegate: Delegado con Instrucciones
Intelligence Community: Comunidad de Inteligencia

Intensity: Intensidad
Interest Group: Grupo de Interés
Interposition: Interposición
Interstate Compact: Compacto Interestatal
In-kind Subsidy: Subsidio de Clase
Iron Curtain: Cortina de Acero
Iron Triangle: Triágulo de Acero
Isolationist Foreign Policy: Politica Extranjera de Aislamiento
Issue Voting: Voto Temático
Item Veto: Artículo de Veto

Jim Crow Laws: No Spanish equivalent.
Joint Committee: Comité Mancomunado
Judicial Activism: Activismo Judicial
Judicial Implementation: Implementacion Judicial
Judicial Restraint: Restricción Judicial
Judicial Review: Revisión Judicial
Jurisdiction: Jurisdicción
Justiciable Dispute: Disputa Judiciaria
Justiciable Question: Pregunta Justiciable

Keynesian Economics: Economía Keynesiana
Kitchen Cabinet: Gabinete de Cocina

Labor Movement: Movimiento Laboral
Latent Public Opinion: Opinión Pública Latente
Lawmaking: Hacedores de Ley
Legislative History: Historia Legislativa
Legislative Initiative: Iniciativa de legislación
Legislative Veto: Veto Legislativo
Legislature: Legislatura
Legitimacy: Legitimidad
Libel: Libelo, Difamación Escrita
Liberalism: Liberalismo
Liberty: Libertad
Limited Government: Gobierno Limitado

Line Organization: Organización de Linea
Literacy Test: Exámen de alfabetización
Litigate: Litigar
Lobbying: Cabildeo
Logrolling: Práctica legislativa que consiste en incluir en un mismo proyecto de ley temas de diversa ídole.
Loophole: Hueco Legal, escapatoria

Madisonian Model: Modelo Madisónico
Majority: Mayoría
Majority Floor Leader: Líder Mayoritario de Piso
Majority Leader of the House: Líder Mayoritario de la Casa
Majority Opinion: Opinión Mayoritaria
Majority Rule: Regla de Mayoría
Managed News: Noticias Manipuladas
Mandatory Retirement: Retiro Mandatorio
Matching Funds: Fondos Combinados
Material Incentive: Incentivo Material
Media: Media
Media Access: Acceso de Media
Merit System: Sistema de Mérito
Military-Industrial Complex: Complejo Industriomilitar
Minority Floor Leader: Líder Minoritario de Piso
Minority Leader of the House: Líder Minorial del Cuerpo Legislativo
Monetary Policy: Politica Monetaria
Monopolistic Model: Modelo Monopólico
Monroe Doctrine: Doctrina Monroe
Moral Idealism: Idealismo Moral
Municipal Home Rule: Regla Municipal

Narrow Casting: Mensaje Dirigído
National Committee: Comité Nacional

National Convention: Convención Nacional

National Politics: Politica Nacional

National Security Council (NSC): Concilio de Seguridad Nacional

National Security Policy: Politica de Seguridad Nacional

Natural Aristocracy: Aristocracia Natural

Natural Rights: Derechos Naturales

Necessaries: Necesidades

Negative Constituents: Constituyentes Negativos

New England Town: Pueblo de Nueva Inglaterra

New Federalism: Federalismo Nuevo

Nullification: Nulidad, Anulación

Office-Block, or Massachusetts, Ballot: Cuadro-Oficina, o Massachusetts, Voto

Office of Management and Budget (OMB): Oficina de Administració y Presupuesto

Oligarchy: Oligarquía

Ombudsman: Funcionario que representa al ciudadano ante el gobierno.

Open Primary: Primaria Abierta

Opinion: Opinión

Opinion Leader: Líder de Opinión

Opinion Poll: Encuesta, Conjunto de Opinión

Oral Arguments: Argumentos Orales

Oversight: Inadvertencia, Omisión

Paid-for-Political Announcement: Anuncios Politicos Pagados

Pardon: Perdón

Party-Column, or Indiana, Ballot: Partido-Columna, o Indiana, Voto

Party Identification: Identificación de Partido

Party Identifier: Identificador de Partido

Party-in-Electorate: Partido Electoral

Party-in-Government: Partido en Gobierno

Party Organization: Organización de Partido

Party Platform: Plataforma de Partido

Patronage: Patrocinio

Peer Group: Grupo de Contemporáneos

Pendleton Act (Civil Service Reform Act): Acta Pendleton (Acta de Reforma al Servicio Civil)

Personal Attack Rule: Regla de Ataque Personal

Petit Jury: Jurado Ordinario

Pluralism: Pluralismo

Plurality: Pluralidad

Pocket Veto: Veto de Bolsillo

Police Power: Poder Policiaco

Policy Trade-offs: Intercambio de Politicas

Political Action Committee (PAC): Comité de Acción Política

Political Consultant: Consultante Político

Political Culture: Cultura Politica

Political Party: Partido Político

Political Question: Pregunta Politica

Political Realism: Realismo Político

Political Socialization: Socialización Politica

Political Tolerance: Tolerancia Política

Political Trust: Confianza Política

Politico: Político

Politics: Politica

Poll Tax: Impuesto sobre el sufragio

Poll Watcher: Observador de Encuesta

Popular Sovereignty: Soberanía Popular

Power: Poder

Precedent: Precedente

Preferred-Position Test: Prueba de Posición Preferida

Presidential Primary: Primaria Presidencial

President Pro Tempore: Presidente Provisoriamente

Press Secretary: Secretaría de Prensa

Prior Restraint: Restricción Anterior

Privileges and Immunities: Privilégios e Imunidades

Privitization, or Contracting Out: Privatización

Property: Propiedad

Property Tax: Impuesto de Propiedad

Public Agenda: Agenda Pública

Public Debt Financing: Financiamiento de Deuda Pública

Public Debt, or National Debt: Deuda Pública o Nacional

Public Interest: Interes Público

Public Opinion: Opinión Pública

Purposive Incentive: Incentivo de Propósito

Ratification: Ratificación

Rational Ignorance Effect: Effecto de Ignorancia Racional

Reapportionment: Redistribución

Recall: Suspender

Recognition Power: Poder de Reconocimiento

Recycling: Reciclaje

Redistricting: Redistrictificación

Referendum: Referédum

Registration: Registración

Regressive Tax: Impuestos Regresivos

Relevance: Pertinencia

Remand: Reenviar

Representation: Representación

Representative Assembly: Asamblea Representativa

Representative Democracy: Democracia Representativa

Reprieve: Trequa, Suspensión

Republic: República

Republican Party: Partido Republicano

Resulting Powers: Poderes Resultados

Reverse: Cambiarse a lo contrario

Reverse Discrimination: Discriminación Reversiva

Rules Committee: Comité Regulador

Rule of Four: Regla de Cuatro

Run-off Primary: Primaria Residual

Safe Seat: Asiento Seguro

Sampling Error: Error de Encuesta

Secession: Secesión

Second Budget Resolution: Resolución Segunda Presupuestal

Second Continental Congress:
Segundo Congreso Continental
Sectional Politics: Política
Seccional
Segregation: Segregación
Selectperson: Persona Selecta
Select Committee: Comité Selecto
Senatorial Courtesy: Cortesia
Senatorial
Seniority System: Sistema
Señiorial
Separate-but-Equal Doctrine:
Separados pero iguales
Separation of Powers: Separación
de Poderes
Service Sector: Sector de Servicio
Sexual Harassment: Acosamiento
Sexual
Sex Discrimination:
Discriminacion Sexual
Slander: Difamación Oral,
Calumnia
Sliding-Scale Test: Prueba
Escalonada
Social Movement: Movimiento
Social
Social Security: Seguridad Social
Socioeconomic Status: Estado
Socioeconómico
Solidary Incentive: Incentivo de
Solideridad
Solid South: Súr Sólido
Sound Bite: Mordida de Sonido
Soviet Bloc: Bloque Soviético
Speaker of the House: Vocero de
la Casa
Spin: Girar/Giro
Spin Doctor: Doctor en Giro
Spin-off Party: Partido Estático
Spoils System: Sistema de
Despojos
Spring Review: Revisión de
Primavera
Stare Decisis: El principio
característico del ley comú por el
cual los precedentes
jurisprudenciales tienen fuerza
obligatoria, no sólo entre las partes,
sino tambien para casos sucesivos
análogos.
Stability: Estabilidad
Standing Committee: Comité de
Sostenimiento
State Central Committee: Comité

Central del Estado
State: Estado
State of the Union Message:
Mensaje Sobre el Estado de la
Unión
Statutory Power: Poder Estatorial
Strategic Arms Limitation Treaty
(SALT I): Tratado de Limitación de
Armas Estratégicas
Subpoena: Orden de Testificación
Subsidy: Subsidio
Suffrage: Sufrágio
Sunset Legislation: Legislación
Sunset
Superdelegate: Líder de partido o
oficial elegido quien tiene el
derecho de votar.
Supplemental Security Income
(SSI): Ingresos de Seguridad
Suplementaria
Supremacy Clause: Cláusula de
Supremacia
Supremacy Doctrine: Doctrina de
Supremacia
Symbolic Speech: Discurso
Simbólico

Technical Assistance: Asistencia
Técnica
Third Party: Tercer Partido
Third-party Candidate: Candidato
de Tercer Partido
Ticket Splitting: División de
Boletos
Totalitarian Regime: Régimen
Totalitario
Town Manager System: Sistema
de Administrador Municipal
Town Meeting: Junta Municipal
Township: Municipio
Tracking Poll: Seguimiento de
Encuesta
Trial Court: Tribunal de Primera
Truman Doctrine: Doctrina
Truman
Trustee: Depositario
Twelfth Amendment: Doceava
Enmienda
Twenty-fifth Amendment:
Veinticincoava Enmienda
Two-Party System: Sistema de
Dos Partidos

Unanimous Opinion: Opinión

Unánime
Underground Economy: Economía
Subterráea
Unicameral Legislature:
Legislatura Unicameral
Unincorporated Area: Area no
Incorporada
Unit Rule: Regla de Unidad
Unitary System: Sistema Unitario
Universal Suffrage: Sufragio
Universal
U.S. Treasury Bond: Bono de la
Tesoreria de E.U.A.

Veto Message: Comunicado de
Veto
Voter Turnout: Renaimiento de
Votantes

War Powers Act: Acta de Poderes
de Guerra
Washington Community:
Comunidad de Washington
Weberian Model: Modelo
Weberiano
Whip: Látigo
Whistleblower: Privatización o
Contratista
White House Office: Oficina de la
Casa Blanca
White House Press Corps: Cuerpo
de Prensa de la Casa Blanca
White Primary: Sufragio en
Elección Primaria/Blancos
Solamente
Writ of Certiorari: Prueba de
certeza; orden emitida por el
tribunal de apelaciones para que el
tribunal inferior dé lugar a la
apelación.
Writ of Habeas Corpus: Prueba de
Evidencia Concreta
Writ of Mandamus: Un mandato
por la corte para que un acto se
lleve a cabo.

Yellow Journalism: Amarillismo
Periodístico

Glossary

A

Acquisitive Model A model of bureaucracy that views top-level bureaucrats as seeking constantly to expand the size of their budgets and the staffs of their departments or agencies so as to gain greater power and influence in the public sector.

Action-Reaction Syndrome For every action on the part of government, there is a reaction on the part of the affected public. Then the government attempts to counter the reaction with another action, which starts the cycle all over again.

Administrative Agency A federal, state, or local government unit established to perform a specific function. Administrative agencies are created and authorized by legislative bodies to administer and enforce specific laws.

Advice and Consent The power vested in the U.S. Senate by the Constitution (Article II, Section 2) to give its advice and consent to the president on treaties and presidential appointments.

Affirm To declare that a judgment is valid and must stand.

Affirmative Action A policy in job hiring that gives special consideration or compensatory treatment to traditionally disadvantaged groups in an effort to overcome present effects of past discrimination.

Agenda Setting Determining which public policy questions will be debated or considered by Congress.

Amicus Curiae **Brief** A brief (a document containing a legal argument supporting a desired outcome in a particular case) filed by a third party, or *amicus curiae* (Latin for "friend of the court"), who is not directly involved in the litigation but who has an interest in the outcome of the case.

Anarchy The condition of having no government and no laws. Each member of the society governs himself or herself.

Anti-Federalist An individual who opposed the ratification of the new Constitution in 1787. The Anti-Federalists were opposed to a strong central government and attacked the failure of the Constitution's framers to include a bill of rights.

Appellate Court A court having jurisdiction to review cases and issues that were originally tried in lower courts.

Appointment Power The authority vested in the president to fill a government office or position. Positions filled by presidential appointment include those in the executive branch and the federal judiciary, commissioned officers in the armed forces, and members of the independent regulatory commissions.

Appropriation The passage, by Congress, of a spending bill, specifying the amount of authorized funds that actually will be allocated for an agency's use.

Aristocracy Rule by the best suited, through virtue, talent, or education; in later usage, rule by the upper class.

Attentive Public That portion of the general public that pays attention to policy issues.

Australian Ballot A secret ballot prepared, distributed, and tabulated by government officials at public expense. Since 1888, all states have used the Australian ballot rather than an open, public ballot.

Authority The features of a leader or an institution that compel obedience, usually because of ascribed legitimacy. For most societies, government is the ultimate authority.

Authorization A formal declaration by a legislative committee that a certain amount of funding may be available to an agency. Some authorizations terminate in a year; others are renewable automatically without further congressional action.

B

"Beauty Contest" A presidential primary in which contending candidates compete for popular votes but the results have little or no impact on the selection of delegates to the national convention, which is made by the party elite.

Bias An inclination or a preference that interferes with impartial judgment.

Bicameral Legislature A legislature made up of two chambers, or parts. The U.S. Congress, composed of the House of Representatives and the Senate, is a bicameral legislature.

Bicameralism The division of a legislature into two separate assemblies.

Block Grants Federal programs that provide funds to state and local governments for general functional areas, such as criminal justice or mental-health programs.

Bundling The practice of adding together maximum individual campaign contributions to increase their impact on the candidate.

Bureaucracy A large organization that is structured hierarchically to carry out specific functions.

Busing The transportation of public school students from areas where they live to schools in other areas to eliminate school segregation based on residential patterns.

C

Cabinet An advisory group selected by the president to aid in making decisions. The cabinet presently numbers thirteen department secretaries and the attorney general. Depending on the president, the cabinet may be highly influential or relatively insignificant in its advisory role.

Cabinet Department One of the fourteen departments of the executive branch (State, Treasury, Defense, Justice, Interior, Agriculture, Commerce, Labor, Health and Human Services, Housing and Urban Development, Education, Energy, Transportation, and Veterans Affairs).

Cadre The nucleus of political party activists carrying out the major functions of American political parties.

Capture The act of gaining direct or indirect control over agency personnel and decision makers by the industry that is being regulated.

Case Law The rules and principles announced in court decisions. Case law includes judicial interpretations of common law principles and doctrines as well as interpretations of constitutional law, statutory law, and administrative law.

Casework Personal work for constituents by members of Congress.

Categorical Grants-in-Aid Federal grants-in-aid to states or local governments that are for very specific programs or projects.

Caucus A closed meeting of party leaders to select party candidates or to decide on policy; also, a meeting of party members designed to select candidates and propose policies.

Charter A document issued by a government that grants to a person, a group of persons, or a corporation the right to carry on one or more specific activities. A state government can grant a charter to a municipality allowing that group of persons to carry on specific activities.

Checks and Balances A major principle of the American governmental system whereby each branch of the government exercises a check on the actions of the others.

Chief Diplomat The role of the president in recognizing foreign governments, making treaties, and making executive agreements.

Chief Executive The role of the president as head of the executive branch of the government.

Chief Legislator The role of the president in influencing the making of laws.

Chief of Staff The person who is named to direct the White House Office and advise the president.

Chief of State The role of the president as ceremonial head of the government.

Civil Law The law regulating conduct between private persons over noncriminal matters. Under civil law, the government provides the forum for the settlement of disputes between private parties in such matters as contracts, domestic relations, and business relations.

Civil Rights Generally, all rights rooted in the Fourteenth Amendment's guarantee of equal protection under the law.

Civil Service A collective term for the body of employees working for the government. Generally, civil service is understood to apply to all those who gain government employment through a merit system.

Civil Service Commission The initial central personnel agency of the national government; created in 1883.

Class-Action Suit A lawsuit filed by an individual seeking damages for "all persons similarly situated."

Class Politics Political preferences based on income level, social status, or both.

Climate Control The use of public relations techniques to create favorable public opinion toward an interest group, industry, or corporation.

Cloture A method invoked to close off debate and to bring the matter under consideration to a vote in the Senate.

Cold War The ideological, political, and economic impasse that existed between the United States and the Soviet Union following World War II.

Commander in Chief The role of the president as supreme commander of the military forces of the United States and of the state National Guard units when they are called into federal service.

Commerce Clause The section of the Constitution in which Congress is given the power to regulate trade among the states and with foreign countries.

Common Law Judge-made law that originated in England from decisions shaped according to prevailing customs. Decisions were applied to similar situations and thus gradually became common to the nation.

Competitive Federalism A model of federalism in which states compete with one another in the provision of goods and services so as to attract "customers"—citizens from other states.

Compliance The act of accepting and carrying out authorities' decisions.

Concurrent Powers Powers held jointly by the national and state governments.

Concurring Opinion A separate opinion, prepared by a judge who supports the decision of the majority of the court but who wants to make or clarify a particular point or to voice disapproval of the grounds on which the decision was made.

Confederal System A system of government consisting of a league of independent states, each having essentially sovereign powers. The central government created by such a league has only limited powers over the states.

Confederation A political system in which states or regional governments retain ultimate authority except for those powers they expressly delegate to a central government. A voluntary association of independent states, in which the member states agree to limited restraints on their freedom of action.

Conference Committee A special joint committee appointed to reconcile differences when bills pass the two chambers of Congress in different forms.

Consensus General agreement among the citizenry on an issue.

Consent of the People The idea that governments and laws derive their legitimacy from the consent of the governed.

Conservatism A set of beliefs that includes a limited role for the national government in helping individuals, support for traditional values and lifestyles, and a cautious response to change.

Conservative Coalition An alliance of Republicans and southern Democrats that can form in the House or the Senate to oppose liberal legislation and support conservative legislation.

Consolidation The union of two or more governmental units to form a single unit.

Constituent One of the people represented by a legislator or other elected or appointed official.

Constitutional Initiative An electoral device whereby citizens can propose a constitutional amendment through petitions signed by the required number of registered voters.

Constitutional Power A power vested in the president by Article II of the Constitution.

Containment A U.S. diplomatic policy adopted by the Truman administration to "build situations of strength" around the globe to contain Communist power within its existing boundaries.

Continuing Resolution A temporary law that Congress passes when an appropriations bill has not been decided by the beginning of the new fiscal year on October 1.

Contracting Out The replacement of government services with services provided by private firms.

Cooley's Rule The view that cities should be able to govern themselves, presented in an 1871 Michigan decision by Judge Thomas Cooley.

Cooperative Federalism The theory that the states and the national government should cooperate in solving problems.

Corrupt Practices Acts A series of acts passed by Congress in an attempt to limit and regulate the size and sources of contributions and expenditures in political campaigns.

Council of Economic Advisers (CEA) A staff agency in the Executive Office of the President that advises the president on measures to maintain stability in the nation's economy; established in 1946.

Council of Government (COG) A voluntary organization of counties and municipalities concerned with areawide problems.

County The chief governmental unit set up by the state to administer state law and business at the local level. Counties are drawn up by area, rather than by rural or urban criteria.

Credentials Committee A committee used by political parties at their national conventions to determine which delegates may participate. The committee inspects the claim of each prospective delegate to be seated as a legitimate representative of his or her state.

Criminal Law The law that defines crimes and provides punishment for violations. In criminal cases, the government is the prosecutor, because crimes are against the public order.

D

De Facto Segregation Racial segregation that occurs because of past social and economic conditions and residential patterns.

De Jure Segregation Racial segregation that occurs because of laws or administrative decisions by public agencies.

Democracy A system of government in which ultimate political authority is vested in the people. Derived from the Greek words *demos* ("the people") and *kratos* ("authority").

Democratic Party One of the two major American political parties evolving out of the Democratic (Jeffersonian) Republican group supporting Thomas Jefferson.

Détente A French word meaning the relaxation of tensions. The term characterizes U.S.–Soviet policy as it developed under President Richard Nixon and Secretary of State Henry Kissinger. Détente stressed direct cooperative dealings with Cold War rivals but avoided ideological accommodation.

Dillon's Rule The narrowest possible interpretation of the legal status of local governments, outlined by Judge John F. Dillon, who in 1872 stated that a municipal corporation can exercise only those powers expressly granted by state law.

Diplomacy The total process by which states carry on political relations with each other; settling conflicts among nations by peaceful means.

Diplomatic Recognition The president's power, as chief diplomat, to acknowledge a foreign government as legitimate.

Direct Democracy A system of government in which political decisions are made by the people directly, rather than by their elected representatives; probably possible only in small political communities.

Direct Primary An intraparty election in which the voters select the candidates who will run on a party's ticket in the subsequent general election.

Direct Technique An interest group activity that involves interaction with government officials to further the group's goals.

Discharge Petition A procedure by which a bill in the House of Representatives may be forced out of a committee (discharged) that has refused to report it for consideration by the House. The discharge petition must be signed by an absolute majority (218) of representatives and is used only on rare occasions.

Dissenting Opinion A separate opinion in which a judge dissents from (disagrees with) the conclusion reached by the majority on the court and expounds his or her own views about the case.

Diversity of Citizenship A basis for federal court jurisdiction over a lawsuit between (1) citizens of different states, (2) a foreign country and citizens of a state or of different states, or (3) citizens of a state and citizens or subjects of a foreign country. The amount in controversy must be more than $75,000 before a federal court can take jurisdiction in such cases.

Divided Government A situation in which one major political party controls the presidency and the other controls the chambers of Congress, or in which one party controls a state governorship and the other controls the state legislature.

Divisive Opinion Public opinion that is polarized between two quite different positions.

Domestic Policy Public plans or courses of action that concern issues of national importance, such as poverty, crime, and the environment.

Dominant Culture The values, customs, language, and ideals established by the group or groups in a society that traditionally have controlled politics and government institutions in that society.

Dual Federalism A system of government in which the states and the national government each remain supreme within their own spheres. The doctrine looks on nation and state as coequal sovereign powers. It holds that acts of states within their reserved powers are legitimate limitations on the powers of the national government.

E

Earned-Income Tax Credit (EITC) Program A government program that helps low-income workers by giving back part or all of their Social Security taxes.

Economic Aid Assistance to other nations in the form of grants, loans, or credits to buy the assisting nation's products.

Elector A person on the partisan slate that is selected early in the presidential election year according to state laws and the applicable political party apparatus. Electors cast ballots for president and vice president. The number of electors in each state is equal to that state's number of representatives in both houses of Congress.

Electronic Media Broadcasting media (radio and television). The term derives from their method of transmission, in contrast to printed media.

Elite An upper socioeconomic class that controls political and economic affairs.

Elite Theory A perspective holding that society is ruled by a small number of people who exercise power in their self-interest.

Emergency Power An inherent power exercised by the president during a period of national crisis, particularly in foreign affairs.

Enabling Legislation A statute enacted by Congress that authorizes the creation of an administrative agency and specifies the name, purpose, composition, and powers of the agency being created.

Enumerated Powers Powers specifically granted to the national government by the Constitution. The first seventeen clauses of Article I, Section 8, specify most of the enumerated powers of Congress.

Environmental Impact Statement (EIS) As a requirement mandated by the National Environmental Policy Act, a report that must show the costs and benefits of major federal actions that could significantly affect the quality of the environment.

Equal Employment Opportunity Commission (EEOC) A commission established by the 1964 Civil Rights Act to (1) end discrimination based on race, color, religion, gender, or national origin in conditions of employment and (2) promote voluntary action programs by employers, unions, and community organizations to foster equal job opportunities.

Equality A concept that all people are of equal worth.

Equalization A method for adjusting the amount of money that a state must provide to receive federal funds. The formula used takes into account the wealth of the state or its ability to tax its citizens.

Era of Good Feeling The years from 1817 to 1825, when James Monroe was president and there was, in effect, no political opposition.

Era of Personal Politics An era when attention centers on the character of individual candidates rather than on party identification.

Executive Agreement A binding international agreement made between chiefs of state that does not require legislative sanction.

Executive Budget The budget prepared and submitted by the president to Congress.

Executive Office of the President (EOP) Established by President Franklin D. Roosevelt by executive order under the Reorganization Act of 1939, the EOP currently consists of nine staff agencies that assist the president in carrying out major duties.

Executive Order A rule or regulation issued by the president that has the effect of law. Executive orders can implement and give administrative effect to provisions in the Constitution, to treaties, and to statutes.

Executive Privilege The right of executive officials to refuse to appear before, or to withhold information from, a legislative committee. Executive privilege is enjoyed by the president and by those executive officials accorded that right by the president.

Expressed Power A constitutional or statutory power of the president, which is expressly written into the Constitution or into statutory law.

F

Faction A group or bloc in a legislature or political party acting together in pursuit of some special interest or position.

Fall Review The time every year when, after receiving formal federal agency requests for funding for the next fiscal year, the Office of Management and Budget reviews the requests, makes changes, and submits its recommendations to the president.

Federal Mandate A requirement in federal legislation that forces states and municipalities to comply with certain rules.

Federal Open Market Committee (FOMC) The most important body within the Federal Reserve System. The FOMC decides how monetary policy should be carried out by the Federal Reserve System.

Federal Question A question that pertains to the U.S. Constitution, acts of Congress, or treaties. A federal question provides a basis for federal jurisdiction.

Federal Register A publication of the executive branch of the U.S. government that prints executive orders, rules, and regulations.

Federal System A system of government in which power is divided by a written constitution between a central government and regional, or subdivisional, governments. Each level must have some domain in which its policies are dominant and some genuine political or constitutional guarantee of its authority.

Federalists Those who supported the adoption of the new Constitution and the creation of the federal union; the first American political party, led by Alexander Hamilton and John Adams.

Feminism The movement that supports political, economic, and social equality for women.

Filibuster In the Senate, unlimited debate to halt action on a particular bill.

Fireside Chat One of the warm, informal talks by Franklin D. Roosevelt to a few million of his intimate friends—via the radio. Roosevelt's fireside chats were so effective that succeeding presidents have been urged by their advisers to emulate him by giving more radio and television reports to the nation.

First Budget Resolution A resolution passed by Congress in May that sets overall revenue and spending goals for the following fiscal year.

First Continental Congress The first gathering of delegates from twelve of the thirteen colonies, held in 1774.

Fiscal Policy The use of changes in government spending or taxation to alter national economic variables, such as the rate of unemployment.

Fiscal Year (FY) The twelve-month period that is used for bookkeeping, or accounting, purposes. Usually, the fiscal year does not coincide with the calendar year. For example, the federal government's fiscal year runs from October 1 through September 30.

Fluidity The extent to which public opinion changes over time.

Focus Group A small group of individuals who are led in discussion by a professional consultant to gather opinions and responses to candidates and issues.

Food Stamps Coupons issued by the federal government to low-income individuals to be used for the purchase of food.

Foreign Policy A nation's external goals and the techniques and strategies used to achieve them.

Foreign Policy Process The steps by which external goals are decided and acted on.

Franking A policy that enables members of Congress to send material through the mail by substituting their facsimile signature (frank) for postage.

Fraternity From the Latin *fraternus* (brother), a term that came to mean, in the political philosophy of the eighteenth century, the condition in which each individual considers the needs of all others; a brotherhood. In the French Revolution of 1789, the popular cry was "liberty, equality, and fraternity."

Front-Loading The practice of moving presidential primary elections to the early part of the campaign, to maximize the impact of certain states or regions on the nomination.

Front-Runner The presidential candidate who appears to have the most momentum at a given time in the primary season.

Functional Consolidation The cooperation of two or more units of local government in providing services to their inhabitants.

G

Garbage Can Model A model of bureaucracy that characterizes bureaucracies as rudderless entities with little formal organization in which solutions to problems are based on trial and error rather than rational policy planning.

Gender Discrimination Any practice, policy, or procedure that denies equality of treatment to an individual or to a group because of gender.

Gender Gap A term most often used to describe the difference between the percentage of votes a candidate receives from women and the percentage of votes the candidate receives from men. The term came into use after the 1980 presidential election.

General Jurisdiction Exists when a court's authority to hear cases is not significantly restricted. A court of general jurisdiction normally can hear a broad range of cases.

General Law City A city operating under general state laws that apply to all local govern-mental units of a similar type.

General Sales Tax A tax levied as a proportion of the retail price of a commodity at the point of sale.

Generational Effect A long-lasting effect of events of a particular time period on the political opinions or preferences of those who came of political age at that time.

Gerrymandering The drawing of legislative district boundary lines for the purpose of obtaining partisan or factional advantage. A district is said to be gerrymandered when its shape is manipulated by the dominant party in the state legislature to maximize electoral strength at the expense of the minority party.

Government A permanent structure (institution) composed of decision makers who make society's rules about conflict resolution and the allocation of resources and who possess the power to enforce those rules.

Government Corporation An agency of government that administers a quasi-business enterprise. These corporations are used when activities are primarily commercial. They produce revenue for their continued existence, and they require greater flexibility than is permitted for departments and agencies.

Government in the Sunshine Act A law that requires all multiheaded federal agencies to conduct their business regularly in public session.

Grandfather Clause A device used by southern states to exempt whites from state taxes and literacy laws originally intended to disfranchise African American voters. It restricted the voting franchise to those who could prove that their grandfathers had voted before 1867.

Great Compromise The compromise between the New Jersey and the Virginia plans that created one chamber of the Congress based on population and one chamber that represented each state equally; also called the Connecticut Compromise.

H

Hatch Act (Political Activities Act) An act passed in 1939 that prohibits the use of federal authority to influence nominations and elections or the use of rank to pressure federal employees to make political contributions. It also prohibits civil service employees from active involvement in political campaigns.

Home Rule City A city with a charter allowing local voters to frame, adopt, and amend their own charter.

Horizontal Federalism Activities, problems, and policies that require state governments to interact with one another.

Hyperpluralism A situation that arises when interest groups become so powerful that they dominate the political decision-making structures, rendering any consideration of the greater public interest impossible.

I

Ideologue An individual whose political opinions are carefully thought out and relatively consistent with one another. Ideologues are often described as having a comprehensive world view.

Ideology A comprehensive and logically ordered set of beliefs about the nature of people and about the institutions and role of government.

Impeachment As authorized by Article I of the Constitution, an action by the House of Representatives and the Senate to remove the president, vice president, or civil officers of the United States from office for crimes of "Treason, Bribery, or other high Crimes and Misdemeanors."

In-Kind Subsidy A good or service—such as food stamps, housing, or medical care—provided by the government to lower-income groups.

Income Transfer A transfer of income from some individuals in the economy to other individuals. This is generally done by way of the government. It is a transfer in the sense that no current services are rendered by the recipients.

Independent A voter or candidate who does not identify with a political party.

Independent Executive Agency A federal agency that is not part of a cabinet department but reports directly to the president.

Independent Expenditures Nonregulated contributions from PACs, ideological organizations, and individuals. The groups may spend funds on advertising or other campaign activities so long as those expenditures are not coordinated with those of a candidate.

Independent Regulatory Agency An agency outside the major executive departments charged with making and implementing rules and regulations to protect the public interest.

Indirect Technique A strategy employed by interest groups that uses third parties to influence government officials.

Inherent Power A power of the president derived from the loosely worded statement in the Constitution that "the executive Power shall be vested in a President" and that the president should "take Care that the Laws be faithfully executed"; defined through practice rather than through constitutional or statutory law.

Initiative A procedure by which voters can propose a law or a constitutional amendment.

Injunction An order issued by a court to compel or restrain the performance of an act by an individual or entity.

Institution A long-standing, identifiable structure or association that performs certain functions for society.

Instructed Delegate A legislator who is an agent of the voters who elected him or her and who votes according to the views of constituents regardless of personal assessments.

Intelligence Community The government agencies that are involved in gathering information about the capabilities and intentions of foreign governments and that engage in activities to further U.S. foreign policy aims.

Intensity The strength of a position for or against a public policy or an issue. Intensity is often critical in generating public action; an intense minority can often win on an issue of public policy over a less intense majority.

Interest Group An organized group of individuals sharing common objectives who actively attempt to influence policymakers in all three branches of the government and at all levels.

Interstate Compact An agreement between two or more states. Agreements on minor matters are made without congressional consent, but any compact that tends to increase the power of the contracting states relative to other states or relative to the national government generally requires the consent of Congress. Such compacts serve as a means by which states can solve regional problems.

Iron Curtain The term used to describe the division of Europe between the Soviet Union and the West; popularized by Winston Churchill in a speech portraying Europe as being divided by an iron curtain, with the nations of Eastern Europe behind the curtain and increasingly under Soviet control.

Iron Triangle The three-way alliance among legislators, bureaucrats, and interest groups to make or preserve policies that benefit their respective interests.

Isolationist Foreign Policy Abstaining from an active role in international affairs or alliances, which characterized U.S. foreign policy toward Europe during most of the nineteenth century.

Issue Network A group of individuals or organizations—which may consist of legislators or legislative staff members, interest group leaders, bureaucrats, the media, scholars, and other experts—that supports a particular policy position on a given issue, such as one relating to the environment, to taxation, or to consumer safety.

Item Veto The power exercised by the governors of most states to veto particular sections or items of an appropriations bill, while signing the remainder of the bill into law.

J

Joint Committee A legislative committee composed of members from both chambers of Congress.

Judicial Activism A doctrine holding that the Supreme Court should take an active role in using its powers to check the activities of Congress, state legislatures, and administrative agencies when those government bodies exceed their authority.

Judicial Implementation The way in which court decisions are translated into action.

Judicial Restraint A doctrine holding that the Supreme Court should defer to the decisions made by the elected representatives of the people in the legislative and executive branches.

Judicial Review The power of the Supreme Court or any court to declare unconstitutional federal or state laws and other acts of government.

Jurisdiction The authority of a court to decide certain cases. Not all courts have the authority to decide all cases. Where a case arises and what its subject matter is are two jurisdictional factors.

Justiciable Dispute A dispute that raises questions about the law and that is appropriate for resolution before a court of law.

Justiciable Question A question that may be raised and reviewed in court.

K

Keynesian Economics An economic theory, named after English economist John Maynard Keynes, that gained prominence during the Great Depression of the 1930s. It is typically associated with the use of fiscal policy to alter national economic variables—for example, increased government spending during times of economic downturns.

Kitchen Cabinet The informal advisers to the president.

L

Labor Movement Generally, the full range of economic and political expression of working-class interests; politically, the organization of working-class interests.

Lawmaking The process of deciding the legal rules that govern society. Such laws may regulate minor affairs or establish broad national policies.

Legislative Initiative A procedure by which voters can propose a change in state or local laws by gathering signatures on a petition and submitting it to the legislature for approval.

Legislative Veto A provision in a bill reserving to Congress or to a congressional committee the power to reject an action or regulation of a national agency by majority vote; declared unconstitutional by the Supreme Court in 1983.

Legislature A government body primarily responsible for the making of laws.

Legitimacy A status conferred by the people on the government's officials, acts, and institutions through their belief that the government's actions are an appropriate use of power by a legally constituted governmental authority following correct decision-making policies. These actions are regarded as rightful and entitled to compliance and obedience on the part of citizens.

Liberalism A set of beliefs that includes the advocacy of positive government action to improve the welfare of individuals, support for civil rights, and tolerance for political and social change.

Liberty The greatest freedom of individuals that is consistent with the freedom of other individuals in the society.

Limited Government A form of government based on the principle that the powers of government should be clearly limited either through a written document or through wide public understanding; characterized by institutional checks to ensure that government serves the public rather than private interests.

Limited Jurisdiction Exists when a court's authority to hear cases is restricted to certain types of claims, such as tax claims or bankruptcy petitions.

Line-Item Veto The power of an executive to veto individual lines or items within a piece of legislation without vetoing the entire bill.

Line Organization With respect to the federal government, an administrative unit that is directly accountable to the president.

Literacy Test A test administered as a precondition for voting, often used to prevent African Americans from exercising their right to vote.

Litigate To engage in a legal proceeding or seek relief in a court of law; to carry on a lawsuit.

Lobbying The attempt by organizations or by individuals to influence the passage, defeat, or contents of legislation and the administrative decisions of government.

Logrolling An arrangement in which two or more members of Congress agree in advance to support each other's bills.

Loophole A legal method by which individuals and businesses are allowed to reduce the tax liabilities owed to the government.

M

Madisonian Model A structure of government proposed by James Madison in which the powers of the government are separated into three branches: executive, legislative, and judicial.

Majority Floor Leader The chief spokesperson of the major party in the Senate, who directs the legislative program and party strategy.

Majority More than 50 percent; full age, or the age at which a person is entitled by law to the right to manage his or her own affairs and to the full enjoyment of civil rights.

Majority Leader of the House A legislative position held by an important party member in the House of Representatives. The majority leader is selected by the majority party in caucus or conference to foster cohesion among party members and to act as spokesperson for the majority party in the House.

Majority Opinion A court opinion reflecting the views of the majority of the judges.

Majority Rule A basic principle of democracy asserting that the greatest number of citizens in any political unit should select officials and determine policies.

Managed News Information generated and distributed by the government in such a way as to give government interests priority over candor.

Mandatory Retirement Forced retirement when a person reaches a certain age.

Matching Funds For many categorical grant programs, money that the state must provide to "match" the federal funds. Some programs require the state to raise only 10 percent of the funds, whereas others approach an even share.

Material Incentive A reason or motive having to do with economic benefits or opportunities.

Media The technical means of communication with mass audiences.

Media Access The public's right of access to the media. The Federal Communications Commission and the courts gradually have taken the stance that citizens do have a right to media access.

Merit System The selection, retention, and promotion of government employees on the basis of competitive examinations.

Military-Industrial Complex The mutually beneficial relationship between the armed forces and defense contractors.

Minority Floor Leader The party officer in the Senate who commands the minority party's opposition to the policies of the majority party and directs the legislative program and strategy of his or her party.

Minority Leader of the House The party leader elected by the minority party in the House.

Monetary Policy The use of changes in the amount of money in circulation to alter credit markets, employment, and the rate of inflation.

Monopolistic Model A model of bureaucracy that compares bureaucracies to monopolistic business firms. Lack of competition within a bureaucracy leads to inefficient and costly operations. Because bureaucracies are not penalized for inefficiency, there is no incentive to reduce costs or use resources more productively.

Monroe Doctrine The policy statement included in President James Monroe's 1823 annual message to Congress, which set out three principles: (1) European nations should not establish new colonies in the Western Hemisphere, (2) European nations should not intervene in the affairs of independent nations of the Western Hemisphere, and (3) the United States would not interfere in the affairs of European nations.

Moral Idealism A philosophy that sees all nations as willing to cooperate and agree on moral standards for conduct.

Most-Favored-Nation Status A status granted by an international treaty by which each member nation must treat other members at least as well as it treats the country that receives its most favorable treatment.

Municipal Home Rule The power vested in a local unit of government to draft or change its own charter and to manage its own affairs.

N

Narrowcasting Broadcasting that is targeted to one small sector of the population.

National Committee A standing committee of a national political party established to direct and coordinate party activities during the four-year period between national party conventions.

National Convention The meeting held every four years by each major party to select presidential and vice presidential candidates, to write a platform, to choose a national committee, and to conduct party business. In theory, the national convention is at the top of a hierarchy of party conventions (the local and state conventions are below it) that consider candidates and issues.

National Politics The pursuit of interests that are of concern to the nation as a whole.

National Security Council (NSC) A staff agency in the Executive Office of the President established by the National Security Act of 1947. The NSC advises the president on domestic and foreign matters involving national security.

National Security Policy Foreign and domestic policy designed to protect the independence and political and economic integrity of the United States; policy that is concerned with the safety and defense of the nation.

Natural Aristocracy A small ruling clique of a society's "best" citizens, whose membership is based on birth, wealth, and ability. The Jeffersonian era emphasized government rule by such a group.

Natural Rights Rights held to be inherent in natural law, not dependent on governments. John Locke stated that natural law, being superior to human law, specifies certain rights of "life, liberty, and property." These rights, altered to become "life, liberty, and the pursuit of happiness," are asserted in the Declaration of Independence.

Necessaries In contract law, necessaries include whatever is reasonably necessary for suitable subsistence as measured by age, state, condition in life, and so on.

Negative Constituents Citizens who openly oppose government foreign policies.

New England Town A governmental unit that combines the roles of city and county into one unit in the New England states.

New Federalism A plan both to limit the national government's power to regulate and to restore power to state governments. Essentially, the new federalism is designed to give the states greater ability to decide for themselves how government revenues should be spent.

Nullification The act of nullifying, or rendering void. Prior to the Civil War, southern supporters of states' rights claimed that a state had the right to declare a national law to be null and void and therefore not binding on its citizens, on the assumption that ultimate sovereign authority rested with the several states.

O

Office of Management and Budget (OMB) A division of the Executive Office of the President created by executive order in 1970 to replace the Bureau of the Budget. The OMB's main functions are to assist the president in preparing the annual budget, to clear and coordinate all departmental agency budgets, to help set fiscal policy, and to supervise the administration of the federal budget.

Oligarchy Rule by a few members of the elite, who generally make decisions to benefit their own group.

Ombudsperson A person who hears and investigates complaints by private individuals against public officials or agencies.

Opinion The statement by a judge or a court of the decision reached in a case tried or argued before it. The opinion sets forth the court's ruling, the law that applies to the case, and the legal reasoning on which the ruling was based.

Opinion Leader One who is able to influence the opinions of others because of position, expertise, or personality. Such leaders help to shape public opinion.

Opinion Poll A method of systematically questioning a small, selected sample of respondents who are deemed representative of the total population. Opinion polls are widely used by government, business, university scholars, political candidates, and voluntary groups to provide reasonably accurate data on public attitudes, beliefs, expectations, and behavior.

Oral Arguments The verbal arguments presented in person by attorneys to an appellate court. Each attorney presents reasons to the court why the court should rule in his or her client's favor.

Oversight The responsibility Congress has for following up on laws it has enacted to ensure that they are being enforced and administered in the way in which they were intended.

P

Pardon The granting of a release from the punishment or legal consequences of a crime; a pardon can be granted by the president before or after a conviction.

Party Identification Linking oneself to a particular political party.

Party Identifier A person who identifies with a political party.

Party Organization The formal structure and leadership of a political party, including election committees; local, state, and national executives; and paid professional staff.

Party Platform A document drawn up by the platform committee at each national convention, outlining the policies, positions, and principles of the party; it is then submitted to the entire convention for approval.

Party-in-Government All of the elected and appointed officials who identify with a political party.

Party-in-the-Electorate Those members of the general public who identify with a political party or who express a preference for one party over the other.

Patronage Rewarding faithful party workers and followers with government employment and contracts.

Peer Group A group consisting of members sharing common relevant social characteristics. These groups play an important part in the socialization process, helping to shape attitudes and beliefs.

Pendleton Act (Civil Service Reform Act) The law, as amended over the years, that remains the basic statute regulating federal employment personnel policies. It established the principle of employment on the basis of merit and created the Civil Service Commission to administer the personnel service.

Picket-Fence Federalism A model of federalism in which specific programs and policies (depicted as vertical pickets in a picket fence) involve all levels of government—national, state, and local (depicted by the horizontal boards in a picket fence).

Pluralism A theory that views politics as a conflict among interest groups. Political decision making is characterized by bargaining and compromise.

Plurality The total votes cast for a candidate who receives more votes than any other candidate but not necessarily a majority. Most national, state, and local electoral laws provide for winning elections by a plurality vote.

Pocket Veto A special veto power exercised by the chief executive after a legislative body has adjourned. Bills not signed by the chief executive die after a specified period of time. If Congress wishes to reconsider such a bill, it must be reintroduced in the following session of Congress.

Police Power The authority to legislate for the protection of the health, morals, safety, and welfare of the people. In the United States, most police power is a reserved power of the states.

Policy Trade-Offs The cost to the nation of undertaking any one policy in terms of all of the other policies that could have been undertaken. For example, an increase in the expenditures on one federal program means either a reduction in expenditures on another program or an increase in federal taxes (or the deficit).

Political Action Committee (PAC) A committee set up by and representing a corporation, labor union, or special interest group. PACs raise and give campaign donations on behalf of the organizations or groups they represent.

Political Consultant A paid professional hired to devise a campaign strategy and manage a campaign. Image building is the crucial task of the political consultant.

Political Culture The collection of beliefs and attitudes toward government and the political process held by a community or nation.

Political Party A group of political activists who organize to win elections, to operate the government, and to determine public policy.

Political Question An issue that a court believes should be decided by the executive or legislative branch.

Political Realism A philosophy that sees each nation acting principally in its own interest.

Political Socialization The process through which individuals learn a set of political attitudes and form opinions about social issues.

The family and the educational system are two of the most important forces in the political socialization process.

Political Trust The degree to which individuals express trust in the government and political institutions, usually measured through a specific series of survey questions.

Politico The legislative role that combines the instructed-delegate and trustee concepts. The legislator varies the role according to the issue under consideration.

Politics According to David Easton, the "authoritative allocation of values" for a society; according to Harold Lasswell, "who gets what, when, and how" in a society.

Poll Tax A special tax that must be paid as a qualification for voting. The Twenty-fourth Amendment to the Constitution outlawed the poll tax in national elections, and in 1966 the Supreme Court declared it unconstitutional in all elections.

Popular Sovereignty The concept that ultimate political authority rests with the people.

Power The ability to cause others to modify their behavior and to conform to what the power holder wants.

Precedent A court rule bearing on subsequent legal decisions in similar cases. Judges rely on precedents in deciding cases.

President *Pro Tempore* The temporary presiding officer of the Senate in the absence of the vice president.

Presidential Primary A statewide primary election of delegates to a political party's national convention to help a party determine its presidential nominee. Such delegates are either pledged to a particular candidate or unpledged.

Press Secretary The individual responsible for representing the White House before the media. The press secretary writes news releases, provides background information, sets up press conferences, and so on.

Property Anything that is or may be subject to ownership. As conceived by the political philosopher John Locke, the right to property is a natural right superior to human law (laws made by government).

Property Tax A tax on the value of real estate. This tax is limited to state and local governments and is a particularly important source of revenue for local governments.

Public Agenda Issues that commonly are perceived by members of the political community as meriting public attention and governmental action. The media play an important role in setting the public agenda by focusing attention on certain topics.

Public Debt, or National Debt The total amount of debt carried by the federal government.

Public Debt Financing The government's spending more than it receives in taxes and paying for the difference by issuing U.S. Treasury bonds, thereby adding to the public debt.

Public Interest The best interests of the collective, overall community; the national good, rather than the narrow interests of a self-serving group.

Public Opinion The aggregate of individual attitudes or beliefs shared by some portion of the adult population. There is no one public opinion, because there are many different "publics."

Purposive Incentive A reason or motive having to do with ethical beliefs or ideological principles.

R

Ratification Formal approval.

Reapportionment The allocation of seats in the House of Representatives to each state after each census.

Recall A procedure allowing the people to vote to dismiss an elected official from state office before his or her term has expired.

Redistricting The redrawing of the boundaries of the congressional districts within each state.

Referendum An electoral device whereby legislative or constitutional measures are referred by the legislature to the voters for approval or disapproval.

Regressive Tax A tax system in which tax rates go down as income goes up.

Relevance The extent to which an issue is of concern at a particular time. Issues become relevant when the public views them as pressing or of direct concern to daily life.

Remand To send a case back to the court that originally heard it.

Representation The function of members of Congress as elected officials in representing the views of their constituents.

Representative Assembly A legislature composed of individuals who represent the population.

Representative Democracy A form of government in which representatives elected by the people make and enforce laws and policies.

Reprieve The presidential power to postpone the execution of a sentence imposed by a court of law; usually done for humanitarian reasons or to await new evidence.

Republic The form of government in which sovereignty rests with the people, who elect agents to represent them in lawmaking and other decisions.

Republican Party One of the two major American political parties, which emerged in the 1850s as an antislavery party. It was created to fill the vacuum caused by the disintegration of the Whig Party.

Reverse To annul or make void a judgment on account of some error or irregularity.

Reverse Discrimination The charge that affirmative action programs requiring preferential treatment or quotas discriminate against those who do not have minority status.

Rule of Four A United States Supreme Court procedure requiring four affirmative votes to hear the case before the full Court.

Rules Committee A standing committee of the House of Representatives that provides special rules under which specific bills can be debated, amended, and considered by the House.

S

Safe Seat A district that returns the legislator with 55 percent of the vote or more.

Sampling Error The difference between a sample's results and the true result if the entire population had been interviewed.

Secession The act of formally withdrawing from membership in an alliance; the withdrawal of a state from the federal Union.

Second Budget Resolution A resolution passed by Congress in September that sets "binding" limits on taxes and spending for the next fiscal year beginning October 1.

Second Continental Congress The 1775 congress of the colonies that established an army.

Sectional Politics The pursuit of interests that are of special concern to a region or section of the country.

Select Committee A temporary legislative committee established for a limited time period and for a special purpose.

Selectperson A member of the governing group of a town.

Senatorial Courtesy In regard to federal district court judgeship nominations, a Senate tradition allowing a senator of the president's political party to veto a judicial appointment in his or her state simply by indicating that the appointment is personally not acceptable. At that point, the Senate may reject the nomination, or the president may withdraw consideration of the nominee.

Seniority System A custom followed in both chambers of Congress specifying that members with longer terms of continuous service will be given preference when committee chairpersons and holders of other significant posts are selected.

Separate-but-Equal Doctrine The doctrine holding that segregation in schools and public accommodations does not imply that one race is superior to another; and that separate-but-equal facilities do not violate the equal protection clause.

Separation of Powers The principle of dividing governmental powers among the executive, the legislative, and the judicial branches of government.

Service Sector The sector of the economy that provides services—such as food services, insurance, and education—in contrast to the sector of the economy that produces goods.

Sexual Harassment Unwanted physical or verbal conduct or abuse of a sexual nature that interferes with a recipient's job performance, creates a hostile environment, or carries with it an implicit or explicit threat of adverse employment consequences.

Social Movement A movement that represents the demands of a large segment of the public for political, economic, or social change.

Soft Money Campaign contributions that evade contribution limits by being given to parties and party committees to help fund general party activities.

Solid South A term describing the tendency of the post–Civil War southern states to vote for the Democratic Party. (Voting patterns in the South have changed, though.)

Solidary Incentive A reason or motive having to do with the desire to associate with others and to share with others a particular interest or hobby.

Sound Bite A brief, memorable comment that easily can be fit into news broadcasts.

Soviet Bloc The Eastern European countries that installed Communist regimes after World War II.

Speaker of the House The presiding officer in the House of Representatives. The speaker is always a member of the majority party and is the most powerful and influential member of the House.

Spin An interpretation of campaign events or election results that is most favorable to the candidate's campaign strategy.

Spin Doctor A political campaign adviser who tries to convince journalists of the truth of a particular interpretation of events.

Splinter Party A new party formed by a dissident faction within a major political party. Usually, splinter parties have emerged when a particular personality was at odds with the major party.

Spoils System The awarding of government jobs to political supporters and friends; generally associated with President Andrew Jackson.

Spring Review The time every year when the Office of Management and Budget requires federal agencies to review their programs, activities, and goals and submit their requests for funding for the next fiscal year.

Stability The extent to which public opinion remains constant over a period of time.

Standing Committee A permanent committee within the House or Senate that considers bills within a certain subject area.

Stare Decisis To stand on decided cases; the judicial policy of following precedents established by past decisions.

State A group of people occupying a specific area and organized under one government; may be either a nation or a subunit of a nation.

State Central Committee The principal organized structure of each political party within each state. This committee is responsible for carrying out policy decisions of the party's state convention.

State of the Union Message An annual message to Congress in which the president proposes a legislative program. The message is addressed not only to Congress but also to the American people and to the world. It offers the opportunity to dramatize policies and objectives and to gain public support.

Statutory Power A power created for the president through laws enacted by Congress.

Strategic Arms Limitation Treaty (SALT I) A treaty between the United States and the Soviet Union to stabilize the nuclear arms competition between the two countries. SALT I talks began in 1969, and agreements were signed on May 26, 1972.

Subpoena A legal writ requiring a person's appearance in court to give testimony.

Suffrage The right to vote; the franchise.

Sunset Legislation A law requiring that an existing program be reviewed regularly for its effectiveness and be terminated unless specifically extended as a result of this review.

Super Tuesday The date on which a number of presidential primaries are held, including those of most of the southern states.

Superdelegate A party leader or elected official who is given the right to vote at the party's national convention. Superdelegates are not elected at the state level.

Supplemental Security Income (SSI) A federal program established to provide assistance to elderly persons and disabled persons.

Supremacy Clause The constitutional provision that makes the Constitution and federal laws superior to all conflicting state and local laws.

Supremacy Doctrine A doctrine that asserts the superiority of national law over state or regional laws. This principle is rooted in Article VI of the Constitution, which provides that the Constitution, the laws passed by the national government under its constitutional powers, and all treaties constitute the supreme law of the land.

T

Tariff A tax on imported goods.

Technical Assistance The sending of experts with technical skills in agriculture, engineering, or business to aid other nations.

Temporary Assistance to Needy Families (TANF) A state-administered program in which grants from the national government are given to the states, which use the funds to provide assistance to those eligible to receive welfare benefits. The TANF program was created by the Welfare Reform Act of 1996 and replaced the former AFDC program.

Third Party A political party other than the two major political parties (Republican and Democratic). Usually, third parties are composed of dissatisfied groups that have split from the major parties. They act as indicators of political trends and as safety valves for dissident groups.

Ticket Splitting Voting for candidates of two or more parties for different offices. For example, a voter splits her ticket if she votes for a Republican presidential candidate and for a Democratic congressional candidate.

Totalitarian Regime A form of government that controls all aspects of the political and social life of a nation. All power resides with the government. The citizens have no power to choose the leadership or policies of the country.

Town Manager System A form of city government in which voters elect three selectpersons, who then appoint a professional town manager, who in turn appoints other officials.

Town Meeting The governing authority of a New England town. Qualified voters may participate in the election of officers and in the passage of legislation.

Township A rural unit of government based on federal land surveys of the American frontier in the 1780s. Townships have declined significantly in importance.

Tracking Poll A poll taken for the candidate on a nearly daily basis as election day approaches.

Trial Court The court in which most cases usually begin and in which questions of fact are examined.

Truman Doctrine The policy adopted by President Harry Truman in 1947 to halt Communist expansion in southeastern Europe.

Trustee In regard to a legislator, one who acts according to his or her conscience and the broad interests of the entire society.

Twelfth Amendment An amendment to the Constitution, adopted in

1804, that specifies the separate election of the president and vice president by the electoral college.

Twenty-fifth Amendment An amendment to the Constitution adopted in 1967 that establishes procedures for filling vacancies in the two top executive offices and that makes provisions for situations involving presidential disability.

Two-Party System A political system in which only two parties have a reasonable chance of winning.

U

U.S. Treasury Bond Evidence of debt issued by the federal government; similar to corporate bonds but issued by the U.S. Treasury.

Unanimous Opinion A court opinion or determination on which all judges agree.

Underground Economy The part of the economy that does not pay taxes and so is not directly measured by government statisticians; also called the subterranean economy or unreported economy.

Unicameral Legislature A legislature with only one legislative body, as compared with a bicameral (two-house) legislature, such as the U.S. Congress. Nebraska is the only state in the union with a unicameral legislature.

Unincorporated Area An area not located within the boundary of a municipality.

Unit Rule All of a state's electoral votes are cast for the presidential candidate receiving a plurality of the popular vote.

Unitary System A centralized governmental system in which local or subdivisional governments exercise only those powers given to them by the central government.

Universal Suffrage The right of all adults to vote for their representatives.

V

Veto Message The president's formal explanation of a veto when legislation is returned to the Congress.

W

War Powers Resolution A law passed in 1973 spelling out the conditions under which the president can commit troops without congressional approval.

Washington Community Individuals regularly involved with politics in Washington, D.C.

Watergate Break-in The 1972 illegal entry into the Democratic National Committee offices by participants in Richard Nixon's reelection campaign.

Weberian Model A model of bureaucracy developed by the German sociologist Max Weber, who viewed bureaucracies as rational, hierarchical organizations in which power flows from the top downward and decisions are based on logical reasoning and data analysis.

Whig Party One of the foremost political organizations in the United States during the first half of the nineteenth century, formally established in 1836. The Whig Party was dominated by the same anti-Jackson elements that organized the National Republican faction within the Democratic (Jeffersonian) Republicans and represented a variety of regional interests. It fell apart as a national party in the early 1850s.

Whip An assistant who aids the majority or minority leader of the House or the Senate majority or minority floor leader.

Whistleblower Someone who brings to public attention gross governmental inefficiency or an illegal action.

White House Office The personal office of the president, which tends to presidential political needs and manages the media.

White House Press Corps A group of reporters assigned full-time to cover the presidency.

White Primary A state primary election that restricts voting to whites only; outlawed by the Supreme Court in 1944.

Writ of *Certiorari* An order issued by a higher court to a lower court to send up the record of a case for review. It is the principal vehicle for United States Supreme Court review.

Index

A

AARP (American Association of Retired Persons)
  material incentives to join, 251–252
  power of, 197, 251–252, 260
ABC, news coverage on, 358
Aberbach, Joel, 465
Abington School District v. Schempp, 121
Abortion(s), 61
  juveniles and, 206
  "partial-birth," 137
  privacy rights and, 32, 136–138
  Roe v. Wade and, 136–137
  special interest groups and, 259
A.C. Nielsen Company, 227
Accidental sample, 244
Accused, rights of
  extending, 141–142
  juveniles as, 207, 208–209
  rights of society versus, 140–145
ACEC (Advisory Commission on Electronic Commerce), 514–515
Achievement tests, 578, 601
ACLU (American Civil Liberties Union), 134, 201, 251, 259
Acquired immune deficiency syndrome. *See* AIDS
Acquisitive model of bureaucracy, 452
Action-reaction syndrome, 525
Actual malice, 132
ADA (Americans with Disabilities Act)(1990), 198–201, 210, 458, 497
Adams, Abigail, 172–173
Adams, John, 97, 173, 441
Adams, John Quincy, 280, 326, 327, 414
Adams, Samuel, 51
Adarand Constructors, Inc. v. Peña, 190
ADEA (Age Discrimination in Employment Act)(1967), 196–197
Adler, David Gray, 428
Administrative agency(ies)
  defined, 451
  independent executive. *See* Independent executive agency(ies)
  independent regulatory. *See* Independent regulatory agency(ies)
  powers of, courts and, 471
  regulations of, as source of law, 480
  Web sites of, 448
Administrative Procedure Act (1946), 432
Adoption, gay males and lesbians and, 206
Advertising
  advocacy, 320, 361
  antidrug, government and, 365
  First Amendment protection and, 128
  negative, 360
  political, 359–361
  reelection goal of incumbent pursued by, 387
Advice and consent, 378–379, 415, 419, 428–429, 489
Advisory Commission on Electronic Commerce (ACEC), 514–515
Advocacy ads, 320, 361

AFDC (Aid to Families with Dependent Children), 517
Affirmation of judgment, 489
Affirmative action, 189–193
  accomplishments of, 192–193
  California Proposition 209 and, 191
  college admissions and, 188
  defined, 189
  future of, 191–192
Afghanistan
  terrorist camps in, American air strikes against, 238, 563
  women's rights in, 178
AFL (American Federation of Labor), 255
AFL-CIO, 255
  Committee on Public Education (COPE) of, 255
  formation of, 255
  Public Employee Department of, 257
Africa
  AIDS and, 571
  regional conflicts in, 570
  United States embassies in, bombing of, 224, 563, 565
African American(s). *See also* Affirmative action; Race
  civil rights movement and, 162–164
  Civil War service and, 157
  college admissions and, 188
  consequences of slavery and, 153–162. *See also* Slaves/slavery
  cultural values and, 20
  equality and, 153–167
  Internet use by, 15
  Million Man March on Washington and, 236
  political participation and, 166–167
  population of, 20, 22, 169
  programs to help, 156
  reparations for, ethics and, 156
  rights of
    civil, 153–167
    limited by majority, 12
    voting, 12, 158, 335
  school integration and, 160–162
  schools with 90% minority enrollment and, 162
  separate-but-equal doctrine and, 58–59, 157–160
  support for Democratic Party and, 223, 236, 289, 339
  on United States Supreme Court, 167, 493
  voter turnout and, 332, 336
Age
  discrimination on basis of, 108, 195, 196–197, 198
  drinking, 104
  Internet use and, 15, 154
  of majority, 207
  political participation and, 197
  right to vote and, 206–207, 259
  voter turnout and, 332
  voting behavior and, 340
Age Discrimination in Employment Act (ADEA)(1967), 196–197

Agenda setting
  by Congress, 381
  defined, 381
  by media, 364
Agnew, Spiro, 442
Agostini v. Felton, 124
Agricultural interest groups, 255
Aguilar v. Felton, 124
Aid to Families with Dependent Children (AFDC), 517
AIDS (acquired immune deficiency syndrome)
  disability and, 199, 200
  national security and, 571
Ailes, Roger, 314
Air pollution, 523–524
Air Pollution Control Act (1955), 523–524
Akinmuwagun, Tayo, 571
Albright, Madeleine K., 177, 550, 567
Alcohol, minimum drinking age and, 104
Alden v. Maine, 108
Algeria, terrorism and, 561
Allen, Joel, 124
Allende, Salvador, 551
Alpine Diamond, 86
AMA (American Medical Association), 249, 257
America. *See* United States
America in Black and White: One Nation Indivisible (Thernstrom and Thernstrom), 193
America Online, Inc. (AOL), 204
  merger with Time Warner and, 256, 353, 365
American Association of Retired Persons. *See* AARP
American Bar Association, 257
American Civil Liberties Union (ACLU), 134, 201, 251, 259
American Conservative Union, 263
American Dairy Association, 252
American Enterprise Institute, 169, 470
American Farm Bureau Federation, 255, 470
American Federation of Labor (AFL), 255
American Federation of State, County, and Municipal Employees, 257
American Federation of Teachers, 257
American flag
  burning of, 128, 482
  desecration of, 56, 128, 482
  flying Texas state flag with, 597
  Pledge of Allegiance to, 16, 17, 233
  proposed constitutional amendments and, 56, 128
American Independent Party, 298
American Institute of Public Opinion, 226
American law, sources of, 480
American Medical Association (AMA), 249, 257
American Nazi Party, 134–135
American Petroleum Institute, 268
American Revolution, 10–11, 17, 36, 38, 521, 523
American Woman Suffrage Association, 174
Americans for Democratic Action (ADA), 262
Americans for Term Limits, 287
Americans with Disabilities Act (ADA)(1990), 198–201, 210, 458, 497

Ames, Aldrich, 551
Amicus curiae brief, 483
Amish people, 16, 18
Amnesty International, 209, 549
AMTRAK (National Railroad Passenger Corporation), 460
Anarchy, 10
Anderson, John, 296, 297
ANDP (Atlanta Neighborhood Development Partnership, Inc.), 168
Andrew W. Mellon Foundation, 192
Andrews, Charles, 34
Andrews, Joe, 286
Angola, 553
Annapolis Convention, 41–42, 43. *See also* Constitutional Convention
Anthony, Susan B., 173–174
    dollar coins with likeness of, 531
Antidrug advertising, government and, 365
Anti-Federalists, 50–51, 278, 292
Anti-Ku Klux Klan Act (Civil Rights Act of 1872), 156–157
Anti-Terrorism and Effective Death Penalty Act (1996), 144
AOL. *See* America Online, Inc.
Appellate courts, 482–483, 589–590
Apple Computer, 94
Appointment power, 415–416, 449, 459–460, 548
Apportionment, 585–586
Appropriation, 472
Arafat, Yasser, 567
Araf-Badr, Camilia, 178
Architectural and Transportation Barriers Compliance Board, 198
Argall, Samuel, 119
Aristide, Jean-Bertrand, 546, 566, 567
Aristocracy
    defined, 10
    natural, 461
Aristotle, 14
Arlington National Cemetery, 435
Armey, Dick, 400
Arms Control and Disarmament Agency, 416
Arterton, Christopher F., 234–235
Arthur, Chester, 441
Articles of Confederation, 39–41, 51, 87, 96, 377, 480, 554
    accomplishments under, 40
    government under, structure of, 40, 43
    weaknesses of, 40–41
Asian American(s)
    cultural values and, 18
    political participation and, 167
    population of, 20, 22
    voting rights of, 167
Assembly, freedom of, 118, 134–135
Assisted suicide, 32, 140, 588
Associated Press, 353
Association for Public Opinion Research, 225, 232
Association of General Contractors of America, 257
Association of Independent Information Professionals, 138
Association of Southeast Asian Nations, 94
Athenian model of government, 10
Atlanta Neighborhood Development Partnership, Inc. (ANDP), 168
AT&T, 365
Attentive public, 553
Austin v. Michigan State Chamber of Commerce, 320

Australia
    common law system in, 479
    federal system of government in, 87
Australian ballot, 328
Authority of government, 8–9
Authorization, 472
Automobile Aerospace, and Agricultural Implement Workers of America, 255
Azerbaijan, violence in, 569

B

Bad-tendency rule, 127
Baer, Kenneth S., 302
Baker, James, 444
Baker v. Carr, 389
Bakke, Allan, 190
Balanced Budget Amendment, 55
Ballot(s)
    Australian, 328
    office-block (Massachusetts), 328
    party-column (Indiana), 328
Ballot initiatives, 191
Baltic republics, 559
Banfield, Edward, 599
Barak, Ehud, 568
Barton, Joe, 438
Beard, Charles, 49, 52
"Beauty contests," 321
Begala, Paul, 314–315
Begin, Menachem, 421
Belarus, Strategic Arms Reduction Treaty (START) signed by, 559
Bell, Daniel, 86
Benjamin, Esther, 438
Berger, Sandy, 550
Berlin Wall, fall of, 560
Bernstein, Carl, 363
Betts v. Brady, 141
Bias
    defined, 367
    in the media, 367–369
    news and, 368
Bicameral legislature, 44
Bicameralism, 377
Bilingual education, 192–194. *See also* English language
Bilingual Education Act (1968), 194
Bill of Rights, 140, 259, 365
    for children, 206
    defined, 17, 32, 57
    incorporation of, into Fourteenth Amendment, 118
    liberties guaranteed by, 117, 118
    ratification of, 52–54
    rationale for, 35
Black Muslims, 164
Black Women Organized for Action, 176
Blackmun, Harry A., 128, 493
Blanket primary, 323
Block grants, 104–105
Blythe, Alan, 587
Board of Education v. Dowell, 161
Board of Regents of the University of Wisconsin System v. Southworth, 131
Boeing Corporation, 549
Boerne, City of v. Flores, 126
Bok, Derek C., 192–193
Bonior, David, 400
Borjas, George J., 170–171

Bork, Robert, 493, 495
Bosnia, 545
    American troops sent to, 5, 418, 428, 547, 570
    ethnic and religious unrest in, 569–570
Bosnia-Herzegovina, creation of, 86
Boston Tea Party, 36, 37, 250
Botswana, AIDS and, 571
Bowen, William G., 192–193
Bowers v. Hardwick, 201–202
Boxer Rebellion, 418
Boy Scouts of America (BSA), 202
Bradford, William, 35
Brady, James, 441
Brady Handgun Violence Prevention Act (1993), 107
Brandeis, Louis D., 88–89, 126, 135
Branti v. Finkel, 462
Brazil, federal system of government in, 87
Breeze, Shirley, 57
Brennan, Thomas, 488
Brennan, William J., Jr., 493
Breyer, Stephen, 493, 497, 499
Bribery, 450
Brief, legal, 483
Brinkley, Alan, 49
Broadcast news, replaced by Internet, 348
Brookings Institution, 167, 497
Brown, Linda Carol, 159
Brown, Oliver, 159
Brown, Ron, 385
Brown v. Board of Education of Topeka, 59, 159–160, 162, 206
Brownback, Sam, 385, 438
Browner, Carol, 467
Bryan, William Jennings, 280, 299
Brzezinski, Zbigniew, 439, 550
BSA (Boy Scouts of America), 202
Buckley v. Valeo, 319, 320
Budget and Impoundment Control Act (1974), 401–402, 434
Bull Moose Progressive Party, 280–281, 298, 299–300
Bundling, 321
Bureau of the Budget, 439
Bureau of the Census. *See* United States Bureau of the Census
Bureaucracy(ies), 447–476
    bureaucrats and. *See* Bureaucrats
    comparison of, 450–451
    defined, 449
    federal
        organization of, 453–459
            illustrated, 454
        president's control of, 416
        size of, 452–453
            illustrated, 453
    incentives for efficiency and productivity and, 464–465
    iron triangles and, 469–472
    issue networks and, 469, 471–472
    lawmaking mandate and, 470–471
    nature of, 449–451
    private, 449–450
    public, 449–450
    reform of, modern attempts at, 463–466
    rulemaking and, 468, 469, 470–471
    size of, 452–453
        illustrated, 453
    staffing, 459–463
    theories of, 451–452
    twenty-first century issues and, 473

"virtual," 448
whistleblowers and, 465–466
Bureaucrats. *See also* Bureaucracy(ies)
bribes to, 450
as politicians and policymakers, 466–472
Burger, Warren, 129, 133
Burger Court and, 498
Burlington Industries v. Ellerth, 179
Burma (Myanmar), sanctions against, 93, 564
Burr, Aaron, 326, 414
Burroughs, Edgar Rice, 129
Burundi, death of president in plane crash and, 570
Bush, George, 128, 198, 291, 442
appointments of
to cabinet, 177
to federal courts, 492, 493, 495, 504
to Supreme Court, 493, 495, 497, 504
armed forces ordered by
into combat without congressional approval, 552
into Middle East, 418, 568–569
into Panama, 418
budget and, 405
divided government and, 281, 393
election of 1988 and, 237, 281, 340, 441
election of 1992 and, 337, 405, 414, 417
federal grants-in-aid and, 105
gridlock and, 393
Haitian "boat people" and, 566
Persian Gulf War and, 238
reregulation and, 458
Soviet Union and, 559
Strategic Arms Reduction Treaty (START) and, 559
tax policies and, 528
Bush, George W., 6, 106, 203, 232, 281, 316, 323, 327, 330, 357, 361, 417, 418, 440, 504
campaign financing controversy and, 242, 427
fund-raising activity and, 427
Social Security policy and, 529–530
Bush, Laura, 357
Business interest groups, 253, 254, 255
Business Roundtable, 253, 255
Business Week/Harris poll, 139
Business-Industry Political Action Committee (BIPAC), 266
Busing, 160–162

C

CAB (Civil Aeronautics Board), 458
Cabinet
defined, 437
departments of. *See* Cabinet departments
kitchen, 437
women in, 177
Cabinet departments, 454, 455, 456
civilian employment in, 416
defined, 455
listed, 416, 456
Cable Reregulation Act (1992), 458
Cable-Satellite Public Affairs Network (C-SPAN), 27, 358, 368
Cabot, John, 33
Cadre, 278
Calcotte, Steven, 53
"Call-in" polls, 244
Cambodia
American invasion of, 418
secret bombing in, 234

Camp David accords, 421
Campaign(s)
changes in, from those earlier, 313
cost of. *See also* Campaign financing
effects of, on voter turnout, 333, 334
financing of. *See* Campaign financing
focus groups and, 316
modern campaign machine and, 312–315
opinion polls and, 315–316
opposition research and, 314
PACs and, 263–264
political consultants and, 314–315
professional, 314–315
twenty-first century issues and, 343
winning, strategy of, 315–316
Campaign financing, 316–321
beyond the limits, 319–321
bundling and, 321
disclosure requirements and, 318
independent expenditures and, 319–321
Internet fund-raising and, 317
limitations on, 318
by public, 318
reform of, 242, 427
regulating, 242, 316–317
soft money and. *See* Soft money
Campbell, Ben Nighthorse, 167
Campbell, Thomas, 438
Campus speech codes, 130–131
Canada
Articles of Confederation and, 41
common law system in, 479
FDR's executive agreements with, 421
federal system of government in, 87
immigration policy in, 171
incarceration rate in, 522
judicial review and, 496
lobbying by, 260
NAFTA and, 537, 549
single-payer health-care system in, 152
Candidate(s), 309–312
choosing, on the Web, 342
for congressional elections, 311, 384–386
contributions to, limitations on, 318
eligibility of, 311–312
free television time for, 308
front-runner and, 323
independent
defined, 277
John Anderson as, 296, 297
Internet and, 283
opposition research and, 314
perception of, 341
professionals as, 311–312
reasons for running and, 310
recruiting, 277
spending by, on own behalf, First Amendment and, 319
third-party, 297–298. *See also* Third party(ies)
twenty-first century issues and, 343
visibility and appeal of, 315
Capital Cities, acquired by Disney, 353, 365
Capital punishment, 141, 144–145, 209
Capture, 457
Caribbean Americans, cultural values and, 18
Carnahan, Jean, 177, 312
Carnahan, Mel, 177, 312
Carnegie Endowment for International Peace, 89
Carothers, Thomas, 89
Carpenter, Candice, 357
Carroll, Lewis, 289

Carter, Jimmy, 327, 413, 439, 491, 550
armed forces ordered into combat by, without congressional approval, 552
cabinet of, 437
Camp David accords and, 421
deregulation and, 457–458
election of 1976 and, 281
election of 1980 and, 227, 230, 281, 338, 340
federal grants-in-aid and, 105
first presidential phone-in television broadcast and, 433
as governor, 583
intelligence community members defined by, 550
legislative record of, 393
mission to North Korea by, 562
People's Republic of China recognized by, 420, 558
return of Panama Canal to Panama by, 420
Strategic Arms Limitation Treaty (SALT II) and, 420
Carville, James, 314–315
Case Act (1972), 421n
The Case for Free Trade and Open Immigration (Hornberger), 171
Case law, 480
Casework, 380
Casillas, Benito, 485
Castro, Fidel, 222, 567, 596
Categorical grants-in-aid, 102
Cato Institute, 171
Caucus, 323
Cayman Islands, online gambling operation resident in, 590
CBO (Congressional Budget Office), 394, 405, 473
CBS
news coverage on, 358
60 Minutes and, 353
CBS News/New York Times poll, 224
CEA (Council of Economic Advisers), 403, 405, 438, 439
Censorship, prior restraint and, 127
Census Bureau. *See* United States Bureau of the Census
Center for Enterprise and Opportunity, 181
Central Intelligence Agency (CIA), 365, 433, 464, 548, 571
computer systems of, attacked by hackers, 552
covert operations of, 551
creation of, 457
embarrassment of, 551, 563
employees of, 550
foreign policymaking and, 551
principal functions of, 457
psychics and, 458
Certiorari, writ of, 487–488
"The Cess Poll," 224
Charter, 593
Chechnya
ethnic movement in, 560
terrorism and, 561
uprising in, 569
Checks and balances, 4, 47–48, 392, 428
defined, 47
illustrated, 47
vertical, 93, 95
Chemical Weapons Convention, 420
Cheney, Dick, 389, 440
Chief diplomat, 419–421

Chief executive, 415–417
Chief legislator, 421–426, 548
Chief of staff, 439
Chief of state, 415
Child Online Protection Act (1998), 84, 129
Children. *See also* Juveniles
    adoption of, gay males and lesbians and, 206
    child-labor laws and, 100, 102
    custody of, gay males and lesbians and, 206
    living in poverty, 519–520
    pornography and, 129
    Social Security numbers and, 276
Chile, CIA involvement in, 551
China, Boxer Rebellion in, 418. *See also*
    People's Republic of China
China Trade Bill, 420, 537, 548, 549
Christian Coalition, 320
    Internet and, 267
Churchill, Winston, 556, 557
CIA. *See* Central Intelligence Agency
CIO (Congress of Industrial Organizations), 255
Citizen(s)
    compliance of, 9
    government information about, 474
    members of Congress versus, 384
    naturalized, 4, 23
    senior. *See* Elderly
Citizens Against Government Waste, 404
Citizens Trade Campaign, 267
Citizenship
    diversity of, 481
    immigrant rights and, 182. *See also*
        Naturalization
Citrus Growers Association, 470
City of Boerne v. Flores, 126
Civil Aeronautics Board (CAB), 458
Civil law, 207
Civil liberties, 115–149
    civil rights versus, 153
    defined, 117
    fear of government and, 117
    twenty-first century issues and, 145
Civil right(s), 151–213
    activists in, new generation of, 168
    African Americans and, 153–167
    civil liberties versus, 153
    civil rights movement and, 162–164
    defined, 153
    disability and, 198–201
    of gay males and lesbians, 201–206
    issues regarding, Rehnquist Court and,
        498–500
    juveniles and, 206–209
    medical care as, 152
    twenty-first century issues and, 182, 210
    women and, 172–181
Civil Rights Act(s)
    of 1866, 156
    of 1872 (Anti-Ku Klux Klan Act), 156–157
    of 1875 (Second Civil Rights Act), 157
    of 1957, 164
    of 1960, 164
    of 1964, 104, 163, 164–165, 189, 198, 497
        Title VII of, 165, 178–179, 180
        Title IX of, 470
    of 1968, 164, 166
    of 1991, 458, 502
    ineffectiveness of, 157–158
Civil Rights Cases, 157
Civil rights movement, 162–164
Civil service
    defined, 415

    history of, 461–463
Civil Service Commission, 463
Civil Service Reform Act
    of 1883 (Pendleton Act), 462
    of 1978, 460, 463, 465
Civil society, Internet and, 89
Civil War, 87, 432
    African American troops in, 157
    crime during, 521
    growth of national government and, 99–100
    slavery and, 98, 99, 154
    states' rights and, 49, 54, 98–100
"Civil War Amendments," 155
Clarke, Wesley, 438
Class politics, 293
Class-action suit, 483–484
Clay, Henry, 280
Clean Air Act
    of 1963, 524
    of 1970, 470
    of 1990, 524
    amendments to (1970), 524
    amendments to (1977), 524
    amendments to (1991), 458
Clear and present danger test, 126
Cleveland, Grover, 423
Climate control, 266
Clinton, Bill, 232, 252, 271, 349, 364, 385,
        403, 502, 571
    Al Gore chosen as running mate by, 440
    appointments of
        to cabinet, 177
        to federal courts, 177, 492, 493, 494,
            504
        to Supreme Court, 177, 493, 504
    armed forces ordered by
        to attack Afghanistan and the Sudan, 563
        attack alleged terrorist bases, 418
        to bomb Serbia, 418
        to Bosnia, 5, 418, 428, 547, 570
        into combat without congressional
            approval, 552
        to Haiti, 418, 546, 547, 566–567
        to Kosovo, 570
    budget and, 405, 535
    character of, 431
    Chemical Weapons Convention approval
        and, 420
    as chief legislator, 423, 425, 426
    China and
        China Trade Bill passage and, 420, 537,
            548, 549
        illegal campaign contributions from
            China and, 427, 564–565
        military equipment sales to China and,
            554, 565
    Comprehensive Nuclear Test Ban Treaty
        defeat and, 561, 562
    deregulation and, 458, 527
    divided government and, 6
    economy and, 291
    election of
        in 1992, 237, 256, 281, 300, 314–315,
            337, 340, 355, 393, 414, 440
        in 1996, 6, 281, 309, 320, 338, 340, 405,
            564–565
        without majority of popular vote, 327, 414
    e-mail and, 423
    Escalante wilderness and, 267, 429
    executive orders and proclamations issued
        by, 429
    executive privilege claim of, 433

    federal grants-in-aid and, 104, 105
    federal mandates and, 107
    foreign policy and, 545, 550
        Bosnia and, 418, 428, 547, 570
        China and. *See* Clinton, Bill, China and
        Cuba and, 567
        Haiti and, 546, 547, 566–567
        Kosovo and, 436, 570
        North Korea and, 562
        Russia and, 561, 562
        sanctions and, 563, 566
    fund-raising activity and, 427, 564–565
    gay and lesbian issues and, 203
    as governor, 88, 583
    gridlock and, 443
    impeachment of, 180, 218, 235, 302, 412,
        431, 435
    Internet taxes and, 514
    kitchen cabinet of, 437
    Lewinsky scandal and, 5, 180, 219, 358,
        382, 406, 430, 431, 433, 435, 436,
        440, 443
    line-item veto and, 424–425
    NAFTA and, 420, 549
    "near" treaties and, 428–429
    "new-age federalism" and, 104
    online chat and, 423
    Paula Corbin Jones lawsuit against, 180,
        436, 443, 486
    popularity of, scandal and, 219, 220
    public opinion of, 429–430, 431
    Puerto Rican nationals convicted of
        plotting terrorism granted clemency
        by, 417
    sexual harassment lawsuit against, 180,
        436, 443, 486
    tax policies and, 528
    videotaped testimony of, 5, 382
    Vietnam recognized by, 420
Clinton, Hillary Rodham, 177, 311, 384, 423
Closed primary, 322
Cloture, 383
CNBC, 359
CNN
    Internet and, 53, 358
    purchase of, by Time Warner, 353
    startup of, 359
CNN.com, 358
CNN-Headline News, 359
Coalition for Women's Appointments, 176
Coattail effect, 328, 386
Code of Federal Regulations, 473
Coelho, Tony, 406
Coercive Acts ("Intolerable Acts")(1774)(Great
    Britain), 36
COG (council of government), 595–596
Cohen, Bernard, 235
Coins, United States
    dollar, Susan B. Anthony, 531
    motto on, 88
Cold War, 222, 556–557
    defined, 557
    end of, 560, 564
Coleman, Norm, 298
College(s). *See also* Education; School(s)
    activity fees used to support opposing
        views and, 131
    admission to, affirmative action and, 188
Color, discrimination on basis of, 101,
    164–165, 165, 189, 198
Columbine High School shootings, 272
Commander in chief, 417–419, 547

Commentaries on the Law of Municipal Corporations (Dillon), 592–593
Commerce clause, 58, 84
  defined, 32, 97
  Gibbons v. Ogden and, 97–98
  reining in of commerce power by Supreme Court and, 107108
  state regulation of the Internet and, 84
Commercial speech, 128
Commission on Civil Rights, 416
Commission plan of municipal government, 596–597
Committee to Reelect the President (CREEP), 317
Common Cause, 259
Common law, 208, 479
Common Sense (Paine), 36–37, 334
Commonwealth of Independent States, 87, 560
Communications Decency Act (1996), 84, 129
Communist Party, 53, 297
Compelling government interest, 125, 190
Compliance of citizens, 9
Comprehensive Nuclear Test Ban Treaty, 561, 562
Concurrent powers, 91, 92–93
Concurring opinion, 489
Confederal Government, 40. *See also* Articles of Confederation
Confederal system, 85
  defined, 87
  flow of power in, 87
Confederate flag, flying of, 99
Confederate States of America, 87, 99
Conference committee, 396
Congo, unrest in, 570
Congress, 375–410. *See also* United States House of Representatives; United States Senate
  107th
    characteristics of, summarized, 385
    party leaders in, 400
    standing committees of, listed, 395
  bicameralism of, 377
  bureaucracy controlled by, 472–473
  campaign-finance reform and, 242
  checks and balances system and. *See* Checks and balances
  checks on courts and, 501–502
  committees of
    investigations, hearings, and review and, 473
    members of, selection of, 397
    power of, 394–395
    structure of, 394–397
    types of, 395–397
  of the Confederation, 40–41. *See also* Articles of Confederation
  conflict resolution by, 381
  Congressional Budget Office (CBO) and, 394, 405, 473
  Congressional Research Service (CRS) and, 394
  Continental. *See* Continental Congress
  creation of, reason for, 377–378
  ethics and, 406
  formal leadership in, 397–400
  functions of, 379–381
  funds appropriated by, 472
  funds authorized by, 472
  General Accounting Office (GAO) and, 394, 473, 519
  gridlock and, 393–394, 443

hearings and, 473
investigations and, 473
iron triangles and, 469–472
lawmaking process of, 379, 401
  illustrated, 402
  president as chief legislator and, 421–426, 548
  and presidential support on congressional votes, 1953 to present, 426
legislative veto and, 381, 429
Library of, Web site of, 391
member(s) of
  African Americans as, 166
  citizenry versus, 384
  constituents served by, 377
  decisions by, 400–401
  election of. *See* Congressional election(s)
  e-mail to, 267
  Hispanic Americans as, 167
  Native American as, 167
  pay of, 391
  perks of, 392–394
  permanent professional staffs and, 393–394
  privileges and immunities of, 394
  representation by, 380–381
  requirement to spend half each year in district and, 376
  safe seats and, 397
  term limits for, 387, 388
  Web sites of, 381, 382
  women as, 173, 176, 178, 198
oversight by, 381, 470
party voting in, 401
powers of, 57–58, 90–91, 378–379
  enumerated, 90, 91, 378–379
  to override presidential vetoes, 423, 425
reapportionment and, 389–391
reason for creating, 377–378
redistricting and, 389–391
Republican Party's control of, 6, 105, 106–107, 256, 281, 387–388, 393, 423, 426, 463, 494
review and, 473
seniority system and, 397
State of the Union address to, 421–422
twenty-first century issues and, 406–407
Congress of Industrial Organizations (CIO), 255
Congressional Budget Office (CBO), 394, 405, 473
Congressional election(s), 384–388
  of 1812, 390
  of 1974, 342
  of 1980, 281
  of 1982, 281
  of 1984, 281
  of 1992, 281, 393
  of 1994, 105, 256, 281, 393, 405, 423, 426
    shakeup in, 387–388
  of 1996, 281, 283, 388, 405
  of 1998, 227, 266, 283, 311, 312, 388, 393, 398, 435
  candidates for, 311, 384–386
  coattail effect and, 328, 386
  midterm, divided government following, 388
  power of incumbency in, 386–387
  voter turnout for, 331
Congressional Research Service (CRS), 394
Congressional Union, 174
Connecticut Compromise (Great Compromise), 44–46, 377

Connor, Eugene "Bull," 163
Consensus, 220–221
Consent of the people, 10–11, 35
Conservatism
  defined, 24
  political beliefs of, 24–25, 240
  vision of government power and, 25
Conservative coalition, 401
Consolidation
  defined, 595
  functional, 595
  of governments, 595–596
Constant dollars, 533
Constituent(s)
  defined, 377
  lobbying by, 266–267
  negative, 550
  service to, by members of Congress, 377, 380
Constitution(s)
  as source of American law, 480
  state, 84, 581
  United States. *See* United States Constitution
Constitutional Convention, 41–48, 58, 88
  delegates to, 42–43, 413. *See also* United States Constitution, framers of
Constitutional convention, 581
Constitutional initiative, 581
Constitutional power. *See* United States Constitution, powers under
Consultants, political, 314–315
Consumer Federation of America, 259
Consumer price index (CPI), 516, 517
Consumer Product Safety Commission, 262
  Internet fraud and, 458
Containment, 557
Continental Congress
  First, 36
  Second, 36, 37–38, 39
Continuing resolutions, 405
Contracting out, 464
Cookies, 138
Cooley, Thomas, 593
Cooley's rule, 593
Coolidge, Calvin, 529
Cooperative federalism, 100–104
Corn Growers Association, 470
Cornwallis, Charles, 39
Corrupt practices acts, 316–317
Corwin, Edwin S., 547
Cott, Nancy, 174
Council of Economic Advisers (CEA), 403, 405, 438, 439
Council of government (COG), 595–596
Council on Environmental Quality, 438
Council on Foreign Relations, 553
Council-manager plan of municipal government, 597
County, 593–594
Court(s). *See also* Judiciary
  agency powers and, 471
  appellate, 482–483, 589–590
  cases in decided using opinion polls, 218
  checks and balances system and. *See* Checks and balances
  checks on, 500–504
  federal. *See* Federal court system
  filing of documents via E-mail and, 486
  judicial activism and, 495–496, 497
  judicial restraint and, 496
  judicial review and, 58–59, 493–495
  judicial traditions and doctrines and, 503–504

jurisdiction of, 481
juvenile, 208
king's *(curiae regis)*(England), 479
policymaking function of, 493–500
state, 588–592
 illustrated, 589
 procedures in, 484
supreme
 state, 590
 United States. *See* United States Supreme
  Court
trial, 482, 483, 588–589
virtual courtroom and, 486
Web sites and, 486
Cox, Christopher, 514
Cox, James M., 354
CPI (consumer price index), 516, 517
Crawford, William H., 414
Credentials committee, 324
Credit claiming, reelection goal of incumbent
 pursued by, 387
CREEP (Committee to Reelect the President),
 317
Crime(s)
in American history, 521–522
"hate," 21
juvenile, 207, 208–209, 522
persons accused of, rights of. *See* Accused,
 rights of
twenty-first century, 521–522
violent, rates of, 521–522
Criminal law, 207
Croatia, creation of, 86
Crocker, Richard, 288
Cronkite, Walter, 433
Crossley, Archibald, 225
"Crowding out," 534
CRS (Congressional Research Service), 394
Cruel and unusual punishment, constitutional
 prohibition of, 144
Crump, Edward, 598
*Cruzan v. Director, Missouri Department of
 Health,* 139
C-SPAN (Cable-Satellite Public Affairs
 Network), 27, 358, 368
Cuba
Clinton administration's policy toward, 567
Cuban missile crisis and, 558
Elian Gonzalez case and, 222, 364, 567, 596
Helms-Burton Act and, 567
local government selective purchasing law
 and, 94
Cuban missile crisis, 558
Culture
dominant, 16–17
political. *See* Political culture
Curiae regis (king's courts)(England), 479
Curtiss-Wright Export Corp., United States v.,
 432
Cybermoney, monetary policy and, 531
Cyberspace, privacy rights in, 138–139. *See
 also* Internet; World Wide Web
Czech Republic, creation of, 86
Czechoslovakia, 86

D

Daily Muse, 358
"Daisy Girl" ad, 359–360
Dale, James, 202
Daley, Richard J., 289, 598, 599
Daley, Richard M., 289

Dangel, Justin, 18
Daschle, Linda Hall, 271
Daschle, Tom, 271, 400
Davidson, Roger, 393
Davis, John W., 292
Davis v. Bandemer, 390
De facto segregation, 160, 161, 162
De jure segregation, 160
Death penalty, 141, 144–145, 209
Debate(s)
presidential, 361–362
in Senate, 383
Debs, Eugene V., 297
The Debt: What America Owes Blacks
 (Robinson), 156
Declaration of Independence, 17–18, 36,
 37–38, 46, 123, 153, 173, 582
Declaration of Sentiments, 173
Defamation of character, 129–130
in writing, 130, 132
DeFazio, Peter, 382
Defense Department. *See* United States
 Department of Defense
Defense Intelligence Agency, 551
Defense of Marriage Act (1996), 205
Defense policy. *See* Foreign policy
DeLay, Randy, 271
DeLay, Tom, 271, 400
Delegate(s)
to Constitutional Convention, 42–43
instructed, 380–381
to national convention
 comparison of, on issues and ideology,
  285
 credentials committee and, 324
 election of, 303
 superdelegates and, 322
Democracy
defined, 10
direct. *See* Direct democracy
elite theory and, 13–14, 15, 269
for the few, 13–14
for groups, 14–16
representative. *See* Representative
 democracy
United States and, 13–15
*Democracy Unbound: Progressive Challenges
 to the Two Party System* (Reynolds), 302
Democratic Party
African Americans' support for, 236, 289,
 339
formation of, 280
Republican Party versus, 290
soft money and, 287, 319
Solid South and, 280, 293, 294, 340
union support and, 263, 289, 337, 340
voters who grew up during Great
 Depression and, 235
Democratic Republicans (Jeffersonian
 Republicans), 49, 279, 280, 292, 461
Demographic factors, voting behavior and,
 337–341
Demographic traits, 236–237
DeMuth, Christopher, 470
Dennis v. United States, 126
Deregulation, 457–458, 527
Desegregation
of military, 223
of schools, 160–162
Détente, 558
Dillon, John F., 592–593
Dillon's rule, 592–593

Diplomacy
as aspect of foreign policy, 546
defined, 545
Diplomatic recognition, 419–420, 548
Direct democracy
dangers of, 10–11
defined, 10
at state level, 586–587
town meeting as, 10, 11, 594
Direct primary, 386
Direct techniques of interest groups, 260,
 261–264
Dirksen, Everett, 164
Disability(ies)
discrimination on basis of, 198–201
persons with
 Americans with Disabilities Act of 1990
  and, 198–201
 "reasonable accommodations" for,
  199–200
 rights of, 198–201
Discharge petition, 395
Discrimination
on basis of
 age, 108, 195, 196–197, 198
 color, 101, 164–165, 165, 189, 198
 disability, 198–201
 gender, 164–165, 175–176, 189, 198. *See
  also* Sexual harassment
 national origin, 101, 164–165, 165, 189,
  198
 pregnancy, 178–179
 race, 101, 158, 164–165, 165, 189, 198.
  See also Affirmative action
 religion, 101, 164–165, 165, 189, 198
dealing with, 211
in housing, 166
reverse, 190, 192
wage, 180–181
Disney Company, 365
Capital Cities acquisition and, 353, 365
Dissenting opinion, 489
Diversity of citizenship, 481
Divided government, 6, 281, 291, 388, 471–472
Divisive opinion, 221
Dixiecrat (States' Rights) Party, 298
DOD. *See* United States Department of Defense
Dole, Elizabeth, 177
Dole, Robert, 271
election of 1996 and, 92, 324, 338
Domestic policy
crime and. *See* Crime(s)
defined, 513
environment and. *See* Environmental policy
homelessness and, 520–521
making. *See* Policymaking, process of
poverty and. *See* Poverty
twenty-first century issues and, 537–538
Dominant culture, 16–17
Dorsey, Lattie, 168
DOT. *See* United States Department of
 Transportation
Douglas, William O., 135, 464
Douglass, Frederick, 154
Dowry killing, 178
Dred Scott v. Sanford, 154, 158
Driver's License Protection Act (1994),
 499–500
Drudge Report, 366
Drugs, dealing with, 587
Dual federalism, 100
Due process clause, 155

Dunne, Finley Peter, 478
Dye, Thomas, 14
Dyton, Jonathan, 42

E

Eagle Forum, 175
Earned-income tax credit (EITC) program, 519
Earth First, 257–258
East Germany, 556. *See also* Germany
Eastern Europe, 559. *See also* Europe
  low-cost labor in, 535
    regional conflicts in, 569–570
    Soviet bloc and, 556–557, 560
Eastman Kodak, 94
Easton, David, 7
E-commerce, national sovereignty and, 526–527
Economic aid, 545
Economic decision making, politics of, 525–533. *See also* Economic policy
Economic interest groups, 253, 255, 257
An Economic Interpretation of the Constitution of the United States (Beard), 52
Economic policy, 528–537
  fiscal policy and. *See* Fiscal policy
  monetary policy and. *See* Monetary policy
  policy trade-offs and, 525
  public debt and. *See* Public debt
  subsidies and, 525–528
  taxes and, 525–528. *See also* Tax(es)
  twenty-first century issues and, 537–538
  world trade and. *See* World trade
Economic Report of the President, 404
Economic status. *See* Income, level of; Socioeconomic status
Editor, letters to, 109
Edmonds, Thomas, 315
Education. *See also* College(s); School(s)
  attainment in
    political opinion influenced by, 233
    political socialization and, 233
    voter turnout and, 332
    voting behavior and, 337
  bilingual, 192–194. *See also* English language
  of public, by Congress, 381
Education for All Handicapped Children Act (1975), 198
Edwards v. Aguillard, 122
EEOC. *See* Equal Employment Opportunity Commission
Egypt
  Camp David accords and, 421
  unitary system of government in, 86
Eighteenth Amendment, 54
Eighth Amendment, 144
Einstein, Albert, 203
EIS (environmental impact statement), 524
Eisenhower, Dwight
  cabinet of, 437
  China and North Korea threatened by, 547
  control of bureaucracy and, 416
  divided government and, 393
  election of 1952 and, 281, 310, 355
  election of 1956 and, 281
  ending Korean War and, 547, 557
  executive agreement with South Vietnam and, 548
  National Guard federalized by, 159, 160, 501
  pact with vice president regarding incapacity and, 442

press conferences and, 434
vetoes by, 423
warning of, regarding military-industrial complex, 553–554
EITC (earned-income tax credit) program, 519
El Salvador, 553
Elastic (necessary and proper) clause, 90–91, 379
Elderly
  benefits of Medicare and Social Security and, 195, 210
  population of, 196
  special protection for, 194–195
Election(s)
  coattail effect and, 328
  conduct of, 328–330
  of delegates to national convention, 303
  landslide, 330, 393
  local, voting in, 330–333
  organizing and running, 277
  state
    of judges, 591–592
    voting in, 330–333
  ticket splitting and, 291
  twenty-first century issues and, 343
  voting in, 330–333
Elector(s)
  choice of, 325
  commitment of, 326–327
  defined, 325
  faithless, 327n
Electoral college, 325–328
  criticisms of, 327
  defined, 48, 295
  electors and. *See* Elector(s)
  proposed reforms of, 327–328
  winner-take-all system and, 295–296
Electorate. *See* Voter(s)
Electronic media. *See also* Radio; Television
  defined, 355
  revolution in, 356
Electronic town meeting, 352
Elementary and Secondary Education Act (1965), 120
Eleventh Amendment, 108, 197
Elite(s)
  defined, 10
  foreign policy influenced by, 553
  power and influence of, 13
Elite theory, 13–14, 269, 515
Elitzer, Daniel, 601
Ellsworth, Oliver, 500
Elrod v. Burns, 462
E-mail
  court filings via, 486
  to First Lady, 423, 444
  to members of Congress, 267
  to president, 423, 444
Emergency power, 432
EMILY's List, 176
E-money, monetary policy and, 531
Employment
  discrimination in. *See* Employment discrimination
  mandatory retirement and, 197
Employment Act (1946), 439
Employment discrimination, 502
  on basis of
    age, 195, 196–197, 198
    color, 101, 165, 189, 198
    disability, 198–201

    gender, 189, 198. *See also* Sexual harassment
    national origin, 101, 165, 189, 198
    pregnancy, 178–179
    race, 101, 165, 189, 198
    religion, 101, 165, 189, 198
  dealing with, 211
Enabling legislation, 466–467, 472
Enforcement Act (1870), 156
England. *See also* Great Britain
  Americans of English origin and, 167
  common law and, 208, 479
  marijuana laws in, 587
Engle v. Vitale (Regents' Prayer case), 120–121
English language
  juror who could not understand, 485
  as official language, 195, 587, 588
  proficiency in, naturalization and, 193
Entertainment, as function of media, 349–350
Enumerated powers, 90, 91, 378–379
Environment, cleaner, working toward, 539
Environmental Council of the States, 467
Environmental Defense Fund, 258
Environmental impact statement (EIS), 524
Environmental interest groups, 254, 257–258
"Environmental justice," 467
Environmental policy, 523–524
  air and water pollution and, 523–524
  major federal environmental legislation and, 523
Environmental Protection Agency (EPA), 416, 451, 455, 470
  air pollution and, 524
  "environmental justice" and, 467
  formation and principal functions of, 457
  Office of Environmental Justice of, 467
  rules of
    cost of compliance with, 524
    making, 468
EOP. *See* Executive Office of the President
EPA. *See* Environmental Protection Agency
Epperson v. Arkansas, 122
Epstein, Leon D., 278
Equal Employment Opportunity Commission (EEOC), 165, 180, 190, 200, 201
  creation of, 459, 466
  principal functions of, 459
Equal Pay Act (1963), 180–181
Equal protection clause, 152, 153, 155, 158, 189, 190, 191, 192, 194, 202, 205, 389, 586. *See also* Civil right(s)
Equal Rights Amendment, 56, 57, 175, 259
Equal time rule, 134, 308, 367
Equality
  African Americans and, 153–167
  defined, 17
  women and, 172–181
Equalization, 102
Era
  of good feeling, 280
  of internationalism, 555–557
  modern, 281
  of personal politics, 280
Escalante National Monument, 267, 429
Eshoo, Ann G., 382
Espionage Act, 126
Espuelas, Fernando J., 357
Establishment clause, 119–125, 578
Ethics
  college activity fees used to support opposing views and, 131

Congress examines its own for
        improprieties and, 406
defiance of federal law and, 596
demands of ethnic nationalism and, 569
exit polls, freedom of the press and, 366
failure of founders to ban slavery and, 46
flying of Confederate and, 99
lobbyists as friends and relatives and, 271
local political machine and, 288
minority clerks hired by Supreme Court
        and, 488
opposition research or dirty tricks and, 314
polls that mislead and, 232
president's character and, 431
reparations for African Americans and,
        156
Ethnic background, voting behavior and,
        338–339
Ethnic nationalism, 569
EU. See European Union
Euro, 527
Europe. See also Eastern Europe; European
        Union
    at close of World War II, 534
    countries in
        bureaucracies in, 450
        economic growth of, 535
        incarceration rates in, 522
        judicial review and, 496
European Community. See European Union
European Union (EU), 94
    confederal system and, 87
    creation of, 86, 534
    lobbying by, 260
    as major trading partner of U.S., 566
    as one economic "nation," 566
    uniform currency (euro) and, 527
Evolution, teaching of, 122–123
Ex post facto laws, 117
Excite.com, 423
Exclusionary rule, 143–144
Executive agreements, 58, 421, 547–548
Executive budget, 401
Executive departments. See Cabinet
        departments
Executive Office of the President (EOP), 416,
        437–439, 454
    Council of Economic Advisers (CEA) of,
        403, 405, 438, 439
    Council on Environmental Quality of, 438
    National Security Council (NSC) of. See
        National Security Council
    Office of Administration of, 438
    Office of Management and Budget (OMB)
        of, 403, 404, 405, 438, 439
    Office of National Drug Control Policy of,
        438
    Office of Policy Development of, 438
    Office of Science and Technology Policy of,
        438
    Office of the United States Trade
        Representative of, 438
    White House Office of, 438
Executive order, 429, 432–433
Executive privilege, 433
Ex-Im Bank (Export-Import Bank of the
        United States), 460
Exit poll(s), 366–367
    freedom of the press and, 366
    Los Angeles Times, 226
Exoo, Calvin F., 368
Export tax, 45–46

Export-Import Bank of the United States (Ex-
        Im Bank), 460
Expressed power, 91, 426
Expression, freedom of. See Speech, freedom of
ezgov.com, 579

F

Fact, questions of, 482
Faction, 277
Fair Deal, 281
Fair Labor Standards Act (1938), 180
Faithless electors, 327n
Fall review, 404
False Claims Act (1863), 466
    1986 amendments to, 465–466
Family, political socialization and, 232–233
Family Research Council, 123
Faragher v. City of Boca Raton, 179
Farrakhan, Louis, 236
Faubus, Orval, 93n, 159, 160, 501, 596
FBI (Federal Bureau of Investigation), 474
FCC. See Federal Communications
        Commission
FCPA (Foreign Corrupt Practices Act)(1977), 450
FDA. See Food and Drug Administration
FDIC (Federal Deposit Insurance Corporation),
        460
FEC. See Federal Election Commission
FECA. See Federal Election Campaign Act
Fed. See Federal Reserve System
Federal Bureau of Investigation (FBI), 474
Federal Communications Commission (FCC),
        308, 365, 367, 455
    broadcasting regulated by, 134
    Howard Stern and, 133
    tax requirement of, 470
Federal court system, 480–485
    appellate courts of, 482–483
    basic judicial requirements and, 481
    checks on, 500–504
    court(s) of
        appellate, 482–483
        procedures in, 484
        trial, 482, 483
        types of, 481–483
    illustrated, 481, 483
    judges of
        appointment of
            for life, 478, 490
            process of, politicization of, 494–495
        candidates to become, nomination of,
            490–493
        impeachment and, 490, 497
        selection of, 489–492
    judicial activism and, 495–496
    judicial restraint and, 496
    judicial review and, 493–495
    judicial traditions and doctrines and,
        503–504
    jurisdiction of, 481
    power of, 500
    trial courts of, 482, 483
    United States courts of appeals of,
        482–483, 490
    United States district courts of, 482, 483, 490
    United States Supreme Court of. See United
        States Supreme Court
Federal Deposit Insurance Corporation (FDIC),
        460
Federal Election Campaign Act (1971)(FECA),
        317–319

1974 amendments to, 263, 318
1976 amendments to, 263, 319
Federal Election Commission (FEC), 296, 297
    creation of, 318, 459
    principal functions of, 459
    reports filed with, by candidates, 318
Federal Food, Drug, and Cosmetic Act, 471
Federal grants-in-aid
    block, 104–105
    categorical, 102
    equalization and, 102
    matching funds and, 102
    record of, 105
Federal Insurance Contribution Act
        (FICA)(1935), 528
Federal mandates, 106–107
Federal Open Market Committee (FOMC), 532
Federal question, 481
Federal Register, 429, 432, 468, 469
Federal Regulation of Lobbying Act (Title III of
        Legislative Reorganization Act)(1946), 268
Federal Reserve System (Fed), 459, 527
    Board of Governors of, 422, 532
    e-money and, 531
    Federal Open Market Committee (FOMC) of,
        532
    independence of, 530, 532, 533, 538
    as monetary authority, 532
Federal system, 85. See also Federalism
    defined, 48
    flow of power in, 87
Federal Trade Commission (FTC), 262
    creation of, 466
    Internet fraud and, 458
    Internet privacy and, 138, 139
    principal functions of, 459
Federal Trade Commission Act (1914), 466
Federal Violence against Women Act (1994),
        498
Federal Water Pollution Control Act (1948),
        523–524
Federalism, 83–112
    arguments against, 90
    arguments for, 88–89
    constitutional basis for, 90–96
    cooperative, 100–104
    dual, 100
    horizontal, 95–96
    issues regarding, Rehnquist Court and, 498
    new, 104–108
    "new-age," 104
    picket-fence, 102
    trends in, 106–108
    twenty-first century issues and, 108–109
The Federalist Papers, 43, 47, 49, 50–51, 58,
        90, 221, 250, 500, 505
Federalists, 49, 50, 52, 278, 280, 292
FedEx, 473
Felton, Rebecca Latimer, 198
The Feminine Mystique (Friedan), 174
Feminism, 174–175
Ferraro, Geraldine, 177, 311
FICA (Federal Insurance Contribution
        Act)(1935), 528
Fifteenth Amendment, 154–155, 158, 164,
        173, 335, 501
Fifth Amendment, 135, 140, 141, 142
Fighting words, 130
Filibuster, 383
Films, First Amendment freedoms and, 133–134
Finland, online gambling operation resident
        in, 590

Fiorina, Morris P., 380
"Fireside chats," 363–364
First Amendment
    candidate spending on own behalf and, 319
    establishment clause of, 119–125, 578
    free exercise clause of, 125–126
    freedom of expression and. See Speech, freedom of
    freedom of religion and, 118–126
    freedom of speech and. See Speech, freedom of
    freedom of the press and, 118, 132–134, 231, 350, 364, 365
    interest group advocacy and, 320
    political patronage and, 289, 462
    privacy rights and, 135
    right of association and, 323
    right to assemble and petition the government and, 118, 134–135, 248, 250, 271
First budget resolution, 405
First Continental Congress, 36
First Lady
    e-mail and, 423, 444
    writing letter to, 444
Fiscal policy
    defined, 530
    lessons in, states and, 603
    politics of, 530–533
    theory and reality of, 530–531
Fiscal year (FY), 403
Fisher, Louis, 428
Fiske, John, 390
Fitzgerald, F. Scott, 519
Flag
    American. See American flag
    Confederate, flying of, 99
    Texas, flying of, with American flag, 597
Flag Protection Act (1989), 128
Fliegelman, Jay, 38
Fluidity, public opinion and, 222–223
FMC Corporation, 466
Focus groups, 316
FOIA (Freedom of Information Act)(1966), 474
Foley, Tom, 388
FOMC (Federal Open Market Committee), 532
Food and Drug Administration (FDA), 249
    Internet fraud and, 458
    regulation of tobacco and, 471
Food stamps, 517, 519
Forbes, Steve, 497
Ford, Betty, 434
Ford, Gerald, 94
    armed forces ordered by into combat without congressional approval, 552
    assumption of presidency by, 434
    cabinet of, 177
    election of 1976 and, 342
    federal grants-in-aid and, 105
    Richard Nixon pardoned by, 417
    service of, without vice president, 441, 442
    vice president nominated by, 441
Ford, Harold, Sr., 385
Ford, Harold E., 385
Foreign Affairs, 557
Foreign Corrupt Practices Act (FCPA)(1977), 450
Foreign governments, lobbying by, 260, 261. See also individual nations
Foreign officials, bribery of, 450
Foreign policy, 543–574
    containment policy and, 557
    defined, 545

domestic sources of, 553–554
era of internationalism and, 555–557
formative years in, 554–555
global economy and, 565–566
isolationist, 555
major themes of, 554–559
makers of, 94, 547–552
morality versus reality in, 546–547
process of, 545
public opinion and, 553
regional conflicts and, 566–570
sanctions and, 553, 563, 564, 566
states as makers of, 94
superpower relations and, 557–559
twenty-first century issues and, 570–571
Foreign Policy, 89
Foreign policy process, 545
Forrester Research, Inc., 154
Founding Fathers. See United States Constitution, framers of
Fourteenth Amendment, 54, 133, 144, 154–155, 164, 501
    due process clause of, 155
    equal protection clause of, 152, 153, 155, 158, 189, 190, 191, 192, 194, 202, 205, 389, 586. See also Civil right(s)
    incorporating Bill of Rights into, 117–118
    privileges and immunities clause of, 155
Fourth Amendment, 32, 58, 135, 140, 143
Fox, Vincente, 419
Fox Television, 353
France
    Alpine Diamond and, 86
    assistance in Rwanda and, 570
    at close of World War II, 556
    Constitutional Council and, 496
    defeat of, in Indochina, 557
    fall of, in World War II, 432
    independence for former colonies of, 569
    judicial review and, 496
    revolution of 1789 and, 10–11, 18
    terrorism in, 561
    unitary system of government in, 85–86
Frankel, Max, 365
Franking, 392–393
Franklin, Benjamin, 37, 42, 43, 46
Fraternity, 18
Fraud
    Internet, 458
    vote, 329–330
Free exercise clause, 125–126
Free Soil Party, 298
Freedom
    of assembly, 118, 134–135
    of expression. See Speech, freedom of
    of the press, 118, 132–134, 231, 350, 364, 365, 366. See also Speech, freedom of
    of religion, 117, 118–126. See also Religion
    of speech. See Speech, freedom of
Freedom of Access to Clinic Entrances Act (1994), 137
Freedom of Information Act (FOIA)(1966), 474
Freeman v. Pitts, 161
Free-PC, 139
Frémont, John C., 280
French and Indian War, 35
Friedan, Betty, 174
Front-loading, 323
Front-runner, 323
Frost, Martin, 400
Frost, Vicki, 1121
FTC. See Federal Trade Commission

Fulton, Robert, 97
Functional consolidation, 595
Fund for a Feminist Majority, 176
Fundamental Orders of Connecticut (1639), 35
Furman v. Georgia, 144
FY (fiscal year), 403

G

Gag order, 132–133
Gallup, George, 225
Gallup Organization
    founding of, 225
    polls of, 20, 52, 122, 162, 167, 175, 177, 225, 227, 231, 234, 237, 238, 239, 315–316
        accuracy record of, 228
        most important problem trend and, 239
        sample size and, 244
Gambling
    on Indian reservations, 585
    online, 590–591
Gandhi, Mahatma, 162
Gannett Company v. De Pasquale, 133
GAO (General Accounting Office), 394, 473, 519
Garbage can model of bureaucracy, 452
Garfield, James A., 441, 462
GATT (General Agreement on Tariffs and Trade), 536
Gault, In re, 206
Gay Activist Alliance, 201
Gay Liberation Front, 201
Gay males and lesbians
    child-custody and adoption issues and, 206
    civil unions for, 205
    in the military, 203–204
    politics and, 203
    rights of, 201–206
    same-sex marriages and, 204–205
Gays and Lesbians for Individual Liberty, 202
Gender
    discrimination on basis of, 164–165, 175–176, 189, 198. See also Sexual harassment
    voting behavior and, 339–340
Gender gap
    defined, 237
    presidential elections and, 237, 339–340
    wages and, 181
General Accounting Office (GAO), 394, 473, 519
General Agreement on Tariffs and Trade (GATT), 536
General Electric Corporation, 466
General jurisdiction, 482
General law city, 593
General Motors (GM), 258
General sales tax, 602
General Services Administration (GSA), 416, 457
Generational effect, 235
Geographic region, voting behavior and, 340. See also Solid South
George III (king of Great Britain and Ireland), 35, 36, 38
Georgia, refusal of, to join the Commonwealth of Independent States, 560
Gephardt, Richard, 400
Germany
    achievement tests of students in, 578
    at close of World War II, 556
    East, 556
    federal system of government in, 87
    legality of homosexuality in, 203

prior review in, 496
unification of, 559
Gerry, Elbridge, 42, 43, 390
Gerrymandering, 390–391, 586
Ghana, unitary system of government in, 86
Gibbons, Thomas, 97
Gibbons v. Ogden, 96, 97–98
Gideon v. Wainright, 141
Gilmore, Jim, 286
Gingrich, Newt, 302, 397, 398, 406
Ginsburg, Douglas, 493
Ginsburg, Ruth Bader, 177, 487, 493, 497, 499
Girl Scouts of America, 438
Gitlow v. New York, 118, 127
Glass ceiling, 181
Global economy, 565–566
Goddard, Taegan, 465
Goldstein, Melissa, 438
Goldwater, Barry, 340, 360, 386
Gonzalez, Elian, 222, 364, 567, 595, 596
Good Samaritan Fund, 438
GOP. *See* Republican Party
Gorbachev, Mikhail, 559, 560
Gore, Albert, 6, 106, 256, 277, 309, 323, 325, 440
   campaign financing controversy and, 242,
     427
   cast vote in budget battle, 405
   fund-raising activity and, 427
   online chat and, 423
   Social Security policy and, 529–530
Government(s)
   aid from, to church-related schools,
     119–120
   anarchy and, 10
   antidrug advertising and, 365
   aristocracy and, 10
   authority of, 8–9
   based on consent of the people, 10–11, 35
   citizens' compliance with, 9
   compelling interest of, 125, 190
   confederal system of. *See* Confederal system
   control of, 48
   council of (COG), 595–596
   county, 593–594
   democracy and. *See* Democracy
   divided, 6, 281, 291, 388, 471–472
   elite and, 10
   elite theory and, 13–14, 15, 269
   fear of, civil liberties and, 117. *See also*
     Civil liberties
   federal system of. *See* Federal system
   information about private citizens and, 474
   Internet connections to, 8, 579
   legitimacy of, 8–9
   limited, 13, 48, 153
   local. *See* Local government(s)
   Madisonian model of, 46–47
   media and, 363–367
   municipal
     defined, 593
     types of plans for, 596–598
   need for, 7–9
   number of, in United States today, 85
   oligarchy and, 10
   online connections to, 8
   operation of, responsibility for, 278
   party-in-, 283, 291
   power of, 9. *See also* National government,
     powers of; State government(s),
     powers of
   regulation by. *See* Government

regulation(s)
   republican form of, 11
   right to petition, 118
   size of, changes in, 86
   state. *See* State government(s)
   totalitarian regimes and, 9, 10
   unitary system of. *See* Unitary system
Government corporation(s), 454, 458–459
   defined, 458
   selected, illustrated, 460
Government in the Sunshine Act (1976), 463
Government Performance and Results Act
   (1997), 464–465
Government regulation(s)
   of campaign financing, 242, 316–317
   deregulation and, 457–458
   environmental. *See* Environmental policy
   of lobbyists, 268–269
   of the media, 364–367
   of online gambling, 590–591
   of polling, 231
   president's powers and, 429
   reregulation and, 458
   self-regulation versus, 139
   of tobacco, 249
Graber, Doris A., 235–236, 361
Gramm, Phil, 318
Gramsci, Antonio, 89
Grand Old Party. *See* Republican Party
Grand Staircase-Escalante National
   Monument, 267, 429
Grandfather clause, 158
Grant, Ulysses, 492
Grants-in-aid. *See* Federal grants-in-aid
Greacen, John, 485
Great Britain. *See also* England
   bureaucracy in, 452
   at close of World War II, 556
   common law system in, 479
   FDR's executive agreements with, 421
   financial markets in, 565
   independence for former colonies of, 569
   India's resistance to colonial system of, 162
   peace talks with Ireland and, 561
   unitary system of government in, 86
   Washington, D.C burned by, 556
   Yalta Conference and, 556
Great Compromise (Connecticut Compromise),
   44–46, 377
Great Depression, 100–101, 103, 108, 141,
   223, 225, 235, 512, 530–531
Great Society, 26, 101, 102
Greece
   American foreign aid to, 557
   ancient, Athenian system of government
     and, 10
   lobbying by, 261
Green Party, 258, 300
Greenback Party, 299
Greenbrier Hotel, 377
Greenpeace Society, 258
Greenspan, Alan, 532
Grenada
   American invasion of, 364, 418
   online gambling operation resident in,
     590–591
Gridlock, 393–394, 443
Griswold v. Connecticut, 135
Groups
   democracy for, 14–16
   interest. *See* Interest group(s)

GSA (General Services Administration), 416,
   457
Guatemala, CIA involvement in, 551
Guiteau, Charles J., 462
Gulf War. *See* Persian Gulf War
Gun control issue, 272
Gun-Free School Zones Act (1990), 107

H

Habeas corpus, writ of, 140
Hackers, government computers attacked by,
   552
Haines, Cynthia, 591
Haiti, 545
   American troops sent to, 418, 546, 547,
     566–567
   Clinton administration's policy toward,
     546, 547, 566–567
   Jean-Bertrand Aristide returned to power
     in, 546, 567
Hamilton, Alexander, 13–14, 59, 414
   Constitutional Convention and, 42, 43, 44
   The Federalist Papers and, 50, 58, 500, 505
Hancock, John, 38
Handbills, 295
"Hang Ten" project, 123
Harding, Warren G., 281, 354, 414, 555
Harlan, John Marshall, 157, 158
Harper's Weekly, 598
Harris poll, 227, 229, 315–316
Harris v. Forklift Systems, Inc., 179
Harris/*Business Week,* 139
Harrison, Benjamin, 327
Harrison, William Henry, 280, 420, 491, 492n
Harriss, United States v., 268
Hastert, Dennis, 398, 400
Hatch, Orrin, 240, 241, 497
Hatch Act (Political Activities Act)(1939), 317,
   463
Hatcher, Richard G., 599
"Hate crimes," 21
Hate speech, 21, 131–132
Hathaway, W. John, 314
Hayes, Rutherford B., 327
Health insurance, 152
Hearst, William Randolph, 355
*Heaven's Door: Immigration Policy and the
   American Economy* (Borjas), 170–171
Hecklers' veto, 130
Helium Program, 463
Helms, Jesse, 428–429
Helms-Burton Act, 567
Hemingway, Ernest, 519
Henry, Patrick, 38
Henry VII (king of England), 33
Herzegovina, 569
Hewlett-Packard Company, 94
Hill, Anita, 180, 493
Hill, Julia "Butterfly," 468
Hispanic American(s)
   bilingual education and, 193–194
   cultural values and, 18, 20
   Internet use by, 15
   political participation and, 22, 167
   population of, 20, 22, 169, 485
   schools with 90% minority enrollment and,
     162
   voting rights of, 167
The History of Women's Suffrage (Stanton), 173
Hitler, Adolf, 496, 556

HIV (human immunodeficiency virus)
   disability and, 199, 200
   national security and, 571
Ho Chi Minh, 557
Hoffa, Jimmy, 255
Holmes, Oliver Wendell, Jr., 126, 496
Holocaust, 156
Home rule city, 593
Homelessness, 520–521
Homer, 38
Homosexuals. *See* Gay males and lesbians
Hong Kong
   China's control of, 224, 564
   economic growth of, 534, 535
"Honor killings," 178
Hoover, Herbert, 295
Hopwood v. State of Texas, 191
Horizontal federalism, 95–96
Hornberger, Jacob G., 171
Hostile-environment harassment, 179
Hotwired, 358
House of Representatives. *See* United States House of Representatives
Housing, discrimination in, 166
Hsing Yun, 320
Human immunodeficiency virus. *See* HIV
Human Life Amendment, 61
Human rights, working for, 572
Human Rights Campaign Fund, 201, 203
Humphrey, Hubert, 298
Humphrey, Hubert ("Skip"), III, 298
Hussein, Saddam, 564, 568
Hyde, Henry, 406
Hyperpluralism, 15, 250

I

"I Love You" computer virus, 552
ICC (Interstate Commerce Commission), 455, 458
Iceland, online gambling operation resident in, 590
Ideologues, 240–242
Ideology
   defined, 24
   of delegates and party voters, 285
   political beliefs and, 24–25, 240–242
   Rehnquist Court and, 496–500
   self-identification and, 240, 241
   Supreme Court nominations and, 492
Illegal immigrants, 170
Immigrants. *See also* Immigration
   American culture adopted by, 20
   continued influx of, 169–170
   flow of, regulating, 170
   illegal, 170
   rights of, citizenship and, 182
Immigration. *See also* Immigrants
   civil rights agenda and, 168–172
   of high-tech workers, 23, 170
   policy regarding, 170–171
   United States population growth and, 23, 25
Immigration and Naturalization Service (INS), 170, 596
Impeachment, 180, 218, 235, 302, 412, 431, 434–435, 490
Implied power, 91
Impoundment of funds, 433–434
In re Gault, 206
Incarceration, rate of, 522
Income

level of. *See also* Socioeconomic status
   Internet use and, 15
   voter turnout and, 332, 336
   voting behavior and, 337–338
   transfer of, 516
   transfer payments as, 517
Income tax, 99–100, 379
Income transfer, 516
Incorporation theory, 118
Incumbency, power of, 386–387
Independent. *See* Candidate(s), independent; Voter(s), independent
Independent executive agency(ies), 454, 455, 457. *See also* Administrative agency(ies)
   defined, 455
   selected, listed, 457
Independent expenditures, 319–321
Independent regulatory agency(ies), 454, 455, 457–458, 459. *See also* Administrative agency(ies)
   capture and, 457
   defined, 455
   purpose and nature of, 455, 457–458
   selected, illustrated, 459
India
   common law system in, 479
   Comprehensive Nuclear Test Ban Treaty not ratified by, 562
   conflicts with China and Pakistan and, 563
   dowry killing and, 178
   federal system of government in, 87
   national unity and, 569
   nuclear weapons and, 261, 551, 562, 563
   resistance to British colonial system and, 162
Indian Claims Commission, 156
Indian reservations, gambling on, 585
Indiana (party-column) ballot, 328
Indirect techniques of interest groups, 260, 264, 266–268
Indonesia
   current economy in, 536
   economic growth of, 535
   fall of President Suharto in, 566
   state selective purchasing law and, 94
INF (Intermediate-Range Nuclear Force) Treaty, 559
Information, political, 18
"Information warfare," 552
Inherent power, 426
Initiative(s)
   constitutional, 581
   defined, 10
   legislative, 586
   state ballot, 191
   voter, 588
Injunction, 97
In-kind subsidies, 517
INS (Immigration and Naturalization Service), 170, 596
Institute of Electrical and Electronic Engineers, 257
Institution(s)
   confidence in, 239
   defined, 6
Instructed delegate, 380–381
Integration, school, 160–162
Intelligence community
   defined, 550
   foreign policymaking and, 550–551
Intensity, public opinion and, 222

Interest group(s), 247–274. *See also* Lobbying; Lobbyist(s); Political action committees
   benefits of, 251
   building alliances and, 267–268
   campaign assistance from, 263, 478. *See also* Campaign financing
   characteristics of, 254
   defined, 249
   democracy for, 14–16. *See also* Lobbying; Political action committees
   incentives to join
      material, 251–252
      purposive, 252
      solidary, 251
   iron triangles and, 469–472
   of professionals, 257
   public pressure generated by, 266
   ratings game and, 262–263
   representative democracy and, 269–270
   role of, 250–251
   selected, characteristics of, 254
   social movements and, 252–253
   special, 259–260, 267
   strategies of, 260–268
   techniques used by
      direct, 260, 261–264
      indirect, 260, 264, 266–268
   twenty-first century issues and, 270–271
   types of, 253–260
Intermediate-Range Nuclear Force (INF) Treaty, 559
Internal Revenue Code, 527
Internal Revenue Service (IRS)
   filing returns electronically and, 448
   information about private citizens and, 136, 474
   Web site of, 448
International Atomic Energy Commission, 562
International Brotherhood of Teamsters (Teamsters Union), 255, 263
International Monetary Fund, 565–566
International Women's Suffrage Alliance, 174
Internet. *See also* World Wide Web
   ADA and, 199
   betting on, state control and, 590–591
   broadcast news replaced by, 348
   candidate use of, 283
   civil society and, 89
   Congressional use of, 381, 382
   digital divide and, 15
   forum provided by, equality and, 17
   fraud conducted via, 458
   free speech and, 53, 60, 84, 367
   governments connected to, 8, 579
   hate speech on, 131–132
   Internet Tax Freedom Act of 1998 and, 513–515
   Library of Congress on, 391
   lobbying contacts reported on, 248
   making money on, 317
   as media, 358
      for new groups, 357
   net-powered generation and, 154
   political information and, 18
   polling on, 227, 229, 244
   pornography on, 129
   privacy rights and, 138–139
   raising campaign money on, 317
   in schools, establishment clause and, 120
   self-regulation and, 139

special interest groups and, 267
Starr report published on, 358, 382
state regulation of, 84
talk-show politics and, 356–358
taxes and, 513–515, 526
use of, 15
　age and, 154
　voting on, 329
Internet Gambling Prohibition Act (proposed), 591
Internet Tax Freedom Act (1998), 513–515
Internships in Washington, DC, 407
Interrogations, videotaped, 142
Interstate commerce, 32, 84, 97
Interstate Commerce Commission (ICC), 455, 458
Interstate compacts, 96
Interstate Oil and Gas Compact (1935), 96
"Intolerable Acts" (Coercive Acts)(1774)(Great Britain), 36
Intrastate commerce, 32, 84, 97
Iran
　CIA involvement in, 551
　"honor killings" in, 178
Iran-contra affair, 417, 439
Iraq, 544
　agreements made after Persian Gulf War and, 564
　"honor killings" in, 178
　Kurdish people persecuted by, 569
　Kuwait invaded by, 568–569
　newspapers censored and shut down by government in, 350
Ireland
　peace talks with Great Britain and, 561
　terrorism and, 561
Ireland, Patricia, 166
Iron curtain, 557
Iron triangles, 469–472
Iroquois Confederacy, 59
IRS. See Internal Revenue Service
Isolationist foreign policy, 555
Israel, 444
　Camp David accords and, 421
　Comprehensive Nuclear Test Ban Treaty not ratified by, 562
　lobbying by, 261
　negotiations with PLO and, 546, 561, 567–568
　opinion polls in, 226
　unitary system of government in, 86
Issue networks, 469, 471–472
Issue voting, voting behavior and, 341–343
Italy
　Alpine Diamond and, 86
　at close of World War II, 556
Item veto, 583
iVillage, 357

J

Jackson, Andrew, 278, 281, 292, 492, 500, 582
　election of 1824 and, 280, 414
　election of 1828 and, 280, 281
　kitchen cabinet of, 437
　patronage and, 461–462
　spoils system and, 461–462
　states' rights and, 98
Jackson, Reverend Jesse, 166, 302
　election of 1984 and, 167, 168
　election of 1988 and, 168
　Rainbow Coalition and, 168, 203

Jacobellis v. Ohio, 129
Jamestown, colony at, 34
Japan, 94, 126, 536
　achievement tests of students in, 578
　atomic bombs dropped on, 418, 556
　at close of World War II, 534, 556
　declaration of war against, 364, 547, 556
　economic growth of, 534, 535
　female professionals in, 178
　financial markets in, 565
　lobbying by, 260
　Pearl Harbor attacked by, 364, 547, 555–556
　terrorism in, 561
　whaling by, 258
Japanese American(s). See also Asian American(s)
　internment camps during World War II and, 426
　reparations for, 156
　rights of, limited by majority, 12
Jarbridge Shovel Brigade, 106
Jarvis, William, 59
Jay, John, 41, 50, 500
Jefferson, Thomas, 41, 52, 59, 119, 352, 441
　Constitutional Convention and, 46
　Declaration of Independence and, 37, 38
　election of 1800 and, 279, 280, 326, 414
　foreign policy and, 554
　inauguration of, 49, 416
　Louisiana Purchase and, 535
　natural aristocracy and, 461, 462
　patronage and, 461, 462
Jefferson, William, 378
Jeffersonian Republicans (Democratic Republicans), 49, 279, 280, 292, 461
Jennings, Peter, 358
Jewell, Malcolm E., 284
Jim Crow laws, 157, 158, 163
Jim Hightower Show, 353
Joan Shorenstein Center on the Press, Politics, and Public Policy, 334
Job Corps, 101
Johnson, Andrew, 156, 423, 434, 491
Johnson, Lyndon B., 281
　affirmative action policies and, 189
　as chief legislator, 421
　civil rights and, 165, 166, 189, 223
　"Daisy Girl" ad and, 359–360
　election of 1964 and, 338, 340, 359–360, 386, 393
　election of 1968 and, 219, 310
　federal grants-in-aid and, 102
　Great Society and, 101
　pact with vice president regarding incapacity and, 442
　Vietnam War and, 219, 310, 418, 428, 548, 558
　"war on poverty" and, 104
Johnson Controls, Inc., 178
Joint committee, 396
Jones, Paula Corbin, 180, 436, 443, 486
Jones v. Clinton, 436
Jordan, "honor killings" in, 178
Journal of the Louisiana Medical Society, 467
Judge(s). See also Court(s); Judiciary
　federal. See Federal court system, judges of state, 591–592
Judicial activism, 495–496, 497
Judicial implementation, 500–501
Judicial review, 58–59, 493–495
Judiciary, 477–507. See also Court(s)

checks and balances system and. See Checks and balances
federal. See Federal court system
judicial activism and, 495–496, 497
judicial restraint and, 496
judicial traditions and doctrines and, 503–504
state, 588–592
　illustrated, 589
twenty-first century issues and, 504
Jurisdiction
　defined, 481
　of federal court system, 481
　general, 482
　limited, 482
Juror(s)
　non-English-speaking, 485
　women serving as, 589
Jury, trial by, 484, 589
Justice Department. See United States Department of Justice
Justiciable controversy, 481
Justiciable question, 389
Juveniles. See also Children
　crimes by, 207, 208–209, 522
　death penalty for, 209
　rights of
　　civil, 206–209
　　criminal, 208–209
　　voting, 206–207

K

Kalb, Marvin, 334
Kanner, Gideon, 494–495
Kasten, Robert, 385
Katzman, Robert A., 497
Kazakhstan, Strategic Arms Reduction Treaty (START) signed by, 559
KDKA-Pittsburgh, 354
Kemp, Jack, 324
Kennedy, Anthony, 498, 499
Kennedy, Dan, 353
Kennedy, Jacqueline, 435
Kennedy, John F., 363, 550
　age of, at election, 414, 418
　burial place of, 435
　as chief legislator, 426
　civil rights and, 223
　Cuban missile crisis and, 558
　election of
　　in 1960, 234, 281, 295, 361
　　without majority of popular vote, 327, 414
　federal forces sent to Mississippi and Alabama by, 160
　first live television presidential press conference held by, 434
　media and, 434
　pact with vice president regarding incapacity and, 442
　Peace Corps created by, 546
　Vietnam War and, 418, 428, 548, 558
Kenya, bombing of American embassy in, 224, 563, 565
Kernell, Samuel, 431
Kerrey, Bob, 528
Key, V. O., Jr., 221
Keynes, John Maynard, 530–531
Keynesian economics, 531
Khrushchev, Nikita, 549–550, 559
Kimel v. Florida Board of Regents, 108, 197
King, Larry, 356, 357

King, Martin Luther, Jr., 162–164, 165, 166, 167–168, 596
King's courts *(curiae regis)*(England), 479
Kissinger, Henry A., 439, 550, 553, 558
Knox, Henry, 414
Korean War, 432, 544
    beginning of, 418, 428, 547, 557
Kosovo, American military action in, 238, 436, 570
Ku Klux Klan, 134
Kurdish people, Iraq's persecution of, 569
Kuwait
    Iraq's invasion of, 568–569
    women's rights in, 178

L

La Follette, Robert, 300
Labor. *See also* Union(s)
    child, 100, 102
    interest groups for, 255, 257
    labor movement and, 255
Labor movement, 255
Labor unions. *See* Union(s)
Ladner, Joyce A., 167–168
Landon, Alfred, 225
Landslide elections, 330, 393
Lane, Carole A., 138
Language, English. *See* English language
Larry King Live, 356, 357
Lasswell, Harold, 7
Lau v. Nichols, 194
Law(s)
    American, sources of, 480
    case, 480
    child-labor, 100, 102
    civil, 207
    common, 208, 479
    criminal, 207
    drug, federal, state actions regarding, 587
    due process of, 155
    ex post facto, 117
    how bill becomes. *See* Congress, lawmaking process of
    Jim Crow, 157, 158, 163
    making. *See* Congress, lawmaking process of; Lawmaking
    Megan's, 143, 350
    "motor-voter" (1993), 330, 335, 344
    questions of, 482
    selective purchasing, 94
    sunset, 464
    sunshine, 463
Lawler, Jim, 123
Lawmaking
    by Congress, 379. *See also* Congress, lawmaking process of
    defined, 379
    president as chief legislator and, 421–426, 548
    by states, process of, illustrated, 585
Lawsuit(s)
    class-action, 483–484
    parties to, 483–485
    standing to bring, 466, 481
League of Conservation Voters, 263
League of Nations, 546
League of Women Voters, 174, 259
Lebanon
    American troops sent to, 418, 419
    bombing of U.S. military housing compound in, 419

Lee, Spike, 164
Lee v. Weisman, 122
Legal Defense Fund, 484
Legal system, changing, 505. *See also* Court(s); Judiciary
Legislation. *See also* Law(s); Statutes
    checks on courts and, 501–502
    enabling, 466–467, 472
    sunset, 464
Legislative initiative, 586
Legislative Reorganization Act, Title III of (Federal Regulation of Lobbying Act)(1946), 268
Legislative veto, 381, 429
Legislature(s)
    bicameral, 44
    checks on courts and, 501–502
    defined, 10
    state. *See* State legislature(s)
    unicameral, 39
Legitimacy of government, 8–9
Lemon v. Kurtzman, 119–120, 121
Lesbians. *See* Gay males and lesbians
Leslie's Weekly, 521
Letter(s)
    to the editor, 109
    to the First Lady, 444
    to the president, 444
Levi Strauss and Company, 438
Lewinsky, Monica, 180, 219, 358, 430, 431, 433, 435, 436, 440, 443
Libel, 130, 132
Liberalism
    defined, 24
    political beliefs of, 24, 240
    vision of government power and, 25
Libertarian Party, 297, 298
Libertarianism, 25
Liberty(ies)
    civil. *See* Civil liberties
    defined, 17
Library of Congress, 394
    Web site of, 391
Libya, 544
    attack of, by American fighter planes, 418
    sanctions against, 564
Liddy, G. Gordon, 357
Lieberman, Joseph, 277, 440
Lightner, Candy, 505
Lightner, Cari, 505
Limbaugh, Rush, 357
Limited government, 13, 48
Limited jurisdiction, 482
Lincoln, Abraham, 6, 99, 153, 155, 157, 280, 321, 413, 434, 547
    cabinet of, 437
    election of
        in 1860, 280, 295
        without majority of popular vote, 327, 414
    Emancipation Proclamation and, 154, 155
    use of emergency power by, 432
Lincoln bedroom, fund-raising activity and, 427
Line Item Veto Act (1996), 424–425, 428
Line organizations, 455
Line-item veto, 423–425, 428
Literacy tests, 4, 158
Literary Digest, 224–225
Litigation, 483. *See also* Lawsuit(s)
Little, Malcolm (Malcolm X), 164
Livingston, Robert, 97, 406
Lobbying. *See also* Interest group(s); Lobbyist(s); Political action committees

by constituents, 266–267
contacts made in, reporting of, 248
First Amendment and, 248, 250
regulation of, 268–269
techniques used in, 261–262
Lobbyist(s). *See also* Lobbying
    defined, 249
    as friends and relatives, 271
    job of, 260
Local government(s)
    consolidation of, 595–596
    contracting out and, 464
    elections of, voting in, 330–333
    employees of, 453
    expenditures of, 600–601
    governing metropolitan areas and, 599–600
    laws of, against gay males and lesbians, 201–203
    learning about, 604
    legal existence of, 592–593
    as maker of foreign policy, 94
    number of, 85, 594
    operation of, 592–600
    paying for, 600–602
    politics in, machine versus reform in, 598–599
    powers of, to levy taxes, 92, 526
    revenues of, 601–602
    twenty-first century issues and, 603
    units of, 593–595
Locke, John, 18, 38
Logrolling, 379
Long, Huey P., 516, 581
Loophole, 525–528
Lopez, Naomi, 181
Lopez, United States v., 107
Loral Corporation, 565
Los Angeles Times, 569
    poll of, 19, 291
        exit, 226
Lott, Trent, 400, 404
Lotteries, 602
Louisiana Purchase, 535, 555

M

Macedonia, creation of, 86
Machado, Richard, 132
MADD (Mothers Against Drunk Driving), 505
Madison, James, 270, 278, 350
    Bill of Rights and, 52–54
    Constitutional Convention and, 42, 43–44, 46–47
    direct democracy and, 11
    The Federalist Papers and, 43, 47, 49, 50, 51, 90, 221, 250
    Madisonian model and, 46–47
Madisonian model, 46–47
Maier, Pauline, 38
Mail
    electronic. *See* E-mail
    franking by members of Congress and, 392–393
    voting by, 328–329
Majority
    age of, 207
    defined, 12
Majority floor leader of the Senate, 399
Majority leader of the House, 398
Majority opinion, 489
Majority rule, 12
Malaysia, economic growth of, 534, 535

Malcolm X (Malcolm Little), 164
Malice, actual, 132
Managed news, 353
Mandatory retirement, 197
Mandela, Nelson, 570
Mapp, Dollree, 143
Mapp v. Ohio, 143
Marbury v. Madison, 58, 493–494, 496
March on Washington for Jobs and Freedom, 163
Marijuana, medical, 587
Marriage, same-sex, 204–205
Marshall, John, 52, 96, 97–98, 104, 500
Marshall, Thurgood, 167, 493
Martin, Luther, 43
Marxism-Leninism, 25
Mason, George, 43, 49
Massachusetts, foreign policy and, 94
Massachusetts (office-block) ballot, 328
Massachusetts Bay Colony, 35, 523
Massachusetts Body of Liberties (1641), 35
Massachusetts Comprehensive Assessment System, 601
Matching funds, 102
Material incentives, 251–252
Mayer, Susan, 520
Mayflower, 34, 35
Mayflower Compact, 34–35, 38, 123
Mayhew, David R., 387, 393
Mayor-administrator plan of municipal government, 597
Mayor-council plan of municipal government, 597–598
McAuliffe, Terry, 286
McCaffrey, Barry R., 365
McCain, John, 232, 302, 317, 323, 334, 361
McCarthy, Eugene, 310
McCulloch, James William, 97
McCulloch v. Maryland, 90, 93, 96–97
McGovern, George, 340, 433
McGovern-Fraser Commission, 321
McKinley, William, 280, 282, 299, 418
McVeigh, Timothy, 204n
McVeigh, Timothy R., 204
Media. *See also* Newspapers; Radio; Television
    access to, public's right to, 367
    bias in, 367–369
    content of, control of by government, 366–367
    defined, 235
    functions of, 349–352
    government and, 363–367
    impact of, on voters, 362
    influence of, on public opinion, 235–236
    Internet as, 358
        for new groups, 357
    monopoly in, 353
    ownership of, controlling, 365–366
    the presidency and, 363–364
    presidential press conferences and, 367, 434
    regulation of, 364–367
    spin doctors and, 361
    twenty-first century issues and, 369
    in the United States, history of, 352–358
Media Network, 357
Mediachannel, 350
Medicaid, 101, 260
Medical care as civil right, 152
Medical marijuana, 587
Medical records, privacy and, 116
Medicare, 195
    benefits of, 195, 210
    creation of, 101, 260

elimination of, 512
    government spending on, 197, 528
    grim future of, 528
    payroll taxes for, 512
    protecting, 290
Megan's laws, 143, 350
Mercer, John Francis, 43
Meredith, James, 160
Merit system, 462
Merit Systems Protection Board (MSPB), 463, 465
Merton, Robert, 598–599
Metropolitan areas, governing of, 599–600
Mexico, 419
    federal system of government in, 87
    NAFTA and, 261, 537, 549
Microsoft Corporation, 449
    government suits against, 256
    joint electronic publishing ventures and, 353
    MSNBC and, 358
    Slate and, 358, 366
Mid-Atlantic Legal Foundation, 259
Middle East
    Persian Gulf War and, 418, 568–569
    regional conflict in, 546, 561
    regional conflicts in, 567–569
Mikulski, Barbara, 400
Military
    desegregation of, 223
    gay males and lesbians in, 203–204
    "information warfare" and, 552
    military-industrial complex and, 553–554
    pilot test of Internet voting and, 329
    president as commander in chief of, 417–419, 547
    women in combat and, 175–176
Military-industrial complex, 553–554
Mill, John Stuart, 407
Miller, Carol, 300
Miller v. California, 129
Million Family March on Washington, 236
Million Man March on Washington, 236
Minnow, Newton, 356
Minor, Virginia Louisa, 173
Minority floor leader of the Senate, 399
Minority leader of the House, 398–399
"Minority-majority" districts, 390–391
Miranda, Ernesto, 141
Miranda v. Arizona, 141–142, 143
Mississippi Summer Project, 165
Missouri Compromise, 154
Missouri v. Jenkins, 161
Missouri Women's Network, 57
Mister Poll, 229
Mitchell, George, 271
Mondale, Walter, 203, 337
Monetary policy
    in age of cybermoney, 531
    defined, 530
    e-money and, 531
    lags and, 532–533
    politics of, 530–533
    theory and reality of, 531–533
Money in Elections (Overacker), 316
Monopolistic model of bureaucracy, 452
Monroe, James, 280, 555
Monroe Doctrine, 555
Moore, Stephen, 171
Moral idealism, 546
Morella, Connie, 394
Morison, Samuel Eliot, 35
Morocco, Barbary pirates and, 554

Morris, Gouverneur, 43
Morrison, United States v., 107–108
Morse, Samuel, 394
Moses, Bob, 168
Mossadegh, Mohammad, 551
Most-favored-nation status, 261, 549, 563–564
Mothers Against Drunk Driving (MADD), 505
"Motor-voter" law (1993), 330, 335, 344
Mott, Lucretia, 173
Mountain States Legal Defense Foundation, 258–259
MSNBC, 358
MSPB (Merit Systems Protection Board), 463, 465
MTV, 336
Muir, John, 257
Municipal home rule, 593
Municipalities
    defined, 593
    government of, 596–598
Murdoch, Rupert, 353
Murphy, Walter, 502
Muslim nations, political parties in, 292
Mussolini, Benito, 496
Myanmar (Burma), sanctions against, 93, 564

N

NAACP (National Association for the Advancement of Colored People), 99, 159, 253, 484
Nader, Ralph, 258, 302
NAFTA (North American Free Trade Agreement), 261, 267, 393, 420, 537, 549
Naked in Cyberspace: How to Find Personal Information Online (Lane), 138
NAM (National Association of Manufacturers), 253, 267, 269
Narrowcasting, 356
NASA. *See* National Aeronautics and Space Administration
Nast, Thomas, 598
National Abortion Rights Action League, 259
National Aeronautics and Space Administration (NASA)
    computers of, attacked by hackers, 552
    formation and principal functions of, 457
    funding of, 472
National American Woman Suffrage Association, 174
National Archives, 56
National Association for the Advancement of Colored People (NAACP), 99, 159, 253, 484
National Association of Automobile Dealers, 252
National Association of Broadcasters, 366
National Association of Counties, 467
National Association of Manufacturers (NAM), 253, 267, 269
National Audubon Society, 251, 257
National Bioethics Advisory Commission, 438
National Broadcasting Company. *See* NBC
National Cattleman's Association, 470
National Center for Children in Poverty, 519
National chairperson, 286
National Chamber (United States Chamber of Commerce), 253, 267, 270
National Coalition to Ban Handguns, 272
National convention(s), 324–325
    amending the United States Constitution and, 56–57
    defined, 284

delegates to. *See* Delegate(s), to national convention
National debt. *See* Public debt
National Education Association (NEA), 257, 263
National Enquirer, 354
National Environmental Policy Act (1969), 524
National Farmers' Union (NFU), 255
National Federation of Business and Professional Women's Clubs, 174
National Foreign Trade Council (NFTC), 94
National Gay and Lesbian Task Force, 201
National government
  antidrug advertising and, 365
  budget of
    budget cycle and, 403
    deficit and, 533–534
    preparation process and, 403–405
    surplus and, 535
  bureaucracy of
    civil service and. *See* Civil service
    congressional control of, 472–473
    organization of, 453–459
      illustrated, 454
  checks and balances system and. *See* Checks and balances
  civil service and. *See* Civil service
  computer systems of, attacked by hackers, 552
  courts of. *See* Court(s); Federal court system; Judiciary
  debt of. *See* Public debt
  deficit and, 533–534
  employees of, 453
  grants-in-aid to states by. *See* Federal grants-in-aid
  growth of, Civil War and, 99–100
  inefficiency in, presidential plans to end, 449
  information about private citizens and, 474
  internships with, 407
  laws of, making of. *See* Congress, lawmaking process of
  nature of, 13–15
  powers of. *See also* Congress, powers of; President(s), powers of
    commerce clause and. *See* Commerce clause
    concurrent, 91, 92–93
    division of, between powers of state governments and
      continuing dispute over, 100–105
      summarized, 91
    enumerated, 90, 91, 378–379
    prohibited, 91, 93
    separation of, 46–47, 48
    preemption by, 93, 95
    public debt of. *See* Public debt. *See also* Public debt
    regulation by. *See* Government regulation(s)
    spending by, 401–405
      impoundment of funds and, 433–434
      on Medicare and Social Security, 197, 528
      "pork barrel projects" and, 404, 428
      shift toward, illustrated, 103
      welfare, 518
National Governors Association (NGA), 514, 583
National Labor Relations Board (NLRB), 459
National Milk Producers Association, 470
National Neighborhood Enterprise Center, 168
National Opinion Research Center, 226

National Organization for Women (NOW), 166, 174–175, 253
National origin, discrimination on basis of, 101, 164–165, 165, 189, 198
National politics, 293
National Public Radio, 352
National Railroad Passenger Corporation (AMTRAK), 460
National Retired Teachers' Association, 197
National Review, 366, 370
National Rifle Association of America (NRA), 9, 260, 268
  gun control issue and, 272
  Internet and, 267, 269
National Right-to-Work Legal Defense Foundation, 259
National Science Foundation (NSF), 457
National Security Act (1947), 439, 545, 550, 551
National Security Agency (NSA), 439, 551
National Security Council (NSC), 436, 438
  creation of, 439, 545, 550, 551
  defined, 439, 545
  foreign policymaking and, 545
  Iran-*contra* affair and, 439
National security policy, 545
National Wildlife Federation, 258
National Woman Suffrage Association, 173, 253
National Women's Party, 175
Native Alaskans, political participation and, 167
Native American(s)
  block grants and, 105
  in Congress, 167
  cultural values and, 18
  political participation and, 153, 167
  political values of, 59
  programs to help, 156
  rights of
    limited by majority, 12
    voting, 167
NATO. *See* North Atlantic Treaty Organization
Natural aristocracy, 461
Natural rights, 38
Naturalization
  constitutional requirement regarding, 23
  proficiency in English and, 193
Nature Conservancy, 258
NBC
  debut of, 354
  news coverage on, 358
NEA (National Education Association), 257, 263
"Near" treaties, 428–429
Nebraska Press Association v. Stuart, 127, 133
Necessaries, 207
Necessary and proper (elastic) clause, 90–91, 379
Negative advertising, 360
Negative constituents, 550
Negotiated rulemaking, 469
Negotiated Rulemaking Act (1990), 469
Netanyahu, Benjamin, 568
Netherlands, drug program in, 587
Net-powered generation, 154
New Deal, 26, 100–101, 103, 281, 289, 290, 339, 436, 463, 464, 495, 530
New England town, 594
New federalism, 104–108
New Jersey plan, 44
New Republic, 370
New York Herald, 352
New York Times, 284–285, 288, 363, 365

on the Internet, 358
  news coverage by, television coverage versus, 359
  Pentagon Papers and, 127
  polling by, 224, 229
  release of Starr report and, 358
New York Times v. United States (Pentagon Papers case), 127
New York Times Co. v. Sullivan, 132
New York Times/CBS News poll, 224
New York Tribune, 352
New York World, 354
New Zealand, common law system in, 479
News
  being a critical consumer of, 370
  bias in, 368
  broadcast, replaced by Internet, 348
  coverage of, management of, 361
  managed, 353
  reporting of, as function of media, 350
news.com, 358
Newspapers, 352–354. *See also* Media; Press
  mass-readership, development of, 353–354
  yellow journalism and, 354
Newsweek, poll of, 21, 242
NFTC (National Foreign Trade Council), 94
NFU (National Farmers' Union), 255
NGA (National Governors Association), 514, 583
NGOs (nongovernmental organizations), 89
Nicaragua, Iran-*contra* affair and, 417
Nicholson, Jim, 286
Nickles, Don, 400
Nigeria, local government selective purchasing law and, 94
Nineteenth Amendment, 173, 174, 335
Ninth Amendment, 135
Nixon, Pat, 434
Nixon, Richard, 327, 439, 442, 493
  Cambodia invasion and, 418
  "Checkers" speech and, 355
  China and, 558, 563
  Committee to Reelect the President (CREEP) and, 317
  divided government and, 393
  election of, without majority of popular vote, 327, 414
  election of 1960 and, 234, 361
  election of 1968 and, 281, 298, 327
  election of 1972 and, 281, 317, 338, 340
  executive privilege claim of, 433
  federal grants-in-aid and, 105
  impeachment proceedings against, 219, 434
  impoundment of funds by, 433–434
  new federalism and, 104
  pardon of, by President Ford, 417
  public opinion and, 234
  resignation of, 219, 281, 363, 434
  service of, without vice president, 441, 442
  Soviet Union and, 558
  Strategic Arms Limitation Treaty (SALT I) and, 558, 559
  Vietnam War and, 418, 428
  War Powers Resolution vetoed by, 419, 552
  Watergate break-in and, 219, 281, 363, 417, 433, 434
Nixon, United States v., 433
NLRB (National Labor Relations Board), 459
Nongovernmental organizations (NGOs), 89
Nonopinion, 221
Nonpolls, 244
North, Oliver, 439

North American Free Trade Agreement
    (NAFTA), 261, 267, 393, 420, 537, 549
North Atlantic Treaty Organization (NATO)
    admission of new members to, 224
    American obligations under, 544
    Bosnia and, 547, 570
    decisions of, Russia's voice in, 428
    Kosovo and, 570
    organization of, 87
    reasons for, 544
North Korea, 545. See also Korean War;
    South Korea
    nuclear weapons development and, 562
    President Eisenhower's threat against,
        547
North Vietnam, American bombing of, 418.
    See also South Vietnam; Vietnam;
    Vietnam War
Northern Ireland, 561
    state selective purchasing law and, 94
Northwest Airlines, 255
Northwest Ordinance (1787), 40
NOW (National Organization for Women),
    166, 174–175, 253
NRA. See National Rifle Association of
    America
NRC. See Nuclear Regulatory Commission
NSA (National Security Agency), 439, 551
NSC. See National Security Council
NSF (National Science Foundation), 457
Nuclear club, 561, 562
Nuclear proliferation, 561, 562
Nuclear Regulatory Commission (NRC), 451,
    455
    principal functions of, 459
Nullification, 99

O

Obscenity, as unprotected speech, 128–129
Occupational Safety and Health Act (1970),
    466
Occupational Safety and Health
    Administration, 429, 466
O'Connor, Sandra Day, 124, 177, 179, 493,
    497–498, 499
Office of Administration, 438
Office of the Attorney General, 452. See also
    United States Department of Justice
Office of Environmental Justice, 467
Office of Management and Budget (OMB),
    403, 404, 405, 438, 439
Office of National Drug Control Policy, 438
Office of the Pardon Attorney, 417
Office of Personnel Management (OPM), 463
Office of Policy Development, 438
Office of Science and Technology Policy,
    438
Office of Special Counsel (OSC), 465
Office of the United States Trade
    Representative, 438
Office-block (Massachusetts) ballot, 328
Ogden, Aaron, 97
Oklahoma City bombing, 24, 204n, 223
Older Americans. See Elderly
Oligarchy, 10
Olmstead v. United States, 135
Olson, David M., 284
Olson, Mancur, 251
Olympics, terrorism and, 561, 563
OMB (Office of Management and Budget),
    403, 404, 405, 438, 439

Ombudsperson, 380
Omnibus Crime Control and Safe Streets Act
    (1968), 142
Onassis, Jacqueline Kennedy, 435
Oncale v. Sundowner Offshore Services, Inc.,
    180
Online gambling, 590–591
Open primary, 322
Operation Head Start, 101
Opinion(s)
    concurring, 489
    consensus, 220–221
    defined, 489
    dissenting, 489
    divisive, 221
    majority, 489
    nonopinion and, 221
    per curiam, 489
    private, public opinion and, 221
    public. See Public opinion
    unanimous, 489
    of United States Supreme Court, 489
Opinion leaders, 235
Opinion poll(s)
    being a critical consumer of, 244
    Business Week/Harris, 139
    "call-in," 244
    campaign use of, 315–316
    campaign-finance reform and, 242
    CBS News/New York Times, 224
    court cases decided using, 218
    defined, 224, 225
    Gallup. See Gallup Organization, polls of
    Harris, 227, 229, 315–316
    Harris/Business Week, 139
    history of, 224–226
    on the Internet, 227, 229, 244
    Los Angeles Times, 19, 291
    misleading, 232
    Mister, 229
    New York Times, 229
    New York Times/CBS News, 224
    Newsweek, 21, 242
    nonpolls and, 244
    political culture and, 237–238
    problems with, 227, 230
    pseudo-, 225
    "push," 232
    regulation and, 231
    sampling error and, 230
    sampling techniques and, 226–227
    technology and, 229
    telephone, 229
    tracking, 316
    Wall Street Journal, 19, 291
OPM (Office of Personnel Management), 463
Opposition research, 314
Oprah, 351
Oral arguments, 488
Oregon v. Smith, 125
O'Reilly, James, 471
Organ donation, policy regarding, 101
Organization for Economic Cooperation and
    Development, 450
Organization of American States, 549
Ornstein, Norman, 328
Osborne v. Ohio, 129
OSC (Office of Special Counsel), 465
Ossian, 38
Oval Office, 418. See also President(s)
Overacker, Louise, 316
Oversight, 381, 470

P

Pacific Legal Foundation, 259
Pacific Lumber Company, 468
Pacific Research Institute, 181
Packwood, Robert, 328, 406
PACs. See Political action committees
Page, Benjamin I., 240
Paine, Thomas, 36–37, 334
Pakistan, 545
    Comprehensive Nuclear Test Ban Treaty not
        ratified by, 562
    conflict with India and, 563
    "honor killings" in, 178
    national unity and, 569
    nuclear weapons and, 261, 551, 562
Palestine, "honor killings" in, 178
Palestine Liberation Organization (PLO),
    negotiations with Israel and, 546, 561,
    567–568
Panama
    American troops sent to, 418
    return of Panama Canal to, 420
Pardon, 417
Parks, Rosa, 162
"Partial-birth" abortions, 137
Party identification
    defined, 300
    trends in, 301
    uncertain future of, 300–301
    voting behavior and, 341
Party identifier, 386
Party organization, 282–289
    defined, 282
    local party machinery and, 288–289
    national, 284–286
    national chairperson and, 286
    national committee and, 286
    patronage and, 289, 427
    state, 287
    theoretical structure of, illustrated, 284
Party platform, 284
Party-column (Indiana) ballot, 328
Party-in-government, 283, 291
Party-in-the-electorate, 282
PATCO (Professional Air Traffic Controllers
    Organization), 257
Paterson, William, 44
Patronage, 289, 427, 461–462, 598–599
Patterson, Thomas, 334, 368
Paul, Alice, 57, 174
Peace Corps, 546
Pearl Harbor attack, 364, 547, 555–556
Peer groups, political opinion influenced by,
    233
Penelas, Alex, 595, 596
Pendergast, Tom, 598
Pendleton Act (Civil Service Reform
    Act)(1883), 462
Penelas, Alex, 595, 596
Pennsylvania Charter of Privileges (1701), 35
Pennsylvania Frame of Government (1682), 35
Pennsylvania Packet & General Advertiser, 354
Pennsylvania Society for the Abolition of
    Slavery, 46
Pentagon, 551. See also United States
    Department of Defense
Pentagon Papers case (New York Times v.
    United States), 127
People's Republic of China, 557
    Comprehensive Nuclear Test Ban Treaty not
        ratified by, 562
    conflict with India and, 563

control of Hong Kong by, 224, 564
control of Internet and, 53, 350
illegal campaign contributions from, 427,
    564–565
most-favored-nation status and, 261, 549,
    563–564
as new world power, 563–565
newspapers censored and shut down by
    government in, 350
nuclear weapons development and, 562
permanent normal trade relations with,
    261, 342, 420, 537, 548, 549
President Carter's recognition of, 420, 558
President Eisenhower's threat against, 547
President Nixon's relations with, 558, 563
Tiananmen Square incident and, 549
UN Convention on the Rights of the Child
    signed by, 209
Vice President Gore's Buddhist Temple
    fundraiser and, 320
Per curiam opinion, 489
Perkins, Frances, 177
Perot, H. Ross
    election of 1992 and, 237, 300, 302, 310,
        356, 388, 393, 414
    election of 1996 and, 300, 302, 310
    Reform Party and, 298, 300
Persian Gulf War, 544, 564, 568–569
    popularity of George Bush and, 238
Personal records, privacy and, 116
Personal Responsibility and Work
    Opportunity Reconciliation Act. See
    Welfare Reform Act
Petrocelli, William, 179
Pew Center for the People and the Press,
    study by, 368
Pfaff, William, 527
Philadelphia Convention, 42, 88. See also
    Constitutional Convention
Philippines
    "I Love You" computer virus and, 552
    unitary system of government in, 86
Phillips, Kevin, 294
Physician-assisted suicide, 32, 140, 588
Picket-fence federalism, 102
Pinckney, Charles, 45, 333
Planned Parenthood v. Casey, 137
Pledge of Allegiance, 16, 17, 233
Plessy, Homer, 157–158
Plessy v. Ferguson, 157–158, 159
PLO (Palestine Liberation Organization),
    negotiations with Israel and, 546, 561,
    567–568
"The Plum Book (Policy and Supporting
    Positions), 459–460
Pluralism, 14–15, 250, 269, 515
Plurality, 326
Pocket veto, 423, 583
Podesta, Anthony, 271
Poindexter, John, 439
Police power(s)
    defined, 92, 580
    rights of accused and, 140, 146
Policy and Supporting Positions ("The Plum
    Book"), 459–460
Policy trade-offs, 525
Policymaking
    agenda and, 513–515
    bureaucrats and, 466–472
    courts and, 493–500
    process of, 513–515
        models of, 515

steps in, 513–515
Political action committees (PACs). See also
    Interest group(s); Lobbying; Lobbyist(s)
    contributions from
        to congressional candidates, 265
        independent expenditures and, 319–321
        soft money and, 266, 319. See also Soft
            money
        top twenty in making, listed, 265
    defined, 263
    growth of, 264
    political campaigns and, 263–264, 319
    women and, 176
Political Activities Act (Hatch Act)(1939), 317,
    463
Political advertising, 359–361
Political appointees, 459–460
Political culture
    defined, 16
    fundamental values of, 17–18
    public opinion and, 237–238
    stability of, 18, 20
    of the United States, 16–18, 20, 294–295
Political events, political attitudes and,
    234–235
Political forum, provided as function of
    media, 351–352
Political information, 18
Political knowledge, public opinion and, 224
Political party(ies), 275–305. See also entries
    beginning with Party; individual parties
    cadre in, 278
    contributions to, 319
    convention of. See National convention(s)
    defined, 277
    differences between, 289–291
    faction of, 277
    functions of, 277–278
    history of, 278–282
    joining, requirement for, 276
    members and, 289–291
    minor. See Third party(ies), minor
    national chairperson of, 286
    national committee of, 286
    organization of. See Party organization
    party voting in Congress and, 401
    patronage and, 289, 427, 461–462
    platform of, 284
    in power, opposition to, 278
    president as chief of, 427–428
    soft money and, 266, 287, 319. See also
        Soft money
    splinter, 298
    theoretical structure of, illustrated, 284
    third. See Third party(ies)
    three faces of, 282–283
    twenty-first century issues and, 301–302
    two-party system and. See Two-party
        system
Political patronage, 289, 427, 461–462,
    598–599
Political press, rise of, 352–353
Political process, public opinion and, 242–243
Political question, 503
Political realism, 546
Political socialization, 232–237
    defined, 16, 232
    influences in, 232–237
    of new generations, media and, 351
Political trust
    defined, 238
    trends in, 238–239

Political withdrawal, as reason for low voter
    turnout, 333
Politics
    in America, in twenty-first century, 26
    city, machine versus reform in, 598–599
    class, 293
    defined, 6–7
    of economic decision making, 525–533
    of fiscal policy, 530–533
    forum for, provided as function of media,
        351–352
    gay community and, 203
    judicial appointment process and, 494–495
    local, learning about, 604
    of monetary policy, 530–533
    national, 293
    sectional, 294
    sexual harassment and, 180, 436, 443, 486
    talk-show, 356–358
    of taxes and subsidies, 525–528
    world, challenges in, 560–570
Poll(s)
    exit, 366–367. See also Exit poll(s)
    opinion. See Opinion poll(s)
Poll taxes, 158
Polsby, Nelson W., 49
Pomper, Gerald M., 284
Poor People's Campaign, 167–168
Popular sovereignty, 13, 48, 496
Population, United States
    distribution of
        by Hispanic origin, 22
        by race, 22
    elderly, by age, 21, 196
    growth of, immigration and, 23, 25
    immigrant, 23, 169
    low-income, 516–517
Populist Party, 280, 299
"Pork barrel projects," 404, 428
Pornography, 129
The Port Authority of New York and New
    Jersey, 96, 594
Portman, Rob, 267
Position taking, reelection goal of incumbent
    pursued by, 387
Poverty
    children living in, 519–520
    civil rights and, 167–168
    defined, 516–517
    "war on," 104
    welfare and, 516–521
Powell, Colin, 167, 438, 550
Powell, Lewis, 190
Power(s)
    appointment, 415–416, 449, 459–460, 548
    concurrent, 91, 92–93
    of Congress. See Congress, powers of
    constitutional. See United States
        Constitution, powers under
    defined, 9
    emergency, 432
    enumerated, 90, 91, 378–379
    expressed, 91, 426
    of federal judiciary, 500
    of government, 9. See also National
        government, powers of; State
        government(s), powers of
    implied, 91
    of incumbency, 386–387
    inherent, 426
    police. See Police power(s)
    political, sources of, 9–10

of president. *See* President(s), power(s) of
  statutory, 426
Prayer in schools, 120–122, 124, 501
Precedent, 479
Preemption, 93, 95
Pregnancy, discrimination based on, 178–179
President(s), 411–446. *See also* individual
      presidents
  attempts to end government inefficiency
      and, 449
  becoming
    constitutional requirements for, 311,
        413–414
    process of, 414
  cabinet and. *See* Cabinet
  checks and balances system and. *See*
      Checks and balances
  checks on courts and, 500–501
  as chief diplomat, 419–421
  as chief executive, 415–417
  as chief legislator, 421–426, 548
  as chief of party, 427–428
  chief of staff to, 439
  as chief of state, 415
  choosing. *See also* Election(s); Electoral
      college; Presidential election(s);
      Presidential primary(ies)
    illustrated, 326
    longest campaign and, 321–325
  as commander in chief, 417–419, 547
  death or incapacity of, 379
  election of. *See* President(s), choosing
  e-mail and, 423, 444
  executive agreements and, 58, 421, 547–548
  executive budget and, 401
  Executive Office of the President and. *See*
      Executive Office of the President
  executive organization and, 436–439
  gridlock and, 393–394, 443
  impeachment and, 180, 218, 235, 302, 412,
      431, 434–435
  impoundment of funds by, 433–434
  leadership of, informal techniques of, 548
  line of succession to, 441–442, 443
  media and, 363–364
  power(s) of
    abuses of, 434–435
    appointment and removal, 415–416, 449,
        459–460, 548
    constitutional, 58, 414, 415, 417–418,
        419, 420, 421–423, 426, 547–548
    diplomatic recognition and, 419–420, 548
    emergency, 432
    executive orders and, 429, 432–433
    executive privilege and, 433
    expressed, 426
    to grant reprieves and pardons, 417
    increase in, 428–429
    inherent, 426
    judicial implementation and, 500–501
    limiting of, by Congress, 419, 428, 552–553
    proposal of treaties and, 419, 420, 428,
        547
    regulatory, 429
    special uses of, 432–434
    statutory, 426
    veto, 422–423
      presidential use of, 1789 to present,
          423, 424. *See also* Veto(es)
  press conferences and, 367, 434
  press secretary and, 363
  public opinion of, 428–431

recall and, 412
  roles of, 414–431
  running for. *See* President(s), choosing
  salary of, 413, 414
  State of the Union address and, 421–422
  as superpolitician, 427–428
  term limit and, 434
  twenty-first century issues and, 443
  Web site of, 423
  White House press corps and, 363
  writing letter to, 444
President *pro tempore* of the Senate, 399,
      442, 443
Presidential election(s)
  of 1800, 279, 280, 326, 414
  of 1824, 280, 326, 327, 414
  of 1828, 280, 281
  of 1836, 441
  of 1840, 280
  of 1848, 280
  of 1860, 280, 295
  of 1876, 327
  of 1888, 327
  of 1892, 299
  of 1896, 280, 282, 299
  of 1904, 299
  of 1912, 280–281, 298, 299
  of 1916, 555
  of 1920, 281, 354
  of 1924, 292, 310
  of 1928, 295
  of 1932, 280, 281, 288, 393
  of 1936, 225, 281
  of 1940, 281
  of 1944, 281
  of 1948, 230, 281, 298
  of 1952, 281, 310, 313, 355
  of 1956, 281
  of 1960, 234, 281, 295, 361
  of 1964, 338, 340, 343, 359–360, 386, 393
  of 1968, 219, 281, 298, 310, 321, 322, 327,
      342, 343
  of 1972, 281, 317, 338, 340, 342, 343, 433
  of 1976, 281, 342
  of 1980, 227, 230, 237, 281, 296, 297, 338,
      339–340, 340, 343, 366
  of 1984, 167, 168, 177, 203, 281, 311, 322,
      337, 338, 340
  of 1988, 168, 203, 237, 281, 340, 441
  of 1992, 237, 256, 281, 300, 302, 310,
      314–315, 330, 336, 337, 340, 355,
      356, 388, 393, 405, 414, 417, 440
  of 1996, 6, 92, 257, 281, 300, 302, 309, 310,
      320, 324, 338, 340, 388, 405, 564–565
  of 2000, 5, 6, 106, 177, 203, 231, 232, 237,
      258, 263, 277, 292, 302, 308, 309,
      313, 316, 317, 323, 325, 328, 330, 334,
      336, 341, 343, 357, 361, 362, 366,
      384, 389, 440, 492
  coattail effect and, 328, 386
  debates and, 361–362
  decided in House of Representatives, 280,
      326, 379
  divided government following, 6, 388
  gender gap and, 237, 339–340
  landslide, 330, 393
  primary. *See* Presidential primary(ies)
  vote by groups in, summarized, 338–339
  voter turnout for, 331
Presidential primary(ies). *See also*
      Campaign(s); Election(s)
  as "beauty contests," 321

blanket, 323
  closed, 322
  defined, 321
  front-loading of, 323
  limited campaign spending for, 318
  open, 322
  public financing for, 318
  reform of, 321–322
  run-off, 323
  as springboard to White House, 323
  Super Tuesday and, 323
  types of, 322–323
Press. *See also* Media; Newspapers
  freedom of, 118, 132–134, 231, 350, 364,
      365, 366. *See also* Speech, freedom of
  political, rise of, 352–353
Press secretary, 363
Primary election(s)
  blanket, 323
  closed, 322
  direct, 386
  open, 322
  presidential. *See* Presidential primary(ies)
  run-off, 323
  white, 158
Printz v. United States, 107
Prior restraint, 127
Prior review, 496
Privacy Act (1974), 136, 474
Privacy rights, 135–140
  abortion and, 32, 136–138. *See also*
      Abortion(s)
  in cyberspace, 138–139
  Freedom of Information Act and, 474
  gay males and lesbians and, 202
  in information age, 135–136
  lobbyists and, 248
  medical records, 116
  personal records and, 116
  "right to die" and, 32, 138–140
Private opinion, public opinion and, 221
Privileges and immunities clause, 155
Privileges and immunities of members of
      Congress, 394
Probability samples, 244
Professional Air Traffic Controllers
      Organization (PATCO), 257
Professionals
  as candidates for office, 311–312
  interest groups of, 257
Profits, making, as function of media, 352
Progressive Party
  Bull Moose, of Theodore Roosevelt,
      280–281, 298, 299–300
  Henry Wallace's, 298
  Robert La Follette's, 300
Prohibition, 54
Prohibition Party, 298
Project Vote Smart, 342
Property, 18
Property tax, 578, 602
Proposition 5 (California), 585
Proposition 13 (California), 588
Proposition 22 (California), 588
Proposition 209 (California), 191
Prynn, William, 132
Psychological factors, voting behavior and,
      341–343
Public agenda
  defined, 350
  setting of
    by Congress, 381

by media, 350–351, 364
Public debt
    burden and, 534
    "crowding out" and, 534
    defined, 533
    disappearing deficit and, 533–534
    financing of, 534
Public debt financing, 534
Public employee interest groups, 257
Public figures, libel and, 132
Public information, reporting of lobbying
        contacts and, 248
Public interest, 258
Public interest groups, 258–259
Public opinion
    check on courts and, 502
    consensus, 220–221
    defining, 219–224
    divisive, 221
    fluidity and, 222–223
    foreign policy influenced by, 553
    intensity and, 222
    measuring. See Opinion poll(s)
    media influence on, 235–236
    political culture and, 237–238
    political knowledge and, 224
    political process and, 242–243
    polling and. See Opinion poll(s)
    power of, 219
    of president, 428–431
    private opinion and, 221
    qualities of, 221–224
    stability and, 223
    twenty-first century issues and, 243
Pulitzer, Joseph, 355
Purposive incentives, 252
"Push polls," 232
Putin, Vladimir, 560

Q

Qaddafi, Muammar, 564
Question(s)
    of fact, 482
    federal, 481
    justiciable, 389
    of law, 482
    political, 503
    poll, 230–231
Quinlan, Karen Ann, 138–139
Quota sampling, 226
QVC, 357

R

Rabin, Yitzhak, 568
Race
    classifications of, problems with, 170–172
    discrimination on basis of, 101, 158,
        164–165, 165, 189, 198. See also
        Affirmative action
    "environmental justice" and, 467
    gerrymandering and, 390–391, 586
    Supreme Court clerks and, 488
    voter turnout and, 332
Radical Republicans, 155, 434
Radio. See also Electronic media; Media;
        Television
    broadcast news on, replaced by Internet, 348
    entertainment on, 349–350
    First Amendment freedoms and, 133–134
    talk-shows and, 236, 356–358

Rainbow Coalition, 168, 203
Rainbow Warrior, 258
Raleigh, Sir Walter, 33
Randolph, Edmund, 44, 414
Random sample, 244
Rankin, Jeannette, 173
Ratification
    of Bill of Rights, 52–54
    defined, 50
    of treaties, 419, 420, 428–429, 547
    of United States Constitution, 50–51, 278
Rational ignorance effect, 333
R.A.V. v. City of St. Paul, Minnesota, 128
Reagan, Ronald, 126, 291, 392, 413, 420, 441,
        553
    age of, at election, 414
    appointments of
        to federal courts, 177, 492, 493, 495,
            497, 504
        to Supreme Court, 177, 493, 495, 497, 504
    armed forces ordered by
        to attack Libya, 418
        into combat without congressional
            approval, 552
        to invade Grenada, 364, 418
        into Lebanon, 418, 419
    attempted assassination of, 441
    deregulation and, 457–458
    divided government and, 392, 393
    economic prosperity under, 235
    election of
        in 1980, 227, 230, 237, 281, 338, 340, 366
        in 1984, 281, 337, 338, 340
    federal grants-in-aid and, 103–104, 105
    on federalism, 90
    as governor, 88, 583
    Intermediate-Range Nuclear Force (INF)
        Treaty and, 559
    Iran-*contra* affair and, 417, 439
    line-item veto and, 423
    PATCO strike and, 257
    political consultants and, 314
    Soviet Union and, 558–559
    strategic defense initiative (SDI) and, 558
    Twenty-fifth Amendment and, 442
Reapportionment, 389–391
"Reasonable accommodations," 199–200
Recall, 10, 587
Reconstruction period, 155, 156
Redistricting, 389–391
Referendum, 10, 586–587, 592, 595
Reform Party, 283, 296, 297, 298, 300, 302
*Regents of the University of California v.
        Bakke,* 190, 191
Regents' Prayer case *(Engle v. Vitale),* 120–121
Registration to vote. See Voting, registration for
Regressive tax, 528
Rehabilitation Act (1973), 198
Rehnquist, William H., 488, 499
    Clinton impeachment trial and, 435
    Rehnquist Court and, 496–500
    on Supreme Court selection of cases, 486
Reid, Harry, 400
Reilly, Kevin, 467
Reinventing Democrats (Baer), 302
Relevance, public opinion and, 223–224
Religion
    discrimination on basis of, 101, 164–165,
        165, 189, 198
    establishment clause and, 119–125, 578
    free exercise clause and, 125–126
    freedom of, 117, 118–126

political opinion influenced by, 234
    school-prayer issue and, 120–122, 124, 501
    voting behavior and, 338
Religious Freedom (School Prayer)
        Amendment, 61
Religious Freedom Restoration Act
        (RFRA)(1993), 125–126, 502
Remandment of court case, 489
Reno, Janet, 364
Reno v. American Civil Liberties Union, 129
Reorganization Act (1939), 438
Report on the Federal Judiciary (Rehnquist), 494
Representation, by members of Congress,
        380–381
Representative assembly, 34
Representative democracy, 11–13, 587
    defined, 11
    interest groups and, 269–270
Representative government, 12
Reprieve, 417
Republic, 11
Republican Party
    Abraham Lincoln and, 155
    control of Congress by, 6, 105, 106–107, 256,
        281, 387–388, 393, 423, 426, 463, 494
    Democratic Party versus, 290
    formation of, 280
    soft money and, 287, 319
    voters influenced by prosperity under
        Reagan and, 235
Reregulation, 458
Resolution of Independence, 37. See also
        Declaration of Independence
Retirement, retirement, 197
Reversal of judgment, 489
Reverse discrimination, 190, 192
Revolutionary War, 10–11, 17, 36, 38, 521, 523
Reynolds, David, 302
Reynolds v. Sims, 389
RFRA (Religious Freedom Restoration
        Act)(1993), 125–126, 502
Riback, Christopher, 465
Rice, Condoleezza, 177
Richards, Ann, 271
Richmond Newspapers, Inc. v. Virginia, 133
"Right to die," 32, 138–140
Right to Life, 259
Right to Work Committee, 260
Rivers, Eugene, 168
Roanoke Island Colony, 33–34
Robinson, Randall, 156
Rock the Vote campaign, 336
Rockefeller, Nelson, 442
Rockman, Bert, 465
Roe v. Wade, 136–137, 504
Rogers, William, 550
Romer v. Evans, 202
Romney, George, 413
Roosevelt, Franklin D., 223, 439, 550
    as chief legislator, 421
    declaration of war against Japan and, 364,
        547
    election of 1932 and, 280, 281, 288, 393
    election of 1936 and, 225, 281
    executive agreements used by, 421, 547
    Executive Office of the President
        established by, 437–438
    federal grants-in-aid and, 102, 103
    "fireside chats" and, 363–364
    Great Depression and, 100–101, 235, 530
    internment of Japanese Americans by,
        during World War II, 426

media and, 363–364
New Deal and, 100–101, 103, 281, 289, 290, 339, 436, 463, 464, 495, 530
"packing" of Supreme Court and, 495
Pearl Harbor speech and, 364, 556
press conferences and, 367
Soviet Union recognized by, 420
use of emergency powers by, 432
vetoes by, 423
woman in cabinet of, 177
Yalta Conference and, 547, 556
Roosevelt, Theodore, 548
age of, upon assuming office, 418
as chief legislator, 421
election of 1904 and, 299
election of 1912 and, 280–281, 298, 299
Roper, Elmo, 225
Roper poll(s), 222, 225, 227, 231, 315–316
Rosenberger v. University of Virginia, 123–124
Ross, Nellie Taylor, 581
Rule of four, 488
Rulemaking, 470–471
environment of, 468
negotiated, 469
Rules Committee, 382, 396–397
Run-off primary, 323
Russell, Benjamin, 390
Russia. *See also* Soviet Union
achievement tests of students in, 578
Comprehensive Nuclear Test Ban Treaty not ratified by, 562
incarceration rate in, 522
negotiations with U.S. on nuclear reduction and, 561, 562
problems with Chechnya and, 560, 569
public opinion and, 222–223
Strategic Arms Reduction Treaty (START) signed by, 559
terrorism in, 561
UN Convention on the Rights of the Child signed by, 209
voice in North Atlantic Treaty Organization (NATO) decisions and, 428
whaling by, 258
Russian Revolution, 420
Rutan v. Republican Party of Illinois, 462
Rutledge, John, 43
Rwanda, 545
death of president in plane crash and, 570
violence in, 569, 570
Ryan, Paul, 385

S

Sabato, Larry J., 330
Sadat, Anwar el-, 421
Safe seats, 397
Salon, 358
SALT I & II (Strategic Arms Limitation Treaty), 420, 558, 559
Sampling error, 230
Samuelson, Paul, 182
Sanchez, Loretta, 313
Sanford, Terry, 102
Santorum, Rick, 400
Saudi Arabia
bombing of American military compound in, 223–224, 563
Persian Gulf War and, 568
SBA (Small Business Administration), 416, 457
Scalia, Antonin, 478, 497, 499

Schlafly, Phyllis, 175
School(s). *See also* College(s); Education
achievement tests and, 578, 601
busing and, 160–162
campus speech codes and, 130–131
choice of, allowed by all states, 578
church-related, government aid to, 119–120, 578
competition among, for students, 578
integration of, 160–162
minority, resurgence of, 162
prayer in, 120–122, 124, 501
school districts and, 594, 595
teaching evolution and, 122–123
technology in, establishment clause and, 120
Ten Commandments posted in, 122, 123
vouchers and, 120, 578
School districts, 594, 595
School Prayer (Religious Freedom) Amendment, 61
Schwartz, Tony, 360
SCLC (Southern Christian Leadership Conference), 162, 253
Scott, Dred, 153, 154
Screen Actors Guild, 257
SDI (Strategic defense initiative)("Star Wars"), 558
Searches and seizures, unreasonable, constitutional prohibition of, 32, 58, 140, 143, 146
SEC. *See* Securities and Exchange Commission
Secession, 99
Second budget resolution, 405
Second Civil Rights Act (Civil Rights Act of 1875), 157
Second Continental Congress, 36, 37–38, 39
Secret Service, 433, 443
Sectional politics, 294
Securities and Exchange Commission (SEC), 451
Internet fraud and, 458
principal functions of, 459
Segregation
de facto, 160, 161, 162
de jure, 160
school integration and, 160–162
Select committee, 396
Selective purchasing laws, 94
Selective Service, 276
Selectpersons, 594
Senate. *See* United States Senate
Senatorial courtesy, 492
Senior citizens. *See* Elderly
Seniority system, 397
Separate-but-equal doctrine, 58–59, 157–160
Separation of powers, 46–47, 48
Separatists, 34–35
Serbia, American bombing of, 418, 570
Service sector, 257
Seventeenth Amendment, 377, 384
Sexual harassment, 179–180, 436, 443, 486
defined, 179
hostile-environment, 179
politics and, 180, 436, 443, 486
Rehnquist Court and, 498–499
Sexual Harassment on the Job (Petrocelli), 179
The Shape of the River: Long-Term Consequences of Considering Race in College and University Admissions (Bowen and Bok), 192–193
Shapiro, Robert Y., 240

Shays, Daniel, 41, 52
Shays's Rebellion, 41, 52
Sheltered homeless, 520
Sherman, Roger, 44–45
Sherman, William T., 156
Shintech Corporation, 467
Side payments, 450
Sierra Club, 257, 484
Sierra Leone, unrest in, 570
Silicon Valley, California, 256
Simpson, Glenn R., 330
Simpson, O. J., 218
Singapore, economic growth of, 534
Sixteenth Amendment, 379
Sixth Amendment, 132, 133, 140, 141
60 Minutes, 353
Slander, as unprotected speech, 129–130
Slate, 358, 366
Slaves/slavery
Civil War and, 98, 99, 154
consequences of, 153–162
United States Constitution and, 37, 44, 45, 46, 52, 153–162
Slovakia, creation of, 86
Slovenia, creation of, 86
Small Business Administration (SBA), 416, 457
Smart card, 531
Smith, Alfred, 295
Smith, Jonathan, 52
Smith v. Allwright, 158
Social contract, 38
Social movements, 252–253
Social Security, 195
benefits of, 518
civil unions for gay couples and, 205
older Americans and, 195, 210, 252, 260
contributors to, declining number of, 529
elimination of, 512
establishment of, 289, 512
funding of, 472
government spending on, 197
grim future of, 528
numbers identifying participation in, newborns and, 276
payroll taxes for, 512
regressiveness of, 528
privatization and, 529–530
problem with, 528–529
protecting, 290
Social Security Administration, 382
information about private citizens and, 136, 474
Web site of, 448
Socialism, 25
Socialist Labor Party, 297
Socialist Party, 297
Socialist Workers' Party, 297
Society, rights of, rights of accused versus, 140–145
Socioeconomic status. *See also* Income, level of
defined, 337
demographic factors and, voting behavior and, 337–341
disparity in, civil rights and, 167–168
political socialization and, 234
voter turnout and, 332, 336
Soft money, 287, 427
defined, 266, 319
impact of, 266
raised by political parties, 266, 287, 319
Solid South

Democratic Party and, 280, 293, 294, 340
    rise of Republican Party and, 294, 340
Solidary incentives, 251
Somalia
    American troops sent to, 428
    human rights and, 572
    UN Convention on the Rights of the Child
        not signed by, 209
Sound bite, 359, 362
Souter, David, 124, 493, 497, 499
South Africa
    economic sanctions against, 553, 564, 570
    first all-race elections held in, 570
    UN Convention on the Rights of the Child
        signed by, 209
South Korea. *See also* Korean War; North Korea
    aid to, from International Monetary Fund,
        565–566
    economic growth of, 535
    lobbying by, 260
South Vietnam. *See also* North Vietnam;
    Vietnam; Vietnam War
    American "advisers" sent into, 558
    executive agreements with, 548
    withdrawal of American forces from, 259
Southern Christian Leadership Conference
    (SCLC), 162, 253
Southern Utah Wilderness Alliance, 267
Southworth, Scott, 131
Sovereign immunity, 197, 498
Sovereignty
    national, e-commerce and, 526–527
    popular, 13, 48, 496
    state, Eleventh Amendment and, 108
Sovereignty at Bay (Vernon), 526
Soviet bloc, 556–557, 560
Soviet Union, 551. *See also* Russia
    beginning of Korean War and, 557
    at close of World War II, 534, 556
    Cold War and, 556–557, 558–559
    Cuban missile crisis and, 558
    détente and, 558
    dissolution of, 86, 222, 545, 559, 560
    former
        Commonwealth of Independent States
            and, 87, 560
        emergence of independent states and, 86
        low-cost labor in, 535
    Franklin Roosevelt's recognition of, 420
    Intermediate-Range Nuclear Force (INF)
        Treaty signed by, 559
    public opinion and, 222–223
    Russian Revolution and, 420
    Soviet bloc and, 556–557, 560
    Strategic Arms Limitation Treaty (SALT I)
        signed by, 558, 559
    superpower relations with United States
        and, 557–559
    Yalta Conference and, 547, 556
Spanish-American War, 515, 555
Speaker of the House, 285, 397–398, 442, 443
Special districts, 594
Speech
    commercial, 128
    freedom of, 17, 84, 117
        campus speech codes and, 130–131
        flag burning and, 128, 482
        Internet and, 53, 60, 84, 367
        lobbyists and, 260
        permitted restrictions on, 126–127
        prior restraint and, 127

hate, 21, 131–132
    symbolic, 128, 482
    unprotected, 128–130
Spencer-Roberts, 314
Spin, 361
Spin doctors, 361
Splinter parties, 298
Spoils system, 461–462
Spring review, 404
Springer, Jerry, 356
Sri Lanka, 438
    revolution in, 569
    terrorism and, 561
SSI (Supplemental Security Income), 518–519
Stability, public opinion and, 223
Stalin, Joseph, 556
Stamp Act (1765)(Great Britain), 36
Standing committee, 395–396
Standing to sue, 466, 481
Stanton, Elizabeth Cady, 173–174
Stanton, Henry B., 173
"Star Wars" (Strategic defense initiative)(SDI),
    558
Stare decisis, 479, 480, 503
Starr, Kenneth, 358, 382, 433, 435, 443
START (Strategic Arms Reduction Treaty), 559
State(s)
    all, school choice allowed in, 578
    ballot initiatives and, 191
    constitutional conventions in, 581
    constitutions of, 84, 581
    courts of. *See* Court(s), state
    defined, 39
    electoral votes of, 325
    government of. *See* State government(s)
    legislature of. *See* State legislature(s)
    lotteries run by, 602
    party organization of, 287
    rights of, 49, 54, 92, 98–100
    secession and, 99
    sovereign immunity and, 197, 498
    sovereignty of, Eleventh Amendment and,
        108
State central committee, 287
State Department. *See* United States
    Department of State
State government(s)
    Bill of Rights extended to, 117–118
    control of Internet betting and, 590–591
    direct democracy and, 586–587
    elections of, voting in, 330–333
    employees of, 453
    executive branch of, 582–583
    expenditures of, 600–601
    governor and
        first woman as, 581
        veto power of, 583
    interstate compacts and, 96
    judiciary of, 588–592
        illustrated, 589
    laws of, against gay males and lesbians,
        201–203
    legislature of. *See* State legislature(s)
    as maker of foreign policy, 94
    paying for, 600–602
    powers of
        concurrent, 91, 92–93
        constitutional, 580
        division of, between powers of national
            government and
            continuing dispute over, 100–105

summarized, 91
    to levy taxes, 92, 526
    police. *See* Police power(s)
    prohibited, 91, 93
    reserved, 91, 92
    preemption by national government and,
        93, 95
    regulation by, of the Internet, 84
    revenues of, 601–602
    twenty-first century issues and, 603
    vertical checks and balances and, 93, 95
State legislature(s), 585–588
    apportionment and, 585–586
    characteristics of, listed, 584
    lawmaking process of, illustrated, 585
State of the Union address, 421–422
States' Rights (Dixiecrat) Party, 298
Statutes, as sources of American law, 480.
    See also Law(s); Legislation
Statutory power, 426
Stern, Howard, 133
Stevens, John Paul, 488, 497, 499
Stevens, Jonathan, 466
Stewart, Potter, 129
Stock market crash, 530
Stokes, Carl B., 599
Stone, Lucy, 174
Stone v. Graham, 123
Stonewall Inn, 201
Strategic Arms Limitation Treaty (SALT I &
    II), 420, 558
Strategic Arms Reduction Treaty (START), 559
Strategic defense initiative (SDI)("Star Wars"),
    558
Street people, 520
Stuart, Gilbert, 390
Subpoena, 165
Subsidy(ies)
    in-kind, 517
    policy of, 525–528
Succession Act (1947), 442–443
Sudan, terrorist camps in, American air
    strikes against, 563
Suffrage. *See also* Voting rights
    defined, 173
    universal, 12
    women's, 173–174
Sugar Act (1764)(Great Britain), 36
Suharto, 566
Suicide, assisted, 32, 140, 588
Suit. *See* Lawsuit(s)
Sullivan, Kathleen M., 49
Sunset legislation, 464
Sunshine laws, 463
Super Tuesday, 323
Superdelegates, 322
Supplemental Security Income (SSI), 518–519
Supremacy doctrine, 44. *See also* Supremacy
    clause
Supreme court(s)
    state, 590
    United States. *See* United States Supreme
        Court
The Supreme Court: How It Was, How It Is
    (Rehnquist), 486
Survey Research Center, 226
Sweden, unitary system of government in, 86
Switzerland
    Alpine Diamond and, 86
    confederal system of government in, 87
    direct democracy in, 10

drug program in, 587
political parties in, 292
Symbolic speech, 128, 482

T

Taft, Helen Herron, 435
Taft, William Howard, 281, 298, 415, 435, 491
Taiwan
  economic growth of, 534, 535
  lobbying by, 261
Talk shows, 356–358
Tammany Hall (Tammany Society), 288, 462, 598
Taney, Roger, 487
TANF (Temporary Assistance to Needy
    Families), 517–518
Tanzania, bombing of American embassy in,
    224, 563, 565
Tariff, 536
Tax(es)
  on exports, 45–46
  fiscal policy lessons and, 603
  general sales, 602
  on imports (tariffs), 536
  income, 99–100, 379
  Internet and, 513–515, 526
  loopholes and, 525–528
  Medicare, 528
  politics of, 525–528
  poll, 158
  powers of state and national governments
    to levy, 92, 526
  property, 578, 602
  rates of, 525–528
  regressive, 528
  simple system of, unlikelihood of, 528
  Social Security, 512, 528
  tariff as, 536
Taylor, Zachary, 280, 491
Teamsters Union (International Brotherhood
    of Teamsters), 255, 263
Technical assistance, 545
Teeter, Bob, 314
Teixeira, Ruy A., 333
Telecommunications Act (1996), 365, 367
Telephone polling, 229
Television. *See also* Electronic media; Media;
    Radio
  broadcast news on, replaced by Internet, 348
  entertainment on, 349–350
  First Amendment freedoms and, 133–134
  free time on, for candidate use, 308
  live
    first presidential news conference on, 434
    first presidential phone-in broadcast on,
      433
  network, declining share of audience and, 356
  Nielsen ratings and, 227
  primacy of, 358–359
  public opinion of president and, 431
  talk-shows and, 356–358
  "V-chip" and, 367
Temporary Assistance to Needy Families
    (TANF), 517–518
Ten Commandments, 122, 123
Tennessee Valley Authority (TVA), 460
Tenth Amendment, 92, 107
Term limits, 387, 388, 434
Terrorism, 24, 144, 561, 563
Texas v. Johnson, 128
Thailand

aid to, from International Monetary Fund,
    565–566
economic growth of, 534, 535
Web-based pharmacies closed down by, 527
Thernstrom, Abigail, 193
Thernstrom, Stephan, 193
Third Amendment, 135
The Third Eye, 336
Third party(ies)
  defined, 296
  minor
    historically important, 296–298
    impact of, 299–300
    role of, in U.S. political history, 296–301
    splinter, 298
  new, providing help to, 297
  time for, 302
Thirteenth Amendment, 154–155, 157
THOMAS, 391
Thomas, Clarence, 167, 180, 488, 489, 493,
    495, 497, 499
Thomasson, Paul, 203
Thompson, Charles, 38
Through the Looking Glass (Carroll), 289
Thurmond, Strom, 400
Tiananmen Square incident, 549
Ticket splitting, 291
Time, 53
Time Life Video, 357
Time Warner, 319
  CNN purchased by, 353
  merger with America Online, Inc. (AOL)
    and, 256, 353, 365
Tinker v. Des Moines School District, 128
Tobacco industry
  campaign contributions and, 319
  cancellation of *60 Minutes* and, 353
  FDA regulation and, 471
  legislation regarding, lobbying and, 249
Tocqueville, Alexis de, 250, 479
Totalitarian regimes, 9, 10
Town manager system, 594
Town meeting, 10, 11, 594
  electronic, 352
Towns, 594
Townships, 594
Tracking polls, 316
Treaties
  "near," 428–429
  ratification of, 419, 420, 428–429, 547
Treaty of Paris (1783), 39
Treaty of Versailles (1919), 420
Trial(s)
  fair, free press versus, 132–133
  impeachment, in United States Senate, 218,
    235, 412, 434, 435
  jury, 484, 589
  rights of accused and, 140–141
Trial courts, 482, 483, 588–589
Trilateral Commission, 553
Truman, Harry S., 203, 413
  armed forces desegregated by, 223
  control of bureaucracy and, 416
  decision to use atomic bombs against
    Japan and, 418, 556
  election of
    in 1948, 230, 281
    without majority of popular vote, 327, 414
  Fair Deal and, 281
  federal seizure of steel plants by, during
    Korean War, 432
  foreign policy and, 546

troops sent to Korea by, 418, 428, 547, 557
Truman Doctrine and, 557
use of emergency power by, 432
vetoes by, 423
Truman Doctrine, 557
Trustee, 380
Turkey
  American foreign aid to, 557
  American missiles near Soviet border and,
    558
  "honor killings" in, 178
Turner Broadcasting, 353
TV. *See* Television
TVA (Tennessee Valley Authority), 460
Twain, Mark, 129
Twain, Shania, 423
Tweed, William "Boss," 288, 598
Twelfth Amendment, 379, 414
Twentieth Amendment, 379
Twenty-fifth Amendment, 379, 442
Twenty-first Amendment, 54
Twenty-fourth Amendment, 158
Twenty-second Amendment, 434
Twenty-seventh Amendment, 56, 57
Twenty-sixth Amendment, 206–207, 259,
    335, 501
Twenty-third Amendment, 48, 325
Two Treatises on Government (Locke), 38
Two-party system
  competition and, voter turnout and, 332
  defined, 292
  historical foundations of, 292–294
  reasons for, 291–296
  self-perpetuation of, 294
  state and federal laws favoring, 296
Tyler, John, 421, 425, 441, 491

U

Uganda, refugees in, 570
Ukraine
  refusal of, to join the Commonwealth of
    Independent States, 560
  Strategic Arms Reduction Treaty (START)
    signed by, 559
UN. *See* United Nations
Unanimous opinion, 489
Unicameral legislature, 39
Uniform resource locators (URLs), 29
Unincorporated areas, 594
Union(s). *See also* Labor
  Democratic Party support from, 263, 289,
    337, 340
  membership in, decline in, 255, 257
Union Oil Company, 524
Unit rule, 287
Unitary system, 85–86
  defined, 85
  flow of power in, 87
United Automobile Workers, 255
United Mine Workers, 255
United Nations (UN), 549
  Convention of, on the Rights of the Child,
    207, 209
  creation of, 86
  Korean War and, 557
  Persian Gulf War and, 568
  Security Council of, 544, 571
  Universal Declaration of Human Rights of,
    152
United Network for Organ Sharing (UNOS), 101
United Parcel Service (UPS), 473

United States
  achievement tests of students in, 578
  British colonization and, 33–36
  bureaucracy in. *See* Bureaucracy(ies)
  changing face of, 20–24
  at close of World War II, 534, 556
  common law system in, 479. *See also*
      Common law
  constitution of. *See* United States
      Constitution
  defense of, 544. *See also* Foreign policy
  ethnic change in, 20–23
  federal system of government in, 87. *See
      also* Federalism
  flag of. *See* American flag
  future of, 19, 26
  government of. *See* National government
  governments in, number of, 85
  incarceration rate in, 522
  NAFTA and, 537, 549
  as nation of joiners, 250–251
  negotiations with Russia on nuclear
      reduction and, 561, 562
  number of governments in, 85
  political change in, 5–6
  political culture of, 16–18, 20, 294–295.
      See also Political culture
  political history of
    crime in, 521–522
    early, milestones in, 35
    federal civil service and, 461–463
    legal restrictions on voting and, 333–335
  politics in, in twenty-first century, 26
  population of. *See* Population, United States
  Strategic Arms Limitation Treaty (SALT I)
      signed by, 558
  Strategic Arms Reduction Treaty (START)
      signed by, 559
  terrorism in, 24, 144
  UN Convention on the Rights of the Child
      not signed by, 209
United States Bureau of the Census, 181
  racial classifications used by, 171–172
United States Chamber of Commerce
    (National Chamber), 253, 267, 270
United States Constitution
  amending, 54–60
  Amendment(s) to. *See also* Bill of Rights
    Third, 135
    Fourth, 32, 58, 135, 140, 143
    Fifth, 135, 140, 141, 142
    Sixth, 132, 133, 140, 141
    Eighth, 140, 141, 144
    Ninth, 135
    Tenth, 92, 107
    Eleventh, 108, 197
    Twelfth, 379, 414
    Thirteenth, 154–155, 157
    Fourteenth. *See* Fourteenth Amendment
    Fifteenth, 154–155, 158, 164, 173, 335,
        501
    Sixteenth, 379
    Seventeenth, 377, 384
    Eighteenth, 54
    Nineteenth, 173, 174, 335
    Twentieth, 379
    Twenty-first, 54
    Twenty-second, 434
    Twenty-third, 48, 325
    Twenty-fourth, 158
    Twenty-fifth, 379, 442
    Twenty-sixth, 206–207, 259, 335, 501

    Twenty-seventh, 56, 57
    American flag and, 56, 128
    Balanced Budget, 55
    Equal Rights, 56, 57, 175, 259
    Human Life, 61
    listed, 55
    ratification of, 55–56
    Religious Freedom (School Prayer), 61
    School Prayer (Religious Freedom), 61
  Article I of, 377, 434
    Section 1 of, 471
    Section 2 of, 153, 377, 389
    Section 3 of, 377
    Section 4 of, 384
    Section 6 of, 394
    Section 8 of, 23, 32, 57–58, 90, 91, 97,
        378, 379, 471
    Section 9 of, 117, 140
    Section 10 of, 86
  Article II of, 426, 434
    Section 1 of, 325, 413, 441–442, 547
    Section 2 of, 378–379, 428, 449, 489,
        547, 548
    Section 3 of, 421–422, 429, 449, 471,
        548
  Article III of
    Section 1 of, 58, 481, 482
  Article IV of
    Section 1 of, 96
    Section 2 of, 96
    Section 4 of, 592
  Article V of, 54, 55–56
  Article VI of, 44, 93, 580
  as basis for American federalism, 90–96
  changing of, through informal methods,
      57–60
  checks and balances system and. *See*
      Checks and balances
  commerce clause of. *See* Commerce clause
  complete text of, 64–81
  cruel and unusual punishment prohibited
      by, 144
  drafting of, 41–48
  due process clause of, 155
  elastic (necessary and proper) clause of,
      90–91, 379
  equal protection clause of, 152, 153, 155,
      158, 189, 190, 191, 192, 194, 202,
      205, 389, 586. *See also* Civil right(s)
  establishment clause of, 119–125, 578
  framers of, 59, 153
    federalism and, 48, 90
    intentions of, 49, 428, 470
    motives of, 52, 325, 377, 413
  free exercise clause of, 125–126
  governmental structure established by, 13
  interpretation of, 32
  limitations on government's activities
      under, 13, 117
  as "living constitution," 32, 60
  naturalization provision of, 23
  necessary and proper (elastic) clause of,
      90–91, 379
  powers under
    of Congress. *See* Congress, powers of
    defined, 96–98, 426
    enumerated, 90, 91, 378–379
    of national government. *See* National
        government, powers of
    of president, 58, 414, 415, 417–418, 419,
        420, 421–423, 426, 547–548
    prohibited, 91, 93

    of state governments. *See* State
        government(s), powers of
  Preamble to, 33, 59
  ratification of, 50–51, 278
  rationale for, 35
  requirements for national office under, 311,
      413–414
  supremacy clause and, 93, 95
  as supreme law of the land, 478, 580
  text of, 64–81
  twenty-first century issues and, 60–61
  unreasonable searches and seizures
      prohibited by, 32, 58, 140, 143, 146
United States courts of appeals, 482–483,
    490
United States Department of Agriculture, 416,
    451, 456
  food plan designed by, 516
  iron triangle and, 469–471
United States Department of Commerce, 199,
    416, 450, 456
  Bureau of the Census of. *See* United States
      Bureau of the Census
  United States Travel and Tourism
      Administration of, 457
United States Department of Defense (DOD),
    416, 456, 548
  contracting out and, 464
  creation of, 551–552
  foreign policymaking and, 551–552
  gay men and lesbians in the military and,
      203–204
  national security policy and, 545
  natural domestic constituency of, 550
  psychics and, 458
  purchasing system of, 469
  strategic materials stockpiled by, 554
  women in combat and, 175–176
United States Department of Education, 416,
    450, 456, 474
United States Department of Energy, 416, 456
United States Department of Health and
    Human Services, 403, 456
  employees of, 549
  organ donor policy and, 101
United States Department of Housing and
    Urban Development, 416, 450, 456, 521
United States Department of the Interior, 416,
    456, 524
United States Department of Justice, 142,
    416, 433, 452, 455, 456, 487
  application of ADA and, 199
  computer systems of, attacked by hackers,
      552
  creation of "minority-majority" districts
      and, 390–391
  Elian Gonzalez case and, 596
  nominating judicial candidates and, 490
United States Department of Labor, 171, 181,
    416, 438, 456
United States Department of State, 416, 456,
    548
  creation of, 455
  employees of, 549
  foreign policymaking and, 549–550
  function of, 549
  national security policy and, 545
United States Department of Transportation
    (DOT), 416, 456
  Internet fraud and, 458
United States Department of the Treasury,
    403, 416, 439, 452, 456

United States Department of Veterans Affairs, 382, 416, 438, 456
  creation of, 455
United States Department of War, 452. *See also* United States Department of Defense
United States district courts, 482, 483, 490
United States Forest Service, 106, 429
United States House of Representatives. *See also* Congress; United States Senate
  campaigning for, cost of, 312, 386. *See also* Campaign(s); Campaign financing
  on C-SPAN, 27
  differences between Senate and, 282–383
    summarized, 383
  discharge petition and, 395
  gerrymandering and, 390–391
  impeachment proceedings in, 412, 434, 435
  leadership in, 397–399, 400
  majority leader of, 398
  member(s) of
    constitutional requirements to become, 311
    election of. *See* Congressional election(s)
    e-mail to, 267
    prestige and, 383
    requirement to spend half each year in district and, 376
    Web sites of, 381, 382
    women as, 173, 176, 312
  minority leader of, 398–399
  "minority-majority" districts and, 390–391
  president elected by, 280, 326, 379, 414
  prestige and, 383
  reapportionment and, 389–391
  Rules Committee of, 382, 396–397
  rules of, 382
  size of, 382
  speaker of, 285, 397–398, 442, 443
  whips in, 399
United States Postal Service, 416, 461
  employees of, 464
  pressure on, to increase efficiency, 473
  principal functions of, 460
United States Reports, 489
United States Senate. *See also* Congress; United States House of Representatives
  advice and consent of, 378–379, 415, 419, 428–429, 489
  campaigning for, cost of, 312, 386. *See also* Campaign(s); Campaign financing
  cloture and, 383
  on C-SPAN, 27
  debate and filibustering in, 383
  differences between House of Representatives and, 282–383
    summarized, 383
  filibustering in, 383
  impeachment trial in, 218, 235, 412, 434, 435
  leadership in, 399, 400
  majority floor leader of, 399
  member(s) of
    Americans for Democratic Action (ADA) ratings and, 262
    constitutional requirements to become, 311
    direct election of, 377, 384
    election of. *See* Congressional election(s)
    e-mail to, 267
    Native American as, 167
    prestige and, 383
    requirement to spend half each year in district and, 376

Web pages of, 381
    women as, 176, 198
  minority floor leader of, 399
  president *pro tempore* of, 399, 442, 443
  prestige and, 383
  ratification of treaties and, 419, 420, 428–429, 547
  rules of, 382
  senatorial courtesy and, 492
  size of, 382
  Supreme Court appointments and, 490, 492–493
  vice president as president of, 399
  vice president elected by, 326, 379
United States Supreme Court, 482–483
  Burger Court and, 498
  caseload and, 489
  cases that reach, 486–487
  certiorari and, 487–488
  civil rights issues and, 498–500
  cooperative federalism and, 104
  deciding cases and, 487–488
  decisions of, 489
  federalist issues and, 498
  judicial activism and, 495–496, 497
  judicial restraint and, 496
  judicial review and, 58–59, 493–495
  judicial traditions and doctrines and, 503–504
  justice(s) of. *See also* individual justices
    African Americans as, 167, 493
    appointment as
      election of versus, 478
      for life, 478, 490
    appointments as, 490–491
    average tenure of, 491
    background of, 491
    chief, impeachment trial and, 435
    women as, 177, 487, 493
  minority clerks hired by, 488
  new federalism and, 107–108
  opinions of, 489
  Rehnquist Court and, 496–500
  rule of four of, 488
  "softened" approach to church-state issues and, 123–125
  2000 elections and, 59, 498
  Warren Court and, 495–496, 498
  at work, 485–489
United States Travel and Tourism Administration, 467
United States Treasury bonds, 533
United States v. Curtiss-Wright Export Corp., 432
United States v. Harriss, 268
United States v. Lopez, 107
United States v. Morrison, 107–108
United States v. Nixon, 433
Universal Declaration of Human Rights, 152
Universal suffrage, 12
University. *See* College(s)
UNOS (United Network for Organ Sharing), 101
Unreasonable searches and seizures, constitutional prohibition of, 32, 58, 140, 143
Unsafe at Any Speed (Nader), 258
UPS (United Parcel Service), 473
Urban League, 253
URLs (uniform resource locators), 29
U.S. Conference of Mayors, 467
U.S. Term Limits, 388
USS Cole, bombing of, 563

V

Van Buren, Martin, 423, 441
Vance, Cyrus, 550
Vanishing Voter study, 334
"V-chip," 367
Ventura, Jesse, 283, 298, 302
Verner, Liipfert, Bernhard, McPherson & Hand, 271
Vernon, Raymond, 526
Versailles Treaty (1919), 420
Veto(es)
  Congress' power to override, 423, 425
  hecklers', 130
  item, 583
  legislative, 381, 429
  line-item, 423–425, 428
  pocket, 423, 583
  by state governor, 583
  veto message and, 422–423
Veto message, 422–423
Vice president(s), 440–443
  becoming, constitutional requirements for, 311
  choosing of, illustrated, 326
  job of, 440–441
  as president of the Senate, 399
  presidential succession and, 441–442, 443
  vacancy in office of, 441, 442–443
Videotaped interrogations, 142
Vietnam
  Bill Clinton's recognition of, 420
  national unity and, 569
  prior to Vietnam War, 557–558
Vietnam War
  brief history of Vietnam preceding, 207, 418, 428, 544, 552, 557–558
  generational effect and, 235
  Pentagon Papers case and, 127
  political attitudes and, 234, 310, 341
  public opinion and, 219, 220, 221–222
  student protest and, 128
  tenth anniversary of end of, survey marking, 224
Vinson, Frederick M., 159
Violence against Women Act (1994), 108
Virginia Company of London, 34, 35
Virginia plan, 44
"Virtual" bureaucracy, 448
Virtual courtroom, 486
VISTA (Volunteers in Service to America), 101
Voice of America, 365
Volunteers in Service to America (VISTA), 101
Vote fraud, 329–330
Voter(s)
  alternative policies presented to, 278
  decisions by, 337–343
  independent
    in 1952, 313
    in 2000, 313
    defined, 277
  initiatives of, 10, 191, 588
  media's impact on, 362
  party, comparison of, on issues and ideology, 285
  plurality of, 326
  registration of. *See* Voting, registration for
  turnout of. *See* Voter turnout
  Vanishing Voter study and, 334
Voter turnout
  campaign effects and, 333, 334

factors influencing, 332, 336
low
    effect of, 331–332
    reasons for, 332–333, 336
political withdrawal and, 333
rational ignorance effect and, 333
Vanishing Voter study and, 334
Voter.com, 18
Voters News Service, 366
Voting
fraud in, 329–330
on the Internet, 329
issue, 341–343
by mail, 328–329
in national, state, and local elections, 330–333
registration for
    defined, 335
    drives and, 166
    legal restrictions on, 333–337
    making convenient, 12
    "motor-voter" law and, 330, 335, 344
    requirements for, 4, 165–166, 259, 344
        current eligibility and, 335–337
ticket splitting and, 291
Voting rights. *See also* Suffrage
African Americans and, 12, 158, 335
age and, 206–207, 259, 335
Asian Americans and, 167
Hispanic Americans and, 167
Native Americans and, 167
women and, 12, 39, 173–174, 310, 335
the young and, 206–207
Voting Rights Act (1965), 164, 165–166, 167, 390–391, 586

W

Wage discrimination, 180–181
Wage gap, 181
Wall Street Journal poll, 19, 291
Wallace, George, 160, 165, 298
Wallace, Henry, 298
Wallace v. Jaffree, 121
War of 1812, 281
War on Poverty Bill (1964), 104
War Powers Resolution (1973), 419, 428, 552
The War Room, 314–315
Ward, Alan, 124
Warren, Earl, 141, 159, 495–496, 498
    Warren Court and, 495, 498
Washington, George, 352–353, 414, 423, 547
    cabinet of, 414, 437
    as commander in chief of Continental Army, 36, 418
    Constitutional Convention and, 43, 44
    farewell address of, 278–279
    foreign policy and, 554
    inaugural address of, 431
    own mail answered by, 436
Washington, Harold, 289
Washington, D.C, burning of, by British, 556
Washington community, 429

Washington Legal Foundation, 259
Washington Post, 363
    Internet and, 358
    Pentagon Papers and, 127
    Watergate break-in coverage and, 363
Washington v. Glucksberg, 140
Water pollution, 523–524
Watergate break-in, 219, 234, 238, 281, 317, 342, 363, 417, 433, 434
Wattenberg, Ben, 169
Watts, J. C., 400
Weaver, James, 299
Weber, Max, 451
Weberian model of bureaucracy, 451
Webster v. Reproductive Health Services, 137
Welfare
    poverty and, 516–521
    programs for, major, 517–519
    spending on, 518
Welfare Reform Act (Personal Responsibility and Work Opportunity Reconciliation Act)(1996), 517–518, 520
    homelessness and, 520–521
Wellstone, Paul, 240, 241, 601
Wesberry v. Sanders, 389
Whig Party, 280
Whip, 399
Whistle-Blower Protection Act (1989), 465
Whistleblowers, 465–466
White, Byron, 202, 493
White, John, 33–34
White, Rick, 382
White House Fellows, 438
White House Office, 438
White House press corps, 363
White primary, 158
William the Conqueror, 479
Wilson, Don, 56
Wilson, James, 43, 48
Wilson, James Q., 599
Wilson, Woodrow, 58, 59
    election of
        in 1912, 281, 298
        in 1916, 555
        without majority of popular vote, 327, 414
    League of Nations and, 546
    Versailles Treaty and, 420
Winfrey, Oprah, 170
Women
    in cabinet, 177
    in combat, 175–176
    in Congress, 173, 176, 177, 178, 198, 311, 312
    equality and, 172–181
    glass ceiling and, 181
    as governors, 581
    jury duty and, 589
    political participation and, 153, 173–177
    rights of
        in other countries, 178
        voting, 12, 39, 173–174, 310, 335
    on United States Supreme Court, 177, 487, 493
    wage discrimination and, 180–181

women's movement and
    feminist, 174–175
    modern, 174–176
    political, early, 173–174
Women's Political Caucus, 176
Woods, Tiger, 170
Woodson, Robert, 168
Woodward, Bob, 363
Woolworth's, 163
Works Progress Administration (WPA), 103
World Antislavery Convention, 173
World Bank, 368
World trade
    America's current competitive position and, 535–536
    freer, 534–537
    global economy and, 565–566
World Trade Center bombing, 563
World Trade Organization (WTO), 86, 89, 94, 368, 536, 549
World War I, 544, 555
World War II, 436, 544
    atomic bombs dropped on Japan and, 418
    fall of France in, 432
    internment of Japanese Americans during, 426
    Japanese attack on Pearl Harbor and, 364, 547, 555–556
    public opinion and, 225–226
    Yalta Conference and, 547, 556
World Wide Web, 29, 60. *See also* Internet
    choosing a candidate on, 342
    cookies and, 138
    court Web sites and, 486
    Library of Congress on, 391
    members of Congress with Web sites on, 381, 382
    President Clinton's videotaped testimony on, 382
    Starr report published on, 358, 382
    White House on, 423
WPA (Works Progress Administration), 103
Wright, Jim, 406
Writ
    of *certiorari,* 487–488
    of *habeas corpus,* 140
WTO (World Trade Organization), 86, 89, 94, 368, 536, 549
Wyatt, Lance, 438

Y

Yalta Conference, 547, 556
Year Books, 479
Yellow journalism, 354
Yeltsin, Boris, 315, 560
Yugoslavia, former, breakup of, 569

Z

Zaire, refugees in, 570
Ziegler, Harmon, 14
Zimbabwe, AIDS and, 571

Photo Credits